Acclaim for *Charl*

"A superb piece of scholarship." —**Daniel J. Boorstin**

"A brilliant portrait of a dominant figure in the American radical tradition."

—**William W. Freehling**, *New York Review of Books*

"[*Charles Sumner*] focuses as tightly as a therapist on its forbidding, fascinating, and complex subject. . . . A highly rewarding study of the tension between political aims and accommodations." —*National Observer*

"The most powerful and moving passage in the book is his description of Sumner's all-night vigil at the bedside of the dying President on April 15, 1865. . . . Close students of the Civil War and Reconstruction will appreciate Donald's massive research, meticulous accuracy, balanced judgments, and incorporation of new interpretations."

—**James M. McPherson**, *New York Times Book Review*

"Donald delineates in rich detail Sumner's conflicts with [Lincoln, Seward, Johnson, Grant, and fellow Republicans]. . . . This is a major biography that thrusts the reader into the heart of some of the most crucial conflicts of our history while drawing a portrait of Sumner that is despairing and tragic in the end." —*Publishers Weekly*

"[*Charles Sumner*] is one of the masterworks of American biography and one in which thorough scholarship is illumined with keen insight and literary grace."

—**Donald E. Fehrenbacher**, *American Historical Review*

"Unquestionably one of the outstanding biographies of the year. . . . [Donald] has caught the flavor of the man. . . . It is a magisterial biography in which details are harnessed to the full flow of the narrative and where the works of the politician are made to harmonize with the character of the man. All of Sumner's qualities have been joined together in this rounded and authentic life." —*New York Times*

"Donald is one of those rare historians who can see both the good and the bad and keep them in balance. He makes no efforts to hide Sumner's faults. . . . Donald has written one of the truly great biographies to be found in American historiography. It will live." —*North Carolina Historical Review*

"This impressive volume . . . is marked by narrative elegance, mastery of evidence, and analytical power. It is in all respects a model of biographic art. . . . The author displays both a warm appreciation of Sumner's virtues (especially his courageous and farsighted fight for Negro rights) and an unblinking recognition of his shortcomings. . . . [A] masterful and definitive study of an extraordinary champion of human rights." —*Journal of American History*

"It is clear that Sumner has fascinated Donald and the fascination is communicated to his readers."

—*New York Herald Tribune*

"[*Charles Sumner*] is biographic art couched in prose of clarity and grace." —*New Leader*

CHARLES SUMNER

CHARLES SUMNER

by

David Herbert Donald

new introduction by the author

DA CAPO PRESS • NEW YORK

Library of Congress Cataloging in Publication Data

Donald, David Herbert, 1920

Charles Sumner / by David Herbert Donald; with new introduction by the author.–1st Da Capo Press ed.

p. cm.

A paperback edition, unabridged republication of "Charles Sumner and the Coming of the Civil War", originally published: New York, 1960; and "Charles Sumner and the Rights of Man", originally published: New York, 1970.

Includes index.

ISBN 0-306-80720-3 (alk. paper)

1. Sumner, Charles, 1811–1874. 2. Legislators–United States–Biography. 3. United States. Congress. Senate–Biography. 4. Antislavery movements–United States. 5. United States–Politics and government–1845–1861. I. Donald, David Herbert, 1920- Charles Sumner and the coming of the Civil War. II. Donald, David Herbert, 1920- Charles Sumner and the rights of man. III. Title. IV. Title: Charles Sumner and the coming of the Civil War. V. Title: Charles Sumner and the rights of man.

E415.9.S9D6 1996

328.73'092–dc20

[B] 96-16124

CIP

First Da Capo Press edition 1996

This Da Capo Press paperback edition of *Charles Sumner* is an unabridged republication of *Charles Sumner and the Coming of the Civil War,* originally published in New York in 1960, and *Charles Sumner and the Rights of Man,* originally published in New York in 1970. It is supplemented with a new introduction by the author, and reprinted by arrangement with him.

Published by Da Capo Press, Inc.
A Subsidiary of Plenum Publishing Corporation
233 Spring Street, New York, N.Y. 10013

Manufactured in the United States of America

TO

THE MEMORY OF MY GRANDFATHER

John Belford

LIEUTENANT

IN THAT BRAVE CIVIL WAR REGIMENT

The First Vermont Cavalry

FOR

Alfred A. Knopf

FRIEND AND PUBLISHER

CONTENTS

PART II

CHARLES SUMNER AND THE RIGHTS OF MAN

ILLUSTRATIONS

PART I

PART II

INTRODUCTION TO THE DA CAPO EDITION

In 1948, when I published my first book, *Lincoln's Herndon,* I began thinking about the next one. After I had considered and rejected several possibilities, Mr. Robert Glauber, an editor at Alfred A. Knopf, suggested that I give serious thought to a biography of Charles Sumner, the great Massachusetts senator and abolitionist. The idea was appealing because it would allow me to combine my interests in biography, political history, and intellectual history.

I quickly discovered that there was no modern biography of Sumner. The authorized four-volume *Memoir and Letters of Charles Sumner*[1] by his close friend E. L. Pierce was valuable because it included many of Sumner's letters, but it was adulatory and dated. Several other, shorter studies[2] all proved thin and wholly uncritical, giving no idea why Sumner was at once the most loved and best hated nineteenth-century American political leader.

I began planning a biography that would cover all of Sumner's long career: his emergence as a reformer and advocate of the abolition of slavery, his part in the formation of

[1] 4 vols.; Boston, 1878–1893.

[2] Jeremiah Chaplin and J. D. Chaplin, *Life of Charles Sumner* (Boston, 1874); C. Edwards Lester, *Life and Public Services of Charles Sumner* (New York, 1874); Archibald H. Grimke, *The Life of Charles Sumner: The Scholar in Politics* (New York, 1892); Moorfield Storey, *Charles Sumner* (Boston, 1900); George H. Haynes, *Charles Sumner* (Philadelphia, 1909); Walter G. Shotwell, *Life of Charles Sumner* (New York, 1910). Of the earlier biographies only Anna Laurens Dawes's *Charles Sumner* (New York, 1892) has any critical edge; it was written by the daughter of a former congressional colleague of the senator.

the Republican party, and his role as the most articulate radical senator of the Civil War and Reconstruction era. The sources proved abundant. In addition to Sumner's *Works,* which the senator himself edited in fifteen volumes, there was a massive collection of his papers and letters in the Houghton Library at Harvard University. Nearly all of Sumner's contemporaries, whether friends or enemies, also left voluminous records. I was then teaching at Columbia University—and after that at Smith College and at Princeton University—but I spent every summer for a decade in Cambridge working my way through these manuscripts.

I had completed about half of the story when I was invited to serve as Harmsworth Professor at the University of Oxford. I felt I ought to accept because this appointment would give me access to nineteenth-century British manuscript collections that contained much Sumner material. I wrote my good friend and publisher Alfred A. Knopf that I planned to put aside what I had written and that I would complete the manuscript after I returned from my year abroad. Concerned, no doubt, that I would never finish the biography, he urged me to send him the chapters that covered Sumner's career up to the outbreak of the Civil War. The result was the publication in 1960 of *Charles Sumner and the Coming of the Civil War.*

Not until ten years later was I able to complete my account of Sumner's career during the Civil War and Reconstruction years. In part, this delay resulted from my discovery during my year at Oxford of much new material on Anglo-American diplomacy. But even more, it stemmed from my belated realization that to understand properly Sumner's role in the Senate required a line-by-line reading of the thousands of pages of the *Congressional Globe* (the predecessor of the *Congressional Record*) for the years between the outbreak of the Civil War in 1861 and his death in 1874. This is not a task that I recommend to anyone else—but I think it is the only way to understand how Congress functioned and what part Sumner played in it. In 1970, when I ended my story, it was published as *Charles Sumner and the Rights of Man.*

Separated by ten years in publication, the two books have rarely been read as a unit, though they were always intended to be parts of one large-scale biography. Now, at last, by reissuing them in a single volume, Da Capo Press has made it possible for readers to view Sumner's life as a whole.

Looking back over the two books, now so happily combined between the same covers, has given me a chance to reassess my biography. Aside from correcting a few minor factual errors and typographical slips, I have left the text unchanged, but if I were rewriting the book now I would make a few alterations that would reflect recent scholarship. For instance, if I were redoing all the footnotes, I would no longer have to list the 114 manuscript collections in the United States, Great Britain, and Canada in which I searched for Sumner letters, but could cite the comprehensive microfilm edition of *The Papers of Charles Sumner*, edited by Beverly Wilson Palmer.[3] In many instances, instead of citing the original manuscripts, I could refer to the carefully edited texts in Palmer's *Selected Letters of Charles Sumner.*[4] Drawing on Dale Baum's *The Civil War Party System: The Case of Massachusetts, 1848–1876,*[5] I could now provide a fuller account of the Bird Club and other political groups that formed the basis of Sumner's political organization in Massachusetts. And, following the recent study by William E. Gienapp,[6] I could present a more complete analysis of the social and economic composition of the Republican party, which Sumner helped create.

Some other changes would reflect a difference in emphasis rather than new research. It is probably true, as one critic has charged, that I have quoted more derogatory comments about Sumner than I have admiring tributes from his contemporaries.[7] In part, this is because the most glowing praise was offered only after Sumner was safely dead, and its sincerity is suspect. But it is also true that Sumner's critics were generally more interesting writers than his admirers. If a biographer, with limited space, has to choose between Carl Schurz's earnest but bland tribute to Sumner's "moral courage" and the "sin-

[3]85 reels; Alexandria, Virginia, 1988.

[4]2 vols; Boston, 1990.

[5]Chapel Hill, 1984.

[6]*The Origins of the Republican Party, 1852–1856* (New York, 1987).

[7]Gilbert Osofsky, "Cardboard Yankee: How Not to Study the Mind of Charles Sumner," *Reviews in American History,* I (1973), 597–599.

cerity of his convictions," and Henry Adams's celebrated remark that Sumner's mind "had reached the calm of water which receives and reflects images without absorbing them; it contains nothing but itself," can there be any doubt as to which he will include? Nevertheless, I wish I had been better able to portray Sumner as his best friends and admirers saw him: amiable, pure, earnest, and affectionate.

I wish, too, that I had written more fully about Sumner's relationships with some of the leading New England thinkers of his day.[8] I have treated at some length the influence that William Ellery Channing exerted on him, but I had too little to say about his friendships with Ralph Waldo Emerson, Bronson Alcott, Orestes Brownson, Margaret Fuller, and other Transcendentalists, and I did not adequately discuss the role that Theodore Parker played as intermediary between Sumner and these reformers.

But there are not many other changes I would make; most of the interpretations I advanced have stood the test of time.[9] Since the publication of these volumes, no one else has felt impelled to write another full-scale biography of Sumner. The only recent biographical sketch has been Frederick J. Blue's *Charles Sumner and the Conscience of the North,*[10] a brief summary, apparently designed for classroom use.

I have, of course, been greatly pleased that my Sumner volumes have been so well received, but I wish they had had more influence on the general interpretation of American his-

[8]See the preliminary exploration of this topic in Bill Ledbetter, "Charles Sumner: Political Activist for the New England Transcendentalists," *Historian,* XLIV (1982), 347–363.

[9]For instance, my account of Sumner's medical history after the Brooks assault is confirmed in nearly every particular by Laura A. White's "Was Charles Sumner Shamming, 1856–1859?" *New England Quarterly,* XXXIII (1960), 291–324. My analysis of the importance that the Brooks assault had in the 1856 election is sustained in William E. Gienapp's "The Crime Against Sumner: The Caning of Charles Sumner and the Rise of the Republican Party," *Civil War History,* XXV (1979), 218–245.

In a highly critical essay, "The Pulitzer Prize Treatment of Charles Sumner," *Massachusetts Review,* II (1961), 749–769, Louis Ruchames did not identify any factual errors in my book, but charged that by selective quotation I misrepresented Sumner's life. This charge was parroted, without independent examination of the evidence, in Paul Goodman's "David Donald's *Charles Sumner* Reconsidered," *New England Quarterly,* XXXVII (1964), 373–387. Both these writers complained that I distorted Sumner's views by quoting only phrases and sentences from his writings, rather than paragraphs and pages. Few other readers, I suspect, will share their eagerness for more of Sumner's prose.

[10]Arlington Heights, Ill., 1994.

tory. I conceived this biography as not just the story of one remarkable man's life but as a case study of the American as reformer in politics, which would illustrate the essential elements required for success in that role. The first and most important of these is the existence of a real, palpable, and threatening evil that demands correction. For Sumner, after some experimentation with other causes, that was slavery.

A second is that a reformer in public life needs to have a profound personal involvement with his cause. This is not to argue that deep psychological problems are the reasons why a man becomes a reformer. Instead, it is a recognition that a life dedicated to unceasing warfare against evil requires more than an intellectual or philosophical commitment. One of the purposes of this biography is to show that Sumner's decision to become a reformer, and his willingness to stick to his cause despite social isolation, hostile criticism, and even physical assault, were deeply rooted in his early family experiences.

A third prerequisite is a body of public thought that can be mobilized against the institution that a reformer attacks. Sumner's greatest strength was his power to energize in support of abolition the widespread, if latent, beliefs of Northerners in the equality of men and the idea of Progress.

Fourth, for a reform to take hold, there have to be cracks or fissures in the established social structure, where seeds of change can take root. In nineteenth-century New England, industrialization and urbanization divided the established leadership and afforded younger people an opportunity to question the traditional politics of deference. In the nation as a whole, the demands of fire-eating Southerners for the extension of their "peculiar institution" of slavery cracked the facade of compromise and allowed the emergence of a Northern spokesman like Sumner, totally dedicated to the principle of human equality.

Finally, if a reformer is to succeed in reshaping public policy, he must have, or develop, skill in political management. Although Sumner always professed to be above political intrigue and management (that detachment was one of the reasons he attracted so many young, idealistic followers), his record shows how dexterously he balanced doctrinal purity and political pragmatism.

Charles Francis Adams may well have been right in terming Sumner a unique figure in American political life, a "statesman *doctrinaire*,"[11] and I trust that these volumes have given adequate attention to the special qualities that made him the most prominent voice for freedom and equality in nineteenth-century American history. But I hope this biography will also suggest that Sumner belongs to a long and distinguished American reform tradition.

DAVID HERBERT DONALD
Lincoln, Massachusetts
April 1996

[11] *Dinner Commemorative of Chas. Sumner and Complimentary to Edward L. Pierce* (Boston, 1895), 46–47.

ACKNOWLEDGMENTS

PART I

DURING the course of my ten years of research on Charles Sumner I have incurred many personal and professional obligations, which it is a pleasure to acknowledge. Perhaps my largest debt is to the staff of the Houghton Library, of Harvard University, where the voluminous Sumner manuscripts are housed. Without the permission of Mr. William A. Jackson to use and quote from these papers, the present book could not have been written, and without the courteous and efficient assistance of Miss Carolyn Jakeman my researches could not have been completed.

The staff of the Massachusetts Historical Society has been equally generous and equally helpful. Mr. Stephen T. Riley, the Director, has been an invaluable guide to that library's rich collections, and Miss Winifred Collins has efficiently handled my most time-consuming requests. I am grateful to the Trustees of the Adams Trust, and to Mr. Lyman Butterfield, the editor-in-chief of the Adams Papers, for permission to quote from the Adams Manuscripts, which I have read in microfilm.

During several summers of research in Washington I have invariably been treated with great kindness by the officials of the Library of Congress. I am particularly indebted to Mr. David C. Mearns, Mr. Robert Land, Dr. Elizabeth McPherson, and Dr. C. P. Powell of the Manuscripts Division; to Mr. Hirst Milhollen and Mr. Milton Kaplan, of the Prints and Photographs Division; and to Colonel Willard Webb, Chief of the Stack and Reader Service.

The full extent of my obligation to the scholars at The National Archives does not appear in this volume, but I must acknowledge my gratitude to Mr. W. Neil Franklin, Chief of the Reader Service, to Mr. C. L. Lokke, of the Foreign Affairs Branch, and to Miss Josephine Cobb, of the Still Picture Branch.

Other librarians, too, have given freely of their time by helping me search out Sumner manuscripts or by solving difficult reference problems. Among those to whom I am particularly indebted for materials incorporated in this volume are: Miss Ellen F. Adams, of the Baker Library, Dartmouth College; Mr. T. D. Seymour Bassett, of the Wilbur Library, University of Vermont; Miss Elizabeth Biggert, of the Ohio State Archaeological and Historical Library; Mr. Carey S. Bliss, of the Henry E. Huntington Library; Miss Alice H. Bonnell, of the Columbia University Library; Miss Dorothy Bridgewater, of Sterling Library, Yale University; Mr. Clarence Brigham, Director of the American Antiquarian Society; Professor Paul H. Buck, Librarian of Harvard University; Miss Margaret E. Butterfield, of the Rush Rhees Library, University of Rochester; Mr. Alexander Clark, of the Firestone Library, Princeton University; Miss Georgia Coffin, of the Cornell University Library; Miss Charlotte D. Conover, of the New Hampshire Historical Society; Mr. Thomas DeValcourt, of the Craigie House Library; Mr. Kimball C. Elkins, of the Harvard University Archives; Mr. William Ewing, of the William L. Clements Library, University of Michigan; Miss Margaret Flint, of the Illinois State Historical Library; Miss Clara E. Follette, of the Vermont Historical Society; Miss Hannah D. French, of the Wellesley College Library; Miss Mary Isabel Fry, of the Henry E. Huntington Library; Mr. Ebenezer Gay, of the Athenaeum, Boston; Mr. Zoltán Haraszti, of the Boston Public Library; Mr. Robert H. Haynes, of the Harvard University Library; Mrs. Alice P. Hook, of the Historical and Philosophical Society of Ohio; Mr. Elmer M. Hunt, of the New Hampshire Historical Society; Miss Edna L. Jacobsen, of the New York State Library; Miss Hazel E. Joselyn, of the Baker Library, Dartmouth College; Miss Lucile Kane, of the Minnesota Historical Society; Mr. William Kaye Lamb, Dominion Archivist, The Public Archives of Canada; Mr. Edward C. Lathem, of the Baker Library, Dartmouth College; Mr. Wilmer R. Leech, of the New York Historical Society; Miss Helen M. McFarland, of the Kansas State Historical Society;

Miss Dorothy McKinley, of the Newberry Library; Mr. Watt P. Marchman, Director of the Rutherford B. Hayes Library; Mr. Walter M. Merrill, Director of the Essex Institute; Mr. Bradley Mitchell, of the Cornell University Library; Mr. Richard W. Morin, Director of the Baker Library, Dartmouth College; Mr. Robert Rosenthal, of the University of Chicago Library; Mr. W. O. Rourke, Director of the Buffalo Public Library; Miss Marian B. Rowe, of the Maine Historical Society; Miss Mattie Russell, of the Duke University Library; Miss Judith E. Sachs, of the Institute for Advanced Study; Miss Margaret Scriven, of the Chicago Historical Society; Mr. Clifford K. Shipton, Custodian of the Harvard University Archives; Mr. Lester G. Wells, of the University of Syracuse Library; Mr. R. N. Williams, II, Director of the Pennsylvania Historical Society; Mrs. Alene Lowe White, of the Western Reserve Historical Society; Mr. Walter Muir Whitehill, Director of the Athenaeum, Boston; Miss Constance Winchell, of the Columbia University Library.

I owe a very special debt of gratitude to my dear friend, Norma Cuthbert, of the Henry E. Huntington Library.

A number of collectors have generously permitted me to examine Sumner manuscripts in their possession: Mr. Charles Sumner Bird (who has since presented the Bird MSS. to Houghton Library); Mrs. E. C. Reeves; Mr. Boyd B. Stutler; and Mr. George H. Wettach. My indebtedness to Mr. Charles M. Segal, who has allowed me to make extensive use of his large collection of Sumner materials, is very heavy. Mr. Herbert W. Sumner, Jr., of Fair Lawn, N.J., and Mrs. Charles Sumner, of Baltimore, have greatly assisted me on genealogical matters.

My professional colleagues have been unvaryingly kind in responding to my numerous appeals for advice and assistance. Especially am I obligated to Professor Bernard Barber, of Barnard College; Professor I. H. Bartlett, of the Massachusetts Institute of Technology; Dean Jacques Barzun, of Columbia University; Dr. Saul Benison, of Columbia University; Mrs. Harry E. Pratt, of the Illinois State Archives; Mr. Bruce Catton, of *American Heritage;* Professor Sigmund Diamond, of Columbia University; Dr. Martin Duberman, of Yale University; Professor Fletcher M. Green, of the University of North Carolina; Professor Walter Harding, of Genesee State Teachers College; Professor Leonard W. Levy, of

Brandeis University; Professor Dumas Malone, of the University of Virginia; Mr. Taylor Milne, Director of the Institute of Historical Research, London; Professor Allan Nevins, of the Henry E. Huntington Library; Dean John G. Palfrey, of Columbia University; Professor Harold Schwartz, of Kent State University; Professor Hans L. Trefousse, of Brooklyn College; Professor Robert K. Webb, of Columbia University; and Professor C. Vann Woodward, of the Johns Hopkins University. Professor Frank Freidel, of Harvard University, has aided me in innumerable ways and most generously made his voluminous notes on the Francis Lieber MSS. available to me.

To many younger scholars I am also profoundly indebted. Three of my own doctoral students at Columbia University did valiant service as research assistants during various stages of this project: Mr. Albert Fein, of Long Island University; Mr. Grady McWhiney, of the University of California (Berkeley); and Dr. Irwin F. Unger, of Long Beach State College. Other Columbia students have kept an eye out for Sumner materials during the course of their own researches: Mr. Richard Abrams, of Columbia University; Mrs. Helene Baer; Mrs. Sylvia Crane; Dr. Stanley P. Hirshson, of Paterson State Teachers College; Dr. Ari A. Hoogenboom, of Pennsylvania State University; Mr. Edward Leonard, of Iona College; Dr. Samuel Shapiro; and Mr. Theodore V. Theobald. Mr. Frank Otto Gatell, a graduate student at Harvard University, has generously shared his findings in the Palfrey MSS. with me.

There are not words adequate to acknowledge my obligation to busy colleagues who took time from their own researches to read this manuscript. My deepest debt is to Professors Richard Hofstadter, of Columbia University, and Allan Nevins, of the Henry E. Huntington Library, who read all of it; I have profited throughout by their detailed and stimulating criticisms. In my early chapters Professor Henry Steele Commager, of Amherst College, caught numerous blunders, and I have drawn heavily upon his profound knowledge of Joseph Story's career. My chapter on Sumner's European travels has benefited from the criticisms of Professor Herman Ausubel, of Columbia University, who has also generously shared with me his researches in English manuscript collections. Dean Roy F. Nichols, of the University of

Pennsylvania, gave me the benefit of his unparalleled expertness in the politics of the 1850's by reading the last half of the book, and the final three chapters have been greatly improved by the close critical reading given them by Professor David M. Potter of Yale University.

Through the kindness of Professor T. A. Larson, I have been privileged to examine the notes collected by the late Professor Laura A. White, of the University of Wyoming, for a projected biography of Sumner. Since I received access to these notes late in the course of my own researches, I found they generally referred to materials I had already examined, yet in a number of cases Miss White's jottings led me to fresh and useful sources.

For advice on medical aspects of Sumner's history I am greatly in debt to Dr. Bronson S. Ray, of the Cornell Medical Center, and to Dr. Julia L. Schneider, of the Neurological Institute of New York.

My publisher, Mr. Alfred A. Knopf, has given me constant encouragement in an undertaking that has at times seemed endless and overwhelmingly difficult.

For subventions without which the travel and research required for this book would have been almost impossible, I am indebted to the following organizations: the American Philosophical Society; the Columbia University Council for Research in the Social Sciences; the George A. and Eliza Gardner Howard Foundation; and the Henry E. Huntington Library. To the Institute for Advanced Study, and to its Director, Dr. Robert Oppenheimer, I am grateful for a stimulating year that provided me the ideal surroundings in which this manuscript was actually drafted.

My wife, Aïda DiPace Donald, has shared with me her research findings in New York newspapers and manuscript collections, and all my chapters have profited by the careful critical reading she gave them.

A great many others have assisted me on the later phases of Sumner's career. I hope to have the opportunity in a future volume to express my indebtedness to them.

PART II

THE dedication of this book will suggest how much I owe to Mr. Alfred A. Knopf, who has encouraged and sustained me during the long period when this book was in preparation. It can, however, only meagerly indicate the respect and admiration I have for this giant figure in the history of American publishing. These feelings I know are shared by my colleagues throughout the historical profession, for the colophon of Alfred A. Knopf has come to be a coveted certificate of excellence. In our time no other man has done so much to promote the writing of serious history in the United States, and no other publisher has insisted that his books be as handsome as they are scholarly.

Without the assistance of many librarians in both Great Britain and the United States, this book could not have been written. To all the staff of the Houghton Library at Harvard University, where the largest collection of Sumner manuscripts is housed, I am deeply indebted, and I want to express particular thanks to Mr. William A. Jackson and Miss Carolyn Jakeman for courtesies extended to me over a long period of time.

Equally extensive is my debt to the indefatigable staff of the Massachusetts Historical Society. Mr. Stephen T. Riley, the Director, has kindly kept me informed of all recent acquisitions relating to Sumner, and Miss Winifred Collins has responded to my most time-consuming appeals for assistance. To the Trustees of the Adams Trust, and to Mr. Lyman H. Butterfield, the editor-in-chief of the Adams Papers, I am grateful for permission to quote from the Adams Manuscripts, which I have read on microfilm.

The officials of the Library of Congress in Washington have been unfailingly cooperative, even when my visits have at times grown so extended as to become sojourns. I am particularly indebted to Mr. Roy P. Basler, Mr. David C. Mearns, Mr. Robert Land, Dr. Elizabeth McPherson, and Dr. C. P. Powell, of the Manuscripts Division, and to Mr. Milton Kaplan and Mr. Hirst D. Milhollen, of the Prints and Photographs Division.

At the National Archives Miss Josephine Cobb, of the Still Picture Branch, Mr. W. Neil Franklin, Chief of the Diplomatic, Legal and Fiscal Branch, Mr. C. L. Lokke, of the Foreign Affairs Branch, and Mr. Buford Rowland, Chief of the Legislative Branch, provided me much assistance.

Other librarians, too, have given freely of their time by helping me search out Sumner manuscripts or by solving difficult reference problems. Among the many to whom I am indebted for materials used in this volume are: Mrs. Margaret Butterfield Andrews, of Rush Rhees Library, University of Rochester; Mr. T. D. Seymour Bassett, of the Wilbur Library, University of Vermont; Miss Elizabeth Biggert, of the Ohio State Archaeological and Historical Library; Mr. Carey S. Bliss, of the Henry E. Huntington Library; Miss Alice H. Bonnell, of Butler Library, Columbia University; Mr. Arna Bontemps, of Fisk University Library; Miss Lila Brady, of the Indiana Division, Indiana State Library; Miss Dorothy Bridgewater, of the Sterling Library, Yale University; Mr. Clarence Brigham, of the American Antiquarian Society; Professor Paul H. Buck, of Harvard University; Mrs. Betty Calloway, of the Center for Advanced Study in the Behavioral Sciences; Mr. Alexander Clark, of the Firestone Library, Princeton University; Miss Georgia Coffin, of the Cornell University Library; Mr. Claude R. Cook, of the Iowa State Department of Archives and History; Miss Norma Cuthbert, of the Henry E. Huntington Library; Mr. Thomas DeValcourt, of the Craigie House Library; Miss Caroline Dunn, of the Indiana Historical Society; Miss Adelaide Eisenhart, of the Milton S. Eisenhower Library, The Johns Hopkins University; Mr. Kimball C. Elkins, of the Harvard University Archives; Mr. William Ewing, of the William L. Clements Library; Miss Margaret Flint, of the Illinois State Historical Society; Miss Clara E. Follette, of the

Vermont Historical Society; Miss Mary Isabel Fry, of the Henry E. Huntington Library; Miss Teresa N. Garfield, of the Fitchburg Historical Society; Mr. Ebenezer Gay, of the Boston Athenæum; Mr. Zoltán Haraszti, of the Boston Public Library; Miss Josephine L. Harper, of the Wisconsin State Historical Society; Mrs. Alice P. Hook, of the Historical and Philosophical Society of Ohio; Mrs. Ione Hoover and Miss Martha J. Hubbard, both of the Milton S. Eisenhower Library, The Johns Hopkins University; Mr. Elmer M. Hunt, of the New Hampshire Historical Society; Miss Edna L. Jacobsen, of the New York State Library; Miss Priscilla Jones, of the Center for Advanced Study in the Behavioral Sciences; Miss Hazel E. Joslyn, of the Baker Library, Dartmouth College; Miss Lucile Kane, of the Minnesota Historical Society; Miss Margaret E. Lough, of the Milton S. Eisenhower Library, The Johns Hopkins University; the Reverend Thomas T. McAvoy, of the University of Notre Dame; Miss Helen M. McFarland, of the Kansas State Historical Society; Miss Dorothy McKinley, of the Newberry Library; Miss Beverly A. McManus, of the Harvard University Archives; Mr. Watt P. Marchman, of the Hayes Memorial Library; Mr. Keith E. Melder, of the Smithsonian Institution; Mr. Bradley Mitchell, of the Cornell University Library; Mr. William T. O'Rourke, of the Buffalo Public Library; Mr. Robert Rosenthal, of the University of Chicago Library; Miss Marian R. Rowe, of the Maine Historical Society; Miss Mattie Russell, of the Duke University Library; Mrs. G. K. Schneider, of the Staten Island Institute of Arts and Sciences; Miss Margaret Scriven, of the Chicago Historical Society; Mr. Clifford K. Shipton, of the Harvard University Archives; Mr. Lester G. Wells, of the University of Syracuse Library; Mr. R. N. Williams, II, of the Pennsylvania Historical Society; Mrs. Alene Lowe White, of the Western Reserve Historical Society; Mr. Walter Muir Whitehill, of the Boston Athenæum; Miss Constance Winchell, of Butler Library, Columbia University.

I have been privileged to use a number of manuscripts and rare published documents in private collections. To Her Gracious Majesty Queen Elizabeth II, I am indebted for access to the Royal Archives at Windsor Castle. The Broadlands Manuscripts, including the papers of Lord Palmerston, were made available to me by Admiral of the Fleet, Earl Mountbatten of Burma. Mr. Charles Sumner Bird permitted me to consult the Bird MSS. before they were presented to the Houghton Library, and Mr. Charles Storey graciously gave me access to the Moorfield Storey MSS. before they went to the Massachusetts Historical Society. Mr. John E. Lodge permitted me to use the Henry Cabot Lodge MSS., and Mr. John G. Palfrey granted me the privilege of reading the Palfrey MSS. Dr. Joseph H. Douglass allowed me to take notes on several important letters from Sumner to Frederick Douglass, and Mr. Alfred D. Chandler, Senior, of Wilmington, Delaware, shared with me his valuable collection of newspaper obituaries of Sumner. Once again Mr. Charles M. Segal generously encouraged me to use his extensive collection of Sumner manuscripts. Other collectors to whom I am greatly indebted include: Mr. Dwight Akers; Mr. H. DeGrasse Asbury; Mrs. Charles S. Hamlin; Mr. Derek Hudson; Mr. Victor Jacobs; Mr. Van Dyk MacBride; Mr. Boyd B. Stutler; Mr. Justin G. Turner; Mr. Frederick Weiser; and Mr. George H. Wettach.

Through the kindness of Professor T. A. Larson I have examined the notes collected by the late Laura A. White, of the University of Wyoming, for a projected biography of Sumner. Wherever possible I have myself consulted the sources used by Professor White, but I have drawn upon her notes from a few manuscript collections that have not been available to me. All such citations are identified in my footnotes as being from the White Notes.

My professional colleagues have been exceedingly generous in sharing with me their own researches and in responding to my frequent appeals for assistance. I am particularly grateful to Professor Herman Ausubel, of Columbia University; to Professor Irving H. Bartlett, of Carnegie-Mellon University; to Professor Carl Bode, of the University of Maryland; to Mr. and Mrs. Michael A. Burlingame, of Connecticut College; to Mr. Roger Butterfield; to Mr. Bruce Catton; to Professor Richard O. Curry, of the University of Connecticut; to Mr. Richard Early; to Professor Albert Fein, of Long Island University; to Professor Frank B. Freidel, of Harvard University; to Professor Frank O.

Gatell, of the University of California, Los Angeles; to William Gillette, of Rutgers University; to Professor Eric F. Goldman, of Princeton University; to Professor Fletcher M. Green, of the University of North Carolina, Chapel Hill; to Professor Stanley P. Hirshson, of Queens College; to Professor Richard Hofstadter, of Columbia University; to Professor Ari A. Hoogenboom, of Brooklyn College; to Professor Larry G. Kincaid, of the University of California, Los Angeles; to Professor Arthur S. Link, of Princeton University; to Professor Dumas Malone, of the University of Virginia; to Professor Grady McWhiney, of Wayne State University; to Mr. Taylor Milne, of the Institute of Historical Research, London; to Mr. Allan Nevins; to Professor Fred Nicklason, of the University of Maryland; to Professor Norman Rich, of Brown University; to Professor Elmo R. Richardson, of Washington State University; to Professor Joe Martin Richardson, of Florida State University; to Professor Richard H. Sewell, of the University of Wisconsin; to Professor Samuel Shapiro, of the University of Notre Dame; to Professor Wilson Smith, of the University of California, Davis; to Professor Hans L. Trefousse, of Brooklyn College; to Professor Frank E. Vandiver, of Rice University; to Professor G. M. Waller, of Butler University; to Dr. R. K. Webb, of the *American Historical Review;* to Professor Alan F. Westin, of Columbia University; to Professor Gordon S. Wood, of Brown University; to Professor C. Vann Woodward, of Yale University; and to Professor J. H. Young, of Emory University.

I wish I knew of some way adequately to thank my colleagues who took time from their own important researches to read and criticize this manuscript. I am grateful to Professor T. Harry Williams, of Louisiana State University, for his wise and encouraging comments upon my Civil War chapters. Professor Richard N. Current, of the University of North Carolina, Greensboro, read the entire manuscript, which is immeasurably strengthened by his substantive and stylistic criticisms. For saving me scores of errors, especially in matters pertaining to diplomatic history, I am indebted to Professor Richard W. Leopold, of Northwestern University, who gave the whole manuscript a close reading. The detailed and incisive comments by

Professor Harold M. Hyman, of Rice University, have helped me in revising the manuscript throughout, and his criticisms were particularly valuable on points of constitutional history and law. To Dr. Aïda DiPace Donald, my wife, I am indebted for her careful, critical reading of the entire work, and I have drawn heavily upon her detailed knowledge of New York politics of the period.

Chapter XII was presented, in an earlier version, to the Seminar of the History Department at The Johns Hopkins University, and I have profited from the criticism of my colleagues and our graduate students upon that occasion.

For efficient typing of this long manuscript I am grateful to Mrs. Thomas R. Grover, of The Johns Hopkins University, and to Mrs. Hildegarde Teilhet and Mrs. Linda Nathan, of the Center for Advanced Study in the Behavioral Sciences.

Mrs. Alice Anderson, of the Institute of Southern History at The Johns Hopkins University, has assisted me in dozens of ways during the last stages of my research and has greatly helped in getting the manuscript ready for the printer.

Miss Heather A. Townshend transcribed numerous letters in the Bright and Cobden MSS. for me, and Mr. Harold E. Samuel searched the Goldwin Smith MSS. at Cornell University for Sumner materials.

In writing on medical aspects of Sumner's later history, I have profited from discussions with Dr. E. Hunter Wilson, of Baltimore.

The encouragement and interest showed by Mr. William A. Koshland, president of Alfred A. Knopf, Inc., has made the labor of completing this book easier. Mrs. Jane N. Garrett has proved the perfect editor; her assistance has been invaluable in seeing it through the press. I want also to thank Mrs. Ann Adelman for her careful copy editing of the manuscript.

For subventions without which the travel and research required for this book would have been almost impossible, I thank the following organizations: the American Council of Learned Societies; the American Philosophical Society; the Columbia University Council for Research in the Social Sciences; the John Simon Guggenheim Foundation; the Henry E. Huntington

Library; and The Johns Hopkins University. The manuscript was finally completed in the ideal surroundings offered by the Center for Advanced Study in the Behavioral Sciences, and I am deeply grateful to Director O. Meredith Wilson and Associate Director Preston Cutler for making my year in California possible.

PART I

CHARLES SUMNER

AND THE

Coming of the Civil War

Charles Sumner in the Early 1850's

NEW YORK PUBLIC LIBRARY

PREFACE

THIS is the first biography of Charles Sumner to be written in fifty years. The neglect of Sumner has not been due to any unawareness of his importance in American history. The more familiar and dramatic episodes of his career spring readily to mind. For example, as Mr. Bruce Catton has recently reminded us in *This Hallowed Ground,*[1] Preston Brooks's assault upon Sumner in the Senate chamber in 1856 may be regarded as the first blow of the Civil War. Students recognize that Sumner's life touched upon virtually every significant movement in mid-nineteenth-century American history. He was an advocate of international peace; leader of educational and prison reform movements; organizer of the antislavery Whigs; a founder of the Republican party; the outstanding antislavery spokesman in the Senate during the 1850's; chief of the Radical Republicans during the Civil War; chairman of the Senate Committee on Foreign Relations during both the war and the Reconstruction years; a principal architect of the congressional program for reconstructing the conquered South; and pioneer in the Liberal Republican movement of 1872. In a period when senators often exercised more influence than presidents of the United States, Charles Sumner was one of the most potent and enduring forces in the American government.

Sumner's role in American history is unique. I can think of few, if any, other instances in which a "statesman *doctrinaire,*" as Charles Francis Adams, Jr., called Sumner—a man inflexibly

[1] New York: Doubleday & Company, Inc.; 1956, pp. 1–7.

committed to a set of basic ideas as moral principles—has exercised political power in the United States. Sumner's career illustrates the problems the man of theories must confront when he becomes the man of action. He was further distinctive in that he alone of his contemporaries moved with equal assurance in the antithetical worlds of New England letters and of Washington politics. He was friend to both Ralph Waldo Emerson and Pierre Soulé. In addition, Sumner was almost the only nineteenth-century American politician who was nearly as widely known in Europe as in his own country. At a time when President Abraham Lincoln had to confess that he had no personal acquaintances abroad, Sumner knew practically every important political leader and literary figure in England, France, Germany, and Italy.

These were some of the reasons why I began research toward a biography nearly ten years ago. At the time I was, fortunately, not aware of the opinion Mr. Edward H. O'Neill, the historian of American biography, had rendered upon Sumner: "He had one of the most complex characters of any man in American public life, a character that requires not only industry but knowledge and genius for its proper interpretation." [2] Of the "genius" allegedly requisite I do not speak, but I can certainly agree that a Sumner biographer must exhibit industry. The published and manuscript records of his career are almost overwhelmingly voluminous. Sumner himself began the editing and publishing of his *Works*, which run to fifteen volumes,[3] but these include, I estimate, less than one half of his public utterances. His papers, which he bequeathed to Harvard University, total somewhere between 40,000 and 60,000 items. Most of these, of course, are letters to Sumner, for the senator's own letters are scattered through dozens of manuscript repositories in the United States, Canada, and Great Britain.

Finding Sumner materials has, indeed, been less a problem than assimilating them. I found, once I had begun this project, that I should have to know not merely something of Massachusetts and national politics, but a good deal of fields where I have

[2] *A History of American Biography* (Philadelphia: University of Pennsylvania Press; 1935), p. 68.

[3] *The Works of Charles Sumner* (Boston: Lee and Shepard; 1870–83). Another edition, misleadingly called *Charles Sumner: His Complete Works* (Boston: Lee & Shepard; 1900; 20 vols.) is in fact only a reprinting, with new introductory material, of the *Works*.

no technical training—constitutional law; rhetoric; medicine; and psychology. The following pages, I fear, reveal that I am still all too inexpert in these matters, but I have tried to learn and, as my acknowledgments will show, I have been fortunate enough to have some of the best teachers in the world to help me.

I wish I could say that I have unraveled the riddle of Sumner and that I am now presenting the "definitive" biography. Of course I make no such claims. Virtually every sentence in the following chapters should have an interjected phrase like "it seems to me," or "to the best of my knowledge," or "in my opinion." Out of charity to the reader I have omitted such qualifiers; out of charity for the author he will supply them for himself.

While I was preparing this book, interested friends—perhaps recalling that a leading American jurist once called Sumner the most objectionable figure in American history—kept asking: "Is your biography going to be a sympathetic one?" I have never, I think, been able to answer the question satisfactorily. Certainly I started my research without conscious preconceptions or partialities. The longer I worked, the less relevant the question of sympathy became. After living with Sumner for a decade, after learning more about him than I know about any other human being, alive or dead—a great deal more, in some respects, than he ever knew about himself—I think of him almost as I would a member of my family. Rarely does it occur to one to ask whether he really "likes" his father or his mother or any other member of his family; these are the people with whom one lives, who are important in his life, and whom he tries to understand.

My purpose has been to understand Sumner and his motives, to recreate a very complex personality, not to hale him for trial before the bar of history. Where he was misinformed, or partially informed, or actually in error, I have not hesitated to set the record straight, but I have not felt it my proper function to sit in moral judgment upon his career, handing down verdicts of either praise or condemnation for his actions.

In trying to explain the motives underlying Sumner's actions, I am not making even an implicit judgment on the causes for which he fought. If—to make an assumption I carefully do *not* make in the following pages—Sumner took up the cause of prison reform solely in order to advance his own political career, his motive in no sense derogates from the desirability of reforming prisons; nor would the unworthiness of his motive keep him from doing valiant service in that worthy cause. In particular, I hope that no one will accuse me of sympathizing with Negro slavery because I have not interjected a little moral discourse after each of Sumner's orations to the effect that he was on the side of the angels. Surely in the middle of the twentieth century there are some things that do not need to be said.

While some readers may feel that I have gone much too far in exploring the depths of Sumner's mind, others may object that I have not explicitly discussed such ultimate questions as the causes of the Civil War. These matters, in my opinion, are beyond a biographer's proper competence. Certainly the debate about whether the Civil War was an "irrepressible conflict" or a "needless war" is not likely to be settled through a study of one participant in the sectional crisis, even of a key figure like Sumner. The more I have learned about the complexities of Sumner's personality and career, the less willing I have grown to generalize about other nineteenth-century American politicians.

If biography is to have a useful function in the historical craft, perhaps it is to steer us away from cosmic and unanswerable questions toward the intricacies of actuality. As André Gide once remarked, it is the part of wisdom to ask not why, but how events happen. I hope that it may be helpful in this biography to examine the way in which a single actor in a historical crisis arrived at his position of power. In 1845 any observer would have predicted that Sumner's chances for political success were much less than those of Robert C. Winthrop or Edward Everett, considerably inferior to those of John Gorham Palfrey or Charles Francis Adams. Yet, as the following chapters show, a series of developments—the Conscience Whig movement; the Free Soil party; the coalition of Democrats and antislavery men; the rise of nativism; the Preston Brooks assault; the factional disputes within the Republican party—sifted out Sumner's rivals and left him the unchallenged spokesman of his own state. The historical philosopher who could explain Sumner's triumph in terms of the interaction of forces, whether of economics, society, or personality, would have to be both daring and wise—and even then, perhaps, he might overlook the part that accident plays in selecting leaders.

I have concluded my book with 1861, when Sumner and his party finally attained power. These chapters form a self-contained unit. The uses to which Sumner and his associates put their power during the stormy Civil War and Reconstruction periods I expect to make the subject of a companion volume at a not too distant date.

A few words need to be added about the documentation of this book. Since, as Edward H. O'Neill correctly observed, Sumner's previous biographers [4] generally omitted "all facts and inferences that might adversely affect the character of their hero," I have placed little reliance upon earlier works, but have tried, wherever possible, to work with the original manuscript sources. I have, however, found a great deal of useful material in the standard four-volume *Memoir and Letters of Charles Sumner,* by Edward Lillie Pierce, his authorized biographer.[5]

Because Sumner's *Works* represent what the senator in the 1870's wished he had said, rather than what he actually said in earlier years, I have usually referred to the manuscripts or to the earliest pamphlet editions of his speeches.

A few liberties have been taken with some of the quotations in this book. Where Sumner, in haste, used "Comm[ttee]," "Gov[t]," "&," etc., I have spelled the words out. For easier reading I have also transposed the persons of a few quotations. Where Sumner

[4] Previous biographies of Sumner include: D. A. Harsha: *The Life of Charles Sumner . . .* (New York: Dayton and Burdick; 1856); Jeremiah and J. D. Chaplin: *Life of Charles Sumner* (Boston: D. Lothrop & Co.; 1874); C. Edwards Lester: *Life and Public Services of Charles Sumner* (New York: United States Publishing Company; 1874); Elias Nason: *The Life and Times of Charles Sumner* (Boston: B. B. Russell; 1874); Anna Laurens Dawes: *Charles Sumner* (New York: Dodd, Mead & Co.; 1892); Archibald H. Grimke: *The Life of Charles Sumner . . .* (New York: Funk & Wagnalls Co.; 1892); Moorfield Storey: *Charles Sumner* (Boston: Houghton Mifflin Co.; 1900); George H. Haynes: *Charles Sumner* (Philadelphia: George W. Jacobs & Co.; 1909); and Walter G. Shotwell: *Life of Charles Sumner* (New York: Thomas Y. Crowell Company; 1910). A biographical essay written by Carl Schurz in the 1890's has recently been published: Arthur Reed Hogue (ed.): *Charles Sumner: An Essay by Carl Schurz* (Urbana: University of Illnois Press; 1951). For a critical appraisal of these and other writings, see Louis Ruchames: "Charles Sumner and American Historiography," *Journal of Negro History,* XXXVIII (1953), 139–60.

[5] Boston: Roberts Brothers; 1878–93. Hereafter cited as Pierce.

may have written "my condition," I have said "his condition." I have also dispensed with most initial and terminal ellipses for quoted materials. Instead of writing: ". . . he was right. . . ." I have simply said: "He was right." In no case, of course, have I tampered with the meaning of any quoted passage.

My footnotes are designed to give sources for specific statements and quotations, not to offer a general bibliography of pre-Civil War history, a task that would require a volume at least as long as the present one. Consequently these notes—though surely more than ample for most readers—do not adequately reflect my indebtedness to scholars who have written on nineteenth-century American history. For nearly every topic discussed in this book I could have referred to the works of Avery O. Craven, Oscar Handlin, Allan Nevins, Roy F. Nichols, James G. Randall, and others as excellent secondary sources. Fortunately the recent publication of the admirable *Harvard Guide to American History* [6] makes such citations here supererogatory.

[6] Edited by Oscar Handlin, et al., Cambridge: Harvard University Press; 1954.

CHAPTER I

A Natural Coldness

"THESE jottings are made for friendly eyes," the newly elected senator from Massachusetts wrote as a postscript to his autobiography, "to be used more or less, or not at all, as shall be thought best." [1] The senatorial contest of 1851 had been the most embittered and prolonged in Massachusetts history, and Charles Sumner wished to repel charges that he was a political nonentity, a mere rhetorician elected through an unholy and corrupt coalition. As his autobiographical notes had this practical purpose, they naturally were not modest, and Sumner's old friend and former Harvard professor, John Gorham Palfrey, to whom he entrusted them, was able to work them into a laudatory newspaper sketch of the new antislavery senator as a statesman whose name would illuminate "the historical page of the triumphs of Freedom in the nineteenth century." [2] Touched by Palfrey's words, which, in fact, merely echoed his own, Sumner was delighted by "that beautiful sketch" of his career. "I felt a throb of gratitude to you," he wrote Palfrey, "but a deep feeling also of my own unworthiness. . . . As a composition your article is all that could be desired. As a token of friendship more than I deserve." [3]

[1] Sumner's MS. autobiography [May 1851], John Gorham Palfrey MSS.

[2] Boston *Commonwealth*, May 16, 1851. Unless otherwise expressly indicated, all newspaper references are to daily editions.

[3] Sumner to Palfrey [May 1851], Palfrey MSS.

• 1 •

Sumner's autobiographical jottings, like Palfrey's published tribute to him, were revealingly reticent. The new Massachusetts senator stated that he had been born in Boston on January 6, 1811, but he had nothing else to say about his boyhood. Neither here nor at any other time did he look back to the good old days when Boston was a compact town of only 40,000 inhabitants, most of whom knew each other by sight. He never told anecdotes of playing in the mud flats of Back Bay, where now some of the proudest houses in Boston rise. He had no tales of wandering on the wharves, thronged with sailing ships manned by rough-voiced sailors shouting in unknown tongues. He never remembered roaming through the markets, sniffing the exotic aroma of tea from the Orient, tasting figs from Smyrna, and sampling barrels of West Indies molasses through straws adeptly inserted through the bungholes. He had no recollections of snowball fights on the Common or of sledding down Beacon Hill across the main thoroughfare of Washington Street in defiance of all traffic. Sumner never had the feeling of his contemporary, Edward Everett Hale, that Boston "was a good place in which to be born, and a good place in which to grow to manhood." [4]

Sumner's autobiography was equally silent on his genealogy. Though he knew that New Englanders had an almost Oriental reverence for their ancestors and delighted in tracing family lineages through assorted Patiences, Ashabels, and Eliphalets back to the founders of Massachusetts Bay Colony, the newly elected senator made no effort to exploit the fact that on both sides of his family he could claim industrious and God-fearing forebears who had settled in New England in the early 1630's. He did not mention that his mother's grandfather had been an extensive landholder, the surveyor of Hanover, in Plymouth County, a town selectman, a member of the Revolutionary Committee on Public Safety, and later a state representative, or that his maternal grandmother was a descendant of Governor William Bradford, of Plymouth.[5] Nor did he refer to the career of his

[4] Hale: *A New England Boyhood* (New York: Cassell Publishing Company; 1893), p. v.

[5] John S. Barry: *A Historical Sketch of the Town of Hanover, Mass., with Family Genealogies* (Boston: Samuel G. Drake; 1853), pp. 319–35. Barry as-

paternal grandfather, Major Job Sumner, who quit his Harvard classes to fight under General Washington and after the Revolution served as United States commissioner to settle the accounts between the Confederation and Georgia.[6]

Any temptation Sumner may have had to proclaim himself the heir of the Puritans in politics was curbed by his knowledge that his father had been born out of wedlock.[7] Inbred, provincial Boston, where such scandals were never forgotten, would be all too likely to rake up the gossip about the dashing Major Sumner's failure to marry Esther Holmes, by whom he begat his one son. Remembering the grandson's fondness for oppressed races, Boston maiden aunts speculated—without any evidence whatever—that the mysterious Esther had been "partly of negro or Indian blood." [8] Prudently the new senator preferred to draw the veil over the whole subject of his genealogy: "It seems to me better to leave it all unsaid." [9]

More surprising was Sumner's silence about his parents. Of his father, Charles Pinckney Sumner, the son merely remarked that he "was a lawyer by profession . . . a person of literary taste and knowledge, of remarkable independence and sterling integrity." [1] The son's coolness reflected the fact that the father was a singularly unlovable man.[2] Presumably he had not always been so formal, so obdurately fixed in his ways. As a student at Harvard he had become a warm friend of young Joseph Story, of Salem, who inspired him to attempt verses in the stately tradi-

---

serted that Sumner's mother, Relief Jacob, was "probably of Jewish descent"; this allegation led Frank Preston Stearns (*Cambridge Sketches* [Philadelphia: J. B. Lippincott Co.; 1905], p. 180) to identify "the Hebrew element in Sumner's nature; the inflexibility of purpose, the absolute self-devotion, and even the prophetic forecast." Such a theory of inherited racial traits is, of course, highly unscientific. But, in any case, the Jewish strain in Sumner's ancestry is dubious. At no point in his career, when virtually every other possible weapon was used against him, were anti-Semitic charges raised.

6 On Job Sumner see Pierce, I, 3–10; Records of the Harvard College Faculty, III, 258, 265; IV, 6, 60; sundry commissions and clippings in C. P. Sumner MSS. On the Sumner genealogy as a whole see William Sumner Appleton: *Record of the Descendants of William Sumner of Dorchester, Mass., 1636* (Boston; 1879).

7 Ibid., p. 176.

8 Robert Carter to E. L. Pierce, Dec. 1, 1877, E. L. Pierce MSS.

9 Sumner's autobiography, Palfrey MSS. Cf. Sumner to George Sumner, July 15, 1842, Sumner MSS.

1 Sumner's autobiography, Palfrey MSS.

2 Pierce, I, 11–30; James Spear Loring: *The Hundred Boston Orators* (2nd ed.; Boston: John P. Jewett and Company; 1853), pp. 325–33.

tion of Alexander Pope's rhymed couplets. The friendship did not expire with college days, and in florid fashion Sumner claimed that he treasured Story's frequent letters as "truly the *balsam of friendship*, . . . infinitely more sacred than that which bedewed the hand of laughterloving *Venus*, when wounded by the sacrilegious shaft of *Diomed*." Under Story's influence he became an ardent Jeffersonian, at a time when only Federalism was respectable in Massachusetts, and he even talked of editing a party newspaper in Boston.[3] But, by the time Charles Sumner was born, his father's feeble fires of rebellion had burned low. "I have now passed more than half the age of man," he wrote in 1811, at the age of thirty-five, "and the ambition of youth is in me now checked by the . . . cautious, and sober thoughts of age." The insecurity of his clouded birth and impoverished childhood, his comparative failure in his law practice, and his financial worries over his growing family he concealed behind an outward front of stiff and stilted formality. Long after the style had changed, he, like Major Thomas Melville, continued to wear a tricornered hat, and he retained to his death the punctilious eighteenth-century etiquette of saluting acquaintances upon the streets by "bowing low, touching his mouth with his hand, and waving it back to his side." His family rarely, if ever, saw him smile.[4]

His wife brought little more warmth to the Sumner household. Tall and stately, with a smooth olive complexion and lustrous brown eyes, Relief Jacob had been a twenty-five-year-old seamstress when she married, and she carried some of her spinster ways into her married life. She did not know how to express affection; not until after her death did Charles learn that she had always cherished a lock of his baby hair. Even her friends remarked that she was "distant" or that she had "the old-school dignity of manner," and she impressed on them her "evident superiority of mind." [5]

Doubtless it was the memory of his own cheerless home

[3] C. P. Sumner: *The Compass. A Poetical Performance at the Literary Exhibition in September, M,DCC,XCV, at Harvard University* (Boston: William Spotswood; 1795); C. P. Sumner to Story [c. 1797], C. P. Sumner MSS.

[4] C. P. Sumner to Thomas Kittera, Aug. 12, 1811, MS., Hist. Soc. of Penn.; Pierce, I, 30.

[5] A. W. N. Howard to Sumner, June 19, 1866, Sumner MSS.; Nason: *Sumner*, pp. 311–12; Boston *Traveller*, Apr. 21, 1874.

that made young Sumner, when a student at Harvard, describe "The present character of the Inhabitants of New England" as one of sobriety, industry, moral purity—and "a natural coldness." [6] The very house in which he was born, on Bartolph (now Irving) Street, was "respectable, and yet only above being humble." Like the two later homes the Sumners occupied on Hancock Street, it lay north of that imaginary line that, as true Bostonians used to say, divided the "bob" from the "nabob" side of Beacon Hill. When Charles was a boy, his father's income was only about $1,000 a year, and only Mrs. Sumner's frugality kept the family from actual want. She could afford only iron knives and forks for tableware, and she sent Charles to school wearing coarse, chunky shoes and cheap sky-blue satinet clothes, "never a nice fitting or handsomely appearing suit." [7]

Sumner's autobiography ignored not merely his undemonstrative parents, but also his brothers and sisters. He himself was a twin; he and his sister Matilda had been premature babies, weighing only three and one-half pounds each, who were scarcely expected to survive. Giving the daughter to a nurse's care, Mrs. Sumner took the boy to feed at breast. Her decision to separate the two children had lasting consequences; there never grew up between Charles and Matilda that closeness of feeling that so often characterizes twins. Though Matilda lived to the age of twenty-one, Charles almost never mentioned her in any of his voluminous letters. When she died, he coolly recalled the anecdote of the Persian matron, who, told by her monarch that she could "save from death *one* of her family and relatives," chose to sacrifice husband and children in order to save her old and decrepit father, "saying that another husband and other children she might have, *but another father never*." [8]

If Sumner hoped that Matilda's death would strengthen his father's affection for him, he was mistaken; there were too many

[6] MS. essay dated June 19, 1830, Harvard Univ. Archives.

[7] E. Buckingham to Pierce, Nov. 27, 1874, Pierce MSS.; Allan Chamberlain: *Beacon Hill: Its Ancient Pastures and Early Mansions* (Boston: Houghton Mifflin Co.; 1925), p. 42; Stearns: *Cambridge Sketches*, p. 182. Sumner indignantly denied reports that he had been "born in affluence and bred in elegance." See his marginal annotations on *Speech of Gerrit Smith (to His Neighbors) in Peterboro, N.Y., June 22d 1872*, in Smith MSS.

[8] Pierce, I, 113.

other rivals in the house. By 1827 Mrs. Sumner had produced nine children [9]—five boys and four girls—and through her skill as a mother and her patience as a nurse she brought them all past the age of adolescence. Toward his younger sisters, born many years after himself, Charles developed a real, if sometimes possessive, affection, but he felt his brothers, so much nearer his own age, as competitors. They seemed to have an easier time with his parents, and not so much was demanded of them. The oldest son, on the other hand, bearing the father's own name, was expected to do the impossible. "Charles," the father formally admonished him, "upon your discretion and good deportment, the happiness of my life will in no trifling measure depend." [1]

Earnestly Charles tried to gain his parents' love by living up to their expectations. But it seemed unfair that he should have to earn affection while it appeared to be heaped undeservingly to Albert and George, Henry and Horace. It was no wonder that Charles early came to find *King Lear* the most satisfying of Shakespeare's plays, for he could identify himself with Cordelia. Throughout his life his most frequently used quotation was the reproach of the mad king, which should have been directed against the faithless and undeserving Goneril and Regan, but instead fell upon the head of the inarticulate Cordelia: "Nothing will come of nothing."

• 2 •

There was only one way in which Charles seemed able to win his father's esteem. He was not a handsome boy, or even a prepossessing one. Growing too rapidly, he had faulty muscular coordination and was poor at all sports except swimming. Boys laughed at him as "Gawky Sumner" and left him out of their play.[2] Shy and lonesome, Charles made up for these defects by becoming bookish. Both at the private school conducted by one of his aunts in the upper floor of the Sumner house and then at the neighborhood public school, teachers found Charles a quiet,

[9] For a list of the children, together with dates of birth and death, see Appleton: *Record of the Descendants of William Sumner*, p. 176.

[1] Aug. 10, 1828, copy, C. P. Sumner MSS.

[2] Stearns: *Cambridge Sketches*, p. 181.

intelligent lad.[3] Their teaching did not interest him, for he wanted to have a classical education like his father's and to understand the Latin phrases with which his parent elegantly larded his conversation. He listened eagerly to the older boys in the neighborhood who attended the Boston Latin School, and, saving up his coppers, he bought the Latin grammar and Liber Primus used in the first class. Without his parents' knowledge, he studied them at home, after school hours, and "came down to his father one morning as he was shaving, and astonished him by reciting and reading Latin."[4] His father, who had intended for Charles to receive only a brief English education, so that he could get to work earlier and help support the family, was touched, and, in August 1821, sent him to the Latin School.

Some of the boys who attended the Boston Public Latin School chafed at the meager educational fare provided by Benjamin Apthorp Gould and his assistants, and were unhappy at having "to commit to memory the uninteresting and unintelligible rules, exceptions, notes, and remarks, of which the school grammar was full,"[5] but Sumner rejoiced in this wonderful opportunity to become a learned man like his father, and for the five years of the course he seems to have been perfectly happy. The formidable list of required Latin classics, including Caesar, Cicero, Tacitus, Sallust, Vergil, and Horace, and the less extensive readings in Greek he managed without difficulty; indeed, he memorized great stretches of them, which he could quote, with or without provocation, to the end of his life. Repeatedly he won prizes for his translations, his Latin hexameters, and other exercises.[6]

At the same time he further emulated his father by becom-

[3] A modern psychologist, on the basis of rather dubious evidence, concludes that Sumner had an I.Q. of between 140 and 145. Catherine Morris Cox: *The Early Mental Traits of Three Hundred Geniuses* (Vol. II of *Genetic Studies of Genius*, ed. by Lewis M. Terman), pp. 731–2.

[4] Richard Henry Dana, Jr., Journal, Sept. 1854, Dana MSS.

[5] Edward Everett Hale (ed.): *James Freeman Clarke: Autobiography, Diary and Correspondence* (Boston: Houghton Mifflin Co.; 1891), p. 26.

[6] Pauline Holmes: *A Tercentenary History of the Boston Public Latin School, 1635–1935* ("Harvard Studies in Education," Vol. XXV; Cambridge: Harvard University Press; 1935), pp. 192, 194, 269–71. For a student debate in which Sumner participated see John O. Sargent, Diary, Mar. 11, 1826, MS., Harvard Univ. Archives.

ing an "ardent student of *history*," rising often before daybreak to read Hume and Gibbon. Imitating his father's antiquarian passion for meticulously tabulating events that had happened on the same day in the past, Charles, at the age of fourteen, drew up an eighty-six-page chronological compendium of English history, including all the kings and their dates:

799 EGBERT succeds [*sic*] to the Kingdom of Wessex the most powerful of the Heptarchy and unites all the kingdoms together and
827 becomes the first king of England.
835 The Danes land in England but are defeated at Hangesdown
838 Egbert dies and is succeeded by ETHELWOLF who dies, and divided his
857 kingdom between his two sons. . . .[7]

The boy's real chance to impress his father, however, came during his final year at the Latin School. With schoolboy curiosity he went to hear Daniel Webster deliver an oration upon the recent deaths of Thomas Jefferson and John Adams. The hall was packed, and Charles could not see the speaker. Taking advantage of his size, the spindly youth dived to the floor and began working his way on his hands and knees to the front of the auditorium. He emerged just as Webster, in tribute to Jefferson, pronounced: "*Felix, non vitae tantum claritate, sed etiam opportunitate mortis.*" "Then I felt proud," Charles later recalled, "for I understood the sentence; and I felt that I too belonged to the brotherhood of scholars." Hurrying home, he told his father of Webster's quotation, and the elder Sumner went to his shelves and checked in the *Agricola* of Tacitus to see if the boy had remembered it accurately. "We were both pleased to find that I had," Charles remembered, even after many years. "He showed the words to me then, in their original application." [8]

Despite the son's obvious eagerness for learning, Charles Pinckney Sumner did not originally plan to send him to college. Even after he had given up his law practice in 1819 to accept slightly more remunerative employment as deputy sheriff of Suffolk County, he felt too poor to send the boy to Harvard. Besides,

[7] Sumner's autobiography, Palfrey MSS.; Julia Hastings to Pierce, Oct. 19, 1874, Pierce MSS.; "A chronological Compendium of English History by Charles Sumner. Copy-right secured Boston MDCCXXV. 1825," Sumner MSS.

[8] Boston *Beacon*, Jan. 26, 1878.

he thought, "The life of a scholar would be too sedentary and inactive for him." Perhaps remembering Major Job Sumner's career, he encouraged Charles to think of a military education, and planned to enroll him as a student proctor in Captain Alden Partridge's "American Literary, Scientific, and Military Academy" at Middletown, Connecticut.[9]

But, on September 6, 1826, a sudden change occurred in the Sumner fortunes. Governor Levi Lincoln appointed Charles Pinckney Sumner sheriff of Suffolk County, which included Boston. It was a lucrative job—at least, more so than any Sumner had ever held—and, on the income of about $2,000 a year, the new sheriff felt able to sell his crowded house on Bartolph Street and rent a larger establishment on Hancock Street. In 1829 he purchased a thirteen-room, three-story house at No. 20 Hancock Street, which became the family's permanent residence. The new sheriff impressively donned his official uniform, which consisted of a tricornered hat, a blue coat with military facings, yellow breeches, white tipped boots, and a neat side sword, and, rejoicing in his unexpected elegance and wealth, even gave dinners twice a year to the governor and judges of the Commonwealth.[1]

His new position made it possible for C. P. Sumner to send his oldest son to college. Confused by the abrupt change, and remembering his father's earlier, repeated injunctions that he must not become a burden on the family finances, Charles continued for a few days to declare that he really would prefer a free appointment to the United States Military Academy at West Point to an expensive education at Cambridge, but his father, in September 1826, enrolled him at Harvard. To Governor Lincoln, his "greatest earthly benefactor," the sheriff gave profuse thanks for making it possible for Charles to follow the steps of his father and grandfather: "Without your favor I should probably not have sent a son to college or emerged from that humility of station from which at the age of forty nine you saw fit to draw me." [2]

[9] Pierce, I, 43.

[1] Between 1831 and 1838 the sheriff's fees totaled $16,745.78. Notarized statements, C. P. Sumner MSS. Edwin Coolidge to Sumner, Mar. 26, 1867, Sumner MSS.

[2] Pierce, I, 43–4; C. P. Sumner to Levi Lincoln, Jan. 21, 1834, copy, C. P. Sumner MSS.

• 3 •

Entering Harvard College marked no decided break in Charles Sumner's life. His father sent him to Cambridge with a Polonius-like letter: "Preserve therefore a good character: associate with those who have it: for those who have it are commonly the greatest proficients in literature and science, and will be not only patient but even gratified with your company. Shun those who have no good character of their own; they will not respect it in you. . . . " etc., etc., for pages and pages.[3] Every Sunday he required Charles to return to Hancock Street and give a report on the week's happenings at college. Sheriff Sumner kept a close watch upon his son's expenses, which ran to $177.86 for room, board, and fees during his first year at Harvard—almost precisely what the college catalogue stipulated as minimal—and he always seemed to know when Charles cut classes. Though by modern standards the boy's record of only three absences out of 580 classes, recitations, and chapel exercises during his first year seems remarkably perfect, his father grimly noted on his report card: "It is of little avail to have expensive and learned professorships established at college if a scholar does not devote his whole time to the duties prescribed." [4]

Even without his father's admonitions Charles could not have become lost at Harvard. The great majority of the 199 undergraduates in 1826 were New England youths like himself, many of them acquaintances from his Boston Latin School days. Certainly there was nothing in the curriculum to confuse him or any of the other thirty-five members of the freshman class. Their schedule was simple and unvarying. Rising for prayers before seven, they had a recitation in Greek and Latin before breakfast, which was at 8:30; their morning recitations in algebra and geometry were followed by dinner at one o'clock; Greek and Latin again occupied them until evening prayers and tea. On Saturdays declamations were substituted for mathematics, and the boys got the afternoon off. If the program was scarcely designed

[3] C. P. Sumner to Charles Sumner [1826], copy, C. P. Sumner MSS.

[4] Receipted bills, Sumner College Memorial Scrapbook, Harvard Univ. Archives; Nason: *Sumner*, pp. 34–5; printed statements of class attendance, 1826–7, Sumner College Memorial Scrapbook. Sumner's expenses reached their maximum, $226.73, during his junior year.

to inspire, neither did it perplex. There was, in fact, a kind of businesslike monotony about the whole proceeding. "No attempt was made to interest us in our studies," remembered James Freeman Clarke, who was in the class ahead of Sumner's. "We were expected to wade through Homer as though the Iliad were a bog, and it was our duty to get along at such a rate *per diem.*" [5]

Sumner, to his own considerable disappointment, proved only a moderately competent student. The Livy and Horace and the smattering of Greek which the learned Professor J. S. Popkin required him to read he could manage easily; any boy trained at Gould's Latin School found these assignments "simply a dull school exercise." But, for mathematics, which made up such a large part of the curriculum, he, like his father, had no aptitude whatever. Nobody tried to explain to him that these studies had any interest or importance; no tutor in conic sections ever suggested "that these were the curves in which the planets and comets moved, and that by learning their laws we were able to determine, a thousand years beforehand, an eclipse of the sun or an occultation of Jupiter." Failing to grasp the first principles of mathematics, Sumner fell far behind as the course progressed. Bored, he left the pages of his algebra text uncut and committed by rote to memory the solutions to enough problems to pass the examinations. In succeeding years, as his class progressed under its rigidly prescribed curriculum to more advanced mathematical studies, Sumner learned even less from his teachers. Once to a professor who pursued him with questions, he replied candidly: "I don't know; you know I don't pretend to know any thing about mathematics." "Sumner!" exclaimed the teacher. "Mathematics! mathematics! Don't you know the difference? This is not mathematics. This is *Physics.*" [6]

It is no wonder that Sumner's standing in his classes was only respectable [7] and that he graduated with no feeling of having undergone an exciting intellectual experience. In his four

[5] *A Catalogue of the Officers and Students of the School in Cambridge, Massachusetts. September,* 1826 (Cambridge: University Press; 1826); Hal Bridges: *Iron Millionaire: Life of Charlemagne Tower* (Philadelphia: University of Pennsylvania Press; 1952), p. 13; Hale (ed.): *James Freeman Clarke,* p. 36.

[6] Hale: *A New England Boyhood,* p. 222; Pierce, I, 47–8.

[7] In his class rank lists (MS., Harvard Univ. Archives), which totaled the grades students received in all subjects, Sumner was never higher than fifteenth or lower than twenty-seventh in a class of about forty students.

years at Cambridge only the occasional lectures of George Ticknor on French and Spanish literature and the sound advice of Edward Tyrell Channing on rhetoric seem to have made any impression on him. If Harvard was in what its historian has called its Augustan Age in these last years of the Presidency of John Thornton Kirkland, Sumner was unaware of it, nor did the coming of a new President, Josiah Quincy, during his senior year immediately raise educational standards. "I am not aware that *any one single thing* is well taught to the Undergraduates of Harvard College," Sumner reflected with some bitterness a few years after he graduated. "Certainly I left it without knowing anything." [8]

Standing well below the first third of his class, Sumner was not elected to Phi Beta Kappa, and he was given such an insignificant part in the 1830 commencement exercises that he wished to decline it. Only firm pressure from his father compelled him to participate, along with three other undistinguished members of the graduating class, in what was called a "conference" on "The Roman Ceremonies, the System of the Druids, the Religion of the Hindoos, and the Superstitions of the American Indians." When his turn came, Sumner, defying all that Professor Channing had taught him about simplicity of rhetoric, announced that the Indians acknowledge "one Supreme Intelligence, who stretcheth forth the Heavens alone and spreadeth abroad the earth by himself—who binds the sweet influences of the Pleiades and looses the bands of Orion"—and so forth for quite a while. His long-suffering auditors, who endured more than six hours of undergraduate oratory that day, did not think Sumner's performance distinguished.[9]

Despite the uninspiring instruction and his inglorious record, Sumner, on the whole, found his Harvard years among the most enjoyable of his life. Though bound by the rigid curriculum and watched by the paternal eye of Sheriff Sumner, he began for

[8] George Ticknor to C. P. Sumner, July 7 [1828], Sumner MSS.; Samuel Eliot Morison, *Three Centuries of Harvard, 1636–1936* (Cambridge: Harvard University Press; 1936), Chaps. IX–XI; Sumner to Joseph Story, Sept. 24, 1839, Sumner MSS.

[9] Sumner's speech, Aug. 25, 1830, MS., Harvard Univ. Archives; "Order of Exercises for Commencement," Aug. 25, 1830, Sumner College Memorial Scrapbook; *Proceedings of the Massachusetts Historical Society*, V (2 ser., 1889–90), 202. Hereafter these *Proceedings* are cited as *MHSP*.

the first time to lead a life of his own. Merely to put on the undergraduate uniform of black-mixed coat and pantaloons ("By black-mixed," the regulations carefully specified, "is understood, black with a mixture of not more than one twentieth, nor less than one twenty-fifth part of white."), with "neck-cloth," hat, shoes, and even buttons of prescribed shape and color,[1] was to commence a new existence in which his family had no share.

He found independence giddily exhilarating and, in his junior year, even staged a private rebellion against the college authorities of a sort he had never had the audacity to attempt at home. Defying the college statutes that undergraduates must wear waistcoats of either "black-mixed" or white, he, perhaps in emulation of Daniel Webster's fancy senatorial costume, sported a vest of buff color. Summoned before the Parietal Board of college professors and tutors who dealt with such heinous infractions of the rules, Sumner coolly denied that the waistcoat was illegal; it "might need the manipulations of a laundress, but it was worn for the lawful color." Giving Sumner warning, the Parietal Board dismissed him, only to learn a few days later that he was still wearing the offending garment. After several additional hearings, during which the board entered upon Sumner's record an "admonition for illegal dress," the professors, wearied by Sumner's stubborn unwillingness to admit that he could be wrong, or perhaps impressed by his ability to argue, in the name of morality and justice, that buff was white, relented and voted "that hereafter Mr. Sumner's vest be considered by this Board white." [2]

Such moments of rebellion in Sumner's college career were few, for most of his days were happy. If he learned little from his teachers, he had the privilege of browsing independently in

[1] *Statutes and Laws of the University in Cambridge, Massachusetts* (Cambridge: University Press; 1826), p. 25.

[2] Boston *Commonwealth*, Feb. 18, 1871; printed statement of class attendance, 1828–9, Sumner College Memorial Scrapbook. This bit of bravado on Sumner's part may have been more of a joke than anything else, for the rest of his college record is remarkably free from infractions of discipline. Aside from being admonished for too frequent absence from public worship and for causing excessive noise on his velocipede (Harvard Faculty Records, XI, 20), he was not otherwise disciplined during four years of college. Miss Eleanor Tilton (*Amiable Autocrat: A Biography of Dr. Oliver Wendell Holmes* [New York: Henry Schuman; 1947], p. 34) errs in stating that Charles Sumner was punished for attending the theater; the offending party was T. H. Sumner, and the punishment was inflicted six months before Charles entered college.

the Harvard Library. During his freshman year he borrowed more books than any other student in his class, books that had little relation to the dull curriculum, but included *Don Quixote*, many of Scott's novels, much of Washington Irving, and some miscellaneous history. During the next three years he continued to read assiduously, becoming especially fond of early English poetry, great stretches of which he committed to memory.[3]

His classmates he found almost as instructive as his books. He appears to have had no friends among the gay, charming Southerners who attended Harvard.[4] Nor did he associate much with the athletes, who performed gymnastic feats in the Delta. Sumner's own physical exertions were confined to his weekly walks into Boston, an occasional attempt at fencing, and an improbable affection for his velocipede, "a heavy, bone-breaking machine, moved not by pedals but by thrusting the feet against the ground," on which, at the expense of a pair of shoe soles, he could race the stagecoach along Massachusetts Avenue.[5] Instead, he found more to his liking the studious New Englanders who were destined to lead their region for the next decade. Sumner probably saw little of Ralph Waldo Emerson, who was listed as a "resident graduate" during his freshman year, but Cornelius C. Felton and Edmund Quincy among the "Senior Sophisters," George S. Hillard and Robert C. Winthrop among the "Junior Sophisters," and Oliver Wendell Holmes, Benjamin R. Curtis, and James Freeman Clarke among the sophomores were to play major roles in his later career, as were John Lothrop Motley and Wendell Phillips, who entered as freshmen in 1827.

Sumner picked his particular "chums," however, from the members of his own Harvard class. Jonathan F. Stearns, of Bedford, whose grandfather had taught Sumner's father, Charlemagne Tower, of Paris, N.Y., John W. Browne, of Salem, and Thomas Hopkinson, of New Sharon, Maine, became the first

[3] Harvard College Library Charge Books, 1826–7, pp. 17, 27; *id.*, 1827–8, p. 34; *id.*, 1828–9, pp. 56–8, 82; *id.*, 1829–30, p. 64. Cf. Sumner's "Common-place Book," Dec. 17, 1829, Harvard Univ. Archives.

[4] There is no reference to Sumner in Arthur H. Cole (ed.): *Charleston Goes to Harvard: The Diary of a Harvard Student of 1831* (Cambridge: Harvard University Press; 1940).

[5] Petition to Dr. Charles Follen, signed by Sumner and many other members of the junior and sophomore classes [Dec. 17, 1827], Harvard College Papers, II, 2 ser., 163; James Kendall Hosmer: *The Last Leaf . . .* (New York: The Knickerbocker Press; 1912), pp. 19–22.

real friends he had ever had, and he learned from them that all social intercourse was not necessarily conducted with the gloomy formality that prevailed in the house on Hancock Street. Secure in the relaxed, affectionate company of these classmates, where there was no moody father or rival brother to pounce upon every careless word or to capitalize upon every failing, Sumner found that he had a hitherto undiscovered talent, conversation.

In fact, he commenced a career, destined to continue for more than half a century, as one of the greatest talkers in American history. Enthusiastically and with relentless persistence, he talked so much that his friends labeled him the "Chatterbox." In "the Nine," a harmless secret society that he and his closest friends formed, he discoursed on English universities, on the "Old English Writers," and like topics. In the Hasty Pudding Club, to which he was elected in his junior year, he was also loquacious, using, on one occasion, "not only the formidable engine of legal argument, but the two edged sword of satire, the poisoned darts of irony, and the barbed shafts of ridicule" in a mock trial of that "notorious felon alias Mr. Blackboard." [6] On an extended walking trip that he and three classmates undertook in the summer of his junior year, tramping across Massachusetts and on to Lake Champlain, he talked, laughed, sang, and talked some more, for nearly three uninterrupted weeks.[7] In the fortnightly junior and senior classes in declamation, held under Professor Channing's frosty eye, he learned to talk in public. Overcoming adolescent squeakiness by letting "his voice down in his throat" and cultivating a bass sonority, he became one of the best declaimers in the class, and his efforts were marked by his "great degree of earnestness" and his "entire freedom from any effort to make a *dash.*" Sumner announced that he was devoted to "the *Divine Art*" of public speaking, and it was scarcely surprising that in one of the college exhibitions of his junior year he was given the part of the "pedantic Orator" in a Greek dialogue, with the significant lines: "For myself I confess the study of oratory—I boast to be 'a speaker of words.' . . . De-

[6] Bridges: *Iron Millionaire*, p. 16; Sumner to J. F. Stearns, Dec. 27, 1829, Sumner MSS.; Pierce, I, 55–6; Secretary's Records, Hasty Pudding Club, IX (June 26, 1829), 22–3. Cf. *id.*, IX, 1–5, 10, 38, 44.

[7] Sumner's pedestrian account of this walking trip, July 13–31, 1829, in the form of a journal is in the C. P. Sumner MSS.

mosthenes and Pericles . . . will be like stars to point out the pathway to glory and their glory will always be the object of my desire."[8]

• 4 •

"I find it hard to untie the spell that knits me so strongly to college life," Sumner wrote more than a month after President Quincy had certified him as a Bachelor of Arts of Harvard College. His four years at Cambridge had given him a mastery of Greek and Latin and a fastidiousness in grammar and style which made him consider form more important than content, and they had left him with a total ignorance of science and mathematics, a desire to live like a gentleman, and an inability to support himself. Sadly he moped about his room in Holworthy Hall until the junior class took over, "parading around, the almost 'undisputed Lords and masters' of what we Seniors a day before alone enjoyed."[9]

Sumner's predicament was not an unusual one; like other Harvard graduates who did not have private fortunes he had to choose a profession. The alternatives were neither numerous nor inviting. The Christian ministry was never a possibility. Like his father, he held vaguely Unitarian views and sometimes attended King's Chapel. Despite all the compulsory chapel sermons at Harvard, he remained "unconvinced that Christ was divinely commissioned to preach a revelation to men and that he was entrusted with the power of working miracles." When pressed, he admitted to believing "that Christ lived when and as the Gospel says—that he was more than man (viz. above all men who had as yet lived) and yet less than God." But these were not subjects on which he thought, or cared to think, much. "I am," he explained to Stearns, "without religious feeling."[1] Medicine, to one as squeamish and as totally ignorant of science as Sumner, was also out of the question as a profession. Remembering his father's uninteresting and unsuccessful legal career, Sumner

[8] Sumner to Charlemagne Tower, Nov. 4, 1830, Tower MSS.; Pierce, I, 58; Translation of Greek Dialogue [Apr. 28, 1829], Sumner College Memorial Scrapbook.

[9] Pierce, I, 80–1.

[1] Sumner to Stearns, Jan. 12, 1833, Sumner MSS.

judged that "a *mere* lawyer" must be "one of the veriest wretches in the world." "Dry items and facts, argumentative reports, and details of pleadings must incrust the mind with somewhat of their own rust." [2] For teaching school, that last resort of the liberal-arts graduate, he quickly learned, after a three weeks' trial, that he had "a natural hydrophobia." To be successful in that "harrassing [*sic*], throat-cutting, mind-dissolving" occupation, he thought, would require him to "gather up all the scraps and rags of patience at his command—ram down into the very bottom of his legs all temper and receive with the meekness of an Ultra-orthodox-Quaker all vexations, crosses, ills to which schoolmaster flesh is heir to." [3]

Sheriff Sumner posed the real difficulty in his son's choice of a career. Though a Harvard graduate, the boy was only nineteen years old, and he desperately wanted to please his dour parent. But, aside from vetoing Charles's romantic notion of leading "a life of letters" and from sourly observing that he ought not to "stand all day idle, dependent upon his Father for support," the Sheriff did nothing either to direct or to encourage his son. "He seems determined to let me shape my own course," Charles reported, with some exasperation, to Stearns; "so that if I am wise, I shall be wise for myself and if I am foolish I alone shall bear it." [4]

Lacking any direction from his father and any preference of his own, Charles decided to spend the year after his graduation at home in individual study. Enthusiastically he planned a program that would remedy the deficiencies of his Harvard training and extend his interests. "I have doomed myself for this year at least to hard labor," he wrote to a classmate. "I intend to diet on study—go to bed late and get up early and leave none of my time unemployed. I have imposed upon myself the task of reading as following—a course of Mathematics, not indeed so thorough as the Cambridge, but one which will give me all I want to know . . . Juvenal and Tacitus (without ponies) —a course of Modern History, Hallam's Middle Ages and Con-

[2] Pierce, I, 86.

[3] Sumner to Stearns, Feb. 13, 1831, Sumner MSS.; Sumner to Tower, Mar. 1, 1831, Tower MSS.

[4] C. P. James to Pierce, Jan. 7, 1877, Pierce MSS.; Sumner to Stearns, Feb. 13, and Aug. 7, 1831, Sumner MSS.

stitutional History, Roscoe's Leo and Lorenzo, Robertson's Charles V etc." "I shall," he pledged, "make labor my pleasure." [5]

This elaborate regimen, so enthusiastically begun, lasted only a month or so. For one thing, the boy had no place to study. At crowded No. 20 Hancock Street there was no privacy, and he was obliged to read in the family parlor, sitting, "like Chance amidst the little chaos around" of "children and chairs, bores and books, andirons and paper." Mathematics, when studied alone, proved no easier than in the classroom. The "*roots* of Algebra," he learned, "when obtained, are but bitter," and after only a month he reported: "I have *ef*fected but little with those *af*fected Equations—indeed I have but little *affection* for them." [6]

Eagerly he welcomed diversions. He spent hours writing long, tedious letters to his friends, so heavily encrusted with quotations from the classics that Browne begged him: "Be less lavish of your classic allusions, for so thickly was your epistle . . . bedizened with these gems that my mineralogy was all at fault —I could neither measure nor sort them." [7] In December 1830 he interrupted his study to dash off an essay on commerce for a contest sponsored by the Boston Society for the Diffusion of Useful Knowledge, and he had the honor of being summoned to the platform, on the evening the awards were announced, to receive the first prize, a set of the *Encyclopedia Americana,* from Daniel Webster himself, who called the author his "young friend."

Bored with study, Sumner for the first time began to take an interest in politics. When Sheriff Sumner entered the Antimasonic movement and publicly attacked the order, in which he had once risen to be a master Mason, as a danger to the republic, "a pillar of ice supporting a superstructure of marble," [8] Charles became an enthusiastic convert to the new party. "My *reason* has enlisted me in Anti-Masonry," he explained to Tower; "my *feelings* have nearly run away with my reason." Though he knew that a genteel Harvard graduate should keep "his mind wholly aloof from politics," it was impossible for him to do so: "My feelings, despite my reason, love them." [9]

[5] Sumner to Stearns, Sept. 28, 1830, ibid.

[6] Pierce, I, 84; Sumner to Stearns, Nov. 24, 1830, Sumner MSS.

[7] Browne to Sumner, Mar. 6, 1831, ibid.

[8] For Sheriff Sumner's many animadversions upon the masons see his manuscript notebook, titled "Miscellany," C. P. Sumner MSS.

[9] Sumner to Tower, June 10, 1831, Tower MSS.

The great disadvantage of all this disorganized activity was that it led nowhere. Sumner was, by his own admission, an ambitious young man; one of his college friends declared that he had "a pervading ambition,—not an intermittent, fitful gust of an affair, blowing a hurricane at one time, then subsiding to a calm, but a strong, steady breeze, which will bear him well on in the track of honor." [1] When he permitted himself to think that he had wasted nearly twelve months, he became the victim of "green-eyed melancholy and sickening musings." He engaged in adolescent brooding about death. "There is a most charming stillness in the grave, contrasted with the busy rolling hum above," he wrote with gloomy inappropriateness to Stearns, who was in the hospital; "no apprenticeship or long pupillage is there demanded." By May 1831 he was ready to admit defeat: "I've passed by a sorry time, progressed but little in those studies which my mind has been the whole while looking to; and enjoyed as little happiness as . . . a sensitive mind could glean from thoughts of negligences and misspent time." [2]

At last, in August, Sumner realized that he must make a choice, if only to appease his father, who stood always in the background silently disapproving his idleness. With considerable reluctance he decided to enroll in the Harvard Law School. His devotion to his new profession, however, was anything but single-minded. "I intend to give myself to the law, so as to read satisfactorily the regular and parallel courses," he explained to Tower, but he added that he intended also "to take hold of some of the classics—Greek, if I can possibly gird up my mind to the work,—to pursue historical studies,—to read Say and Stewart; all mingled with those condiments to be found in Shakespeare and the British poets." [3]

[1] Pierce, I, 83.

[2] Sumner to Tower, June 10, and May 27, 1831, Tower MSS.; Sumner to Stearns, Mar. [22], 1831, Sumner MSS.

[3] Pierce, I, 88.

CHAPTER II

You Were Meant for Boston

SUMNER's three years in the Harvard Law School, he declared later, were "the happiest of my life." Originally reluctant to study the law, he soon discovered that it was his "true profession; the one in which the mind is the most sharpened and quickened, and the duties of which, properly discharged, are most vital to the interests of the country." He promptly gave up his vague hopes for a literary career and diverted his energies, with single-minded intensity, to his new occupation. The law, he found, offered him not merely personal satisfaction and professional advancement; it also opened for him a new circle of friends and gave him an entree into the best Boston society. After only one year in law school he was certain that he had found himself. "I become more wedded to the law, as a profession, every day that I study it." [1]

• 1 •

The principal agent in this remarkable transformation was Joseph Story, the associate justice of the United States Supreme Court, who had infused new life into the Harvard Law School when he accepted the Dane professorship in 1829. Under Story's prodding, the college added John H. Ashmun to the faculty as Royall professor of law, purchased a sizable legal library, and

[1] Pierce, I, 108, 111, 117.

commenced work on a new building to house the classes and library of the reinvigorated professional school. Enrollment quickly increased. Benjamin R. Curtis, future justice of the Supreme Court, Timothy Walker, later one of the most influential lawyers in Ohio, Thomas Hopkinson, who had held the highest rank in Sumner's undergraduate class, and George S. Hillard, shortly to become Sumner's close friend and partner, were among those who flocked to Cambridge during these first years of the Story-Ashmun regime. By the time Sumner entered, in September 1831, enrollment in the law school totaled forty-two.[2]

Sumner joined the law school with doubts about his profession and reservations about Story, who, he thought, was often guilty of "mawkish sentimentality" and "bad taste." [3] But, once he heard the Dane professor lecture, all his doubts vanished. Never had Sumner encountered anybody so captivating as the little pink-faced, cherubic professor who combed his pixie-like wisp of curling blond hair on his forehead as he talked to his students. Story seemed actually interested in teaching. The sullen taciturnity of Sumner's father, the mechanical grading of his recitations by Harvard teachers had never been anything like this. Story did not ask students to repeat answers to routine questions upon the assigned text; he illuminated every line of it with a running commentary, linking together his prodigious knowledge of the law, his broad acquaintance with literature, his personal experience in the Supreme Court, and his political prejudices in an altogether hypnotic and totally convincing fashion.

Immediately Story became Sumner's hero. Sumner admired his erudition, his enthusiasm, his gaiety, his incessant and brilliant conversation, his concern for his students, which "warmed the classes with ardor in their studies." Story he thought the ideal teacher, "always ready and profuse in his instructions, anx-

[2] The best accounts of Story's life are William Wetmore Story: *Life and Letters of Joseph Story . . .* (Boston: Charles C. Little and James Brown; 1851), and Henry Steele Commager: "Joseph Story," *The Gaspar G. Bacon Lectures on the Constitution of the United States* (Boston: Boston University Press; 1953), pp. 33–94. On the Harvard Law School the standard works are Charles Warren: *History of the Harvard Law School and of Early Legal Conditions in America* (New York: Lewis Publishing Company; 1908), and *The Centennial History of the Harvard Law School, 1817–1917* (Harvard Law School Association; 1918).

[3] Sumner to Stearns, Sept. 25, 1831, Sumner MSS.

iously seeking out all the difficulties which perplexed the student and anticipating his wants, leaving no stone unturned by which the rugged paths of the law might be made smoother." Consequently the students, Sumner reported to Charlemagne Tower, "love him more than any instructor they ever had before. He treats them all as gentlemen, and is full of willingness to instruct. . . . The good scholars like him for the knowledge he distributes; the poor (if any there be), for the amenity with which he treats them and their faults." [4]

Identifying himself completely and enthusiastically with the judge, Sumner ran into the danger, common to all students of great teachers, of becoming a caricature of his professor. When Story was charmed by Fanny Kemble, the young English actress who moved Boston to flurries of tears, Sumner, in whom anything artistic was an acquired taste, promptly dropped his law studies to attend the theater. If Story was impressed by the earnest, learned German expatriate, Francis Lieber, to whom he introduced Sumner, his student promptly annexed Lieber as an admired friend, whose works he humbly praised and whose career he sought to forward by soliciting for him honorary degrees from Harvard, contracts with publishers, and puffs in the Boston newspapers. Lieber asked Sumner to serve as "part friend, part agent" for him in Boston, but the young lawyer promptly replied: "I will be *all* friend, and do for you as well as I can." Pleased by such adulation, Lieber told his wife: "Sumner, is one of the finest men I know of; he . . . studies hard and *deep*, and is withal enthusiastically devoted to me. He verily loves me." [5]

For Sumner, who had for so many years sought but never secured his father's approbation, winning Story's approval became a chief goal in life. The professor had merely to suggest some reading, to hint of some research, and Sumner dashed out

[4] *American Jurist,* XIII (Jan. 1835), 114; Pierce, I, 112.

[5] Sumner to Lieber, June 28, Aug. 25, and June 8, 1835, Sumner MSS.; Lieber to Matilda Lieber, Aug. 12, 1837, Lieber MSS. Sumner wrote the article praising Lieber in the Boston *Advertiser,* Aug. 24, 1835. Sumner met Lieber in Washington in 1834. For carefully documented accounts of his friendship with Lieber see Frank Freidel: "Francis Lieber, Charles Sumner, and Slavery," *Journal of Southern History,* IX (Feb. 1943), 75–93; and Freidel: *Francis Lieber: Nineteenth Century Liberal* (Baton Rouge: Louisiana State University Press; 1947), pp. 109–10, 141–2, 201–2, and *passim.*

to do it. As Story thought that a student should not parrot textbooks, but should investigate legal precedents for himself, Sumner dug assiduously in the law library. "In my studies," he reported proudly, "[I] never relied upon the textbooks, but went to the original sources, read all the authorities and references, whether treatises or decided cases—made myself acquainted more or less, with every work of the common law, from the Year Books in uncouth Norman down to the latest reports—could go into the Law Library of many thousand volumes, and, if every volume was in its place, could find any volume desired in the dark." As Story thought lawyers should be acquainted not merely with cases, but with the broad literature of the law, Sumner tried to learn "the names of all the authors who have treated on the different branches of the law, their various degrees of merit, and how to consult them"; he read and digested the most important books, paid less attention to slighter works, and gave "a transient glance along the pages of others, like a dog drinking at the Nile as he runs." [6]

When Story announced that a good lawyer must also be broadly versed in literature, Sumner promptly agreed: "A lawyer must know every thing. He must know law, history, philosophy, human nature; and . . . he must drink of all the springs of literature." His lawyer's commonplace book he filled not merely with usable quotations from the fathers of the common law, but with extracts from St. Augustine, Thomas Gray, Leibnitz, Thomas Burton, Edmund Burke, and Alexander Pope. Sometimes there seemed to be so much work ahead that his eyes would be blinded with reading. "Volumes upon volumes are to be mastered, of the niceties of the law," he explained to Tower; "and the whole circle of literature and science and history must be compassed. For what is a lawyer, brim-full, though his head may be, with statutes and precedents and points, if he lacks that elegance and taste which will set off his own mind and infuse itself into every thing which passed through it." So diligently did Sumner set himself to studying that his friends became seriously concerned about his health, and his father was obliged to enter one of his stately reproaches: "Charles, while you study the law,

[6] Sumner's autobiography, Palfrey MSS.; *American Jurist*, XIII (Apr. 1835), 388–9.

be not too discursive; study your prescribed course well. That is enough to make you a sound lawyer. You may bewilder your mind by taking too wide a range." But, Sumner, now under an influence more potent and more agreeable than his father's, continued avidly to read.[7]

In a day when the requirements of the Harvard Law School were not notably stringent, Sumner's exertions were naturally considered remarkable. Although his classes recited but three times a week when Story was away in Washington and but once a day even when Story was in Cambridge, and although there were no fixed standards of attendance and no written examinations, Sumner worked as though "every moment, like a filing of gold, ought to be saved." In his room in Divinity Hall, the most secluded of the college buildings, he saw few friends except Browne and Hopkinson, of his undergraduate class, who were also reading law; he seldom went into society; he rarely even returned to his home in Boston. Instead, he studied. He completed not merely all the prescribed books for the regular two-year course, but also the works recommended for supplementary reading "as far as the leisure and progress of the students may permit" and even most of the titles listed on the "parallel course," which were suggested "chiefly for private reading." [8]

Sumner's enthusiastic diligence won him the recognition he craved. Everybody agreed that this lanky, pale-faced youth, whose bloodshot eyes, muddy complexion, and harsh, constant cough indicated too serious application to his studies, would make a name for himself. His classmate Browne reported that after only a year of study Sumner had become "to the law what he used to be for history,—a repertory of facts to which we might all resort." Professor Ashmun, that precise opposite of Story, whose teaching relied less upon inspirational excitement than on "exactness of learning, . . . acuteness of mind and untiring perseverance" in drill, accepted the assiduous young student as a friend and almost an equal. Simon Greenleaf, Ash-

[7] Sumner to Stearns, Sept. 25 [1831], Sumner MSS.; Sumner's Commonplace Book, ibid.; Sumner: "The Lawyer's Commonplace Book," MS., Harvard Univ. Archives; Sumner to Tower, Sept. 29, 1831, Tower MSS.; Pierce, I, 98–9; C. P. Sumner to Sumner, Apr. 4, 1832, copy, C. P. Sumner MSS.

[8] Pierce, I, 111. Compare the list of books Sumner read during law school, 1831–4, in his "Lawyer's Commonplace Book," pp. 435–8, with the prescribed lists in Warren: *Harvard Law School,* I, 436–7.

mun's successor, grew equally fond of this eager, serious youth, whose 120 pounds seemed scarcely to cover his six-foot, two-inch frame, but whose burning zeal for the law was untiring.[9]

Most important of all, Sumner's goodhearted simplicity and eagerness to please promptly gained him the "affectionate intimacy and confidence of Story himself." Sumner became a regular visitor at the Story house, where the professor welcomed him "with a beaming face, and treated him almost as if he were a son." During Story's long absences in Washington, Sumner continued to drop in frequently to cheer up the lonely Mrs. Story and to give Latin lessons to young William Wetmore Story, for whom he developed an almost paternal affection.[1]

Story came to respect as well as to like the young man. Very early he was impressed by Sumner's organized industry. "He has a wonderful memory," he told President Quincy's family; "he keeps all his knowledge in order, and can put his hand on it in a moment." Rather than see so promising a student leave Cambridge after only two years of professional training, Story encouraged him to remain a third by naming him librarian of the law school, in which capacity Sumner was given "the pleasantest room in Cambridge," in the newly constructed Dane Hall, and by persuading the corporation to pay him $160 for cataloguing the law library.[2]

Soon Story entrusted Sumner with various small professional duties. When the judge had to go to Washington for the Supreme Court sessions, he turned over the proofreading of his *The Conflict of Laws* to his student, secure in the knowledge that Sumner would check all the quotations and citations and prod the printer into more rapid action.[3] So eager was Sumner to serve that the judge found it necessary to warn him: "You will

[9] Pierce, I, 99; *American Jurist,* XIII (Jan. 1835), 114; Sumner's autobiography, Palfrey MSS.; Sumner's passport, signed by Edward Everett, Nov. 18, 1835, C. P. Sumner MSS.

[1] Sumner's autobiography, Palfrey MSS.; Pierce, I, 108, 105–6; Sumner to Story, Jan. 20 [1834], Story MSS.; Andrew F. Rolle: "A Friendship across the Atlantic: Charles Sumner and William Story," *American Quarterly,* XI (Spring 1959), 40–57.

[2] Pierce, I, 103; Story to Sumner, July 12, 1833, Sumner MSS.; Sumner to Story, Dec. 18, 1833, Harvard Coll. Papers, VI, 2 ser., 69; Harvard Coll. Records, VII (1827–36), 342.

[3] Sumner to Story, Jan. 20 [1834], Story MSS. See also numerous letters from Sumner to Charles Folsom, concerning proofreading and indexing Story's books, Folsom MSS.

have to learn, that those, who are willing to labour for others, will never want ample employment, especially if their services are gratuitous; and you must begin to be chary of your intellectual, as well as physical strength." Still, knowing Sumner's fondness for obliging his friends, he continued to call on him for assistance. "There are not many, of whom I would venture to ask the favor of troubling themselves with my affairs," he told Sumner, "but I feel proud to think, that you are among the number, and I have . . . a heritable right to your friendship." [4]

Sumner, for his part, rejoiced at every opportunity to be of service. Every favor he performed gave him another excuse to write one of his long, affectionate letters to "My dearest Judge Story." "My happiness is materially dependent upon your regard and favorable estimate of my trifling labors," he ingenuously confessed. He was actually sorry to complete the proofreading and indexing of *The Conflict of Laws* because "it dissolves for the time the connection of confidence which, in my vanity, I imagined to be expressed, towards me, thereby." "Indeed," he added, "my whole relation to you has been, from the first, one of unlimited obligation on my part. Not a day—not an hour passes without some perception of your kindness coming into my mind. I can never express towards you the fullness of my feelings." [5]

• 2 •

"For *once* . . . I have felt desolated and alone," Professor Greenleaf wrote Story in January 1834. "Sumner . . . has left me. I stoutly refused *ever* to bid him farewell." Though Sumner had reluctantly departed from Cambridge, he was not, in fact, cutting his ties with the law school, but carrying out a program advised by his professors. As Story and Greenleaf thought that a young attorney should, after his theoretical training, get practical experience in the office of some established lawyer, Sumner went, with Story's strong letter of recommendation, to study with Benjamin Rand, of Boston, whom he found "a thorough lawyer and at the same time a liberal lawyer—a jurisconsult." [6]

[4] Story to Sumner, Feb. 4, 1834, Sumner MSS.; Story: *Story*, II, 119–20.
[5] Sumner to Story, Jan. 20, and 30, Feb. 12, and undated [1834], Story MSS.
[6] Greenleaf to Story, Jan. 23, 1834; Sumner to Story, Jan. 20 [1834], ibid.

Following another of Story's suggestions, that a lawyer should not merely practice, but should contribute to the literature of his profession, Sumner, as early as July 1833, had commenced writing for *The American Jurist,* the best legal periodical in the United States at the time. As he settled into Rand's office, his contributions became more frequent. Some of his articles, such as a technical essay on "Can the assignee of a Scotch bond maintain an action in his own name in the courts of this country?" attracted favorable critical notice. In May 1834 he became joint editor of the journal, and his duties were heavy. To fill up the July issue, for instance, he himself had to write "upwards of 100 pages of pretty heavy print"—"no small labor," he thought.[7]

Then, too, Story and Greenleaf thought that a beginning lawyer should gain as broad an acquaintance as possible with his nation's judges and political leaders, and at their suggestion Sumner obediently made his first visit to Washington in 1834. Setting out in February, he stopped off in New York to call on Chancellor James Kent, whose *Commentaries* gave him a place alongside Story's in American jurisprudence, and the fastidious young attorney found the old judge "lively and instructive, but grossly ungrammatical." On his way through Maryland Sumner had his first sight of Negro slaves. "My worst preconception of their appearance and ignorance did not fall as low as their actual stupidity," he reported to his family. "They appear to be nothing more than moving masses of flesh, unendowed with any thing of intelligence above the brutes. I have now an idea of the blight upon that part of our country in which they live."

In Washington Sumner made the Supreme Court the center of his interest. Though few causes of importance were being argued, Sumner listened attentively as Francis Scott Key pleaded a case in which he relied "upon a quickness and facility of language rather upon research" and as Webster replied in a fashion that indicated he had not studied the case, even though half a million dollars was involved. The justices were more impressive, and Sumner, whose friendship with Story gave him "almost . . . a place in the court,—*persona standi in judico,* as Lord Stowell

[7] *American Jurist,* XI (Jan. 1834), 101–15; Sumner's autobiography, Palfrey MSS.; Henry Moore to Sumner, May 14, 1834, Sumner MSS.; Sumner to Tower, July 17 [1834], Tower MSS.

would say," not merely observed them on the bench, but also had the privilege of dining with them regularly at their boarding house, where they discussed judicial business over postprandial Madeira. Sumner admired most of all the venerable chief justice, John Marshall, now within a year of his death, whom he found "a model of simplicity . . . naturally taciturn, and yet ready to laugh; to joke and be joked with." [8]

Compared with the court, everything else in Washington seemed vulgar. President Andrew Jackson did not impress Sumner; "the old tyrant," he reported, "seemed to have hardly nerve enough to keep his bones together." In Congress he found Henry Clay's eloquence "splendid and thrilling" and admired John C. Calhoun, who seemed "more than an orator . . . an honest and able man, having earnestly at heart all that he was uttering, and indifferent to the guise of his thought, so he could make them understood." Even so, little about the congressional proceedings attracted Sumner's interest, and after the court adjourned, he found "nothing but dust and dullness" in Washington, "the one sweeping in volumes up and down the Avenue and the other pervading the Capitol." Under the tutelage of Story, who had conveniently forgotten his own earlier career as a Jeffersonian partisan and had now become John Marshall's chief support in the Supreme Court,[9] Sumner developed, during his Washington trip, a decided aversion to politicians and to "the unweeded garden in which they are laboring." "The more I see of *politics*," he reported, in words that echoed Story's, "the more I learn to love *law*." As he left the capital, he shook the dust off his feet. "I probably shall never come here again," he announced. "I have little or no desire ever to come again in any capacity." [1]

By the fall of 1834 Sumner's advisers felt that he was ready to begin his professional career. In September, having had his title to the degree of Bachelor of Laws from Harvard College certified by President Quincy, his diligence in legal studies endorsed by Greenleaf, and his "most unblemished character" vouched for

[8] Pierce, I, 132, 134–7, 141; Boston *Commonwealth*, Mar. 7, 1874.

[9] The change in Story's opinions, however, had been neither so abrupt nor so marked as historians have sometimes pictured it. Commager: "Joseph Story," pp. 35–7, 58–9.

[1] Pierce, I, 136, 137, 139, 141–2; Sumner to Story, Mar. 20, and 21 [1834], Story MSS.

by Rand, Sumner was admitted to the bar.[2] Immediately he formed a partnership with George S. Hillard, another of Story's favorite pupils, rented an office at No. 4 Court Street, and hung out his shingle. On October 13 he had his first case, a minor suit in the Boston municipal court. The Boston *Atlas* kindly noted Sumner's first appearance at the bar and remarked that he was "said to be more deeply read in the law than any other individual of similar age." [3]

It is difficult to judge how successful Sumner's practice was during the next three years. No business records exist of the Hillard and Sumner partnership; court dockets are fragmentary and unrevealing; later reminiscences are not entirely reliable. In his autobiography Sumner himself claimed that his early practice was "considerable," that he promptly began earning an "income larger than that of any other person at the time so young in his profession," and that as a result of his successes, he "was soon invited into lucrative partnership with *three* eminent members of the profession." Theophilus P. Chandler, who had an office in the same building as Hillard and Sumner, agreed that Sumner's practice was both successful and increasing. The fact that only a year after Sumner was admitted to the bar, the United States District Attorney for Massachusetts, Andrew Dunlap, invited him to become his partner, to handle all his cases before the court of common pleas, the municipal court, and perhaps the district court, suggests that the young attorney's abilities were widely recognized.[4]

On the other hand, there are indications that Sumner was less than overwhelmed with business. The remaining, scattered legal papers for these years suggest that most of his cases were small matters—the drawing of a will, the settling of an estate, etc.—and even these appear not to have been numerous.[5] Clients could tell that Sumner was not at his best in the court-

[2] Harvard College Papers, VI, 2 ser., 224; certificate signed by Greenleaf, Jan. 6, 1834, and certificate signed by Rand & Ashe, Sept. 2, 1834, MSS., American Antiquarian Society; certificate signed by J. G. Kendall, Sept. 3, 1834, Sumner MSS.

[3] Oct. 14, 1834.

[4] T. P. Chandler to Pierce, Jan. 24, 1879, Pierce MSS.; Sumner to Story [Jan. 1835], Story MSS.

[5] E.g., Sumner to Gustavus S. Drane, Oct. 24, 1835, MS., Segal Coll.; Boston *Commonwealth,* Nov. 1, 1862.

room, for he thought too slowly to succeed at cross-examination and relied too heavily upon cited precedents to impress a jury. The envious claimed that he owed whatever business he did attract chiefly "to Judge Story's friendship and favor." He did not argue a case before the Massachusetts Supreme Judicial Court until 1837, and even after that, his appearances were rare.[6] Three years after he commenced practice, Sumner, in what may have been a bit of unintentional autobiography, advised a friend just admitted to the bar not to be discouraged by a seeming want of success. "The *first* year is no criterion," he argued. "Many of the *first years* of our first lawyers have been passed in the direst desolation, without the chance ray from a single client to enlighten their darkness." [7]

Sumner occupied his considerable spare time with professional writing, which he found more congenial than practice. He, Hillard, and Luther S. Cushing, whose office was just above Sumner's, now edited *The American Jurist*, and for almost every quarterly issue Sumner turned out long articles and shorter reviews on such topics as "Are Challenges to Jurors in Massachusetts Determinable by Triors?" "The Advocates Library in Edinburgh," and "The Juridical Writings of Sir James Mackintosh." [8] He also found time to write on legal subjects for the *North American Review* and the *American Monthly Review*.[9] Sumner's plan to edit, in fifteen or twenty volumes of 800 pages each, "the whole series of modern and ancient British chancery reports, in a condensed form," was interrupted when Dunlap, who was dying of tuberculosis, asked him to complete his *Practice in Admiralty*. Without interrupting his own practice, Sumner found time to check all of Dunlap's citations, to read the proofs twice, to prepare over one hundred pages of appendices, including sum-

[6] Theophilus Parsons to Sumner [Apr. 1836], Sumner MSS.; 19 Pickering 202.

[7] Sumner to "My dear George," Aug. 6, 1837, MS., Yale Univ. Sumner's attempt to add to his income by buying stock in a speculative land company failed, and he was left in debt. Sumner to W. C. Russell, Aug. 25, Sept. 4, and 20, 1835. Sumner MSS. He was obliged to borrow $1,100 from his father during his first few years at the bar. Will of C. P. Sumner, Apr. 5, 1839, Docket No. 32,151. Probate Court Office, Suffolk Co., Boston.

[8] J. C. Perkins to Sumner, Nov. 3, 1837, Sumner MSS.; printed circular, enclosed in Sumner to James Kent, Apr. 30, 1836, Kent MSS.; *American Jurist*, XII (Oct. 1834), 330–40; XIII (Apr. 1835), 382–9; XIV (July 1835), 100–34.

[9] *North American Review*, XLV (Oct. 1837), 482–4, 502–4; XLVI (Jan. 1838), 300–1; *American Monthly Review* (Boston), III (Apr. 1833), 315–27; (May 1833), 430–3.

maries of the rules of United States admiralty courts and a collection of practical forms to be used in admiralty proceedings, which Sumner himself worked up from British and American usage, to make the index, and to write a biographical preface about Dunlap, who died before the book appeared.[1] Early in 1835 Sumner, appointed reporter for the United States Circuit Court by Judge Story, who sensed that the young man was not making a living at his practice, undertook an even more time-consuming task. During the next two years he gathered, edited, and oversaw the publication of two volumes that were known as *Sumner's Reports;* a third volume appeared in 1841.[2]

If Sumner's friends were not worried because these literary activities diverted him from actual practice at the Massachusetts bar, where such giants as Rufus Choate were gaining both impressive incomes and national reputations and where younger attorneys like Benjamin R. Curtis were rapidly establishing themselves, it was because they planned a different future for him. Even while he was in law school, Sumner's classmates had predicted that through "the confidence, esteem, and friendship of that truly great man," Story, Sumner would find his "employment probably in the science of the law" and would thus escape its "drudgery." The hope was one that Sumner himself earnestly shared. He had hated to leave the law school. "I could spend my life, I believe, in this, as some call it, monkish seclusion," he confessed. Sumner's professors encouraged his aspiration. Greenleaf was "full of lamentations" when Sumner left the school in 1834, and Story, who missed his young friend even more, promised him: "If the Law School succeeds I am sure you will be with us again at no distant period." [3]

In fact, only a year after his graduation, Sumner was invited to return to the Harvard Law School. In 1835, when Story

[1] *American Jurist,* XIII (Apr. 1835), 490–1; Dunlap to Sumner, Feb. 14, 1835, Sumner MSS.; Sumner to Dunlap, June 8, 1835, Dunlap MSS.; Sumner to Benjamin W. Stone, Aug. 15, 1836, ibid.; Sumner to C. S. Daveis, Aug. 8, 1836, Daveis MSS.; Dunlap's *A Treatise on the Practice of Courts of Admiralty . . .* (2nd ed.; New York: Jacob R. Halsted; 1850), pp. viii–xii. Sumner received $500 for his labors on Dunlap's book.

[2] Richard Peters to Sumner, June 6, 1835, Sumner MSS.; Sumner's contract with Hilliard, Gray & Co., Mar. 11, 1836, ibid. The title page read: *Report of Cases Argued and Determined in the Circuit Court of the United States for the First Circuit, By Charles Sumner, Reporter of the Court.*

[3] Pierce, I, 100, 119; Story to Sumner, Feb. 4, 1834, Sumner MSS.

was obliged to remain for longer than usual in Washington, President Quincy asked Sumner to teach his courses. The invitation came at just the time Dunlap offered him a partnership, but Sumner had no difficulty in making his choice. "The situation [in the law school], in a pecuniary point of view and on divers other accounts is far less acceptable than that offered by you," he explained to Dunlap; "yet my sense of duty, of respect to those who have treated me kindly, and some of my tastes and predilections do not allow me to decline it." Not only in 1835, but in the following year as well Sumner served as instructor in the law school, and in 1837, when both Story and Greenleaf were absent, he was for a time in sole charge of the Harvard Law School.[4]

Sumner lectured principally upon the Law of Evidence, using Starkie as a text, "expounding and commenting on the subject, step by step, and saying everything which occurred to him by way of illustration from the cases, from practice, history and legal anecdote," and upon the Law of Nations, "discussing the principles of International Law, the rights of war, of neutrals and the duties flowing therefrom, now running along the narrow lines which separate the cases with regard to domicil and the various kinds of property liable to capture, and now rejoicing in historical illustration or in some of the more expansive principles which are to be found in the elementary writers." One does not know how much his students learned, but the lecturer received invaluable training for a future career in the Senate Committee on Foreign Relations. Sumner also gave "some most righteous judgments in the moot-court," then, as always, an essential feature of a Harvard legal education. With every year of teaching he thought he gained "new confidence, as well as facility, and, perhaps, capacity." [5]

Though Sumner reported that the students were "in admirable order, most ardently engaging in work, and zealous after knowledge," he seems to have made no striking impression upon them. Doubtless many were disappointed that a novice was attempting to fill the place of Story and Greenleaf. Probably they

[4] Sumner to Dunlap [Jan. 1835], Dunlap MSS.; Sumner's autobiography, Palfrey MSS. Harvard paid Sumner $275 for his teaching services in 1835, $225 in 1835–6, and $150 in 1837. Harvard College Papers, VII, 2 ser., 99, 550; VIII, 204, 238.

[5] Sumner to Story, Jan. 18, and 25, and Feb. 5, 1837, Story MSS.

also recognized that Sumner, like every beginning teacher, was only one assignment ahead of his students. Necessarily "he confined his talk to the given pages in the text book, but . . . did not question the students or so develop the lecture as to present anything new outside of the text book, or compel the students, by his method, to hard and close study of the lesson." Still, they found him "a ready and agreeable talker," and, on the whole, he was "very popular with the students." [6]

Whatever the students thought, Sumner's professors valued his services. Hearing through Greenleaf of Sumner's "complete, and every way gratifying" success, Story as early as 1835 wrote him frankly: "I hope this is but the beginning, and that one day you may fill the chair which he or I occupy, if he or I, like autocrats, can hope to appoint our successor." Greenleaf shared his colleague's hope and wrote Sumner, a little later: "Our earnest desire is to have you occupy an additional professor's chair, with Judge Story and myself, bringing into our institution all that power and all the affluence of your mind, to bear upon the great and increasing number of young men who come to us for instruction."

Their wish was also Sumner's desire. "You have thrown out some hints with regard to my occupying a place with you and the Judge at Cambridge," he replied to Greenleaf. "You know well that my heart yearns fondly to that place, and that in the calm study of my profession I have ever taken more delight than in the pert debate at the bar." [7]

• 3 •

Story's influence shaped not merely Sumner's professional career, but also his pattern of thought, his outlook on life, and even

[6] Most of these comments come from students who heard Sumner lecture in 1843, when he again replaced Story, but they are doubtless applicable to his earlier teaching experience as well. Warren: *Harvard Law School,* II, 26, 56.

[7] Story: *Story,* II, 189; Pierce, I, 380; II, 9. Sumner later claimed that he "in 1835 was invited by President [Quincy] to the professorship of Moral Philosophy and political Economy in Harvard University—declined—afterwards was again pressed, and asked if I would not entertain it, if coupled with a permanent professorship in [the] Law School—declined." Sumner's autobiography, Palfrey MSS. I have been unable to find anything to support this recollection, and as there is considerable evidence to indicate that he desired just such a professorship, I am inclined to think his memory was at fault.

his gestures and his mannerisms. He did his best to mold his favorite pupil into the safe, conservative, respectable pattern of Boston Whiggery. The merchants of State Street began to speak of Sumner as a promising young man, who combined a proper respect for law and a belief in the indispensability of the legal profession [8] with a suitable disdain for popular politics and an outright contempt for the Jacksonian Democrats. Even in literature he exhibited a wholesome reverence for the classics and an ability to quote almost too extensively from the Latin sages. He held the reassuring conviction that the essays of the dangerous transcendentalist, Ralph Waldo Emerson, contained "exquisite sentences, images and phrases, but [were] a maze without a plan." The young lawyer seemed to hold no dangerous ideas on the subject of property, so basic to the Whig creed. Instead, he belittled the sermons of William E. Channing, who was beginning to advocate needed social reforms, as wanting "in the forms of logical discussion, and the close, continuous chain of reasoning," and even contributed an article to the *North American Review,* arguing that "the enterprise and generosity of the merchants" of the United States were the best contemporary manifestation of the "spirit of chivalry." [9] Clearly Sumner was doing all he could to fulfill the prophesy of a classmate, who dissuaded him from even thinking of locating his law office in another state. "I have always supposed that the place of your ultimate destination was certain," he had told Sumner. "You were made for Boston." [1]

As yet, however, Sumner's general acquaintance in Boston society was still limited. Though both Story and Hillard sponsored him, Sumner seemed an odd figure to those Bostonians who sedulously imitated English manners and considered conversation a fine art. "He was tall, thin, and ungainly in his movements, and sprawled rather than sat on a chair or sofa," William Wetmore Story recalled. "Nothing saved his face from ugliness but his white gleaming teeth and his expression of bright intelligence

[8] *North American Review,* XLV (Oct. 1837), 503.

[9] Sumner to Mrs. George Bancroft, Jan. 24, 1849, Bancroft MSS.; Pierce, I, 157; *North American Review,* XLVI (Jan. 1838), 115–16. Cf., however, T. Wemyss Reid: *The Life, Letters, and Friendships of Richard Monckton Milnes, First Lord Houghton* (New York: Cassell Publishing Company; 1891), I, 237–9.

[1] Pierce, I, 100.

and entire amiability." Everybody recognized Sumner's "simplicity, his perfect *naturalness*," as well as his intelligence, but it was not at all clear that these compensated for his social deficiencies.

Though Sumner talked incessantly to his close friends, he had no general conversation. He admitted that he had "no knowledge of music, and but little, scarcely any, ear for it," that he was ignorant "of the principles of art and of its history." Even poetry was "with him more an acquired taste than a natural one." He cared nothing for sports and could not talk of fishing, shooting, and rowing, or of horses and dogs. His intensity and seriousness dampened light conversation. He had no sense of humor; a censorious father and rival brothers had taught him that it was dangerous ever to let down his guard and that to laugh at himself was an admission of error. "He was," young Story declared, "totally put off his balance by the least *persiflage;* and, if it was tried on him, his expression was one of complete astonishment. He was never ready at a retort, tacked slowly, like a frigate when assaulted by stinging feluccas, and was . . . almost impervious to a joke." Oliver Wendell Holmes exaggerated only a little when he declared that if one told Sumner that the moon was made of green cheese, he would say: "No! it cannot be so," and proceed to give weighty reasons to the contrary.[2]

Sumner's most serious social handicap was his inability to converse with women. As a college senior he had been too timid to be introduced to President Quincy's youngest daughter, Anna, who had attained the venerable age of eighteen; he dared only to look on her "from afar with awe."[3] Now that he was a promising young lawyer, he still did not know how to act or what to say. He was not hostile to women. In fact, he held highly romantic notions about love, marriage, and the family. He firmly believed "that the only true love is love at first sight." Marriage, he was certain, would be a life of perpetual rapture. "One beautiful look of love from a wife or child must start a more exquisite thrill of happiness than comes from any distinction, literary or politi-

[2] Ibid., I, 106–7, 127, 237, 241; John T. Morse, Jr.: *Life and Letters of Oliver Wendell Holmes* (Boston: Houghton Mifflin Co.; 1896), II, 202–3.

[3] Pierce, I, 103. Sumner did, however, later overcome his shyness and converse with the Quincy sisters. M. A. DeWolfe Howe (ed.): *The Articulate Sisters* . . . (Cambridge: Harvard University Press; 1946), pp. 238–9.

cal." But, in such a partnership, he thought that a woman should know her role. "A female's place is at home," he somewhat heavily instructed his young sister Jane when she was but fourteen years old, "not abroad in the excited scenes of the world," and her principal charm should be the ability "to listen intelligently." [4]

But, Boston ladies showed a disconcerting unwillingness to listen. They wanted to talk themselves, to make witty remarks, and to engage in flirtatious conversation. Such creatures fascinated Sumner, but they were beyond his comprehension. How, to so awesome a being as a Boston lady, could one bare his soul? Could he ever dare to squeeze the universe into a ball and roll it to some overwhelming question? How his classmates mustered the courage to enter "Cupid's Tribunal" baffled him. Such delight was not for him, he grew convinced; it would be his fate to "tarry at the gate, beholding his associates enter one by one, waiting for Time when tired of detaining him to let him in." So terrifying were these formidable females that Sumner tried to avoid them. "It was in vain for the loveliest and liveliest girl to seek to absorb his attention," William Story declared. "He would at once desert the most blooming beauty to talk to the plainest of men." [5]

If Sumner was not at home in mixed society, he was exceptionally popular among men of his own age, who found him sincerely sympathetic, eager for friendship. Besides, as an unmarried man, he was always available. After graduating from the law school, he had moved from his father's crowded, gloomy house, and he and Luther Cushing rented a furnished room and took their meals at a restaurant. Later Sumner found living quarters in the Albion Hotel, on the corner of Beacon and Tremont streets, where his friends could always find him ready for a talk, a walk out to Cambridge—though he strode along at such a rate that few tried this more than once—or a midnight supper in one of the oyster houses.

"Among my chief delights have been my friends," Sumner declared in his autobiography. He had many of them, especially among his colleagues at the bar, nearly all of whom had a genuine affection for this serious, studious young man. Gradually he

[4] Sumner to Story, Feb. 12, 1837, Story MSS.; Sumner to Lieber, Oct. 13, 1837, Lieber MSS.; Sumner to Jane Sumner, Mar. 4, 1834, Sumner MSS.

[5] Sumner to Tower, Dec. 17, 1832, Tower MSS.; Pierce, I, 106–7.

Sumner as a Young Man

Miniature (2" x 2½") by an unknown artist

MASSACHUSETTS HISTORICAL SOCIETY

Boston about 1830: A View from Dorchester Heights

MASSACHUSETTS HISTORICAL SOCIETY

built a smaller circle of specially cherished intimates. One, naturally, was his law partner, Hillard, whose dreamy, poetic look and delicate, sickly constitution suggested that literature rather than law should have been his vocation.[6] Another was Henry Wadsworth Longfellow, Ticknor's successor at Harvard, whom Sumner met while lecturing at the law school. Between the poet and the lawyer there grew up an instant affection, which ripened into the most enduring friendship of Sumner's life.[7] Frail, ailing Henry R. Cleveland, who served for a time as proctor at Harvard before feeble health compelled him to lead a life of idleness, served as a sounding board for his more loquacious and excitable friends. Sumner thought him wholly admirable, combining "the choicest qualities of the heart and head—a truth and purity of character, as unsullied as the lawn of the altar, with a temper which is never ruffled and a constancy which never fails."[8] In marked contrast was Sumner's fifth special friend, Cornelius C. Felton, tall and stout, certainly the most jovial professor of Latin ever to teach at Harvard or anywhere else. His "*fat*, and . . . his *fun*," Sumner thought, made Felton an ideal companion, and his "exilerating [*sic*] laugh, and his constant flow of wit and kindliness" kept his friends from too much morbid introspection.[9]

Sumner, Hillard, Longfellow, Cleveland, and Felton grew so attached to each other that they formed a kind of informal society, which they styled "The Five of Clubs." At their Saturday dinner meetings they discussed the many interests they had in common. In 1837 they were all less than thirty years old, and all except Hillard were still unmarried. All aspired to be accepted in Boston society, and, even though they lacked the wealth and the family connections to move easily among the Winthrops, the Curtises, and the Searses, they were recognized as promising

6 Francis W. Palfrey: "Memoir of the Hon. George Stillman Hillard," *MHSP*, XIX (June 1882), 339–45.

7 The best account of Longfellow during these early years of his friendship with Sumner is Lawrance Thompson: *Young Longfellow (1807–1843)* (New York: The Macmillan Co.; 1938).

8 Sumner to Sarah Perkins, June 9, 1837, copy, Henry Wadsworth Longfellow MSS.; *A Selection from the Writings of Henry R. Cleveland. With a Memoir by George S. Hillard* (1844), pp. v–li.

9 Sumner to George Washington Greene, Mar. 31, 1843, Greene MSS.; Hillard: "Remarks on Felton's Death," *MHSP*, V (1862), 446–57; William Watson Goodwin, in *The Cambridge Historical Society Publications, II: Proceedings, October 23, 1906–October 22, 1907*, pp. 117–30.

young men who might someday be admitted to the socially elect. But, it was chiefly their love of literature which drew the five together. Though only Longfellow was able to make a career for himself as a man of letters, the other four friends had also originally aspired to become writers, and, despite other occupations, all did make minor contributions to American literature. Eagerly they read and criticized each other's manuscripts, and loyally they published laudatory reviews of each other's books. These articulate friends thought so well of themselves that newspapers began to refer to them derisively as "The Mutual Admiration Society." [1]

Younger than any of his close friends, Sumner in the 1830's was the most endearing and ingratiating of the five. Nothing about him at the time suggested the inflexible zeal and moral terrorism of his later reform career. On the contrary, he was totally dependent upon his friends for affection and praise. A phrenologist who analyzed Sumner's character in 1835 by measuring the bumps on his head—and doubtless by collecting current opinion and gossip about him—declared that his "self esteem" was much too small; he was "not self poised and independent" enough. "You must rouse up your self respect," the phrenologist urged, prescribing that he overcome his shyness by attempting to speak in public. "You would be mild, bland, respectful, and pleasing," he promised Sumner, "if you could feel self-confidence enough to get well under weigh [*sic*]." Sumner's intimates would have agreed with this analysis. If Sumner could only overcome his diffidence and his willingness to be exploited by others, they believed he might make a name for himself. Longfellow was certain that Sumner's "very lovely character" was "full of talent; with a most keen enjoyment of life; simple, energetic, hearty, good." [2]

• 4 •

Completely under Story's influence, Sumner in the 1830's seemed well on the way to becoming a Boston Brahmin, yet, paradoxically, it was Story's ideas that kept him from quite fitting

[1] Samuel Longfellow: *Life of Henry Wadsworth Longfellow With Extracts from his Journals and Correspondence* (Boston: Houghton Mifflin Co.; 1891), I, 253–4.

[2] Ibid., I, 304; Memorandum by T. Jones, Nov. 12, 1835, Sumner MSS.

into the dominant pattern of Boston society. Now growing old and conservative, the judge tended to think of himself as the defender of nationalism and of property, the friend of Webster and of Marshall, and to forget that in his younger days he had been suspected of harboring dangerous, almost Jacobinical ideas. But, Sumner, as a worshipful student, treasured every word the judge had ever written and adopted every opinion he had ever expressed—including some that Story had himself discarded.

In his legal writings, for example, Sumner began to advocate certain mild reforms that Story had once endorsed in his lectures, and, in his thorough-going fashion, carried them to an extreme the judge had never contemplated. Remembering Story's defense of the "intricate, but . . . exquisitely finished system" of equity jurisprudence, Sumner, in his very first essay for *The American Jurist*, challenged the State Street merchants' reverence for the common law by suggesting that equity proceedings were more reliably just. In subsequent articles he pushed the idea further, urging American lawyers to import "new principles from the broad field of ethics" and quoting with approval an English judge's dictum: "Principles of private justice, moral fitness and public convenience, when applied to a new subject, make common law without a precedent." [3]

It was even more heretical for Sumner to prefer the commentators on French and Roman law to Blackstone and Chitty, those twin gods of Court Street. He recalled reading Story's pious wish, expressed in an article published in 1817, "that the time is not far distant, when [the writings of such jurisconsults as] Pothier and Emerigon and Valin will be accessible in our native tongue to every lawyer, and will be as familiarly known to them as they now are to the jurists of continental Europe," and decided that a knowledge of the civil law should be considered a mark of "enlarged liberality and intelligence." Even in petty municipal cases he attempted, to the considerable confusion of his clients and the judges, to introduce concepts from continental jurisprudence. In his Harvard lectures, too, Sumner exhibited what he proudly called a "tincture of *Radicalism*" in preferring the simple, all-inclusive rules of the civil code to the obscure

[3] William Wetmore Story (ed.): *The Miscellaneous Writings of Joseph Story* (Boston: Charles C. Little and James Brown; 1852), p. 540; *American Jurist*, X (July 1833), 227–37; XI (Apr. 1834), 321.

common law, "so shingled over with exceptions, that the rule can hardly be observed." [4]

Enthusiastically Sumner adopted Story's view that the law should be succinct and simple, but what was a moderate opinion in the judge became, in Sumner, a dogma. Story, for instance, had always been in favor of codifying Massachusetts law, so as to bring some measure of order into the conflicting, confused, and repetitious legislation of the Commonwealth. By the 1830's, though he still spoke of codification "with great ardor . . . and with confidence in its practicability," he derided the possibility of drawing up "a positive code, which shall be adequate to the business and rights and modifications of property in any one single age, unless the legislature can foresee every possible as well as every probable combination of circumstances applicable to every subject-matter in that age," and thought it best to advocate "only the reduction to a positive code of those general principles, . . . which . . . are now capable of a distinct enunciation." Sumner, on the other hand, treasured the judge's younger, more radical opinion that codification was not only possible, but might be "within the reach of a single mind successfully to accomplish," and he favored reducing the common law to the regularity and simplicity of the Code Napoleon. When the Massachusetts legislature in 1836 set up a commission, with Story at its head, to investigate the possibilities of codification, Sumner was delighted. He urged the judge, in naming his fellow commissioners, to "use the *young*," as "the old are prejudiced" against thorough-going legal reform. One of the young men he had in mind was Charles Sumner.[5]

To detect these faint notes of dissent in Sumner's think-

[4] Story (ed.): *Story's Miscellaneous Writings*, pp. 78, 281; *American Jurist*, XI (Jan. 1834), 265; XIV (Oct. 1835), 313; Sumner to Story, Jan. 18, 1837, Story MSS. It was doubtless this same "radicalism" that caused Sumner to disagree with Story's conservative opinion in the Charles River Bridge case. *MHSP*, XXXV (1901–2), 210–11.

[5] Sumner to Theophilus Parsons, undated [1836], MS., Boston Public Lib.; Story (ed.): *Story's Miscellaneous Writings*, pp. 239, 707, 709; Sumner to K. A. J. Mittermaier, Mar. 27, 1837, Sumner MSS.; Sumner to John A. Kasson, July 12, 1849, Charles Aldrich Coll.; Story to Edward Everett, Mar. 17, 1836, Everett MSS.; Parsons to Everett, Mar. 17, 1836, ibid.; Parsons to Sumner [Apr. 1836], Sumner MSS. On codification see Oscar and Mary Flug Handlin: *Commonwealth: A Study of the Role of Government in the American Economy: Massachusetts, 1776–1861* (New York: New York University Press; 1947), pp. 213–14; Leonard W. Levy, *The Law of the Commonwealth and Chief Justice Shaw* (Cambridge: Harvard University Press; 1957), pp. 196–202.

ing would have required a closer attention to his trivial court cases and his technical legal essays than any busy merchant of Boston was prepared to give, but Sumner's decision in 1837 to interrupt both his law practice and his teaching in order to travel in Europe was unmistakable evidence that this promising young lawyer did not accept the values of Boston as absolute. Nearly everybody was shocked by his plan. His father sourly disapproved. Puzzled by his willingness to throw up his promising prospects, his colleagues at the bar urged: "Do not think of going to Europe, until you shall become the head of your profession, as you will become, and rich, as you will be." Professor Greenleaf shook his head at Sumner's want of wisdom. President Quincy, remembering all too well that George Bancroft had returned from his European trip an effeminate dandy, told Sumner brusquely: "You will come home with a cane, moustaches and an additional stock of vanity—that's all." [6]

What was worse, Story disapproved. Sumner found the judge's position incomprehensible. It had been Story who originally caused him to fall "in love with *Europa*" [7]—just as it had been Story who had been the source of Sumner's quiet legal heresies. The judge had indeed taught that the well-rounded lawyer should travel abroad, but he himself never left the United States.

Story's views on the value of travel might change, but not Sumner's. Easily influenced initially to adopt an idea, he was, as the Harvard Parietal Board had discovered, inflexibly stubborn. By using almost the same words Story had employed in his lectures, he sought to bring the judge around. "Do . . . think of my strong desire, which dates back to my earliest days of memory—amounting almost to an instinct—to visit those scenes memorable in literature and history and to see, so far as it may be given to one so humble as myself, the great men that are already on the stage," he begged Story; "think, then, of the desire, which has arisen in maturer years, of obtaining a knowledge of languages, of observing the manners, customs and institutions of

[6] Richard Peters to Sumner, Dec. 29, 1836, Sumner MSS.; Sumner to Story, Feb. 10, 1840, ibid.

[7] Sumner to Lieber, Jan. 17, 1837, ibid. As a student in the law school, Sumner had pledged: "I will bond my services to any one for five years, who will furnish me with means sufficient to go to Europe and travel from one to two years in the old countries." N. F. Bryant to Pierce, Apr. 2, 1878, Pierce MSS.

other people than my own, particularly of noting in France and Germany the administration of justice and the course of legal institutions and in England frequenting Westminster Hall and drinking at the very bubbling fountain of the common law."

Rather against his own judgment, Story allowed himself to be convinced that Sumner planned to travel "not for *display* but for *purposes* of *education*," and he agreed to lend his young friend $1,000 for his journey. Samuel Lawrence, the textile magnate, and Congressman Richard Fletcher, a wealthy Boston lawyer, put up similar amounts.[8]

With his money in hand, Sumner turned to soliciting letters of introduction. From all his friends who had European acquaintances, even from friends of friends who had been abroad, he sought letters. By the time he was ready to leave, Sumner had "letters, under which a mail would groan." Story, Fletcher, C. S. Daveis, of Maine, David Hoffman, of Baltimore, and Horace Binney wrote to English lawyers and judges in his behalf; Caleb Cushing and Edward Everett to English politicians; Channing, Longfellow, Emerson, and Washington Allston to men of letters; Lieber to his many acquaintances in France, Germany, and Italy. "My supply of introductions is bountiful," Sumner at last reported; "the door of English life, law and literature [is] wide open to me."[9]

Sumner had hoped to sail in October 1837, but business detained him until December. As the time for departure grew near, he became increasingly excited about his prospects and increasingly troubled by the audacity of his course. Toward midnight of his last day on land, he wrote a troubled letter to Story, whose words had originally inspired the trip, but whose opinion of it was still far from favorable: "Your confidence and friendship are a life-blood to me. I hope these may not desert me. And may God grant that I may return from Europe with increased knowledge and added capacity for usefulness. If I do not, then, indeed, shall I have travelled in vain."[1]

[8] Sumner to Story, July 13, 1837, Story MSS.; Samuel Lawrence to Pierce, Jan. 3, 1876, Pierce MSS.

[9] Sumner to Lieber, Nov. 19, 1837, Sumner MSS.; Sumner to Daveis, Aug. 4, 1837, Daveis MSS.; Sumner to Longfellow, Aug. 18, 1837, Longfellow MSS.; Sumner to Jared Sparks, Oct. 28, 1837, Sparks MSS.; Sumner to Kent, Nov. 7, 1837, Kent MSS.; Sumner to Story, Nov. 7 [1837], Story MSS.

[1] Sumner to Story, Dec. 7, 1837, Story MSS.

CHAPTER III

The Life of Life

I TREMBLE with hope, anticipation and anxiety," Sumner wrote as he was about to begin his European tour.[1] His worry was entirely justified. One hundred years ago the physical perils that attended a trip abroad were numerous. On the transatlantic crossing, wooden sailing ships often suffered disastrously from fires or storms. Fortunately, the *Albany*, upon which he sailed from New York in December 1837, was a safe, swift ship, requiring but twenty days to reach Europe. Though the voyage was tranquil, Sumner suffered considerably from seasickness, which prostrated him before he lost sight of land. "Literally 'cabbined, cribbed and confined' in my berth I ate nothing, did nothing, and read nothing for three days," he reported to his Boston friends, with an invalid's interest in his own health. For more than a week after that he was too feeble to appear at the public table.

Isolated and lonely, he began to question the wisdom of this bold, almost rash, step he had taken "contrary to the advice of dear friends." Perhaps he had lost forever his chance to build a successful law practice. After all, he could not "throw off his clients and then whistle them back, 'as a huntsman does his pack.' "

[1] Sumner to Daveis, Dec. 7, 1837, Daveis MSS. Sumner's European trip is the most elaborately documented part of his life. His voluminous letters and detailed travel journals contain fascinating descriptions of most of the important leaders in British and Continental society, politics, and literature of the period. Fortunately many of these letters and most of Sumner's journal, except for a few passages considered slanderous or risqué, were printed in E. L. Pierce's *Memoir and Letters of Charles Sumner,* I, 213–380; II, 1–147. My purpose in this chapter is not to repeat this travelogue, but to discuss the effect of European travel upon Sumner's personality.

But, with better health and an appetite that returned "like a Bay of Fundy tide," he became more cheerful. Soon he was able to read, to study French, to walk the wet decks, and to play whist and chess with the other passengers. By the time the captain spied land, on Christmas night, Sumner's spirits were high. Each wave in the English channel seemed "to have a tale of interest or of glory." At any moment, he fancied, he might "catch a glimpse of Admiral Drake, slowly proceeding on his circuit of the globe, or of Robinson Crusoe, when as a runaway apprentice he left Hull, or Nelson sweeping on to the victories of the Nile and Trafalgar." He could hardly wait to go ashore. Joyfully he exclaimed: "The life of life seems to have burst upon me." [2]

• 1 •

From the moment Sumner set foot in France he was prepared to admire everything. The docks at La Havre, bearing the inscription *An IX. Bonaparte 1er Consul,* were like a romantic introduction to the glories of French history. The room he rented for his first night in Europe, with its "floor of hexagon tiles partially covered with a neat rug-like carpet; with a bed plump and neat as imagination could picture, with a crimson coverlet and curtains," was wonderfully "un-American." The diligence, which carried him along the winding Seine to Rouen, was distinctively and excitingly French. The old cathedral at Rouen, with its thousands of historical associations, "its heaven-kissing spire, . . . its stained windows and the dim religious light, . . . its innumerable arches, . . . its altars, and above all its tombs and inscriptions," was alone enough, he declared, to repay the cost of his trip. The pictures in Rouen's rather mediocre museum had "a finish, a grace, an expression and subtlety of colouring" which made him "recall the collections of America as mere daubs." Everything about France, he concluded, breathed of antiquity. France was "all *old cheese,* mouldy, rotten and worm-eaten, but full of pregnancy and strength, as compared with the curdled milk of America." [3]

[2] Sumner to Hillard, Dec. 25, 1837, and Dec. 14, 1838, Sumner MSS.; Pierce, I, 214–15, *MHSP*, XV (2 ser.), 211–12; Sumner to Lieber, Mar. 9, 1838, Sumner MSS.

[3] Pierce, I, 217; *MHSP*, XV (2 ser.), 215; Sumner's Travel Journal, Dec. 29–30, 1837, Sumner MSS.

Only one thing interfered with his incipient love affair with France—his inability to master the French language. Though he had studied French at Harvard and had carefully reviewed his grammar before coming abroad, he discovered when he reached Paris that his "French was no more fit for use than a rusty gun-barrel." Calling upon Jean-Jacques Gaspard Foelix, the editor of the *Revue Etrangère de Législation et d'Economie Politique,* to whom he had a glowing letter of introduction, Sumner presented himself: "*Je m'appelle* Charles Sumner." Baffled by the accent, Foelix asked the stranger whether he had seen Mr. Sumner lately. The contretemps convinced Sumner that he should give up all idea of entering French society until he learned to make himself understood. With characteristic thoroughness, he employed not one, but two tutors, and spent hours each day in "laborious *artificial* conversation" with them. Every morning, in the hope of accustoming his ear to the spoken language, he sampled lectures at the Sorbonne or at the Collège de France. Evenings he went to the theater or opera, attempting to follow the rapid and elusive French in a libretto. His progress at times was discouraging. "That letter *u*," he exclaimed; "my lips refuse to utter it. I stumble over it constantly; and despair of being able to compass it." [4]

Debarred "from the society and scenes of this great metropolis" by his awkward linguistic handicap, Sumner, like many a more recent tourist, found consolation in sight-seeing in the company of fellow Americans. A true Bostonian, he gravitated naturally toward the New Englanders in Paris. He was delighted to find that the George Ticknors, who had just completed a triumphant tour of the Continent, were temporarily settled in the French capital, and the fact that Sumner brought them news and letters from Boston gave him an excuse to spend every evening of his first week in Paris at their lodgings. Soon he discovered even more congenial company in Dr. George Shattuck, another young Bostonian, who was completing his medical education in France. Sumner was so lonely that Shattuck was able to drag him to the Ecole de Médecine, where he saw "skeletons etc,

[4] Pierce, I, 227; Sumner to Henry R. Cleveland, Jan. 30, 1837 [the date should be 1838], Cleveland MSS.; Sumner to Hillard, Jan. 6, 1837 [i.e., 1838], Sumner MSS.

all of which most thoroughly disgusted him," and to the great hospital, the Hôtel Dieu, where, in spite of his shrinking "from the sight of the knife, and the gush of blood," he witnessed "several operations for the stone" and where he nearly fainted among those "shambles of death," the dissecting rooms.[5]

Gratefully concluding that Providence made him a lawyer and not a doctor, Sumner soon found it pleasanter to stride about the streets of Paris alone. Used to compact little Boston, he was astonished to find the distances so gigantic. The galleries of the Louvre, for instance, were so vast that he spent "four hours in walking through them, not stopping to study anything." He longed for time to investigate every street, every building of Paris. He walked along the boulevards with his "mind swimming with the excitement." "Great as my anticipations were," he reported to Hillard, "they were greatly surpassed." [6]

Of course this very conventional young American from Puritan New England found much in France to shock him. On Sumner's first day in Paris, and a Sunday at that, he dashed out to visit Frascati's, the largest gambling hell in the metropolis, which the law was about to close permanently. He found it very exciting to see the roulette table, surrounded by intent gamblers, and to watch the card games, where gold and silver were "spread on the table to a vast amount," but he cautiously refrained from betting so much as a franc. Nor were the young women moving from table to table—"undoubtedly Cyprians," Sumner thought—more enticing, though they possessed "considerable personal attractions." Life in Paris gave Sumner a series of such titillations, unaccompanied by temptations. A singularly pure young man with romantic notions of womanhood, he found "the immorality and total depravity" of the city at once fascinating and revolting. "It is a perfect Sodom," he assured Hillard, "without religion and without any morality between the sexes." [7]

Living abroad gave Sumner a new perspective on American society. Like most Bostonians, he had been provincially conceited

[5] Sumner to Hillard, Jan. 6, 1837 [i.e., 1838], and Jan 13, 1838, Sumner MSS.; George Ticknor, Journal, Jan. 1, 1838, Ticknor MSS.; Sumner's Travel Journal, Jan. 10, and 31, Feb. 15, Mar. 21, 1838, Sumner MSS.

[6] Sumner's Travel Journal, Jan. 10, 1838, Sumner MSS.; Sumner to Hillard, Jan. 13, and 30, 1838, ibid.

[7] Pierce, I, 225; Sumner to Hillard, Mar. 8, and Jan. 30, 1838, Sumner MSS.

when he sailed for Europe. If he did not precisely believe that Boston was the hub of the universe, he did think that David Sears's house on Beacon Street was the ideal type "of a palace, the Athenaeum Gallery, of a collection of paintings, and the plaster casts in the Athenaeum reading-room, . . . of a collection of antiques." Paris taught him a lesson. "Never," he warned Hillard, only two weeks after arriving in France, "exalt any building in Boston . . . to the dignity of a *lion*, especially in the presence of a foreigner. . . . Otherwise, rest assured he will laugh in secret at the national vanity which could exalt such petty things into objects of curiosity." Sumner began to suspect that other American beliefs were parochial. Though the sight of two or three Negroes, "dressed quite *à la mode*, and having the easy jaunty air of young men of fashion" as they sat among the other students at the Sorbonne struck him as very strange, he promptly decided that French tolerance was superior to American racial proscription. "It must be," he concluded, "that the distance between free blacks and the whites among us is derived from education, and does not exist in the nature of things." [8]

Preoccupied with learning the French language and with sight-seeing, Sumner almost forgot that he had come abroad with the serious purpose of studying the civil law, perhaps in anticipation of a Harvard professorship when he returned. To be sure, he had almost, from the day of his arrival, dropped in occasionally upon law lectures at the Sorbonne and at the Collège de France, but his purpose was not so much to pursue a course of study as to gain some personal impressions of the chief French jurists and to improve his command of the language. During his first two months he never got around to visiting the French Chamber of Deputies or to attending the Paris courts.

Not until March did Sumner apply himself vigorously to studying the French legal system. Though he still spoke falteringly and "in defiance of all the rules of Grammar and pronunciation," he was now able to follow conversation easily, and he began to present his letters of introduction to such lawyers as Michel Chevalier, who had made an investigation of the American railroad system and later published a report of his travels, the Baron de Gérando, the peer who was engaged in preparing

[8] Sumner to Hillard, Jan. 13, 1838, Sumner MSS.; Pierce, I, 241–2.

a massive treatise on philanthropy, and Jean Marie Pardessus, an internationally recognized authority on maritime law. Through their intercession he was assigned "a comfortable and honorable seat" at the Cour d'Assises and the Cour de Cassation, where for several weeks he followed cases carefully, drew diagrams of the courtrooms for his journal, and recorded strange or interesting details of French legal usage.[9]

Favorably predisposed toward continental jurisprudence, Sumner was impressed by what he saw. To his older friends at home, to be sure, he reported his opinions on the French law with circumspection. Story, who urged him to be skeptical of "all the visionary notions of Reformers" and to "value old principles more and innovation less," was doubtless pleased to hear that Sumner thought a French court "a laughable place," "a theatre, and all the judges, advocates, and parties 'merely players.' " In Paris, Sumner wrote the judge, "the learning of the profession is of the most shallow kind," and added: "Without vanity . . . I have several times felt that my acquaintance with the literature of French jurisprudence, and with the character and merits of its authors, was equal if not superior to that of many of the Frenchmen with whom I conversed." But, to Hillard, Sumner wrote his true opinion that the French Code, so grossly calumniated in America, offered "much greatly to admire." Doubtless a combination of French and English procedures would make the most desirable legal system, but, he concluded: "I am . . . *convinced,*—that if I were compelled to adopt the *whole* of either, without admixture, I should take the *French.*" It was clear that Professor Greenleaf's hope that Sumner would come back from Europe "cured of some *over*-tendencies to excess in legal reform" would not be realized. Instead, Sumner boasted: "I shall return, not simply a codifier, but a *revolutionist;* always ready however, I trust, to be illuminated by the superior wisdom of my friends." [1]

Though Sumner in his long letters to Story still spoke of his studies in Paris as leading ultimately to "a work presenting a *comparative view of the judicial institutions* of France, England, and America, particularly with a view to the theory of proofs and the

[9] Sumner to Hillard, Jan. 30, Mar. 21, and Apr. 10, 1838, Sumner MSS.

[1] Story to Sumner, May 22, 1838, ibid.; Pierce, I, 277, 288, 292; Sumner to Hillard, Apr. 10, 1838, Sumner MSS.; Greenleaf to Lieber, May 5, 1838, MS. bound in Vol. IX of "Pamphlets on Crime," Univ. of California Lib.

initiation of causes," in his heart he realized that preparing such a book "would take months, perhaps years." During his brief stay in Paris he did not, of course, secure anything like the formal training in the civil law necessary for such a scholarly study, though he had toured the courts with the same sight-seeing enthusiasm he had given the galleries of the Louvre, the studio of David, the abattoir and the morgue. By May, when it came time for him to leave France, he had quietly changed the purpose of his European trip. Leaving Paris behind "with the liveliest regret, and . . . with a thousand things undone, unlearned and unstudied," he headed for England to "find a *vacation,*—the first I have had for years." [2]

• 2 •

"Land of my studies, my thoughts, and my dreams!" Sumner rapturously saluted England. "There, indeed, shall I 'pluck the life of life.'" Arriving in London on May 31, he was almost at once swept into the exciting round of English social life. By accepted convention, each of his numerous letters of introduction entitled its bearer to one dinner invitation, but Sumner proved so personable that many of his hosts insisted upon entertaining him again and again. Justice John Vaughan, for example, to whom Sumner presented a letter from Story, gave a dinner so that Sumner could meet some other British judges. Charmed by his American guest's behavior, he invited Sumner to accompany him to the Old Bailey, where he sat beside the judge during the hearings, and asked him to dine with the other magistrates of that court. "I received you first on Story's account," Vaughan exclaimed to the young American, "but I keep you on your own; I like you very much; indeed, if a judge may say so, I have an affection for you, by G—d." [3]

As one invitation led to another, Sumner found "every moment of his time . . . absorbed and his mind almost in a *fever*" of social excitement. "Aroused prematurely in the morning to dress for breakfast," then one of the most fashionable forms of British entertaining, he kept active in his giddy social whirl until

[2] Pierce, I, 290, 294, 295.
[3] Ibid., I, 294; Sumner to Story, July 12, 1838, Sumner MSS.

long after midnight. For want of time he abandoned the travel journal with which he had so methodically begun his journey, but his immensely detailed letters to his Boston friends were now crammed with references to lords and ladies, barons and earls, lord chancellors, and even an occasional duke or two. He became an honorary member of the Garrick, the Travellers', the Athenaeum, and the Alfred clubs; the last, he boasted, was "the most exclusive in London," and he was "the only untitled honorary member" of it. At Westminster Hall, after declining repeated invitations to sit on the bench, he was assigned a seat in the Sergeants' row at the Court of Common Pleas and in the Queen's Counsel row at the Queen's Bench. He was admitted to the floor of the House of Commons, and in the House of Lords he had a regular place assigned him, on the steps of the throne, where he could remain even during divisions. For the coronation of the young Queen Victoria, for which admission to Westminster Abbey was so eagerly sought that seats sold at the scalper's rate of twenty-five guineas each, Sumner had no fewer than three tickets—one from a privy councillor and another from the Marquis of Lansdowne—and he was able to give two away with "terrible éclat." [4]

Soon Sumner knew everybody in the small world of London society. He was impressed by Sir Robert Peel, "polished, graceful, self-possessed, candid, or apparently candid, in the extreme," and thought poorly of Lord John Russell, who reminded him of a pettifogging attorney, since he wriggled as he spoke, "played with his hat, [and] seemed unable to dispose of his hands or his feet." At one breakfast he heard that "perfect model of a judge," Lord Denman, condemn the judicial wig as "the silliest thing in England," and at the next he heard Justice James Allan Park exclaim that this sentiment "was all a piece of Denman's coxcombry —that he wished to shew his person." Through Emerson's introduction he met Thomas Carlyle, who seemed to him "like an inspired boy," whose "thoughts . . . came from his apparently unconscious mind, couched in the most grotesque style, and yet condensed to a degree of intensity." With Walter Savage Landor, "about 55, with an open countenance, firm and decided, with a

[4] Sumner to Story, June 27, 1838, Sumner MSS.; Sumner to Hillard, June 14, 1838, ibid.; Lieber to Matilda Lieber, Aug. 1, 1838, Lieber MSS.

head grey and inclining to baldness" and "dressed in a heavy frock-coat of snuff colour, trowsers of the same and boots," he argued the comparative merits of Napoleon and Washington. At dinner at Lord Lansdowne's he encountered a sharp-voiced, articulate man of "about 40, rather short, and with a belly of unclassical proportions," who proved to be Thomas Babington Macaulay, just back from India and about to commence his history of England. "My acquaintance is most extensive—extensive beyond my most sanguine anticipations," Sumner reported complacently to Lieber. "All that is eminent in the law I know well, as well as some of the most prominent men in politics and in the church." [5]

The end of the London social and legal season in July was only the beginning of Sumner's conquest of Britain. During the summer, at the invitation of the presiding judges, he "travelled a part of the Home Circuit with Lord Denman, the Western with Baron Parke, the North Wales with Mr. Justice Vaughan, and the Northern with Baron Alderson." When he reached Chester, where Vaughan was holding assizes, the judge addressed him from the bench and called him to his side, where he sat for two hours. At Liverpool he dined one day "with the city corporation at a truly aldermanic feast in honor of the judges; the second, with the judges, to meet the bar; the third, with the Mayor at his country seat; the fourth, with the bar; the fifth, with Mr. Cresswell (the leader and old reporter) . . . , the sheriffs, etc."; the sixth, with John Arthur Roebuck, the young Radical who was later to become the Confederacy's best, if not wisest, friend in England. The English judges and lawyers, he found, were "indeed, a band of brothers," and they treated him not "as a young man, or a *junior brother*, but every way as an *equal*." By September, when the courts adjourned, he could boast that he had seen "more of the English bar and of its practice, than ever before fell to a stranger." [6]

Sumner did not confine his interests to lawyers and courts.

[5] Pierce, I, 316; Sumner to Story, July 12 [continued July 17], and Aug. 18, 1838, Sumner MSS.; Sumner to Hillard, June 14, and July 3, 1838, ibid.; Sumner to Lieber, Sept. 3, 1838, ibid.

[6] Sumner to Benjamin Rand, Sept. 4, 1838, MS., Mass. Hist. Soc.; Sumner to Story, Aug. 12, 1838, Sumner MSS.; Pierce, I, 343; Sumner to Hillard, Dec. 4, 1838, Sumner MSS.; Sumner to Richard Fletcher, Sept. 10, 1838, Segal Coll.

In August he stopped off at Combe Florey for a visit with Sydney Smith, whom he considered "one of the most remarkable men of England," despite his baffling sense of humor. The witty clergyman was so pleased with this "remarkably agreeable modest well behaved American lawyer" that he sent Sumner with a glowing letter of introduction to his fellow founder of the *Edinburgh Review*, the Lord Advocate Sir John A. Murray. At Rydal Mount, Wordsworth entertained Sumner with tea and "sensible, instructive and refined" conversation. At Brougham Hall the eccentric Henry Brougham startled his American visitor by speaking "in the most disparaging terms of the aristocracy" and by lacing his conversation with " 'God!' 'good God!' 'by God'—'damned' etc.," and then impressed him by dashing off a letter in correct Latin and scrawling a Greek ode without referring to a dictionary.[7]

Almost as interesting as lawyers and literary lions to Sumner were English noblemen who had nothing but birth and wealth to recommend them. In Yorkshire he visited Baron Wharncliffe at Wortley Hall, set in a park of 1,800 acres, where deer grazed, and Sumner found the family, for all its wealth and titles, abounding in "good sense, pure Toryism, simplicity and affectionate intercourse." At Wentworth House he was the guest of Earl Fitzwilliam, who showed him an establishment so vast that there were stables for one hundred horses, and conservatories and aviaries which made the Boston Botanical Garden seem small. On a brief trip to Dublin, he was entertained by the Lord Lieutenant of Ireland, Lord Morpeth, oldest son of the Earl of Carlisle. At Holkham House the Earl of Leicester showed Sumner his priceless Vandykes, Titians, and Rubenses, but his guest was more interested in the "crabbed hand-writing" on "the darksome notes and memoranda" which the Earl's ancestor, Edward Coke, had left in the library.[8]

By the time Sumner returned to London in November, he was a social lion. He knew everybody—or everybody wanted to know him. George Shattuck, who came over from Paris and visited him, was astonished to find that Sumner, in the course of

[7] Sumner to Sarah P. Cleveland, Aug. 6, 1838, copy, Longfellow MSS.; Smith to Murray, Aug. 16, 1838, MS., J. Pierpont Morgan Lib.; Sumner to Hillard, Sept. 6, and 8, 1838, Sumner MSS.

[8] Sumner to Story, Oct. 24, 1838, Sumner MSS.; Sumner to Hillard, Oct. 27, 1838, ibid.; Sumner to Greenleaf, Nov. 2, 1838, ibid.

only six months in England, had become "acquainted with all [the] distinguished . . . whigs, tories, radicals, judges, literary men of all grades and classes, scientific, professional men." The acquaintance that I have is truly *prodigious,*" Sumner himself exclaimed; "it is almost *unmanageable.*" [9]

His days were "a constant succession of kindnesses and attentions of the most flattering and gratifying character," he proudly wrote Story, "such as belong to a *Crown Prince*, rather than to a person so humble as myself." He was the guest of the Lord Mayor of London at the Guildhall dinner. At Windsor palace he was given a private view of Victoria's rooms, "never shown except during the Queen's absence," and was privileged to hear "the gals" in waiting upon Her Majesty complain "that there is nothing but stale eggs in the Castle." He had breakfast with Samuel Rogers, the aged poet, who explained that it took him ten times as long to write a sentence of prose as it did Wordsworth to write one in verse. Henry Hallam, the historian, had him to dinner, and Harriet Martineau to an evening party. Richard Monckton Milnes, the poet, became a close friend. He accepted an invitation to visit the meretricious Countess of Blessington and see her famous and scandalous ménage at Gore House, but snubbed two of her attendant friends, Disraeli, whom he thought "one of the most vulgar fops I ever saw," and Bulwer, with "his flash *falsetto* dress, with high-heel boots, a white great coat . . . and a flaming blue cravat." Sir Charles Vaughan welcomed him to All Soul's College at Oxford, and William Whewell entertained him at Cambridge.[1]

By February 1839, when he began to think of leaving England, Sumner was almost exhausted, and complained that he was beginning "to tire of company and society." "I have sounded it in all its depths and shallows," he explained to Hillard. "I have seen it in some of its most splendid and fashionable, as well as literary and intellectual phases." But, though he claimed to be bored, he could not drag himself away until the end of March. After all, he found, "the blood does dance to sit at meat with men gifted and good, and more still, with ladies cultivated, refined and beautiful

[9] Sumner to Story, Aug. 18, 1838, ibid.; Shattuck to Miss E. E. Shattuck, Feb. 21, 1839, Shattuck MSS.

[1] Sumner to Story, Aug. 18, 1838, Sumner MSS.; Sumner to Hillard, Nov. 16, Dec. 4, and 28, 1838, ibid.

—to see the shifting shadows that crowd the countenance and catch the various conversation, perhaps to mingle in it and find your voice not unheeded." [2]

· 3 ·

Sumner left England in a shower of compliments. Lord Denman, urging him to return, declared: "No one ever conciliated more universal respect and good will." Lord and Lady Holland, Lord Lansdowne, and the Earl of Leicester declared that their homes were always open to him. Sydney Smith thanked him for coming, and added that it was an honor to be "thought well of on the other Side of the World by a Gentleman as honourable—and as enlightened" as Sumner. When Lord Brougham heard that Sumner was leaving, he exclaimed: "O God! must you go!" "Do you wonder that I quit England full of love and friendly feeling?" Sumner asked his American friends.[3]

They did not, but a good many did wonder at the extraordinary reception he had received. Sumner's social campaign in Britain, the historian Prescott concluded, was "more brilliant . . . than was ever achieved by any of his countrymen before." Felton wrote proudly: "Probably no other private American gentleman has enjoyed opportunities equal to yours." Sumner himself was almost as astonished as pleased by his social success. Could all this really be happening to "Charles Sumner, a poor scribe and lawyer of Boston?" he sometimes asked himself. Why should he, a "poor lawyer, hardly recognized at home, or if recognized, only received as a young man," be accepted upon intimate terms by "the very leaders and Queen's Counsel, the *elite* of the English bar" and by fashionable English society as well? [4]

It is not too difficult to learn the secret of Sumner's success. He had come to England at a most opportune time. In another decade the ubiquitous American tourist with his letters of introduction would become a bore and a nuisance, but as yet only a few, eminent Americans, such as Washington Irving and George

[2] Sumner to Hillard, Dec. 14, 1838, ibid.

[3] Denman to Sumner, Feb. 27, 1839, Sumner Autograph Coll.; Smith to Sumner, Aug. 16, 1838, ibid.; Pierce, II, 80–1.

[4] George Ticknor: *Life of William Hickling Prescott* (Boston: Ticknor and Fields; 1864), p. 364; Felton to Sumner, Nov. 5, 1838, Sumner MSS.; Sumner to Hillard, June 14, and Aug. 12, 1838, ibid.

Ticknor, had knocked at the doors of English society.[5] Furthermore, English attitudes toward America were generally friendly, as in the 1830's the only source of friction between the two countries was the Maine boundary line, about which, Sumner quickly found, nobody in England seemed to know or care.

Though the English were in a receptive mood and though Sumner's letters of introduction initially opened doors for him, he had to rely upon his own social resources to stay inside of them. These were, in fact, impressive. He was obviously of English descent. His appearance as well as his name lent truth to his repeated protestation that when an American like himself went to England, "he was coming home,—coming, as it were, to his father's hearthstone." [6] This visitor looked not merely English, but handsome and personable as well. The lankness, clumsiness, and muddy complexion which had marred Sumner's adolescence had now disappeared, and with his regular features, smooth olive skin, dark brown flashing eyes, perfectly regular white teeth, and shock of dark brown hair, he looked like a strikingly healthy, vigorous young giant. The excellent tailors to whom he had immediately resorted had persuaded him to discard some of his more exuberant American clothing, and in his expensive, unobtrusive wardrobe he seemed almost English.

Yet, of course, the fact that Sumner was not English was one of his chief social assets. His hosts found that everything was delightfully new to him. The most demanding Englishman could not ask for a more assiduous sight-seer, or one in a more "constant state of astonishment and delight." Sumner's willingness to be pleased irritated choleric Thomas Carlyle, who defined Sumner as "the most completely nothin' of a mon that ever crossed my threshold,—naught whatsoever in him or of him but wind and vanity," but most Englishmen found it only proper that a visiting American should be impressed by all things British, and concluded that Sumner was "an amiable, sensible, high-minded, well-informed gentleman." [7]

[5] Robert E. Spiller, *The American in England during the First Half Century of Independence* (New York: Henry Holt & Co., Inc.; 1926).

[6] Pierce, I, 347.

[7] Ibid., I, 306, 309; Sara Norton and M. A. DeWolfe Howe: *Letters of Charles Eliot Norton with Biographical Comment* (Boston: Houghton Mifflin Co.; 1913), I, 422.

They found his naïveté delightful, and took pleasure in shocking this serious-minded young American. A true New Englander, Sumner was astonished to learn that Englishmen played cards for money. "Sober persons," he reported, with puzzlement, "make the sum six-pence on each *point*, a term which I do not understand, though I have gained several points as I have been told." He was upset, too, by the prevalence of swearing among the members of the English upper classes. Even more disconcerting was the lack of reticence upon subjects absolutely prohibited in Boston society. Sumner was greatly embarrassed when the Lady Georgiana Wortley told him that Lady John Russell "had gone to Brighton *to lie in*," and was covered with confusion when Lady Anson asked if he had "seen in Edinburgh the small room in which Mary Queen of Scots was *confined* with James." Most shocking of all was to hear Lady Morgan, in the presence of a young niece, assert "that it was time men should begin to think of children in the selection of their wives, and that they should be influenced by the same consideration that governed them when they *bought* a *mare to breed from*." [8]

But, if Sumner was easily shocked, he was even more easily taught. He promptly learned that "one would sooner commit the unpardonable sin than appear in boots" and that "every day should be *clean-shirt* day." Noting that the English aristocrats avoided using titles or even "Mr." except when addressing strangers, Sumner made their usage his lifelong habit. Willingly he accepted reproof from Englishmen. At a dinner party when Sumner mentioned that George Washington's "ashes still reposed at Mt. Vernon," he took with good grace Landor's chiding: "Why will you, Mr. Sumner, who speak with such force and correctness, employ a word which in the present connection is not English. Washington's body was never *burnt*—there are no ashes—say, rather, *remains*." Sumner's hosts found him uniformly enthusiastic in doing whatever they had planned for his entertainment, however strange it seemed to him. In Northumberland, though it was pouring rain, he uncomplainingly accompanied Archdeacon T. H. Scott in splashing out over the moors to hunt grouse; though their dogs started several coveys, neither man

[8] Sumner to Hillard, Oct. 27, and Nov. 16, 1838, and Jan. 23, 1839, Sumner MSS.

got a single bird all day, but Sumner shot a hare, which he formally entered in his host's game book. On a Christmas visit to Lord Fitzwilliam at Milton Hall, Sumner went fox hunting, again in a dreary rain, remained on horseback, at the imminent risk of life and limb, for seven or eight hours each day, received a bad fall, but cheerfully enjoyed the whole affair.[9]

The English found Sumner as reserved as he was agreeable. He was careful never to push himself forward. Though he presented many of his American letters of introduction, he was punctilious in not asking his English acquaintances for favors. "I have followed a rigid rule . . ." he explained. "*I have not asked an introduction to a single person—I have not asked a single ticket, privilege, or any thing of the kind from any body—I have not called upon anybody* (with one exception) *until I had been first called upon or invited.*" Yet, he noted proudly: "I doubt if there is a man in England that I could not have been introduced to simply by expressing a bare wish." [1]

Sumner was also discreet. Some previous American travelers, notably James Fenimore Cooper and N. P. Willis, had published books on their Europen adventures which amounted to an invasion of the privacy of those who had entertained them. Carefully Sumner made it known that he "came abroad in no book-making spirit." As anything he wrote would present either an untrue picture of the men he had met or an offensive portrait that would tell all the truth, he would publish nothing at all. "For instance," he asked Hillard, who was urging him to do a book of travel essays, "could I say of O'Connell that he is a vulgar looking man with a foul breath; of Brougham, that he has a glorious head, but little heart, and that withal he has a vein of insanity, which, indeed, existed in his father and in a still-living sister, a fact unknown to the public at present entirely?" [2]

Gradually Sumner's English friends recognized that he had, apart from enjoying British society, only one purpose, to promote "the diffusion of the writings of any American calculated to in-

[9] Sumner to Hillard, July 3, Aug. 24, Sept. 6, and Dec. 25, 1838, ibid.; Sumner to George Sumner, Sept. 6, 1839, ibid.; T. H. Scott to Sumner, Feb. 5, 1839, Sumner Autograph Coll.

[1] Sumner to Story, July 15, 1838, Sumner MSS.; Sumner to Hillard, Aug. 12, 1838, ibid.

[2] Sumner to Hillard, Aug. 12, 1838, ibid.

spire respect . . . [for] liberal institutions." He advocated his friends' books with a zeal he did not show for himself. He tried to interest English publishers in Motley's poor novel, *Morton's Hope,* in Palfrey's lectures on Jewish antiquities, and in Richard Hildreth's *The Slave,* which anticipated *Uncle Tom's Cabin* by many years. Through his friendship with Monckton Milnes he secured the publication of the first serious article devoted to Emerson in a British periodical. He persuaded an English firm to bring out an edition of Lieber's *Political Ethics.* But most of all he tried everywhere to promote the reputation of Judge Story. In France he started a movement to elect Story to the Institute, even preparing himself a memoir of the judge in French; in England he saw that his important friends at the bar read and reviewed Story's works. "I perpetually keep in view," he wrote the judge, "the making of our jurisprudence known in England." [3]

Englishmen might have found these exertions for American law and letters objectionable in another person, but Sumner so clearly admitted the overwhelming superiority of the English in these, as in all other fields, that no one could take offense. Increasingly Sumner was becoming an Anglophile. He spent a good deal of his time abroad being embarrassed for his country and for his countrymen. From his English vantage point American politics seemed "inconceivably petty," smaller than "Tom Thumb's 'pint-pot.' " Like his English friends, he was horrified by the reports of frontier violence and vigilante gangs that appeared in the news from the United States. This American disregard of law, he sharply told Story, had "a gigantic importance" abroad, and he could not understand how reputable men at home could "stand by and smile, while the law is prostrated." [4]

When compared with Great Britain, Sumner concluded, the United States was lamentably lacking in culture. American social life was narrow and censorious. "One who mingles in the broad society of London and Paris," he informed Longfellow, rather loftily, "must be reminded, by sad contrast, of the narrow imper-

[3] Sumner to Story, Sept. 28, and Nov. 16, 1838, ibid.; Sumner to Richard Bentley, Dec. 3, 1838, Longfellow MSS.; Bentley to Sumner, Dec. 6, 1838, Sumner Autograph Coll.; James Pope-Hennessy, *Monckton Milnes: The Years of Promise, 1809–1851* (London: Constable; 1949), p. 115; Sumner to David B. Warden, May 28, 1838, Jan. 15, 1839, and Mar. 12, 1840, Warden MSS.

[4] Sumner to Hillard, Dec. 11, 1838, and July 26, 1839, Sumner MSS.; Sumner to Story, Oct. 4, 1838, ibid.

tinence that characterizes our town, where the colour of a gentleman's coat, and the habit of his shirt-collar or cravat are cardinal topics of criticism." His fellow citizens were as lacking in independence as in taste. "Americans are sheep," Sumner scornfully decided, "and follow the bellweather." American colleges were shockingly deficient when compared to European universities. "When shall we have an institution in America, where a person may get an education?" he querulously asked. By European standards, the professions in the United States were ill-trained. The American bar, compared with the French and the English, was "the poorest, most illiterate, and ungentlemanlike, of all the three." Even the use of language in the United States was slovenly, Sumner complained, when a great writer like Longfellow could in the middle of a beautiful poem "commit that *Americanism—'side-walk.'*" All in all, Sumner summarized, as he was about to leave England: "Here, civilization has gone further than with us," an opinion which was in no small measure responsible for the warmth of his welcome in Britain.[5]

• 4 •

Though Sumner's friends in Boston jokingly referred to him as "the Earl," they were seriously troubled by the insistent note of anti-Americanism which kept creeping into his letters. Greenleaf feared that he would "be so 'improved' by travel" that he would not return "the simple, whole-souled, transparent, generous fellow we all love," and Longfellow wondered whether Sumner, when he came home, would not "find it somewhat hard, to put his Pegasus into a yoke." [6]

Indignantly Sumner rejected suggestions that travel had weakened his loyalty to the United States. "Grateful I am that I am an American," he insisted, "for I would not give up the priceless institutions of my country (abused and perverted as they are), the purity of morals in society, and the universal competence which prevails, in exchange for all that I have seen

[5] Sumner to Longfellow, Jan. 24, 1839, Longfellow MSS.; Sumner to Hillard, July 26, 1839, and Mar. 18, 1840, Sumner MSS.; Sumner to Story, Sept. 24, 1839, ibid.; Sumner to William F. Frick, Aug. 4, 1839, ibid.; Sumner to Benjamin Rand, Feb. 20, 1839, MS., Mass. Hist. Soc.

[6] Lieber to Hillard, Sept. 8, 1839, Lieber MSS.; Greenleaf to Lieber, Apr. 11, 1838, ibid.; Longfellow to Hillard, Aug. 16, 1838, photostat, Longfellow MSS.

abroad." "I am not yet entirely perverted by Europe," he protested, a bit too emphatically. "I have not ceased to be an American." [7]

To prove his point, and to counteract some of his earlier, more extreme pro-English statements, he wrote his Boston friends, rather repetitiously, that America was in many ways superior. "In England what is called society is better educated, more refined, and more civilized than what is called society in our country," he admitted, but "The true pride of America is in her middle and poorer classes, in their general health and happiness, and freedom from poverty, in their facilities for being educated, and in the opportunities to them of rising in the scale there." [8]

Doubtless Sumner sincerely believed these patriotic sentiments, but it is hard to see that he had any evidence to support them. Though he had an intimate and remarkable acquaintance among the English aristocracy, bar, and intelligentsia, though he had friends among all political parties and counted no fewer than four Cabinet members as personal friends, Sumner had, as some of his English acquaintances reminded him, seen "little of the middle ranks and masses" while abroad.[9] Interested in historic sights and aristocratic estates, he was insensitive to the less happy aspects of life in the early Victorian age. He visited no factories. He lived for months in London unaware of the slums around him. He showed no concern over the British government's failure to provide general elementary education, medical care, or sanitation. In fact, Sumner's animadversions against English society reflected not so much his experience abroad as his desire to appease his worried friends in Boston. His remark that the superiority of the American masses more than counterbalanced the excellence of the British upper classes was not really a profound reflection derived from his wide experience; it was a direct quotation of a remark he had heard Charles Buller make in a London drawing room and, what is more, it was the familiar theme of Francis J. Grund's *The Americans,* which Sumner had praised in the *North American Review* before he ever left Boston.[1]

[7] Pierce, I, 326; Sumner to Hillard, Mar. 9, 1839, Sumner MSS.

[8] Sumner to Hillard, Mar. 1, 1839, Sumner MSS.

[9] Joseph Parkes to Sumner, June 2, 1840, ibid.; W. S. Gilly to Sumner, Nov. 26, 1838, ibid.

[1] Similarly, Sumner's occasional remarks that the British ought to equalize suffrage and that primogeniture, "the worst thing in England," should be

Whatever he might tell his American friends, Sumner was, in fact, completely in love with England. Not even the raw London winter, with "murky, foggy days,—freighted with colds, catarrhs, and death," could disenchant him. He felt that he was living "in a land of imagination and not of reality," and he continued to enjoy his stay right up to the day for his departure to the Continent. When his English friends expressed envy because he was going to the sunny, warm south, he replied, with genuine feeling: "England is the *Italy* of an American." Leaving Britain, he explained, was for him "like quitting a *second country*." [2]

Almost immediately upon his arrival in France, Sumner found his affection toward England tested against loyalty to his own country. He learned that the United States minister, Lewis Cass, and many other Americans residing in Paris were seriously excited over the danger of a war between Great Britain and the United States. When in England, Sumner had been so absorbed by society that he was only casually aware that the perennial dispute over the Northeastern Boundary had erupted again, and he could not believe that anyone could take seriously "the undignified, illiterate and blustering" proclamation of the governor of Maine, claiming title to the whole area in dispute. Embarrassed that his countrymen were behaving so badly, Sumner had announced: "I would rather give up the whole state of Maine, and of Massachusetts to boot than to go to war." [3] But in Paris he discovered that the dispute, which he had so easily brushed aside, was indeed a dangerous one, and his loyalties were divided.

Believing that "*peace* is the duty of nations before all things," Sumner, at Cass's suggestion, immediately commenced research upon the points at dispute between England and America and within a very few days produced a long and learned essay that attempted to settle impartially the rival boundary claims. The article showed that whatever Sumner had learned in Europe, he had not forgotten his law; it was a careful, scholarly, perspicuous

abolished so as "to break the aristocracy," are not real social criticism on his part, but are merely echoes of the ideas of his friends among the moderate Radicals, Joseph Parkes and George Grote. Sumner to Hillard, Jan. 12, 1839, ibid.; Sumner to Story, Mar. 18, 1839, ibid.

[2] Pierce, II, 52, 81; Sumner to Story, June 27, 1838, and Mar. 9, 1839, Sumner MSS.

[3] Sumner to J. O. Sargent, Mar. 15, 1839, J. O. Sargent MSS.; Sumner to Richard Fletcher, Mar. 20, 1839, copy, Sumner MSS.

statement of the main points in the intricate and prolonged dispute. More significant was the fact that Sumner, after all the flattering attentions he had received in England, found himself enthusiastically "stating the *American side*" of the argument. "I endeavored to look at it candidly," he naïvely explained to Lord Morpeth, "and I cannot resist coming to the conclusion that we are right." Delighted at this *"most complete and satisfactory statement of our side that had ever appeared,"* Cass had it published in *Galignani's Messenger*, which was widely circulated throughout Europe.[4]

Having convinced himself of the justice of the American claim, Sumner was sure he could persuade his recent hosts in England to agree with him. The British he had found to be an eminently reasonable people. If Americans would only cease their vulgar agitation and base their case upon a "clear, correct and dignified ground," he was certain they would overcome the general ignorance and indifference of the English. Characteristically, Sumner did not believe that the accredited American diplomats abroad could influence British opinion; the United States minister in London, Andrew Stevenson, was, after all, a man of no particular social standing, who certainly had never been admitted to the circles in which Sumner had moved. Against the advice of both Cass and Stevenson, Sumner tried to settle the Maine boundary dispute by personal diplomacy. Buttonholing every influential English politician who came to Paris during these weeks, widely distributing his *Galignani* article to his British friends, and writing "to some *thirty* persons of influence in British politics, soliciting their attention to this subject," Sumner was sure his exertions would help keep the peace. "I thought," he explained to Stevenson, "considering what I had seen and enjoyed there, that nobody was more called upon to contribute his mite to the great cause of peace than myself." [5]

Leaving Paris at the end of April 1839, Sumner did not tarry to observe the consequences of his shirt-sleeve diplomacy. Had he done so, he might have realized that his friendships, valuable as they were as a social and intellectual bridge between America

[4] Sumner to Hillard, Apr. 15, 1839, Sumner MSS.; Pierce, II, 87.

[5] Sumner to Everett, Mar. 18, 1839, Everett MSS.; Sumner to Stevenson, Apr. 10, and 19, 1839, Stevenson MSS.; Cass to Stevenson, Apr. 10, 1839, ibid.; Sumner to Sir Charles Vaughan, Apr. 19, 1839, Vaughan MSS.

and England, were not an effective means of settling grave political issues between the two nations. He could have observed, too, that his arguments, however lucid or accurate, were ineffectual in persuading the English government to act against its national interest. But these were lessons Sumner would only learn, with a shock, some twenty years later, during the Civil War.

• 5 •

"I have supped full of society, and am tired of bright lights," Sumner had announced as he left London for Italy. "I have scores of letters to all sorts of people on my *route*, but am sated with society, and shall look at *things*." The month he delayed in Paris in order to write on the boundary dispute kept him from breaking his resolve, for he arrived in Italy during the hot summer months when "everybody" was leaving it. "Man's season was over," he remarked sententiously, "but I may truly say, God's was come." [6]

Sumner rejoiced that he had come at the slack social season, for he could devote his unlimited energy to serious sight-seeing. With the same thoroughness he had once demonstrated in cataloguing the Harvard law library, he set himself to mastering the language, literature, and history of Italy. Every day he followed a strict schedule: "rose at 6½ o'clock; threw myself on my sofa, with a little round table near well-covered with books—read undisturbed till about 10, when the servant brought on a tray my breakfast—two eggs done *sur le plat,* a roll and cup of chocolate . . . rang the bell, and my table was put to rights, and my reading went on—often till 5 and 6 o'clock in the evening, without my once rising from the sofa. . . . At 5 or 6 got up, stretched myself—dressed to go out—dined in a garden under a mulberry tree, chiefly on fruits, salads, and wine . . . walked. . . . After an ice-cream . . . to my books again. . . ."

During his four months in Italy he tried to read everything. He studied, in the original, all of Dante, Tasso, Boccaccio, Manzoni, and Alfieri, and most of Machiavelli, Guicciardini, Goldoni, and Foscolo as well, generally working with several "different editions, and going over a monstrous mass of notes and annotations."

[6] Sumner to Hillard, Apr. 15, and Mar. 1, 1839, Sumner MSS.; Sumner to George Ticknor, Sept. 15, 1839, Ticknor MSS.

By October he thought himself master of the language. "There is no Italian which I cannot understand without a dictionary; there is hardly a classic in the language of which I have not read the whole, or considerable portions." [7]

With his time so employed, Sumner found his stay in Italy all too short. He tried to hoard his hours by ignoring as much as possible of modern Italy, which depressed him. Like most American tourists, he was annoyed that he could not leave his rooms "without being surrounded with half a dozen squalid wretches, with most literally scarcely a rag to cover their nakedness." As bad as the poverty was the superstition. At a single village church he was proudly shown "the skeletons of *twenty five* saints dressed in silk, . . . a part of a cushion that belonged to the Mother of the Virgin Mary and also a part of a sandal of *Joseph*." This "perversion of Christianity," he decided in disgust, was an "uncouth imposture," and he willingly turned to "the thrilling . . . antient classical sites and things." [8]

For company in his sight-seeing Sumner looked to the little colony of Americans resident in Italy. With Bostonian fastidiousness he spotted other American tourists—a record crowd of 375 poured into Rome in 1839—by "their dirty shirts—their nasal conversation—their want of the manner either of the scholar or the man of the world," and in their presence pretended to speak only French and Italian. But a semipermanent resident like George W. Greene, the American consul at Rome, who was both a grandson of General Nathanael Greene and a friend of Longfellow, was different. Promptly concluding that "our country has not *five* men his peers" in scholarship, Sumner annexed Greene as his constant companion and cicerone during his three months in Rome. Together they walked each evening to the Forum, or to St. Peter's, or out to one of the gates of Rome; they used to sit together for hours on a broken column along the Via Sacra or a rich capital in the Colosseum and reconstruct in fancy the history that had passed before these mute marbles.[9]

Greene introduced Sumner to the numerous American artists then living in Italy. At Florence he met Horatio Greenough,

[7] Sumner to Hillard, Sept. 29, 1839, Sumner MSS.; Pierce, II, 118.

[8] Sumner to Hillard, May 19, 1839, Sumner MSS.; Sumner to Story, Sept. 4, 1839, ibid.

[9] Sumner to Hillard, Sept. 29, 1839, ibid.

and, recognizing the famous sculptor as a "high priest of the Temple of Art," approached him as "a mere neophyte, one of the humblest worshippers, who kneel between the posts of the door." Greenough proved not to be a formidable personage after all, but "a wonderful fellow—an accomplished man," and Sumner, who was unable to distinguish between personal and aesthetic feelings, concluded that he was "master of his art, . . . the most accomplished artist alive." Soon he ventured, almost as an equal, to offer suggestions about the details of Greenough's "masterly" but startlingly nude statue of George Washington.[1] Sumner found Hiram Powers less impressive than Greenough, for the Cincinnati artist had "not gone beyond bust-making" and his works seemed "quite pretty, but rather tame and insignificant." Far more interesting was the relatively obscure Thomas Crawford, to whose studio in Rome Greene brought Sumner. Greatly taken by Crawford personally, excited at the idea of discovering a hitherto unknown, and convinced by Greene that the "Orpheus" on which Crawford was working would be "one of the most remarkable productions that have come from an artists of his years in modern times," Sumner promptly started a campaign to have his friends in Boston purchase or publicize the sculptor's works. "If you cannot order a statue," he told Longfellow, "you can at least write an article." [2]

Absorbed in his studies of literature, history, and art, Sumner broke away from Italy with great reluctance. "I regret that I left so many things unseen, and saw so little of many others worthy to be studied and pondered,—food for thought and imagination," he wrote Greene in farewell. Like many another American visitor to that enchanting land, he had fancies of going back to the United States, "collecting together some of the savings of a few years," and returning to Italy to "live in the sight of all that is fine in art, and under this beautiful sky, and die in peace."

[1] Ibid.; Sumner to Greenough, Nov. 8, 1839, and Jan. 8, 1839 [the date should be 1840], photostats of MSS. in the possession of Mrs. Sylvia Crane, New York City. See also Otto Wittman, Jr.: "The Italian Experience (American Artists in Italy, 1830–1875)," *American Quarterly*, IV (Spring 1952), 3–15, and Van Wyck Brooks: *The Dream of Arcadia: American Writers and Artists in Italy, 1760–1915* (New York: E. P. Dutton & Co., Inc.; 1958), esp. Chaps. iii–viii.

[2] Pierce, II, 111–12; Sumner to Hillard, July 26, 1839, Sumner MSS.; Sumner to Longfellow, July 26, 1839, Longfellow MSS.; Sumner to W. H. Prescott, June 28, 1839, Prescott MSS.

As unconscious evidences of his wish to remain, Sumner carelessly left belongings behind him at every place he stopped during his last few weeks in Italy: "a silk handkerchief at one, a cambric one at another, a shirt at another, and an umbrella at a fourth; to say nothing of a pair of gloves." [3]

Uncertainty about his future, as well as love for Italy, was behind his reluctance to depart. "I begin to tremble about myself," he confessed to Story. "I look with great anxiety to my professional prospects." Cheerfully he tried to predict that when he got back to Boston, he could easily "renew the labors which I have for the while forsaken" and "grasp resolutely the plough which I have left in the furrough [*sic*]," but, in more realistic moods, he recognized that his European trip had permanently affected his prospects at the bar. "I think of that tide, whose ebb I declined to take, which might have floated me on to fortune—that is, to worldly success," he wrote Greenleaf ruefully, "and I fear that I have lost it forever." Ahead of him now could lie only a life of "unchanging drudgery" at "the great grindstone of the law." [4]

These distressing reflections hung darkly over the remaining few months of Sumner's European travels. Not even the fact that Prince Metternich showered him with civilities in Vienna, that the Crown Prince of Prussia received him in Berlin, or that in Heidelberg the jurists Mittermaier and Thibaut welcomed him as an equal and addressed him as "*Herr Professor*" could make him forget that he had so shortly to return to America. In his heart he wanted to stay in Germany "all the winter, pursuing his studies, and mingling in this learned and gay world," but Story, Greenleaf, and Hillard all urged him to come home. Even more pressing was the advice of his pocketbook. "I have spent more than five thousand dollars," he calculated, "and I cannot afford to travel longer." Reluctantly he admitted that it was time to "close this charmed book." [5]

Returning to England in March 1840, Sumner had a final fling in English society. London he found "more mighty, magnifi-

[3] Sumner to Greene, Dec. 30, 1839, Greene MSS.; Sumner to Hillard, Sept. 29, 1839, Sumner MSS.; Pierce, II, 118.

[4] Sumner to Story, Sept. 24, 1839, Sumner MSS.; Sumner to Greenleaf, Nov. 2, 1838, and Jan. 21, 1839, ibid.; Pierce, II, 126.

[5] Sumner to Story, Feb. 10, 1840, Sumner MSS.; Sumner to Hillard, Dec. 25, 1839, and Mar. 18, 1840, ibid.; Pierce, II, 133.

cent, and fascinating than ever." He had not been forgotten during his travels on the Continent, and his friends overwhelmed him with invitations. He had time to visit only a few—"the Lansdownes, Duke and Duchess of Sutherland (the most beautiful woman in the world), Mrs Norton, Lady Seymour (both beautiful in the extreme); [Abraham] Hayward, Sydney Smith, [Nassau] Senior, Fonblanque, Milnes, . . . the [George] Grotes, Charles Austin (more brilliant than ever), the Wortleys, etc." But "I must leave all this," he sternly told himself. "If I do not force myself away, I shall not be able to go." [6]

Sailing from Portsmouth on April 3, Sumner spent the slow four-week voyage reflecting upon his past triumphs and future prospects. His very wardrobe proclaimed that he was now a cosmopolitan man. His "trowsers, waist-coats, frock-coat, and blue evening coat" came "from London—black evening coat from Berlin . . . boots from Paris—where else can boots be made? . . . huge *pelt-stiefel* from Vienna and distant Hungary—hat from Rome—*thick* travelling-cap from New York—*thin* one from Marseilles—surtout from Paris—cloak from Boston—the good old cloak, that has 'braved the battle and the breeze' so long." His thoughts were of a similarly composite character. Though he protested that he was "still a *believer* in our institutions," he could not help thinking that, when compared to Europe, America looked "sad enough—vulgar, petty, grovelling." He professed eager anxiety to return to his professional life, "to plunge at once . . . in *medias res*," but he also admitted that he anticipated "mortification, disappointment, perhaps defeat." Difficult as it would be "to step from the pinnacle of this world's society to . . . the stern realities of American life," he was certain that he had benefited by his travels. "My tour has stimulated my ambition," he told Lieber, "taught me my ignorance—and enabled me to direct my future studies." [7]

[6] Sumner to Hillard, Mar. 18, and 28, and Feb. 11, 1840, Sumner MSS.

[7] Sumner to Story, Mar. 24, and Feb. 10, 1840, ibid.; Sumner to Hillard, Feb. 8, 1840, ibid.; Sumner to Lieber, Sept. 12, 1839, Lieber MSS.

CHAPTER IV

The Iron Curtain

"MY EUROPEAN drama is wound up," Sumner lamented as he returned to Boston. "The iron curtain has fallen upon it." Even before he left Europe, he had begun to dread going back to his "lot . . . of stern uninteresting employ, vulgar contacts dealing with magnified trifles, inhaling bad air, moiling in formal documents, trudging, drudging." His misgivings, he now discovered, had been more than justified. Boston was not London, and the Athenaeum not the Uffizi. Sadly Sumner complained of "the littleness of American life." His only solace was in his "recollections —thoughts—thick-coming fancies." Each morning as he dressed, he returned in imagination to the scenes of his European triumphs, and as he walked down Beacon Hill to his office, he let his mind wander back to "the memory of his Roman life—the happiest days he ever passed." [1]

• 1 •

There was, one might think, no good reason for Sumner's discontent. He returned from Europe in fine health and excellent appearance. A strikingly handsome young man, whose London tailor dressed him to perfection, Sumner was the rage among adolescent girls in Boston, who swooned over him as "fascinating" and nicknamed him "Hyperion." [2] Some of their older sisters thought him equally glamorous.

[1] Sumner to Lieber, July 6, 1840, Sumner MSS.; Sumner to Cleveland, Aug. 27, 1839, Cleveland MSS., Richard Monckton Milnes to Sumner, Aug. 24 [1840], Sumner MSS.; Sumner to Samuel Gridley Howe, May 31, 1844, ibid.

[2] Anna R. Palfrey to Mrs. John G. Palfrey, Nov. 19, 1840, Palfrey MSS.; Anna R. Palfrey to Sarah H. Palfrey, Nov. 20, 1840, ibid.

Joseph Story

Painting by Chester Harding

MASSACHUSETTS HISTORICAL SOCIETY

Sumner in 1839

Bust by Thomas Crawford

MASSACHUSETTS HISTORICAL SOCIETY

Boston was ready to welcome Sumner enthusiastically. Among the stanchly pro-English residents of Beacon Hill, Sumner's almost royal reception abroad more than counterbalanced his humble origins and gave him a "halo never acquired by domestic sanctity." Everybody wanted to hear of his European adventures. George Ticknor, who had moved in the same elevated social circles abroad—and who consequently knew how difficult they were of access—invited Sumner to his mansion on Park Street and had the traveler "sitting up with him night after night, till 12 o'clock," retelling his successes. Wanting to hear Sumner's story while it was still fresh, Samuel Lawrence begged him to spare a day for a visit to Lowell. Even Ralph Waldo Emerson emerged from his transcendental brooding to invite Sumner to Concord. It was not a happy encounter. Sumner, who professed complete incomprehension of what, if anything, transcendentalism meant, regretted that "the great mystagogue" failed to lead out "his winged griffins to take us into the Empyrean," and Emerson, equally disappointed, thought that his "talkative countryman" had "brought nothing home but names, dates, and prefaces." [3]

But for most Bostonians these were quite enough, and they rejoiced in hearing Sumner relive his social successes abroad. Nathan Appleton, the great textile manufacturer, welcomed him as an equal. At Charles P. Curtis's mansion on Mt. Vernon Street Sumner was a dinner guest-of-honor along with Daniel Webster, Jeremiah Mason, and Rufus Choate. The historian Prescott, whose *Ferdinand and Isabella* Sumner had helped to publicize abroad, commenced a lifelong friendship for the young traveler. To symbolize his social acceptance, Sumner became a regular attendant at Mrs. Ticknor's weekly soirees, where, he reported smugly: "There is always a circle of the best people in our town." [4]

Sumner's domestic life was also more satisfactory than before his trip. The worst of his family difficulties had been re-

[3] Henry Adams: *The Education of Henry Adams* (New York: Modern Library, Inc.; 1931), p. 30; C. S. Daveis to Sumner, May 21, 1840, Sumner MSS.; Samuel Lawrence to Sumner, May 9, 1840, ibid.; Sumner to Longfellow [Aug. 9, 1840], Longfellow MSS.; Felton to Longfellow, Aug. 7, 1840, ibid.; *The Correspondence of Thomas Carlyle and Ralph Waldo Emerson, 1834–1872* (Boston: James R. Osgood and Company; 1883), I, 300.

[4] *MHSP*, XLIV, 338; Sumner to Cleveland, Apr. 3, 1841, copy, Longfellow MSS.

solved when his father died while Sumner was in Italy. The relations between Charles and his father had steadily worsened during the 1830's. As Sheriff Sumner grew older, he became more morose and domineering, and the very word "home" came to have sad connotations for his son. During the more than two years Sumner spent abroad, he exchanged few letters with his family. "Where Charles is now and what his designs [are] I am ignorant," the sheriff had to confess in January 1839. When the news of his father's death reached Charles a few months later, he professed "unfeigned sorrow," but added rather coolly: "I cannot affect to feel entirely the grief that others have on such a bereavement." His closest friends did not write him letters of condolence. "What your father has been to you, you have not disguised from me," Cleveland said frankly. "That you are not as deeply afflicted by his death as you would have been if he had been like a father to you I cannot suppose." [5] When Sumner returned to Boston, he went, not to the hotel where he had previously lived, but back to No. 20 Hancock Street.

Altogether Charles found his new domestic arrangements the most satisfactory he had ever known. Mrs. Sumner, to whom the sheriff had left his entire estate, was, to be sure, a bit parsimonious and tended to make the house a "large rookery that is perpetually cawing" by entertaining too many of the "old crones" who were her relatives, but she was a good manager and was willing to foot Charles's bills. The two surviving Sumner daughters helped make the house cheerful, for during Charles's absence Mary had become a delicate and handsome young woman and Julia a bright girl of thirteen. Sumner took a strong interest in both, and he offered to surrender any future share in his father's legacy in order to give them the best education the country could afford. He was proud to escort Mary to concerts and social affairs and even unbent to play with "Jule," as he called his youngest sister. "There was," said Julia many years later, "a world of love and tenderness within him,—often hidden under a cold

[5] Sumner to Hillard, Dec. 8, 1837, Sumner MSS.; C. P. Sumner to George Sumner, Jan. 19, 1838 [the date should be 1839], copy, C. P. Sumner MSS.; Pierce, II, 109; Cleveland to Sumner, May 2, 1839, copy, Longfellow MSS. Sumner's letters have been carefully mutilated to excise nearly all references to his difficulties with his father.

exterior, or apparently crusted over with a chilling coat of reserve." [6]

The absence of Sumner's two older brothers from the house on Hancock Street unquestionably made life easier for him. Albert, who had married a rich widow, had his own luxurious mansion in New York and a summer place at Newport. George had sailed to Europe as supercargo on a trading vessel that docked in Russia. By a combination of charm, effrontery, and good fortune he met Tsar Nicholas, whose kindly attentions launched the young American upon his travels in Europe, Asia, and Africa.[7] Charles watched his brother's social progress with a mixture of approval and irritation. Though he conceded that George was remarkably intelligent, he felt that he lacked "respect for education and educated men" and feared he might publish a book of travels, "which may give a young man some notoriety, but which a man of established character would hardly like to own." As George reached Italy and announced plans for visiting France and England as well, Charles became worried and asked Greene to give a confidential report on his brother's appearance and manners. "Brother as he is," Charles announced, "I shall not presume to present him to my friends in . . . these countries unless I feel assured that he is *entirely presentable*." [8] Presentable or not, George was to remain in Europe for the next fifteen years, and Charles had no rival in his own house.

There seemed no good reason why professionally as well as personally Sumner should not be content in Boston. His office at No. 4 Court Street was waiting for him, as was his law partner and closest friend, Hillard. During the first four months after his return from Europe, he engaged in no legal business, except to substitute for Hillard for a few days, but, with the opening of the fall term of court, he settled back into his office routine. He made it a point to be at his desk punctually at nine o'clock in the morning and to remain at work until two; then, after an hour and a

[6] Sumner to George Sumner, Jan. 1, 1844, and July 13, 1839, Sumner MSS.; Julia Sumner Hastings to Pierce, Nov. 10, 1874, Pierce MSS.; Pierce, II, 158.

[7] Robert C. Waterston: "Memoir of George Sumner," *MHSP*, XVIII (1880–1), 189–223.

[8] Sumner to Greene, Jan. 4, 1840, Greene MSS.; Sumner to Hillard, Sept. 29, 1839, Sumner MSS.; Sumner to George Sumner, July 8, 1838, ibid.

half for lunch, he returned to his office, where he stayed until night. "Never at any time, since I have been at the bar," he proudly reported to Lieber, "have I been more punctual and faithful. Po[c]ket that, ye croakers! who said that Europe would spoil me for office-work." Hillard agreed: "Sumner is behaving like a very good boy, nailed to his desk like a bad cent to a grocer's counter—not that the parallel holds throughout." [9]

After an absence of twenty-nine months, Sumner had, of course, to start his law practice almost anew, but clients were soon flocking to his office. Some were referred to him by Greenleaf, whose practice was heavy. Others came because of Sumner's erudition in the more esoteric branches of legal lore.[1] A few probably thought his intimacy with Story might be helpful in cases tried before the Federal Circuit Court. Through the influence of his English friends, the British consul in Boston, T. C. Grattan, retained Sumner to defend a number of cases where English vessels were sued for searching alleged American slave traders off the coast of Africa.[2] But the most important part of Sumner's practice came from such leading merchants as Thomas and Edward Wigglesworth, Henry Lee, T. C. Thwing, Stephen H. Perkins, Nathan and Samuel Appleton, G. R. Minot, and Zachariah Silsbee, who thus gave practical evidence that Sumner had arrived in Boston society.[3]

Only a month after returning to practice, Sumner was able to report that he was doing very well. He had, he announced complacently, "already disposed of one weighty matter, say ($50,-000)," by giving his opinion on a legal point that had escaped all other Boston attorneys to whom the case had been submitted. At the December 1841 term of the United States District Court he appeared in twenty-four cases to defend Boston merchants and won them all.[4] At the same time he was arguing eleven cases

[9] Sumner to Lieber, Sept. 23, 1840, Sumner MSS.; Hillard's postscript on Sumner to Sarah P. Cleveland, Oct. 2, 1840, copy, Longfellow MSS.

[1] *Law Reporter,* III (Feb. 1841), 383–6; IV (Dec. 1841), 301–3; IV (Jan. 1842), 342–9.

[2] Ibid., IV (May 1841), 33–4; J. C. Perkins to Pierce, Nov. 16, 1875, Pierce MSS.

[3] U.S. District Court, Record Books, XXV, 251, 256–61, 263–5, 270–4, 278–9, etc. (MS., Federal Records Center, Dorchester).

[4] Sumner to Cleveland, Sept. 23, 1840, copy, Longfellow MSS.; U.S. District Court, Docket Book, December 1841, Nos. 32–6, 38–40, 42 (MS., Federal Records Center, Dorchester); U.S. District Court, Record Books, XXV, 251–79, *passim.*

before the United States Circuit Court, where he often served as junior counsel to such leaders of the bar as Greenleaf, Franklin Dexter, and Charles G. Loring.[5] Sumner was not modest about his legal merits, and he assessed his fees accordingly. "I charged one client yesterday as *part* of my fee in one case $600," he told Lieber in December 1841. "He had the grace to say that it was no more than he expected and not so much as I deserved." [6]

Sumner was promptly recognized as an expert in certain special branches of his profession. Everybody admitted that "in what may be called the literature of the law, the curiosities of legal learning," he had no rival in Boston. In cases involving British and Continental precedents other attorneys often drew upon his prodigious memory. He was at his best in suits that hinged upon historical research, as, for instance, in the much litigated dispute over the Massachusetts–Rhode Island boundary. Serving as junior counsel to Rufus Choate, he diligently ransacked musty volumes of town records to learn just what had been the original bounds of the Bay Colony. In cases where Sumner thought some basic principle of justice was at stake he showed himself relentlessly persistent. Retained in litigation over a patent for friction matches, Sumner concluded that his opponents were "ignorant, impudent and unprincipled," and, in suits that stretched over a period of five years, fought them as though he were defending the nation's fundamental liberties.[7]

When Sumner had time to relax after his work, he found his intimate friends in "The Five of Clubs" as congenial as ever. Longfellow, Cleveland, Felton, and Hillard had held only occasional meetings while Sumner was abroad, but when he reappeared in Boston, all the old warmth of friendship was instantly rekindled. Night after night they gathered in "delightful Gaudiolum" to hear Sumner retell his adventures. On one occasion Sumner "discoursed in one continuous flow" from four o'clock in the after-

[5] U.S. Circuit Court, Docket Book, Term beginning October, 1841, Nos. 25–6, 31–2, 43, 93, 99–103 (MS., Federal Records Center, Dorchester).

[6] Sumner to Lieber, Dec. 10, 1841, Sumner MSS.

[7] *Law Reporter,* VII (May 1844), 58; Fanny Appleton Longfellow, Journal, Jan. 6, 1844, Longfellow MSS.; Jared Benson, Jr., to Sumner, Dec. 27, 1852, Sumner MSS.; Samuel Gilman Brown: *The Works of Rufus Choate with a Memoir of His Life* (Boston: Little, Brown & Co.; 1862), I, 74; Sumner to Hillard [Sept. 25, 1841], Sumner MSS.; Pierce, II, 149–50. See the elaborate legal documents in William Brooks versus Ezekiel Byam et al., before the United States Circuit Court, 1841–5 (MS., Federal Records Center, Dorchester).

noon until eleven at night, when Hillard protested that listening to him was "like being under Niagara," but the friends vicariously enjoyed even the minutiae of Sumner's travels.[8]

Quickly "The Five of Clubs" fell back into the pattern of regular Saturday meetings. In addition, of course, Sumner saw Hillard every day. Nearly every Sunday he drove out to Cambridge to visit Longfellow. More rarely he went to Pine Bank, Cleveland's home, to which illness more and more confined him. From the Feltons he had a standing invitation: "Whenever you have no other engagement, . . . jump into the omnibus, and come out." With their growing intimacy, the friends adopted nicknames for each other. Cleveland was "Hal"; Felton, "Corny"; Longfellow, partly because he was so short, "Longo." Sumner to his friends was "Charley," sometimes "Carl" or "Karliken," but most often, in tribute to his triumphs among the European nobility, "Don Carlos."

Without the slightest restraint, the friends talked over everything together. They listened to Longfellow read his poetry before he had it published, so as "to tread with iron heel" upon it and "winnow out the chaff." With Cleveland they sympathized in his illness, and with Hillard, that "young Hamlet in our own times with a dark destiny hanging over him," in his unhappy marriage and frustrated aspirations for a literary career. They shared the joy of Felton, who always seemed "perfectly happy just like a child with both hands full of flowers," and they echoed when he gave one of his "resounding laughs, containing at least one hundred cubic feet of laughter." [9] And to Sumner his friends gave what he needed most of all—unreserved affection and unqualified praise.

• 2 •

During the first few months after his return from Europe, Sumner seemed to settle securely into his niche in Boston society. Bos-

[8] Longfellow, Journal, Apr. 6, May 9, and 12, 1840, Longfellow MSS.

[9] Felton to Sumner, Oct. 26, 1840, Sumner MSS.; Longfellow to Sumner [Oct. 1841], Longfellow MSS.; Longfellow to Cleveland, Jan. 4, 1843, photostat, ibid.; Longfellow to Greene, Aug. 6, 1838, ibid.; Hillard to Longfellow, July 2, 1842, ibid.; Hillard: "Memoir of Cornelius Conway Felton," *MHSP*, X (1867–9), 367.

tonians began to think of him as a man with a promising future. He would be, they felt, a leader in Massachusetts, less, perhaps, in the tradition of Daniel Webster and Rufus Choate, both vigorous lawyer-politicians, than in that of Edward Everett or George Ticknor, scholarly gentlemen with European connections.[1]

Some Bostonians, to be sure, felt that Sumner had been spoiled by his European success. After listening to Sumner hold forth for hours upon his adventures, Fanny Appleton, the daughter of the textile magnate, judged that he was "*tant soit peu gâté* by the great civilities he has met with in England, at least for his own happiness and contentedness in this limited society and sphere," and wondered: "Has he any thing in his head beside a marvellous memory and a quantity of musty law-learning hanging to it to give him such renown and astonishing success?" Even Longfellow was at first inclined to think that Sumner's head had been a little turned by European applause, and deplored Sumner's "un-American" sneers at Boston, his "Flings at the College," and his " 'Jeringen! bring me my gaiters' style of conversation." [2]

Tongues began to wag more rapidly when Sumner, only a few months after his return, paid a public call on Fanny Ellsler, the dancer who exhibited to Boston with equal nonchalance her tight-clad legs and her "manager," who was notoriously reputed to be her lover. Sumner further drew all the hornets of scandal about his ears by taking Fanny on a drive through the countryside.[3]

In fact, Boston was needlessly alarmed. Sumner had called on Fanny not in order to shock society, but to honor letters of introduction which Harriet Grote and other English friends had written about the dancer. After Boston was scandalized, he continued to see her through sheer stubborn bravado, but he was doubtless relieved when she moved on to engagements elsewhere, for he was careful never again to put himself in such a compromising role.

1 Adams: *Education of Henry Adams*, p. 30.

2 Fanny Appleton to Lieber, June 12, 1840, Longfellow MSS.; Longfellow, Journal, May 7, and June 2, 1840, ibid. Cf. William Kent: *Memoirs and Letters of James Kent* (Boston: Little, Brown & Co.; 1898), p. 261.

3 Sumner to Lieber, Sept. 22, 1840, Sumner MSS.; Sumner to Cleveland, Sept. 23, 1840, copy, Longfellow MSS. Cf. Sumner to Henry Wikoff, Oct. 11, 1844 [misdated 1834], in J. C. Derby: *Fifty Years Among Authors, Books and Publishers* (New York: G. W. Carleton & Co.; 1884), p. 373.

Though Sumner did not desire to disrupt Boston society, he did wish to impress it, and his letters from his friends in Europe gave him frequent opportunities. Henry Reeve, Tocqueville's translator and friend, made Sumner his only transatlantic correspondent and assured him: "You are continually talked of in Europe." The George Grotes, Joseph Parkes, and other moderate Radicals wrote him in almost every mail. Sydney Smith continued a cordial exchange of letters, reminding Sumner: "You occupy a large corner of Mrs. Sydney's heart." In one transatlantic mail, received just after the English elections of 1841, Sumner was both amused and pleased to count "four letters, all from MP's, who have lost their seats." His friends were proud of his European fame, and they rejoiced with him when the *London Quarterly Review,* in December 1840, announced that Sumner's recent triumphs in Britain offered "decisive proof that an American gentleman, without official rank or wide-spread reputation, by mere dint of courtesy, candour, an entire absence of pretension, an appreciating spirit, and a cultivated mind, may be received on a perfect footing of equality in the best English circles, social, political, and intellectual." [4]

In playing his part as a bridge between European and American society, Sumner spent a great deal of his time serving as cicerone to visiting foreigners, who came introduced by letters from his English acquaintances. Sometimes his guests were private gentlemen of no great consequence, who wanted merely to see the sights of Boston and be entertained for dinner. More often they were celebrities, for whom Sumner exerted himself. When Lord Ashburton's suite visited Boston, during the course of negotiating the Webster-Ashburton Treaty, Sumner was chosen to give them a special tour of the city. He also took Sir Charles Lyell out for an evening drive, and when the English geologist saw fireflies for the first time, Sumner obligingly caught a hatful for him.[5]

In 1841, when Lord Morpeth decided to visit America, Sum-

[4] Reeve to Sumner, Nov. 1, 1840, Sumner MSS.; Harriet Grote to Sumner, Jan. 31 [1841], ibid., Sumner to Nathan Appleton, Aug. 4 [1841], Appleton MSS.; *London Quarterly Review,* XLVII (Dec. 1840), 19. The article was by Abraham Hayward.

[5] Sumner to Story [1841], Story MSS.; Thomas Brown to Sumner, Mar. 27, 1844, Sumner MSS.; Abbott Lawrence to Sumner, Aug. 29 [1842], ibid.; Sumner to Hillard, July 15, 1842, ibid.

ner virtually suspended all business for several weeks in order to entertain his friend. On the day Morpeth landed, Sumner gave him a conducted tour of Boston. They climbed to the top of the State house, where Sumner pointed out "the various spots illustrated in the early progress of the War of independence with the proper feelings of a true and liberal American." Then they visited the legislature, toured the courts, where Sumner presented his guest to Story, inspected the city hall, and met the mayor. "In the course of the walk," Morpeth recorded in his diary, "Sumner introduced me far and near." After dinner, Sumner took the Englishman for a drive through the suburbs, calling on the Clevelands, taking coffee with the Storys, and inspecting historical sights along the route. In the evening Sumner presented his friend to the Great Panjandrum of Boston Society, George Ticknor.[6]

This was but the first of many strenuous days of sight-seeing and visiting. Boston took at once to Morpeth. He was, as Longfellow said, "a very pleasant, jolly, sociable, ruddy-faced man, with gray hair, blue coat, and red waistcoat,—a laughing bachelor of forty." Besides, he was an English lord. Everybody wanted him for parties, receptions, and dinners, and everywhere he went, Sumner stood in useful attendance, identifying names and faces for him and reminding him of whether he had previously met the guests to whom he was introduced. When Morpeth left Boston at the end of December, he could not part from such a "fast and firm friend" without emotion. The following fall, after Morpeth had concluded his tour of America, Sumner again dropped all business to spend a final week in New York with the Englishman. They had, as Prescott laughingly said, "a perpetual wake,—wake, indeed, for you don't seem to have closed your eyes night or day. Dinners, breakfasts, suppers, 'each hue,' as Byron says, 'still lovelier than the last.' "[7]

When Charles Dickens came to America in 1842, he, too, made Sumner his guide and friend. A strikingly contrasted pair

[6] Morpeth, Diary, Oct. 21, 1841, copy, Houghton Lib. Cf. Morpeth's *Travels in America* . . . (New York: G. P. Putnam's Sons; 1851), pp. 8–14.

[7] Longfellow: *Longfellow,* I, 410; Charles Francis Adams: *Richard Henry Dana: A Biography* (Boston: Houghton Mifflin Co.; 1890), I, 29–30; Morpeth, Diary, Dec. 27, 1841, and Sept. 25–9, 1842, MS., Houghton Lib.; Ticknor: *Prescott,* p. 373.

they made as they strode over the cobblestones of Boston: Sumner, tall, serious, and intent, dark-haired and olive-skinned; Dickens, gay and free-and-easy, with his "fine bright face, blue eyes, and long dark hair." Together they climbed Copp's Hill and inspected the monument on Bunker Hill; they went with Longfellow to hear Father Taylor, prototype of Melville's Father Mapple, preach; they repeatedly dined, wined, and ate midnight oyster suppers together. Sumner served as a kind of social shield for Dickens and protected him from some of the cruder importunities of his admirers. As Dickens left for the West, he begged his new friend to accompany him, for, as he reported to their English friends: "Sumner is of great service to me." [8]

Sumner's friendly exertions were not confined to Englishmen. He continued to promote the fortunes of the still poor and unrecognized American sculptor, Thomas Crawford, whom he had met in Rome. Recognizing that a reputation in England would give an American artist great prestige, he pressed Sir Charles Vaughan and other British acquaintances to commission Crawford to make portrait busts. After much exertion, he persuaded Ticknor, the Lawrences, and other wealthy Bostonians to purchase Crawford's "Orpheus" for the Athenaeum, at a cost of $2,500. He himself superintended the repair of minor damages the statue suffered in being shipped across the Atlantic, vetoed the idea of exhibiting it in the Athenaeum's usual gallery, where the cross lights would kill its effect, and persuaded the directors to erect a little house on the grounds, where the statue could be shown against mahogany brown walls and in diffused lighting. As Boston gaped appreciatively over Crawford's curiously unbalanced figure of Orpheus, accompanied by its melancholy Cerebus, which looked embarrassed over its superfluity of heads, Sumner sought further to assist his friend by publishing a glow-

[8] Henry James: *William Wetmore Story and His Friends from Letters, Diaries, and Recollections* (Boston: Houghton Mifflin Co.; 1903), I, 58; Longfellow: *Longfellow*, I, 414; Edward F. Payne, *Dickens Days in Boston* (Boston: Houghton Mifflin Co.; 1927), pp. 7, 29, 42–3, 45–9, 59, 61; Edgar Johnson: *Charles Dickens: His Tragedy and Triumph* (New York: Simon and Schuster, Inc.; 1952), I, 360, 367–8, 371, 373; Walter Dexter (ed.): *The Letters of Charles Dickens* (Bloomsbury: The Nonesuch Press; 1938), I, 379, 406. For Sumner's similar attentions to the actor Macready, see William Toynbee (ed.): *The Diaries of William Charles Macready, 1833–1851* (London: Chapman and Hall, Ltd.; 1912), II, 235, 238–40.

ing account of his sculpture in the Boston *Advertiser* and in the New York *Democratic Review*.[9]

Not all of Sumner's efforts for his friends were equally successful, but they were sincere and enthusiastic. He continued to batter his French acquaintances with proposals to elect Justice Story to the French Academy.[1] For his crusty friend Francis Lieber, who was teaching at South Carolina College, which Sumner considered an exile "undisturbed by the foot of civilization," he ran errands, bought books, and interviewed publishers. Lieber, who was, as Rufus Choate said, "the most fertile, indomitable, unsleeping, combative and propagandising person of his race," relentlessly exploited Sumner's good nature and drew interminably upon his time, yet he was greatly aggrieved when his every letter was not promptly answered, his too frequent proposals for publishing books proved impracticable, and his nudging hints that he ought to receive a chair at Harvard were not acted upon. Finally even Sumner was goaded by Lieber's reproaches into protesting "that in judging my conduct, my desire to serve you, at all times and in all ways, *you do me injustice*," but his good nature quickly reasserted itself, and, making allowance for Lieber's loneliness, he reassured him: "Remember I shall always be over-happy in doing anything I can for you." [2] It was no wonder that in Boston men said: "Charles Sumner's friends are like other men's brothers." [3]

• 3 •

Despite all these indications that Sumner could settle comfortably into Boston society, surrounded by a warm circle of admiring friends, he was an unhappy man. After the immediate exaltation of returning to America and telling of his European adventures wore off, he fell more and more into moods of self-pity and loneliness. His friends described him as "rather depressed, and

[9] Sumner to Ticknor, Sept. 15, 1839, Ticknor MSS.; Sumner to Hillard, July 26, 1839, Sumner MSS.; Pierce, II, 304; Boston *Daily Advertiser*, May 8, 1844; *The United States Magazine, and Democratic Review*, XII (May 1843), 451–6.

[1] Sumner to Warden, June 20, 1841, Warden MSS.

[2] Sumner to Lieber, Dec. 10, 1840, May 12, 1841, and Jan. 20, 1842, Sumner MSS.; Choate to Sumner, Jan. 7, 1842, ibid.

[3] John Kenyon to Sumner, Dec. 29 [1844], ibid.

weary with the great Ixion wheel of life," and he felt that he was a black cistern of melancholy. "You cannot fathom the yawning depths of my soul," he exclaimed to Longfellow. "I am *alive;* that is, continue to draw breath, and stride through the streets. But what is this? I am becoming every day duller and duller; I have nothing to say to any body. I am like an extinct volcano." [4]

Some part of Sumner's depression was probably caused by financial worries. Before he went to Europe, he had incurred a debt of $1,200 in an unfortunate land speculation, and he had borrowed $3,000 more from Story, Fletcher, and Samuel Lawrence in order to go abroad. As soon as Sumner returned to law practice, he began applying his earnings to these debts, but he seemed never to make quite enough. Finally in 1844 he gave up the struggle and persuaded his mother to pay his creditors.[5]

It soon became obvious that Sumner was not making a brilliant success of his legal career. In exceptional cases he excelled, but he had little interest in routine common-law practice. "I paid the bill of costs, without understanding it," he confessed to a colleague at the end of a case, "and I sometimes believe that it is not in my power to understand anything, which concerns such matters." Prospective clients found him uninterested as well as uncomprehending. His desk was almost constantly surrounded by admiring, talking literary acquaintances. Longfellow and Felton made his office their regular headquarters when they came into Boston, and Lieber, on his frequent summer visits from South Carolina, was at No. 4 Court Street from morning until night. Sumner would suspend business for a morning to debate with the elder Richard Henry Dana whether Washington Allston had written the finest poetry of modern times. Even if a client found Sumner alone, he was unlikely to win his full attention, for at the slightest provocation Sumner would launch into a long-winded reminiscence of his European adventures, recalling "in a dreamy way the irrelevant as well as the relevant incidents . . . connected with it." [6]

[4] Sumner to Cleveland, Apr. 3, 1841, copy, Longfellow MSS.; Longfellow, Journal, Apr. 10, 1844, ibid.; Sumner to Longfellow [May 12, 1843], ibid.; Sumner to Howe, undated, Sumner MSS.

[5] Sumner to Cleveland, Sept. 23, 1840, Cleveland MSS.; Samuel Lawrence to Sumner, Apr. 2, 1844, Sumner MSS.; Pierce, I, 199.

[6] Sumner to J. C. Perkins, June 14, 1844, Sumner MSS.; Mellen Chamberlain, Jr., Diary, Apr. 12, and Nov. 15, 1847, MS., Boston Public Lib.; Sumner to

Though Sumner's friends tried to convince themselves that he only needed time to rise to the head of the bar, prospective clients knew better, and they took their business to hard-working, untraveled lawyers like Benjamin R. Curtis, C. G. Loring, and Benjamin F. Butler, or to the deans of the profession, Choate and Jeremiah Mason. Despite his brilliant beginning in 1841, Sumner's business fell off sharply. He seems to have had no cases before the Federal District Court in Boston during the next five years. Nor was he listed as attorney in any cases before the Supreme Judicial Court of Massachusetts during these years. Even before the United States Circuit Court, where his friendship with Judge Story might be presumed to have some weight, he had little practice. From the eleven cases he argued in the fall term of Story's court in 1841 his business declined to three in 1842 and then to two in 1843; after that, except for the friction match case which was continued until 1845, his name does not appear on the docket books. Two years after he came home from Europe, Sumner's practice was so small that he happily accepted an appointment, procured through Story's influence, as a United States commissioner in bankruptcy proceedings, and he and Hillard made their "living on the blood and tears of those victims." [7]

More quickly than his friends, Sumner recognized that his future as a practicing lawyer would be, at best, one of unrewarding mediocrity. "Though I earn my daily bread," he confessed to Lieber in 1840, "I lay up none of the bread of life. My mind, soul, heart are not improved or invigorated by the practice of my profession; by overhauling papers, old letters, and sifting accounts, in order to see if there be any thing on which to plant an action. The sigh will come, for a canto of Dante, a Rhapsody of Homer, a play of Schiller." [8]

Lacking clients, Sumner occupied his time in seeing the third volume of his *Reports* through the press. When Judge Story fell sick, Sumner took his place in the Harvard Law School for a

---

Hillard, Aug. 5 [1840], Sumner MSS.; Edwin Percy Whipple: *Recollections of Eminent Men* . . . (Boston: Houghton Mifflin Co.; 1893), pp. 209–13.

[7] Docket Books of U.S. Circuit Court and U.S. District Court (MS., Federal Records Center, Dorchester); Francis Bassett to Sumner, Feb. 2, 1842, Sumner MSS.; Hillard to Lieber, Mar. 24, 1842, Lieber MSS. It is possible, of course, that Sumner served as junior counsel in some cases during these years when his name was not listed on the docket books.

[8] Sumner to Lieber, Sept. 23, 1840, Lieber MSS.

fortnight in 1840 and again in 1843. He employed his abundant leisure and extensive energy in writing articles and reviews for the *Law Reporter* which unconsciously revealed how little he was interested in the details of daily practice. He expressed pain that an editor of Sir James Mackintosh's *A Discourse on the Study of the Law of Nature and Nations* had given notes translating the numerous, difficult Latin quotations in the work as, he observed snobbishly: "Few persons will attempt the text, who can desire any such assistance as is here volunteered." Reviewing the latest volume of New Hampshire supreme-court reports, he ignored all points of law and fretted about the judges' "use of a barbarism, like 'loaned.' " "The verb *to loan* in all its inflections," he ruled, "is not only vicious in respect of taste, but it is superfluous. We trust it will be discountenanced from the bench." [9]

However satisfying, such legal diversions were decidedly not remunerative, and Sumner began to think that a public office might prove more profitable than private practice. Alexander H. Everett, who had some influence with the administration of President James K. Polk, tried to get Sumner appointed Chief Clerk in the Department of State, but James Buchanan, the new Secretary, declared that he was "rather unwilling to appoint a gentleman, with whom he had no personal acquaintance." Story, too, tried to assist his impecunious friend by having him chosen reporter of the United States Supreme Court, and Sumner was enthusiastic about the job, which would give him "$3,000 for two months' work, . . . besides an opportunity of taking business in the highest court of the country." Announcing that he disliked "most cordially the *principle* and *practice* of office-seeking" and that he had "no disposition to join that 'army offensive,' which is perpetually crying 'Give, give,' " he nevertheless solicited the support of Justice John McLean. "I could not decline to present myself, in a proper way, and on a proper occasion, as one of the candidates for the office." But illness kept Story from attending the Supreme Court in 1842–3, and there was little other support for Sumner's candidacy. Through what he characteristically concluded was "a cabal among the loco [foco] judges of the Su-

[9] Report of Treasurer, Mar. 31, 1841, Harvard Coll. Papers, X, 2 ser., 213; Harvard Coll. Records, VII (1837–46), 197; Sumner to Lieber, July 11, 1843, Sumner MSS.; *Law Reporter*, VI (Dec. 1843), 380; VII (May 1844), 48–51. Cf. also Sumner's essay on "The Number 'Seven,' " ibid. VI (Apr. 1844), 529–41.

preme Court," a new reporter of Democratic antecedents was appointed.[1]

• 4 •

But Sumner's financial insecurity was not the real cause of his unhappiness. After all, he was a bachelor with moderate living expenses; his legal work did bring in some income, he had free room and board, and he could always call on his mother's help in real emergencies. Sumner's comparative failure at the bar was less a cause than a symptom of his deeper, more mysterious discontents.

When Sumner returned from Europe, he found that for the first time in his life he was obliged to stand alone, without the guidance and support from some older man who could give direction to his career. His father was dead. Justice Story remained a good friend, but no longer exhibited the same paternal interest in Sumner's career. There was no estrangement between the two, but they were gradually drifting apart. During Sumner's two years abroad, Story had grown older and feebler, and his interests had become centered on the new crop of students who were attending the Harvard Law School. He had been troubled by Sumner's legal "radicalism," which echoed his own early but now rejected views, and concerned over his decision to go abroad; now he was puzzled by Sumner's failure to succeed at his practice. When Sumner went to see the judge in Cambridge, he always found the warmest welcome; but there were no more prophecies about a Harvard law professorship for him.[1a]

For a time it seemed that Samuel Gridley Howe would take Story's place in Sumner's life. Sumner had known Howe casually since 1837, when the two men, at considerable personal risk, helped quell an anti-Irish riot on Broad Street, but not until his return from Europe were they thrown frequently together. Howe,

[1] A. H. Everett to Sumner, Mar. 26, 1846, Sumner MSS.; Sumner to McLean, Feb. 2, 1843, McLean MSS.; Sumner to Cleveland, Feb. 17, 1843, Cleveland MSS.; McLean to Story, Jan. 25, 1843, Story MSS.

[1a] When Story died a few years later, Sumner cooly observed that his passing "has been keenly felt by friends, the profession and the public; but, in this busy life, new interests arise to take the place of those that have disappeared, and the world soon learns to forget its benefactors." Sumner to Lord Morpeth, Mar. 29, 1846, Carlisle MSS.

who was more than a decade older in years and seemingly a generation older in experience, seemed positively heroic to Sumner. The younger man thrilled to hear Howe's tales of fighting for the Greeks in their war for independence and of assisting the Poles in their revolution against Prussia. Now the distinguished head of the Perkins Institute for the Blind, Howe was still a knight-errant of reform, and Sumner worshipfully concluded that his new friend possessed "intelligence and experience of no common order, all elevated and refined by a chivalrous sense of honor, and a mind without fear." [2]

At Sumner's urging, Howe was made a member of "The Five of Clubs," replacing Cleveland, who went to Cuba for his health, but Sumner spent more time with him than with all the other members, who were either married or lived outside of Boston. "Bachelors both," Sumner explained, "we drive and ride together—and pass our evenings far into the watches of the night in free and warm communion." At loose ends when summer came and other friends were out of town, he and Howe used every evening to "mount their horses or jump into a gig and career through the country for two hours," returning to eat ices and strawberries and to "chat, wherein, are remembered things, experiences and hopes of all sorts, [which] absorb the remainder of the evening." Often they spent the night together at Howe's quarters in South Boston, and "Chev" (as intimates nicknamed Howe) had fond memories of Sumner, "his straps unbuttoned, his waistband also, his feet in my red slippers, a glass of orvieto in his hands, his sweet smile on his lips . . . as he used to sit in my easy chair." When they went to bed, they left the door between their rooms open, so that they could continue their conversation into the drowsy hours.[3]

The two friends addressed each other in terms of intimacy verging upon endearment. When "Chev" was out of town, Sumner felt desolate and wrote him: "I lack the consciousness of

[2] Laura E. Richards (ed.): *Letters and Journals of Samuel Gridley Howe* (Boston: Dana Estes & Company; 1909), II, 97–8; Sumner to Lieber, May 12, and June 3, 1841, Sumner MSS.

[3] Sumner to Lieber, June 27, and July 13, 1842, Sumner MSS.; Howe to Sumner, Feb. 2, 1844, Howe MSS. For a perceptive study of Howe, which casts much light on Sumner, see Harold Schwartz: *Samuel Gridley Howe, Social Reformer, 1801–1876* (Cambridge: Harvard University Press; 1956).

your presence, and the sense of security, which it gave me." Howe fondly reassured him: "I love thee better than thou ever lovedst me—better even I believe than any of the numerous friends who spring up around thee wherever thou plantest thy foot." With as much truth as humor Hillard reported on the progress of Sumner's new friendship. "He is quite in love with Howe and spends so much time with him that I begin to feel the shooting pains of jealousy." [4]

Seeing Howe as "the soul of disinterestedness," who had "purged his character from all considerations of *self*," Sumner tried to imitate his friend in his career of bettering society. Admiringly he observed the Doctor's work with the blind, and faithfully he visited the Perkins Institute to observe the progress he was making with the education of the deaf-blind girl, Laura Bridgman, even though Laura privately complained: "Sumner is not gentle like Dr. . . . Why does Dr want Sumner to come here if he is not gentle. . . . I do not love or like Sumner. . . ." Howe called Sumner's attention to the important work Horace Mann was doing to rejuvenate the public schools of the Commonwealth, and Sumner enthusiastically endorsed Mann's ideas of nonsectarian education: "Let us put an iron heel upon the serpent of religious bigotry trying to hug our schools in its insidious coil." With his civic interests aroused, he became secretary of the Emigration Society, designed to ease the problems of the Irish immigrants who were beginning to pour into Boston, joined the Prison Discipline Society, and attended the meetings of the Peace Society.[5]

Though powerfully influential, Howe could not quite fill the place that Sumner's father and later Judge Story had played in his life. For one thing, Howe resolutely refused to be an older man directing a young friend's career. On the contrary, he insisted that it was he who derived inspiration from Sumner. "It has never been my lot to know a man more perfectly loyal to truth, right and humanity," he assured his friend. "You are my junior by

[4] Sumner to Howe, June 25, 1850, MS., Huntington Lib.; Howe to Sumner, May 4, 1843, Sumner MSS.; Hillard to Longfellow, May 16, 1842, Longfellow MSS.

[5] Schwartz: *Howe*, p. 108; Sumner to Howe, May 31, 1844, Sumner MSS.; Sumner to R. H. Dana, Sr., Feb. 22 [1842], Longfellow MSS.

many years, but to you I owe many of the feeble aspirations which I feel for progress upwards and onwards in my spiritual nature." [6]

Howe also had other aspirations, which needed, and received, no encouragement from Sumner. He fell in love. In the summer of 1841 Julia Ward, oldest daughter of a prosperous New York merchant, visited Boston, and Howe was immediately captivated. With a perfect oval face, creamy complexion, blue eyes, and startlingly red hair, Julia was as beautiful as she was talented; she wrote poetry, read French, German, and Italian, and sang operatic arias so well that friends called her Diva. Though he was eighteen years her senior, Howe promptly commenced a serious courtship and during the next two years made frequent visits to New York.[7]

With friendly generosity Howe wanted Sumner to share his experience of falling in love. After all, there were three daughters in the Ward household, the "Three Graces of Bond Street," and if Howe had singled out Julia for himself, Sumner could choose the dark, exotic-looking Louisa or the gentle, self-effacing Annie. The fact that Sumner was thirty-one and that Annie and Louisa were seventeen and eighteen, respectively, seemed no insuperable barrier to the Doctor; there was a greater disparity between his and Julia's ages.

Willingly Sumner allowed himself to be carried along—up to a point. He accompanied Howe in his pilgrimages to "the Trinity of Bond Street," and helped attend the Ward sisters wherever they went. He unbent amazingly. When Felton gave a party for Julia and her friend Mary Dwight, Sumner was actually flirtatious. After dinner, Julia reported, "Sumner got Mary and me under a curtain, held it down, called us his dear wives, and said it was the commencement of his domestic bliss." In December 1842 Sumner, Howe, and Felton all went to New York to greet Longfellow, who was returning from Europe, and the Ward sisters welcomed them with much rejoicing. The three maidens, the two Harvard professors, the veteran of the Greek wars, and Sumner played blindman's buff, and, Sumner reported coyly: "Who

[6] Richards: *S. G. Howe*, II, 252.

[7] Schwartz: *Howe*, Chap. viii; Louise Hall Tharp: *Three Saints and a Sinner* (Boston: Little, Brown & Co.; 1956), Chap. viii.

should I catch . . . but the lovely Louisa? and who should catch me, in the same game, but the same paragon of loveliness?" Felton shrewdly noted the "unerring skill [with which] Howe caught Julia, and Sumner, Louisa; and . . . the length of time they spent in determining who their captives were; a question they did not presume to decide until they had made the most minute phrenological examination of their beautiful heads." Encouraged, Howe had "strong hopes that Charley may be warmed by the star second in magnitude in the Constellation of Bond Street." [8]

Sumner shyly assured his friends that there was ground for these hopes. He spoke rapturously of "warm hearted, simple and affectionate" Louisa and of "gentle, simple, sweet, confiding" Annie. When Lieber visited Boston in 1843, he found that Sumner had no other topic of conversation. "We spoke so much of love, and my soul turned to that so spontaneously," Sumner apologized, "that whenever I sought to wake another cord, it was in vain." A devoted wife, he decided, would be better than "an Indian argosy." "I would walk on foot round the earth, to find a woman who would love me with . . . truth," he exclaimed. "Oh! with what ardour I would pour my gushing affections into her soul," he wrote, with grimly inappropriate imagery, "as the Parthians filled the head of Crassus with the gold he loved too well." [9]

For all his protestations, Sumner took no steps toward finding a wife. Once he realized that Louisa Ward was no sisterly adolescent, but a marriageable young woman, he declared frankly: "I have no desire in that quarter," and he was relieved when she went to Europe, where she shortly met her future husband, Sumner's friend Crawford. Available women did not interest Sumner. He declined to begin a correspondence with one female admirer, and he showed total indifference to the highly eligible Mary Dwight, whom his friends constantly threw at his head. But, on a trip to Philadelphia, he reported that he "met the most fascinating woman I have ever seen in America—

[8] Sumner to Lieber, Sept. 5, 1841, and Dec. 8, 1842, Sumner MSS.; Julia Ward to Annie and Louisa Ward [1842], Howe MSS.; Felton to Cleveland, Nov. 28, 1842, copy, Longfellow MSS.; Howe to Lieber, Aug. 17, 1842, Lieber MSS.

[9] Sumner to Lieber, July 18, and Dec. 8, 1842 [Sept. 1843], and Aug. 31, 1841, Sumner MSS.; Sumner to Longfellow, July 10, 1842, Longfellow MSS.

beautiful as morning, with the *esprit* of France . . . and the glowing soul of the South." But he discovered: "Alas! she is married—to a senator in Congress." He was similarly bewitched by the former Euphemia Van Rensselaer, of New York, a "peerless creature." "I fell in love with that beautiful creature," he gushed to Howe. "The first moment I saw her I felt that she had a warm heart, a pure and etherial [*sic*] nature, a clear intellect, and a soul as graceful as her person." She, too, was quite happily married. So regularly did the pattern recur that Lieber concluded sagely: "The truth is you dont wish for love, but delight in amatory cro[a]king. . . . How else is it that you are always, not once, smitten with women out of reach?" [1]

Friends were genuinely concerned about the "cage of celibacy" in which Sumner was trapped. Felton's and Hillard's select "committee upon his domestic relations" was a little more than a joke. Felton urged Sumner to get married before he turned into "a solitary monument, in the deserts of life, like one of the strong Sphinxes, in the wastes of Aegypt, buried all but the *head,* in the unfruitful, parched and parching sands . . . staring out upon the appalling loneliness with deadened eyes." Howe thought Sumner was simply too timid. "You do love," he argued, "you are all love—you have more of love in you than any man I ever knew." Action was all that was required. "Go straight up to Beacon Street; walk around the Common; seek out the sweetest girl you meet; join her at the second round, and offer yourself to her; insist upon her accepting you, and carry off her troth before you are thrice around." [2]

But Julia Ward, with shrewd feminine intuition, knew the case was hopeless and said that Sumner had "*no heart.*" Though Sumner indignantly protested: "I have a *heart*—it is not my fault if all its throbbings have been in vain," her judgment came near the mark. Easily falling in love with ineligible women, he set up impossible standards for those whom he might win. Sam Ward, Julia's worldly wise brother, diagnosed Sumner's difficulty. "He is

[1] Sumner to Fanny Longfellow, Oct. 20, 1843, Longfellow MSS.; Louisa Bullard to Charles Eliot Norton, May 19, 1843, Norton MSS.; Sumner to Hillard, Jan. 29, 1841, Sumner MSS.; Sumner to Howe, Oct. 1, 1843, ibid.; Lieber to Sumner, Oct. 15, 1843, Lieber MSS.

[2] Sumner to Palfrey [Oct. 1845], Palfrey MSS.; Felton to S. G. and Julia Howe, May 23, 1843, copy, Howe MSS.; Felton to Sumner, Apr. 2, 1844, Sumner MSS.; Howe to Sumner, Feb. 2, 1844, Howe MSS.; Richards: *S. G. Howe*, II, 193–4.

like the Sultan in the Arabian tale who sent a mirror out to reflect the face of an unsullied virgin—He requires nevertheless that he should be master—superior in intellect." Sumner was in fact protecting himself against possible rejection and humiliation. In his father's embittered household he had learned that he must never let down his guard; yet how could he fall in love or propose marriage without opening himself to scorn or even ridicule? Perhaps it might have been easier could he have courted a girl in humble station, like his mother, but the society in which he now moved demanded that his wife be educated, intelligent, and probably wealthy. These were the very women Sumner found most frightening, for they inspired in him, he confessed, "a certain awe, and a sense of [their] superiority, which makes me . . . anxious to subside into my own inferiority, and leave the conversation to be sustained by other minds." [3]

Reluctantly, broodingly, he watched others take the step he dared not take. It was a bitter blow when Howe became engaged to Julia in February 1843. "God bless you both! You will strengthen each other for the duties of life; and the most beautiful happiness shall be yours," he exclaimed in his letter of congratulations, but privately he was deeply troubled: "I am about to lose a dear friend; for the intimate confidence of friendship may die away, when love usurps the breast, absorbing the whole nature of a man." He could only hope that Howe would not entirely forget him and that in time Julia might come to accept him, too. Though Julia promptly assured Sumner that he had not lost but gained a friend by the engagement, she had deeper reservations. At her wedding reception "her natural roguery broke out, and seeing Sumner bent over, and intently engaged in talking to a lady, she could not help slipping two or three silver spoons into his coat pocket." Then, jestingly, she accused him of attempting to steal something belonging to herself.[4]

[3] Sumner to Lieber, Sept. 22, 1842, Sumner MSS.; Ward to Longfellow, Jan. 14, 1842, Longfellow MSS.; Sumner to Hillard, Sept. 12, 1844, Sumner MSS.

[4] Laura E. Richards and Maud Howe Elliott: *Julia Ward Howe, 1819–1910* (Boston: Houghton Mifflin Co., 1916), I, 76; Sumner to Samuel Ward, Feb. 21, 1843, Howe MSS.; Julia Ward to Sumner [Feb. 21, 1843], Sumner MSS.; Longfellow to Sarah P. Cleveland [Apr. 19, 1843], photostat, Longfellow MSS. Vexed by the amount of time Howe spent writing letters to Sumner during their honeymoon, Julia exclaimed: "Sumner ought to have been a woman and you to have married her." Howe to Sumner, Sept. 11, 1844, Howe MSS.

• 5 •

"I am all *alone—alone*," Sumner lamented, as Howe's marriage and honeymoon trip to Europe left him without that paternal counsel he needed to direct his life. Howe wrote him "strangely confidential" letters from Europe, announcing: "The torrent of affection which is continually flowing from my heart toward the new object of my love diminishes not by one drop the tide of feeling which swells within my bosom at the thought of thee dear Sumner: I love thee not less because I love her more," but Sumner was inconsolable. "My friends fall away from me," he grieved. "I lead a joyless life, with very little sympathy." [5]

During the tense months of Howe's courtship and marriage Sumner had grown to be an increasingly difficult person to live with. At home he was almost as domineering as his father had been. Constantly he reproached and scolded his younger brothers and sisters who remained at home. Only Mary, now a tall, gentle girl of nearly twenty, escaped his censorious advice, perhaps because it was already clear that she was gradually dying of tuberculosis. But Horace, the youngest brother, "a very good youth, of moderate capacity and no ambition and little energy," but with "an affectionate temper, [an] unworldly disposition and [a] feminine purity and delicacy of feeling," was a constant vexation to his drivingly ambitious brother.[6] Henry, who felt that Charles's meddling had thwarted one of his love affairs, lived in open enmity with his older brother, to whom he refused to speak.[7] Little Julia was subjected to nothing more than tedious admonitions about education and cleanliness until she grew up and began to have ideas of her own. Then Charles objected so strenuously to

[5] Sumner to Lieber, July 13, and Oct. 6, 1843, Sumner MSS.; Fanny Longfellow, Journal, Mar. 26, 1844, Longfellow MSS.; Howe to Sumner, May 13, 1843, Howe MSS.

[6] Hillard to Lieber, July 23, 1850, Lieber MSS.; undated clipping from Boston *Journal*, Pierce Scrapbooks; Sumner to George Sumner, May 15, 1844, Sumner MSS.; Sumner to George Sumner, June 19, 1849, Segal Coll. Horace was for a time a member of Brook Farm; then he worked a year or two on a New Hampshire farm; finally he was shipped off to Italy, where it was hoped he would strengthen his health and broaden his limited intelligence. In Italy he became a friend of the Marchioness Ossoli (Margaret Fuller). (Horace Sumner to "Dear Madame Ossoli," undated, Fuller MSS.) Returning to America on the same ship, they were both lost off Fire Island, July 19, 1850. Sumner to Henry David Thoreau, July 31, 1850, MS., Abernethy Lib., Middlebury Coll.

[7] Sumner to George Sumner, June 1, July 16, and Oct. 7, 1846, and Nov. 16, 1847, Sumner MSS. Henry died in South Orange, N.J., May 5, 1852.

her engagement to the "plain but sensible" Dr. John Hastings that he forbade the physician to visit the house, and Julia had to make a scene in order to win her right to receive her lover when and how she liked.[8]

Lonely and discouraged, Sumner grew increasingly sensitive. He began to suspect that people were saying unkind things about him, and, except when he was with his few intimate friends, he stalked through Boston's streets as though he were in panoply of prickly, defensive armor. He conducted social intercourse with extreme punctiliousness. "He would never submit to any discourtesy from others," Peleg W. Chandler remembered, "and required that they should observe the rules which he rigidly adhered to himself." When David Sears, one of the richest and most influential men in Boston, heard a distorted account of something Sumner supposedly had said reflecting upon the Sears family, Sumner icily refused to explain or to make amends. "Mr. Sears owes me an ample apology, for allowing me to be talked of in such a way," he stonily informed Hillard, and he stood on his dignity until Sears, learning the truth from other sources, wrote him a formal letter expressing regret at the misunderstanding.[9]

Soon Sumner convinced himself that he was surrounded by dangerous enemies in Boston society. Though he had been an intimate of the Ticknors since his return from Europe, he came to think, for reasons that are not at all clear, that Ticknor had "a peculiar prejudice and ill will" toward him. Once Sumner suspected a slight, he magnified every occurrence, real or fancied, into an insult. The turn of a phrase in conversation, the casual laughter that might drift out as he entered one of Ticknor's soirees would be enough to persuade him that there was a conspiracy against him. Sumner's close friends reproached him for being too sensitive. "Here you are, a man with full grown powers, circled by loving friends, with every thing to stimulate you, and above all with the priceless blessing of fine health," Cleveland chided. "Will you be driven to despondency by the apparent

[8] Julia Ward Howe to "Aunt Lou," Oct. 28, 1853, Howe MSS.; Pierce, II, 157. Julia, who married Hastings in 1854, was the one member of the family who outlived Charles. She died in California, May 29, 1876.

[9] Pierce, II, 254; Sumner to Hillard, Jan. 24, and 27, 1841; Prescott to Sumner, Jan. 25, and 27, 1841; Sears to Sumner, Jan. 14, 1841, Sumner MSS.

treachery of a few friends, or the tittering nonsense of a few girls." But Sumner was implacable. The gulf between him and the Ticknors, he felt, was "growing broader every day." Soon he convinced himself that Ticknor, whom he had earlier considered the chief ornament of Boston arts and letters, was "the impersonation of *refined* selfishness." While men like Howe were doing good works, Sumner sneered, Ticknor "sits in his rich library, and laps himself in care and indulgence, *doing* nothing himself, treating unkindly the works of those who *do*, looking down upon all, himself having no claim to be regarded, except as a man of *promises*—never, in a life no longer short, redeemed." In a society so small and closely knit as Boston's, such remarks quickly got back to Ticknor's ears, and the essential justice of Sumner's characterization made them rankle. By 1843 friends warned Sumner not to call at Park Street, lest he be shown the door.[1]

Unhappy at home and in society at large, Sumner sought comfort in the company of his closest friends, but even here, it seemed, fate was constricting his circle. Felton was too wholesome and hearty to give Sumner much sympathy in his black moods. Hillard was preoccupied by his own unhappiness, Cleveland was dying in Cuba, and Howe was honeymooning in Europe.

Only Longfellow was left, and at Craigie House in Cambridge, where Sumner's visits were so regular that he was known as "the Sunday *male*," the two friends read together and talked long and affectionately. Sumner could take solace in the fact that Longfellow, too, had suffered reverses. He had fallen in love with Fanny Appleton, daughter of Nathan Appleton, when they met in Germany in 1836. Her black eyes and dark auburn hair had driven the young Harvard professor into importunate wooing, which met with prompt rejection. Longfellow's loss was Sumner's gain, for the two could now pool their loneliness.[2]

But Sumner was soon to be deprived even of this comfort. In 1842 Longfellow sailed for Europe to recover his health and his spirits. Soon he reported to Sumner a significant dream: the two men were in bed together, and when Sumner mentioned "a

[1] Sumner to Longfellow, May 14, 1842, Longfellow MSS.; Cleveland to Sumner, Apr. 7, 1843, Cleveland MSS.; Sumner to Lieber, Jan. 29, 1844, Sumner MSS.; Howe to Sumner [Apr. 10, 1843], Howe MSS.

[2] Julia Ward Howe to Longfellow, undated, Longfellow MSS.; Thompson: *Young Longfellow*, pp. 235–8, 250–62; Edward Wagenknecht: *Longfellow: A Full-Length Portrait* (New York: Longmans, Green & Co., Inc.; 1955), pp. 223–7.

certain person's name," Longfellow fell on Sumner's neck and wept, exclaiming: "I am very unhappy." In the dream Sumner was "buried up to his neck in sand," but Longfellow was not—as he promptly demonstrated when he returned to America and won Fanny Appleton's hand, leaving his friend buried in his celibacy.[3]

When Longfellow announced his approaching marriage, Sumner, already prostrated by Howe's recent wedding, could only conceal his dismay by pretending to be dull and indifferent to his friend's great happiness. He compelled himself to write Fanny his "most sincere, most cordial, most affectionate congratulations," but he was, in fact, heartbroken and desolate. "Howe has gone," he reproached Longfellow, "and now you have gone, and nobody is left with whom I can have sweet sympathy. . . . What shall I do these long summer evenings? And what will become of those Sabbaths, sacred to friendship and repose?" The Longfellows, who had no intention of giving up their friends just because they were married, took pity on Sumner and invited him to accompany them on their wedding trip to the Catskills. He accepted, and, on the train, read to the newlyweds Bossuet's funeral orations.[4]

Sumner tried to forget his unhappiness in work. He treated his body, as Lieber remarked, "like an iron pot which may be night and day over fire," without remembering even that would wear out. By the fall of 1843, the disastrous year in which both Howe and Longfellow were married, Sumner's friends were worried about his health; the fact that his sister Mary was dying of tuberculosis and that his brother Henry was coughing blood indicated the danger. Howe begged him to abandon "that morbid and unnatural state of mind which made you careless of whether you should live or die," and, as a physician, sternly directed him to stop "working hard all day, eating and drinking without regard to time or quality, or quantity; sitting up two thirds of the night, using up the whole store of nervous power accumulated by one night's sleep, and anticipating that of the next day by forced loans." [5]

[3] Longfellow to Sumner, June 24, 1842, copy, Longfellow MSS.

[4] Sumner to Longfellow [May 12, 1843]; Sumner to Fanny Appleton, May 11, 1843; Fanny Longfellow to Sumner [July 1843]; Fanny Longfellow, Journal, Aug. 8, 1843, ibid.

[5] Lieber to Hillard, Nov. 11, 1844, Lieber MSS.; Howe to Sumner, Dec. 1843, Howe MSS.

But Sumner, instead of cutting down his load, increased it. In April 1844, against his better judgment and as though to punish himself, he signed a contract with Little & Brown to edit twenty volumes of Francis Vesey's chancery reports. For the sum of $2,000 he agreed to furnish copy for a volume every fortnight; as there were twenty-seven printers in the Little & Brown plant waiting to set the books in type, there could be no delay. Felton exclaimed that Sumner would have to "take the veil" and retire from the world while he performed this Herculean task. "I imagine you wearing a shirt set sharp with steel pens by day; and at night, catching brief snatches of rest in proof-sheets, with black-letter folios for your pillows," he punned, "while, like Saint Antony [*sic*], you are haunted by Devils, and tempted by the lucious forms of imaginary oysters, in every variety." [6]

The labor was indeed arduous, for Sumner attempted to annotate Vesey with citations to later English and American chancery cases and to add biographical sketches of the English judges and lawyers mentioned in the reports. For two months he was able to keep up the work and saw four volumes through the press. The physical strain did not relieve his mental depression, for Longfellow found him "in a desperate mood of *Werterismus*, wishing that some one would shoot [him] through the heart." In June his body rebelled, and he went to bed with a cold and fever. Attempting to resume work too soon, he had a serious relapse, and his physicians diagnosed tuberculosis, which was killing pallid, delicate Mary, confined in the room adjacent to his.[7]

Though there were, in fact, no apparent symptoms of consumption, Sumner's doctors were ready to declare his case hopeless. His friends came to Hancock Street to pay him final visits and to offer what kindly services they could. "There are so few like him upon earth," mourned Sam Ward, "that I cannot believe God really means to deprive humanity of so noble an example of all that is good and high-minded and pure." [8]

[6] J. C. Perkins to Pierce, Nov. 16, 1875, Pierce MSS.; Little & Brown to Sumner, Apr. 1, and 2, 1844, Sumner MSS.; Felton to Sumner, Apr. 10, 1844, ibid.; Longfellow, Journal, Apr. 4, 1844, Longfellow MSS.

[7] *Law Reporter*, VII (May 1844), 57–8; Longfellow, Journal, July 3, 1844, Longfellow MSS.; Hillard to Sarah P. Cleveland, July 31, 1844, copy, ibid.; Pierce, II, 308.

[8] Ward to Longfellow, July 28, 1844, Sumner MSS. Cf. Ticknor: *Prescott*, p. 241.

At the end of July, to everyone's surprise, Sumner began to mend. Relieved by the news that his Harvard classmate, J. C. Perkins, had agreed to take over the labor of editing Vesey, he began to feel that his physicians' verdict had been premature, and decided that his disease was only "a slow, nervous fever, brought on by sitting and studying at his desk, till after the clock struck two at night." His mood of depressed loneliness lifted when he learned of how his numerous friends had gathered around his bedside. As Hillard said: "It was worth while to approach the gates of the grave, to have such assurances of affection and regard as was [*sic*] showered upon him." [9]

Accustomed to the most vigorous health, Sumner felt that recovery should come overnight. Obliged to "assume the character of an invalid, watch the wind and skies, wrap up his throat, . . . take medicines, and listen to the vacillating opinions of his physicians," he suspected that he might, after all, be suffering from some dread ailment. "I begin to feel . . . that I have a shattered constitution," he confessed to Howe, "and that health has flown from me, perhaps forever." Death he did not fear, but throughout his life he had a terror that some lingering illness would leave him "but half a man." [1]

A fall vacation in the Berkshires helped take his mind off his symptoms, and while he rode horseback, flirted mildly with the neighboring belles, and played at archery with Fanny Kemble, his body gradually recuperated. By late November he was back at his office, editing the remaining volumes of Vesey and appearing in courts. He celebrated his recovery by appearing in the friction match case, in which he had taken so strong an interest, and his ten-hour summation speech to the jury was evidence that he was physically as strong as ever.[2] But he continued to suffer from his deep spiritual malaise.

[9] Pierce, II, 309; Sumner to Sarah P. Cleveland, July 31, 1844, copy, Longfellow MSS. There is not sufficient evidence to warrant a medical diagnosis of Sumner's illness. For similar "identity crises" in the lives of other young men about Sumner's age, see Erik H. Erikson: *Young Man Luther* (London: Faber and Faber Ltd., c. 1958), pp. 38–45.

[1] Sumner to Howe, Aug. 27, 1844, Sumner MSS.

[2] Sumner had edited Vols. I–IV of Vesey before his collapse. Perkins edited Vols. V, VII–X, and XII, and Charles B. Goodrich, Vol. XI. Sumner, after his recovery, edited Vols. VI and XIII–XX. Sumner to Tower, Dec. 4, 1844, Tower MSS.

CHAPTER V

An Outrageous Philanthropist

SUMNER'S "spirits are not good I am sorry to say," Hillard reported several months after he seemed fully recovered from his breakdown, "and life seems to have less and less attractions for him as he grows older." Failing to win professional success, failing to keep the social approbation on which he thrived, and, worst of all, failing to find security from these blows in domestic happiness, Sumner became bored, frustrated, and lonely. The reverses he had suffered during the four years since his return from Europe would have disconcerted any man; to Sumner they were catastrophic. "To me friendship, sympathy and kindness are a peculiar necessity of my nature," he recognized, "and I can have few losses greater than the weakening of any of these bonds." The death of his sister Mary, the only member of his family for whom he had a deep attachment, pointed up the meaningless of his own life. "I dwell often on the image of her beauty, of her sweet nature, and of her most serene soul," he wrote a few months after her funeral, "and feel that it would have been far better, had the health, which was unexpectedly renewed in my veins, been bestowed upon her in my stead." [1]

Genuinely troubled by Sumner's unhappiness, his friends tried to cheer him up. Henry and Fanny Longfellow welcomed

[1] Hillard to Sarah P. Cleveland, Dec. 1, 1844, copy, Longfellow MSS.; Sumner to Longfellow, May 14, 1842, ibid.; Sumner to Sarah P. Cleveland, Jan. 31, 1845, Cleveland MSS.

him as a regular weekend guest at Craigie House; Hillard endlessly sympathized with him; Felton regaled him with oysters and outrageous puns. Howe, when he got back from Europe, favored more active measures. He thought it best to divert Sumner's interest from his personal problems into the constructive channels of civic reform.

• 1 •

Philanthropy was not something new to Sumner in 1844. Ever since his return from Europe he had been under the influence of William Ellery Channing, the father of organized benevolence in Boston. It is difficult to explain the enormous influence this frail, aging spokesman for liberal religion exercised over New Englanders of Sumner's generation. Certainly it was not his appearance that won him a following. As Longfellow unkindly remarked, Channing "is one of the funniest looking individuals you meet in the streets; as he wears a blue camlet wrapper, silver-bowed spectacles; a shawl round his neck, and an enormous hat, coming down over his eyes and ears, like an extinguisher." Nor was he in the conventional sense an orator, for "his voice was soft and musical, not loud or full in its tones," and he carefully refrained from rhetorical display. Quiet, sickly, and cautious, Channing was a philosopher whose ideas had neither great originality nor brilliance. Yet he managed to be, as Emerson said, the "Bishop" for the "New" in Massachusetts thought and society.[2]

Learning of Channing's enormous European reputation while abroad, Sumner was prepared to overcome his initial distrust of the minister, and when Hillard, who was secretary of the Federal Street congregation, brought his friend to the informal weekly discussions Channing held at his Mount Vernon Street mansion, Sumner was totally captivated. In Channing he found an older man, of the same generation as his father and Justice Story, whom he could revere as "one of the purest, brightest, greatest minds of this age." Unlike Sheriff Sumner, Channing was

[2] Longfellow to his father, Jan. 3, 1841, Longfellow MSS.; Sumner: *The Scholar, The Jurist, The Artist, The Philanthropist* . . . (Boston: William D. Ticknor and Company; 1846), pp. 65–6. For Channing's enormous influence in New England, see Gladys Brooks: *Three Wise Virgins* (New York: E. P. Dutton & Co., Inc.; 1957), and Arthur W. Brown: *Always Young for Liberty* (Syracuse: Syracuse University Press; 1956), Chap. xv.

"a saint-like character," always kindly and benevolent. Unlike Story, the minister did not become conservative as he grew older, but instead "as he advanced in life, his enthusiasm seemed to brighten, his soul put forth fresh blossoms of hope, his mind opened to new truths," namely, social reforms.[3]

Where Channing led, Sumner followed. He adopted all of the minister's arguments; he shared his concern over prison reform, education, international peace, and Negro slavery. It seemed to him positively heroic that the great Unitarian should continue to battle for social justice despite his age and obviously failing health. When Channing died in 1842, Sumner felt his loss more deeply than he had the death of his own father. Channing's "soul was of rectitude and courage 'all compact,'" he wrote. "What seemed to me a sight almost sublime, was this weak old man, almost fading out of life, with a voice affected by the debility of his frame, uttering words that pass mountains and seas, overcoming the impediments of distance and boundaries, and . . . pleading trumpet-tongued for humanity, for right, for truth."[4]

During Channing's lifetime, Sumner's own activities in social reform had been unobtrusive. Perhaps the very fact that he was a loved, respected member of the minister's circle kept him from being angry with society. Certainly Channing exercised a restraining hand upon his disciples, warning "that there is danger of pushing principles to extreme" and "that there must be a compromise between the Ideal and the Actual." Under such moderate guidance, Sumner had been a reformer only in the limited sense that he shared Howe's interest in the deaf and dumb and Mann's concern with education. He had also published letters in the "respectable daily," the Boston *Advertiser,* defending the British navy's right to search suspected American slave traders, and he had assisted Channing in preparing *The Duty of the Free States,* a pamphlet that attacked Secretary of State Webster's conten-

[3] Pierce, II, 223, 227; Sumner: *The Scholar, The Jurist, The Artist, The Philanthropist,* p. 67.

[4] Henry Marion Hall (ed.): "Longfellow's Letters to Samuel Ward," *Putnam's Monthly,* III (Nov. 1907), p. 166. On Channing as a social reformer, see William H. Channing: *Memoir of William Ellery Channing . . .* (Boston: Wm. Crosby and H. P. Nichols; 1848), III, Chaps. iii–v, and David P. Edgell: *William Ellery Channing: An Intellectual Portrait* (Boston: Beacon Press; 1955), pp. 150–201.

tion that the American flag protected even a slave ship on the high seas. But further Sumner was not prepared to go, and, despite numerous invitations, he took no public position as leader of any reform cause.[5]

By 1844, however, his reluctance had vanished. Irritated at the "toryism and donnishness" of Boston society, he was becoming increasingly restive. Both his European successes and his American failures taught him that a social order dominated by George Ticknor was not necessarily utopian. The darker his own personal prospects became, the greater grew his willingness to recognize a duty to improve society.[6]

The first reform cause in which Howe involved him was the common-schools controversy. Horace Mann was in serious trouble. His *Seventh Annual Report* charged that the famous Boston public schools were dulling students' minds through rote memorization and injuring their bodies through daily atrocious floggings. Outraged, the Principals' Association of Boston published an attack upon Mann's report. Angry and unwell, Mann issued a "Reply" to "this association—alias *Club* for eating and drinking and telling bawdy stories." As all Boston eagerly watched the fight, the embattled teachers published a "Rejoinder," and Mann retaliated with an "Answer to the 'Rejoinder.' "[7]

Always fond of losing causes, Howe plunged into the controversy on Mann's side, and, doubtless thinking that it would distract Sumner's mind from his woes, he brought his best friend along with him. He worked out a plan to have Mann's backers chosen to the Boston School Committee in the fall elections;

[5] Boston *Advertiser*, Jan. 4, and Feb. 10, 1842. See the reply of J. C. Perkins, ibid., Jan. 21, 1842. On this controversy see Hugh G. Soulsby: *The Right of Search and the Slave Trade in Anglo-American Relations, 1814–1862* ("Johns Hopkins University Studies in Historical and Political Science," Vol. XI, No. 2; Baltimore: The Johns Hopkins Press; 1933), esp. pp. 58–77. On Sumner's interest in the *Creole* affair see George Ticknor: *Life, Letters, and Journals* (Boston: James R. Osgood and Company; 1876), II, 199; Pierce, II, 194, 202, 205, 208, 210; Channing to Sumner, May 24, 1842, Sumner MSS.; Boston *Advertiser*, Apr. 18, 1842; Sumner to Lord Morpeth, Jan. 18, and Mar. 29, 1842, Carlisle MSS.

[6] Pierce, II, 214; III, 3–4. Cf. Eric Hoffer: *The True Believer: Thoughts on the Nature of Mass Movements* (New York: New American Library of World Literature, Inc.; 1958), pp. 22–3.

[7] Louise Hall Tharp: *Until Victory: Horace Mann and Mary Peabody* (Boston: Little, Brown & Co.; 1953), p. 203; Francis Bowen to Sumner, Dec. 14, 1844, Sumner MSS. The best treatment of the common schools controversy is in Schwartz: *Howe*, Chap. ix.

then, with a whip over the obdurate schoolmasters, they could insist upon progressive teaching methods. For Ward 4 Howe put up Sumner, despite vigorous objections from East Bostonians, who also belonged to that ward, against a candidate of "so little popularity, with the people." Though Howe's machine pushed Sumner's nomination through the Whig convention, the dissidents afterward ran a candidate of their own, a Baptist clergyman from East Boston. With the normal Whig majority split, Sumner was defeated in this his first trial for elective office.[8]

As Sumner was not elected to the school committee, he could have no part in Howe's 1845 campaign of harrying the Boston schoolmasters, but now that his interest was aroused, he did all he could elsewhere to assist Mann. In January he persuaded twenty-four leading Boston merchants and literary figures to sign a public letter he drafted praising Mann's "noble ardour, . . . marvellous application, undissipated and unwearied, [and] various labors, shrinking from no details or drudgery of duty." Mann's gratitude for this "most beautiful and touching letter" spurred Sumner to further exertions. Along with four other admirers of Mann's he petitioned the state legislature to appropriate $5,000 to construct normal schools, one of Mann's favorite projects, which the Boston principals were ridiculing; the five petitioners promised to match the state grant with an equal sum raised by private subscription.[9]

When the governor signed the bill in March, Sumner was sure there could be no difficulties ahead. Westfield, Bridgewater, and Northampton all were ready to pledge $1,000 if selected as a normal school site; Theodore Lyman had secured promises of another thousand; and Charles Brooks, one of Sumner's fellow petitioners, said he could raise the remainder on the Boston exchange "*in five minutes*." Fearing to delay the enterprise and hoping to assist Mann, then in the bitterest stage of his quarrel with the Boston teachers, Sumner borrowed the needed $5,000 on his own personal note, and presented the sum to the Board of Educa-

[8] Schwartz: *Howe*, pp. 127–9; Henry Greenleaf Pearson: *The Life of John A. Andrew: Governor of Massachusetts, 1861–1865* (Boston: Houghton Mifflin Co.; 1904), I, 45–6; Pierce, II, 324–5.

[9] Draft of a letter to Mann in Sumner's writing [Jan. 13, 1845], Sumner MSS.; Mann to the Members of the Committee, Jan. 13, 1845, ibid.; Mary Mann to Sumner [c. Jan. 20, 1845], ibid.; Boston *Post*, Jan. 28, 1845.

tion, relying upon the subscribers and the other friends of the common schools to repay him.

It was a noble gesture, but once Sumner had paid the money, the others lost interest and the subscriptions stopped coming in. The buildings went up, the normal schools opened, and Mann paid tribute to the "active and leading agency" that Sumner had "had in executive measures which have led to this beneficial result." But Sumner was once again heavily in debt. When his note was due, more than a year after the buildings had been finished, he could not pay it. In anger, he turned upon the others who had helped sponsor the project. "It seems to me rather hard that I should be thus left in the lurch by our committee, and particularly by individuals on it who have never contributed their full quota, and who are themselves rich, too. I . . . am less able than any member of the committee to pay this deficiency out of my own pocket. . . . It seems to me, therefore, that I may properly devolve upon the members of the committee . . . the duty of meeting this deficit." [1]

• 2 •

Such an initial experience in reform might have dampened the zeal of anyone except Sumner, but, in his unhappy mood, he found defeat almost as satisfying as victory. From Channing he had learned to expect reverses when the spirit of benevolence came into conflict with "the infinite, intense thirst for gain and accumulation" prevalent in Massachusetts. The "stone-blindness of the multitudes" was no cause for defeatism. "Amidst the disappointments which may attend individual exertions," Sumner argued, in words that paraphrased Channing's, "let us recognize . . . that whatever is just, whatever is humane, whatever is good, whatever is true . . . in the golden light of the Future, must prevail." [2]

Unquestioningly Sumner shared Channing's faith in prog-

[1] Sumner to Mann, June 5, and 13, 1845, Mann MSS.; Pierce, II, 327–38.

[2] Channing: *Channing*, III, 55, 264; Sumner: *The Law of Progress* . . . (Boston: William D. Ticknor & Company; 1849), p. 44. I am deliberately disregarding chronology in the following discussion of Sumner's philosophy of reform. His opinions did not change between 1844 and 1850, and his more carefully considered utterances, which were made later in this period, give the best insight into his pattern of thought.

ress. From his own personal dark defeatism he found solace in the bright future of humanity. Like Channing, he rejected the "want of faith in improvement . . . found . . . chiefly among what are called 'the better classes.'" He chafed impatiently at the Beacon Hill residents who lamented that commercial supremacy was shifting to uncultured New York, that political power had fallen to the unwashed Jacksonian masses, and that Boston itself was being invaded by hordes of Catholic Irish. He dissented from Joseph Story's mournful opinion: "The Republic is daily sinking. . . . I have lost my confidence in the practical administration of our government. . . . I am in utter despair . . . I can see little or no ground of hope for our country." Such a melancholy want of faith in man, he agreed with Channing, sprang from a want of faith in God, and he thrilled to the great preacher's challenge: "In such a world, who shall set limits to change and revolution?"[3]

Convinced by Channing, Sumner believed that "man, as an individual, is capable of indefinite improvement, so long as he lives." Eagerly he welcomed all advances in knowledge which might promote human betterment. For a time he shared with Mann and Howe an enthusiasm for phrenology, as the pseudo science justified a challenge to the "granite, felspar, hornblende, and mica State Orthodoxy" of Massachusetts.[4] If phrenology was right, "surrounding circumstances" had "an important, if not controlling influence" in shaping men. It must be, Sumner concluded, with his usual passion for carrying an argument to its logical extreme, the external circumstances of climate which made the Ethiopian black and the New Englander white, and it was no less true "that the minds of persons . . . take their complexion from predominating influences; and the forms even of . . . the character are modified by external circumstances." If environment made man, evil could be eliminated. By creating a society where "knowledge, virtue, and religion prevail," even "the

[3] Channing: *Channing*, III, 132–3; Story to Sumner, Jan. 16, 1839, and Feb. 6, 1842, Sumner MSS.; Story: *Story*, II, 518–20.

[4] Sumner to Longfellow, May 15, 1842, Longfellow MSS.; Mary Mann: *Life of Horace Mann* (Boston: Walker, Fuller, and Company; 1865), pp. 111, 124, 132; Harold Schwartz: "Samuel Gridley Howe as a Phrenologist," *American Historical Review*, XVII (Apr. 1952), 644–51. Cf. John D. Davies: *Phrenology, Fad and Science: A 19th-Century American Crusade* (New Haven: Yale University Press; 1955), esp. p. 3.

most forlorn shall grow into forms of unimagined strength and beauty." [5]

But the reformer, Sumner believed, must not be concerned with individuals; "the good of the whole human family, its happiness, its development, its progress" should be his objective. From Channing he borrowed unquestioningly the postulates that "states and nations . . . were amenable to the same moral law as individuals" and, therefore, that *"what is wrong for an individual is wrong for a state."* [6]

In an elaborate address delivered at Union College in 1848, Sumner summarized his thinking on reform. Citing Leibnitz, Descartes, Pascal, Turgot, and Condorcet as prophets, he announced "The Law of Progress" as "a *discovery* of our age." "The tocsin of monarchy and injustice of all kinds," progress ordained that indefinite improvement be "the Destiny of man, of societies, of nations, and of the Human Race." The lesson of history was "Onward forever." [7]

As the "Age of Humanity" was waiting in the wings, it was the duty of the reformer to usher it on stage. From Channing, who had supplied so much of his philosophy of progress, Sumner derived his view of the proper role of the reformer. As a first step a would-be philanthropist must make certain that he himself was uncontaminated by any legal or moral connection with the evils he wished to destroy. "Let us wash our hands of the great guilt" became the constant refrain of Sumner's speeches.[8] Pure himself, the reformer must then stir up public opinion, "which insensibly operates every where, like the gentle droppings of water and produces mighty results." Others would join him in proclaiming a *"moral blockade"* against the wrong, and, as "the soul of all effective laws is an animating public sentiment," the laws that

[5] Sumner to George Putnam, Apr. 1848, author's copy, Sumner MSS.; Sumner: *Law of Progress,* p. 32.

[6] Sumner: *The Scholar, The Jurist, The Artist, The Philanthropist,* pp. 55, 59.

[7] Sumner to Greene, May 10, 1848, Greene MSS.; Sumner: *Law of Progress,* pp. 12, 28. A recent scholar calls the "Law of Progress" address "the most adequate and significant treatment of the subject" to appear in America during Sumner's generation. Arthur Alphonse Ekirch, Jr.: *The Idea of Progress in America, 1815–1860* (New York: Columbia University Press; 1944), p. 258.

[8] E.g., Sumner: *Works,* I, 157. Cf Channing's justification of his petition for the abolition of slavery in the District of Columbia: "I wished by some public act to disclaim all participation in the national guilt. . . ." Channing: *Channing,* III, 187.

tolerated evil would themselves be changed. To charges of utopianism, Sumner replied firmly: "The Utopias of one age have been the realities of the next." [9]

• 3 •

Though Sumner himself thought that his ideas had revolutionary implications, few of his contemporaries were alarmed by his views.[1] If rarely heard on Beacon Hill, the word "progress" came naturally to the lips of Americans of Sumner's generation. For years Bostonians had heard orators expatiate on "The Progresive Character of Mankind" or "Progressive Improvement in the Condition of Man." [2] Sumner's views seemed a bit extravagant, but quite pardonable in a young man, especially as he was careful to exclude Comte, Saint-Simon, and Fourier from the legitimate prophets of progress, which, in his opinion, must not "shake *property.*" Besides, Sumner announced, his law of progress "shews that all change must come gradually—I am tempted to add peacefully." [3]

Far from being disturbed, respectable Bostonians approved of Sumner's growing interest in civic affairs, and to indicate their commendation, Mayor Thomas A. Davis and his council invited the young lawyer to deliver the city's 1845 Fourth of July oration. It was a considerable honor, for Boston's city fathers had made it a practice since 1783 to assign the principal speech on these occasions to "young men of promising genius." Harrison Gray Otis, John Quincy Adams, and Josiah Quincy had delivered the oration in earlier years; more recently Charles Francis Adams, Hillard, and Mann had made their formal bows before the Boston public in this fashion.[4]

[9] Sumner to Lieber, Oct. 26, 1837, Lieber MSS.; Sumner: *The Scholar, The Jurist, The Artist, The Philanthropist,* p. 59; Sumner: *The War System of the Commonwealth of Nations . . .* (Boston: Ticknor, Reed, and Fields; 1849), pp. 8, 29.

[1] Lieber, to be sure, grumbled that Sumner's "Law of Progress" oration was "peculiarly superficial" because the speaker had not "paid sufficient attention to retrograde nations and times." Lieber to Hillard, May 19, 1850, Lieber MSS.; Lieber's undated note on the cover of *The Law of Progress* in The Johns Hopkins Univ. Lib.

[2] Alexis de Tocqueville: *Democracy in America,* ed. by Phillips Bradley (New York: Vintage Books, Inc.; 1956), II, 78; Ekirch: *Idea of Progress,* pp. 67, 73.

[3] Dawes: *Sumner,* pp. 104–6; Sumner to George Sumner, May 16, 1848, Sumner MSS.; Sumner to Greene, May 10, 1848, Greene MSS.

[4] Davis to Sumner, Apr. 24, 1845, Sumner MSS.; Pierce, II, 338–9. Prior to 1783 the annual oration had been delivered on March 5, to commemorate the

Inexplicably, Sumner was reluctant to accept. As he later recalled, he "*peremptorily declined*" at first and agreed only when the mayor himself suggested that he had "kept aloof from public affairs in an unbecoming manner." Even after he had promised to give the oration, he had inner misgivings about the assignment. He delayed so long before commencing his preparation that Felton had repeatedly to remind him that his "numerous and distinguished audience" might determine his entire future career. Not until the middle of June did he settle down to real work, when he began "reading books like Briareus, fifty abreast," but even so, his manuscript was completed only on the eve of the holiday.[5]

In accepting the invitation to speak, Sumner had informed the mayor that his topic would be International Peace. His choice was not an unexpected one, as for years he had had an active, though quiet, interest in the peace movement. One of his earliest memories was of an address Josiah Quincy delivered before the Peace Society in the Old South Church; though only nine years old at the time, Sumner received from it "a deep and lasting impression" of the horrors of war. Shortly after he left college, hearing an address by William Ladd strengthened Sumner's antiwar convictions. His trip abroad intensified his dislike of militarism. He found European military installations and fortifications shocking and thought it would be better if the millions of soldiers were out "building . . . railways and other internal improvements, instead of passing the day in carrying superfluous muskets." When he returned to the United States, he joined the Peace Society, which Channing had helped found, and became a member of its executive committee. With most Bostonians he shared a concern over American saber-rattling in the 1840's, and he deplored with equal vigor the "insidious" plan of the South to annex Texas and carve from it "great slaveholding States" and the abominable intrigue to seize the disputed Oregon Territory, "not worth a groat to us." "For myself," he declared in private letters, "I hold all wars unjust and un-Christian." [6]

Boston Massacre. For a complete list of the speakers to 1852 see Loring: *The Hundred Boston Orators.*

[5] Sumner to George Putnam, Apr. 1848, author's copy, Sumner MSS.; Felton to Sumner [June? 1845], ibid.; Hillard to Sarah P. Cleveland, June 15, 1845, copy, Longfellow MSS.

[6] Sumner to Putnam, Apr. 1848, author's copy, Sumner MSS.; Ralph Volney Harlow: *Gerrit Smith, Philanthropist and Reformer* (New York: Henry Holt &

If the Boston city officials knew of these opinions, they were not at all perturbed by them, but went ahead with their plans for a customary rousing holiday celebration. Even nature seemed to co-operate. July 4 was a beautiful, cool day, and a partial newspaperman reported: "We doubt whether any part of our blessed country showed a fairer sight than the Boston common on the morning" of the holiday. "Magnificent flags" hung along the streets, and the ships in the harbor displayed colorful pennants. The United States warship *Ohio*, visiting in the port, "was beautifully dressed with flags, from the tops of her tall masts to the water's surface."

At about 10:30 the city authorities, led by the mayor and the orator of the day, began the procession from City Hall. They were followed by representatives of the Sons of Temperance, the Catholic Sunday Schools, the Veteran Cod Association, the Irish Charitable Relief Society, and by throngs of gaily dressed school children. More than 2,000 persons filed into Tremont Temple to hear the oration. On the platform, behind the speakers' chairs, was a choir of one hundred schoolgirls, dressed in white, ready to sing the national anthem. The Washington Light Guards, the uniformed officers of the Massachusetts militia, and officers of the United States army and navy occupied the seats just in front of the platform. After introductory prayers, the Declaration of Independence was "most effectively and impressively read." The celebration seemed to be going off "beautifully and harmoniously."[7]

Then Sumner rose to deliver his oration, which he titled "The True Grandeur of Nations." Carefully dressed for the occasion in a long-tailed blue coat with gilt buttons, white waistcoat, and white trousers, he had never looked so well in his life. Tall, erect, his clean-cut features saved from sternness by the smile that occasionally lit up his intelligent face, the thirty-four-year-old lawyer seemed to many of his audience the perfection of manly beauty.[8] With great ease and spirit he began: "It is in

Co., Inc.; 1939), p. 107; Pierce, II, 82, 278, 301, 314; Sumner to Howe, Dec. 31, 1843, Sumner MSS.

[7] Boston *Post*, July 7, 1845.

[8] *Dinner Commemorative of Charles Sumner and Complimentary to Edward L. Pierce. Boston, December 29, 1894* (Cambridge: John Wilson and Son; 1895), p. 23; Fanny Longfellow to Nathan Appleton, July 5, 1845, Longfellow MSS.

obedience to an uninterrupted usage in our community that, on this Sabbath of the Nation, we have put aside the common cares of life and seized a respite from the neverending toils of labor, to meet in gladness and congratulation, mindful of the blessings transmitted from the Past, mindful also, I trust, of the duties to the Present and the Future." [9] As the deep voice rolled out the swelling periods, Sumner's hearers settled themselves comfortably to listen.

Abruptly they were startled. After denouncing the annexation of Texas as an attempt "in this land of boasted freedom, to fasten by new links the chains which promise soon to fall from the limbs of the unhappy slave" and branding the American demand for Oregon as "a presumptuous assertion of a disputed claim to a worthless territory," Sumner bluntly announced his theme: "IN OUR AGE THERE CAN BE NO PEACE THAT IS NOT HONORABLE: THERE CAN BE NO WAR THAT IS NOT DISHONORABLE."

For nearly two hours the orator, ignoring the uneasy whisperings of the military men just in front of him and the occasional hisses from the crowd, proceeded to develop this proposition. Speaking entirely from memory, except when he referred to his notes for statistics, he enumerated the evils of war. This "monstrous and impious usage" was "utterly ineffectual to secure or advance" justice; it produced only "wasted lands, ruined and famished cities, and slaughtered armies." What was even worse, it destroyed human nature, for war was "a temporary adoption, by men, of the character of wild beasts, emulating their ferocity, rejoicing like them in blood."

Why, then, were wars still fought? Sumner asked. Partly because men had a mistaken belief in their necessity; partly because they relied upon the "feeble tapers that glimmer in the sepulchres of the Past," rather than upon "those ever-burning lights" of present progress. Still another reason was the support the Christian Church gave to warfare. A mistaken view of honor and "a selfish and exaggerated *love of country*" also perpetuated

[9] Unless otherwise noted, all quotations in the following paragraphs are from the contemporary pamphlet edition of *The True Grandeur of Nations* (Boston: William D. Ticknor and Company; 1845), which is considerably different from the often revised and somewhat subdued version that appears in Sumner: *Works*, I, 1–132. The manuscript of Sumner's address (Sumner MSS., Houghton Lib.) differs in only slight verbal matters from the pamphlet version.

the martial spirit. "Our country, be she *right or wrong*," announced Sumner, was "a sentiment dethroning God and enthroning the Devil."

But perhaps the weightiest cause of conflict was "the costly *preparations* for war, in time of peace." With their armies and navies, their cannon and their fighting ships, nations were like "the wild boar in the fable, who whetted his tusks on a tree in the forest, when no enemy was near, saying that in time of peace he must prepare for war." Even the United States government, Sumner noted, spent more than seven times as much for "*peaceful preparations for war*" as for "all other purposes whatsoever."

And for what purpose were these warlike preparations? the orator continued. The army of the United States, trained in "farcical and humiliating exercises," performed no useful function. Its officers were educated at that "seminary of idleness and vice," West Point. Similarly, the navy had no purpose, for it would be "an unavailing defence against any serious attack." As for the militia, he announced, addressing himself directly to the officers in front of him, though they might dress "in padded and well-buttoned coats of blue, 'besmeared with gold,' surmounted by a huge mountain-cap of shaggy bear skin, and with a barbarous device, typical of brute force, a tiger, painted on oil-skin tied with leather to their backs," they were not even competent to put down a street riot, much less to defend a nation.

Americans, Sumner concluded, must recognize that the true grandeur of nations lies, not in warfare, but "in moral elevation, enlightened and decorated by the intellect of man." Then would come the "true golden age." "Then," declared the orator in a final burst of rhetoric, "shall the naked be clothed and the hungry fed. Institutions of science and learning shall crown every hill-top; hospitals for the sick . . . shall nestle in every valley; while spires of new churches shall leap exulting to the skies. . . . The eagle of our country, without the terror of his beak, and dropping the forceful thunderbolt from his pounces, shall soar with the olive of Peace, into untried realms of ether, nearer to the sun."

Immediately following the oration, Sumner, the city officials, and the invited guests repaired to Faneuil Hall for the customary July 4 dinner, and here the animosity that had been accumulating while the orator spoke exploded. Thirteen toasts were given, and nearly all the responses showed hostility toward Sumner and his ideas. Even his friend Palfrey announced that "he was not, on the fourth of July, willing to forget that Massachusetts sent one soldier for every three to the armies which fought the battles of independence." J. C. Park, of the state senate, bitterly attacked Sumner for the inappropriateness of his oration and for the rudeness with which he had assailed the military men present, the invited guests of the city, as "so many lions, tigers, or other wild beasts." Adjutant General Oliver praised the American Revolution as a defensible and desirable war, which "gave to the world a new nation, . . . permitting to each man the right to think, act and speak whatever he lawfully may, he himself being the best and only judge of the fitness of time, place and presence." The allusion was not missed.

The most weighty of all the rebukes came from Congressman Robert C. Winthrop, who spoke authoritatively for the Whig oligarchy of Massachusetts. Feeling that Sumner "seemed to contemplate non-resistance and dissolution of the Union," he replied to a toast by bluntly stating his own doctrine: "Our Country, whether bounded by Sabine or Del Norte—still our Country—to be cherished in all our hearts—to be defended by all our hands."

To keep the audience from becoming vicious, the toastmaster, Sumner's friend P. W. Chandler, decided "to throw the whole thing into broad farce" and "began by criticizing the oration, and asked what more or better you could expect from an old bachelor. How could a man who never knew anything of domestic broils feel competent to speak of war? What were the discomforts of a camp to a washing day at home?" This kind of coarse nonsense tickled the crowd, and Chandler even got some applause for the toast: "The orator of the day. However much we may differ from his sentiments, let us admire the simplicity, manliness and ability with which he has expressed them."

Sumner rose and "said he would not follow the apple of discord which he appeared to have thrown out." Instead he replied with another toast: "The youthful choristers of the day—May their future lives be filled with happiness, as they have filled our hearts to-day with the delights of their music." [1]

[1] Boston *Post*, July 7, 1845; Winthrop to J. H. Clifford, Jan. 7, 1846, copy, Winthrop MSS.; Chandler to Pierce, Aug. 27, 1877, Pierce MSS.

· 4 ·

His Fourth of July oration, Sumner objectively reported a few weeks later, "was delivered to a large and applauding audience, and has been received . . . by some persons with very great favor, and by others with condemnation. It is admitted on all sides to be bold and fearless, and many who condemn its sentiments praise its style." [2]

Many influential persons were outraged by "The True Grandeur of Nations." Samuel A. Eliot, former mayor of the city and treasurer of Harvard College, stiffly remonstrated with Sumner for sacrificing "a reputation for good judgment and civility" to "the applause of thousands of excited and enthusiastic persons." He summarized the opinion of Beacon Hill: "The young man has cut his own throat." A "Citizen of Boston" published an irate pamphlet attacking Sumner as a theorist, questioning his taste in presenting a Peace Society oration on such an occasion, ridiculing his "harsh and unpolished . . . involved and obscure" style, and riddling his faulty logic and history. L. M. Goldsborough, of the United States navy, angrily challenged Sumner's statistics on American expenditures for armaments and branded the oration as a "collation of irrelevant shreds and patches . . . exceedingly deficient in manliness, originality, and accuracy." The Boston *Post* rebuked Sumner for his "mixture of monomania, sophistry and presumption" in delivering on the Fourth of July "a discourse appropriate perhaps for an insane Quaker in his dotage." [3]

Many of Sumner's friends were distressed by his oration. Nathan Appleton, a practical man whose income depended upon the importation of Southern cotton into the port of Boston, was unwilling "to leave our harbors unprotected and to rely for safety on the character of non-combatism." Like President Quincy,

[2] Sumner to Sarah P. Cleveland, Aug. 15, 1845, copy, Longfellow MSS.

[3] Eliot to Sumner, Aug. 19, 1845, Sumner MSS.; Allan Nevins: *Ordeal of the Union* (New York: Charles Scribner's Sons; 1947), I 393; *Remarks Upon an Oration Delivered by Charles Sumner Before the Authorities of the City of Boston, July 4th, 1845. By a Citizen of Boston* (Boston: Wm. Crosby & H. P. Nichols; 1845), esp. pp. 8, 15; Goldsborough: *A Reply . . . to an Attack Made Upon the Navy of the United States, . . . In which a Brief Notice is Taken of the Recent Fourth of July Oration, Delivered at Boston, by Charles Sumner* (Portsmouth: C. W. Brewster; 1845), esp. pp. 18, 22; Boston *Post*, Aug. 21, 1845.

he was troubled by the extremism of Sumner's views, but conceded: "It is sometimes necessary to 'cut beyond the wound' . . . to go for the whole in order to get half." Remembering "the Poles, and the negroes at the South," Horace Mann thought there were some cases where "people would be justified, before the holiest tribunal, for declaring and waging even the most exterminating [*sic*] war." "By all those who fought and bled at Marathon; by those who fought at Morgarten and Bannockburn; by those who fought and bled at Bunker's Hill," Prescott denied Sumner's proposition that all wars were dishonorable. Lieber sneered at Sumner as "a new Archangel Michael with a flybrush instead of a sword," and Chancellor Kent gave opinion that Sumner's oration, though "beautifully classic and eminently benevolent," revealed his mind to be "diseased manifestly . . . on certain subjects." [4]

Two dissents cost Sumner more pain than all the other criticism combined. Justice Story, now within a few weeks of his death, read the oration and disagreed with Sumner. Too kindly to be harsh upon a favorite pupil, whom he had treated as a member of his family and had once destined to be his successor in the Harvard Law School, Story admitted the justice of Sumner's strictures upon war and praised his "exalted mind . . . and enlarged benevolence." But he added firmly: "In my judgment war is under some . . . circumstances not only justifiable, but an indispensable part of public Duty. . . . In the extent, to which you press your doctrines, they are not in my judgment defensible." Congressman Winthrop, quasi-official representative of the Massachusetts Whig party, also vigorously dissented. He wrote Sumner that his toast at the July 4 dinner had been no offhand remark; defensive wars were justifiable, and the American Revolution had been worth its cost in blood.[5] The doors of both Boston and the Harvard Law School were closing in Sumner's face.

Sumner gained some comfort from the fact that many peo-

[4] Appleton to Sumner, Aug. 11, 1845, Sumner MSS.; Mann to Sumner, Sept. 8, 1845, ibid.; Ticknor: *Prescott*, p. 377; Lieber to Sumner, June 25, 1845, Lieber MSS.; C. H. Van Tyne (ed.): *The Letters of Daniel Webster* . . . (New York: McClure, Phillips & Co.; 1902), p. 334. Many of the letters Sumner received on this occasion are printed in W. C. Ford (ed.): "Sumner's Oration on the 'True Grandeur of Nations,' July 4, 1845," *MHSP*, L (1916–17), 249–307.

[5] Story to Sumner, Aug. 11, 1845, Sumner MSS.; Winthrop to Sumner, July 9, 1845, ibid.; Sumner to Winthrop, July 6, 1845, Winthrop MSS.

ple did approve his peace doctrines. Requests for copies of the oration poured in from all parts of New England, from New York, and from as far west as Kentucky and Ohio. Many of his enthusiastic correspondents were embattled, doctrinaire reformers, a group with whom he had hitherto had little contact. Such antislavery crusaders as William Lloyd Garrison, Gerrit Smith, and J. M. McKim praised the oration. Theodore Parker, the hard-hitting Unitarian heretic, barred from most of Boston's pulpits because of his daring social and theological ideas, initiated a correspondence with Sumner, lauding him "for so nobly exposing the evils of war, its worthlessness and its waste." The principal figure in the American Peace Society, Elihu Burritt, the learned blacksmith, who was now organizing a world crusade to outlaw war, wrote Sumner simply: "The cause of Peace dates principally from your oration." [6]

The Peace Society immediately asked to republish the oration, and it rapidly went through six editions. A copy was sent to each member of Congress, in the hope that it might help avert a threatened war with England over the Oregon boundary. Abroad, too, the speech had a large audience. In Liverpool the Peace Society published an edition of 7,500 copies, sending them to the Queen, the Duke of Wellington, Sir Robert Peel, and other notables. Five or six editions were printed in London, and near the Royal Exchange, news venders hawked it as ha'penny a copy as "Sumner's Speech agin war with England." [7]

From two continents grateful words of praise rolled in. "That oration will live," a Boston admirer predicted. "It will be a text-book for hundreds. . . . Should you never do anything else, than you have now done—you will not have lived in vain." [8]

Sumner pretended to be indifferent to both the censure and the praise his oration elicited. In fact, however, he shrank sensitively under the unaccustomed criticism. During the weeks fol-

[6] Parker to Sumner, Aug. 17, 1845, Sumner MSS.; Burritt to Sumner, Nov. 19, 1845, ibid.

[7] John W. Tatum to Sumner, Mar. 9, 1854, ibid.; Christina Phelps: *The Anglo-American Peace Movement in the Mid-Nineteenth Century* ("Columbia University Studies in History, Economics, and Public Law," No. 330, New York: Columbia University Press; 1930), p. 71; Merle E. Curti: *The American Peace Crusade, 1815–1860* (Durham: Duke University Press; 1929), pp. 121–2; William Hayden to Sumner, June 19 [1846], Sumner MSS.

[8] R. C. Waterston to Sumner, July 7, 1845, Sumner MSS. Merle Curti (*American Peace Crusade*, p. 120) agrees that the oration had an "epoch-making significance in the history of the peace movement."

lowing July 4 he spent much of his time writing long, troubled letters explaining and defending his positions. To add to his discomfort he developed boils—one, as Felton pointed out, "on the shoulder, just where the epaulette is worn, and another on the side, where the sword hangs." [9]

He was genuinely surprised by the storm he had stirred up. He had intended nothing more than an oratorical display of fairly common opinions that he earnestly shared. Neither now, or at any time during his later career, did he make any great claim to be an original thinker. A hostile critic complained with some justice that the oration contained "nothing new in its sentiments, its arguments, or its illustrations," though he went too far in calling it "a birds-nest built out of materials gathered from all quarters, and without any great scrupulousness or delicacy as to their quality or value." Even an admirer pointed out that Sumner's oration contained the same ideas as Channing's sermons.[1] Channing had observed that war "turns man into a beast of prey"; Sumner called war "a temporary adoption, by men, of the character of wild beasts." "Justice and force have little congeniality," Channing preached; Sumner, weighing war's "sufficiency as a mode of determining justice between nations," found "that it is a rude appeal to force or a gigantic game of chance, in which God's children are profanely dealt with as a pack of cards." Channing and Sumner used identical words in condemning any American conflict with England as a civil war between brothers. On other points Sumner echoed the ideas, and sometimes the very words, of William Ladd, William Jay, and other advocates of international peace.[2]

Nor was Sumner's oration distinguished for its logical force. The historical incidents, classical quotations, and statistics on military expenditures which he cited were, properly speaking, not arguments at all, but illustrations of generalizations so obvious as to require no proof.[3] Everybody agreed that wars are un-

[9] Felton to Longfellow, Aug. 9, 1845, Longfellow MSS.

[1] *Remarks upon an Oration Delivered by Charles Sumner . . . By a Citizen of Boston*, pp. 8–9; John Tappan to Sumner, July 5, 1845, Sumner MSS.

[2] *The Works of William E. Channing* (Boston: James Munroe and Company; 1841), IV, 55; V, 118; Sumner: *True Grandeur of Nations*, pp. 9, 81. Sumner acknowledged his borrowing in his elaborate annotations.

[3] R. Elaine Pagel and Carl Dallinger: "Charles Sumner," in William Norwood Brigance (ed.): *A History and Criticism of American Public Address* (New York: McGraw-Hill Book Co.; 1943), pp. 751–76.

fortunate, bloody, and undesirable; everybody knew that preparations for war are expensive. The oration was the earliest public demonstration of Sumner's propensity for what might be called illogical logicality, his tendency to extend a principle to its utmost limits. Given the assumption that war is bad, Sumner thought it followed that all wars are equally bad. As a nation, like an individual, should do only what is good, the United States should always and under all circumstances eschew war.

No one could have taken Sumner's "The True Grandeur of Nations" as a practical guide to world peace. Except for passing references to a possible congress of nations and to international arbitration, Sumner said nothing about how wars were to be prevented. The oration was a perfect example of Channing's technique of reform through verbal exorcism, through public disapproval of an institution considered wrong. On the practical question of how even this verbal outlawing of war could be secured, Sumner's sole advice was: "*Believe* that you can do it, and you *can* do it." [4]

If it is not hard to understand why the oration exasperated so many of Sumner's hearers, the acclaim it received from reformers is also easy to explain. To the leaders in the peace crusade, whose writings had been distinguished more for good intentions than for good grammar, "The True Grandeur of Nations" seemed a marvel of learning and rhetoric. Sumner lent reputability to the peace movement, for he spoke as one who had "enjoyed the rare advantages of having graduated at Harvard; studied law with Justice Story; and, withal, basked in the allurements of foreign climes." [5]

The eloquence of the address, too, made a tremendous impression upon his audience. Sumner's emphasis upon Christian truths, his simple faith that a nation must obey the same moral law as an individual, his invocation of faith, justice, and duty reminded his older listeners of the half-forgotten principles on which New England had originally been founded; his appeal to progress inspired the young. If the ideas in the oration were not new, the rhetoric in which they were clad was fresh and original. One cannot, of course, separate the oration from the orator. Sum-

[4] Sumner: *Works*, I, 129.

[5] Goldsborough: *A Reply . . . to an Attack Made Upon the Navy*, p. 22.

ner's handsome presence, his obvious sincerity, his deep, convincing voice, his flashing eye kindled with righteousness—all gave magic to words that read coldly upon the printed page.

The circumstances under which Sumner delivered his oration lent it additional interest and importance. "Had it been delivered before a Peace Society," Sumner's sharpest critic declared, "we should never have raised our . . . voice against it." But Sumner spoke, it seemed, in the very mouth of the cannon. Since he was, as Wendell Phillips once remarked, like "a cat without smellers," it was not, in fact, so much audacity as insensitivity to the weight and edge of his own words that led Sumner to look the city's military guests in the eye and denounce "the pride, pomp and circumstance of glorious war" or to point to the frowning guns of the warship in the harbor and ask: "What is the use of the Navy of the United States?" But his listeners thought it an act of high moral courage. "You mistake your vocation, my dear Sumner," one of his friends wrote him. "You should be a soldier and a general—The bravery which led you to declare such a doctrine on such a day would secure you laurels and arches." As the Boston essayist E. P. Whipple summarized: "The great success of Sumner was due to the fact that this oration was studiously framed so as to be utterly *in*appropriate to the occasion." [6]

• 5 •

Though Felton warned that Elihu Burritt and his peace reformers were "sentimental idiots . . . with their cant and fee-faw-fum," Sumner relished their praise, which was all the more grateful because respectable Boston disapproved of him. He pledged eternal devotion to a cause he had hitherto only cautiously endorsed, and, holing up in Felton's Cambridge house for several weeks, carefully revised his oration, adding citations, appendices, arguments, and footnotes in Greek, Latin, French, and Italian. "You have no idea what an arsenal of peace arms my home has become," Felton joked. "Lives of William Penn, Sermons on War, tracts of the American Peace Society, journals anti-everything, Scriptural arguments, estimates of the costs of navies and

[6] *Remarks upon an Oration Delivered by Charles Sumner . . . By a Citizen of Boston*, p. 30; B. D. Silliman to Sumner, Sept. 8, 1845, Sumner MSS.; Whipple: *Recollections of Eminent Men*, p. 213.

armies, besides a great many smaller arms—the pistols, hand grenades, cutlasses and so forth of the Peace Establishment—are arranged in every part of the house—upstairs, downstairs, in the attic, and in the cellar." [7]

During the next four years Sumner rarely neglected an occasion to depict the grandeur of peace and the horror of war. In 1846 he devoted a large part of his Phi Beta Kappa oration at Harvard to lauding Channing for understanding "that the fairest flowers cannot bloom in soil moistened by human blood." The following summer he urged the students at Amherst to recognize that as all God's "children are brethren, . . . ALL WAR BECOMES FRATRICIDAL." In newspaper letters he protested against the governor's appearing in church accompanied by an "escort of his fellow-citizens, dressed in strange harlequin garments, and with burnished weapons of war," and he implored the Massachusetts clergy not to "lend themselves to the fanfaronade of a militia celebration" on the traditional Artillery Election Day.[8]

Sumner's most ambitious contribution to the peace crusade was a long oration titled "The War System of the Commonwealth of Nations," which he delivered to the American Peace Society in 1849. Very proud of this address, Sumner was convinced that he had not merely cogently restated all the old arguments against war, but had put the peace movement on a "thoroughly *practicable* foundation." Actually, he mostly summarized, with rhetorical flourishes, the conventional peace advocates' picture of war as a "damnable profession—a trade of barbarians," and urged, in almost precisely the same words William Ladd had used years before: "The most complete and permanent substitute for War would be a Congress of Nations, and a High Court of Judicature organized in pursuance thereof." [9]

If Sumner made any contribution to the ideas of the peace movement, it was his theory that war should be outlawed through international law. For years he had been struck by the

[7] Felton to Sumner [July? 1845], Sumner MSS.; Felton to Longfellow, Aug. 9, 1845, Longfellow MSS.

[8] Sumner: *The Scholar, The Jurist, The Artist, The Philanthropist*, pp. 63–4; Sumner: *Fame and Glory* . . . (Boston: William D. Ticknor and Company; 1847), p. 38; Boston *Chronotype*, Nov. 7, 1847; Boston *Semi-Weekly Courier*, Dec. 20, 1847.

[9] Sumner to George Sumner, June 19, 1849, Segal Coll.; Sumner to Amasa Walker, June 29, 1849, Walker MSS.; Sumner: *The War System*, pp. 20, 60. Cf. William Ladd: "Essay on a Congress of Nations . . . ," in *Prize Essays on a Congress of Nations* (Boston: Whipple & Damrell; 1840), p. 521.

fact that the law of nations recognized war as a means, even if a last, unhappy means, by which countries could secure their rights. This, in Sumner's opinion, was comparable to the barbarous usage of permitting individuals to resort to force, as in dueling, to redress wrongs. Just as municipal law outlawed violence between citizens, and the American Constitution outlawed violence between states, so should international law ban war as "impious, monstrous and unchristian." Once the law of nations was changed, war would disappear, and with it "forts, navies, armies, military display, military chaplains and military sermons." [1] The difficulties involved in changing international law or in yielding national sovereignty to some international organization never occurred to Sumner. He was concerned with principles, not with mechanics.

Thoroughly pleased with his own efforts in behalf of peace, Sumner was distressed that so few of his close friends took him seriously as a thinker on international affairs. Only Hillard and Longfellow really approved his course; Richard Henry Dana, Jr., spoke for the rest when he declared that Sumner's views on peace were "in inextricable confusion." When they questioned Sumner, he was repeatedly obliged to modify his positions. Though he insisted that he was voicing Christian principles in denouncing war, he maintained that the strength of his argument was "entirely independent of the texts of the Gospels." Though he repeatedly praised the Quakers for understanding that force availed nothing against "*unarmed virtue* and *truth*," he declared that he was not a nonresistant. He thought a purely defensive war unlikely, "at least in our age, and with reference to our country," but, when closely cross-examined, he was obliged to admit that nations, like individuals, did have the right to self-defense. "If sorrowfully, necessarily, the sword may be taken as the instrument of Justice," Sumner finally restated his position, "it can never be *the Arbiter of Justice*." In effect, this meant that Sumner thought all war was horrible and that he opposed aggressive wars.[2]

[1] *MHSP*, L, 264; Sumner to George Putnam, Apr. 1848, author's copy, Sumner MSS.; Sumner: *War System*, pp. 13, 23.

[2] Dana to Julia Ward Howe, Feb. 9, 1876, Howe MSS.; Sumner: *The War System*, p. 6; Sumner to Winthrop, July 6, 1845, Winthrop MSS.; *MHSP*, L, 262; Sumner to Everett, Sept. 7, 1846, Everett MSS.; Sumner to R. H. Dana, Jr., [August 1845], Dana MSS.; Sumner's undated memorandum, enclosed in Amasa Walker, to Sumner, June 4 1849, Sumner MSS.

However much Sumner's friends approved these more cautiously stated views, his Peace Society associates were greatly disappointed in his watered-down opinions. While publicly praising Sumner's "War System" oration as "the mightiest word for peace that has yet been spoken," the pacifist editor of the *Christian Citizen* privately rebuked Sumner for lowering the standard of the Peace Society by admitting the possibility of a defensive war. In the eyes of extreme nonresistants Sumner was becoming merely another man who favored peace, not a Peace Society man.[3]

Though Sumner continued to announce that the outlawing of war was "the question of *our age*," especially important because the economies of disarmament offered European nations the only practical way of curing their ills and "of meeting *socialism*," he drifted away from the peace movement after 1849. The European Revolutions of 1848 caused him to see that inflexible advocacy of peace often meant support of the reactionary status quo. In these contests between tyranny and liberty, he announced, "all our sympathies must be with Freedom, while, in our sorrow at the unwelcome combat, we confess that victory is only less mournful than defeat." Retaining a nominal affiliation with the peace movement down into the 1850's, and occasionally sponsoring international mediation or arbitration, Sumner gradually came to feel that this cause was less important than other reforms. "One evil at a time," he said, and turned to other crusades.[4] When war came in 1861, America's foremost peace advocate solidly supported the military measures of the Union government.

• 6 •

Even before Sumner became famous as a peace advocate, he had become fiercely involved in a dispute over penal reform. Like all

[3] Curti: *American Peace Crusade*, p. 122; Thomas Drew to Sumner, June 11, and 20, 1849, Sumner MSS.; Sumner to Amasa Walker, June 11, 1849, Walker MSS. On factionalism in the peace movement see Curti: *American Peace Crusade*, Chap. iv, and Alice Felt Tyler: *Freedom's Ferment: Chapters in American Social History to 1860* (Minneapolis: University of Minnesota Press; 1944), pp. 409–13.

[4] Sumner to George Sumner, May 16, 1848, Sumner MSS.; Sumner to Joshua R. Giddings, Aug. 20, 1849, Giddings-Julian MSS.; Sumner: *The War System*, p. 66; Sumner: *Works*, II, 393–7; Sumner to Henry Richards, Apr. 4, 1854, Sumner MSS.; G. C. Beckwith to Sumner, Feb. 21, 1861, ibid.

the other crusades in which Sumner engaged, improvement of prisons was considered a perfectly respectable interest even by eminently conservative Bostonians. Since 1825 the Boston Prison Discipline Society, which was run by its influential secretary, Louis Dwight, issued reports "that served as penal textbooks for governors, legislators, and prison officers throughout the country." Such Boston leaders as A. A. Lawrence and John T. Bigelow belonged to the society, subscribed generously to its funds, and attended its public meetings each spring during Anniversary Week, when Dwight reported on the cheering progress of the good cause.[5]

Though Sumner was too young to take any active role in these proceedings until the 1840's, his interest in penal reform, like his concern for education and international peace, had been aroused many years earlier. As editor of *The American Jurist* he had entered into correspondence with such penologists as Lieber, Alexis de Tocqueville, N. H. Julius, of Prussia, and Joseph Adshead, of England. After his return from Europe, his "friend, and . . . idol," Channing, urged him to take a more vigorous interest in prisons, and Sumner accompanied Dorothea Dix, another of the great minister's disciples, on her visits to expose the shocking state of Massachusetts jails and asylums.[6]

If Sumner's ideas about penal reform derived largely from Channing, his impetus for action, once again, came from Howe. Shocked to find that, after decades of agitation by the Boston Prison Discipline Society, the idiots, the feeble-minded, and the insane of Massachusetts were still being herded into noisome jails along with hardened criminals, Howe concluded that the reform society itself needed reformation. As early as 1842 he and Sumner eyed the well-paid secretaryship of the society as an ideal haven for their friend Lieber, who was discontented in his South

[5] Blake McKelvey: *American Prisons: A Study in American Social History Prior to 1915* (Chicago: University of Chicago Press; 1936), Chap. i, esp. pp. 9–10; Stewart Holbrook: *Dreamers of the American Dream* (Garden City, N.Y.: Doubleday & Company, Inc.; 1957), pp. 240–3.

[6] Pierce, II, 227; Channing: *Channing*, III, 25–9; Francis Tiffany: *Life of Dorothea Lynde Dix* (Boston: Houghton Mifflin Co.; 1890), p. 75; Helen E. Marshall: *Dorothea Dix: Forgotten Samaritan* (Chapel Hill: University of North Carolina Press; 1937), p. 95. On European interest in American prisons see Frank Thistlethwaite: *The Anglo-American Connection in the Early Nineteenth Century* (Philadelphia: University of Pennsylvania Press; 1959), pp. 88–9.

Carolina exile, and contemplated making "a severe onslaught on the incumbent." [7]

Not until the collapse of his personal happiness and his severe physical breakdown in 1844 could Sumner be persuaded actively to enter upon a crusade to oust Dwight. When he turned his full attention to the Boston Prison Discipline Society, he found, in his new mood of pessimism and disillusionment, that Dwight embodied everything that was wrong about Boston: he was a part of the inbred ruling aristocracy; he was "*lazy* to the last degree"; he was provincial and bigoted; he knew "nothing of the European mind." [8] Dwight's narrow-mindedness, Sumner thought, was clearly exhibited in his attitude toward the rival systems of prison discipline which prevailed in the United States in the 1840's. In the separate system, best exemplified in the Eastern Penitentiary at Cherry Hill, Philadelphia, each prisoner was confined in an absolutely isolated, separate cell. The rival congregate system, developed at Auburn and Sing Sing, New York, also isolated prisoners in separate cubicles at night, but during the day they marched, in lock step, and worked together, but with all communication prohibited by the ever present threat of the lash.[9] The bitter rivalry between the partisans of the two systems had deep emotional undertones. As the Pennsylvania plan was so much more expensive than the Auburn system, the argument involved the perennial battle between the idealistic reformer and the practical administrator concerned with money. As European governments tended to admire the separate system while American states more often followed the congregate plan,

[7] Howe to Lieber, Aug. 17, and Sept. 5, 1842, Lieber MSS. On Howe and prison discipline see Schwartz: *Howe*, pp. 147–9. Sumner at this point joined the Prison Discipline Society and donated $2.00. *Eighteenth Annual Report of the Board of Managers of the Boston Prison Discipline Society* (Boston: Damrell and Moore; 1843), p. 109.

[8] Sumner to Howe [July 27, 1846], Sumner MSS.; Sumner to Francis Wayland, May 30, 1845, Wayland MSS.

[9] Tyler: *Freedom's Ferment*, pp. 265–85; O. F. Lewis: *The Development of American Prisons and Prison Customs, 1776–1845* (Albany; 1922); Harry Elmer Barnes: *The Evolution of Penology in Pennsylvania* (Indianapolis: The Bobbs-Merrill Company, Inc.; 1927); Negley K. Teeters and John D. Shearer: *The Prison at Philadelphia Cherry Hill: The Separate System of Prison Discipline, 1829–1913* (New York: Columbia University Press; 1957), esp. pp. 201–23. By modern standards both systems were strikingly inhumane. If the Auburn plan seemed ideally devised for turning out hardened criminals, the Pennsylvania system, as Barnes remarks (p. 291), could make serious pretensions only to converting its inmates into Robinson Crusoes, "broken and unoffending hermits."

the controversy became partly one between cosmopolitanism and nationalism.

An idealist who prided himself upon never counting the cost, an internationalist who was much influenced by such European penologists as Tocqueville, Sumner was horrified to find that Dwight had committed the Boston Prison Discipline Society to unrelenting warfare against the Pennsylvania system and that his reports had become an arsenal for advocates of the Auburn plan. After unsuccessfully attempting to remonstrate with the secretary in private, he decided that Dwight must go.

The first stage of Sumner's assault upon the unsuspecting Dwight came during the annual meeting of the Prison Discipline Society at Park Street Church in May 1845, which promised to be the usual cut-and-dried affair. Dwight, "a stout person, with a hard, red face and a dogmatic manner," read extracts from his report, and John T. Bigelow made some animadversions upon the Pennsylvania system. At this point, when the customary formal motion to accept the secretary's report was expected, Sumner rose and claimed the floor. Unceremoniously he "mounted upon the rail of his pew, and passed rapidly from pew to pew till he stood upon the platform." Most of the audience did not recognize the tall and rather slender young man, "with a shock of black hair not very carefully arranged, dressed in a blue frock-coat, buttoned, with a velvet collar," and even Francis Wayland, the president of the society, had to inquire his name.

Not waiting for an introduction, Sumner seized the lectern and launched into an arraignment of Dwight and his report. He showed "how the Pennsylvania system was regarded by all the governments of Europe . . . and argued that it was not right for the Boston Prison Discipline Society to continue to malign and misrepresent a system which most of the members had had no means of examining." For half an hour he continued, carrying his audience with him. Though Dwight retorted angrily, Sumner's motion to refer the secretary's report to a select committee was adopted; furthermore, the committee, to which both Sumner and Howe were appointed, was authorized to visit Philadelphia and inspect the system Dwight had so energetically condemned.[1]

During the months following his unexpected appearance

[1] Pierce, III, 81–2; Boston *Post,* May 28, 1845; Howe to Lieber, May 28, 1845, Lieber MSS.; G. B. Emerson to Dorothea L. Dix, May 27, 1845, Dix MSS.

before the Prison Discipline Society, Sumner continued his agitation against Dwight and won some converts for his views. Thus far he had surprised, but not alienated, Boston society. A large body of expert opinion agreed with him that the Pennsylvania system was greatly preferable, and even a stalwart conservative like Nathan Hale, editor of the Boston *Advertiser,* thought Dwight wrong in serving as an advocate of the Auburn plan.[2] In October 1845 the special committee spent three days at the Eastern Penitentiary, and Sumner returned more than ever convinced of the virtues of the separate system. Although the Society refused to print Howe's minority report praising the Pennsylvania plan, many Bostonians still had an open mind. Even George Ticknor was willing to concede that Howe's report was a "most important one," and A. A. Lawrence talked of subsidizing its publication.[3]

Sumner's extremism soon alienated most of this good will. He insisted upon pushing his arguments to the uttermost. As all penologists thought that criminals should not be permitted to contaminate each other through conversation, he argued that the Pennsylvania system, being more separate than the Auburn system, was superior "on grounds of reason, independent of experience." "If separation be desirable," he asked with his usual logic, "should it not be complete?"[4]

Even more disturbing to most Bostonians was Sumner's newly discovered propensity to engage in personalities with those who disagreed with him. At the May 1846 meeting of the Prison Discipline Society he launched into an hour-long attack upon Dwight. Ostensibly paying tribute to the secretary's labors for the convict, he in fact minimized them in his repeated ironical references to Dwight's "indefatigable" exertions. Angrily Sumner drew up his indictment: Dwight had suppressed communications hostile to the congregate system; he had misquoted authorities; he had ignored the painstaking reports of foreign observers; he had misrepresented European penology. "If the

[2] Dorothea L. Dix: *Remarks on Prisons and Prison Discipline in the United States* (Philadelphia: Joseph Hite & Co.; 1845), pp. 76–7; Francis Lieber: *A Popular Essay on Subjects of Penal Law . . .* (Philadelphia; 1838), p. 90; Schwartz: *Howe,* pp. 147–9; Hillard to Dorothea L. Dix, Feb. 9, 1846, Dix MSS.

[3] Sumner to Lieber, Dec. 15, 1845, Sumner MSS.; Sumner to A. A. Lawrence, June 29, 1846, Lawrence MSS.; Ticknor: *Life, Letters and Journal,* II, 228.

[4] Sumner: *Works,* I, 165–71, 173.

facts and authorities to which I have referred, were withheld intentionally," Sumner charged, "it was most uncandid; if through ignorance, the ignorance was gross." Dwight's reports were "lies," "*wilful and unwarrantable perversions of truth.*"

All Boston was shocked by the intemperance of Sumner's vituperation. Something, it seemed, had transformed this hitherto exceptionally agreeable, accommodating young man into a master of invective, whose words, uttered with fierce moral indignation, had the power to wound. Many observers thought they detected Sumner's real animus when he interrupted his tirade against Dwight to take an entirely gratuitous fling at Winthrop, whose July 4 toast still rankled: " 'Our country, right or wrong' is a cry that rises from the hoarse conclaves of politics. Let its spirit never intrude into any association like ours. Let none of us say, 'Our Society, right or wrong.' " [5]

Appointed to a committee to investigate Dwight's alleged misdeeds, Sumner and his friends spent much of the summer of 1846 agitating against the secretary. When Dwight's supporters refused to participate in the inquiry, Sumner and Hillard, who had persuaded President Wayland to go along with them, drew up a report showing up Dwight as "one of those singular individuals whose self esteem leads them to believe they are religious, honest and industrious, while in reality they are selfish, jesuitical and lazy." Not content with undermining Dwight at home, Sumner roused up his European friends against him. When Dwight attended the Frankfurt International Penitentiary Congress during the summer, Sumner's allies "out-generaled" him and prevented him from stating his case abroad; when he stopped in England on his way home, English penologists, all acquaintances of Sumner, snubbed the secretary.[6]

All these maneuvers were merely preliminary to the next annual meeting of the society, which opened in Tremont Temple on May 25, 1847. Dwight's report was more than ever hostile

[5] Hillard to Dorothea L. Dix, June 30, 1846, Dix MSS.; Boston *Advertiser*, May 28, 1846; Boston *Courier*, May 30, 1846; Sumner to Wayland, May 30, 1846, Wayland MSS.

[6] Howe to Lieber, July 30, 1846, Lieber MSS.; Richard Rathbone to Sumner, July 3, 1846, Sumner MSS.; N. H. Julius to Sumner, July 8, 1846, ibid. George Sumner, who was in Paris, published a letter at this time defending the separate system on the basis of recent French experiments in penology. *Mr. Sumner's Letter* (City of Boston, *City Document*, No. 11; 1846).

to the Pennsylvania system, and for the third consecutive year Sumner rose to reply. Loftily he moved that the secretary's report be tabled and that, instead, the society adopt resolutions announcing that it was not "the pledged advocate of the Auburn system" and praising the directors of the Eastern Penitentiary as "sincere, conscientious and philanthropic fellow-laborers." [7]

This time Dwight and his friends were prepared to put down Sumner as a brash interloper. Dwight himself opened the counteroffensive; Francis C. Gray was ready with facts and reasons to uphold the congregate system; and J. T. Stevenson, a representative of the textile manufacturers of Lowell, with whom Sumner was already at odds politically, ridiculed Sumner's logic. Most weighty of all was Eliot, "pompous and Boston personified," who was, as he reminded his hearers, a man of considerable importance—a former mayor of the city; treasurer of Harvard College; senator of the Commonwealth; treasurer of the Society. He did not need to remind them that he spoke not merely for himself, but for his large family connections—the Dwights, the Guilds, the Willises, the Curtises, the Ticknors—and for Boston respectability itself.[8]

The debates stretched over eight evenings (May 25–June 23) and as they became increasingly embittered, they attracted an enormous amount of public attention. On some nights more than 2,000 persons filled Tremont Temple, ostensibly to hear the merits of rival prison systems discussed, in reality to watch the antagonists "bait each other like dogs and bulls." "Night after night . . . the discussions have proceeded," one regular attendant reported, "until they are become the only evening amusement of the city." [9]

The drama of the debate lay in the fact that Sumner, nearly unaided, was taking on in a single fight all the organized powers that ruled Boston. He had alienated most of the moderates in the society and now had virtually no supporters besides Howe and Hillard. As the debates progressed, Howe spoke up

[7] E. D. Cheney to Pierce, Jan. 16, 1877, Pierce MSS.; Boston *Semi-Weekly Courier*, May 27, 1847.

[8] Elaborate accounts of the debates were carried in the Boston *Advertiser*, June 1, 1847, and in the Boston *Whig*, June 10, 12, 19, and 23, 1847.

[9] Mary Lesley Ames (ed.): *Life and Letters of Peter and Susan Lesley* (New York: G. P. Putnam's Sons; 1909), I, 151.

manfully, but he was no orator, and newspapers correctly belittled his efforts as "petulant, rambling, discursive, touching everything and discussing nothing." Hillard was even less effective, for after a newspaper ridiculed the irritable, scolding tone of his one speech as the prerogative of a person who appeared "to be mid-way between the sexes" and who had, therefore, "the right of exercising the privilege of the softer portion of humanity" whenever he felt testy, he lapsed into silence.[1]

Even without allies Sumner put up a magnificent fight, but as the debates wore on, his temper grew increasingly acerb. With renewed bitterness he repeated all his old charges against the society; even the loyal Hillard had to admit that his friend was "not altogether conciliatory." Toward Eliot, Sumner manifested positive venom. Striking through the treasurer at the Boston oligarchy, Sumner riddled Eliot's "vanity or self-esteem" which had led him to intermeddle in subjects of which he was ignorant, and, borrowing "something of his frankness, without his temper," sharply deflated his pretensions to be a philanthropist. Turning on the platform so as to face Dwight directly, Sumner now explicitly charged that the secretary was lazy, inefficient, and extravagant. It would be hard, Sumner argued, to show that the society was doing "any thing of much importance beyond the publication of its annual report, a pamphlet of about one hundred pages." "Between its flimsy covers," Sumner shouted derisively, "is all that we have done." Flapping the pages of Dwight's offending report high in the air above his head, he sneered: "Our three thousand dollars have been wrapt here as in a napkin."[2]

As the protracted debate went on, arguments wore threadbare and the audience drifted away. At last somebody proposed as a compromise that the society would pledge itself not to advocate any special system of prison discipline. Sumner accepted the resolution; his opponents refused to concede anything. Finally, on July 22, in a surprise move, made after most of the members had left the hall for the evening, one of Eliot's relatives proposed to lay the whole question on the table. There, despite entreaties

[1] Boston *Semi-Weekly Courier,* June 7, 1847; Boston *Post,* June 4, and 9, 1847.

[2] Longfellow, Diary, June 18, 1847, Longfellow MSS.; George Bemis, Diary, June 29, 1847, Bemis MSS.; Hillard to Lieber, June 10, 1847, Lieber MSS.; Sumner: *Works,* I, 496–7; Boston *Semi-Weekly Courier,* June 3, 1847; Pierce, III, 89.

from Sumner, it remained. The next year, in a move designed to illustrate the solidity of Boston society, George Ticknor and George T. Curtis were elected to the board of managers of the society, Eliot was made president, and Dwight, who was suffering from a nervous breakdown, was re-elected secretary, a post he continued to hold until his death in 1854. In 1848, at Ticknor's suggestion, it was voted to hold no further public meetings of the Boston Prison Discipline Society.[3]

Sumner felt that he had accomplished something by his foray. Prison authorities in Philadelphia praised him; the New York Prison Discipline Society invited him to make an address; Tocqueville, Julius, and Adshead all supported his views in Europe. "The weight and influence of the Society abroad have already been broken—partly through our exertions," he reported, adding, with grim jubilation: "Mr. Dwight, the secretary, has become insane, whether incurably so or no, I do not know." [4]

But for these victories, if such they were, Sumner had a price to pay. Sumner's "inconceivable effrontery," his "brazen audacity," and his "vituperative declamation" made him a marked man. For his "close twisted cord of charge, imputation and innuendo, so scandalously interwoven" against Dwight, respectable Boston had an explanation: "The only supposition which will relieve him from the charge of being a malignant defamer of other men's reputation, is that of having a disordered intellect." "The scorpion sting of that speech," the newspapers predicted, "will be turned on its author." [5]

Far more than his activities for education or peace, Sumner's efforts in the prison-discipline dispute caused him to be banned from Boston society. For Beacon Hill George Ticknor said the last word. The principles of the Boston oligarchy, he announced, were "right, and its severity towards disorganizers, and social democracy in all its forms, is just and wise. . . . Unsound opinions must be rebuked, and you can no more do that, while you treat their apostles with favor, than you can discourage bad

[3] Boston *Advertiser*, Aug. 5, 1847; Sumner to George Sumner, May 30, 1848, Sumner MSS.

[4] Sumner to George Sumner, May 30, 1848, Sumner MSS.; Sumner to Alexis de Tocqueville, Sept. 15, 1847, ibid.

[5] Boston *Post*, June 2, 1847.

books at the moment you are buying and circulating them." [6] Though Ticknor lived until 1871, he never again spoke to Sumner.

Boston had an even sharper way of making Sumner feel its disapproval. On September 10, 1845, Joseph Story died, and a new Dane Professor had to be chosen for the Harvard Law School. It was a post about which Sumner had dreamed for years. Both Story and Greenleaf had virtually promised it to him; his trip to Europe had really been undertaken to fit him for teaching civil and international law. After Story's funeral, Sumner published in the Boston *Advertiser* an eloquent tribute to his departed friend—which incidentally happened to point up his own qualifications as friend of "the chief jurists of our time, in the classical countries of jurisprudence, France and Germany." His mail was full of letters that assumed that he would be named to the chair.[7] But Daniel Webster was said to oppose the appointment, and President Edward Everett acquiesced in the Corporation's unanimous choice of William Kent, son of the New York Chancellor.

Nor when Kent resigned after only two years was the post offered to Sumner. Chief Justice Lemuel Shaw declared that Sumner, in his temporary teaching assignments in the law school, "had not . . . rendered himself and his services acceptable to the students." [8] But in a private letter to Lieber, Kent explained the Corporation's action: "Sumner has become an outrageous Philanthropist—neglecting his Law, to patch up the world—to reform prisoners and convicts—put down soldiers and wars—and keep the solar system in harmonious action. . . . The conservative Corporation of Harvard College . . . consider Sumner in the Law-school, as unsuitable as a Bull in a china-shop." [9]

[6] Ticknor: *Life, Letters, and Journals*, II, 235.

[7] Sumner: *Works*, I, 144; John Jay to Sumner, Nov. 8, 1845, Sumner MSS.; Charles Sedgwick to Sumner, Nov. 28, 1845, ibid.; Sumner's autobiography, Palfrey MSS.

[8] Theodore Sedgwick to Sumner, Oct. 29, 1845, Sumner MSS.; Everett to Sumner, Aug. 22, 1846, ibid.; Lemuel Shaw to Everett, Sept. 14, 1849, Harvard College Papers, XV, ser. 2, 133.

[9] Kent to Lieber, June 15, 1847, Lieber MSS.

CHAPTER VI

Let the Lines Be Drawn

"MY NAME," Sumner modestly declared in 1845, "is connected somewhat with two questions, which may be described succinctly as those of peace and slavery. To these may be added prison-discipline." In all three reform movements the pattern of his participation was precisely the same. He started by holding ideas most New Englanders shared. Through the influence of Channing, his views on international peace, on prison discipline, and on slavery came to be more carefully thought out and more articulately expressed, but not until personal unhappiness increased Sumner's sensitivity to social injustice did he take an active part in agitating these issues. Once he appeared before the public, he was attacked, and the more he was criticized, the more inflexible his opinions became. Carrying his ideas to extremes, he alienated moderate opinion and placed himself, as George Ticknor announced, "outside the pale of society." [1]

• 1 •

For as long as Sumner could remember, he had detested slavery. His father taught him that Negroes deserved not merely freedom, but equality and happiness as well. "It will do us no good to make the blacks as free as the whites," Sheriff Sumner de-

[1] Sumner to George Putnam, Apr. 1848, author's copy, Sumner MSS.; Pierce, III, 119.

clared, "unless we learn to have good feelings toward them, and treat them as well." Reading Lydia Maria Child's *An Appeal in Favor of that Class of Americans Called Africans,* a tract published in 1833, further helped convince Sumner of the injustice of both slavery and racial discrimination. He found his first actual sight of slaves, on his trip to Washington in 1834, shocking, and he was outraged by the bullying proslavery tone Calhoun's disciples adopted during the 1830's. In 1836 he wrote to Lieber: "We are becoming abolitionists at the North fast." [2]

Sumner's European travels had further strengthened his belief that the United States must abolish slavery.[3] Everywhere abroad he was told that slavery was his country's disgrace. At the Collège de France he heard a savant declare "that all the races of men have a common origin, [and] that of course they must be substantially alike at present," and at the Sorbonne he saw a practical illustration of this theory in the easy intermingling of Negroes and whites in the same law classes. In Italy at the Convent of Palazzuola, where he and Greene spent a few quiet days, he noted the "freedom, gentleness, and equality" with which the friars treated "an Abyssinian, very recently arrived from the heart of Africa, whose most torrid sun had burned upon him." When Sumner returned to America, he made all his friends cognizant of his "hatred of slavery." [4]

His views were anything but unique, for virtually everyone in Massachusetts shared them. Though the Democratic leaders of the state, dependent upon pro-Southern national administrations for patronage, were quiet on the question of slavery, every influential Massachusetts Whig spoke out openly against the

[2] C. P. Sumner's notebook titled "Miscellany," p. 78, C. P. Sumner MSS.; Lydia Maria Child to Sumner, July 7, 1856, Sumner MSS.; Sumner to Lieber, Jan. 9, 1836, ibid.

[3] Sumner to J. O. Sargent, Nov. 20, 1838, J. O. Sargent MSS. Years later John Forster circulated a rumor that Sumner, on his European trip, had been an apologist for slavery. Norton and Howe (eds.): *Letters of Charles Eliot Norton,* I, 422. Sumner's contemporary letters, such as that to Sargent, refute the charge. Sumner himself explicitly denied the story and suggested that Forster had probably remembered some words of George Sumner. John Bigelow: *Retrospections of an Active Life* (New York: Doubleday, Page & Company; 1913), IV, 76.

[4] Pierce, I, 247–8; II, 261; Theodore Sedgwick to Sumner, Oct. 11, 1842, Sumner MSS. Bitterly Sumner rejected the pretensions of Calhoun and his followers: "The Southerners, and slave-owners are Chinese in character; theirs is the celestial empire; and all who do not buy and sell human sinews are outer barbarians." Sumner to Lord Brougham, May 15, 1844, Brougham MSS.

South's peculiar institution. "I regard slavery as one of the greatest evils, both moral and political," Daniel Webster asserted in his famous reply to Hayne. Abbott Lawrence, Webster's rival for the control of Massachusetts Whiggery, announced that he had been "born an abolitionist," that "we were all abolitionists." In 1837 the Whig-dominated Massachusetts Senate, with near unanimity, adopted resolutions opposing the admission of additional slave states and demanding, in the name of "the principles of the Revolution and humanity," the abolition of slavery in the District of Columbia.

Massachusetts men differed, of course, on the best way to oppose slavery. Conservatives feared that direct agitation against slavery would undermine the Constitution and hoped that the slow processes of time would bring freedom to the Negro. A large segment of moderate opinion followed Webster, who admitted that "domestic slavery of the Southern States is a subject within the exclusive control of the States themselves," but frankly announced his "unwillingness to do anything that shall extend the slavery of the African race on the continent, or add other slaveholding States to the Union." Only a handful of extremists agreed with William Lloyd Garrison, who called for an immediate end to slavery throughout the land.[5]

Sumner was not one of these Garrisonians. Though he had subscribed for the *Liberator* since 1835, he did not approve its "vindictive, bitter, and unchristian" tone. Secure in the respectable, Whiggish society of Boston, Sumner appears never to have met Garrison before 1845. "Of the many abolition meetings held in Boston" during these martyr years of the antislavery movement, Garrison himself stated: "Mr. Sumner's presence was never recognized at any one of them. Why he never came—at least among the curious to hear—I know not." [6]

[5] Claude Moore Fuess: *Daniel Webster* (Boston: Little, Brown & Co.; 1930), II, 32, Boston *Whig*, June 19, 1846; Henry Wilson: *History of the Rise and Fall of the Slave Power in America* (Boston: Houghton Mifflin Co.; 1872), I, 370, 591.

[6] Garrison to Pierce, Oct. 25, 1876, Pierce MSS.; Garrison to Edmund Quincy, Aug. 16, 1872, Garrison MSS., Smith Coll. In the 1870's, angry with Sumner, Garrison doubted that he had ever subscribed for the *Liberator*, but more reliance can be placed on Sumner's positive contemporary statement: "The earliest newspaper that I remember to have subscribed for was the Liberator." Sumner to George Putnam, Apr. 1848, author's draft, Sumner MSS. Cf. Wendell Phillips, in *Twenty-First Annual Report Presented to the Massachusetts Anti-Slavery Society* . . . (Boston; 1853), p. 122; Sumner to Lord Morpeth, Jan. 29, 1847, Carlisle MSS.

Sumner's indifference to Garrisonianism did not mean a coolness to the cause of antislavery. In this, as in all other reform impulses, he followed Channing, who defied conservative Boston opinion in praising Garrison's followers as "advocates of the principles of freedom, justice, and humanity," but was himself unwilling to become an abolitionist. Unable to endorse the Garrisonians' blanket indictment of all slaveholders, to adopt their motto of "Immediate Emancipation," or to approve their "showy, noisy mode of action," Channing agreed that slavery was "radically essentially evil" and argued that Northerners should first dissociate themselves from this great sin and then plead the cause of the slave before that "grand moral tribunal, before which all communities stand, and must be judged." Under this "moral blockade" slaveholders would come to realize that they were condemned by "those great principles of justice and charity, with which the human heart is everywhere beginning to beat." [7]

Sumner's ideas on slavery were essentially an elaboration of Channing's. Unlike the Garrisonians, who denounced the Constitution as a proslavery document and desired no union with slaveholders, Sumner prided himself upon his "strong attachment to the Constitution and the Union." "Thank God!" he exclaimed, "the Constitution of the United States does not recognize man as *property*." "The laws that sanction slavery are *local* and *municipal* in their character," he argued. Antislavery men, therefore, could not properly "seek, either through their own Legislatures or through Congress, to touch slavery in the States where it exists."

Opponents of slavery should not, on the other hand, "feel called upon to suppress their sympathy for the suffering slave." Sumner himself urged Longfellow to publish his "Poems of Slavery," and he tried in 1842 to get Boston lawyers to pledge that they would boycott claimants who attempted to recover fugitive slaves on Massachusetts soil. "The moralist, the statesman, the orator, the poet, all in their several ways and moods," he argued, should express their disapproval of slavery and thus "surround the Southern States with a *moral blockade*."

There were also more direct ways in which antislavery men

[7] Channing: *Remarks on the Slavery Question, in a Letter to Jonathan Phillips, Esq.* (Boston: James Munroe and Company; 1839), pp. 5, 11–12; Brown: *Always Young for Liberty*, pp. 222–41.

could strike at the South's peculiar institution. Barred by the Constitution from attacking the domestic institutions of the slave states, they could properly and legally act wherever slavery was "a *national* evil, for which . . . the *nation* and all its parts are responsible." Specifically, as United States law established slavery in the District of Columbia and in the territories, regulated the interstate and coastal slave trade, and controlled the rendition of fugitive slaves, these were legitimate objects for Northern action. Another possibility, he noted ominously, lay in the fact that "the Constitution may be amended so that it shall cease to render any sanction to Slavery."

In 1846 Sumner summarized his antislavery position:

> I think Slavery a sin, individual and national; and think it the duty of each individual to cease committing it, and, of course of each State, to do likewise. Massachusetts is a party to slave-holding, and is responsible for it, so long as it continues under the sanction of the Constitution of the United States. I would leave it to the *local* laws of each State. If the South persists in holding slaves let it not expect Massachusetts to aid or abet in the wrong. I cannot be a slave-holder; nor can I help upholding [i.e., to uphold] slaveholding.[8]

• 2 •

Up until his illness of 1844 Sumner, though he did not conceal these antislavery opinions, took no part in agitating the issue. He did not "express in public his opposition to Slavery," he explained, because "there never had . . . been any occasion in which he was disposed to participate," because he could not "coincide in views with those who conducted the Anti-Slavery movement," and because he "had no relish for the strife of politics." [9]

He had been, in fact, quite content with the course Massachusetts Whig leaders were following on questions concerning slavery. He was enthusiastic about John Quincy Adams's "grand" fight against the Gag Rule, which choked off antislavery petitions

[8] Sumner to George Putnam, Apr. 1848, author's copy, Sumner MSS.; Pierce, II, 204; Sumner to Joshua R. Giddings, Dec. 21, 1846, Giddings MSS.; Boston *Advertiser*, Jan. 10, 1843; Sumner to Cleveland, Nov. 28, 1842, copy, Longfellow MSS.; Sumner to Maria Weston Chapman, Nov. 30 [1842], Weston MSS.; *MHSP*, LVII, 196. In Chap. IX, *infra,* I have given a more elaborate analysis of Sumner's antislavery theories.

[9] Sumner to George Putnam, Apr. 1848, author's copy, Sumner MSS.

Henry Wadsworth Longfellow

MASSACHUSETTS HISTORICAL SOCIETY

Samuel Gridley Howe

MASSACHUSETTS HISTORICAL SOCIETY

Cornelius C. Felton

MASSACHUSETTS HISTORICAL SOCIETY

George S. Hillard

Painting by William Hillard, c. 1865
MASSACHUSETTS HISTORICAL SOCIETY

FRIENDS IN THE FIVE OF CLUBS

Sumner in 1846

Woodcut from a crayon drawing made by Eastman Johnson

THE LIBRARY OF CONGRESS

to the House of Representatives. The ex-President, he cheered, "has rallied the North against the South, has taught them their right, and opened their eyes to the *bullying* (I dislike the word, as much as the thing) of the South." Though he deplored Webster's proslavery *Creole* letter and feared that he lacked "sympathy with the mass,—with humanity, with truth," his record seemed "clear, massive and statesmanlike" when compared with the "weakness and bad faith" of President John Tyler or the proslavery platform of the Democratic presidential candidate, James K. Polk, that "pot house politician, vulgar, ignorant, wayward." [1]

But, in 1844 a national emergency, which coincided with Sumner's personal crisis, shocked him out of his complacency and brought him actively into politics. Like Channing, he had for several years watched with growing concern the movement to annex the Republic of Texas to the United States. Neither he nor his Whig contemporaries in Massachusetts could see the annexation scheme in the calm second glance of history; he failed to comprehend that the migration of American settlers into Mexican territory had been but a part of the national westward movement, that the Texas revolution had been inspired by genuine grievances against Mexico, and that annexation was not the result of a proslavery conspiracy. Instead, he believed that Southern slaveholders, by playing upon the "prejudice, selfishness, and vanity" of President Tyler, had persuaded him to sign the treaty of annexation, and he rejoiced when the Senate rejected that "ditch-delivered drab." Tyler's subsequent maneuver to annex Texas through joint resolutions of the two houses of Congress Sumner thought clearly unconstitutional, but he feared that if elected, Polk, that "4th rate lawyer," would acquiesce in the proslavery scheme.[2]

In all these opinions Sumner was in complete agreement with the leaders of the Massachusetts Whig party. The movement to annex Texas deeply stirred the latent antislavery sentiment of New England. Not merely the Liberty party, which cam-

[1] Sumner to Lieber, Feb. 21, 1841, and July 18, 1842, ibid.; Pierce, II, 223; Sumner to Horatio Greenough, Sept. 16, 1841, copy, Sumner MSS.; Sumner to George Sumner, Feb. 28, 1846, ibid.

[2] Sumner to Howe, May 31, 1844, ibid.; Sumner to George Sumner, June 1, 1844, ibid.

paigned in 1844 upon a platform explicitly repudiating annexation, fought the Texas scheme; all segments of Massachusetts Whiggery did likewise. Abbott Lawrence, Nathan Appleton, and other cotton manufacturers attempted in March 1844 to start a free-state protest against annexation, and dropped their project only because of the difficulty of securing co-operation from Whigs in other states. When the Massachusetts General Court assembled in January 1845, it voted that the Commonwealth would "never by any act or deed give her consent to the further extension of slavery to any portion of the world." Even more significant was an allegedly nonpartisan public meeting held in Faneuil Hall on January 29, where an enthusiastic crowd adopted resolutions denouncing "the iniquitous project in its inception and in every stage of its progress, its means and its end, and all the purposes and pretenses of its authors." [3]

Sumner attended this anti-Texas rally, and he enthusiastically applauded its resolutions. There for the first time he heard Garrison, whose words "fell in fiery rain" upon the audience, and he noted that even in this Whig-controlled assembly there was "a very respectable number . . . in favor of a dissolution of the Union, in the event of the Annexation of Texas." As the joint resolution for annexation was pushed through Congress in February 1845, Sumner felt that anti-Texas sentiment had lifted public opinion "to a new platform of Anti-Slavery." By fall he reported to Lieber: "The Anti-Slavery element is becoming the controlling power in our state, and, I doubt, if any person could be sent [to Congress] who was not in favor of earnest efforts for the abolition of slavery under the Federal Constitution." [4]

Even while Sumner was predicting "Massachusetts will never give her vote for another slaveholder," the Whig opposition to Texas began to dwindle. All along, astute observers had noted that the most conspicuous figures in the anti-Texas movement were not the regular party chieftains, but a group of younger, more idealistic, and generally somewhat disaffected "Young Whigs." Such men as Charles Francis Adams, the son and grand-

[3] Martin Bauml Duberman: "Charles Francis Adams, 1807–1851" (unpublished Ph. D. dissertation, Harvard Univ.; 1957), pp. 250–1; Wilson: *Slave Power*, I, 622–3. Webster helped draft the resolutions, but was not present at the meeting.

[4] Sumner to Story, Feb. 5, 1845, Sumner MSS.; Sumner to Lieber, Nov. 19, 1845, ibid.

son of Presidents of the United States, Stephen C. Phillips, a Salem merchant with political aspirations, John G. Palfrey, formerly professor of theology at Harvard and currently Secretary of State to the Commonwealth, Henry Wilson, the Natick cobbler turned politician, and Hillard, who aspired to membership in the state legislature, appeared most frequently as spokesmen of the group, with which Sumner early identified himself. But Webster, Choate, Everett, Winthrop, Abbott Lawrence, and Nathan Appleton, the real leaders of Massachusetts Whiggery, rarely took public part in these protests. These practical politicians quickly recognized that they were facing an accomplished fact; after Congress passed the annexation resolution, what was the point of further resistance? Factious opposition would only serve to split the Whig party and to alienate Southern congressmen at just the time when President Polk was urging a downward revision of the tariff seriously injurious to New England manufacturing. More important in the minds of some Massachusetts Whigs than even the manufacture of cotton was the manufacture of a Whig presidential candidate for 1848, as both Webster and Abbott Lawrence aspired to the White House.[5]

Still a political amateur, Sumner was insensitive to these shifting currents of expediency. For him it was enough that the annexation of Texas was wrong; the authoritative spokesmen for the Massachusetts Whig party had said so. Characteristically he had committed himself to a principle, and he continued with it to extreme conclusions long after it was abandoned by its originators. In "The True Grandeur of Nations" oration on July 4, 1845, Sumner thought that he was merely announcing good Whig doctrine in condemning as "mean and cowardly" both the annexation and the war that threatened to result from it. So like a Whig stump speech were parts of Sumner's address that some in the audience thought he was making a bid for public office. When old John Quincy Adams read the "highly wrought, learned, ingenious diatribe," he concluded: "Mr. Sumner takes a lofty flight and promises to be a politician." [6]

But at the dinner following the speech, Winthrop bluntly

[5] Pierce, III, 105. On the "Young Whig" movement I have greatly profited by reading Mr. Frank Otto Gatell's admirable "'Conscience and Judgment': The Bolt of the Massachusetts Conscience Whigs," a seminar paper prepared under the direction of Professor Frederick Merk at Harvard University.

[6] J. Q. Adams, Diary, Aug. 13, 1845, Adams MSS.

announced that Sumner was out of step. "Our country—whether bounded by Sabine or Del Norte . . . ," he toasted, rebuking not merely the orator of the day, but all of the "Young Whig" group.

The switch in the official Massachusetts Whig position placed Sumner's friends in a serious dilemma. Genuinely concerned over the expansion of slavery, and deeply troubled over the approaching war with Mexico, they hoped even after annexation to continue "an agitation against the admission of Texas as a *Slave State*,"[7] but to do so in the face of Winthrop's explicit warning might mean cutting themselves off from the Whig party, to which they were bound by ancient ties of loyalty and from which they, in the overwhelmingly Whiggish state of Massachusetts, must expect any future public honors or offices.

Moreover, continued agitation of the Texas issue would inevitably throw the "Young Whigs" into closer contact with the despised and distrusted abolitionists, who had plans for exploiting the anti-Texas sentiment for their own ends. The "Young Whigs" had invited Garrison and his followers to participate in the original Faneuil Hall rally in order to demonstrate that all elements in Massachusetts were opposed to annexation. When the Garrisonians in return asked them to speak at a nonpartisan rally designed to continue the anti-Texas agitation, the "Young Whigs" had difficulty in declining. Once publicly connected with the abolitionist-sponsored movement, Adams, Palfrey, Wilson, and Sumner found it necessary to become increasingly active in it, lest it be taken over by the Garrisonians, who hoped to divert the aroused public interest into their own program for the immediate abolition of slavery and the dissolution of the Union.

Too prominently associated with the anti-Texas drive to retreat, too distrustful of their new abolitionist allies to be silent, the "Young Whigs" behaved as a kind of junto. They thought of themselves as "conspirators," bound by a firm discipline. Palfrey, the senior statesman of the little group, handed down rulings on the duties "our brotherhood" demanded, and Charles Francis Adams, whose cool, balanced mind planned their strategy, required that the members chasten their "personal views . . . into entire obedience to the sacrificing nature of our mission."[8]

[7] Sumner to Lieber, Nov. 19, 1845, Sumner MSS.

[8] C. F. Adams, Diary, Dec. 3, 1846, and Apr. 12, 1847, Adams MSS.

Sumner was a willing and prominent member of the group. Winthrop's rebuke, far from abashing him, increased his stubborn opposition to Texas and to any war with Mexico. As he had no conscious political aspirations, he hesitated less than did Wilson, Adams, Palfrey, or Phillips in challenging the Whig oligarchy of Massachusetts. With antislavery views more advanced than those of most of his new friends, he was not embarrassed to associate with the abolitionists, and his warm friendship with Wendell Phillips, Garrison's right-hand man, made him an ideal go-between. In the conspiratorial tone of the "Young Whig" enterprise, its secrecy, and its danger, Sumner found a sense of security, of belonging to a group with a mission.[9] Enthusiastically he began pushing the "Young Whig" ideas to an extreme, and his political allies were disturbed by his radical tone. Adams thought that, "too much led by his visions," Sumner needed "constantly the guiding and superintendence of a man more worldly wise." [1]

But even Adams was forced to admit that if Sumner had "not sufficient every day steadiness of mind to do well the work of infantry," he performed "with success as a pioneer." He helped organize and edit the little newspaper the anti-Texas leaders published, *The Free State Rally and Texas Chain-Breaker*, and he served efficiently on a state committee appointed in the fall of 1845 to arouse Massachusetts opinion against the admission of Texas as a slave state. In planning the large rally of anti-Texas Whigs, abolitionists, and Liberty party men, to be held in Faneuil Hall on November 4, Sumner was particularly active. When the spokesmen of the mutually distrustful co-operating groups were unable to agree upon resolutions to be adopted at the meeting, Sumner produced a compromise draft, eloquently denouncing "this wicked scheme" of annexation, undertaken "for the atrocious purpose . . . of increasing the market for human flesh," the consummation of which would "cover the country with disgrace, and make us all responsible for crimes of gigantic magnitude." [2]

The long-heralded meeting took place on a dark and stormy

[9] Cf. Eric Hoffer: *The True Believer*, pp. 60–1.

[1] C. F. Adams, Diary, Mar. 1, 1847, Adams MSS.

[2] Ibid., Mar. 8, 1847; *Free State Rally* . . . , Nov. 20, 1845, p. 2; draft of resolutions in Sumner's handwriting [c. Nov. 4, 1845], Palfrey MSS.; Sumner: *Works*, I, 149 ff.

night—weather suitable for so foul a plot, Democrats claimed. There was, nevertheless, a respectable attendance, and, with Charles Francis Adams in the chair, the proceedings, carefully divided among the sponsoring groups, went off smoothly. After Palfrey read the resolutions Sumner had drafted, Garrison, Wendell Phillips, and the Reverend W. H. Channing spoke for the abolitionists, H. B. Stanton for the Liberty party, and Hillard and Sumner for the Conscience Whigs. "All in very tolerable temper," Adams noted in his diary, with his customary restraint, "and some in a high style of oratory." [3]

For Sumner the occasion was far more important than Adams's arid diary record indicated. Testing his aptitude for oratory, which he had discovered only on July 4, he made his first political speech. It was brief and effective. He begged his hearers to put "aside all distinctions of party" and to subordinate all political and economic questions to "the supreme requirements of religion, morals, and humanity," and he proposed again Channing's idea of a moral blockade against evil. He did not suggest interference "with any institution of the Southern States," or modification of "any law on the subject of Slavery anywhere under the Constitution." But, to admit slaveholding Texas to the Union would implicate his dearly loved Massachusetts in wrong. "By welcoming Texas as a Slave State we make slavery our own original sin." "Let us wash our hands of this great guilt," he urged. "God forbid that the votes and voices of Northern freemen should help to bind anew the fetters of the slave! God forbid that the lash of the slave-dealer should descend by any sanction from New England! God forbid that the blood which spurts from the lacerated, quivering flesh of the slave should soil the hem of the white garments of Massachusetts." [4] Antislavery in Massachusetts had found a new voice.

• 3 •

It was not a voice welcomed by conservative Boston Whiggery. The regular party leaders now openly discountenanced further agitation of the Texas question. Abbott Lawrence announced:

[3] C. F. Adams, Diary, Nov. 4, 1845, Adams MSS.

[4] Sumner: *Works*, I, 152, 155–7.

"A majority of the people have decided in favor of annexation, and . . . Texas now virtually composes a part of our Union." Pointing to the presence at the Faneuil Hall rally of "a great number . . . of those who have distinguished themselves as members of the abolition party," Nathan Appleton refused to give further support to the anti-Texas movement. "I consider the question settled," he declared. Whig leaders blocked Henry Wilson's attempt to push anti-annexation resolutions through the state senate, and were unmoved by E. Rockwood Hoar's spirited pronouncement: "It is as much the duty of Massachusetts to pass resolutions in favor of the rights of man as in the interests of cotton." If obliged to be either "Cotton Whigs" or "Conscience Whigs"—as the "Young Whigs" henceforth designated themselves—Boston leaders had no hesitation in making a choice. Shortly after the Faneuil Hall meeting, Edmund Dwight took Sumner aside, told him of the party's decision to discourage further discussion of the Texas issue, and "gave him very good advice not to go into this abolition movement in disguise." [5]

Warning Sumner to cease agitating the Texas issue was the most certain way of making him do just the opposite. In his opinion the regular Whig leaders were blind to the proslavery plot that was being hatched. In December Texas was admitted to the Union, a slaveholding state. In April 1846 General Zachary Taylor's men, marching into territory claimed by both the United States and Mexico, were fired upon. War, announced President Polk, had begun through the shedding of American blood upon American soil, and American armies started to slice off great segments of Mexico's northern empire.

In New England it was an unpopular war, and Conscience Whigs, who had hitherto been a tiny minority, suddenly found they had many supporters, especially in the strongly antislavery rural districts of Massachusetts. Taking advantage of the aroused public opinion, Palfrey, Adams, S. C. Phillips, Wilson, and Sumner prepared to renew and expand their agitation against slavery. In May they purchased a nearly derelict Boston daily newspaper, *The Whig*, as organ for their faction, which had been inhospitably

[5] Abbott Lawrence to C. F. Adams, Nov. 17, 1845, copy in Adams's Diary of the same date, Adams MSS.; Appleton to C. F. Adams, Palfrey, and Sumner, Nov. 10, 1845, author's copy, Appleton MSS.; Wilson: *Slave Power*, II, 117–18; C. F. Adams, Diary, Nov. 22, 1845, Adams MSS.

treated in the *Advertiser* and the *Atlas,* the two principal Boston Whig papers, and had received only grudging recognition in the more tolerant *Courier.* Palfrey and Phillips contributed three fifths of the capital; Adams, in addition to putting up the rest of the money, agreed to serve as editor; and Sumner and Wilson, who were both poor, promised to write for the newspaper.[6]

"The Whig principles of Massachusetts, such as they have been declared at every authorized assembly of the party since 1840, will be . . . the guides of this paper," Adams announced in his inaugural editorial on June 1, 1846. He and his friends were trying to lose the taint of disunionism acquired during the previous year by association with the Garrisonians and to establish themselves as true Whigs. "We do not believe," Adams announced firmly to a correspondent who proposed that the free states separate from the slaveholding South, "that a division would be productive of permanent benefit to either party, whilst on the other hand, it would originate innumerable evils to both." Even more positive was the *Whig's* rebuke to the Liberty party men, with whom Sumner and his associates had formerly worked so amiably. Third parties, Adams asserted editorially, "are productive of a much greater share of evil to the community, than they can be of good. . . . We . . . never did and cannot now put any confidence in Mr. [James G.] Birney," the Liberty party's presidential candidate.[7]

The real purpose of the newspaper, of course, was not so much to demonstrate that the Conscience Whigs were still Whigs, but to prove that they were the only true Whigs in Massachusetts. Relentlessly Adams ridiculed the professed antislavery sentiments of such regular party leaders as Abbott Lawrence and Nathan Appleton. "Thinking more of sheep and cotton than of Man," "truckling to expediency in every thing, for the sake of . . . slaveholding gold," these two cotton textile manufacturers, Adams asserted, had used their influence "to keep down in Massachusetts the growing restlessness under the domination of the slave power." They had sabotaged the movement "for a general union of the members of all parties . . . in opposition to the annexation of Texas." To Lawrence and his money-making

[6] C. F. Adams, Diary, May 23, 1846, Adams MSS.

[7] Boston *Whig,* Aug. 20, and July 9, 1846.

schemes, "wholly unworthy of the noble aim of the Pilgrim race," the *Whig* attributed "the manifest degeneracy which prevails among . . . our politicians, a tone which blusters about the rights of sheep and falls into the softest whisper when dealing with the rights of man." [8]

However scathing or eloquent, the *Whig's* attacks upon Appleton and Lawrence lacked any real urgency, for neither of the manufacturers held public office in 1846; their control over the Whig party in Massachusetts, though real, was tacit and informal and beyond the reach of public opinion. To make their attack felt, Adams and his allies needed a more immediate target, and they found one in Congressman Winthrop. With his ancient family, great wealth, excellent education, and undeviating loyalty to the Whig party, Winthrop was obviously being groomed as successor to Daniel Webster and Edward Everett; the weight of his responsibilities had already made him, as Tom Appleton thought, "the dullest and most unelastic of companions, the perfection of prudence and respectability." Neither great nor strong, Winthrop was, in Hillard's words, "a man of decencies, decorums and proprieties." [9] In his cold, formal way he held antislavery principles, and he lived by them as well as an ambitious politician, who would ultimately need Southern votes for national office, could. Originally opposed to the annexation of Texas, Winthrop was placed in a serious dilemma by the declaration of war against Mexico. Through Democratic parliamentary ingenuity, the bill providing necessary supplies for Taylor's army had a preamble asserting that the war they were fighting had been caused by Mexican aggression. As a Northern antislavery man, Winthrop could not conscientiously vote for the preamble, but as a Whig politician who remembered the fate of the Federalists who had opposed the War of 1812, he could not refuse to vote supplies. Fourteen of his Massachusetts colleagues in the House voted against the bill, but Winthrop, together with one other congressman from Essex County, finally decided to support it.[1]

[8] Ibid., July 3, and 31, Aug. 7, and 21, and Sept. 18, 1846.

[9] T. G. Appleton to Nathan Appleton, Aug. 4 [1850], Appleton MSS.; Hillard to Lieber, Sept. 9, 1850, Lieber MSS.

[1] The best accounts of Winthrop are Robert C. Winthrop, Jr.: *Memoir of Robert C. Winthrop* (Boston: Little, Brown & Co.; 1897), and Daniel D. Levenson: "Robert C. Winthrop: A Study of a Whig Conscience" (unpublished honor's thesis, Harvard Univ.; 1954).

At last Adams had his issue. Winthrop, the *Whig* announced on July 16, had "set his name in perpetual attestation of a falsehood"; he had given "a positive sanction of the worst acts of the Administration." The attack ruffled Boston; Adams began to hope that people might even subscribe to the *Whig* for such spicy reading. But when the *Advertiser* issued a massive rebuttal of the *Whig's* changes against Winthrop, Adams called for help.[2]

At this point Sumner entered the controversy. To defend Adams and the *Whig*, he renewed the assault upon Winthrop. Unctuously protesting high regard for the congressman and faith in his integrity, Sumner, under the pseudonym "Boston," announced boldly that Winthrop, in voting for the war bill, had "told a lie" and had committed "gross disloyalty to Truth and Freedom." A week later he continued the attack, again under his pseudonym, this time in the columns of the *Courier*. Taking the questionable charges made in his first letter as proved, Sumner now went on to make even more serious accusations. Winthrop, he proclaimed, had voted for *"an unjust war, and national falsehood, in the cause of slavery"*; he had supported what was unquestionably "the darkest act in our history." [3]

The violence of these assaults took Winthrop by surprise. He was ready for the hostility of Charles Francis Adams, who, he thought, aspired to replace him in Congress. But the mysterious "Boston" articles, written by "an accomplished person [who] does his work with elegance," made him writhe. Speculation suggested Wendell Phillips or Theodore Parker as author, but Winthrop thought both lacked the polish and finesse of his assailant. For a time he suspected Hillard. It was with reluctance that he came to believe that the author was Sumner, who in April 1846, only six months earlier, had been Winthrop's guest in Washington and had "parted with many expressions of obligation on his part, which would seem at odds with . . . so much personal unkindness." [4]

After gossip had identified Sumner as author of the "Boston" articles and "A True Whig" replied to him in the *Courier*, he thought it expedient to explain his motives directly to Winthrop.

[2] Pierce, III, 114; C. F. Adams, Diary, July 15–16, 1846, Adams MSS.

[3] Boston *Whig*, July 22, 1846; Boston *Courier*, July 31, 1846.

[4] Winthrop to J. H. Clifford, July 24, Aug. 2, and 3, 1846, copies, Winthrop MSS.

The congressman must believe, Sumner declared in a personal letter, that the articles were written "under the impression of duty." Their anonymity, he rather feebly protested, was "less from any disposition to withhold my name, than because that is the customary [use] made with communications" in the newspapers. "I hope," Sumner concluded, "in doing what I have done, I have not in any way been disloyal to those pleasant relations, which I have always had the happiness of cherishing with you, and which I trust may always continue." [5]

Hurt, Winthrop replied that Sumner's articles were "ungenerous and unjust"; he had been "grossly and wantonly wronged by them." He objected to their "intentional offensiveness . . . , and their obvious design, not to sustain a principle or vindicate the truth, but to rob him, personally, of that 'spotless reputation, which is the purest treasure mortal times afford.'" Coolly he ended his reply by sharing Sumner's regret at the interruption of their "pleasant relations" and with a vague "hope that circumstances may occur, which may enable us to restore them without sacrifice of self-respect on either side." [6]

Never willing to yield a point, Sumner prepared a reply to Winthrop's "very crusty and illtempered" letter. He denied any personal animus toward the congressman. Winthrop's toast at the July 4, 1845, dinner had originally aroused Sumner's suspicions. "I would have cut off my right hand rather than utter such a sentiment," Sumner passionately exclaimed. Winthrop's toast was promptly followed by his vote "for an *unjust war.*" Adams had felt obliged to discuss the issue in the *Whig*, the *Advertiser* had made support of Winthrop's vote a party test, and Sumner had entered the controversy at the urging of the editor of the *Courier*. He hoped that it was not too late for Winthrop to put behind him the pinchbeck "notability, acquired in the displays of party politics" and to exercise his powers "in the highest causes of Humanity and Right." [7]

Three days after Sumner sent this private letter to Win-

[5] Boston *Courier*, Aug. 1, 1846; Sumner to Winthrop, Aug. 5, 1846, Winthrop MSS.

[6] Winthrop to Sumner, Aug. 7, 1846, Sumner MSS.

[7] C. F. Adams, Diary, Aug. 10, 1846, Adams MSS.; Sumner to Winthrop, Aug. 10, 1846, Winthrop MSS. The editor of the *Courier* denied that he either incited or approved Sumner's articles. J. T. Buckingham to Winthrop, Oct. 13 [1846], Winthrop MSS.

throp, his third "Boston" article appeared in the *Courier*. Winthrop, Sumner now announced, was a modern Pontius Pilate. "Mr. Winthrop's vote was wrong," "Boston" protested. "It was wrong by the law of nations, and by the higher law of God. . . . It cannot be forgotten on earth; it must be remembered in heaven. Blood! blood! is on the hands of the representative from Boston. Not all great Neptune's ocean can wash them clean." [8]

Furious, Winthrop retorted with a letter that terminated all relations with Sumner for the next sixteen years. Sumner's articles, he declared, were full of "the coarsest personalities" and "the grossest perversions"; they assailed not merely Winthrop's acts, but his motives and his integrity. "I am willing to believe that you have not weighed the force of your own phrases," Winthrop added, with unusual perspicacity. "Your 'periculosa facilitas' has betrayed you. Your habitual indulgence in strains of extravagant thought and exaggerated expression, alike when you praise and when you censure, has, perhaps, impaired your discrimination in the employment of language." But, after such abuse, Winthrop could not maintain social relations with Sumner. "My hand," he said bluntly, "is not at the service of any one, who has denounced it, with such ferocity, as being stained with blood." [9]

The Conscience Whigs' assault upon Winthrop was only a part of their larger effort to seize control of the state-party machinery. They planned their strategy with care and secrecy. Looking ahead to the Massachusetts Whig convention announced for September 1846, they took great pains to see that their faction was well represented at the primary meetings that chose the members of the state assembly. The regular party leaders were surprised, for the newspapers noted with puzzlement how many "gentlemen who were never before seen in a political caucus, took part in the proceedings." At the Boston primary meeting, when Abbott Lawrence made the conventional Whig talk about the need for a higher tariff and internal improvements, the Conscience group sent Sumner to the stand to reply. It was, he announced, "the first meeting of the kind he had ever attended," but he was not abashed by the novelty of his situation. Lawrence

[8] Boston *Courier*, Aug. 13, 1846.

[9] Winthrop to Sumner, Aug. 17, 1846, Sumner MSS.

"had spoken for the material interests of the community—and no man, he was sure, could better do it." But Sumner, for the Conscience Whigs, had another, higher theme, "the moral interests which were at stake." The Whig party was one of freedom, he declared; at the approaching convention the Massachusetts party must reassert "the essence of Whig principles . . . the idea that all men were created free and equal." The regular party leaders managed to control a majority of the delegates named to the state convention, but Sumner, Adams, Hillard, and a handful of other young insurgents also secured places.[1]

With seats in the Boston delegation, a newspaper behind them, and much support in the strongly antislavery rural districts, the Conscience Whigs carefully planned their tactics in the state convention, which met in Faneuil Hall on September 23. The Cotton Whig leaders had arranged for Winthrop to be called to the stand while the committee on resolutions was preparing the platform. Secretly the Conscience Whig junto organized a counter demonstration, a demand from the floor to have Sumner speak. As the delegates cheered their respective spokesmen, the two factions engaged in a tug of war, and the admirably organized Conscience Whigs won.

Bounding to the platform, Sumner enunciated the "Antislavery Duties of the Whig Party." Strikingly dressed in his blue waistcoat and white trousers, his voice passionate with sincerity, Sumner implored his fellow delegates to put the Declaration of Independence, the Constitution, and the Union ahead of "obsolete ideas" like the protective tariff and internal improvement. "The Whigs," he announced, "are, or ought to be, the party of Freedom." Their watchword must be "REPEAL OF SLAVERY UNDER THE CONSTITUTION AND LAWS OF THE NATIONAL GOVERNMENT." They should seek to abolish slavery in the District of Columbia, to end slavery in the national territories, to terminate the slave trade, to refuse admission to new slave states, and to amend the Constitution so as to reach slavery elsewhere. Their leaders "must not be Northern men with Southern principles, nor Northern men under Southern influence." Their motto should not be 'Our party, *howsoever bounded,*' " he added, in a gratuitous gibe at Winthrop, "but 'Our party, bounded always by the Right.' "

[1] Boston *Whig*, Sept. 10, 1846; Boston *Courier*, Sept. 11, 1846.

Sumner concluded by urging Webster to join the Conscience group, adding to his titles as "defender of the Constitution" and "Defender of Peace" another, higher title, "never to be forgotten on earth or in heaven,—*Defender of Humanity.*" [2]

When Winthrop got the floor after this elaborate and effective speech, he refrained from discussing "some incidental questions connected with this war," on which "there have been differences of opinions among friends at home," and entered upon a pallid and ineffectual review of Democratic financial measures, objectionable to New England manufacturers. The longer he spoke, the more certain it appeared that the Conscience Whigs would stampede the convention.

Promptly and shrewdly the Cotton Whigs replanned their strategy. While Winthrop was speaking, they inserted strong antislavery plans into their proposed platform. Though the determined Conscience Whigs attempted to move a substitute set of resolutions, most members of the convention could not distinguish between the rival platforms. Further to distract attention, the Cotton Whigs, at the crucial moment of the debates, staged a demonstration to bring Daniel Webster to the stand, "under an elaborate attempt to down every thing with acclamation." Puzzled and confused, the majority of the delegates followed the regular party leaders, rejected the Conscience Whig resolutions, and enthusiastically applauded Webster's plea for party solidarity: "For my part, in the dark and troubled night that is upon us, I see no star above the horizon promising light to give us, but the intelligent, patriotic, united Whig Party of the United States." [3]

Depressed by the failure of the Conscience Whigs, Sumner was by no means ready to give up his crusade against Winthrop. When Boston Whigs unanimously renominated the congressman, he toyed with accepting the Liberty Party nomination to run against him, but Adams's advice that "it would not do for him to go out and in the Whig party at pleasure" made him abandon the idea. Instead, he convinced himself that it was his duty to publish a summary and review of his controversy with Winthrop. In a long public letter to the congressman, this time issued over Sumner's own signature, he branded Winthrop's vote for the war

[2] Boston *Courier*, Sept. 24, 1846; Sumner: *Works*, I, 304–16.

[3] Boston *Whig*, Sept. 24–5, 1846; C. F. Adams, Diary, Sept. 23, 1846, Adams MSS.

bill as not merely "the most wicked in our history," but "one of the most wicked in all history." "Rather than lend your hand to this wickedness," Sumner objurgated the congressman, "you should have suffered the army of the United States to pass submissively through the Caudine Forks of Mexican power,—to perish, it might be, like the legions of Varus." [4]

After such a letter, Sumner could hardly have been surprised when a group of the younger Conscience Whigs in Boston, led by John A. Andrew, decided to bolt the party and offer him an independent nomination to Congress. Discreetly out of town when the nomination was made, Sumner found that his friends in the junto doubted its wisdom, as his enemies could now claim that personal ambition had all along been behind his letters attacking Winthrop. Hastily he withdrew, announcing: "I have never on any occasion sought or desired public office of any kind. . . . My tastes are alien to official life; and I have long been accustomed to look to other fields of usefulness." Howe, who realized that the contest was hopeless, took Sumner's place as the independent nominee. The abortive demonstration cost Winthrop hardly a vote; instead, it stimulated his friends and the Whig party generally to extraordinary efforts, and he was triumphantly re-elected.[5]

• 4 •

"That a man who but yesterday professed to be my friend, and who was filling my ears with all sorts of phrases of devotion and admiration, should turn upon me with such ferocity, denounce me so publicly and grossly, and pursue me with such relentless malignity," Winthrop thought, "is almost inconceivable." The other leaders of the regular Whig party in Massachusetts had no such difficulty in conceiving Sumner's motives. Bostonians of the George Ticknor sort said openly that Sumner had "taken his position on reform questions in order to get a notoriety and prominence, greater than he could get otherwise so soon" and that he

[4] C. F. Adams, Diary, Sept. 29, and Oct. 2, 1846, Adams MSS.; Sumner: *Works*, I, 317–29.

[5] Andrew to Sumner, Oct. 30, 1846, Sumner MSS.; "To the Voters of Massachusetts," photostat of a broadside in Levenson: "Winthrop," facing p. 64; Boston *Whig*, Oct. 30–1, and Nov. 2, 1846; Boston *Courier*, Nov. 2, 1846; Schwartz: *Howe*, pp. 160–1; Edward Everett to A. H. Everett, Oct. 30, 1846, letterbook copy, Everett MSS.

was trying "to make himself thus early the chief of a growing party, and get earlier into power than he could by other tracks which are occupied by older men." Congressman George Ashmun attributed the entire Conscience Whig movement to the personal ambitions of its leaders. "If [S. C.] Phillips could be made Governor, [Judge Charles] Allen Senator, and Adams Representative from Suffolk, with such small chance for anything less which might fall to Sumner," he cynically suggested, "the trouble [over antislavery in the Whig party] would be at an end." [6]

Indignantly the Conscience Whigs denied such unworthy motives, and none more passionately than Sumner. "I have no personal motive to gratify in this controversy," he assured Winthrop. "I seek no office of any kind for myself, or for any friend." Though Sumner's own repeated assertions that he was not, and never would be, an office-seeker may be discounted, it is harder to dismiss the unanimous testimony of his close friends that Sumner was, as the critical Hillard said, "perfectly disinterested" in his antislavery agitation. Not even opponents could suggest any specific office for which Sumner was ambitious. Some credence must be given to Sumner's own considered opinion that his reform activities had hampered, rather than forwarded, his opportunities for political advancement. With dignity he answered a critic who suggested that self-promotion was his goal:

> At the time my "position was taken in the Reform questions" few persons of my age in this community could behold wider openings for himself than I could, and few had declined more various opportunities. I was connected by relations of amity and confidence with those whose influence would have been most important to one seeking personal advancement. . . . I had often been solicited to take part in public affairs, and by members of different political parties. I had been thought of as a proper person for offices, academic, professional, judicial and diplomatic. . . . Surely, if mine were the ambition that has been suggested, I should not have neglected these advantages; most certainly I should not have renounced them, in pursuit of a vulgar notoriety.[7]

[6] Winthrop to J. H. Clifford, Feb. 14, 1847, copy, Winthrop MSS.; George Putnam to Sumner, Jan. 26, 1848, Sumner MSS.; Ashmun to Winthrop, Sept. 27, 1846, Winthrop MSS.

[7] Sumner to Winthrop, Aug. 10, 1846, Winthrop MSS.; *MHSP*, XVII, 195; Hillard to Dorothea L. Dix, Nov. 26, 1846, Dix MSS.; Sumner to George Putnam, Apr. 1848, copy, Sumner MSS.

Far from consciously plotting an easy route to power, Sumner was surprised to find himself a controversial figure and a leader of a political faction. In his own eyes he was a moderate and a man of good will. Reluctantly, but necessarily, he had stepped forward to defend Right at a time when the leaders of his party appeared about to endorse Wrong. In the controversies that followed, he had tried to keep his temper. He had, he thought, made it his inflexible rule *"never to question the motives of others."* "Well aware that where freedom of thought exists, differences must ensue," Sumner informed a critic, "I have always desired that these should be tempered by mutual kindness and forbearance, so that we might all at least 'agree to disagree.' "[8]

It is easy to understand why Sumner's enemies were infuriated by what they took to be his cant, which they found more objectionable than his criticisms, but Sumner was not being consciously disingenuous. A child of provincial New England, where small beer poets were compared to Shakespeare, and where poor George Hillard, who published a travel journal and an edition of Spenser's poems, was termed one of the sweetest and most enduring writers of the English language, Sumner shared his section's propensity for superlatives. Brought up under the spell of Daniel Webster and Edward Everett, he fell easily into the orator's natural tendency to use the exaggerated contrasts that made for rounded periods. When he praised, he seemed, as Lieber caustically observed, unable to "reign [*sic*] in the prancing steed of laudation." He compared his friend Channing to Pascal, the lexicographer John Pickering, to Erasmus. Similarly, when Sumner condemned, he condemned utterly. Totally insensitive to the power of his own words, he could not see why Winthrop should be so angry at having his vote called not merely bad, but *"the worst act that was ever done by a Boston representative."*[9]

But something more than mere rhetorical extravagance is required to account for the tone that pervades Sumner's early speeches. Edward Everett, noting the timing of Sumner's belated

[8] Sumner to George Putnam, Apr. 1848, author's copy, Sumner MSS.

[9] Lieber to Sumner, June 14, 1846, Lieber MSS.; Lieber's notes in his copy of Sumner's *The Scholar, The Jurist, The Artist, The Philanthropist,* in the Univ. of California Lib.; Freidel: *Lieber,* p. 238; Sumner to Nathan Appleton, Aug. 11, 1846, Appleton MSS.

entry upon the reform stage, tartly judged that his crusading zeal resulted from his failure to get Story's chair in the Harvard Law School.[1] Such an explanation is, of course, far too simple, yet it is true that a whole series of personal disasters and professional failures during the early 1840's had turned Sumner against the Boston society he once so admired. His inner state of mind was reflected in the rhetoric of his orations, in the frequent images of destruction and mutilation which recurred in his speeches. His references to "nations, now prostrate on the earth with bloody streams running from their sides," to "Blood! blood! . . . on the hands of the representative from Boston," to the "blood which spurts from the lacerated, quivering flesh of the slave," are ample, if unintentional, evidence of the deep anger that drove him on. It was not chance that singled out Robert C. Winthrop as the first object of Sumner's attack; perhaps his real offense lay less in his vote on the Mexican War than in the mere fact that he was a Winthrop.

Whatever the motives that initially brought Sumner into the political field, pride and stubbornness kept him there. When Winthrop and his allies unexpectedly took offense at the "Boston" letters, Sumner would not admit that he was to any degree at fault. All he had done, in his own estimation, was "gently and kindly to put [Winthrop] right; not defend him; not let him deceive himself into the belief that he has done anything but *wrong*." Sumner had not greatly changed since the Harvard Parietal Board attempted to prove to him that his buff waistcoat was not white. As William Kent shrewdly observed: "Sumner is a man of the loveliest temper and kindest and most generous heart; but he is Utopian as Horace Greele[y], and obstinate as a mule." [2]

That a man as dependent as Sumner upon approbation should defy Boston society was, however, something that stubbornness could not alone account for. If his former acquaintances snubbed him, his activities in the Conscience Whig group gave him a fresh sense of power and a new feeling of belonging. He seemed actually to enjoy his role as political pariah and social outcast. "The great questions to which he is giving himself," Hillard

1 Everett, Diary, May 10, 1856, Everett MSS.

2 Sumner to Nathan Appleton, Aug. 11, 1846, Appleton MSS.; Sumner to Longfellow, [Aug. 1846], Longfellow MSS.; William Kent to James Kent, Nov. 14, 1846, Kent MSS.

noted shrewdly, "have, at least, one salutary effect: that of breaking the spell of self-brooding melancholy which hung over him." [3]

Sumner's antislavery activities cost him some friends, but they also won him a new, fatherly adviser. Ex-President John Quincy Adams, now ending his long, controversial career, had apparently hardly known Sumner before he delivered "The True Grandeur of Nations." Though Adams could not approve of Sumner's pacifism, he did, out of sheer love of combat, rejoice that the young speaker had "set all the vipers of Alecto ahissing, by proclaiming the Christian Law of universal Peace and Love." Sumner's slashing attacks upon the Boston Brahmins further endeared him to the old President, for all the Adamses shared a suspicious hostility toward State Street. Finding in Sumner's eloquence and audacity something akin to his own notoriously bad temper and stubborn disposition, the elder Adams began to praise him as a young man who would "contribute largely to redeem the spirit of the free people of the Union from the dastardly servility to the slave-monger oligarchy into which they have . . . almost unconsciously fallen." [4]

Always responsive to praise, Sumner became Adams's adoring admirer. He had always extolled the ex-President's "unquestioned purity of character, and remarkable attainments, the result of constant industry," but in earlier years, when under the influence of Beacon Hill, he had objected "most strenuously to his manner, and to some of his expressions and topics, as unparliamentary and subversive of the rules and order of debate." Now he rejoiced in the very violence and vituperation with which Adams conducted his congressional campaign against slavery. Whenever the old President was in Quincy, Sumner came out to sit at his feet, and he undiscriminatingly adopted all of Adams's opinions, from his enthusiastic nationalism to his injunction that a statesman should "*Never accept a present.*" Throughout the remainder of his career Sumner was to echo Adams's doctrines that the Declaration of Independence, with its pledge of universal human equality, was as much a part of the public law of the land as the Constitution; that an antislavery congressman was not obliged

[3] Hillard to Lieber, July 3, 1849, Lieber MSS.

[4] J. Q. Adams, Diary, Aug. 13, 1845, Aug. 27, and 31, 1846, Adams MSS.; J. Q. Adams to Sumner, Aug. 29, 1846, Sumner MSS. Cf. C. F. Adams to Pierce, June 6, 1877, Pierce MSS.

to uphold the fugitive slave acts, as "in swearing to support the Constitution, he swore to support it as he understood it, and not as other men understood it"; and that in the event of civil war the federal government could use martial law to abolish slavery.[5]

The aging ex-President was delighted by so diligent a student, whose enthusiastic admiration was in contrast with the cool detachment of his own son, and he earnestly urged the younger man to enter public life. When Sumner objected that he "was unwilling to renounce literature," Adams predicted: "You will enter public life; in spite of yourself." In some senses he regarded Sumner as his successor. "I see you have a mission to perform," he saluted his disciple at the beginning of his political career. "I look from Pisgah to the promised Land. You must enter upon it." [6]

• 5 •

There was little in the election returns of 1846 to justify President Adams's prediction. The Conscience Whigs were so soundly defeated that Sumner, during the next six months, was able to carry on his antislavery agitation only through incidental remarks in the course of his peace crusade, his prison discipline fight, and his several addresses before lyceums. He was particularly proud of his success in insinuating his political opinions from the lecture platform to groups that customarily banned discussion of current issues. In an ostensibly historical discourse on "White Slavery in the Barbary States," delivered before the Mercantile Library Association, he compared *"the old mercantile interest"* that had once prevented the English from exterminating slavery in Tripoli with New England's traffickers in cotton, and likened the Algerine pirates to the Southern slaveholders.[7]

[5] Sumner to Howe, Dec. 31, 1843, Sumner MSS.; Sumner to Lieber, Feb. 21, 1841, ibid.; David L. Child: *Homes of American Statesmen* (New York: Alfred W. Upham; 1860), p. 333; Sumner to Joshua R. Giddings, Dec. 21, and 30, 1846, Giddings MSS.; Sumner: *Duties of Massachusetts at this Crisis. A Speech . . . delivered at the Republican Convention at Worcester, Sept. 7, 1854* (Boston; 1854), p. 6. On Adams's political ideas see George A. Lipsky: *John Quincy Adams: His Theory and Ideas* (New York: Thomas Y. Crowell Company; 1950), esp. Chap. xii, and David Donald: "Abraham Lincoln: Whig in the White House," in Norman A Graebner (ed.): *The Enduring Lincoln* (Urbana: University of Illinois Press; 1959), pp. 63–6. The definitive study of Adams's career as congressman and antislavery leader is Samuel Flagg Bemis's masterly *John Quincy Adams and the Union* (New York: Alfred A. Knopf, Inc.; 1956).

[6] Sumner's autobiography, Palfrey MSS.; Child: *Homes of American Statesmen*, p. 333; J. Q. Adams to Sumner, Aug. 29, 1846, Sumner MSS.

[7] Sumner: *Works*, I, 389, 460–1.

"In Sumner's alphabet just now there are only two words Slavery and Mexican War," Hillard complained in February 1847. "He does nothing but write paragraphs for the newspapers and letters without number. Business he utterly neglects and the only persons he sees with any interest are those with whom he is in communication on these points." Sumner's practice virtually disappeared, and with it his interest in the law. Looking back a bit sentimentally upon his "early days of precocious judical enthusiasm," he was obliged to admit that his mind had flowed completely into other channels.[8]

Increasingly Sumner's Court Street office became "a sort of *reunion* for the ultra liberals" of Massachusetts. Almost every day Adams, Wilson, Phillips, Allen, and other Conscience Whig leaders dropped in for long conferences, and Hillard, who had law business to attend to, gave up the outer office to his partner and retreated to the back room. State legislators of pronounced antiwar or antislavery opinions began showing up at these sessions, and Sumner in turn started to attend their caucuses in the State House. As most of these were rural legislators without great legal lore or literary gifts, they often asked him to draft their motions and bills. For example, it was Sumner who drew up the resolutions that served as a platform for the Conscience Whigs in the legislature; they denounced the Mexican War as "a war of conquest, so hateful in its objects, so wanton, unjust, and unconstitutional in its origin and character," called for "the country to retire from the position of aggression which it now occupies towards a weak, distracted neighbor," and demanded that the national government undertake "all constitutional efforts for the destruction of the unjust influence of the slave power, and for the abolition of slavery within the limits of the United States."[9]

Sumner also became a kind of middleman between the Massachusetts Conscience Whigs and the national leaders of the political antislavery movement. He was in confidential correspondence with Salmon P. Chase, of Ohio, and John P. Hale, of New Hampshire, both of whom were trying to fuse the antislavery elements of all parties into a new national organization. On his frequent trips to New York, he came to know John A. Dix, John Bigelow, William Cullen Bryant, and other leaders of the "Barn-

[8] Hillard to Lieber, Feb. 16, 1847, Lieber MSS.; Pierce, III, 55, 75–6.

[9] Howe to Lieber, Mar. 15, 1847, Lieber MSS.; Boston *Whig*, Sept. 17, 1847.

burners," the dissatisfied antislavery Democrats who followed ex-President Martin Van Buren. Closest of all Sumner's new political friends was Joshua R. Giddings, of Ohio, who was John Quincy Adams's chief lieutenant in the antislavery struggles in the national House of Representatives. Through Gidding's frequent letters Sumner was able to keep his Massachusetts associates informed of the latest Washington political gossip, the rumors about the next presidential candidates, and the strategy of the tiny but vocal antislavery minority in Congress.[1]

Naturally Sumner's chief political interest during 1847 was in Massachusetts, where an embittered rivalry between two groups of Conservative Whig leaders gave the Conscience Whigs an unexpected opportunity. Hoping to be the Whig presidential candidate in 1848, Webster made a stately tour through the South, wooing slaveholders' votes and in the process, Sumner thought, humbling himself and stultifying his state.[2] But, even while Webster was angling for the nomination, a group of moneyed Whigs in his own state, headed by Abbott Lawrence and Nathan Appleton, were resolved that he would never get it. They were tired of paying Webster gratuities to keep him in public office; they felt that he had sacrificed the interests of their textile industry to his own selfish ambition; and, at least in the case of Lawrence, they considered themselves worthy of the offices that Webster had so long pre-empted. If unencumbered by Webster, they thought they could speedily come to terms with Southern and Western Whigs on the really important issues of tariffs, internal improvements, and banking. Tired of defeat and remembering that the one successful Whig candidate had been a military man, they looked to the Mexican War to produce their nominee. After the victory at Buena Vista on February 22, General Zachary Taylor was their man, with Abbott Lawrence for Vice-President.[3]

[1] Both George W. Julian: *The Life of Joshua R. Giddings* (Chicago: A. C. McClurg and Company; 1892), and Richard W. Solberg: "Joshua Giddings: Politician and Idealist" (unpublished Ph. D. dissertation, Univ. of Chicago; 1952) contain detailed accounts of the Sumner-Giddings friendship. The former includes many of the letters the two men exchanged.

[2] Sumner to Lieber, May 3, 1847, Sumner MSS.

[3] Surprisingly little has been written about the Webster-Lawrence antagonism, which began when Webster refused to resign from John Tyler's cabinet and was exacerbated by Webster's jealousy of Henry Clay in 1844. As the leading figures in both factions were careful to maintain a public semblance

The Conscience Whigs, holding a balance between these rival regular factions, found themselves courted by both, and in their political inexperience they had difficulty in keeping their independent position. Early in 1847 Webster's spokesmen approached them with an invitation to join in preventing the renomination of Senator "Honest John" Davis, whose untimely loquacity during the previous session of Congress had killed the Wilmot Proviso, which was designed to exclude slavery from all lands acquired by the Mexican War. Sumner and his friends rejoiced to think that Webster shared their condemnation of Davis's "vacillation and treachery," but they soon learned that his real purpose was to strike at Lawrence through his henchman, Davis.[4]

At the same time, the Lawrence faction showed unusual kindness to the Conscience Whigs. A full year after most Beacon Hill doors were closed to Sumner, Abbott Lawrence still entertained him and his antislavery associates. After Webster's friends determined to force an endorsement of his presidential candidacy through the state Whig convention in 1847, Lawrence's attentions to the conscience junto became increasingly assiduous. When Sumner, Adams, Phillips, Palfrey, and Allen were chosen by primary meetings to attend the state convention, the Conscience Whigs naïvely attributed their success to the carelessness or stupidity of the regular Whig managers, but in fact the Lawrence group was happy to have them serve as hatchet men against Webster.[5]

When the convention met in Springfield on September 29, the Webster men were apparently in full control. Desirous of a

---

of agreement, little appeared in the newspapers about their differences. But see A. B. Darling: *Political Changes in Massachusetts, 1818–1848* ("Yale Historical Publications," Vol. XV, New Haven: Yale University Press; 1925), pp. 325–6; James Schouler: "The Whig Party in Massachusetts," *MHSP*, L (1916–17), 39–53; Hamilton Andrews Hill: *Memoir of Abbott Lawrence* (Boston; 1883), pp. 73–9.

[4] Sumner to Giddings, Feb. 1, and 5, 1847, Sumner MSS.; C. F. Adams, Diary, Feb. 6, and 8, 1847, Adams MSS.

[5] This judgment is admittedly based only upon inferential evidence. C. F. Adams in his diary (Sept. 15, 1847, Adams MSS.) attributed the "unexpected victory" of the Conscience leaders to "some error in tactics" on the part of their opponents and to the disturbing presence of liquor dealers at the caucus. He could not explain, however, how the regular party leaders, who were presumably defeated when Sumner, Adams, et al., were elected delegates, were able promptly to regain control of the caucus and squash resolutions proposed by Sumner which would have embarrassed Taylor's supporters. For a report of the caucus proceedings see the Boston *Advertiser*, Sept. 16, 1847.

unanimous endorsement of Webster as Massachusetts' favorite son, they were willing to forget "their horror at the youthful Anti-Slavery *escapades* of the juvenile portion of the party" and to permit Sumner and his friends to speak at great length, provided they did not disturb Webster's chances. But by prearrangement the Conscience Whigs, with the tacit approval of Lawrence's backers, upset the program by moving that it was "inexpedient to recommend a nomination of candidates for the Presidency and Vice Presidency." To appease the strong antislavery element that backed the motion, Webster's friends on the platform committee worked desperately to produce a set of resolutions acceptable to the Conscience minority. While they labored, Webster himself took the stand, and, keeping a careful eye on the door through which the committee must return to the convention with their compromise scheme, he delivered one of the most remarkable and agile speeches of his career. The longer the committee delayed, the more articulate Webster's antislavery opinions became. By the end of two hours, the *Liberator* gibed, a miracle had occurred. "He who had gone up, as men thought, the Oldest of the Old Whigs, came down again younger than the Youngest! His youth was renewed like the eagle's. . . . He had never been an Old Whig at all. He had always indulged in a Conscience. The Wilmot Proviso was not Mr. Wilmot's, after all, but Mr. Webster's thunder." [6]

Thus far Sumner and his friends had unwittingly served Lawrence well. Even though the convention finally accepted a resolution endorsing Webster, they had compelled him to make antislavery statements that would certainly injure him in the South, and they had demonstrated that Massachusetts was anything but unanimously behind her favorite son.

But, having used the Conscience Whigs to destroy Webster, the Lawrence faction was now ready to discard them. When Palfrey moved "That the Whigs of Massachusetts will support no men as candidates for the offices of President and Vice President, but those who are known by their acts or declared opinions to be opposed to the existence of Slavery," Lawrence's friends, who had sat complacently silent while Webster was under attack, furiously

[6] C. F. Adams, Diary, Sept. 29, 1847, Adams MSS.; Boston *Advertiser*, Sept. 30, 1847; *The Liberator*, Oct. 8, 1847.

fought back, lest the resolution jeopardize the chances of the slaveholding Zachary Taylor. In the acrimonious debate, Sumner again clashed directly with Winthrop. While Sumner was speaking, the congressman made a "sullen and impudent interruption," and Sumner flashed back with scornful denunciation of one who could "say, with detestable morality, 'Our party, *right or wrong.*'" "Loyalty to principle is higher than loyalty to party," Sumner warned. "Whatever the final determination of this Convention, there are many here to-day who will never yield support to any candidate, for Presidency or Vice-Presidency, who is not known to be against the extension of Slavery, even though he have freshly received the sacramental unction of a 'regular nomination.'"[7]

Defeated by the Lawrence machine, the Conscience Whigs did not fully understand what had happened to them. Puzzled by the fact they were able to destroy the genuinely antislavery Webster, but were impotent against the proslavery Taylor, they feebly explained their final failure by the early departure from the convention of country delegates, who supposedly went home to milk the cows. Regardless of the causes of the fiasco, they were sure of the consequences. The Conscience Whigs left Springfield, aware that they could never attend another Whig convention.

Sumner, for one, did not leave the party with great reluctance. He had never been "an ultra Whig," but he had hoped that the old party would become an antislavery organization. His quarrel with Winthrop had disillusioned him, and as early as January 1847 he had thought it "more than probable that we shall be obliged to enter the next Presidential contest with our own candidate." A new political movement might extricate the Conscience group "from our present uncomfortable position, of political association with those who really hate us more [than] they hate the Locofocos."[8] "Let the lines be drawn," he urged after the Springfield convention. "The sooner the better."[9]

[7] Boston *Whig*, Oct. 1, 1847; Linus B. Comins to Sumner, Mar. 22, 1861, Sumner MSS.; Sumner: *Works*, II, 61–2.

[8] "Locofoco" was originally a term applied to the antimonopoly wing of the New York City Democrats, but by the 1840's Whigs used it as a smear word for all members of the Democratic party.

[9] Sumner: *Works*, II, 76; Sumner to Giddings, Jan. 6, 1846 [the date should be 1847], and Dec. 1, 1847, Giddings MSS.

CHAPTER VII

Glacial Solitude

I AM TIRED of the anomalous position which is forced upon dissenting Whigs here in Massachusetts," Sumner exclaimed a few months after his defeat in the Springfield convention. "Let us have an open field, and direct battle, instead of private assassination and assault which is our lot here—suspected, slandered, traduced by those who profess to call themselves Whigs." If the Conscience Whigs would face the fact that they had no future in a party dominated by Abbott Lawrence and Nathan Appleton, they would look elsewhere for political allies. "Unexpected combinations" with other antislavery groups, of Democratic, Liberty, and even abolitionist antecedents, might be worked out. Even if a new political party could not be formed immediately, Sumner thought, "all of us, who are in earnest in our opposition to slavery, should cultivate kindly relations with each other—in view of some future association." [1]

• 1 •

Though the Conscience leaders as early as 1847 were prepared to bolt the Whig party rather than support a slaveholding candidate, and though the Cotton Whigs announced that their departure would be a welcome "sluice way through which, the Whig party could run off a good deal of cumbersome material, and thereby purify itself," [2] the farewells were protracted and acrimonious.

Undeterred by the triumph of the Lawrence faction in the

[1] Sumner to Chase, Oct. 1, 1847, and Feb. 7, 1848, Chase MSS., Lib. of Cong.
[2] T. N. Brewer to William Schouler, May 1848, William Schouler MSS.

state convention of 1847, the Conscience Whigs continued to attack Winthrop, now especially vulnerable as he was the Whig candidate for speaker of the national House of Representatives. After consulting with other members of the junto, Palfrey, who had recently been elected to Congress, joined with one or two other antislavery Whigs to vote against Winthrop, and his action almost cost Massachusetts the speakership.

Though respectable Boston felt "ineffable contempt and disgust" at Palfrey's course, Sumner rejoiced in his "courage, firmness and *conscience.*" [3] When the *Atlas* and the *Advertiser* attacked Palfrey for his vote, the Conscience clique came to his defense. Adams and S. C. Phillips praised Palfrey in the *Whig,* and Sumner in anonymous letters in the *Courier* extolled his independence and integrity as among the state's "brightest possessions, more precious far than all the distinctions of office, or the rewards of political success." [4]

The venom with which the Cotton Whigs replied indicated that they had already singled out Sumner as the most dangerous, and perhaps the most exposed, of the Conscience leaders. The editor of the influential Boston *Atlas,* William Schouler, publicly ridiculed Sumner's "cant," his "inordinate vanity and self-conceit," his "puerile self-consequence," his "vagrant theories, and transcendental abstractions," and, most of all, his "personal malignity" in attacking Winthrop.[5]

"I feel the bitter personality of this attack upon myself more than I thought I should ever again feel anything a newspaper could say," Sumner admitted to Palfrey.[6] His friends appeared indifferent to the "envenomed" attacks Schouler was making. Phillips finished his series of articles against Winthrop and fell silent. Adams supported Sumner vigorously until February, when John Quincy Adams died. Touched by Winthrop's obviously sincere admiration of his father and by his many kindnesses to the Adams family, he then dropped the quarrel.

[3] Sumner to Palfrey, Dec. 8, and 10, 1847, Palfrey MSS.; Ezra Lincoln to William Schouler, Dec. 12, 1847, William Schouler MSS. For a thorough study of the Palfrey-Winthrop controversy see Frank Otto Gatell: "Palfrey's Vote, the Conscience Whigs, and the Election of Speaker Winthrop," *New England Quarterly,* XXXI (1958), 218–31.

[4] Boston *Semi-Weekly Courier,* Dec. 23, 1847.

[5] Boston *Atlas,* Jan. 3, 27, and 29, 1848.

[6] Sumner to Palfrey, Jan. 27, and 31, 1848, Palfrey MSS.

Desperately casting about for assistance, Sumner turned to Giddings, that "master of us all in antislavery matters." The Ohio congressman told him a new reason why Palfrey had been correct in opposing Winthrop: "At a meeting of the Whig members of the House of Representatives, held on the morning on which our present war with Mexico was declared, Mr. Winthrop made a speech urging the whole party to vote for the war. While the bill was pending in the House, he went among his colleagues and personally urged them to sustain the bill, containing one of the most flagrant falsehoods ever uttered by a deliberative body." Without trying to check the facts, Sumner rushed into print with Gidding's charges.[7]

He paid for his precipitancy. Informed by Winthrop himself that Giddings's accusation was false, Schouler, in the *Atlas*, bluntly branded Sumner's story as a lie and connected it with the "vindictiveness" and "malignity" of his previous attacks. Frantic, Sumner begged Giddings for proof of his charges. But Giddings delayed; then he expressed qualms about appearing publicly in the controversy; and finally he sent along a weak collection of statements from congressmen who disagreed as to whether a caucus had been held, whether Winthrop had been present, and whether he had spoken in favor of the war bill. Even Sumner had to admit that Giddings's proofs were "less strong than he had anticipated." Schouler triumphantly noted that they were "frivolous." "As for Sumner," wrote one wealthy Boston merchant at the end of the controversy, "the more I hear about him, . . . the more difficult it is for me to believe him to be an honest man." [8]

• 2 •

In attacking Winthrop, Sumner and his allies were really striking at the Cotton Whigs who were promoting the nomination of Zachary Taylor for President in 1848. None of the Conscience group could support the slaveholding Taylor, and Sumner, with his peace principles, was especially hostile to any military man. In his curiously naïve way he called on Abbott Lawrence, promi-

[7] Boston *Whig*, Jan. 15, 1848.

[8] Boston *Atlas*, Jan. 27, and Mar. 17, 1848; Sumner to Giddings, Feb. 3, 10, and 11, and Mar. 25, 1848, Giddings MSS.; J. H. Clifford to Winthrop, Mar. 27, 1848, Winthrop MSS.

nently mentioned as a likely running mate for Taylor, in the hope of convincing him that the general was not entitled to the Presidency.

"I am your friend," Sumner informed the manufacturer. "I have faith in the sincerity, the goodness and generosity of your nature. I do not believe you actuated . . . by a desire for the Vice Presidency . . . ; and I now plead with you to withdraw from this movement in which you are involved."

Genially Lawrence replied: *"What can I do about it;* I AM IN UP TO THE EYES."

Righteously Sumner retorted: "Get out of it. . . . It is never too late to begin to do right." [9]

But it was hard even for the Conscience Whigs to know what was right for 1848. They were opposed to Taylor, but the other possible candidates for the Whig nomination all had weaknesses. General Winfield Scott had antislavery sentiments, but Sumner objected to him as another "instrument of this atrocious war." Justice John McLean, of the United States Supreme Court, was popular among conservatives, but the Conscience group doubted his antislavery zeal. For a time Sumner was enthusiastic about Senator Thomas Corwin, who had eloquently denounced the Mexican War, but the Ohioan proved reluctant to commit himself to the rigid antislavery doctrines of the Conscience group. The newly elected senator from New Hampshire, John P. Hale, was entirely willing to endorse their principles, but he had no general popularity and was tainted by his previous acceptance of a Liberty nomination. Conscience Whig leaders began to think that the most attractive possibility to defeat Taylor was Daniel Webster, whose campaign they had so effectively sabotaged only the previous year. Henry Wilson openly announced that Webster was his first choice for the Presidency, and even Sumner had an occasional "fit" of "the mania of Mr. Webster," until Charles Francis Adams reconvinced him that Webster lacked moral principles.[1]

[9] Sumner to Nathan Appleton, Aug. 31, 1848, copy, Sumner MSS.

[1] Sumner to Giddings, May 6, 1848, Nov. 1, 1847, and July 28, 1847, Giddings MSS.; Sumner to Lieber, Mar. 22, 1847, Sumner MSS.; Sumner to S. P. Chase, Feb. 7, 1848, Chase MSS., Lib. of Cong.; Sumner to Thomas Corwin, Sept. 7, 1847, copy, Sumner MSS.; Sumner to Giddings, Feb. 19, 1847, ibid.; Sumner to Palfrey [Apr. 23, 1848], Palfrey MSS.; Wilson to Webster, May 31, 1848, Webster MSS., Dartmouth Coll.; Adams, Diary, Mar. 29, 1848, Adams MSS.

Even while hoping that the Whig convention would come up with a candidate of acceptable antislavery views, the Conscience leaders were exploring the possibilities of uniting the dissatisfied Whigs, the Liberty party men, and the antislavery Democrats into a third party. Sumner joyfully welcomed the prospect of such a union. "Let us all join in earnest labor," he urged, "not against *each other*—but against *Slavery*." To the dismay of his more cautious associates, he came actually to desire the disruption of the Whig party. "The truth is," Charles Francis Adams sourly remarked, "Sumner is impulsive and ardent and this carries him perpetually to an extreme." [2]

Sumner played an important role in the informal pre-convention discussions of a united antislavery front. As he held no political position and had no known political aspirations, he could talk with Democrats and Liberty men with less likelihood of committing the other members of his group; at the same time, the other Conscience Whigs knew that his tendency to converse "upon abstract points" concerning lofty principles "would keep him out of the range of imprudence as to passing events." [3] There was also the practical consideration that Sumner, alone of the Conscience group, had close friends among the "Barnburners," the New York antislavery Democrats, and could discuss the possibilities of fusion in intimacy and privacy with "Prince John" Van Buren, son of the ex-President, John Bigelow, and William Cullen Bryant.[3a] In addition, Sumner's agitation in behalf of edu-

[2] Boston *Whig*, Jan. 19, 1847; Sumner to Giddings, Jan. 22, 1847, Giddings MSS.; Adams, Diary, Jan. 21, 1848, Adams MSS. Frank Otto Gatell's " 'Conscience and Judgment'; The Bolt of the Massachusetts Conscience Whigs," *The Historian*, XXI (1958), 18–45, is the best study of the formation of the Free Soil party in Massachusetts.

[3] C. F. Adams, Diary, Jan. 20, 1848, Adams MSS.

[3a] New York Democrats who were enthusiastic about reform were called "Barnburners" in allusion to the fable of a man who burned his barn in order to get rid of the rats. Their conservative opponents were called "Hunkers" because they allegedly forgot their principles in hungering after office. The story of New York politics in the 1840's is very complex, but in a general way it can be said that the Barnburners, who rallied about Martin Van Buren and his son, were strongly opposed to slavery. Alienated by President Polk's course, they formed the backbone of the Free Soil party in New York in 1848. After 1849 most of them returned to the Democratic party. Some Barnburners were later to become prominent in the Republican party, though others, most notably the Van Burens, remained stanchly Democratic. Herbert D. A. Donovan: *The Barnburners* (New York: New York University Press; 1925); William Trimble: "Diverging Tendencies in New York Democracy in the Period of the Locofocos," *American Historical Review*, XXIV (1919), 396–421; Ernest P. Muller: "Preston King: A

cation, peace, and prison reform had won him many admirers in the Liberty party, and John Greenleaf Whittier, who was not only a poet, but a principal political leader among Massachusetts abolitionists, had become one of his warmest friends.[3b]

The importance of such personal contacts became apparent as the two national parties began to break up during the summer of 1848. When the Democrats nominated Lewis Cass in May, antislavery men repudiated him as a tool of the South, and the New York "Barnburners" bolted the party. Throughout New England, antislavery Whigs, anticipating Taylor's success in the Philadelphia convention, were preparing to join the insurgent movement. There was going to be "an organized revolt at the North," Sumner predicted. "We in Massachusetts are maturing it in advance; the same is doing in Ohio. If so, there will be a new party, having some *principles*, and looking to the good of Humanity." [4]

When the Whig convention brushed aside antislavery protests and nominated Taylor, the Conscience junto swiftly moved to create a new party. Sumner and Adams promptly circulated a call for a convention to meet at Worcester on June 28; all Massachusetts voters opposed to both Taylor and Cass were invited. During the few weeks before the convention, planning for the new party consumed all of Sumner's time. Through Giddings and Dr. Gamaliel Bailey, the editor of the *National Era* in Washington, he tried to synchronize developments in Massachusetts with antislavery movements in other states. Spurring along the "Barnburners," Sumner helped persuade ex-President Martin Van Buren to write letters that, despite their customary ambiguity, could be interpreted as endorsing antislavery. He persuaded Whittier that Hale, the Liberty candidate, was hopeless as a coalition leader and must be withdrawn.[5]

Political Biography" (unpublished Ph. D. dissertation, Columbia Univ.; 1957); Walter L. Ferree: "The New York Democracy: Division and Reunion, 1847–1852" (unpublished Ph. D. dissertation, Univ. of Pennsylvania; 1953); Martin Lichterman: "John Adams Dix, 1798–1897" (unpublished Ph. D. dissertation, Columbia Univ.; 1952).

[3b] J. Welfred Holmes: "Whittier & Sumner: A Political Friendship," *New England Quarterly*, XXX (1957), 58–72.

[4] C. F. Adams, Diary, May 27, 1848, Adams MSS.; Sumner to George Sumner, May 30, 1848, Sumner MSS.

[5] Sumner to Palfrey, June 8, 1848, Palfrey MSS.; Boston *Whig*, June 19, 1848; John Albree (ed.): *Whittier Correspondence from the Oak Knoll Collections, 1830–1892* (Salem: Essex Book and Print Club; 1911), pp. 97–100.

Sumner, as Hillard cynically observed, expected the union of antislavery factions to produce "a new political Jerusalem," and he attended the Worcester convention in a spirit of dedication to a noble cause. The crowd was impressively large, and it responded enthusiastically to vigorous speeches by Giddings, Adams, and Charles Allen. When Sumner was called to the platform, he was powerfully stimulated by his audience and made one of the most effective addresses of his life. A revolution was occurring in American politics, he announced. All the old party issues—the tariff, the bank, internal improvements—were dead. Neither of the old parties dared face the one real remaining issue —the extension of slavery into territory recently acquired from Mexico. Nobody could expect anything from the Democrats under Cass. From the Whig party more might have been anticipated, but it had been perverted from its true principles by a "secret influence which went forth from among ourselves." Taylor's nomination had been procured by a "conspiracy" between Southwestern and Northeastern politicians, "between the cotton-planters and flesh-mongers of Louisiana and Mississippi and the cotton-spinners and traffickers of New England,—between the lords of the lash and the lords of the loom." Consequently, it was time to abandon both the old parties and form a new organization based upon the truth and the right. Then would a new era dawn. "Politics and morals, no longer divorced from each other, become one and inseparable in the holy wedlock of Christian sentiment." [6]

It was well for Sumner that he had the power of self-deception, for the great crusading army he thought he was organizing was, even in Massachusetts, a mongrel assortment of disgruntled Conscience Whigs, a few Webster followers, furious that their chief had been spurned at Philadelphia, some patronage-hungry Democrats, assorted Liberty men, and other disaffected persons. In other states the amalgam was even more curious. In New York the Free Soil forces, under their veneer of antislavery, were mostly the followers of Martin Van Buren, who, as President, had discountenanced the abolition of slavery in the District of Co-

[6] Hillard to "My dear Rogers," Dec. 29, 1847, MS., Mass. Hist. Soc.; Boston *Courier*, June 29, 1848; Boston *Atlas*, June 29, 1848; Boston *Whig*, June 29, 1848; Boston *Advertiser*, June 30, 1848; C. F. Adams, Diary, June 28, 1848, Adams MSS.; Sumner: *Works*, II, 81, 87.

Robert Charles Winthrop

Painting by George P. A. Healy

MASSACHUSETTS HISTORICAL SOCIETY

George Ticknor

MASSACHUSETTS HISTORICAL SOCIETY

Daniel Webster

THE NATIONAL ARCHIVES

SPOKESMEN OF BEACON HILL

lumbia and had upheld the right of Southern postmasters to burn abolitionist mail. None of these discords and inconsistencies troubled Sumner; he was marching to Zion.

At the national Free Soil convention, which met in Buffalo in early August, Sumner's role was an unimportant one. He was not a delegate, because the Massachusetts representation had to be carefully apportioned among former Whigs, former Democrats, and former Liberty men, and none of these groups considered Sumner as representing their distinctive interests. Nevertheless, he attended the convention as a spectator and watched the enthusiastic delegates nominate Van Buren for President. When there was some talk of inviting Sumner to address an open-air rally, he declined, as he was unaccustomed to speaking without first having memorized a carefully prepared script, and fled, with Charles Francis Adams's oldest son, to Niagara Falls. During their absence Adams was nominated Vice-President.[7]

Returning to Massachusetts with the delegation, Sumner prepared to stump the state in defense of the Free Soil ticket. Everywhere his arguments were the same. The Democratic nominee, Cass, did "not represent the principle of *Freedom.*" The Whig candidate was a successful general, but a man ignorant and inexperienced in civil affairs. In contrast was the Free Soilers' Martin Van Buren, that "veteran statesman, sagacious, determined, experienced, who, at an age when most men are rejoicing to put off their armor, girds himself anew, and enters the lists as champion of Freedom." Obliged to admit that antislavery men had hitherto consistently opposed the ex-President, Sumner rationalized manfully: "It is not for the Van Buren of 1838 that we are to vote, but for the Van Buren of *to-day.*" Men were less important than principles, anyway, and the Free Soil party was "The Party of Freedom," long desired by John Quincy Adams and William Ellery Channing. "Their spirits hover us, and urge us to

[7] R. H. Dana, Diary, July 18, 1848, Dana MSS.; Adams: *Dana,* I, 135–6. On his way to Buffalo, Sumner conferred with New York politicians and, with their approval, tried to interest Edward Everett and John McLean in the second place on a ticket with Van Buren. Everett firmly refused to leave the Whig party, and McLean entrusted his fortunes at the convention to Salmon P. Chase. Sumner to McLean, July 31, 1848, McLean MSS.; Francis P. Weisenburger: *The Life of John McLean: A Politician on the United States Supreme Court* (Columbus: Ohio State University Press; 1937), p. 136; Sumner to Everett, July 31, 1848, Everett MSS.; Everett to Sumner, Aug. 4, 1848, Sumner MSS.; J. A. Briggs to Pierce, Feb. 6, 1877, Pierce MSS.; Adams, Diary, Aug. 9, 1848, Adams MSS.

persevere," Sumner concluded his addresses. "Let us be true to the moral grandeur of our cause." [8]

The Free Soilers discovered that politics demanded organization as well as oratory. Patricians like Dana and Phillips made excellent speeches, but the necessary behind-the-scenes work called for a shrewd, opportunistic politician like Henry Wilson. Though most of the Conscience group scorned Wilson because of his reputation for deviousness and his low social standing, Sumner, who welcomed all allies from all quarters, had no repugnance to working with him. He helped Wilson organize the first Massachusetts state convention of the new party, which met on September 7, and became the chairman of its state central committee.[9]

Inevitably when district conventions met and named candidates for Congress, Sumner was invited to run in the Boston district. As in 1846, he hesitated. To run against Winthrop would reopen all the old quarrels of the past two years; it would renew suspicions that he had been acting for revenge or for personal advancement. Sumner "stands now, as he himself feels, at just the most critical point of his life," Longfellow noted on October 22. "Shall he plunge irrevocably into politics, or not? . . . From politics, as a career, he still shrinks back. When he has once burnt his ships there will be no retreat. He already holds in his hands the lighted torch." [1]

In fact, though Sumner still protested vigorously that he had no desire for office, that his life had other objectives, that he contemplated some great historical work that would occupy his future time (though he never commenced one),[2] his protestations were wearing thin. This time feelings of duty, ambition, and revenge obliged him to accept the nomination in a platitudinous letter declaring: "Morals is the soul of all true politics." [3]

Thoroughly absorbed in politics, Sumner was not discouraged when the Free Soil ticket carried no state in the fall elections and won no electoral votes. "The public mind has been

[8] Outline of a speech delivered at various places during the 1848 campaign, Sumner MSS.; Boston *Republican*, Oct. 19, 1848; Sumner: *Works*, II, 144–5.

[9] Boston *Advertiser*, Sept. 8, 1848; Boston *Republican*, Sept. 8, 1848.

[1] Longfellow, Diary, Oct. 22, 1848, Longfellow MSS.

[2] Sumner to Samuel Lawrence, Nov. 29, 1848, copy, Sumner MSS.

[3] Boston *Republican*, Oct. 28, 1848.

stirred on the subject of slavery to depths never before reached," he argued cheerfully; "and much information with regard to the Slave-Power has been diffused in quarters heretofore ignorant of this enormous tyranny." Not even Winthrop's victory in the congressional election, held on November 14, just after the presidential balloting, checked Sumner's enthusiasm. He had known from the start that his candidacy was hopeless, and he found some consolation in the fact that the Free Soiler tickets in Massachusetts drew a respectable vote. "If we have not reached the anticipations of the more sanguine," he wrote Giddings, "we have disappointed all the calculations of our enemies. We have . . . taken our place, before the Cass party, as the *second* party. First we are in principles; I trust we shall soon shew ourselves *first* in numbers." [4]

• 3 •

"I have spoken a great deal . . . and with a certain effect," Sumner reviewed the 1848 campaign in a letter to his brother. "As a necessary consequence, I have been a mark for abuse. I have been attacked bitterly; but I have consoled myself by what J. Q. Adams said to me . . . 'No man is abused whose influence is not felt.' " [5]

He could have no doubt that Beacon Hill felt his influence. Nathan Appleton, a kinsman by marriage and father-in-law of Sumner's best friend, Longfellow, had tried to maintain his friendship with Sumner even when other Boston doors were closed to the young agitator, but he found intolerable the accusation that a conspiracy of Southern slaveholders and New England cotton millers, "the lords of the lash and the lords of the loom," had brought about Taylor's nomination. Curtly Appleton, who was both one of the largest textile manufacturers in the United States and a firm supporter of Taylor's candidacy, asked whether Sumner had any evidence for such a charge or whether it was "a mere rhetorical flourish." For several weeks Sumner refused to reply because of Appleton's lordly tone; then he composed a long review of the evidence which sustained his accusa-

[4] Sumner to Chase, Nov. 16, 1848, Chase MSS., Lib. of Cong.; Sumner to Giddings, Nov. 10, 1848, Giddings MSS.

[5] Sumner to George Sumner, Nov. 15, 1848, Sumner MSS.

tion.[6] Appleton found in the reply only reports, impressions, newspaper columns and gossip—"very *skimble skamble stuff,* in the way of evidence"—and declared that Sumner had not proved any "conspiracy," much less an "unholy" one. In the past, Appleton added, he had watched Sumner's course "more in sorrow than in anger." Now the time for charity had passed; he could only regard Sumner as a malignant liar. Henceforth when the textile manufacturer visited his daughter at Craigie House, Longfellow carefully warned Sumner to stay away.[7]

Another old friend, Samuel Lawrence, who had once helped finance Sumner's trip to Europe, also took umbrage at the "lords of the loom" conspiracy charge. "How an intelligent Massachusetts man could have given utterance to these words," Lawrence wrote angrily, "is beyond my comprehension . . . you appear in the eyes of your friends as a demagogue." Once again Sumner tried to defend himself; his objective in political life, he said, was not to advance himself, but "to introduce into politics the principles of Christianity." Savagely Lawrence retorted: "Your desire 'to intro[duce] into Politics the principles of Christianity' is so strong that . . . you have joined a Faction whose leaders . . . are [Henry] Wilson . . . and Mr. Martin Van Buren!!!!" "You and I never can meet on mutual ground," Lawrence concluded. "I can contemplate you only in the character of a Defamer of those you profess to love, and an enemy to the permanency of this Union." [8]

Even Sumner's more intimate friendships were disrupted by politics. Of the Five of Clubs only Howe fully sympathized with Sumner's Free Soil activities; Longfellow, though deeply antislavery, was uninterested in political warfare; and Hillard and Felton were on the Whig side. With little of the old comradely spirit left, the club sometimes failed to meet for months on end. "A pity these meetings should be so interrupted," Longfellow lamented. "Nothing but politics now! Oh where are those genial days, when literature was the theme of our conversation!" [9]

[6] For copies of both sides of this correspondence, which stretched from July 4 through August 31, 1848, see the Sumner-Appleton MSS.

[7] Appleton to Sumner, Sept. 4, 1848, copy, Appleton MSS.; Longfellow to Sumner [June 1849], Longfellow MSS.

[8] Lawrence to Sumner, Nov. 7, and Dec. 4, 1848, Sumner MSS.; Sumner to Lawrence, Nov. 29, 1848, copy, ibid.

[9] Longfellow, Diary, Dec. 27, 1845, and Sept. 17, 1848, Longfellow MSS.

Though Felton continued to protest undying affection for his "Dearly Beloved Charley," he found it increasingly difficult to get along with Sumner. When Sumner announced that William Lloyd Garrison was "an angel, that we are entertaining unawares," Felton, related by marriage to the most conservative families in Boston, snapped back that Garrison was "a demon." Unable to bear contradiction, Sumner accused the professor "of no longer sympathizing with him"; Felton, in turn, complained that Sumner was "running into all manner of extravagances and vitiating his naturally sweet disposition." Year by year their relations grew worse. When Felton tried to defend the Whig view of political affairs, Sumner treated him like a heckler in an audience, "rushing and sweeping over him in argument, as if he were nobody," and the outraged Harvard Latinist protested that he could not and would not "stand this over-bearing and down-bearing proceeding any longer." Sumner, he complained, was becoming so intolerant as "to think that difference from his opinions can only proceed from a bad head or a corrupt heart." "It almost seems," he added bitterly, "as if the *love of man* meant [to Sumner] the *hatred of men*." In 1850, when Sumner charged him with being "vindictive, bitter and unchristian" toward the friends of true liberty, Felton exclaimed that he would not endure "language . . . that gentlemen should not address to housebreakers and pickpockets," and broke off social intercourse.[1]

Hillard, too, was drifting away from Sumner. He had sympathized with Sumner's earlier views; he had admired the moral fervor of "The True Grandeur of Nations," supported Sumner in the prison discipline controversy, and helped rally anti-Texas sentiment in 1845. But, as Sumner became increasingly rabid on these subjects, Hillard, restrained by frail health, a gentle and conciliatory disposition, and his friendship for the Ticknors, held back.[2] With genuine anguish he watched Sumner become increasingly absorbed in politics, for he did not think his partner well fitted for a life of action. "Sumner," he astutely observed, "is

[1] Ibid., Dec. 26, 1845, May 16, 1847, and Dec. 19, 1849; Felton to Sumner, Jan. 27 [1846], Sumner MSS.; Sumner to Felton, Apr. 9, 1850, copy, Sumner MSS.; Felton to Palfrey, Sept. 13, 1850, Palfrey MSS.; Felton to Howe, Apr. 11, 1850, Howe MSS.

[2] Hillard analyzed his own weaknesses in letters to Lieber, Sept. 28, 1835, and Jan. 6, 1860, Lieber MSS.

so much occupied with thoughts of how the world is to be made better, that he does not pause to consider and observe what the world really is."[3]

As Sumner regarded anything short of unqualified approval as little less than a personal affront, he came to regard Hillard with increasing coolness. In the spring of 1847, when Hillard was seriously ill and confined to his house for eight days, Sumner did not take time to visit him.[4]

A few months later Hillard sailed to Europe for his health, and, upon his return, he moved his law practice to new quarters. "Sumner was so absorbed in politics," he explained, "and his office was such a rendezvous for abolitionists, free soilists and all other *ists,* that it was quite impossible to think of doing any business there." He did not break off all contact with Sumner, but kept up a thin, formal relationship. "We have made up our fagots for life, and we will not wrangle or 'establish raws' upon subjects on which we shall never agree," he told Sumner, "but will respect each other's intellectual rights and accept each other's convictions as facts."[5]

• 4 •

Though Sumner spoke of himself as being excluded from virtually every house on Beacon Hill and loudly bewailed his social isolation, he was not, in fact, without friends. Even in the best Boston society there were a few families, like the Josiah Quincys, the John Lodges, and the W. H. Prescotts, who continued to welcome him.

If politics excluded Sumner from the Ticknor circle, they made him the more welcome in the Adams family.[6] While the old President was alive, he always greeted Sumner with tremulous enthusiasm. Charles Francis Adams was naturally more reserved, but he encouraged Sumner to come out to Quincy for

[3] Hillard to Lieber, Nov. 25, 1846, ibid.

[4] Hillard to Lieber, Feb. 16, 1847, ibid.

[5] Hillard to Lieber, Dec. 5, 1848, ibid; Pierce, III, 250–1.

[6] Sumner also became increasingly intimate with Theodore Parker and Ralph Waldo Emerson, who invited him to edit the new transcendalist journal, *The Massachusetts Quarterly Review.* Theodore Parker to Sumner [1846], Sumner MSS.; Rusk (ed.): *Emerson Letters,* III, 391–4; Ralph L. Rusk: *The Life of Ralph Waldo Emerson* (New York: Charles Scribner's Sons; 1949), p. 324.

dinner every Friday or Saturday. To the older Adams boys, John, Henry, and Charles Francis, Jr., the embattled Sumner, fighting for the cause of Truth and Virtue, was a heroic figure, a "boy's ideal of greatness; the highest product of nature and art." Of course, upon occasion, they grew restive under Sumner's moralizing and took advantage of his want of humor. At dinner once Sumner attempted "in his rather direct way" to instill into young Henry Adams a love for historical study. "Why, Henry," he said solemnly, "I am sure you would never let a slice of pudding stand in your way to a slice of history!" When John pertly replied: "You bet your life, Mr. Sumner, he wouldn't let it stand in the way *long*," Sumner's face presented a picture of puzzled bafflement. But, for all Sumner's seriousness, they admired him greatly; years later Charles Francis Adams, Jr., declared that he "owed far more to Charles Sumner than to all of the Harvard professors put together." [7]

With the Howes, too, Sumner continued on terms of closest intimacy. Julia, to be sure, sometimes found it a strain to have to prepare the kind of "neat little dinner" he liked—"soup, salmon, sweetbreads, roast lamb and pigeon, with green peas, potatoes *au maitre d'hotel,* spinach, and salad, . . . pudding and blanc-mange, then strawberries, pineapple, and ice-cream, then coffee, etc." More than once she was vexed when Sumner persuaded her husband to go out campaigning, leaving her alone in South Boston with a houseful of small children. She used to sing to her babies:

Rero, rero, riddety rad;
This morning my baby caught sight of her Dad.
Quoth she, "Oh Daddy, where have you been?"
"With Mann and Sumner, a-putting down sin!"

Still, she admitted Sumner's purity of character and true friendship for her husband and concluded that he was "funny, but very good and kind."

Her children adored Sumner—as children nearly always did. They scrambled over his massive frame and called him "the harmless giant." For years one of the Howe daughters used Sum-

[7] Henry Adams: *Education,* p. 31; *Pierce Dinner,* p. 40; Charles Francis Adams: *Charles Francis Adams, 1835–1915: An Autobiography* . . . (Boston: Houghton Mifflin Co.; 1916), p. 37.

ner's stately figure as a unit of measure, saying "that a thing was so much higher or lower than Mr. Sumner." [8]

Howe himself remained everything Sumner could desire in a friend—devoted, sympathetic, adulatory. He rejoiced when Sumner was victorious, and comforted him when he was in despair. "I know not where you may be, or what you may be about," he wrote once when Sumner was sulking during a depressed mood, "but I know what you are *not* about; you are not seeking your own pleasure, or striving to advance your own interests. You are, I warrant me, on some errand of kindness, some work for a friend or for the public." [9]

When Sumner wished to assume a less Olympian pose, he could always go out to the Longfellows' house in Cambridge. Giving Sumner unquestioning admiration and love, the Longfellows tried to divert his mind from politics. On his regular Sunday visits he inspected the improvements Longfellow was making at Craigie House, and he was especially charmed by the new shower bath the poet installed in his dressing room. Standing nude under it, ready to pull the string, he would announce to Longfellow: "This is a kind of Paradise."

"And you a kind of Adam!" replied the poet.

"With all my ribs," laughed Sumner, attempting a rare witticism, and then he let the deluge descend.[1]

The Longfellow children, too, loved Sumner, and no sooner did he settle into his favorite rocking chair at Craigie House than one of the three little daughters would snuggle in his lap. They liked his stately attempts at humor, and giggled hysterically when he would ceremoniously open a door for one of the tiny children with a grand wave of his hand and a sonorous "*In presequas*." The Longfellow boys were a bit more restive under Sumner's solemnity, and objected strongly to his elephantine humor in taking a child's hand, grinding his thumb into the back of it until the pain was unbearable, and then releasing it with a laugh.

The entire Longfellow family at times found Sumner inex-

[8] Richards and Elliott: *Julia Ward Howe*, I, 121, 127–8, 152; Richards: *S. G. Howe*, II, 228.

[9] Richards: *S. G. Howe*, II, 189–91.

[1] Longfellow, Diary, June 14, 1846, Longfellow MSS. Ernest Longfellow, who did not like Sumner very much, erroneously remembered that he stepped into the shower fully clad and got drenched. *Random Memories* (Boston: Houghton Mifflin Co.; 1922), p. 22.

pressibly, if unintentionally, funny, and they long remembered the occasion when Sumner, strolling in the garden after dinner, decided to pet a calf tethered in the yard. In his "bucolic moment of enthusiasm for the fascinations of rural life," Sumner—"he who knows not grass from grain," Longfellow laughed—seized the rope and pulled the calf nearer and nearer, saying "Come here! Come here!" With a sudden leap the "idyl[l]ic animal" sprang away; "there is a glimmer of gray gaiters high in air, and prone lies the philanthropist on the sod." "So much for cockney ruralizing," laughed Fanny, while Henry mercilessly compared Sumner's position with that of the Free Soil party. Dignity gravely wounded, Sumner turned majestically upon young Charlie, who was guffawing wildly: "When a friend meets with an accident you ought not to laugh at him; you ought to pity, and sympathize with him!" [2]

Still, their laughter was in good fun, not in malice, for Sumner was truly welcome at Craigie House. "I am delighted to see him so often," Longfellow wrote in his diary; "the face of a friend, and such a friend! is what one cannot see too much of; never enough." [3]

In spite of such a circle of genuine friends, Sumner never ceased to grieve that Boston society had turned against him. "There was a time," he once remarked when driving down Beacon Street, "when I was welcome at almost every house within two miles of us, but now hardly any are open to me." Though he was still "rarely without a pocket-full of letters from duchesses or noblemen in England," he now had no one to read them to. He felt absolutely alone. "His solitude was glacial," Henry Adams remembered, "and reacted on his character. He had nothing but himself to think about." [4]

The role of martyr came easily to Sumner. Since childhood he had felt that he was discriminated against, imposed upon, and unjustly attacked. "I cannot but think how many *rubs* it is my for-

[2] Annie Longfellow Thorp: "A Little Person's Little Memories of Great People" (MS. in the Longfellow MSS.); Ernest Longfellow: *Random Memories*, p. 21; Longfellow, Diary, Nov. 4, 1849; Fanny Longfellow to Mary and Tom, Nov. 5, 1849, Longfellow MSS.

[3] Longfellow, Diary, June 12, 1846, ibid. Cf. Fanny Longfellow's affectionate references to Sumner. Edward Wagenknecht (ed.): *Mrs. Longfellow: Selected Letters and Journals of Fanny Appleton Longfellow*, pp. 124, 152, and 175.

[4] Henry Adams: *Education*, pp. 30–1.

tune to receive," he lamented. Surely no one else suffered quite so much, and so undeservedly. When gossip spread the story that his brother George was a Russian spy, Sumner, instead of denouncing the canard, merely reflected that George's trials were nothing compared to "the fiery torrents" to which he himself had been exposed. The malignant powers of evil seemed to have concentrated their forces upon him. "Why," he sadly questioned, "if . . . I render no evil, and say no evil, am I the mark for so much? I cannot turn my bosom away from my most intimate friends without receiving a shaft. I begin to feel a distrust of everybody. Nobody is true; and all the words of kindness which drop, like fresh coin, from the lips of those I meet, are counterfeit." [5]

But, instead of collapsing under what he regarded as a combination of persecutors, this holy, blissful martyr thrived upon his torments. When left alone to the "tranquil pursuits and tranquil pleasures" he claimed he craved, Sumner was often ill. But, as soon as he became active in politics and became Boston's " 'caput lupinum' against whom every body was throwing a stone," his health amazingly was restored. Hillard's analysis of Sumner was, as usual, shrewd: "His mind and character require the stimulus of something outward and exoteric, some strong pressure, to take him out of himself and prevent him from a morbid habit of inactive brooding. He is a man of moral enthusiasm; made to identify himself with some great Cause and accept and surrender himself to it unconditionally." [6]

Despite his embattled isolation, which he interpreted as social martyrdom for the sake of high principle, Sumner was happier than he had been for years. He received much comfort from his friends—and perhaps even more from his enemies. "Amidst these troubles," he admitted, "I think I have found a higher satisfaction than I have experienced in any former period of my life, derived partly from the intensity of occupation but more from the intimate conviction that I was doing my duty." [7] "The world with ignorant or intolerant judgment may condemn," he added smugly; "the countenances of companions may be averted; the

[5] Sumner to Palfrey, Feb. 22, 1848, Palfrey MSS.; Sumner to Greene, July 28, 1849, Greene MSS.; Sumner to Howe [Apr. 24, 1845], Sumner MSS.

[6] Hillard to Lieber, Apr. 14, 1847, Dec. 5, 1848, and Mar. 28, 1849, Lieber MSS.

[7] Sumner to Mrs. George Bancroft, Jan. 24, 1849, Bancroft MSS.

hearts of friends grow cold; but the consciousness of duty done will be sweeter than the applause of the world, than the countenance of companion, or the heart of friend." [8]

• 5 •

The outcome of the 1848 election posed political as well as personal problems for Sumner. Massachusetts Free Soil leaders were sharply divided over the future course of their party. The more distinguished Conscience Whigs, such as Adams, Phillips, and Dana, wanted the party to maintain an absolutely independent course, without "*making terms*" with either Democrats or Whigs.[9] They were proud of the nearly 40,000 votes the new party had attracted in its first presidential contest. Its following was well distributed throughout the state. Van Buren had received an absolute majority of votes in forty-one of the Commonwealth's 312 towns, drawing his heaviest support from the Worcester area in central Massachusetts, which was unhappy at being forcibly drawn into the economic orbit of Boston. Free Soil voting, moreover, followed a pattern that offered considerable promise for the future. Instead of supporting Sumner's theory that antislavery votes came from the declining rural sections of Massachusetts, the election returns showed that the party had won pluralities in only six towns in the three western, most rural counties, but had carried such growing industrial centers as Worcester, Leicester, Fitchburg, and Grafton. Nor, even within the cities, was the Free Soil vote a limited, one-class following. In Boston, for example, Sumner's vote was widely scattered, coming about equally from rich and poor wards, from native American and heavily Irish precincts. There was, in other words, opportunity in Massachusetts for a broadly based, permanent Free Soil party to develop, if only it kept itself unentangled.[1] "The truth is," said Adams, one of the

[8] Sumner to Samuel Lawrence, Nov. 29, 1848, copy, Sumner MSS.

[9] Dana, Diary, Sept. 9, 1849, Dana MSS.

[1] MS. election returns for gubernatorial and presidential races, 1848, Mass. State Archives; Boston *Republican*, Nov. 15, and 22, 1848. I have found no significant statistical correlation between the percentage of Free Soil votes and the size of towns, their relative rank as manufacturers of woollens, cotton goods, or shoes, or the percentage of foreign-born inhabitants. A ward-by-ward statistical analysis of Sumner's vote in Congressional District No. 1 (Boston) similarly reveals no significant relationship between Free Soil vote and the wealth of the inhabitants (calculated upon the basis of the number of persons per housing

chief advocates of a permanent, independent third party, "the democratic and Whig parties are the Scylla and Charibdis of our principles and we must guard equally against both." [2]

When men like Adams, Phillips, Palfrey, and Dana permitted themselves to contemplate any political alliance, they looked naturally back toward the Whig party, from which they had originally come. They still had friends in the old party. Some of the original Conscience group, like Horace Mann, had never severed Whig connections; fearing to imperil both his much needed congressional salary and his work in Massachusetts education, he had remained neutral in the 1848 presidential campaign. Now that the election was over, Mann counseled the healing of the breach between Free Soilers and Whigs. "With what power such men as Phillips and Palfrey . . . and Sumner, could act upon the whigs," he argued persuasively, "if they did not stand in a hostile attitude toward them?" Even the Cotton Whigs, perturbed by the 1848 defection, were willing to forget the past and welcome the erring brothers home. Winthrop, who had suffered most from the Boston antislavery politicians, wanted to leave the door open to reconciliation; "silence is the best policy," he urged.[3]

But some of the less socially prominent Free Soil politicians, men like Henry Wilson, John B. Alley, Francis W. Bird, and E. L. Keyes, who had performed the ward-by-ward work of organizing the party in 1848, hoped for a very different sort of alliance. Recognizing that practically all the conspicuous orators in the Massachusetts Free Soil movement had come from the Whig party, they also knew that fully forty-five per cent of its voters were former

unit), the number of Irish residents, or the number of foreign-born voters. I do not suggest that the Free Soilers won many converts among the Irish, who later became bitter opponents of all antislavery groups, but in 1848 relatively few Irish were allowed to vote. Francis DeWitt (comp.): *Abstract of the Census of the Commonwealth of Massachusetts . . . 1855* (Boston: William White; 1857); Francis DeWitt (comp.): *Statistical Information Relating to Certain Branches of Industry in Massachusetts . . . 1855* (Boston: William White; 1856); *Report and Tabular Statement of the . . . State Census of Boston, May 1, 1850 . . .* (City Document, No. 42, Boston: John H. Eastburn; 1850). For a careful study of the Irish in Boston politics during this whole period see Oscar Handlin: *Boston's Immigrants, 1790–1865: A Study in Acculturation* (Cambridge: Harvard University Press; 1941), Chap. 7.

[2] Adams, Diary, Oct. 8, 1850, Adams MSS.

[3] Mann to Samuel Downer, Mar. 21, 1850, Mann MSS.; Winthrop to Everett, Jan. 31, 1849, Everett MSS.

Democrats, whose antislavery was merely one plank in their platform of opposition to all special privilege everywhere.[4] "Our beloved Commonwealth is at present governed by as perfect a monied aristocracy as ever existed," one of these embattled equalitarians wrote Palfrey; "wealth and not men governs." These voters were never going to join the Whig party. Instead, they felt, the Free Soilers should combine with the Democrats to "check and alleviate this evil" of moneyed monopoly.[5]

Sumner's position in this intraparty struggle over the future of the Free Soil movement was crucial. As one of the original Conscience leaders, who had repeatedly announced: "I am willing to be in a *minority* in support of our principles," [6] he could have given decisive strength to an independent third-party movement. As he had occupied such a prominent position during three years of warfare against the Cotton Whigs, his colleagues who wished to re-cement the Whig party would first have to gain his consent. To those who favored a coalition with the Democrats, Sumner was even more important. His support would break the united front of old Conscience Whig leaders—Adams, Palfrey, Phillips, Dana, and the rest—opposed to such a fusion. As "the classical ornament of the anti-slavery party," [7] Sumner with his learning and his legal knowledge would give dignity to such a coalition, and his strong personal following among the young men, the women, and the clergymen of the Commonwealth would add to its strength. During the months after the 1848 election, therefore, Sumner was "approached by all parties." [8]

He found all three possibilities attractive. He liked the idea of an independent party; he secretly hankered for a restoration of his ties with Boston Whiggery; but he also thought well of a coalition with the Democrats. Never more than a "weak and passive Whig," he had always leaned slightly toward Democratic economic policies, so far as he understood them. As early as 1837

4 William Gleason Bean: "The Transformation of Parties in Massachusetts . . . from 1848 to 1860" (unpublished Ph. D. dissertation, Harvard Univ.; 1922), pp. 32–3. (Hereafter cited as Bean: "Party Transformations.") For somewhat different figures see Darling: *Political Changes in Massachusetts*, pp. 354–7.

5 James Russell to Palfrey, Dec. 15, 1848, Palfrey MSS.

6 Sumner to Giddings, Feb. 1, 6, and 25, 1847, Sumner MSS.

7 Henry Adams: *Education*, p. 31.

8 Adams, Diary, May 14, 1850, Adams MSS.

he had disagreed with Judge Story's opinion in the Charles River Bridge case, which upheld the rights of corporate monopoly, and had agreed with the Jacksonian view of Chief Justice Taney that economic opportunity should be available to all.[9] More than most Massachusetts Whigs, he had always had friends in the Democratic party, in his own state, in New York, and, most recently, in Ohio, where Salmon P. Chase had just been elected to the Senate by a Democratic-Free Soil coalition.[1] With his growing ambition, Sumner must have realized that an independent antislavery party had no chance to win offices, that he could look to the Whig hierarchy for no future favors, and that fusion with the Democrats could be politically profitable, as it had paid off in the election of Free Soilers to Congress from Connecticut and Vermont, as well as from Ohio.

Shortly after the election of 1848 Sumner began making statements he once would have condemned as Jacksonian demagoguery. He shocked his friends by declaring that American democracy had more to fear "from the corruption of wealth than from mobs." He grew enthusiastic about the European revolutions of 1848, of which he regarded the Free Soil movement as an American counterpart, and hoped that they would destroy the outrageous social and economic injustices that had, to tell the truth, seemed anything but outrageous to him only a few years earlier when he visited England.[2]

Borrowing from the Jacksonian Democrats the idea of equal opportunity and from the French revolutionary spirit the phrase "Equality before the Law," Sumner in 1849 challenged the legality of segregated schools in Boston. In the famous Roberts case, Sumner pointed out the obvious physical inferiority of the school provided for Negroes, but he rested his argument chiefly upon the harmful psychological and sociological consequences of segregation. Anticipating Supreme Court decisions made more than a century later, he argued that both white and Negro children suffered from attending separate schools. Whatever facili-

[9] *MHSP*, XXXV (1901–2), 210–11.

[1] Albert Bushnell Hart (ed.): *Diary and Correspondence of Salmon P. Chase* (*Annual Report of the American Historical Association*, 1902, Vol. II), pp. 183–4; Sumner to Chase, Feb. 27, 1849, Chase MSS., Lib. of Cong.

[2] Pierce, III, 230; Sumner to Longfellow [Jan. 26, 1850], Longfellow MSS.; Sumner to George Sumner, Oct. 23, 1849, Sumner MSS.

ties were provided, "the separate school is not an equivalent. . . . The matters taught in the two schools may be precisely the same, but a school devoted to one class must differ essentially in spirit and character from that Common School known to the law, where all classes meet together in Equality."[3] Though Chief Justice Lemuel Shaw and the Supreme Judicial Court did not adopt these arguments, based as they were on philosophical and psychological grounds rather than on common-law precedents, Sumner was content with his fight. As Palfrey said: "When a question of vast social and constitutional bearings can be thus brought to the responsible decision of the Courts of Justice, there is good hope that the right will prevail." Only six years later the Massachusetts legislature, dominated by Sumner's friends, outlawed racial segregation in all public schools in the Commonwealth.[4]

In his new, equalitarian mood, Sumner did not mind that Whigs branded his opinions as "nothing more or less than old fashioned Jacobinism, or new-fashioned loco-focoism, dressed up in more gentlemanlike habiliments than they were wont to wear." He welcomed "any associates from any quarter." He was sure that the Free Soilers could trust "the instincts of *personal freedom*" among the Democrats to bring them ultimately to the cause of antislavery.[5]

As chairman of the Free Soil state executive committee, Sumner was in a position to help steer the party into the coalition with Democrats, so much desired by Henry Wilson. In an address, "To the Friends of Freedom in Massachusetts," issued just

[3] Sumner: *Works*, II, 327–76. Two recent, careful scholars conclude that "Sumner's argument before Shaw deserves to be included in a volume of great documents on American democracy, for its nobility of sentiment, literary excellence, and grasp of principles which have been validated by modern sociology." Leonard W. Levy and Harlan B. Phillips: "The *Roberts* Case: Source of the 'Separate but Equal' Doctrine," *American Historical Review*, LVI (1956), 510–18.

[4] For Shaw's decision in the *Roberts* case see Helen Tunnicliff Catterall (ed.): *Judicial Cases Concerning American Slavery and the Negro* (Washington: Carnegie Institution; 1936), IV, 512–14. Sumner served without fee in the Roberts case. For further details on this significant case see: Sumner to George Sumner, Dec. 10, 1849, Sumner MSS.; Chase to Sumner, Dec. 14, 1849, ibid.; *The Liberator*, XX (Apr. 26, 1850), 67; XIX (Dec. 7, 1849), 1951; *Eighteenth Annual Report, Presented by the Massachusetts Antislavery Society . . . 1850* (Boston; 1859), p. 48; Palfrey to Sumner, Dec. 12, 1849, Palfrey MSS.

[5] Boston *Republican*, Nov. 12, 1849; Felton to Palfrey, Sept. 13, 1850, Palfrey MSS.; Dana, Diary, Sept. 8, 1849, Dana MSS.

after Taylor's victory in 1848, he stressed that the basic principle of Free Soil was "dear to real Democrats from its connection with the name of Thomas Jefferson," and regularly during the next twelve months he praised "the united regenerated Democracy of the North." [6]

By the 1849 Free Soil state convention Sumner and Wilson were prepared to take the party into a formal alliance with the Massachusetts Democrats. While Wilson managed the floor of the convention, Sumner, as chairman of the committee on resolutions, urged the delegates in opposing slavery not to forget another sort of tyranny, the "selfish, grasping, subtle" money power of the Commonwealth. His resolutions favored "a cheaper system of postage; the abolition of all unnecessary offices and salaries; the election of Post Masters and all other civil officers . . . by the people; the retrenchment of the expenses and patronage of the Federal Government; the improvement of Rivers and Harbors; and . . . the free grant to actual settlers, of reasonable portions of the public lands," and concluded with a fling at "the tendency of the legislation of the Commonwealth to consolidate wealth in corporations." The phrases could have been borrowed from any radical Democratic manifesto of the previous decade, and Massachusetts Whigs saw in Sumner's resolutions "an insidious appeal to class prejudices—an attempt to rouse the hatred of the poor against the rich, and to organize the vulgar passions of envy and jealousy into political action." But, under Wilson's skillful management, the convention, despite some reluctance on the part of Adams and some other former Whigs, swallowed the resolutions without gagging.[7]

When the Massachusetts Democrats, sore because the Southern wing of their party had deserted Cass in 1848 and supported Taylor, simultaneously adopted resolutions affirming opposition "to slavery in every form and color" and declaring that Congress had no power to institute slavery in the territories acquired from Mexico, the groundwork for coalition between the two parties in Massachusetts had been laid.[8]

[6] Boston *Semi-Weekly Republican,* Dec. 28, 1848, and July 25, 1849.

[7] Sumner: *Works,* II, 282–321; C. F. Adams, Diary, Sept. 11–12, 1849, Adams MSS.; Boston *Semi-Weekly Republican,* Sept. 15, 1849; Felton to Palfrey, Sept. 13, 1850, Palfrey MSS.

[8] Bean: "Party Transformations," p. 36.

CHAPTER VIII

A One-Idead Abolitionist Agitator

AS A MORAL movement, our cause naturally appeals to good men of all party complexions," Sumner wrote, just before the 1849 Massachusetts elections. "With us fusion is complete." The election returns proved him a bad prophet. Arrangements for the Democratic-Free Soil coalition had been hastily and imperfectly made, and only in some of the eastern counties were formal fusion tickets placed before the voters. Free Soilers of Whig background were distrustful of what the Boston *Atlas* called a "corrupt bargain" with their life-long political adversaries. Democrats, too, were suspicious of their new allies. The Whigs carried the state by a heavy plurality, and Free Soil votes declined five per cent from 1848. The only comfort for the coalitionists was the fact that the Democratic and Free Soil votes if combined made up fifty-two per cent of the total. Fusion had not worked, but it was still possible.[1]

• 1 •

National events played directly into the hands of the Massachusetts coalitionists. The Free Soilers had watched unsympathetically as the Taylor administration proved itself incompetent to handle the delicate issues arising from the Mexican War. Dis-

[1] Sumner to Chase, Sept. 18, and 25, 1849, Chase MSS., Lib. of Cong.; Boston *Atlas*, Oct. 22, and 25, and Nov. 1, 1849; MS. election returns, 1849, Mass. State Archives.

counting Southern threats of secession, they, like many Massachusetts Democrats and Whigs, thought that the compromise measures Henry Clay proposed in January 1850 were quite unnecessary concessions to the slaveholders. Sumner was especially aggrieved by the harsh new fugitive slave bill, which was a part of the compromise, and he urged Free Soilers not to "sacrifice one jot or tittle of our principles" even to conserve the Union.[2] Naturally, therefore, antislavery men were horrified when Daniel Webster, on March 7, endorsed Clay's proposals in a massive oration designed to foster national feeling and allay sectional strife.

For once Massachusetts was virtually unanimous in disapproving the course of her distinguished senator. Antislavery men compared his placating of the Southerners to "the ineffable meanness of the lion turned spaniel in his fawnings on the masters whose hands he was licking for the sake of the dirty puddings they might have to toss to him." Sumner agreed that Webster was an "archangel ruined" or "a traitor to a holy cause," comparable only to Judas Iscariot, Strafford, or Benedict Arnold.[3] It was more significant that Boston Whiggery, though, of course, in gentlemanly tones, disapproved of Webster's course as "madness." The powerful Boston *Atlas* openly criticized the Seventh of March speech; not a member of the Massachusetts congressional delegation defended the Senator's views; Winthrop said Webster's speech "would have killed any Northern man except himself." [4]

Angered by opposition to his opinions, Webster vigorously backed the compromise measures and publicly informed Massachusetts that it must conquer its "prejudices" against a strong fugitive slave act. He was furious over Winthrop's mild dissent from his position, and announced that he would "much prefer to see a respectable Democrat elected to Congress, than a professed Whig, tainted with any degree of Free Soil doctrines, or aboli-

[2] Sumner to Palfrey, Feb. 15, 1850, Palfrey MSS.; Adams: *Dana*, I, 172; Boston *Semi-Weekly Republican*, Mar. 2, 1850.

[3] Nevins: *Ordeal of the Union*, I, 291; Pierce, III, 213–14.

[4] T. N. Brewer to William Schouler, Mar. 8, 1850, William Schouler MSS.; Godfrey Tryggve Anderson: "The Slavery Issue as a Factor in Massachusetts Politics from the Compromise of 1850 to the Outbreak of the Civil War" (unpublished Ph. D. dissertation, Univ. of Chicago; 1944), p. 12; Everett, Diary, May 2, 1850, Everett MSS.

tionism." After the sudden death of Taylor, when the new President Millard Fillmore named Webster Secretary of State, adherence to the compromise measures became the test of genuine Massachusetts Whiggery.[5]

The result was to close the door to any possible return of Free Soil dissidents to the Whig party. On the contrary, Webster did all he could to oust from the party men like Horace Mann, who were infected with the antislavery heresy. When the governor appointed Winthrop to succeed Webster in the Senate, and a new election for congressman had to be held in the Suffolk district, Webster personally intervened to keep the Boston Whigs from naming an uncommitted candidate, who might be acceptable to the Boston *Atlas* and other dissidents, and forced the selection of Samuel A. Eliot, Sumner's opponent in the prison discipline quarrels, who was known to endorse every one of the compromise measures, including the fugitive slave act.[6]

To oppose Eliot, the Boston Free Soilers once more nominated Sumner. He had not the slightest hope of winning, for he considered Webster's Seventh of March speech as part of the wave of reaction sweeping over both America and Europe after the liberal strivings of 1848. Still, he announced, his sense of duty did not permit him to refuse any service to the cause of liberty. Other Free Soilers showed a remarkable indifference to his candidacy. A scheduled rally at Faneuil Hall had to be canceled because the invited speakers, "pleading it was no use to waste their breath in such uphill work," did not attend, and his entire campaign consisted of newspaper publication of a rather tepid letter of endorsement by Richard Henry Dana, Jr., and a more vigorous one from David Wilmot. Sumner received fewer than 500 votes.[7]

Eliot's victory, which showed that Webster was firmly in control of Massachusetts Whiggery and that reconciliation with

[5] Webster to "My Dear Sir" [Aug. 11, 1850], Webster MSS., Dartmouth Coll.; Phil Shelton to S. Draper, May 9, 1850, Thurlow Weed MSS.; Webster to Fillmore, Oct. 14, 1850, Fillmore MSS.

[6] Boston *Atlas*, Aug. 14, 1850; Samuel Downer to Mann, Aug. 7, 1850, Mann MSS.

[7] Sumner to William Bates and James W. Stone, Aug. 12, 1850, MS., Boston Public Lib.; Samuel Downer to Mann, Aug. 16, 1850, Mann MSS.; Adams, Diary, Aug. 14, 1850, Adams MSS.; Boston *Traveller*, Aug. 17, 1850; Boston *Atlas*, Aug. 20, 1850.

the Conscience junto was ruled out, strengthened Wilson's desire for a fusion with the Democrats. During the summer of 1850 Sumner's office was the scene of frequent and often acrimonious meetings of the Free Soil leaders. As the fall elections would determine the naming not merely of the next governor, lieutenant governor, president of the state senate, and speaker of the house of representatives, but also of the United States senator to succeed Winthrop, Wilson wanted a formal coalition with the Democrats. Virtually all the original Conscience Whig leaders, who considered Massachusetts Democrats "the shameless apologists of . . . extreme profligacy," condemned such a scheme as "a renunciation of all moral character." So strong were Adams, Dana, and Palfrey against fusion that Wilson, rather than split the party, finally dropped his plan, and on September 10 the caucus compromised on a milk-and-water resolution "forbidding the central organization [of the Free Soil party] from any action [in support of coalition], . . . and leaving the individuals in the minor elections to act as they may deem most advisable." [8]

In all these negotiations Sumner's role was ambiguous. A far better politician than even his friends believed, he knew the advantages of rowing toward his objective with muffled oars. Though aware of Sumner's theoretical faith in the instincts of the Democracy, Adams, Dana, and Palfrey thought that he was opposed to coalition; he always said that any union with the Democrats must be upon the basis of Free Soil principles. He wrote a letter to Wilson, intended to be read at the Free Soil caucus, discouraging "any departure from our customary course, which did not enlist the sympathies of all who have thus far acted together in our movement." He thought it "a step of questionable propriety for our State Committee . . . to enter into an arrangement . . . with the Democrats as to the disposition of offices," and announced that he was "unwilling to be a party to any such bargain." [9]

But, even while making public disclaimers, Sumner was quietly co-operating with Wilson's plans. He left town so as not to be present at the September 10 caucus, where he would have

[8] Samuel Downer to Mann, Aug. 21, 1850, Mann MSS.; Adams, Diary, Aug. 10, and Sept. 10, 1850, Adams MSS.

[9] Sumner to Wilson, Sept. 9, 1850, in Boston *Journal*, Mar. 16, 1874.

had to show his hand, and his letter opposing coalitions, a convenient thing to have on record and one which Wilson carefully preserved, was deliberately not read to the assembled Free Soil leaders. Sumner's closest political friends, who were the most active promoters of the coalition, let the party work horses know, unofficially but definitely, that he was behind the plan.[1]

Adams judged that Sumner, in these maneuvers, exhibited "some want of character," but it is more realistic to assume that he was, as he later admitted, "swept along by the current without looking at these things as he should have done."[2] Uncertain in his own mind about the propriety of a coalition, he found it easy to agree both with Adams's theory and with Wilson's practice.

Unconsciously, personal considerations swung him over to Wilson's side. In all plans for dividing the spoils with the Democrats, the Free Soil managers expected to secure the full-term United States senatorship, and as early as August 1850 Sumner was mentioned as the most likely nominee, the only prominent Conscience Whig whom Democrats could stomach. Careful never to mention his aspirations, Sumner began behaving suspiciously like a candidate. Protesting that public office was not within the field of his ambition, he nevertheless admitted that it "can be welcome when it comes entirely unsought," and reflected that the Senate chamber was "a mighty pulpit from which the truth can be preached."[3] In case anyone had forgotten that Sumner had never been a strong Whig and had often co-operated with the Democrats, the two handsomely bound volumes of his speeches, which he published at this strategic time, proved the point.[4] And, on a long summer's evening at Swampscott beach, he allowed John Greenleaf Whittier to convince him that if duty called, he could not refuse to have his name considered for high office.[5]

At the state Free Soil convention, which met in Boston on

[1] Samuel Downer to Mann, Sept. 3, 1850, Mann MSS.; Adams, Diary, Sept. 2, and Nov. 16, 1850, Adams MSS.

[2] Adams, Diary, Oct. 12, 1850, and Jan. 12, 1851, Adams MSS.

[3] Sumner to Greene, Nov. 2, 1849, Greene MSS.; Sumner to George Sumner, Apr. 18, 1849, Sumner MSS.; Sumner to Howe, Aug. 27, 1850, ibid.; Pierce, III, 212.

[4] *Orations and Speeches* (2 vols.; Boston: Ticknor, Reed, and Fields; 1851).

[5] Nason: *Sumner*, p. 142; Whittier to Pierce, Feb. 16, 1878, Pierce MSS.; Samuel T. Pickard: *Life and Letters of John Greenleaf Whittier* (Boston: Houghton Mifflin Co.; 1907), I, 351, 355–6; John A. Pollard: *John Greenleaf Whittier: Friend of Man* (Boston: Houghton Mifflin Co.; 1949), pp. 217–19.

October 3, Sumner made what was virtually an announcement of his candidacy in a speech that attempted simultaneously and somewhat contradictorily to prove that he was willing to co-operate with the Democrats and that his antislavery principles were simon-pure.[6] His theme was the new Fugitive Slave Act, adopted with the approval of Daniel Webster. One of the worst measures in history, it ranked with the tyranny of Appius Claudius, Louis XIV, Charles I, and George III. President Millard Fillmore in signing it had sunk to the "depths of infamy." "Better far for him had he never been born; better far for his memory, and for the good name of his children, had he never been President!" Sumner proclaimed. The fugitive slave bill—Sumner would never call it an act of Congress because he thought it unconstitutional and hence void—would never be executed in Boston. Public opinion, "like the flaming sword of the cherubim at the gates of Paradise, turning on every side, . . . shall prevent any SLAVE-HUNTER from ever setting foot in this Commonwealth."

Turning from the wrongs of the past to a program for the future, Sumner called for the abolition of the fugitive slave laws, the end of slavery in the District of Columbia, the exclusion of slavery from all the national territories, the abolition of the domestic slave trade, and the overthrow of the slave power in politics, "so that the Federal Government may be put openly, actively and perpetually on the side of Freedom." To these labors he welcomed "men of all parties and pursuits, who wish well to their country, and would preserve its good name." Of their candidates the people should demand not party allegiance, but "tried character and inflexible will." "Three things at least they must require; the first is *back-bone;* the second is *back-bone;* and the third is *back-bone.*" [7]

[6] Sumner seems to have made virtually the same speech at the Free Soil convention in Boston on October 3, 1850 (*Orations and Speeches,* II, 396–420) and at the Faneuil Hall rally to ratify the Free Soil nominations on November 6 (*Works,* II, 398–424; Boston *Traveller,* Nov. 11, 1850). The speech combined phrases and ideas he had repeatedly tested on previous public occasions (Cf. *Works,* II, 423; Boston *Republican,* Nov. 12, 1849). The quotations in the following paragraphs are from *Orations and Speeches,* II, 403, 408, 412, 415, 418, and 420.

[7] Here again Sumner was using a catchy phrase he had often previously tested. Cf. Pierce, III, 214, 219, 278. He must have been disconcerted by the fact that Joshua Leavitt, who preceded him in addressing the Free Soil convention, also stressed the need for "backbone."

Sumner's speech was received with vast enthusiasm, partly because he was known to be in favor of coalition, but the Adams-Palfrey-Dana bloc was still strong enough to block Wilson's plans for running a joint ticket with the Democrats.[8] In the campaign that followed the nominations, state-wide fusion was quietly abandoned; Democrats and Free Soilers in many towns co-operated in selecting candidates for local offices, but technically and officially their alliance extended no further. When the votes were counted, the Whigs had a heavy plurality, but the Democrats and Free Soilers together had a slight majority of all votes. As no candidate for governor or lieutenant governor received a majority, the election fell to the state legislature, where no party had clear control.

• 2 •

If the state government was to be organized, two of the three parties had to work together. Delighted with the outcome of the election, Wilson, Keyes, and Bird reverted to their idea of sharing offices with the Democrats. During the six weeks following the election, there was much buzzing back and forth between Free Soil and Democratic headquarters, and a plan was readied for presentation to the legislative caucuses of the two parties, held on the last day of 1850. With Free Soil backing, the Democrats would elect their candidate for governor, George S. Boutwell, the lieutenant governor, the speaker and other officers of the House of Representatives, a majority of the governor's council; in addition they would receive the short-term United States senatorship, the few remaining weeks of Webster's term which Winthrop was filling. The Free Soilers would get the presidency of the state senate, the remaining members of the governor's council, and the six-year United States senatorship, commencing March 4. On January 7 a Free Soil caucus, by a vote of eighty-four to one, nominated Sumner senator, and the following day the Democrats, with only six dissenting votes, accepted him.[9]

[8] Adams, Diary, Oct. 3, 1850, Adams MSS.

[9] For a detailed history of the coalition see Henry Wilson's article in the Boston *Commonwealth*, Jan. 30, 1851. Two senatorial elections were before the legislature, one short-term, to replace Winthrop, whose appointment expired with the assembling of the legislature, the other for the same seat for the six-year term beginning March 4, 1851. Robert S. Rantoul, a Democrat, was elected for the short term.

As the details of these arrangements became public, Massachusetts erupted in a blaze of denunciation of this "contemptible coalition," which was "usurping power in opposition to the will of a majority of the people." It is hard to believe that this tone of outraged surprise was genuine. Insiders had known even the details of the proposed coalition as early as August 1850. Despite the official silence of the Free Soil convention, their campaign sheet, which Bird edited, had openly announced that the antislavery men would give state offices to the Democrats if they could have the triumph of electing a Free Soiler to the seat of Daniel Webster. The Democratic state convention had explicitly endorsed coalition. These plans certainly were not concealed from the Whigs. The Whig state central committee, on November 8, had issued a circular urging every Massachusetts businessman "to use all the influence he can over those in his employ, or in any way under his control" to crush the Democratic-Free Soil coalition at the polls. Throughout the campaign, Whig papers grimly anticipated that Free Soilers would support a series of Democratic reform measures—amending the state constitution, limiting the hours of workingmen, changing the charter of Harvard College—in order to exclude Winthrop from the Senate and choose "some one inferior in ability and influence" in his stead.[1]

Nor was the identity of that "some one" much in doubt. Sumner's name was mentioned during the canvass as the likely Free Soil candidate, and when he heard the election returns, he told Longfellow that he would probably be the next senator. On the day after the election, Seth Webb, Jr., one of Sumner's young Free Soil admirers, dashed off a note to him:

> I called to tell you *such* good news. We have
> carried everything in the state—senate sure,
> house nearly certain, Governor, *Senator* and all—
> You are bound for Washington this winter.[2]

1 Springfield *Republican*, Jan. 10, 1851; Boston *Advertiser*, Jan. 10, 1851, and Oct. 9, 1850; Samuel Downer to Mann, Aug. 22, 1850, Mann MSS.; Boston *Commonwealth*, Jan. 14, 1851; Bean: "Party Transformations," p. 57; Thomas Henry O'Connor: "Cotton Whigs and Union: The Textile Manufacturers of Massachusetts and the Coming of the Civil War" (unpublished Ph. D. dissertation, Boston Univ.; 1958), p. 125; Boston *Atlas*, Oct. 12, 1850.

2 Longfellow, Diary, Nov. 10, 1850, Longfellow MSS.; Seth Webb, Jr., to Sumner [Nov. 1850], Sumner MSS.

If the surprise over the division of spoils was somewhat spurious, the anger was entirely real. Henry Wilson's maneuver had the effect of splitting all three of the state parties. The Whigs had the least difficulty assuming a public attitude toward the coalition. Their newspapers denounced it as "a combination of opposing elements, like oil and water," having "no principle in common but the spoils of office." The most "dishonorable, disgraceful and immoral" means were being used to make Sumner senator; if he should be elected, his only claim to his seat would be "that he was ignobly shuffled through the forms of an election, by the machinery of a political gambling table." [3]

In private, however, the Whig position was a good deal more complex. Though about 165 Whigs in the House of Representatives could be counted on to support Winthrop in ballot after ballot, most were less than enthusiastic about their candidate. The Boston wing of the party was "heart and soul" behind Daniel Webster, who demanded total acquiescence in the Compromise of 1850 and blamed Winthrop's failure to endorse the Fugitive Slave Act for the Whig defeat at the polls. Indeed, Winthrop seemed so badly tinged with abolitionism that some of Webster's supporters actually preferred Sumner, "on the desperate grounds of *the worse, the better*." Keeping a close watch on Massachusetts affairs and purging from federal office any daring souls who supported Sumner, Webster himself wished to lead Massachusetts Whigs into a new political organization "of Union men of all parties." Hence Webster's supporters showered social attentions upon Governor Boutwell, whose inaugural message gratifyingly endorsed the compromise, and praised the "highly honorable" course of Democrats opposed to the coalition.[4]

More numerous, but less highly placed, were the Massachu-

[3] Boston *Advertiser*, Jan. 7, and 18, 1851; Boston *Courier*, Jan. 16, 1851.

[4] E. M. Wright to H. L. Dawes, Nov. 27, 1850, Dawes MSS.; Webster to Fillmore, Apr. 13, 1851, and Nov. 18, 1850, Fillmore MSS.; A. A. Lawrence to Charles Devens, Feb. 17, 1851, copy, Lawrence MSS.; Moses Stuart to Webster, Apr. 18, 1851, Webster MSS., Dartmouth Coll.; Winthrop to Julius Rockwell, July 31, 1851, Julius Rockwell MSS.; Webster to Peter Harvey, May 4, 1851, copy, Everett MSS.; Edward Casneau to J. A. Andrew, Mar. 30, 1861, Andrew MSS.; Van Tyne (ed.): *Webster Letters*, p. 445; Boston *Courier*, Jan. 17, 1851; A. A. Lawrence to Boutwell, Jan. 17, 1851, copy, Lawrence MSS.; Boutwell to Lawrence, Jan. 23, 1851, ibid.; Samuel Bridge to Caleb Cushing, Feb. 19, 1851, Cushing MSS.; *The Liberator*, XXI (Jan. 24, 1851), p. 13.

setts Whigs who felt that Webster's course was ruinous, that Winthrop could never be elected, and that an understanding should be reached with Free Soilers of Whig background. George Morey, chairman of the Whig state central committee, speaking for the majority of the Whigs outside of Boston, spread the word that many Whigs might be willing to support Charles Francis Adams for the Senate.[5]

Democratic difficulties were equally intense and far more difficult to conceal. Without question, most Massachusetts Democrats favored coalition as "the only means available to break down a dynasty of wealth and aristocracy, such as existed no where else in this country; and the only mode of securing a new constitution, and certain important reforms in [the] state legislation; and by changing the public officers throughout the state, to equalize political power, and teach a class of men for the first time that their right to office was not hereditary and perpetual." The United States senatorship was not of great importance to these Democrats, but, of the possible Free Soil nominees, Sumner was their "decided favorite," as party managers promised that he was sound on *"all the great measures of Democracy,* from Jefferson's time downward." [6]

But a powerful, articulate Democratic minority, led by Caleb Cushing, objected to sending "a red-hot Abolitionist, . . . like a firebrand, for six years, into the senate chamber of the United States." Shrewdly keeping quiet during the preliminary negotiations, Cushing gave tacit consent to the coalition until the Free Soilers helped elect Boutwell governor; he then called his friends into a separate caucus and announced that the election of a "one-idead abolitionist agitator" like Sumner would be a "death-stab to the honor and welfare of the Commonwealth." Cushing's thirty-odd "Indomitables" held the balance of power between Sumner and Winthrop. For a time Cushing considered promoting his own election to the Senate; then he planned to run the conservative Whig, Edward Everett; but mostly he used his power, with

[5] Adams, Diary, Nov. 16, 1850, and Feb. 6, 1851, Adams MSS.; Springfield *Republican,* Jan. 31, 1851.

[6] Samuel Downer to Mann, Dec. 15, 1850, and Jan. 9, 1851, Mann MSS.; Whiting Griswold in Boston *Post,* Mar. 20, 1855; Springfield *Republican,* Feb. 8, 1851. Cf. Fred Harvey Harrington: *Fighting Politician: Major General N. P. Banks* (Philadelphia: University of Pennsylvania Press; 1948), pp. 10–13.

great effect, to intimidate the coalitionist Democrats. Under his pressure, backed by stern letters from Cass and other leading Democrats, Boutwell, who had been elected by Free Soil votes, announced: "I am not pledged to elect Mr. Sumner, I am not pledged to defeat him. The subject is in the control of the Legislature." [7]

The Free Soilers were better able to keep their legislative delegation in line behind the coalition, but behind the scenes they, too, were seriously split. For the former Democrats in the party, ex-Governor Marcus Morton objected that Wilson seemed determined "to exclude every Freesoil democrat from any important office." The senatorship was Morton's special grievance. Sumner, who "had genius but not the soundest judgment . . . learning but not practical knowledge," was a Whig. Privately Morton lobbied with the Free Soilers of Democratic extraction, and publicly he urged the legislature to reject all "*caucusses* [*sic*], *compromises* and *coalitions*." [8]

Considerably more influential was the continuing opposition of the former Conscience Whigs who had all along fought coalition and who resented Wilson's leadership of the Free Soil party, S. C. Phillips exhibited "considerable jealousy" over the pertinacity with which Sumner's name was pressed for the senatorship, to the exclusion of older and more prominent members of the party, like himself.[9] Palfrey, too, continued to fight the coalition. Scheduled to become editor of the new Free Soil newspaper, the *Commonwealth*, which was to start publication in Boston on January 1, 1851, Palfrey, in December, circulated a printed letter to all members of the incoming General Court. He opposed voting for Boutwell; he thought the importance of having an anti-

[7] Samuel Dexter Bradford: *Works* (Boston: Phillips, Sampson & Company; 1858), p. 294; T. J. Whittemore to Cushing, Nov. 29, 1850, Cushing MSS.; Boston *Post*, cited in Boston *Advertiser*, Jan. 8, 1851; Boston *Transcript*, Mar. 13, 1851; Everett, Diary, May 15, 1851, Everett MSS.; Boutwell: *Reminiscences of Sixty Years in Public Affairs* (New York: McClure, Phillips & Co.; 1902), I, 119. Cf. Claude M. Fuess: *The Life of Caleb Cushing* (New York: Harcourt, Brace & Co.; 1923), II, 100–4.

[8] Marcus Morton, Letterbooks, III, 60, 62, 89, 90–1; Morton: *Letter Addressed to the Free Soil and Democratic Members of the Legislature of Massachusetts* (Taunton; 1851), p. 7; Boston *Commonwealth*, Mar. 18, 1851. In a letter to Sumner (Mar. 12, 1851, Sumner MSS.) Morton denied lobbying against his election.

[9] Springfield *Republican*, Jan. 1, 1851. Cf. Phillips to Sumner, Jan. 9, and 12, 1851, Sumner MSS.; Adams, Diary, Jan. 9, 10, and 12, 1851, Adams MSS.

slavery senator "overrated," as his influence would be "very much crippled" by the manner of his election, and his protests against slavery would in any case "be crushed under an overwhelming proslavery majority" in Washington. He counseled the Free Soilers to keep their principles untarnished and to wait for another election.[1]

Palfrey's attack not merely disrupted plans for the *Commonwealth,* which had hastily to be entrusted to the less skillful editorial team of Bird, Richard Hildreth, and Elizur Wright, but it almost split the Free Soil party. His letter was known to have the support both of Richard Henry Dana and of Charles Francis Adams,[2] who was at a critical moment in his career. Disliking the state-wide coalition, and confessing a "lurking jealousy of Sumner's purity of purpose," Adams thought that he could probably be elected to the Senate himself with Whig support. After some soul-searching, he concluded that it would not be fitting for an Adams to be party to such a scheme: to Sumner, "who is rising in the world a little abrasion of this sort will do no harm, whilst to me who am constantly contrasted with my predecessors, it would be discreditable." Finally convincing himself that Sumner was not intriguing for the office, Adams issued a public letter in which he rejoiced that the present arrangement would elect "one of our ablest and most honest and most inflexible advocates" to the United States Senate, replacing "one, whose loose private and wavering public career has done more . . . to shake the principles and unsettle the highest policy of puritan New England than that of any man known to its history." [3]

• 3 •

In all these crosscurrents of politics, Sumner maintained an attitude of reserve bordering upon indifference. "I was brought forward contrary to my express desires," he wrote his brother. "The nomination was forced upon me." Phillips or Adams, his "seniors

[1] Palfrey: *To the Members of the General Court of Massachusetts for the Year 1851*, a pamphlet marked "Confidential."

[2] Adams and Dana "entirely concurred" in Palfrey's reasoning, but did not favor the distribution of his letter. Adams, Diary, Dec. 26, 1850, Adams MSS.

[3] Adams, Diary, Nov. 14, and 16, 1850; *The Liberator*, XXI (Jan. 17, 1851), p. 9.

and betters" in the Free Soil movement, should have been the party's standard-bearer. "I never directly or indirectly suggested a desire for the place, or even a willingness to take it," he told John Bigelow. "I do not desire to be senator." [4]

Though he had "implicit faith in the propriety of the Coalition," he kept "aloof from all the arrangements at the State House, making no suggestion on any points or persons." Unwilling to solicit the endorsement even of the Free Soilers, he was immovably averse to wooing the Democrats. Four separate Democratic committees called on him. To all he replied: "I do not desire to be Senator. . . . I would not move across the room to take the post. . . . It must seek me—and . . . if it finds me, it will find me *an absolutely independent man,* without any pledge or promise." [5]

With outward equanimity Sumner chronicled the fluctuations in his own fortunes as the two houses of the legislature began their separate ballotings. On the first ballot in the House of Representatives, on January 14, Democratic defections kept him five votes from a majority, and his position did not improve during the next two days, when four additional ballots were taken. Though Wilson was furious, Sumner remained bright and cheerful. He thought the chance for his election now "lost beyond recovery," but declared he felt "no personal disappointments." [6]

When the state senate elected Sumner on January 22, he became cautiously optimistic.[7] But the five ballots held in the House of Representatives on January 23–24 showed that he was still far from election. The Whigs held firmly for Winthrop; the Free Soilers voted unanimously for Sumner, as did most of the Democrats; but between twenty-five and thirty "Indomitable" Democrats, following Cushing, threw away their votes upon other candidates.

While practically all public business in Massachusetts was

[4] Sumner to George Sumner, Feb. 23, 1851, Sumner MSS.; Frank Preston Stearns: *The Life and Public Services of George Luther Stearns* (Philadelphia: J. B. Lippincott Co.; 1907), p. 84; Pierce, III, 233; Bigelow: *Retrospections,* I, 105–6.

[5] Sumner to Dana, [1851], Dana MSS.; Sumner to Mann, Jan. 11, 1851, Mann MSS.; Bigelow: *Retrospections,* I, 106; Boston *Traveller,* Apr. 21, 1874.

[6] Springfield *Republican,* Jan. 15, 1851; Boston *Commonwealth,* Jan. 16, and 20, 1851; Adams, Diary, Jan. 14, 1851, Adams MSS.; Bigelow: *Retrospections,* I, 106.

[7] Richards, *S. G. Howe,* II, 335.

suspended, politicians of all factions attempted to rally their forces. Believing Boutwell "a timid, cunning, time-serving *trimmer*," Free Soilers tried to bully him into support of the coalition, by which his own election had been secured. At the same time they hoped to rally public opinion behind their candidate by publishing fulsome articles in the *Commonwealth* about Sumner's qualifications for office, his unquestioned Americanism, and his reverence for the Constitution and the Union. The Whigs, more practically, started a fund, for which Amos A. Lawrence, Ezra Lincoln, and William Appleton subscribed, to relieve Whig members of the legislature whose businesses at home were suffering during the protracted sessions of the General Court. The fund, Lawrence piously explained, was "not intended to be used for influencing any member in an improper manner," but he confided to Congressman Eliot: "Everything is being done to prevent Sumner's election . . . that can be." [8]

When voting resumed on February 7, Sumner still lacked two votes of election. A week later, on the fourteenth ballot, his strength had declined, and he needed nine votes. Despondent, Sumner wrote a letter to Wilson urging "the friends of Freedom in the Legislature . . . to transfer their support to some other candidate, faithful to our cause." "I have searched my heart, and have its response," he wrote to George at this time. "I do not desire to be Senator. My ambition is to live without office." [9]

Not one of Sumner's friends, and, indeed, few of his opponents, doubted that he was remaining creditably aloof from the election contest. Hillard, now a leading Whig politician, admitted that his former partner "behaved very well" by refusing "to retract any thing, to modify any thing or to promise any thing." Charles Francis Adams, who was not given to kindliness, agreed that it was "impossible for any body to have acquitted himself more honorably under circumstances of great trial." Palfrey, strongly opposed to the whole coalition scheme, wrote Sumner: "No one acquainted with your course in this matter, can ever say that it has not been most high and honorable." [1]

[8] Ibid., II, 338; Boston *Commonwealth*, Feb. 3–6, 1851; Ezra Lincoln and H. J. Gardner to A. A. Lawrence, Feb. 10, 1851, Lawrence MSS.; Lawrence to Ezra Lincoln, Samuel A. Eliot, and William Appleton, Feb. 10, 1851, copies, ibid.

[9] Sumner: *Works*, II, 430; Sumner to George Sumner, Feb. 23, 1851, Sumner MSS.

[1] Hillard to Lieber, Jan. 31, 1851, Lieber MSS.; Adams, Diary, Mar. 16, Apr. 1, and 24, 1851, Adams MSS.; Palfrey to Sumner, Feb. 25, 1851, Palfrey MSS.

At the same time that they credited the purity of Sumner's intention, practically nobody really believed his protestations of not wanting the senatorship. The eagerness with which he followed every detail of the coalition negotiations seemed to Adams to make "his pretensions of utter indifference rather ridiculous." "He is," Adams shrewdly remarked, "manifestly wound up" in desiring the office, "without being himself conscious of it." [2]

There is, in fact, considerable evidence to indicate that Sumner genuinely desired the senatorship and that he did all he honorably could to attain it. Even while he asserted that the senatorship properly belong to Adams or Phillips—both, incidentally, impossible candidates, as they opposed the coalition and were unacceptable to the Democrats—he admitted: "I feel that it would, to a certain extent, be a vindication of me against the attacks to which . . . I have been exposed." Sumner's refusal to dicker with Caleb Cushing reflected his high-spirited independence; but it also showed his political sagacity, as to keep Adams, Palfrey, Phillips, and Dana in the party, he had to convince them that he would maintain Free Soil principles uncontaminated. In January, to counter Marcus Morton's charge that he was a disunionist, Sumner wrote a letter for circulation among the legislators, announcing that he proposed "to wait and work patiently under and through the Constitution" in fighting slavery. The next month, when the Negro Shadrach was seized on the streets of Boston as a fugitive slave, Sumner cautiously declined to assist Dana in defending him because, he frankly admitted, of "the effect it might have on the pending senatorial election." But, when it became clear that Massachusetts opinion was outraged by the arbitrariness and cruelty of the arrest, Sumner apparently decided that high principle was good politics. In the next fugitive slave case, in early April, he instantly came to the defense of Thomas Sims and helped, unsuccessfully, to plead for his release.[3]

Doubtless Sumner was sincere in his February 22 letter, offering to withdraw from the senatorial contest, but he must have

[2] Adams, Diary, Feb. 7, and 29, 1851, Adams MSS. Cf. H. W. Beecher, in New York *Tribune*, May 31, 1856.

[3] Pierce, III, 233; Sumner: *Works*, II, 429; Adams: *Dana*, I, 183; Boston *Courier*, Apr. 12, 1851. On the Sims case see Leonard W. Levy: *Chief Justice Shaw and the Law of the Commonwealth* (Cambridge: Harvard University Press; 1957), pp. 92–104.

known that his declination would not be accepted. Though a number of Free Soilers began to murmur: "If we cant get Sumner, we must go for some one whom we can elect," everybody recognized that Phillips, the only other candidate seriously mentioned, would draw even fewer Democratic votes than Sumner. The Free Soilers, as Adams pointed out, had no choice but "to sustain their candidate until they get assurances from either side that they can elect another, who will suit them." Sumner's withdrawal was, accordingly, suppressed.[4]

Unresolved and apparently unresolvable, the senatorial deadlock continued through March and well into April. The House of Representatives took occasional votes, but Sumner came no nearer a majority. Violent charges and countercharges were hurled back and forth in the legislature. The Free Soilers blamed that "slimy snake" Marcus Morton for the stalemate, and Henry Wilson published a blast at the ex-governor's "croaking, paltering . . . duplicity." On both sides there were accusations of corruption. The Whigs were charged with employing their vast resources to buy up legislators, and the coalitionists, in return for votes for Sumner, were said to have pledged a $2,000,000 state loan to the Troy and Greenfield Railroad, which was trying to tunnel under the Hoosac Mountain in order to give northwestern Massachusetts direct railroad connections with New York and the West.[5]

The truth of such charges, so freely made through the protracted balloting, is difficult to ascertain. Wealthy Whigs did subscribe funds to charter special trains for bringing in absent members of the legislature, to pay their expenses while in Boston, and to stir up anticoalition sentiment in town meetings, but the amounts involved were so small and the records of the transactions were so publicly kept that it is hard to think of this as actual bribery.[6] The story connecting the Free Soilers with the Hoo-

[4] Charles Allen to Sumner, Feb. 7, 1851, Sumner MSS.; Richards: *S. G. Howe*, II, 341; Howe to Palfrey, Feb. 13, 1851, Palfrey MSS.; Adams, Diary, Mar. 19, 1851, Adams MSS.

[5] Richards: *S. G. Howe*, II, 344; Boston *Commonwealth*, Feb. 22, Mar. 18, and 25, 1851; Boston *Transcript*, Mar. 14, 1851; Springfield *Republican*, Apr. 2, 1851; Boston *Advertiser*, Apr. 3, 1851.

[6] Ezra Lincoln to A. A. Lawrence, Mar. 7, 1851, Lawrence MSS.; memorandum, listing donors and amounts, Mar. 14, 1851, ibid. The sum subscribed was only $500.

sac tunnel scheme, which was to drain the Massachusetts treasury for the next quarter of a century, is almost certainly false. In private correspondence both Whigs and "Indomitable" Democrats declared that the report deserved "no Credit whatever." [7]

A larger issue was the Whig contention that the coalition itself was corrupt. If the charge was correct, the guilt of the Free Soilers was not palliated by the fact that similar coalitions were occurring in other states. Nor was it an extenuating circumstance that some of the Whigs had themselves contemplated just such a coalition with the Free Soilers or that Webster wished a union with conservative Democrats. Nor were Sumner's skirts cleared by the fact that he had not personally arranged or intrigued for his nomination. After all, as William Kent caustically reminded him, he could not have been run against his will, or, as gruff Francis Lieber put it, a man whose house is being used as a brothel is not innocent because he claims ignorance of that fact.[8]

But the Whig accusation was based upon two premises—that the senatorship was the chief goal of the coalition, and that the Free Soil and Democratic parties shared no principles—and neither was true. Most of the Democrats thought reform of the Massachusetts state government the essential object of the coalition; they were willing to surrender the senatorship to the Free Soilers because it was not important or useful in their plans of state reform. Many of the Massachusetts Free Soilers had originally been Democrats, and they shared that party's hostility to the "money power" in the Commonwealth, and, on the other hand, the Democrats—like practically all citizens of Massachusetts—shared the Free Soilers' opposition to the further extension of slavery. It seemed equitable, therefore, that the Democrats, interested in state reform, should get the state offices, and the Free Soilers, interested in the national question of slavery, should get the senatorship. The resulting union had about as much coherence of principle as any major American party ever does—and rather more than the Whig party in Massachusetts

[7] W. A. Hawley to H. L. Dawes, Apr. 5, 1851, Dawes MSS.; D. N. Carpenter to Caleb Cushing, Apr. 21, 1851, Cushing MSS.

[8] William Kent to Sumner [Oct. 1851], Sumner MSS.; Lieber to Hillard, Jan. 30, 1852, Lieber MSS.

had at this time. Inexpedient and unwise the coalition may have been, but not corrupt.[9]

If the Whig charge that the coalition was "unprincipled" was not tenable, the Free Soil counterclaim that some weighty principle of antislavery was involved in Sumner's election was equally dubious. Whatever idealism the Free Soilers may have had in the beginning had disappeared by the time two dozen ballots were taken, each followed by higgling for office and spoils. As their moral fervor effervesced, Free Soil leaders behaved, said Hillard, "like a woman, who has sold her person for money, going the next morning and . . . saying 'I was a virgin and I agreed to sleep with you for so many dollars and I have slept with you and now I want you to pay me.' "[1]

With diminishing hopes and waning enthusiasm, the struggle continued through April. The Webster Whigs were immovable, wanting nothing more than to prevent any election at all, expecting that the fall elections would bring in an anticoalition legislature.[2] Cushing, whose wing of the Democratic party depended upon national patronage, was equally inflexible; the fall elections meant nothing to him. But the majority of the Democrats and the Free Soilers were becoming desperate; in only a few weeks the legislature would have to adjourn, without having passed any significant legislation, without having secured any state reforms, and without even having elected a senator. On such a record, defeat would be certain in November.

When balloting was resumed on April 23, there were slight indications that a break might be in sight. During the three weeks since the last vote, Free Soilers had been agitating to have town meetings instruct their representatives to vote for Sumner, and at least one Whig, the member from Fall River, obeyed the instructions and was now ready to vote for the coalition candidate. There may have been some outside influence brought on Whig representatives; Thurlow Weed, the Whig boss of New York, was said to have persuaded a few Massachusetts Whigs to vote for Sumner because, as part of a bargain, Free Soilers had

[9] The soundest treatment of the coalition and the senatorial election is Bean: "Party Transformations," Chap. 4.

[1] Hillard to Lieber, Jan. 31, 1851, Lieber MSS.

[2] B. R. Curtis to Webster, Feb. 23, 1851, Curtis MSS.; Abbott Lawrence to Nathan Appleton, Feb. 14, 1851, MS., Houghton Lib.

induced New York "Barnburners" to allow Hamilton Fish to be chosen senator from New York. Not a few Whigs were responsive to such pressure because Webster was now demanding that they abandon Winthrop and vote for a more thoroughgoing advocate of the Compromise of 1850. Rather than kill their party by backing a supporter of the Fugitive Slave Act, these Whigs preferred to see Sumner elected.[3]

With so many subtle forces at work, the political experts were prepared for a shift of votes on the twenty-first ballot, and when it was taken, shortly after noon on April 23, it was announced that Sumner had received 195 votes, a majority of the votes cast, and was elected. Free Soil representatives went "as crazy as a parcel of school boys just entered upon a vacation," and all over the city their supporters began to celebrate. While Sumner was having dinner with the Adamses at their Mt. Vernon Street home, visitors began pouring in to congratulate him. But, as the legislature did not adjourn, doubts about the election began to rise, and young Henry Adams was sent off to the Statehouse to learn the facts. He found that one printed ballot bearing Sumner's name had also been lightly penciled "John Mills, of Springfield." Under Whig pressure this doubtful ballot was given to Mills, the votes were recounted, and Speaker N. P. Banks announced that there was still no choice. As Henry Adams told the news, the Adams family lamented, but "Sumner did not to appearance change a muscle nor a tone." "In self-command," the elder Adams noted admiringly, "he certainly is fit for a politician much more than I am." [4]

The House of Representatives took two more ballots that day, all marked by great irregularities. On one of them there were two more votes than there were legislators. Coalitionists accused Whigs, and Whigs blamed coalitionists. Whoever was at fault, Sumner was no nearer election.

On April 24 the legislature reassembled in an atmosphere of great tension. On the twenty-fifth ballot there were again two

[3] George F. Hoar: *Autobiography of Seventy Years* (New York: Charles Scribner's Sons; 1903), I, 186; John Bigelow to Sumner, Apr. 2 [1851], Sumner MSS.; Springfield *Republican*, Apr. 25, 1851; Thomas M. Foote to Millard Fillmore, May 2, 1851, Fillmore MSS.; Adams, Diary, Apr. 23, 1851, Adams MSS.

[4] Boston *Advertiser*, Apr. 23, 1851; Springfield *Republican*, Apr. 24, 1851; Adams, Diary, Apr. 23, 1851, Adams MSS.

more votes than there were representatives present. After much wrangling, the house adopted a Whig proposal that on future ballots each member must cast his vote in a sealed envelope, so that it would be impossible for these extra ballots to be slipped in. Shortly after noon, the twenty-sixth ballot was taken. This time Sumner received 193 of the 385 votes cast, a majority of precisely one, and was declared elected.[5]

While great excitement prevailed at the State house, Henry Adams, who had been watching the voting attentively, slipped out and ran home to inform his parents of the triumph. Sumner was there, seated at the dining table with the Adams family. Breathless, Henry told his glorious news. "It was," he reflected more than half a century later, "probably the proudest moment in the life of either." [6]

While Whigs gloomily remained indoors, throngs of Free Soilers and Democrats began to congregate in the streets. By nightfall perhaps 10,000 people were milling about the *Commonwealth* office on the corner of Washington and State streets; the three upper stories of the building were illuminated, flags were stretched across the streets, and one hundred rockets were sent up to announce the victory. Henry Wilson spoke in praise of the election he, more than any other person, had brought about, and when hecklers interrupted him with shouts for Daniel Webster, the Union, and the Constitution, he turned on them with the taunt: "The victory this day consummated dates from the 7th of March, 1850, when that great man stood up in the Senate and repudiated the long-cherished sentiments of Massachusetts." In

[5] "Election of U. S. Senators in Massachusetts, 1788–1895," in *Massachusetts Year Book,* II (1896), 43–4. After close study of all the extant voting records, I am obliged to conclude with "Warrington" (Springfield *Republican,* Jan. 31, 1863): "It is impossible to tell how the election was finally effected, that is to say, by what change of vote." As all the ballots were secret, as a number of blank ballots were cast, and as there were several absentees, no one can say which person cast the deciding vote that gave Sumner his majority. The calculation of the *Advertiser* (Apr. 25, 1851) that one Whig and two "Indomitable" Democrats voted for Sumner on the last ballot seems plausible. In that case, there is room for the rival claims of Nathaniel Doane, of Harwich, a Whig; of Henry A. Hardy, of South Danvers, a Democrat (Boston *Commonwealth,* Jan. 31, 1863); and of Israel Haynes, of Sudbury, a Democrat (affidavit of Leander Haynes, Jan. 3, 1895, Pierce MSS.)—all of whom said they cast the deciding ballot.

[6] Henry Adams: *Education,* p. 51.

the privacy of his diary, Charles Francis Adams vindictively agreed that the election marked

> the downfall of Mr. Webster. Nothing in the ordinary course of events will now avail to set him up again before nature shall remove him. His career on the whole has been rather that of a mountebank than of a statesman; a moral character degraded by the lowest sensualities and by the upmost rapacity. . . . Not a fit emblem of puritan Massachusetts. Sumner will come much nearer to it.

"The event of this day," Adams predicted, "constitutes probably an era in the present movement." [7]

Massachusetts Whiggery agreed. Webster himself was "grieved and mortified" by the results, and there were long faces and deep swearing in State Street. The day after the election some men, and more children, wore black crepe on their sleeves to commemorate the death of pure government in the Commonwealth. Whig newspapers, almost without exception, deplored the election, through the blackest of frauds, of an impractical theorist opposed to the principles of the American Constitution.[8] Nathan Appleton thought Sumner's election was "the most fatal blow to . . . popular suffrage that [had] been inflicted," and Winthrop felt that Sumner, despite his "professions of purity and disinterestedness," had "done more to demoralize and debauch the young men of our State by his example and by his success, than any man of modern days." In an effort to challenge the validity of Sumner's election, or at least to neutralize in advance any influence he might exert in the Senate, Benjamin R. Curtis drew up a public indictment, signed by all the Whig members of the legislature, denouncing the coalition as "a factious conspiracy," at once immoral and illegal.[9]

7 "The Diary of William Read, a Boston Physician, April, 1851," *Proceedings of the Bostonian Society,* 1902, p. 38; Boston *Commonwealth,* Apr. 25, 1851; Adams, Diary, Apr. 24–5, 1851, Adams MSS.

8 Webster to Stephen M. Allen, June 11, 1851, Webster MSS., Dartmouth Coll.; Hillard to Lieber. Apr. 24, 1851, Lieber MSS.; Nevins: *Ordeal of the Union,* I, 392; Henry Adams: *Education,* p. 51; extracts from the *Atlas, Advertiser,* and *Courier* in Boston *Globe,* Mar. 13, 1874.

9 Nathan Appleton to Fanny Longfellow, May 23, 1851, Appleton MSS.; Winthrop to Hamilton Fish, Apr. 29, 1851, Fish MSS.; Winthrop to Everett, May 21, 1851, Everett MSS.; Everett to B. R. Curtis, May 1, 1851, ibid.; Samuel Hooper to Franklin Haven, May 4 [1851], Webster MSS., Houghton Lib.; Curtis: *To the People of Massachusetts* (Boston; 1851). Curtis (p. 8) argued that the

In the storm of triumph and abuse, Sumner gave not the slightest evidence of personal exultation over the result. Escaping as soon as he could from his congratulating visitors, he fled to the privacy of Longfellow's house in Cambridge, where he remained in retirement during the victory celebrations. Thoroughly exhausted by the prolonged contest, he seemed "more saddened than elated" by success. Sumner thrived under persecution, and flourished when battling overwhelming odds; victory had a flat taste. The responsibilities of his new position already seemed oppressive, and just after the election, he told a young friend: "I am by no means sure this result is best, either for the country or for me." "Most painfully do I feel my inability to meet the importance which has been given to this election and the expectation of enthusiastic friends," he lamented. "If I should fail through faithlessness," he declared, "I feel that I should go far to destroy all confidence in man." [1]

---

coalition was "a misdemeanor, punishable by indictment." Everett tried to persuade Henry Clay to present the Whig protest to the United States Senate. Everett to Clay, Dec. 3, 1851, Everett MSS. Cf. Benjamin R. Curtis, Jr. (ed.): *A Memoir of Benjamin Robbins Curtis* . . . (Boston: Little, Brown & Co.; 1879), I, 138–50.

[1] Longfellow, Diary, Apr. 24–5, 1851, Longfellow MSS.; Fanny Longfellow to Nathan Appleton, May 4, 1851, ibid.; Sumner to Epes Sargent, Apr. 29, 1851, Epes Sargent MSS.; Sumner to C. M. Ellis, Apr. 28, 1851, MS., Mass. Hist. Soc.; A. B. Muzzey: *Reminiscences and Memorials* . . . (Boston: Estes and Lauriat; 1883) p. 224; Pierce, III, 247; Sumner to Mann, Apr. 28, 1851, Mann MSS.

CHAPTER IX

The Slave of Principles

"YOUR PARTING benediction and God-speed, mingling with mother's, made my heart overflow," Sumner wrote his sister Julia as he left for Washington in November 1851 to begin his first session of Congress. "For myself, I do not desire public life; I have neither taste nor ambition for it; but Providence has marked out my career, and I follow." [1] During the months since his election his repugnance for a political career had increased, for he realized that his position in Washington would be ambiguous and difficult. He had been chosen by a coalition widely condemned as unprincipled and immoral. A Free Soiler, he would be a member of a tiny and despised minority in the Senate. With no previous experience in any legislative body, he would be obliged to carry on his antislavery agitation against the opposition of veteran parliamentarians, and at a time when all outstanding national issues appeared to have been settled and when all the leaders of both major parties discountenanced further sectional controversy.

Even the purely formal ceremony of being sworn in as senator, when the first session of the Thirty-Second Congress assembled on December 1, suggested the embarrassments that lay ahead of Sumner. Each of the other five new senators had his credentials presented, as was customary, by his senior colleague from his own state. But "Honest John" Davis, the other Massachusetts senator, perhaps mindful of Webster's fury, overslept

[1] Pierce, III, 259.

that morning, and Sumner was obliged to turn to Michigan's Lewis Cass, his oldest personal acquaintance in the Senate. All the other new senators were introduced with "I beg leave to present . . ." or "I desire to present. . . ." Cass merely announced: "I have been requested to present the credentials of Charles Sumner, a Senator elect from the State of Massachusetts." [2]

• 1 •

Bostonians, said Oliver Wendell Holmes, "all carry the Common in our heads as the unit of space, the State House as the standard of architecture, and measure off men in Edward Everetts as with a yardstick." Comparing Washington with this ideal, Sumner found it sadly wanting. "I am sick at heart with what I see here," he complained only a few weeks after assuming his new duties. "The tone of society . . . is inexpressibly low." There was, in fact, little to commend Washington in the 1850's. From the broken-down hackney coaches that served for public transportation to the huge unfinished Capitol building, everything seemed impermanent and incomplete. "The whole place looks run up in a night," a British observer wrote, "like the cardboard cities which Potemkin erected to gratify the eyes of his imperial mistress on her tour through Russia; and it is impossible to remove the impression that, when Congress is over, the whole place is taken down, and packed up again till wanted." [3]

Making the best of the capital's poor offerings, Sumner rented a bedroom and sitting room in a private house on New York Avenue, between Fourteenth and Fifteenth streets, for which he paid thirty-five dollars a month. As the rooms were "well appointed for Washington, retired, and yet conveniently situated," he felt himself "better lodged than any member of Congress, who has not a house of his own." [4]

Moving to Washington did not alter Sumner's routine of liv-

[2] *Cong. Globe*, 32 Cong., 1 Sess., 2–3.

[3] Morse: *Holmes*, II, 157; Sumner to Dorothea L. Dix, Dec. 26, 1851, Dix MSS.; Edward Dicey: *Six Months in the Federal States* (London: The Macmillan Co.; 1863), I, 93–9. Dicey's description, written during the 1860's, was equally applicable to the previous decade.

[4] Charles Eames to Sumner, Sept. 28, 1851, Sumner MSS.; Sumner to George Sumner, Apr. 19 [1852], ibid.

ing. Rising about seven o'clock each morning, he invariably took a cold-water bath in his hat-shaped tub, shaved with cold water, and set to work as soon as he had dressed. Between eight thirty and nine he had breakfast served him in his rooms, a hearty meal of tea, toast, eggs, fruit, and pancakes and butter. He did not eat again until the evening meal, which in Washington was between four and six. After first trying the food at Willard's Hotel, he arranged a regular mess with Count Sibbern, the Swedish minister to the United States, and Judge John A. Rockwell, of Connecticut, at a nearby French restaurant. Sumner's tastes were simple, but far from ascetic. A porterhouse steak, dressed with oysters and accompanied by bread and butter and a glass of claret, was his standard dinner, though he also liked corned beef and cabbage. Not all the temperance preachments of Horace Mann could make him abstain from wine, but he almost never touched hard liquor. Though he might occasionally light an after-dinner cigar to keep a guest from feeling uncomfortable, he did not smoke or chew tobacco.[5]

Promptly Sumner fell into an unvarying schedule of work. Walking the mile between his lodgings and the Capitol, he made it a point to be in his place each morning when the Senate was called to order, and to stand during the chaplain's prayer. Once in his seat, he remained there, following the debates closely and permitting nothing to distract his attention. Of course, as a freshman member belonging to a third party, he did not have the frequent business visitors who beseiged the more influential senators and summoned them into the corridors for whispered conferences. Nor were the insignificant committee assignments given him—the lowest ranking positions in the revolutionary claims and canals and roads committees—a drain on his time. With little to do but listen and study, Sumner tried to learn the rules of debate and the temper of his associates.

The Senate in 1851 was not a distinguished body. Calhoun

[5] A. B. Johnson: "Recollections of Charles Sumner," *Scribner's Monthly*, VIII (1874), 474–5; Johnson: "Charles Sumner," *Cosmopolitan*, III (1887), 407; IV (1887), 48; G. M. Samson: "Senator Sumner in his Washington Home," Pierce MSS.; Sumner to Longfellow, Jan. 11, 1852, Longfellow MSS.; Sumner to George Sumner, Apr. 19 [1852], Sumner MSS.; Mann to Samuel Downer, Feb. 10, 1852, Mann MSS.

was dead; Clay put in a single appearance, on the day Sumner was sworn in, but took no part in the debates; Webster was in the State Department. Thomas Hart Benton, who had just been defeated for re-election, told Sumner "that he had come to the Senate too late. All the great issues and all the great men were gone. There was nothing left but snarling over slavery, and no chance whatever for a career." [6] As Sumner settled into the Senate seat formerly occupied by Jefferson Davis, of Mississippi, the faces around him seemed to confirm Benton's prognosis. Such mediocrities as Solomon W. Downs, of Louisiana, Thomas J. Rusk, of Texas, and Charles T. James, of Rhode Island, made up most of the Senate.

Besides Sumner, there were only two other Free Soil senators. He doubted the integrity of John P. Hale, of New Hampshire, whose Senate career was more remarkable for his "long speeches, loud professions, Scriptural quotations, funny anecdotes, vehement denunciations" than for any legislative achievements, and could never work closely with him. Salmon P. Chase, of Ohio, with whom Sumner had been co-operating since 1848, was a more reliable ally. Sumner thought him "a tower of strength," whose mere presence would "confirm the irresolute, quicken the indolent, and confound the trimmers," and was pleased to have his Senate seat just in front of Chase's, on the Democratic side of the chamber.[7]

Sumner made only a few friends among the other Northern senators. Cass was too old and too selfish to be more than formally courteous, and Stephen A. Douglas, the leader of the Western Democrats, struck Sumner as a vulgar upstart. The New York senators he liked. In William H. Seward he found "those congenial sentiments, on things higher than party" which made "a peculiar bond of friendship." Though Sumner feared that Seward placed loyalty to the Whig party ahead of antislavery principles, he knew he had a firm ally in Mrs. Seward, who was an outright abolitionist. The aristocratic and wealthy Hamilton Fish,

[6] Haynes: *Sumner*, p. 139.

[7] John T. Morse, Jr. (ed.): *Diary of Gideon Welles, Secretary of the Navy under Lincoln and Johnson* (Boston: Houghton Mifflin Co.; 1909), I, 150; Adams, Diary, Nov. 27, 1852, Adams MSS.; Sumner to Chase, Feb. 7, and 27, 1849, Chase MSS., Lib. of Cong.

of New York, who was also serving his first term, was very cordial to Sumner. Though in private Fish had deplored the defeat of Winthrop, he graciously made Sumner feel almost a member of his Washington household.[8]

Oddly enough it was the Southerners whom Sumner found the best company in Washington. They seemed not to hold his antislavery opinions against him—after all, many Northerners made antislavery speeches when running for Congress—but welcomed him with gracious cordiality. Before long Sumner boasted that Pierre Soulé, the extreme state-rights senator from Louisiana, was his best friend in the Senate: "We deeply sympathize and stand firmly together." Soon he was also on excellent terms with Andrew Pickens Butler, whose seat adjoined Sumner's. The good-natured South Carolina senator took a fancy to his new colleague and frequently asked him to verify classical quotations he planned to use in his speeches. In his stiff Boston way Sumner grew fond of the old man, with his genial red face and his long silver-white hair standing on end, as though charged with electricity; he condescended to say that "if he had been a citizen of New England [Butler] would have been a scholar, or, at least, a well educated man." [9]

Even with Southern women, who dominated Washington society, Sumner was initially popular. They puzzled him, for their lighthearted repartee often went over his humorless head. To a friend who noted his inability to reply to a Southern belle's quips, Sumner confessed as they were walking home after the party: "I have *l'esprit d'escalier* and my retorts do not come until I am well-nigh down the flight of stairs." But, in formal calls, where he could arrange his thoughts in advance, he shone. Carefully not obtruding his antislavery views upon his Southern hostesses, he discoursed with "much Greek fire" and numerous "set pieces." Mrs. Jefferson Davis recalled that he talked learnedly to her of "the Indian mutiny, lace, Demosthenes, jewels, Seneca's morals,

[8] Sumner to Seward, Oct. 22, 1851, Seward MSS.; Fish to Winthrop, Apr. 26, 1851, Winthrop MSS.

[9] Lieber to Hillard, Mar. 2, 1852, Lieber MSS.; Carl Schurz: *The Reminiscences of Carl Schurz* (New York: Doubleday, Page & Company; 1917), II, 35; Ben: Perley Poore: *Perley's Reminiscences of Sixty Years in the National Metropolis* (Philadelphia: Hubbard Brothers; 1886), I, 408–9; James Redpath to Elias Nason, Apr. 10, 1874, MS. owned by Mr. Boyd B. Stutler.

intaglios, the Platonian theory," and once gave her "quite an interesting résumé of the history of dancing." [1]

Though Sumner was sometimes lonely in Washington and often missed the Longfellows and the Howes, he was soon caught up in a faster social whirl than had been his fortune in Boston since 1845. In a single week during his first month in the Senate, for instance, he dined, in succession, with the French minister, President Fillmore, Francis P. Blair, Robert Walsh, and Henry A. Wise.[2] He thrived upon the attentions and compliments that came his way, and his Boston friends found him growing "more egotistical than ever." It was not without cause that the Earl of Carlisle (Lord Morpeth) had warned Sumner after his election to the Senate: "Do not ever get dry, and big, and pompous, like some whom you . . . find your neighbors there." [3]

• 2 •

Sumner was resolved to prove himself no one-idead abolitionist agitator, but a practical, businesslike senator. He spent as much time as possible studying Luther Cushing's *Manual of Parliamentary Procedure*, the *United States Statutes at Large*, and the previous Senate debates recorded in the *Congressional Globe*. As his correspondence increased, he took pride in answering all important letters in his own hand, scrawling off a few widely spaced lines in immediate reply to most inquiries. Normally Sumner worked in his rooms from nine in the evening until midnight, but, when preparing a speech, he would often write all night. With his powerful physique he seemed never to tire, and after a bath and a complete change of clothing, he felt able to work on through the next day.[4]

Sumner was not "anxious to make a display in Congress"

[1] Marian Gouverneur: *As I Remember* . . . (New York: D. Appleton and Company; 1911), p. 243; Varina Howell Davis: *Jefferson Davis* . . . (New York: Belford Company; 1890), I, 557–8.

[2] Sumner to Longfellow [Dec. 28, 1851], Longfellow MSS. Blair was the Democratic strategist, former editor of the *Globe;* Walsh, a literary man who had once edited the *National Gazette;* Wise, a naval officer and Edward Everett's son-in-law.

[3] Adams, Diary, May 23, 1852, Adams MSS.; Carlisle to Sumner, Feb. 29, 1851, Sumner MSS.

[4] *Pierce Dinner*, pp. 58–9; Johnson: "Recollections," *Scribner's Monthly,* VIII (1874), 475–6.

during his first session,[5] but he felt called upon to make his maiden speech as early as December 10. The occasion was the arrival in America of Louis Kossuth, exiled leader of the Hungarian revolution. Whether because of the pathos of the Hungarian cause, Kossuth's unexpected eloquence in English, or the exile's handsome appearance (considerably aided by the black wig that concealed his grizzled hair), Americans went wild about him. Everybody wanted to give him an official welcome to the capital of the United States, but in the Senate the resolutions of greeting became involved with Southern fears that Kossuth was antislavery and with reverence for George Washington's noninterventionist teachings.

Sumner decided that his voice could help settle the controversy, and he made what Charles Francis Adams called an "admirably delivered and very impressive" speech. First he welcomed Kossuth as the servant of Freedom: "Whosoever serves this cause, wheresoever he may be, in whatever land, is entitled . . . to the gratitude of every true American bosom, of every true lover of mankind." But what he gave with one hand, he promptly took away with the other. An official reception for Kossuth, he argued, must not be understood as "encouraging any idea of belligerent intervention in European affairs"—precisely the objective on which Kossuth had come to America.[6]

Though Howe, veteran of Greek and Polish revolutions, protested that this was "the speech of Lawyer Sumner, Senator Sumner—not of generous, chivalrous, high-souled Charles Sumner," champion of liberty, Sumner's first Senate speech was generally received with favor. The friendly Massachusetts *Spy* declared that "his bland manners and deep toned melodious voice" had disarmed all criticism and left "an impression for scholarship, good sense, and soul." [7] Even the Boston *Atlas*, a stanchly Whig paper, joined in the chorus of praise.

"If I were disposed to regard my speech in other light than as a *duty done*," Sumner wrote home complacently, "I might be pleased with what is addressed to me." The elders of the Senate

[5] Ticknor: *Prescott*, p. 355.

[6] Adams, Diary, Dec. 10, 1851, Adams MSS.; Sumner: *Works*, III, 3–9.

[7] Richards: *S. G. Howe*, II, 360; Massachusetts *Spy* (weekly edition), Dec. 31, 1851. C. F. Adams approved the speech; Henry Wilson was disappointed in it.

crowded about him as he finished, beaming congratulations. Southerners like Henry S. Foote, of Mississippi, joined James Shields, of Illinois, in praising the new senator, and Cass condescended to say that he was not ashamed to have presented Sumner's credentials. "Many have told me," Sumner proudly wrote Howe, "that they never saw any senator listened to with superior attention than I was throughout." [8]

Having found his voice, Sumner did not wait long to use it again. In January 1852, when the Senate was discussing a proposed land grant to build a railroad in Iowa, Sumner, to everybody's surprise, joined in the debate as a defender of the project. Doubtless remembering Webster's exposition of New England's friendship for the West, in his Second Reply to Hayne, Sumner announced that it was becoming that he, as "a Senator from one of the old States," should speak in behalf of Iowa. Previously coached by his messmate, Judge Rockwell, he argued that the Western states suffered because the United States government kept the public lands exempt from taxation. As federal gifts of land for schools, asylums, and other purposes did not repay these states for their loss in taxes, they had a claim in equity for grants such as the one under discussion.[9]

This time Sumner's speech did not escape criticism. Senators from the landless states were unenthusiastic about legislation that would benefit only the West. Senator Joseph R. Underwood, of Kentucky, declared that all Sumner's statistics and computations were wrong; in addition, his comparison of the United States public lands to English crown lands, which were taxed, was un-American. "The Yankees are great inventors and great manufacturers," the Kentuckian sneered, "but such a mental invention, such a mental manufacture as this, I never met with before." [1]

Taking to heart Winthrop's warning that Sumner was "a Jesuit of the first water," who must not be given "the *prestige* of acknowledged success, in order to make him all the more dangerous to us," the Massachusetts Whig press energetically de-

[8] Sumner to Dana, Dec. 14, 1851, Dana MSS.; Sumner to Howe, Dec. 14, 1851, Sumner MSS.

[9] Sumner: *Works*, III, 12–32; Sumner to Palfrey, Feb. 11, 1852, Palfrey MSS.

[1] *Cong. Globe*, 32 Cong., 1 Sess., Appendix, 222, 225.

nounced Sumner. The *Atlas* pronounced his speech "uninteresting and heavy, . . . unsound and visionary"; the *Advertiser* called his ideas "entirely novel, and . . . extremely questionable." A correspondent of the latter paper, claiming that Sumner was favoring the Western states at the expense of New England, concluded: "We have sent into the national councils men of such universal philanthropy that our own immediate interests would seem to be the last in their concern." [2]

"I am not disturbed by Boston criticism," Sumner retorted angrily, though his letters reveal that he was writhing under the attacks. Peevishly he complained that nobody in Massachusetts had really studied his speech; only the *Commonwealth,* which had a tiny circulation, had bothered to print it. Earnestly he tried to convince such doubting friends as Adams, Palfrey, and Prescott that his argument was "original and unanswerable." His, he insisted, was "the most important speech for the West uttered in Congress for 10 years." [3]

• 3 •

Sumner's "Justice to the Land States" speech was, in fact, neither so gross a betrayal of New England as his opponents charged, nor so daring a vindication of justice as Sumner himself thought. The subject of public lands was not one about which he had thought very deeply or cared very much. He spoke on the land question in order to impress his fellow senators with his "reserve, familiarity with the place, and the discussion of other subjects" than slavery.[4]

He attempted to make his speech a model of rhetoric, an example of the proper style and argument for congressional oratory. Considering an appearance upon the Senate floor a public performance, he carefully prepared every detail in advance. Like Daniel Webster, he thought he should "present his best thoughts,

[2] Winthrop to John Davis, Dec. 13, 1851, Davis MSS.; extracts from Massachusetts newspapers in Boston *Commonwealth,* Jan. 31, Feb. 4, Mar. 11, and 22, 1851.

[3] Sumner to Longfellow, Feb. 2, 1852, Longfellow MSS.; Sumner to Epes Sargent, Mar. 13, 1852, Epes Sargent MSS.; Sumner to Howe, Feb. 1, 1852, Sumner MSS.

[4] Sumner to Howe, Feb. 14, 1852, Sumner MSS.

his best manner, [and] his best garb when he addressed his fellow-men." At a time when most senators wore black frock coats, Sumner affected light-colored English tweeds; his "favorite costume was a brown coat and light waistcoat, lavender-colored or checked trousers, and shoes with English gaiters."

Sumner's manner was as carefully chosen as his clothing. "Habit," he used to say, "is everything," and he declared he "never allowed himself, even in the privacy of his own chamber, to fall into a position which he would not take in his chair in the Senate." The irreverent might wonder how he looked in a nightshirt, but adherence to this rule made Sumner one of the most conspicuously dignified figures in the Senate chamber. Six feet two inches tall, weighing about 185 pounds, with a broad chest and well-knit figure, he looked the senator incarnate.

In most of his speeches in Congress, Sumner assumed the faintly condescending air of a pedagogue instructing backward children, and as he explained the rudimentary principles of justice to his colleagues, he customarily stood with his left hand on his hip, his right hand toying with an eyeglass. When he became more excited, his most frequent movement was to toss his high-piled, luxuriant brown hair back from his forehead by a swift motion of his head. His gestures were forceful rather than graceful, and Longfellow criticized him for standing "like a cannoneer . . . ramming down cartridges." [5]

Like most of his Senate colleagues, Sumner had little facility in extemporaneous debate, and both pride and belief in the importance of his ideas impelled him to write out and memorize his principal addresses. The later rumor that Sumner rehearsed his speeches at night before a full-length mirror, employing a Negro servant to hold a lamp so that he could better practice his gestures, had no foundation in fact and was probably not intended seriously. Very often, however, when committing a speech to memory, he would mutter phrases to himself, pacing back and forth in his bedroom or lying on his bed. With his incredibly fast and accurate memory, he was able to learn by heart pro-

[5] Noah Brooks: *Washington in Lincoln's Time* (New York: The Century Co.; 1895), pp. 24–5; "Lord Acton's American Diaries," *The Fortnightly Review*, CXVII (1922), 75; Mrs. W. S. Robinson: *"Warrington" Pen-Portraits . . .* (Boston: Lee and Shepard; 1877), p. 57; Dawes: *Sumner*, p. 224; Longfellow, Diary, Mar. 2, 1847, Longfellow MSS.

longed passages, even those including statistics and elaborate legal citations.[6]

Sumner's oratory was highly formal, in a style that was already considered a little old-fashioned. Professor Edward T. Channing, at Harvard, had taught him that orators should follow the classical Greek and Latin pattern of exordium, narration, partition, proof, refutation, and peroration, and nearly all his addresses used precisely this structure.[7] From Professor Channing, too, he had learned that an orator must always have "his points fixed and always visible, his statements almost laboriously distinct," and even in a short, minor effort like his speech on public lands he clearly listed his principal propositions before proceeding to develop them. As a result, virtually all Sumner's addresses had a blocky quality; the careful enumeration of points to be made, the repetition of those points in the course of the argument, and the recapitulation of the same points in the summary gave clarity at the expense of fluency and grace. Sumner was aware of this effect and cultivated it. He advised Horace Mann to follow the same pattern: "Let your points be clear; and the arrangement careful—divided, and sub-divided. These resting places help the understanding of a long document." [8]

To his sentence structure Sumner gave the same careful attention he devoted to his outline. In an age of oratorical solemnity, nobody expected him to be conversational. He deliberately strove to achieve a sonority of expression comparable to that of Edmund Burke, his model in oratory. Sumner's long, complex sentences, with their high proportion of Latin derivatives, gave his addresses a style "that would have been more at home in the days of Cicero and Quintilian than in contemporary life." [9] Early in his public-lands speech, for instance, he declared:

I have no inclination to go into these matters at length, even if I were able; but entertaining no doubt as to the requirements of policy and

[6] Brooks: *Washington in Lincoln's Time*, p. 25; A. B. Johnson to Pierce, Nov. 27, 1894, Pierce MSS.; E. L. Pierce in *Century Magazine*, XLIX (1895), 792.

[7] The best discussion of Sumner's oratory, to which I am much indebted, is Pagel and Dallinger: "Charles Sumner," in Brigance (ed).: *History and Criticism of American Public Address*, II, 751–76.

[8] Edward T. Channing: *Lectures Read to the Seniors in Harvard College* (Boston: Ticknor and Fields; 1856), p. 71; Sumner to Mann, June 23, 1850, Mann MSS.

[9] Pagel and Dallinger: "Charles Sumner," p. 764.

of justice in the present case, and in all like cases, seeing my way clearly before me by lights that cannot deceive, I hope in a few words to exhibit these requirements and to make this way manifest to others.

Though long, Sumner's sentences were considerably shorter than those of the orotund Rufus Choate and Daniel Webster.[1] The thundering clauses, the intricately balanced phrases, and the poetic effusions of these orators Sumner belittled as "scarlet, green-baize, holyoke flower stuff," and he tried to follow Channing's advice and keep his metaphors to a minimum.[2] In his speech on the public lands, for instance, he allowed himself only one real flight of rhetoric, predicting that if the projected railroad was built, the Missouri River, that "distant giant stream, mightiest of the earth, leaping from its sources in the Rocky Mountains, will be clasped with the Atlantic in the same iron bracelet."

In selecting his words, Sumner applied the same standards of restraint. He joined Professor Channing's war to defend the purity of the English language, and sternly scorned neologisms and technical terms. Such phrases as "poke fun" or "folks" he considered hopelessly vulgar.[3] Endlessly he revised his speeches, first in manuscript, again when they appeared in the *Congressional Globe,* and still further when he included them in his published collections of orations. In a single paragraph of an 1855 address, for example, he altered "glimpses" to "glances," "utterances" to "tones," "complete" to "carry through," and "different aspects" to "different heads." [4] Sumner felt that the care he took

[1] As a sample, I have found that Sumner in the introduction and peroration of his public-lands speech and of his Kansas-Nebraska speech averaged 33 words per sentence. Choate's average sentence contained 37 words. John W. Black: "Rufus Choate," in Brigance (ed.): *American Public Address,* I, 546. Wendell Phillips, the only orator of his generation who was colloquial and informal, averaged only 22.98 words per sentence. Raymond H. Barnard: "An Objective Study of the Speeches of Wendell Phillips," *The Quarterly Journal of Speech,* XVIII (1932), 578.

[2] Sumner to Longfellow [Nov. 1848], Longfellow MSS.

[3] Channing: *Lectures,* pp. 218–32; Richards: *S. G. Howe,* II, 389–90. In the Longfellow MSS. there is a set of proofs of *Evangeline,* bearing numerous marginal verbal corrections and suggestions by Sumner, which show his minute attention to purity of style.

[4] The manuscript of Sumner's "The Antislavery Enterprise" address is in the New York Historical Society; an early revision of the paragraph occurs in Sumner: *Recent Speeches and Addresses* (Boston: Higgins and Bradley; 1856), pp. 479–80; Sumner's final revision is in his *Works,* IV, 10–11.

in such matters was very important; he was proud to be a purist.

Instead of using vivid words or ornate sentences, Sumner relied for rhetorical effect upon four other devices. He used statistics to an extent that no modern audience would endure. In his brief address on public lands, for example, he rattled off the number of acres of public lands in the United States, their rate of sale, the amount of state taxes that might have been levied against them, and the total of federal grants to schools, universities, and asylums in the Western states. As a second device, he relied heavily upon quotations, especially from the classics, from English literature, and from medieval historians. Apparently he felt that no speech, however brief, was complete without one good Latin quotation. Though his political advisers in Massachusetts warned him that every Latin phrase he used cost him a vote, and though Hillard complained that his quotations often had no more relevance than the mysterious "Selah" of the Psalmist, Sumner was unwilling to conclude even a lesser effort such as the public-lands speech without a resounding

> *Quam bene Saturno vivebant rege; priusquam*
> *Tellus in longas est patefacta vias.*[5]

Sumner's speeches also gained force from rhetorical exaggeration, though it is hard to know when he was consciously extravagant and when he had convinced himself of his own statements. In his public-lands speech he announced that the projected railroad would make "the distant post of Council Bluffs . . . a suburb of Washington." Welcoming Kossuth, he compared the Hungarian to William Wallace, William Tell, and George Washington, and asserted that the exile's recent reception in England had been grander than any victory won by Julius Caesar or William the Conqueror. Finally, Sumner's oratory drew strength from the epithets he coined. A very high proportion of the antislavery men's armory of slogans came from Sumner's speeches: "Freedom National," "The Backbone Party," "The Crime Against Kansas," "The Barbarism of Slavery," and the like.

Though enemies like Winthrop complained that Sumner's

[5] J. W. Stone to Sumner, Dec. 16, 1851, Sumner MSS.; Hillard to Lieber, Dec. 30, 1851, Lieber MSS. Helpfully, Summer gave the Senate his source (Tibullus, *Eleg. Lib.*, I.iii.35,36) and translated for the nonscholars: "How well they lived while Saturn ruled—before the earth was opened by long ways!"

speeches were "stuffed full of sentimental commonplaces and exaggerated truisms and inflated affectations," and though less scholarly opponents of slavery like Ben Wade and Zach Chandler sneered at Sumner as one of "them literary fellers," whose oratory had "no bones in it," [6] the Massachusetts senator came to be recognized as the most eloquent congressional spokesman of the antislavery cause. No doubt a large part of Sumner's contemporary repute stemmed simply from the fact that he was a vigorous, handsome man who boldly dared speak out with impassioned sincerity against the majority. Doubtless, too, the high seriousness with which Sumner regarded himself and his mission contributed to his following; he agreed entirely with Professor Channing that an orator "must have a deep and sustained interest in what he is saying" and that he "must believe that he is uttering what others ought to hear and take to heart." [7] If a sense of humor is a handicap in American political life, Sumner was singularly unencumbered. Considering the earnestness of the warfare against the slavery, he could not understand how Wendell Phillips permitted humorous remarks to crop up in his speeches. "Did you ever see a joke in one of my speeches?" he sternly asked a young friend.

"No sir, I think I never did," was the unhesitating reply.

"Of course you never did," returned Sumner triumphantly. "You might as well look for a joke in the book of Revelations." [8]

With his high seriousness, Sumner seemed to true believers a reincarnation of some Old Testament prophet. Unlike Seward, who seemed constantly verging on frivolity, or Chase, whose personal ambition stained his eloquence, or Wade, who was crude and unclassical, Sumner carried absolute conviction to antislavery men. "What a glittering far-darting irresistable [*sic*] Ethuriel lance you have poised in the lists to tilt with the foes of Freedom!" wrote one of these admirers after Sumner's first antislavery speech in the Senate. "From the depths of my soul I say that your oration came like a new morning to one who was wandering

[6] Winthrop to John Davis, Dec. 13, 1851, Davis MSS.; Gouverneur: *As I Remember*, p. 241; Nevins: *Ordeal of the Union*, I, 395. Benjamin F. Wade was senator from Ohio (1851–69); Zachariah Chandler was senator from Michigan (1857–75, 1879).

[7] Channing: *Lectures*, p. 71.

[8] C. H. Brainerd: "Reminiscences of Charles Sumner," unidentified clipping, Sumner Scrapbooks.

in darkness; and so lighting up the Constitution that the Fathers gave, as to call forth all my reverence for them and for you." [9]

• 4 •

To elicit such encomiums, however, Sumner had to speak on subjects more stirring than public lands. He presumably had been elected to the Senate in order to vindicate the cause of antislavery. Though he repeatedly refused to give any pledges to politicians, he had made a deep moral commitment by promising Theodore Parker and the antislavery radicals that as senator he would be "in morals, not in politics." In a rather unnecessary public letter accepting his office, he had announced, as from on Mt. Sinai: "Since true politics are simply morals applied to public affairs, I shall find constant assistance from those everlasting rules of right and wrong which are a law alike to individuals and communities." [1]

While Massachusetts conservatives eagerly watched Sumner's course for evidences to support their predictions that he would "betray the very men who have elevated him, give the lie to all his own professions and promises, and acknowledge that he has been an agitator merely for the purpose of obtaining office," antislavery men were equally worried lest he prove the accuracy of Hosea Biglow:

So, wen one's chose to Congriss, ez soon ez he's in it,
A collar grows right round his neck in a minnit,
An' sartin it is thet a man cannot be strict
In bein' himself, wen he gits to the Deestrict,
For a coat thet sets wal here in old Massachusetts,
Wen it gits onto Washington, somehow askew sets.[2]

Both groups of observers thought they had evidence that Sumner, now that he was entrenched in his office for six years, was cooling toward antislavery. Just after his election, he paid a courtesy call upon Millard Fillmore—that same Fillmore whom

[9] Benjamin F. Presbury to Sumner, Sept. 14, 1852, Sumner MSS.

[1] John Weiss: *Life and Correspondence of Theodore Parker* (New York: D. Appleton and Company; 1864), II, 111; Sumner: *Works*, II, 440.

[2] Winthrop to Everett, May 21, 1851, Everett MSS.; James Russell Lowell: *The Biglow Papers* . . . (Cambridge: George Nichols; 1848), p. 49.

he had once assigned to the "depths of infamy" for signing the Fugitive Slave Act—when the President visited Boston. In the fall elections of 1851 he refused to take an active part in supporting the coalition that had just chosen him to the Senate.[3]

Once in Washington, Sumner seemed to be edging his way into the Democratic party. He favored "fraternizing fully with Democracy" in the 1852 campaign, and was reported to desire the disbanding of the Free Soil party.[4] Even after the Whigs nominated a strong antislavery candidate, Winfield Scott, Sumner thought Massachusetts Free Soilers should keep themselves "*absolutely uncommitted,*" because he looked "for light from the Democratic side." When the Democrats nominated the proslavery Franklin Pierce, Sumner still refused to support Scott, and backed the third-party candidacy of John P. Hale, which was admittedly hopeless, but which might prevent the Whigs from regaining control of the Massachusetts legislature.[5]

While these undercover political maneuvers were known only to a few of Sumner's intimates, every Massachusetts antislavery man was conscious of Sumner's slowness to make a demonstration in the Senate against slavery. Garrisonians thought they had provided him with the perfect occasion when they sent him a petition demanding the release of Drayton and Sayres, two antislavery men imprisoned in the Washington jail for having attempted to smuggle some fugitive slaves out of the District of Columbia.

Sumner failed to present the petition to the Senate. Wendell

[3] Massachusetts *Spy* (Worcester), Oct. 1, 1851; *The Liberator,* XXI (Oct. 3, 1851), 160; Sumner to George Sumner, Sept. 30, 1851, Sumner MSS.

[4] Everett to Abbott Lawrence, Jan. 6, 1852, copy, Everett MSS.; F. P. Blair to Martin Van Buren, Jan. 2, 1852, Van Buren MSS.; George Allen: *Reminiscences* (Worcester: Putnam and Davis; 1883), pp. 99–100. E. L. Pierce (III, 314) brands Allen's recollections as "not authentic," but they do at least prove that contemporaries thought Sumner was ready to abandon the Free Soil party.

[5] Sumner to Amasa Walker, Jan. 9, 1852, Walker MSS.; Sumner to Henry Wilson, Jan. 10, 1852, Wilson MSS.; Sumner to Mann, June 4, 1852, Mann MSS.; Sumner to F. W. Bird, June 20, 1852, Bird MSS. At the same time, however, Sumner wrote: "My hope is to have a third candidate, by whose support we may openly declare our principles, but of democratic inclinings so as to draw from Democrats rather than Whigs, and thus, so far as we can, consistently with our principles, discriminate in favor of Scott." Sumner to Howe, July 4, 1852, Sumner MSS. Consequently he urged Chase to run. Chase to E. S. Hamlin, July 19, 1852, Chase MSS., Lib. of Cong. There seems no reason to accuse Sumner of duplicity; he was simply so thrilled at being for the first time on the "inside" of presidential politics that he veered from side to side, and his letters reflected the views of the person he had most recently been talking to.

Phillips warned him that antislavery men were restive, and *The Liberator* expressed "surprise and regret," but he still did not act. At the April 1852 meeting of the Norfolk County Antislavery Society, Garrison himself introduced resolutions declaring that the senator's silence was "inexplicable," and, though Phillips and one or two others tried to defend Sumner, a vote of censure was adopted. Garrison followed it by a sharp assault in *The Liberator,* titled: "Inquiry after a 'Back-Bone.'" After four and one-half months in the Senate, he pointed out, Sumner had "yet to utter his first word of disapproval of slavery in general, or the Fugitive Slave Law in particular"; he had failed even to present the Drayton-Sayres petition, though it had been in his hands for nearly three months.[6]

In fact, Sumner was working hard to get Drayton and Sayres released by presidential pardon. Realizing that any public clamor would be the surest way of preventing Fillmore from acting, he withheld the Garrison petition. While the case was before the President, Sumner could make no public statement about it, and could not, indeed, even reply to petitioners so notoriously indiscreet as the Garrisonians. Fillmore moved with exasperating slowness, and not until August 11 did he sign the pardon. Fearing that Southerners would attempt to rearrest the two prisoners, Sumner, just as soon as the pardon was issued, hastened to the jail, put Drayton and Sayres in a carriage under the protection of an armed friend, and sped them on their way to the North and to freedom.[7]

The *Commonwealth* could now claim that Sumner had demonstrated that "efficient and practical private action" was preferable to "mere public agitation, which would, perhaps, have retarded instead of advancing . . . liberation" of Drayton and Sayres, but the Garrisonians were unappeased. They cared less for the liberty of Drayton and Sayres than for a denunciation of slav-

[6] Wendell Phillips to Sumner, Mar. 15, and Apr. 27 [1852], Sumner MSS.; *The Liberator,* XXII (Mar. 19, 1852), 47, and XXII (Apr. 23, 1852), 66; W. I. Bowditch to Sumner, Apr. 22, 1852, Sumner MSS.

[7] Boston *Commonwealth,* Aug. 24, 1852; Sumner to George Bemis, Apr. 17, 1852, Bemis MSS.; Sumner: *Works,* III, 49–63; Sumner to Howe, May 21, 1852, Sumner MSS.; J. H. Clay Mudd to Caleb Cushing, June 30, 1856, Cushing MSS.; Sumner to Pierce, May 7, 1852, Sumner MSS. Walter C. Clephane: "Lewis Clephane: A Pioneer Washington Republican," *Records of the Columbia Historical Society,* XXI, 267–9.

ery from the Senate. In November 1850, at Faneuil Hall, they reminded Sumner, he had pledged instant action against the Fugitive Slave Law; now "Almost seven months has he sat in the U.S. Senate, yet not a syllable has he uttered against that Bill; though men, women and children are hunted daily, and ruthlessly shot down or dragged back to bondage." On all other subjects—public lands in Iowa, abolition of the grog ration in the navy, inexpensive international postage—he was eloquent; only on slavery did he maintain his "strange, extraordinary and inexcusable silence." "Surely," Garrison shrilled, "this is 'the play of Hamlet, with the part of Hamlet omitted by particular request.'" Even Phillips, who tried to sustain his friend, was obliged to condemn his course as "impolitic and wrong," and Theodore Parker warned that "poor Sumner" was in "imminent deadly peril": "If he does not speak, then he is *dead—dead—dead!*" [8]

These attacks were the more annoying to Sumner because conservative Whigs seized upon them as evidence that he cared less for humanitarian reform than for his own political advancement. At Boston dinner tables Edward Everett sneeringly commented upon the new senator's silence, and Hillard, hearing that Southern senators liked Sumner, smartly remarked: "*Yes! now they find he is a man that will never do them any harm.*" Winthrop, vindictive toward the "perfect lickspittle" who was his successor in the Senate, in the early summer published a volume of *Addresses and Speeches* containing a supplementary note that ridiculed Sumner's "mysterious and prudent silence." "It is quite too late for him," Winthrop jeered, "to explain away this signal 'disloyalty to Freedom,' as he has been accustomed to call it; . . . the fact will remain on the record, in most ridiculous, or, as some will think, in most lamentable contrast, both with his ferocious attacks upon others, and with his fervent professions for himself." [9]

At first Sumner's Free Soil friends were willing to let him choose his own time for speaking out against slavery. Though they warned the senator not to get lost in a "dismal Sahara of si-

[8] Boston *Commonwealth,* Aug. 12, 1852; Phillips to Sumner, Apr. 27 [1852], Sumner MSS.; *The Liberator,* XXII (June 11, 1852), 94; XXII (June 18, 1852), 98; Weiss: *Parker,* II, 213.

[9] Everett, Diary, July 6, 1852, Everett MSS.; Parker to Sumner, Aug. 4, 1852, Sumner MSS.; Winthrop to J. H. Clifford, Nov. 20, 1851, copy, Winthrop MSS.; Winthrop: *Addresses and Speeches on Various Occasions* (Boston: Little, Brown & Co.; 1852), pp. 770–1.

lence," they were not greatly troubled by Garrison's original assault. But as summer drew on and Sumner still did not speak, Howe and Frank Bird began to grumble about his silence, and Adams said that the party had made a mistake in expecting Sumner to be "a leader when he was only an orator." At the end of June, Wilson wrote Sumner bluntly: "You must not let the session close without speaking. Should you do so you would be openly denounced by nine tenths of our people." [1]

Behind Wilson's agitation lay deep-seated Free Soil disgruntlement over the operation of the coalition. Antislavery men in the legislature had faithfully co-operated with the Democrats in passing laws dealing with corporations, banks, and mechanics' liens. But the Democrats had failed to help then enact the personal liberty bill that Sumner and Dana had drafted to protect fugitive slaves; they had failed to adopt resolutions attacking the Fugitive Slave Act; they had failed to do anything about slavery. To justify the coalition to their antislavery followers, Free Soil leaders could point to only one achievement—the election of Sumner to the Senate. And now silent Sumner seemed to be selling them out. "Do not for Heaven's sake fail to speak, cost what it may of effort and trouble," Wilson implored him. "I tell you frankly that our people are in a state of disappointment and almost of despair. . . . For God sake do not keep us in this state longer than you can help it. . . ." [2]

Sumner had, as a matter of fact, intended all along to speak on the question of slavery, and his failure to do so early in the session reflected not dereliction of duty, but an inexperienced political judgment. "In view of the singular misapprehension of my character and position, and of the fact that I have several years before me in which to labor," he explained to his friends, "I desire by early caution and reserve, and by strengthening myself on other subjects, to place myself in a position to speak from a vantage-ground when at last I do speak." He expected to attack the Fugitive Slave Act "*last* of all in this session." [3]

[1] J. W. Stone to Sumner, Jan. 25, 1852, Sumner MSS.; Wilson to Sumner, Mar. 9, and June 29, 1852, ibid.; Bird to Sumner, July 3, 1852, ibid.; Richards: *S. G. Howe*, II, 382–3; Adams, Diary, May 5, 1852, Adams MSS.

[2] R. H. Dana, Jr., to Sumner, fragment of a letter written about June 1852, Sumner MSS.; Wilson to Sumner, Aug. 3, 1852, ibid.

[3] Sumner to Palfrey, Feb. 11, 1852, Palfrey MSS.; Sumner to Howe, Feb. 14, 1852, Sumner MSS.

His plan was thoroughly unrealistic. First of all, it failed to take into consideration the anxieties of his Massachusetts constituents. Had be been a senator of many years' service, his plea that antislavery men should trust his judgment might have carried weight. But, in a freshman senator, silence gave strength to doubts about the coalition and fortified Free Soilers who had felt all along that Adams, Palfrey, or S. C. Phillips should have been their party's choice.[4]

Furthermore, Sumner misjudged himself and his capacities. It proved hard to find an opportunity for an antislavery oration. "Subjects of debate here are like waves on the beach," he complained. "You expect to leap into one, which comes rolling on, but it has already given way or been lost in another." The longer he delayed, the more difficult it became to speak out. When both major parties, in the spring of 1852, adopted platforms condemning further agitation of the slavery question, he realized that an attack on the Fugitive Slave Act would precipitate a fierce brawl. Sumner, who had uttered many a violent word from the platform, had rarely engaged in face-to-face debate, and he was unsure of his powers. Moreover, he was, as Horace Mann said, "amazingly sensitive to praise," and hated to lose the esteem of the Senate and the friendship of the Southerners whom he had taken such pains to cultivate. Dejected and unhappy as June and his hoped-for time to attack slavery approached, Sumner became ill with diarrhea, undoubtedly of nervous origin, and for a fortnight was too feeble to precipitate a debate.[5] The two following weeks afforded him no opportunity to get the floor.

Finally, on July 27, under enormous pressure from his constituents, Sumner moved the immediate repeal of the Fugitive Slave Law of 1850. The next day, when he asked consent to speak on his motion—a permission required by the Senate rules, but customarily extended as a matter of courtesy—the very senators whom he had considered his warmest friends objected. Butler declared that Sumner's resolution was "merely a pretense to give him an opportunity to make an oratorical display before the

[4] For sharp Free Soil criticisms of his course see Wilson to Sumner, Aug. 3, 1852, ibid., and Theodore Parker to Sumner, Aug. 4, 1852, ibid.

[5] Sumner to George Sumner, Apr. 1, 1852, ibid.; Sumner to Howe, July 4, 1852, ibid.; Mann to Howe, July 27, 1852, Mann MSS.; Mann to Samuel Downer, July 27, 1852, ibid.; Mann to Mary Mann, Aug. 10, 1852, ibid.

Senate, and . . . wash deeper and deeper the channel through which flow the angry waters of agitation." Other Southerners warned that Sumner's motion was "equivalent to . . . a resolution to dissolve the Union." For the northern Democrats, Douglas announced that he would not "extend any act of courtesy to any gentleman to . . . fan the flames of discord that have so recently divided this great people." By a vote of thirty-two to ten the Senate refused Sumner permission to speak.[6]

Massachusetts antislavery papers were indignant against "this insult to the State of Massachusetts," which should make every citizen's "blood curdle with shame, or boil with indignation." Sumner's correspondents branded the Senate's action as "characteristically mean," "contemptible," and Seward fumed that it was "wicked and base." The Southerners, announced the *Commonwealth*, "dare not hear him, because they dread their own consciences."[7]

However consoling such balm, Sumner was "mortified and dejected" by his defeat. Nor were his spirits cheered when Cass, Soulé, Fish, and several other senators who had voted against hearing him sidled up and expressed their regrets. They had toward him the best will in the world, they declared, but their party platforms bound them not to permit further agitation of the slavery question during the presidential campaign. Senator James M. Mason, of Virginia, was more forthright. After silencing Sumner, he told the Massachusetts senator patronizingly: "You may speak next term."

"I must speak this term," Sumner replied firmly.

"By God, you shan't," Mason retorted.

"I will," promised Sumner, "and you can't prevent me."[8] His boast was mostly bravado, for the session was near its end and he was not likely to have another opportunity.

Sumner's unsuccessful attempt to speak failed to silence his critics in Massachusetts. Garrison's denunciations became so vituperative that Seward urged him to restrain his indignation. The

[6] *Cong. Globe*, 32 Cong., 1 Sess., 1934, 1950–3.

[7] Boston *Commonwealth*, July 31, and Aug. 2, 1852; E. A. Stansbury to Sumner, July 29, 1852, Sumner MSS.; John Jay to Sumner, July 30, 1852, ibid.; Frederick W. Seward: *Seward at Washington . . . 1846–1861* (New York: Derby and Miller; 1891), p. 190.

[8] Pierce, III, 292; Dana, Diary, Sept. 11, 1852, Dana MSS.

Democratic Boston *Post* called Sumner's motion a "contemptible dodge," intended to avoid a real discussion of slavery, and the Worcester *Palladium* agreed that Sumner "went into the matter cat-footed," without real intent of forcing a vote on the Fugitive Slave Law. Even the pious protest of the *Commonwealth* that "No well-informed man has any reason to distrust Mr. Sumner's devotion to the cause of freedom" lost its force when the same paper demanded that he "introduce at once a bill for the repeal of the Fugitive Slave Law, and let the slave drivers take, if they dare, the responsibility of silencing him." [9]

Sumner squirmed restlessly under the criticism. Distressed "by the evident impatience of distant friends . . . and the extravagant expectations" they had of him, he angrily reminded the Free Soilers that he had never sought the senatorship, that he had taken it "only as an independent man," unfettered by any claims or pledges. But, in the privacy of a letter to his brother George, he recognized that he had lost his "native independence of position, by becoming the holder of a public office," and that he must speak.[1]

Anxiously he sought an opportunity to deliver his prepared speech. Every subject in the world seemed to come before the Senate except slavery. "My ship is in a *terrible calm,*" he wrote Whittier, "like that of the Ancient Mariner." His one opportunity was likely to come just at the end of the session, when he might be able to move an amendment to the civil appropriations bill and claim, as a matter of parliamentary right, an opportunity to speak in defense of his motion. Such a course, Sumner recognized, would have dangers: if the presiding officer failed to recognize him, or if he ruled his amendment not germane to the bill under discussion, there would be no other chance to speak this session. To allay Southern suspicions, Sumner cultivated an air of resignation; he cleared off all the books and papers from his desk and gave no hint that he had an antislavery speech in the top drawer. "*But I shall speak,*" he promised his friends in confidence. "For a long time I have been prepared to handle the Fugi-

[9] *The Liberator,* XXII (Aug. 13, 1852), 130; Theodore Parker to Seward, Aug. 11, 1852, Seward MSS.; Boston *Commonwealth,* Aug. 2, 6, and 9, 1852.

[1] Sumner to Longfellow [Aug. 1852], Longfellow MSS.; Sumner to Dana, Aug. 13, 1852, Dana MSS.; Sumner to George Sumner, Aug. 18, 1852, Sumner MSS.

tive Slave Bill at length. By the blessing of God it shall be done." [2]

On August 26, as the Senate was debating the appropriations bill, Senator Hunter, for the appropriations committee, introduced an amendment for payment of "the extraordinary expenses" incurred by officials in enforcing the laws of the United States. The presentation of this amendment, designed to cover the expense of executing the Fugitive Slave Act, was precisely the opportunity for which Sumner had been waiting. Promptly he submitted an amendment of his own, to the effect that no part of any appropriation should be spent for carrying out the Fugitive Slave Act, "which said act is hereby repealed." [3]

Seizing the floor, he demanded to be heard "not as a favor, but as a right," and quickly launched into his prepared oration. No political platforms could keep him from discussing slavery, he boasted: "The slave of principles, I call no party master." [4] These principles impelled him to denounce the inconsistent, absurd, tyrannical effort to crush opposition to the Fugitive Slave Bill. He would, he promised, reveal that bill in its true enormity and prove that by the original intentions of the founders of the republic, slavery was a sectional institution and freedom national.

• 5 •

During the months while he prepared and memorized his "Freedom National" speech, Sumner had considered and reconsidered the best strategy for attacking slavery. Undoubtedly he was tempted to adopt an extreme abolitionist position. Sumner had a streak of what Lieber called "jacobinical abstraction"; he was the "statesman *doctrinaire*," who seized upon a single idea and carried it to its most extreme conclusion. He liked to fancy himself the descendant of the Separatists of the English revolution, who uncompromisingly contended "for religious, intellectual, and political emancipation." As their heir, he boldly announced that slavery was wrong. "There is no offense against religion, against morals, against humanity, which, in the license of this enormity, may not stalk 'unwhipt of justice.'" Therefore it must be de-

[2] Sumner to Whittier, Aug. 13, 1852, copy, Whittier MSS.; Dana, Diary, Sept. 11, 1852, Dana MSS.

[3] *Cong. Globe*, 32 Cong., 1 Sess., 2,371.

[4] The entire speech is in Sumner: *Works*, III, 95–196.

stroyed. Constitutional provisions and congressional enactments which tried to support this barbarous evil were offenses "against the Divine Law" and must not be obeyed. If it was argued that the rights of slaveholders had been settled by numerous laws and precedents, Sumner answered: "*Nothing . . . can be settled which is not right.*" If it was argued that insuperable practical difficulties forbade emancipation, he replied simply: "The Antislavery Enterprise is right; and the right is always practicable." [5]

Yet, however intense Sumner's Come-Outer spirit, he could never join Garrison and Phillips in denouncing the Constitution as a proslavery document and desiring the disruption of the Union. The basic influences upon his life had all been conservative. His father had taught him unquestioningly to respect the law. Judge Story had inculcated a lawyerlike reverence for precedents, and his *Commentaries on the Constitution* permanently impressed upon Sumner the values of American nationalism. W. E. Channing had urged him to follow a cautiously conservative course, even in reform. John Quincy Adams had been one of the great American nationalists.

With such teachers it was natural that Sumner should think of himself not as a radical extremist, but as a "Conservative Reformer," an American equivalent of Edmund Burke. Sumner even fancied he bore a physical resemblance to the great Irishman, and, later in life, insisted upon having his collected *Works* issued in bindings precisely like those of the standard American edition of Burke's. On questions where he had no great emotional stake, he often spoke with a genuinely conservative accent. He urged Massachusetts reformers seeking to alter the state's ancient constitution to remember that "Institutions are formed *from within, not from without.*" "They spring from custom and popular faith, silently operating with internal power," he added in the best Burkean manner, "not from the imposed will of a lawgiver." He could become eloquent in defending prescriptive usage. The Missouri Compromise, for instance, whatever its original merits, had "by long acquiescence become part of our fundamental law, irrepealable by common legislation." Similarly he refused to vote

[5] Lieber to Hillard, Jan. 16, 1851, Lieber MSS.; *Pierce Dinner*, p. 47; Sumner: *Works*, III, 191, 271–2, 291; II, 413; IV, 24.

against a subsidy to the notorious Collins steamship line on the ground that though he would not favor initiating such a grant, it was unwise and unfair constantly to agitate an already settled question. He was given to reminding his hearers that there were often "proper occasions for compromise." [6]

The difficulty with applying a conservative attitude to the slavery question was the fact that history, precedent, and law all seemed to favor the continuation, or even the extension, of the South's "peculiar institution." For over sixty years the Congress had protected slavery in the coastal slave trade, had admitted new slave states, had guaranteed slavery in the District of Columbia, and had authorized the seizure of fugitive slaves in the North; for over sixty years the courts had upheld all these acts. It was not clear how any disciple of Burke, believing in the organic growth and slow evolution of institutions, could act against slavery.

Sumner's task was to make conservative means lead to radical ends. He had to show that the supporters of the Compromise of 1850, who spoke of themselves as conservative unionists, were in fact extreme sectionalists, while the antislavery agitators, so often accused of radical sectionalism, were the true nationalists. His "Freedom National" speech carefully formulated these ideas and outlined his antislavery philosophy and program; in other speeches during the next decade he was to elaborate the points he made in this 1852 address, but he never varied his basic approach.[7]

To establish his argument, Sumner analyzed both the general question of federal protection of slavery and the specific problem of fugitive slave laws "in the light of history and of reason." In effect, he appealed from history drunk to history sober. Not merely precedents of the last sixty years, but the broader perspectives of American growth since the seventeenth century were relevant. The American nation, as Sumner saw it, had originated in the conflict between Puritan and Cavalier in England, a struggle between right and wrong, democracy and aristocracy. The

[6] A. B. Johnson: "Charles Sumner," *Cosmopolitan*, IV (1887), 40; Sumner to J. T. Fields, July 7, 1866, Fields MSS.; Sumner to Longfellow, July 8, 1869, Longfellow MSS.; Sumner: *Works*, III, 252–3, 315; New York *Times*, Mar. 2, 1855.

[7] For this reason I am presenting, in the following pages, a composite analysis of Sumner's antislavery thought, citing, without chronological differentiation, speeches made between 1848 and 1855.

contest was continued in the New World. The founders of New England, especially the builders of that "just and generous Commonwealth," Massachusetts, carried on the Puritan tradition; the fathers of Virginia had the vices of the Cavaliers, which multiplied after the introduction of Negro slaves. New England had inspired the American Revolution; her troops had won the nation's independence despite "the imbecility of Southern States," palsied by slavery. In the ardor of revolution the best of the Southerners came to see that slavery was pernicious; Jefferson, Washington, Madison, and Patrick Henry had favored abolition.[8]

The United States was thus born in an atmosphere of freedom for all men. The Declaration of Independence, that "Great Charter of our country," which embodied "in immortal words, those primal truths to which our country pledged itself with baptismal vows as a Nation," proclaimed liberty to all. The Northwest Ordinance, by which the Founding Fathers carefully excluded slavery from all the western territories then owned by the federal government, attested their devotion to liberty. So also did the Constitution, which carefully did not mention the words "slave" or "slavery," but which instead incorporated the Declaration of Independence in its preamble, pledging to "promote the general welfare, and secure the blessings of Liberty to ourselves and our posterity." When Washington was inaugurated, "Slavery had no national favor, existed nowhere on the national territory, beneath the national flag, but was openly condemned by Nation, Church, Colleges, and Literature of the time."[9]

From this high point of virtue there had, of course, been a decline. "The generous sentiments which filled the early patriots, giving to them historic grandeur, gradually lost their power." The slave masters "availed themselves of this indifference." In collaboration with the Northern "mercantile interests," they used "the skillful tactics of party" and "succeeded, through a long succession of years, in obtaining the control of the National Government, bending it to their will." The United States, as a result, was "not now what it was in the beginning"; "it has shrunk in character."[1]

[8] Sumner: *Works*, III, 133, 230, 386, 396.

[9] Ibid., III, 111, 127, 292.

[1] Sumner: *The Landmark of Freedom: Speech . . . in the Senate, February 21, 1854* (Washington; 1854), p. 11.

John Quincy Adams

THE NATIONAL ARCHIVES

Henry Wilson

THE NATIONAL ARCHIVES

Charles Francis Adams

MASSACHUSETTS HISTORICAL SOCIETY

RIVAL MASSACHUSETTS FREE SOILERS

The remedy lay not in ending the Union, as the Garrisonians proposed, but in reverting to the policy of the Founding Fathers. Once the national government resumed its true position and gave no positive countenance to slavery, the South's "peculiar institution" must cease in the national territories, in the District of Columbia, and in the coastal slave trade; there would be no more slave states admitted; and "The Union Flag of the Republic will become once more the flag of freedom, and at all points within the national jurisdiction will refuse to cover a slave." [2]

When Americans cleared their minds of proslavery fallacies, Sumner thought they would see that the Constitution, as well as the Founding Fathers, spoke for liberty. He did not accept the tenuous reasoning that led Lysander Spooner and a few other antislavery men to argue that the Constitution, properly interpreted, actually abolished slavery throughout the United States.[3] Sumner was never willing to admit that in time of peace "the National Government has power under the Constitution to touch Slavery in the States." But he did insist, following Lord Mansfield's opinion in the Sommersett case (1772), which ended slavery in England, that the institution was "so *odious, that nothing can be suffered to support* it but POSITIVE LAW." Once men recognized the "essential barbarism" of slavery, no one could "be so absurd as to imagine, infer, suppose, conjecture, surmise, fancy, guess or presume that Slavery can have any sanction in words [of the Constitution] which do not plainly and unequivocally declare it." [4]

There were, Sumner boldly contended, no such words. Concealing the nationalistic views he had learned from Story and from John Quincy Adams, he, like most other antislavery politicians, resorted to an extremely strict interpretation of the Constitution to prove his point. As the Tenth Amendment stated that the powers of the United States government are "not general or universal, but special and particular," Congress could not establish slavery in the national territories or protect it in the District

[2] Sumner: *Works:* III, 129. Cf. *supra*, pp. 133–4.

[3] Lysander Spooner: *The Unconstitutionality of Slavery* (Boston: Bela Marsh; 1860), Chap. 8; William Goodell: *Views of American Constitutional Law, and Its Bearing upon American Slavery* (2nd ed.; Utica: Lawson & Chaplin; 1845), p. 77; Dwight L. Dumond (ed.): *Letters of James Gillespie Birney, 1831–1857* (New York: D. Appleton-Century, Inc.; 1938), II, 834.

[4] Sumner to A. P. Brown, Sept. 9, 1860, Garrison MSS., Boston Public Lib.; Sumner: *Works,* III, 105.

of Columbia without some explicit grant of power, and this did not exist in the Constitution. Any attempt of Congress to exercise jurisdiction over such matters was a threat to "all the rights of the States." Sumner called upon the Northern state governments to resist such "intrusive and offensive encroachment on State Rights"; he praised the Virginia Resolutions of 1798; and once or twice he even used Calhoun's word and asked for "nullification" of the Fugitive Slave Law. Slavery in America, he argued, was a creature of municipal or state law, with which the national government could have nothing to do.[5]

Not even the clause of Article IV providing for the rendition of fugitives, the constitutional basis of the fugitive slave laws of 1793 and 1850, gave the United States government power to protect slavery. Both these laws were, first of all, unconstitutional because they violated the Fifth Amendment, guaranteeing that no person could be deprived of life, liberty, or property without due process of law, and the Seventh Amendment, providing for jury trials. But, in fact, no conceivable fugitive slave law could be constitutional, because Article IV only recognized the right of rendition, but did not give Congress power to enforce that right. The fugitive slave clause was designed to promote interstate comity; it was "merely *a compact between the States, . . . conferring no power on the Nation.*" The existing fugitive slave acts must be stricken from the statute books, and "*Each State, in the exercise of its own judgment, will determine for itself the precise extent of obligation assumed.*" [6]

It is extremely difficult to judge the validity of these arguments, which Sumner made the basis of his antislavery agitation throughout the 1850's. There is much justification for his view that the framers of the Constitution did not intend to protect slavery, much less extend it to the national territories.[7] But Sumner did not adequately distinguish between the private opinions of the Founding Fathers and their public actions toward slavery, and he incorrectly identified their mild antislavery sentiments

[5] Sumner: *Works*, III, 125–6; Weiss: *Parker*, II, 140; Sumner to Byron Paine, Jan. 18, 1856, Paine MSS. Lieber thought that Sumner had become "*a genuine nullifier.*" Lieber to Hillard, Oct. 28, 1852, Lieber MSS.

[6] Ibid., III, 186–8.

[7] Allan Nevins: "The Constitution, Slavery and The Territories," in *The Caspar G. Bacon Lectures on the Constitution of the United States, 1940–1950* (Boston: Boston University Press; 1953), pp. 95–141.

with the abolitionism of later decades. His contention that slavery had to be the creature of positive law and that in the United States it depended upon local, not national, legislation found support in the opinions of leading Southern and Northern judges,[8] but it did not necessarily follow that the federal government had to adopt an antislavery attitude. Practically all the Southerners in the Senate argued from the same premise that the federal government had no power to intervene against slavery anywhere.[9] Sumner's arguments against the constitutionality of the fugitive slave acts, though ingenious, were never sustained by the courts. Massachusetts Chief Justice Lemuel Shaw, United States Supreme Court Justices Joseph Story, Levi Woodbury, and John McLean, and Chief Justice Roger B. Taney were among those who upheld the validity of the 1793 and 1850 fugitive slave laws.[1]

Critics noted that there was nothing new in Sumner's antislavery arguments. Sumner's stress on the antislavery views of the Founding Fathers had been common Liberty party propaganda; Salmon P. Chase made the same case in 1845. His argument that the federal government had no constitutional right to protect slavery had been a mainstay of Joshua R. Giddings's speeches for years and was a plank in the 1848 Free Soil national platform. Sumner's ideas about the unconstitutionality of the fugitive slave laws had been anticipated by Robert Rantoul, his predecessor in the Senate, and his due-process and jury-trial arguments could be traced back further, to Chase's briefs in the Matilda case of 1837 and the Van Zandt case of 1846.[2] Sumner

[8] E.g., 18 Pickering, 211, 215; J. C. Hurd: *The Law of Freedom and Bondage in the United States* (Boston: Little, Brown & Co.; 1858), I, 576.

[9] It was not until later, when Southerners sought a federal slave code for all the territories, that they argued that slavery was "the common law of the thirteen States of the Confederacy at the time they burst the bonds that united them to the mother country." Hurd: *Law of Freedom and Bondage*, I, 573.

[1] Shaw, in 7 Cushing 285; Story, in 16 Peters 539; Woodbury, in 5 Howard 229; McLean, in 2 McLean 611; Taney, in 21 Howard 506. It should be noted, however, that in none of these cases did the Court decide upon the precise issues Sumner posed. A recent close student concludes, with Sumner, that "the provisions of the clause dealing with fugitives from service patently vest no power in Congress to which that body . . . might give effect by legislation." Levy: *The Law of the Commonwealth and Chief Justice Shaw*, p. 99.

[2] Cf. Salmon P. Chase and Charles Dexter Cleveland: *Anti-Slavery Addresses of 1844 and 1845* (London: Sampson Low, Son, and Marston; 1867), pp. 76–7; Joshua R. Giddings: *Speeches in Congress* (Boston: John P. Jewett and Company; 1853), pp. 336–7; Kirk H. Porter and Donald Bruce Johnson (eds.): *National Party Platforms, 1840–1956* (Urbana: University of Illinois Press; 1956), p. 13; Luther Hamilton (ed.): *Memoirs, Speeches and Writings*

himself recognized that most of his ideas were derivative; his mind, he frankly admitted, was "a cistern, not a fountain." It was, therefore, unkind of Wendell Phillips, addressing the American Antislavery Society, to claim that with the possible exception of one minor point, Sumner had introduced "no train of thought or argument, and no single fact in the whole ["Freedom National"] speech, which has not been familiar in our meetings and essays for the last ten years." Horace Mann gave a fairer appraisal of Sumner's role as an antislavery thinker: "The subject has been so extensively discussed already that he has an immense amount of material put into his hands. This position will require not originality . . . but skill in using, and this is his *forte*." [3]

It was not Sumner's constitutional arguments that gave strength to his antislavery addresses, but his vision of an emancipated America. He sought first to arouse "an enlightened, generous, humane, Christian public opinion" in the free states, so that the whole North would join in the "moral blockade" against slavery. Then the United States government, under Northern leadership, would withdraw its protection from the hated institution, and the "Slaveholding Oligarchy, banished from the National Government, and despoiled of ill-gotten political consequence, without ability to punish or reward," would sink into impotence. Slavery itself might "linger in the States as a local institution," but eventually "the citizens of the Slave States, where a large portion have no interest in Slavery," would realize that just as "A blade of grass would not grow where the horse of Attila had trod," so could no "true prosperity spring up in the foot-prints of the slave." The non-slaveholding whites, then, would force "open the gates of

---

of Robert Rantoul, Jr. (Boston: John P. Jewett and Company; 1854), pp. 740–1; Jacobus ten Broek: *The Antislavery Origins of the Fourteenth Amendment* (Berkeley: University of California Press; 1951), p. 38; Salmon P. Chase: *Reclamation of Fugitives from Service: An Argument . . . in the Case of Wharton Jones vs. John Van Zandt* (Cincinnati: K. P. Donough & Co.; 1847), pp. 89–92. Lysander Spooner: *A Defence for Fugitive Slaves . . .* (Boston: Bela Marsh; 1850) also anticipated many of Sumner's arguments. Practically all Sumner's points had been included in Horace Mann's Feb. 28, 1851, speech in the House of Representatives (Mann: *Slavery: Letters and Speeches* [Boston: B. B. Mussey & Co.; 1851], pp. 390–472), but numerous letters in the Mann MSS., 1849–50, show that Sumner was the source of his legal arguments and citations.

[3] Thomas Wentworth Higginson: "Charles Sumner," *The Independent*, XXVI (Apr. 2, 1874), 1; *Twenty-First Annual Report of the American Antislavery Society* (Boston; 1853), p. 111; Phillips to Sumner, Mar. 7, 1853, Sumner MSS.; Mann to Howe, July 27, 1852, Mann MSS.

Emancipation in the Slave States." To assist in this redemption, Sumner was willing to compensate the slave owners at national expense; nothing was due to them, but, so great was his hatred of slavery, he "could not hesitate to build a Bridge of Gold, if necessary for the retreating fiend." [4]

After emancipation, the South would once again come into fraternal relations with the rest of the nation, abandoning its sectional institutions and prejudices. Soon, too, the "profane assumptions of race" would disappear, though Sumner was careful to declare that he did not wish "to change human nature, or to force any individual into relations of life for which he is not morally, intellectually, and socially adapted," and that one must not assume "that a race, degraded for long generations under the iron heel of bondage, can be taught at once all the political duties of an American citizen." Though Sumner was willing to explore plans "for opening our neighboring tropical lands to the colonization of people of the African race," he thought that most of the Negroes, free and contented, would remain in the South as "a dependent and amiable peasantry." [5]

• 6 •

During the three and three-quarters hours Sumner held the Senate floor in delivering his "Freedom National" speech, the galleries filled with spectators who had heard that an important oration was being given, and many members of the House of Representatives thronged the Senate floor. Webster, though old and ill and within two months of death, came in to listen. Sumner triumphantly noticed his presence and gloated that he, not the Secretary of State, was now the spokesman of Massachusetts. Rest-

[4] Sumner: *Works,* II, 312; III, 133, 459, 540; IV, 27, 32; Sumner to A. F. Rockwell, Mar. 23, 1854, Rockwell MSS., Lib. of Cong. Mann had used the "Bridge of Gold" phrase in 1850. Mann: *Slavery,* p. 278; it was derived from Byron's: "a golden bridge is for a flying enemy" (*The Deformed Transformed,* pt. II, sc. 2).

[5] Sumner: *Works,* III, 509; IV, 24; Sumner to J. R. Lowell, Dec. 14, 1857, Lowell MSS.; Boston *Times,* Apr. 12, 1874. Frederick Douglass complained that Sumner failed to recognize "the entire manhood and social equality of the colored people." Douglass to Sumner, Apr. 24, 1855, Sumner MSS. There is no necessary inconsistency between Sumner's position on Negro equality in his Senate speeches and his Roberts argument. He wished to remove all *legal* barriers that sustained racial discrimination, not to enforce social equality for the Negro.

lessly Webster moved from one side of the chamber to another, and after about an hour, he left, black and scowling.

Throughout the long speech the attention of the audience was unbroken, and as Sumner reached his peroration, many ladies in the gallery, and at least one senator as well, were in tears. Gracefully concluding with some "words of Oriental piety" —"Beware of the groans of the wounded souls. Oppress not to the utmost a single heart; for a solitary sigh has power to overset a whole world"—Sumner resumed his seat amid "unbounded" applause.[6]

Immediately Senator Jeremiah Clemens, of Alabama, rose to urge that no reply be made to Sumner's remarks: "The ravings of a maniac may sometimes be dangerous, but the barking of a puppy never did any harm." But Senator George E. Badger, of North Carolina, irritated apparently as much by the manner as the content of Sumner's address, attacked this "elaborate oration, carefully written, studied, committed to memory, and interspersed in various parts with curious quotations from modern learning and ancient lore, and every now and then dignified and adorned with Latin quotations, which, when the Senator did not condescend to translate them into English, I presume were very unintelligible to most of the members of this body." As the constitutionality of the fugitive slave laws had been unchallenged since 1793, Sumner's speech was designed for "mischievous purposes," not for the promotion of constructive legislation. "Never, sir, since I have been a member of this body," the veteran senator declared, "has the Senate witnessed such an exhibition."

Though leaders of both parties wanted to cut off the debate, it inevitably broadened. Stephen A. Douglas asserted that Sumner was not attacking the Fugitive Slave Act; he was assaulting the Constitution. Senator John B. Weller, of California, announced that this was the first abolitionist speech he had ever listened to and, as it was "so handsomely embellished with poetry, both Latin and English, so full of classical allusions and flourishes," he had found it more palatable than he had fancied possible; but he could see no purpose in Sumner's speech unless it was to incite riots in the Northern states.

[6] Horace Mann to Mary Mann, Aug. 27, 1852, Mann MSS.; Dana, Diary, Sept. 11, 1852, Dana MSS.

Sumner was not entirely without defenders. Hale told the Senate that in this one speech Sumner had placed "himself side by side with the first orators of antiquity, and as far ahead of any living American orator as freedom is ahead of slavery." And Chase loyally defended his friend's speech as opening "AN ERA in American history."

Gradually the debate widened into a general discussion of the approaching presidential election. Sumner, exhausted by his oration, said very little more. When at last a vote was taken on his motion to repeal the Fugitive Slave Act, there were only four "ayes"—Hale, Chase, Ben Wade, and himself.[7]

[7] *Cong. Globe*, 32 Cong., 1 Sess., Appendix, 1,113–25. A number of other genuine antislavery men in the Senate—Seward, Fish, Hannibal Hamlin, etc.—refrained from supporting Sumner's motion lest it imperil the chances of Whig presidential candidate Winfield Scott. For Badger's reactions to the speech see Lawrence F. London: "George Edmund Badger: His Last Years in the United States Senate, 1851–1855," *North Carolina Historical Review*, XV (1938), 231–50.

CHAPTER X

Outside of Any Healthy Political Organization

SUMNER believed that his "Freedom National" oration was a triumph. When the debate ended, Democratic Senator James Shields, of Illinois, complimented him warmly, and John H. Clarke, a Rhode Island Whig, declared that the speech would "be a text-book when they were dead and gone." William H. Polk, of Tennessee, who may have been pulling Sumner's leg, said that the address "was the greatest triumph of genius, he had ever known," and Soulé, who claimed to be "familiar with all the efforts of Wilberforce, and others against slavery in the British Parliament," vowed that Sumner's oration was the greatest of them all. Avid for praise, Sumner passed these remarks along to his friends. "Be assured I receive these things with humility," he assured Longfellow as he related the more extravagant of these compliments. "I am satisfied to labor in the cause and not in vain." [1]

In Massachusetts, as well as in the Senate chamber, the speech seemed to have made a great impression. Such conservative papers as the Boston *Atlas, Advertiser, Courier,* and *Post* did

[1] Bigelow: *Retrospections,* I, 126; Sumner to Longfellow [Aug. 1852], Longfellow MSS.

not print it or even deign to comment upon it editorially, but Bay State voters read it in full in the *Commonwealth*, the *National Era*, or the New York *Post*, or purchased the pamphlet version, which quickly ran through five editions. The oration was "glorious," Henry Wilson wrote; it was "masterly," said Wendell Phillips. It seemed to restore him "to his full tide of popularity with the masses" of Massachusetts Free Soilers. When Sumner went home in September, they staged a rally at the door of his Hancock Street house and welcomed the returning hero "with the heartiest and most enthusiastic plaudits, long continued." "Now," rejoiced Theodore Parker, "you have done yourself Justice and put yourself out of the reach of attack from friend or foe." [2]

Tired from the long session, Sumner wanted to bask in his new popularity and to rest for three months until the next session of the Senate began. He looked forward to having dinner with his close friends, to meeting Arthur Hugh Clough, the visiting English poet, to sea-bathing with the Longfellows at Newport, to a cool, leisurely trip up Lake Champlain into Canada.

Instead, he found himself beset by importunate demands to aid the coalition in the fall elections. Free Soilers were at first plaintive, then strident, in their reproaches when, after making a brief appearance before the state Free Soil convention on September 15, he persisted in his vacation plans. "Every motive of interest, of gratitude, and of humanity" ought to impel him to support his own party, one angry correspondent wrote the *Commonwealth*. "Cannot Sumner . . . submit to some personal inconvenience in defence of the glorious truths embodied in our platform?" asked another. Howe warned that party leaders strongly felt: "That you ought 'to take the stump.' That the party has claim upon you in faith, honor. That you cannot disregard the claim with[out] risking your hold upon the confidence and regard of the party. That many influential men are already disaffected towards you in consequence of your reluctance to come forward. . . . That some who tried hard to secure your election to Congress swear they would work as hard to put you out."

[2] Boston *Commonwealth*, Sept. 6, and 10, 1852; John Bigelow to Sumner, Sept. 5, 1852, Sumner MSS.; J. W. Stone to Sumner, Dec. 27, 1852, ibid., Wilson to Sumner, Sept. 5, 1852, ibid.; Phillips to Sumner, Sept. 3 [1852], ibid.; Samuel Downer to Mann, Aug. 28, 1852, Mann MSS.; Parker to Sumner, Aug. 27, 1852, Sumner MSS.

More briefly, but bluntly, Henry Wilson said that Sumner was wrong to remain silent. When the Whigs regained control of the Massachusetts government in the fall elections, Free Soilers blamed Sumner.[3]

For the next eight years Sumner's life was to exhibit this same pattern: after doing everything he could to battle slavery in the Senate, he returned to Massachusetts only to find that distrust of his motives was as widespread as ever. Each demonstration he made against slavery was followed by renewed, ever more strident calls for further agitation. He could never satisfy his critics.

Though Sumner grew "very sore" under these incessant demands, and thought that each of his major addresses should have sufficiently demonstrated his antislavery zeal, his peculiar political position inevitably exposed him to such criticism. He was not sufficiently identified with any group to have its unqualified confidence. Whigs, of course, hated him and considered his antislavery protestations a pious front for self-promotion. So did the conservative, anticoalitionist Democrats. Abolitionists never fully trusted him because he did not meet their tests for doctrinal purity. Even the Free Soilers doubted his loyalty. As the chief recipient of benefits from the coalition, Sumner could never fully win the confidence of the small but influential group of anticoalitionists, such as Adams, Palfrey, Phillips, and Dana, who were trying to oust Wilson, that "third rate man, with the arts of a first rate demagogue," and restore the party to its original independent stand. At the same time, Wilson and his associates, recognizing that Sumner's friendships and social ties bound him to the Adams clique, demanded that he repeatedly demonstrate his loyalty to the coalition by "active participation in their hopes, their fears, their reverses and their successes." [4]

• 1 •

The Senate session of 1852–3 afforded few opportunities for such demonstrations. In the quiet, lame-duck term, which opened on

[3] Boston *Commonwealth,* Oct. 27, and Nov. 2, 1852; Howe to Sumner [Oct. 1852], Howe MSS.; Pierce to Sumner, Dec. 6, 1852, Sumner MSS.

[4] The best account of the intraparty Free Soil feuds is in C. F. Adams's Diary. See entries for Sept. 6, and 11, and Nov. 10, and 25, 1852; also Samuel Downer to Mann, Feb. 16, 1853, Mann MSS.

December 7, the only interesting development was the plan of Southern expansionists to purchase Cuba from Spain. Though Sumner was thoroughly conversant with the scheme, he could not make a public protest, for all the debates were held in secret session, and he vainly attempted to have the rule of secrecy lifted. Aside from advocating the abolition of the grog ration in the navy, proposing lower international postage rates, and securing a small pension to a Massachusetts widow of a Revolutionary war veteran, Sumner had nothing to do. He could not even make a show of busy-work in committees, for he and Chase received no assignments because both Democratic and Whig caucuses agreed that they were "outside of any healthy political organization." [5]

Obliged to be silent, Sumner came under renewed attacks at home. The Garrisonians, discovering that his "Freedom National" speech had upheld the Constitution, decided that he was no better than Webster. Indeed, said Parker Pillsbury to the Massachusetts Antislavery Society: "Webster's fall was not so deplorable as that of Charles Sumner." Charles Francis Adams, concluding that Sumner was a prisoner of his own reputation, fearful of making another speech on slavery lest it fail to live up to the first, thought he "was never formed to be a political leader." Even more harshly Palfrey concluded that Sumner's mission in Washington had "failed by reason of his own reputation, and of his social tendencies, which relax his energies." When resolutions were introduced in the General Court deploring Sumner's exclusion from committee assignments as a slap at the sovereign state of Massachusetts, Wilson's faction let them die, declaring: "We are fools to defend those, who wont defend us or themselves." [6]

Sumner became petulant under these strictures. He was sure that his motives were pure; he knew that he was doing all that anybody could. His critics failed to recognize that he kept constant vigil in the Senate against proslavery plots. They did not understand that a senator had to have an occasion to make a ma-

[5] Everett, Diary, Dec. 22, 1852, Everett MSS.; Sumner: *Works*, III, 212–15; Pierce, III, 320.

[6] *Twenty-First Annual Report Presented to the Massachusetts Anti-Slavery Society* . . . (Boston; 1853), p. 86; A. G. Browne to Sumner, Feb. 14, 1853, Sumner MSS.; Samuel Downer to Mann, Feb. 16, 1853, Mann MSS.; Adams, Diary, Apr. 23, and 26, 1853, Adams MSS.

jor address and that each of his important antislavery orations required weeks to prepare and commit to memory. They did not realize that corruption, intemperance, and slavery were the dominant trinity in Washington, against which his efforts too often proved unavailing. His assailants had forgotten that he never wanted to come to the Senate, that he was not a politician; they ignored all that he had already done and said in Congress for the cause of freedom, even "though not ripening in any immediate fruit." "If among my discouragements," he wrote in soreness of spirit, "shall be alienation or distrust at home, I will try to bear this, and keep on in my duty." [7]

Sore and sensitive, Sumner did not re-examine his own course to see whether he might possibly have been at fault; he never outgrew the bitter lesson of his childhood that it was dangerous to admit the possibility of error. Nor did he reply directly to his critics. Characteristically, he vented his anger upon a bystander, much as a child in a temper tantrum will beat the wall or the floor. There was no little truth in the shrewd remark of a Boston spinster that Sumner was a "specimen of prolonged and morbid juvenility." [8]

Independent-minded, crusty Francis Lieber became the object of Sumner's wrath. For years the two men had gradually been drifting apart. Lieber thought Sumner's peace orations vapid, illogical, and impractical, and his antislavery agitation nothing less than Jacobinical. He regretted his friend's election to the Senate as "bad for Sumner, for Boston . . . for Congress, for the Union, for the country." [9]

Though Sumner was not a man to suffer dissent gladly, he tried for a long time to keep up his friendship with Lieber. As his Senate duties occupied more and more of his time, he wrote fewer and briefer letters; often he would only mark a few lines in a newspaper or pamphlet which he thought might specially interest the South Carolina professor.

All this, to Lieber, was perfectly insulting. Sumner's hasty notes he thought worse than no letters at all. All too often the

[7] Dana, Diary, Apr. 25, 1853, Dana MSS.; Sumner to Charles List, Dec. 5, 1852, Robie-Sewall MSS.

[8] Hillard to Lieber, Dec. 24, 1850, Lieber MSS.

[9] Lieber to Hillard, May 4, and Apr. 28, 1851, ibid.; Lieber to Sumner, May 20, 1851, ibid.

newspapers the senator forwarded contained marked passages lauding himself to the skies. To Lieber, who was fond of comparing himself to Grotius and Montesquieu, such egotism was disgusting. Equally revolting and more dangerous were the shocking articles "about ill-treated negroes marked with thick lines" which Sumner kept sending. They not merely endangered Lieber's standing in South Carolina; they seemed to brand Lieber himself as responsible for the slave system. "Is it nothing to me that Fate has put me hither and that I pass my life with a smarting pain the whole day and year," Lieber indignantly protested to Hillard; "have I made slavery? Have I praised it?" After nearly three years of being pelted with antislavery missives, Lieber, in 1853, asked Sumner to stop. Government reports and personal letters he would always welcome, but, he told Sumner: "If you have really no time to write to me, pray do not remind me of you in that peculiar manner." [1]

His protest reached Sumner as he was suffering most acutely from Massachusetts criticism and was looking for somebody to attack. Swiftly he retorted that Lieber had no right to complain, as he had become "the apologist of slavery."

Lieber was furious, but, remembering that "Sumner uses words as boys do stones," to "break windows and knock down flowerpots, while he all the time plays the offended," he wrote denying that he was a defender of slavery.

With the icy reserve Sumner always assumed when he was furious, he replied curtly that he was "right glad" if indeed Lieber was not a slavery apologist. Lieber refused to answer so offensive a communication and broke off the correspondence and the friendship.[2]

• 2 •

Sumner's irritability was by no means assuaged by the fact that after a long, frustrating session of Congress, he was obliged to come home in the summer of 1853 and take an active part in

[1] Lieber to Dorothea L. Dix, Apr. 18, 1858, ibid.; Lieber to Hillard, Mar. 16, 1853, ibid.; Lieber to Sumner, May 2, 1853, ibid.

[2] Lieber to Hillard, May 29, and June 7, 1853, ibid. For a careful, perceptive analysis of the reasons for the break between the two see Freidel: *Lieber*, pp. 265–6.

Massachusetts politics. Defeated in the 1852 elections by the Whigs, the coalition had nevertheless managed to carry its proposal for calling a convention to amend the ancient constitution of Massachusetts. Howe convinced Sumner that serving in this convention would restore his popularity with the Free Soilers, and Wilson staged his election as a delegate from Marshfield, where Webster had lived.[3]

When the convention met at the State house in May, Sumner was conspicuously present, and Wilson had him named chairman of the committee on the Bill of Rights. Several times he presided over the assembly when it met in committee of the whole. Not until June 21 did he take an active part in the debates, making during the concluding weeks "two beautiful, classical, high-toned orations" on the Bill of Rights and the system of representation. But, unfamiliar with the issues and puzzled by the swiftness with which the debates ranged from one strange topic to the next, he exercised little influence in the convention. "Sumner has held his own as an orator," Richard Henry Dana, Jr., noted. "As a debater, a worker, an influential member, he has not succeeded. He takes but little active part, and seems to have a fear of taking the floor, except on leading subjects, and after great preparation."[4]

But it was not so much personal inadequacy as political embarrassment that limited Sumner's role. This convention of 1853, though numbering among its members such extraordinary talents as Choate, Dana, Anson Burlingame, N. P. Banks, Wilson, and Benjamin F. Butler, and including three state governors, two United States senators, ten congressmen, and seventy-nine members of the state senate, was anything but an impartial, judicious effort to improve the venerable constitution of 1780. Sponsored by the leaders of the recently defeated coalition, the convention was in fact a political move designed to break down the dominance of the Whig party in the state. As Boston, voting as a single election district, regularly sent a solid phalanx of forty-four

[3] Howe to Sumner, Feb. 1, 1853, Howe MSS.; Wilson to Sumner, Mar. 5, 1853, Sumner MSS. The fact that Wilson ran Sumner in Marshfield, where he was chosen in preference to Webster's own son, suggests that Wilson was aware of Sumner's mild flirtation with the antislavery Whigs (Adams, Diary, Nov. 10, and 25, 1852, Adams MSS.) and was deliberately arranging a victory that Whigs could only regard as an insult to Webster's memory. Hillard to Lieber, Mar. 1853, Lieber MSS.

[4] Boutwell: *Reminiscences*, I, 227; Adams: *Dana*, I, 247.

Whig members to the General Court, coalition leaders resolved to divide all cities into several election districts. Because Whig mill owners were intimidating their employees, the coalitionists wanted to institute the secret ballot. As the coalitionists knew that their strength was in the central and western parts of the Commonwealth, while the Whigs generally carried the larger cities of the eastern section, they planned to reshuffle the system of representation so as to give two thirds of the representatives to the one half of the state's population living in towns smaller than 4,500 inhabitants. All in all, it is difficult to resist the conclusions of opponents that the coalitionists intended to produce "a party Constitution, not a state Constitution." [5]

While the coalitionists wanted to use the Constitutional Convention of 1853 to strike at Whiggery, they also hoped to consolidate their power within their own parties. Boutwell made of the convention an excuse for seizing control of the Massachusetts Democratic machine. Wilson, too, used it in an attempt to force the old Conscience Whigs like Adams, Palfrey, and E. Rockwood Hoar—none of whom was elected to the convention—out of the Free Soil party. Both Wilson and Boutwell gained support from the Troy and Greenfield Railroad interests, which were willing to exchange votes of delegates from northwestern Massachusetts in exchange for state loans to construct the Hoosac tunnel.[6]

In this web of interests and ambitions, Sumner's position was acutely uncomfortable. If he opposed coalition plans for revising

[5] The best analyses of the convention are: James Schouler: "The Massachusetts Convention of 1853," *MHSP*, XVIII (2 ser.; 1903), 30–48; Samuel Eliot Morison: "History of the Constitution of Massachusetts," in *A Manual for the Constitutional Convention, 1917* (Boston: Wright & Potter Printing Co.; 1917), pp. 41–63; Bean: "Party Transformations," Chap. 6; Samuel Shapiro: "Richard Henry Dana, Jr.: A Biography" (unpublished Ph. D. dissertation, Columbia Univ.; 1958), Chap. 6; Jean Carol Kenney: "An Analysis of Political Alignments in Massachusetts as Revealed in the Constitutional Convention of 1853" (unpublished M.A. thesis, Smith Coll.; 1951). See also: A. Poole (comp.): *Poole's Statistical View of the Convention . . .* (Boston: White and Potter; 1853); Michel Brunet: "The Secret Ballot Issue in Massachusetts Politics from 1851 to 1853," *New England Quarterly*, XXV (1952), 354–62; *Discussions on the Constitution Proposed to the People of Massachusetts by the Convention of 1853* (Boston: Little, Brown & Co.; 1854). The detailed convention proceedings may be consulted in *Official Report of the Debates and Proceedings in the State Convention, Assembled May 4th, 1853, to Revise and Amend the Constitution of the Commonwealth of Massachusetts* (Boston: White & Potter; 1853).

[6] *Discussions on the Constitution*, p. 203. Cf. Edward C. Kirkland: "The Hoosac Tunnel Route: The Great Bore," *New England Quarterly*, XX (1947), 88–113.

the constitution, he would be turning against the very men who elected him to the Senate—and Henry Wilson never permitted him to forget his debt to them. If he supported the revisions, he would take on "the responsibility of a set of schemes about which he was never even consulted." If he remained silent, everybody would think him incompetent.[7]

With his remarkable talent for rationalization, Sumner managed to convince himself that expediency and justice coincided, and he squarely endorsed most of the coalition's proposals. He came out enthusiastically for the Hoosac tunnel as "a glory to the Commonwealth, and a mighty channel of trade and travel." He contrived, with less enthusiasm, to support the coalitionists' plans to take representation away from Boston and give it to the central and western towns. The true basis for representation, Sumner declared in a speech to the convention on July 7, should ideally be founded "absolutely upon equality" so as to make "all men, in the enjoyment of the electoral franchise, whatever their diversities of intelligence, education, or wealth, and wheresoever they may be within the borders of the Commonwealth, whether in small town or in populous city, absolutely equal at the ballot-box." But, he swiftly backtracked, this system of equal representation could not be advantageously instituted "unless supported by the permanent feelings and conditions of the people." As the practice of giving Massachusetts small towns disproportionate influence had sprung "from custom and popular faith, silently operating with internal power, not from the imposed will of a lawgiver," he announced in Burkean rhetoric, no radical change in the admittedly inequitable system should be tried at present, but instead the rural towns should be given even more representation so as to protect the Commonwealth against the "commercial feudalism" of the big cities.[8]

Even after this public demonstration of loyalty, coalition leaders, perhaps still convinced that he was inwardly disaffected, drove him with a tight checkrein. When Sumner tried to make a flowery little speech on the origins of the Bill of Rights, most of the delegates were ready to listen, but coalitionists, headed by

[7] Longfellow, Diary, May 3, 1853, Longfellow MSS.; Sumner to W. W. Story, Aug. 2, 1853, MS., Huntington Lib.; Adams, Diary, June 4, 1853, Adams MSS.

[8] *Debates of the Massachusetts Convention,* III, 20–1; Sumner: *Works,* III, 229–58.

Boutwell and Bird, invoked the fifteen-minute limit imposed upon debaters. Then, to demonstrate their power to the senator, they relaxed the rule so that he could finish, but Sumner, peeved, peremptorily refused to continue with his prepared address.[9]

Wilson and the other Free Soil managers rather hoped that Sumner would take no part in the campaign to ratify the new constitution, so that they would have an excuse for reading him, along with Palfrey and Adams, out of the party. But Sumner surprised them by undertaking the most extensive speaking tour he had made since 1848. He made eighteen major addresses, speaking in every section of the state and reaching, as he believed, "more persons than have ever before been addressed in the same time by one man in Massachusetts." Though his address was long and technical, his hearers stayed through more than two hours of his oratory and even applauded as he announced ponderously: "I have now refuted, as I think, the twelfth argument brought against a new constitution. I pass to the thirteenth objection." [1]

Whatever effect Sumner may have had upon his audiences, he at least succeeded in convincing himself of the merits of the new constitution, and with all the zeal of a new convert he keenly resented criticisms of the reforms it proposed. The opposition of "the Boston cabal, whose home is State Street, and whose breath is Silver Grey Websterism," he had anticipated. He was not seriously disturbed when Attorney General Caleb Cushing issued a "ukase," condemning the coalition as "a fatal error" and warning Massachusetts Democrats that continued support of "persons engaged avowedly in the persistent agitation of the slavery question" would be considered "hostile in the highest degree to the determined policy of the [Pierce] Administration." Nor was he surprised that the Boston Irish, under Bishop John B. Fitzpatrick, mobilized to fight a new constitution that would have banned state support for sectarian schools.[2] But, when some of his old

[9] *Debates in the Massachusetts Convention,* III, 373–6; Schouler: "The Massachusetts Convention of 1853," p. 39.

[1] Pierce to Sumner, Jan. 23, 1854, Sumner MSS.; Sumner to Seward, Nov. 15, 1853, Seward MSS.; Thomas Wentworth Higginson: *Part of a Man's Life* (Boston: Houghton Mifflin Co.; 1905), p. 86.

[2] Sumner analyzed the opposition to the new constitution in letters to Seward, Nov. 15, 1853 (Seward MSS.), to Whittier, Nov. 21, 1853 (Albree: *Whittier Correspondence*, pp. 121–2), and to E. L. Pierce, Dec. 18, 1853 (Sumner MSS.). Cf. Handlin: *Boston's Immigrants*, pp. 204–5.

Free Soil allies expressed doubts about the proposed constitution, they came too close to the very questions Sumner had suppressed in his own mind, and he turned upon them with disproportionate bitterness.

Charles Francis Adams was the first to feel his anger. In November Adams explained to the citizens of Quincy his reasons for opposing the new constitution; it had little to commend it, and the inequitable system of representation was alone enough to condemn it. In a pointed reference, Adams claimed that his "honored friend, Charles Sumner," had started out with the impregnable principle of "*democratic equality of numbers,*" but, allowing himself to be led astray by "the siren song of expediency," had "bowed his neck to the iron rod of party." Sumner was indignant, and not until Dana persuaded Adams to explain that he did not mean to "imply the smallest disrespect" to Sumner or any "dereliction of principle," did the two men resume social relations, and then for months they were on a rather distant footing.[3]

More angry and more lasting was Sumner's rupture with his old friend Palfrey, who was bitter that the coalitionists did not run him for governor, and hurt that he had not been chosen to the convention. Denying that he was imputing any dishonorable motives to the framers of the new constitution, Palfrey, signing himself "A Free Soiler from the Start," published a pamphlet vigorously attacking that document. Deeply hurt, Sumner complained to Dana of Palfrey's inexplicable course, but toward the offender himself he maintained an icy silence until after the election and the defeat of the new constitution. Ready to weep over the defeat of a plan that "would have broken the back-bone of the Boston oligarchy, the stumbling-block of all reform and especially of all Anti-slavery," Sumner blamed this "severe calamity" upon Palfrey, who, he said, could hardly "by any future services repair the wrong he has done to our cause." Palfrey's tentative efforts toward reconciliation were rebuffed, and for a long while after Sumner returned to Washington, he ignored the friendly notes Palfrey continued to send him. Finally, after Palfrey had gone to what he considered "the very verge of humiliation," Sumner con-

[3] Clipping from Boston *Advertiser,* in Adams, Diary, Nov. 4, 1853; Dana, Diary, Nov. 20, and 27, 1853, Dana MSS.; Adams to Sumner, Nov. 21, 1853, copy, Adams MSS.; Adams, Diary, Nov. 21–2, 24, 1853, ibid.

sented to resume relations, though he frankly informed his friend "that it seems to me that Freedom in Massachusetts has received from you a more deadly blow than from any other living citizen of our Commonwealth." The coolness between the two men continued, and their old cordiality was not revived for years.[4]

When the new session of Congress opened in December 1853, Sumner's political fortunes were at a new low. The coalition that had elected him to office had again been defeated, this time so decisively that the plan for Free Soil–Democratic fusion in Massachusetts was finally abandoned. The recent campaign caused many of the old Conscience Whig group to doubt, as did Adams and Palfrey, Sumner's political morality and to suspect that he lacked "the main requisite, sagacity and penetration." The Whigs continued in control of the state government, and Edward Everett, the new Whig senator from Massachusetts, was able to prevent Sumner from receiving any responsible committee assignments.[5] "Eheu! Eheu!" Sumner lamented. "For a while we must eat our political bread in great humility."

• 3 •

"This Congress is the worst—or rather promises to be the worst—since the Constitution was adopted," Sumner wrote in December 1853; "it is the 'Devil's Own.' " He and Chase were now the only Free Soil members in the heavily Democratic Senate, and so hopeless was their position that rumors of Sumner's impending resignation were widely circulated.[6] As the session got under way, it was clear that his only role would be the frustratingly negative one of opposing every proposal of the Pierce administration and

[4] See the copies of the following letters in the Palfrey MSS.: Palfrey to Sumner, Nov. 29, 1853, Jan. 3, June 1, 13, and 23, 1854; Sumner to Palfrey, June 6, and 14, 1854; also Palfrey to Dana, Sept. 12, 1854, copy, ibid.

[5] Adams, Diary, Nov. 28, 1853, Adams MSS. As the Democrats gave Chase committee assignments at this session, Seward proposed that the Whig caucus include Sumner in its lists. Everett objected that he "could not consent to his being regarded as a Whig." Eventually the Whigs left vacant two posts at the foot of the committees on pensions and on enrolled bills, which the Democrats filled with Sumner's name. Seward: *Seward at Washington, 1846–1861*, p. 212; Everett, Diary, Dec. 10, 1853, Everett MSS.

[6] Pierce, III, 361; Buffalo *Commercial Advertiser*, Jan. 7, 1854; Boston *Commonwealth*, Dec. 12, 1853.

of everlastingly introducing petitions for cheaper international postage.[6a]

Sumner grew morose and sensitive. He quarreled bitterly with Everett, and only the tact of Mrs. Hamilton Fish patched up the dispute.[7] With suspicious eye he observed his fellow senators, certain that every move indicated a proslavery plot.

In January 1854 his worst suspicions seemed to receive corroboration. Stephen A. Douglas, the Democratic chairman of the Senate committee on territories, introduced a measure for organizing a territorial government for Nebraska. The new territory, which included both the present states of Kansas and Nebraska, was one from which slavery had been excluded by the Missouri Compromise of 1820, but Douglas's bill provided that "all questions pertaining to slavery in the Territories, and in the new States to be formed therefrom, are to be left to the decision of the people residing therein," and that the states to be formed from the territory, when applying for admission to the Union, should be received "with or without slavery" as their constitutions provided.

Instantly alarmed, Sumner proposed an amendment that would reaffirm the Missouri Compromise ban on slavery in the Nebraska territory. His maneuver was a hopeless one, intended to arouse public opinion against Douglas's bill; in fact, his amendment may have inadvertently been a disservice to freedom, as it also alerted Southern senators to the ambiguities of Douglas's proposal. Yielding to their pressure, Douglas, on January 23, introduced a substantially revised version of his bill, providing for two separate territorial governments in the region, and specifically asserting that the prohibition on slavery in the Missouri Compromise was "inoperative" because it had been "superseded by the principles of the legislation of 1850." [8]

[6a] In private conversation Sumner suggested adding an arbitration clause to a proposed commercial treaty between Great Britain and the United States, but both Secretary of State William L. Marcy and British minister J. F. Crampton agreed that, however desirable, the amendment would be defeated if Sumner sponsored it. Crampton to Earl of Clarendon, Jan. 1, 1854, Clarendon MSS.

[7] Sumner to Mrs. Fish, Jan. 9, 1854, copy, Fish MSS.; Everett to Mrs. Fish, Jan. 9, 1854, copy, ibid.

[8] The Missouri Compromise, which admitted Missouri to the Union as a slave state, prohibited slavery in all the rest of the territory acquired by the Louisiana Purchase which lay north of 36°30′. Thus it had been agreed since 1820 that Kansas and Nebraska would be organized as free territories. The

Even before the measure assumed its final form, Sumner was spreading the alarm that "the Nebraska bill opens anew the whole slavery question." He did not, actually, know very much about these territorial questions, nor had he hitherto exhibited any passionate concern over the fate of Nebraska. Assuming that the Missouri Compromise forever barred slavery from the region, he had failed to vote for its organization as a free territory in the previous Congress.[9] Nor did Sumner have any comprehension of the "whole broad complex of reasons, half-reasons, and quarter-reasons" behind Douglas's measure: "the disorganized, discontented state of the Democratic party, lacking both leader and policy; the obligation resting upon 'Young America' for bold, trenchant action; his own legitimate ambition to become President; the demand of the Northwest for a Pacific Railroad, with the consequent necessity for settling the Kansas-Nebraska country to furnish its future path; the fear of Missouri slaveholders lest they be surrounded on three sides by freesoil territory; [Missouri Senator David R.] Atchison's stubborn assertion that he would let Nebraska 'sink in hell' before he would see it organized on a basis excluding slaveholders with their property; and Atchison's ability to rally a solid block of Southern Senators behind him." [1] But to Sumner most of these factors were not merely unknown; they were irrelevant. All that mattered was that Douglas's bill permitted slaves in territory hitherto dedicated to liberty.

He needed no further evidence of the atrocity of Douglas's proposal, and even before the Southerners pushed the "Little Giant" into an explicit repeal of the Missouri Compromise, Sum-

Compromise of 1850 permitted the inhabitants of the New Mexico territory and the Utah territory, acquired through the War with Mexico, to decide the question of slavery for themselves by promising: "That, when admitted as a State, the said territory . . . shall be received into the Union, with or without slavery, as their constitution may prescribe at the time of their admission." Douglas claimed that by endorsing this principle of "popular sovereignty" in 1850, Congress had tacitly overruled the Missouri Compromise prohibition on slavery. For a defense of Douglas's argument see Harry V. Jaffa: *Crisis of the House Divided: An Interpretation of the Issues in the Lincoln-Douglas Debates* (New York: Doubleday & Company, Inc.; 1959), pp. 133–46.

[9] Pierce, III, 361. Sumner, Chase, and Seward all failed to vote when the Nebraska organization bill was defeated by a small margin on March 3, 1853. *Cong. Globe*, 32 Cong., 2 Sess., 1,117.

[1] Nevins: *Ordeal of the Union*, II, 102, 106. Cf. James C. Malin: *The Nebraska Question, 1852–1854* (Lawrence, Kans.; 1953); Roy F. Nichols: "The Kansas-Nebraska Act: A Century of Historiography," *Mississippi Valley Historical Review*, XLIII (1956), 187–212.

ner joined with Chase, Giddings, and three other antislavery congressmen to draw up an "Appeal of the Independent Democrats in Congress to the People of the United States." This skillful paper, written by Chase from a rough draft supplied by Giddings and then given a final literary revision by Sumner,[2] was a brilliantly effective piece of antislavery propaganda. Arraigning the bill "as a gross violation of a sacred pledge; as a criminal betrayal of previous rights; as part and parcel of an atrocious plot to exclude from a vast unoccupied region immigrants from the Old World and free laborers from our own States, and convert it into a dreary region of despotism, inhabited by masters and slaves," the "Appeal" begged free-state residents who thought of settling in the West, the German-born immigrants who had hopes of finding farms there, and Christians and Christian ministers everywhere to oppose the "monstrous plot." Douglas, so the "Appeal" charged, was actuated by "the mere hazards of a presidential game"; hoping to win Southern support, he was willing "permanently [to] subjugate the whole country to the yoke of a slaveholding despotism."

While the "Appeal" was secretly being distributed, Douglas moved for prompt consideration of his bill. Sumner and Chase, disturbed by the apparent apathy in the North and wishing their address to have a maximum effect, requested Douglas to delay the debate for a week, ostensibly so that they could give it further study, and the Illinois senator courteously agreed.[3] That same afternoon the "Appeal" appeared in Washington newspapers, and Douglas, learning that the very senators who had so blandly asked for delay were circulating what he considered gross libels upon himself and his favorite measure, grew choleric over their hypocrisy.

When the debate opened on January 30, he shrewdly turned his wrath to political purposes. By identifying all opposition to his measure with the intemperate and sometimes inaccurate "Ap-

[2] Julian: *Giddings*, p. 311.

[3] The best accounts of the Kansas-Nebraska debates are in Nevins: *Ordeal of the Union*, II, Chaps. 3–4; George Fort Milton: *The Eve of Conflict: Stephen A. Douglas and the Needless War* (Boston: Houghton Mifflin Co.; 1934), Chaps. 7–9; Albert J. Beveridge: *Abraham Lincoln, 1809–1858* (Boston: Houghton Mifflin Co.; 1928), II, Chap. 3.

peal," and by singling out the two Free Soil senators as the leaders of that opposition, he tried to consolidate behind him moderate opinion in both North and South. Ten times in his opening speech he denounced Chase and Sumner as the "abolition confederates." They were, he shouted, "the pure, unadulterated representatives of Abolitionism, Free Soilism, Niggerism in the Congress of the United States." He stigmatized the "Appeal of the Independent Democrats" as "an abolition manifesto," "a negro movement," "a wicked fabrication," "a gross falsification," "an atrocious falsehood."

Pushing ahead with driving, galloping speed, Douglas would not permit his enemies to explain their course. An interruption from Chase he brushed aside, as the senator, he claimed, had "violated all the rules of courtesy and propriety." He allowed Sumner barely a moment to declare that in signing the "Appeal" he had been judging "the act, and not its author" and that he still considered the measure "a soulless, eyeless monster—horrid, unshapely, and vast." [4]

In the ensuing bitter and vituperative debate, which occupied the Senate for most of the next month, Douglas ably marshaled on his side many moderate Northern senators and all but two of the slave-state senators. From the outset it was clear that, backed by the patronage of the Pierce administration, the bill would easily pass the Senate.

Because of Douglas's tactics, leadership of the opposition fell not to conservative Whigs, like Edward Everett, or even to Whigs of known antislavery views, like Seward, who gave one stiff, formal oration against the measure, but had little more to do with the debates, but to Chase and Sumner. Chase led the attack in an able speech that, in effect, was an amplification of the "Appeal." Knowing that it was impossible to defeat the bill in the Senate, he hoped to expose its inconsistencies and implications, to induce moderates to speak out against it, and, chiefly, to delay proceedings until Northern sentiment could be aroused. "It is *Slavery* that renews the strife," he asserted; he hit strongly at Douglas's argument that the Compromise of 1850 "superseded" the Missouri Compromise; and he denied that Douglas's "great

[4] *Cong. Globe*, 33 Cong., 1 Sess., 282.

principle" of squatter sovereignty could settle the territorial question. "What kind of popular sovereignty is that which allows one portion of the people to enslave another portion?" he asked.

Aside from raising minor questions about Indian tribes in the Nebraska territory, other opponents of the bill closely imitated Chase's argument. "You have seen them on their winding way," Douglas taunted, "meandering the narrow and crooked path in Indian file, each treading close upon the heels of the other, and neither venturing to take a step to the right, or left, or to occupy one inch of ground which did not bear the foot-print of the Abolition champion."

Sumner, both because he wanted moderate senators to voice their opposition to the Kansas-Nebraska bill first and because he was always slow in preparation, did not take the floor until February 21. By this time, he thought, Douglas's arguments had "been already amply refuted by able Senators." Nevertheless, he plunged ahead and, taking as his text a verse from Deuteronomy: "Cursed be he that removeth his neighbor's landmark," he titled his oration "The Landmark of Freedom." Declaring that the Kansas-Nebraska bill had been "precipitated . . . upon the Senate, at a moment of general calm, and in the absence of any controlling exigency, and then hurried to a vote in advance of the public voice," he condemned it, first of all, as "the infraction of solemn obligations originally proposed and assumed by the South . . . as a covenant of peace." The South had profited by the Missouri Compromise; the slave states of Missouri and Arkansas attested that. But now, "with the consideration in its pocket, it repudiates the bargain which it forced upon the country." In the second place, Douglas's bill, by permitting the extension of slavery, was "a flagrant and extravagant departure from the original policy of our fathers," and Sumner recapitulated his argument that the Founding Fathers had dedicated the nation to antislavery principles.

Douglas's bill, he concluded, was another of "the melancholy tokens of the power of slavery, under our political system." Slavery "loosens and destroys the character of Northern men, even at a distance—like the black magnetic mountain in the Arabian story, under whose irresistible attraction the iron bolts, which held together the strong timbers of a stately ship, were drawn out, till the whole fell apart, and became a disjointed wreck." Comparable was the Northern man from whom slavery had drawn the iron of principle; he became "that human anomaly—*a Northern man with Southern principles.*" After a burst of applause from the galleries, Sumner quickly ended. Douglas and his allies could pass the bill, he prophesied, but they could not settle the slavery question by their act. "Sir"—he repeated his favorite maxim—"*nothing can be settled which is not right.*" [5]

Douglas promptly replied to Sumner's charges. Giving little attention to Sumner's unquestionably correct arguments that the Compromise of 1850 was not intended to supersede the Missouri Compromise and that Douglas's bill did reopen the floodgates of sectional controversy, the "Little Giant" adroitly seized upon weaknesses in his opponent's case. The Missouri Compromise, he pointed out, was not a "compact," as Sumner had claimed; it was an act of Congress which could be repealed by any succeeding Congress. If prescription sanctified the Missouri Compromise, Douglas sharply observed, the same might be said of the Fugitive Slave Law, which Sumner wanted repealed. It was "truly refreshing," he bitingly remarked, to hear a man like Sumner, who had protested so earnestly against the compromise measures of 1850, now bear testimony "to their beneficial effects in restoring peace, harmony, and fraternity to a distracted country." Sumner's attempt to attribute abolitionist views to the Founding Fathers Douglas dismissed casually as another of those "mere essays against slavery." [6]

Nor was the "Little Giant" one to endure a personal affront in silence. Sumner's hit at "a Northern man with Southern principles" had sounded very telling in the course of his speech, but, a short time later, when Douglas, bristling with anger, demanded to know whether the senator had intended a personal reference, Sumner sat silent. "He says nothing," Douglas gloated; "he has not the candor to admit it nor the courage to deny it." Then, triumphantly, he reminded the Senate that the phrase was not

[5] Sumner: *Landmark of Freedom*, pp. 2, 4, 8–9, 13, 14.

[6] *Cong. Globe*, 33 Cong., 1 Sess., Appendix, 326; James Ford Rhodes: *History of the United States from the Compromise of 1850 . . .* (New York: The Macmillan Co.; 1893), I, 454.

new with Sumner; it had been conspicuously applied to Martin Van Buren—Sumner's candidate for the Presidency in 1848.[7]

The bitterness of Douglas's rebuttal indicated that "The Landmark of Freedom" had made a considerable impression. Even proslavery Senator Badger, of North Carolina, congratulated Sumner upon his "master-piece of oratory; perfect in its arrangements, in its historical elucidation and in its eloquent delivery"—though adding that it lacked "one thing; it was on the wrong side." Conservative Whigs like Edward Everett and William Seaton, editor of the *National Intelligencer*, thought the speech "extremely pertinent and conclusive." Chase called it "a splendid effort," and Seward enthusiastically praised it as "very brilliant, magnificent and effective." Complacently Sumner wrote Longfellow: "I have occasion to be satisfied with the reception of my speech." [8]

Particularly cheering was the news of its reception in Massachusetts. Though the Hunker newspapers of Boston failed to comment editorially on Sumner's speech, even they felt obliged to print the flattering telegraphic reports of its enthusiastic reception. The *Commonwealth* published a large extra edition containing the speech, and it was promptly exhausted by the universal and extraordinary demand. Massachusetts readers who could not get the *Commonwealth* read the speech in full in the New York *Herald*, the New York *Tribune*, and the New York *Times*. Sumner's oration was read to factory hands in Millbury, Massachusetts, as they worked, and extracts from it appeared in the *Transcript*, which fashionable Bostonians saw at tea time. "Since the introduction of this infamous bill into the Senate," Charles Francis Adams wrote the senator, "your position here has undergone a most sensible change, even those who have been most opposed to you, now acknowledge that you speak the voice of Massachusetts." [9]

Most gratifying of all was the change of opinion that seemed

[7] Everett, Diary, Apr. 6, 1854, Everett MSS. Sumner himself had been using the phrase since 1846. See *supra*, p. 147.

[8] Boston *Commonwealth*, Mar. 1, 1854; Sumner to Longfellow, Mar. 2, 1854, Longfellow MSS.; Everett, Diary, Feb. 21, 1854, Everett MSS.; Chase to Pierce, Mar. 12, 1854, Sumner MSS.; Seward: *Seward at Washington, 1846–1861*, p. 223.

[9] J. D. Baldwin to Sumner, Feb. 26, 1854, Sumner MSS.; A. H. Waters to Sumner, Mar. 4, 1854, ibid; Dana to Sumner, Feb. 26, 1854, ibid.; Adams to Sumner, Mar. 14 [1854], ibid.

to be occurring in Massachusetts Whiggery. Massachusetts conservatives had supported the Compromise of 1850 only because of Webster's assurance that it was necessary to save the Union.[1] Now it appeared that the South was plotting to extend slavery not merely to remote New Mexico, but to the fertile plains of Kansas, where Massachusetts farmers had expected to find free land, and Massachusetts manufacturers new markets.[2] Angrily Whigs cried that the price of Union was too great. At a Faneuil Hall meeting, held the day after Sumner spoke, Winthrop announced, to great applause, that he could not now support all the compromise measures of 1850—meaning the Fugitive Slave Law—and Samuel A. Eliot denounced the Kansas-Nebraska bill as "a deliberate breach of the plighted faith of the nation." [3]

In their new mood, Boston Whigs had little patience with their cautious, conservative representative, Edward Everett, whom they had sent to the Senate to checkmate Sumner. Indisposed to controversy, Everett hesitated long before declaring himself on the Kansas-Nebraska bill, and when he did come out in opposition, his muted attacks on the measure and his great courtesy toward Douglas made his efforts seem feeble when compared to the forceful directness of Chase, Seward, and Sumner. Everett's course, his own brother-in-law grumbled, proved him "stuff not good enough to wear in rainy weather, though bright enough in sunshine." Even a loyal Whig like Hillard thought Everett's speech "like a boned turkey—the knife goes clean through." When Everett, afflicted by kidney stones, was obliged to leave the Senate chamber during the long evening session of March 3, when the bill finally passed, Boston Whigs said that he had shirked the vote, and cruelly laughed that a man with so much gravel should be without grit.[4]

As Everett declined, Sumner rose. Daily he received dozens of enthusiastic letters, many from constituents who had hitherto

[1] But, for some economic considerations that made the Compromise palatable to them see David D. Van Tassel: "Gentlemen of Property and Standing: Compromise Sentiment in Boston in 1850," *New England Quarterly*, XXIII (1950), 307–19.

[2] Cf. Philip S. Foner: *Business and Slavery: The New York Merchants and The Irrepressible Conflict* (Chapel Hill: University of North Carolina Press; 1941), Chap. 5.

[3] New York *Tribune*, Feb. 24, 1854.

[4] Pierce, III, 370; Hillard to Lieber, Mar. 2, 1854, Lieber MSS.; George Sumner to Sumner [Mar. 1854], Sumner MSS.

opposed his course. With charming naïveté he took handfuls of the complimentary messages over to the Sewards and read them aloud, so that his friends could see that he was truly loved and wanted by Massachusetts.[5]

Strengthened by such support, he began to thrive under the attacks made upon him on the Senate floor, and more than once ventured, without having prepared and memorized a formal speech, to enter into the debates. Courteously but firmly he corrected Senator Butler, who misrepresented the status of slavery in colonial Massachusetts, and with more acerbity he denied Senator Moses Norris's allegation that he had counseled violence in resisting the fugitive slave laws.

By the time the Kansas-Nebraska bill came up for final vote in the Senate, Sumner felt ready to tangle with Douglas himself, but he found the "Little Giant" a more formidable foe than his subordinates. In a memorable Senate session that lasted for seventeen consecutive hours, Douglas reached a height of eloquence and vindictiveness. Summarizing the arguments for his bill, Douglas refuted the charges made by its opponents. Toward Sumner and Chase, whom he held responsible for the anti-Nebraska sentiment sweeping through the North, he was overbearingly insolent. When Sumner tried to explain his views on the Missouri Compromise, Douglas shouted him down and, with temper flaring, denounced him and Chase: "You degrade your own States. . . . You have stimulated [the people] to these acts [of opposition to the Nebraska bill], which are disgraceful to your State, disgraceful to your party, and disgraceful to your cause." If Sumner dared impeach his motives, Douglas snarled: "I must be permitted to remind the Senator from Massachusetts that I did not enter into any combinations or arrangements by which my character, my principles, and my honor, were set up at public auction or private sale in order to procure a seat in the Senate of the United States!"

Sumner, who always shrank "instinctively from any effort to repel a personal assault," rose to deny that he had come "into this body by any waiver of principles; by any abandonment of my principles of any kind; by any effort or activity of my own, in any degree."

[5] Seward: *Seward at Washington, 1846–1861*, p. 226.

Douglas sneeringly rejected his explanation: "As well might the receiver of stolen goods deny any responsibility for the larceny, while luxuriating in the proceeds of the crime, as the Senator to avoid the consequences resulting from the mode of his election while he clings to the office." "I regret," Douglas added unctuously, "that the Senator should now, by a violation of all the rules of courtesy and propriety, compel me to refresh his mind upon these unwelcome reminiscences." [6]

Though Sumner had announced that he intended once more to enter the debate in opposition to the bill, he now took Seward's advice and did not speak again. At 4:55 in the morning of March 4, the Senate passed Douglas's bill, by a vote of thirty-seven to fourteen, with Sumner's vote in the negative. It was still dark when Sumner and Chase left the Capitol together, but Douglas's sympathizers in the city were firing cannon to celebrate his triumph. "They celebrate a present victory," said Chase, turning to his companion, "but the echoes they awake will never rest till slavery itself shall die." [7]

· 4 ·

"The North, through this Administration, is delivered bound, hand and foot to the South," Sumner grieved, but as long as he felt that Massachusetts was behind him, he was not despondent. "For a while Freedom is defeated," he admitted, "but I turn to the country and to God and do not despair." [8]

His opportunity to make another onslaught against slavery came when Mrs. Harriet Beecher Stowe, acting upon a hint in the "Appeal of the Independent Democrats," devoted some of her royalties from *Uncle Tom's Cabin* to the collection of a "*united clerical protest of New England*" against the Nebraska act.[9] Solemnly, "in the name of Almighty God, and in his presence," the clergymen denounced Douglas's bill as "a great moral wrong, . . . a breach of faith, . . . a measure full of danger to the Union, and

[6] *Cong. Globe*, 33 Cong., 1 Sess., Appendix, 234, 309, 332, 335–6.

[7] Sumner to S. Hale, Mar. 22, 1854, MS., N. H. Hist. Soc.; Pierce, III, 361; J. W. Schuckers: *The Life and Public Services of Salmon Portland Chase* (New York: D. Appleton and Company; 1874), p. 156.

[8] Sumner to R. C. Waterston, Mar. 21, 1854, Waterston MSS.; Sumner to J. Wingate Thornton, Mar. 9, 1854, Segal Coll.

[9] Mrs. Stowe to Sumner, Feb. 23, 1854, Sumner MSS.

exposing us to the righteous judgements of the Almighty." When completed, the petition formed a scroll 200 feet long. To avoid the imputation that this was an abolitionist manifesto, its sponsors asked Edward Everett to present it to the Senate. With a notable want of enthusiasm, he did so, and even when Douglas sprang up to denounce "political preachers" who were "desecrating the pulpit, and prostituting the sacred desk to the miserable and corrupting influence of party politics," Everett presented a cautious apology, rather than a manly defense of the petitioners.

Sumner looked on in anger, but while his colleague had the petition in charge, he felt that he should not intervene. But when Everett, ill and unhappy, went home to Boston and, a few weeks later, resigned his seat, Sumner saw his chance. Eagerly he welcomed some late signatures to the clergymen's petition, and on May 25, when the Senate prepared to give its final approval to the Kansas-Nebraska bill, as amended in the House, he gained the floor, ostensibly to present the petition, actually to vindicate the preachers who signed it. He would not, he announced, attempt "anything like a defence of the clergy. They need no such thing at my hands. There are men in the Senate justly eminent for eloquence, learning, and ability; but there is no man here competent, except in his own conceit, to sit in judgment on the clergy of New England." The Senators who had been "so swift with criticism and sarcasm" against these petitioners might profit by their example. Perhaps Senator Butler, who was "not insensible to scholarship, might learn from them something of its graces." Perhaps Senator James M. Mason, of Virginia, who found "no sanction under the Constitution for any remonstrance from clergymen, might learn from them something of the privileges of an American citizen." Perhaps Douglas himself, "who precipitated this odious measure upon the country, might learn from them something of wisdom."

Predicting the direst consequences from the Kansas-Nebraska act, Sumner announced that it was "at once the worst and the best which Congress ever acted": "It is the worst bill, inasmuch as it is a present victory of Slavery. . . . It is the best bill on which Congress ever acted; for it . . . annuls all past compromises with Slavery, and makes all future compromises impossible. Thus it puts Freedom and Slavery face to face, and bids them grapple. Who can doubt the result?" [1]

The very next day gave an answer to Sumner's question. On May 26 a throng of citizens assembled in Faneuil Hall to protest the arrest of a pitiable fugitive slave named Anthony Burns. Incited by Wendell Phillips and Theodore Parker, they mobbed the courthouse, where Burns was imprisoned, and tried to force an entrance. They were repelled, but only after they had killed one of the temporary guards appointed by the United States marshal. Promptly President Pierce ordered troops to Boston, and on June 2 they escorted the trembling fugitive through the crepe-hung streets lined with hostile spectators down to the ship that waited to carry him back to Virginia and to slavery.[2]

Sumner's enemies blamed him for the outbreak. Ignoring the fact that telegraphic reports of his speech did not reach Boston until the day after the Burns riot, they pointed to his prediction that the Nebraska bill would "broadcast through the land, dragons' teeth, which . . . will . . . fructify in civil strife and feud." Sumner, claimed the pro-administration Washington *Union*, had given the command for the Burns mob. The Washington *Star* warned: "If Southern gentlemen are threatened and assaulted, while legally seeking to obtain possession of property for the use of which they have a solemn constitutional guaranty, . . . *certain Northern men now in our midst* will have to evince a little more circumspection . . . in their walk, talk, and acts. . . . *Let Sumner and his infamous gang* feel that he cannot outrage the fame of his country, counsel treason to its law, incite the ignorant to bloodshed and murder, and still receive the support and countenance of the society of this city, which he has done so much to vilify." [3]

New England grew excited over the implicit threat. The seizure of Burns and the attempt to intimidate Sumner, wrote one formerly conservative Boston Whig, had unified "the good

[1] Henry M. Dexter to Pierce, Apr. 15, 1885, Pierce MSS.; Sumner: *Final Protest for Himself and the Clergy of New England against Slavery in Kansas and Nebraska* (Washington; 1854), pp. 4–6.

[2] The best account of the Burns case is Samuel Shapiro: "The Rendition of Anthony Burns," *Jou~nal of Negro History,* XLIV (Jan. 1959), 34–51.

[3] Sumner: *Works,* III, 348.

men of all parties in a common sentiment of hostility to the encroachments of the slave power." Joseph Hawley, future governor of Connecticut, offered to come to Washington and defend Sumner. "I have revolvers and can use them," he announced. "Should you fall," one admiring correspondent told the senator, "you will . . . kindle a fire of freedom that will blaze and burn the length and breadth of the land the light of which will irradiate the fartherest corners of the earth."[4]

Confident in the support of his constituents, Sumner paid little attention to the threats—except to see that they received suitable publicity. Not even a Southern attempt to insult him in the restaurant where he regularly dined frightened him. "The Administration organs tried to stir a mob against me," he calmly told Mrs. Seward, "and some evil-disposed persons expressed a desire to put a bullet through my head; but I was never for a moment disturbed." He continued to walk unarmed from his lodgings to the Capitol, and to friends who urged him to take precautions, he replied: "I am here to do my duty and shall continue to do it without regard to personal consequences."[5]

Far from deterring Sumner, the threats made him the more eager to renew his war on slavery. Feeling "humbled in the dust" by the outcome of the Burns case, he planned again to demand the repeal of the odious Fugitive Slave Act. Then he would move "for the complete annulling by the North of all the other compromises." "Slavery will be discussed with us *as never before*," he promised Theodore Parker.[6]

Sumner did not have an opportunity to make the formal oratorical assault he had intended, however, for inadvertently his new colleague, Julius Rockwell, Everett's successor, started a fresh debate on slavery when he presented a petition of 2,900 Massachusetts citizens asking repeal of the Fugitive Slave Law. Southern senators objected to its reception because some of its signers had been members of the Burns rescue mob, who, "with

[4] George Livermore to Sumner, June 1, 1854, Sumner MSS.; Joseph R. Hawley to Sumner, May 31, 1854, ibid.; C. S. Macreading to Sumner, June 2, 1854, ibid.

[5] Sumner to Mrs. W. H. Seward, June 17, 1854, Seward MSS.; Sumner to Longfellow [June 2, 1854], Longfellow MSS.

[6] Sumner to James Freeman Clarke, June 10, 1854, Clarke MSS.; Sumner to Dana, June 4, 1854, Dana MSS.; Bigelow: *Retrospections,* I, 136; Weiss: *Parker,* II, 140.

Sumner during His First Term in the Senate

THE NATIONAL ARCHIVES

Salmon P. Chase

Stephen A. Douglas

Edward Everett

William H. Seward

SENATE LEADERS OF THE 1850's

THE NATIONAL ARCHIVES

treason in their hearts, and with knives in their hands," had resisted "the constituted authorities of the country."

Intervening to assist his colleague, Sumner boldly answered Southern threats that repeal of the fugitive slave laws would dissolve the Union. "If the Union be in any way dependent on an act . . . so revolting in every regard," he announced, "then it ought not to exist." He himself would continue "with joy and satisfaction" to work for repeal of the obnoxious law. As for the signers of the petition, something must be pardoned them because they were citizens of Massachusetts. Could Massachusetts, the home of Faneuil Hall, where John Adams and Joseph Warren had thunderously spoken for liberty, of Bunker Hill, of Lexington and Concord, be expected to tolerate the "disgusting rites" by which a "slave-hunter from Virginia" doomed a fellow man to bondage? Just as Massachusetts had annulled the Stamp Act, so would it refuse to enforce the Fugitive Slave Law.[7]

While Sumner was speaking, Butler came into the Senate chamber, and as he listened to Sumner's conclusion, he grew angrier and angrier. Seizing the floor, he denounced Sumner's speech as one "whose whole style, tone, and character does not become *a Senate.*" "If we repeal the fugitive slave law," Butler demanded, turning to Rockwell, "will the honorable Senator tell me that Massachusetts will execute the provision of the Constitution without any law of Congress? . . . Would they send fugitives back to us after trial by jury, or any other mode?" As Rockwell remained silent, Butler turned upon Sumner. "Will this honorable Senator tell me that he will do it?"

"Does the honorable Senator ask me if I would personally join in sending a fellow-man into bondage?" Sumner replied. " 'Is thy servant a dog, that he should do this thing?' "[8]

Furious, Butler began berating Sumner for saying that it was "a dog's office to execute the Constitution of the United States." Promptly Mason, of Virginia, joined him, shouting that Sumner had "rudely, wantonly, grossly assailed" the dignity of the Senate by his "vapid, vulgar declamation," the utterance "of a fanatic, one whose reason is dethroned." Pettit, of Indiana,

[7] Sumner: *Defense of Massachusetts* . . . (Washington; 1854), pp. 3–6.

[8] Wendell Phillips had earlier made effective use of this same biblical quotation. Oscar Sherwin: *Prophet of Liberty: The Life and Times of Wendell Phillips* (New York: Bookman Associates, Inc.; 1958), p. 219.

cried that Sumner ought to be expelled for declaring that he would spit on his solemn oath to support the Constitution, an oath Sumner had sworn "upon the holy Evangelists of God, kissing the book, giving seal and sanction" to the asseveration.

"Never!" Sumner interjected angrily. "Never!"

"You . . . said you would not maintain the Constitution of the United States—" Pettit retorted.

From his seat, Sumner interrupted: "I said I recognized no obligation in the Constitution of the United States to bind me to help to reduce a man to slavery." [9]

"Sir," Pettit addressed the chair, "I am inclined to believe that, in a moral point of view, that Senator cannot find one beneath himself. . . . He . . . has sunk . . . to a depth of humiliation and degradation which it would not be enviable for the veriest serf or the lowest of God's creation to occupy."

Two days later, on June 28, when the debate was resumed, Pettit renewed his assault upon Sumner, and Stephen Mallory, of Florida, joined him. Even more vindictive was Clement C. Clay, Jr., of Alabama, who called Sumner a "serpent," a "filthy reptile," a "leper," a Uriah Heep, and urged that he be ostracized and placed "in that nadir of social degradation which he merits."

Forcefully Sumner defended himself. He was not faithless to his oath to support the Constitution. "No such thing. Sir, I swore to support the Constitution *as I understood it;* nor more, nor less." For his interpretation of his oath he could cite not merely his own mentor, John Quincy Adams, but that Democratic sage, Andrew Jackson. Sumner thought the Constitution imposed no duty upon him, either as an individual or as a senator, to assist in returning fugitive slaves. Remembering the Southerners' aversion to the slave trade, he asked scathingly: "How many there are, even in this body, if, indeed, there be a single Senator, who would stoop to any such service? Until some one rises and openly confesses his willingness to become a Slave-

[9] The Senate spent much time two days later discussing precisely what words Sumner had used. This version is the one Sumner himself gave to the Senate reporter. Pettit charged that Sumner had falsified the Senate's records. Southern senators pretended to believe that Sumner had declared he had no obligation to obey the Constitution of the United States. What he clearly meant —and, according to most Northern senators, what he said—was that he did not recognize that the Constitution imposed upon him a duty to return fugitive slaves. *Cong. Globe,* 33 Cong., 1 Sess., 1,549–51, 1,557.

Hunter, I will not believe there can be one." Pausing dramatically, he waited, but no Southerner volunteered.[1]

Throughout his reply Sumner maintained a tone of bitter personal vindictiveness, coupled with a hauteur infuriating to his opponents. Intending to be "as severe as an overseer's lash," he rebuked the "plantation manners" of Butler and of Mason; doubtless "in the characteristic fantasy of the moment" they fancied themselves not in the United States Senate, but on "a plantation well stocked with slaves, over which the lash of the overseer had full sway." Sneeringly he turned upon Mason, who, "with imperious look, and in the style of Sir Forcible Feeble," had tried to question Sumner's interpretation of the Fugitive Slave Law. As father of that "soulless monster," Mason might be presumed to know something about its constitutionality; in fact, he was ignorant of all knowledge of law. Knowing "something of his conversation, something of his manners, something of his attainments, something of his abilities, something of his character," Sumner boldly invited comparison of his own legal knowledge and personal character with those of the Virginian's. From Pettit, Mallory, and Clay, Sumner turned away scornfully. They were "best answered by silence; best answered by withholding the words which leap impulsively to the lips." [2]

When Sumner sat down, Clay sprang to his feet to declare that he, for one, was willing to accept Sumner's challenge; he had the moral courage to declare that he would assist in the rendition of a fugitive slave. Sumner turned upon him witheringly: "Then let the Senator say the immoral courage." [3]

As the debate ended, there was serious talk of attempting to expel Sumner for perjury and treason, but a quiet canvass showed that sufficient votes could not be obtained. Unquestionably Sumner emerged from the controversy with new stature. Hitherto he had been regarded merely as an elaborate and learned orator; now he had proved that, when aroused, he could fight back in debate. Henceforth Southern senators tended to leave him alone in respectful silence, while cutting him socially. The very next day he presented another petition for the repeal

[1] Sumner: *Defense of Massachusetts*, pp. 8–9.

[2] Ibid., pp. 7, 12–14, 15–16; Sumner to Earl of Carlisle, Oct. 30, 1854, Carlisle MSS.

[3] *Cong. Globe*, 33 Cong., 1 Sess., 1,554.

of the Fugitive Slave Act, and this time his Southern opponents, to get rid of the subject, quietly referred it to the appropriate committee.[4]

Respect from the South was matched by an overwhelming demonstration of affection and trust from the North. Sumner's "matchless eloquence and power," the New York *Times* announced, had carried the day; "his triumph was complete." "You have given the heaviest blow you ever struck to the slave-holding Oligarchy," Wilson congratulated him. "Dont I feel proud to think that I had a humble part in placing you in the Senate?" "You have done gallantly," Dana echoed. "You don't know how rejoiced I am that a Northern gentleman and scholar has met them in the true spirit of a cavalier." [5]

Flushed with praise, Sumner had never been so radiantly happy, so completely triumphant. Though exhausted by the long session and by the heat of the Washington summer, he was, nevertheless, for the first time in his Senate career, anxious to spend his vacation campaigning in Massachusetts. Surely the North was now aroused. It was time to forget "all past differences on Tariff, Internal improvements and other things" and form "a *Grand Junction* party" in the North which would "take the control of the Government." [6]

• 5 •

"I find myself 'a popular man,' " Sumner reported enthusiastically upon his return to Boston. "If my election to the Senate were now pending before the million of educated people whom I now represent, I should be returned without any opposition." All over the North, Free Soilers, Whigs, and antislavery Democrats were combining into anti-Nebraska coalitions, and a "fusion" convention of Massachusetts antislavery elements in July adopted the name "Republican." "At last there seems to be an awakening of the North," Sumner confidently exclaimed. "Good!" [7]

[4] Ibid., pp. 1,567–68.

[5] New York *Times*, June 30, 1854; Wilson to Sumner, July 2, 1854, Sumner MSS.; Dana to Sumner, July 2, 1854, ibid.

[6] Sumner to Howe, July 22, 1854, ibid.; Bigelow: *Retrospections*, I, 135; Sumner to Amasa Walker, Apr. 26, 1854, Walker MSS.

[7] Pierce, III, 406; Sumner to Mrs. W. H. Seward, June 17, 1854, Seward MSS.

At the regular nominating convention of the new party, held in Worcester in September, Sumner lashed out at the national administration in what even his critics admitted was an "eloquent, and forcible, and bitter" address. Avoiding Latin phrases and quotations from the classics, he branded the Kansas-Nebraska act as an atrocity paralleled only by the Burns case, where Federal authorities had converted the Boston courthouse "into a fortress and barracoon," guarded by "heartless hirelings" and "a prostituted militia." Against such proslavery aggressions, there must be union of all true Northern men. Neither Democrats nor Whigs could effectively battle the slave power. "Unseduced and unterrified," Northern voters must go forth "As *Republicans* . . . to encounter the *Oligarchs* of Slavery." [8]

Elated by applause and carried away by his own oratory, Sumner saw in the Republican convention at Worcester the vanguard of the armies of freedom; it was instead, as Adams acidly noted, merely "a drum and fife [corps] without followers." Democrats, deterred by Cushing's "ukase" from further collaboration with antislavery men, did not join the new organization. It did not embrace all of the Free Soilers, for Wilson, who was running for governor, tried to exclude Adams, Palfrey, Dana, and other former Conscience leaders from the new party. Nor did many Massachusetts Whigs join the Republicans. Opposed to the Kansas-Nebraska act, they distrusted Sumner's extreme views and suspected Wilson's "party *alliances* and *manoeuvres*." Like Seward in New York and Abraham Lincoln in Illinois, more than one Massachusetts antislavery man decided: "I can do my duty more efficiently and sincerely as the parties now stand . . . as a Whig than in any other way." [9]

So feeble was the enthusiasm for the new party that Republican leaders did not dare let Sumner campaign for its candidates, fearing that they could not attract audiences for him. The senator had come home from Washington "full of fight on the Slavery

[8] Boston *Advertiser,* Sept. 8, 1854; Sumner: *Duties of Massachusetts at This Crisis* . . . (n.d.).

[9] Adams to Bird, Oct. 16, 1854, copy, Adams MSS.; Bird to Sumner, Apr. 16, 1854, Sumner MSS. On Free Soil factionalism see A. G. Browne to Sumner, Feb. 22, 1854, Sumner MSS.; Dana to Sumner, Feb. 26, 1854, ibid.; Adams to G. Bailey, Sept. 2, 1855, copy, Adams MSS. For the Whig position see Boston *Advertiser,* Sept. 8, 1854; C. G. Loring to Sumner, Mar. 14, 1854, Sumner MSS.; T. D. Eliot to Sumner, Sept. 13, 1854, ibid.

question" and expecting to take the stump, but he found himself idle and unwanted as the election drew near.[1]

The November election returns revealed the reason behind the apathetic Republican campaigning. Henry Wilson had sold his party out. Becoming aware that a new secret organization, technically known as the Order of the Star Spangled Banner, but generally called Know-nothings, was combining the discontented factions of all parties into a powerful anti-immigrant, anti-Catholic movement, Wilson had joined a nativist lodge and had thrown his strength behind Henry J. Gardner, the Know-nothing candidate for governor. In return he secured a pledge that, if successful, the Know-nothings would elect him to the Senate as Sumner's colleague. Gardner received an unprecedented majority of nearly 33,000 votes, and the new legislature consisted of one Whig, one Democrat, one Republican—and 377 Know-nothings. Surely, wrote Rufus Choate, "Any thing more low, obscene, feculent, the manifold heavings of history have not cast up. We shall come to the worship of onions, cats and things vermiculate." [2]

Though Sumner was surprised by the extent of the Know-nothing victory, he had, of course, been aware for some time of the existence of the nativist movement. Some of his strongest political supporters had been active in it, for there had always been a strong nativist tinge to Massachusetts antislavery. From the beginning, Free Soilers had objected not merely to slaveholders in the South, but to Northern manufacturers and businessmen, economically tied to the South's "peculiar institution," who were altering the structure of New England society. Sumner's 1848

[1] Samuel Downer to Mann, Oct. 26, 1854, Mann MSS. Sumner occupied his spare time preparing an elaborate lecture on Granville Sharp, the English abolitionist. Sumner: *Works*, III, 479–519.

[2] Robinson: *Pen Portraits*, p. 63. Of the extensive literature on the Know-nothing movement in the North, I have found the following most helpful: Ray Allen Billington: *The Protestant Crusade, 1800–1860* (New York: The Macmillan Co.; 1938), Chaps. 15–16; Handlin: *Boston's Immigrants*, Chap. 7; Bean: "Party Transformations," Chaps. 8–10; Bean: "Puritan Versus Celt, 1850–1860," *New England Quarterly*, VII (1934), 70–80; George H. Haynes: "A Chapter from the Local History of Knownothingism," *New England Magazine*, XV (1896–7), 82–96; Haynes: "A Know Nothing Legislature," *Annual Report of the American Historical Association*, 1896, I, 177–87; Harry J. Carman and Reinhard H. Luthin: "Some Aspects of the Know-Nothing Movement Reconsidered," *South Atlantic Quarterly*, XXXIX (1940), 213–34.

theory of a conspiracy between the Lords of the Loom and the Lords of the Lash precisely expressed the dual suspicions of Massachusetts antislavery men. From hostility to manufacturing and corporations it was an easy step to opposition to cities and their working-class population. The transition was easier because by the 1850's factory workers in Massachusetts were predominantly immigrants. During the decade after 1846 over 100,000 Irish entered the Bay State; by 1855 they formed twenty-five per cent of Worcester's population and a majority of Boston's. Cruelly exploited by American employers, compelled to live in virtual ghettos, clinging to Catholicism, the Irish became a visible symbol of the forces that were transforming an unwilling New England.

Both temperamentally and intellectually Sumner disliked this nativist movement, which he feared might "break up the whole Northern combination and . . . give the South another lease of national ascendency." After the election of 1854, he talked confidentially with Adams and S. C. Phillips about rebuilding a fresh, independent antislavery party in Massachusetts, uncontaminated by Wilson and other Know-nothings. When the nativist legislature in 1855 elected Wilson to the Senate, Sumner was not a little regretful.[3]

But, whatever he said in private, Sumner took great care not to offend the powerful new order. Recognizing that most Massachusetts antislavery men, and practically all his special political backers, were now Know-nothings, he refrained, even in private letters, from condemning its course. Mildly and unaccusingly he explained the Know-nothing success in Massachusetts: "The people were tired of the old parties and they have made a new channel." Bolder politicians came out bluntly against the nativist party; Stephen A. Douglas, for instance, condemned it as early as July 4, 1854. But Sumner held his peace and, in January 1855, presented to Congress, without explanation or disclaimer, a petition of Massachusetts citizens seeking to impose a tax of $250 per head on immigrants. When a leading Unitarian

[3] Sumner to "My Dear Sir," Dec. 7, 1854, MS., Univ. of Chicago; Adams, Diary, Sept. 16, and Nov. 16, 1854, Adams MSS.; S. C. Phillips to Sumner, Nov. 15, 1854, Sumner MSS.; W. H. Whitcomb to Sumner, Jan. 16, 1855, ibid.; Everett, Diary, Feb. 9, 1855, Everett MSS.; Pierce to Mann, Jan. 18, 1855, Mann MSS.

minister urged Sumner to become Massachusetts' champion not merely against slavery, but against nativist bigotry, he received no reply.[4]

Sumner's silence showed how worried he was becoming about his own political future. Governor Gardner was no sooner elected than he began scheming to use his office, and the Know-nothing movement, to secure his own election as Sumner's successor. As Sumner could not conscientiously advocate nativist principles, and as, in any case, he had delayed too long to assume leadership in the Know-nothing movement, he was once again in the exposed position of a senator without a political machine behind him.

The new session of Congress, which assembled in December 1854, offered him no chance to recover his fortunes. There were no angry sectional contests, which would give him opportunities for enunciating principles or for assaulting the South. On only one day did the debates turn to the slavery question. Sumner seized his chance to declare that "no temptation, no inducement," could induce him "in any way to sanction the return of any man to Slavery," but after the heated quarrels of the previous session, that was hardly news. Deciding that the best thing he could do would be to follow a friend's advice and present "matters of business" to the Senate so as to demonstrate that he knew "a great many things outside . . . of peace and war, and slavery," he started introducing resolutions for the payment of bounties to fisheries, the erection of a new marine hospital in Boston, and the guaranteeing of wages to seamen in case of shipwreck.[5]

Feeling his popularity slipping, Sumner became increasingly unhappy as the session drew to an end and he had no opportunity to recover lost ground. In such a mood, even his good friends found him unbearable. When Seward, eager to promote New York constituents' interests in an election year, asked him to support a subsidy for the Collins Steamship Line, Sumner declared

[4] Sumner to Mrs. Hamilton Fish, Nov. 15, 1854, Fish MSS.; Adams, Diary, Oct. 25, 1854, and Mar. 24, 1855, Adams MSS.; *Cong. Globe*, 33 Cong., 2 Sess., 178; John Weiss to Sumner, May 8, 1855, Sumner MSS.

[5] Sumner: *The Demands of Freedom Speech . . . in the Senate . . . February 23, 1855* (n.d.), p. 8; P. W. Chandler to Sumner, Feb. 17, 1855, Sumner MSS.

that there was not sufficient economic justification for the measure. Then Seward urged him to vote for the measure as a personal favor. Loftily Sumner replied that he had not been sent to the Senate to get Seward re-elected. Losing his self-command, Seward exclaimed: "Sumner, you're a damned fool." The two men did not speak for months.[6]

Returning North in March, as the term ended, Sumner tried to rally public opinion behind him by delivering a lecture on "The Antislavery Enterprise: Its Necessity, Practicability, and Dignity." After giving the address in several smaller Massachusetts cities, and in Auburn and Albany, New York, he delivered it in May at the huge Metropolitan Theater in New York City, which was crammed with enthusiastic listeners. Shout upon shout of applause greeted Sumner as he stepped to the lectern, and his audience was carried away by his "magnificent presence, . . . physically as well as mentally a giant, and symmetrical as his own orations, the grand organ-music of his voice, bearing to the heart the intense conviction that it comes deep out of the heart; the calm strength of his delivery, breathing the conscious assurance of eventual victory; the thunderbursts of eloquence."[7]

Sumner's brilliant and successful appearance in New York may have convinced him that "a general union of the antislavery elements on a broad foundation" was in the offing, but when he returned to Massachusetts, he was disillusioned. Bay State politics were "in a perfect muss." One objective reporter listed some of the turbulent ingredients: "Whig party nowhere. Democratic very small. Free Soil small. Republican small. Antipope and antislave large. Rum party pretty large, very active. Temperance pretty large, and doubtfull [*sic*]—pure Native Americanism small, and active. Catholic perfectly quiet." A new secret order called Know-Somethings, opposed to the Know-nothings, but also devoted to upholding Freedom, Protestantism, and Temperance, helped confuse the situation. "There is material to work upon,"

[6] Worthington Chauncey Ford (ed.): *Letters of Henry Adams (1858–1891)* (Boston: Houghton Mifflin Co.; 1930), p. 87; Sumner to Hamilton Fish, Apr. 28, 1855, copy, Fish MSS. Characteristically, Sumner did vote for the bill, after all, and even published a little speech explaining his stand. *Cong. Globe*, 33 Cong., 2 Sess., Appendix, 313; New York *Times*, Mar. 2, 1855.

[7] Sumner: *Works*, IV, 1–51; newspaper reaction clipped in *The Liberator*, XXV (May 18, 1855), 79; XXV (May 25, 1855), 81. Because of unusual public demand, Sumner repeated his lecture in Manhattan and gave it also in Brooklyn.

a veteran politician concluded sardonically. "No man knows what will come out of it." [8]

So uncertain was the political situation, Sumner decided that he had a clear duty—to remain aloof from all factions by making a prolonged trip to the West. After stopping to see his old friend Horace Mann at Antioch College, and visiting Chase in Cincinnati, Sumner crossed into Kentucky, where he made his first real acquaintance with the South's "peculiar institution," which he had so often denounced. Guided by Cassius M. Clay, the Kentucky antislavery leader, he saw the bluegrass country at the loveliest time of the year, and he found much he could admire and much he could never forget. The magnificent pastures and the cattle made a strong impression on him, and he was astonished to find the slave quarters so snug and comfortable. But, at Lexington he watched a slave auction on the courthouse steps, where a Negro was "compelled to open his mouth and show his teeth, like a horse"; his stagecoach was delayed so that the driver could "help lick a nigger"; at a hotel meal he had "to witness the revolting spectacle of a poor slave, yet a child, almost felled to the floor by a blow on the head from a clenched fist." Prudently keeping his reactions to himself, he traveled south to Mammoth Cave, then to Nashville, and on to St. Louis.[9]

Willingly leaving the slave states behind him, Sumner took a slow steamboat trip up the Mississippi River, stopping off at numerous places. At Davenport, Iowa, his horse ran away, and the buggy in which he was riding "was dashed against the projecting rails of a zig-zag fence, with such tremendous force that it whirled some ten or twelve feet into the air, and turning several complete somersets, came down upon the ground with . . . Sumner under its wreck." Suffering only from bad bruises, he continued to Minneapolis, where he made quite a favorable impression even upon his political opponents. At Milwaukee he visited Sherman M. Booth, who was contesting the constitutionality of the Fugitive Slave Act, and was cordially welcomed by his "hosts of admiring friends." After short trips to Chicago and to

[8] Samuel Downer to Mann, Aug. 25, 1855, Mann MSS.

[9] Sumner to William Schouler [June 1855], Segal Coll.; Pierce, III, 417–19; Sumner: *Works*, IV, 64. During the 1855 campaign the Boston *Post* charged that Sumner, while in Kentucky, had been so impressed by the "perfect happiness and contentment" of the Negroes that "he could but confess that his previous belief concerning slavery had been . . . wholly incorrect." Sumner promptly issued "a point-blank contradiction." Boston *Post*, Nov. 15–16, and Dec. 14, 1855.

Detroit, where he again flirted with Senator Cass's handsome, marriageable daughter, he made a steamboat tour of the Great Lakes before returning to New England for a brief vacation in the White Mountains. Not until September 6 did he return to Boston, having traversed eleven free states and three slave states.[1]

Prolonged as his vacation had been, it was not long enough to permit him to escape from the complexities of Massachusetts politics. Some changes, to be sure, had occurred during his absence. The defeat of the Know-nothings in the Virginia gubernatorial election gave promise that political nativism was but a transient phenomenon, and more and more politicians mustered courage to denounce it. In Massachusetts the new party, with its unwieldy majority of untrained legislators, had, despite a remarkable record of constructive, democratic achievements, lost favor, partly because of a notorious investigation of the state's convents and nunneries. So unpopular was the party by early summer of 1855, Charles Francis Adams observed, "that a disavowal of sympathy with them *now* would be liable to the suspicion of being prompted by a wish to escape odium." [2]

Wilson had reverted to his original strong antislavery position and, resenting Southern domination of the Know-nothing party, led an exodus of Northern nativists from the party's national convention. Upon his return to Massachusetts, he started elaborate negotiations to bring together all groups known to be opposed to slavery. Gardner, willing to accept support from any quarter, promised to join in the hope of securing re-election as governor. Wilson extended a special invitation to Winthrop, as the leader of conservative Whiggery, "to take the lead in forming a victorious Republican party." For a while it looked as if antislavery Whigs, anti-Nebraska Democrats, Know-nothings, and Free Soilers would all combine at the convention called for Worcester on September 20.[3]

[1] Ibid., July 21, 1855; James Shields to Hamilton Fish, Nov. 25, 1855, Fish MSS.; Milwaukee *Sentinel*, July 17–18, 1855; Theodore Calvin Pease and James G. Randall (eds.): *The Diary of Orville Hickman Browning* ("Collections of the Illinois State Historical Library," Vol. XX, Springfield: Illinois State Historical Lib.; 1925), I, 192; W. Preston to Hamilton Fish, Sept. 5, 1855, Fish MSS.; Sumner to Gerrit Smith, Aug. 28, 1855, Smith MSS.

[2] Adams to G. Bailey, Apr. 15, 1855, copy, Adams MSS.

[3] For details on the break-up of the Know-nothing party and the origins of Massachusetts Republicanism see Bean: "Party Transformations," Chap. 11; Wilson: *Slave Power*, II, Chap. 32.

Sumner had kept himself studiously ignorant of these developments during his long vacation, but, on his return, he faced a difficult decision. Fearing both the "corrupt tactics" of Governor Gardner, who was seeking re-election as a steppingstone to the Senate, and the hostility of Wilson, who was promising men like Winthrop "the honors of success" if they joined the fusion movement, he anticipated that either the success or the failure of the Worcester convention might imperil his Senate seat. Firmly he declined to attend.[4]

The Republican convention proved not to be so dangerous as Sumner had expected. Winthrop and the Boston Whigs refused to attend, chiefly because they distrusted Wilson and Sumner. Lacking another candidate, Wilson swore renewed fidelity to Sumner's interests, and pledged: "If I live and God gives me power Sumner goes back to the Senate." [5] Through Wilson's management and Dana's shrewd parliamentary maneuvering, the convention adopted a platform that contained no nativist appeals, and, after a hard fight, it passed over Gardner and nominated Julius Rockwell for governor.

When Gardner bolted the Republican party and ran as a Know-nothing candidate, Sumner clearly had no choice but to campaign for Rockwell. His decision was made easier by the fact that the nativist movement had drastically changed its composition since 1854; now it no longer drew chiefly from the antislavery small towns of the interior, but from the conservative Whigs of eastern Massachusetts. Late in the campaign he delivered an address at nine principal cities throughout the state. "Are you for Freedom, or are you for Slavery?" he asked his audiences. To combat the slave power, which he could now describe firsthand, Massachusetts could not rely upon the Democratic party, which was sustaining "the tyrannies and perfidies of the Slave Oligarchy," or upon the Whigs, "the Rip Van Winkles of our politics." Nor could the Know-nothings lead in the fight for freedom. Boldly, if belatedly, Sumner attacked the party for its policy of racial and religious proscription. "I am not disposed to place any check upon the welcome to foreigners," he declared. "Ourselves the children of the Pilgrims of a former generation, let us not

[4] Adams, Diary, Sept. 6, and 17, 1855, Adams MSS.; Wilson: *Slave Power*, II, 433.

[5] Boutwell: *Reminiscences*, I, 118; H. Kriesman to Sumner, Sept. 18, 1855, Sumner MSS.

turn from the Pilgrims of the present. . . . A party, which, beginning in secrecy, interferes with religious belief, and founds a discrimination on the accident of birth, is not the party for us." Only the Republican party, whose cornerstone was Freedom, whose "broad, all-sustaining arches" were Truth, Justice, and Humanity, was "the fit shrine for the genius of American Institutions." [6]

Although friendly newspapers spoke of the "rapturous applause" Sumner received, the hostile press was probably more accurate in describing the cool reception given the "modern Cicero." The Republican "fusion" party proved, as an opponent had predicted, "a mere resuscitation of the Radical Free-Soil party with an impotent *infusion* of a portion of the Whigs." [7] In 1855, as in the previous year, the new party made a poor showing at the polls, and Gardner, combining nativism and Whiggery, was re-elected.

"It is humiliating that this American faction should have thus triumphed," Sumner lamented. The Know-nothing victory threatened to become a personal humiliation, for Gardner's friends began loudly demanding that both Sumner and Wilson "voluntarily" resign from the Senate or be "instructed out of their seats . . . made to feel the embarrassment of their position, representing . . . a faction which never had a majority or even a plurality of the votes of the people of Massachusetts, and which the people have condemned anew with indubitable emphasis at the recent election." Gardner talked of asking the legislature to choose a new United States senator—preferably himself—even though Sumner's term did not expire until 1857.[8]

"Gardner is after your place," Theodore Parker warned Sumner as the Senate met in December 1855. "He has one eye . . . on the *Senatorship*. His chances are not contemptible. . . . The more decided your course is against slavery, and the further you depart from the Hunkers, the more secure is your position." [9]

But, for weeks the new session of Congress gave Sumner no

[6] Sumner: *The Slave Oligarchy and Its Usurpations* . . . (Washington: Buell & Blanchard [1855]).

[7] Pierce, III, 421; Sumner: *Works*, IV, 62; Boston *Post*, Oct. 30, and Nov. 3, 1855; J. H. Clifford to Winthrop, Aug. 31, 1855, copy, Winthrop MSS.

[8] Sumner to Seward, Nov. 11, 1855, Seward MSS.; Adams, Diary, Nov. 9, 1855, Adams MSS.; Boston *Advertiser*, Nov. 10, 1855; Boston *Post*, Nov. 17, 1855; Hillard to Lieber, Nov. 19, 1855, Lieber MSS.

[9] Weiss: *Parker*, II, 158.

opportunity to distinguish himself. During the long stalemate in the choice of a speaker of the House of Representatives, which held up all important business for two months, he had to content himself with behind-the-scenes negotiations. In December 1855 he went into conference with Chase, representing the Western "Independent Democracy," N. P. Banks, of the Northern Know-nothings, and Francis Preston Blair, Sr., of the "Barnburner" faction, on the "means for an organization of the AntiNebraska forces for the presidential election." Though carefully reticent on presidential possibilities, he talked with John Charles Frémont, that daring "pathmarker of the West," who was often mentioned as the most likely nominee of the new Republican party. Enthusiastically Sumner endorsed the "strong and yet moderate, conservative and yet progressive" declaration of principles adopted at the preliminary Republican convention, which assembled at Pittsburgh on February 22.[1]

Though politicians knew of these activities, the general public in Massachusetts was unaware of them and thought that Sumner was doing nothing in the Senate. Boldly the Boston *Courier* taunted "our mute representative," and even Sumner's friends began, rather despairingly, to hope "that his long silence is only ominous to the foes of freedom." [2]

Frustrated in Congress, Sumner closely watched Gardner's plot to stage a premature election of his successor. The Boston *Courier* enthusiastically supported the governor's plan, and the Democratic *Post*, welcoming dissension among its opponents, egged it along. Though the Boston *Atlas* and the Boston *Advertiser* manfully battled the scheme, and though Sumner's closest advisers in the State house advised him that Gardner was not likely to succeed, the senator was worried. "Do not believe me too sensitive," he assured Howe. "I am the representative of a great cause and a powerful party, both of whom suffer when I suffer." [3]

[1] Seward to Thurlow Weed, Dec. 31, 1855, Weed MSS.; William Ernest Smith: *The Francis Preston Blair Family in Politics* (New York: The Macmillan Co.; 1933), I, 323–4; Gamaliel Bailey to Chase, May 8, 1856, Chase MSS., Hist. Soc. of Penn.; Boston *Post*, Apr. 3, 1856; Sumner to Henry J. Raymond, Mar. 2, 1856, Raymond MSS.

[2] Boston *Courier*, Mar. 5, 1856; Thomas Baldwin to Seward, Apr. 11, 1856, Seward MSS.

[3] Boston *Courier*, Mar. 15, 1856; Boston *Post*, Mar. 11, 1856; Seth Webb, Jr., to Sumner, Mar. 19, 1856, Sumner MSS.; J. W. Stone to Sumner, Mar. 20, and

Unable to make an antislavery demonstration, Sumner again tried to win his constituents' confidence by paying even more assiduous attention than ever to their desires and petitions. Never before did he so carefully distribute public documents and the free flower seeds to which congressmen were entitled. Never before had he so persistently presented Massachusetts claims and memorials. Never had he so energetically prepared bills that would directly benefit his home state—bills for the construction of a new customs house at Plymouth, for the improvement of the Taunton River, for the protection of Cape Cod harbors, etc., etc.

But somehow mere attention to business did not restore Sumner's waning fortunes. Neither did his attempt to start a major foreign policy debate by challenging the President's right to abrogate a treaty with Denmark excite much enthusiasm. Equally unpromising was Sumner's attempt to remind his constituents of his past services by publishing a volume of his *Recent Speeches*. Despite prodding from Howe and Longfellow, who subsidized the publication, Ticknor & Fields were reluctant to issue the volume unless they could include, as Howe reported to Sumner, "something which they can *call* a last speech . . . [to] help sell the book." [4]

The advice of publishers and politicians for once coincided. If Sumner was to regain his political strength in Massachusetts, he had once again to agitate the slavery question. Providentially, a burning issue came to hand, for the mails brought in reports of proslavery aggressions and outrages in the newly organized territory of Kansas. In the middle of March, when Douglas, with his "vulgar swagger," ushered in the debate on Kansas, Sumner instantly resolved that he would reply, in an "elaborate speech," using "plain words." Confidentially he reassured Theodore Parker: "I shall pronounce the most thorough philippic ever uttered in a legislative body." [5]

28, 1856, ibid.; Adams to Sumner, Apr. 1, 1856, ibid.; Dana to Sumner, Mar. 14, 1856, ibid.; J. B. Alley to Sumner, Mar. 14, 1856, ibid.; Sumner to Howe, Dec. 28, 1855, ibid.

[4] Howe to Sumner, Apr. 2, 1856, ibid.

[5] Sumner to Gerrit Smith, Mar. 18, 1856, Smith MSS.; Sumner to Longfellow, Apr. 7, 1856; Weiss: *Parker*, II, 179.

CHAPTER XI

The Crime Against Kansas

TRULY—TRULY—this is a godless place," Sumner lamented as the Thirty-Fourth Congress got under way. The friends of Freedom seemed thoroughly demoralized by the "Know Nothing madness." "In the House we are weak," Sumner reported; "in the Senate powerless." Stephen A. Douglas, whom Sumner thought "a brutal vulgar man without delicacy or scholarship [who] looks as if he needed clean linen and should be put under a shower bath," was undisputed master of the Democratic majority in the Senate. Aspiring for the Presidency, Douglas appeared ready to support any proslavery aggressions. "We have before us a long season of excitement and ribald debate," Sumner predicted, as Douglas opened the discussion of Kansas affairs in March 1856, "in which the Truth will be mocked and reviled." [1]

For months Sumner's mails had been full of urgent letters about the ominous developments in Kansas. As his correspondents gave him the story, the peaceable settlers in that remote frontier area were industrious Northerners, especially those brought out under the sponsorship of the New England Emigrant Aid Company. They had formed "an association of sincere benevolence, faithful to the Constitution and laws, whose only fortifications are hotels, school-houses, and churches; whose only weapons are saw-mills, tools, and books; whose mission is

[1] Sumner to Gerrit Smith, Mar. 18, 1856, Smith MSS.; Sumner to John P. Hale, Mar. 1, 1856, Segal Coll.; James Redpath to Elias Nason, Apr. 10, 1874, MS. owned by Mr. Boyd B. Stutler.

peace and good will." But, the South, determined to create a new slave state in Kansas, had banded together "murderous robbers from Missouri," "hirelings, picked from the drunken spew and vomit of an uneasy civilization," commanded by that Catiline, former Senator David R. Atchison, of Missouri. They had invaded the territory "as an 'army with banners,' organized in companies, with officers, munitions, tents, and provisions, as though marching upon a foreign foe, and breathing loud-mouthed threats that they would carry their purpose, if need be, by the bowie-knife and revolver." Under their reign of terror a hideous proslavery government had been set up with the support of the proslavery President Pierce. Outraged by this brutality and usurpation, high-minded free-state immigrants had formed their own rival free-soil government at Topeka.[2]

With the coming of spring, Sumner's Kansas correspondents anticipated fresh outbreaks of violence. Our "citizens are in arms to defend the dearest rights of Americans," one embattled Northern immigrant warned. "Preparations of the most warlike kind are in progress," wrote another, "men enrolled, munitions of war collected in the western counties of Missouri, for the purpose of invading Kansas. My dear sir—HELP US." [3]

Completely trusting these private sources of information, Sumner was indignant when Douglas presented the Democratic version of these same events to the Senate. According to the "Little Giant," Kansas was a land where immigrants, chiefly and naturally from the adjacent slave state of Missouri, had been peacefully settling since the adoption of his Kansas Nebraska Act in 1854. But, the New England Emigrant Aid Company, an abolitionist conspiracy, had brought in hordes of antislavery men, armed with Sharps rifles and pledged to use them against the peaceful Southerners. Despite this interference, despite the attempt of the abolitionist interlopers to set up an unconstitutional government, the legitimate settlers of Kansas had organized a

[2] Sumner: *Kansas Affairs: Speech . . . in the Senate of the United States, May 19, 1856* (New York: Greeley & McElrath; 1856), pp. 8–9, 11, 18. All subsequent references to *The Crime Against Kansas* are to this contemporary pamphlet edition, published at the New York *Tribune* office and widely circulated.

[3] Henry P. Waters to Sumner, Topeka, Dec. 6, 1855; Mrs. Hanna Ropes to Sumner, Lawrence, Jan. 22, 1856; Samuel F. Tappan to Sumner, Jan. 18, 1856—all MSS. in Kansas Hist. Soc.

territorial government, drawn up a body of fundamental law, which naturally borrowed from the code of Missouri and included protection for slaveholders, and now they sought recognition from Congress. Only a partisan desire to continue sectional strife into the coming presidential campaign could keep Congress from approving at once this "Law and Order" government in Kansas and from crushing out its abolitionist rivals.

Certain that Douglas's picture of events in Kansas was totally incorrect, Sumner did not pause to consider that his own version of happenings on that remote frontier might be equally distorted. Like the rest of the senators, he was unaware that the Kansas struggle involved not merely freedom and slavery, but also land speculations, bitter rivalries over the location of the territorial capital, and personal ambitions of would-be congressmen from the territory. He did not understand that there was no ineradicable hostility between Southern pioneers in this region, virtually all of whom were non-slaveholders, and free-state settlers, who wanted forever to ban free Negroes from Kansas. Disorder there was, and some bloodshed, but up to 1856 there had been scarcely more of either than was normal on any frontier.[4]

At any time it would have been difficult for congressmen to arrive at such an objective view of the Kansas difficulties; certainly it was impossible for them to do so in 1856, a presidential year. As the Democrats were committed to the principles of popular sovereignty, and as Douglas was one of the principal presidential possibilities, they had little choice but to uphold the "Law and Order" party and to brand the rival free-state government of Kansas as revolutionary. On the other hand, the opponents of the administration, who were slowly coalescing into the new Republican party, had little in common except hostility to popular sovereignty; they necessarily argued that it was unsuccessful in Kansas, the territory where it had been most conspicuously applied.[5]

Outraged by the bullying tone in which Douglas began the

[4] James C. Malin: *John Brown and the Legend of Fifty-Six* ("Memoirs of the American Philosophical Society," Vol. XVII, Philadelphia: The American Philosophical Soc.; 1942); James G. Randall: *Lincoln the President: Springfield to Gettysburg* (New York: Dodd, Mead & Co.; 1945), I, 83, 92.

[5] Andrew Wallace Crandall: *The Early History of the Republican Party, 1854–1856* (Boston: Richard G. Badger; 1930), Chap. 3.

debate, Sumner was delighted when Seward promptly countered by a demand for the immediate admission of Kansas as a free state under the Topeka constitution. As the discussion grew angrier and extended over several weeks, he was heartened to find more and more Northern senators joining in the attack on Douglas.

From the opening of the debate Sumner had planned a plea for Kansas, "that distant plundered territory," but it was not until nearly two months later that he claimed the Senate floor. In the interval he had been preparing an elaborate oration that he intended not merely as a defense of the free-state government of Kansas, but as a vindication of himself and of Massachusetts. Remembering the slurs Southerners had cast upon his state in the Kansas-Nebraska debates two years earlier, he borrowed from the Library of Congress histories of North Carolina, South Carolina, and Georgia, so as to be prepared to exhibit the past failings of the South. Recalling the enormous popular acclaim he had received from his sharp attacks on Butler, Mason, and Douglas in those same debates, he carefully included a personal assault upon each of these enemies, and, so that his quotations would be correct, he borrowed the Library of Congress's *Don Quixote*.[6]

[6] Sumner to Longfellow, Apr. 7, 1856, Longfellow MSS.; Receipts for Books, Library of Congress Records, 1855–7, pp. 49, 181. My imputation of motives here is admittedly speculative, yet it is hard to find any other reason why Sumner assailed these three senators in "The Crime Against Kansas." Douglas, to be sure, had been the leading administration spokesman during the debates, but Mason had said little, and Butler, who had spoken more often, had maintained a gravely solemn tone. The speech itself contains considerable internal evidence to show that Sumner, as he wrote it, was thinking back to the acrimonious 1854 debates. Attacking Douglas, he said: "But I go back now to an earlier occasion, when . . . he threw into this discussion . . . personalities most discreditable to this body." In his final fling at Mason, Sumner mentioned: ". . . on a former occasion I did something to exhibit the plantation manners which he displays." I cannot accept Butler's conclusion that Sumner's "mortified vanity, arising from former conflicts, was the cause of the attack" upon these three senators (*Cong. Globe*, 34 Cong., 1 Sess., 1,403–4), for Sumner and his friends thought he had come off triumphant in the earlier fray. Ben: Perley Poore, a not too trustworthy friend, claimed that Sumner told him the attack on Douglas, Mason, and Butler was a necessary "demonstration to satisfy those who had elected him" (Poore to Pierce, Nov. 18, 1875, Pierce MSS.), but such candid cynicism was not all like Sumner.

There is no reason to believe that Sumner intended to invite physical retaliation for his hard words. He wanted to be as frank as possible "within the limits of parliamentary propriety" (*Crime Against Kansas*, p. 6). Unaware of the power of his own words, he could not anticipate how offensive they would seem to his opponents. Long afterward he used to ask his secretary "with perfect simplicity what it was in the speech . . . that Butler's friends objected to. . . ." (Dawes: *Sumner*, p. 113).

Feeling that the occasion was "the greatest . . . that has ever occurred in our history," Sumner wanted the form as well as the content of his oration to measure up to the challenge. Painstakingly he wrote out his speech, which in a printed version runs to 112 pages, working in not merely the usual citations from British parliamentary debates, the *Congressional Globe*, and the *Statutes at Large*, but also quotations from Florus, Cicero, Livy, Vergil, Dante, and Milton. He tested the cadences of his elaborately balanced sentences:

> A few short months only [he planned to say, early in the oration] have passed since this spacious mediterranean country [Kansas] was open only to the savage, who ran wild in its woods and prairies; and now it has already drawn to its bosom a population of freemen larger than Athens crowded within her historic gates, when her sons, under Miltiades, won liberty for mankind on the fields of Marathon; more than Sparta contained when she ruled Greece, and sent forth her devoted children, quickened by a mother's benediction, to return with their shields or on them; more than Rome gathered on her seven hills, when, under her kings, she commenced that sovereign sway, which afterwards embraced the whole earth; more than London held, when, on the fields of Crecy and Agincourt, the English banner was carried victoriously over the chivalrous hosts of France.

For his peroration he closely imitated a passage from Demosthenes's "On the Crown," which he had just borrowed from the Library of Congress.[7] Then he thoroughly memorized the entire oration so that he would not have to refer to his manuscript once during his delivery. After reading the whole address to Seward —ostensibly to get the New Yorker's advice; actually, one suspects, to practice before an audience—he had the congressional printer set it up in type. He was ready to denounce "The Crime Against Kansas."

• 1 •

"Mr. President," Sumner commenced sonorously when he gained the floor at one o'clock on the afternoon of May 19. "You are now called to redress a great transgression. Seldom in the history

[7] Cf. Sumner: *Crime Against Kansas*, p. 22, and Demosthenes: *De Corona and de Falsa Legatione* (The Loeb Classical Lib., London: William Heinemann; 1926), pp. 155, 157. Receipts for Books, Library of Congress Records, 1855–7, p. 49.

of nations has such a question been presented. . . . A crime has been committed, which is without example in the records of the past. . . . It is the rape of a virgin territory, compelling it to the hateful embrace of slavery. . . ."

Long heralded, Sumner's speech had drawn an unusually large audience. "Not only were the galleries thronged to their utmost capacity with ladies and gentlemen, but all the doorways were completely blocked up with listeners," the New York *Post* correspondent reported. "It seemed even as if the members of the other House had adjourned to crowd the lobbies of the Senate. No such scene has been witnessed in that body since the days of Webster." Virtually every member of the Senate was in his seat as Sumner began. During the first few minutes, while Sumner announced his intention to exhibit the proslavery conspiracy against Kansas in its brutal nakedness, "without a single rag, or fig-leaf, to cover its vileness," Douglas, Isaac Toucey, of Connecticut, and Robert Toombs, of Georgia, made an ostentatious pretense of being totally preoccupied with letter writing or engaged in loud and distracting conversation, but as the orator launched into his fierce indictment, they subsided and, along with the rest of the crowded chamber, listened intently.[8]

During the three hours Sumner spoke on May 19 he exposed "The Crime Against Kansas," which, he insisted, originated in "the *One Idea*, that Kansas, at all hazards, must be made a slave State." It was for this very purpose that the Missouri Compromise had been repealed and that "swindle," the Kansas-Nebraska Act, passed. The word "swindle," Sumner apologized, had "not the authority of classical usage," but it had "the indubitable authority of fitness," as no other word could adequately express "the mingled meanness and wickedness of the cheat." Under its malign operations, Atchison, that "connecting link between the President and the border ruffian," had invaded Kansas with his Missouri banditti, and there had "renewed the incredible atrocity of the Assassins and of the Thugs." Douglas's "Popular Sovereignty" had thus "ended in Popular Slavery." [9]

The apologies for this hateful atrocity, Sumner continued,

[8] Washington Correspondence of New York *Evening Post,* May 21, 1856, in W. S. Thayer MSS.; New York *Tribune,* May 21, 1856.

[9] *Crime Against Kansas,* pp. 6–8, 11, 12, 15.

were "four in number, and four-fold in character." First was Douglas's "Apology *tyrannical,*" that the proslavery legislature in Kansas had been properly authenticated by law and, "whatever may have been the actual force or fraud in its election, . . . the whole proceeding is placed under the formal sanction of law." Such an argument, Sumner contended, placed "the certificate above the thing certified" and gave "a perpetual lease to violence and fraud, merely because at an ephemeral moment they were unquestioned." The "Apology *imbecile,*" that there was an "alleged want of power in the President to arrest the Crime," Sumner refuted by noting that Pierce had found no such constitutional obstacle to enforcing the fugitive slave acts in the Burns case. "Where there is a will, there is a way." The "Apology *absurd*" cast the blame for Kansas disorders upon an alleged free-soil Kansas Legion, a "poor mummery of a secret society." Finally, the "Apology *infamous*" blamed the New England Emigrant Aid Company for the civil war threatening the territory. The company, Sumner declared, not quite accurately, "supplied no arms of any kind to anybody." [1] Its planned emigration was entirely legal—just as legal as was Massachusetts' determination to support freedom in the territory. "I am proud to believe," Sumner concluded his first day's remarks, "that you may as well attempt, with puny arm, to topple down the earth-rooted, heaven-kissing granite which crowns the historic sod of Bunker Hill, as to change her fixed resolves for Freedom everywhere, and especially now for freedom in Kansas." [2]

When Sumner resumed on May 20, he examined "*the various remedies proposed*" for the Kansas difficulties, which, by careful rhetorical planning, were four-fold like the apologies he had just discussed. To "the *Remedy of Tyranny,*" President Pierce's proposal to compel obedience to the "Law and Order" government, Sumner replied that he would "not consent to wad

[1] In response to Sumner's inquiry, the secretary of the company told him "the company had never sent, or paid for sending guns, cannon, pistols or other weapons to Kansas." If the company was technically innocent, its directors and officers individually contributed heavily to supplying the Kansas migrants with rifles. W. H. Iseley: "The Sharps Rifle Episode in Kansas History," *American Historical Review,* XII (1906–7), 546–66. The best modern account of the New England Emigrant Aid Company is Samuel A. Johnson: *The Battle Cry of Freedom* (Lawrence: University of Kansas Press; 1954).

[2] *Crime Against Kansas,* pp. 15–20, 22.

the National artillery with fresh appropriation bills, when its murderous hail is to be directed against the constitutional rights of my fellow-citizens." The "*Remedy of Folly*," the suggestion that the free-state settlers should be deprived of their arms, would "trample on one of the plainest provisions of constitutional liberty." If Congress adopted "the *Remedy of Injustice and Civil War*," the proposal that the "Law and Order" legislature be authorized to call a constitutional convention, it would, Sumner protested, "put the infant State . . . to suckle with the wolf, which you ought at once to kill." This solution would "be the beginning of civil war." There remained, then, only the "*Remedy of Justice and Peace*," Seward's proposal to admit Kansas immediately as a free state. This remedy, Sumner argued, was justified "on every ground of precedent, whether as regards population or forms of proceedings; also on the vital principle of American institutions; and, lastly, on the absolute law of self-defense." [3]

Such was the argument of Sumner's "Crime Against Kansas" oration, and if the address had contained nothing more, it could hardly have been reckoned among the senator's more notable productions. But, in addition, Sumner felt it necessary to "say something of a general character"—"not," as he admitted, "belonging to the argument"—"in response to what has fallen from Senators who have raised themselves to eminence on this floor in championship of human wrongs," and he included his carefully rehearsed personal attacks upon Senators Douglas, Butler, and Mason.

On the first day Sumner spoke, he branded Senator Butler, who was absent in his native South Carolina, as the Don Quixote of slavery, who "has chosen a mistress to whom he has made his vows, and who, though ugly to others, is always lovely to him; though polluted in the sight of the world, is chaste in his sight . . . the harlot, Slavery," and labeled Douglas "the squire of Slavery, its very Sancho Panza, ready to do all its humiliating offices." [4]

Many senators were surprised at the venom of Sumner's remarks, but, largely because of the complexity and confusion of the Senate rules, no one called the speaker to order. Douglas,

[3] Ibid., 22–4, 28.
[4] Ibid., pp. 3, 5.

pacing irritatedly across the rear of the Senate Chamber, muttered: "That damn fool will get himself killed by some other damn fool." [5]

On the second day of his oration, Sumner continued and extended his personal references. Once again he attacked the absent Butler. Uncharitably referring to the effects of the slight labial paralysis from which the elderly South Carolina senator suffered, Sumner charged that he "with incoherent phrases, discharged the loose expectoration of his speech" upon the representatives of free Kansas. "There was no extravagance . . . which he did not repeat; nor was there any possible deviation from truth which he did not make. . . . But the Senator touches nothing which he does not disfigure—with error, sometimes of principle, sometimes of fact. He shows an incapacity of accuracy. . . . He cannot ope his mouth, but out there flies a blunder." Yet, this senator, Sumner complained, had dared rush "forward in the very ecstasy of madness" to compare his State of South Carolina, with "its shameful imbecility from Slavery," to the free territory of Kansas. "Were the whole history of South Carolina blotted out of existence, from its very beginning down to the day of the last election of the Senator to his present seat on this floor, civilization might lose—I do not say how little, but surely less than it has already gained by the example of Kansas, in its valiant struggle against oppression."

Sumner concluded with a rapid assault upon Senator James M. Mason, "who represents that other Virginia, from which Washington and Jefferson now avert their faces, where human beings are bred as cattle for the shambles." [6]

As Sumner resumed his seat, Cass, dean of the Senate, rose solemnly to pronounce Sumner's speech "the most un-American and unpatriotic that ever grated on the ears of the members of this high body." Douglas followed with a complaint that Sumner had merely rehashed old arguments, adding nothing new to the debate but "personal assaults and . . . malignity" and a series of "classic allusions, each one only distinguished for its lasciviousness and obscenity—each one drawn from those portions of the

[5] *Cong. Globe*, 34 Cong., 1 Sess., 1,477 ff., esp. 1,483. (All subsequent references to the *Congressional Globe* in this chapter are to the proceedings of this session.) Milton: *Eve of Conflict*, p. 233.

[6] *Crime Against Kansas*, p. 29.

classics which all decent professors in respectable colleges cause to be suppressed, as unfit for decent young men to read." [7] These "libels" and "gross insults" were the more objectionable as they did not rise in the give-and-take of debate, but had been "conned over, written with cool, deliberate malignity, repeated from night to night in order to catch the appropriate grace." "Is it his object to provoke some of us to kick him as we would a dog in the street, that he may get sympathy upon the just chastisement?" Douglas asked.

Mason rose loftily to explain: "I am constrained to hear here depravity, vice in its most odious form uncoiled in this presence, exhibiting its loathsome deformities in accusation and vilification against the quarter of the country from which I come . . . because it is a necessity of my position, under a common Government, to recognize as an equal, politically, one whom to see elsewhere is to shun and despise."

Regaining the floor for a rebuttal, Sumner made one of his rare impromptu efforts, doubtless allowing the excitement of his oratorical success to carry him further than he had originally intended. Cass, his oldest acquaintance in the Senate, he passed over in silence. "To the Senator from Illinois I should willingly leave the privilege of the common scold—the last word," Sumner continued, but Douglas should "remember hereafter that the bowie-knife and bludgeon are not the proper emblems of senatorial debate. . . . I say, also, to that Senator . . . that no person with the upright form of man can be allowed—" and he hesitated.

Douglas blustered: "Say it."

"I will say it," Sumner went on; "no person with the upright form of man can be allowed, without violation of all decency, to switch out from his tongue the perpetual stench of offensive personality. . . . The noisome, squat, and nameless animal, to which I now refer, is not the proper model for an American Senator. Will the Senator from Illinois take notice?"

"I will," Douglas retorted; "and therefore will not imitate you, sir."

[7] This charge against Sumner, which historians have often repeated, had no basis in fact. There was nothing obscene about any of his allusions, or anything lascivious about his quotations. It is hard to believe that Douglas, a rough Westerner, was so shocked by a word like "harlot."

"Mr. President," Sumner replied haughtily, "again the Senator has switched his tongue, and again he fills the Senate with its offensive odor."

Turning finally upon Mason, Sumner reminded him that "hard words are not argument; frowns not reasons; nor do scowls belong to the proper arsenal of parliamentary debate."

Reporters understood Mason to mutter: "The Senator is certainly *non compos mentis,*" and the debate closed.[8]

• 2 •

"Mr. Sumner has added a cubit to his stature," the New York *Tribune* declared, as the debate ended. Letters of praise began pouring in. About half of them lauded "the inspiring eloquence and lofty moral tone which characterized and ran through this triumphant senatorial achievement," and the rest rejoiced in the way Sumner "*Lashed Those Demagogues.*" "Your speech," the loyal Longfellow wrote, "is the greatest voice on the greatest subject that has been uttered." [9]

Many politicians, however, were troubled by the harshness of Sumner's language. Seward had advised Sumner to eliminate all his personal attacks and disapproved also of his gratuitous assault against the honor of South Carolina. Even Republican stalwarts like Wilson and Ben Wade regretted the vindictiveness of Sumner's tone. "Language equally intemperate and bitter is sometimes heard from a notorious parliamentary blackguard," Edward Everett thought, "but from a man of character of any party I have never seen any thing so offensive." [1]

Most Democrats and nearly all Southerners were outspokenly hostile. The Washington *Star* declared that Sumner's "personal vilification and abuse of Senator Butler . . . caused a blush of shame to mantle the cheeks of all present who respect the character of the body before whom it was uttered; because it was wholly unjust and untrue, and, in style, far better suited to

8 *Cong. Globe,* Appendix, 544–7; New York *Tribune,* May 21, 1856.

9 New York *Tribune,* May 20–1, 1856; New York *Evening Post,* May 21, 1856; W. W. Leland to Sumner, May 21, 1856, Sumner MSS.; Longfellow to Sumner, May 28, 1856, copy, Longfellow MSS.

1 *Cong. Globe,* Appendix, 664; Everett, Diary, May 25, 1856, and June 18, 1857; A. G. Riddle: *The Life of Benjamin F. Wade* (Cleveland: The Williams Publishing Co.; 1888), p. 242.

some low doggery." In street-corner conversations in Washington, always a hotbed of proslavery interests, Southerners could discuss only the insults Sumner had offered the South and the redress that should be taken. One Tennessee Congressman announced: "Mr. Sumner ought to be knocked down, and his face jumped into." [2]

The danger that these sentiments might erupt in personal violence against Sumner was not lost upon his friends. Troubled by Douglas's question: "Is it his object to provoke some of us to kick him . . . ?" Representative John A. Bingham, a Republican from Ohio, warned Wilson just after the speech to protect his colleague. Wilson gathered Anson Burlingame and Schuyler Colfax, both Republicans in the House, and told Sumner: "I am going home with you to-day—several of us are going home with you."

Unafraid, and rather vexed by what he considered unnecessary precautions, Sumner replied: "None of that, Wilson." He slipped out a side door of the Capitol unattended, accompanied Seward, who was on his way to catch the omnibus, a few blocks, and then walked to his lodgings alone.[3]

But the alarm of Sumner's friends was not excessive. Though no attacks were made upon him on May 20, Southerners were still angrily discussing his speech. A South Carolinian, it was said, "could not go into a parlor, or drawing-room, or to a dinner party, where he did not find an implied reproach that there was an unmanly submission to an insult to his State and his countrymen." [4]

Congressman Preston S. Brooks, of South Carolina, flinched sensitively under these reproaches. Now serving his second term in the House of Representatives, Brooks was not known as one of the Southern fire-eaters. He had pursued a moderate course during the Kansas-Nebraska debates of 1854 and was even taunted in his home state for being "a little too national." A man of very moderate ability, his one claim to fame was his half-humorous proposal that congressmen be required to check their firearms in the cloakroom before appearing on the House floor. Six feet tall and weighing about 170 pounds, with a proud military bearing that

[2] *Star*, quoted in Boston *Post*, May 24, 1856; *Cong. Globe*, Appendix, 631–2; *Alleged Assault upon Senator Sumner* (*House Report, No. 182*, 34 Cong., 1 Sess.), p. 66. Hereafter this document is cited as *Sumner Assault.*

[3] *Sumner Assault*, pp. 25, 42.

[4] *Cong. Globe*, Appendix, 632.

reminded observers of his Mexican War service, and a handsome, though rather juvenile, face, the thirty-six-year-old Brooks had won many friends in Congress "by his obliging disposition and his conciliatory temper, not less than by his cordial and agreeable manners." But, under his placid exterior, there burned a smoldering hatred of abolitionists, a proud devotion to the South and to South Carolina, an intense loyalty to his family, and a determination to live by the code of a gentleman.[5]

Along with many other representatives, Brooks had gone over to the Senate chamber on May 19, when Sumner began his oration, and he remained long enough, apparently, to hear Sumner call Butler, who was Brooks's cousin, the Don Quixote of slavery. Of Sumner's remarks on the second day Brooks knew only by report, but that apparently was enough to convince him that the Massachusetts senator had "insulted South Carolina and Judge Butler grossly." By the code of Southern chivalry Butler, when he returned from South Carolina, would be obliged to flog Sumner. Realizing that his cousin was old and that Sumner was "a very powerful man," Brooks concluded: "I felt it to be my duty to relieve Butler and avenge the insult to my State." But with curious deliberateness he waited until he could read the published version of Sumner's speech, on May 21, before definitely deciding to take action.[6]

Finding the speech as offensive as rumor had reported, Brooks determined to proceed according to the Southern code duello. Though he believed Sumner's remarks clearly slanderous, he did not even think of bringing legal action. No Southern gentleman considered a law suit the proper redress for a slur upon his own good name or upon that of a member of his family. Though Brooks had fought a duel in his youth, he did not consider challenging Sumner to a fight. In the first place, he knew that Sumner

[5] James E. Walmsley: "Preston S. Brooks," in Allen Johnson and Dumas Malone (eds.): *Dictionary of American Biography* (New York: Charles Scribner's Sons; 1929), III, 88; Harold S. Schultz: *Nationalism and Sectionalism in South Carolina, 1852–1860* . . . (Durham: Duke University Press; 1950), pp. 115–16; *Cong. Globe*, Appendix, 876.

[6] *Cong. Globe*, Appendix, 886; Brooks to his brother, J. H. Brooks, May 23, 1856, in Robert L. Meriwether (ed.): "Preston S. Brooks on the Caning of Charles Sumner," *South Carolina Historical and Genealogical Magazine*, XII (1951), 2 [hereafter cited as "The Caning of Sumner"]; *Sumner Assault*, pp. 61–2; "Statement by Preston S. Brooks," May 28, 1856, *MHSP*, LXI (1927–8), 221.

would not accept, as "the moral tone of mind that would lead a man to become a Black Republican would make him incapable of courage." Secondly, he thought that Sumner might report the challenge to the police, in which event Brooks would become liable "to legal penalties more severe than would be imposed for a simple assault and battery." But chiefly Brooks refrained from challenging Sumner because, according to the code of the Old South, a duel must be between social equals; to call Sumner out to the field of honor would be to give him, in Southern eyes, a social respectability he could not otherwise attain.[7]

"To punish an insulting inferior," the Southern code ruled, "one used not a pistol or sword but a cane or horsewhip." Brooks coolly explored these possibilities. "I . . . speculated somewhat as to whether I should employ a horsewhip or a cowhide," he declared later; "but knowing that the Senator was my superior in strength, it occurred to me that he might wrest it from my hand, and then . . . I might have been compelled to do that which I would have regretted the balance of my natural life." In other words, "it was expressly to avoid taking life that I used an ordinary cane." The instrument he selected was a gutta-percha walking stick, presented to him several months earlier by a friend. Weighing eleven and one-half ounces, the cane had a gold head; it tapered from a thickness of one inch at the large end to three quarters of an inch at the small, and had a hollow core of about three eighths of an inch.[8]

Having selected his weapon, Brooks had merely to pick the time and place for chastising Sumner. On Wednesday morning, May 21, he chose a seat in the Capitol grounds, waiting for Sumner to pass on his way to the Senate, and paced back and forth between it and the steps of the Capitol. Meeting him as he turned away from the steps, Representative Henry A. Edmundson, of Virginia, hailed him: "You are going the wrong way for the discharge of your duties." Brooks asked his friend to walk with him, and as they paced along, he declared that "Sumner had been very

[7] Brooks, in the Carolina *Times*, Aug. 30, 1856, clipping in Parker-Sumner Scrapbook; *Cong. Globe*, Appendix, 832. Cf. Charles S. Sydnor: "The Southerner and the Laws," *Journal of Southern History*, VI (1940), 3–23; and Jack Kenny Williams: "The Code of Honor in Ante-Bellum South Carolina," *South Carolina Historical Magazine*, LIV (1953), 113–28.

[8] *Cong. Globe*, Appendix, 832; *Sumner Assault*, pp. 73, 75.

insulting to his State, and that he had determined to punish him, unless he made an ample apology." "It was time," he continued, "for southern men to stop this coarse abuse used by the Abolitionists against the southern people and States, and . . . he should not feel that he was representing his State properly if he permitted such things to be said." Edmundson asked how he could be of assistance. "I wish you merely to be present, and if a difficulty should occur, to take no part in it," Brooks replied. "Sumner may have friends with him, and I want a friend of mine to be with me to do me justice." The two representatives remained at their observation post until twelve thirty, but when Sumner did not appear, they concluded that their prey had eluded them, and they walked into the Capitol.

Foiled, Brooks spent the rest of the day brooding about the "insult" to his state and his family, and he grew more than ever resolved that "it ought to be promptly resented." That night he told Representatives Lawrence M. Keitt and James L. Orr, both close political associates from South Carolina, of his purpose "to 'disgrace' the Senator with the South by a flagellation." What they advised is not known, but Brooks left them resolved "that he could not overlook the insult." So angry that he slept scarcely at all, he was up early the next morning to seek his revenge.

By eleven o'clock he was waiting in the porter's lodge at the entrance to the Capitol grounds, again ready to intercept Sumner as he entered the building. He planned to assault the senator there, if Sumner followed his customary practice and walked to the Capitol; if he came by carriage, Brooks intended to cut through the grounds, run up the flight of steps and through the Capitol so as to meet him in the space behind the building where the carriages stopped. Passing by the lodge on his way to the House, Edmundson spied Brooks and greeted him: "You are looking out." When Brooks explained his plan, the Virginia congressman cannily suggested a flaw: "The exertion and fatigue of passing up so many flights of steps would render him unable to contend with Mr. Sumner, should a personal conflict take place," especially as "no doubt Mr. Sumner was physically a stronger man than himself." [9]

[9] *Sumner Assault,* p. 59; *MHSP,* LXI, 221–3; Boston *Commonwealth,* Feb. 22, 1873.

Perhaps the reasoning convinced Brooks, or perhaps he concluded, as the noon hour for the convening of Congress approached, that he had again missed his quarry. In either case, he walked along with Edmundson up to the Capitol rotunda, where the Virginian went to his duties in the House, and Brooks "determined to keep [an] eye on Mr Sumner." He found the Senate in session, but both houses were scheduled to adjourn at an early hour because of the recent death of Representative John G. Miller, of Missouri. While Senator Henry S. Geyer pronounced a eulogy upon his deceased colleague, Brooks stood in the lobby on the opposite side of the main aisle from where Sumner was sitting.

As the House adjourned earlier than the Senate that day, Edmundson came over to the Senate chamber, where he saw Brooks and where, in the vestibule, he met Keitt and proposed that they leave. "No," said Keitt, "I cannot leave till Brooks does," and he disappeared behind the screen back of the Vice-President's chair, where he began talking with one of his constituents.[1]

At 12:45 the Senate adjourned, and most of the members left the chamber, though several stood talking in the vestibule and in the cloakroom. Sumner stayed at his desk, pen in hand, franking copies of his "Crime Against Kansas" speech. Several visitors tried to interrupt him, but he promptly and briefly dismissed them, declaring that he was busy.[2]

Impatiently Brooks awaited his opportunity. Until the room could be cleared, he took a desk in the back row of the chamber, across the aisle and three seats removed from Sumner. Wilson, when leaving, caught his eye, recognized him, and gave a polite bow. When Edmundson came up and jokingly asked Brooks if he were now a senator, the South Carolinian, fuming with anger, replied that he could not approach Sumner while there were ladies present, and he pointed to a pretty but persistent female conversationalist who had taken a seat in the lobby not far from where Sumner was sitting. He had already tried, unsuccessfully, to get the sergeant-at-arms to remove the lady. Finally, exclaiming that "he would stand this thing no longer," he rose and went into the vestibule, where he planned to send a message asking Sumner to

1 *MHSP*, LXI, 221–3; *Sumner Assault*, pp. 60, 63; *Cong. Globe*, 1,292.
2 *Sumner Assault*, p. 23.

come outside. Edmundson, following him, argued that such a move would do no good, as Sumner undoubtedly would only send for Brooks to come to his desk. When Edmundson stopped to speak to a friend, Brooks went back into the Senate, where Sumner was still busily writing.[3]

Finding the lobby at last clear of women, Brooks proceeded upon his errand. Operating, as he thought, "under the highest sense of duty," he approached the front of the desk where Sumner still sat behind a large pile of documents, "writing very rapidly, with his head very close to the desk," his armchair drawn up close and his legs entirely under the desk. With cool self-possession and formal politeness, Brooks addressed him: "Mr. Sumner." [4]

Sumner did not get up, but merely raised his head to identify his visitor. Nearsightedness, for which he was too vain to wear glasses, made the figure before him indistinct, but perfect vision would not have warned him, as he did not know Brooks by sight.[5]

"I have read your speech twice over carefully," Brooks began in a low voice. "It is a libel on South Carolina, and Mr. Butler, who is a relative of mine—" [6] As Sumner seemed about to rise, Brooks interrupted himself to give Sumner "a slight blow" with the smaller end of his cane. Stunned, Sumner instinctively threw out his arms to protect his head, and Brooks felt "compelled to strike him harder than he had intended." He began to rain down blows, and, he boasted: "Every lick went where I intended." In the excitement, Brooks forgot that he had set out only to flog Sumner, and began to strike him on the head "as hard as he could." [7]

Dazed by the first blow, Sumner of course could not remember that in order to rise from his desk, which was bolted to the

[3] Ibid., pp. 42, 60, 79.

[4] The Carolina *Times*, Aug. 30, 1856, in Parker-Sumner Scrapbook; Sumner: *Works*, IV, 269; *Sumner Assault*, p. 57.

[5] H. W. Beecher, in New York *Tribune*, May 31, 1856; *Sumner Assault*, p. 26.

[6] It is difficult to determine precisely what words Brooks used. The version here given is that remembered by Sumner himself, who asserted that Brooks began striking while uttering these words; he also recalled that Brooks had used the phrase "old man." *Sumner Assault*, pp. 23–4. Brooks claimed that he used more elaborate phraseology: "Mr. Sumner, I have read your Speech with care and as much impartiality as was possible and I feel it my duty to tell you that you have libeled my State and slandered a relative who is aged and absent and I am come to punish you for it." "Caning of Sumner," p. 2. For other variants see *MHSP*, XLI, 221–3; *Sumner Assault*, p. 81. I accept Sumner's version both because the senator's memory was remarkably precise and because the phrasing is shorter and less "literary." In any case, the difference is not great, for Brooks admitted that he struck before he ended his sentence.

[7] *MHSP*, LXI, 222; *Sumner Assault*, pp. 27, 35.

floor by an iron plate and heavy screws, he had to push back his chair, which was on rollers.[8] Perhaps half a dozen blows fell on his head and shoulders while he was still pinioned. Eyes blinded with blood, "almost unconsciously, acting under the instinct of self-defence," he then made a mighty effort to rise, and, with the pressure of his thighs, ripped the desk from the floor. Staggering forward, he now offered an even better target for Brooks, who, avoiding Sumner's outstretched arms, beat down "to the full extent of his power." So heavy were his blows that the gutta-percha cane, which he had carefully selected because he "fancied it would not break," snapped, but, with the portion remaining in his hand, he continued to pour on rapid blows. The strokes "made a good deal more noise after the stick was broken than before. They sounded as if the end of the stick was split." [9]

As soon as Sumner was free from the desk, he moved blindly "down the narrow passage-way, under the impetuous drive of his adversary, with his hands uplifted." As "Brooks continued his blows rapidly with the part of the stick he held in his hand," Sumner lost consciousness and "was reeling around against the seats, backwards and forwards." "His whole manner seemed . . . like a person in convulsions; his arms were thrown around as if unconsciously." Knocking over another desk, diagonally in front of his own, he seemed about to fall when Brooks reached out and with one hand held Sumner up by the lapel of his coat while he continued to strike him with the other. By this time the cane had shivered to pieces. Sumner, "entirely insensible" and "reeling and staggering about," was about to fall in the aisle. "I . . . gave him about 30 first rate stripes," Brooks summarized. "Towards the last he bellowed like a calf. I wore my cane out completely but saved the Head which is gold." [1]

The beating had taken place in less than one minute. The sound made by Brooks's cane had at once attracted the attention of everyone who remained in the Senate chamber, and most of them began rushing toward the fracas. Representatives Ambrose S. Murray and Edwin B. Morgan, who had been in con-

[8] I have been permitted to inspect Sumner's desk and chair, which are preserved in the Massachusetts Historical Society, through the courtesy of the Director, Mr. Stephen Riley.

[9] *Sumner Assault*, pp. 23–4, 32, 35, 56, 65, 79; *MHSP*, LXI, 222.

[1] *Sumner Assault*, pp. 27, 32, 37, 38, 40, 71, 80; "The Caning of Sumner," pp. 2–3.

versation behind the screen that separated the Senate seats from the vestibule, were the first to arrive. While Morgan caught Sumner, Murray seized Brooks by the arm while in the act of striking, and tried to draw him back from his foe.[2]

While Brooks struggled against this unexpected interference, the elderly Whig senator from Kentucky, John J. Crittenden, came up the aisle, expressed his "disapprobation of such violence in the Senate chamber," and warned Brooks: "Don't kill him." Brooks, apparently realizing that he had far exceeded his original purpose, muttered: "I did not intend to kill him, but I did intend to whip him." [3]

Just as Crittenden was warning Brooks, Keitt, who had been near the clerk's desk at the outset of the attack, bounded up the center aisle, with his "small cane . . . lifted above his head, as if he intended to strike." "Let them alone, God damn you," he shouted at Crittenden.[4]

By this time Toombs, of Georgia, had come up, and he warned the infuriated Keitt not to strike Crittenden. He did nothing, however, to restrain Brooks, still struggling to escape from Murray and renew the assault on Sumner; "I approved it," said Toombs later. Nor did Douglas, summoned from the anteroom by the scuffling, interfere. He at first thought of trying to "help put an end to the affray," he declared, but "it occurred to my mind, in an instant, that my relations to Mr. Sumner were such that if I came into the Hall, my motives would be misconstrued, perhaps, and I sat down again." [5]

In a few seconds, friends led Brooks off into a side room, where they washed a small cut he had received above his eye from the recoil of his stick. Minutes later he and Keitt were walking together down Pennsylvania Avenue.[6]

Meanwhile, Morgan, who had arrived at the same moment as Murray, had caught Sumner so that he was "saved . . . from falling as heavily upon the floor as he would otherwise have done." While Brooks was being led off, Sumner, partially supported by Morgan, lay "at the side of the center aisle, his feet in the aisle, and he leaning partially against a chair." He remained "as sense-

[2] *Sumner Assault*, pp. 38–40, 48.
[3] Ibid., pp. 30, 33, 49, 57; Boston *Commonwealth*, Feb. 22, 1873.
[4] *Sumner Assault*, pp. 29, 58.
[5] *Cong. Globe*, 1,305.
[6] *Sumner Assault*, pp. 50, 71.

less as a corpse for several minutes, his head bleeding copiously from the frightful wounds, and the blood saturating his clothes." [7]

Within a few minutes Sumner regained consciousness. One of the pages gave him a glass of water, and somebody suggested that he should be carried to a sofa in the anteroom. Sumner said that he thought he could walk, requested that his hat be found and that the documents on his desk be taken care of, and, leaning upon Morgan and another man, stumbled into the anteroom. His face was covered with blood as he passed Louisiana Senator John Slidell, who "did not think it necessary to . . . make any advances toward him" or to express any sympathy. A few minutes later Dr. Cornelius Boyle, who had been hastily summoned, dressed the wounds, which were still bleeding profusely, and put two stitches in each.[8]

Just as the doctor was finishing, Wilson, who had heard of the attack and had rushed back to the Capitol, arrived, and, helping Sumner into a carriage, took him to his lodgings and put him to bed. Sumner's "shirt around the neck and collar was soaked with blood. The waistcoat had many marks of blood upon it; also the trowsers. The broadcloth coat was covered with blood on the shoulders so thickly that the blood had soaked through the cloth even through the padding, and appeared on the inside; there was also a great deal of blood on the back of the coat and its sides." [9]

About an hour later Dr. Boyle came to Sumner's rooms to make a more thorough examination. He told the anxious friends waiting there "that such was the condition of Mr. Sumner it was absolutely necessary that he should be kept quiet, for he could not tell the extent of his injuries at that time." [1]

Before falling into a dazed sleep, Sumner remarked: "I could not believe that a thing like this was possible." [2]

• 3 •

Arrested on a charge of assault, Brooks was immediately freed under a $500 bail, and he became the hero of the extreme pro-

[7] Ibid., 38–40; *Cong. Globe*, 1,305; Morgan, in New York *Tribune*, May 31, 1856.

[8] *Sumner Assault*, pp. 35–6, 41–2, 51; *Cong. Globe*, 1,305.

[9] *Sumner Assault*, p. 26.

[1] Ibid., p. 67.

[2] Johnson: "Recollections of Charles Sumner," *Scribner's Monthly*, VIII (1874), 482.

slavery clique. Armed and menacing, Southern fire-eaters talked of imitating Brooks's example, and made violent threats against other Northern leaders. "It would not take much to have the throats of every Abolitionist cut," Brooks thought. "If the northern men had stood up," Keitt wrote scornfully a few days later, "the city would now float with blood. . . . Everybody here feels as if we were upon a volcano." Southerners said that if Congress dared discuss Brooks's actions, the House of Representatives would "ring with vollies [*sic*] from revolvers." [3]

The Senate made no move to redress Sumner's injury. The Republican caucus, which met shortly after the assault, decided that it would be best not to make a party issue of the attack and that Massachusetts congressmen should not take the lead in any investigation. With these party injunctions restraining his natural indignation, Wilson took the floor on May 23 and made a brief, factual explanation of his colleague's absence. He submitted no motion, but left it "to older Senators" to devise "measures to redress the wrongs of a member of this body, and to vindicate the honor and dignity of the Senate." There was a pause, and nobody stepped forward. As the President pro tempore was about to go on to other business, Seward moved for the appointment of an investigating committee. Elected by the Senate, it contained not one Republican. Its report, made on May 28, declared that "this assault was a breach of the privileges of the Senate," but, as Brooks was a member of the other house, "it is not within the jurisdiction of the Senate, and can only be punished by the House of Representatives." [4]

Meanwhile, the House, less dignified but more active, had already appointed an investigating committee of its own, a majority of whose members were Republicans, and it began taking the testimony of twenty-seven witnesses, starting with Sumner himself, who was interviewed at his lodgings.

While Congress was investigating, the public had already made up its mind. For most Northerners, news of the attack upon Sumner came as an electrifying shock. The deep sense of Northern outrage can best be judged not from the reactions of party

[3] "The Caning of Sumner," p. 3; Schultz: *Nationalism and Sectionalism*, pp. 117–18; H. A. Wise to Everett, May 31, 1856, Everett MSS. Cf. Wilson in *The Collector*, XLII (1927), 525.

[4] *Cong. Globe*, 1,279, 1,317.

politicians, whose responses could be anticipated, but in the letters and diaries of unimportant citizens. "The instant Papa told me," one Massachusetts maiden wrote, "it seemed exactly as if a great, black cloud was spread over the sky. . . . I keep always thinking about it, and no matter what I am doing I have a sort of consciousness of something black and wicked." "Mr. Brooks is a very naughty man," little Mary Rosamond Dana, daughter of Sumner's friend, decided, "and if I had been there I would have torn his eyes out and so I would now if I could." "We are in great indignation here," a Connecticut schoolgirl told her parents. "I don't think it is of very much use to stay any longer in the High School, as the boys would better be learning to hold muskets, and the girls to make bullets." [5]

Hundreds wrote Sumner of their sympathy. "My life is at your service," declared one New Yorker. "The news of the most foul, most damnable and dastardly attack . . . perfectly overwhelmed me with indignation and rage," a Chicago German wrote. "Even if they succeed in killing you now, you have achieved renown with posterity," another correspondent comforted Sumner. "You are glorious now," still another echoed. "The crown of martyrdom is *yours*. . . . 'Every noble crown is, and ever has been, a crown of thorns' and *you* have been found meet to wear the one the Savior wore—Oh thank God and murmur not." As is always the case in times of deep emotional stress, dozens of writers resorted to tried phrases that in other circumstances would have seemed clichés. The assault "made my blood boil." I should have "fought like a tiger for you." "My blood is boiling." "This murderous outrage . . ." ". . . the mean and dastardly attack on your person." "The blood boils in my veins." ". . . this detestably cowardly assault." "For four days my blood overboils. . . ." ". . . my warmest sympathy." ". . . the cowardly assault upon your person." As Horace Mann simply summarized: "We are not only shocked at the outrage committed upon you, but we are wounded in your wounds, and bleed in your bleeding." [6]

[5] Lilian R. Clarke to Sumner [May 1856], Sumner MSS.; Mary R. Dana to Sumner [June 1856], ibid.; A. Augusta Dodge (ed.): *Gail Hamilton's Life in Letters* (Boston: Lee and Shepard; 1901), I, 123.

[6] Mann to Sumner, May 27, 1856, Sumner MSS. The other quotations in the above paragraph are phrases chosen at random from the hundreds of letters Sumner received between May 21 and May 26, ibid.

Virtually every Northern city held a public meeting to protest the assault. There were rallies not merely in New York, Philadelphia, and Boston, not merely in Albany, Cleveland, Detroit, New Haven, Providence, and Rochester, but in Newmarket, New Hampshire, Lockport, New York, Rahway, New Jersey, Berea, Ohio, Burlington, Iowa, and in dozens of other towns.[7] The New York meeting, on May 30, was the most conspicuous of these gatherings. "It was the most remarkable and significant assembly I ever attended," one of Sumner's correspondents told him; "4000 of the most substantial citizens of N. York spoke as *one man* in terms and tones which would make Southern sneaks and bullies tremble in their shoes." "A vast crowd, earnest, unanimous, and made up of people who don't often attend political gatherings" thronged the Tabernacle. Though an effort had been made to keep the meeting out of radical antislavery men's hands by asking New York merchants, of Whig background, to preside, the audience was ready for strong talk. Whenever William M. Evarts, who read the resolutions, mentioned Sumner's name, "Peal after peal, cheer after cheer, succeeded each other like the discharge of heavy artillery," and there was "a spontaneous outburst of groaning and hissing at the sound of 'Preston S. Brooks.' "[8]

In Massachusetts, naturally, the feeling ran deepest. "When the intelligence of the assault on Mr. Sumner . . . reached Boston," declared Edward Everett, who was not given to exaggeration, "it produced an excitement in the public mind deeper and more dangerous than I have ever witnessed. . . . If a leader daring and reckless enough had presented himself, he might have raised any number of men to march on Washington."[9]

For a moment it seemed as if political lines and past differences had been obliterated in Massachusetts. "There is a great de-

[7] New York *Herald*, May 31, 1856; Boston *Advertiser*, May 26, 1856; New York *Tribune*, May 30, and June 2–3, 9, and 11, 1856; Rochester *Democrat*, May 31, 1856; *Zachariah Chandler: An Outline Sketch of His Life and Public Services* (Detroit: The Post and Tribune Company; 1880), pp. 119–20; Francis and H. L. Wayland: *A Memoir of the Life and Labors of Francis Wayland . . .* (New York: Sheldon and Company; 1867), II, 154; *Annals of Cleveland, 1818–1935*, XXXIX, items 2,847–8, 2,854; William Salter: *The Life of James W. Grimes . . .* (New York: D. Appleton and Company; 1876), pp. 80–1.

[8] G. P. Putnam to Sumner, May 30, 1856, Sumner MSS.; J. A. Briggs to George Sumner, May 31, 1856, ibid.; Allan Nevins and Milton Halsey Thomas (eds.): *The Diary of George Templeton Strong* (New York: The Macmillan Co.; 1952), II, 276; New York *Herald* and New York *Tribune*, May 31, 1856.

[9] Everett to Horace Maynard, Oct. 3, 1857, copy, Everett MSS.

sire for a public meeting to express the outraged feelings of all classes of our citizens," one Bostonian reported to Sumner. The organizers of the Faneuil Hall rally on May 24 were careful to invite men of all political views. A dense throng, estimated at 5,000 persons, crowded in and around the ancient building, to hear Governor Henry J. Gardner declare that he would "rise above party feeling and party bias" and stand by Sumner "as a representative of Massachusetts, under every circumstance, in this, his hour of trouble"; to listen to Hillard, long estranged from Sumner politically, pronounce the attack the "act of an assassin" and, "after a friendship of twenty years," praise Sumner as "a most amiable, gentle and kindly man"; and to roar approval of resolutions condemning Brooks's attack "not only as a cowardly assault upon a defenceless man, but as a crime against the right of free speech and the dignity of a free State." [1]

This appearance of unanimity was superficial; it was too much to expect that all the antagonisms Sumner had aroused could be forgotton in a moment. Fletcher Webster, the embittered son of Daniel Webster, said cynically that if Sumner "would indulge in such attacks . . . he ought at least to take the precaution of wearing an iron pot on his head." Some of the conservative Curtis family muttered, when they heard the news: "Served him right," and "I wish they had killed him." Sumner himself received a very few letters from Northerners who announced: "I am happy that one man was found who chastised you, but . . . you did not get one half what you merit." [2]

The political implications of the Brooks assault were immediately apparent. The chance fact that Brooks's attack had occurred almost simultaneously with a Southern raid on the free-state town of Lawrence, Kansas (May 21, 1856), gave the Republicans the perfectly matched themes of "Bleeding Sumner" and "Bleeding Kansas" for the coming presidential campaign. Astute observers like Secretary of State William L. Marcy predicted that the Sumner-Brooks affair, as ceaselessly exploited in the New

[1] George White to N. P. Banks, June 10, 1856, Banks MSS.; J. W. Stone to Sumner, May 22, 1856, Sumner MSS.; J. A. Dresser to Sumner, May 25, 1856, ibid.; Boston *Advertiser*, May 25, 1856.

[2] Charles T. Congdon: *Reminiscences of a Journalist* (Boston: James R. Osgood and Company; 1880), p. 85; R. E. Apthorp to Sumner, May 29, 1856, Sumner MSS.; "A Pennsylvanian who is opposed to Slavery" to Sumner, May 25, 1856, ibid.

York *Tribune* and other antislavery newspapers, would cost the Democratic party 200,000 votes in the fall election. On the very day after the beating, Sumner received a telegram from Michigan: "Every blow from the ruffian Brooks gives ten thousand [votes] to liberty." New Jersey Republicans reported that the assault on Sumner was the only force galvanizing antislavery opinion. Sourly Winthrop concluded: "Brooks and Douglas deserve statues from the Free-Soil party. The cane of the former and the Kansas Bill of the latter . . . have secured a success to the agitators." [3]

Republican strategists tried to take full advantage of the popular indignation. Perhaps a million copies of Sumner's "Crime Against Kansas" speech were distributed. The New York *Tribune* printed them at twenty cents a dozen, twenty dollars a thousand. Desiring the people to read Sumner's speech, Republican managers were, nevertheless, anxious not to have too much discussion of his arguments. By stressing the Brooks assault itself, they felt, Northern differences of opinion could be minimized and "the instincts, passions and sense of liberty of the free states" could be "roused against the enormous pretensions and villainous acts of the South." The main point to stress, the Springfield *Republican* urged, was: "The remedy for ruffianism resides in a united North. Old party names must be forgotten, old party ties surrendered." [4]

Massachusetts Republican leaders shrewdly capitalized upon the intense popular excitement. Keeping abolitionists and the recognized leaders of their party from taking too active a role in the protest rallies, they tried to give the impression that "prominent men of all parties" joined in condemning the assault. Then, as the movement was allegedly nonpartisan, they could exert immense pressure upon those who refused to participate in it. When Edward Everett, for example, declined to serve as vice-president of the Faneuil Hall rally on the ground that he had retired from politics, his refusal was widely publicized as a tacit endorsement

[3] Rochester *Democrat*, Sept. 3, 1857; J. G. Hudson to Sumner, May 23, 1856, Sumner MSS.; Everett to H. A. Wise, June 2, 1856, Everett MSS.; "Wales" to N. P. Banks, July 21, 1856, Banks MSS.; Ruhl Jacob Bartlett: *John C. Fremont and the Republican Party* ("Ohio State University Studies: Contributions in History and Political Science," No. 13, Columbus: Ohio State University Press; 1930), p. 61.

[4] Pierce, III, 458; E. P. Whipple to George Sumner, June 14, 1856, Sumner MSS.; George S. Merriam: *The Life and Times of Samuel Bowles* (New York: The Century Co.; 1885), I, 148.

of Brooks, his lecture invitations throughout New England were canceled, and he had to make a public statement of his "decided condemnation of the outrages." Conservative Whigs fumed impotently under the Republicans' pressure. "It is not enough that you agree with them," ex-governor Emory Washburne complained, "you must say your creed in their words with their intonation and just when they bid you or they hang or burn you as a heretic." [5]

Sumner's friends used Massachusetts indignation over the assault to bolster his shaky political prospects. The news of the attack reached Boston just in time to give Sumner's supporters a face-saving victory over Governor Gardner, who was trying to emasculate the personal liberty law Sumner had helped draft. By astute management Republicans forced through the legislature resolutions not merely condemning Brooks's actions, but endorsing "Mr. Sumner's manliness and courage in his earnest and fearless declaration of free principles, and his defence of human rights and free territory." John A. Andrew almost gave their game away when he blurted out at the Faneuil Hall rally that in order to secure "liberty of speech—nay, liberty itself," Sumner must be reelected, for Republicans were unobtrusively working toward precisely that end. "Providence itself seems to be on the side of the republican party," Hillard lamented. "Sumner is not merely their champion but their martyr, and his election for the next six years is now certain." A New Yorker, more prescient, declared that Sumner "is made by this act, senator for life." [6]

Sumner's political opponents tried to minimize the effects of the assault by balancing their denunciation of Brooks with criticism of Sumner. The Boston *Post*, a Democratic paper, forthrightly called Brooks's action "disgraceful," but it also complained of "the bitter tirade of personality, the wanton vituperation of high personal character, the absolute vulgarity of language" in Sumner's speech. The Boston *Courier*, an inveterate opponent of Sumner's, declared: "The member from South Carolina transgressed every rule of honor which should animate or restrain one gentleman in his connexions with another, in his ruffian assault

[5] Everett, Diary, May 24, 28, and 31, and June 2, 1856, Everett MSS.; Frothingham: *Everett*, p. 405; Washburne to Winthrop, June 7, 1856, Winthrop MSS.

[6] Bean: "Party Transformations," pp. 331–3; Boston *Advertiser*, May 26–7, 1856; *Cong. Globe*, Appendix, 630; Hillard to Lieber, May 28, 1856, Lieber MSS.; James E. Harvey to John McLean, May 30, 1856, McLean MSS.

upon Mr. Sumner," but added that "The Crime Against Kansas" speech was "excessively insulting and provoking, and not only highly indiscreet in sentiment and language, but unjustifiable, in any view in which it can be regarded." [7]

The significant thing, however, is the fact that virtually every Northern public man, however much he disapproved of Sumner or his speech, expressed sharp condemnation of Brooks. Even George Ticknor called the assault "brutal," and Winthrop exclaimed: "But how could any highminded and honorable man, as Mr. Brooks is represented to be considered in Carolina, have taken such a mode and place of redress, and have proceeded to such extreme violence!" The strength and unanimity of Northern opinion can best be gauged by the actions of that wily, unprincipled Democratic operator, Benjamin F. Butler. While the other members of the Massachusetts delegation to the Democratic national convention, passing through Washington in late May, carefully had nothing to do with Sumner, Butler, more sensitive to public opinion, paid a conspicuous visit of sympathy to the wounded senator, openly praised him as "a chivalric citizen of the Puritan commonwealth," and denounced Brooks as "a coward and an assassin." [8]

• 4 •

Simultaneously the opposite pattern of public opinion was appearing in the South. Brooks, virtually unknown before the assault, suddenly found himself a sectional hero. "Every Southern man sustains me," he confidently wrote his brother. "The fragments of the stick are begged for as *sacred relicts* [*sic*]." His constituents in Newberry, at a public meeting on May 24, voted the congressman a "handsome gold headed cane" and endorsed his action:

> Our Senators and Representatives in Congress have for a series of years patiently submitted to these tirades of calumny and vituperation, and they have in vain attempted to meet insults by argument and reason. . . . The aggravated insults given by the Senator from Massachusetts . . . furnish an ample justification of our Representative.

[7] Boston *Post*, May 24, 1856; Boston *Courier*, May 24, and 26, 1856. Cf. D. D. Barnard to Hamilton Fish, May 26, 1856, Fish MSS.

[8] Ticknor: *Life, Letters and Journals*, II, 296; Winthrop to John J. Crittenden, June 3, 1856, Crittenden MSS.; Conger: *Reminiscences*, pp. 89–90; Lowell *Evening Advertiser*, June 10, 1856; Butler to F. P. Rice, Feb. 15, 1886, Butler MSS.

Charleston, South Carolina, merchants contributed to buying Brooks a cane, inscribed: "Hit him again." "One of Carolina's truest and most honored matrons" wrote Brooks that "the ladies of the South would send him *hickory* sticks, with which to chastise Abolitionists and Red Republicans whenever he wanted them." In Columbia the governor of South Carolina headed the subscription list for "a splendid silver pitcher, goblet and stick" to be presented to Brooks, and even the slaves in the South Carolina capital collected money to buy him "an appropriate token of their regard." At the University of Virginia, students arranged to send Brooks a cane that should "have a heavy gold head, which will be suitably inscribed, and also bear upon it a device of the human head, badly cracked and broken." [9]

In their private correspondence, as well as in their public utterances, Southerners almost unanimously supported Brooks's actions. "Were I in the House I should certainly propose a vote of thanks to Mr. Brooks," Braxton Bragg, of Louisiana, wrote a friend. "You can reach the sensibilities of such dogs only through . . . their heads and a big stick." Paul Hamilton Hayne, the Southern poet, thought that Sumner, far from being "a martyr," should rather have been willing to "burn a hundred years in Hell than submit to a Public indignity—and *such* an indignity." "The Yankees seem greatly excited about Sumner's flogging," Toombs sneered. "They are afraid the practice may become general and many of [their] heads already feel sore. Sumner takes a beating badly." [1]

"In the main," announced the Richmond *Enquirer*, "the press of the South applaud the conduct of Mr. Brooks, without condition or limitation." A very few Southern papers boldly denounced the assault. The obscure Minden (Louisiana) *Herald* forthrightly condemned Brooks. The Memphis *Bulletin*, after complaining that

[9] "The Caning of Sumner," p. 3; Schultz: *Nationalism and Sectionalism*, p. 119; Columbia *South Carolinian*, May 28, 1856; Richmond *Enquirer*, May 30, 1856; Thomas Shelton Fox to W. H. Fox, June 1, 1856, John Fox MSS.

[1] Ulrich Bonnell Phillips (ed.): *The Correspondence of Robert Toombs, Alexander H. Stephens, and Howell Cobb* (*Annual Report of the American Historical Association*, 1911, Vol. II), p. 365; Bragg to "Dear General," May 31, 1856, George Hay Stuart MSS.; Hayne to Horatio Woodman, Sept. 8, 1856, Woodman MSS. Cf. Wilson: *Slave Power*, II, 490; J. F. H. Claiborne: *Life of John A. Quitman* . . . (New York: Harper & Brothers; 1860), II, 318–20. Of course, Southern opinion was not really unanimous, but the few Southerners who expressed regret over Brooks's actions did so privately. For example see Felton to Sumner, Nov. 8, 1860, Sumner MSS.; Everett, Diary, June 9, 1856, Everett MSS.; Phillips (ed.): *Toombs Correspondence*, p. 336.

Sumner was "a low, grovelling, wicked demagogue," called the attack "wholly inexcusable upon any grounds whatever." Especially in border cities like Baltimore, Louisville, and St. Louis some newspapers branded the "wanton and unjustifiable" assault as an "outrage and desecration" of the Senate chamber which called for "the prompt expulsion . . . of Mr. Brooks." [2]

A great many more Southern newspapers criticized not the principle upon which Brooks acted, but the time, place, and manner of its execution. Some Southern editors doubted the chivalry of attacking "a man whilst seated at his desk engaged in writing, and who has not had time to place himself face to face with his opponent." "The Senate Chamber is not the arena for exhibitions of this character," the Wilmington (North Carolina) *Herald* chided. "It is a shock to every man's sense of right and propriety to think of . . . a Senator in his seat subjected to such ignominious and hostile treatment," the Mobile *Advertiser* agreed. The Macon (Georgia) *Telegraph* argued that Brooks's action would give "a stronger impetus to Black Republicanism than anything else which could be imagined of a hundred times its importance." [3]

These Southern reservations came mostly from Whig editors, largely in the border states and in the larger port cities along the Mississippi River and the Gulf of Mexico. Perhaps they reflected Southern conservatives' positive dislike for Brooks's rash deed, their distrust of fire-eating, and their hope for peaceable adjustment of sectional conflicts, but it is notable that they were arguments against the policy, not the principle, of the Brooks assault. Southern dissenters, like the Northerners who had private reservations about Sumner's speech, were obliged to give at least lip service to the dominant sentiment of their section.[4]

[2] Richmond *Enquirer*, June 2, 1856; Minden (La.) *Herald*, clipped in Sumner Scrapbooks; Memphis *Bulletin*, Baltimore *Clipper*, Baltimore *Sun*, and Baltimore *Maryland*, all quoted in New York *Herald*, June 11, 1856.

[3] Charlottesville (Va.) *Advocate*, and Mobile *Advertiser*, quoted in New York *Herald*, June 11, 1856; Huntsville *Southern Advocate*, and Macon *Telegraph*, quoted in Avery O. Craven: *The Growth of Southern Nationalism, 1848–1861* (Vol. VI of *A History of the South*, ed. by Wendell H. Stephenson and E. Merton Coulter, Baton Rouge: Louisiana State University Press; 1953), pp. 233–5; Wilmington *Herald*, clipped in Parker-Sumner Scrapbook.

[4] Avery O. Craven in *The Growth of Southern Nationalism* has made a careful analysis of Southern newspaper reactions to the Brooks assault, which I have found valuable. But Professor Craven's very laudable desire to show the diversity of Southern opinion has led him, as it seems to me, to give disproportionate space to the newspapers that did not approve the attack. In quoting from

That feeling was one of enthusiastic approval of Brooks. Aside from a momentary deviation by the Charleston *Mercury*, every South Carolina newspaper unqualifiedly praised the assault. "*A Good Deed*," exclaimed the Richmond *Whig*. "The only regret we feel is, that Mr. Brooks did not employ a horsewhip or a cowhide upon his slanderous back, instead of a cane." "We consider the act good in conception, better in execution, and best of all in consequences," the Richmond *Enquirer* said. "These vulgar abolitionists in the Senate . . . must be lashed into submission. Sumner, in particular, ought to have nine-and-thirty early every morning. He is a great strapping fellow, and could stand the cowhide beautifully." "Far from blaming Mr. Brooks," added the Richmond *Examiner*, "we are disposed to regard him as a conservative gentleman, seeking to restore to the Senate that dignity and respectability of which the Abolition Senators are fast stripping it." The *South-Side Democrat*, of Petersburg, Virginia, expressed gratitude for "the *classical* caning which this outrageous Abolitionist received . . . at the hands of the chivalrous Brooks," and another Petersburg editor concluded: "If thrashing is the only remedy by which the foul conduct of the Abolitionist can be controlled . . . it will be very well to give Seward a double dose at least every other day until it operates on his political bowels." [5]

With public opinion so aroused, congressional discussion of the Brooks assault inevitably became a field day for the excited, the oratorical, and the politically ambitious. When Wilson in the Senate denounced the "brutal, murderous, and cowardly assault," Butler, who had hurried to Washington in order to defend his young relative as "a man acting under sensibility and under the dictates of high honor," interrupted with: "You are a liar!" Two days later Brooks challenged Wilson to a duel, but the Massachusetts senator scornfully declined, declaring that dueling was "the lingering relic of a barbarous civilization, which the law of the country has branded as a crime." [6]

---

them, he does not give sufficient recognition to the rhetoric demanded of Southern editors everywhere except in a few border cities. They were free to question the time, place, and expediency of Brook's actions, but not his correctness in following the code duello.

[5] Schultz: *Nationalism and Sectionalism*, p. 119; Richmond *Whig* and Petersburg *Intelligencer*, clipped in Parker-Sumner Scrapbook; Richmond *Enquirer*, June 2, 1856; Richmond *Examiner*, May 30, 1856; Petersburg *South-Side Democrat*, May 24, 1856.

[6] *Cong. Globe*, 1,306, and Appendix, 631; Wilson: *Slave Power*, II, 486;

In the House the debates presented an even more threatening aspect. On June 2 the investigating committee, by a strict party vote, recommended the expulsion of Brooks and the censure of both Edmundson and Keitt; the minority, two Southerners, declared that the House had no jurisdiction and should express no opinion on the subject. The reports excited heated debate. Every member of the South Carolina delegation in Congress felt it his duty to defend Brooks. Republicans filled the pages of the *Congressional Globe* in reply. The angriest of the Northern speeches was that by Anson Burlingame, a friend of Sumner's, whose Boston constituency seemed likely to repudiate him in the fall election. Defiantly he charged that Brooks had stealthily approached Sumner and had struck him down "as Cain smote his brother." When Brooks promptly challenged him to a duel, Burlingame accepted—but picked as the location the Canadian side of the Niagara Falls, to which Brooks could not go unless he defied the mobs that would threaten him in New York and Philadelphia.[7]

After protracted, bitter argument, the motion to expel Brooks came to a vote on July 14. It passed the House by 121 to 95, but as the requisite two-thirds was lacking, Brooks was not expelled. The next day the House acquitted Edmundson and censured Keitt. After making defiant speeches, both South Carolina representatives promptly resigned, returned to their constituencies, and were triumphantly re-elected. Brooks was at length fined $300 in the district court at Baltimore for his assault.

• 5 •

The vote on Brooks's expulsion revealed an ominous pattern: every Southern congressman but one voted against expulsion. The vote was a crystallization of what had become apparent in the debates. "In determining this question," one troubled representative found, "members from the South are rallying in a body to one legal conclusion, while members from the free States are concentrating with like unanimity in the other direction, as if there was any-

---

Elias Nason and Thomas Russell: *Life and Public Services of Henry Wilson, Late Vice-President of the United States* (Boston: B. B. Russell; 1876), p. 188.

[7] *Cong. Globe*, Appendix, 656; James E. Campbell: "Sumner—Brooks—Burlingame, or, The Last of the Great Challenges," *Ohio Archaeological and Historical Quarterly*, XXXIV (1925), 435–73, an article sharply hostile to Burlingame.

thing in climate, latitude, or longitude, which ought to control the judgment of a lawyer in determining a legal question." [8]

The same polarization had already appeared in newspaper opinion and in public and private reactions to the assault. To thoughtful observers it was apparent that something dangerous was happening to the American Union when the two sections no longer spoke the same language, but employed rival sets of clichés to describe the Brooks-Sumner affair.

In Southern parlance, Preston Brooks had inflicted a caning, or a whipping, upon that blackguard Sumner in order to chastise him for his unprovoked insults to the hoary-headed Senator Butler and for his foul-mouthed denunciation of South Carolina.[9] There was no conspiracy, and Brooks had no coadjutors. He acted not for political reasons, but solely to redress a personal wrong. In caning Sumner, he neither violated the privileges of the Senate nor broke the Constitutional guarantee of free speech to congressmen.[1] His weapon was nothing but a common walking stick, such as gentlemen frequently use. After sufficiently warning Sumner, Brooks lightly struck him across the face with a blow that was but a tap, intended to put him on his guard. As Sumner promptly rose to defend himself, Brooks naturally applied the stick with more force. After the first blow, Sumner bellowed like a bull calf and quickly fell cringing to the floor, an inanimate lump of cowardice. Though Sumner suffered only flesh wounds, he absented himself from the Senate because of mortification of feeling and wounded

[8] *Cong. Globe,* Appendix, 822.

[9] Virtually every word in these next paragraphs might well be put in quotation marks, or in multiple quotation marks, for all the key phrases constantly recurred in the public and congressional discussions of the attack.

[1] Though my purpose here is to show what men thought and felt, I am obliged to add that this contention was most dubious. Brooks's defenders argued that the Senate was not in session when he struck Sumner; that he chastised the senator not for words uttered in debate, but for libelous words printed in advance of delivery and read, not heard, by Brooks; and that in any event senatorial privilege, as guaranteed in the Constitution (Art. I, sec. 6) does not cover defamation of character. But American courts have consistently ruled (4 Mass. 27; 103 U.S. Reports 200; 341 U.S. Reports 367) that the immunity of congressional speech is absolute. See Leon R. Yankwich: "The Immunity of Congressional Speech—Its Origin, Meaning and Scope," *University of Pennsylvania Law Review,* XCIX (1950–1), 960–77. But, for dissenting views see *Stockdale* v. *Hansard* (112 Eng. Rep. 1,112); Story's *Commentaries on the Constitution,* sec. 863; Justice W. O. Douglas, in *Tenney* v. *Brandhove* (341 U.S. Reports 381), and Oliver P. Field: "The Constitutional Privileges of Legislators," *Minnesota Law Review,* IX (1924–5), 442–6.

pride. Brooks, with conspicuous gallantry, promptly reappeared in the House of Representatives, ready to face all accusers.

In Northern language, the affair bore an entirely different aspect. Bully Brooks had made a brutal assault upon Sumner with a bludgeon. The act had no provocation; on the contrary, Sumner for years had silently endured a harsh stream of unparliamentary personalities from Butler and other defenders of the slave power.[2] The alleged cause of the assault, Sumner's speech, was marked by the classic purity of its language and the nobility of its sentiments. The fearlessness of Sumner's ideas had, in fact, been what singled him out for assassination. Brooks was the mere tool of the slave-holding oligarchy. While fellow conspirators gathered around him to prevent interference, the South Carolinian stealthily approached Sumner and committed his brutal and barbarous outrage upon an unarmed man. Though Sumner courageously tried to defend himself,[3] the ruffian took advantage of his defenseless position and of the surprise, beat Sumner senseless, and continued to strike him after he collapsed on the floor. For most Northerners a versifier in the New York *Evening Post* summarized the matter:

Who, like a caitiff, base and low,
Came treacherously upon his foe,
And stunned him with a murderous blow?
Preston Brooks!

. . .

[2] Wilson and Representative W. S. Damrell, of Massachusetts, both made elaborate attempts to prove that in the matter of personalities Butler was the aggressor. (*Cong. Globe,* 1,400–3, and Appendix, 872–5). They showed that Butler in previous debates had referred to Sumner as a "plunging agitator," a "rhetorical advocate," guilty of "sickly sentimentality" and of "flagrant misrepresentation" of history and that he had once declared: "I know [Sumner] is not a tactician, and I shall not take advantage of the infirmity of a man who does not know half his time exactly what he is about." On the whole, however, their argument is not convincing. Butler had indeed said sharp things about Sumner, but they were intended to make him appear ridiculous, not to assail his moral character; in any case, they were made in the course of extemporaneous debate when Butler may have been carried away by his own rhetoric. Sumner's attack on Butler, on the other hand, was carefully and deliberately prepared in advance, and it made inexcusable personal references to Butler.

[3] After some Northern papers expressed "contempt for a man who has not spunk enough for either resistance or revenge," Sumner's friends heavily stressed this point. Sumner later declared that he would "most certainly" have defended himself "to the best of my ability, and the last extremity," had he been able. Letter of Jane G. Swisshelm to New York *Tribune,* Aug. 23, 1856, clipping in Sumner Scrapbooks. According to Wilson, as Sumner was led bleeding from

Who, when his victim senseless lay,
Cold and inanimate as clay,
His brutal hand refused to stay?
Preston Brooks!

While Brooks's coadjutors triumphantly led their champion out of the Senate, Sumner lay prostrate and suffering, his head a mass of beaten flesh, a martyr to the cause of Liberty and Free Speech.

Northern spokesmen drew a significant contrast between the character of the assailant and the assailed. Brooks, they said, was a coward. When Burlingame called his bluff by accepting his challenge to a duel, the South Carolinian quickly showed his true metal:

To Canada Brooks was asked to go,
To waste a pound of powder or so,
But he quickly answered, No; No; No.
For I'm afraid, afraid, afraid,
Bully Brooks's afraid.

What else could one expect, Ralph Waldo Emerson asked, from a product of the slave system, where man was but "an animal, given to pleasure, frivolous, irritable, spending his days in hunting and practising with deadly weapons to defend himself against his slaves and against his companions brought up in the same idle and dangerous way?" Sumner, on the other hand, was the ripe product of Northern scholarship and culture. No enemy could accuse him of "drunkenness, nor debauchery, nor job, nor peculation, nor rapacity, nor personal aims of any kind." Sumner, declared Emerson, in the words Bishop Burnet had applied to Isaac Newton, was "the whitest soul I ever knew."

When the two sections no longer spoke the same language, shared the same moral code, or obeyed the same law, when their representatives clashed in bloody conflict in the halls of Congress, thinking men North and South began to wonder how the Union could longer endure. "I do not see how a barbarous community and a civilized community can constitute one state," Emerson gravely declared. "I think we must get rid of slavery, or we must get rid of freedom." [4]

---

the Senate chamber, he declared: *"When I recover I will meet them again, and put it to them again."* Boston *Courier*, June 10, 1856.

[4] Rusk: *Emerson*, p. 389; *The Liberator*, XXVI (June 6, 1856), 91.

CHAPTER XII

The Vacant Chair

While Congress and the public were angrily debating the Brooks assault, Sumner was trying to regain his health. It was more than three years before he was able regularly to resume his Senate duties. During this unhappy period he wandered restlessly from one health resort to another, fretting impatiently at the slowness of his recovery and experimenting with any cure, however rigorous, that might promote it. These three years were filled with exciting developments in national politics: James Buchanan was inaugurated; the Supreme Court handed down the Dred Scott decision; Douglas broke with the administration over its Kansas policy; Abraham Lincoln challenged the "Little Giant" in his home state; John Brown's raid sent panic through the South. On all these subjects Sumner's voice was unheard in the Senate chamber. His only consolation for his enforced abstinence from politics was his conviction that "to every sincere lover of civilization his vacant chair was a perpetual speech." [1]

• 1 •

When Sumner was led bleeding from the Senate chamber on May 22, 1856, nobody anticipated that his recovery would be thus protracted. To be sure, his injuries were painful. He had three wounds on his head: one very slight and requiring no medical attention; another on the left side, "two and a quarter inches long, cut to the bone—cut under, as it were, and very ragged"; and still another on the right side, "rather in front," not quite two inches long, cut also to the bone. In addition, he had bruises on both his

[1] Sumner: *Works,* IV, 409.

hands, on his arms, and on his shoulders, and there was a heavy black bruise across his thighs, made as he wrenched his desk from its bolts.[2]

During the first three days after the assault, Sumner seemed to be recovering rapidly. Though he remained in bed most of the time, under the care of his brother George, who hastily came down from Boston to act as nurse, Dr. Cornelius Boyle, his physician, thought that he was "doing very well." Sumner's injuries, the doctor told congressional investigators a few days later, were "simply . . . flesh wounds"—"nothing but flesh wounds." They did not, he declared, "necessarily confine him one moment. . . . Mr. Sumner might have taken a carriage and driven as far as Baltimore on the next day [after the beating] without any injury." [3]

Dr. Marshall S. Perry, who was sent down from Boston by wealthy Republican manufacturer George L. Stearns so as to be sure Sumner would receive the best medical treatment, also found the patient in very satisfactory shape on May 25. The wound on the left side of his head had nearly healed, but "in the one on the right side there was perhaps an inch, or three quarters of an inch, which had not adhered." Troubled by "a pulpy feeling" on the right side of Sumner's head and by the senator's "unnaturally excited state," Perry recommended that he keep very quiet and get complete rest.

On the following day Sumner still appeared to be progressing satisfactorily, though the wound on the right side of his head began suppurating. He felt able to make a statement to the House investigating committee, which called at his rooms. That evening Dr. Boyle "applied collodion, which prevented the escape of pus." He was still "pretty comfortable" on the morning of May 27, though he complained of more pain. Giddings, who visited him that afternoon, found him sitting up. "His countenance appeared natural, and his conversation was cheerful." With little or no fever, he "insisted that he would resume his seat in a few days." [4]

That evening he suffered a relapse. Dr. Perry found him

[2] *Sumner Assault,* pp. 51, 55.

[3] Ibid., pp. 51–3.

[4] *Sumner Assault,* pp. 68–9; undated statement of Dr. Perry, Sumner MSS.; Perry: *Case of Hon. Charles Sumner* (a communication to the Boston Society for Medical Improvement, Dec. 8, 1856; 7-page pamphlet in Parker-Sumner Scrapbook), pp. 1–2; *Cong. Globe,* 34 Cong., 1 Sess., Appendix, 1,119.

with "more fever than at any time before, skin hotter than natural —pulse between 80 and 90, fuller and harder than at any time before." During the evening his pain, "principally confined to the posterior part of the head," became quite intense, and, restless and uneasy, he passed a sleepless night. The next morning Dr. Boyle found Sumner "excited and feverish, his pulse about a hundred." The glands on the back of his head and neck had begun to swell. Almost certainly septicemia had set in. Dr. Boyle decided that the patient's discomfort resulted from the "cuticle" (a solution of gun cotton and chloroform) he had applied to the wound on the previous day, and, removing it, found "about a tablespoonful of pus, . . . which had gathered under the scalp." He then poulticed the wound, and Sumner, under an opiate, was able to get several hours of sleep.[5]

At this point George Sumner dismissed Dr. Boyle. He felt that the treatment of his brother had been unskillful, and perhaps he was displeased when the doctor told congressional investigators that his patient suffered only "flesh wounds."[6] Dr. Perry took complete charge of the case, and he promptly called in Dr. Harvey Lindsly, a Washington physician, as consultant. They permitted the wound to suppurate freely, and soon Sumner felt "very nearly free from pain in the head—more calm and composed than he had been." On May 29 George was able to write Longfellow: "The crisis has passed and our noble fellow is safe."[7]

During the next two weeks Sumner "was very weak, had some fever, especially when excited, and was confined mostly to his bed." He felt debilitated; he "lost flesh and strength, his appetite was irregular, and his nights wakeful—sometimes lying awake all night, or when sleeping, disturbed." Anemia had probably followed his septicemia.[8] Sumner no longer complained of much pain from the wounds on his head, which were healing over, but he began exhibiting other, more disturbing symptoms. A

[5] Perry's Statement, Sumner MSS.; *Sumner Assault*, pp. 69–70.

[6] George Sumner claimed that he dismissed Boyle before hearing of his testimony. *Cong. Globe*, 34 Cong., 1 Sess., 1,438. Southerners insisted that he did so because Boyle would not exaggerate the nature of Sumner's wounds. Ibid., Appendix, 806; New York *Herald*, June 22. 1856.

[7] Perry's Statement, Sumner MSS.; George Sumner to Longfellow, 4 a.m., Thursday [May 29, 1856], Longfellow MSS.

[8] For this diagnosis, as for much of the other medical opinion incorporated in this chapter, I am indebted to Dr. Julia L. Schneider, of the Neurological Institute of New York.

neuralgic pain in the back of his head came on in paroxysms. He had "a feeling of oppressive weight or pressure on the brain," which he repeatedly described as "a 56-pounds weight" upon his skull. "Increased sensibility of the spinal cord, and a sense of weakness in the small of the back" made his walking so irregular and uncertain that "after slight efforts he would lose almost entire control of the lower extremities." [9]

By the middle of June, Sumner was able to move to Francis P. Blair's tree-shaded home at Silver Spring, on the outskirts of Washington, where he could escape some of the capital's mid-summer heat. For a while he "lay 22 hours out of the 24 on his back," but by June 23 he was "able to totter a mile around the garden . . . hoping daily for strength which comes slowly." But Silver Spring was too close to Washington. When Sumner went into the capital, on June 25, he overexerted himself and had a relapse. When he remained at the Blairs', numerous visitors came to see him, and he was "exhausted by his efforts to entertain them." On July 4 Seward found him much prostrated, his elasticity and vigor gone, moving "like a man whose sight is dimmed, and his limbs stiffened with age." [1]

It was clear that Sumner needed less exciting and more salubrious surroundings, and, after arranging his affairs in Washington, he left for the North. At Philadelphia he consulted the distinguished physician, Dr. Caspar Wister, who found that Sumner was in "a condition of extreme nervous exhaustion, his circulation feeble, and in fact every vital power alarmingly sunken." At Dr. Wister's advice, he went to Cape May, where for a week he seemed to do very well, though the water was too cool for bathing, but an unaccountable setback sent him seeking other remedies. In early August he found the secluded health resort of Dr. R. M. Jackson, high in the mountains at Cresson, Pennsylvania, where he was put on a regimen of "judicious diet, mild tonic agents, constant exercise in the open air on horse back or in a carriage." [2]

[9] Perry: *Case of Sumner,* p. 2.

[1] Smith: *Blair Family,* I, 348–9; Sumner to Howe, June 23 [1856], Sumner MSS.; A. B. Johnson to George Sumner, July 7, 1856, ibid.; Seward: *Seward at Washington, 1846–1861,* p. 282.

[2] Wister to M. S. Perry, Oct. 14, 1856, in Perry: *Case of Sumner,* p. 3; R. M. Jackson to Henry Wilson [Sept. 1856], Sumner MSS.

Sumner still gave some outward evidence of illness. Though his general health seemed "partially restored, his appetite reasonably good, and his mind ever glowing," he "had the appearance of a man who had been sick for a length [of] time, and was still extremely unwell." He had lost weight; his lips and face were pale; there was "a slight redness around the cicatrices of the recently healed cuts, also some morbid sensibility on pressure." Most conspicuous of all was his "tottering and uncertain gait"; he had difficulty in rising from a chair, and he walked like a man "creeping through a darkened chamber under the influence of a paroxysm of nervous headache." [3]

With the invigorating mountain air, the exercise, and Dr. Jackson's mild remedies, these outward symptoms gradually began to disappear, leaving Sumner to wrestle with more subtle and frightening warnings of illness. Walking (but not horseback riding) or the slightest mental exertion continued to produce the sense of pressure on the top of his head. His thigh muscles continued to be weak. When fatigued, he often involuntarily relived the trauma of the assault. His secretary described his symptoms: "At times he feels as tho' the blows were raining upon his head again; then will feel a numbness in the scalp; then again acute pains; then a sense of exhaustion that prevents any physical or mental effort." [4]

Restless and unable to sleep at night, Sumner feared that these symptoms might mean that he was losing his mind. He had always dreaded incapacitating disease more than death itself.[5] Now, he told Giddings: "I sometimes am led to apprehend that I may yet be doomed to that heaviest of all afflictions, to spend my time on earth in a living sepulcher." George Sumner's indiscreet reminiscences of mental cases he had seen in Paris hospitals undoubtedly contributed to Sumner's state of mind. So did Dr. Wister's disclosure that he was uncertain as to whether Sumner's brain "was deranged *organically* or only *functionally.*" "Had it been the former," Sumner wrote Howe, "then, as you know, death would have been my best friend." [6]

[3] Rochester *Democrat,* Aug. 19, 1856; R. M. Jackson to Henry Wilson [Sept. 1856], Sumner MSS.; Jane G. Swisshelm to New York *Tribune,* Aug. 23, 1856, clipping in Sumner Scrapbooks.

[4] A. B. Johnson to George Sumner, July 7, 1856, Sumner MSS.

[5] See above, p. 97.

[6] *Cong. Globe,* 34 Cong., 1 Sess., Appendix, 1,119; Sumner to Howe, July 2, and Sept. 26, 1856, Sumner MSS.

In this state of anxiety, Sumner closely watched his symptoms, and every weakness, every ache, every bout of insomnia reinforced his troubled conviction that his brain was affected. After a month he found the isolation of Cresson unbearable and, against Dr. Jackson's advice, he returned to Philadelphia. He explained that he wanted to be nearer his Senate duties; perhaps he also wanted something to distract his mind.

The change brought only partial relief. Though he felt very comfortable some days, his nerves were "still painfully sensitive," his nights were often sleepless, and his "legs and arms seemed all jangled." "I left the Mountain prematurely," he confessed to Dr. Jackson, "before my system had hardened into health, and have had some weakness and nervous sensibility since, incapacitating me for work." Dr. Perry, who re-examined Sumner at the end of September, concluded: "From the time of the assault to the present, Mr. Sumner has not been in a situation to expose himself to mental or bodily excitement without the risk of losing his *life*." [7]

• 2 •

These sufferings, of course, did not go unobserved. Newspaper correspondents followed Sumner from one health resort to another and filled Northern newspapers with stories of interviews with "the Martyr Senator." So great was popular enthusiasm for Sumner that the New York *Tribune* and the Cleveland *Leader* urged that he be named as the vice-presidential candidate on the Republican ticket, along with John C. Frémont, who was slated to fill the first place. At the Republican national convention in June Sumner received thirty-five votes in the balloting for vice-presidential nominees—a sizable tribute, though considerably less than the number cast for Illinois's Abraham Lincoln or for New Jersey's William L. Dayton, who was nominated.[8]

Sumner had no desire to be Vice-President, but he was "much in hopes that some benefit to the anti-slavery cause might

[7] Sumner to Dana, Sept. 16, 1856, Dana MSS.; Sumner to Howe, Sept. 11, 1856, Sumner MSS.; Sumner to R. M. Jackson, Oct. 11, 1856, MS. owned by Mrs. Edward C. Reeve, Clearfield, Pennsylvania; Statement of Dr. M. S. Perry, Sept. 30, 1856, Sumner MSS.

[8] New York *Tribune*, June 17, 1856; Buffalo *Commercial Advertiser*, June 18, 1856; Cleveland *Leader*, June 11, 1856; New York *Herald*, June 20, 1856.

accrue from the affair" with Brooks. With his faith in the power of oratory, he longed to take the stump for the Republican candidates, but his physicians absolutely forbade all public appearances. The advice of Republican politicians agreed with that of the doctors; they shrewdly realized that Sumner whole had less popular appeal than Sumner wounded. Reluctantly the senator abandoned his hope of campaigning. "Never before could I exert so much influence by speaking," he lamented in October; "and now nearly five months have been consumed—a large slice of human life—and I have been compelled to silence." He was obliged to content himself with writing spirited public letters endorsing "those candidates who are openly and unequivocally hostile" to the criminal plot "to subjugate Kansas and install the slave Oligarchy in the permanent control of the National Goverment."[9]

Massachusetts Republicans wanted to take the fullest advantage of public interest in Sumner. They did not support his vice-presidential candidacy because they were unwilling to lose so overwhelmingly popular a figure from state politics. Instead they talked for a time of capitalizing upon Sumner's martyrdom by running him for governor; thus simultaneously they could give "a tremendous rebuke of S. Carolina and the South" and could kill off the sinister Henry J. Gardner. Only the senator's firm refusal quashed the scheme.[1]

Within limits Sumner was willing to help his party. As it seemed probable that Anson Burlingame was going to be defeated in his fight for re-election, Sumner, who privately distrusted the young congressman and thought that by accepting Brooks's challenge he had "deliberately discarded the standards of Northern civilization to adopt the standards of Southern barbarism," staged an affectionate interview with him at Cresson, where newspaper correspondents thought that the senator and

[9] Seward: *Seward at Washington, 1846–1861*, p. 272; Sumner to Wendell Phillips, Oct. 7, 1856; MS. in private hands (photostat supplied through the courtesy of Prof. Irving Bartlett, of M. I. T.); Sumner to the chairman of the meeting at Faneuil Hall, Oct. 29, 1856, photostat in Alexander William Armour MSS. Cf. Sumner to W. M. Whitehead et al., Oct. 10, 1856, C. G. Leland MSS.

[1] Adams, Diary, June 16–17, 1856, Adams MSS.; John Bigelow to Sumner [Aug. 22, 1856], Sumner MSS.; E. D. Moore to Wilson, Aug. 9, 1856, ibid. See also James Lodge to Sumner, June 10, 1856, ibid.; Boston *Post*, Aug. 4, 1856; J. G. Fuller to N. P. Banks, Aug. 14, 1856, Banks MSS.; Anderson: "Slavery Issue," p. 210.

the representative acted "like father and son." [2] When not even a strong public letter endorsing Burlingame seemed sufficient, Sumner yielded to heavy pressure and, against the advice of his physicians, returned to Boston, ostensibly to receive a giant public reception, actually to promote the chances of Republican candidates.

On November 3 most of Boston joined enthusiastically in what the newspapers called "an earnest, heartfelt ovation to the ORATOR, STATESMAN, the SCHOLAR, and 'CHAMPION OF FREEDOM.'" The procession started from the Brookline house of Amos A. Lawrence, who for the time forgot his political hostility to Sumner, and moved to the Boston city line, where the aged Josiah Quincy, on the same spot where he had welcomed Lafayette as the honored guest of the city in 1824, greeted Sumner "as one to whom the deliverance, which we hope may yet be destined to our country will be greatly due." Then the parade proceeded toward Beacon Hill. Many homes and stores were decorated with greetings: "MASSACHUSETTS LOVES, HONORS, AND WILL SUSTAIN HER NOBLE SUMNER"; "Welcome, thrice Welcome"; "May 22, 1856" (in black); "WELCOME, FREEDOM'S DEFENDER." As Sumner's carriage passed, "spontaneous cheers would rise from the crowds, and ladies waved their handkerchiefs, making a very animated scene."

At the State house Governor Gardner welcomed the senator. This, he took pains to declare, was "no political ovation," but he pledged that Massachusetts "does stand by you today. She will stand by you tomorrow; (enthusiastic cheers) and she will stand by you, in her defense, forever (loud cheering)."

Sumner, who still looked "like an invalid—pale and suffering from weakness," replied "in a very low tone, and was evidently laboring under great physical disability." After only a few sentences he had to stop, and handed the remainder of his intended remarks to the reporters for newspaper publication. His ostensibly nonpartisan address of thanks for the welcome he had received actually made two principal points: that Sumner, though still an invalid, expected soon to "be permitted, with unimpaired vigor, to resume all the responsibilities of his position";

[2] Sumner to Giddings, July 22, 1856, Sumner MSS.; Jane G. Swisshelm to New York *Tribune*, Aug. 23, 1856, clipping in Sumner Scrapbooks.

and that the opponents of the Republican party in Massachusetts were "in sympathy, open or disguised, with the vulgar enemy, quickening everywhere the lash of the taskmaster, and helping forward the Satanic carnival" of slavery.[3]

Though Sumner suffered a relapse immediately after this public appearance and once again reported his "brain, shoulders and back all sensitive," his exertions were not in vain. Frémont received an overwhelming majority in Massachusetts. Burlingame was re-elected by the narrowest of margins. What was more important, an immense amount of enthusiasm had been generated for Sumner himself. As the Boston *Atlas* explained: "The personal appearance of Mr. Sumner, so haggard and careworn, the eye, once so beaming, now languid, the healthful cheek, now pale and thin, and the dark lines around the brow, chilled the hearts of all who beheld him. . . . Strong, athletic men, unaccustomed to emotion, drew stifled breaths, and were not ashamed to let it be known that they, too, suffered with Mr. Sumner." All this emotion had an immediate political point, as when the Boston *Herald*, hitherto opposed to Sumner, now changed its policy and urged: "If now we were a member of the legislature, we would be unwilling to enter upon any business after the organization, till Charles Sumner was re-elected to the seat where he was assaulted; we should not care what his political opinions were; if we disagreed with them ten thousand times more than we ever did, still would we give him our earnest and hearty support." [4]

Though Sumner professed total indifference to his re-election, he was in fact very keenly interested. He kept a close watch on the intrigues of Gardner, again re-elected governor in 1856 with Republican connivance, of Burlingame, and of others who aspired to succeed him. Though he sometimes talked in private of resigning his Senate seat, in order to go to Europe and regain his

[3] This account is based upon Sumner: *Works*, IV, 368–85, the Boston *Advertiser*, Nov. 4, 1856, Boston *Herald*, Nov. 2, 1890, and reports in the Boston *Bee*, *Journal*, *Transcript*, *Atlas*, *Courier*, and *Traveller*, clipped in Sumner Scrapbooks. I cannot verify the story that all but two of the houses on Beacon Street were tightly shuttered during the reception to show disapproval of Sumner. Dawes: *Sumner*, p. 120.

[4] Sumner to Howe, Wednesday [1856], MS., Huntington Lib.; Boston *Herald*, Nov. 5, 1856.

health, he always accompanied such suggestions with a reminder of "Gardner's intrigues, and the prospect of putting into the vacancy a lower toned and unfaithful man." He spoke of his willingness to give up his office if only Charles Francis Adams could be his successor—a choice he well knew was politically impossible—and then quickly permitted himself to be persuaded that resignation would embarrass his party. Learning that Gardner was promoting a rumor that he was an incurable invalid, the senator quietly dropped a passage from his remarks at the Boston reception suggesting "the probability that he might not be able to take his seat the next session," and, though actually very unwell, he announced, just as the new legislature assembled in January 1857, that he would resume his duties by the end of the month. "All of us must persevere," he wrote to correspondents who expressed sympathy for his continued feebleness, "and I assure you that I have no intention of abandoning the field of duty in which I have been placed." [5]

Sumner could remain publicly aloof from the re-election contest because his friends were working assiduously for him. The most effective of these was that "*straight* and *impracticable* Republican," Frank Bird, a paper manufacturer of East Walpole, who, as a friend said, could not "be coaxed, bought, told nor bullied." Active in antislavery politics since 1848, Bird had started having lunch every Saturday with John A. Andrew, the young Free Soil lawyer, James W. Stone, one of the Free Soil ward bosses in Boston, and William S. Robinson, the Boston correspondent of the Springfield *Republican,* in order to talk over political prospects. Other antislavery stalwarts, such as Howe, George L. Stearns, and Wilson, had joined them, and, moving to Parker's Hotel, they held a kind of irregular weekly antislavery caucus, attended by as many of its thirty or forty members as might be in town and might want to share the simple Saturday lunches, which cost each man a dollar, with wine extra. By 1856 the "Bird Club," as the group was called, exerted an immense, if informal, influence in Massachusetts politics, and fortunately for Sumner it enthusiastically supported his re-election by nomi-

[5] Adams, Diary, Oct. 11, Nov. 8, 13, and 20, and Dec. 25, 1856, Adams MSS.; Sumner to E. C. Dawes, Dec. 11, 1856, MS., William L. Clements Lib.

nating pro-Sumner candidates for the legislature, by spying out Gardner's plots, and by careful canvassing of the legislators.[6]

When the new legislature met in January 1857, Bird's planning brought prompt results. Announcing that "there was one particular thing for which the members of the present Legislature were sent here, and that was to choose a United States Senator," the Republicans in the House of Representatives forced a vote on January 9, even before Governor Gardner could send in his inaugural message, which they feared might contain distracting proposals. Out of the 345 votes cast, Sumner received all but twelve. Four days later, against protests over their unseemly haste, Republicans in the Senate adopted a rule for viva-voce voting on the senatorial election, and, as public opinion could thus be brought to bear upon each member, Sumner received the unanimous vote of the upper house.[7]

Welcoming the vote as a "sign, that the people of Massachusetts, forgetting ancient party hates, have at last come together in support of a sacred cause, compared with which the fate of any public servant is of small account," Sumner began his second six-year term in the Senate in his favorite role of the statesman called by popular acclaim to his duties. "The election here has not cost me one moment's solicitude," he assured Seward. "I sought nobody, and said nothing, pursuing now the course which I adopted six years ago. . . . What has been done has been the utterance of the State, without a hint from me." [8]

• 3 •

If Sumner's health was of great concern to his friends, both personal and political, it was of equal interest to his opponents, who from the beginning found something suspicious about his invalidism. As it was part of the standard Southern interpretation of the assault that Brooks had only "chastised" Sumner with a "light

[6] Howe to Palfrey, Aug. 10 [1859], Palfrey MSS.; John A. Andrew's endorsement, on P. W. Chandler to Andrew [Mar. 1862], Andrew MSS. On Bird and the "Bird Club" see: Stearns: *Cambridge Sketches*, pp. 162–79; Schurz: *Reminiscences*, II, 130; Pearson: *Andrew*, I, 58–60; Harrington: *Banks*, p. 41; Boston *Commonwealth*, July 29, and Aug. 5, 1865, Nov. 5, 1870.

[7] Clippings from Boston *Advertiser* and Boston *Atlas*, Sumner Scrapbooks.

[8] Sumner: *Works*, IV, 394; Seward: *Seward at Washington, 1846–1861*, p. 296.

walking cane," proslavery congressmen never accepted as a fact that Sumner had been seriously injured. Their suspicions were confirmed when Dr. Boyle testified to the House investigating committee on May 27 that Sumner's injuries were "nothing but flesh wounds." When Senator Butler spoke in defense of Brooks on June 12, he argued: "For anything that appears in that testimony, if [Sumner] had been an officer of the Army, and had not appeared on the next day [after the attack] on the battle-field, he would have deserved to be cashiered." [9]

After Republicans made "Bleeding Sumner" one of the principal issues in the 1856 presidential campaign, supporters of both Buchanan, the Democratic nominee, and Fillmore, the American candidate, openly charged that the senator was shamming. His wounds, they noted, offered a most convenient political martyrdom. As Sumner was not too ill in June to prepare a carefully revised edition of "The Crime Against Kansas," the Boston *Courier* decided that he was "playing the political possum." In July the Washington *Union*, the official organ of the Pierce administration, charged that Sumner's wounds were entirely healed, but that he stayed away from the Senate because of "his wounded pride and his irrepressible anger and indignation." The Boston *Post* suggested that Sumner's doctors were conspiring to picture the senator as an invalid until just prior to election, when he could reappear before the public and capitalize "very much upon the interest his protracted absence from public duty [would] excite to see and hear him, for party effect." By fall the Washington *Union* had uncovered an even worse plot: physicians were "nursing the disease, lest it should die a natural death," because Sumner was "resolved not to recover until after the next Senatorial election in Massachusetts." Noting that Sumner miraculously recuperated just in time to address the citizens of Boston on the day before the elections, the Philadelphia *News* concluded: "The Senatorial sophomore has no doubt done more by playing possum than if he had stumped the entire North with re-hashes and plagiarisms from Demosthenes." [1]

Sumner was furious over these accusations. "While thus

[9] *Cong. Globe*, 34 Cong., 1 Sess., Appendix, 625. Cf. ibid., 806.

[1] Boston *Courier*, June 21, 1856; Boston *Post*, Aug. 21, 1856; Washington *Union*, and Philadelphia *News*, quoted in *The Liberator*, XXVI (July 25, 1856), 118, and XXVI (Nov. 28, 1856), 189.

suffering for more than four months," he exclaimed in September, "I have been charged with the ignoble deed of *shamming illness!* It seems to me, if any thing could add to the character of the original act it is this supplementary assault on my character." Republican politicians were also seriously troubled over these slanders, which seemed to attract much credence in the Northwest, and they urged Sumner to collect affidavits from his other physicians to counteract the influence of Dr. Boyle's damaging testimony. Wilson helped Sumner gather statements from Dr. Lindsly, Dr. Wister, Dr. Perry, and Dr. Jackson, all declaring that Sumner's brain had "received a shock from which it might not recover for months" and all emphatically affirming that Sumner was unable to resume his Senate duties. This combined medical statement, Sumner himself declared in private, "was specially intended for Indiana, where the calumny had been employed; and . . . it was necessary that it should be circulated before the Election. . . ." [2]

The publication did not down the suspicion of fraud. Throughout the next three years, while Sumner was generally absent from the Senate, hostile newspapers carried occasional stories that he was "malingering" with a "sham sickness." Sumner, declared the New York *Atlas* in 1858, "is rapidly acquiring the reputation of a charlatan, who, preceded by his servant in motley, with a trumpet and drum, cries his injuries and sufferings in the cause of freedom as saleable wares, for the purpose of putting money in his purse." "This most ridiculous of humbugs," announced another editor, "fairly stinks in the nostrils of the American people." [3]

This accusation, which has found some defenders among later historians of pronounced antiabolitionist sympathies,[4] rests upon very flimsy evidence. The only medical testimony that sup-

[2] Sumner to Mrs. Hamilton Fish, Sept. 27, 1856, Fish MSS.; Lyman Trumbull to George Sumner, June 13, 1856, Sumner MSS.; W. H. Furness to R. M. Jackson, Oct. 10, 1856, MS. in the possession of Mrs. Edward C. Reeve; Sumner to R. M. Jackson, Oct. 11, 1856, ibid. The statements of Drs. Lindsly, Perry, Wister, and Jackson, all dated in September 1856, are in the Sumner MSS.

[3] New York *Atlas,* quoted in *The Liberator,* XXVIII (July 2, 1858), p. 105; Richmond *Whig,* Dec. 27, 1856; Charleston *Courier,* quoted in Boston *Advertiser,* Sept. 16, 1858.

[4] E.g., Milton: *Eve of Conflict,* pp. 236–7. Avery Craven: *The Coming of the Civil War* (New York: Charles Scribner's Sons; 1942), pp. 367–8, is slightly less hostile to Sumner.

ports it is the statement of Dr. Boyle, a Southern physician, strongly opposed in politics to Sumner and very friendly to both Senator Butler and Preston Brooks. Even if Dr. Boyle had been an unprejudiced observer, his testimony as to Sumner's superficial wounds, lack of fever, etc., would have only limited medical value, for it was given on May 27, before septicemia was apparent. In his frequently overlooked testimony on the following day, Dr. Boyle added that Sumner had begun to run a fever, that infection had set in, and that he had prescribed opiates.[5] If Dr. Boyle's testimony is accepted in its entirety, it proves only what no one ever denied: that Sumner seemed to be recovering quite satisfactorily during the first few days after the assault, but that infection set in on the evening of May 27.

Opposed to Dr. Boyle's slight evidence are elaborate, sworn statements by the four physicians who were in charge of Sumner's case from May 27 until the end of the year. Dr. Harvey Lindsly declared that when he came on the case, Sumner was unable to resume his public duties, and that he had urged him to go to the seashore or to the mountains to recuperate. Dr. Caspar Wister, of the eminent Philadelphia family of physicians, opposed in politics to Sumner, made an early diagnosis that Sumner's recovery depended upon his "entire abstraction from all excitement" and, on re-examining him in late September, held that he was "still an invalid," requiring constant medical care. Dr. R. M. Jackson, who was a Democrat, swore that Sumner was "still extremely unwell" when he came to the Pennsylvania mountains and that he left Cresson prematurely, "still an invalid." Dr. Marshall S. Perry, one of the most respected doctors in Boston, was positive that Sumner was so badly injured that mental or bodily exertion would cost him his life.[6]

[5] *Sumner Assault,* pp. 50–4, 71. When George Sumner peremptorily dismissed Dr. Boyle, the physician grew very angry at what he considered a slur upon his professional integrity, and tried to collect other evidence to prove that Sumner had not been dangerously injured. The best he could do was to get an offhand remark from Dr. Lindsly to the effect that there was "not much the matter" with Sumner—an opinion that Dr. Lindsly presently contradicted in a affidavit—and a letter from Dr. Thomas Miller, who helped drain Sumner's wounds on May 30, declaring that he did not think "Mr. Sumner in any danger." *Cong. Globe,* 34 Cong., 1 Sess., 1,414.

[6] The statements of these four doctors, dated Sept. 22–30, 1856, are in the Sumner MSS. Dr. Jackson, who was postmaster at Cresson, was removed by the Pierce administration for his statement that Sumner was an invalid. Sumner to R. M. Jackson, Dec. 20, 1856, in the possession of Mrs. Edward C. Reeve.

There is a notable lack of evidence to support the theory that Sumner was pretending to be ill. Certainly not one word he ever uttered or wrote, even to his closest friends and to his brother, could be interpreted as lending support to such a charge. If there was a plan to have Sumner feign sickness until after the 1856 elections, somebody must have been in on the plot. But there is not a known scrap of evidence, in the correspondence of any of his friends, in the papers of any Republican leader, or even in any belated reminiscence, which lends credence to the theory. If there was a plot, it was one of the best kept secrets in American history.

Those who charged Sumner with shamming relied upon logic as defective as their evidence. If he was pretending invalidism in order to aid the Frémont campaign or to promote his own re-election to the Senate—and there is no question but that his illness was skillfully exploited for both purposes—surely by January 1857 the game should have been over and Sumner should have resumed his seat. In fact, Southerners were puzzled at his failure to do so. Recognizing that after 1856 neither Sumner nor the Republican party had anything to gain by continuing a charade of this kind, proslavery men changed their attack and, during the next two years, attributed Sumner's absence from Washington to embarrassment at having been detected in his sham or to cowardice.[7]

• 4 •

If the charge that Sumner was malingering must be dismissed as illogical theorizing upon insubstantial evidence, it must be admitted that the precise nature of Sumner's ailment was mysterious.[8] He looked well in the face, his voice was as firm and manly as usual, his intellect was bright and strong; but, when he tried to rise from his chair, he had to reach out for support, and he

[7] E.g., Lieber to Hillard, Dec. 13, 1856, Lieber MSS.

[8] In the following discussion of Sumner's medical problems, I have been fortunate to secure the advice of two leading specialists, Dr. Bronson S. Ray, of the Cornell Medical Center, and Dr. Julia L. Schneider, of the Neurological Institute of New York. Giving generously of their time, both Dr. Ray and Dr. Schneider read through a 30-page memorandum I had prepared, listing in objective fashion Sumner's symptoms and the treatments prescribed for them. The judgments of these two eminent specialists, made quite independently and without any consultation between themselves, coincided at every point.

Preston S. Brooks

The Brooks Assault

NEW YORK PUBLIC LIBRARY

"walked with a cane and quite feebly, instead of his peculiarly vigorous stride." His progress toward recovery was disturbingly unpredictable. "Sometimes I think at last it has come," he wrote in January 1857, "and then before the day is over I am admonished that I can do but little." [9]

Disturbed over these setbacks, he postponed returning to Washington until late February, when Massachusetts businessmen demanded that he vote on the new tariff bill. Republican colleagues greeted Sumner warmly as he resumed his seat, as did the two Democratic senators from Rhode Island; the rest, including Douglas, Toombs, Slidell, and Cass, "passed and repassed Mr. Sumner's seat and neither gave nor received a look of recognition." After casting the deciding vote against a proposed increase in import duties on raw wool, a proposal naturally opposed by Massachusetts woolen manufacturers who desired cheap raw materials, Sumner felt too unwell to continue in his place. "I have sat in my seat only one day," he reported to Theodore Parker on March 1. "After a short time the torment to my system became great, and a cloud began to gather over my brain. I tottered out and took to my bed." [1]

He decided to go to Europe for his health. Delaying in Washington only long enough to be sworn in on March 4, the beginning of his second Senate term, he sailed from New York three days later. Though he was seasick, his other symptoms began to disappear. By the end of the voyage he could rise from a seat without difficulty, and, aided only by a cane, he walked the decks for hours.

Landing at Le Havre on March 21, Sumner spent the next seven months in an exhausting round of visiting and sight-seeing.[2] The twenty years that had passed since his first trip to Eu-

[9] Lydia M. Child to Whittier, Jan. 2, 1857, Child MSS.; Mary Thatcher Higginson (ed.): *Letters and Journals of Thomas Wentworth Higginson, 1846–1906* (Boston: Houghton Mifflin Co.; 1921), p. 78; Sumner to William Schouler, Jan. 6, 1857, James Schouler MSS.

[1] W. B. Spooner to Sumner, Feb. 24, 1857, Sumner MSS.; John E. Lodge to Sumner, Mar. 4, 1857, ibid.; Washington correspondence of Boston *Traveller*, Feb. 27, 1857, clipping in Sumner Scrapbooks; Pierce, III, 519. For Sumner's votes on the tariff bill see *Cong. Globe*, 34 Cong., 3 Sess., Appendix, 354, 356, 358. Cf. Edward Stanwood: *American Tariff Controversies in the Nineteenth Century* (Boston: Houghton Mifflin Co.; 1903), II, 97–108.

[2] Sumner kept a rather bare, day-by-day account of his itinerary in his Travel Journal, MS., Wellesley College. The essential portions were printed in Pierce, III, 529–55.

rope had dimmed none of his enthusiasm for historic sights or his admiration for eminent persons. Though some of the friends he had made on his former visit were dead, there were still many who remembered him and who flooded him with calls and invitations. Guizot, Lamartine, Drouyn de Lhuys, Michel Chevalier, Tocqueville, and Turgenev welcomed him in Paris. In London he had barely registered at Maurigy's Hotel, in Regent Street, when Lord Brougham and Lord Chancellor Cranworth called. The Duchess of Sutherland entreated him to make Stafford House his home; her daughter, the Duchess of Argyll, took a fond interest in Sumner's health, and, with her husband, persuaded him to pay a visit to Inverary. Nassau Senior, George Grote, Henry Reeve, Charles Kingsley, William Makepeace Thackeray, and Thomas Babington Macaulay entertained him. He met Lord Palmerston, who "seemed to have the gift of perpetual youth," lunched with Lord John Russell, and dined with William E. Gladstone. He renewed his acquaintance with Richard Cobden and met John Bright for the first time.

During the entire trip Sumner kept up a rigorous schedule of sight-seeing which would have exhausted a man half his age. Despite a cold that persisted for the two months he remained in Paris, he saw everything and everybody in the French capital. On May 24 he went on a tour of the French provinces and visited Orleans, Blois, Chambord, Tours, Angers, Nantes, La Haye, Poitiers, Bordeaux, Bayonne, Toulouse, Lyons, and Dijon—as well as a number of intervening places—in something less than three weeks. Then followed two months of frenzied social life and sight-seeing in London. Returning to the Continent, Sumner then went to Rheims, Strasbourg, Basle, Berne, Lucerne, Turin, the Hospice of St. Bernard, Geneva, Heidelberg, Frankfurt, Cologne, Amsterdam, the Hague, and Brussels, all within a month and without missing one of the starred attractions in his Baedeker. Returning to London for a week in September, during which he had five dinner engagements, Sumner then traveled to Manchester, Leeds, Edinburgh, Glasgow, Aberdeen, and Llandudno before sailing from Liverpool on November 7.[2a]

The mere recital of this exhausting peregrination is enough

[2a] For detailed accounts of these English engagements, see six letters from Sumner to Baron Hatherton, Aug. 10–Nov. 7, 1857, Hatherton MSS.

to prove that Sumner, while in Europe, was not severely troubled by the effects of the Brooks assault. Though he occasionally complained that his health was "not yet firm" and that he had "a morbid sensibility of the spinal system," everybody reported that he looked remarkably well. Young Henry James never forgot his disappointment when Sumner turned up in Paris "with wounds by that time rather disappointingly healed," and not even the senator's "visible, measurable, unmistakeable greatness" could quite compensate for that defect.[3]

Toward the end of his European tour, however, Sumner's health received a setback, which was of psychological rather than physiological origin. Convinced that he had received "injuries to the brain" during Brooks's assault, he was uncertain about whether he should resume his place in the Senate when the new session of Congress began in December. Instead of asking the advice of any of several distinguished British physicians, he solicited the opinion of George Combe, whose writings on phrenology he had at a much earlier day admired. Combe, who was not a doctor and who was now nearly seventy years old, wrote out an account of what he took to be Sumner's symptoms and submitted them to Sir James Clarke, the Queen's physician. Clarke, without making any examination himself—indeed, without even seeing Sumner—gave as his considered judgment: "I have no hesitation in affirming, that, if he returns to mental labor in less than a year from this time he will soon become a permanent invalid, if he does not lose his life." Passing the diagnosis along to the senator, Combe added his personal opinion that Sumner's "brain, although apparently functionally sound, . . . would give way under the pressure of public life in America."[4]

Bearing these medical warnings always in mind, Sumner returned to America torn between conflicting desires. With all his conscious will he wanted to reappear in the Senate and further to expose the villainies of the slavocracy. From the very

[3] Sumner to Longfellow, Apr. 2, 1857, Longfellow MSS.; Sumner to Mrs. W. H. Seward, July 23, 1857, Seward MSS.; *The Liberator*, XXVII (Oct. 30, 1857), 175; Edward Waldo Emerson: *The Early Years of the Saturday Club, 1855–1870* (Boston: Houghton Mifflin Co.; 1918), p. 306.

[4] Sumner to Bird, Sept. 11, 1857, Bird MSS.; Combe to Clarke, Oct. 8, 1857, copy, Combe MSS.; Clarke to Combe, Oct. 9, 1857, ibid.; Combe to Henry D. Rogers, Oct. 19, 1857, Sumner MSS.

day after the Brooks assault he had expressed "the constant wish . . . that he might be speedily restored so as to take his seat again in the Senate, from which . . . he had never before been absent for a single day." Compelled to be silent during the 1856 presidential campaign, he vowed on the day of his re-election to the Senate that he would return to Washington and "paint in its true colors, that institution, whose barbarism had with its own peculiar instrument enforced silence upon him." He told Theodore Parker that he expected to deliver an oration "in the Senate which shall tear Slavery open from its chops to its head—from its bully chops down to its coward heel!" "If I ever get back to Washington," he promised Thomas Wentworth Higginson, "the speech that I shall make when I do get there . . . will be to my last speech in the Senate of the United States as first proof brandy to molasses and water." [5]

Perhaps the very frequency and intensity of such statements suggest the inner reluctances that Sumner also felt about returning to the Senate. The more Sumner committed himself to delivering another powerful attack on slavery, the less he could forget the likely consequences. All along he had been convinced that a new attempt would be made against his life. He believed such letters as that signed by "A South Carolina Plug Uglie," who wrote "to say if you value your life not to visit Washington the coming session. . . . You may take the whole of Boston as your body guard but it wont make a damn bit of difference I am willing to sacrifice my life for the honor of my native state." "I suppose I shall be shot," Sumner told Higginson as he talked of going back to his seat. "I don't see what else is left for them to do." [6] Now to these fears the English physicians added another and, in his eyes, even greater danger—one that had never been entirely absent from his thoughts—the likelihood that if he re-

[5] Harvey Lindsly to Wilson, Sept. 22, 1856, Sumner MSS.; J. W. Atwood to Sumner, June 21, 1860, ibid.; Weiss: *Parker*, II, 218; Worcester correspondence of New York *Tribune*, Jan. 17, 1857, clipping in Sumner Scrapbooks. Sumner was unhappy that Higginson revealed these intentions. Sunmer to "My dear friend," Jan. 25, 1857, MS., Yale Univ. Lib.

[6] "A South Carolina Plug Uglie" to Sumner, Nov. 23, 1857, Sumner MSS.; Worcester correspondence of New York *Tribune*, Jan. 17, 1857, clipping, Sumner Scrapbooks. Cf. Lydia Maria Child: *Letters* . . . (4th ed.; Boston: Houghton Mifflin Co.; 1884), p. 88; Wilson to Sumner, Jan. 29, 1857, Sumner MSS.; Ames: *Life . . . of Peter and Susan Lesley*, I, 319.

turned to the Senate, it would be "at the peril of his intellect." [7]

When the new session of Congress opened in December 1857, Sumner was able to force himself to attend, but he could not take much interest in politics. The feud between President Buchanan and Senator Douglas over the Kansas question, which threatened to split the Democratic party, attracted only his most cursory attention; like any other invalid, he was concerned chiefly with his own health. He found that listening to the Senate debates jangled his nervous system. After only a few days of attendance he felt "the weight spreading over his brain." He thought that it might help if he kept away from the Senate, though remaining within call if his vote was needed, but still he grew no better. [8]

Tense and worried by his absence from duty during the day, he now spent sleepless nights, for a bladder condition, probably prostatitis, obliged him to rise three or four times during each night. Sumner connected this new affliction—quite incorrectly, and contrary to Dr. Perry's very sound diagnosis—with the injuries produced by Brooks's assault. Here was just one more bit of evidence that the English doctors had been correct, and he began worrying even more about having "paralysis or softening of the brain." "I cannot work with the mind, except in very narrow limits," he wrote the Duchess of Argyll in despair. "To sit in the Senate is exhausting, even though I renounce all special interest in the debate and leave every thing to others. This is hard—very hard. It is hard to be so near complete recovery and still to be kept back." [9]

On December 20 Sumner left Washington, and he remained away during most of the next five months. As soon as he left the "vileness and vulgarity" of the capital, he noted a considerable improvement in his health. To occupy his time he started studying engravings, a large collection of which had just been presented to Harvard College, and his enthusiasm and energy in his new recreation exhausted his friends. "Verily, he goes thoroughly through the work," Longfellow complained. "For

[7] Adams, Diary, Nov. 20, 1857, Adams MSS.

[8] Pierce, III, 558–9.

[9] M. S. Perry to Sumner, Dec. 10, and 18, 1857, Sumner MSS.; Sumner to Duchess of Argyll, Dec. 22, 1857, Argyll MSS.

my part I cannot take in so much at once." But, guided by Dr. Louis Thies of Harvard, Sumner examined every engraving at the college. Then he studied private collections, first in Boston, then in New York and Philadelphia.[1]

Once Sumner was away from Washington, his interest in public affairs picked up. He longed to show that the continuing "injustice, cruelty and meanness" of Buchanan's Kansas policy was "the natural fruit of slavery—which makes men unjust, cruel and mean." He yearned also to denounce William Walker's filibustering expedition against Nicaragua as a new attempt to spread slavery. He worried fretfully over Southern schemes to seize Cuba. In letter after letter he urged the Duchess of Argyll and his other English friends to have the British government persuade Spain to emancipate the slaves in Cuba, for such an action would end the illegal American slave trade, stop filibustering in the Caribbean, and "humble forever the whole slave-interest in the United States." [2] When Lord Napier, the British minister in Washington, failed to agree with Sumner, but instead fraternized with the Southern Democrats, Sumner pungently reported his deficiencies to English friends. When Napier was recalled in 1858, the American press gave Sumner the credit.[3]

Every time Sumner had to go to Washington, all his old symptoms returned. In February 1858 Wilson summoned him to the capital for a few days to vote against Buchanan's Army Bill, "giving soldiers to a wicked Government" for use in Kansas, but, though Sumner tried to spend most of his time in the Smithsonian Institution and in the Library of Congress, the strain was too great and he had to return to New York. Brought down again in April, he arrived too late to give his vote for the free-state cause in Kansas, but, during the several days he remained, the

[1] Sumner to Longfellow, Feb. 22, 1858, Longfellow MSS.; Longfellow, Diary, Jan. 22, and 26, 1858, ibid.

[2] Sumner to Gerrit Smith, Jan. 17, 1858, Smith MSS.; Sumner to Duchess of Argyll, Jan. 12, 1858, Argyll MSS.; Sumner to Duchess of Sutherland, Apr. 30, 1858, ibid.; Sumner to Nassau Senior, June 22, 1858, MS., Huntington Lib.; Sumner to Lord Brougham, Apr. 21, and June 30, 1858, Brougham MSS.

[3] Sumner to Duchess of Argyll, Dec. 22, 1857, Jan. 12, and Feb. 15, 1858, Argyll MSS.; Duchess of Argyll to Sumner [Mar. 1858] and June 19 [1859], Sumner MSS.; New York *Times*, Dec. 16, 1858; A. B. Johnson to Sumner, Apr. 21, and 26, 1858, Sumner MSS. Sumner denied the rumor that he brought about Napier's recall. "I could never think of any such interference . . . even if its impotence were not too glaring." Sumner to Seward, Apr. 19, 1858, Seward MSS.

tense bitterness of the Senate debates once again affected him. Without warning his old enemy struck. While reading in the stacks of the Library of Congress, he was called to the Senate to cast a vote. Perhaps he rose too quickly or walked too rapidly to the Senate chamber, for the afternoon found him prostrate with exhaustion. For the next three or four days he suffered back ailments and could rise from his chair only with great difficulty. At Wilson's insistence, he again left Washington. "All my plans are clouded," Sumner gloomily wrote Howe. "I had hoped to do something—indeed to strike a blow before this session closed." "Two years gone already! How much more!" [4]

Dr. Wister, whom Sumner consulted again in Philadelphia, found his condition serious and warned that he "must resolutely renounce all idea of doing any thing till next winter." The advice confirmed Sumner's fears. "The English physicians understood my symptoms better than I did," he once more began to think. There must be a "deep-seated disease," the softening of the brain and the paralysis suggested by Sir James Clarke.[5]

"Never before was I so uncertain what to do or where to go," Sumner lamented. He had no faith in his American doctors. Dr. Perry's diagnosis that his symptoms were caused by his "generous diet and little exercise," by his urinary complaint, and by that "depressing passion," fear, which acted "sadly upon the nervous system," seemed shallow to him. Both Dr. Perry and Dr. Wister advised him to go abroad again, but, after all, he had tried that remedy. "Where shall I go? What do?" he desperately queried. "Europe? where in Europe? baths there? water-cure there? extensive travel there? Switzerland and baths there? . . . the Pyrenees, and baths there? . . . Spain? Russia? . . . Where shall I go and what do? I know not, nor can I divine." [6]

• 5 •

When Sumner sailed again for Europe on May 22, 1858, all his friends and most of his enemies were convinced that his sena-

[4] Sumner to Longfellow, Feb. 22, 1858, Longfellow MSS.; Boston *Advertiser*, Apr. 3, 1858; Sumner to Howe, Apr. 16–17, 1858, Sumner MSS.

[5] Sumner to Duchess of Argyll, June 1, 1858, Argyll MSS.; Sumner to Pierce, Apr. 24, 1858, Sumner MSS.

[6] M. S. Perry to Sumner, Apr. 29, 1858, Sumner MSS.; Sumner to Longfellow, May 10, 1858, Longfellow MSS.

torial career was closed. People said that his case was hopeless; the fact that, on the train from Washington, he allowed his pocket to be picked of a $2,000 note of Longfellow's suggested that "his mind was somewhat weakened." Shedding hypocritical tears over "Mr. Sumner's physical infirmity," the Boston *Courier* joined the Boston *Herald* in demanding that a senator so incapacitated should resign.[7]

Sumner's appearance at this time justified the most ominous forebodings. He walked only with the greatest difficulty. "When he tried to move forward he was compelled to push one foot slowly and gently forward but a few inches, and then drag the other foot to a level with the first, holding his back at the same time to diminish the pain that he had there." Only after moving about for fifteen minutes or so in this slow and stiff fashion did the pain abate, so that he would walk more easily. More disturbing was the fact that "he could not make use of his brain at all. He could not read a newspaper, could not write a letter. He was in a frightful state as regards the activity of the mind, as every effort there was most painful to him. It seemed to him at times as if his head would burst; there seemed to be some great force within pushing the pieces away from one another."[8]

His physicians did not agree on the causes of these distressing complaints. After some hesitation, Dr. Wister finally concluded that there was "no evidence of organic disease." Sumner suffered, he thought, from "extreme nervous prostration"; "the injuries he originally received on the floor of the Senate had been aggravated by the peculiar condition of his nervous system at the time, a condition induced by severe mental and nervous tension from the loss of sleep for several consecutive nights, also by the peculiar susceptibility of his temperament, which is highly nervous." Dr. Jackson, on the other hand, was certain that Brooks's blows had caused "either congestion, or concussion followed by congestion, or positive inflammation of the brain or its investing membranes" and that Sumner's "brain and spinal cord had been the seat of a grave and formidable lesion." Though not so posi-

[7] Howe to M. F. Conway, June 27, 1858, Howe MSS.; Hillard to Lieber, Apr. 27, and May 26, 1858, Lieber MSS.; Boston *Courier*, May 24, 1858; Anderson: "Slavery Issue," p. 242.

[8] Dr. Charles Edward Brown-Séquard, in New York *Tribune*, Mar. 18, 1874.

tive, Dr. Perry also believed "that the base of the brain, as well as the spinal cord, has been the seat of some serious lesion." But, when Sumner was examined in Paris, his physician was emphatic in declaring that he "never had a brain affection" and that he "had no paralysis." [9]

It is difficult to appraise the medical validity of these conflicting statements. Unfortunately Sumner never had a complete neurological examination, for he never consulted Dr. S. Weir Mitchell, of Philadelphia, the one specialist in the United States competent to make such a study. As Sumner's friends refused to permit an autopsy of his brain and spinal cord after his death in 1874, the question of his injuries can never be settled with absolute certainty. Fortunately, however, Sumner kept such elaborate records of his health, his physicians' opinions, and even his medical prescriptions that modern neurologists and brain specialists can agree on the nature of his affliction.

These physicians declare that Sumner's reactions during the first few days after the Brooks assault were precisely what they would expect in a patient who had received a nasty blow on the head.[1] He did not have either a fractured skull or a concussion, for he did not suffer the severe headaches, changes in state of awareness, and somnolence which accompany brain traumas; instead, his condition was feverish and excited. Septicemia developed in his wounds and left him considerably debilitated, perhaps suffering from anemia. The symptoms of which he subsequently complained—pressure on the skull, weakness of the spine, difficulty in walking—could not, from a neurological point of view, possibly have been the results of blows he received on his head or even of a spinal lesion. The urinary condition that caused Sumner so much distress had no medical connection with the Brooks assault. At the same time no physician who has

[9] Wister to Wilson, Sept. 25, 1856, Sumner MSS.; Perry: *Case of Sumner*, pp. 5–7; C. E. Brown-Séquard to J. Collins Warren, Mar. 21, 1874, MS., Mass. Hist. Soc.; *Boston Medical and Surgical Journal*, Mar. 26, 1874.

[1] Sumner's remarkably complete medical record includes diagnoses by Drs. Boyle, Wister, Lindsly, Jackson, Perry, Brown-Séquard, and George Hayward; prescriptions and medical instructions given Sumner by Brown-Séquard, Hayward, Perry, and Jackson; and elaborate day-by-day accounts of Sumner's appearance and symptoms by Sumner himself, by interested friends, and by political and personal opponents.

studied the voluminous medical documents in Sumner's case has the least suspicion that Sumner was malingering; his sufferings were intense and genuine.

The diagnosis, then, is that Sumner was not shamming, but that his ailments were not, neurologically, the result of Brooks's beating. Cases of this sort are far from rare in medical history, and modern specialists classify Sumner's illness as "post-traumatic syndrome," in which numerous symptoms without objective causes follow a traumatic experience, such as an accident (physical trauma) in which the patient is not seriously injured. The precise nature of such a post-traumatic syndrome is not entirely clear; most neurologists believe it to be largely psychogenic. Patients suffering from such symptoms have great difficulty in reassuming their obligations to their families, their friends, and their employers.

In Sumner's case it is clear that the Brooks assault produced psychic wounds that lingered long after the physical injuries had disappeared. The pressure he felt on his head was a mental reenactment of the beating. Bearing in mind that the attack occurred in 1856, one is not so puzzled that he felt the weight on his skull to be precisely fifty-six pounds. The pain in his thighs was reminiscent of his tearing up his desk as he sought to rise under Brooks's lashing. It is at least suggestive that the senator who had for years been demanding a political party with "Backbone" should suffer mysterious spinal complaints. All these symptoms occurred chiefly, though not exclusively, when Sumner turned his mind to public affairs or tried to return to his Senate duties. The incredibly unprofessional and unscientific warnings of his English physicians that mental exertion might permanently impair his brain added to his tension on these occasions, as did his strong belief that the Southerners would shoot him. Hitherto Sumner had driven himself with his inflexible will to maintain impossibly high standards, despite overwork and mental strain; now he was faced with rebellion on the part of his body and of an unconscious segment of his mind.

As the ordinary remedies of rest and exercise were ineffectual for a malady of this sort, Sumner did not know what further steps to take for recovery; he was ready for desperate measures. In June 1858 an American merchant residing in Paris suggested that he visit Dr. Charles Edward Brown-Séquard, the French-American physician who was already famed for his pioneer work in the dissection of the spinal cord and for his discovery of the vasomotor nerves. Though Brown-Séquard was not then in general practice, he welcomed a case so interesting and important as Sumner's. "There is," he wrote the senator, "hardly a single human being,—my own family included,—whom I would so heartily rejoice to relieve from pain or disease, as Mr. Charles Sumner." [2]

On June 10 Brown-Séquard gave Sumner a three-hour examination. After noting his more obvious symptoms, the doctor tested the sensitivity of Sumner's spine, first with ice, then with boiling water, and finally with an esthesiometer, and he repeated his experiments again and again to ascertain the precise range of the disease in the spine and the neck. He found two "exquisitely tender" spots on the spine, one "situated at the junction of the cervical and dorsal regions, the other at that of the dorsal and lumbar." The brain itself he declared "free of any serious remaining injury," though there was still "an effusion of liquid about the brain and . . . a slight degree of congestion, chiefly if not only confined to the membrane around the brain." [3]

Sumner had instant and complete faith in this "most careful, skilful, learned and devoted physician," whose every word was reinforced by his worldwide reputation. He felt enormously relieved to be assured, by such an authority, that his brain was unaffected. He could easily accept Brown-Séquard's explanation, in simple, everyday language, of the symptoms from which he suffered. His back ailments, the doctor told him, were "the effect of what is called *contre-coup*. Mr. Sumner being seated and inclined over his desk at the time of the assault, the blows on his head took effect by *counter-stroke,* or communicated shock in the spine." "It is the nature of this disease," he added, "that, when the blow is struck upon the head, especially when the person struck is in a sitting posture, that the shock follows the spinal column until it reaches what is termed the point of resistance. Here the shock stops, and at this point there arises the germ of

[2] Brown-Séquard to Sumner, June 9, 1858, Sumner MSS.

[3] Sumner to Nassau Senior, June 22, 1858, MS., Huntington Lib.; Sumner to Longfellow, June 27, 1858, Longfellow MSS.; *Boston Medical and Surgical Journal,* May 21, 1874; New York *Tribune,* July 9, 1858.

future trouble." It was, Brown-Séquard explained, just like trying to drive a nail into very hard wood; the blow of the hammer bent not the head of the nail, but the weakest spots in its shaft. So, the thick bones of the skull had protected Sumner's brain, but the shock had injured the spine at the two points that were now so sensitive. The upper irritation was "the cause of the whole mischief as regards the function of the brain"; the lower "caused the pain which gave the appearance of paralysis" in the legs.[4]

Having diagnosed the case, Brown-Séquard proposed a cure. "Fire" was his remedy. If he applied counter-irritants to the two sprains, these would "produce the absorption of the excess of fluid effused about the brain, and diminish the congestion of the membranes of this organ," and would thus lessen "the degree of pain, if not altogether render the sensibility normal, so as to allow walking and other movements to take place without pain." The most effective counter-irritant, Brown-Séquard told his patient, was the moxa, a treatment of Japanese origin, in which the naked skin was burned with inflamed agaric (*amadou*), cotton wool, or some other very combustible substance. The medical records do not show which form of moxa Brown-Séquard favored, but the standard one in use at the time was formed of "cotton, rendered downy by carding, and made into a roll an inch long, and from half an inch to two inches in diameter." The treatment, Brown-Séquard warned, would be most painful, but without it Sumner must remain "a permanent invalid, always subject to a sudden and serious relapse." [5]

Brown-Séquard's "examination and report gave me such confidence," Sumner wrote Howe, "that I put myself at once in his hands." He asked the doctor when he could apply the first moxa.

"To-morrow, if you please," said Brown-Séquard.

[4] Sumner to Mrs. W. H. Seward, June 27, 1858, Seward MSS.; New York *Tribune*, July 9, 1858; Brown-Séquard, in New York *Tribune*, Mar. 18, 1874, and in Meadville *Republican*, Mar. 20, 1874. At another time Brown-Séquard suggested a slightly different origin of these "two sprains of the spine." "The upper one was caused by the blows on the head, the lower by the violent effort which Mr. Sumner made to rise during the assault." *Boston Medical and Surgical Journal*, May 21, 1874.

[5] Sumner: *Works*, IV, 330; Sumner to Longfellow, June 27, 1858, Longfellow MSS.; New York *Tribune*, June 23, 1858. On the moxa then used see *Cyclopedia of Practical Medicine* (1833), I, 492.

"Why not this afternoon?" countered Sumner eagerly.

The doctor prepared to give his patient chloroform to ease the pain. Sumner objected: "If you say positively that I shall derive as much benefit if I take chloroform as if I do not, then of course I will take it; but if there is to be any degree whatever of amelioration in case I do not take it, then I shall not take it." Believing that the greater Sumner's pain, the better his chances of recovery, Brown-Séquard did not give him the anesthetic, but burned the moxa on his bare back.[6]

During the next thirteen days Brown-Séquard gave Sumner the moxa treatment five additional times, each time without anesthetic. "I have never seen a man bearing with such fortitude as Mr. Sumner has shown, the extremely violent pain of this kind of burning," he declared at the time, and many years later he still felt that he had submitted Sumner "to the martyrdom of the greatest suffering that can be inflicted on mortal man." Sumner bore the pain stoically. "The torment is considerable," he wrote Howe, in marked understatement, "but that is over in 5 or 10 minutes. But then come the annoyances and inflammations which . . . are incident to burns. Of course, I walk with pain; lie down with pain; rise with pain." [7]

After six moxae Brown-Séquard gave his patient a two-month respite from burning, but, in the ninety-degree heat of Paris, Sumner got little benefit from the rest. The six open suppurating wounds resulting from his burns kept him in torment. "For 5 weeks," he lamented, "I have not been able to lie on my back or to turn over in my bed." He began complaining that the fire had driven his pains into one of his legs, which was "sadly disabled." [8]

On July 20 the meaning of that last symptom appeared. In the middle of the night "neuralgic, constringing and oppressing" pain in his chest woke him up. He could neither lie down nor stand up. Finally he managed to prop himself up with cushions in a chair, so as to get a little relief. Alone in his hotel, unattended except by servants, he had to wait in this position from

[6] Sumner to Howe, June 24, 1858, Sumner MSS.; Sumner: *Works*, IV, 330–1; New York *Tribune*, Mar. 18, 1874.

[7] New York *Tribune*, June 28, 1858, and Mar. 18, 1874; Sumner to Howe, June 24, 1858, Sumner MSS.

[8] Sumner to Longfellow, July 19, 1858, Longfellow MSS.

four o'clock in the morning until six in the evening, when Brown-Séquard arrived. Finding the pain "almost without precedent," the doctor attributed it to "the original concussion" of the Brooks assault and rather proudly decided that Sumner's case was "one of the most interesting in the history of science." Giving Sumner opiates for immediate relief, he prescribed belladonna and decided to postpone indefinitely further moxa treatments.[9]

Sumner was apparently entirely satisfied with Brown-Séquard. If he had any doubts about his treatment, they were dispelled when George Hayward, a Boston physician then practicing in Paris, not only endorsed it, but reported that four of "the most eminent medical authorities in England," Sir Benjamin Brody, Sir James Clarke, Sir Henry Holland, and Dr. Lawrence, also approved it. Many of Sumner's American friends, however, were very dubious about Brown-Séquard and his remedies. Dr. Perry was sure that "a life of perfect repose would be more beneficial . . . than the application of hot irons." Howe, who was a doctor himself, thought that his friend had fallen into the hands of quacks who were "certainly tormenting and injuring him in the pursuit of a baseless theory."[1]

From a medical point of view, Brown-Séquard's critics were entirely correct. His neurological examination of Sumner had been wholly inadequate, and his diagnosis of spinal sprains brought about by *contre-coups* was medical nonsense. The moxa treatment was, therapeutically, no treatment at all; it was merely a terribly painful experience. Application of moxae could no more give permanent benefit to a brain or spine injury than could a strong liniment. Brown-Séquard's theory that the constrictive pressure in Sumner's chest was somehow an extension of the spinal injury "through the avenue of the nearest network of veins . . . from the spinal column to the heart" is anatomically ridiculous.[2] In fact, Sumner had his first attack of angina

[9] Sumner to Howe, July 22, 1858, Sumner MSS.; New York *Tribune*, Aug. 10, 1858.

[1] Sumner to Seward, July 19, 1858, Seward MSS.; Hayward to Sumner, Nov. 20, 1862, Sumner MSS.; G. R. Russell to Sumner, Aug. 15, 1858, ibid.; Howe to Palfrey, Sept. 2, 1858, Palfrey MSS.; Howe to Sumner, July 11, 1858, Howe MSS.

[2] Meadville *Republican*, Mar. 20, 1874. Brown-Séquard had the grace to admit that "this theory did not admit of demonstration." *Boston Medical and Surgical Journal*, Mar. 26, 1874.

pectoris, perhaps brought on by—though not caused by—the shock and discomfort of the moxa treatment; Brown-Séquard quite properly prescribed belladonna for it.

If from a physiological point of view Brown-Séquard's treatment—which, it must be remembered, was in keeping with the most advanced medical thought of the time—was worse than worthless, it is possible that it benefited Sumner in other ways. His sufferings, which were widely publicized in American newspapers, gave the lie, once and for all, to charges that he was shamming; moreover, the same very real and demonstrable pain freed Sumner himself from his worried sense of guilt at being absent from his post of duty. He even gained some psychic income from his torture. While his back was being burned, he allowed his mind to wander, and he "thought sometimes of St. Lawrence on the gridiron—sometimes of Prometheus with the vulture at his liver, and also of many others in the list of fire-sufferers." Identifying himself with the martyrs of the past, he erased any unconscious doubts about the correctness of his course; never again in the future would he feel lost without the unstinted approbation of his peers. Having, as Prescott observed, enjoyed "quite contrary to usage—the crown of martyrdom during his own lifetime," Sumner came to be, even in his own eyes, less a fallible human being than a symbol of a righteous cause. He found it easy to suppress any expression of resentment against Preston Brooks, who, in this new mood, seemed only "the unconscious agent of a malign power." Not even the death of the South Carolina congressman of an agonizing disease in March 1857 evoked a bitter word from Sumner. "The Almighty has settled this," he told a friend, "better than you or I could have done." [3]

Secure in his faith that his and the Almighty's ways were identical, Sumner began to mend. Gradually the sores on his back healed, and he could ride comfortably in a carriage. His

[3] Sumner to Howe, July 1, 1858, Bird MSS.; Ticknor: *Prescott,* p. 423; Pierce, III, 524; J. L. Bennett to Sumner, June 7, 1860, Sumner MSS. Still Sumner did speak of the assault as attempted "murder" (Earl of Carlisle, Diary, Oct. 29, 1857, Carlisle MSS.), and his devoted secretary declared: "Mr. Sumner largely refrained from talking of Brooks, except to say he had no more personal feeling against him than against the stick he used—but I was sensible that he was not unwilling to have me talk of him." A. B. Johnson to Pierce, Feb. 12, 1886, Pierce MSS.

"neuralgia," as Brown-Séquard persisted in calling his angina pectoris, was an ever present danger; on a little excursion to St. Germain in August he suffered "those terrible pains" in his chest four times. Still he could now receive callers, make occasional visits, and listen to lectures. At the end of the summer he went to Aix-en-Savoie to try the famous mineral baths. After his experience with Brown-Séquard, he found the treatment of hot and cold douches a positive luxury. The regimen palled after about a month, and he "rushed through Switzerland," visited Milan, Verona, Padua, and Venice all too briefly, and then came north by way of Vienna, Prague, Dresden, and Berlin. "All my time," he explained, "has been devoted simply to regaining my lost health." [4]

• 6 •

On his return to Paris in November 1858, Sumner received disquieting political intelligence from home. A number of Massachusetts citizens were becoming bored by what they considered the undue length of Sumner's martyrdom. Henry David Thoreau recorded that one Massachusetts woman, with feeble curiosity, asked: "How is that young man who had his head hurt? I haven't heard anything about him for a good while." Others felt that they had heard far too much about Sumner's wounds, treatments, and sufferings. "We hope," declared the stanchly Republican New York *Times*, "that Mr. Sumner's friends will not consider it necessary hereafter to send bulletins of his health to the Press upon the arrival of every steamer; these . . . are getting to be monotonous." [5]

By the summer of 1858 a strong sentiment had developed that Sumner ought to resign. Republicans as diverse as Howe, Charles Francis Adams, and William Pitt Fessenden shared it.[6] Active leadership in the movement, however, fell to Governor

[4] Sumner to Felton, Aug. 5, 1858, Sumner MSS.; Sumner to Longfellow, Sept. 15, 1858, Longfellow MSS.; Sumner to Duchess of Argyll, Dec. 2, 1858, Argyll MSS.; Sumner to Lyman Trumbull, Sept. 12, 1858, MS., Illinois State Hist. Lib.

[5] Bradford Torry (ed.): *The Writings of Henry David Thoreau* (Boston: Houghton Mifflin Co.; 1906), XII, 447; New York *Times*, Dec. 16, 1858.

[6] Howe to Sumner, May 18 [1858], Howe MSS.; Adams, Diary, Dec. 18, 1858, Adams MSS.; Fessenden to Hamilton Fish, Dec. 18, 1858, Fish MSS.

N. P. Banks, that "bobbin boy of Waltham," who had managed to secure the combined nominations of the Republican and American parties in 1857 and to defeat the obnoxious Henry J. Gardner.[7] Ambitious and necessitous, Banks was hardly inaugurated before he began to think longingly of the security of a six-year Senate term. To others Sumner's vacant chair might be a "perpetual speech"; to Banks it was a perpetual reminder of a political opportunity.

As Sumner's popularity was still great, Banks moved stealthily. First he carefully disseminated a rumor that Sumner had already submitted his resignation. Then, at the Republican state convention in September 1858, Banks's friends presented an apparently innocuous resolution to the effect that "It is the first duty of a Representative to attend the sessions of the body of which he is a member." Actually Banks had written the resolution himself and wanted it to serve as a trial balloon. If it met with popular approval, the governor would interpret it as applying to the absent senator; if there was popular resentment against it, he could swear that it was intended to refer only to the state legislature.[8]

Frank Bird, who hated Banks as much as he loved Sumner, was instantly alert to the plot. He countered Banks's ambiguous resolution with another, very positive one: "That . . . Charles Sumner, though separated from us by the broad Atlantic—seeking in foreign lands for the restoration of health, impaired by ruffian violence in the Senate House—has our undivided affection, our high regard, and our constant prayer for his speedy restoration to health." Faced with such a challenge, Banks's stratagem failed—but not his desire to become senator.[9]

Sumner, who had been completely out of touch with American news for months, was distressed to hear of Banks's intrigues. Though Republican leaders in Boston assured him that the plot to replace him was "confined to the meanest hunkers and the

[7] On Banks's rise to power see Harrington: *Banks*, pp. 42–4; Bean: "Party Transformations," pp. 357–64; clippings from Massachusetts newspapers for 1857 campaign, W. S. Robinson Scrapbooks.

[8] Howe to Sumner, Nov. 6, 1858, Howe MSS.; Bird to Sumner, Sept. 14, 1858, Sumner MSS.; A. G. Browne to Sumner, Sept. 14, 1858, ibid.; Anderson: "Slavery Issue," p. 242.

[9] The Worcester *Spy* (Dec. 29, 1858) and the Boston *Advertiser* (Sept. 18, 1858) denounced Bank's intrigue as "inconsiderate and premature."

smallest of trading politicians with the exception of a very few cold-blooded and selfish scamps like Banks," Sumner also bore in mind the advice of his personal supporters: " 'Political friends' are ungrateful scoundrels, and if they huzza you to day they will talk of your successor tomorrow." [1]

Sumner refused to allow Banks's "heartless" plot to force him into resigning. He needed his Senate salary for his medical and traveling expenses; [2] his best friends urged him not to resign; he could not surrender his seat without also giving up faith in his permanent recovery. Most important of all, he now completely identified his own personal prospects with the future of the antislavery cause. "If my position were merely political, I should resign at once," he assured Howe, "but I am unwilling to renounce the opportunity of again meeting the enemies of freedom in the Senate. My resignation would delight the slave-drivers, and . . . it would pain, the true Anti-Slavery men of the country. . . . That delight and that pain shall not come from me." [3]

Unwilling to resign, Sumner still felt unable to resume his duties. In November 1858 he issued a new public statement of his disabilities and prospects. Dr. Brown-Séquard and Dr. Hayward now brought in the eminent physician, Armand Trousseau, as a consultant; the three declared that Sumner "was still suffering from the injuries he received more than two years and a half ago," that they considered it "unadvisable for him to return to his public duties during the present winter," but that they had "great confidence, *that he would surely recover.*" The timing of the statement suggests that it was designed to check Banks's

[1] Bird to Sumner, Sept. 14, 1858, Sumner MSS.; A. G. Browne to Sumner, Sept. 14, 1858, ibid., G. R. Russell to Sumner, Aug. 15, 1858, ibid.

[2] C. F. Adams to J. T. Furness, Jan. 17, 1858, copy, Adams MSS. Sumner continued regularly to draw his Senate pay while absent in Europe. The expenses of his European travels were large. During his 1858–9 trip alone he had a letter of credit on the House of Baring for £2000; apparently he spent all of this and owed the bankers at the end of his trip $206.40 more. His financial records, with numerous receipted bills for large purchases of hand-tailored clothing, *objets d'art*, etc., are in the Sumner MSS. Howe, as numerous letters to Sumner in the Howe MSS., 1858–9, indicate, managed his finances while he was abroad.

[3] Sumner to Howe, Nov. 24, 1858, Sumner MSS. Cf. Sumner to Carlos Pierce, July 19, 1858: "It is hard to endure pain long continued; but it is harder still to see life glide away and precious opportunities disappear . . . and there is a new pang added by the baseness of men." MS. in the possession of Mr. George H. Wettach, Fair Lawn, N. J.

plot; the carefully balanced wording indicates that the doctors had been asked to speak of the senator's injuries as serious, but not permanently incapacitating.[4]

Though Brown-Séquard wanted to resume the moxa treatments, the three doctors finally agreed that Sumner should spend the winter in retirement in southern France. He selected the placid university town of Montpellier, where he would be almost completely isolated from disturbing news from America. "Away from care, responsibility or excitement," he settled into a three-month round of "*ventouse seches* and *capsules* and *pilules*." Though not entirely free from angina pectoris, and obliged to spend much of his time in bed, he enjoyed this "most retired and tranquil life." He found the climate "exquisite,—a perpetual spring"; the promenades were "the finest in France"; the professors at the university were "charming." [5]

Best of all, his health was improving. Though overexertion occasionally produced some of his old symptoms, he suffered no real relapses during his quiet winter. By spring he was feeling almost well again. "Many gloomy hours I have passed, and much pain I have endured," he triumphantly wrote Howe in March 1859. "But I believe this is past." [6]

By April he felt able to visit Italy. In Naples he met George Bemis, a young and sympathetic Boston lawyer, and they joined forces in sight-seeing. Though Bemis wrote home that the senator was "not a well man yet," as he had to use a cane, became tired if he walked a considerable distance, and still had "to disturb himself three or four times" each night because of his bladder condition, the lawyer's diary shows that Sumner was capable of vigorous exertions. They visited museums, inspected the cathedral, went out to Vergil's grotto, climbed Vesuvius, drove to Herculaneum and Pompeii, took a horseback trip to St. Elmo, during which Sumner "indulged himself in a glass of goat's milk, much to the amusement of the by-standers," and went through the royal palace, including even the coach house.

All the while Sumner talked and talked. He discussed litera-

[4] New York *Tribune*, Dec. 16, 1858.

[5] Sumner to W. W. Story, Dec. 11, 1858, MS., Huntington Lib.; Sumner to Duchess of Argyll, Feb. 10, 1859, Argyll MSS.; Sumner to Longfellow, Mar. 4, 1859, Longfellow MSS.

[6] Sumner to Howe, Mar. 8 [1859], Sumner MSS.

ture with Bemis—"e.g., Hannibal's campaign, Italian writers, French and Italian morals, Manzoni's Promesi Sposi—love, including some of Sumner's experiences—Society, wherein Sumner told . . . a great deal of his English and foreign acquaintances—Law, including Sumner's relations with G. T. Curtis, B. F. Hallett, R. C. Winthrop, G. S. Hillard, etc.—Persons, including Prescott, Bancroft, Lord Brougham, Bunsen, de Tocqueville, Judge Fletcher etc., etc. . . . criminal law theories . . . curious chapters in Franklin's history . . . English peculiarities of pronunciation . . . Lord Palmerston's intrigues and marriage . . . Michelet on Amour (Love). . . ." Bemis, the good listener, reported that Sumner, as he left Naples, "spoke as if he had enjoyed our intercourse."[7]

Then Sumner spent three glorious weeks in Rome, where William Wetmore Story, the artist son of Justice Story, accompanied him to the galleries and the churches and the art studios. Sumner's enthusiasm exhausted the Storys, the Robert Brownings, and the Nathaniel Hawthornes, for what he lacked in appreciation of art he made up with zeal. Leaving reluctantly, he wrote Story: "Rome haunts me perpetually, and I wish to ask you a hundred questions which I forgot."[8]

He arrived in northern Italy just as Napoleon III's troops were driving out the Austrians. At Turin he rejoiced equally in the courage and hope he found among all classes in the Kingdom of Savoy and in the firm competence of Count Cavour, who granted him a private interview. "Three cheers for Italy," Sumner exclaimed as he left the capital of the Piedmont, "and may the Austrian empire cease to exist."[9]

Back in Paris in June, Sumner had another examination by Brown-Séquard and went on another round of sight-seeing. Theodore Parker, who had come to Europe in what proved to be a vain hope of combatting the tuberculosis that afflicted him, found him "the same dear old Sumner as he used to be before that scoundrel laid him low." "He walks on those great long legs of

[7] Bemis to Jonathan Bemis, Apr. 23, 1859, Bemis MSS.; Bemis, Diary, Apr. 19, and 24, 1859, ibid.

[8] Sumner to W. W. Story, May 14, 1859, MS., Huntington Lib.; James: *Story*, II, 40–1.

[9] James: *Story*, II, 36–41; Sumner to Duchess of Argyll, May 20, 1859, Argyll MSS.

his at the rate of four or five miles an hour; his countenance is good, good as ever; he walked upright and sits upright; all the trouble has vanished from his brain. . . ." [1]

As the time for his departure drew near, Sumner dreaded leaving the "Elysium" of Europe for an America "befouled by slavery." Even the Italians, oppressed by centuries of despotism, were proving themselves more worthy of liberty than the "Americans with four millions of slaves, and with a leaven of slaveholding tyrants, and foreign immigrants who cannot speak our language." Sumner joined his European friends in laughing at the notion that slaveholding America could claim "All men are created equal"; he was so bitter against his country that one irate fellow citizen thought him "Mrs. Trollope in disguise." [2]

Anticipating his return to Washington, where he would be "amidst tobacco-spitting, swearing slave-drivers, abused by the press, insulted so far as it is possible, pained and ransacked by the insensibility about him to human rights and the claims of human nature," Sumner tried to enjoy every moment of his last months abroad.[3] An exciting fling in London society, six weeks at the salt-water baths near Le Havre, a brief tour of Brittany, a final few days in Paris, where he spent about $1,500 in buying, generally at outrageous prices, bronzes, china, books, engravings, manuscripts, and other alleged antiques, and a short, happy trip through rural England completed his European travels. On November 5 he sailed from Liverpool.

"I return," he wrote to Bemis, "with mingled feelings—happy in the consciousness of health regained, and yet with a certain solicitude as to how I can stand the strain and tug of the work and responsibility before me." Of the nature of that work and the extent of his responsibility he had no doubt. While suffering from the moxa treatment, he had sworn: "If health ever returns I will repay to slavery and the whole crew of its supporters every wound, burn, . . . ache, pain, trouble, grief which I have suffered. That vow is registered." [4]

[1] Weiss, *Parker*, II, 294–5.

[2] Sumner to Longfellow, July 19, 1858, Longfellow MSS.; Weiss, *Parker*, II, 336; F. Schrœder to Hamilton Fish, July 7, 1859, Fish MSS.

[3] James: *Story*, II, 45.

[4] Sumner to Bemis, Nov. 5, 1859, Bemis MSS.; Sumner to Howe, July 22, 1858, Sumner MSS.

CHAPTER XIII

If Mr. Lincoln Stands Firm

"WHAT A DIFFERENCE between this place and Rome!" Sumner lamented as he returned to Washington in December 1859. The American capital looked more than ever bare and grotesque. At one end of Pennsylvania Avenue rose the architecturally improbable Capitol with its unfinished dome; at the other, Clark Mills's "caricature" of General Jackson imperturbably saluting from the saddle of an anatomically impossible horse. Sumner blushed when courtesy required him to show the sights of Washington to visiting Englishmen. Constantly he wished for "A walk in the streets of Rome, a stroll on the Pincian, a visit to the Vatican, a sight of St. Peter's—oh, for an hour, one brief hour, of any of these!" [1]

Politically, too, Washington seemed worse than ever. Embittered by John Brown's raid on Harpers Ferry, the Southerners had become more extreme in their defense of slavery. Even a moderate like Jefferson Davis demanded federal protection for slavery in all the territories. Albert Gallatin Brown, the other senator from Mississippi, boldly announced that "slavery is a great moral, social, and political blessing—a blessing to the slave, and a blessing to the master." Senator Mason, of Virginia, agreed "that the condition of African bondage elevates both races," and

[1] James: *Story*, II, 48; Boston *Commonwealth*, Mar. 7, 1874; Gordon N. Ray (ed.) *The Letters and Private Papers of William Makepeace Thackeray* (Cambridge: Harvard University Press; 1946), III, 195.

R. M. T. Hunter, from the same state, argued: "There is not a respectable system of civilization known to history, . . . whose foundations were not laid in the institution of domestic slavery." [2]

Southern hostility toward Sumner had not diminished during his years of absence. Some young Virginians talked of kidnapping him for the purpose of offering him some physical indignity. "We see plainly that you are spoiling fast for another licking," a "Southern Mazzini or Plug Ugly" wrote him, "and it is quite evident that you are flattering yourself with the idea that no Southerner dare lay hands on *you* for fear of mighty vengeance of the northerners in defence of their sand-box dollybaby Senator. . . . What in Hell do we care for the Vengeance of the Yankees. Why a dissolution and a fight is what we are after. And if giving you *another pummelling* will be the means of bringing it about then here gos [*sic*] it." [3]

"This is a barbarous place," Sumner felt. "The slave-masters seem to me more than ever *barbarians*—in manner, conversation, speeches, conduct, principles, life. All things indicate a crisis." [4]

• 1 •

Sumner was slow to resume an active part in the sectional contest. His health, he felt, was still precarious. Unable to reconcile himself to the fact that at forty-eight years of age he did not have the vigor of an adolescent, he worried because he could no longer race along the streets at a pace that approached a gallop and because he was obliged to walk, rather than run, up the steps of the Capitol.[5]

His role in the Republican party was as uncertain as his health. During his absence Republican leaders seemed to have become more concerned with respectability than with human rights. Feeling sure of the antislavery vote in the 1860 elections,

[2] *Cong. Globe*, 36 Cong., 1 Sess., 596, 1,004, and Appendix, 106.

[3] Sumner to J. A. Andrew, Dec. 9, and 12, 1859, Andrew MSS.; "Southern Mazzini" to Sumner, Apr. 19, 1860, Sumner MSS.

[4] Sumner to "My dear Sir," Mar. 24, 1860, Segal Coll.; James: *Story*, II, 48.

[5] George Sumner to Chase, Nov. 20, 1859, Chase MSS., Hist. Soc. of Penn.; Richards: *S. G. Howe*, II, 477.

they were cultivating a moderate stand in order to win over former Whigs and Know-nothings. They went out of their way to condemn John Brown's raid; Seward repressed his "irrepressible conflict" doctrine and talked blandly of differences between "capital states" and "labor states"; there was even doubt about whether the Republicans, in their national convention of 1860, would dare endorse the Declaration of Independence. Sumner cared nothing for the protective tariff, the land grants to agricultural colleges, the chartering of a Pacific railroad, and other economic legislation with which Republicans now concerned themselves.

Even when Congress discussed questions relating to slavery, Sumner's consuming interest as a senator, he found himself unfamiliar with issues. He knew only what the newspapers told him about John Brown's raid, which had occurred before he returned from Europe. Sumner's attention had been so centered upon his own suffering that he apparently forgot that he had once met Brown, in early 1857, when the Kansas free-state leader, already notorious for the bloody massacre of Southerners on Pottawatomie Creek, visited him in Boston and asked to see the coat he was wearing when Brooks assaulted him. Painfully Sumner had hobbled to his closet and handed the garment, still stiff with blood, to Brown, who closely examined it and "said nothing . . . but . . . his lips compressed and his eyes shown like polished steel."[6] Sumner had forgotten, too, his endorsement of Hugh Forbes, the Englishman who had served for a time as Brown's drillmaster, but had broken with him over his plan to seize the Harpers Ferry arsenal.[7]

Sumner found it hard to make up his mind about Brown's raid, which occupied so much of the time of the Thirty-Sixth Congress. Convinced that Brown was "almost mad" and that "of course his act must be deplored," he could not help admiring "the singular courage and character shewn by its author," in whom he found "much of the Convenanter, the Puritan and even the early Christian martyr." "For a practical statesman, believing

[6] James Redpath to Elias Nason, Apr. 10, 1874, MS. owned by Mr. Boyd B. Stutler; Springfield *Republican*, Feb. 6, 1857. Cf. Nason: *Sumner*, pp. 250–1; James Freeman Clarke: *Anti-Slavery Days* . . . (New York: R. Worthington; 1884), pp. 153–4; Clarke: *Memorial and Biographical Sketches* (Boston: Houghton Mifflin Co.; 1878), 101–2.

[7] Sumner to Rev. Dr. Francis, Oct. 24 [1858], Washburn MSS.

slavery a wrong, the subject is not without its difficulties," he confessed. "Not, indeed, that I hesitate to judge the *act;* but how can I refuse my admiration to many things in the *man?*" He refrained from entering the debates on Brown's raid, giving as his reason his doctor's advice against overexertion.[8]

Such silence was what Republican managers most wanted from Sumner as the presidential election of 1860 drew near. Hoping to widen the split in the Democratic party, they feared any word or act which might give Stephen A. Douglas an opportunity to step forward as the defender of the South. Almost as fervently they hoped that nothing would be said in the Senate to alienate any of the Northern Whigs and Know-nothings who seemed ready to join the Republicans. So obvious was the Republican desire to play down antislavery agitation that Sumner grew distressed over "the hollowness of our own professing friends." "Half of our republicans need conversion to first principles," he decided.[9]

Sumner was willing to go along with his party leaders, however, at least until after the Republican nominee was selected. He had no thought of being a candidate himself. "It is hard for a person, who has been in the Senate, exposed to bitter opposition and also to jealousies and rivalries, to rally for himself the whole party," he realized, "and perhaps the very brilliancy of his position is against him. He is too much known, and the neutral men, whose votes are wanted, cannot sustain him." [1] Like most Republicans, he expected the Chicago convention to nominate William H. Seward, and he was well pleased with the prospect. Though he regretted that Seward's recent speeches had become increasingly conservative on slavery questions, he recognized that the New Yorker was trying "to plead the good cause, and at the same time to avoid disturbing the prejudices of those who differed from him," and he remained confident of Seward's basic soundness.[2]

[8] Sumner to Duchess of Argyll, Dec. 20, 1859, Argyll MSS.

[9] Sumner to Palfrey, Apr. 26, 1860, Palfrey MSS.; Stearns: *Stearns*, p. 214.

[1] Sumner to Duchess of Argyll, May 22, 1860, Argyll MSS. Sumner was explaining the reasons why the Republican party failed to nominate Seward, but his words also applied to himself.

[2] Adams, Diary, May 7, 1860, Adams MSS.; Sumner to W. W. Story, May 8, 1860, MS., Huntington Lib.; Sumner to Duchess of Argyll, Mar. 2, 1860, Argyll MSS.

To Sumner's surprise, however, the Republican convention, which met at Chicago on May 16, passed over Seward and nominated Abraham Lincoln, of Illinois, who was personally unknown to Sumner—and, indeed, to most Eastern Republicans. To the Duchess of Argyll, who watched American politics closely, he tried to show the nomination in the best possible light. Lincoln, he assured her, was "a good honest Anti-Slavery man," who would bring strength to the party in the Northwest and in Pennsylvania, where Seward's chances would have been doubtful. "Those who know him speak of him as a person of positive ability and of real goodness," he added, though he was obliged to admit that the nominee had "very little acquaintance with Government" and was quite ignorant of foreign affairs. Still, he added cheerfully: "We think he will be the next President." [3]

Sumner thought that the nomination of Lincoln, whose views on slavery were believed to be moderate, required an explicit, radical restatement of Republican doctrines. Any hesitation he might have had on the ground of expediency was removed when he learned that the Democrats had irreparably split, with Douglas the nominee of the Northern wing of that party, John C. Breckinridge that of the Southern. The existence of a feeble fourth ticket, calling itself Constitutional Unionist, which sought to rally conservative Whigs behind John Bell and Edward Everett, made Republican success more certain. Winning the election was now less Sumner's concern than keeping his party faithful to its principles.

• 2 •

Political considerations dictated the timing of Sumner's new assault upon the South, but the intention had been fixed in his mind ever since the Brooks assault. So evident was the vindictive-

[3] Sumner to Duchess of Argyll, May 22, 1860, Argyll MSS. I have found nothing to confirm the belated reminiscence of Blair Lee that Sumner, meeting his mother on the streets of Washington just after Lincoln's nomination, said: "Mrs. Lee, we are wholly ruined." (Smith: *Blair Family,* I, 485.) Sumner's letter consoling Seward upon the loss of the nomination (May 20, 1860, Seward MSS.) certainly reflects disappointment, but not despair. In the balloting at Chicago for presidential nominees, Sumner himself received a single vote, from a Kentucky delegate. *Proceedings of the First Three Republican National Conventions of 1856, 1860 and 1864 . . .* (Minneapolis: Charles W. Johnson; 1893), p. 149.

ness he had stored up that even loyal friends like Howe and Longfellow thought he was "too full of fight," and they warned him "against saying a word not qualified by benevolence and charity." [4] Others urged him not to make any reference to his sufferings when he spoke and to ignore his Southern assailants. "You have floored those dirty fellows," T. P. Chandler advised, "and I would not stop to piss on them while they are down." [5]

Sumner was not to be diverted by these appeals. "There is a time for every thing," he informed Howe severely, "and when crime and criminals are thrust before us they are to be met by all the energies that God has given us by argument, sarcasm, scorn and denunciation. The whole arsenal of God is ours, and I will not renounce one of the weapons—not one!" [6]

With his mind fully made up, Sumner waited for an opportunity to claim the Senate floor. A bill for the admission of Kansas as a free state afforded a suitable occasion, and on June 4, at precisely twelve o'clock, he appeared in the Senate in full evening dress, including white gloves, to launch into his four-hour oration on "The Barbarism of Slavery."

The news that Sumner was to speak had attracted a respectable, but not crowded, audience to the Senate galleries, and at the same time had driven most of the Democratic members to absent themselves conspicuously from the chamber. Gathering at the bars in the Senate lobby, they made a considerable amount of noise as Sumner spoke. Senator Louis T. Wigfall, a Texas fire-eater, strolled ominously up and down the aisle near the speaker, his "dark, deeply-set eyes, glaring from beneath his heavy, shaggy brows" at Sumner. Douglas squirmed restlessly in his seat, and Mason exhibited his exasperation by chewing an immense quantity of tobacco, so that by the end of the oration, his quids lay around him in a semicircle.[7]

There was great curiosity to see whether Sumner's strength would be equal to another long oration, and there was an even more sensitive interest to learn whether he would refer to him-

4 Richards: *S. G. Howe,* II, 445.

5 Chandler to Sumner, Feb. 24, 1860, Sumner MSS.

6 Sumner to Howe [Jan. 1860], Sumner MSS.

7 Undated clipping from Cincinnati *Commercial,* Pierce Scrapbooks; Boston *Atlas & Bee,* June 5, 1860; New York *Herald,* June 6, 1860; George Sumner to Longfellow [June 1860], Longfellow MSS.

self and his own sufferings. Quietly he began: "I have no personal griefs to utter. . . . I have no personal wrongs to avenge; only a barbarous nature could attempt to wield that vengeance which belongs to the Lord. The years that have intervened and the tombs that have been opened since I spoke have their voices too," he declared, in his only public reference to the recent deaths of Preston Brooks and Andrew P. Butler. "Besides, what am I—what is any man . . . compared with the Question before us?"[8]

Without further preliminary he launched into his elaborate philippic, which marked an innovation in his oratorical technique. Hitherto he had carefully memorized each major speech and had addressed his remarks to his fellow senators in the hope of influencing their votes. Now he did not wish to overtax his strength by committing to memory an address that, when published, filled forty-two closely printed columns of the *Congressional Globe*. Moreover, experience had taught him that "no senator is reached by any argument" and that his orations could have an effect only if "addressed somewhat as harangues to the whole country." As he intended them "for circulation as tracts," he wanted them to be "full and almost scholastic in form" and to have "more of the completeness and elaborateness of an article, with, however, the form of a speech." Consequently he made no concessions whatever to his listeners, but read all the 35,000 words of his address, including elaborate statistics and lengthy quotations, from galley proofs he held in his hand.[9]

As if recognizing that his new technique lacked brilliance in delivery, Sumner compensated by resorting to increased violence of language. Over half his oration was a refutation of Southern senators' claims that slavery was a beneficent institution, productive of a high civilization. Sumner retorted bluntly that a slave society was no civilization at all. "Barbarous in origin; barbarous in its law; barbarous in all its pretensions; barbarous in the instruments it employs; barbarous in consequences; barbarous in spirit; barbarous wherever it shows itself, Slavery must breed Barbarians." The real character of Southern slavery appeared

[8] Sumner: *The Barbarism of Slavery* . . . (Washington: Thaddeus Hyatt; 1860), p. 1.

[9] Sumner to Theodore Tilton, June 22, 1860, Tilton MSS.; Sumner to Duchess of Argyll, July 31, 1860, Argyll MSS.

in the laws regulating the "peculiar institution." A Southern Negro might "be marked like a hog, branded like a mule, yoked like an ox, maimed like a cur, and constantly beaten like a brute; all according to law." Moreover, "by the license of Slavery, a whole race is delivered over to prostitution and concubinage, without the protection of any law."

The practical consequences of slavery were as barbarous as its laws. In relentless statistical detail Sumner compared the populations and the economies of the free and the slave states. He found that through the influence of slavery "population, values of all kinds, manufactures, commerce, railroads, canals, charities, the post office, colleges, professional schools, academies, public schools, newspapers, periodicals, books, authorship, inventions" in the South were "all stunted." Mercilessly he singled out South Carolina for scorn. Despite that state's lofty pretensions to culture, a smaller percentage of her white population than of the Massachusetts free Negroes attended school.

Even more shocking, Sumner found, was the influence of slavery upon the character of the slaveholders. "Every Slave-master on his plantation is a Bashaw, with all the prerogatives of a Turk." "Six thousand skulls of infants are said to have been taken from a single fish-pond near a nunnery, to the dismay of Pope Gregory," Sumner asserted. "Under the law of Slavery, infants, the offspring of masters 'who dream of Freedom in a slave's embrace,' are not thrown into a fish-pond. . . . They are sold."

How could one expect civilized leaders to emerge from such a society? Naturally these "modern imitators of Cain" in the Southern United States adopted "the bludgeon, the revolver, and the bowie-knife" as their constant companions; naturally they turned to the cowardly duel; naturally they desired "the suppression of all freedom of speech or of the press." Naturally, too, these slaveholders, when they became members of Congress, heaped "reproach, contumely, violence even unto death" upon anyone who disagreed with them. Sumner reviewed the history of the violence committed by these congressional "bludgeon-bearers of Slavery"—conspicuously omitting any reference to 1856.

These Southern slaveholders were not merely barbarians; they seemed to rejoice in their degraded condition. "No New Zealander exults in his tattoo, no savage of the Northwest exults in his flat head, more than the Slave-master in these latter days . . . exults in his unfortunate condition."

In the second, much briefer section of his oration, Sumner contested the Southern argument that slaveholders had a right to take their "property" into the national territories. "There is no sanction for such pretension; no ordinance for it, or title," he asserted. The Southern claim of superiority for the white race, if true, was no justification for extending slavery. "If the African race be inferior, as is alleged, then is it the unquestionable duty of a Christian Civilization to lift it from its degradation, not by the bludgeon and the chain . . . but by a generous charity." The argument that the Bible justified slavery was both ridiculous and unhistorical. The Southern contention that the Constitution protected their peculiar property was equally unfounded; the Constitution contained "not one sentence, phrase, or word—not a single suggestion, hint, or equivocation, even" to justify such a proslavery interpretation. The true principle, Sumner concluded, in almost the same words used in his first antislavery speech in Congress in 1852, was to make "Freedom *national* and Slavery *sectional*" by establishing everywhere under federal jurisdiction "the law of impartial Freedom without distinction of color or race." [1]

As Sumner concluded, Senator James Chesnut, of South Carolina, rose to explain why the Southern senators had listened quietly to Sumner's diatribe. "After ranging over Europe, crawling through the back doors to whine at the feet of British aristocracy, craving pity, and reaping a rich harvest of contempt," Sumner, "the incarnation of malice, mendacity, and cowardice," had reappeared in the Senate, neither wiser nor better for his experience. Unwilling "to increase the devotees at the shrine of this new idol," the Southerners were "not inclined again to send [him] forth the recipient of punishment howling through the world, yelping fresh cries of slander and malice."

[1] All quotations in the above paragraphs are from Sumner: *The Barbarism of Slavery*. See pp. 3–6, 12, 14–18, 20, 24–5, 27–8, 31. On Sumner's use of the Civilization-Barbarism antithesis to characterize the sectional struggle see Charles A. and Mary R. Beard: *The American Spirit: A Study of the Idea of Civilization in the United States* (*The Rise of American Civilization*, Vol. IV, New York: The Macmillan Co.; 1942), pp. 301–7.

Sumner, though very weary from his exertions, replied that he planned to print Chesnut's remarks in an appendix to his speech as another illustration of the barbarism he had just described.[2]

• 3 •

Washington seethed with excitement as the news spread of Sumner's fresh, bitter attack upon the South. Wherever Southerners gathered, they asked each other whether "Sumner's got it yet." Four days after the oration a drunken clerk from the patent office forced his way into Sumner's chamber and threatened that his friends would cut the senator's "d——d throat before the next night."

Alarmed, the Massachusetts delegation to Congress rallied to protect their senator, and some Kansas admirers constituted themselves his bodyguard. Though in "a state of not unnatural excitement" over the danger, Sumner refused to arm himself and tried to dissuade protectors from carrying firearms. But, for more than three weeks they kept the senator closely guarded. "Two men sleep on the floor of my front room," he reported to Longfellow; "they have watched me at leaving the Senate, and, if not by my side, have kept within a short distance, so as to be near if any attack should come. All this has been done without any hint from me, and hardly with my approval. . . . Think of such precautions in a place which calls itself civilized!" [3]

Events proved that Sumner was more in need of protection from his Northern friends than from his Southern enemies. Of course the Southerners were irritated by his speech, and probably most agreed with the editor of the New Orleans *Crescent* that Sumner was "a pestilent knave and low demagogue, who, from the meanest of motives, is trying to create sectional hatred in the country." But the vituperativeness of Sumner's analysis

[2] *Cong. Globe*, 36 Cong., 1 Sess., 2,603–4.

[3] Clippings from New York *Evening Post* and other newspapers, Sumner Scrapbooks; *The Liberator*, XXX (June 18, 1860), 94; A. B. Johnson to George Sumner, June 6, 1860, Sumner MSS.; Adams, Diary, June 9, 1860, Adams MSS.; Sumner to Longfellow, June 29, 1860, Longfellow MSS. The story that Sumner himself asked the Massachusetts delegation to defend him (Dawes: *Sumner*, pp. 146–7) is untrue. A. B. Johnson to Pierce, Aug. 8, 1892, Pierce MSS.

of slavery made it possible for many Southerners to dismiss his speech as just another abolitionist harangue, no more worthy of consideration than the rantings of Garrison or Wendell Phillips.[4]

In the North, however, Sumner's oration could not be so easily dismissed. The senator was, after all, a principal figure in the Republican party. He could claim, with justice, to have been one of the founders of the party; his sufferings at the hands of Preston Brooks had been potent Republican ammunition in 1856; now, as one of the senior Republicans in the Senate, he was certain to be a powerful figure if Lincoln was elected. Surely he spoke not for himself alone, but for his party.

Such an interpretation was precisely what most Republican leaders feared. Few Republicans in Congress approved his speech. "As a bitter, denunciatory oration, it could hardly be exceeded in point of style and finish," Senator James W. Grimes, of Iowa, thought. "But . . . it sounded harsh, vindictive, and slightly brutal. . . . His speech has done the Republicans no good." Party leaders outside of Congress were equally disturbed by Sumner's incendiary tone. When the senator sent a copy to Abraham Lincoln, the presidential nominee cagily acknowledged it in a noncommittal note: "I have not yet found time to peruse the speech; but I anticipate much both of pleasure and instruction from it."[5]

Republican newspapers were outspoken in criticizing the speech. Horace Greeley could not find room for the oration in his New York *Tribune* (though he later printed it in his weekly edition, which circulated in the strongly antislavery rural areas of the North and the West). Faintly praising it as "doubtless a strong and forcible speech," the *Tribune* editor wished "he had made it on some other bill than that providing for the Admission of Kansas," which it would, in fact, help to defeat. The New York *Times* was even more unsympathetic. Judging that Sumner had devoted his "four leisure years . . . to collecting every instance of cruelty, violence, passion, coarseness, and vulgarity recorded as having happened within the Slave States," it asked: "Aside from

[4] Dwight Lowell Dumond (ed.): *Southern Editorials on Secession* (New York: The Century Co.; 1931), pp. 129, 131.

[5] Salter: *Grimes*, p. 127; Roy P. Basler (ed.): *The Collected Works of Abraham Lincoln* (New Brunswick: Rutgers University Press; 1954), IV, 76.

Republican Reaction to "The Barbarism of Slavery" Speech, 1860

THE LIBRARY OF CONGRESS

Sumner at the Outbreak of the Civil War

THE NATIONAL ARCHIVES

its utter irrelevancy to the Kansas Question, what general good can be hoped from such envenomed attacks upon the Slave States?" [6]

Even Massachusetts Republicans received "The Barbarism of Slavery" coolly. The Boston *Advertiser*, a former Whig journal that now represented the conservative wing of the Republican party in eastern Massachusetts, thought well of the "careful and patient labor" which had gone into the speech, but asked "whether the occasion called for such a display of power, whether the object of attack needed such ponderous blows." The Springfield *Republican*, the most powerful party paper in western Massachusetts, was more blunt: "We do not think Charles Sumner a statesman and we doubt if he ever can become one, or has any bent in that direction." [7]

Sumner's opponents gleefully attacked the speech. Boston patricians, ousted from political power, but still cherishing their hatred of Sumner, which they now could exhibit only in carping at his use of classical quotations or in repeatedly blackballing him for membership in the Massachusetts Historical Society,[8] welcomed the oration as evidence "no less [of] his total unfitness for public station than [of] his utter inaptitude for political warfare." The Boston *Courier*, for which his former friend Hillard now wrote, branded the speech as "an insidious and faithless blow at the Constitution." Boston Democrats denounced the "pedantry, egotism, fortuitous hypothesis, malice, rhapsody, and verbosity" which characterized the address, and Catholic papers, alarmed by Sumner's gratuitous reference to alleged immoralities

[6] New York *Tribune*, June 5, 1860; New York *Times*, June 6, 1860. For other, similar newspaper reactions see Sumner: *Works*, V, 132–7.

[7] Boston *Advertiser*, June 6, 1860; Springfield *Republican*, quoted in Laura A. White: "Charles Sumner and the Crisis of 1860–61," in Avery Craven (ed.): *Essays in Honor of William E. Dodd* (Chicago: University of Chicago Press; 1935), p. 139.

[8] When Sumner declared that Senator Mason's conduct as chairman of the committee investigating John Brown's raid reminded him of what "an ancient poet said of a judge in hell, that he punished first and heard afterwards,—'*castigatque auditque*'" (Sumner: *Works*, IV, 450), the Boston *Courier* professed to be terribly shocked at his "offensive and insulting language . . . unfit to be employed by any person worthy of such a place." *The Liberator*, XXX (Apr. 27, 1860), 65. C. F. Adams repeatedly sponsored Sumner for membership in the Historical Society, but Winthrop always blocked his election. Adams, Diary, Dec. 10, 1857, Mar. 11, and Dec. 9, 1858, and Feb. 1, 1859, Adams MSS.

in monasteries, agreed that "a speech more destitute of statesmanship, in every point of view, was never given to the public in any form." [9]

James Gordon Bennett, the pro-Southern editor of the New York *Herald,* was more cunning that these forthright opponents of Sumner's. He printed "The Barbarism of Slavery" in full on the front page of the *Herald* and day after day gave it a great play. Bennett argued that Sumner, who possessed "the philosophical acumen of Mr. Seward, without his cautious reserve as a politician; the honesty of Lincoln, without the craft of a candidate in nomination [;] and literary culture, political zeal, and the gift of eloquence," was "in the very foremost rank as a leader and exponent of the black republican ideas." Hence Sumner's oration revealed the true plans of his party, whose success in November would mean "carnage and the flames of war," "swords dripping with fraternal gore, torches put to the homes of brothers, desolation spread over happy and prosperous States, for opinion's sake." [1]

Sumner angrily resented these criticisms. Neither the attacks of the Southerners, whom he now considered beyond the reach of reason, nor the jibes of Northern Democrats, those open compurgators of Preston Brooks, troubled him so much as the "cold shoulderism, heartlessness, dirty-water and paving stones" with which Republicans had received his ideas. Indignantly he denied the charge, which even *The Times* of London echoed, that he had spoken in a spirit of "personal irritability." "The Barbarism of Slavery" was "almost a necessity," he explained defensively; he had avoided "all personality and . . . absolutely all allusion to his own experience." Of course he had used strong language, but it was not his words but the facts that branded slavery as barbaric. Critics failed to see the symbolic purpose in his speech: he was no mere senator, but the Spokesman of a Righteous Cause, who had acted "to vindicate Freedom of debate

[9] *The Liberator,* XXX (June 22, 1860), 97; Sumner: *Works,* V, 136; Anderson: "Slavery Issue," pp. 286–7.

[1] New York *Herald,* June 5–6, 1860. After building Sumner up, Bennett proceeded joyfully to demolish him, arguing, with some justice, that the crimes he attributed to slavery were unrepresentative and that he ignored "the record of divorces, elopements . . . the overcrowded prisons; the penal hospitals . . . the notorious insecurity of life in the great cities," and other evidences of "barbarism" in the North. Ibid., June 7, 1860.

struck down in my person; and this I wished to do not by words and mere declamations, but by a speech, which, as a practical exercise of this right, should be a precedent and an example." [2]

Instead of praise for this service, Sumner felt that he was rewarded with obloquy and indifference. "Perhaps no person has ever received so many attacks—with so little of real assistance in his defence," he complained. "Others, who have become equally obnoxious, have had earnest [newspaper] presses to beat back the enemy. I have none; not one that does not give the enemy something to hurl at me." "Perhaps," he added, in his martyr tone, "I deserve it. At all events, I have labored for the truth, and I accept the consequences." [3]

With the new, inner security Sumner had developed during his long illness, he was undeterred by criticism. "*That* speech," he vowed, "will yet be adopted by the Republican party." Long after Congress adjourned, he remained in sweltering Washington franking thousands of copies for distribution all over the country. Determined to maintain the offensive, he accepted an invitation to speak before the Young Men's Republican Club of New York, the radical anti-Seward wing of the party, on July 11. Aside from adding juicy details on "the roasting of slaves alive at the stake" in the South, a tribute to Lincoln, "whose ability, so conspicuously shown in his own State, attracted at once the admiration of the whole country," and a prediction that with Republican success slavery would die "as a poisoned rat dies of rage in its hole," he mostly repeated the argument of "The Barbarism of Slavery." By reiteration he hoped to gain broader acceptance of his ideas, so as to maintain the Republican principles "in purity and power." [4]

Loyally Sumner's friends supported his efforts. Howe solicited subscriptions on the streets of Boston in order to finance a wide distribution of the speech. Frank Bird mailed a copy to each voter in his district. E. L. Pierce interviewed every editor in his congressional district and secured pledges that they would back

[2] Sumner to Elizur Wright [June 1860], copy, Wright MSS.; Robinson: *Pen Portraits*, p. 91; *The Times* (London), June 18, 1860; Sumner to Duchess of Argyll, July 31, 1860, Argyll MSS.

[3] Sumner to Theodore Tilton, July 21, 1860, Tilton MSS.

[4] Sumner to Howe, June 12, 1860, MS., Huntington Lib.; Sumner to Pierce, July 6, 1860, Sumner MSS.; Sumner to Theodore Tilton, July 21, 1860, Tilton MSS.; Sumner: *Works:* V, 210, 225, 229.

Sumner's stand. Then the Bird Club backed resolutions in the Massachusetts House of Representatives praising the senator "for his recent manly and earnest assertion of the right of free discussion on the floor of the United States Senate" and approving "the thorough, truthful and comprehensive examination of the institution of Slavery embraced in Mr. Sumner's recent speech." "There was," Howe reported with delight, "much *squeaming* among the party hacks at the State House about endorsing the speech; and they only lacked the pluck—(not will) to refuse to do it." But, under the remorseless pressure of Bird's machine, both houses of the legislature passed the resolutions by overwhelming majorities. Triumphantly Pierce wrote Sumner: "If the politicians disown you, they will have to disown Massachusetts—for Massachusetts will sustain both you and your speech—and you will without question be reelected at the expiration of your present term." [5]

After a few weeks, Sumner's exertions to circulate and publicize his speech began to pay off. Though the more sophisticated Republican Eastern cities had repudiated it, the rural areas of the North and West welcomed it. To these Republicans, whose antislavery principles were ingrained, Sumner's address was an assurance that their party stood for something more significant than enacting a protective tariff, building a Pacific railroad, or even electing a presidential candidate. Practically every small-town newspaper in Massachusetts, most of those throughout the rest of New England, and a great many others stretching out to the western frontier—in fact, wherever New Englanders had settled—enthusiastically praised both the speech and the senator. Equally significant were the hundreds of adoring letters which poured in upon Sumner. While Republican chieftains, with the notable exception of Salmon P. Chase, were silent, insignificant members of the party thanked Sumner for his oration "in the name of our common humanity, in the name of justice, in the name of righteousness and of the God of all excelence [*sic*]. "Behind you," pledged a Pittsburgh admirer, "stand a mil-

[5] Howe to Sumner, June 5, and 15, 1860, Howe MSS.; Bird to Sumner, June 30, 1860, Sumner MSS.; Pierce to Sumner, June 20–1, 1860, ibid.; "Resolves Relating to Freedom of Speech," passed by the Massachusetts legislature, and transmitted to Sumner, June 16, 1860, ibid.

lion of your fellow-citizens in whose hearts your speech finds an echo." [6]

So great was the reaction in Sumner's favor that the same party managers who treated him coolly in June warmly solicited his aid in August. The congressional Republican committee decided to circulate "The Barbarism of Slavery" as a campaign document at two dollars a hundred. Thurlow Weed, who, like Seward, had been aghast at the impolicy of the speech when it was delivered, now begged Sumner to campaign through upstate New York. From Illinois, Maine, and Ohio Sumner received urgent invitations to speak. So popular was the senator now that a mere letter from him, supporting the candidacy of Republican J. M. Ashley in Ohio, was credited with playing a major role in defeating the Democratic candidate.[7]

Sumner refused to campaign outside of Massachusetts, for he had urgent business at home. The murmur of criticism evoked by his "Barbarism of Slavery" speech reminded him that he must reassert leadership in his own state Republican party—a task the more urgent as his own re-election to the Senate was only two years away. As the Republicans were certain to carry Massachusetts by an overwhelming majority in 1860, Sumner and his friends thought the occasion most opportune to weed out party leaders whose antislavery zeal was dubious.

Governor N. P. Banks, handsome, dapper, and plausible, was marked for slaughter. Ever since Banks had intrigued for Sumner's seat, the senator's friends had been undercutting him. They had not been able to keep him from winning renomination in 1859, but they kept the choice from being unanimous. With Sumner's tacit connivance, they undermined the governor's hopes for the Republican presidential nomination in 1860 by splitting the Massachusetts delegation and making John A. Andrew, Sumner's warm partisan, chairman. Banks decided to retire temporarily from politics in order to become resident director of the Illinois Central Railroad, but he had his eye on 1864 and wanted to leave the Massachusetts Republican party in friendly

[6] Sumner preserved clippings from dozens of small-town newspapers in his scrapbooks. For extracts from the correspondence evoked by the speech see Sumner: *Works*, V, 146–73. Hundreds of other letters are in the Sumner MSS.

[7] Ashley to Sumner, Oct. 13, 1860, Sumner MSS.

hands. Consequently he kept his decision not to run again for governor a secret until his henchmen could organize support for the nomination of his friend, Congressman Henry L. Dawes. Then, only five days before the state convention was to meet at Worcester, he publicly announced his withdrawal in a statement carefully timed to reach the rural districts, where Sumner's friends were strongest, too late to influence the choice of delegates.

But, William Claflin, a member of the Bird Club and a state senator, got wind of Banks's intention one day before he made his public announcement and, though it was late at night, went at once to Sumner's house on Hancock Street. "Give me my boots," exclaimed Sumner when he heard the news. "John A. Andrew must be the next governor of Massachusetts." During the next five days Sumner and the members of the Bird Club were incessantly active, buttonholing delegates, arranging caucuses, planning tactics. Strongly as they desired Andrew's nomination, Sumner's faction had in mind something "more important than the mere nomination of governor"; they intended to purify the Republican party in Massachusetts, to endow it with "the spirit of liberty"—and to align it squarely behind Sumner himself.[8]

When the Republican convention met at Mechanic's Hall in Worcester on August 29, every detail had been prearranged, including Sumner's carefully delayed appearance, at which the delegates rose and cheered. Before the nominations began, the senator was invited to address the meeting. After the enthusiastic shouts of welcome died out, Sumner launched into a vindication of the Republican party against "the Proslavery non-committalism of Bell, the Proslavery dogma of Breckinridge, and the Proslavery dodge of Douglas." Ostensibly standing aloof from the gubernatorial nomination the convention was about to make, Sumner, in fact, warmly endorsed Andrew. "Let not fidelity to those principles which give dignity and glory to Massachusetts, and to our common country, be an argument against him," he urged, referring to the unnamed candidate; in obvious reference

[8] For an excellent account of these maneuvers see Harrington: *Banks*, pp. 47–51. See also Pearson: *Andrew*, I, 120–1; C. M. Ellis to Sumner, Aug. 25 [1860], Sumner MSS.

to Andrew, who had approved of John Brown and had subscribed money to defend the raiders, Sumner cited the verses of Jonathan Swift:

> *That stupid cant, "He went too far," despise,*
> *And know that to be brave is to be wise.*

Partly by preconvention maneuvering, partly by Sumner's oratory, the Bird Club frustrated Banks's efforts to name his successor, and the convention chose Andrew by a vote of 723 to 327.[9]

Enthusiastically Sumner threw himself into the campaign to elect Andrew, whose "unquestioned abilities, extensive attainments, and rare aptitude for affairs" would make him an ideal governor. Almost every day he addressed Republican rallies in speeches that had a force and directness markedly in contrast with his Senate oratory. The choice before the voters, he said, was simply that between Northern civilization and Southern barbarism, between the doctrines of John Quincy Adams and those of John C. Calhoun, between the Mayflower and the first "Slave-Ship, with its fetters, its chains, its bludgeons, and its whips." "Choose ye, fellow-citizens, between the two."[1]

In November the voters of Massachusetts chose. By almost unprecedented majorities they elected John A. Andrew governor and gave their electoral votes to Abraham Lincoln for President.

• 4 •

In the secession crisis that followed Lincoln's election in 1860 Sumner's course was an erratic one.[2] Though he later recalled

[9] Contemporary newspaper accounts of the convention are clipped in the W. S. Robinson Scrapbooks. Cf. Sumner: *Works,* V, 240–68.

[1] Sumner: *Works,* V, 277, 286; Boston *Advertiser,* Nov. 6, 1860.

[2] The following pages cover the period treated in Laura A. White's "Charles Sumner and the Crisis of 1860–61," the only portion of a projected biography Professor White published before her death. In her critical and stimulating essay Miss White argued that "Sumner's central idea at this time seems to have been . . . the *permanent* separation of all slave states and the organization of two confederacies—one slave, one free." I cannot agree with this interpretation for the following reasons: (1) I am unwilling to trust the anonymous Washington newspaper correspondents, particularly those of the venemously anti-Sumner New York *Herald,* upon whom Miss White heavily relied; (2) I agree with Professor Frank Maloy Anderson (*The Mystery of 'A Public Man': A Historical Detective Story* [Minneapolis: University of Minnesota Press; 1948]) that "The Diary of a Public Man" (*North American Review,* CXXIX (1879), 125–40, 259–73, 375–88, 484–96), upon which Miss White depended, is "a semi-fictional

that he had, from the very beginning, insisted that the Federal Union must be preserved, even at the cost of coercing the seceding states, contemporary evidence shows that his ideas were confused and contradictory. Like most Republicans, he failed at the outset to understand the seriousness of the crisis. He had heard threats of disunion so often that he had ceased to credit them. Like Greeley, Seward, and Thurlow Weed, Sumner, during the 1860 campaign, had sneered at Southern talk of disunion as mere "weapons of political warfare," "threats, and nothing more," "one supreme absurdity." [3]

Even after Sumner arrived in Washington in December 1860, and learned that South Carolina, Georgia, Florida, Alabama, Mississippi, Louisiana, and Texas would almost certainly be out of the Union before Lincoln could be inaugurated, he found it difficult to decide what policy to pursue. A sincere advocate of peace, he could not share Ben Wade's enthusiasm for forcing the Southern states back into the Union, or join Zachariah Chandler in asserting: "Without a little blood-letting this Union will not . . . be worth a rush." The other alternative, further concessions to the South, was even less palatable. If the history of the United States taught anything, Sumner felt, it was that appeasement of slaveholders was impossible. The Missouri Compromise, the Compromise of 1850, the Kansas-Nebraska Act had all been abdications of Northern principle in order to placate the South, but the slaveholders remained insatiable. Concessions, furthermore, would demoralize the forces of freedom in the North. "The enmity of Slavery may be dangerous," Sumner warned, "but its friendship is fatal." [4]

production," which "ought not to be regarded as a reliable source"; (3) I have found new materials in the Adams MSS. and the Argyll MSS., which, of course, were not available to Miss White, contradicting her thesis; (4) I believe that Miss White, by confining her researches to Sumner alone, failed to realize that his position on peaceful secession was very similar to Greeley's, which David M. Potter has so incisively analyzed: "When confronted by a choice between compromise and peaceable secession, Greeley chose peaceable secession; but when confronted by a choice between war and peaceful secession, Greeley chose war" ("Horace Greeley and Peaceable Secession," *Journal of Southern History*, VII [1941], 145–9). (5) It seems to me that Miss White confused Sumner's prophecies about the spread of secession with a desire to see it spread.

[3] Boston *Advertiser*, Oct. 9, 1860; Sumner: *Works*, V, 296, 305. In the following pages I am heavily indebted to Professor David M. Potter's admirable monograph, *Lincoln and His Party in the Secession Crisis* (New Haven: Yale University Press; 1942).

[4] Sumner: *Works*, V, 342.

Tentatively Sumner brought himself to think that the temporary secession of the Gulf states might not be a bad thing. He never went as far as President-Elect Lincoln, who said that he was "rather glad of this military preparation in the South" because it would "enable the people the more easily to suppress any uprisings there which [the secessionists'] misrepresentations . . . may have encouraged,"[5] but he did recognize that secession—"the mild phrase for treason"—might have compensations. Withdrawal of the congressional delegations from the Deep South would make it easier for the Republicans to gain complete control of the national government. Perhaps during the absence of the slaveholders the United States could take advantage of the unrest in British North America, and Sumner again toyed with one of his oldest and most persistent ideas, the "magnificent project of the . . . acquisition of Canada."[6]

What was more important, the seceding Southerners, sailing off into independence "with the black flag at the mast-head," would promptly find that "Slavery could not gain" from their venture. They would learn that "the civilization of the Christian world, speaking with the innumerable voices of the press, and constituting a Public Opinion of irresistible energy," was hostile to the creation of a new slave power. Europe would "refuse to recognize it in the Family of Nations." Out of the Union, and unprotected by federal armies, these states of the Deep South would inevitably face "servile insurrection, ending in Emancipation—perhaps, as in Santo Domingo." As a lover of peace Sumner shuddered at this prospect. "Much as I desire the extinction

[5] Quoted in Potter, *Lincoln and His Party,* p. 141.

[6] Everett, Diary, Jan. 29, 1861, Everett MSS. The New York *Herald* charged that Republicans actually desired "to prevent the seceding States from returning to the Union, and to force the rest of the slave States out of it, . . . with a view of annexing the British colonies, which would have nothing to do with the confederacy so long as slavery was tolerated within its borders, but which, with that insuperable objection removed, will be glad to unite . . . with their Anglo-Saxon brothers" (Feb. 4, 7, and 17, 1861). Cf. Gardner Brewer to Sumner, Jan. 30, 1861, Sumner MSS. For Canadian opinion on annexation see Helen G. MacDonald: *Canadian Public Opinion on the American Civil War* ("Columbia University Studies in History, Economics, and Public Law," Vol. CXXIV, New York: Columbia University Press; 1926), p. 85 ff. As early as 1849 Sumner wrote Richard Cobden of the "inevitable . . . annexation to the United States" of Canada. Pierce, III, 42. He told the Earl of Carlisle that the acquisition of Canada by the United States "would 'redress the balance,' which has been turned in favor of Slavery by the annexation of Texas." Sumner to Earl of Carlisle, Jan. 8, 1850, Carlisle MSS.

of slavery," he protested, "I do not wish to see it go down in blood." Yet he could not resist a certain grim satisfaction in watching the slaveholders "rush upon their destiny." All in all, then, he began to think that a temporary secession of the Gulf states could be endured quite cheerfully. "The difficulties in the way of the *seceders* are so great," he wrote Howe in December 1860, "that I fear we shall not get rid of them *long enough.* My desire is that 4 or 5 should go out *long enough* to be completely humbled and chastened and to leave us in the control of the Government." [7]

"If the secession can be restrained to the 'Cotton States,'" Sumner wrote the Duchess of Argyll shortly after Congress convened, "I shall be willing to let them go. But can it be stopped there?" That "if" and that question were weighing on all minds. Sumner was convinced that a proper Northern policy could keep the slave states of the Upper South peaceably in the Union until the Gulf states, after an unsuccessful attempt at independence, asked readmission. Considering "the whole slave-holding class as a combination of ruffianism and bluster, whiskey-drinking and tobacco-chewing," Sumner, as Charles Francis Adams, Jr., shrewdly observed, thought that the secessionists of the Upper South would, "like petulant, passionate children, prone to violence," yield in face of Northern firmness. Convinced that "the large mass of people even in the Slave States do not desire disunion," Sumner felt that the Republicans must strengthen the hands of such Southern antislavery men as the Blairs in Maryland and Missouri, and Cassius M. Clay in Kentucky. The potential unionist majority in the Upper South must not be "debauched" by concessions or compromises. To the suggestion that his policy might make the Southerners resort to arms, Sumner exclaimed: "Never! They are too crafty! Bullies! Braggarts! They would be assassins some of them if they dared—but fair fight, never!" [8]

Positive that he had worked out a proper policy for coping with secession, Sumner was appalled to discover that Congress

[7] Sumner: *Works,* V, 304, 482–3; Sumner to Duchess of Argyll, Dec. 14, 1860, Argyll MSS.; Sumner to Howe, Dec. 16, 1860, Sumner MSS. Cf. Ellis Yarnall: *Wordsworth and the Coleridges . . .* (New York: The Macmillan Co.; 1899), p. 8.

[8] Sumner to Duchess of Argyll, Dec. 14, 1860, Argyll MSS.; C. F. Adams, Jr.: *Autobiography,* pp. 85–6; Sumner: *Works,* V, 302; W. H. Russell: "Recollections of the Civil War," *North American Review,* CLXVI (1898), 241–2.

was seriously considering compromise as a means of relieving the crisis. Senator Crittenden, Henry Clay's successor, proposed irrevocable constitutional amendments that, among other things, would guarantee slavery in "all the territory of the United States now held, or hereafter acquired, below the latitude of 36° 30′." Stephen A. Douglas was working indefatigably to support compromise. So strong was the desire for adjustment that the House of Representatives appointed a Committee of Thirty-three and the Senate a Committee of Thirteen to work out remedies for the sectional crisis.

Believing that his own program would ensure peace, liberty, and union, Sumner gave no countenance to such talk of appeasement. He was unmoved by appeals from the Boston mercantile community, hard hit by the cutting off of Southern cotton. If businessmen failed to support his plan, Sumner announced that he would appeal to the soundly antislavery elements in Massachusetts, "the farmer, the mechanic, the laborer." He refused to believe impressive evidence that popular sentiment even in his own state favored compromise. In Boston itself a rowdy mob showed its sympathies with the South by breaking up a meeting commemorating the execution of John Brown, manhandled some Negroes who were in attendance, threatened Wendell Phillips's life, and hooted at Sumner's house in Hancock Street. At local elections held in December the Republican vote fell off sharply; the party lost Worcester and Newburyport and had far smaller strength in Boston, Charlestown, and Lowell. Boston workingmen favored compromise and bitterly condemned Sumner for opposing it. Mammoth petitions supported Crittenden's proposals; in Boston, with only 19,000 voters, 14,000 persons endorsed the compromise amendments.[9]

To all such agitation Sumner professed himself totally indifferent. To the intense irritation of the sponsors of the Crittenden petition, he declared that most of the Massachusetts signers must have been "seduced" by the Kentucky senator's rep-

[9] Sumner: *Works,* V, 473; Maria Weston Chapman to Sumner [Dec. 1860], Sumner MSS.; Mary Scrugham: *The Peaceable Americans of 1861* ("Columbia University Studies in History, Economics, and Public Law," Vol. XCVI, New York: Columbia University Press; 1921), pp. 70–1; Mrs. Chapman Coleman: *The Life of John J. Crittenden* (Philadelphia: J. B. Lippincott & Co.; 1873), II, 238–40, 262.

utation and have "put their names to a petition which . . . they did not, in all respects and in all its bearings, fully understand." Anyway, as most of the signers lived in the cities, especially in Boston, they did not represent the true spirit of the Commonwealth, "for it is only when you get off those pavements, away from the paving stones, that you find the true sentiment of Massachusetts." [1]

Naturally Sumner showed no sympathy for the committee of distinguished Bostonians who arrived in Washington to present their huge petition, patriotically wrapped in a United States flag, in favor of the Crittenden compromise, and the choice of Edward Everett, A. A. Lawrence, and Robert C. Winthrop to head the group was scarcely designed to win his confidence. When Sumner met members of the committee accidentally on the evening of their arrival, he scornfully refused to speak to Winthrop, but told the others that their petition was "mere *wind*, —nothing better than a penny-whistle in a tempest." During the next few days, while the committee tried to drum up support for the compromise, Sumner ignored their existence. Not until Edward Everett cunningly played upon the senator's vanity by telling him that he alone could introduce a successful compromise bill did Sumner unbend to the extent of explaining, in an incoherent, excited fashion that Everett thought "approaching to insanity," his own program for solving the crisis. Not even Everett's flattery could induce him to support Crittenden's proposals. Sententiously he explained: "You are mistaken in supposing that I might have success with compromise, if I could bring it forward. If I am strong with the North, it is because of the conviction that I cannot compromise; but the moment I compromised, I, too, should be lost."

Toward Winthrop, Sumner remained implacable. When Winthrop and Everett, as former members, were admitted to the Senate chamber, where most of the members they had known in previous years cordially welcomed them, Sumner came up, thrust himself between the two men on the sofa where they were seated, and, rudely turning his back upon Winthrop, proceeded to talk

[1] George T. Brown and others to Sumner, Feb. 13, 1861, copy, Crittenden MSS.; C. B. Allen to J. J. Crittenden, Feb. 13, 1861, ibid.; Sumner: *Works*, V, 472, 474; White: "Sumner and the Crisis," p. 167.

with Everett. Eager to do anything he could to help promote compromise, Winthrop had other members of the committee tell Sumner that he was willing to forget the past. Loftily Sumner refused to speak to him until he made an apology. "I did not understand *for what* the apology was to be," Winthrop noted in his journal, "but as I had always considered him as the offending party I had nothing further to do but to forgive him (as I did) and let him go." [2]

If the Massachusetts Union-savers found Sumner intractable, President Buchanan learned that he was immovable. Convinced that "The President is a traitor, who lets the vessel drift to destruction," Sumner did not willingly speak to Buchanan, but, when Governor Andrew requested him to have a formal interview with the President, he reluctantly went to the White House on February 2. The feeble Buchanan was distraught by the crisis; believing that no state had the right to secede and that the federal government could not coerce a seceded state, he longed for compromise and, though he probably knew it was in vain, tried to influence Sumner. When the senator had completed his official business, he remained to ask: "Mr. President, what else can we do in Massachusetts for the good of the country?"

There was a pause. Then Buchanan heavily sighed: "Much, Mr. Sumner—no state more."

"What?"

"Adopt the Crittenden propositions," said Buchanan.

"Is that necessary?"

"Yes."

Firmly Sumner replied: "Massachusetts has not yet spoken directly on these propositions; but . . . such are the unalterable convictions of her people, they would see their state sink below the sea and become a sandbank before they would adopt those propositions acknowledging property in man." [3]

[2] For a day-by-day account of the committee's reception in Washington see Winthrop's "Memorandum, January 1861," Winthrop MSS. See also Everett, Diary, Jan. 29, 1861, Everett MSS.; Sumner: *Works*, V, 444; George W. Curtis, in *A Memorial of Charles Sumner* (Boston; 1874), pp. 141–2.

[3] Sumner to Thomas Gaffield, Dec. 29, 1860, MS., Huntington Lib.; Sumner to Andrew, Feb. 3, 1861, Andrew MSS.; Springfield *Republican*, Feb. 6, 1861.

• 5 •

Sumner gained a certain fierce satisfaction from such encounters with political opponents, to whom he owed nothing and from whom he could expect less, but he grieved to find that members of his own party were also endorsing concessions to the South. It was bad enough for moderate Republicans like John Sherman to advocate compromise, or for Thurlow Weed, whom Sumner dismissed as "a *politician*—not a *statesman*," [4] to talk of extending the Missouri Compromise line. But, when leading spokesmen of the party, hitherto distinguished for their antislavery principles, also favored yielding to the South, Sumner became almost frantic over their backsliding.

He found Seward's position both incomprehensible and unpardonable. The foxy New Yorker, who was expected to become the "premier" of the incoming Lincoln administration, was too clever to expose his hand, but everybody believed that he was co-operating with Douglas and Crittenden to work out a new compromise scheme. Hoping to win Sumner over, Seward asked his opinion of the major policy statement he planned to make in the Senate on January 12, favoring a modification of the Northern personal liberty laws, guaranteeing by constitutional amendment that Congress would never interfere with slavery in any state, and endorsing a somewhat obscure plan that appeared to mean that the New Mexico–Arizona territory would be admitted as another slave state. Sumner was appalled. He thought that Seward's speech would encourage the fire-eaters of the Deep South and undermine the strong unionism of the border states. These concessions would cost the country everything. He pleaded with Seward, "he . . . prayed him, besought him, implored him by his past record, his good name, his memory hereafter," to delete "every word of compromise, concession, or offer to the traitors." All Seward needed to do was "simply to declare that Mr. Lincoln would be inaugurated on the 4th March, President of the United States, and to rally the country to his support." [5]

[4] Sumner to Andrew, Jan. 8, 1861, Andrew MSS.

[5] C. F. Adams, Jr.: *Autobiography*, p. 81; Sarah Forbes Hughes (ed.): *Letters and Recollections of John Murray Forbes* (Boston: Houghton Mifflin Co.; 1899), I, 186; Sumner to Andrew, Jan. 17, 1861, Andrew MSS. For a discussion of Republican intraparty strife, by an admirer of Seward, see Henry Adams: "The Great Secession Winter of 1860–61," *MHSP*, XLII (1909–10), 660–87.

When Seward ignored the advice and made his speech, Sumner became frantic with anxiety. He could not sleep nights; his health was impaired; his concern over compromise became obsessive. He "talked like a crazy man," the hostile Charles Francis Adams, Jr., remembered, "orating, gesticulating, rolling out deep periods in theatrical, whispered tones,—repeating himself, and doing everything but reason." He could not be diverted from his concern over Seward's defection; at an interruption of his monologue he did not go off the track, but "merely gave a bump and a jerk, and went on fiercer in his utter disregard of logic and policy." Seward, he declaimed, had "never been aware of the real peril"; Seward "had throughout the session been demented, . . . wholly ignorant of the true nature of the question and of the feeling of the South." Seward "was demoralizing the North. If he had but held firmly to his position, and refused all parley with secessionists, all would have been well. An appeal should have been made to the loyal, Union-loving feeling of the border Slave States, and all would have been well." Firmness would have kept the North united; it would have held the border states in the Union; it would have brought the Gulf states back with their pride humbled and their slaves freed. "I am sure," Sumner whispered excitedly, "I am certain—I see my way so clearly; such a glorious victory was before us; right was with us, God was with us—our success was sure did we only hold firmly to our principles." [6]

Disturbed by Seward's course, Sumner became positively frenetic when he discovered that the compromise spirit was spreading to the Massachusetts congressional delegation and that his old friend Charles Francis Adams was infected. Adams, of all men, in Sumner's opinion should have rejected concessions to the slavocracy. He was a Massachusetts man. He was a man of principle. The son of John Quincy Adams, the grandson of John Adams, Charles Francis was, in Sumner's opinion, "as great a man as his father or his grandfather," [7] and he should have exhibited their moral stamina. He owed much to Sumner, who had overridden the opposition of Wilson and other party hacks to

[6] C. F. Adams, Jr.: *Autobiography*, pp. 79–82; Sumner to Andrew, Jan. 17, 1861, Andrew MSS.

[7] Charlton Yarnall (ed.): *Forty Years of Friendship* . . . (London: The Macmillan Co., Ltd.; 1911), p. 66.

force his nomination to Congress in 1858. He should have reflected Sumner's ideas, for the senator took great pains to indoctrinate him every Sunday when he had dinner with the Adams family.

Instead, Adams, starting from premises identical to Sumner's, arrived at precisely opposite conclusions as to how the secession crisis could be handled. Whereas Sumner thought firmness would develop the unionist sympathies of the border states, Adams, who was a member of the Committee of Thirty-three from the House, concluded that the moderate old Whigs like Crittenden were the only border-state unionists who had any political power and that they would be repudiated by their states unless they could show that the North was willing to make concessions. Adams concluded that Sumner's policy of "rigid dignity and listless inactivity," of "railing at the rebellion and repulsing all sympathy with the hesitating and timid but honest citizens of the slave states," could only lead to the secession of the border states and the Confederate capture of Washington before Lincoln's inauguration. First in the House committee, then in a major speech on January 31, Adams indicated the concessions that he, along with others in the Seward wing of the Republican party, was willing to make to the border states: modification of the personal liberty laws; a constitutional amendment prohibiting federal interference with slavery in the states; admission of New Mexico as a slave state.[8]

To Sumner all these concessions seemed derelictions of principle. The Massachusetts personal liberty law, which he and Dana had originally drawn up, which had been saved from repeal by the Brooks assault, was "one of the glories of our Commonwealth"; moreover, its repeal would *"not have the slightest influence in satisfying the slave states."* To admit New Mexico as a slave state would be *"a fatal dismal mistake,"* "an abandonment of principle." It did not matter if, as Adams argued, the number of slaves in New Mexico would always be small. *"To sanction the enslaving of a single human being,"* Sumner passionately believed, "is an act which cannot be called small, unless the whole

[8] This analysis of Adam's course in the secession crisis is based on his unpublished diary and on his letterbooks of the period. See, especially, his Diary, Dec. 20, 1860, and his letter to Dana, Feb. 9, 1861, Adams MSS.

moral law which it overturns or ignores is small." To add an amendment guaranteeing slavery would undermine the basis of Sumner's entire antislavery argument, that the Constitution nowhere recognized property in man. "Ignoble will it be in us," he argued, "to concede beyond the Constitution, which . . . embodies all that our fathers would concede." [9] Worst of all, even if the North humiliated itself by making the concessions Adams proposed, the slaveholders, "Punic in faith, Punic in character," would not be satisfied. *"They are all essentially false, with treason in their hearts, if not on their tongues."* [1]

Vainly Sumner tried to convince Adams of the error that he and Seward were making. But, Adams, busy with the practical work of the Committee of Thirty-three, never really tried to understand the senator's plan for coping with the secession crisis and tended to dismiss him as an impractical theorist. Since Sumner, as Henry Adams said, could "no more argue than a cat" and was unable to reason with his friend, he orated at him. His formerly peaceful Sunday dinners with the Adams family now became occasions of violent political wrangling. One Sunday after Seward's speech, for example, Sumner and Senator Preston King, of New York, dined with the Adamses, and, after the ladies retired, fat, amiable King in his genial way deplored the plan to admit New Mexico as a slave state. Sumner sustained him in round, rhetorical periods. As the discussion grew warmer, with King and Adams each attacking the other's logic, Sumner interposed "with a re-assertion of our being right, and that the South must be made to bend." Sharply Adams rebuked him: "Sumner, you don't know what you're talking about. Yours is the very kind of stiff-necked obstinacy that will break you down if your persevere." [2]

Offended, Sumner did not answer Adams; he thought that events were already doing so. Prior to December 21, when Adams had first endorsed the admission of New Mexico as a slave state, only South Carolina had seceded; during the six weeks following that concession Mississippi, Florida, Alabama, Georgia, Louisi-

[9] Sumner to Dana, Jan. 20, 1861, Dana MSS.; Sumner to H. L. Pierce, Jan. 29, 1861, MS., Houghton Lib.; Worthington C. Ford (ed.): "Sumner's Letters to Governor Andrew, 1861," *MHSP*, LX (1926–7), 227–8; Hughes: *Forbes*, I, 186.

[1] Sumner to Andrew [Jan. 1861], Andrew MSS.

[2] Ford (ed.): *Letters of Henry Adams*, pp. 79–80.

ana, and Texas had moved toward secession, and Virginia and Tennessee were about to summon conventions. With a feeling approaching satisfaction, Sumner observed the progress of disunion during the month of January; these developments were precisely what he had predicted would result from compromise of any sort. The cotton states were lost already, he told Governor Andrew. "Virginia will go, and will carry with her Maryland and Kentucky." "*They will all go.*" [3]

Pleased to have his prophecies fulfilled, willing to believe the worst of the "barbarous" slaveholders, Sumner seemed at times to look "forward to the violence and slaughter of civil war, with the consequences of insurrection in the South almost with a grim satisfaction." He was entirely willing to credit Edwin M. Stanton, Buchanan's new attorney general, who told him in excited, conspiratorial tones: "that every thing was bad as could be—that Virginia would certain secede—that the conspiracy was the most wide-spread and perfect—that all efforts to arrest the movement there by offers of compromise . . . were no more than that" (snapping his fingers). Stanton, who more than anybody else in Washington seemed to have a "strong . . . grasp of the whole terrible case," further convinced Sumner that the Peace Conference, which Virginia had summoned to meet in the capital on February 4, was intended not to preserve the Union, but "to constitute a Provisional Government which was to take possession of the capital and declare itself the nation." [4]

Adams's and Seward's concessions, Sumner reflected bitterly, had already undermined Southern unionism and had frustrated his own plan for coping with the crisis. All the North could do now was to maintain its principles and await events. There must be no further Republican gestures toward compromise; they would be futile in restraining the slave states, but would be potent in demoralizing the North. But, while the North remained inflexible, it must take no move that could be considered aggressive; it must not even send troops to defend the national capital, for that would provoke bloodshed. "If possible," Sumner coached

[3] Sumner to Andrew, Jan. 8, 1861, Andrew MSS.

[4] Adams, Diary, Jan. 6, 1861, Adams MSS.; Sumner to Andrew, Jan. 26, 1861, Andrew MSS.; Henry Wilson: "Jeremiah S. Black and Edwin M. Stanton," *Atlantic Monthly,* XXVI (Oct. 1870), 466.

Andrew, "we must avoid civil war; indeed, to avert this dread calamity, I will give up, if necessary, territory and state; but I will not give up our principles." [5]

With Seward and Adams among the compromisers, Sumner felt that he must exert his every power to keep Massachusetts Republicans firm against all concession to the South. His letters home became constantly shriller in his effect to counteract Adams's influence. Almost daily he wrote Governor Andrew not to concede so much as a "pepper-corn" to the slaveholders. "My earnest prayer," he informed his Boston friends, "is that the state where I was born, and which I now honorably represent may not join in the surrender of those principles which constitute her glory." The italics and the exclamation marks with which Sumner peppered his numerous letters during the secession crisis attest the passion he felt on this subject. "Pray," he besought Andrew, "keep Massachusetts sound and *firm*—FIRM—FIRM—against every word or step of concession." [6]

• 6 •

Had Sumner's conflict with Adams been a purely intellectual difference, it could have been smoothed over, but behind their arguments lurked wounded personal feelings and latent political rivalries. Adams inevitably was irked by his role as Sumner's protégé in Washington. The senator's ponderous homilies, his ostentatious culture, his rhetorical flourishes, his unvarnished egotism all became increasingly insufferable. Adams, who could never forget his distinguished ancestry, found intolerable Sum-

[5] Sumner to Andrew, Jan. 8, 1861, Andrew MSS. I do not agree with Miss Laura A. White's conclusion ("Sumner and the Crisis," p. 156) that this statement proves that Sumner desired a permanent disruption of the United States. As a peace advocate he wanted to avert war; as an antislavery man he feared compromise more than secession. I know of no authenticated statement by Sumner indicating that he ever considered the *permanent* division of the nation possible or desirable. There is no reason to accept statements in the New York *Herald* to the contrary, and the opinion of William B. Read, of Philadelphia, that "Sumner and his peculiar school [were] preaching peace and recognition" of the Confederacy (Read to Joshua Baring, Apr. 25, 1861, House of Baring MSS.) is based on nothing but hearsay.

[6] Sumner to Dana, Jan. 20, 1861, Dana MSS.; Sumner to Charles G. Loring, Jan. 26, 1861, Loring MSS.; Sumner to Andrew, Jan. 17, 1861, Andrew MSS. Cf. Ford (ed.): "Sumner's Letters to Andrew."

ner's conviction that "his great services, his superiority in education, his oratorical power, his political experience, his representative character at the head of the whole New England contingent, and, above all, his knowledge of the world, made him the most important member of the Senate." [7]

Sumner, for his part, bore his differences with Adams with unusual docility until he thought his own political position was imperiled. He had been disturbed to find that Adams was the only member of the Massachusetts delegation in either house given a place on the committees formulating compromise proposals. The fact that the Massachusetts newspapers that had always been most suspicious of Sumner voiced such hearty approval of Adams's course during the secession crisis was alone enough to arouse the senator's apprehensions, and Boston talk about Adams as an ideal candidate to oppose Sumner in 1862 did nothing to allay them.[8]

Always secretive when his own personal prospects were at stake, Sumner moved cautiously against Adams, giving no overt cause for hostility. In January, when a strong Massachusetts movement developed for putting Adams into the cabinet, the letter making the recommendation to President-Elect Lincoln was circulated to every other member of the delegation before it reached Sumner. Rather than cause an open break, Sumner "most sincerely and cordially" endorsed Adams's candidacy—but a close friend of Lincoln's reported: "Not quite *all* the Massachusetts delegation are for Mr. Adams," and Wilson, who was working very closely with Sumner, wrote Lincoln that he would "cheerfully bow" to a decision "passing over Massachusetts" for a cabinet post.[9]

[7] Henry Adams: *Education,* p. 102.

[8] White: "Sumner and the Crisis," pp. 140, 165–6; John E. Lodge to Sumner, Mar. 4, 1861, Sumner MSS.

[9] Letter signed by all members of the Massachusetts delegation to Abraham Lincoln, Jan. 4, 1861, R. T. Lincoln MSS.; Leonard Swett to Lincoln, Jan. 5, 1861, ibid.; Wilson to Lincoln, Jan. 5, 1861, ibid. There is nothing to suggest that Sumner himself wished to go into the cabinet at this time, though there was some newspaper speculation that he might become Secretary of State. William E. Baringer: *A House Dividing: Lincoln as President Elect* (Springfield: The Abraham Lincoln Association; 1945), pp. 45, 86–7. New England conservative Republicans for months had been organizing to defeat any such possibility. L. E. Chittenden to Thomas H. Dudley, Nov. 1, 1860, Dudley MSS.

Conscious of his own rectitude, Adams did nothing to placate Sumner. On January 28 he drew up a letter urging Governor Andrew to send delegates to the Peace Conference recently summoned by Virginia, and persuaded most of the other Massachusetts congressmen to sign it. Perhaps it was not entirely by accident that he approached Sumner last. Angered at again being confronted with a *fait accompli,* worried by Stanton's information that the proposed conference was really "a treacherous and violent assemblage, which . . . was to be the nucleus of the assault upon the city," and prickly with pride because he had just written Andrew not to send delegates, Sumner hotly refused to sign. After exchanging sharp words with his friend, Adams mailed the letter anyway and went back to his seat in the House. Sumner promptly followed and called aside one Massachusetts representative after another to convince them of the error they had committed. Adams inevitably was drawn into one of these conversations, and, flying into a passion, he denounced Sumner's course as "insulating Massachusetts." The next day Sumner tried to renew the discussion, declaring that he was "much pained" by Adams's expressions, which seemed to cast doubt upon the purity of his motives, but Adams, though expressing regret that he had offended the senator, refused to budge from his position.[1]

Two days later, when Adams made his important speech in the House endorsing compromise, Sumner was conspicuous by his absence. The following Sunday, for the first time since the session opened, he did not dine with the Adamses. Though the Adams family tried to conciliate him, he coolly rebuffed them. "To bring him round is impossible," Henry Adams exclaimed. "God Almighty couldn't do it. . . . He will stand on his damned dignity." Twice more, at Mrs. Adams's urgent insistence that it was necessary to quash public reports of a quarrel, Sumner had dinner with his former friends, and late in March he called on them at Quincy, where, finding Charles Francis Adams away on business, he condescended to inform Mrs. Adams that he believed "Mr. Adams meant to be honest" in his mistaken course. But their friendship was already dead. Sumner, as usual, con-

[1] Sumner to Andrew, Jan. 26, 1861, Andrew MSS.; Adams, Diary, Jan. 28–9, 1861, Adams MSS.; Ford (ed.): *Letters of Henry Adams,* pp. 85–6.

cealed his feelings about the break, but Adams recorded in his diary that he had "a sense of relief," as Sumner had "ceased to be an agreeable companion." [2]

Adams tried to keep the public pretense that his differences with the senator were not over important principles, but were "mainly as to policy," but Sumner thought otherwise and promptly began to undermine Adams's position in the Massachusetts Republican party. After their quarrel, he entered into the debates on the Crittenden resolutions for the first time and, hoping to rally public opinion against Adams, demanded "plainly and unequivocally . . . two things, all-sufficient for the present crisis . . . : first, that the Constitution of the United States, as administered by George Washington shall be preserved intact and blameless in its text, with no tinkering for the sake of Slavery; and, secondly, that the verdict of the people last November, by which Abraham Lincoln was elected President of the United States, shall be enforced without price or condition." [3] On March 4 his vote helped finally defeat the Crittenden Compromise.

For once Sumner did not rest in his belief that a good speech was an action; he sent out dozens of letters to his friends in Massachusetts, carefully not mentioning Adams by name, but ardently opposing every one of the compromise proposals Adams supported. Those who favored amending the personal liberty law—like Adams, his correspondents were supposed to add—he termed men who placed "*property* above *Human Freedom.*" Congressmen who talked of compromise—again like Adams, Sumner's readers were expected to supply—failed to understand that "all propositions of adjustment, unless they assume the form of absolute 'surrender' are absolutely in vain." After stirring up anti-Adams opinion at home, Sumner then turned his attention to the other members of the Massachusetts delegation in Congress. Confidentially he assured them that Adams and Seward were "Ishmaelites," that the former was now condemned everywhere

[2] Adams, Diary, Jan. 31, Feb. 3, and 7, and Apr. 27, 1861, Adams MSS.; Ford (ed.): *Letters of Henry Adams*, p. 87; Pierce, IV, 3; C. F. Adams, Jr.: *Autobiography*, pp. 102–3; Frederic Bancroft (ed.): *Speeches, Correspondence, and Public Papers of Carl Schurz* (New York: G. P. Putnam's Sons; 1913), VI, 286.

[3] Adams to Bird, Feb. 11, 1861, copy, Adams MSS.; Boston *Advertiser*, Feb. 6, 1861; Sumner: *Works*, V, 471; *Cong. Globe*, 36 Cong., 2 Sess., 863.

in the Bay State as "weak-kneed," and that were he now running for re-election, he could not "get a corporal's guard to vote for him." [4]

On the specific question of sending Massachusetts commissioners to the Peace Conference, Sumner acted adroitly. In newspaper interviews, which he could always repudiate, he branded the proposed convention as "part of the treasonable conspiracy against the general government." In private letters to his personal followers he warned that the conference would be "a *first step* toward 'surrender.' " At his suggestion E. L. Pierce and other members of the Bird Club published editorials attacking Adams's proposal to send delegates. But, uncertain about just how great the appeal of a peace conference would be in Massachusetts, and recognizing that Governor Andrew was under heavy pressure, Sumner carefully did not test his strength by demanding that the governor refrain from appointing Massachusetts commissioners. Instead, he advised Andrew "to keep the delegation a *Unit*" by appointing only delegates hostile to compromise. The result was that though Adams won a small victory when the governor appointed commissioners, the delegates were completely under Sumner's influence when they got to Washington. He saw to it that they were protected from contact with compromise, including contact with Adams himself, and could later report with joy that they were satisfactorily intransigent in the Peace Conference.[5]

As Sumner's campaign against Adams got under way, his friends, perhaps without direct inspiration from the senator himself, planned to push it further. By February it was too late to urge Sumner for a seat in the cabinet; anyway, everybody already knew that not Adams, but Gideon Welles, of Connecticut, would be the one New Englander called to Lincoln's council. But, as Adams was now frequently suggested as United States minister to England, Sumner's intimates began to wonder whether this important assignment could not go to a person more worthy. His

[4] Sumner to H. L. Pierce, Jan. 29, 1861, MS., Houghton Lib.; Sumner to Dana, Feb. 1, 1861, Dana MSS.; Samuel Hooper to N. P. Banks, Feb. 1, 1861, Banks MSS.

[5] New York *Evening Post*, Jan. 30, 1861; Boston *Transcript*, clipped in Stephen Higginson to Sumner, Jan. 31, 1861, Sumner MSS.; Sumner to William Claflin, Feb. 4, 1861, Claflin MSS.; Sumner to Andrew, Jan. 28, and Feb. 20, 1861, Andrew MSS.; Adams, Diary, Feb. 8, 1861, Adams MSS.

brother George took the most active role in soliciting letters of recommendation, but John E. Lodge and Longfellow also did their part. They put pressure on Senators Wilson and Fessenden to support Sumner's appointment, and they persuaded Governor Andrew and former Governor Boutwell that Sumner, with his advantages and experience, would "*begin* a diplomatic career in England, as far forward, as most men would leave off, at the end of four years." [6]

Sumner himself stood carefully aloof from the movement. "I shall neither say or do anything on the matter," he coyly told Andrew, "but I shall continue in position to act hereafter, as I have always tried to do, according to the requirements of duty." But George Sumner more forthrightly declared: "There is no doubt now the thing would be *agreeable* to Charles—but ACTION is wanted." [7]

• 7 •

The fate of Sumner's efforts to block Adams both on compromise and on the English mission lay in the hands of Abraham Lincoln. Anxiously he looked toward Springfield. The little news that reached him about the President-Elect seemed encouraging. His brother George, who was lecturing in the West, wrote him that Lincoln had pledged not to let the Republican party become "a mere sucked egg, all shell and no meat,—the principle all sucked out." Though Sumner himself was not in correspondence with the incoming President, he doubtless had heard that Lincoln was privately advising other congressmen to "entertain no proposition for a compromise in regard to the *extension* of slavery," as "the tug has to come, and better now, than any time hereafter." Hopefully Sumner read the speeches Lincoln made during his circuitous February journey to Washington. Along with Fessenden and other Republicans opposed to compromise, he pre-

[6] George Sumner to Longfellow [Mar. 12, 1861] and Mar. 18, 1861, Longfellow MSS.; Lodge to Sumner, Mar. 4, and 8, 1861, Sumner MSS.; *MHSP*, LXII, 209–10; Longfellow to Fessenden, Feb. 26, 1861, photostat, Longfellow MSS.; Andrew to Abraham Lincoln, Mar. 12, 1861, Appointment Papers, Department of State Records; Boutwell to Lincoln, Mar. 18, 1861, ibid.; Andrew to Wilson, Mar. 11, 1861, copy, Andrew MSS.

[7] Sumner to Andrew, Mar. 10, 1861, Andrew MSS.; George Sumner to Longfellow [Mar. 12, 1861], Longfellow MSS.; New York *Herald*, Mar. 13, 1861.

pared to exercise his utmost charm upon the President-Elect when he arrived. "If Mr. Lincoln *stands firm,*" Sumner told Andrew, "I do not doubt that our cause will be saved. All that we hear testifies to his character." "But," he reflected, *"he is a man!"* [8]

On the day after Lincoln reached the capital, Sumner called on him at Willard's hotel. In the antechamber he frostly met Charles Francis Adams, also bent on influencing the President-Elect. Both men had their interviews, and both left puzzled. Adams went away feeling that this "tall, illfavored man, with little grace of manner or polish of appearance" had nevertheless "a plain, goodnatured, frank expression which rather attracts one to him." Sumner was "greatly amazed" to find Lincoln so wanting in the dignity, the social poise, the breadth of culture requisite for a President. Now and then he noticed in Lincoln's conversation "flashes of thought and bursts of illuminating expression which struck him as extraordinary," but he was baffled by his droll Western sense of humor. When the President-Elect, admiring the senator's height, offered to "measure backs" to determine who was the taller, Sumner, unamused, stiffly replied that this was "the time for uniting our fronts against the enemy and not our backs." After they parted, Lincoln is supposed to have said: "I have never had much to do with bishops where I live, but, do you know, Sumner is my idea of a bishop." Sumner, on his part, "could not get rid of his misgivings as to how this seemingly untutored child of nature would master the tremendous task before him." [9]

Eagerly Sumner waited for Lincoln's inaugural address to reveal the policy of the new administration. Though March 4, 1861, was a raw day, Sumner stood in the dust-laden, rasping wind to witness the swearing in of the first Republican president. Rejoicing that the inauguration had come off without disturbance from Southern sympathizers and even more that Lincoln's address, though ambiguous in parts, offered the South no new compromise proposals, Sumner strode home from the Capitol in

[8] Pierce, IV, 16; New York *Herald,* Feb. 23, 1861; Sumner to Andrew, Feb. 20, 1861, Andrew MSS.

[9] Adams, Diary, Feb. 24, 1861, Adams MSS.; Schurz: *Reminiscences,* II, 240–1; Ben: Perley Poore, in Allen Thorndike Rice (ed): *Reminiscences of Abraham Lincoln by Distinguished Men of His Time* (New York: *North American Review;* 1888), 223. Cf. the "Diary of a Public Man," quoted in Anderson: *The Mystery of "A Public Man,"* pp. 215–18.

high spirits. To Charles Francis Adams, Jr., who met him, he remarked: "I do not suppose Lincoln had it in his mind, if indeed he ever heard of it; but the inaugural seems to me best described by Napoleon's simile of 'a hand of iron and a velvet glove.'"[1]

Happy in his belief that Lincoln's first inaugural had killed off Adams's "demented" scheme of appeasing the South, Sumner was willing to accept, without too much grumbling, the new President's attempts to placate the pro-compromise wing of the Republican party through patronage. He offered no resistance when Lincoln thwarted a last-minute move he and other antislavery Republicans made to block Seward's nomination as Secretary of State. Nor did he protest when Adams was named minister to Great Britain. He recognized that the nomination was not intended as a slap at himself; Lincoln had apparently made up his mind before the recommendations for Sumner reached him, and he appointed Adams simply because Seward insisted on it.[2]

If either of these rebuffs wounded Sumner's vanity, he was pacified by his selection as chairman of the Senate Committee on Foreign Relations, a post which he was to make more important than that of any ambassador and more influential than that of most Secretaries of State. Even the usually hostile New York *Herald* had to admit that Sumner dserved the chairmanship: "He is probably one of the most accomplished linguists in the United States, and his present relations with the foreign ministers are of the highest social order."[3]

Partly because Sumner was suspected of being "grouty" over the English mission, Lincoln gave him as free a hand as possible in other patronage. "Sumner's influence is very potential—more than any body's else put together," Congressman John B. Alley warned a Massachusetts office-seeker. Though the senator constantly lamented that he was powerless to aid his true antislavery friends, he actually controlled an extraordinary number of the

[1] Charles Francis Adams, Jr.: "Lincoln's First Inauguration," *MHSP*, XLII (1908–9), 148–50; Adams: *Autobiography*, pp. 97–8.

[2] Aaron Goodrich to Frederick W. Seward, Feb. 20, 1861, Seward MSS.; Wilson to Andrew, Mar. 14, 1861, Andrew MSS.; Seward to Lincoln, Mar. 11 [1861], R. T. Lincoln MSS. Sumner telegraphed Adams the news when the Senate confirmed his appointment. Adams, Diary, Mar. 20, 1861, Adams MSS.

[3] New York *Herald*, Mar. 7, 1861. "That you should displace Mason as the head of Foreign Relations!" Dana exulted. "Who would have dreamed it in 1856 . . . ?" Dana to Sumner, Mar. 9, 1861, Sumner MSS.

federal offices in Massachusetts, and he filled them not with Bostonians, but with Republicans from the central and western counties, which had always been the source of his political strength. The new collector of customs at Boston, who hired more employees than any other federal office-holder in the state, was John Z. Goodrich, of Stockbridge, in far western Massachusetts. His previous services to the party would probably have gained him his appointment in any event, but Sumner's intervention was given credit for his final selection.[4]

Of almost equal political importance to Sumner was the postmaster at Boston, whose office employed 127 clerks. When Lincoln asked Sumner to fill the office, the senator, unaccustomed to handling patronage, laughed that it was "an elephant on his hands," but he took the greatest care to select a postmaster who would be politically useful. Avoiding all the outstanding Republican candidates, as their loyalty to him personally was doubtful, Sumner chose John G. Palfrey, his political ally since Free Soil days. Palfrey's plaintive appeals for an appointment, his literary eminence, and his complete trustworthiness no doubt were the influences determining Sumner's selection, but he also took into account Howe's observation: "It is not in *you* to ask or wish any thing of a post master that the Doctor [Palfrey] would not accede to." [5]

In making foreign appointments, Sumner's influence was equally powerful. Believing that "it is of incalculable importance, that our cause should be represented at every European Government with all of character, skill and persuasion which we can command," Sumner repeatedly urged Lincoln to appoint American men of letters to diplomatic posts. Though he did not succeed in securing a consulate for Herman Melville, he did promote the appointments of George Perkins Marsh as minister to Italy and of John Lothrop Motley as minister to Austria. Restive under the frequent claims Sumner made for Massachusetts citizens, Lincoln protested: "I suppose you . . . think your State

[4] Bigelow: *Retrospections,* IV, 275; Alley to William Schouler, Apr. 14, 1861, William Schouler MSS.; Sumner to Elizur Wright, Mar. 7, 1861, Wright MSS.; New York *Herald,* Mar. 27, and Apr. 6, 1861; Stearns: *Stearns,* p. 244.

[5] New York *Herald,* Mar. 14, 1861; C. F. Adams, Jr.: *Autobiography,* pp. 101–3; Sumner to Bird, Mar. 10, 1861, Bird MSS. See also letters from the following in the Sumner MSS.: Andrew, Mar. 11, and 21, 1861; Dana, Mar. 13, 1861; John B. Alley, Mar. 15, 1861; Pierce, Apr. 2, 1861; Howe, Mar. 13 [1861].

could furnish suitable men for every diplomatic and consulate station the Government has to fill," but he gave to Massachusetts, and to Sumner, a very large share.[6]

Sumner professed to be "weary, disheartened and unhappy" at having to participate in these struggles for power. "From early morning till late at night I see nothing but the contest of politicians, and the incapacity of men in power," he lamented, "and I long for my old place in Opposition, free, open, unembarrassed." As a matter of fact, there is a good deal of evidence to show that he found it wonderfully exciting to be in power and at the center of events. Even if the office-seekers were as thick as "the buffaloes on the plains at the foot of the Rocky Mountains," he liked to help give out jobs, for he could now end the ostracism that Southerners had too long imposed upon the enemies of slavery. He also enjoyed having a friendly administration in the White House, and he grandly showed his constituents over the executive mansion and introduced them to the President. Best of all, he liked to know the latest gossip, and he regaled his dinner companions with tales of how Lincoln "was meddling with every office in the gift of the Executive" and how Mrs. Lincoln had interfered with the selection of a naval officer at the Boston customs house.[7]

Absorbed by the distribution of the spoils, Sumner virtually abandoned his earlier, excited attention to the problems of secession. As he knew nothing of Seward's elaborate, abortive efforts to arrange for the surrender of Fort Sumter, in Charleston harbor, to the Confederates, Sumner thought that the Lincoln administration had given up all thought of compromise. Consequently he was willing to trust the President. When Senator Wade at a secret Senate caucus on March 11 proposed to demand that Lincoln hold Fort Sumter even if it cost 100,000 lives, Sumner helped quash the resolution, declaring that evacuation

[6] Sumner to Bird, Mar. 10, 1861, Bird MSS.; Jay Leyda: *The Melville Log* (New York: Harcourt, Brace & Co.; 1951), II, 634–9; George William Curtis (ed.): *The Correspondence of John Lothrop Motley* (New York: Harper & Brothers; 1889), II, 30–1; Sumner to Duchess of Argyll, Nov. 11, 1861, Argyll MSS.; J. B. Alley, in Rice (ed.): *Reminiscences of Abraham Lincoln*, pp. 577–9.

[7] Sumner to Howe, Apr. 7, 1861, Sumner MSS.; Sumner to Elizabeth Peabody, Apr. 7, 1861, Mann MSS.; Sumner to Longfellow, Jan. 23, 1861, Longfellow MSS.; New York *Herald*, Apr. 11, 1861; C. F. Adams, Jr.: *Autobiography*, pp. 102–3; Adams, Diary, Mar. 16, 1861, Adams MSS.

of the forts was a purely military question, in which the Senate had no right to meddle.[8]

In the complex sequence of events which led up to the Confederate attack on Fort Sumter, on April 11, Sumner played no role.[9] Early recognizing that "Everything tends . . . to a break-up of the Union," [1] he was not surprised when the Southerners rashly precipitated war. His regret at hearing the news was tinctured with irony that he, "loving Peace, vowed to Peace, should be called to take such great responsibility in an awful ghastly civil war." "My system," he told Longfellow, "would have made it unnecessary." [2]

If Sumner had been given to self-criticism, the firing on Fort Sumter might have caused him to ponder what part he himself had played in bringing on the sectional conflict. In the minds of many Southerners, extremists like Sumner were responsible for the break-up of the Union. As a Conscience Whig, he had helped kill the national Whig party, which had once bound together conservatives of both North and South. As Free Soil senator, he had seized every opportunity to attack the South and to embitter sectional feelings. As Republican martyr, he had been instrumental in keeping his party committed to an antislavery course and in scotching efforts at compromise. "By degrees," as Carl Sandburg has remarked, "Sumner had come to stand for something the South wanted exterminated from the Union; he was perhaps the most perfect impersonation of what the South wanted to secede from." [3]

He might also have reflected upon the role that chance had played in elevating him to his prominent position. He had stumbled into politics largely by accident. He rose to leadership in the Massachusetts Free Soil movement as much through the unavailability of his rivals as through his own talents and exertions. Can-

[8] Rudolph Schleiden, Despatch No. 34, to the Hanseatic government at Bremen, Mar. 12, 1861, Lib. of Cong.

[9] See the thorough analyses of the Sumter crisis in Randall: *Lincoln the President* (New York: Dodd, Mead & Co.; 1945), I, Chap. xii; Kenneth M. Stampp: *And the War Came* (Baton Rouge: Louisiana State University Press; 1950), Chap. xiii; Allan Nevins: *The War for the Union* (New York: Charles Scribner's Sons; 1959), I, Chap. iii.

[1] Pierce, IV, 17.

[2] Sumner to Longfellow, Apr. 17, 1861, Longfellow MSS.

[3] Carl Sandburg: *Abraham Lincoln: The War Years* (New York: Harcourt, Brace & Co.; 1939), I, 104.

didate of a minority party, he was first chosen to the Senate through the devious workings of a political coalition. At nearly any point during his first five years in office, had he been up for re-election, he would almost certainly have been defeated. Then Preston Brooks's attack gave him his second term in the Senate and thereby assured him seniority and prestige within the Republican party. Never chosen by direct popular vote for any office, Sumner, by 1861, nevertheless had become one of the most powerful men in the United States.

But Sumner was not introspective, and he would brusquely have dismissed both these lines of thought. In his own mind he bore no responsibility whatever for the coming of the Civil War. The voice of puritanism in politics, he had merely spoken out for Truth and Justice. Not he, but the treasonable leaders of the South, madly intent upon defending their barbarous institution, had caused the war. Nor would Sumner have agreed that he owed his own commanding political position to chance. True, he would admit that high office had been thrust upon him, without his solicitation and even against his will. But the fact that despite the intrigues of the Boston magnates, the propaganda of the newspaper editors, and the maneuvers of the politicians, Massachusetts had twice chosen him senator proved that the plain people of the Commonwealth were sound on the slavery question.

Far from brooding over the past, Sumner looked toward the future. At once he recognized that the coming of the Civil War, despite all its attendant horrors, would solve many problems. No longer would he have to endure the arrogance of Southern slaveholders in the United States Senate. No longer would he have to fight to keep members of his own party firm against compromise. No longer need he fear a movement to write slavery into the Constitution. Indeed, the war offered new opportunities for the antislavery crusade. As soon as Sumner heard of the firing on Fort Sumter, he instantly thought back to John Quincy Adams's teaching that emancipation was one of the President's war powers. At once he went to the White House, pledged Lincoln his support, "heart and soul," and indicated his own program for winning the Civil War: "I . . . told him . . . that under the war power the right had come to him to emancipate the slaves." [4]

[4] Yarnall: *Wordsworth and the Coleridges*, pp. 7–8. Cf. Julian: *Giddings*, p. 385.

PART II

CHARLES SUMNER

AND THE

Rights of Man

Sumner at the Outbreak of the Civil War

HARVARD UNIVERSITY ARCHIVES

PREFACE

THIS book is an account of the career of Charles Sumner during the Civil War and Reconstruction period. It is long because Sumner's activities during those years were influential and deserve extended discussion. The principal antislavery spokesman in the United States Senate, Sumner in the early years of the war prodded Abraham Lincoln to emancipate the slaves. Once that was done, he insisted that the President protect the freedmen in their liberty. In the postwar period Sumner worked unceasingly to guarantee the political and civil rights of Negroes in the South and to eliminate racial discrimination throughout the United States. Equally important, though less familiar, was Sumner's role in the direction of American diplomacy from 1861 to 1871. As chairman of the Senate Committee on Foreign Relations, he often exercised influence as great as that of the Secretary of State. Devoted to international peace, Sumner countered William H. Seward's belligerent propensities and, through his wide and powerful circle of correspondents abroad, discouraged European powers from meddling in the American conflict. After the war Sumner blocked the ill-advised plans of Andrew Johnson and Ulysses S. Grant for annexing territory in the Caribbean, but he was instrumental in persuading the Senate to approve the purchase of Alaska. Though Sumner's influence in foreign policy was usually exerted in the direction of peace, he was also responsible, through two major addresses in 1863 and 1869, for whipping up American ill-will against Great Britain over the Alabama Claims issue.

Though the importance of these activities justifies the

writing of Sumner's life, I did not undertake his biography on this account. I became interested in Sumner because he was a man of ideas. After closely studying Sumner for more than twenty years, I do not argue that he had great originality or remarkable literary gifts, but I do believe that he was a major figure in American intellectual history. Such diverse contemporaries as Ralph Waldo Emerson and Francis Lieber so regarded him, and historians would do well to follow their example. Sumner had a comprehensive and systematic political philosophy, which was based on the simple premise that all men are created equal. He felt that the role of government was to secure to all its citizens equal rights, without regard to race or color or sex or national origin or religion. To bring about such a truly democratic society, Sumner, unlike most of his contemporaries, was not content to see government play the negative role of prohibiting violations of rights; he wanted the national government to take positive steps to promote education, science, and the arts. Throughout his speeches he contrasted "civilization" and "barbarism," [1] for it was his hope that after the tragedy of Civil War the United States would emerge as a truly civilized society.

Yet it was not the importance of Sumner's ideas, or the sympathy which I have for them, that caused me to persist in my researches on this complex and often difficult man. After all, many other men of letters and men of learning in nineteenth-century America shared his aspirations. What is unique about Sumner is the way he implemented his principles. Despite the prevailing climate of anti-intellectualism, the American man of ideas in his generation had several ways to make an impact upon public policy: Emerson chose to remain a contemplative critic of society; Wendell Phillips championed lost causes; E. L. Godkin and George William Curtis served as journalistic gadflies to American complacency; Lieber and Charles Eliot Norton helped mobilize Northern opinion during the war through the

[1] On the importance of this polarity in American thought, see the neglected but exceedingly valuable work by Charles A. and Mary R. Beard: "The American Spirit: A Study of the Idea of Civilization in the United States," *The Rise of American Civilization*, Vol. IV (New York: The Macmillan Co.; 1942), especially pp. 301–7.

pamphlets they wrote and edited for the Loyal Publication Society; Joseph Henry put his scientific knowledge at the disposal of the Lincoln administration; and, in the postwar years, Henry Adams served as closet adviser to a generation of American statesmen. Only Sumner had a successful career in politics. He alone was responsible to a constituency of voters, and he alone had to battle for his ideas in the Congress of the United States. Between the age of Thomas Jefferson and that of Woodrow Wilson, Sumner was the one American who had equal claim for distinction in the world of the intellect and the world of politics.

Much of this book is necessarily an account of how Sumner—stereotyped by his enemies as a dreamy-eyed abstractionist, a single-minded ideologist—was able to hold his powerful place in the Senate during a critical period in our history. I have tried to show how shrewdly he balanced political forces. In Lincoln's administration he had to play off the President against the Secretary of State; in Johnson's and Grant's, to counter the weight of the executive branch of the government with that of the legislative. Within the Senate he had to draw upon the respect his colleagues had for his expertness on foreign policy to secure a hearing for his proposals in behalf of freedom and equality. So long as his position in the national government was strong, he could scotch discontent among Massachusetts Republicans. The antislavery vanguard condoned his occasional concessions to expediency because he was in a position to do so much good in Washington, and even Massachusetts businessmen forgave Sumner's radicalism on Negro rights because he was so sound on questions of currency and foreign policy. Sumner's skill in preserving this equilibrium enabled him to keep his position in the Senate, and his hold on public opinion, long after most of the other early Republican leaders had dropped out of sight.

I trust that readers will understand that I am presenting an analysis of Sumner's techniques for remaining in power, not an explanation of his motives for so doing. This biography is not a political interpretation of Charles Sumner (i.e., an argument that he was motivated principally by the desire for political office and power). Long before the events traced in this book, Sumner's personality had been permanently shaped, and in a previous study, *Charles Sumner and the Coming of the Civil War,*[2] I described the forces that molded him. In the present volume—which is a completely self-contained work and may be read without reference to the earlier book—I attempt to show how a man with Sumner's ideas and motives was able to operate within the American political system.

It may also be proper for me to remind readers that this is a biography, not a general history of the Civil War and Reconstruction era. I have included only such material as I believe necessary for an understanding of Sumner's career. The following pages, therefore, do not summarize the provisions of, say, the Civil Rights Act of 1866 or the Treaty of Washington, important as these matters may be.

Nor have I thought it necessary in this book to discredit again hoary racist stereotypes about the Civil War and Reconstruction period. For more than a generation historians have rejected the notion that Reconstruction was what Claude G. Bowers called "the tragic era," during which malignant Radicals—like Sumner—thrust the good whites of the South under the control of knavish and barbaric blacks. I assume that my readers will know that this old interpretation is wholly untenable. Lest there be any obscurity about my own position, perhaps I ought to say that I do indeed believe that the postwar years formed a tragic era—tragic in the sense that we failed to adopt Sumner's principles and failed to reconstruct our whole society on the basis of equal rights for all. This is a position that I have argued consistently in a series of books and articles [3] since 1944, and I do not think it useful to repeat myself here.

Instead, I hope this book may encourage some new ways of looking at the period in which Sumner lived. In particular, I have sought to help readers see how the political, diplomatic,

[2] New York: Alfred A. Knopf; 1960.

[3] David Donald: "The Scalawag in Mississippi Reconstruction," *Jour. So. Hist.*, X (1944), 447–60; "Why They Impeached Andrew Johnson," *Am. Heritage*, VIII (Dec. 1956), 20–25 ff.; *Lincoln Reconsidered: Essays on the Civil War Era* (New York: Alfred A. Knopf; 1956); *The Politics of Reconstruction, 1863–1867* (Baton Rouge: Louisiana State University Press; 1965); with J. G. Randall: *The Civil War and Reconstruction*, 2nd ed. (Boston: D. C. Heath and Company; 1961).

military, social, economic, and intellectual developments of these years were complexly interrelated. Too often historians have presented these matters in a curiously isolated, topical fashion. The diplomacy of the Civil War–Reconstruction years, for instance, is sometimes discussed as though foreign policy were formulated without regard to domestic affairs. In tracing Sumner's work in the Foreign Relations Committee, which absorbed a major share of his time and energy and gave him a base of power from which to push his domestic programs, I have constantly tried to show the political matrix in which foreign policy was formed. Similarly, historians sometimes discuss Congressional policy toward the South and the freedmen as if public opinion and the political process in the Northern states had little to do with the shaping of Reconstruction plans. Again, I have repeatedly explained how Sumner's stand on emancipation and equal rights was related to his own political situation, within both the national Republican party and his home state.

In the following pages I have generally limited my footnote citations to the sources for specific quotations contained in the text. I refer to secondary works when they are based upon source materials that I have not been able to consult, when they give an extended or variant discussion of a topic to which I can give only passing attention, or, in a few instances, when they contain egregious factual errors concerning Sumner. My footnotes, then, obviously do not reflect my debt to the many historians and biographers of the Civil War period from whose work I have learned so much. For any seeming discourtesy I must offer the apology that I have only limited space for annotations. I ought also to explain that I have tried to give interested readers a comprehensive and critical evaluation of the vast scholarly literature in the annotated bibliography of my revision of J. G. Randall's *The Civil War and Reconstruction.*[4]

[4] Second edition, revised (Boston: D. C. Heath and Company; 1969), pp. 703–834. I offer a more selective listing in *The Nation in Crisis, 1861–1877* (New York: Appleton-Century-Crofts; 1969). My footnotes include citations to a few important books and articles published since I completed these two bibliographies. I wish that in preparing the present study I had been able to consult the authoritative study of *The United States and France: Civil War Diplomacy* (Philadelphia: University of Pennsylvania Press; 1970), by Lynn M. Case and Warren F. Spencer, but it appeared after my book was in press.

I confess, though, that I have had another reason in thus restricting my references to the writings of previous scholars. American historians, I think, spend too much time quarreling with each other. Some members of the profession make a career out of exposing errors or fallacies in the writings of their predecessors—as though, alas, all books did not contain both. Others devote all their energy to categorizing historians into "schools" of interpretation, or to "explaining" their limitations in terms of their geographical origins, social position, and the like. So repeatedly have specialists in the Reconstruction period dissected its historiography that even undergraduates now prattle about the Dunning school of historians, the Marxist school, and the Revisionist school—without, usually, having read any of the books by any of these writers. In times past I did my share of this sort of historical cannibalism. Increasingly, however, I have grown disenchanted with this essentially negative approach to history. In writing my biography of Charles Sumner, I have deliberately tried not to renew, much less to settle, old arguments among scholars. Instead, this book is an attempt to get on with the historian's main task, that of rediscovering the past.

—D. D.

Center for Advanced Study in the Behavioral Sciences
Stanford, California
April 24, 1970

CHAPTER I

More Than "One Idea"

NOT since the assassination of Abraham Lincoln had so many Americans mourned. At the news of Charles Sumner's death the Michigan state legislature unanimously adopted resolutions expressing grief, and in Charleston, South Carolina, once the hotbed of secession, flags were lowered to half-mast. The mayors of Philadelphia and New York begged to have the body lie in state in their cities. Residents of Boston thronged to Faneuil Hall to hear tributes to the dead, and the governor of Massachusetts proclaimed a statewide day of mourning.

In Washington grief was intense. During the early morning of March 11, 1874, Negro residents in the capital, learning of the Senator's serious heart attack, began to gather in quiet groups outside his house on Vermont Avenue and H Streets, just across Lafayette Park from the White House, and by midday the streets were jammed. At the other end of Pennsylvania Avenue, the Senate, meeting at noon, immediately suspended business out of respect for its dying member, and the House of Representatives, after desultory discussion interrupted by frequent medical bulletins from Sumner's bedside, adjourned promptly at the news of his death. The next day Congress voted to set aside Friday, March 13, for funeral services in the Capitol.

At nine o'clock that morning the funeral procession left Sumner's house.[1] A delegation from Congress was supposed to be in the lead, but quietly the Negro mourners, marching five abreast, took their place at the head of the line. Though the day was raw and blustery, thousands were waiting at the Capitol when the coffin was placed in the rotunda on the black catafalque where Lincoln's body had rested. It was the first time in American history that a Senator's memory had been so honored. For three hours a dense throng of the idle, the curious, and the grief-stricken filed by the open coffin to look at the cold, livid, discolored face that, beneath the transparent glass, looked like that of a drowned man. At twelve-thirty the body was brought into the Senate Chamber, where the President of the United States and his cabinet, the justices of the Supreme Court, the members of the diplomatic corps, and the Senators and Representatives were waiting. As five thousand spectators tried to crowd into the galleries, the anterooms, and the corridors, every chair in the Senate chamber was filled except one, Sumner's own seat, heavily draped in black.

After the service the casket, guarded by the sergeant-at-arms of the Senate and escorted by delegations from both houses of Congress, traveled by non-stop special train to New York, to the disappointment of crowds that had assembled at Wilmington and at Philadelphia to pay their final respects. After an overnight halt, the funeral train moved on to Massachusetts. Beginning at Springfield there were throngs gathered at every railroad station to watch the black train speed east, and church bells tolled along the entire route. In Boston the crowd, too large for the police to control, surged onto the railway tracks and followed the cortege up Beacon Hill to the State House. There in the dimly lit Doric Hall, the governor waited. Speaking for the Congressional delegation, Henry B. Anthony, the President pro

[1] For details on the funeral services in Washington and Boston, see Edward L. Pierce: *Memoir and Letters of Charles Sumner* (Boston: Roberts Brothers; 1894), IV, 599–605 [hereinafter cited as Pierce]; *A Memorial of Charles Sumner* (Boston; 1874), pp. 867–89; Springfield *Republican*, Mar. 14 and 17, 1874; A. Augusta Dodge (ed.): *Gail Hamilton's Life in Letters* (Boston: Lee and Shepard; 1901), II, 744–5; and J. J. Ingalls to his wife, Mar. 13, 1874, Ingalls MSS. Unless otherwise expressly indicated, all newspaper references in these notes are to daily editions.

tempore of the Senate, addressed him: "May it please your Excellency, we are commanded . . . to render back to you your illustrious dead. . . . With reverent hands we bring to you his mortal part that it may be committed to the soil of the renowned Commonwealth which gave him birth. Take it; it is yours. The part which we do not return to you is not wholly yours to receive, nor altogether ours to give. It belongs to the country, to mankind, to freedom, to civilization, to humanity."

The next day, March 15, the coffin, now sealed, lay in state in the Doric Hall, attended by soldiers from the all-Negro Shaw Guard, which had proved its heroism at Fort Wagner during the Civil War. A large floral crown hung just above the head of the coffin, and beneath it a snow-white dove, apparently in the very act of alighting. On the coffin itself lay a shield bearing the motto: "Don't Let the Civil Rights Bill Fail." Perhaps as many as five thousand people were waiting outside when the doors of the State House were opened, and by afternoon the crowd had grown so large that women began to faint in the closely packed lines. Walking silently, two or three abreast, nearly forty thousand persons passed by the catafalque during Sunday and the morning hours of Monday.

With all business in Boston suspended on Monday, the streets were packed with the mourners and the curious, and the police had difficulty in clearing the route of the funeral procession from the State House to King's Chapel, selected because it had once been the place of worship attended by the mother of the Senator, who himself had belonged to no church. Spectators pushed close to touch the casket, to eye the delegations from Washington, and to count off the pallbearers: Henry Wadsworth Longfellow, Ralph Waldo Emerson, and John Greenleaf Whittier, representatives of the literary culture of New England; Robert C. Winthrop and Charles Francis Adams, embodiments of the patrician leadership of Massachusetts; and five former governors, during whose terms in office Sumner had represented the state in the United States Senate.

After the Episcopal service for the dead, the funeral procession slowly formed anew to escort the remains to the cemetery. At the head were the Vice President of the United States, the members of the Massachusetts delegation to Congress, the governor of the state, the mayor of Boston, and the president and overseers of Harvard College. At the rear were two thousand representatives of Negro fraternal groups. As the huge cortege inched down Beacon Street to turn onto the Charles River Bridge, it produced a gigantic traffic snarl, and for forty-five minutes the hearse was stalled in front of a house with tightly drawn blinds. Behind them stood the divorced wife of the dead Senator, who looked down at the coffin and said: "That is just like Charles; he never did show tact." [2]

Finally the procession lurched on, across the bridge, through Cambridge, past Harvard College, and out to the cemetery at Mount Auburn. All along the five-mile route crowds lined the streets. As dusk was falling and the graveside prayers were said, the male choir sang: *"Inter vitae scelerisque purus."*

• 2 •

Popular interest in the dead Senator was insatiable. Virtually every newspaper in the United States, as well as many abroad, carried an obituary editorial. Reporters wrote of his daily routine as Senator, of his recent divorce, of his final hours. The press publicized the provisions of his will, which divided most of his one-hundred-thousand-dollar estate equally between his surviving sister, who lived in California, and the Harvard College Library. Some periodicals offered steel engraved portraits of Sumner in order to attract new subscribers. Music publishers sold at least three different Sumner funeral marches.[3]

With the nineteenth century's seemingly endless appetite for oratory, audiences assembled again and again to hear Sumner extolled. At a huge public meeting in the Music Hall on March 18 Bostonians listened to an elaborate eulogy by Carl Schurz, the German-American who was Sumner's closest associate in the Senate during his final years. Both houses of Con-

[2] Caroline H. Dall to E. L. Pierce, May 6, 1893, Pierce MSS.; C. K. Bolton to Gamaliel Bradford, Feb. 13, 1915, MS., Houghton Library. Cf. New York *Herald*, Dec. 29, 1889.

[3] These have been preserved in the remarkable sheet-music collection of Mr. Lester S. Levy, of Baltimore, who kindly gave copies to me.

gress set aside April 27 to hear tributes to Sumner. On June 9 there was another large gathering at Boston's Music Hall, this time sponsored by the Massachusetts state government, at which Whittier read a funeral ode on Sumner and George William Curtis, crusading editor of *Harper's Weekly,* delivered a commemorative oration. Within the year at least four books containing these collected tributes and eulogies were published.[4]

Nearly all the orators repeated the story of Sumner's life.[5] They told of his industrious years at Harvard, where he had been the favorite law student of Justice Joseph Story; they recounted the extraordinary social successes he had achieved during the more than two years he spent in Europe in the 1830's; and they recalled his stunning first public appearance in Boston when, at the age of thirty-four, he had delivered on July 4, 1845, his oration on "The True Grandeur of Nations," announcing that there was no justifiable war, no dishonorable peace. Most speakers told of Sumner's painful decision in the 1840's to join with Charles Francis Adams, John Gorham Palfrey, Richard Henry Dana, Jr., and a few others in breaking with the Whig party over the annexation of Texas and recalled how these "Conscience Whigs" had coalesced with other antislavery men to form the Free Soil party. They discussed Sumner's first election to the Senate in 1851, by a coalition of Free Soilers and Democrats, and recalled how courageously, as a member of the tiny antislavery minority in Congress, he had demanded that the United States recognize that freedom was national, slavery sectional. Nearly every eulogist told how Sumner in 1856 because of his orations against slavery was assaulted upon the floor of the

[4] *A Memorial of Charles Sumner* (Boston; 1874); *A Memorial of Charles Sumner from the City of Boston* (Boston: Printed by the order of the City Council; 1874) [hereinafter cited as *Boston Memorial*]; *Memorial Addresses on the Life and Character of Charles Sumner, (A Senator of Massachusetts,) Delivered in the Senate and House of Representatives* . . . (Washington: Government Printing Office; 1874); William M. Cornell (ed.): *Charles Sumner: Memoir and Eulogies* (Boston: James H. Earle; 1874).

[5] Perhaps the best of these obituary biographies was that appearing in the Boston *Commonwealth,* Mar. 14, 1874. For a full narrative of Sumner's life up to 1861, see my *Charles Sumner and the Coming of the Civil War* (New York: Alfred A. Knopf; 1960). Edward L. Pierce: *Memoir and Letters of Charles Sumner* (4 vols.; Boston: Roberts Brothers; 1878–93) is the best of the older biographies and remains invaluable because it reprints so many of Sumner's letters.

Senate by Representative Preston S. Brooks of South Carolina and how he had spent three years recovering from those wounds. More recent history the eulogists assumed to be familiar to their listeners, and for the most part they passed over in less detail Sumner's labors as chairman of the Senate Committee on Foreign Relations for ten years and his unceasing efforts to secure to Negroes all the rights of man.

In both public eulogies and private appraisals contemporaries agreed that the United States had lost one of its truly great men.[6] Sumner was "the greatest of our Senators and of our Citizens alike," concluded Senator Timothy O. Howe of Wisconsin, who had been politically at odds with the Senator for several years. Whittier lauded Sumner's "tireless devotion to duty, his courage, his proved scorn of meanness and greed and fraud, his almost austere truthfulness, his unbending integrity, stainless honor and tender regard for the rights of all." The Springfield *Republican,* frequently critical of Sumner in the past, began its obituary: "The noblest head in America has fallen, and the most accomplished and illustrious of our statesmen is no more." A Massachusetts legislator went the newspaper one better: "Not only has America lost her greatest and best statesman, but the world has lost its ablest and most devoted friend." [7]

At the same time, a note of puzzlement kept appearing in the numerous tributes to Sumner, as though the speakers were not sure on what basis his claim to greatness rested. Those who paid tribute to Sumner's industry, to his sincerity of purpose, to his incorruptibility in an age of spoilsmen knew that these traits, admirable as they were, hardly warranted ranking the Senator among the greatest of statesmen. No more did his erudition, amounting at times to pedantry, entitle him to the esteem of

[6] There were some exceptions to this chorus of praise, the most notable being that from Charles Francis Adams. In a public letter Adams lauded Sumner's "personal integrity, unassailable by any form of temptation, however specious" (*Boston Memorial,* p. 63), but in his private diary he wrote: "He was selfish and untrue, professing indifference and concealing his intrigues, professing great friendship and confidence with me and covering his real tracks entirely" (Adams: Diary, Mar. 21, 1874, Adams MSS.).

[7] Howe to Grace Howe, Mar. 13, 1874, Howe MSS.; Whittier to Henry Wilson, Mar. 10 [*sic*], 1874, MS., Friends Historical Lib., Swarthmore College; *Memorial of Charles Sumner,* p. 56.

countrymen who honored Abraham Lincoln and Ulysses S. Grant as popular heroes. Some years earlier eulogists might have attributed Sumner's fame to his oratory, but in recent times his style had fallen into disfavor. Even in funeral orations speakers felt obliged to complain that his speeches made an "almost barbaric display of literary wealth gleaned from all languages and gathered from all lands," and a friendly newspaper observed that had Sumner "had a large family to look after . . . or large professional clientage taking up his odd moments, his speeches would have gained more in directness and force than they would have lost in affluence of learning." [8]

No one tried to explain Sumner's fame in terms of legislation which he had pushed through Congress. His Senate colleague, George S. Boutwell, with humorous exaggeration grumbled that after nearly a quarter of a century in Congress Sumner had been instrumental in the adoption of only one law —a measure permitting Mongolian immigrants to be naturalized.[9] Though the leading proponent in Congress of Negro rights, Sumner had not been the author or the sponsor of the Thirteenth, Fourteenth, or Fifteenth amendments; indeed, he had gravely objected to all three measures. Everybody agreed, declared Massachusetts Congressman Nathaniel P. Banks, that Sumner had "no claim to respect or to honor upon the mere measures that are placed on the statute book." As Senator John Sherman more tactfully put it, Sumner was "often so eager in the advance that he did not sufficiently look to practical measures to secure the progress already made." [1]

A large number of the eulogists concluded that Sumner's fame rested upon the special role he had so long played in American public life, that of the idealist in politics. Some misconceived that role so completely as to claim that he had been above politics. Blessedly he "knew nothing of management and party manoeuvre," declared one speaker, and another admirer

[8] *Memorial Addresses on Charles Sumner,* p. 107; Boston *Morning Journal,* Mar. 14, 1874. I have slightly changed the punctuation in the *Journal* quotation.

[9] Boutwell: *Reminiscences of Sixty Years in Public Affairs* (New York: McClure, Phillips & Co.; 1902), II, 47.

[1] *Boston Memorial,* p. 55; *Memorial Addresses on Charles Sumner,* p. 45.

insisted: "He never packed a caucus, pulled a wire, or rolled a log." [2] Such assertions of Sumner's political innocence must have come as a surprise to the members of the Massachusetts legislature, which for four consecutive terms had chosen him to the Senate; they could remember how Sumner had systematically undercut every political rival in Massachusetts and how his lieutenants, especially Francis W. Bird and the other members of the "Bird Club," had pressured the legislators into endorsing Sumner's policies and repeatedly reelecting him.

The most perceptive commentators recognized that Sumner's political role was far more complex. If his elections rested in the hands of legislators who were not notably indifferent to party, his popular support came from idealistic groups, such as the clergymen, the women, and especially the young voters of Massachusetts, who were hostile to the institutions and the compromises of American political life. Even the members of the Bird Club, which met every Saturday afternoon at Young's Hotel in Boston, were apolitical politicians; Bird himself, as Governor John A. Andrew once remarked, could not be "coaxed, bought, told nor bullied." [3] Such men wanted their Senator to be "the embodiment of the moral idea, with all its uncompromising firmness, its unflagging faith, its daring devotion"; indeed, as Carl Schurz tried to show, Sumner could be their "leader only because he was no politician." [4]

No acting was necessary for Sumner to play the part of "statesman *doctrinaire*," [5] especially during the years before the

[2] *Boston Memorial*, p. 115; *Memorial of Charles Sumner*, p. 54.

[3] Andrew's endorsement on a letter from P. W. Chandler [Mar. 1862], Andrew MSS. On the Bird Club, see Henry G. Pearson: *The Life of John A. Andrew, Governor of Massachusetts, 1861–1865* (Boston: Houghton Mifflin and Company; 1904), I, 58–60; *The Reminiscences of Carl Schurz* (New York: Doubleday, Page & Company; 1907–09), II, 130; and Frank P. Stearns: *The Life and Public Services of George Luther Stearns* (Philadelphia: J. B. Lippincott Company; 1907), pp. 162–79. On the anti-institutionalism of American reformers, who made up the vanguard of Sumner's support, see my essay, *An Excess of Democracy* (Oxford: Clarendon Press; 1960); Stanley M. Elkins: *Slavery* (Chicago: The University of Chicago Press; 1959), pp. 140–222; and, especially, George M. Fredrickson: *The Inner Civil War: Northern Intellectuals and the Crisis of the Union* (New York: Harper & Row; 1965), *passim*.

[4] *Boston Memorial*, pp. 116–17.

[5] The phrase is that of Charles Francis Adams, Jr., in *Dinner Commemorative of Charles Sumner and Complimentary to Edward L. Pierce* (Cambridge: John Wilson and Son; 1895), p. 46.

Civil War. Manly and impressive, when he rose to his full six feet and two inches, tossed back his mane of dark brown hair, already showing a little gray, and pointed out the barbarism of slavery, he seemed principle personified. Psychologically as well as physically he fitted the role. His boyhood inability to live up to the expectations of his dour father or to win the love of his undemonstrative mother left him chronically unable to relish success; after each victory, a contemporary noted, he felt obliged to sound "the trumpet-note of an ever higher endeavor." [6] In early years Sumner had flogged himself with his dissatisfaction, even over triumphs won, but during his sufferings after the Brooks assault he came to count himself among the holy company of the martyrs and never again questioned his own motives or regretted his own actions. Thenceforth he blamed the hollowness of victory upon the inadequacies of others, whose low political instincts preferred compromise to consistency.

Once the Republican party came to power in 1860 Sumner found his political role more difficult to sustain. It had been easy to be indifferent to applications for patronage when he knew that a Democratic President would ignore his recommendations, and it had been simple to scorn all compromise when his voice and his vote carried no weight. An influential member of the victorious party was, however, in an entirely different position, obliged to make small concessions and day-by-day compromises if he was to participate effectively in the governing of the country.[7] Some veteran antislavery leaders, like Salmon P. Chase, became so absorbed with this process as to neglect principle; others, like Joshua R. Giddings, unable to adjust to the responsibilities of power, were quietly pushed out of positions of prominence. Neither Sumner's temperament nor his constituency permitted him to follow Chase's course, and he was equally

[6] *Memorial of Charles Sumner*, p. 157.

[7] One may describe the problem which Sumner—and, indeed, the whole abolitionist wing of the Republican party—faced during the Civil War and reconstruction in terms of routinization of charisma. See Max Weber's familiar essay on that subject in Robert K. Merton and others (eds.): *Reader in Bureaucracy* (Glencoe, Ill.: The Free Press; 1952), pp. 92–100. I have found it more rewarding to think of an alternation between what Talcott Parsons has called "symbolic" and "instrumental" leadership roles. Parsons: *The Social System* (Glencoe, Ill.: The Free Press; 1951), pp. 400–6.

unwilling to be driven from public life. From 1861 on, therefore, his career was marked by awkward attempts to reconcile the expectations of his constituents and the demands of the Republican national administrations, by frequent shifts from the role of sectarian leader to that of responsible party member, by precarious efforts to balance principle and power. In 1874 Sumner was almost the only surviving original Republican leader who could still command, even in diminished form, broad respect throughout the country as well as influence within his party.

• 3 •

At the outbreak of the Civil War it was by no means clear how contradictory and conflicting were the pressures that operated upon Sumner. Like most of his fellow Republicans, he seemed to have taken to heart Jacob Collamer's warning that "whenever a party is the dominant party, and in the possession of power, it may require a very different measure of duty from each individual that composes that party from what it would when they were in the minority."[8] Returning to Boston shortly after the attack upon Fort Sumter, Sumner did his best to be conciliatory and statesmanlike. Making light of the threat that a mob had made upon his life when he passed through Baltimore, he stressed instead the attack that Maryland plug-uglies had made upon the Massachusetts Sixth Volunteer Regiment as it rushed south to defend the national capital, and he linked this bloodshed of April 19 with that which, exactly eighty-six years earlier, had opened the Revolutionary War. In the great outpouring of Northern patriotism that followed President Lincoln's call for troops, Sumner discouraged memories of past partisanship. He went out of his way to shake hands with his old enemy, Robert C. Winthrop, with whom he had had no social relations for fifteen years, when that Massachusetts conservative leader presented a flag to a volunteer regiment on the Boston Common.[9] At about the same time Sumner renewed his friendship with Francis Lieber, the

[8] *Cong. Globe*, 37 Cong., 2 Sess., p. 2251.
[9] Winthrop to George F. Hoar, Aug. 13, 1879, Hoar MSS.

German-born publicist and jurist, from whom he had long been estranged by the slavery controversy but who now, as professor at Columbia College in New York City, again became an arsenal of legal learning for the Senator.

When Lincoln called Congress into extraordinary session on July 4, Sumner hoped that both houses might meet in secret to pass the few bills necessary to prosecute the war and that the brief, businesslike session would hear not "a single speech or one word of Buncombe." [1] Though the proceedings were open to the public, Sumner did his best to keep them low-keyed and efficient. During the five-week session he made not one major speech, even after the appalling Federal defeat at Bull Run, and his few remarks were brief, amiable, and to the point. Although towering, arrogant Senator John C. Breckinridge, soon to join the Confederates, attacked him as "the chief author of the public misfortunes" from which the country was suffering, he was not goaded into reply; and when Andrew Johnson of Tennessee pushed through resolutions declaring that the war was not being undertaken to overthrow slavery, Sumner continued to hold his peace, merely registering his opposition by not voting. In two bills which he himself introduced for the confiscation of rebel property, he carefully avoided any mention of slavery, and he went so far as to remark, when presenting an abolitionist petition, that this subject could not now be practically treated by Congress.[2]

Instead of agitating the slavery issue, Sumner turned his energies to the shaping of American foreign policy, for the Republican caucus in March had made him chairman of the prestigious Senate Committee on Foreign Relations. The assignment was one for which Sumner, with his wide acquaintance abroad and his extensive reading in history and international law, felt himself particularly suited. The fact that as chairman of this committee he succeeded James M. Mason, the Virginia Senator

[1] Sumner to Lieber, June 23, 1861, Sumner MSS. Though there are Sumner papers in several libraries, all citations to the Sumner MSS. in this book are, except where otherwise expressly identified, to the huge, basic collection in the Houghton Library at Harvard University.

[2] *Cong. Globe*, 37 Cong., 1 Sess., pp. 380, 257, 265, 78.

who had been father of the 1850 fugitive slave act, doubtless gave him an added sense of satisfaction. The chairmanship not merely gave Sumner power; it afforded him, for the first time in his career, a chance to share in the normal give-and-take of political life. On all questions relating to sectionalism and slavery his position was so well known that if he made any concession to practicality or acquiesced in the will of the majority of his party, friends would mourn and foes would gloat that he was selling out his principles; but in foreign affairs, especially since so much of his work would have to be done in the privacy of committee and in the secret sessions of the Senate, he had a freer hand. At any rate, the assignment was one that he welcomed and cherished, for as he wrote Lieber, the chairman of the Senate Foreign Relations Committee was more influential than any member of the cabinet and, indeed, was in power and responsibility inferior only to the President of the United States.[3]

In a businesslike, conciliatory way Sumner set about his duties as chairman. Entitled to name the clerk of the committee, who also served as the chairman's private secretary, he carefully consulted the Democratic minority members before selecting Ben: Perley Poore, of Newburyport. Though a Massachusetts man, Poore had not been a political friend of Sumner's, and Stephen A. Douglas, the ranking Democratic member of the committee, greeted his appointment with relief: "I feared Sumner would send to Boston for a d—d free nigger for clerk, and I shall be delighted to have you in the committee room." Sumner's gesture was not merely generous but politically shrewd, for Poore, who wrote under the name "Perley," was one of the most influential Massachusetts newspaper correspondents in the capi-

[3] Eleanor E. Dennison: *The Senate Foreign Relations Committee* (Stanford University, Calif.: Stanford University Press; 1942), pp. 11–12. The records of the Senate Foreign Relations Committee for the years when Sumner was chairman (1861–71) are scant and unrewarding. Though I have, of course, studied these few surviving papers in the National Archives, my account of the workings of the committee is based upon the unpublished correspondence of its members, and especially upon Sumner's own frequent and candid letters. I have also studied the numerous reports of the committee, often drafted by Sumner, which were published in the serial set of United States government documents. The *Senate Executive Journal* gives a frustratingly abridged report of the secret sessions in which treaties and conventions were debated, but it supplies an accurate and full tally of how members voted.

tal and henceforth generally brought the powerful Boston *Journal* to support the Senator's course.

Sumner conducted the meetings of his committee with dignity. One of his first acts as chairman was to banish from the committee room the buffet which had long stood in the corner, freely stocked with liquor. Next the open box of cigars disappeared from the mantel. Holding regular, formal meetings, he followed a careful agenda. Since the Democrats on the committee —at first Douglas and Breckinridge; but after the death of the former and the resignation of the latter, Trusten Polk of Missouri—were vigorous opponents of abolitionism, and since the Republican members were mostly conservative men like Orville H. Browning, Lincoln's stuffy Illinois friend who succeeded Douglas, Sumner had to avoid appearing to dominate the proceedings. In presenting items for consideration, he asked the opinion of each member, almost deferentially, and usually kept his own views to himself until the end of the discussion. Nevertheless, since he alone had the knowledge and the time to give close study to the questions before the committee, his word on foreign affairs came gradually to be accepted both in the committee and in the Senate itself.[4] Before many months Sumner could candidly write to Lieber that he was, in fact, doing all the work of the committee.

That work, though not so onerous as the labors of his colleague Henry Wilson, whose Committee on Military Affairs had to screen every army appointment and promotion submitted by the President, or of Maine's Senator William Pitt Fessenden, whose Committee on Finance dealt with both tax and appropriation bills, was both time-consuming and responsible. To the Committee on Foreign Relations went the name of every presidential nominee for diplomatic office. Sumner on his trips abroad had seen the damage done by patronage appointments, and he felt it was "of incalculable importance, that our cause should be represented at every European Government with all of the character, skill and persuasion which we can command." [5] To this end he not merely scrutinized the qualifications of all

[4] "Perley," in Boston *Commonwealth*, Mar. 25, 1871; Pierce, IV, 630–4.
[5] Sumner to Bird, Mar. 10, 1861, Bird MSS.

presidential nominees; he actively solicited Lincoln to name men of literary and intellectual distinction to posts abroad. In the selection of Charles Francis Adams, once a close friend and antislavery associate but now a bitter opponent, as minister to Great Britain Sumner had no part; that was the choice of Secretary of State William H. Seward. Nor did Sumner influence the appointment to France of William L. Dayton, the 1856 Republican vice-presidential candidate. But he did persuade the President to name George Perkins Marsh, the noted philologist, to head the Italian mission. He also secured the ministry at Vienna for the historian John Lothrop Motley. A number of his personal friends and veterans in the antislavery cause became consuls.[6]

By the time Congress adjourned in early August, Sumner's course caused some of his constituents to think that he was so sobered by the responsibilities of power as to put aside his crusade against slavery. He had, it seemed, followed the advice of Boston businessman George Morey: "Avoid . . . all reference to antislavery questions and old issues and assume a high—conservative—statesmanlike tone. Plant yourself on the grounds that the great issue now is, whether there shall be such a thing as a firm, strong and efficient government, under which *law* and *order* shall be maintained. . . ." [7] To symbolize approval of Sumner's new-found moderation, the Phi Beta Kappa Society at Harvard College, where his name had hitherto aroused suspicion if not contempt, elected him vice president.

Rewarding Sumner for his conversion to conservatism was, of course, premature, for he had no intention of abandoning the principles he had so long advocated or the constituency that had so devotedly supported him. Had he done so he would have committed political suicide. If he seemed to soften his agitation against slavery in the months after Sumter, it was because he was now convinced that his goal would soon be attained. The opinion of John Quincy Adams that emancipation was one of the war powers did much to reconcile Sumner, who had first made his name in the peace crusade, to the outbreak of hostilities. As

[6] For a review of these appointments see Harry J. Carman and Reinhard H. Luthin: *Lincoln and the Patronage* (New York: Columbia University Press; 1943), Chap. 4.

[7] June 15, 1861, Sumner MSS.

soon as he learned of the Confederates' attack he informed Lincoln that now "under the war power the right had come to him to emancipate the slaves." [8]

Though Lincoln did not act at once, Sumner felt sure that he would ultimately understand that "Slavery will go down in blood," and he did his best to persuade the President. Returning to Washington in late May, Sumner approved the cautious policy Lincoln had thus far pursued, but he urged the President to be ready to strike at slavery when the proper time came. Union defeat at Bull Run convinced Sumner that the moment had come to proclaim emancipation, but he could not get the President to move.[9] Vexed by Lincoln's slowness, Sumner nevertheless recognized that he was "a deeply convinced and faithful anti-slavery man" and felt he would soon be obliged to act.[1]

This conviction accounted for the note of euphoria in Sumner's correspondence during the bleak months of 1861 when it seemed that the nation was dissolving. Convinced that good would come from ill, that emancipation would result from the proslavery conspiracy, he announced: "Others may despair; I do not. Others may see gloom; I cannot." "I fancy that you agree with me in thinking these times the best we have had since—for many a year," he wrote an old antislavery colleague on Septem-

[8] Donald: *Sumner*, p. 388. A day or two before, learning from the President that the fort would be provisioned and held, Sumner told Lincoln: "Then the War Power will be in motion, and with it great consequences." Charles Sumner: *Works* (Boston: Lee and Shepard; 1870–83), VI, 30. This is the edition of Sumner's writings which he himself collected and edited, and he lived to see half the volumes through the press. In the following pages I have cited this collection except where in editing his speeches and writings Sumner made significant alterations. Wherever possible I have collated the *Works* with the original manuscripts or at least with the contemporary pamphlet editions of Sumner's writings.

[9] Sumner: *Works*, VI, 30–1. After the defeat at Bull Run there were attempts to blame Sumner, along with other outspoken antislavery Senators, for pressing Lincoln to order the unprepared Union army forward. New York *Herald*, June 20, 1861; Worthington C. Ford (ed.): *A Cycle of Adams Letters, 1861–1865* (Boston: Houghton Mifflin Company; 1920), I, 22. In fact, Sumner made no attempt to guide military policy but left that subject to his colleague, Wilson. Whenever correspondents sent him suggestions about strategy and weapons, he forwarded them to the proper authorities with a note—e.g.: "I have not the knowledge which enables me to express an opinion on the military question, but I think it merits attention." Sumner to Lincoln, Oct. 25, 1863, Lincoln MSS.

[1] Schurz: *Reminiscences*, II, 240–1; Sumner to Duchess of Argyll, June 4, 1861, Argyll MSS.

ber 3. Soon afterwards he predicted to George William Curtis: "It is a glorious moment—with grander moments at hand." [2]

• 4 •

Sumner's confidence in Lincoln derived in large part from working with him to shape Union diplomacy. At the time of his inauguration the President was unversed in foreign affairs. According to Lord Lyons, the British minister in Washington, Lincoln appeared to possess a comprehensive "ignorance of everything but Illinois village politics." He was expected to turn over control of foreign policy to his Secretary of State, William H. Seward, who openly boasted that because of "the utter absence of any acquaintance with the subject in the chief [executive]," his would be the guiding hand in Union diplomacy.[3]

By April, however, Lincoln had become aware that his Secretary of State might prove a very dangerous guide. In a confidential memorandum titled "Some thoughts for the President's Consideration," Seward on April 1 proposed that the United States should seek explanations from Spain, France, Great Britain, and Russia and, if the replies were not satisfactory, should declare war against the first two of these powers. Not a momentary aberration, this remarkable document was the outgrowth of policies which Seward had matured during the secession crisis, when he conceived the notion that he could arouse latent Unionist sentiment in the South by diverting attention from sectional issues. In early February he confided to Rudolph Schleiden, the minister of the Hanseatic League in Washington, "that nothing would give [him] so much pleasure as to see a European Power interfere in favour of South Carolina—for . . . then he should 'pitch into' the European Power, and South Carolina and the seceding states would soon join him in doing so." Behind Seward's policy lay his strong faith in American patriotism; he was

[2] Sumner to Julius Rockwell, Sept. 3, 1861, Rockwell MSS.; Curtis to C. E. Norton, Dec. 6, 1861, Curtis MSS. All references to the Curtis MSS. are, except where otherwise expressly identified, to the large collection in the Houghton Library.

[3] Lyons to Lord John Russell, April 9, 1861, Russell MSS.; Charles Francis Adams: Diary, Mar. 16, 1861, Adams MSS.

confident that an attack upon any part of the United States by a foreign power would make "all the hills of South Carolina pour forth their population to the rescue." Behind it may also have been the calculation that Southern planters would rather rejoin the Union than see the North seize Cuba, the last feasible area for Southern expansion, free the slaves on that island, and, by producing cotton and sugar with free labor, compete with Confederate staples in the European market.[4]

Quietly burying Seward's fantastic proposal in the files, the President began looking for a more reliable adviser in foreign affairs. It was inevitable that he should turn to Sumner, whose position on the Foreign Relations Committee, whose acquaintance with international law, and whose standing in the Republican party made him the one possible counterweight to Seward. Lincoln knew that the two men had long been at odds, for Sumner through the 1850's grew increasingly dubious about Seward's commitment to the antislavery cause and during the secession crisis almost hysterically denounced Seward's support of compromise with the South. During the early weeks of Lincoln's administration Sumner disagreed with the Secretary of State over appointments, and he vigorously objected to Seward's decision to blockade the Southern ports, a step which Sumner feared would amount to virtual recognition of the Confederates as belligerents. Sumner was also unhappy over the Secretary's truculent despatches directing Union representatives abroad to have no further dealings with any governments that might recognize the Confederacy.

There is nothing to indicate that Lincoln ever showed Seward's April Fool's Day memorandum to Sumner, but from Schleiden and other ministers in Washington the Senator learned the drift of the Secretary's thinking. Sumner also had a virtual spy in the State Department in the person of the eccentric Polish exile, Count Adam Gurowski, for whom he had secured a

[4] Lyons to Russell, Feb. 4, 1861, Russell MSS.; Allan Nevins: *The War for the Union: The Improvised War, 1861–1862* (New York: Charles Scribner's Sons; 1959), pp. 62–3. For analyses of Seward's policy, see Frederic Bancroft: *The Life of William H. Seward* (New York: Harper & Brothers Publishers; 1900), II, Chaps. 29–30; Glyndon G. Van Deusen: *William Henry Seward* (New York: Oxford University Press; 1967), Chaps. 19–20.

job as a translator. These sources informed him that the "*policy of insincerity,*" which he labeled "*Sewardism,*" had so "crept into our foreign relations . . . that there is not a foreign minister who does not distrust our Secretary." By the time Sumner returned to Massachusetts in late April he knew enough to tell his closest friend, Henry Wadsworth Longfellow, that he did "not like Seward, nor his policy," since he was "not frank and straightforward; only a cunning contriver of little plots; and not a true man." [5]

Not until Sumner went back to Washington for ten days at the end of May did Lincoln directly enlist him as his foreign policy adviser. During the intervening weeks Seward had continued to assail the European powers so strongly that Lord Lyons reluctantly concluded "that it may be impossible to deter this Government from offering provocations to Great Britain, which neither our honour nor our interest will allow us to brook." [6] On May 21 the Secretary wrote to Charles Francis Adams a despatch apparently designed to bring on war. Responding to the news of Queen Victoria's proclamation of neutrality, which recognized that a state of war existed in North America and acknowledged the Confederacy as a belligerent—but not as an independent nation—Seward directed Adams to demand that the British government acquiesce in the blockade of the Southern coast, acknowledge that the United States had the right to treat captured Confederate privateers as pirates, and promise that it would henceforth have no intercourse, official or unofficial, with Confederate emissaries. The penalty would be war "between the European and the American branches of the British race," a war like that of the Revolutionary era, which could only result in suffering for Britain and triumph for the United States. This "bold remonstrance," as Seward himself called it, Adams was directed to read to Lord John Russell, the British Foreign Minister.[7]

[5] Sumner to R. H. Dana, Jr., April 14, 1861, Dana MSS.; Longfellow: Journal, April 29 and May 13, 1861, Longfellow MSS.

[6] Lyons to Russell, May 20, 1861, copy, Lyons MSS.

[7] J. G. Randall: *Lincoln the President: Springfield to Gettysburg* (New York: Dodd, Mead & Company; 1945), II, 35–7.

When Lincoln received this bellicose document, he showed it to Sumner. With shocked outrage the Senator read the despatch, and he enthusiastically approved Lincoln's proposal to excise the more offensive passages and to mark the entire document as being for Adams's information only, not to be read or presented at the British Foreign Office. Trying to learn what lay behind this explosion of Seward's, Sumner hastened to visit both Lord Lyons and Henri Mercier, the French minister. Both told him of the Secretary's repeated denunciations of the European powers, attacks stronger in his dinner-table conversation than in his despatches. Calling on Seward himself, Sumner found him raving about the French and British recognition of Confederate belligerency. "God damn them, I'll give them hell," the Secretary shouted. "I'm no more afraid of them than I am of Robert Toombs." Feeling authorized by the confidence the President had just shown, Sumner warned Seward: "The issues of peace and war between England and America do not rest with you, and henceforth every statement put forth from Washington concerning European powers will be carefully watched." Back at the White House, he told Lincoln of his interview with the Secretary of State and urged: "You must watch him and overrule him." [8]

Raging that there were now too many Secretaries of State in Washington,[9] Seward continued his bellicose course. He ignored many of Lincoln's suggestions for toning down his despatch to Adams. Though he marked it, as the President had directed, confidential, for the minister's use only, he already intended to publish it, along with all the other diplomatic correspondence however indiscreet or personal, in the massive annual compilations which the State Department began to issue in the fall of 1861. In his uninhibited social intercourse with Washington diplomats the Secretary was so unrestrained in denouncing Great Britain and France that Lyons on June 6 felt obliged to warn his government that "a sudden declaration of war by the

[8] Edward Everett: Diary, Aug. 31, 1861, Everett MSS.; Moncure D. Conway: *Autobiography* (Boston: Houghton Mifflin and Company; 1904), I, 350–1. I have deleted the italics in quoting from Conway.

[9] Montgomery Blair to Gideon Welles, Dec. 12, 1873, Welles MSS.

United States against Great Britain appears to me by no means impossible." [1]

Fearfully Sumner observed this "new madness" into which Seward had fallen, and when he returned to Boston in June he told his friends that the Secretary of State, "distrusted and overruled in the Cabinet, and disliked and distrusted by the diplomats," was "pursuing a course of correspondence, language and manner, calculated to bring England and France to coldness if not to open rupture." [2] Sumner's distress became greater when he received a confidential letter from his old friend, the Duke of Argyll, now a member of the British cabinet, warning against the reckless spirit which Seward was exhibiting, against the high-handed and offensive things he was saying, and especially against the Secretary's apparent opinion "that the English people cant and wont take offence at *anything* the America Government may do to their ships—or their people." [3]

Anxiously Sumner attempted to fathom the Secretary's inexplicable and dangerous course. He himself was convinced that the best policy for the Union was to inflict as little injury as possible on the powerful British manufacturers who depended upon Southern cotton and to ally "to the North the Anti-Slavery Party in England, as a counterpoise to the allurements held out by the South to the trading and manufacturing interests." [4] He could only conclude that the Secretary of State must be mad. Seward, he declared some years later, "lost his head when he lost the [Republican] nomination at Chicago and has done nothing but blunder since." [5]

It seems never to have occurred to Sumner that Seward might be not crazy but cunning. The Secretary's irritable jingo-

[1] Lyons to Russell, June 6, 1861, Papers of the [British] Foreign Office: United States, Public Records Office (hereinafter cited as F. O. 5, PRO). For a discussion of the embarrassments rising from Seward's publication of despatches, see [William B. Reed]; *A Review of Mr. Seward's Diplomacy, by a Northern Man* (Philadelphia; 1862), pp. 3–9.

[2] Sumner to Hamilton Fish, May 22, 1861, copy, Fish MSS.; R. H. Dana, Jr., to C. F. Adams, June 4, 1861, Adams MSS.

[3] Argyll to Sumner, June 4, 1861, Sumner MSS.

[4] Lyons to Russell, May 20, 1861, copy, Lyons MSS. The British minister was here quoting an unnamed "eminent Senator, well acquainted with Europe" —obviously Sumner.

[5] Sumner to W. W. Story, Dec. 16, 1866, MS., Huntington Lib.

ism was carefully calculated, so that the British and French would do nothing that might upset such a seemingly volatile official. Remembering that "the first business of a statesman and Minister here is to keep the confidence of his own countrymen," Seward also hoped that his belligerence would strengthen the Lincoln government in the North and possibly that his unwearying appeal to American nationalism might serve, when hostilities ceased, to rally moderate men, mostly former Whigs, of South and North behind a new political party that would repudiate alike the excesses of the antislavery Republicans and the extravagances of the pro-Southern Democrats. "At heart always inclined to peaceful and moderate counsels" in foreign affairs, Seward asserted in confidence that he could not afford to "lessen his means of usefulness" by appearing conciliatory toward European powers. Indeed, he wrote to Adams, who was concerned over his chief's reported bellicosity toward Lord Lyons: "You could do no greater harm, than by inducing an opinion that I am less decided in my intercourse with the British Minister than I am reputed to be or less determined to maintain the pride and dignity of our Government." [6]

Ignorant of Seward's intent, Sumner consulted with Boston friends like Edward Everett, who had served both as minister to Great Britain and as Secretary of State, and Richard Henry Dana, Jr., who was a close student of international law, in an effort to plumb the Secretary's policy. Unquestionably he talked too freely and too much. When word of these conversations filtered back to Washington, it served further to poison relationships between the Secretary and the Senator.

Dana wrote Adams that the Senator had fiercely denounced Seward and added: "I have reason to believe that his correspondence with England, (which is large, and in influential quarters) . . . is in the same style." [7] In fact, Dana had no evidence at all for his statement, for Sumner's letters to his many European friends in 1861 contained no animadversions upon Seward but

[6] Seward to Adams, July 9, 1861, Adams MSS.; Lyons to Russell, July 20, 1861, Russell MSS. For Seward's later plans for a regrouping of political forces, see LaWanda and John H. Cox: *Politics, Principle and Prejudice, 1865–1866* (New York: The Free Press of Glencoe; 1963), Chaps. 1–2.

[7] Dana to Adams, June 4, 1861, Adams MSS.

stressed the pacific intentions of the Washington administration.[8] It was not Sumner who aroused British suspicions of Seward; it was Lord Lyons.[9] But when Adams, bitterly hostile to Sumner, received Dana's letter, he fully believed the accusation against Sumner and promptly wrote Seward that the "prevailing tone of distrust of your policy and motives" was largely attributable to "the very hostile manner in which one of the Senators of my state is in the constant habit of speaking about you every where in private." The Secretary of State, in turn, credited Adams's misstatement and added to the minister's ill will by reminding him: "If I could have listened favorably to energetic remonstrances from the *cidevant* friend to whom you refer against your appointment, he and I might still have been friends."[1]

· 5 ·

Sumner enjoyed being a responsible member of the Lincoln administration. For a Senator who had served ten years in the minority, it was headily exciting to have instant access to the President, to read the secret telegrams at the War Department, to exercise minute surveillance over the State Department. After

[8] During the first nine months of 1861 there were no attacks upon Seward in Sumner's frequent letters to John Bright, Richard Cobden, W. E. Gladstone, the Duke and Duchess of Argyll, and other British friends. Indeed, the Secretary of State was rarely mentioned. In writing to the Duchess of Argyll on June 4, 1861, Sumner did refer to "a sinister influence" near the President, only to add that it was "now checked" (Argyll MSS.). Not until October 15 did Sumner make his first explicit reference in his trans-Atlantic correspondence to his differences with Seward: "Several times I have been obliged to oppose the Secretary of State, who has been disposed to a course of much harshness" (Sumner to Bright, Oct. 15, 1861, Bright MSS.). Of course there is no doubt that influential Britons knew indirectly of Sumner's low opinion of Seward. Both Dana and Everett helped pass along the news, and Sumner made indiscreet remarks about the Secretary to the American correspondent of *The Times* of London. William H. Russell: *My Diary North and South* (Boston: T. O. H. P. Burnham; 1863), pp. 377–8 and 386–7. See also the charges against Sumner in the New York *Herald*, Dec. 31, 1861, and in Thurlow Weed to Seward, Dec. 31, 1861, Seward MSS.

[9] Lyons begged the Foreign Minister to ask the Duke and Duchess of Argyll "to make Mr. Sumner aware of the real perils to which Mr. Seward and the Cabinet are exposing the Country." Lyons to Russell, May 21, 1861, Russell MSS.

[1] Adams to Seward, June 21, 1861, Seward MSS.; Seward to Adams, July 9, 1861, Adams MSS. See also C. F. Adams: Diary, June 21, 1861, and C. F. Adams to C. F. Adams, Jr., June 21, 1861, Adams MSS.

Seward's "bold remonstrance," Lincoln gave Sumner a virtual veto over foreign policy. Before Congress assembled in July he authorized the Senator to go through all the foreign correspondence since the inauguration; he asked Sumner's advice on that part of his message to Congress dealing with foreign affairs; and he repeatedly consulted with him on legal questions relating to the blockade.[2] When it became known that Sumner was, in effect, setting up his own state department at the opposite end of Pennsylvania Avenue, his presence at diplomatic dinners and soirées became as indispensable as that of Seward. Visiting foreigners in Washington, like Prince Napoleon, a cousin of Napoleon III, naturally sought out Sumner, because he was the only Senator who spoke fluent French, because he had such a wide acquaintance abroad, and because he exercised power.[3]

For that power there was, however, the price of tacit acquiescence in the policies of the Lincoln administration. So long as Sumner remained in Washington, he did not find that price too high. To be sure, Seward continued in the State Department, but under Sumner's watchful eye he grew "mild and gentle" in his conduct toward foreign powers.[4] Lincoln did not act to free the slaves, but more and more people agreed that slavery could not survive the war, and General Benjamin F. Butler, the former Massachusetts Democratic Congressman, pointed out a practical road to emancipation by freeing as "contrabands" the slaves who fled to his lines. Though the Union had still to win a major victory, young George B. McClellan was reorganizing the army after the disaster at Bull Run, and Sumner was convinced that the general was "a greater soldier than any, on this Continent, and as a strategist unsurpassed." [5]

Once Sumner returned to Massachusetts, he came to feel that power came at too high a cost. The minor concessions, the day-by-day adjustments so necessary for the running of a government, could be explained to him in Washington, but back in

[2] Sumner to J. G. Palfrey, June 26, 1861, Palfrey MSS.; Sumner to Dana, June 20 and July 18, 1861, Dana MSS.

[3] Camille Ferri Pisani: *Prince Napoleon in America, 1861*, trans. by Georges J. Joyaux (Bloomington, Ind.: Indiana University Press; 1959), p. 102.

[4] Sumner to Dana, June 30, 1861, Dana MSS.

[5] John E. Lodge to Sumner, May 9, 1862, quoting Sumner, and Sumner to Lieber, Aug. 24, 1861, both in Sumner MSS.

Boston they appeared to threaten a serious betrayal of principle. He began to suspect that there might be "peril from some new surrender to Slavery." With alarm he learned that Simon Cameron, the Secretary of War, in overturning Butler's "contraband" order, had announced: "It is the desire of the President that all existing rights in all the States be fully respected and maintained." Anxiously he read a speech that Secretary of the Interior Caleb B. Smith made at a Providence, Rhode Island, clambake: "The Government of the United States has no more right to interfere with the institution of Slavery in South Carolina than it has to interfere with the peculiar institution of Rhode Island, whose benefits I have enjoyed." Most alarming of all was the decision of the President himself to overrule the proclamation of General John C. Frémont ordering the property of all rebels in Missouri confiscated and "their slaves, if any they have, hereby declared freemen." Since Lincoln was not nearby to explain his fear that Frémont's proclamation would drive the border states out of the Union, Sumner put the worst construction upon his action. "To me the President's letter is full—too full of meaning," Sumner lamented to Lieber. "Our President is now a dictator, imperator,—which you will; but how vain to have the power of a god and not to use it godlike." [6]

Letters from abroad added to Sumner's disenchantment with the Lincoln administration. From Turin Marsh wrote that, though Italians were disposed to favor the Union, Lincoln's failure to strike down slavery caused many to feel "that the professions of the Republican party were but words." The capable career diplomat at Brussels, Henry S. Sanford, reported that European sympathy for the North was based upon the expectation that the war would lead to emancipation and that by fall, when cotton supplies would run low, there would be "a terrific *howl*" against the blockade of Southern ports. Germans, declared Theodore S. Fay, who had served as minister to Switzerland, increasingly believed "that we are not fighting against slavery and the African [slave] trade *at all*, but to preserve our financial

[6] Sept. 17, 1861, ibid.

despotism over the South." Still more disturbing were Sumner's letters from Great Britain, where even Harriet Martineau, whose writings in the London *Daily News* presented the Northern case to a large British public, could coolly remark that the Union had "no general intention, or wish, to abolish slavery." John Bright, the strongest defender of the Union in British public life, warned Sumner that support for the Northern cause was dwindling but predicted that if the United States government directly attacked slavery there would then "be no power in this country able to give any support to the South." [7]

At the same time Sumner came to realize that there were political disadvantages in being a member of Lincoln's team. Already people in Massachusetts were talking about the 1862 elections, which would choose a legislature that must either reelect Sumner or select a successor. The antislavery men who formed the backbone of Sumner's political following were troubled by his failure to attack slavery and by his willingness to follow Lincoln's conciliatory policies. Chronically suspicious of all men in power, they might easily be persuaded that even Sumner had sold out.

Their defection, it was clear, would not be compensated for by greater support from the Whiggish, moderately antislavery wing of the Massachusetts Republican party. So virulent were the animosities of the past, nothing Sumner could ever say or do would win their hearty approval. His work with the Lincoln administration in 1861 did not convince them of his statesmanship; it merely alerted them to the possibility that his hold upon the abolitionist element might be weakening. Always hostile, they had long sought an opportunity to unseat Sumner. During the secession crisis they had denounced Sumner's intransigence and had rallied behind Charles Francis Adams's plan of compromise. As early as February the chairman of the Republican state committee, William Claflin, warned Sumner of "a desperate ef-

[7] See the following letters in the Sumner MSS.: from Marsh, July 26, 1861; from Sanford, July 19, 1861; from Fay, Aug. 22 and Sept. 3, 1861; and from Martineau, Aug. 2, 1861. Bright's letter is in *Mass. Hist. Soc. Proceedings*, XLVI (1912–13), 93–7.

fort, under the surface," to force him from the Senate. "*This* Legislature," wrote John E. Lodge a month later, "would elect you unanimously for the Senate. The *next* one [to meet in January 1862] is doubtful—and the *next still* [which would have the actual choice of a Senator] is more so." [8]

Aware that Sumner's friends controlled the machinery of the Massachusetts Republican party, these conservatives welcomed the idea that in the national crisis loyal men should abandon all former party labels and join in a new Union party, or People's party, which presumably they could dominate. The first public step toward party realignment occurred in September, when at a large rally in Faneuil Hall Benjamin F. Hallett, who had led the Massachusetts delegation to the 1860 Democratic convention, opposed party nominations for the coming elections, since partisan candidacies could "do no good for the country and may do harm." Hallett urged all Massachusetts voters to support candidates who believed the sole purpose of the war was "the re-establishment of the supreme Government of the Union in all the States and Territories." About the same time, the Constitutional Unionists, who had supported John Bell and Edward Everett in 1860, announced a willingness to confer with both Democrats and Republicans "in reference to an abandonment of existing party organizations, and the calling of a People's Convention to nominate State officers." [9]

Though these plans were aimed directly at preventing the reelection of John A. Andrew, the energetic abolitionist war governor of Massachusetts, and indirectly at choosing a conservative Senator the following year, there was little Sumner could overtly do to check them. Many voters thought it entirely reasonable in time of war to forget about parties and to rally behind the Union. If Sumner denounced such a move, he would be thought to be acting in his own self-interest, and he was acutely aware how much his hold upon young and idealistic voters depended upon his being above the sordid concerns of practical politics. If,

[8] Claflin to Sumner, Feb. 7, 1861, Sumner MSS.; Lodge to Sumner, Mar. 4, 1861, ibid.

[9] Edith Ellen Ware: *Political Opinion in Massachusetts During Civil War and Reconstruction* (New York: Columbia University; 1916), pp. 76–9. I have omitted italics from the Hallett quotation.

on the other hand, he tried to cooperate in the Union party movement, he would surely lose.

Claflin's invitation to address the Republican state convention, which met at Worcester in October, offered Sumner an escape from his dilemma. His address, one of the briefest and most forceful of his career, was a passionate effort to prove that "the pretended right of secession" was inextricably linked with the barbarous institution of slavery. "Rebellion is Slavery itself, incarnate, living, acting, raging, robbing, murdering, according to the essential law of its being." Hence that it was idiocy to talk about a war to preserve the Union without abolishing slavery, "the main-spring of the Rebellion." "MILITARY NECESSITY, *in just self-defence*," required the United States government to abolish it, and martial law—that "higher agency . . . which is at the same time under the Constitution and above the Constitution" —gave it ample powers to act. If the national government would simply throw slavery "upon the flames madly kindled by itself," Sumner predicted, "the Rebellion will die at once." [1]

Though the speech brought down upon Sumner's head the customary obloquy from Democratic newspapers, which declared that he should be ducked in a horse pond or confined to a straightjacket,[2] it was one of the most successful he ever made. By linking the prosecution of the war with the elimination of slavery, he warned the Lincoln administration that it must reckon with the abolitionist sentiment of Massachusetts as well as with the proslavery feeling of Kentucky. By insisting upon emancipation as a Northern war aim, he helped to strengthen the cause of the Union abroad.

At the same time he succeeded in scotching the idea of a coalition party in Massachusetts. Though Dana, who was emerging as the strategist of the conservative Republicans, defeated at Worcester a resolution which called upon Lincoln to abolish slavery,[3] and though the Boston *Advertiser* and the Springfield

[1] Sumner repeated these arguments in a public lecture delivered in Boston, New York, and other cities in November. Sumner: *Works*, VI, 7–29, 71–114.

[2] For an anthology of representative press clippings, see ibid., VI, 38–53.

[3] Ford (ed.): *Cycle of Adams Letters*, I, 54; Philip D. Jordan (ed.): *Letters of Eliab Parker Mackintire of Boston* (New York: The New York Public Library; 1936), pp. 146–7.

Republican grumbled that Sumner did not speak for the whole party, his speech so completely identified Republicans with opposition both to slavery and secession as to make cooperation with other parties impossible. The Boston *Courier*, voice of the Bell-Everett faction, declared that by inviting Sumner to speak at Worcester Republicans had proved themselves insincere in talking of coalition. Sumner's "unquestionable Anti-slavery ultraisms" had killed the whole idea of a Union party.

That was precisely what Sumner had intended. As the old party lines held firm, the Republicans again swept to victory in the fall elections, and Andrew was reelected governor. Sumner's personal following was more devoted than ever. For the first time since the outbreak of the war, his mails were again filled with tributes from antislavery men. Abolitionist Samuel E. Sewall reported that almost everybody he knew thought the speech "eloquent, statesmanlike, and timely." "You have shown the way," declared Lewis Tappan, "and the only way." "I could not take the hazard of advising you to make [the speech]," wrote his old friend Wendell Phillips, "though I told you in your circumstances I should; but now you've done it, I can say it was *wise* and *well*,—your duty to the country, to the hour, yourself, the slave—to your fame as a statesman, and your duty as a leader." [4]

• 6 •

It was not immediately clear how Sumner's speech at Worcester would affect his relations with the Lincoln administration. Recognizing that the Senator was advocating policies directly contrary to those of the President, Nahum Capen, the former postmaster of Boston, urged Seward, who was responsible for arresting disloyal citizens in the North, to take official cognizance of the speech, since "such discourses . . . do more to paralyse the strong arm of government than all other adverse influences here in the North." Others thought less of arresting Sumner than of reading him out of the party. Anticipating such a rupture, Postmaster General Montgomery Blair reassured Lin-

[4] See the sampling of Sumner's correspondence printed in Sumner: *Works*, VI, 54–64.

coln that few, even in Massachusetts, would follow Sumner's extreme leadership.[5]

A diplomatic crisis kept Sumner from having to choose between strengthening his political position at home and cooperating with the national administration. On November 8, 1861, the U.S.S. *San Jacinto,* commanded by Captain Charles Wilkes, stopped a British mail packet, the *Trent,* and forcibly removed two Confederate emissaries, James M. Mason and John Slidell, who were sailing to take up their diplomatic duties in London and in Paris. An immense surge of enthusiastic approval swept through the North. Secretary of the Navy Gideon Welles approved Wilkes's action; Governor Andrew gave Wilkes a public dinner after he reached Boston, where the prisoners were confined at Fort Warren, in the harbor; when the House of Representatives met in December it promptly voted him a gold medal. Lawyers and jurists shared in the frenzy, and in Massachusetts men like Edward Everett, Dana, and Theophilus Parsons of the Harvard Law School pronounced the American action fully justified under international law.

When the news reached Boston, a friend rushed up to Sumner, who was just getting off the train from Providence, and asked for his reaction to the seizure. After learning the details of what had happened, he said promptly: "Then we will have to give them up." At dinner that evening, where most of the guests were exultant over this American triumph, he quietly but decidedly repeated his prediction: "They will have to be given up." Realizing that any statement he might make would be premature and might be in conflict with the views of the national administration, he kept silent in public, but in the tense weeks ahead there is nothing to indicate that he ever wavered from his belief that Mason and Slidell must be released.[6]

[5] Capen to Seward, Oct. 31, 1861, Seward MSS.; Blair to Lincoln, Oct. 7, 1861, Lincoln MSS.

[6] George P. Hayward to E. L. Pierce, Jan. 12, 1884, Pierce MSS.; G. H. Monroe in Hartford *Courant,* Nov. 22, 1873. In "Charles Sumner and the *Trent* Affair," *Journal of Southern History,* XXII (1956), 205–20, Victor H. Cohen correctly notes that these recollections were recorded many years after the event and agrees with Anna Laurens Dawes (*Charles Sumner* [New York: Dodd, Mead and Company; 1892], p. 165) that Sumner, "feeling that Captain Wilkes had won a great triumph, . . . was at first desirous of upholding him." For this view, however, I have found little evidence. To be sure, on November 17 Sumner sent

In private he warned Minister Dayton in Paris that he anticipated a "groundswell from Europe on account of the arrest of Mason and Slidell" and predicted that peaceful settlement would "require all possible patience on our part." [7] To help achieve that settlement he, like many other Bostonians, began looking carefully into precedents in international law, and his brother George, now bedridden with a mysterious degenerative disease, offered to assist him. According to Anthony Trollope, who was visiting at this critical juncture, even the young ladies of Boston prattled at parties about rulings of Grotius and Vattel which justified Wilkes, and it was hardly surprising that the Sumner brothers unearthed two precedents which appeared to support the captain's action. With characteristic irresponsibility, George dashed off to the Boston *Transcript* a letter summarizing his researches, and it was promptly reprinted in other newspapers. The Senator, who did not know of his brother's letter and did not see it until it was in print, simply forwarded the citations to the Secretary of State, noting that one of them seemed dubious.[8] In writing his British friends, Sumner expressed a hope that there would be no difficulties over the incident, since Wilkes had apparently followed English precedent, but most strongly he entreated: "Pray keep the peace." [9]

Returning to Washington on November 30, Sumner was distressed to discover that relations between the United States and Great Britain had deteriorated so seriously as to make peace-

---

Seward citations of two precedents which might uphold Wilkes's action, but he did not endorse these precedents. His brother George in a public letter did approve them, but the Senator explicitly stated that he did not see that letter until it was published. The two brothers often differed on legal and political questions. On the other hand, Monroe published his statement in 1873, when Sumner was still alive and when he had many enemies who would have rejoiced in exposing his past errors; none did so. It is perhaps significant, too, that Charles Francis Adams, Jr., who, like all the Adamses was sharply critical of Sumner, was obliged to conclude that the Senator's "attitude and bearing . . . throughout those trying days" were "above criticism" (*Mass. Hist. Soc. Proceedings*, XLV [1911–12], 63). No voice was raised in the Massachusetts Historical Society to contradict him. The report that Sumner accompanied Montgomery Blair to the White House on November 16 in order to urge the immediate release of Mason and Slidell is incorrect. Earl Schenck Miers (ed.): *Lincoln Day by Day* (Washington; Lincoln Sesquicentennial Commission; 1960), III, 77.

[7] Dec. 6, 1861, Dayton MSS.

[8] Sumner to Seward, Nov. 17, 1861, Miscellaneous Letters, Department of State Records.

[9] Sumner to Duchess of Argyll, Nov. 18, 1861, Argyll MSS.

ful settlement difficult. Increasingly he was puzzled by the attitude of the British government toward the American conflict. He did not know Lord Palmerston, the Prime Minister, personally, but he had expected sympathy from the other members of the triumvirate that dominated the cabinet. Russell, the Foreign Minister, who had little impressed Sumner at first sight in 1838 but who had later come to seem "one of the greatest men I have seen in England," ought surely, as a reformer and a friend of liberty, to side with the Union, yet from him came no "word . . . shewing sympathy with a constitutional Government struggling with a wicked rebellion founded upon a principle long ago repudiated by the people of England." No more friendly was W. E. Gladstone, the Chancellor of the Exchequer, whom Sumner had visited at Hawarden in 1857 and had judged in personality, in broad literary culture, and in humanitarian sympathies almost the ideal statesman. Palmerston believed the Confederates would ultimately win their independence; Russell thought that secession was legally justified and that Sumner was actuated by "a spirit of vengeance" for the Brooks assault in trying to coerce the reluctant South back into an unwanted Union; Gladstone confused the aspirations of the Confederates with the longings of the Italians for national independence. Day after day, the influential *Times* of London, which seemed to speak for the Palmerston government, published pro-Southern editorials which Sumner believed were "better for the rebel slave-drivers than an army."[1]

To Sumner these views would not have been surprising had they stemmed from a Tory government representing aristocratic families naturally sympathetic to the South. Nor would they have been unexpected had the government spoken for the British workingmen unemployed after the blockade cut off Southern cotton. But for a Liberal government in Britain to favor the Confederacy seemed to him inconceivable. Surely Britons misunderstood the nature of the American conflict.

From the outbreak of the war Sumner set himself earnestly to the task of enlightening his friends abroad. He scornfully

[1] Sumner to Duchess of Argyll, June 4, 1861, and Nov. 11, 1861, ibid.; Russell to Lyons, Oct. 26, 1861, copy, Russell MSS.

dismissed Gladstone's notion that the Southerners, like the Italians or the Poles, were simply fighting for their national existence; the secession of the South was the result of a conspiracy of fewer than twenty men. Insistently he denied that the protective Morrill tariff of 1861 gave the British reason to favor the South, but in the interest of "moderation, conciliation, and good will" he opposed further increases in tariff duties during the July session of Congress. Recognizing that cutting off Southern cotton would produce hardship abroad, he hoped that Britons would realize that in the long run their prosperity was "linked with that of our Northern States." [2]

Most of all he sought to enlist British antislavery opinion on the Northern side. On his two long trips abroad he had come to know the most prominent British abolitionists, especially those in the circle around the beautiful and philanthropic Duchess of Sutherland, the sister of Sumner's warm friend the Earl of Carlisle (formerly Lord Morpeth) and the mother of the generous and devotedly antislavery Duchess of Argyll. So strong was British aversion to slavery, Sumner was convinced, that once the American conflict was understood as a war for emancipation all thought of aiding or recognizing the South must die. Privately Palmerston, who was not noted for effusions of philanthropic spirit, came to the same conclusion, judging that it would be "repugnant to English Feelings and Principles" to "mix ourselves up with the acknowledgement of Slavery and the Principle that a slave escaping to a free Soil State, should be followed and claimed and recovered like a Horse or an ox." [3]

The difficulty in persuading Britons that "Slavery is the single cause" of the war, Sumner understood, derived from the failure of the Union government to take effective action for emancipation. Lincoln announced that he had no intention of touching slavery in the Southern states; the Congress voted that the objective of the war was to restore the Union, not to free the slaves; Seward instructed American diplomats that the Union

[2] *Cong. Globe*, 37 Cong., 1 Sess., p. 316; Sumner to Duchess of Argyll, June 4, 1861, Argyll MSS.

[3] Palmerston to Edward Ellice, May 5, 1861, copy, Broadlands MSS. Cf. Palmerston to Russell, Dec. 30, 1861, Russell MSS.

government had no plans to interfere in the South's domestic institutions. All these were steps which Sumner had deplored, mostly because they were wrong, partly because they would adversely influence public opinion abroad. But he felt that, even if the Union government because of its written Constitution, the complex federal system, and the limitations of practical politics, could not yet fully avow its antislavery policies, foreigners ought to understand that the whole purpose of the war was "to prevent the foundation of a piratical nation whose cornerstone shall be Slavery." They ought to see that they were witnessing "one of the great epochs of Human History," for the victory of freedom in the United States would lead throughout the world to "the probable destruction of African Slavery (which cannot stand any where if destroyed here.)" To impress this truth abroad had been one of Sumner's purposes in delivering his Worcester address.[4]

Now, however, it seemed that the effect of that speech, and of Sumner's whole campaign of foreign correspondence, would be lost as the British seemingly forgot about slavery in an explosion of wrath over the *Trent* affair. "You may stand for this but damned if I will!" Palmerston blazed when he heard the news in cabinet meeting. To handle the emergency he appointed a special cabinet war committee, headed by George Cornewall Lewis, hitherto a strong supporter of the Union cause. Eight thousand British troops were readied for shipment to Canada, the fleet was put on the alert, and export of munitions to the United States was stopped. "It all looks like war," Russell wrote gloomily; Lewis echoed: "inevitable war." The Foreign Minister directed Lord Lyons to ask for the release of Mason and Slidell and an apology as well; in a private note he instructed the British minister to withdraw from the United States unless these conditions were met within seven days.

Sumner did not, of course, know the details of these British plans, but his overseas correspondents gave him an alarmingly clear picture of the danger of war. Richard Cobden, the distinguished British Liberal leader, warned that Wilkes's action, whether legal or not, would certainly encourage the hopes of

[4] Sumner to Duchess of Argyll, Nov. 11, 1861, Argyll MSS.; Sumner to Martin F. Tupper, Nov. 11, 1861, Tupper MSS.

those who wished to embroil Great Britain in the war. John Bright wrote Sumner that the law officers of the Crown had ruled that the seizure of Mason and Slidell was illegal, and he reported that the cabinet had held two meetings on the crisis. Speaking both for herself and for her husband, the Duchess of Argyll bluntly called the seizure "the maddest act that ever was done, and, unless the [United States] government intend to force us to war, utterly inconceivable." [5]

Gravely troubled, Sumner at once took his correspondence to the White House, where he found Lincoln much moved and astonished by these reports and by the demand for release of the prisoners which Lord Lyons on December 19 had just made to Seward. During the next week Sumner met with the President almost daily, and the two men anxiously assessed the consequences that would flow from war with Great Britain. The British navy would not merely break the Union blockade of the South but would bottle up Northern ports and sweep the Union fleet from the seas. France would join in recognizing the independence of the Confederacy in order to forward Napoleon III's dream of a Latin empire in Mexico. Once the South, with British and French assistance, won its freedom, English manufacturers would be smuggled across the border into the North, and ultimately "the whole North American continent [would become] a manufacturing dependency of England." [6]

To avoid these disastrous consequences, Lincoln pledged to Sumner: "There will be no war unless England is bent upon having one." Vexed that European governments seemed determined to misunderstand the pacific temper of his foreign policy, the President offered to ignore bureaucratic channels and diplomatic protocol and talk to the British minister face to face. "If I could see Lord Lyons," he told Sumner rather wistfully, "I could show him in five minutes that I am heartily for peace." Sumner warned that such a step would be an impropriety, one that would certainly ruffle the Secretary of State. Instead he suggested submitting the question to arbitration, either by the sovereign of

[5] Cobden to Sumner, Nov. 29, 1861, Sumner MSS.; *Mass. Hist. Soc. Proceedings*, XLV (1911–12), 148–50; XLVII (1913–14), 108.

[6] Sumner to Lieber, Dec. 24, 1861, Sumner MSS.

Sumner during the Lincoln Administration

MASSACHUSETTS HISTORICAL SOCIETY

Sumner and Longfellow in 1863

THE NATIONAL ARCHIVES

Prussia or by a group of learned publicists. Seizing upon Sumner's idea, Lincoln began drafting such a proposal. Remembering Sumner's distrust of Seward, Lincoln promised that he himself would scrutinize whatever reply was finally given to Lord Lyons, "word for word, in order that no expression should remain which could create bad blood anew." [7]

Temporarily reassured, Sumner grew alarmed once more when he read the letters brought by the next packet from Britain. Though in fact by mid-December British opinion had considerably softened, war had appeared imminent when Bright and Cobden wrote him on December 6 and 7. Both great British Liberals feared a lack of firm leadership in the United States, and Bright warned: "I need not tell you who are much better acquainted with modern history than I am, that Nations *drift* into wars, . . . often thro' the want of a resolute hand at some moment early in the quarrel." Both urged the United States to make "a courageous stroke, not of arms, but of moral action, in order to avert war." Bright favored submitting the issue to arbitration, just as Sumner had suggested to Lincoln, and Cobden urged the unconditional release of the prisoners; but both hoped that any settlement would be accompanied by "a complete abandonment of the old code of maritime law as upheld by England and the European powers" and the substitution of the rule that henceforth all "private property at sea should be exempt from capture." "You know that I write . . . with as much earnest wish for your international welfare as if I were a native and a citizen of your country," Bright concluded. Cobden was more personal: "I write to you of course, in confidence, and I write to you what I would not write to any other American,—nay what it would be perhaps improper for any other Englishman than myself to utter to any other American but yourself." [8]

When Sumner asked for an opportunity to present these

[7] Edward Waldo Emerson and Waldo Emerson Forbes (eds.): *Journals of Ralph Waldo Emerson* (Boston: Houghton Mifflin Company; 1910–14), IX, 380; Roy P. Basler (ed.) *The Collected Works of Abraham Lincoln* (New Brunswick, N.J.: Rutgers University Press; 1953), V, 62–4 [hereinafter cited as Lincoln: *Works*]; Ephraim D. Adams: *Great Britain and the American Civil War* (London: Longmans, Green and Company; 1925), I, 231, note.

[8] Cobden to Sumner, Dec. 5 and 6, 1861, Sumner MSS.; *Mass. Hist. Soc. Proceedings*, XLV, 152.

views to the President and the Secretary of State,[9] he was invited to attend a critical meeting of the cabinet, held at ten o'clock on Christmas morning in the White House. In part, no doubt, Lincoln wanted him present in order to convince Wilkes's supporters in the cabinet that there was a real danger of war with Great Britain. Inviting Sumner to the meeting served also to protect the Lincoln administration from attack in Congress. Since Sumner had suggested arbitration of the case, a course which Lincoln himself had seriously considered, it was expedient to secure his prior consent if any other policy was to be followed. Whether Sumner argued the case for arbitration at the Christmas Day meeting is not recorded, but if he did, he was soon persuaded that Mason and Slidell must be immediately given up, since the threatened war with Great Britain resulted in a "paralysis upon all our naval and military movements against the Rebellion." Convinced "that upon our decision depended the dearest interest, probably the existance [*sic*], of the nation," Sumner agreed with the members of the cabinet that Seward should proceed with a despatch announcing the release of the two Confederates.[1]

Two nights later, after an elaborate dinner at Seward's, which was marred only by the fact that John J. Crittenden could not hold his tobacco spittle and expectorated upon the carpet, Sumner and the other members of the Foreign Relations Committee went to Seward's room to hear the final version of the Secretary's reply to Lord Lyons.[2] Sinking down into his leather chair, tossing one leg over its arm, and lighting a potent black cigar, the wiry little Secretary read his letter aloud, in his curiously muffled voice. One of the best despatches Seward ever wrote, this remarkable document revealed the Secretary's fondness for strutting before an American audience and his basic contempt for international law. "It is sometimes a good thing,"

[9] Undated pencil note from Sumner to "Mr. Seward or the President," misdated Sept. 1, 1863, by a cataloguer, but almost certainly written on Dec. 24, 1861, Lincoln MSS.

[1] Howard K. Beale (ed.): *The Diary of Edward Bates, 1859–1866* (Washington: Government Printing Office; 1933), pp. 213–14; Theodore C. Pease and James G. Randall (eds.): *The Diary of Orville Hickman Browning* (Springfield, Ill.: Illinois State Historical Library; 1925), I, 518–19; Sumner to Bright, Dec. 30 [1861], Bright MSS.

[2] Browning: *Diary*, I, 519; Frances A. Seward: Diary, Dec. 27, 1861, Seward MSS.

he declared scornfully, "not to know too much of it." [3] He argued that Mason and Slidell were indeed contraband of war, that Wilkes had the right to stop and search the *Trent,* and that he was entitled to capture the ministers and their despatches. But the law of nations required him not to remove the men from the ship but to take the entire vessel to a United States port for a hearing before a prize court. Wilkes's error stemmed from the fact that he followed British precedents during the Napoleonic wars, when American ships had been boarded and seamen had been impressed, precedents against which the United States always vigorously objected. In asking for the release of these two men, Great Britain was giving tacit endorsement of American principles, and the demand could not be refused without repudiating "an old, honored, and cherished American cause." Mason and Slidell would, therefore, be cheerfully liberated—though, Seward added, "if the safety of this Union require the detention of the captured persons it would be the right and duty of this government to detain them." [4]

• 7 •

"The case of the Trent *is settled,*" Sumner wrote jubilantly to Bright late that night. Also settled was the fact that Sumner, despite his Worcester speech, was still a trusted adviser of the Lincoln administration. Less certain now, however, was the extent of his control over foreign policy, for Seward emerged from the *Trent* affair with an enhanced reputation both at home and abroad. Throughout the crisis the Secretary had behaved with perfect propriety, and, despite British forebodings, he had been more prompt in the cabinet discussions to make concessions than Sumner himself. The President might reasonably wonder whether it was still necessary for Sumner to exercise what Cobden described as "a veto in a certain sense over Seward." [5]

[3] Auguste Laugel: *The United States during the Civil War* (Bloomington, Ind.: Indiana University Press; 1961), pp. 313–14.

[4] For a critical analysis of Seward's despatch, see Bancroft: *Seward,* II, 237–53. Cf. the verdict of Charles F. Adams, Jr., (*Mass. Hist. Soc. Proceedings,* XLV, 74), that Seward's despatch was "clever," not "great."

[5] Cobden to John Slagg, Dec. 6, 1861, copy, Cobden MSS.

Sumner felt it was, for he thought the Secretary betrayed a lamentable ignorance in his conduct of foreign relations. Agreeing with Seward's decision to free Mason and Slidell, he believed that the Secretary had arrived at his conclusion by the wrong path. In drafting his despatch, Seward had apparently known only of the November 12 opinion in which the British law officers had advised the Palmerston government that Wilkes had the right to take the *Trent* to a United States port but not to remove the Confederate emissaries from her; consequently the Secretary had concentrated on this single technical flaw in Wilkes's proceedings. Sumner, however, had access to a later opinion of the Queen's legal advisers, dated November 28, which flatly asserted that any interference with Confederate civilians who were on board "a merchant-ship of a neutral Power pursuing a lawful and innocent voyage" was "illegal and unjustifiable by international law." Consequently, Sumner realized, American naval commanders who followed the procedures which the Secretary had outlined might easily precipitate other crises as dangerous as that over the *Trent*.[6] Even if there were no incidents of this sort, Sumner felt that "the deepseated distrust of our Secretary of State" would lead to new diplomatic incidents unless Europe could be convinced that there was a steadier hand guiding American foreign policy.[7]

Congressional opposition to releasing the Confederate emissaries gave Sumner the opportunity to show how the Secretary of State should have acted. Even before the surrender was announced, John P. Hale, the veteran antislavery Senator from New Hampshire, warned that giving up Mason and Slidell would "reduce us to the position of a second-rate Power, and make us the vassal of Great Britain." On January 7, 1862, Democratic Representative Clement L. Vallandigham of Ohio protested

[6] For texts of the law officers' opinions, see James P. Baxter, III (ed.): "Papers Relating to Belligerent and Neutral Rights, 1861–1865," *American Historical Review*, XXXIV (1928), 84–7. An English politician, Edward Twistleton, sent extracts from both opinions to William Dwight, of Springfield, Massachusetts, who promptly forwarded them to Sumner. Sumner told Lord Lyons of having the opinions before him as he spoke on the *Trent* affair on January 9. Lyons to Russell, Feb. 3, 1862, Russell MSS. Cf. Palmerston to Russell, Feb. 19, 1862, ibid.

[7] Sumner to Lieber, Dec. 25, 1861, Sumner MSS.

against the unmanly capitulation to the British and predicted that for this national humiliation the Lincoln administration would have to pay a terrible price. To Sumner a more troublesome voice was that of Representative Benjamin F. Thomas, a Massachusetts conservative now occupying Charles Francis Adams's seat, who argued that "England has done to us a great wrong in availing herself of our moment of weakness to make a demand which, accompanied as it was by 'the pomp and circumstance of war,' was insolent in spirit and thoroughly unjust." [8]

"The fire-eating speeches already made and to be expected, seem to require an answer," Sumner told Lieber. "I flatter myself that I can state the case honorably for us." [9] Borrowing from the Library of Congress the works of Grotius, Hautefeuille, Wheaton, and other writers on international law, he carefully prepared an elaborate hour and three-quarters speech on "The Trent Case, and Maritime Rights," which he announced he would deliver to the Senate on January 9.

Despite the inclement weather, Sumner's address, which had been widely heralded in the newspapers, attracted a large audience. Nearly every Senator was present; Secretaries Chase and Cameron occupied seats on the Senate floor; the French, Russian, Austrian, Prussian, Danish, and Swedish ministers were in the diplomatic gallery, and only protocol kept Lord Lyons from attending. Entering quickly through a side door, Sumner had dressed for the occasion with more than his usual fastidious elegance. Like an actor who plans each movement for best effect, he elaborately removed his olive-green gloves, arranged his papers, and took his seat as the Senate was called to order.[1] Leaning back in his chair, with his head stooping slightly over his broad chest and his hands resting gracefully upon his crossed legs, he looked very much like an English country gentleman. His "great, sturdy, English-looking figure, with the broad, massive forehead, over which the rich mass of nut-brown hair,

[8] *Cong. Globe,* 37 Cong., 2 Sess., pp. 176–7, 208–10; John Y. Simon: "Congress Under Lincoln, 1861–1865" (unpublished Ph.D. dissertation in history, Harvard University; 1960), p. 305.

[9] Dec. 19, 1861, and Jan. 8, 1861 [i.e., 1862], Sumner MSS.

[1] New York *Herald,* Jan. 10, 1862; undated clipping by M. C. A[mes]., from Springfield *Republican,* in Sumner Scrapbooks.

streaked here and there with a line of grey, hangs loosely; the deep blue eyes, and the strangely winning smile, half bright, half full of sadness," contributed to this impression; so did his tailored English clothing, which, in a day when most public men favored funereal frockcoats, was likely to consist of "a brown coat and light waistcoat, lavender-colored or checked trousers, and shoes with English gaiters." Without saying a word during the hour while the Senate transacted its customary morning business, he was the most conspicuous figure in the chamber.[2]

At precisely one o'clock he rose to deliver his speech.[3] On three grounds he concluded that Wilkes's seizure of Mason and Slidell had been illegal and unwarranted. First, in an argument paralleling that of Seward's despatch, he contended that American usage did not authorize Wilkes to remove the envoys until the *Trent* had been brought before an American prize court, for a naval officer was not a judge. When impressing sailors from American ships during the Napoleonic wars, Great Britain had always upheld the opposing view, but now, Sumner rejoiced: "In return for the prisoners set free, we receive from Great Britain a practical assent, too long deferred, to a principle early propounded by our country, and standing forth on every page of our history." Second, Sumner contended, even had Wilkes taken the *Trent* into port, it would have been improper to remove the envoys, because according both to the principles of international law and to the provisions of numerous American treaties only military and naval personnel, not civilians, were liable to seizure. Finally, Sumner held, the vessel was not subject to seizure on the ground that it carried Confederate despatches for under American practice, endorsed by many publicists, despatches were not contraband.

"Mr. President," Sumner concluded, "let the Rebels go. Two

[2] Edward Dicey: *Six Months in the Federal States* (London: Macmillan and Co.; 1863), I, 236–7; Noah Brooks: *Washington in Lincoln's Time* (New York: The Century Co.; 1893), pp. 23–5.

[3] The manuscript of the speech, which I have followed, is in the Chicago Historical Society. The published version in Sumner's *Works* (VI, 153–218) has been considerably revised, with many verbal changes and the addition of long sections on how international law governed blockades and on whether the neutral destination of the *Trent* affected the legality of the seizure. For Sumner's literary borrowings, see Receipts for Books, 1861–1863, Library of Congress Records, p. 73.

wicked men, ungrateful to their country are let loose with the brand of Cain upon their foreheads." By opening the prison doors the United States was reinforcing the principles of international law. In demanding the release of Mason and Slidell, Great Britain had tacitly renounced her "early, long-continued tyranny" and could now join with the United States in "rendering the ocean a highway of peace, instead of a bloody field." Henceforth the "statutes of the sea, thus refined and elevated, will be the agents of peace instead of the agents of war." Reaching his peroration, with his right hand pointing high and his face flushed with excitement, Sumner concluded: "In this work our country began early. . . . And now, the time is come when [Great Britain] this [former] champion of belligerent rights has 'changed his hand and checked his pride.' Welcome to the new-found allegiance!"

As drama, Sumner's oration was highly effective, and when he sat down friends thronged about him, congratulating both him and themselves that the country had found so learned an advocate, able to reconcile the unpleasant necessity of the present with the glorious precedents of the past.[4] Indeed, as a statement of international law, Sumner's speech was superior to Seward's despatch, which Hamilton Fish characterized as being: "In style, . . . verbose and egotistical; in argument, flimsy; and in its conception and general scope . . . an abandonment of the high position we have occupied as a nation upon a great principle."[5] Certainly Sumner's position—directly contradictory to that of the Secretary of State—that neither ambassadors nor despatches were subject to seizure on the high seas was far more likely to avert future incidents.

[4] There was much general praise for Sumner's speech (e.g., Theodore Dwight Woolsey: *Introduction to the Study of International Law* [6th ed.; New York: Charles Scribner's Sons; 1899], p. 399, note) but little close analysis of his reasoning or precedents. Heinrich Marquardsen: *Der Trent-Fall* (Erlangen: Ferdinand Enke; 1862), is still the most careful study of the international law involved in the whole affair, but it does not give full consideration to Sumner's arguments. Nor, except by implication, did Dana in his elaborate note on the *Trent* affair in his edition of Henry Wheaton: *Elements of International Law* (8th ed.; Boston: Little, Brown, and Company; 1866), pp. 644–61; but Dana at the time strongly criticized Sumner's reasoning (Dana to C. F. Adams, Jan. 19, 1862, Adams MSS.), and if closely studied his discussion seriously challenges Sumner's basic arguments.

[5] Pierce, IV, 54.

Few noticed that there were serious flaws in Sumner's statement of international law. Like Seward and like most subsequent historians, he thoroughly confused the entirely legitimate right of searching neutral vessels for contraband in time of war with the obnoxious right of search for vagrant seamen claimed by the British in time of peace. As the Duke of Argyll remarked: "It is curious that Sumner should not see, what is obvious from his own statement of the case, that we might (logically) resume that practice [of impressment] tomorrow without acting inconsistently with anything we have said or done in the case of the Trent." [6] Moreover, Sumner's argument that the seizure of Mason and Slidell was illegal because of American treaties stipulating that only military and naval personnel could be removed from neutral vessels was, as Joel Parker showed at the time and as Dana proved later, fallacious.[7] The United States had no such treaty with Britain. Besides, as Secretary Chase warned, Sumner's argument on this point was potentially embarrassing to the Lincoln administration, since it directly contradicted the position just taken by the Secretary of State.[8]

"The applause accorded to this really great production," announced the usually critical New York *Herald*, "is universal and unqualified." Praise poured in on Sumner from literary men like James Russell Lowell and Charles Eliot Norton; from lawyers like Theophilus Parsons and George T. Bigelow, the Chief Justice of Massachusetts; from diplomats like James E. Harvey, the United States minister to Portugal, and John Bigelow, the American consul at Paris. In London Charles Francis Adams complained that Sumner had derived his argument almost entirely from his own despatches, and from an Adams such a left-handed compliment was a tribute. Even Dana, who disagreed with Sumner's reading of international law, was obliged to report that the *Trent* speech was "the best thing for his popularity that he had done. It was the first opportunity he has had to

[6] Argyll to C. F. Adams, Jan. 25, 1862, Adams MSS. Cf. Montague Bernard: *Notes on Some Questions Suggested by the Case of the "Trent"* (Oxford: John Henry and James Parker; 1862), p. 7, note.

[7] [Joel Parker]: "International Law," *North American Review*, CXCVI (1862), 5–6. Cf. Bernard: *Notes on . . . the "Trent,"* p. 19.

[8] David Donald (ed.): *Inside Lincoln's Cabinet: The Civil War Diaries of Salmon P. Chase* (New York: Longmans, Green and Co.; 1954), p. 59.

speak without offending half the nation." "You have done a capital thing toward conciliating the favor and good-will of our State Street gentlemen," a Boston lawyer told Sumner, and a Salem friend wrote: "At last you have satisfied even the commercial community, and they acknowledge that you have more than 'one idea.' "[9]

[9] New York *Herald,* Jan. 10, 1862; Dana to Adams, Jan. 19, 1862, Adams MSS.; Sumner: *Works,* VI, 228–42.

CHAPTER II

Riding the "Nigger" Hobby

IN Sumner's mind keeping the peace abroad was connected with freeing the slaves at home. Repeatedly he tried to convince Lincoln that by issuing an emancipation proclamation he could kill Confederate chances of recognition in Europe. In December, when it seemed that all the foreign powers chorused condemnation of the United States for Captain Wilkes's rash action, Sumner did not fail to point the moral: "Now, Mr. President, if you had done your duty earlier in the slavery matter, you would not have this trouble on you. Now you have no friends, or the country has none, because it has no policy upon slavery. . . . But if you had announced your policy about slavery, this thing could and would have come and gone and would have given you no anxiety." [1]

Though Lincoln made no move toward emancipation, Sumner was careful to avoid any break with an administration which, he was convinced, must ultimately adopt an antislavery policy. Even in his Worcester speech, announcing that emancipation was the North's best weapon against rebellion, he refrained from condemning Lincoln's failure to use this terrible swift sword. "I calmly deliver the whole question to the judgment of those on whom the responsibility rests," he declared, "content-

[1] Edward Everett Hale: *Memories of a Hundred Years* (New York: The Macmillan Company; 1904), II, 192.

ing myself with reminding you that there are times when *not to act* carries with it greater responsibility than *to act.*" "I do not say now in what way or to what extent, but only that we must strike," he repeated in his November lecture in New York. Though Sumner himself wanted immediate, uncompensated emancipation, he refrained from attacking the President's plan of paying the slavemasters. "Never should any question of money be allowed to interfere with human freedom," Sumner announced grandly. "Better an empty treasury than a single slave." [2]

Though Massachusetts abolitionists grew restive, Sumner could justify his working with the administration. Even in the confused early months of the war he was able to score small but significant gains for the antislavery cause. During the summer session of Congress, for example, Robert Morris, a Negro lawyer of Boston, who wanted to send his son abroad for further education, asked Sumner to secure him a passport. In person the Senator carried to the Secretary of State the application describing his constituent as having "dark brown complexion and woolly hair." "This will never do," exclaimed Seward; "it wont do to acknowledge colored men as citizens." For several minutes the Secretary, no doubt to Sumner's inward satisfaction, fussed and fidgeted; Seward knew that granting the passport would cost the New York Republicans votes in the fall elections but that denying it would alienate the abolitionists. Finally he asked: "Why can't you ask for his passport as a friend of *yours?*" At first inclined to make an issue of principle, Sumner finally decided that there was more to be gained by avoiding a head-on confrontation with Seward and agreed. So a passport was issued to Morris, omitting any physical description but noting that he was vouched for by the Senator from Massachusetts. It was the first granted to a member of that race which Chief Justice Roger B. Taney in the Dred Scott decision had declared not to be citizens of the United States.[3]

[2] Sumner: *Works,* VI, 24–5, 107, 28.

[3] Lydia M. Child to J. G. Whittier, Sept. 22, 1861, Child MSS.; Sumner: *Works,* V, 497–8. The account in Stearns: *Life . . . of George Luther Stearns,* p. 267, is confused.

In October 1861 Sumner had gained another small but important victory for the antislavery cause. While General Thomas W. Sherman and Commodore Samuel DuPont were preparing a large Union expedition to move against Port Royal in South Carolina, War Secretary Cameron, convinced that "we should make no head-way until we let the negroes loose," consulted Sumner in preparing the officers' instructions. Promptly the Senator specified that slaves who fled to the Union lines must not be surrendered but should be welcomed and put to work, "even in a military way." These orders, Sumner exulted, "must practically give Freedom" to South Carolina Negroes; they were "the equivalent to Emancipation." [4]

By the time Congress reassembled in December, Sumner was confident that further blows against slavery were in the offing. Early in the session he and the President had a long discussion of emancipation, and Lincoln told him: "Well, Mr. Sumner, the only difference between you and me on this subject is a difference of a month or six weeks in time."

"Mr. President," replied Sumner, "if that is the only difference between us, I will not say another word to you about it till the longest time you name has passed by." [5]

Sumner kept his word, but meanwhile he did all he could to build up antislavery sentiment in Congress. When the Senate discussed the new internal revenue bill, he insisted that it ought to include a special tax upon slaveowners. When recognition of the new state of West Virginia came up for consideration, he insistently fought the plan for gradual emancipation included in its constitution, because, he said, "it takes but little slavery to make a slave State with all the virus of slavery." [6] Earnestly he denounced Northern generals like Henry W. Halleck and Don Carlos Buell who refused to admit fugitive slaves to their lines and who even allowed masters to reclaim those who managed to flee to freedom. When he learned that Massachusetts officers

[4] "Chas. Sumner's Minutes of Instructions for Naval Expedition of Oct. 61," MS., Wisc. State Hist. Soc.; Allan Nevins and Milton H. Thomas (eds.): *The Diary of George Templeton Strong* (New York: The Macmillan Company; 1952), II, 192; Sumner to Duchess of Argyll, Nov. 11, 1861, Argyll MSS.

[5] Hale: *Memories of a Hundred Years*, II, 191. Cf. Sumner to Dana, Dec. 14, 1861, Dana MSS.

[6] *Cong. Globe*, 37 Cong., 2 Sess., p. 2942.

and men were involved in this foul business, he felt especially outraged.[7] He drove out to the camp of a Massachusetts regiment near Washington to demand the resignation of the colonel who had returned fugitive slaves, and in the Senate he passionately attacked Brigadier-General Charles P. Stone, who had imposed "this vile and unconstitutional duty upon Massachusetts troops." [8]

Sumner even made obituary eulogies the occasion for promoting abolitionism. The death of Senator Kinsley Bingham, who had occupied the seat next to Sumner's, offered an opportunity to urge emancipation.[9] The funeral services for E. D. Baker, killed in the badly managed skirmish at Ball's Bluff, afforded an even better occasion, with the President himself in the audience, for Sumner to denounce "Slavery, the barbarous enemy of our country, the irreconcilable foe of our Union, the violator of our Constitution, the disturber of our peace, the vampire of our national life, . . . the assassin of our children, and the murderer of our dead Senator." [1]

So vigorously and so frequently did Sumner speak on the slavery issue that Massachusetts conservatives sneered that he was constantly "riding the 'nigger' hobby," [2] and some evolved complex explanations for his persistence. Remembering that Sumner had always been an advocate of peace and that he had had difficulty "in justifying support of the Constitution with its slave clauses," Dana concluded that "War, in order to sustain a Constitution that itself needs justification is too much for him"; consequently Sumner "relieves his conscience by proclaiming this to be a holy crusade to abolish Slavery." [3]

[7] Sumner to Andrew, July 9, 1861, Andrew MSS.; Andrew to Sumner, July 17, 1861, copy, ibid.; Boston *Post*, July 29, 1861.

[8] Sumner: *Works*, VI, 146. Shortly afterward Stone wrote a public letter branding Sumner as "a well known coward" who was guilty of slander. Stone to Sumner, Dec. 23, 1861, Sumner MSS. There is no reason to doubt Sumner's assertion that he was "an absolute stranger" to the subsequent arrest of Stone (Sumner: *Works*, VI, 149), for the general had made many enemies through his unfortunate conduct of the engagement at Ball's Bluff. There is every reason, however, to believe that Sumner rejoiced in the exemplary punishment of a soldier so forgetful of his antislavery duties.

[9] Sumner to Mrs. Kinsley Bingham, Oct. 20, 1861, copy, Bingham MSS.

[1] Sumner: *Works*, VI, 136.

[2] C. F. Adams, Jr., to C. F. Adams, Dec. 22, 1861, Adams MSS.

[3] Dana to C. F. Adams, Nov. 25, 1861, ibid.

In fact, Sumner's purposes were by no means so complex, for he was not given to introspection and never questioned his own motives. Though he described himself as "almost a Quaker in principle," [4] he had no difficulty in accepting a war that would surely put an end to slavery. His speeches were not intended to convince himself but to ready Congress and the public for what the President had promised to do.

Though the *Trent* crisis kept Lincoln from moving against slavery during the first three weeks in December, Sumner knew he was maturing a plan for gradual, compensated emancipation, and he predicted that it would be "a proposition of greater magnitude than was ever yet submitted to a deliberative assembly." As soon as Mason and Slidell were released, he begged the President: "I want you to make Congress a New Year's present of your plan." For a time Sumner believed he had prevailed upon Lincoln, but then the President's friends in Kentucky thought the proposal untimely and there was further delay. Still, he drew comfort from Lincoln's statement "that he was now convinced that this was a great movement of God to end Slavery and that the man would be a fool who should stand in the way." [5]

During the month-long illness of Lincoln's son, Willie, who died on February 20, Sumner forebore pressing the distracted President, but he continued to be hopeful. The naming of Edwin M. Stanton as Secretary of War to succeed Cameron, whose administration was tainted with corruption, renewed Sumner's confidence in the antislavery principles of the administration. He knew Stanton, who, even while a member of James Buchanan's cabinet, had confidentially consulted with him during the secession crisis; and he was certain that the new Secretary did "not agree with those who want the war so managed as to save slavery no matter what else may result" but "believed that the war should be prosecuted to save the Union and that everything necessary should be made to contribute to its suc-

[4] Sumner to Bright, Dec. 23, 1861, Bright MSS.

[5] Sumner to Orestes Brownson, Feb. 2, 1862, Brownson MSS.; Sumner to William Claflin, Dec. 29, 1861, Claflin MSS.; Moncure D. Conway to Ellen Conway, Mar. 17 [1862], Conway MSS.

cess." "The new Secretary of War *is with us,*" he jubilantly informed a friend. "I know him personally and well." [6]

On March 6, 1862, Sumner learned that his confidence in the Lincoln administration was finally justified. Early that morning, even before he was dressed, he received an urgent summons to the White House. "I want to read you my message," Lincoln told him when he reached his office. "I want to know how you like it. I am going to send it in today." First the President read the manuscript aloud; then Sumner went over it himself. He had some reservations about some of the language—especially the word "abolishment"—but concluded that Lincoln's style was "so clearly . . . aboriginal, autochthonous" that it would not bear verbal emendation. Delighted with the content of the message, which pledged the cooperation and the financial assistance of the federal government to any state that began gradual, compensated emancipation, Sumner could hardly bear to part with the manuscript, which he went over again and again until Lincoln was obliged to say: "There, now, you've read it enough, run away. I must send it in to-day," and then gave it to his secretary for copying.

As "the only Senator consulted from the beginning to the end," Sumner had had to pledge himself to secrecy, and he returned to the Capitol barely able to contain himself. Impatiently he waited until Lincoln's secretary brought the message to the Vice President's desk, and then he jubilantly heard it read. In his rejoicing there was, however, one note of regret. "I might have made some preparation for a speech of welcome to it," he said later.[7]

• 2 •

When Sumner read through the draft of Lincoln's message of March 6, 1862, the first emancipation proposal ever submitted

[6] Frank A. Flowers: *Edwin McMasters Stanton* (New York: Western W. Wilson; 1906), p. 117; Sumner to Orestes Brownson, Feb. 2, 1862, Brownson MSS.

[7] Hale: *Memories of a Hundred Years,* II, 193–6; Sumner: *Works,* VI, 391–2.

by a President to Congress, he nodded approvingly until he came to the sentence: "Should the people of the insurgent districts now reject the councils of treason, revive loyal state governments, and again send Senators and Representatives to Congress, they would, at once find themselves at peace, with no institution changed, and with their just influence in the councils of the nation, fully re-established." Rather than argue with the President, Sumner tried to recast the offensive sentence, but Lincoln, in a hurry to have the document copied, chose instead to bracket it for deletion.[8] Neither President nor Senator, it was clear, was yet ready for a confrontation over what was to prove the most explosive issue of the entire war: what was to happen to the seceded states once peace was restored.

Sumner had already been brooding over this problem. In retrospect, his concern in the winter of 1861–62 over the terms to be imposed upon the South seems incredibly premature, but at the time it appeared probable that the war would end within a few months. McClellan had magnificently reorganized the Union forces in the East, and, although Sumner along with many other Congressmen complained of his delays, he would be ready to take the field by early spring. In the West General George H. Thomas's victory at Mill Springs seemed to open up eastern Kentucky and Tennessee to the advance of Union armies, and Ulysses S. Grant's spectacular capture of Fort Henry and Fort Donelson broke the entire Confederate line of defense and promised the speedy occupation of the Mississippi Valley. Elsewhere, the Port Royal expedition had already reestablished the Union flag on the seacoast of South Carolina, and another joint army-navy expedition was preparing to seize historic Roanoke Island and New Bern in North Carolina. As early as January Sumner learned of an even larger flotilla which was being readied to sail against New Orleans, the largest city of the Confederacy. All around the Southern coast the blockade was tightening, and, after the *Trent* affair was settled, prospects for European recognition of the Confederacy had dimmed. Logic decreed that the Civil War ought to end with resounding Northern victory not

[8] Hale: *Memories of a Hundred Years,* II, 194; Lincoln: *Works,* V, 146, n.7.

later than midsummer of 1862. In February, Seward, the chronic optimist, told Sumner he had "authentic information from Virginia that the Rebellion will be over there in 4 weeks."[9]

To Sumner peace threatened dangers no less than war. "Assuming that our military success is complete, and that the rebel armies are scattered," he wrote Lieber, to whom he often turned for advice on law and policy, "what next? Unless I am mistaken, the most difficult thing of all—namely, the re-organization." Unlike Seward and many other Republicans, who believed that there was in the South a powerful latent Unionism which Northern victory would revive, Sumner had already concluded that in the Gulf states there was no responsible and loyal white population, and he "spoke with great despondency of the low ebb of Union feeling in the border States." He judged that Northern victory would not result in Southern willingness to return to the Union but instead would produce in the South "a bitter, sullen, rebellious, and probably conspiring faction,—breeding discontent and breathing a hatred the malignity of which will have been intensified by defeat."[1]

With growing concern, therefore, he observed the tendency of the Lincoln administration to think of a peace which would merely restore the status quo ante bellum. Ending the war on such terms would, in Sumner's view, simply return to the national government the imperious and embittered slavemasters of the South, who would join with the Democrats of the North and once more dictate national policy. All the gains antislavery men had made during the war would be swept away. Anxiously and ambivalently, then, Sumner watched the progress of the Northern armies, for each victory might bring peace but might also "hurt THE cause at home."[2]

So complex were the problems of peace that Sumner at times thought them insolvable. Being, as he confessed to the Duchess of Argyll, "no idolator of the Union,"[3] in depressed

[9] Sumner to Bird, Feb. 19, 1862, Bird MSS.

[1] Sumner to Lieber, Mar. 29, 1862, Sumner MSS.; Lately Thomas: *Sam Ward: "King of the Lobby"* (Boston: Houghton Mifflin Company; 1965), p. 304.

[2] Sumner to Sidney H. Gay, Feb. 18, 1862, Gay MSS.; Sumner to Bird, Feb. 19, 1862, Bird MSS.

[3] April 7, 1863, Argyll MSS.

moments he toyed with the paradoxical possibility that the North ought to conquer the South and then acquiesce in its separation. Anything would be better than another generation of Southern dominance of the national government.

The only solution, he concluded, was the "subjugation of these states with Emancipation," since the Southern slavocracy could never return to power once its peculiar institution was destroyed.[4] But this policy would contradict all the Republican campaign promises not to touch slavery where it already existed and would violate Sumner's own assurance that Congress had no right to interfere with slavery in a State.[5] Casting about for a way to reconcile past pledges with presently needed policies, Sumner came up with a set of resolutions that he introduced in the Senate on February 11. The states of the Confederacy, he argued, through their acts of secession and treason, had forfeited their status in the Union; they had committed suicide, becoming, "according to the language of the law, *felo de se*." In consequence, the land and inhabitants of these former states now fell back "under the exclusive jurisdiction of Congress," just as any other territory of the United States did. In this national territory all "peculiar local institutions" automatically ceased to exist unless sanctioned by act of Congress; slavery, which could not exist without positive law, was therefore abolished throughout the seceded states. Congress now had the duty to "*assume complete jurisdiction of such vacated territory, . . . and . . . to establish therein republican forms of government under the Constitution.*"[6]

Contrary to the claims of Sumner's admirers, there was little or nothing new in these "state-suicide" resolutions. As early as May 21, 1861, Lord Lyons had reported widespread talk in Washington of reducing the seceded states "to the condition of what are called 'Territories' . . . under the absolute control of the President and Congress of the United States." In the July

[4] Sumner to Lieber, Mar. 29, 1862, Sumner MSS.

[5] *Cong. Globe*, 37 Cong., 2 Sess., p. 1811. Before the war Sumner announced that he did not believe that in times of peace "the National Government has power under the Constitution to touch Slavery in the States." Sumner to A. P. Brown, Sept. 9, 1860, Garrison MSS.

[6] Sumner: *Works*, VI, 301–5.

session of Congress Senator Edward D. Baker, soon to die at Ball's Bluff, declared that Congress had the right to reduce the Confederate states "to the condition of Territories, and send from Massachusetts or from Illinois Governors to control them." In December Treasury Secretary Chase argued that the seceded states had "lapsed into the condition of a Territory with which we could do what we pleased."[7] There was nothing original in Sumner's contention that in such territories slavery, lacking the sanction of positive law, must expire. This was a familiar part of the prewar antislavery argument, which Sumner himself had done much to publicize in his 1852 speech titled "Freedom National, Slavery Sectional."[8] Nor was there anything novel in Sumner's assertion that Congress had authority to reorganize the South's political—and social—order, under the constitutional provision guaranteeing to each state a republican form of government. For two decades before the war antislavery men had argued that no government which recognized slavery could be republican in form. Very recently the aged New England jurist, Timothy Farrar, a former law partner of Daniel Webster, insisting that "the provisions of the Constitution are . . . adequate to all the purposes for which it was made," found in the guarantee clause a mandate for permanent, not temporary, national guardianship wherever needed.[9]

Sumner's resolutions juxtaposed and combined these three hitherto separate lines of thought, gave them the authority that derived from sponsorship by a major Republican Senate leader, and made the whole easy to identify by the catchy phrase "state suicide." They offered the first comprehensive and radical program for reconstructing the South.

Instantaneous and almost unanimous disapproval greeted

[7] Lyons to Russell, May 21, 1861, F. O. 5, PRO; *Cong. Globe*, 37 Cong., 1 Sess., pp. 45, 69, 141; Donald (ed.): *Inside Lincoln's Cabinet*, pp. 50–1. See also Herman Belz: *Reconstructing the Union* (Ithaca, N.Y.: Cornell University Press; 1969), Chap. 3.

[8] Donald: *Sumner*, pp. 227–32.

[9] Charles O. Lerche, Jr.: "Congressional Interpretations of the Guarantee of a Republican Form of Government during Reconstruction," *Journal of Southern History*, XV (1949), 192–4; Jacobus ten Broek: *Antislavery Origins of the Fourteenth Amendment* (Berkeley: University of California Press; 1951), pp. 18, 49–51; Harold M. Hyman (ed.): *New Frontiers of the American Reconstruction* (Urbana, Ill.: University of Illinois Press; 1966), p. 30.

his resolutions. Where newspapers could not ignore his proposals, they condemned them. The Democratic Boston *Post* argued that by threatening the South with social revolution Sumner's resolutions were "strongly calculated to strengthen the rebellion"; "for a man to hold to this policy and to say that he stands by the Constitution," it added, "is an insult to the common sense of men and a mockery before high heaven of the oath he has taken to support this Constitution." "Senator Sumner is playing into the hands of the Southern secessionists by declaring that they no longer belong to the Union," agreed the independent but anti-abolitionist New York *Herald,* guessing that what the Senator really wanted was "political and social amalgamation, and some forty blacks in both houses of the national legislature." [1]

Congressional response was equally hostile. Speaking as a representative of the border states, Senator Waitman T. Willey of western Virginia protested that Sumner was attempting "by one fell swoop of his pen to blot ten or twelve States out of the Union forever, to remit them back to a territorial condition." "No recruiting officer," he predicted, "will have such power to replenish the thinned ranks of the rebel army as these propositions." Senator Joseph A. Wright from Negrophobic Indiana agreed that Sumner's resolutions had "done more harm to the Union cause than the addition of fifty thousand soldiers to the rebel army." More weighty was the criticism of highly respected, cautious Senator John Sherman of Ohio, who called the proposals "substantially an acknowledgment of the right of secession" and declared that he could therefore "draw no distinction between the resolutions of the Senator from Massachusetts and the doctrines that are proclaimed by Jefferson Davis." Even New Englanders dissented strongly from Sumner's views. William Pitt Fessenden of Maine announced flatly that "the opinions of the honorable Senator from Massachusetts are his own, for which he alone is responsible." [2]

As usual when under attack, Sumner began preparing an elaborate speech to defend his position, but this time he did not deliver it. Possibly the overwhelmingly hostile reaction to his

[1] Boston *Post*, Feb. 14 and 28, 1862; New York *Herald*, Feb. 13 and 25, 1862.
[2] *Cong. Globe*, 37 Cong., 2 Sess., pp. 1300, 1302, 1469, 1493, 1472.

resolutions deterred him. More probably the approaching contest in Massachusetts over his reelection warned him not to make unnecessary enemies at this time. For the moment, therefore, he contented himself with writing several public letters to be read at antislavery rallies, in which he referred to "the territory once occupied by certain States, and now usurped by the pretended Government" of the Confederacy and argued that in the South "the State, with its unnatural institutions, has ceased to exist." Though prudence compelled him to be silent on reconstruction, he in no way changed his basic views, and he felt obliged therefore to challenge the sentence in Lincoln's emancipation message which promised speedy, unconditional restoration of the Southern states to the Union. Between the Senator and the President there was no pact, but Lincoln deleted the offending sentence and Sumner indefinitely postponed making his speech on state suicide.

• 3 •

So long as both the President and the Senator were prepared to minimize their differences, they worked as an effective team. It took Lincoln's initiative and Sumner's careful management to secure passage on June 5, 1862, of an act authorizing diplomatic relations with the Negro republics of Haiti and Liberia, which the United States had hitherto refused fully to accredit, largely because Southerners were afraid these countries would send black ministers to mingle in Washington society.[3] Similarly Sumner and the State Department cooperated on the treaty with Great Britain that finally stamped out the Atlantic slave trade. Present when Seward and Lyons signed the document on April 7, 1862, Sumner realized that it could precipitate explosive debate, for Americans were still wrought up over the *Trent* affair and, in the treaty provisions for stopping and searching slave ships on the high seas, might find reminders of the British impressment of American seamen before the War of 1812. Cautiously and patiently he set to work persuading members of his own Foreign

[3] Sumner to Lieber, Feb. 10, 1862, Sumner MSS.; Sumner to Andrew, April 22, 1862, Andrew MSS.; Sumner: *Works*, VI, 449–70.

Relations Committee to back the treaty, and then, selecting his moment carefully, he induced the Senate to approve it on April 24 without a single dissenting vote. "*Laus Deo!*" Sumner exclaimed, and he sped from the Senate Chamber to the State Department, where he roused Seward from a nap on the office couch. "Good God!" exclaimed the Secretary as he learned of the unanimous ratification; "the Democrats have disappeared. This is the greatest act of the Administration." Reporting the news to Lord Lyons that evening, Sumner was moved to tears of joy, not merely over the approaching end of an ancient evil but over the seeming groundswell of antislavery sentiment throughout the North.[4]

Rarely were Sumner's relations with the administration so amicable, however, for he found Lincoln so "slow, with an immense *vis inertiae*, and . . . without experience in public affairs," that he needed constant prodding.[5] Most of Sumner's encounters with the President tended, therefore, to fall into a repetitious pattern. For example, when Sumner learned that Lincoln was delaying for a few days before signing a bill for compensated emancipation in the District of Columbia, he descended upon the White House to ask: "Do you know who at this moment is the largest slave-*holder* in this country? It is Abraham Lincoln; for he holds all the three thousand slaves of the District, which is more than any other person in the country holds." "Why, Mr. President," Sumner went on, warming to his task, "I cannot see how you dare trust yourself to sleep to-night. . . . Suppose you should die, to-night, do you think your spirit could look back upon this great act of justice unperformed and feel that Abraham Lincoln had done his duty." [6]

Similarly, a few weeks later, when Sumner learned that Edward Stanly, whom Lincoln appointed provisional governor of North Carolina, had closed down a school for Negro children at New Bern, he again sought out the President. Not finding him at the White House, he tracked him to the War Department and

[4] Sumner to Lieber [April 25, 1862], Sumner MSS.; Lyons to Russell, April 25, 1862, Russell MSS. Cf. Conway W. Henderson: "The Anglo-American Treaty of 1862 in Civil War Diplomacy," *Civil War Hist.*, XV (1969), 308–19.

[5] Sumner to Duchess of Argyll, Aug. 11, 1862, Argyll MSS.

[6] Sumner: *Works*, VI, 393; Springfield *Republican*, April 25, 1873.

there charged the tired and irritable Lincoln with countenancing, through Stanly, an action unworthy of a civilized nation.

"Do you take me for a School-Committee-man?" impatiently exclaimed Lincoln, who had hitherto known nothing of the affair.

"Not at all," retorted Sumner; "I take you for the President of the United States; and I come with a case of wrong, in attending to which your predecessor, George Washington, if alive, might add to his renown."

When even after such a rebuke Lincoln failed promptly to overrule Stanly, whom the Senator considered "a marplot, summoned by Seward from California, instructed by him and acting in conformity with his ideas," Sumner introduced in the Senate a sharply worded resolution declaring that Stanly's post of military governor was one "unknown to the Constitution and laws of the Union," created "in derogation to the powers of Congress." [7]

After the beginning of May 1862 such clashes between Sumner and Lincoln became increasingly frequent. By that time the prospects for Union victory, which had gleamed so brightly during the winter, had faded. In the West Grant's victory at Shiloh was so costly that Sumner thought some of the Union generals "ought to be shot—according to all the laws of war." Then Halleck took over the campaign with a snail-like progress toward Corinth. Union capture of New Orleans in April had no significant military results. In the East McClellan insisted upon sailing off with his magnificent army to attack Richmond from the Peninsula, and Lincoln frankly told Sumner that the general "had gone to Yorktown very much against his judgment, but that he did not feel disposed to take the responsibility of overruling him." Sumner, who had earlier clashed with McClellan over whether advancing Union armies should free the slaves, became convinced that the general was "utterly incompetent!—incompetent to command more than fifty men, and if he can command fifty, he can't command fifty-one." Only disaster seemed to lie ahead. "I see no cheerful omens," Sumner wrote Dana. "Victory is possible; but not success—at present. There must be more

[7] Sumner: *Works*, VII, 112, 119–20; Sumner to "My dear Sir," Dec. 27, 1862, MS., New York Public Library.

suffering, debt and bloodshed—to be followed by a famine throughout the slave states."[8]

Inevitably he blamed the failures upon the President's refusal to proclaim emancipation. Once fearful that Lincoln might not free the slaves before Union victory was achieved, he now worried that he might not free them in time to avert defeat. Absolutely convinced that there was only "*one way to safety,* clear as sunlight,—pleasant as the paths of Peace,"[9] Sumner never ceased begging Lincoln to strike down slavery. On July 4, 1862, he twice went to the White House "to urge the reconsecration of the day by a decree of emancipation." On his first visit Lincoln seemed to think that he might declare the slaves in eastern Virginia free, though a general decree of emancipation would be "too big a lick." Two hours later, Sumner returned again to urge: "You need more men, not only at the North, but at the South, in the rear of the Rebels: you need the slaves." By that time the President had changed his mind. He could see no merit in issuing a proclamation he could not enforce, he told Sumner; anyway, if he issued it, "half the officers would fling down their arms and three more States would rise." Sumner thought him "plainly mistaken" and told him so, but Lincoln would not budge.[1]

Since the President refused to act, Sumner increasingly hoped that Congress would. The Republicans, with huge majorities in both houses of Congress after the withdrawal of the Southern Senators and Representatives, certainly had the numbers to pass any legislation they desired. During the brief, businesslike session in the summer of 1861 they had exhibited a remarkable unanimity, but in the regular December session marked differences of opinion and sharp clashes of personality had begun to appear in the party. On December 9 a Senate caucus discussing a proposal to confiscate rebel property, includ-

[8] Sumner to Andrew, April 22 and May 1 [?], 1862, Andrew MSS.; George B. McClellan: *McClellan's Own Story* (New York: Charles L. Webster & Company; 1887), p. 33; James D. Green to Nahum Capen, Aug. 10, 1871, copy, Mass. Hist. Soc.; Sumner to Dana [May 31, 1862], Dana MSS.

[9] Sumner to Mrs. Josephine S. Griffing, April 11, 1862, MS., Columbia University.

[1] Louis M. Starr: *Bohemian Brigade* (New York: Alfred A. Knopf; 1954), p. 125; Sumner: *Works,* VII, 215; Sumner to Bright, Aug. 5, 1862, Bright MSS.

ing slaves, broke up angrily after a wrangle between what Senator Howe called "timid, hesitating and unresolved" conservatives and "turbulent, passionate and reckless" radicals. In the vanguard of the second group was Sumner, who, according to Howe, "after brooding over his wounds for years, now day after day hurls back the blows he received from Preston Brooks upon the devoted body of slavery." [2]

During the early months of the session these groups were not clearly defined, either in membership or in program. Indeed, on many questions Republicans were not divided. All Republicans agreed that the Union must be preserved, that the President must be sustained, and that the war must be prosecuted until victory. Most felt that the President was too cautious, too inexperienced, and too deferential to border-state sentiment. As the winter dragged on, nearly all grew impatient with General McClellan's slowness. All were opposed to slavery.

They differed, however, over how best to eradicate the peculiar institution. Some took Sumner's extreme position that the war afforded a providential opportunity for immediately exterminating slavery, at least in the rebellious states; a few thought that slavery ought not to be touched until after the Union was restored; most adopted positions somewhere in between. There were as yet no distinct factional lines, and the differences among Republicans were rarely in evidence in roll-call votes during the early months of the session.[3]

By the summer of 1862, however, as Union armies failed to make significant progress and as Congressmen grew "exhausted, tired, and fatigued by the protracted session," [4] disagreements among Republicans became more sharply focused. It was possible to identify Sumner, Wilson, Benjamin F. Wade of Ohio, Lyman Trumbull of Illinois, and a few others as "Radicals" (or "Jacobins," as their enemies preferred to call them), while Browning, James R. Doolittle of Wisconsin, Edgar Cowan of Pennsylvania, and James Dixon of Connecticut were known as "Conservatives" (or "Moderates," as they preferred to call them-

[2] T. O. Howe to Grace Howe, Dec. 31, 1861, copy, Howe MSS.

[3] Allan G. Bogue: "Bloc and Party in the United States Senate: 1861–1863," *Civil War History*, XIII (1967), 211–41.

[4] *Cong. Globe*, 37 Cong., 2 Sess., p. 2734.

selves). The line between the two groups was not easy to trace, for neither faction had any formal organization. There was much movement back and forth between groups on specific issues, and on most matters of practical, everyday legislation, such as the tax bill, the homestead act, and federal support for a transcontinental railroad, Republicans continued to vote together with great unanimity.

The May debates over the Second Confiscation Act showed that the most readily recognizable characteristics of the Radical Republicans were distrust of the President of the United States and confidence that Congress could take the lead in conducting the war. Sponsored by Lyman Trumbull, that cold, calculating former New Englander who had never thought very highly of his fellow Illinoisan in the White House, this measure provided for the confiscation, after sixty days' warning, of the property of all Southerners who supported the rebellion and for the liberation of their slaves, who were declared "forever free of their servitude." Here, in effect, was a direct warning that if Lincoln would not strike down slavery, Congress would.

In the heated debates over the confiscation bill, Sumner emerged as the most extreme advocate of the duty of Congress to lead. He arrived at this position with some difficulty and reluctance. To be sure, he had endorsed the confiscation proposal in its early stages as "the death-blow of Slavery," [5] but, knowing that the bill was distasteful to the President, he did nothing to push it during the winter months when the war seemed to be going well. Unlike Trumbull, who was a careful constitutional lawyer concerned with preserving Congressional prerogatives, Sumner cared very little who exercised the power to free the slaves. Brought up in the broadly nationalistic school of Joseph Story and John Quincy Adams, he did not specially venerate the principle of the separation of powers. What he wanted was results. He would have been entirely content to have the Supreme Court strike down the "musty, antediluvian, wicked statutes" which protected slavery,[6] but he knew better than to expect much from a judiciary headed by Taney.

[5] William Stuart to Russell, July 15, 1862, copy, Stuart MSS.
[6] Sumner: *Works*, VI, 411, 416.

Sumner had originally preferred to have the President proclaim emancipation, believing that the chief executive could act quickly and effectively and that he could abundantly justify his action as an exercise of the war powers. But Lincoln's decision to overrule Frémont's emancipation proclamation in September 1861 caused Sumner to doubt whether he would ever take drastic action, and he began to fear that "Slavery shall only be touched by Act of Congress." [7] This view, however, immediately involved him in difficulties, because of his repeated pledge "against any interference with Slavery in the States." [8] Only by asserting that Congress also could act under the war powers could he consistently advocate emancipation through legislation. So long as there was a possibility that Lincoln might move against slavery, Sumner was careful not to claim for Congress exclusive control of the war powers, preferring to obscure the issue by arguing that they were "deposited with the legislative branch, being the President, Senate, and House of Representatives, whose joint action becomes the supreme law of the land." [9]

When it became clear in the late spring of 1862 that Lincoln was not going to order general emancipation, Sumner decided that full control of the war powers rested in Congress alone, and on May 19 he made a major address earnestly supporting Trumbull's confiscation bill as a legitimate exercise of those powers.[1] Protesting rather too earnestly his "determination to uphold the Constitution, which is the shield of the citizen," Sumner tried to brush away the "fine-spun constitutional theories" of Senators who questioned the power of Congress to seize property and free slaves. In a line of reasoning which paralleled the subsequent ruling of the Supreme Court in the Prize cases, Sumner argued that the United States had a dual relationship toward the Confederates; it could act against them and their property both because they were rebels subject to criminal law and because they were simultaneously "enemies outside of the Constitution," subject, therefore, to the laws of war. As prece-

[7] Sumner to Lieber, Sept. 17, 1861, Sumner MSS.

[8] ". . . I have always been against any interference with Slavery in the States. . . ." Sumner to Duchess of Argyll, Aug. 11, 1862, Argyll MSS.

[9] Sumner: *Works*, VI, 45.

[1] Ibid., VII, 11–77.

dents for Trumbull's bill he listed no fewer than eighty-eight statutes passed by the American states during the Revolutionary War to confiscate the property of Tories. It was elementary justice, he argued, to seize the property of individual Southerners, because *"every rebel who voluntarily becomes an enemy is as completely responsible in all his property, . . . as a hostile Government or Prince."*

Sumner's manner as well as his argument showed how rapidly he was shifting from his earlier role as Senate supporter of the administration. During the opening months of the 1861–62 session he had tried being conciliatory, both with the President and with the Conservatives in Congress, but he learned that such a tactic did not pay. As the summer heats became oppressive in Washington his temper grew shorter, his speeches more personal, and his self-righteousness more evident. Those cowardly Senators who wanted to weaken the force of the confiscation bill, he remarked scornfully, were like the character in one of Charles Dickens's novels who said: "Take a glass of water, put into it a little piece of orange peel, and then make believe very hard and you will have a strong drink." [2] Anybody opposed to the bill in its original form, he announced angrily, was a friend and supporter of slavery.

Such extreme language invited counterattack, for even gentle Jacob Collamer complained that Sumner, like the Southern Democrats who had dominated the Senate in former days, was trying to crack the plantation whip over the Republican party. Fessenden, too, exploded angrily at Sumner and Trumbull for rejecting any amendment to the confiscation bill "that does not exactly suit their own notions," and he wrote home: "If I could cut the throats of about half a dozen Republican Senators . . . Sumner would be the first victim, as by far the greatest fool of the lot." [3]

If fellow New Englanders reacted so sharply to Sumner's tactics, he could expect much worse from Conservative leaders in his party, and on June 25 he got it. In a three-hour speech,

[2] *Cong. Globe*, 37 Cong., 2 Sess., p. 2251.

[3] Ibid., pp. 2251, 2253; Eric L. McKitrick: *Andrew Johnson and Reconstruction* (Chicago: The University of Chicago Press; 1960), p. 272.

both learned and passionate, Orville Browning ripped into Sumner's arguments for confiscation. Seizing the property of individuals in the Confederate states was "a violation of all the laws of civilized warfare." It was ironical that Sumner, who had so eloquently in his speech on the *Trent* affair urged the immunity of private property from search and seizure at sea, should now advocate those abhorred practices on land. Even if confiscation were authorized under international law, Browning continued, Congress had no right to act, for "Congress has no powers which are peculiar to a state of war. . . ." Sumner's argument to the contrary was so "heterodox, and dangerous, and indefensible" that, should it be embodied in legislation, the Constitution would be overthrown. Exercise of the war powers clearly belonged to the President in his role as commander-in-chief; for Congress to claim these powers was an encroachment upon "a coordinate department of the Government." "The Constitution," announced Browning, "invests it with no such prerogative." The real issue, therefore, was not so much whether rebel property should be confiscated "but one of far greater magnitude, namely, who shall conduct the active operations of war, and determine upon and enforce military necessities?" If Sumner and Trumbull had their way, Browning predicted, the President would be reduced "to pitiable dependence upon the will of Congress." The true constitutional doctrine was: "The part to be performed by the President must be performed by him alone. Congress can neither do nor control the doing of it." [4]

Browning's speech had every indication of being the opening gun of a Conservative counteroffensive against Sumner and his fellow Radicals, and it attracted added interest from the possibility that the White House was behind the attack. To be sure, Browning denied that he was speaking for anyone except

[4] *Cong. Globe*, 37 Cong., 2 Sess., pp. 2917–24. On the general problem as to whether the Constitution authorizes the President or the Congress to exercise the war powers, see Clarence A. Berdahl: *War Powers of the Executive in the United States* (Urbana, Ill.; 1921), and J. G. Randall: *Constitutional Problems under Lincoln* (Urbana, Ill.: University of Illinois Press; 1964), Chap. 2. Randall notes (p. 42) that judicial interpretation has tended to "support . . . the Sumner, rather than the Browning, view" of the extent of legislative war powers; such an interpretation has not, however, followed Sumner's ideas on the limits of the executive war powers.

himself, but everybody knew that he was Lincoln's closest personal friend in Congress, a longtime intimate from the Illinois years, who almost daily visited the executive mansion. That Browning was acting in concert with other Conservatives was indicated when Dixon immediately followed him with a denunciation of Sumner's state-suicide resolutions, which, it was known, had "excessively annoyed" the President.[5] Thus Sumner's views on confiscation, on the war powers, and on reconstruction all came under fire at once.

Both Dixon and Browning spoke with a personal venom that seemed calculated to drive Sumner into an open break with the President's policies. Sumner, suggested Browning, "hates slavery more than he loves the Constitution, and . . . to reach and throttle the one he is willing to march over the prostrate form of the other." Picking out Sumner's rather pretentious statement in his May 19 speech that he felt "humbled" to be obliged at this late date to recapitulate the arguments in favor of confiscation, Browning sneered: "It must be a happy state of mind which enables one to abase himself for the shortcomings of his neighbors, and thank God that he is not as other men. He who has attained to such a state of perfection as to justify him in doing so, must be approaching his apotheosis, and rapidly verging to the point where he shall be withdrawn from contaminating contact with the world."

If Browning and Dixon intended to open wounds in the Republican party they succeeded. Hale immediately jumped into the debate, boldly asserting that the "plain, good English" of the Constitution justified confiscation, despite any citations from "black-letter lawyers of ancient or modern times" that Browning might adduce. More directly to the point, Wade, turning his intense, unblinking black eyes upon Browning, denounced the "miserable, slavish doctrine" that "the President of the United States was by some mysterious power invested with despotic authority to trample upon the rights of the people and the rights of Congress."[6]

[5] Gideon Welles: "Administration of Abraham Lincoln," *Galaxy*, XXIII (1877), 150.

[6] *Cong. Globe*, 37 Cong., 2 Sess., pp. 2928–9.

Never ready in impromptu debate and desiring not to create a schism until after the ratification of the slave trade treaty, Sumner made no reply to Browning until June 27. Then, repeating his argument that both municipal and international law justified confiscation, he insisted that Trumbull's bill was "as constitutional as the Constitution itself." Forced by the debate to clarify his views on the war powers, Sumner repudiated Browning's claim that they belonged to the President alone as "irrational and unconstitutional, . . . absurd and tyrannical." No longer could there be any ambiguity about his own position. "I claim for Congress all that belongs to any Government in the exercise of the Rights of War," he announced. As for the President, to whom he had once looked for the country's salvation, Sumner now concluded: "He is only the instrument of Congress, under the Constitution." [7]

• 4 •

Sumner's stand further endeared him to Massachusetts abolitionists, the most dependably loyal group among his constituents. The debates over the confiscation bill, exclaimed Mrs. Lydia Maria Child, one of the earliest antislavery propagandists, proved anew how Sumner towered "in moral majesty, a whole head and shoulders above others, at this trying crisis." She was proud that her Senator was "the politician who has *never* compromised a principle, either for fear or favor." "The impossibility of tempting him from the straight line is why his enemies hate him so," she believed "and [why] friends are so ready to complain of him as impracticable." Shrewdly she concluded: "If he *were* practicable, in *their* sense, the moral Samson would soon be shorn of his strength." [8]

Others among Sumner's backers would have preferred that he linger a bit longer in the harlot's house of practicality before emerging as leader of the opposition to his own party's President. A formidable campaign was already under way to elect in November 1862 a legislature that would not return Sumner to the

[7] Sumner: *Works*, VII, 138–9.

[8] Lydia M. Child to "My Precious One," June 9, 1862, Shaw Family Papers.

Senate, and Sumner's more alert political friends knew he was in the most serious danger of his career. Democrats could, of course, be counted upon to oppose his reelection; in a permanent minority in Massachusetts, they were always ready to cooperate with any other dissidents to secure the defeat of an abolitionist Senator. Equally implacable were those former Whigs who had voted for John Bell and Edward Everett in 1860, some of whom were animated by fierce personal hostility toward Sumner. Robert C. Winthrop, for instance, could not forget that his own distinguished political career had been cut short when the legislature in 1851 chose Sumner to the Senate instead of him.

There was a grave danger that by overtly criticizing the President Sumner might give other powerful interests in Massachusetts the pretext to join these outright opponents. Businessmen, especially those in the Boston area, had long been critical of the Senator, feeling that their interests were not being served in Washington as they had been in the days of Daniel Webster. Rarely did they have a specific complaint against Sumner, but they tended to blame him for the slowing down of New England cotton mills because of the shortage of Southern cotton and for the disappearance of the New England merchant marine from the seas because of Confederate raiders. Since Sumner's important work in the direction of foreign affairs was largely done behind the scenes, they thought he did nothing but incessantly agitate the slavery issue. The present deplorable state of affairs, they complained, had risen "because we have left the conduct of public affairs to men of one idea, . . . idealists and sentimentalists." "Massachusetts," announced the Boston *Courier*, "no longer wants men to represent her who see one thing so clearly that they can see nothing else." [9]

Lawyers, too, tended to disapprove of Sumner's course. Trained to revere precedent, they grew genuinely alarmed over what they took to be his fast-and-loose construing of the Constitution. They found in that document no authority for his revolutionary proposals to abolish slavery by decree and to reduce eleven Southern states to the condition of territories. The principal spokesman of these legal conservatives was Joel Parker,

[9] Boston *Courier*, Oct. 8, 1862.

Abraham Lincoln

THE NATIONAL ARCHIVES

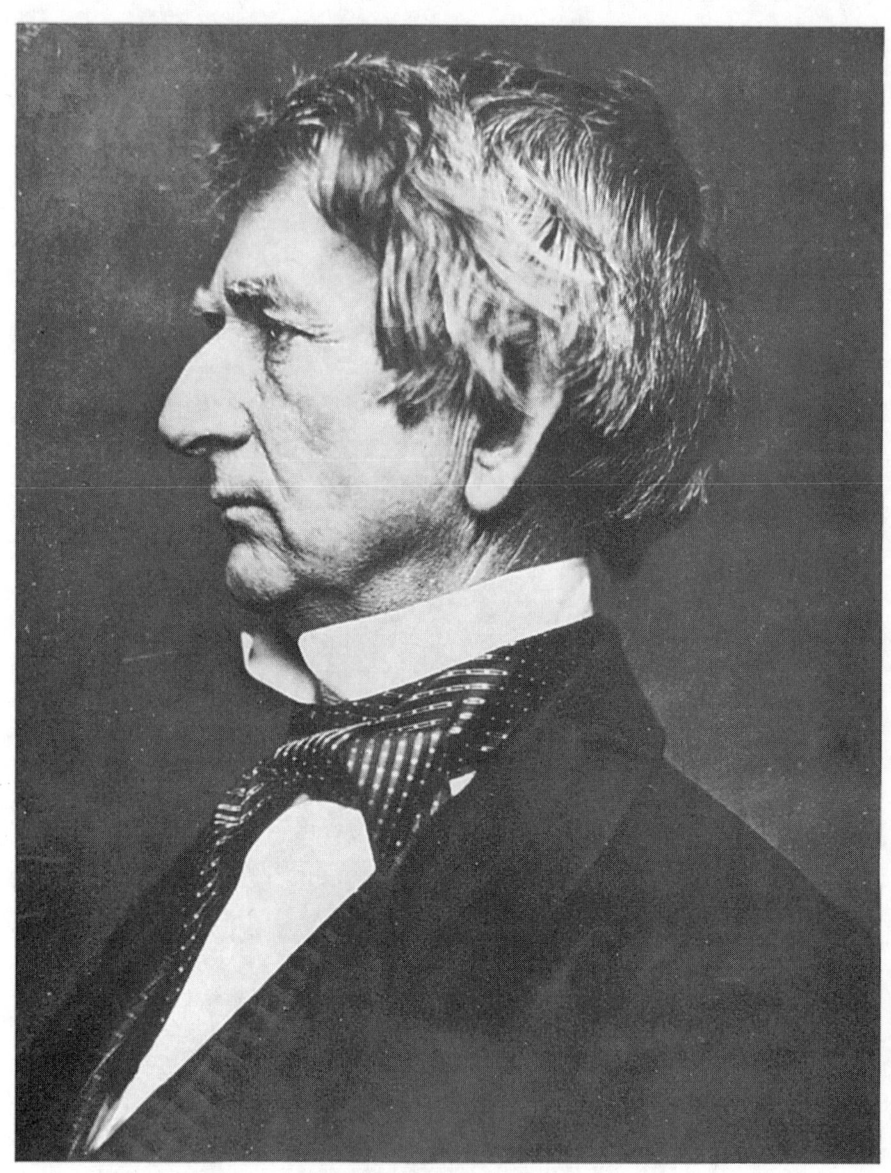

William Henry Seward

THE NATIONAL ARCHIVES

Royall Professor in the Harvard Law School, who bitterly attacked Sumner's constitutional theories in a long essay in the January 1862 issue of the *North American Review*.[1] There was, he argued, no constitutional basis for claiming that emancipation was a legitimate Union war weapon. To be sure, as Federal troops penetrated the South the commanders might free some slaves "as an incident to military occupations and operations," but general "proclamations for emancipation, from whatever source, will be of no avail. The President and Congress," Parker announced, "have no more authority to emancipate the slaves, than the writer of this article."

To Sumner's more devoted followers Parker's powerful and well-reasoned article simply proved the existence of a "plot which the pro-slavery politicians in this State have been at work upon all winter to supersede Mr. Sumner." They suggested that the professor himself had "an itching for a seat in the Senate." Sumner's more astute advisers, however, warned that his recent course in the Senate had tended to alienate "all the respectability and eminent gravity of Boston and its vicinity." Even the ultra-abolitionist Wendell Phillips, whose patrician birth made him almost the only antislavery spokesman who kept in touch with Brahmin opinion in Boston, counseled in May that Sumner ought to let all "side and second questions *relating to slavery* . . . gently slip for the present."[2]

The opposition of Democrats and embittered former Whigs and the distrust of many businessmen and lawyers were political perils of which Sumner long had been aware, but what made the 1862 elections especially dangerous was the disaffection toward him within the Republican party. There seemed to be a widespread belief that Sumner no longer had "so strong a position as he once had" with his constituents, since he had not been "altogether judicious" in his agitation for abolition and since "his *personel* [did not] bring him within the popular embrace." A good many voters simply thought he had served so long in the

[1] Reprinted as *The Domestic and Foreign Relations of the United States* (Cambridge: Welch, Bigelow, and Company; 1862).

[2] New Bedford *Standard*, quoted in *The Liberator*, XXXII (May 9, 1862), 75; Ware: *Political Opinion in Massachusetts*, p. 115, note; Phillips to Sumner, May 10, 1862, Sumner MSS.

Senate as to be out of touch with the interests of Massachusetts and concluded, as did one of Governor Andrew's correspondents, that "rotation in office is . . . a pretty safe basis for our institutions." [3]

Especially ominous was Andrew's indifference toward Sumner's reelection. The governor resented having to stand in the shadow of the Senator, to whom he owed his first election. Conceited and dogmatic, Andrew felt that his tremendous exertions in raising and supplying Massachusetts troops went unnoticed while Sumner's speeches made the headlines. He was aggrieved because Sumner and Wilson did not fully support him in his frequent controversies with the War Department, and he tended to agree with his agent in Washington that "Our Senators . . . are not worth a cent for any interest outside there [*sic*] own." Sumner, he thought, spent too much of his time promoting theoretical proposals concerning emancipation and reconstruction and not enough in advocating practical bills that would help Massachusetts troops at the front. Aware of Sumner's growing unpopularity, Andrew was petulant because the choice of Senator had to be involved in the fall elections, when he was seeking a merited third term as governor, and he felt that he would probably have to carry Sumner on his back to victory. Declaring that he was too busy running the state to take part in politics, Andrew decided to sit out the election.[4]

With Andrew neutral, other Massachusetts Republicans felt free to work against Sumner. Western Massachusetts had long felt slighted because both of the state's Senators came from the Boston area, and some politicians promoted the candidacy of Representative Henry L. Dawes of Pittsfield, whose efforts to root out corruption in the Lincoln government, they claimed, were but "imperfectly and coldly seconded by men who would talk . . . at any time on abstract philanthropy and democracy." [5] Though not prepared to commit himself to Dawes, Samuel

[3] Charles Ingersoll to Andrew, June 20, 1862, Andrew MSS. By *"personel"* Ingersoll probably meant "personality."

[4] Simon: "Congress under Lincoln," pp. 404–5; Frank E. Howe to Andrew, Jan. 27, 1862, Andrew MSS.; Mrs. W. S. Robinson: *"Warrington" Pen-Portraits* (Boston: Lee and Shepard; 1877), p. 411.

[5] Dana to Dawes, May 10, 1862, Dawes MSS.

Bowles, editor of the Springfield *Republican,* which was the best and most influential paper in the state, was sharply critical of Sumner. Planning to go to Europe during the summer of 1862, Bowles promised that his substitute, Josiah G. Holland, would use the *Republican* to fight Sumner's reelection.[6]

In the eastern part of the state there was also Republican disaffection toward Sumner, especially among those who had once joined with him in the Free Soil party. Some resented the fact that Sumner alone of those who had dared to disrupt the Whig party was rewarded by high office and public renown; others were unhappy that Sumner had pushed so far beyond the limited Free Soil platform in his campaign for abolition. Richard Henry Dana, Jr., now in one of his moods of high conservatism, emerged as the strategist of this group of Sumner's opponents. Dana, long a close personal friend of the Senator, had worked with him in politics since the breakup of the Whig party, and Sumner had been instrumental in securing his appointment as United States District Attorney. Nevertheless, Dana actively plotted to replace the Senator with his greatest enemy, Charles Francis Adams, now minister to Great Britain.[7]

Formidable in itself, the opposition to Sumner's reelection drew added strength from his enemies in the administration at Washington. From the outset many of Sumner's Massachusetts critics regarded their battle against his reelection as part of a nationwide effort to curb the Radical element in the Republican party, and they naturally turned to the Secretary of State for assistance.[8] Circumspect, Seward could take no public part in the move to unseat Sumner, but his political crony and principal editorial supporter, Thurlow Weed, actively intervened in the Massachusetts contest. Fearing, as did Seward, that when the Confederacy collapsed Sumner and his fellow Radicals would "become rampant" and commit excesses which would encourage

[6] C. C. Chaffee to Dawes, April 8, 1862, ibid. Bowles's biographer attempted to disassociate the editor from the move to unseat Sumner and to put all the responsibility upon Holland (George S. Merriam: *The Life and Times of Samuel Bowles* [New York: The Century Co.; 1885], I, 357–9), but the contemporary evidence refutes this view.

[7] Samuel Shapiro: *Richard Henry Dana, Jr., 1815–1882* (East Lansing, Mich.: Michigan State University Press; 1961), pp. 124–7.

[8] E.g., John H. Clifford to Seward, Feb. 25, 1862, Seward MSS.

"the Democracy . . . [to] seek Power in the old way," Weed regularly criticized Sumner in his Albany *Evening Journal* and damned "the more than incendiary, the scarcely less than infernal spirit" which he represented in the Senate. Begging the citizens of Massachusetts "to withdraw their support from, and their confidence in, an impracticable Senator," Weed's paper bluntly opposed Sumner's reelection: "Massachusetts is patriotic and sensible. She should choose as Senator, in this hour of peril, a man of practical sense. In this quality, Mr. Sumner is eminently deficient." [9]

• 5 •

Facing a severe challenge, Sumner responded with political astuteness. Recognizing that his most earnest supporters in Massachusetts were those who backed him precisely because they did not think him a politician, he publicly professed complete indifference as to how he might fare in the next election. As always in such a crisis, he talked of withdrawing from public life. "There is a diabolism in Massachusetts," he wrote Andrew, in an effort to arouse the governor's sympathies. "I sometimes think that, if I were out of the way it would be less rampant." [1]

He was, however, very careful not to put himself out of the way. Instead, he and his close friends took a series of steps intended to secure his reelection. In June the Boston *Journal*, Ben: Perley Poore's paper, published what purported to be a personal letter from Sumner to an unidentified friend, rebuking his correspondent's impatience with Lincoln's failure to abolish slavery and assuring him of the President's "sincerity of . . . purpose to do what he can to carry forward the principles of the Declaration of Independence." "Could you—as has been my privilege often—," Sumner went on, thus suggesting his intimacy with Lincoln, "have seen the President, while considering the great questions on which he has already acted, beginning with the invitation to Emancipation in the States, then Emancipation

[9] Weed to Seward, Mar. 9, 1862, ibid.; Albany *Evening Journal*, quoted in Boston *Courier*, July 23 and Oct. 30, 1862.

[1] May 28, 1862, Andrew MSS.

in the District of Columbia, and the acknowledgment of the Independence of Hayti and Liberia, even your zeal would be satisfied. . . ." "Stand by the Administration," the letter concluded.[2]

The document was a curious one. Not one word in it was false, for Sumner truly was pleased with the steps Lincoln had taken against slavery; but it was not the whole truth, for it revealed nothing of the Senator's mounting impatience with the slow, legalistic Chief Executive. The timing, too, was odd, coming, as it did, just before Sumner put himself at the head of the Congressional critics of Lincoln and just before he announced that the President was the tool of Congress. Finally, the recipient of the letter was, and has remained, unknown. Wickedly the New York *Herald* conjectured that Sumner's mysterious "friend" was none other than Massachusetts Congressman John B. Alley, who, it claimed, sat at the table while Sumner wrote the letter to him and then released it to the papers.

Publication of the letter was a clever political maneuver, intended, as conservatives suggested, to "hedge on the charge of antagonism to the President." Though a few irate abolitionists thought it a "flunkeyish manifesto," designed to put Sumner back in Lincoln's good graces, most readers accepted its statement of basic agreement between Senator and President. It undercut conservatives' claims that they, rather than Sumner, supported Lincoln's policies.[3]

As another step to promote his reelection Sumner let his Massachusetts friends know of his concern about the "wicked," if not "diabolical," Massachusetts press. To be sure, a number of small country weeklies backed Sumner, but the major newspapers in the state were hostile. The Democratic Boston *Post* and the Whiggish Boston *Courier* were virulent opponents; the Springfield *Republican* openly sought to replace him; and the Republican Boston *Daily Advertiser* seemed to Sumner "almost as bad as the *Courier*."[4] No Boston paper but the insignificant

[2] Sumner: *Works,* VII, 117.

[3] New York *Herald,* July 13, 1862; Adam Gurowski to Andrew, June 16, 1862, Andrew MSS.; Springfield *Republican,* June 16, 1862.

[4] Sumner to Andrew, May 28, 1862, Andrew MSS.

Traveller made a practice of publishing his speeches. Sumner passed along his bitter sense of being unable to reach the people to his old friend, Samuel Gridley Howe, who assembled the members of the Bird Club to consider the problem. "There is not a newspaper in Boston," said Howe, with only a little exaggeration, "that will publish one of Sumner's speeches, or say a good word for him."

"Then," said George L. Stearns, a wealthy Boston manufacturer of lead pipes who had long backed antislavery causes, "we must have a paper of our own and I will put a thousand dollars in it as a sinking fund."

"I cannot do that," replied Howe, "but I will give three hundred."

Other members of the club also contributed, and they agreed that the new journal should be called *The Commonwealth,* after the defunct Free Soil paper which had supported Sumner's original election to the Senate in 1851. James M. Stone became the first editor. Sumner himself was not asked to contribute money, but, though he had repeatedly rebuked those who used for private purposes the Congressional privilege of free postage, he franked a thousand envelopes in which the first issues of the *Commonwealth* were mailed out on September 6.[5]

Sumner also made sure that federal officeholders in Massachusetts would not work against his reelection. Under the new Internal Revenue Act each Congressional District in a state was to have a tax assessor and a tax collector, and it was immediately clear that these powerful officials, who had to visit every ward and every hamlet, would exert great political influence. Former Massachusetts Governor George S. Boutwell, soon to become chief of the whole internal revenue system in Washington, alerted Sumner to "the importance of so guiding the appointments that our enemies may not have the opportunity of canvassing the State at the public charge." Sumner's supporters thought he ought to warn Secretary Chase not to appoint "untrustworthy men," "men who have merely worked with us because we are in the majority." The danger stirred even Governor Andrew from

[5] Stearns: *Life . . . of George Luther Stearns,* pp. 263, 268.

his lethargy, for it threatened his reelection; he worried that conservatives might "secure a large representation in this agency, so that by means of their influence with the people (and in traveling from town to town) they can poison the minds of prominent citizens" and help defeat "Republicanism in this Commonwealth." Sumner always recoiled from such direct appeals to play the practical politician distributing the spoils, but he worked privately with Chase to make sure that only his reliable supporters, mostly veteran antislavery men, received appointments. "I note the raging of the Hunkers," he reassured Andrew. "But with the Governor and the 2 Senators a unit—and the organization with us—are they not powerless?" [6]

Meanwhile his Massachusetts friends were making sure that "the organization" remained with him. Since the chairman and the treasurer of the Republican state committee directly controlled the expenditure of between ten and twenty-five thousand dollars in each election campaign and influenced the use of even larger amounts raised by local party units, it was imperative that these officials be vigorous supporters of Sumner's reelection. But they were chosen by a Republican convention called to nominate candidates for the governorship and other state offices. Since United States Senators were still elected by legislatures, Sumner's name would not be on the ballot in November; indeed, since in Massachusetts senatorial aspirants customarily pretended total indifference to the process by which they were selected, there was no need for Sumner's name even to be mentioned at the state convention. It was quite possible, therefore, that the party machinery could fall into hands indifferent to his prospects.

To forestall this possibility, Bird met with W. S. Robinson —the influential Boston correspondent of the Springfield *Republican,* whose politics differed markedly from those of his editor —Adin Thayer, and one or two other members of the Bird Club near Plymouth during the summer to plan their strategy. Recognizing that the principal threat to Sumner would not be a Demo-

[6] Boutwell to Sumner, April 14, 1862, Sumner MSS.; James W. Stone to Sumner, May 31, 1862, Chase MSS., Lib. of Cong.; Stone to Andrew, May 31, 1862; Andrew MSS., Andrew to Sumner, June 9, 1862, Sumner MSS.

cratic or a Bell-Everett candidate but a moderate Republican around whom all the anti-Sumner forces would rally, they decided to make Sumner's reelection the test of party orthodoxy in Massachusetts by having the Republican state convention endorse him as its one and only choice for the Senate. Since the tactic had never been tried before in Massachusetts, it was, as Robinson wrote, "a bold and somewhat risky plot," which was sure to encounter opposition. In order to confuse opponents as much as possible, the planners chose as their convention spokesman young J. Q. A. Griffin, of Charlestown, known to be able and intelligent but not yet closely identified with Sumner's ideas.[7]

No amount of strategy could prevent the fight which erupted at the Worcester convention on September 9. Sumner's opponents were present in numbers.[8] Their strength became evident when Griffin, after the preliminary ceremonies, moved the customary appointment of a committee on resolutions. Dana jumped up to deny the need for such a committee. The only purpose of this convention, he claimed, was the renomination of Governor Andrew and the rest of the state ticket, which everybody present favored; but if any resolution was called for, it was simply that "Massachusetts, with all her heart and soul and mind and strength, will support the President of the United States in the prosecution of this war."

Countering Dana's maneuver, Griffin endorsed this sentiment but added that he was for supporting "the fearless legislator in his duty" as well as the soldier in the field. He then proposed a resolution extolling "the preeminent merits and services of our Senators in the Congress of the United States," expressing "warm approbation" of Sumner's course, and explicitly commending him "to the suffrages of his fellow citizens" in the forthcoming election.

In the angry debate which followed, it was evident that Sumner's partisans were more numerous and better organized

[7] Robinson: *"Warrington" Pen-Portraits*, p. 126; undated clipping from Boston *Post*, in Frank W. Bird Scrapbooks, owned by Mr. Charles Sumner Bird; George F. Hoar: *Autobiography of Seventy Years* (New York: Charles Scribner's Sons; 1903), I, 301–2.

[8] My account of the Worcester convention is based upon stories in the Boston *Advertiser*, Sept. 11, 1862, Boston *Courier*, Sept. 11, 1862, and Boston *Commonwealth*, Sept. 13, 1862.

than their opponents. Finally, to cut off the controversy, George F. Hoar moved that both Dana's and Griffin's resolutions should be referred to a special committee, with orders to combine them and to add an "expression of this Convention that it is the duty of the U. S. Government, in the further prosecution of the war, to strike the rebellion where it is weakest"—i.e., to abolish slavery.

While the committee on resolutions deliberated, the convention proceeded to renominate Andrew by acclamation and to name the other members of the state ticket. At this point Sumner was expected to make a speech, but, worrying over the rapid deterioration of his brother's health and following his "instincts . . . against going where [his] name was to be brought in question," he stayed away from the convention. Instead he sent a letter to be read that deplored "the rancors and animosities of party," urged further antislavery measures *"to hamstring this Rebellion"*—and made no reference at all to Abraham Lincoln or his administration.[9]

When the resolutions committee then reported, it was clear how closely it followed the Senator's lead. For the majority Griffin proposed that "Massachusetts with all her heart and strength will support the Government of the United States in the prosecution of this war," but, like Sumner's letter, his resolution carefully refrained from mentioning, much less endorsing, the President of the United States. Other resolutions demanded that slavery be "exterminated," that Andrew be reelected, and that Sumner, "a statesman, a scholar, a patriot, and a man of whom any Republic in any age might be proud," be returned to the Senate. Vainly conservatives protested the deliberate silence about the President of the United States; vainly Dana presented a minority report denying the convention's authority to name a candidate for the Senate; vainly Dr. Charles G. Loring argued that "there were persons in this Commonwealth who, from their more practical ability . . . *might* be able to represent this Commonwealth with more force, and more . . . advantage than Mr. Sumner." Sumner's friends hissed down all opposition, rejected

[9] Sumner to J. Q. A. Griffin, Sept. 11, 1862, MS., Wellesley College Lib.; Sumner: *Works*, VII, 187–90.

all amendments to Griffin's resolutions, and whooped through an adjournment before anybody could change his mind. The Republican party entered the fall campaign with Sumner's reelection as its principal issue.

· 6 ·

The action of the Worcester convention divided Sumner's critics. Those who were members of the Republican party, and especially those who held public office under that party, had little choice but to cease open opposition to his reelection. Dana, recognizing that he might lose his profitable post as United States District Attorney, sought out Sumner to make his peace. "I must say, to his honor," Dana reported on the interview, "that he did not quarrel with me. He was intensely *exercised* . . . and thought me on the perilous edge of the pit of perdition, and thought he had a claim on me for a vigorous support. Indeed, he has set his heart on a re-election, with a passion passing the love of women. He [is] a fanatic in his own cause." Still, with so much at stake, Dana could only fall in line, writing to Sumner: "I sincerely say that you have always treated me with extreme kindness and even forbearance, when I have differed from or failed to support you, in certain things you hold dear." [1]

For others, not constrained by personal loyalty or patronage ties, the resolutions of the Worcester convention were the signal to start a new party. On August 28, before the Republicans met, a group of "conservative gentlemen" from Boston, Salem, and Lowell had already gathered privately to "consider the best method of overcoming the radical element in Massachusetts at the polls." [2] Among the leaders were former Whig governor John H. Clifford, former Know-Nothing Governor Henry J. Gardner, the editor of the Catholic Boston *Pilot,* and Leverett Saltonstall, the influential lawyer. Just three days after the Republican convention endorsed Sumner, these and other conservatives issued an address "To the People of Massachusetts," which urged that

[1] Dana to Adams, Oct. 26, 1862, Adams MSS.; Dana to Sumner, Sept. 13, 1862, Sumner MSS.

[2] Lowell *Weekly Journal,* Aug. 29, 1862.

"Party and party names must be abandoned in this crisis." At a time when Robert E. Lee's army was crossing the Potomac to invade Maryland, the North must have but "one purpose, one aim." "No discussions about political, social, or party measures and dogmas . . . should be tolerated." Capitalizing upon the Republicans' calculated slight to Lincoln, the address urged that "the hands of the president, the chosen and only head of the nation, must be strengthened by the people"; Massachusetts must not "turn from him in coldness or palsy his efforts with a feeble and half confidence." [3]

Within ten days more than a thousand voters, representing some of the oldest and most influential families in Massachusetts, endorsed this appeal and, along with it, a call for a "Convention of the People" to be held in Faneuil Hall on October 7. This "People's Party," as the movement became known, posed a formidable threat to Republican success in November and to Sumner's reelection in January. It had effective leadership from men like Josiah G. Abbott, who drafted the original address, and Joel Parker, who headed the list of signers. It capitalized upon the general feeling that Sumner had been neglecting the practical, business interests of the state. It took advantage of the growing war weariness and drew strength from the widespread report that Sumner had failed to support McClellan and the other Union generals in the field. It appealed to the strong anti-Negro prejudice prevalent throughout the North, even in Massachusetts. Claiming that Sumner desired a servile insurrection in the South, a writer in the *Courier* believed that he also looked toward racial amalgamation in the North; indeed, one could observe the practical result of Sumner's policies in his own Beacon Hill ward in Boston, where "a negro—stalwart in frame—uncontaminated by any mixture of white blood in his veins" was seen "lounging up the street with a white female; his arm encircling her neck in close embrace—and she by no means reluctant." But most of all the People's movement drew strength from the belief that Sumner and the Massachusetts Republican leaders were opponents of the President of the United States.

[3] Boston *Courier*, Sept. 22, 1862; Springfield *Republican*, Sept. 25, 1862.

Once the masses of the Republican party "perceive that they are being used by a set of men who are in virtual opposition to the government," the conservatives predicted, "they will revolt . . . [and] join in any honest movement to destroy the old party, cast down its idols, and begin anew." [4]

Sumner was scared. Genuinely believing, as Dana scornfully reported, "that if *any* other man . . . should be elected in his place, it would be felt at the antipodes,—that the cause of liberty the world over would be put back a century, and Freedom would shriek," [5] he sadly viewed the possibility that Massachusetts would once more fall under the control of Hunkers, callous to the plight of the Negro, indifferent to the rights of man. During September as the People's movement gained strength, he grew more gloomy and despondent, and friends heard him sigh from time to time: "Poor Country—poor, poor Country!" [6]

On September 22 Abraham Lincoln came to his rescue by issuing the Emancipation Proclamation. It was the move for which Sumner had so long prayed in vain that he grew to despair of it. Nothing Sumner had been able to say or do during the long session of Congress, which ended on July 17, had induced Lincoln to act. Nor, though he had stayed on in Washington for a few days after adjournment to urge emancipation, could he secure any definite promise of future action. Vaguely Lincoln declared "that, in the last resort, *every agency* must be employed," but the sum of his conversation with Sumner had been: "*wait—time* is essential." Nor had Sumner been able to secure a positive pledge of emancipation when he returned to Washington in mid-August, in order to help Chase select politically reliable appointees for the internal revenue service. Lincoln, he learned, had actually drawn up an emancipation proclamation and had discussed it with the cabinet, but Seward had persuaded him "that 'we *mustn't issue it* till after a victory.'" Angrily Sumner "protested against the delay, and wished it to be put forth—the sooner the better—without any reference to our military

[4] Boston *Courier*, Sept. 13, 1862; Springfield *Republican*, Sept. 19, 1862.

[5] Dana to Adams, Oct. 26, 1862, Adams MSS.

[6] Longfellow: Journal, Sept. 14, 1862, Longfellow MSS.

condition," but the President would not agree.[7] Without hope of ever getting action from the chief executive, Sumner increasingly rested his hopes for emancipation upon the confiscation act, which promised to free the slaves of those still in rebellion after September 17. This measure, Sumner concluded, would prove "an effective edict of Emancipation," no matter what Lincoln might do.[8]

When Lincoln did issue his proclamation, Sumner, like many other antislavery men, may have had a moment of regret, recognizing that the President was really postponing emancipation for another hundred days, while freeing the slaves under the confiscation act would presumably have begun immediately.[9] But if Sumner had reservations, he silenced them immediately, for he recognized that Lincoln had handed him a superb political weapon. The whole People's movement rested on the claim that Massachusetts Republicans differed in policy from the President. Now the Emancipation Proclamation offered Sumner the chance to get right with Lincoln. Scheduling a rally at Faneuil Hall on the day before the People's Party convention was to meet, Sumner made an exultant speech. "For myself," he announced, "I accept the Proclamation without note or comment. . . . I place myself, with the loyal multitudes of the North, firmly and sincerely by the side of the President, where, indeed, I have ever been."[1]

The People's Party convention met the next day in an air of anticlimax and anticipated defeat. Bravely their speakers denounced "miserable meddling politicians interfering with our noble men and generals in the field" and pledged "an unconditional support of the Government, in all the measures known to civilized warfare." With seeming enthusiasm the convention

[7] Sumner to Duchess of Argyll, Aug. 11, 1862, Argyll MSS.; Sumner to B. F. Wade, Aug. 11, 1862, MS., Ill. State Hist. Soc.; George Bemis: Diary, Nov. 13, 1862, Bemis MSS.; William Stuart to Russell, Aug. 22, 1862, Stuart MSS.; Sumner to Bright, Oct. 28, 1862, Bright MSS.

[8] Sumner to B. P. Poore, Sept. 23, 1862, MS., Chicago Hist. Soc.

[9] Simon: "Congress under Lincoln," pp. 535–6.

[1] Sumner: *Emancipation! Its Policy and Necessity, as a War Measure for the Suppression of the Rebellion* (n.p., n.d.). The same passage, slightly modified, appears in Sumner: *Works,* VII, 204.

named a slate of candidates for state office, headed by Brigadier General Charles Devens, recently conspicuous as a hero in the Peninsula campaign but, to antislavery men, notorious as the United States marshal who sent the shivering fugitive Thomas Sims back to slavery in 1851. Having objected so strongly that the Republican convention had no power to endorse Sumner for the Senate, the People's Party leaders could not consistently ask their convention to name a candidate to compete with him.[2]

The probable fate of the People's movement became evident during the Democratic convention held at Worcester on the following day. Adopting the slate of candidates nominated by the People's convention, Democratic leaders indiscreetly let it slip out that they had all along been behind the new party; they had "coaxed" and "admonished" the "conservative republicans to call that meeting [the People's Party convention] in Faneuil Hall." "These men of the people's party are going to unite with us hereafter," one blunt Democratic politician explained; "there is nowhere else that they can go." [3]

This too ardent embrace from the Democrats strangled the People's movement, but its failure was already foreordained. Pledged to uphold the President of the United States against the assaults of his Radical enemies, People's politicians discovered on September 22 that Lincoln and Sumner stood on the same ground. Dedicated to preserving the Constitution with all its niceties, they found themselves backing an administration that believed the war powers were all-encompassing. Pledged to oppose partisan rule, they found themselves tools of the Democrats.

Many leaders in the anti-Sumner movement lapsed into silence. Clifford, for instance, announcing that he was "not willing to be sold out to the half-Secession Democracy," declined to take any further part in the canvass and refused to stand as People's candidate for the state senate. Others continued to fight,

[2] *Proceedings of the Convention of the People of Massachusetts, Holden at Faneuil Hall, Boston, October 7, 1862* (Boston: C. J. Peters; 1862); Boston *Courier*, Oct. 8, 1862.

[3] Boston *Advertiser*, Oct. 10, 1862.

but in an underhanded fashion. After accepting the People's nomination for the legislature, Charles J. Hinsdale, of the Punkett Wollen Company of Hinsdale, wrote confidential letters as an ostensible Republican urging "that we ought to have a more practical statesman to represent our state in Congress" than Sumner.[4]

As a last effort to block Sumner's reelection, the Springfield *Republican* urged the four major papers in the state—the Boston *Post*, the Boston *Advertiser*, the Boston *Courier*, and the *Republican* itself—to unite in endorsing either Charles Francis Adams or Nathaniel P. Banks, "our first-class, commonsense, practical men—statesmen both." [5] Even this last hope of the anti-Sumner men was promptly shot down. Though the members of the Adams family had not abated their detestation of Sumner, "so convinced that he alone sees the clear way, so absolute in his opinions and wholly devoid of charity to others," they recognized that the *Republican's* proposal was nothing but a desperate attempt on the part of Massachusetts "fogies" to regain power. The minister's son, John Quincy Adams, Jr., issued a statement declaring that Charles Francis Adams's "ideas of usefulness and duty incline him rather to remain at his post than to desire any change of position" and that, in consequence, "he most explicitly declines to be a candidate . . . for the Senate of the United States." [6]

After this, the People's Party campaign degenerated into farce. As the respectable politicians withdrew from the movement, a half-lunatic, half-genius named George Francis Train took over. The heir of a prominent Massachusetts shipbuilding family, who had made a name for himself in Great Britain by building street-railroads and by denouncing the aristocracy, Train had returned to America in September to save his native land from "the Fanatics, Charles Sumner, Henry Wilson, Wendell Phillips and William Loyd [*sic*] Garrison," who were, he

[4] Clifford to R. C. Winthrop, Oct. 19, 1862, copy, Winthrop MSS.; Mountaineer" [Charles Wright]: *An Appeal for Rectitude in Primary Politics* (Boston: Alfred Mudge & Son, Printers; 1863), pp. 8–9.

[5] Springfield *Republican*, Oct. 16, 1862.

[6] Ford (ed.): *A Cycle of Adams Letters*, I, 172; J. Q. Adams, Jr., to C. F. Adams, Jr., Oct. 10, 1862, Adams MSS.; Boston *Advertiser*, Oct. 28, 1862.

charged, conspiring "TO RUIN OUR GREAT AMERICAN EMPIRE." Failing in an effort to disrupt Sumner's speech at Faneuil Hall on October 6, Train hired the large Boston Music Hall ten days later for a meeting of his own, where he pledged he would "dissect and cut up Charles Sumner, inch by inch." Before an audience that came to be amused, the buffoon charged that Sumner did not represent "the true sentiments and instincts of the people of Massachusetts," since he suffered from "a deep seated nigger cancer." Sumner could "speak of nothing but the 'sublime nigger' "; his speech in Faneuil Hall "was nothing but the nigger at the beginning, nigger in the middle, and nigger at the end." If Sumner were honest in his beliefs, he would take "the negro to his home, and the negro woman to his bed." Asking the audience whether they "lived in the Old Bay State or in the Nigger State," Train generously disclaimed any plans to succeed Sumner. "I am too young to take Charles Sumner's place in the Senate," he announced, giving his age as thirty-three, "else I would be elected by acclamation." [7]

Though the danger was over, Republicans continued to campaign in earnest during the final six weeks before the election. They made rather unconvincing efforts to prove that Sumner was a business-minded Senator who took a profound interest in the economic well-being of his constituents. They recalled his past sufferings in the fight against slavery by circulating a pamphlet called *The Sumner Memorial,* which reprinted 1856 newspaper accounts of "The Ruffian Assault upon Charles Sumner in the Senate Chamber," and the *Commonwealth* regularly referred to the opposition as the "Brooks party." In public letters Horace Greeley paid tribute to Sumner's "stern uprightness," and Whittier argued that his "defeat would weaken the Government at home, and its influence abroad, discourage the loyal and true in other States, and give a thrill of joy to the traitors in arms against the Union." [8]

[7] Boston *Post,* Oct. 17, 1862; Boston *Advertiser,* Oct. 14, 1862; Willis Thornton: *The Nine Lives of Citizen Train* (New York: Greenberg; 1948), pp. 130–1.

[8] *The Independent,* Oct. 16, 1862; *The Liberator,* XXXII (Oct. 24, 1862), 170.

Behind the scenes the whole Republican party organization in Massachusetts worked for Sumner's reelection. Quietly the newly appointed internal revenue assessors and collectors threw their weight behind the Senator. Workmen in the Charlestown navy yard got word "that the men employed there will be required to favor Charles Sumner's reelection to the U. S. Senate, or resign." Candidates for the legislature were asked to give public pledges that they would vote for Sumner if elected. Instructions from Republican county committees to party workers concluded: "Above all, see to it that your candidate for Representative to the General Court [i.e., the state legislature], will support CHARLES SUMNER for the U. S. Senate, and then use every exertion to elect him." [9]

Intent upon making the election a mighty referendum endorsing emancipation, Sumner himself campaigned strenuously. "I will speak every night till the election . . . ," he promised,[1] and he crisscrossed the state, appearing at Worcester, Woburn, Salem, Gloucester, Lowell, Greenfield, Pittsfield, Springfield, Fitchburg, and Haverhill. Everywhere he charged that the Democratic and the People's parties were falsely labeled. While the United States was engaged in fighting a civil war, there could be only two parties: "the party of our country, with the President for its head, and Emancipation its glorious watchword; and the party of Rebellion, with Jefferson Davis for its head, and no other watchword than Slavery." [2] Union, Emancipation, Lincoln, and Sumner were identical; opposition to any one of them was nothing short of treason.

With the lines so drawn, the outcome could not be in doubt. "The game is up," conceded the Springfield *Republican* on October 30; "as between Mr. Sumner and any man who is likely to be nominated against him, now, we should go for Mr. Sumner decidedly." So too did the voters. On November 4 fifty-nine percent of the Massachusetts voters chose Andrew to be gover-

[9] Boston *Post,* Sept. 24, 1862; Springfield *Republican,* Oct. 11, 1862; printed letter from D. L. Morril, Secretary, Headquarters Republican County Committee Worcester, Oct. 20, 1862, in Sumner Scrapbooks.

[1] Sumner to "My dear Sir," Oct. 12, 1862, MS., Boston Pub. Lib.

[2] Sumner: *Works,* VII, 236.

nor again and selected an overwhelmingly Republican legislature pledged to give Sumner a third term in the Senate.[3] As the returns poured in on election night, triumphant Republicans marched from door to door to serenade the successful candidates. Nearly a thousand assembled in front of Sumner's house on Hancock Street and loudly called upon him to speak. The "unarmed guerilla bands of Jefferson Davis here in Massachusetts have been routed," he announced, to their cheers and applause. "The cause of the President, of the Government, of the Republic, and the cause of Liberty itself, has triumphed."[4]

[3] This represented a two percent decline in the Republican vote since 1860. It has not been possible to make a meaningful statistical analysis of the election returns, since, though Sumner's reelection was the principal issue before the voters, his name could not appear on the ballots. In general the vote for the Republican state ticket, headed by Andrew, was nearly as large as that in 1860 but was markedly below the sixty-seven percent which Andrew received in 1861, when Democratic opposition was nominal. A computer program correlating these votes with various social, economic, ethnic, and religious indices reveals few changes in group-voting patterns between 1860 and 1862, but the aversion of the Irish toward the Republicans seemed to have intensified. There was in 1862 a marked decline in both the number and the percentage of Republican votes cast in western Massachusetts, particularly in Berkshire, Franklin, Hampden, and Hampshire counties—the area where the Springfield *Republican* had the greatest influence—though all remained safely Republican. When the legislature assembled in January, however, the votes cast against Sumner's reelection came largely from areas which had always been hostile to him and to Republicans. Of the 38 votes given to other candidates, 12 came from Boston and all but 5 of the rest came from surrounding towns. Seven of these 38 legislators represented towns which had given Andrew a majority in the 1862 gubernatorial election.

[4] Boston *Advertiser,* Nov. 5, 1862.

CHAPTER III

Remove Him!

"REMOVE him!" began the lead editorial in the Boston *Commonwealth* on December 6, 1862. "William H. Seward stands before the American people today as the enemy of the public. . . . We have had enough of his paralizing [*sic*] influence on the army and the President; let the Watchword of the Hour be, *Remove Seward from the Cabinet!*" As usual, the *Commonwealth* reflected Sumner's views, and the Senator was to make its "watchword" his unchanging objective throughout the next session of Congress.

Step by step Sumner's relations with Seward had deteriorated until an open break was inevitable. Once close friends and colleagues in the antislavery movement, they had seriously disagreed over the handling of the secession crisis and over the conduct of foreign relations. Sumner felt that Seward, being "merely . . . a politician, . . . did not see the elemental forces engaged" in the Civil War and "failed to see this war in its true character" as a struggle for human freedom everywhere. This moral obtuseness, Sumner thought, explained Seward's holding up of the issuance of the Emancipation Proclamation in August. The same blindness to principle permitted Seward to sit idle and inactive during the crucial fall elections in New York, when the voters rejected a dedicated antislavery candidate for governor and chose instead a Democrat, Horatio Seymour. It also was behind Seward's tacit encouragement of that "enormous mischief-maker," Thurlow Weed, in his attempt to block Sumner's bid for reelection. Convinced that Seward had "neither wisdom or courage," Sumner resolved that he must be ousted from the government, else the nation would face only "gloom and tragedy." [1]

When the Thirty-Seventh Congress began its third session on December 1 Sumner found that most Republicans shared his forebodings. The party had been badly shaken by the fall elections, which gave the Democrats control of important states like New York, Pennsylvania, New Jersey, and Indiana and nearly doubled the number of Democratic Representatives who would have seats in the next Congress. Though some Republicans from closely divided states blamed the disaster upon the President's antislavery policy, more agreed with Sumner in attributing it to the "hesitation of the Administration to adopt the policy of Emancipation," which had encouraged the Democrats to rally. "A more determined policy months ago would have prevented them from shewing their heads," Sumner judged. "The President himself has played the part of the farmer in the fable who warmed the frozen snake at his fire." [2]

Repeated failure of the Union armies added to Republican discontent with the Lincoln administration. Though Antietam had been called a Union victory, General McClellan, whom Sumner called "our military incubus," failed to follow it up. In November Lincoln replaced McClellan with Ambrose E. Burnside, whose inadequacy for high command was equaled only by his recognition of his incompetence. "I am not sure that Burnside is capable," Sumner wrote anxiously to John Bright, asking whether it might be possible to "send us an Englishman who will handle . . . two hundred thousand men." His fears proved all too justified when, two weeks after Congress reassembled, Burnside blundered into the bloody fiasco at Fredericksburg.[3]

[1] Sumner to Bright, Oct. 28 and Nov. 18, 1862, Bright MSS.; Sumner to Horace Greeley [1863], Greeley MSS., New York Pub. Lib.; Sumner to Chase, Nov. 7, 1862, Chase MSS., Lib. of Cong.

[2] Sumner to Bright, Oct. 28, 1862, Bright MSS.

[3] Sumner to Duchess of Argyll, Nov. 12, 1862, Argyll MSS.; Sumner to Bright, Nov. 18, 1862, Bright MSS.

From all over the North there came a roar of discontent with the Lincoln administration. Much of it was directed at the President himself. "I do not believe in Mr. Lincoln at all . . . ," Orestes A. Brownson wrote Sumner. "He is thick-headed; he is ignorant; he is tricky, somewhat astute in a small way, and obstinate as a mule." We have "a cowardly imbecile at the head of the Government," raged one of Sumner's Cincinnati correspondents. "Old Abe will do nothing decent till driven to it by a force which would save all the devils in hell," Bird grumbled. Lincoln's resignation, wrote a Bostonian, "would be received with *great satisfaction*," and it might "avert what . . . will otherwise come viz a *violent and bloody revolution at the North*." Other critics, believing it impossible to force the President to resign, demanded that Lincoln be required to listen to new advisers. "A storm is rising," warned John Jay "that presently will not be stilled by any thing less than an entire reconstruction of the Cabinet." [4]

Even before Fredricksburg Sumner had come to that conclusion. Upon returning to Washington he learned that the United States was facing a formidable crisis in foreign affairs, and he thought that Seward, in addition to all his other failings, was badly handling it. It is not clear how soon Sumner learned of the exceedingly dangerous plan for European mediation in the American Civil War brought before the British cabinet in October 1862, but in early December Bright told him about the proposal, which had temporarily failed because of dissension within Palmerston's cabinet, reluctance of Tory leaders in Parliament to support intervention, and unwillingness of the Russian government to participate. It took no inside information, however, to know of Gladstone's indiscreet speech at Newcastle on October 7, announcing that Jefferson Davis had succeeded in making a nation in the South, or of the fitting out in British shipyards of Confederate raiders that were sweeping the Union merchant marine from the seas. In the face of such dangers the American Secretary of State appeared to be doing nothing.

[4] Letters to Sumner from Brownson, Dec. 26, 1862; W. Grant, Dec. 24, 1862; Bird, Dec. 24 [1862]; George F. Williams, Dec. 17, 1862; Jay, Dec. 18, 1862—all in Sumner MSS.

Indeed, Sumner thought Seward was doing worse than nothing, for he discouraged the antislavery forces in Britain, the truest friends of the North. Sumner was outraged to discover in the volume of *Papers Relating to Foreign Affairs,* which Seward published in the fall, a despatch the Secretary had written to Charles Francis Adams on July 5, 1862, denouncing both "the extreme advocates of African slavery [in the United States] and its most vehement opponents," the abolitionists, for "acting in concert together to precipitate a servile war—the former by making the most desperate attempt to overthrow the federal Union, the latter by demanding an edict of universal emancipation as a lawful and necessary . . . way of saving the Union." Neither at the time nor later did anybody know what was in Seward's mind in writing such a despatch at the very time that Lincoln was considering an emancipation proclamation, nor is it clear why Seward thought it desirable to publish this confidential document, which any abolitionist was bound to consider offensive.[5] Conceivably the Secretary, who never gave up the notion that a restored Union ought to be governed by a moderate party which excluded Southern fire-eaters on the one side and ultra-abolitionists on the other, thought the fall elections were a signal for a new political alignment. Whatever Seward's purposes, he could hardly have done more to alienate Sumner than by thus restating a policy which, the Senator felt, "had turned Europe against us and still keeps 4 millions of slaves the invaluable allies of our enemies." [6]

Sentiment against Seward, which had been bubbling even before Congress assembled and had grown hotter after the news of Fredericksburg, boiled over when the Secretary made known his intention to send Thurlow Weed abroad again as an unofficial roving ambassador.[7] Such public recognition of the "audacious

[5] *Papers Relating to Foreign Affairs, 1862* (Washington: Government Printing Office; 1862), I, 124. None of Seward's biographers has a satisfactory account of the writing and publication of this despatch. Frederic Bancroft (*Life of Seward,* II, 365) asserts that "nothing less than an accident would seem to account for its publication." Glyndon G. Van Deusen (*Seward,* p. 344) states that "Seward himself edited the publication of the dispatches for 1862."

[6] Sumner to S. H. Gay [Nov. 1862?], Gay MSS.

[7] Sister Mary M. O'Rourke: "The Diplomacy of William H. Seward during the Civil War" (unpublished Ph.D. dissertation, University of California, Berkeley, 1963), p. 204.

but deceptive" Weed, who was, Sumner thought, "one of the marplots of our history," symbolized all that was wrong with the Lincoln administration—its slowness, its incompetence, its reliance upon tricky politicians, its unwillingness to take a stand on principle. Angered finally into action, Republican Senators held a caucus in the Senate reception room immediately after adjournment on December 16.[8] It required no poll to show that nearly all were disheartened by the failures of the administration, and a large number of Senators, fed information by the ambitious and earnestly antislavery Secretary of the Treasury Chase, concluded that Seward was responsible for the recent disasters. Charging that the Secretary of State was opposed to the vigorous prosecution of the war, Morton S. Wilkinson of Minnesota claimed that Seward "controlled the President and thwarted the other members of the Cabinet." Fessenden also felt that Seward exerted "a back stairs and malign influence which controlled the President," and James W. Grimes demanded "that the Senate should go in a body and demand of the President the dismissal of Mr. Seward." Even the conciliatory Collamer complained "that the President had no Cabinet in the true sense of the word," that he "did not consult his Cabinet councilors, as a body, upon important matters," and that, indeed, he appeared to believe that the best policy was to have no policy.

Adjourning without action, the caucus reconvened the following day. "Many speeches were made," Browning recorded in his diary, "all expressive of want of confidence in the President and his cabinet. Some of them denouncing the President and expressing a willingness to vote for a resolution asking him to resign." Attempting to sum up the sentiment of the caucus, Ira Harris of New York proposed a resolution "that in the judgment of the Republican members of the Senate, the public confidence

[8] My account of the Republican caucus and of the subsequent meetings with Lincoln is based upon Francis Fessenden: *Life and Public Services of William Pitt Fessenden* (Boston: Houghton Mifflin and Company; 1907), I, 231–48; Browning: *Diary,* I, 596–601; Howard K. Beale and Alan W. Brownsword (eds.): *Diary of Gideon Welles* (New York: W. W. Norton & Company, Inc.; 1960), I, 194–9; and Howard K. Beale (ed.): *The Diary of Edward Bates* (Washington: Government Printing Office; 1933), pp. 269–70. The best secondary account is J. G. Randall: *Lincoln the President* (New York: Dodd, Mead & Company; 1945), II, 241–9.

in the present administration would be increased by a reconstruction of the Cabinet." When John Sherman objected, fearing this resolution might force his fellow Ohioan Chase out of the cabinet, Sumner entered the discussion for the first time by offering a substitute: "*Resolved,* that a committee be appointed to wait upon the President . . . and urge upon him changes in conduct and in the Cabinet which shall give the administration unity and vigor." After some discussion, during which Harris's motion was amended so as to call for only the partial reconstruction of the cabinet, the Republican caucus adopted both his and Sumner's resolutions by a unanimous vote, and then, to present these views to Lincoln, named a committee consisting of Collamer, Harris, Grimes, Fessenden, Wade, Trumbull, Samuel C. Pomeroy of Kansas, James M. Howard of Michigan, and Sumner.

At 7:00 P.M. on December 18 the committee called upon the haggard and depressed Lincoln to present their case. News of the action of the Republican caucus had already leaked out, and both Seward and his son, the Assistant Secretary of State, had submitted their resignations and were packing their bags. Other resignations were impending, and it seemed probable that the entire government would have to be reconstituted. Considering the accusations against Seward "a lie, an absurd lie, that could not impose upon a child," Lincoln was convinced that the Republican Senators were really aiming at him. "They wish to get rid of me," he told Browning, "and I am sometimes half disposed to gratify them."

Neither disappointment nor anger was evident, however, as the President greeted his visitors urbanely and listened while Collamer, the chairman of the committee, read their statement urging the reorganization of the cabinet. Wade, Howard, Grimes, and Fessenden then followed with individual statements, "expressing their entire want of confidence in Secretary Seward" and complaining that "the conduct of the war . . . was left in the hands of men who had no sympathy with it or the cause." To most of these charges Lincoln made no reply, but he did produce a large bundle of papers, from which he read several letters to prove that the government had always sustained General McClellan to the fullest extent.

When Sumner's turn came, he "commented freely upon Mr. Seward's official correspondence, averring that he had subjected himself to ridicule in diplomatic circles at home and abroad; that he had uttered statements offensive to Congress and spoken of it repeatedly with disrespect in the presence of foreign ministers [and] that he had written offensive dispatches which the President could not have seen or assented to." Sumner instanced the July 5 despatch to Adams, which linked abolitionists with secessionists as equal foes of the Union.

Claiming to have no recollection of this particular despatch, the President replied that the full cabinet did not consider diplomatic despatches but that Seward usually read them aloud to him before sending them.

After further animadversions against Seward by Trumbull, the meeting adjourned inconclusively, with the President professing to be pleased by the tone and temper exhibited by the committee, promising to study carefully the resolutions, and exhibiting, according to Fessenden, remarkably good spirits, as though content with the outcome of the interview.

When the members of the Senate committee—all except Wade, who scornfully refused to have anything more to do with such a weak-willed President—returned to the White House the next night at 7:30, they learned the reason for Lincoln's cheerfulness. During the day he had called his cabinet members together, informed them of complaints about "lukewarmness in the conduct of the war," told them that the Republican Senators appeared to believe that whenever the President "had in him any good purposes, Mr. S[eward]. contrived *to suck them out of him unperceived,*" notified them of Seward's resignation, and summoned them to meet with the Senate delegation at the White House that night. As the Senators and the Secretaries—all, of course, except Seward—met in the anteroom to Lincoln's office, they exchanged glances of wild surmise. More than one cabinet member recognized the ambiguity of his position. Postmaster General Montgomery Blair, for instance, so hated Seward that he longed for his resignation, but he recognized that in any general reorganization of the cabinet he too would have to leave. Self-righteous Secretary of War Stanton, convinced that only he would bring order to the war department and energy to the battlefield, feared that if Radicals forced Seward to withdraw, Conservatives might compel him to follow. Most difficult of all was the role of Chase, from whom the Senators had learned details of Lincoln's failure to consult with his cabinet. If he reaffirmed what he had told the Radicals, he would be exposed as a disloyal subordinate, but if he stood by the President, he would be known among the Senators as a liar. As the meeting began in the President's office, Chase angrily protested "that he should not have come here had he known that he was to be arraigned before a committee of the Senate."

Suavely the President opened the proceedings by reading the resolutions Collamer had presented the night before, commenting with severity upon some passages but admitting that for want of time the cabinet had not been very regular in its consultations. But, he declared, he "was not aware of any divisions or want of unity" in the cabinet; "though they could not be expected to think and speak alike on all subjects, all had acquiesced in measures once decided." In that acquiescence he emphatically included Seward, who, he asserted, was "earnest in the prosecution of the war." Closing his remarks in a conciliatory vein, Lincoln asked each member of the Senate committee to state whether he still believed Seward should be dismissed.

Before the Senators could respond, Chase, feeling a desperate need to clarify his position, declared that he "fully and entirely" endorsed what the President had just said and averred —contrary to what he had been telling Radical Senators for months—"that there had been no want of unity in the Cabinet."

With their principal source discredited, Collamer, Fessenden, and Howard weakened in their opposition to Seward and declined reply to the President's question, and Harris did an about-face, declaring: "Seward's retirement would . . . be calamitous in the State of New York." Pomeroy, Grimes, and Trumbull continued to favor Seward's removal. When Lincoln called on Sumner, he again put his opposition to Seward on the narrow ground of the alleged misconduct of foreign relations; once more he reviewed "some bad passages in Mr. S[eward]'s late published correspondence. Blamed him for the *publication,* as unnecessary and untimely, and denounced, as untrue S's charge that the extremes had united to stir up servile insurrection."

It was one o'clock in the morning before everybody had had a chance to express his views. Though no vote was asked for or taken, it was clear to all the participants that Lincoln, by confronting cabinet and cabal, had neatly split the opposition. As the disgruntled Senators left the White House, they grumbled that Lincoln would probably make no change in his cabinet.

• 2 •

Though the cabinet crisis of December 1862 might easily have led to a permanent rupture between Lincoln and Sumner, it did not. In managing the confrontation so as to checkmate Seward's foes, the President acted, as Secretary of the Navy Gideon Welles noted, with such "great tact, shrewdness, and ability" as to leave little room for personal resentment. On the next day, he welcomed Chase's resignation as a counterweight to that of Seward, announced that he could afford to lose neither of these invaluable advisers, and kept the cabinet intact. Sumner, too, behaved with discretion. Though vexed by Lincoln's slowness, he felt pity rather than anger toward the beleaguered President, recognizing, as he wrote Longfellow, that "he wants to do right and save the country."[9] In the committee's meetings with Lincoln he carefully made no reflection upon the President's motives and indulged in no general condemnation of his policy. While censuring Seward's despatches, he made clear his conviction that Lincoln could not have seen, much less have approved, the offending documents.

Even had Sumner been so inclined, he could not at this point afford a break with the President. Though Lincoln had

[9] [Dec. 1862], Longfellow MSS.

already issued his preliminary emancipation proclamation and had promised a final edict on January 1, 1863, conservative Republicans were mounting a powerful campaign to dissuade the President from taking that irrevocable step. Every day his mails were filled with appeals to move slowly. The fall elections, conservatives argued, showed how far the country was from being ready to change a war for the Union into a war for freedom. So numerous were the voices of dissent that Lincoln himself told Sumner that he now feared "'the fire in the rear'—meaning the Democracy especially at the Northwest—more than our military chances." [1]

Aware of this pressure and having little confidence in Lincoln anyway, many antislavery men believed that the proclamation of emancipation would never be issued. Daily Sumner received mournful letters from abolitionists protesting that Lincoln's anticipated backing down would make "the country a byword and a scorn before the whole world through all time." Even the more generously disposed of the abolitionists feared that if Lincoln did muster the courage to act, "the emancipation proclamation will fail miserably through this lack of executive skill and power." [2]

Sumner himself thought that it was important for Lincoln to have a strong antislavery voice constantly at his ear. As soon as he learned of Republican defeats in the November elections he realized that the President would be under great pressure to withhold the final emancipation edict, and he rushed a letter to him urging "the most unflinching vigor, in the field and in council." "Our armies must be pressed forward," he insisted, "and the proclamation must be pressed forward. . . ." In the interval before Congress met he feared that Seward and Weed might persuade Lincoln to renege upon his promise. For a time he thought of making another trip to Washington in order to screw up the President's courage but concluded that he probably could accomplish nothing. "Alas for our poor country!" he lamented. All he could do was to encourage antislavery men to

1 Sumner to Lieber, Jan. 17, 1863, Sumner MSS.

2 George C. Beckwith to Sumner, Dec. 22, 1862, and John D. Baldwin to Sumner, Dec. 30, 1862, Sumner MSS.

"strengthen an [*sic*] popular sentiment [for the final emancipation] by argument persuasion, appeal[s] of all kinds." [3]

In retrospect it is clear that Sumner's fears were exaggerated and that Lincoln played upon them to keep the Senator from drifting too far into opposition. The President knew that the plan announced in his December 1862 message to Congress for compensated emancipation and the subsequent colonization of freedmen would offend Sumner, but he also calculated that Sumner would swallow his protest because the message reaffirmed the goal of emancipation: "In *giving* freedom to the *slave*, we *assure* freedom to the *free*. . . . We shall nobly save, or meanly lose, the last best, hope of earth." While the cabinet crisis was brewing Lincoln conspicuously consulted with Sumner about emancipation, assuring him "repeatedly of his purpose to stand by his [preliminary] Proclamation" and reminding Sumner that it was "hard to move him from a position . . . once taken." If Sumner had residual ill feelings after the meeting between Senate committee and cabinet on December 19, they were assuaged when Lincoln called him to the White House on Christmas Day to consult about the wording of the final proclamation. The President willingly accepted his suggestion that emancipation be justified not merely as a step required by military necessity but also as "an act of justice and humanity, which must have the blessings of a benovolent God." In the same interview Lincoln told Sumner that he was finally ready to enlist Negro troops and that he planned to use them "to hold the Mississippi River and also other posts in the warm climates, so that our white soldiers may be employed elsewhere." [4]

There was another interest beside emancipation which Sumner protected by remaining on good terms with the President. Unlike most observers, he did not think that the December

[3] Sumner to Lincoln, Nov. 8, 1862, Lincoln MSS.; Sumner to Chase, Nov. 7, 1862, Chase MSS., Lib. of Cong.; Sumner to S. H. Gay, Dec. 10, 1862, Gay MSS.

[4] Sumner to Harriet Beecher Stowe [Dec. 25, 1862], MS., Chicago Hist. Soc.; Sarah Forbes Hughes (ed.): *Letters and Recollections of John Murray Forbes* (Boston: Houghton, Mifflin and Company; 1899), I, 352–3. When Lincoln did issue the proclamation, he included a final sentence invoking "the gracious favor of Almighty God." "The last sentence was actually framed by Chase," Sumner declared, "although I believe that I first suggested it both to him and to the President." *Mass. Hist. Soc. Proceedings,* XLIV, 597.

19 meeting had ended the cabinet crisis or had removed the need for stronger leadership. "Our country, great and glorious, is acephalous," he lamented in early January 1863. "Oh! for the intelligent, courageous and great counsels needed for the work!" [5] Prepared to credit Lincoln with good, if rather ineffectual, intentions, he and his friends continued to blame Seward for all the disasters to the Union cause. "Old Abe has called him back—the more fool he," declared the *Commonwealth* scornfully when it learned that Seward was being retained in the cabinet; "but it will not do,—Mr. Seward this day is in the cart and sitting on his political coffin." [6] Sumner himself indulged in his sharpest, most personal attacks upon the Secretary after the cabinet crisis appeared to have been settled. "From the beginning he has had no true conception of our case," he wrote Bright frankly; "he regarded this tremendous event [of civil war] with levity; . . . he has filled his conversation and his writing with false prophecies; . . . he has talked like a politician, and . . . he has said things and kept up relations, shewing an utter indifference to his old party associations." [7]

Surely, now that the immediate crisis was over, even Lincoln, with all his slowness and his hostility to change, would have to remove Seward, who was without friends in the House of Representatives, in the Senate, or in the cabinet itself. To assist the President in seeing the light, Sumner leaked the story of the Republican Senate caucus and of the meetings with the President to James W. White, a partisan anti-Seward judge of the New York supreme court, and authorized him to secure signatures from his Massachusetts supporters to a petition urging a speedy change in the cabinet. Partly as a result of White's energetic activities, Sumner was able to report on January 23: "The pressure for the expulsion of Seward increases—by letters, and fresh arrivals." [8] Two days later the New York *Herald* predicted "that if a change should not be made before the 4th of March,

[5] Sumner to Orestes A. Brownson, Jan. 4, 1863, Brownson MSS.; Sumner to Cephas Brainerd, Jan. 9, 1863, Segal Coll.

[6] Dec. 27, 1862.

[7] Sumner to Bright, Mar. 16, 1863, Bright MSS.

[8] White to Bird, Jan. 8, 1863, Bird MSS.; Sumner to Lieber, Jan. 23, 1863, Sumner MSS.

Congress . . . will pass resolutions declaring a want of confidence in the present Cabinet."

Whenever there was talk of reconstituting the cabinet, Sumner was mentioned as the likely successor to Seward. There were, of course, some obstacles to such a switch. Before descending upon Lincoln, the members of the committee representing the Senate Republican caucus had agreed to "a self-denying ordinance so far as taking office was concerned," [9] and Sumner would have to be released from this pledge. There were also Sumner's Massachusetts supporters to be thought about, especially those who had just fought so hard to return him to the Senate. On the whole, however, his political friends thought voters would understand and approve if he decided to leave the Senate for the cabinet, since appointment as Secretary of State would be a deserved "recognition of his fitness to direct the diplomatic affairs of the country, a fitness indicated not only by his general abilities and culture, but by his special familiarity with the currents of opinion in Europe, derived from travel and correspondence." "The suggestion of his name was, in truth," declared the Washington *Republican,* "the general recognition of the eminent suitability of his appointment." [1]

Sumner himself was not averse to going into the cabinet. Of course he could make no public announcement that he was willing, for he knew how much of his strength derived from appearing to be the disinterested statesman, indifferent to public office but called to power by his constituents. In private correspondence, however, he let the mask slip a little. "I see great difficulties in organizing a true and strong Cabinet," he wrote Orestes A. Brownson in early January. "Who will you take?" Then he made a Freudian slip: "Some at least that you select would not object, especially if in the Senate," and, half-realizing what he had unwittingly said, hastily went back and deleted the "not." [2] To Longfellow he was more candid. "Many talk and write to me about going into the cabinet," he reported. "Of course, I should not shrink from any duty required of me by my country

[9] Fessenden: *Fessenden,* I, 238.
[1] Quoted in Boston *Commonwealth,* Jan. 10, 1863.
[2] Jan. 4, 1863, Brownson MSS.

at such a moment of peril." "But," he quickly covered himself, "I much prefer my present place." [3]

• 3 •

So long as there was a possibility that Sumner might go into the cabinet, he had to keep on good relations with the President, but he did not have to exercise the same self-restraint when dealing with Seward. At the height of the cabinet crisis in December, Sumner abruptly canceled his acceptance of a dinner invitation from Baron Gerolt, so that he would not have to sit at the same table with the Secretary of State. During the next three months the two men did not meet socially.[4] If possible Sumner transacted his business at the State Department with the veteran chief clerk, William Hunter, but when he was obliged to see Seward, the men often exchanged sharp words. On one occasion when Sumner ventured to suggest that the United States ought to have a more gentlemanly secretary of legation in London than Charles Wilson, a political appointee who made it his daily practice to go to his club, throw his legs on the table, and coarsely abuse England and the English, Seward flew into a rage and shouted that Sumner "knew nothing of political (meaning party) claims and services" but was trying to cut Wilson's throat. Nothing Sumner could say or do calmed the Secretary, who became ever "more violent, and louder in his declarations that Charley Wilson was a clever fellow and should be retained." Only Sumner's hasty withdrawal ended the angry interview, and a surface peace returned when both men apologized.[5]

For most of the winter, illness gave Sumner the perfect excuse for avoiding Seward. Doubtless because of overexertion in the Massachusetts campaign, the angina pectoris which he had not experienced since the outbreak of the war returned, and in November he was again obliged to take the belladonna pills

[3] [Dec. 1862], Longfellow MSS.

[4] Alvan F. Sanborn (ed.): *Reminiscences of Richard Lathers* (New York: The Grafton Press; 1907), pp. 188–9; Frances A. Seward: Diary, April 5, 1862–April 30, 1863, Seward MSS.

[5] Welles: *Diary,* I, 300–1; Sumner to Seward, May 9, 1863, Seward MSS.; Seward to Sumner, May 12, 1863, Sumner MSS.

Dr. Charles E. Brown-Séquard prescribed. The discomfort persisted, however, and in January Sumner reported that it was complicated by "a cold which has settled especially in the lower part of the bowels, giving me pain and breaking my rest." [6] Though Sumner continued to attend the Senate, he spent much of the time resting on a lounge at the rear of the chamber. He declared that he was not well enough to attend the annual dinner which the Sewards gave the diplomatic corps in February.

Bad health did not keep him from suspiciously watching the Secretary of State, and in January he became greatly alarmed over what he considered the mishandling of American relations with France. From the outset of the war he thought that Seward had failed to distinguish between the positions of the British and the French governments. When dealing with Great Britain the true Union diplomacy was to appeal to the universal antislavery opinion which, if properly roused, could compel a change in policy or topple the Palmerston government. In France, on the other hand, though liberals like Alexis de Tocqueville, Henri Martin, Count Agenor de Gasparin, and Edouard Laboulaye stalwartly supported the Union cause, public opinion was relatively powerless to influence Napoleon III. The Union government ought, therefore, not to forget that Napoleon favored disunion, looked kindly upon the Confederacy, and hoped to establish a puppet monarchy in Mexico; but it should make no public move that would offend the French ruler, who was, Sumner said, such "a mystery . . . [that] no one could penetrate his designs." [7]

Early in 1863 Sumner's hope to avoid any challenge to Napoleon III was endangered both in the Senate and in the State Department. Unable to watch the landing of French troops in Mexico with the same equanimity as a New Englander, James A. McDougall, the California Democrat, on January 19 introduced resolutions condemning the French intervention as "not merely unfriendly to this Republic, but to free institutions everywhere; and . . . as not only unfriendly, but as hostile." When McDou-

[6] Sumner to Howe [Feb. 1863], Sumner MSS.

[7] Browning: *Diary*, I, 613–14.

gall tried to bring his resolutions to the Senate floor, Sumner asked: "Sir, have we not war enough already on our hands, without needlessly and wantonly provoking another?" Persisting, McDougall argued that Sumner must be "smitten with judicial blindness" not to see that the French presence in Mexico was already so dangerous "that we have nothing of value to lose by a French war" but instead "everything to gain." By characteristically overstating his case, the California Senator gave credence to Sumner's charge that his resolutions would "excite the hostility of France, and give to the Rebellion armies and fleets, not to mention that recognition and foreign intervention which we deprecate." "There is," Sumner said bluntly, "madness in the proposition."[8] Convinced that the United States could not fight two wars at a time, the Senate in early February tabled McDougall's resolutions.

Sumner found the State Department harder to keep in line than the Senate. At the same time that Napoleon III was planning to make Maximilian Emperor of Mexico, he continued to contemplate direct intervention in the American Civil War, and, though rebuffed by both Great Britain and Russia in earlier attempts to play the peacemaker, he offered in January 1863 the services of France as mediator between the Union and Confederacy. When Henri Mercier, the French minister, presented Napoleon's plan in Washington, Union fortunes were at the nadir. In the East, Burnside's army bogged down so hopelessly in the futile "mud march" that Lincoln had to remove that inept commander; in Tennessee W. S. Rosecrans's forces were immobilized for six months after the indecisive battle at Murfreesboro; and, farther West, the Confederates killed or wounded 1200 of W. T. Sherman's men when they attempted a direct assault on Vicksburg. Throughout the North peace sentiment was rising, and influential spokesmen like Horace Greeley begged the President to stop the senseless slaughter.

Seward thought that Napoleon's offer of mediation, coming at this bleak moment, offered an unequaled opportunity to rally

[8] Sumner: *Works*, VII, 258, 260; *Cong. Globe*, 37 Cong., 3 Sess., Appendix, pp. 99–100.

the American national spirit. Sensing that the Emperor's proposal was an empty gesture, since it was not backed by the other great powers, the Secretary of State rejected it in the bluntest language permissible in diplomatic discourse: ". . . this Government has not the least thought of relinquishing the trust which had been confided to it by the nation . . . ; and if it had any such thought, it would still have abundant reason to know that peace proposed at the cost of dissolution would be immediately, unreservedly, and indignantly rejected by the American people."

Fearing such an out-of-hand rebuff would give Napoleon just the pretext for intervening in favor of the Confederacy, Sumner deplored Seward's handling of the mediation offer. He did all that he could to counter the Secretary's bluntness. When Mercier, after talking with Greeley and others in New York, consulted Sumner on January 18, 1863, the Senator spent a long evening exploring with him all the implications of the French proposal. Though Sumner was no more willing than Seward to countenance foreign intervention, he was careful not to offend Mercier. The military situation was indeed grave, he admitted, and without military success in the spring, the Union government might be reduced to impotence. But, he warned, the United States must and would have that final chance to gain its victory, so that if the Emperor pressed for mediation now, his offer would surely be rejected. Persuaded that Sumner might favor mediation at some future date, Mercier the more easily accepted his present hostility to it. Further to soothe the minister's feelings, Sumner, along with some other members of the Senate Committee on Foreign Relations, made a point of calling on Mercier, "so as to protest by their presence against the attitude our Secretary of State has deemed proper to assume." [9]

For a time it seemed possible that Seward's bellicose rejection of French mediation might lead to a renewed demand for his resignation from the cabinet. Believing that Seward deliberately precipitated this "difficulty with the French Minister from

[9] Mercier to Drouyn de Lhuys, Jan. 19, 1863, cited in Daniel B. Carroll's unpublished biography of Mercier, pp. 432–3; New York *World*, quoted in undated clipping from New York *Times*, Sumner Scrapbooks.

an unworthy motive, a desire to retain his official seat, his possession of which was becoming very precarious," Judge White thought the time had come for a general attack on the Secretary. He asked Sumner to help by listing "a few instances of what you consider Seward's most important diplomatic failures and follies." Sumner responded by telling how Seward in 1861 had pledged that slavery would not be touched whatever the outcome of the war and how he in 1862 had linked the abolitionists and the Southern secessionists as equally subversive of the Union. Thus fortified, White published in the New York *Tribune,* under the signature "Truth and Justice," a blistering review of Seward's diplomacy. Like Sumner, White was careful to exonerate the President, while attacking the Secretary of State, for he alleged that Seward frequently sent despatches abroad without consulting Lincoln.

Promptly Henry J. Raymond, Seward's close political ally, secured a statement from the Secretary and published it in his New York *Times:* "Every dispatch that was not merely and technically formal that I have ever sent abroad has been fully submitted, in words and substance, to the President, and read by him or to him before it was sent." This presidential approval explicitly extended to Seward's 1861 despatches concerning slavery. Furthermore, Seward told Raymond, it included "even this dispatch to yourself." [1]

Charged with an outright lie, White desperately sought Sumner's help. "May I state in the Tribune," he begged, "that the President had assured *you,* that a certain dispatch [i.e., that to Adams on July 5, 1862, linking abolitionists and secessionists], not coming within the definition, 'merely and technically formal,' which you pointed out to him in the printed volume, had not been seen by, or known to him before it appeared . . . ?" By authorizing such a statement, White felt, Sumner would halt the wild career of the Secretary of State, who was "more responsible than any other man for the formidable dimensions to which the Rebellion has grown." "Let me add my prayer . . . ," entreated Sidney H. Gay of the *Tribune* staff, "that you will sustain us in

[1] White to Sumner, Feb. 19, 1863, Sumner MSS.; New York *Times,* Feb. 25 and 27, 1863.

this controversy with *The Times*. . . . It will do more than any thing that has been done to unseat the Secretary." [2]

Though—as even Raymond admitted in private [3]—the facts were precisely what White stated them to be, Sumner declined publicly to enter the lists against the Secretary of State, now that he had invoked the President's authority to cover his course. Sharply he reminded White that information about these despatches had been passed along to him "*confidentially*." It was unfair, he protested, to involve him in this controversy; after all, the other Senators who had met with Lincoln on December 18 and 19 knew the facts as well as he did. "I must reserve to myself the power to determine when I will enter into a personal controversy," he concluded. "While I have had positive opinions, I have not seen that any thing was to be gained to the cause, worthy of the sacrifice, if I should enter into a personal contest with certain parties." [4]

By the middle of February it was clear that Seward had once again ridden out the storm. When the French government quietly accepted his scornful rejection of mediation, the Secretary's popularity reached a new high, and, as the New York *Herald* gloated, certain antislavery Senators were "much crestfallen." [5] White, unable to document his accusations, was obliged to resort to verbal abuse of the Secretary as "unstable in mind," "whimsical and capricious, . . . intellectually vagrant." Jubilantly the New York *Times* tore White's charges to shreds and dared the men behind him to come out in the open. "There are some hundreds of ambitious gentlemen—Senators and others—who have taken pains to inform the President and the rest of mankind, from time to time," that Seward was incompetent, the *Times* sneered. "Why do not these gentlemen put the case before the world as they think it should be? . . . Some of them [it noted pointedly] can speak from the Senate. If they could *prove* their ability to do better than Mr. Seward has done, very

[2] White to Sumner, Feb. 27, 1863, and Gay to Sumner, Feb. 27, 1863, Sumner MSS.

[3] H. W. Raymond (ed.): "Extracts from the Journal of Henry J. Raymond," *Scribner's Monthly*, XIX (1880), 710.

[4] Sumner to [James W. White], Mar. 1, 1863, MS., Univ. of Chicago Lib.

[5] Feb. 14, 1863.

probably Mr. Lincoln would meet their wishes and give them his place. Why not try it?"[6]

Sumner, in fact, was preparing to do just that. When the Senate in March received copies of the correspondence concerning French mediation, he anxiously noted that Seward's despatch threatened danger at home as well as abroad. In rejecting the good offices of the French, Seward suggested that peace could easily be restored in the United States, not through intervention of a foreign power but simply through the return of Southern Senators and Representatives to Washington, where Congress would provide "a constitutional forum for debates between the alienated parties." As usual, Seward left his meaning purposefully obscure, but Sumner thought the Secretary was renewing the pledge he had given Mercier in April 1862 that Southern leaders, when they laid down their arms, "would be cordially welcomed back to their Seats in the Senate, and to their due share of political influence." So loosely worded an offer might prove exceedingly dangerous, especially after Congress adjourned, and Sumner began to look for a formula which at least would commit both the chief executive and the Congress to continuing the war until victory and at best might result in the ousting of Seward.[7]

Drawing upon Lieber for advice, Sumner drafted a set of resolutions announcing that future attempts at foreign intervention would be considered not merely "unreasonable and inadmissible" but "unfriendly" to the United States, because this "unprovoked and wicked Rebellion" sought to destroy the American republic only in order to establish "a new government . . . with Slavery as its acknowledged cornerstone." To block any possibility that Seward might attempt a negotiated peace while Congress was in recess, the resolutions resoundingly pledged that "the war will be vigorously prosecuted, according to the humane principles of Christian nations, until the Rebellion is overcome."[8]

As a restatement of Union war aims, Sumner's resolutions

[6] Mar. 2, 1863.

[7] New York *Herald*, Mar. 3, 1863; despatch of Baron Stoeckl, Feb. 18, 1863, copy in White Notes.

[8] Sumner: *Works*, VII, 308–11.

were useful enough, though Mercier observed that they would be readily ignored whenever peace sentiment became dominant in the North. As a weapon against Seward they had even more limited effectiveness. To persuade his Foreign Relations Committee to adopt the resolutions during the last busy days of the session, Sumner had to make a number of modifications and deletions and to phrase his proposals in Aesopian language which even the proslavery Senator Garrett Davis of Kentucky would approve. In presenting this formulation to the Senate itself, Sumner took pride in announcing that it proceeded from "the spontaneous deliberations of the Senate Committee on Foreign Relations, without any hint or suggestion from the Secretary of State, or from any member of the Administration." As debate proceeded, however, Sumner, in order to muster votes for the propositions, was obliged to assure his colleagues that they had "the entire and most cordial approval of the Secretary of State." [9] Seward must have been wryly amused.

· 4 ·

Sumner distrusted Seward's policy toward Great Britain even more than that toward France. Though by 1863 there was little serious prospect that the British government would intervene in behalf of the Confederacy, there was a real danger that it might drift into war with the Union. Despite explicit legal prohibitions, British shipyards continued to build and outfit ships for the Confederate navy. The vessel which became the C.S.S. *Florida* had sailed from British docks in March 1862, and in July the more powerful *Alabama* had escaped the surveillance of Crown officers and now preyed upon Union commerce. To Charles Francis Adams's protests that Great Britain was becoming the arsenal of the Confederacy, Russell gave evasive answers, and to claims for damages caused by these raiders he haughtily replied that "Her Majesty's Government cannot admit [such demands] to be founded on any grounds of law or of justice." During the winter of 1862–63 it grew clear that another major diplomatic

[9] Sumner to Lieber, Mar. 13, 1863, Sumner MSS.; *Cong. Globe*, 37 Cong., 3 Sess., p. 1498.

crisis was approaching. The gunboat *Alexandra,* destined for the Confederacy, was nearing completion, and the Laird brothers were constructing two huge ironclad rams, designed to permit the Southerners to sink the wooden ships of the Union navy and lift the blockade.

Seward's plan for coping with the crisis was characteristically devious. On the one hand, he cultivated close personal relations with Lord Lyons and gradually convinced that pompous bachelor that he really wanted to keep the peace. Aware of Lyons's earlier suspicions, Seward went out of his way to avoid friction. In April 1863, when Lyons asked that the mails captured aboard the *Peterhoff,* a British-owned vessel sailing for Matamoras, Mexico—where, according to American sources, her contraband cargo would be transshipped to Texas—be forwarded to their destination unopened, Seward readily complied. Both Secretary of the Navy Welles and Sumner were appalled by his action, which prevented positive proof that the *Peterhoff*'s goods were intended for the Confederacy and thus threatened the effectiveness of the blockade. Believing that Seward was acting against the best American and British precedents in international law, both men took their case to Lincoln himself, but they got little satisfaction. "Very ignorant or very deceptive," the President permitted himself to be "imposed upon, humbugged" by Seward, who warned that opening the *Peterhoff* mails might bring on war, and he sustained his Secretary of State.[1] If Sumner had needed further evidence that Seward lacked "good sense and also a knowledge of International Law," this too willing acquiescence in such British demands would have provided it. "The country," he lamented, "is in much more danger from W.H.S. than from Jeff. Davis." [2]

Even while being overly agreeable to the British, Seward was pursuing another policy, which can best be characterized as blackmail. At his request, Grimes, chairman of the Senate Com-

[1] Welles: *Diary,* I, 285–9, 292; Adam Gurowski: *Diary, from November 18, 1862, to October 18, 1863* (New York: Carleton, Publisher; 1864), pp. 208–9. See also James P. Baxter, III, "Some British Opinions as to Neutral Rights, 1861 to 1865," *Am. Jour. of International Law,* XXIII (1929), 524–7. The fullest modern treatment of the *Peterhoff* affair is Stuart L. Bernath: *Squall Across the Atlantic* (Berkeley: University of California Press; 1970), Chap. 5.

[2] Sumner to Lieber, May 3 and 10, 1863, Sumner MSS.

mittee on Naval Affairs, revived a bill authorizing the President to issue letters of marque. In justifying the measure, which would permit the owners of private vessels to capture enemy property upon the high seas, Grimes warned that the Confederates were "now building in England a fleet of vessels designed to break our blockade of their coast." "If," he added threateningly, "the President shall find himself environed with new difficulties, involved in new complications, I wish him to have the power to 'let slip the dogs of war' against any new enemy that may declare against us."

Seward took care that the British government understood the connection between issuing letters of marque and allowing further Confederate raiders to escape. He did not have to spell out to Russell how a fleet of Union privateers could adversely affect Great Britain, for the learned Sir William Harcourt, who wrote under the pen name "Historicus" for *The Times* of London, had just explained that under international law a blockade could be maintained not only by a fleet offshore of the Confederacy but by a "cruising squadron" anywhere on the high seas.[3] In despatches to Adams Seward gave the British the far from comforting assurance that except in "extreme circumstances" he would give warning to Britain and other neutral powers whose commerce might be "incidentally or indirectly affected" by privateers before he actually issued the letters of marque.

To Sumner this policy seemed a blunder more dangerous, because less reparable, than Seward's too frequent concessions to the British on minor matters of international law. Privateers, he forcefully argued, were supposed to prey upon the commerce of an enemy; but, since the Confederacy was "absolutely without commerce," inevitably these "rovers of the sea would be driven to prey upon neutral commerce, and to involve us with the great neutral Powers of the world." Bitterly he fought Grimes's bill, and he besought friends like Greeley to help him save "the country from the scandal of Privateers when they can do no good." "Let [the] Government hire any good merchant-ships, and then offer a bounty for catching one of our hostile sea-rovers," he

[3] [Harcourt]: *Letters by Historicus, on Some Questions of International Law* (London: Macmillan and Co.; 1865), pp. 99–108.

suggested as an alternative plan. "But do not let us take the odium of *Privateering* when all that you propose to do can be better done in some other way." [4]

When the Senate, ignoring his pleas, passed the privateering bill on February 17, 1863, and the House also adopted it two weeks later, Sumner turned to the President and earnestly begged him to take no action under the new law. "Here are my reasons," he wrote Lincoln:

> (1) It is not practical. . . .
> (2) It may *possibly* involve us with Foreign nations.
> (3) It is counter to the opinion and aspirations of the best men in our history.
> (4) It is condemned by the Civilization of the age.
> (5) It will give us a bad name.
> (6) It will do this without any corresponding good.
> (7) It will constitute a precedent which we shall regret hereafter and the friends of Human Progress will regret every where.
> (8) It will pain our best friends in Europe.[5]

Impressed, Lincoln invited Sumner to argue his case at the next cabinet meeting, but Sumner was, as always, disinclined to engage in open combat with Seward. As the embittered Count Gurowski complained: "He goes about and laments against Seward's policy, and never had the courage to attack it like a man in the Senate." Even less was he prepared to challenge the Secretary's policies in his presence. At a series of cabinet meetings in late March and early April, however, his views were strongly represented by Attorney General Bates and by Welles, to whom he had described the plan for privateers as "unpractical, unreasonable . . . [and] unquestionably barbarous." Though both Seward and Chase argued for issuing letters of marque, Welles killed the project by ridiculing it as "the idle scheme of attempting to spear sharks for wool." [6]

[4] Sumner: *Works*, VII, 281; *Cong. Globe*, 37 Cong., 3 Sess., p. 1024; Sumner to Greeley [Feb. 1863], Greeley MSS., New York Pub. Lib.

[5] Mar. 18, 1863, Lincoln MSS.

[6] Sumner: *Works*, VII, 300; Gurowski to Andrew, April 10, 1863, Andrew MSS.; Sumner to Welles, Mar. 11, 1863, copy, Welles MSS., Henry E. Huntington Lib.; Bates: *Diary*, p. 284; Welles: *Diary*, I, 246–61.

"My policy has at last prevailed," Sumner boasted at the end of April. "There will be no letters [of marque], at least for the present. Mr. Seward has been obliged to yield."[7] Seward's reactions are not a matter of record, but whether he had in fact suffered a defeat was questionable. Since his objective was not to issue letters of marque but to intimidate the British, he may have taken a quiet but malicious pleasure in the fact that Sumner's vociferous opposition to privateering was a splendidly effective way of underscoring his threat.

• 5 •

Sumner thought Seward's policy toward Great Britain of overt concession and covert threat was desperately wrong. His own approach to Anglo-American relations was simple and forthright. First the United States should maintain all its rights under international law. In the *Peterhoff* case, for instance, the Union government ought to have kept and opened the captured mails not only because it needed these documents to prove the Confederate destination of the cargo but because excellent British and American precedents authorized such action. If necessary the American government should assist the British in understanding and enforcing international law. Though some of Lincoln's cabinet thought it was enough to give the British warning that the Laird rams were being built for the Confederates, Sumner favored taking a more active role in preventing their escape. It had become a question of peace or war, he insisted; "I would not stand upon any form; . . . I would employ agents, attorneys, and counsel; institute law proceedings,—in short, do all that we thought the British government ought to do, so far as we might be able to do, whether in courts or out of courts."[8]

At the same time Sumner wanted to arouse public opinion abroad in favor of the Union. Bypassing Seward, he conferred with Lincoln on ways to stimulate the widespread antislavery sentiment among British workingmen, thousands of whom were unemployed because of the shortage of Southern cotton, cut off

[7] Sumner to Duchess of Argyll, April 26, 1863, Argyll MSS.
[8] Sumner to Duchess of Argyll, April 21, 1863, ibid.

by the Union blockade. At his urging Lincoln drafted, for possible use in pro-Union rallies in Great Britain, a resolution equating the Southern cause with slavery. "England must declare that a slavemonger State cannot be recognized," Sumner insisted in transmitting the President's words to John Bright. "To this England must come logically, according to her history; and the sooner the better." [9]

Recognizing, however, that the governing classes in Great Britain were only slightly influenced by even the largest public meetings in support of the Union, Sumner attempted through correspondence to make British leaders accept the Northern point of view. With the possible exception of Edward Everett, Sumner was more widely known, and more highly respected, in Great Britain than any other American of his day, and he knew that his words would be listened to, even in the cabinet itself. In writing his friends abroad, Sumner deliberately played the role of advocate and defender of the Union cause—the role which he thought an effective Secretary of State should have played. Though at home he had been protesting, at least since the fall of 1861, against Lincoln's slowness to move against slavery, in his overseas letter he consistently maintained that the cause of the Union was the cause of freedom. Though he constantly feared that Seward would cook up a compromise, he regularly reassured his British friends that there could be no peace without Union victory.

In turn, some of Sumner's British correspondents used their letters to explain and defend their government's policy, even when they did not fully agree with it. When Sumner wrote the Duke of Argyll that the British government was at fault for allowing the *Alabama* to escape, the Duke, who was now Lord Privy Seal, drafted a sharp denial that the raider was " 'British' in any sense which involves the British Government in responsibility." To make sure that his reply was authoritative, he circulated both Sumner's letter and his answer, to Gladstone and other cabinet members. The marginal annotations Argyll made on Sumner's letters showed, however, that he saw the justice of the

[9] Lincoln: *Works,* VI, 176–7; Sumner to Bright, April 21 and May 25, 1863, Bright MSS.

Senator's accusations. Transmitting the correspondence to Gladstone he noted privately: "He is right—and . . . the maintenance of peace between nations is incompatible with the [British government's] refusal to recognise it as an international obligation that such proceedings should be stopped." [1]

If Sumner's trans-Atlantic correspondence was not completely candid, its objectives were entirely clear. He sought first of all to convince the rulers of Britain that the Civil War would ultimately end in Northern victory. Recognizing that Palmerston, Russell, and Gladstone believed Southern success was inevitable and that even many warm friends of the Union feared that after years of bloodshed the North would give up its vain attempt to subdue the South, he kept repeating: "There is no thought in the Cabinet or the President of abandoning the contest. *Of this be sure.*" To the Duke of Argyll, who reasoned that "the moment a war becomes *hopeless,* it becomes wrong," Sumner stanchly replied: "We all believe that, there can be but one end to the war,—sooner or later; and that is the triumph of the Government and the establishment of Peace on the extinction of Slavery. . . . Therefore, the war is not *hopeless.*" [2]

Sumner's unwavering confidence helped to prevent British intervention in the American conflict. In the late summer of 1862, while the British cabinet was considering Russell's proposal of mediation, to be followed by recognition of the Confederacy, Argyll received another of Sumner's letters reaffirming the fixed determination of the North to continue the struggle despite any reverses. "It is evident," Argyll wrote in forwarding Sumner's letter to Gladstone, "whatever may be *our* opinion of the prospects of 'the North' that they do not yet, at least, feel any approach to such exhaustion as will lead them to admit of Mediation; and that they are firmly possessed with the idea that it is a Life or Death struggle, in which no terms of compromise are to them, conceivable." Believing that there should be no

[1] Henry G. Pearson (ed.): "Letters of the Duke and Duchess of Argyll to Charles Sumner," *Mass. Hist. Soc. Proceedings,* XLVII (1913–14), 75; Argyll to Gladstone, April 24 and May 28, 1863, Gladstone MSS.; Argyll's marginal notes on Sumner's letter to him of May 10, 1863, Argyll MSS.

[2] Sumner to Bright, Aug. 5, 1862, Bright MSS.; *Mass. Hist. Soc. Proceedings,* XLVII, 75; Sumner to Argyll, May 10, 1863, Argyll MSS.

British intervention unless it was acceptable to the North, Argyll joined with George Cornewall Lewis and other members of the cabinet to oppose, and finally to reject, Russell's scheme for mediation.[3]

Sumner's second objective in his overseas correspondence was to emphasize that the war would end slavery. He never ceased to regret Seward's failure at the outbreak of the war to appeal to antislavery opinion abroad, for he agreed with Richard Cobden that if the North stood openly for freedom, "recognition of the South, by England, whilst it bases itself on negro slavery, is an impossibility." He constantly reminded his British friends, therefore, that the Civil War was a struggle between freedom and slavery. Bluntly he scolded his correspondents for failing to recognize the clear moral issue. "I am mortified and humiliated to see England ranging herself daily more and more with a vulgar Oligarchy of slave-drivers, who, if once independent, will open the slave-trade," he wrote Bright. "Is this the fare to which Englishmen invite their country? Opinion with you seems to be growing worse and worse—more utterly prejudiced and senseless. The English heart seems to be given to the brutal slave-masters."[4]

Vainly Sumner's correspondents reminded him that, according to the official statements of the President of the United States and his Secretary of State, the North was warring "not against Slavery, but against rebellion," and that, therefore, it was "not entitled to claim that personal sympathy which a pure anti-slavery contest would undoubtedly awaken." Though Sumner at home made exactly the same argument, he retorted that Britons were allowing themselves to be misled by words. If instead of calling the Southern rebels "Confederates" they would speak of "woman-whippers and children-sellers," if instead of labeling James M. Mason minister plenipotentiary of the Confederacy they branded him as "the author of the Fugitive Slave Bill,"

[3] Argyll to Gladstone, Aug. 26, 1862, Gladstone MSS. On the mediation crisis of 1862 I have profited by reading the senior thesis written at Princeton University by Jeffrey B. Morris and I have also studied the Palmerston, Gladstone, Russell, Hammond, and George C. Lewis manuscripts as well as the Royal Archives at Windsor Castle.

[4] "Letters of Richard Cobden to Charles Sumner, 1862–1865," *Amer. Hist. Rev.*, II (1897), 309; Sumner to Bright, Nov. 12, 1862, Bright MSS.

who, "when a Senator was struck down on the floor of the Senate, . . . wrote a letter *publicly approving the act,*" they could more easily conceive the moral dimensions of the contest. Then, too, they would realize the "grim insensibility" of their presumed "neutral" policy. "Neutrality between slave-pirates and those who are trying to put them down!" Sumner exclaimed. "Here is a confusion of morals under a seeming propriety of form." [5]

Finally, Sumner wanted his letters to warn the British of the real danger of war. They needed to understand that building Confederate vessels in British shipyards was virtually the equivalent of fitting out "an English expedition of war, practically under the patronage of the English Government." Once the *Alexandra* and the Laird rams sailed, war would have "already begun, with hostilities all on one side." Even if the United States government was in no immediate position to return the fire, Great Britain ought to realize that Americans would not quickly forget her unneutral course. After the rebellion was crushed, Sumner warned, it would be a "difficult piece of statesmanship . . . to keep from instant war with England," a war in which not merely five hundred thousand Irish-Americans—"all the old Democrats whose false sympathies England latterly cultivates" —but "the best educated, the best-principled, and the wealthiest of the land" would willingly fight.[6]

Once the British comprehended the dimensions of the danger, Sumner was sure they would compel their government to reconsider its course. They would require Russell to rephrase his diplomatic despatches, which were "bad and mischievous, and . . . intended to provoke." They would make the Foreign Minister retract his "cold and unsympathizing" remarks about the Emancipation Proclamation. They would insist that both Russell and Gladstone repudiate their public statements about the inevitable dissolution of the Union, because such declarations tended,

[5] *Mass. Hist. Soc. Proceedings*, XLVII, 79; Sumner to Duchess of Argyll, April 13 and June 29, 1863, Argyll MSS.; Sumner to W. L. Garrison [Mar. 8, 1863], Garrison MSS. The "Senator . . . struck down" was, of course, Sumner himself, in 1856.

[6] Sumner to Duchess of Argyll, Mar. 24, April 7, and April 26, 1863, Argyll MSS.

"first, to encourage the slave-mongers . . . and, secondly, by an infirmity of human nature, to bind these ministers, who had thus made themselves prophets, to desire the verification of their prophecy." Most of all, they would demand that their government recognize that "from the beginning there has been but one side to this terrible conflict." [7]

If Sumner's tone in his almost daily letters in 1863 to Bright, Cobden, Gladstone, and the Argylls was strident, it was because Great Britain seemed to be drifting steadily toward a collision with the United States. The decision of the Palmerston government in April to have the *Alexandra* seized offered a momentary reprieve, but when the Court of Exchequer on June 22 ruled that her builders had not violated the British Foreign Enlistment Act, the fate of both the *Alexandra* and the Laird rams was left in doubt. At the same time James Arthur Roebuck, acting in collaboration with the French government, moved in Parliament that the independence of the Confederacy be recognized. Though the ensuing debate was mainly adverse to the Southern cause and Roebuck had finally to withdraw his motion to avoid certain defeat, the tone of the discussion was anything but friendly to the Union government. Speaking for the Palmerston ministry, Gladstone reaffirmed his belief that "the main result of the contest was not doubtful" and that Confederate independence was inevitable. He added that if the Union should entirely crush the South it would be a disaster to freedom everywhere.

Eagerly Sumner had welcomed the seizure of the *Alexandra* as a sign that the British did not mean to make war upon the United States—at least, as he wrote Bright, "for the present." Then came news of the court's order to free the ship and of the parliamentary debates on the American question. "These reports from Europe make us feel, that you are determined to make us suffer more, to spend more money and to sacrifice more lives," he angrily protested to the Duchess of Argyll. He thought that in the parliamentary debates "Gladstone dealt with the whole ques-

[7] Sumner to Bright, April 7 and Mar. 30, 1863, Bright MSS.; Sumner to Duchess of Argyll, April 13, 1863, Argyll MSS.

tion as if there was no God." The British government ought to recognize that every "proffer of mediation in our affairs, . . . and every report of such an idea, must tell for the slavemongers." "Your Government," Sumner lamented to Bright, "recklessly and heartlessly seems bent on war." [8]

• 6 •

Even while anxiously watching the dangers from abroad, Sumner in mid-1863 worried about a new peril at home: Union victory. Defeat he had learned to live with. For more than a year his letters had chronicled with monotonous regularity the reverses inflicted upon the Federal forces, and he developed the rationalization that "these delays and disasters were needed in order to compel emancipation." As he watched the Army of the Potomac stumble to another disaster at Chancellorsville, the gigantic naval preparations directed against Charleston miscarry, and Grant's army apparently disappear in the trackless swamps opposite Vicksburg, he even came to think there was a divine purpose in these defeats. "They have been the chastisement and expiation imposed by Providence for our crime towards a long-suffering race," he explained to the Duchess of Argyll. "We have more to suffer; we have deserved it for our hardness of heart." Not a conventionally religious man, in the sense of belonging to a church, Sumner had unquestioning faith in a Providence that governed human affairs, and he voiced a fatalism much like that expressed in Lincoln's Second Inaugural. But, like Lincoln, he remained serenely confident in adversity: "We must lose other battles, and bury more children; but the result will be attained." [9]

The news of Union victories at Gettysburg and Vicksburg in early July might have been expected to lift Sumner's spirits, but it did not. "The God of battles seems latterly to smile upon us,"

[8] Sumner to Bright, May 25, July 21, and Aug. 4, 1863, Bright MSS.; Sumner to Duchess of Argyll, June 8, 1863, Argyll MSS.

[9] Sumner to Duchess of Argyll, Nov. 12 and 17, April 7 and 17, 1863, Argyll MSS.

he wrote his trusted political lieutenant, Edward L. Pierce. "I am content that he should not smile too much. There must be more delay and more suffering,—yet another 'plague' before all will agree to 'let my people go'; and the war cannot, must not, end till then." Though such words came strangely from one who thought himself almost a pacifist, they did not reflect just a passing mood. "*We are too victorious,*" Sumner expressed the same idea to Bright. "I fear more from our victories than from our defeats." [1]

The object of Sumner's fear was the same sinister figure who, he thought, threatened to provoke war with France and with Great Britain: William H. Seward. He was convinced that the Secretary of State, who had favored compromise in the secession crisis, who had assured slaveholders in 1862 that their representatives would be welcomed back in the Capitol, and who had again in January 1863 promised that Southern Senators and Representatives could restore peace by returning to Washington, was contemplating some new appeasement of the Confederates. On July 7, after hearing the news from Vicksburg, Seward made a curious and pregnant speech, in which he reviewed his course since the secession crisis and declared he was going to make the brave Andrew Johnson of Tennessee his "associate and leader," even though Johnson "tolerated and excused, if he did not justify slavery." Seward concluded: "The country shall be saved by the republican party if it will, by the democratic party if it choose, without slavery if it is possible, with slavery if it must." Echoed and amplified by Thurlow Weed in the Albany *Evening Journal*, who called abolitionists "the worst enemies of the colored man," Seward's speech seemed, as the London *Star* suggested, to consider Lincoln's emancipation proclamation "as a trick to be revoked" now that victory was at hand.[2]

Greatly perturbed, Sumner wrote Lincoln that Seward's remarks "had a tendency to excite distrust" and that there was

[1] Pierce, IV, 142; Sumner to Bright, July 31, 1862, Bright MSS.

[2] George E. Baker (ed.): *The Works of William H. Seward* (Boston: Houghton Mifflin and Company; 1884), V, 486; Thurlow Weed Barnes: *Memoir of Thurlow Weed* (Boston: Houghton Mifflin Company; 1884), p. 436.

general "consternation at the idea that the Proclamation can be forgotten or abandoned." It was this fear of "that devil of Compromise" which made Sumner exclaim that Union armies were "too victorious." "If the Rebellion should suddenly collapse," he explained to Bright, "democrats, copperheads, and Seward would insist upon amnesty and the Union, and 'no question asked about Slavery.'" The danger, he admitted, might not be great; "but any such danger is terrible. The longer our triumph is postponed, the more impossible this becomes." [3]

Sumner planned to redeem the time. Throughout the 1862–63 session of Congress he had sought so completely to vest freedmen with their rights as citizens that they could never be reenslaved. It was for this reason that he persistently demanded the enrolling of Negro troops and personally interceded with Lincoln to support officers like General Rufus Saxton who promoted the enlistment of freedmen in the army. "Tell Saxton to push his colored troops," he wrote Pierce, who was serving as a Treasury agent in the Sea Islands. "There is salvation that way." [4] There was salvation also in seeing that the freedmen became owners of land, preferably of land formerly belonging to Confederates. Repeatedly Sumner urged that the ex-slaves on the Sea Islands be given title to the tracts they had been cultivating since their masters fled before the Union army. It was only just that these valuable plantations should be divided among the former slaves rather than be sold at public auction, for in that event they "would be purchased by speculators, so that the colored population that had during the last year been working on the lands, would be excluded from the enjoyment of them." It was also highly expedient to have such a division of lands, for the Confederates were far less likely to consider compromise if their plantations had been divided among the freedmen. In February, though unwell, Sumner proposed a bill which combined his interest in arming the slaves with his concern for giving

[3] Sumner to Lincoln, Aug. 7, 1863, Lincoln MSS.; Sumner to Bright, July 21 and Aug. 4, 1863, Bright MSS.

[4] Julia L. Butterfield (ed.): *A Biographical Memorial of General Daniel Butterfield* (New York: The Grafton Press; 1904), pp. 156–8; Sumner to Pierce, July 1, 1863, Sumner MSS.

them land; it authorized the President to enroll 300,000 black troops, who when discharged should receive homesteads on lands confiscated from the rebels.[5]

Though Sumner was not able to persuade Congress to adopt his bill, he had more success in influencing the Secretary of War. On March 16 Stanton created the American Freedmen's Inquiry Commission, to "investigate the condition of the colored population and to report what measures will best contribute to their protection and improvement, so that they may defend and support themselves." The mandate was so sweeping that Sumner thought briefly of going on the Commission himself, but, finding his services needed in the Senate, he persuaded Stanton to appoint the "excellent and admirable" Robert Dale Owen, James MacKaye, and his old friend Samuel Gridley Howe. He was happy when the Commission, after an elaborate investigation, recommended the creation of an agency to supervise the freedmen and urged that "ultimately . . . the freemen should become owners in fee of the farms and gardens they occupy."[6]

While working positively to help the freedmen, Sumner sought to block any measures that might serve as a precedent for compromise with slavery. In February he joined with Fessenden and Wilson to fight Lincoln's cherished plan for gradual compensated emancipation in Missouri. Sumner saw the bill as a model for subsequent settlements with the slave states in rebellion and vigorously denounced it. "Alas, that men should forget that God is bound by no compromise," he exclaimed, "and that, sooner or later, He will insist that justice shall be done! . . . Palsied be the tongue that speaks of compromise with Slavery!" Finding little support for his demand that Missouri adopt immediate emancipation, Sumner proposed to reduce the authorized

[5] *Cong. Globe*, 37 Cong., 3 Sess., p. 508; Sumner: *Works*, VII, 263–4. For a superb account of the Port Royal experiment, with many references to Sumner's continuing interest in the project, see Willie Lee Rose: *Rehearsal for Reconstruction* (Indianapolis, Ind.: The Bobbs-Merrill Company, Inc.; 1964).

[6] Sumner to Bird, Mar. 19, 1863, Bird MSS.; Sumner to Howe, Feb. 3 and April 9, 1863, Sumner MSS.; Sumner to Andrew, Dec. 28, 1862, Andrew MSS. For discussions of the important work of this Commission see John G. Sproat: "Blueprint for Radical Reconstruction," *Journal of Southern Hist.*, XXIII (1957), 25–44, George R. Bentley: *A History of the Freedmen's Bureau* (Philadelphia: University of Pennsylvania Press; 1955), Chap. 2, and Richard W. Leopold: *Robert Dale Owen* (Cambridge: Harvard University Press; 1940), pp. 360–4.

compensation from three hundred to two hundred dollars for each slave. Such an amendment he knew would be unacceptable to the Missourians, who would therefore reject the whole plan and block a settlement that Seward might have used as a basis for a negotiated peace.[7]

All the while Sumner tried to mobilize public opinion against any compromise with the Confederates. As one step in firming up antislavery sentiment he arranged for the publication of a new edition of his 1860 speech on "The Barbarism of Slavery," designed especially to reach those who had previously failed to read his denunciation of the South. He reminded his audience that in the Civil War they were witnessing another stage in the age-old conflict between barbarism and civilization: "On the one side are women and children on the auction-block; families rudely separated; human flesh lacerated and seamed by the bloody scourge. . . . On the other side is the Union of our Fathers with the image of 'Liberty' on its coin and the sentiment of Liberty in its Constitution. . . ." In such a contest, Sumner warned, there could be no word of compromise that did not speak "openly for Barbarism." [8]

An even more effective way of blocking a possible negotiated settlement would be to get Northerners interested in peace terms. Seward and Weed could talk grandly about compromise, but there was bound to be serious disagreement in the North over how and when the Confederate states were to be readmitted. Long convinced that there could be no genuine peace without "the whole reconstruction of Southern Society," [9] Sumner put out his own plan as a rallying point for those opposed to compromise. His article, "Our Domestic Relations," which appeared in the influential *Atlantic Monthly,* was a revision of a speech he

[7] Sumner: *Works,* VII, 267–77. Sumner denied that he was responsible for the defeat of the plan, claiming that it failed because of "careless management" and adding: "I regret this sincerely because it would have made Emancipation in Missouri sure, and thus would have begun the work in the Border States." Sumner to Bright, Mar. 16, 1863, Bright MSS. He knew, however, that Missourians would not accept immediate emancipation but continued throughout the debate to insist upon it, and he knew from reliable informants that the two-hundred-dollar limit he proposed was altogether too low. J. M. Forbes to Sumner, Feb. 17, 1863, Sumner MSS., and Edward Archibold to B. F. Wade, Feb. 15, 1863, Wade MSS.

[8] Boston *Commonwealth,* Sept. 11, 1863.

[9] Sumner to Bright, Oct. 28, 1862, Bright MSS.

had planned to make in 1862 defending his "state-suicide" resolutions. Recognizing that his proposals had aroused an intensely unfavorable response in February 1862, he now skirted the issue whether the Southern states were alive or dead, declaring it was "a topic fit for the old schoolmen or a modern debating society." The really practical matter was to decide who was to control the process of reconstructing those states and how they were to be treated. On the first point Sumner argued that direction of the process belonged to Congress rather than the President. Thus far, Lincoln had followed the "Cromwellian policy" of appointing military governors for the conquered Southern states "without direct sanction in the Constitution or existing laws." "If the President, within State limits, can proceed to organize a military government to exercise all the powers of the State," Sumner argued, "surely Congress can proceed to organize a civil government within the same limits for the same purpose. . . ."

Since "the whole broad Rebel region is *tabula rasa,* or 'a clean slate,' where Congress, under the Constitution of the United States may write the laws," it ought to "do whatever is needful within Rebel limits to assure freedom and save society." Promising that "Congress will blot no star from the flag," Sumner suggested that it could and should divide the lands of the South "among patriot soldiers, poor whites, and freedmen." Thus "those citizens in the Rebel States who throughout the darkness of the Rebellion have kept their faith will be protected, and the freedmen rescued from hands that threaten to cast them back into Slavery."[1] Thus too the demon compromise, that inevitable accompaniment of early victory, could be exorcised.

• 7 •

While Sumner was preparing his article on "Our Domestic Relations" for the printer, he was also writing a speech, designed in more than title to be its companion, on "Our Foreign Relations." Back in February 1863, when hopes for ousting the Secretary of State had been high, anti-Seward Republicans of New York had asked him to undertake this review of American diplomacy, but

[1] Sumner: *Works,* VII, 493–546.

he was not able to give it much attention until summer, after Congress adjourned. Beginning his research in Washington, he continued work after he returned to Boston in mid-July.

The atmosphere in Massachusetts was hardly conducive to calm and impartial reflection upon foreign affairs. Anti-British sentiment ran high in New England, which had suffered heavily from the Confederate devastation of the Union merchant marine. Residents of Massachusetts, more than those in any other part of the country, worried over the probable escape of the Laird rams, now nearing completion, and feared that once these powerful vessels joined the Confederate navy the coastal towns of New England would be plundered.[2] Massachusetts intellectuals like Dana, Palfrey, and Longfellow, who had once thought of England as a mother country, were now bitter over the aid she had given the Confederacy, and they spoke "with sorrow unspeakable and astonishment of her course." Outraged by what seemed to be palpable British violations of international law, Massachusetts lawyers engaged in close and acrimonious review of the errors of the Palmerston government, and one of them, George Bemis, plied Sumner with the latest legal citations adverse to British policy.[3]

Sumner's own mood coincided with this angry, unhappy mood in Massachusetts. He had returned from Washington despondent. Congress had not done its full duty in protecting the Negro, yet because of continuing ill-health he had been unable to exercise effective leadership. Lincoln had failed to reorganize his cabinet, and Sumner bitterly wondered whether "our condition could be improved by any probable change" the President might be willing to accept.[4] Union victories only brought renewed talk of compromise with slavery.

Personally as well as politically the summer of 1863 was an unhappy time for Sumner. He felt more than ever isolated.

[2] New Englanders were especially fearful on this point. In the Lincoln Papers there are one or two letters from New Yorkers and Pennsylvanians expressing this fear, but from the Boston area there are many, including strong appeals from Governor Andrew to both the President and the Secretary of the Navy.

[3] Bemis: Diary, Aug. 29, 1863, Bemis MSS.; Sumner to Bemis [Sept. 1, 1863], ibid.; Sumner to Duchess of Argyll, June 29, 1863, Argyll MSS.

[4] Sumner to "My dear Sir," July 4, 1863, MS., New York Pub. Lib.

Death was reducing the small company of his close friends. The tragic accident in which Fanny Longfellow burned to death not merely made a gap in Sumner's circle but left her husband, Sumner's oldest and closest friend, remote and unconcerned with public affairs. When John E. Lodge died, Sumner lost his only strong supporter on Beacon Hill, though his widow, Anna, continued to be a loyal confidant and Henry Cabot Lodge, his son, was a suitably awed young admirer.

Sumner felt lonely even in his home on Hancock Street. During the winter of 1861 his elderly mother had fallen ill and ever since had been almost completely bedridden, tortured by insomnia and frequently too exhausted even to talk. Sadder was the condition of his only surviving brother, George, whose fluent, clever, and sometimes pretentious chatter had once enlivened the house. Boundlessly energetic and endlessly loquacious, George had never been able to find a focus for his considerable abilities until the war gave him a cause worth fighting for. After the firing on Fort Sumter he was constantly busy, writing pro-Union columns for the London *Morning Post,* sending Seward unsolicited advice on international law, informing Chase about his duties, assisting Andrew in mobilizing Massachusetts troops. While supervising the loading of troops, he was accidentally hit in the knee by a railroad car. Though the injury at first did not seem serious, it resulted in a paralysis that subsequently extended to his entire right leg. Unable to diagnose the ailment, his physician prescribed the water cure at Northampton and urged absolute rest "in order to tone up the system." "Oh that I had only had a leg off at Bull Run," George exclaimed bitterly, "instead of being thus keeled up, with more of annoyance and less of hope of speedy usefulness." Making little progress, he returned to Hancock Street in the summer of 1862, now so paralyzed that a manservant had to care for all his needs. During the following winter the disease, which the Senator believed "arose from some subtle weakness in the constitution," extended up the right side and arm, and it became apparent that he could no longer be treated at home, where his presence troubled his ailing mother. Taken to a sunny room in the Massachusetts General Hospital overlooking the Charles River, George grew visibly weaker during the summer of 1863, and the Senator, on his daily visits to his brother's bedside, realized that soon he would be entirely alone in the world.[5]

Sumner's unhappiness and depression were everywhere apparent in the forty-thousand-word analysis he wrote during July and August of "the perils to our country, foreshadowed in the action of foreign powers since the outbreak of the war."[6] In substance there was little that was new in this forbidding document. Believing that the most serious threat to peace lay in the likely escape of the Laird rams, he devoted his speech largely to a review of British policies which had led up to this anticipated breach of international law. As in the past, Sumner stressed British, rather than French, actions hostile to the Union cause, both because he thought the immediate danger was from Great Britain and because he knew nothing he might say would affect Napoleon III's policy.

The fatal mistake of the British, he contended, was their original failure to understand the moral issue of the American Civil War. From this failure derived their miscalled neutrality. The British should have understood, he wrote bitterly to the Duchess of Argyll, that "It is one thing to supply ships to an organized Government fighting for Civilization and to put down a slave-monger State crawling into existence; and a very different thing to supply ships to help build this slave-monger State. One must forget that God is God, not to see the difference."[7]

Because of this moral obtuseness, Sumner argued, the British in 1861 had made their "precipitate, unfriendly, and immoral concession" of belligerency to the Confederates, and this action, he increasingly believed, was the source of "great wrong to us—destined to enter into future diplomacy."[8] Sumner had

[5] On George Sumner, see the memoir in *Mass. Hist. Soc. Proceedings*, XVIII, 189–223; Nicholas B. Wainwright (ed.): *A Philadelphia Perspective: The Diary of Sidney George Fisher* (Philadelphia: The Historical Society of Pennsylvania; 1967), p. 253; Joseph Parkes to Lord Brougham, Aug. 13, 1861, Brougham MSS.; George Sumner to Horatio Woodman, Jan. 1, 1862, Woodman MSS.; George Sumner to Andrew [Jan.] 8 [1862], Andrew MSS.; Longfellow to G. W. Greene, Jan. 1 and April 27, 1863, Longfellow MSS.; Charles Sumner to W. L. Gage, MS., Harvard Univ. Sumner's only surviving sister, Mrs. Julia Hastings, lived in California.

[6] The revised text of the speech is in Sumner: *Works*, VII, 333–471.

[7] Sumner to Duchess of Argyll, May 19, 1863, Argyll MSS.

[8] Sumner to Theodore Tilton, Oct. 23, 1863, MS., New York Hist. Soc.

not always so viewed the Queen's proclamation of neutrality. At the outset of the war he, like the Queen's law officers, like the stanchest supporter of the Union abroad, and like virtually every subsequent student of international law, appears to have felt that the proclamation was necessary,[9] and it was even rumored that in December 1861 he would make a speech expressing "his entire satisfaction with the position of England and France." [1] Gradually, and perhaps unwittingly, he had come around to accepting Seward's argument that recognition of the Confederates as belligerents was "in derogation of the law of nations and injurious to the dignity and sovereignty of the United States." Having made this view his own, Sumner characteristically pushed the argument to its extreme. By mid-1863 he concluded that the Queen's proclamation was the fountain from which all subsequent evil had flowed. The high-handed British attitude in the *Trent* affair, the gratuitous British protests when the Union tried to block up the Charleston harbor, the "irritating tendency" of Russell's diplomatic correspondence, the unneutral speeches of the Foreign Minister and of Gladstone—all these were the results of the original sin. So, too, now was the threatened "fitting out in England of a *naval expedition* against the commerce of the United States."

As though aware this was a shaky argument, Sumner sought to bolster his position by introducing a proposition novel to international law. Though any concession of belligerent rights, especially to a slave power, was "a blunder, if not a

[9] For a well-informed contemporary British view, see Montague Bernard: *A Historical Account of the Neutrality of Great Britain during the American Civil War* (London: Longmans, Green, Reader, and Dyer; 1870), Chap. 7. See also Henry Wheaton: *Elements of International Law*, ed. R. H. Dana, Jr. (8th ed.; Boston: Little, Brown and Company; 1866), pp. 34–8; John Bassett Moore: *A Digest of International Law* (Washington: Government Printing Office; 1908), I, 184–93; Charles C. Hyde: *International Law* (2nd ed.; Boston: Little, Brown and Company; 1945), I, 198–202; H. Lauterpacht: *Recognition in International Law* (Cambridge: Cambridge University Press; 1948), Chaps. 12–15, esp. pp. 177–8; Ti-Chiang Chen: *The International Law of Recognition*, ed. L. C. Green (New York: Frederick A. Praeger, Inc.; 1951), Chaps. 20–27. A recent statement is that of D. P. O'Connell (*International Law* [London: Stevens & Sons Limited; 1965], I, 161): ". . . the status of *de facto* government includes the capacity to wage civil war, and recognition is no more than the acknowledgment of the legal fact."

[1] C. F. Adams, Jr., to C. F. Adams, July 2, 1861, Adams MSS.; C. F. Adams, Jr., to Abigail B. Adams, Sept. 29, 1861, ibid.

crime," he argued that the British had been flagrantly unneutral in their "concession of *belligerent rights on the ocean,*" because the Confederates—whatever their situation on land—in 1861 had no open ports, no fleet, no maritime commerce, no sailors, and no prize courts. Since the South was "incompetent to exercise *belligerent jurisdiction* on the ocean," it followed that the ships built for the Confederacy, in Britain and elsewhere, should have been treated by the British government as "mere gypsies of the sea, disturbers of the common highway, outlaws, and enemies of the human race."

Very proud of this distinction between ocean and land belligerency, Sumner continued to elaborate and argue it for nearly a decade. The idea appears to have been suggested to him when the Duke of Argyll in April 1863 defended the action of the British government in the case of the *Alabama* but suggested that the time might be near when "the present understanding of international law on this subject" ought to be reviewed. "I doubt," the Duke continued, "whether a Government which is unable to keep open one single port of its own seaboard ought to be allowed to exercise the rights of a *naval* belligerent." Hastily he added: "But no such doctrine as this has ever been laid down hitherto. . . ." [2] In his speech Sumner sought to repair that omission. Unable to cite any British or American precedent or to quote any publicist who distinguished between land and naval belligerency, he had to rest his case on abstract justice; indeed, his most telling documentation was a reference to the "deserts of Bohemia" in Shakespeare's *Winter Tale.* In the protracted postwar diplomatic correspondence concerning the Alabama Claims his argument was not followed by any party, and it finds no place today in international law.[3]

But what Sumner's speech lacked in the way of law and precedent, he supplied in indignant rhetoric reflecting his angry, isolated mood. He accused the British government of "flagrant oblivion of history and of duty." He sneered that the British were

[2] *Mass. Hist. Soc. Proceedings,* XLVII, 75.

[3] See Dana's statement of the tests for determining whether recognition of belligerency is justified in his edition of Wheaton: *Elements of International Law,* p. 35, and the modern formulation of those tests in Lauterpacht: *Recognition in International Law,* pp. 175–6.

deliberately aligning themselves with a new nation "which not only tolerates Slavery, but, exulting in its shame, strives to reverse the judgment of mankind, making this outrage its chief support and glory." He jeered at the anticipated diplomatic union between that "virtuous lady," Queen Victoria, and Jefferson Davis, "once patron of 'Repudiation,' now chief of Rebel Slavery." If Britain and France persisted in their failure to see that the South was a *"bordello,* . . . [a] mighty house of ill-fame which the Christian powers are now asked for the first time to license," if, instead, they continued in their "adulterous dalliance with Slavery," Sumner threatened retaliation in due time: "Should our cases be reversed, there is nothing England and France now propose, . . . which it will not be our equal right to propose when Ireland or India once more rebels, or when France is in the throes of its next revolution."

During the six weeks while Sumner was preparing this speech he wrote few letters and gave almost no indication of the reasons that impelled him to prepare an address so long on invective, so short on law. The document itself shows that he had difficulty keeping his material in focus. Not merely was the speech excessively long, but it lacked real unity. First he offered a prolonged discussion of American grievances, real and fancied, against Britain and France. Next a thirty-eight-page section tried to show England's history bound that country never to intervene in a foreign war so as to encourage slavery. After this tedious historical review, Sumner was obliged to admit that precedent on this point "sometimes . . . was against the rights of men, sometimes . . . in their favor," but concluded firmly that "if intervention in behalf of slavery was not contrary to the Law of Nations, it ought to be." There followed an extended argument that it was a violation of international law to recognize any insurgent government so long as civil war was going on—with the exception that such recognition was excusable *"where sincerely made for the protection of Human Rights."* His final section on ocean belligerency appeared to be an afterthought, unconnected in substance or in logic with the rest of the lecture. In language, too, the speech was murky. His pages were full of digressions and irrelevancies, and his sentences grew to serpentine length, one running on to 529 words. It was scarcely surprising that Sumner found himself unable to memorize the speech, as he customarily did on important occasions, complaining that his "brain, exhausted perhaps by labor, did not grapple with the text." [4]

Such confusion of language and thought suggests that Sumner himself was not fully aware of his own purposes in writing his speech. During the acrimonious controversy that arose after he delivered it, he stressed that he had hoped to effect a change in British foreign policy. "My special aspiration was to reach the people of England and France, and their cabinets also," he explained to Chase. He told Greeley that his purpose was "to show how completely England was committed against slavery, so that all logic and consistency required her to set her face as flint against any paltering with slavery." To the Duchess of Argyll he wrote: "There was the cause of Freedom—and of Peace between our two countries—both put in jeopardy by the uncertain, irritating and offensive policy of Lord Russell. *The time had come to tell him so plainly.*" His hope, then, was "to have England retrace her steps." [5]

The difficulty in accepting this explanation, which appears to have come as an afterthought to Sumner himself, is that the speech is an indictment, not a plea for reconciliation. If Sumner sought to bludgeon the British into being peaceful, he showed a remarkable misconception of their national temper. His rhetorical flings were the more offensive because he damned the errors of the British so much more strongly than those of the French and because he failed adequately to recognize the dedicated services performed by friends of the Union abroad or to acknowledge the long-suffering patience of the Lancashire unemployed. Such an "elaborate enumeration of the injuries which we have suffered from the hands of England and France," Edward Everett told him candidly, "would be appropriate as a manifesto or a declaration of war; but unless that is intended, it seems calculated to do mischief."

[4] Sumner to Chase, Aug. 30, 1863, Chase MSS., Lib. of Cong.

[5] Sumner to Chase, Sept. 21, 1863, ibid.; Sumner to Greeley, Sept. 21, 1863, Greeley MSS.; Sumner to J. R. Giddings, Oct. 5, 1863, Giddings MSS.

In replying to Everett, Sumner exposed a different purpose for the speech. He enumerated British failings at such length, he explained, "because, although there was a general impression that England had greatly wronged us, few persons knew the particulars." [6] A close study of his text shows that it was, indeed, directed at an American, not a British, audience. In Sumner's earliest explanation of the speech he declared frankly that his main purpose was "to instruct my own fellow-countrymen." "It seemed to me," he wrote Lieber, "that the country needed light; that the people were groping from ignorance of what England had done, and also from ignorance of law and history applicable to our case." So far as Sumner knew when he mounted the platform in New York on September 10, the Laird rams were about to sail for the Confederacy, and he had therefore determined "(1) if possible, by appeal and exposition, to prevent the war; or, if war came, then (2) to have a vindication of my country." [7]

Vindication of the country would also be a vindication of Charles Sumner. His speech was, in fact if not in conscious intent, a carefully calculated gamble, planned during his personal and political despondency of the past summer. If, after his denunciation of Great Britain, the Palmerston government should order the seizure of the Laird rams, Sumner could claim the credit and could contrast the success of his candid diplomacy with the failure of Seward's covert policy. If, on the other hand, the rams sailed for the Confederacy, Sumner's bellicose speech would put him at the head of an aroused and angry people ready for war with Great Britain. The critical British chargé d'affaires in Washington, William Stuart, considered Sumner's "fanatical and mischievous" speech so blatant a play for popularity that it must be his "Card for the Presidency" in 1864. Even his former friend, Harriet Martineau, judged that Sumner had, "for himself, declared war against England" as his "bid for the Presidentship." [8]

[6] Everett: Diary, Sept. 26, 1863, Everett MSS.

[7] Sumner to Chase, Sept. 21, 1863, Chase MSS., Lib. of Cong.; Sumner to Lieber, Sept. 15, 1863 and [May 1864], Sumner MSS.

[8] Stuart to Russell, Sept. 14, 1863, Stuart MSS.; Harriet Martineau to Henry Reeve, Sept. 29, 1863, MS. in private hands.

It was not the presidency that was in Sumner's mind as he appeared before a throng of three thousand patient listeners in Cooper Union and read what one hopes were extracts from his speech, which in any case went on for nearly four hours. In "Our Foreign Relations," as in "Our Domestic Relations," which appeared simultaneously in the *Atlantic*, the object was to checkmate William H. Seward and kill forever compromise with slavery.

CHAPTER IV

Equality Before the Law

SUMNER had omitted one possibility from his calculations. If the British government seized the Laird rams after his Cooper Union speech, he could claim that he, rather than Seward, was responsible for preserving the peace. If the British let the ships go, Sumner was in a better position than the Secretary of State to stand at the head of the outraged American people demanding war. But he could not reckon upon the fact that Russell ordered the ships detained on September 8, 1863—just two days before Sumner spoke in New York.[1]

Since there was no working trans-Atlantic cable, the news was slow in reaching the United States, and in the interval Sumner basked in the overwhelmingly favorable reaction to his speech. The New York *Tribune* was glowing in its praise. The New York *Herald* delighted in Sumner's "exposure and denunciations of the hypocritical pleadings and false pretences of the British Government." Though the New York *Times,* friendly to Seward, reserved comment until it could hear from Washington, it devoted nearly half of the entire September 11 issue to publishing the address in full. In Boston, though the Democratic *Post* was as usual hostile and the conservative *Advertiser* spent more time in summarizing than in commending the speech, the *Journal* lauded the "fairness, candor, earnestness and ability" of

[1] For a rhetorical analysis of the speech, and some details on the circumstances in which it was delivered, see Richard A. Ek: "Charles Sumner's Address at Cooper Union," *Southern Speech Journal,* XXXII (1967), 169–79.

Sumner's address, and the *Transcript,* the respectable evening daily, commended "Mr. Sumner's comprehensive views of International Law, the extensive learning with which he enriches the discussion of it, his convincing logic and kindling eloquence." Daily Sumner's mail was filled with letters praising "this eloquent exposition, so full of righteous indignation, terrible denunciation, exhaustive research, unanswerable argument,—so abundant, so powerful, and so eloquent in the cause of humanity." [2]

When the news spread that the British had already seized the rams and that there would be no war, the reaction to Sumner's speech became more critical. Horace Greeley had second thoughts and concluded that Sumner's too emphatic rejection of any possible mediation was in conflict with "those Peace doctrines whereof Mr. Sumner was once so able and distinguished an advocate." Doubtless with some guidance from Washington, the New York *Times* complained that during the past session of Congress there had been "not a solitary debate, in fact not a solitary speech, of any weight, upon the subject of our foreign wrongs" and concluded that "Mr. Sumner's [Cooper Union] speech, clear and cogent as it is, would have had far greater influence had it been delivered from his seat in the Senate." Democratic papers now gleefully ridiculed Sumner's denunciation of Great Britain and France. "Sir Humphrey Davy once swore at the North pole and spoke disrespectfully of the Equator," jeered the New York *World,* "and we fear that Palmerston and Napoleon may be capable of snapping their fingers at Mr. Sumner."

Then British reactions to the speech began to come in, and they were all hostile. Scornfully dismissing "the enormous mass of words with which Mr. Sumner had overlaid a very simple and intelligible subject," *The Times* of London set the tone in condemning the speech as "based neither on law nor on fact, but upon his own sympathies and antipathies, which he is pleased to assume must also be ours." Except for John Bright's paper, the London *Morning Star,* virtually every other British paper ex-

[2] See the summary of press opinion and of Sumner's correspondence in Sumner: *Works,* VII, 474–83.

pressed much the same opinion. "Of all things least likely to happen," lamented Harriet Martineau in the London *Daily News,* which had hitherto tried to promote good relations with the United States, "we should have thought, was this speech from the man who spoke it." Sumner had had an opportunity to appeal for peace, Miss Martineau continued, but "he has employed it to lash the irritations of his fellow-citizens into rage, and to obscure and pervert the facts of history . . . by his own judgment and passion."

"Alas, that it has come to this," lamented the Duchess of Argyll, when she could bring herself to write Sumner again; "that you should have felt it right to charge England as you have done in a public assembly. Was the fire not hot enough already?" Cobden, too, asked *"cui bono?"* and felt Sumner should have appealed to the "masses in England, led by so much of the intellect and the moral and religious worth of the kingdom." These were the muted responses of old friends; those less partial to Sumner or less familiar with his long services to the antislavery cause spoke out more bluntly. W. E. Forster, who had battled repeatedly in Parliament against attempts to recognize Confederate independence, thought Sumner's speech "makes it very uphill work for your friends here; because it gives a colour to the argument . . . that you are determined to revenge yourselves upon us when you can." Another strong supporter of the Union, Professor Goldwin Smith of Oxford, felt Sumner's "indiscriminate condemnation of the whole English people" could only discredit and discourage allies of the North. A former friend of Sumner's, the Liberal Joseph Parkes, thought this "wrong-headed, perverse, wordy declamation against England" almost called for "another caning on the floor of Congress." [3]

Ironically, the chief result of Sumner's "Our Foreign Relations" speech was to strengthen the two men it had been chiefly

[3] *Mass. Hist. Soc. Proceedings,* XLVII, 83; *Am. Hist. Rev.,* II, 313–14; T. Wemyss Reid: *Life of the Right Honourable William Edward Forster* (4th ed.; London: Chapman and Hall, Limited; 1888), I, 360–1; Goldwin Smith to Lieber, Oct. 3, 1863, Lieber MSS.; Parkes to Lord Brougham, Sept. 29, 1863, Brougham MSS. For adverse reports on the speech by American diplomats abroad, see H. S. Sanford to Seward, Oct. 1, 1863, Seward MSS., and James S. Pike to Fessenden, Oct. 12, 1863, Pike MSS., copy in White Notes.

designed to injure. As part of the tottery, faction-ridden Palmerston government, Russell had hitherto not felt strong enough to curb Confederate activities in Britain lest he be accused of being a tool of the United States. Sumner's denunciation of the Foreign Minister eliminated that possibility, and Russell made sure that it received wide publicity by replying in a speech at Blairgowrie on September 26. Sumner's address was so long that he had not been able to read it all, he said sneeringly, but he deplored the portions he had read of "what is called an oration, heaping up accusation after accusation, and misrepresentation after misrepresentation, all tending to the bloody end of war between these two nations." At the same time Russell went out of his way to compliment Seward, the other, but concealed, object of Sumner's onslaught: "The Government of America discusses these matters very fairly with the English Government. Sometimes we think them quite in the wrong; sometimes they say we are quite in the wrong; but we discuss them fairly, and with regard to the Secretary of State I see no complaint to make." Two months after Sumner's speech, Charles Francis Adams recorded that it continued to have unanticipated consequences: "The absurd prejudices against our administration, with which I had first to contend, are now nearly gone. Mr. Seward is no longer regarded as the *bet*[*e*] *noir*, intending all sorts of shocking insults to the British lion." [4]

As Seward's successor in the role of the most unpopular American in Great Britain, Sumner writhed unhappily. Ever since the Brooks assault he tended, when criticized, to think of himself as a martyr to principle, like St. Stephen or, more frequently, St. Sebastian. "I shall be attacked brutally," he predicted, even before the full extent of British anger became known; "indeed, I have taken the foreign shafts all into my own bosom. . . ." "Of course, I am abused," he plaintively wrote the Duchess of Argyll. "I expected it. I expected a sheaf of spears in my own bosom." [5]

[4] *The Times* (London), Sept. 28, 1863; Adams to Palfrey, Nov. 10, 1863, copy, Adams MSS. Cf. Adams: Diary, Sept. 29, 1863, ibid.

[5] Sumner to Chase, Sept. 21, 1863, Chase MSS., Lib. of Cong.; Sumner to Duchess of Argyll, Oct. 26, 1863, Argyll MSS.

At first he insisted that his speech had been misunderstood abroad. Not enough people had read it in full, and most had relied upon distorted extracts or summaries. At Sumner's urging friends overcame Seward's reluctance and persuaded the State Department to send out post-free copies of the speech to all members of Parliament, all consuls and vice consuls of the United States, and editors of most British newspapers.[6] At the same time, John Bigelow, the American consul at Paris, supervised publication of an abridged French version of the speech.[7]

Finding that fuller knowledge brought fuller criticism, Sumner tried to explain and defend his speech. He insisted that, despite all the strictures, his address had brought about his intended result, the maintenance of peace between the United States and Great Britain. "I rejoice in the good . . . which impartial minds assure me has been done in England and in France," he wrote the Duchess of Argyll. "It was a duty to be done, and I am glad to have done it," he told the Duke. "Of course, you will not do again the things which I charge. Lord Russell will stop writing pert notes; he will stop unfriendly criticism; he will stop unneutral speeches; he will stop unfriendly prophesies; he will stop . . . future Alabamas. . . ."[8]

Sumner's tone was, however, too emphatic; it suggested that he did not really believe his own words. A better index of his feelings was his initial reaction to Russell's speech at Blairgowrie. The Foreign Minister's remark that, according to international law, there was nothing to prevent the British government from recognizing a slave power like the Confederacy was evidence that Russell was persisting in his abominable course, and

[6] F. W. Ballard to Seward, Sept. 16, 1863, and W. H. Seward to Ballard, Sept. 17, 1863, both in State Department, Miscellaneous Letters, The National Archives. Apparently Sumner's friends did not believe Seward's promise to distribute copies of the speech, for they made arrangements to send others by direct, private mail to Great Britain. Ballard to Sumner, Oct. 12, 1863, Sumner MSS. In later years this distrust was translated into the mistaken recollections that Seward had refused to send the speeches abroad in the diplomatic pouches. Cephas Brainerd to Sumner, June 26, 1873, ibid. See also Gurowski: *Diary, from November 18, 1862, to October 18, 1863* (New York: Carleton, Publishers; 1864), p. 334.

[7] Bigelow: Diary, Sept. 28 and 30, Oct. 2 and 14, 1863, Bigelow MSS.

[8] Sumner to Duchess of Argyll, Oct. 26, 1863, and to Duke of Argyll, Nov. 10, 1863, both in Argyll MSS.

Sumner planned once more to attack him "in a grave quiet speech of an hour," preferably delivered again in New York.[9] Lieber and other friends apparently dissuaded him, however, from continuing a controversy that could not redound to his credit, and the death of George Sumner on October 3 provided a convenient and legitimate excuse for keeping quiet.

Once more Sumner's effort to take over control of American foreign policy had failed. Shrewdly Seward sensed that failure even before Sumner himself, and only two days after the Cooper Union speech the Secretary wrote a note exquisitely combining congratulation with condescension. "You have performed a very important public service in a most able manner and in a conjunction when I hope that it will be useful abroad and at home," Seward declared—at just the moment that he was doing all in his power to keep copies of the angry speech from being sent abroad. Remembering his own efforts earlier in the war to arouse patriotic sentiment through foreign adventures, the Secretary added a bit patronizingly: "You are on the right track, rouse the nationality of the American People. It is an instinct upon which you can always rely when the conscience that ought never to slumber is drugged to death." [1]

• 2 •

Meanwhile, Sumner's ideas on reconstruction came under sharp attack. Though his *Atlantic* article on "Our Domestic Relations" was published anonymously, everybody promptly identified the author and made him a target. The most careful rebuttal of Sumner's arguments appeared in the Washington *National Intelligencer*, which called his claim for Congressional supremacy over the conquered South clearly unconstitutional. The long, thoughtful essay, replete with legal citations, raised most of the arguments conservatives were to use during the next four years of debate over the Southern question. States could not commit

[9] Sumner to Lieber, Oct. 15, 1863, Sumner MSS.; Sumner to G. W. Greene, Oct. 26, 1863, Greene MSS.

[1] Draft of a letter to Sumner, Sept. 12, 1863, Seward MSS.

treason; individuals could. The federal government had no power to act upon states, only upon individual citizens in states. To argue, as Sumner did, that Southern states had forfeited their rights through rebellion was to concede the very point for which the Confederates were fighting—the right to secede. "Let us, then," urged the *Intelligencer*, "not with singular inconsistency emulate the misconduct of those whom we seek to punish for their disregard of the Constitution by disregarding it ourselves."

After attacking the constitutional bases of Sumner's reconstruction plan, the *Intelligencer* went on to explore its social implications. What was going to happen to the former slaves of the South? If freedmen were recognized as citizens of the United States, might they not claim the right to vote and even to hold office? Did Sumner and his friends really want "a piebald Senate and House of Representatives, composed of 'black spirits and white,' to regulate the destinies of the great American nation?" Feeling that these consequences were too horrendous to contemplate, the *Intelligencer* also shuddered at the only alternative: If the freedmen could not control their own political destinies, would they not inevitably fall back into the power of the "superior race" in the South? And, since the abolition of slavery would end the three-fifths clause of the Constitution, would not those Southern whites return to the Union with their political power actually augmented as a result of their rebellion?

The more conservative members of the Republican party echoed these objections. Avoiding personalities, Seward made clear his disagreement: "I am willing that the prodigal son shall return. The doors, as far as I am concerned, shall always be open to him." Seward's friend, Henry J. Raymond, who was editor of the New York *Times* and would soon become chairman of the Republican National Committee, was more explicit. In a widely circulated speech at Wilmington on November 6, 1863, he told Delaware Republicans that the Constitution "has almost nothing to do with States as such," since it "does not impose positive obligations upon States, but only upon their individual citizens." Therefore, "a State cannot be disfranchised any more than it can be hung." Individual rebels might be guilty of treason, but "every citizen of every State is entitled today to every civil right which he enjoyed before the Rebellion broke out, unless he has forfeited it by some crime . . ."[2]

The most vigorous attack upon Sumner's reconstruction theory came from Montgomery Blair, who spoke not merely for himself but for the powerful Blair family with influence in all the border states. On October 3 the hatchet-faced Postmaster General warned a group of Unconditional Unionists meeting at Rockville, Maryland, that the country faced further grave dangers. Now that the rebellion of the "nullifiers" was near an end, freedom was "menaced by the ambition of the ultra-Abolitionists, which is equally despotic in its tendencies, and . . . alike fatal to republican institutions." The aims of the "Abolition party" were *"amalgamation, equality* and *fraternity"*; they "would make the manumission of the slaves the means of infusing their blood into our whole system."

The first step in their scheme, Blair revealed, was "to declare the State Governments vacated" in the South, and he found evidence of an abolitionist conspiracy in the simultaneous advocacy of this idea in the Washington *Chronicle*, the *Missouri Democrat*, and the *Atlantic Monthly*. Viewing Sumner's unsigned article on "Our Domestic Relations" as "the programme of the movement," Blair thought its thesis was "abhorrent to every principle on which the Union was founded." Its author was evidently "hostile at heart to free debate, and to . . . the checks and balances of our complicated system of National and State Governments." The "extreme anxiety evinced in certain quarters" to prevent the speedy restoration of the Union suggested to Blair that there was afoot "something of a design to command a great event in prospect by revolutionary means." The President, he concluded, would have cautiously to "steer his course through the strong conflicting tides of two revolutionary movements—that of the nullifiers, to destroy the Union . . . , and that of the ultra-abolitionists, which has set in to disfranchise the South on the pretext of making secure the emancipation of the slaves."[3]

[2] Francis Brown: *Raymond of the Times* (New York: W. W. Norton & Company, Inc.; 1951), pp. 245–7.

[3] *Speech of the Hon. Montgomery Blair (Postmaster General), on the Revolutionary Schemes of the Ultra Abolitionists, and in defence of the Policy of the President* (New York: S. W. Lee; 1863), pp. 3, 5–7, 19.

In other circumstances Sumner might have denounced Blair's speech or have coldly cut off all communication with the Postmaster General. He had, however, a certain fondness for the whole Blair family, who had treated him kindly at their house in Silver Spring when he was recovering from the Brooks assault, and he knew their faithfulness to the antislavery cause. He also knew that, despite their conservatism, old Francis P. Blair, Montgomery Blair, and General Frank Blair were fiercely hostile to Seward; indeed, the Blairs' animus toward the Secretary of State was so intense that they were willing to see Sumner take his place in the cabinet. But most of all Sumner knew that he had just experienced a series of disastrous defeats, in both foreign and domestic controversies, and that he could not now afford to make more enemies. Permitting himself to believe that Blair, alone of American politicians, had not known the authorship of the *Atlantic Monthly* essay, he quietly admonished the Postmaster General in a private letter against exaggerating "controversies among friends." [4] "Of course you desire to get the rebel regime back under the national government," he gently argued. "So do I. Of course you desire that it shall be loyal and true. So do I. *Now I am for any way that will best accomplish this result.* Are not you? Where then is the difference?"

Refusing to be soothed, Blair replied that his differences with Sumner were "wide as the poles." He stressed an issue that was going to be endlessly argued throughout the controversy over reconstruction: "You assume that good and true white men in the South are not more numerous than the vote of Old Sarum —I . . . say the great body of our people are as good and as loyal as yours [in the North]. . . ." The result of Sumner's proposals would be "substantially to enslave the white people [of the South], beginning with the abolishment of the Constitutions of ⅓ of the States." Blair did concede that Sumner, however wrong, was not guilty of "the besotting Egotism" which in his speech he had attributed to abolitionists like "that profane wretch," Wendell Phillips.

[4] For both sides of this correspondence, see Blair to Sumner, Oct. 24 and Nov. 28, 1863, Sumner MSS., and William E. Smith: *The Francis Preston Blair Family in Politics* (New York: The Macmillan Company; 1933), II, 244–5.

Sumner declined to be baited. Blandly he wrote Blair again that he felt they were really in agreement upon such basic matters as the necessity for "the complete suppression of the rebellion," the "return of our system to perfect harmony under the National Government," and the "protection of the Union men and their freedom." "Of course," he added, "this cannot be done constitutionally by military or presidential power"; therefore, the duty fell on Congress.

Blair got the last word by denying any need for Congress to meddle in the reconstruction process. Since a law passed by one Congress could be repealed by the next, it was "safer" for freedom to stand on the Jacksonian ground that "an executive act within the sphere of duty of the President is valid and will be maintained by all the power of the Executive military and otherwise, despite of Congress Legislatures or Judges of any kind." "I wish," Blair closed the correspondence on a plaintive note, "you could regard this subject from my Jackson Stand point. It is altogether the best and surest foundation to build on."

If Sumner was not willing to change his mind, neither was he prepared to continue the quarrel. He was now at one of the lowest points in his long public career. His advice on foreign policy had proved wrong, his plan for reconstruction had been severely mauled, and his old antagonist was more securely than ever ensconced in the State Department. It was time to devise a new strategy.

• 3 •

In the first session of the Thirty-Eighth Congress Sumner found few opportunitites to recoup his political fortunes. Just before Congress assembled in December 1863, the huge iron dome of the Capitol was completed, and all Washington turned out to watch the gigantic statue of Liberty hoisted in sections to crown the edifice. Like the builders, Congressmen had a sense that their work, too, was finished. They had raised armies and equipped navies; they had mobilized the economy of the nation; they had set the country upon an antislavery course. Though there was much detailed legislative work to be done, there was no need for bold new policies. "Never before since I have been in Congress," Sumner reported in December, "has it come together in such tranquility. . . . The battle of 'ideas' has been fought—in the last Congress. It only remains that we should carry forward the 'ideas' that have been adopted." [5]

As Congress settled down to business, Sumner found his role an unenviable one. Most of the serious work of the Senate has always been carried on in its committees, and the reports of those groups, and particularly the opinions of their chairmen, carry great weight. As head of the prestigious Committee on Foreign Relations, Sumner could expect, and did usually receive, "implicit obedience . . . to all his requests" dealing with diplomatic affairs.[6] But in the winter of 1863–64 his committee had few important topics to consider. Because patronage had already been distributed, only a handful of minor diplomatic appointments were referred to it. Though Sumner's committee continued to meet regularly, the only treaties it discussed dealt with such matters as claims of the Hudson's Bay Company, dues imposed by the King of Belgium for use of the Scheldt,[7] and commercial relations with the United States of Colombia.

The one significant action of the Foreign Relations Committee during the whole session was negative. In January 1864 McDougall revived, in a more belligerent fashion, his resolution condemning French intervention in Mexico with the proviso that the United States should declare war unless French troops were withdrawn by March 15. At the same time some Republican Senators favored recognizing Maximilian's regime, in the hope that it would then cut off Confederate supplies pouring through Mexico. Equally opposed to "any concession to this new-fangled imperialism" and any action that would afford Napoleon "any excuse for hostility—or recognition [of the Confederacy]—or breaking the blockade," Sumner killed both proposals in his

[5] Sumner to Bright, Dec. 15, 1863, Bright MSS.

[6] *Cong. Globe,* 38 Cong., 1 Sess., p. 1110.

[7] Aware that King Leopold was hostile to the Union and feeling that he was demanding an exorbitant amount for the Scheldt dues, Senators first voted to reject a proposed treaty of commerce with Belgium, which Sumner favorably reported, but after three days of lobbying he persuaded them to reconsider and approve the treaty. *Senate Exec. Jour.,* XIII, 416, 423.

committee.[8] In April Henry Winter Davis's resolution condemning "any monarchical government erected on the ruins of any republican government in America, under the auspices of any European power," though unanimously approved in the House of Representatives, met the same fate. In vain McDougall tried to bring these proposals to the Senate floor, recognizing that in Sumner's committee they lay "buried, not five fathoms deep, but certainly as well buried as if . . . put into the tombs of the Capulets." "I have been circumscribed, circumbounded, and surrounded by the Committee on Foreign Relations," the Californian protested, but his colleagues made it clear that on such questions they were "governed by the recommendation of the Committee on Foreign Relations." [9]

In turn, the chairmen of other Senate committees expected the same deference from Sumner. His colleague Wilson, who was often referred to as the "military Senator from Massachusetts," took charge of bills relating to the army. Hale and Grimes managed the naval bills. Trumbull was head of the powerful Judiciary Committee. Fessenden and Sherman looked after revenue measures. With the exception of Hale, all these men were competent and experienced, and on measures in which they took a strong interest, their voices usually prevailed. If one of their bills directly affected Sumner's constituents, they were willing to listen to his views. For instance, John Sherman said that it was Sumner's "potent voice" which defeated a section of the proposed omnibus tax bill raising rates on manufactures; though the provision promised to bring in fifty million dollars of much needed revenue, Sumner was able to persuade the Senate that it fell too heavily upon New England factories.[1] But if he tried to make general improvements in these bills, the chairmen resented his interference.

Of all the committee chairmen, Fessenden was fiercest in defense of his prerogative, and he grew especially angry when Sumner tried to tamper with his revenue or financial bills. Indus-

[8] Sumner to N. Niles, April 2, 1864, Segal Coll.; Sumner to Lieber, May 4, 1864, Sumner MSS.

[9] *Cong. Globe*, 38 Cong., 1 Sess., pp. 3495, 3339, 1113.

[1] Ibid., p. 3512.

trious to the point of physical and nervous exhaustion, Fessenden thought of himself as the embodiment of practicality in the Senate, and he was temperamentally averse to Sumner's idealism and lofty rhetoric. Like Trumbull a close student of history and law, he revered precedents and deplored Sumner's tendency to appeal to Truth, Justice, and Liberty rather than to the Constitution. Perhaps a bit envious of Sumner's position as the leading Senator from New England, Fessenden would tolerate no interference from a man whom he considered "cowardly, mean, malignant, tyranical [*sic*] [and] hypocritical." When Sumner showed a tendency to introduce his general principles and his platitudes in the discussion of financial questions, the Maine Senator resolved that he must be stopped. "I must tomahawk him in self defense," Fessenden wrote home, in one of his dyspeptic moods. "I would gladly let the dirty dog alone if I could, but to bear his insolence, and suffer his malignity to have full swing would only be to destroy myself." [2]

Sumner's effort to amend the proposed national banking act gave Fessenden his chance. Strongly favoring the creation of a national banking system, Sumner took alarm at the politically necessary concession, supported by the finance committee, which gave the states power to tax certain assets of the new banks. In his memory this provision tolled a reminiscent bell, and, leading off with a quotation from Milton, he reminded his colleagues at length that John Marshall in McCulloch *v.* Maryland (1819) affirmed that the power to tax involves the power to destroy. He, therefore, opposed granting the states this dangerous privilege. "If I err in this conclusion," he eloquently announced, "I err on the side of my country and in a patriotic purpose. . . . This is not the time to think of anything less than our whole country."

Dryly Fessenden commented that he had no special objection to having the business of the Senate interrupted by Sumner's "running commentary upon a decision of the Supreme Court . . . with which those of us who are lawyers might be supposed to be tolerably familiar, in connection with a little

[2] Browning: *Diary*, I, 588; Charles A. Jellison: *Fessenden of Maine* (Syracuse: Syracuse University Press; 1962), pp. 177–8.

poetry," but said that it should be mentioned that the McCulloch case has "no earthly application as a matter of law to the question now before us." In his sneering, waspish voice Fessenden gibed: ". . . it is not to be assumed . . . we must sit at the feet of the honorable Senator from Massachusetts to learn what is practical in matters of legislation, especially in matters relating to finance."

When Sumner complained that Fessenden was indulging in personal abuse, the Maine Senator scornfully replied that he always began "to whine about personalities when anyone demonstrated the flimsiness of his arguments," and he challenged Sumner to point out anything unparliamentary in his remarks. In fact, as a Washington reporter noted, there was not much in Fessenden's speech which could be proved to be a direct attack upon Sumner, "yet the manner, the bearing and the occasional sarcasm were personal and intended to be so." For "so distinguished, so sensitive and so conceited a man as Mr. Sumner," the reporter predicted, the insult would probably prove unforgivable. Indeed, after this encounter, the two most powerful Senators from New England were never again on cordial terms.[3]

Other Senate committee chairmen shared Fessenden's resentment, though not necessarily his acerbity, when Sumner took too great an interest in measures which were in their charge. His efforts to engage in the general debate met with repeated rebuffs. The cantankerous Adam Gurowski, now thoroughly alienated from Sumner, caught the mood of the Senate when he jeered at his former friend's "learned . . . appeals to Shakspeare on the question of a mint for Oregon or Philadelphia," and his "doctor-like . . . sentences about finances and political economy," which seemed almost to invite attack "from opponents, who . . . expose his arrogant assumptions and superficiality."[4]

With little else to do, Sumner turned his attention to devising bills to establish a training program for consuls, for codifying the United States statutes, for chartering a federally spon-

[3] *Cong. Globe,* 38 Cong., 1 Sess., pp. 1873, 1894–6; Springfield *Weekly Republican,* May 7, 1864.

[4] Gurowski: *Diary: 1863–'64–'65* (Washington: W. H. and O. H. Morrison; 1866), pp. 219–20.

sored railroad between Washington and New York, and for establishing a federal civil service system, but none of his proposals attracted much attention or enthusiasm. The newspapers gave his bills scant attention, and he complained to Lieber: "There is very little disposition now to print or reprint any thing that does not describe a battle." For Sumner who, as George F. Hoar unkindly remarked, sometimes seemed to think that the Rebellion "was put down by speeches in the Senate, and that the war was an unfortunate and most annoying, though trifling disturbance, as if a fire-engine had passed by," the situation was uncomfortable and depressing. Toward the end of the session, which stretched on into July, he wrote Longfellow a bleak summary of his labors: "After constant work, it seems as I can accomplish nothing . . . all about there seem to be enmities and jealousies, springing up to devour me." "Life is weary and dark," he lamented, "full of pain and enmity. I am ready to go at once." [5]

As always in such depressed moods, Sumner became even more self-centered than usual. Diverting his eyes from his failures, he lifted them to the loftier realm of principle. Morose and shut out, he was less inclined than ever to be conciliatory toward his colleagues, who, as the session dragged along and the badly ventilated Senate chamber grew fetid with heat and blue with cigar smoke, had repeatedly to object to his "dogmatical tone" in debates. Even mild-mannered Lafayette Foster from Connecticut reminded Sumner "that the divine prerogative has not yet been vouchsafed to him of saying, 'Let there be light, and there was light.' "

Such criticism made Sumner all the more aloof and intractable. To Foster he replied: "The Senator asks the laws of God to be set aside and the laws of Satan to be installed instead." [6] The identification of his own opinions with those of the Deity became daily more apparent. Increasingly he seemed to think of himself as speaking from Mount Sinai. When his old friend Julia Ward Howe visited Washington in the spring of 1864, she recorded that the Senator had attained a new height of self-centeredness.

[5] Sumner to Lieber, May 4, 1864, Sumner MSS.; Hoar: *Autobiography of Seventy Years* (New York: Charles Scribner's Sons; 1903), I, 212; Sumner to Longfellow, May 21 and June 18, 1864, Longfellow MSS.

[6] *Cong. Globe*, 38 Cong., 1 Sess., pp. 327–8, 1746, 1751.

Asked whether he had yet seen the actor Edwin Booth, Sumner loftily replied, "Why, n-no, madam—I, long since, ceased to take any interest in *individuals!*"

"You have made great *progress*, Sir," the sharp-tongued Julia retorted, "*God* has not yet gone so far—at least according to the last accounts." [7]

• 4 •

Sumner's unhappiness stemmed in part from the small role he was permitted to play in the final abolition of slavery. Though Lincoln had issued his Emancipation Proclamation, ardent abolitionists were far from satisfied, since the presidential edict applied only to slaves in areas beyond the reach of the Union armies and since, even in the areas where it did apply, it might be struck down by the Supreme Court. Early in 1863 Elizabeth Cady Stanton and Susan B. Anthony had organized the Women's Loyal National League, which hoped to secure a million signatures to petitions demanding the complete abolition of slavery through an amendment to the Constitution. During the summer the project picked up support from other antislavery men, including some who had hitherto denounced the Constitution. In November William Lloyd Garrison begged Sumner, as the leading antislavery Senator, to advocate a Congressional "edict abolishing slavery throughout the country as the only method of securing permanent peace and preserving the unity of the republic." [8]

On the way to Washington Sumner conferred with the abolitionist Henry C. Wright, in an attempt to concert these antislavery voices, and he drafted a resolution which Wright presented at the American Anti-Slavery Society convention on December 3: "That the voice of the people is heard through petitions to Congress, and this Convention earnestly recommend that this voice be raised in petitions for an Amendment of the

[7] Bates: *Diary*, p. 371. Cf. Laura E. Richards and Maude H. Elliott: *Julia Ward Howe, 1818–1910* (Boston: Houghton Mifflin Company; 1916), I, 205.

[8] James M. McPherson: *The Struggle for Equality* (Princeton, N.J.: Princeton University Press; 1964), pp. 125–7; Garrison to Sumner, Nov. 12, 1863, Sumner MSS.

Constitution, declaring that slavery shall be forever prohibited within the limits of the United States." The abolitionists expected Sumner to present their demands to Congress.[9]

Anticipating a flood of petitions, Sumner on January 13, 1864, asked the Senate to create a special committee "to take into consideration all propositions and papers concerning slavery and the treatment of freedmen." As a matter of course, he became its chairman. The Senate's action, he proudly reported to the Duchess of Argyll, "marks an epoch of history." "Only a short time ago such a Committee would not have been authorized. A few years ago the proposition would have created a storm of violence." "I hope very soon," he confided, "to report . . . an amendment of the Constitution abolishing slavery throughout the U. States."[1] Before doing so, however, he needed the petitions that Mrs. Stanton and Miss Anthony had promised, and they were unexpectedly slow in arriving. To give the new committee something to do and to establish a precedent for future action, he and his friends began quietly referring occasional and incidental memorials urging abolition to his Select Committee on Slavery and Freedmen.

Finally, on February 9, the first batch of petitions from the Women's Loyal National League was ready. Though falling far short of the goal of a million signatures, the documents were so bulky that no one man could carry them. Dramatically two tall Negroes bore the massive roll into the Senate chamber and deposited it upon Sumner's desk. He proudly presented this "Prayer of the Hundred Thousand," signed by men and women "from all parts of the country, and from every condition of life: from the seaboard . . . and from the Mississippi and the prairies of the West . . . ; from the . . . educated and uneducated, rich and poor, of every profession, business, and calling in life, representing every sentiment, thought, hope, passion, activity, intelligence, that inspires, strengthens, and adorns our social system." Hoping that Congress would "pass, at the earliest

[9] Sumner: *Works*, VIII, 351; Susan B. Anthony to Sumner, Dec. 13, 1863, and Elizabeth Cady Stanton and Miss Anthony to Sumner, Feb. 4, 1864, both in Sumner MSS.

[1] Feb. 8, 1864, Argyll MSS.

practicable day, an act emancipating all persons of African descent held to involuntary service or labor in the United States," he asked that the gigantic petition be referred to the select committee of which he was chairman.[2]

Sumner attempted to follow up this success by introducing a proposed constitutional amendment declaring that "all persons are equal before the law, so that no person can hold another as a slave." The phrase, "equal before the law," was one of which Sumner was proud. During his early years of study abroad he had come upon it in the 1791 French Declaration of Rights, and he believed that he was the first to introduce the words, "*equality before the law*" into American jurisprudence. Of course, he observed, conservatives might object to the phrase, for it did "not come from England; for the idea itself finds little favor in that hierarchical kingdom." Still the meaning, if not the words, was a familiar part of the American legal tradition, for the phrase gave "precision to that idea of human rights which is enunciated in our Declaration of Independence." [3] He moved that his proposed amendment be sent, along with the petition, to his select committee.

Promptly the Senate showed that, while it was willing to allow Sumner his moment of drama in presenting the gigantic appeal, the practical work of drafting a constitutional amendment would fall into other hands. He encountered the objection that his proposed amendment ought to go before the Senate Judiciary Committee, which traditionally considered all changes in the Constitution. Sumner was entirely aware of this usage but knew that his proposal would receive scant consideration from a committee which Lyman Trumbull so completely dominated; indeed, it was in the hope of bypassing the Judiciary Committee that he had moved the creation of his own select committee with a mandate "broad enough to cover every proposition relating to slavery." His strategem was, however, too apparent to other Senators, who had no intention of challenging the hegemony of

[2] Sumner: *Works,* VIII, 81–2.

[3] Sumner: *Universal Emancipation without Compensation* (Washington: H. Polkinghorn, Printer; 1864), pp. 14–15.

the chairmen of the major standing committees, and they consigned Sumner's proposed antislavery amendment, along with many others, to Trumbull's committee.

As a result Sumner, though probably the Senator best known for his antislavery views, had almost nothing to do with the framing or passage of the constitutional amendment ending slavery. Not consulted by Trumbull, he could not know the pressures under which the Judiciary Committee worked or understand the compromises that they felt obliged to reach. Consequently when the proposed Thirteenth Amendment was reported to the Senate, he found it sadly deficient and, though without much hope of success, moved a stronger substitute. Out of things, Sumner began to wonder whether a constitutional amendment could possibly be adopted. Since there were not enough dependable antislavery votes in the House of Representatives, he warned his colleagues not to operate "under the illusion that we settle this question by an attempt, for it will be an attempt only, at a constitutional amendment"; [4] they had better give their time instead to the more practical and specific antislavery measures which he was pressing. At the end of March, when the Senate began serious debate upon the emancipation amendment, Sumner unexpectedly held up a vote by announcing that he wished to speak on the proposition but had not yet had time to prepare.

When he was ready, on April 8, his elaborate discourse had almost nothing to do with the amendment approved by the Judiciary Committee but did reveal a major shift in Sumner's own antislavery thinking. A Senator who had once hoped to kill slavery by containing it in the Southern states, Sumner moved with the outbreak of war to advocating emancipation within rebel territory, even while admitting that there was no constitutional right in time of peace to strike down slavery in the states. Now, however, he proceeded one step further: Since the rebellion was slavery incarnate, and since the peculiar institution in the Confederacy drew strength from lingering slavery in the states loyal to the Union, the time had come to abolish slavery everywhere in the United States. Since slavery could not exist

[4] *Cong. Globe*, 38 Cong., 1 Sess., p. 1178.

without positive law and since there was "nothing in the Constitution on which Slavery can rest," all vestiges of the peculiar institution should be swept away immediately. Long ago the courts of the United States could and should have ended slavery throughout the land, had they not permitted themselves to become "barracoons" and the Supreme Court of the United States "the greatest barracoon" of all.[5] Congress, too, could eradicate slavery. No amendment was necessary; it could act under the general welfare clause, the Fifth Amendment, and the provision guaranteeing each state a republican form of government. Emancipation would long since have been achieved, Sumner informed the Senate, had the three branches of the federal government remembered the cardinal rule: *"Nothing against Slavery can be unconstitutional."*

Since the President had not acted, the courts were debauched, and Congress was timid, Sumner reluctantly agreed that a constitutional amendment might now be desirable. But, instead of endorsing the work of the Judiciary Committee, he urged his own version declaring equality before the law. Should that be considered too extreme, at least the Senate should eliminate from the proposed amendment the implication that slavery as punishment for crime was tolerable in the United States. Sumner had little hope for succeeding in either of his proposals and made them largely for the record. When Trumbull protested that he was being too "pertinacious about particular words" and Howard begged him "to dismiss all reference to French constitutions or French codes, and go back to the good old Anglo-Saxon language employed by our fathers in the [Northwest] ordinance of 1787," Sumner withdrew his proposals, weakly explaining: "I offered them sincerely with a desire to make a contribution to perfect the measure."[6] Along with other Senate Republicans he then voted for Trumbull's constitutional amendment, which, however, failed to receive the requisite two-thirds majority in the House.

The debates on the Thirteenth Amendment revealed a pat-

[5] At the advice of Lieber and other friends, Sumner omitted these phrases from the version of the speech published in his *Works*, VIII, 35–401.

[6] *Cong. Globe*, 38 Cong., 1 Sess., pp. 1488–9.

tern that characterized Sumner's relationship to most of the significant legislation passed during the ten remaining years of his life. In the coming decade he, perhaps more than any other individual, would be responsible for arousing public concern over emancipation, the freedmen, and the restoration of the Southern states, but his resolutions dealing with these matters would go to committees in which he had no voice. Invariably Sumner found the legislation recommended by these committees too weak, and in Senate debates would often be as critical from his radical perspective as Democrats were from the opposing viewpoint. In a showdown Sumner nearly always voted with the majority of Republican Senators, but when their measures proved not to be efficacious, he rarely failed to remind them, in a superior tone, that he had foreseen their weakness and foretold their failure. Inevitably his unpopularity among his colleagues grew, and with it his feeling of isolated self-righteousness. As a result, Gurowski shrewdly noted, Sumner's position was peculiarly an exposed one. "He is attacked by political enemies and is obnoxious, nay, at times nauseous, to men of the same party principles as his. He stands alone; is roughly handled by the opponents . . . in similar ways he is often thus treated by . . . political friends. Nay! by his petty schoolmaster-like conceit, and by the everlasting pompous display of his rhetorical superficiality and undigested erudition, he averts from him the best men in the Senate; the truest Republicans and anti-slavery apostles at times are forced to put him down." [7]

• 5 •

Having little to do in the Foreign Relations Committee, excluded from playing a major part in the workaday business of the Senate, prevented from shaping the constitutional amendment to end slavery, Sumner during the winter of 1863–64 found another outlet for his enormous energies. While his colleagues were still debating over how to end slavery, he worried about how to protect the rights of the freedmen. This was not a new concern for Sumner. Long before the war he had battled racial

[7] Gurowski: *Diary, 1863–'64–'65*, p. 219.

discrimination in the North even while attacking slavery in the South, and in 1849 he had brought the celebrated Roberts case to end segregated schools in Massachusetts. He knew that so long as Negroes had no land, no jobs, no education, no legal rights, emancipation would be a mockery. In the early years of the war, until the abolition of slavery itself was assured, he made only a few moves, tentative and mostly unsuccessful, to guarantee equal rights, but now, when victory seemed near, he acted with greater urgency. Since the subject was one which clearly fell within the purview of his Select Committee on Slavery and Freedmen, he could not be accused of poaching upon the territory of other powerful committee chairmen.

His first objective was to "remove from the statute-books odious provisions in support of Slavery." [8] For instance, laws regulating the coastwise slave trade ought to be repealed. The trade was dead and, with the Thirteenth Amendment in prospect, could never be revived, but it was important that the United States statute books should not be defiled by words that licensed such an ignoble business. More important to Sumner personally was the repeal of the fugitive slave laws, since indignation over the infamous 1850 act had been partly responsible for his original election to the Senate and since his speeches against that act in the 1850's had first established his commanding stature as an antislavery leader. Because slavery was almost extinct, the fugitive slave laws were not, Sumner admitted, at the present moment of any considerable value to anybody, but he felt they ought to be repealed both to purify the law books and to clear the name of the United States abroad, for "foreign nations have pointed with scorn to a republic which could legalize such indecencies." [9]

"Greatest of all in practical importance" of Sumner's efforts to cleanse the statutes was his proposal to prohibit racial discrimination in testimony accepted by federal courts. Hitherto, usage in United States courts had followed that of the states in which they were held, with the result that Negro witnesses were systematically excluded, especially in the South. If this practice

[8] Sumner: *Works*, IX, 34.
[9] Ibid., VII, 120, 169.

was continued after peace was restored, freedmen would be wholly unable to protect their lives or property in the courts. Vainly Sumner had tried in 1862 to reverse this "melancholy, disastrous, discreditable" practice, but he had only succeeded in securing the right of Negroes to testify in proceedings brought under the emancipation act for the District of Columbia. Now, however, with growing antislavery sentiment in Congress and with his own select committee as a sounding board, he moved more forcefully to forbid any United States court from excluding the testimony of any witness on account of his color.[1]

Not content with repealing discriminatory laws, Sumner also sought positively to protect the equality of free Negroes. Angered by the Jim Crow streetcar system in the District of Columbia, which required all blacks to ride on the exposed platforms of cars or else to wait long periods for specially marked, segregated vehicles, Sumner in the previous session of Congress had succeeded in banning such discrimination on one of the minor street railways, but the major lines obdurately continued to exclude or to segregate blacks. The practice of compelling even old Negro women and wounded black soldiers to wait in the rain or snow for Jim Crow cars struck Sumner as "a disgrace to this city, and a disgrace to the National Government, which permits it under its eyes." He called for a flat edict prohibiting racial discrimination on all lines operating within the District.[2]

At the same time he demanded equal treatment for black men serving in the Union armies. The 1862 act which authorized the President to recruit Negro troops had set their pay scale lower than that of white soldiers and had failed to provide the same enlistment bounty offered whites. Largely as a result of Governor Andrew's indignant protests, the issue came up in Congress, where, after the demonstration of the bravery of black troops at Fort Wagner, there was little opposition to equalizing their pay as of January 1, 1864. Strong hostility, however, developed to proposals which would make this increase retroactive to the date when these black troops enlisted. As chairman of the

[1] Sumner to Duchess of Argyll, July 4, 1864, Argyll MSS.; Sumner: *Works*, VI, 442–3, 502–3; VII, 152–61; VIII, 176–216.

[2] Ibid., VIII, 103–13.

Senate Committee on Military Affairs, Wilson took the lead in the attempt to secure justice for Negro soldiers, many of whom belonged to Massachusetts regiments, and Sumner vigorously backed him. To pleas that retroactive payments might bankrupt the treasury, he replied simply: "Is not the money due?" "I would," he added, "have my country above doing injustice, least of all injustice to a people of a race too long crushed by injustice." [3]

Sumner's exertions in behalf of Negro rights during the Thirty-Eighth Congress brought upon him fiercer and more widespread criticism than any he had encountered since his attacks upon slavery in the early 1850's. Many friends of the Negro accepted Sumner's objectives but questioned his timing. A correspondent in the *Liberator* complained that Sumner was misusing his precious strength in raising so many peripheral issues when the main question, "the one all-comprehensive measure for the abolition of the slave system," was not yet adopted. To Sumner's hurt protest, Garrison replied with praise for any exertions, "whether by wholesale or in detail, to cripple or exterminate the great abomination of our land," but he nevertheless made clear his opinion that the first priority should be "concentrated effort upon the proposition to abolish slavery." [4]

Other critics questioned the practicality of Sumner's moves. Most of his bills and resolutions, he admitted in private, would have little effect beyond removing offensive and obsolete laws from the statute books. Thus everybody recognized that the fugitive slave laws were moribund; though repeal might favorably influence world opinion, Sumner himself confessed that "its practical importance at home is not great, except that every blow at Slavery is practically important." [5] The only discernible results of Sumner's exertions, Cowan remarked, was to divide the Republicans in the Senate and to help "destroy the political power which his party now enjoys." Ironically calling Sumner's argument for repeal "learned, learned beyond comparison," Doolittle lamented: "I sometimes almost fear that he is so learned he has

[3] Ibid., 93. See Dudley T. Cornish: *The Sable Arm* (New York: Longmans, Green and Co.; 1956), pp. 184–93.

[4] Garrison to Sumner, April 19, 1864, Sumner MSS.

[5] Sumner to Lydia M. Child, Aug. 7, 1864, MS., Ill. State Hist. Soc.

lost all practical sense." Grimes and Trumbull made the same objection to Sumner's bill outlawing segregation on Washington streetcars. Since under the common law, the streetcar companies had no power to discriminate against Negroes, they asked why Sumner wished to "reenact what is already the law; what he himself admits to be the law." When Sumner replied that most Washington Negroes were too poor to go to court and defend their rights, his critics pertinently inquired whether fresh legislation would change that situation. Democratic Senator Powell of Kentucky wondered why, if Sumner was "such a vehement friend of this down-trodden race," he showed his devotion only in the Senate and only in words; "as he is a lawyer, why did he not undertake their case, and propose to argue it for them before the courts?" [6]

Sumner's manner alienated other Senators. Fessenden, for instance, was as much in favor of equal pay for Negro troops as Sumner himself but, always concerned with finances, he was troubled by the retroactive provisions of Sumner's bill, so loosely worded as to make it "manifestly a strange one, covering nobody could tell whom, one that it was impossible to reduce to a certainty." When Sumner brushed aside Fessenden's objections, announcing that the case was one of "such absolute and overwhelming justice that the Senate ought not to postpone it for a single day," the Maine Senator snapped: "The honorable Senator from Massachusetts has a fashion of deciding rather *ex cathedra* . . . . upon what is just and what is unjust, and rather a fashion to leave us to infer that he thinks everybody who differs from his opinion is disposed to do injustice." Similarly, Reverdy Johnson, learned in the law and deeply respectful toward the Supreme Court, was outraged when Sumner proclaimed that any and all decisions of the Court upholding the fugitive slave laws were attempts to prove that two and two equal five. When Sumner indulged in such hyperbole, Johnson protested, he "leaves this mundane sphere of earth and gets into the skies, goes off to authority above us." [7]

It was, however, the substance of Sumner's proposals that

[6] *Cong. Globe*, 38 Cong., 1 Sess., pp. 2247, 3128, 3132–4.
[7] Ibid., pp. 871–2, 1714.

most aroused hostility, for the suggestion that Negroes should be treated as equal to white men woke some of the deepest and ugliest fears in the American mind. Democrats, as a matter of course, fought all of his bills, believing, as Thomas A. Hendricks of Indiana declared early in the session, that his intention was "that by the action of the Federal Government the social as well as the political equality of the negro is to be forced upon the white race." Merely to raise this possibility was, to Democrats, to demonstrate the error of Sumner's course. "God has made the negro inferior," announced William A. Richardson of Illinois, "and . . . laws cannot make him equal." Just so, agreed Hendricks; since history shows the white race constantly progressing upward and the black race steadily deteriorating, he could not be "convinced that the negro is the equal of the white man." "Let us not try to improve upon nature," chimed in Reverdy Johnson.[8]

So preposterous did Sumner's ideas seem to many Democrats that they could not believe he was serious. His bills, thought Powell, were just an electioneering device, designed to give "gratification to that ultra-radical sentiment" in New England by permitting Sumner "to say that such and such laws have been passed in favor of the negro," even though everybody realized they were both absurd and ineffectual. "We are all politicians or have been," Powell observed charitably. "The Senator's staple is this fanatical idea. He wants this little hobby to ride through Massachusetts on, and to feed a fanatical flame there." "He can fool nobody with this kind of thing," Powell concluded, and his colleague, Garrett Davis, agreed that Sumner might as well go all the way and "petition the Congress to change the negroes into white people." [9]

Knowing how widespread anti-Negro sentiment was in the North, Democrats planned to make the fullest propaganda advantage of Sumner's equal rights proposals in the forthcoming presidential election. When Sumner prepared an elaborate majority report from his special committee recommending the repeal of the fugitive slave laws, the Democratic minority submitted a caustic dissent, warning that rescinding these statutes

[8] Ibid., pp. 554, 2802, 839, 1157.

[9] Ibid., pp. 838, 3134, 2727.

would "encourage . . . the migration of negroes . . . from those parts of the country where they are most suitably placed" to the North, where, "despised, oppressed, hated; ostracised from honorable employments; hutted in the purlieus of cities and the outskirts of towns," they would produce "corruption" and "the debasement of social life." [1]

Sumner's bills also produced factionalism within the Republican party, where the old division between Radicals and Conservatives had been dropping out of sight since emancipation became the party's official policy. Moderates, who had begun the war to support the Union, found it hard enough to add Liberty as a war objective; now Sumner was demanding that they go even further and make a commitment to Equality as well.[2] "Merely to raise the question of negro social as well as political equality," as Doolittle confessed, was frightening to these conservatives, many of whom represented states containing large numbers of the despised and feared free Negroes. Since Sumner came from a state where there were few black men, Cowan of Pennsylvania argued, he simply had no understanding of what it was like to live in "a community surcharged with an idle, dissolute, vicious, ignorant negro population just emerged from slavery." The only way to preserve white civilization in such circumstances was to have strict rules about the mingling of the races. Segregated streetcars, argued Henry S. Lane of the virulently anti-Negro state of Indiana, were "precisely the best and most convenient mode for the transmission of passengers, white and black," for it was "better they be kept separate." Reflecting the fact that the West had always been antislavery rather than pro-Negro, Grimes of Iowa agreed that the best Negroes in the District of Columbia did not want to ride in desegregated cars but preferred to be "permitted to occupy undisturbed the cars which the company have dedicated to their use." The real outrage in the situation, therefore, was not segregation

[1] *Senate Report* No. 24, 38 Cong., 1 Sess., p. 32.

[2] See C. Vann Woodward: "Equality: The Deferred Commitment," in his *Burden of Southern History* (rev. ed.; Baton Rouge, La.: Louisiana State University; 1968), pp. 69–88.

but "the interference of white men with the cars devoted to the exclusive use of colored people." [3]

The arguments Sumner used to defend his Negro rights measures helped make the breach between Moderate and Radical Republicans wider. He insisted that opposition to equal rights stemmed from the "odious prejudice bequeathed by Slavery, having its origin in Slavery, and in nothing else." Those who differed with him were, therefore, defenders of the peculiar institution, since anti-Negro sentiment was "nothing but the tail of Slavery." He was not surprised, he announced, that Senator Waitman T. Willey of West Virginia tacitly admitted "his willingness to be a slave-hunter" by opposing the repeal of the fugitive slave acts; that was what one expected from a representative of a slave state. Northern Senators who failed to support Sumner's bill were more contemptible; ignoring the antislavery principles of their constituents, they were indirectly aiding the cause of the Confederates. Cowan bitterly protested against Sumner's tactic of libeling everybody who disagreed with him "as rogues and knaves and villains advocating . . . the cause of the enemies of the country," and he begged his fellow Republicans, in the name of common decency, to stop Sumner's abuse. Equally outraged, Willey, who had risked his life to make West Virginia a free state loyal to the Union, defended himself: "While the honorable Senator, with his great abilities, and learning, and eloquence, has been talking about the freedom of slaves, I have been actually setting slaves free. How many has he set free?" [4]

Relentlessly Sumner pushed on with his equal rights bills, even though they caused divisions in the Republican party. On all possible occasions he demanded that they be debated and voted upon. If one of his measures was defeated as an independent bill, he moved it as amendment to some other measure. Should anybody object that the amendment was not relevant, he replied grandly: "Such is its intrinsic justice that I can hardly imagine any bill on which according to the rules of the Senate it

[3] *Cong. Globe*, 38 Cong., 1 Sess., pp. 1844, 2247, 837, 3133–4.

[4] Sumner: *Works*, VIII, 459–69, 115; *Cong. Globe*, 38 Cong., 1 Sess., pp. 2975, 2247.

could be out of place." If one of his proposals was defeated in the committee of the whole, he warned his colleagues: "I shall take every occasion to call the bill up, and press its consideration upon the Senate." Then, when the Senate resumed general sessions, he would reintroduce his bill and start the entire debate anew. When he feared final defeat, he stalled for time and tried to arouse antislavery opinion throughout the North. "Will you not help clean the statute-book of all support of slavery?" he entreated Parke Godwin of the New York *Post*. "Pray help us." If, however, he had the votes, he was ruthless in pushing for prompt action. When Senators explained that absent colleagues wanted to speak on his measures, he replied: "The public business cannot wait." When others tried to amend one of his bills, he announced: "I regard it as perfect." [5]

By March 1864, according to Reverdy Johnson's calculations, "at least one half of the business of the session, so far as the Senate is concerned," had been taken up with Sumner's equal rights proposals. To some of his colleagues his pertinacity seemed obsessive; he cared for nothing else. "No matter what becomes of the white man; let him go; let him starve; let him fight your battles; send him to the front, and leave the negro behind; let his wife and children perish wherever they may be; but you must take care of the negro." [6] A cruel cartoon of the period showed Sumner, dreamy-eyed and mystical, giving coins to a Negro child while ignoring the pleas of a ragged little white girl, who protested: "I'm not to blame, for being white, Sir!"

The results of Sumner's efforts in behalf of equal rights during this session of Congress were more evident in the growing factionalism of the Republican party than in bills passed. On the issue of equal pay for black troops, he and Wilson were obliged, after protracted controversy, to settle for a compromise which Sumner called "the little end of nothing." [7] The Senate passed his bill forbidding discrimination in Washington street-

[5] Ibid., pp. 871, 3177; Sumner to Godwin, April 23, 1864, Bryant-Godwin MSS.

[6] *Cong. Globe*, 38 Cong., 1 Sess., pp. 1156, 2801–3.

[7] Ibid., p. 2852; Sumner to Andrew, April 30, 1864, Andrew MSS.; Marvin R. Cain: *Lincoln's Attorney General: Edward Bates of Missouri* (Columbia, Mo.: University of Missouri Press; 1965), p. 234.

cars by a majority of one, but the measure died in the House. Sumner succeeded, however, in outlawing the coastal slave trade and in opening federal courts to black witnesses, for both laws were signed by the President on July 4, 1864.

More important to Sumner was the repeal of the fugitive slave laws, for which he pushed with incredible doggedness, defeating finally all efforts to pigeonhole or to emasculate his proposal. After sitting out Garrett Davis's angry denunciation of his "hollow claims of devotion to justice, to philanthropy, to benevolence, to the lifting up of a downtrodden race" as merely a facade to hide "the disgraceful efforts of the people of Massachusetts to get possession of the rich cotton and sugar and rice lands of the South, and to compass for . . . their own enrichment the labor of the freed negro," [8] Sumner demanded a final vote. By 27 to 12 the Senate approved the measure, which had already passed the House. "All fugitive slave Acts were to-day expunged from the statute-book," Sumner jubilantly wrote Longfellow, noting the precise time as 4:10 P.M. on June 23. "This makes me happy. . . . Thus closes one chapter of my life. I was chosen to the Senate in order to do this work." [9]

[8] *Cong. Globe,* 38 Cong., 1 Sess., Appendix, p. 133.
[9] Longfellow MSS.

CHAPTER V

Making His History

SUMNER's efforts in behalf of Negro rights received neither encouragement nor assistance from the White House. Lincoln, he complained to Bright, "does not know how to help or is not moved to help. . . . I do not remember that I have had any help from him in any of the questions which I have conducted—though a word from him in certain quarters would have saved me much trouble."

Indifference was only one of the President's qualities which distressed Sumner. He lacked "practical talent for his important place." He was not a good administrator; he did not systematically consult with his cabinet; he did not always read the papers that came to his desk. In military matters, too, Lincoln was a failure. Having "neither faculty or despatch in business," he was unable to make hard decisions. In inertia and indecisiveness he resembled "Louis XVI more than any other ruler in history." It was because the President had "no instinct or inspiration" that the war dragged on through 1864. "It should have been over long ago," Sumner believed.[1]

Since Sumner held such a low opinion of the President, he might have been expected to lead the growing movement within the Republican party to replace Lincoln as its nominee in 1864,

[1] Sumner to Bright, Sept. 27, 1864, and Jan. 4, 1863 [i.e., 1864], Bright MSS.; Pierce, IV, 200.

but in fact he remained cautiously neutral. He discouraged all talk of presidential candidates. "We must not electioneer just yet for anyone," he wrote a friend in March. "Our business now is to crush the enemy in the field." "Dont trouble yourself on the Presidential question," he enjoined Lieber. "Silence." "The more I reflect upon the Presidential question," he explained to Orestes Brownson, "the more I regret its premature discussion. The country ought not now to be diverted from the war, and the means . . . and principles by which it is to be sustained and our cause advanced. . . ." He regretted that the Republican national convention had been scheduled to meet in June, for he felt: "The Presidential Question should be kept back as long as possible—at least until the end of summer." "Of course I say nothing about candidates," he repeated in May. *"That question ought not to be touched now."* [2]

Sumner's reticence infuriated some of his friends, who were determined to have a more energetic and a more earnestly antislavery Republican nominee than Lincoln. To their chagrin Sumner refused to say a word in favor of any of the numerous candidates suggested as alternatives. He continued almost daily to stop by Chase's house for breakfast and ten or fifteen minutes of talk about public affairs, but his name was conspicuously missing from the list of prominent Republicans backing the ambitious Treasury Secretary's bid for the presidency. Convinced that Lincoln's popular appeal was "not deep or firm," Wendell Phillips bitterly protested that "Sumner &c by their *silence* let opinion crystallize round his measures as wise and safe," when "one word of the right stamp would root out his hold on the masses." "The opposition to Old Abe *must* be open—in the press and in Congress," agreed Frank Bird. "The country *must* know why you gentlemen who have so long lauded the President should not now support him." [3]

Sumner's reticence in view of his known reservations about Lincoln caused some to speculate that he dreamed of the White

[2] Sumner to Mary L. Booth, Mar. 18, 1864, MS., Boston Univ.; Sumner to Lieber, Feb. 14, 1864, Sumner MSS.; Sumner to Brownson, Mar. 22, 1864, Brownson MSS.; Sumner to Charles E. Norton, May 2, 1864, Norton MSS.

[3] Phillips to Moncure D. Conway, Mar. 16, 1864, Conway MSS.; Bird to Sumner, Feb. 29, 1864, Sumner MSS.

House himself. The Senator, concluded the abolitionist F. B. Sanborn, was "not heartily for Lincoln; he is for Sumner," adding that he was "a candidate but without hope of success." The atrabilious Gurowski judged that Sumner was deliberately keeping aloof from both the Lincoln and Chase presidential movements in order to be "ready to gently, gracefully, and by force of his irresistible rhetoric, conciliate on his person—a la Henry VII —the deadly hatred and antagonism of all" Republican factions. Sumner, Gurowski added, "imagines that he will become the man of the last, the eleventh hour, and be nominated for the Presidency in Baltimore." [4]

For such speculations there was no foundation. Unlike Chase, Sumner wrote not one word which any reader could interpret as indicating his availability, and his trusted lieutenants took no steps to promote his candidacy, such as advocating his nomination in the *Commonwealth* or trying to pledge Massachusetts delegates to support him. Indeed, Sumner was too astute a politician not to understand that if he sought the presidency he would undermine his main source of strength; his hold upon his idealistic following depended in great measure upon his known indifference to personal advancement. A cartoon prominently displayed in Massachusetts store windows during 1864 symbolized his role; it showed a tall cliff, at the base of which presidential candidates were busily posting placards and uttering catch phrases while Sumner, atop a long ladder, composedly painted in bold letters upon the rock: "Amendment of the Constitution." "There was," one of Sumner's correspondents from the early days of the antislavery struggle wrote him of the cartoon, "something in your quiet air up above all the tumult below which struck me as very true and very much to your honor." [5]

If Sumner's silence as the time for the Republican convention approached did not indicate self-seeking, it did suggest the extreme difficulty of his political situation. The failure of his

[4] Sanborn to Conway, May 3, and Mar. 31, 1864, Conway MSS.; Gurowski: *Diary, 1863–'64–'65*, pp. 129, 240. Gideon Welles's charge that Sumner had "vague and indefinite dreams of himself" as President was not a contemporary remark but one later added by the acidulous Secretary of Navy. Welles: *Diary*, I, 503.

[5] Rufus P. Stebbins to Sumner, April 6, 1864, Sumner MSS. Cf. George Livermore to Sumner, Mar. 1, 1864, ibid.

bids in 1863 to take over the direction of Republican foreign and domestic policy had seriously undermined his influence in Washington, and he could not afford to be the champion of another unsuccessful cause. None of the candidates suggested as rivals to Lincoln looked like a winner. Given a free choice, Sumner, as Gideon Welles surmised, probably would have preferred Chase, but the early collapse of the Secretary's candidacy and his official withdrawal from the race made his chance of success at Baltimore slim. Unlike Phillips, Bird, and some other antislavery men in Massachusetts, Sumner could not support the movement that led to the nomination of John C. Frémont by the "Free Democracy" in Cleveland on May 31. Such a third-party candidacy could only strengthen the Democrats; anyway Sumner had learned when trying to get Frémont an independent command in 1863 that the general was petty, obstructionist, and protocol-conscious.[6] Some anti-Lincoln Republicans favored General Benjamin F. Butler, the former Democrat who had once backed Jefferson Davis for the presidency, but Sumner thought poorly of that incompetent commander's military record. Ulysses S. Grant, warmly endorsed by such incongruous allies as the Missouri Radicals and the conservative New York *Herald*, doubtless had "a military genius," but his political views were so uncertain that Sumner, along with other antislavery Senators, had reservations about promoting him to the newly created rank of lieutenant general.[7]

In comparison with such rivals, Lincoln looked less unsatisfactory. At least he was educable. After many and, to Sumner's mind, unnecessary delays, he did issue the Emancipation Proclamation, and then stood by it. After much urging, he reluctantly agreed to enroll Negro troops, but once they saw action he came to share Sumner's confidence "that colored troops are to have the glory of finishing the war." In August 1863 the President went so far as write a public letter praising the work of black soldiers who fought "with silent tongue, and clenched teeth, and steady eyes, and well-poised bayonet" and declaring that use of these

[6] On this episode see Lincoln: *Works*, VI, 242–4.

[7] *Mass. Hist. Soc. Proceedings*, LVI, 480; Sumner to Lieber, Dec. 28, 1863, Sumner MSS.; Cornelius Cole: Diary, Mar. 10, 1864, Cole MSS.

Negro troops constituted "the heaviest blow yet dealt to the rebellion." Sumner thought Lincoln's "true and noble letter" so admirably stated the case "that all but the wicked must confess its force."[8] He could think of worse prospects than four more years with such an apt pupil.

To Lincoln, no doubt, this student-teacher relationship seemed a little different. Probably Gurowski was correct in judging that the President often found Sumner's visits to his White House office in order to exhort, implore, and demand "not very entertaining." Perhaps, though, he was amused by the ease with which he could outmaneuver Sumner. Early in 1863, for instance, the Senator came to the White House upset by rumors that General Quincy Adams Gillmore was to supersede Rufus Saxton in command of Federal troops about to attack Charleston; Saxton, who had worked earnestly in behalf of the Sea Island blacks, was one of the abolitionists' favorite generals, and anyway he outranked Gillmore.

"You say, Mr. Senator, that they are both Brigadier-Generals?" asked Lincoln, as Sumner ended his protest.

"Yes; and General Saxton is the ranking officer."

"Will it be entirely satisfactory to you, Mr. Senator, and all your friends, and General Saxton, if the ranking officer is in command."

"Perfectly so, Mr. President."

"Very well," said the President. "I will arrange it. I will have General Gil[l]more made a Major-General."

Discomfited but estopped from further argument, Sumner left the White House, and Lincoln, with a twinkle in his eye, remarked to an onlooker at the little scene: "We have to manage all sorts of ways to get along with this terrible war position."[9]

At other times Lincoln manipulated Sumner by allowing the Senator seemingly to extract from him concessions which he had already decided to yield. For example, Sumner's arguments had almost nothing to do with the President's decision to use Negro troops—but he knew the advantage of allowing the Sena-

[8] Sumner to an unidentified correspondent, June 9, 1863, Lincoln Collection, Brown Univ.; Sumner to Lincoln, Sept. 7, 1863, Lincoln MSS.

[9] Gurowski: *Diary . . . 1862, to . . . 1863*, p. 224; Julia L. Butterfield (ed.): *A Biographical Memorial of General Daniel Butterfield*, pp. 156–8.

tor to think his voice had been decisive. "Don't I get along well with Sumner," Lincoln once asked another Congressman; "he thinks he manages me." [1]

Sometimes Lincoln felt he could manage Sumner only as one does an unruly child—by ignoring him. When well-meaning friends observed that Sumner was advocating reconstruction measures that ran counter to those of the administration and urged Lincoln to try to influence him, Lincoln replied: "I can do nothing with Mr. Sumner in these matters. While Mr. Sumner is very cordial with me, he is making his history in an issue with me on this very point. . . . I think I understand Mr. Sumner; and I think he would be all the more resolute in his persistence . . . if he supposed I were at all watching his course. . . ." [2]

If the generally amicable relationship between Sumner and Lincoln resulted in part from calculation—on both sides—it also reflected the basic compatibility of the two men. Though repeatedly baffled by Lincoln's sense of humor and appalled that the President in a state paper could use a phrase like "turned tail and ran," Sumner respected Lincoln's earnest antislavery convictions, acknowledged his good intentions, and sympathized with his difficulties in coping with the impossible duties of a wartime President. Lincoln, for his part, recognized Sumner's seriousness of purpose and his services to the antislavery cause. When Sumner was around, he tried to curb his passion for storytelling, and he even took his feet down from his desk when Sumner came into the White House office.[3]

The fact that Mrs. Lincoln developed a great liking for the handsome bachelor Senator made it easier for Sumner and the President to get along with each other. Feeling isolated in Washington society, which ignored when it did not ridicule her, Mary Lincoln was touched by the attentions that the Senator, knowing what it was to be an outcast in snobbish and pro-Southern Washington, paid her. By the winter of 1863–64 the two had

[1] Anna L. Dawes: *Charles Sumner* (New York: Dodd, Mead and Company; 1892), p. 180.

[2] John G. Nicolay and John Hay: *Abraham Lincoln: A History* (New York: The Century Co.; 1890), X, 84–5.

[3] Benjamin P. Thomas: *Abraham Lincoln* (New York: Alfred A. Knopf; 1952), pp. 475–6.

become fast friends. They wrote each other notes in French; they went for carriage drives; they lent each other books; he let her read his correspondence from European notables, and she sent him bouquets from the White House conservatory.[4] So frequently did Sumner receive White House invitations that on one occasion the President felt obliged to write him:

> Mrs. L. is embarrassed a little. She would be pleased to have your company again this evening, at the Opera, but she fears she may be taxing you. I have undertaken to clear up the little difficulty. If, for any reason, it will tax you, decline, without any hesitation; but, if it will not, consider yourself already invited, and drop me a note.[5]

Doubtless the flurry of invitations the Lincolns extended to Sumner during the winter of 1863–64, just at the time when other Republicans were thinking of Chase or Frémont for the presidency, was not without political motivation. As Lieber cynically wrote the Senator: "I suppose all this civility to you in the White H. is to help getting L. right with the N. Engl. antislavery people." Whatever the intention, the result was that the Senator and the Lincolns got to know and understand each other better. Sumner, Mary Lincoln recalled later, "was a constant visitor at the W[hite] H[ouse]. both in office and drawing room—he appreciated my noble husband and I learned to converse with him, with more freedom and *confidence* than any of my other friends." Lincoln, too, found that the Senator could be a pleasant companion. Those who saw Sumner only as the "cold and haughty looking" abolitionist fanatic might find it hard to believe, but Mrs. Lincoln declared that her husband and the Senator used to talk and "laugh together like *two* school boys." [6]

Though Sumner cooperated with Lincoln and enjoyed his company, he did not work for his renomination. He was not one of the President's loyal lieutenants who saw to it that the state

[4] Ruth P. Randall: *Mary Lincoln: Biography of a Marriage* (Boston: Little, Brown and Company; 1953), pp. 355–7.

[5] Lincoln: *Works*, VI, 185.

[6] Lieber to Sumner, Feb. 4, 1864, Lieber MSS.; Mary Lincoln to Mrs. J. H. Orne, Nov. 28, 1869, MS., W. H. Townsend Collection; Mary Lincoln to Alexander Williamson, Aug. 19, 1866, MS., Henry E. Huntington Lib.

delegations were pledged to Lincoln's renomination long before the Republican national convention met in Baltimore on June 7. Instead, he remained completely silent and completely neutral. When Charles Eliot Norton asked his opinion about the nomination, he replied: "I say nothing upon it here and take no part in any of the controversies. My relations with the President are of constant intimacy, and I have reason to believe that he appreciates my reserve." [7]

• 2 •

Though Sumner played no part in the 1864 Republican national convention, rumor was to assign him a devious, almost a conspiratorial, role in its proceedings. To no one's surprise the convention promptly and almost unanimously renominated Lincoln but then, dropping the incumbent, Hannibal Hamlin, named Andrew Johnson as its candidate for Vice President. The move was part of the general effort to improve the party's image. The Baltimore convention was officially not a Republican but a National Union convention, because party leaders wanted to broaden its appeal and to erase the stigma of being narrowly sectional. Similarly the selection of a vice-presidential candidate who was a Southern Democrat—albeit, a Southerner opposed to secession and a Democrat now divorced from his party—suggested a broad coalition of all political groups devoted to preserving the Union.

To the disappointed Hamlin and the members of his family, this explanation was too simple. Ignoring the fact that Hamlin came from a state certain to cast its electoral votes for Lincoln, that he had no discernible political following elsewhere, and that, in any case, he was suspected of "using his influence against Lincoln wherever practicable," [8] they believed that Johnson's nomination was the result of a conspiracy in which Sumner played a central part. Sumner, they argued, had two major enemies in Washington: Fessenden in the Senate and Seward in the State Department. He knew that if Hamlin was not renomi-

[7] May 2, 1864, Norton MSS.

[8] Carl Sandburg: *Abraham Lincoln: The War Years* (New York: Harcourt, Brace & Company; 1939), III, 86.

nated for the vice presidency he would return to Maine politics and try to unseat Fessenden. At the same time he calculated that the convention, passing over Hamlin, might choose a New Yorker as its vice-presidential candidate—say, Daniel S. Dickinson, a lifelong Democrat who now vigorously supported Lincoln's policies. Since it would clearly be politically unwise to have both the Vice President and the Secretary of State from New York, Seward would have to resign. Then Sumner would have a clear field in Washington.[9]

The plot, however, did not quite work out as planned. The New England delegations, where Sumner had the greatest influence, did show surprisingly feeble interest in renominating Hamlin at Baltimore. The hostility of the Massachusetts men at the convention was probably responsible for his defeat. Overriding the preference of both Senator Wilson and Governor Andrew, the Massachusetts delegation followed the lead of William Claflin and, as Andrew later complained, "foolishly and in a very poor spirit threw overboard Mr. Hamlin."[1] By voting that "the interests of the party demanded the nomination of a War Democrat," the Massachusetts caucus strengthened Seward's enemies among the New York delegates, who were determined to force the Secretary from the cabinet by nominating Dickinson.[2] But Seward's friends were alert. Anticipating just such a move, they had worked in the early stages of the convention to seat delegates from Tennessee, Louisiana, and Arkansas, who were sure to vote for Andrew Johnson. Now, dropping Hamlin, Weed and Raymond worked on the other New York delegates also to back the Tennessean, and New York's vote determined the choice of

[9] Charles E. Hamlin: *The Life and Times of Hannibal Hamlin* (Cambridge: Riverside Press; 1899), pp. 465–7. Other studies which have followed this version of the 1864 nomination include Jellison: *Fessenden*, pp. 178–9, and George F. Milton: *The Age of Hate* (Hamden, Conn.: Archon Books; 1965), pp. 33–6. H. Draper Hunt: *Hannibal Hamlin of Maine* (Syracuse, N.Y.: Syracuse University Press; 1969), pp. 185–7, also accepts this tale of Sumner's "Machiavellian scheme" but adduces no new evidence. This most recent biographer of Hamlin, however, correctly stresses Lincoln's influence and Johnson's popularity as the determining forces in the decision at Baltimore. I know of no reliable evidence to support the claim (Milton: *Age of Hate*, p. 24) that Sumner in 1863 approached Hamlin with a "tender" of the Republican nomination for President.

[1] Andrew to Charles Ingersoll, Mar. 23, 1865, copy, Andrew MSS.; Boston *Daily Advertiser*, Aug. 7, 1865.

[2] Chicago *Tribune*, June 8, 1864.

the convention.[3] Thus Sumner's scheme to defeat Fessenden and Seward, it was claimed, miscarried, and Sumner was responsible, however circuitously, for the fact that during the reconstruction era his principal enemy occupied the White House as Lincoln's successor.

There are, however, difficulties in accepting this Hamlin version of how Johnson came to be nominated. Almost certainly it exaggerates Sumner's influence among New England Republicans. At the time, the defection of the Connecticut delegation from Hamlin was attributed not to Sumner but to the conservative Gideon Welles.[4] Not even among Massachusetts delegates was Sumner's the dominant voice. In fact, he had rather less control over the group that went to Baltimore than usual because many of his special friends had already broken with the Republican party and come out in favor of Frémont. Rather than following Sumner's lead, they complained of his failure publicly to denounce Lincoln, who, they said, was so degraded that if "we should run a gorilla for Vice President . . . the beast might well complain at being put in so degrading a position." [5]

There are only three bits of evidence that have been adduced to prove that Sumner even tried to influence the vote of the Massachusetts delegation at Baltimore. In 1891 Josiah H. Drummond, a Maine delegate to the 1864 convention, recalled that Sumner had come up from Washington to urge the Massachusetts delegation to stand firm against renominating Hamlin.[6] The following year the story reappeared in Anna L. Dawes's biography of Sumner. Lacking specific details, this version may be an abridgment of Drummond's account, or it may possibly embody the recollections of Miss Dawes's father, the long-term Massachusetts Congressman Henry L. Dawes.[7] Then in 1899

[3] DeAlva S. Alexander: *A Political History of the State of New York* (New York: Henry Holt and Company; 1909), III, 94; Glyndon G. Van Deusen: *Thurlow Weed, Wizard of the Lobby* (Boston: Little, Brown and Company; 1947), pp. 307–8.

[4] Welles: *Diary*, III, 47.

[5] Charles C. Hazewell to Sumner, Mar. 7, 1864, Sumner MSS. Not even the Boston *Commonwealth* consistently reflected Sumner's views during 1864. See the issue of May 13, 1864. Its failure to support Sumner outraged some of its original backers. W. S. Robinson to Sumner, May 28 [1864], Sumner MSS.

[6] Portland *Evening Express*, July 16, 1891.

[7] Dawes: *Sumner*, pp. 200–1.

Hamlin's son reproduced what purported to be remarks uttered "a few days after the Baltimore convention" by Frank B. Fay, a member of the Massachusetts contingent at Baltimore, to the effect that "Mr. Sumner appealed to the Massachusetts delegates, and insisted that they should advocate the nomination of a war Democrat for Vice-President." [8] All these accounts are suspect. All were published long after the event—after both Sumner and Hamlin were dead. Fay's remarks have been preserved only indirectly, with no specification as to when, where, or how Sumner is supposed to have addressed the Massachusetts delegation. Miss Dawes's account is based upon unspecified "contemporary anecdotes"; it attempts to show that Sumner exercised his influence over the Massachusetts delegates "largely without their knowledge." Drummond's recollections, being more precise, are easier to test. Of the hundreds of contemporaries who wrote letters, of the scores of newspapermen who covered the convention, of the dozens of memoir writers, he alone remembered Sumner's presence in Baltimore, and even he did so in a qualified way, admitting: "As far as I could ascertain no man from Maine had any interview with him."

It is hard to form a conclusive judgment about a negative issue, but the evidence overwhelmingly indicates that Sumner did not go to Baltimore, did not speak to the Massachusetts delegates, and did not urge that Hamlin be dropped. His personal and political correspondence of the time contains not a hint of his views about the vice presidency. In the papers of his political friends there are no references to his support of or opposition to any candidate for that office. Nor in later years did Sumner's supporters reminisce about his role in Johnson's nomination. Even though many of Sumner's backers in 1864 came sharply to differ with him during the Reconstruction era, no one ever charged that he was personally responsible for the selection of Johnson.[9]

[8] Hamlin: *Hamlin*, p. 480.

[9] In March 1865, when Washington was aghast at Johnson's intoxication while delivering his inaugural address as Vice President, Governor Andrew's aide in the national capital speculated that, since the Massachusetts delegation had been responsible for Johnson's nomination, "Sumner as a Massachusetts man, perhaps thought that he *himself* shared" some of the blame. (A. G. Browne, Jr., to Andrew, Mar. 21, 1865, Andrew MSS.) Since both Andrew and

Aside from lacking reliable proof, the story of Sumner's involvement in an elaborate intrigue to oust Hamlin is entirely out of character for the Senator. Sumner was a better politician than most of his contemporaries recognized, and he also had a firmer grip of political reality than even he himself liked to admit. Because his own position depended upon his aloofness from political machinations, he would never have risked involvement in a plan so cumbersome and so certain to be disclosed. Though he doubtless would have preferred to see Hamlin rather than Fessenden in the Senate, he also knew that the Vice President had only a small following in Maine; he was able to offer negligible competition when Fessenden, after a brief period as Secretary of the Treasury, came up for reelection in 1865. Finally, though Sumner had long been distrustful of Seward, by 1864 the acrimony between the two men had abated as the dangers of foreign intervention lessened. Now the two former rivals could joke together about Lincoln's limitations in foreign policy. "There was a great cry last year on the question whether the President read despatches *before they are sent*," Seward told Sumner in May—in obvious but amicable reference to the cabinet crisis in which the Senator had played such a large part—"but I am sure he never reads a d—nd one which we receive."[1]

• 3 •

In 1864 it was not in foreign but in domestic policy that Sumner saw Lincoln's gravest limitations. The President appeared to take little interest in protecting the rights of the freedmen. He had, of course, issued the Emancipation Proclamation, and Sum-

---

the aide were bitterly critical of Sumner at this time, it is significant that there was no suggestion that Sumner had played a personal role in the selection of Johnson. A few months later the New York *Commercial Advertiser* carried the story that "Mr. Sumner and his friends did not want Mr. Hamlin renominated, because they wished him . . . to supersede Mr. Fessenden . . . ; therefore they supported Andy Johnson for the vice presidency," and the Springfield *Weekly Republican* (June 10, 1865) reprinted the column without comment. In 1866 the Washington correspondent of the Boston *Commonwealth* flatly denied that Sumner had anything to do with Hamlin's defeat and declared: "'The nomination of Mr. Johnson was the fruit of Thurlow Weed's labors at Baltimore" (Mar. 17, 1866).

[1] Sumner to Lieber, May 4, 1864, Lieber MSS.

ner was delighted that in his December 1863 message to Congress he gravely reaffirmed his pledge to stand by that edict. He had also enrolled black men in the Union armies, and his annual message highly praised their work. But in the same message he expressed a willingness to see the Southern states adopt "any provision" which, recognizing the permanent freedom of the blacks, would prevent "a total revolution of labor" throughout the South by special regulation of the Negroes "as a laboring, landless, and homeless class."

Sumner had long been concerned over the possible reestablishment of "Slavery under an *alias*," whether of peonage or of forced labor. He knew that the freedmen were now clustered in large, disorderly, and disease-ridden refugee camps on the outskirts of Union army posts.[2] They lacked the land, the equipment, and the training to support themselves by independent farming, and as soon as peace returned they must inevitably fall back under the control of the Southern master class. Already, as members of the American Freedmen's Inquiry Commission warned him, the former slaveholders were planning to "establish some new system of serfdom." Since "the hideous spirit of Slavery" was still alive throughout the Southern states, the commissioners urged him to press legislation to secure "*some proper and just guarantee of the civil freedom and rights of the colored man.*"[3]

It was not Sumner, however, who first introduced the bill establishing a Freedmen's Bureau. Knowing the Senate committee system, he understood that such a proposal would be buried unless he was in a position to take official charge of it, yet it was not until the middle of January 1864 that he could persuade the Senate to establish the Select Committee on Slavery and Freedmen, of which he became chairman. Even then he wanted public sentiment to be aroused before he acted, and he waited impatiently for the report of the American Freedmen's Inquiry Commission exposing the desperate plight of the freedmen in the refugee camps. But the commissioners were slow and did not get

[2] Bentley: *History of the Freedmen's Bureau,* pp. 16–36; McPherson: *The Struggle for Equality,* Chap. 8.

[3] James McKaye to Sumner, Jan. 20 and Feb. 5, 1864, Sumner MSS.

their final report to the Senate until late June 1864. Meanwhile, Representative Thomas D. Eliot of Massachusetts had already introduced a bill creating a special bureau, as part of the War Department, to look after the freedmen.

Even after the House passed Eliot's bill on March 1 and the Senate referred it to Sumner's special committee, he could do little to advance the measure. Despite Eliot's plea that any alteration would imperil the bill in the House, only Howard and Sumner favored reporting it without change to the Senate; the other five members of the committee were strongly critical of Eliot's proposal. "Charles 5th could not make his clocks go alike," Sumner lamented, "and I have had a similar experience with the Committee. . . ."[4]

Each member of the committee had his own objections to Eliot's bill, but a large majority joined in "inflexible opposition" to placing the Freedmen's Bureau under the control of the War Department. Their reasons are not entirely clear. Since this majority included the Democrats and the moderate Republicans on the committee, but not Sumner or Howard, it is unlikely that the proposed transfer of the bureau to the Treasury Department was intended to strengthen the presidential chances of Salmon P. Chase by giving him control of this additional patronage.[5] Had such been the purpose, moreover, it is hard to understand why its proponents allowed the measure to languish without Senate action throughout March, April, and May, only to bring it before the Senate in June, when Lincoln's renomination was already secured. Nor was the shift intended to assure Radical control over the new agency, for Secretary of War Stanton was as much in the good graces of antislavery men as Chase. In all probability the change stemmed from the opinion of the American Freedmen's Inquiry Commissioners that supervision of the freedmen and control of the confiscated plantations and abandoned lands on which they must work ought to be under the same authority.[6] Since the Treasury Department already controlled the lands and

[4] Sumner to G. W. Curtis, April 13, 1864, Curtis MSS. Cf. T. D. Eliot to Sumner, July 24, 1864, Sumner MSS.

[5] For this argument see Bentley: *History of the Freedmen's Bureau*, pp. 39–43.

[6] R. D. Owen to Sumner, Jan. 16, 1864, Sumner MSS.

the War Department was not prepared to take them over, it seemed logical to put the Freedmen's Bureau also under Treasury supervision.

Vexed by the dissension within his committee, Sumner himself had no strong feelings as to which department should prevail. Since the majority wanted to change Eliot's bill, he tried his hand at drafting a proposal upon which they could all agree, giving the Treasury Department control of the new agency.[7] Loosely constructed and poorly worded, his draft never got past a second reading, and perhaps Sumner did not intend it to, though he apologized: "It was the best thing I could do." After this failure, the committee authorized him to report out Eliot's bill, but with an amendment giving the Treasury, not the War, Department control of the Freedmen's Bureau. Sumner accepted the change as the only way to keep his committee behind him. "*I seek the best that is practicable,*" he explained to a critic. "For myself I am ready to take any bill and trust to the corrective of good sense in its administration and [to] future legislation." [8]

When the Senate finally got around to debating the Freedmen's Bureau bill in June, Sumner anticipated that the major opposition would come from Democrats but was astonished to find many antislavery men opposed to the measure. Friends of the Negro claimed that it would put all the freedmen under the control of "unscrupulous knaves" appointed in Washington. Grimes objected that the bill authorized "nothing more nor less than peon slavery," since it allowed bureau officials to supervise the freedmen's labor contracts. T. O. Howe protested that the Commissioner of Freedmen would have "the right to control the action and the efforts of all these freedmen," including the power to compel them "to occupy and cultivate these lands" in the South.[9]

These objections, Sumner protested, were "absolutely novel," something "not anticipated by the Committee," and he assured critics with some asperity that there was "no bureau of the Government constituted with more care, or surrounded with

[7] Senate Bill No. 227, 38 Cong., 1 Sess.

[8] Sumner to G. W. Curtis, April 13, 1864, Curtis MSS.; Sumner to C. E. Norton, May 2, 1864, Norton MSS.

[9] *Cong. Globe*, 38 Cong., 1 Sess., pp. 2972, 3331.

more safeguards against abuse." To find tyranny in this measure, he asserted in a rare attempt at wit, Senators "must be as critical as the German theologian who found heresy in the Lord's Prayer." [1]

Able to refute specific criticisms of the bill, Sumner did not understand that opponents were raising a more general objection, which in the Reconstruction era would come to be of great significance. The issue involved how much the government owed to the freedmen in the way of special care and protection. Sumner thought emancipation was a hoax unless the federal government saw that the blacks in the South secured jobs, land, and education. But for many Northerners, especially those brought up in the Jacksonian tradition hostile to all special privilege, it seemed a dangerous precedent to create a government bureau not just to combat the immediate problems of disease and starvation but to supervise the whole transition from slavery to freedom. The American Freedmen's Inquiry Commission itself urged that the Freedmen's Bureau be only a temporary organization, to "be replaced as soon as possible by equal laws equally administered." In a separately published report Samuel Gridley Howe stressed this laissez-faire view more strongly: "The negro does best when let alone . . . we must beware of all attempts to prolong his servitude, even under pretext of caring for him. The white man has tried taking care of the negro, by slavery, by apprenticeship, by colonization, and has failed disastrously in all; now let the negro try to take care of himself." Grimes's objection to Sumner's bill echoed the same sentiment: "Are they free men, or are they not? If they are free men, why not let them stand as free men. . . ?" [2]

The full implications of these questions were not evident in 1864, when virtually everybody agreed that something must be done to relieve the suffering, poverty, and actual starvation among freedmen in the South. On June 28 the Senate finally passed the Freedmen's Bureau bill by a strictly partisan vote, with Republican critics of the measure pointedly abstaining. The

[1] Sumner: *Works*, VIII, 508, 499, 504.

[2] McPherson: *The Struggle for Equality*, pp. 186–7; *Cong. Globe*, 38 Cong., 1 Sess., p. 2972.

House, however, refused to agree that the bureau should come under the Treasury Department and, with some recriminations between Eliot and Sumner, [3] the end of the session postponed the whole project. At no point during the debates had the President expressed an opinion on the bill or urged action to prevent the famine and plague that threatened the refugee camps.

• 4 •

No more satisfactory to Sumner was Lincoln's policy of reconstruction, though in this area it was action, not the failure to take action, to which he objected. He found the President's course the more discouraging because earlier in the congressional session he had seemed to be on the right track. Like most other Radical Republicans, Sumner had generally approved Lincoln's December 1863 message, promising pardon and amnesty to the Confederates and encouraging the formation of loyal governments in the South when as few as ten percent of the 1860 voters agreed henceforth to support the Union.[4] By speaking of the need to "re-establish" the "subverted" governments in the South, the President came close to endorsing the Radical view that the Confederate states had dropped into a territorial status; as Sumner later declared, in a commentary upon the message: "We do not *reestablish* a government which continues to exist." By invoking the constitutional provision guaranteeing to each state a republican form of government as his legal basis for imposing conditions, including emancipation, upon the seceded states, Lincoln adopted the argument which the Radicals increasingly came to prefer, because they thought it would justify sweeping changes in the South. To be sure, the ten percent plan was not entirely to Sumner's liking, but Lincoln carefully noted that "whether members sent to Congress from any State shall be admitted to seats, constitutionally rests exclusively with the respective Houses, and not to any extent with the Executive." The President further stressed that his reconstruc-

[3] Eliot to Sumner, July 24 and Aug. 1, 1864, Sumner MSS.

[4] Herman Belz: *Reconstructing the Union*, pp. 155–66, is an excellent analysis of the message, which corrects the older view that Lincoln's program was a conservative one.

tion program was provisional and flexible: "Saying that reconstruction will be accepted if presented in a specified way, it is not said that it will never be accepted in any other way." Finally, and most important to Sumner, Lincoln included a ringing reaffirmation of the Emancipation Proclamation and a vow never to commit such "a cruel and an astounding breach of faith" as dishonoring that pledge of freedom.

While the clerk read the message, John Hay, the President's secretary, observed that most of the Radicals were nodding in approval and that Sumner was beaming. The next day the Senator continued to speak of it with great gratification. "It satisfies his ideas of proper reconstruction," Hay felt, "without insisting upon the adoption of his peculiar theories." So pleased indeed was Sumner that he authorized the correspondent of the Chicago *Tribune* to announce that he was "fully and perfectly satisfied" with Lincoln's message. "There may be differences about the details of the admissions of the States," he noted; "but . . . these will drop out of sight, and nothing remain but the great principle of the irrevocability of the proclamation." [5]

Far from dropping out of sight, these "details of the admissions of the States" within a few weeks proved a major source of controversy between the President and the leaders of his party in Congress. After initially working on legislation that would implement Lincoln's plan, Radical leaders in January 1864 abruptly changed course when they discovered the direction in which the President was heading. Placing General N. P. Banks in complete control of reconstruction in Louisiana, Lincoln supported his plan to reconstitute the government of that state under its antebellum constitution, with only the proslavery clauses stricken out. If Banks's efforts succeeded, there would be few significant changes in Louisiana. Political power would continue to rest with the planters, after they took an oath of future loyalty to the

[5] Hay: Diary, Dec. 9–10, 1863, photostat of MS., Mass. Hist. Soc.; Boston *Commonwealth*, Jan. 8, 1864. In his recollections the newspaper correspondent Noah Brooks (*Washington in Lincoln's Time* [New York: The Century Co.; 1895], p. 163) wrote that Sumner was so displeased with the message that during the reading he slammed his books and documents about on his desk and upon the floor "in a boyish and petulant manner." I am at a loss to explain this report, so sharply at variance with Hay's contemporary record and with Sumner's letters of the time.

Union, and with the army officers who cooperated with them; Banks set up a labor system that tied the freedmen to the plantations; and there was even a possibility that slavery might be continued, since New Orleans and the surrounding parishes had been excepted from the Emancipation Proclamation.

To Sumner, as to many other Radicals, such a program of reconstruction negated all the gains made during the war. Under this policy, as soon as the slaveholders repented of their folly in seceding, they would resume control of their state governments and return to the seats of power in Washington. Convinced that the Southern slavemasters would "never again be loyal to the Union" but would remain "a disaffected element, always ready to intrigue with a foreign enemy," Sumner was unwilling ever to trust them again. "The only Unionists of the South are black," he firmly believed, and they formed the cornerstone upon which loyal governments in that section must be built. To prepare for this result it had been necessary first to free and to arm the slaves. Next it was essential to see that the freedmen received land and education. Finally—though Sumner was not yet prepared publicly to announce his objective—it would be essential "to extend the suffrage to the Negroes . . . as a counteracting power to that of their former masters." [6]

With no seat on the Senate Committee on Territories, which had the duty of perfecting reconstruction legislation, Sumner was not in a position to originate congressional policy toward the South, but while the committee debated he stood guard against any action which even indirectly or inadvertently might serve as a precedent for readmitting the Southern states under their ante-bellum leadership. Thus he joined with Radical Senator Wilkinson of Minnesota in fighting a proposal to organize Montana territory with a government elected under universal white manhood suffrage. He wanted to enfranchise every adult male. When Reverdy Johnson objected that his proposal was clearly unconstitutional, since the Dred Scott decision had declared Negroes were not citizens, Sumner again dismissed that court opinion as being "as absurd and irrational as . . . a re-

[6] Wainwright (ed.): *A Philadelphia Perspective,* p. 467; Sumner: *Works,* VII, 229.

versal of the multiplication table." Boldly he asserted "the right of Congress to interpret the Constitution without constraint from the Supreme Court." To objections from Trumbull that the question of Negro suffrage in Montana was "the merest abstraction" and from Doolittle that "There is not a negro in the territory, and probably will not be for years," he replied that the same arguments had been used to support the loathsome Kansas-Nebraska act in 1854. Anyway, it made no difference whether there were or ever would be blacks in Montana; his real objective was to set a precedent by requiring impartial suffrage. "It is something to declare a principle . . . ," he urged.[7]

Unable to persuade his colleagues to apply his principle to faraway Montana, Sumner made another fight for impartial suffrage in May, when the Senate was amending the charter of the city of Washington. Wade, who was in charge of the bill, announced that he was "utterly opposed to any restriction upon the voting of any intelligent person in the community, whatever his color or condition," but he also argued that since the charter changes were urgently needed it was "impracticable to act . . . now" to give Washington Negroes the vote. Sumner protested against this counsel of expediency. Since the disfranchisement of Negroes was the result of slavery, since he was "against Slavery, wherever it shows itself, whatever form it takes," it was his "duty to vote against all propositions creating any discrimination of color." To the anger of his colleagues, who wanted to get on with legislative business and end the protracted session, he threatened to attach a Negro suffrage amendment not only to the District of Columbia bill but to "any other bill . . . to which the question may be germane." After prolonged debate he lost his fight to enfranchise Washington Negroes, but not until he had an opportunity to explain his persistence. The issue involved more than a few voters in the District of Columbia; it concerned the entire "question of human rights everywhere throughout this land, involving the national character and its good name forever more." [8] More specifically it involved the suffrage requirements

[7] Ibid., VIII, 237–9, 242; *Cong. Globe*, 38 Cong., 1 Sess., p. 1705.

[8] *Cong. Globe*, 38 Cong., 1 Sess., pp. 2486, 2543; Sumner: *Works*, VIII, 459–69.

in the Southern states, where the President and his agents were setting up reconstructed governments.

In another move designed to prevent the return of ante-bellum Southern leaders to power, Sumner in January earnestly insisted that Senators be required to take the "iron-clad oath," affirming past, as well as future, loyalty to the federal government. Prescribed by Congress in July 1862, as a means of securing loyalty among civil servants and military officers, the oath probably could not be constitutionally required of members of the Senate, whose qualifications are set forth in the Constitution. But Republicans, in a great show of loyalty, took the oath at the beginning of the special session in March 1863, and Sumner contended that all other Senators must do so too. In the December session he renewed the pressure upon the one non-juring Democratic Senator, James A. Bayard of Delaware, and after protracted debate persuaded the Senate to insist upon the loyalty test. Bayard then took the oath and promptly resigned, telling the Senators they had inflicted "a vital wound upon free . . . government."[9] It was clear that Sumner's objective was not so much to oust Bayard, whose loyalty nobody questioned, but to establish a precedent barring leaders in the rebellion from returning to the Senate.

Finally, while eagerly waiting for the congressional committees to perfect an alternative scheme of reconstruction, Sumner and his fellow Radicals refused to seat Senators chosen by the governments Lincoln sponsored in the South. From the Radical point of view it was fortunate that the test was not presented by Louisiana, where a sizable number of Unionists backed the regime fostered by Banks, or by Tennessee, which supplied the Republican vice-presidential candidate, but by Arkansas, a state still largely under Confederate control, where the provisional government was clearly the creation of the Federal military authorities. Though it was obvious from the outset that the Senate would not seat William M. Fishback, who had been elected by this regime, Sumner delayed the customary reference of his credentials to the Judiciary Committee so that he could

[9] See the admirable treatment of this episode in Harold M. Hyman: *Era of the Oath* (Philadelphia: University of Pennsylvania Press; 1954), pp. 26–31.

make a speech, which was directed less against Arkansas than against Louisiana, less against Fishback than against Abraham Lincoln. Conceding that "in the absence of Congressional action" what the President had done in Arkansas was "to a certain extent, proper, if not necessary," he hinted of grave dangers that might result from Lincoln's course. In the event of a tie in the electoral college after the approaching presidential election, the choice would fall to the House of Representatives, where each state would cast one vote. In that event the puppet government of Arkansas, if readmitted to representation in Congress, would have a voice "affecting the result as weighty as that of Massachusetts, New York, or Illinois." To avert such possibilities, Congress must take over the whole question of reconstruction, over which it had "all needful power." "Congress and not the President must decide when the restoration has taken place." [1]

Urging Congress to make haste slowly so far as the President's program was concerned, Sumner pointed out that the House of Representatives had already approved a superior plan of reconstruction proposed by Henry Winter Davis and that the Senate Committee on Territories had it under consideration. When Wade reported the bill from committee, however, Sumner found it not altogether to his liking, for it limited suffrage in the Southern states to whites. Aware that it was an election year and that Negro suffrage was decidedly unpopular throughout the North, he refrained from making a speech opposing the measure. Indeed, throughout the long session, even while trying to set precedents for impartial suffrage, he had resisted Democrats' attempts to bait him into discussing "the equality of races, or their fortunes in the future" or into ranging "over the whole field of history, or morals, or of politics." [2] Instead, he quietly joined with four other Radical Senators in moving to strike the word "white" out of the suffrage clause. Though the attempt failed, he voted for the Wade-Davis bill, both because it made emancipation an absolute condition for the readmission of any Southern state and because it explicitly affirmed the power of Congress to control the reconstruction process.

[1] Sumner: *Works*, IX, 14, 4–5, 20.
[2] Ibid., VIII, 112.

Uncertain whether Lincoln would approve the bill, Sumner, along with a few other Radical Senators, tried to keep Congress in session so that the President would have no chance to use a pocket veto. Though suffering from such a severe cold that he spoke with difficulty, he kept raising issue after issue which he insisted the Senate ought to consider before adjourning. He pointed out that he had as much reason as any other Senator to desire to end the session and leave the capital: "Born on the sea-shore, accustomed to the sea air, I am less prepared than many of my friends to endure the climate here. I feel sensibly its sultry heats. . . ." But he was prepared to sacrifice comfort for duty.[3]

Most Congressmen were tired out, however, and the Senate adjourned on July 4, 1864, with the Wade-Davis bill not yet approved or disapproved. As the session ended, the President came down to the Capitol to sign some of the measures passed during the final hours. Sumner, along with Boutwell and Zachariah Chandler, hovered about him, anxious to see whether he would approve the reconstruction act. When Lincoln pushed it aside without his signature, Chandler protested, but the President noncommittally observed: "This bill was placed before me a few minutes before Congress adjourned. It is a matter of too much importance to be swallowed in that way." It was not until four days later that Sumner learned Lincoln would kill the bill by his pocket veto, which, however, he accompanied with a declaration that the bill set forth "one very proper plan" which any Southern state could follow if it liked. "The refusal of the President to sign the great bill which placed Freedom under the safeguard of an Act of Congress, causes me great grief," Sumner wrote the abolitionist Parker Pillsbury. "I am inconsolable." [4]

• 5 •

At the end of what one Senator called "the most exhausting session that has ever been held since the foundation of the

[3] Ibid., IX, 61.

[4] Tyler Dennett (ed.): *Lincoln and the Civil War in the Diaries and Letters of John Hay* (New York: Dodd, Mead & Company; 1939), p. 204; Sumner's letter quoted in Pillsbury to Theodore Tilton, July 10, 1864, Tilton MSS.

Government,"[5] Sumner was tired and dispirited. Worn out by seven months of almost daily attendance in the Senate, unable to shake off his cold, depressed by the heats of Washington, he had an overwhelming sense of defeat. Congress had failed to do its duty: it had not adopted the Thirteenth Amendment, not created the Freedmen's Bureau, not taken control of reconstruction, not secured to the black man equality before the law.

The Union armies, too, had failed. "This war stretches on fearfully," he wrote the Duchess of Argyll on the final day of the congressional session. "The blood and treasure we lavished to subdue *belligerent slavery* are beyond precedent. But so great and audacious a crime, sustained by European aid, resists with a natural diabolism."[6] After fierce battles in the Wilderness and at Spotsylvania, Grant was thrown back at Cold Harbor and shifted his army to the James River, where he settled in for a protracted siege of Petersburg and Richmond. At the same time, Confederate troops under Jubal A. Early swarmed up the Shenandoah Valley, poured across Maryland, and reached the edge of Washington itself. In the West Joseph E. Johnston's Confederates skillfully fended off Sherman's advance into Georgia, and the Federal assault at Kenesaw Mountain on June 27 resulted in eight times as many Union as Confederate casualties. In the Mississippi Valley, Banks's expedition up the Red River met with costly defeat, and that unfortunate general was happy to retreat to the protection of the Union gunboats on the Mississippi. "I am sick and weary," Sumner wrote as he prepared to leave for Boston on July 10, "and see little promising in the future, unless Grant's promises are fulfilled."[7]

The President was the greatest failure of all. He had shown himself inefficient in conducting business, incapable in military matters, ignorant in foreign affairs, and indifferent to the rights of the freedmen; yet he was now running for reelection as the candidate of Sumner's own party. The Senator was wholly disenchanted with him. Shortly after returning to Massachusetts, he told Longfellow and A. A. Lawrence that the country needed

[5] *Cong. Globe,* 38 Cong., 1 Sess., p. 3451.
[6] July 4, 1864, Argyll MSS.
[7] Sumner to Lieber, July 10, 1864, Sumner MSS.

more than anything else "a president with brains; one who can make a plan and carry it out." His opinion of Lincoln, he informed members of the Saturday Club, was "at least not higher than it was three years ago." [8]

Remaining in the Boston area during the summer, Sumner had an opportunity to confer with other Republicans who were equally disaffected toward Lincoln. Salmon P. Chase, no longer Secretary of the Treasury, was vacationing in the vicinity, for, once the Baltimore nominations were made, Lincoln had unceremoniously accepted his frequently tendered resignation. In August, Pomeroy, one of the original promoters of the Chase presidential movement, came to Massachusetts, as did Wade, who had just joined Winter Davis in an angry blast against Lincoln's pocket veto of the reconstruction bill. As a newspaper correspondent shrewdly surmised, the gathering of such prominent Radicals "boded no good to Father Abraham." [9]

Out of their conferences emerged a remarkable and unprecedented plan to replace Lincoln, already the official nominee of his party, with another candidate from that same party who would be more positive and energetic, who would be more deeply committed to equal rights, and who would, presumably, have a greater chance of success. The plan drew its strength from the nearly universal conviction, in the midsummer of 1864, that Lincoln could not be reelected, a conviction shared not merely by Radicals but by Conservatives like Thurlow Weed and Henry J. Raymond, and, indeed, by Lincoln himself. To avoid the defeat which seemed inevitable, the Boston Radical conferees, along with similar groups in New York and in Ohio, planned first to hold a meeting of all prominent anti-Lincoln Republicans, then to call upon both Lincoln and Frémont to abandon the hopeless presidential contest, and, finally, to hold a new Republican convention to select a fresh candidate.[1]

[8] William Lawrence: *Life of Amos A. Lawrence* (Boston: Houghton, Mifflin and Company; 1888), p. 195; Sara Norton and M. A. DeWolfe Howe: *Letters of Charles Eliot Norton* (Boston: Houghton, Mifflin and Company; 1913), I, 279.

[9] Unidentified clipping enclosed in Thurlow Weed to Seward, Aug. 10, 1864, Seward MSS. For Sumner's summer meetings with Chase, see Donald (ed.): *Inside Lincoln's Cabinet*, pp. 241, 243, 251.

[1] William F. Zornow: *Lincoln & the Party Divided* (Norman, Okla.: University of Oklahoma Press; 1954), pp. 114–17.

Though sympathetic to this plan, Sumner carefully refused to commit himself to it. He did not mind having it known that he regretted the Republican convention had been held so early. "The whole subject might have been postponed till September," he declared, "when we should have seen more clearly who ought to be the candidate." Yet when it came to an outright break with Lincoln, he held back. "Into the darkness of the Presidential contest I am not prepared to enter," he wrote Mrs. Child in early August. So cagey was he that he refrained, even in private, from commenting upon the Wade-Davis manifesto, which denounced the President for killing the reconstruction bill. Davis complained that Sumner acknowledged receiving the manifesto by sending him two copies of his own speech "on the Arkansas Senator—but not one word about the Protest!"[2]

When the disaffected Republicans met in the home of New York Mayor George Opdyke on August 18, Sumner was not present, though he kept himself fully informed as to their proceedings and knew of their plan to hold a second, more decisive meeting on August 30. "I do not yet see the Presidential horizon," he explained on the day after the August 18 gathering to Lieber, who had attended. "I wait for the bluelights of [the Democratic nominating convention at] Chicago, which will present the true outlines." Though some of Sumner's closest friends, including Howe and Bird, took their lead from the New York meeting and published a call for both Frémont and Lincoln to abandon the hopeless race and allow a united effort behind a new candidate, the Senator himself continued to be noncommittal. "He hesitates till he knows more than I can tell him," Bird wrote in some exasperation; he promised to talk the presidential question over with Boutwell; but he agreed to nothing.[3]

On the day before the August 30 meeting, which was held in the home of David Dudley Field in New York, Sumner explained his position to Andrew, who was expected to attend. "You know well that I have regretted that the Republican Con-

[2] Sumner to Mrs. Child, Aug. 7, 1864, MS., Ill. State Hist. Lib.; Belz: *Reconstructing the Union*, p. 231.

[3] Sumner to Lieber, Aug. 19, 1864, Sumner MSS.; Gideon Welles: *Lincoln's Administration: Selected Essays*, ed. Albert Mordell (New York: Twayne Publishers; 1960), pp. 185–6; Bird to Andrew, Aug. 26, 1864, Andrew MSS.

vention was called at so early a day," he reminded the Governor, who was also strongly critical of Lincoln. "Its action seemed to me ill-considered and unseasonable." If nominations made at Baltimore could be regarded as "merely temporary," Republicans could now call a new convention, which "might nominate a candidate who would surely be elected." So far Sumner entirely agreed with the anti-Lincoln plot, but then he hedged. No new nomination could hope for success without "the concurrence of Mr. Lincoln." Would the President step aside? "I can imagine a patriotism," Sumner announced loftily, "which setting aside all personal considerations, and looking singly to the good of the country at this trying moment, should insist upon another appeal to the people in Convention." "But," he added cautiously, "I see no way of meeting the difficulties from the candidacy of Mr. Lincoln, *unless he withdraws patriotically and kindly, so as to leave no breach in the party.*" [4]

In writing to John Austin Stevens, who served as the secretary for the New York group of Radical Republicans, Sumner was even more oracular:

> It is clear that all who love their country, and wish to see it free, must act together. There must be no division.
>
> To this end we must all be ready to make sacrifices.
>
> It may be that Mr. L. will see that we shall be stronger and more united under another candidate. But if he does not see it so, our duty is none the less clear to unite in the opposition to the common enemy.[5]

To add to the ambiguity, and to prevent his views from becoming public, Sumner was careful not to write Stevens until September 1—the day after the meeting in New York.

To Lieber, who was puzzled by his course, Sumner explained that he had "declined to sign any paper or take part in any action" that could be construed as being overtly hostile to the President. He recognized that nothing could be "done *except through Mr. L. and with his good will*" and that "any *adversary* proceeding would disaffect him, and his friends, so as to destroy

[4] Aug. 29, 1864, Andrew MSS.
[5] New York *Sun*, June 30, 1889.

the *unity of the party.*" "If Mr. L. does not withdraw," he predicted, "then all who now disincline to him must come into his support." [6]

As a political prophet Sumner showed himself more sagacious than the Radicals who assembled at New York. Within a few days of their meeting two developments completely undercut the movement to replace Lincoln as Republican nominee. Just before the Radicals gathered at Field's house, the Democratic national convention in Chicago nominated General George B. McClellan for President on a platform that called the war a failure. "Lincoln's election would be a disaster," Sumner told an abolitionist friend when he heard the news, "but McClellan's damnation." Then, on the day after the New York meeting, Sherman's army marched into Atlanta. "The Chicago platform and our victories have settled the Presidential election beyond question," Sumner wrote Bright at the end of September, "and we all see the beginning of the end." "To my mind the election seemed already decided," he declared.[7]

In the anticipated Republican victory Sumner was determined to have a part. Up till now wholly inactive in the campaign, he took to the platform in September to hail Sherman for shattering "the very key-stone of the Rebel arch" and, using the same rhetoric he had employed in 1862, to call McClellan's supporters "nothing else than unarmed guerilla bands of Jefferson Davis." Still he carefully refrained from praising the President. "Candidates and men, no matter who, are all insignificant by the side of the cause," he assured a Faneuil Hall rally on September 28. The only questions before the voters were: "Are you for Freedom, or are you for Slavery?" and "Are you for your country, or are you for the Rebellion?" [8]

In October Sumner found reason to speak more positively of his party's nominee. After a prolonged illness Chief Justice

[6] Sept. 3, 1864, Sumner MSS. For a further explanation of Sumner's course, see his letter to Cobden in Pierce, IV, 199–200.

[7] J. G. Randall and Richard N. Current: *Lincoln the President: Last Full Measure* (New York: Dodd, Mead & Company; 1955), p. 225; Sumner to Bright, Sept. 27, 1864, Bright MSS.; New York *Sun*, June 30, 1889. Cf. William B. Parker: *The Life and Public Services of Justin Smith Morrill* (Boston: Houghton Mifflin Company; 1924), p. 160.

[8] Sumner: *Works*, IX, 65–82.

Taney died on October 12, and as soon as Sumner heard the news he wrote Lincoln of his joy in this "victory for Liberty and for the Constitution." Sumner had long anticipated the day when the office of Chief Justice would become a bulwark of freedom, instead of a prop for slavery. As early as December 1863, when Taney fell ill, he had urged Lincoln to appoint Chase to the Court, and he received what he took to be a promise that it would be done. Now he renewed his plea for the former Secretary of the Treasury as "an able, courageous, and determined friend of Freedom, who will never let Freedom suffer by concession or hesitation." Believing that the appointment of Chase would "complete our great reformation by purifying the Constitution and by upholding those measures through which the Republic will be saved," Sumner urged Lincoln to nominate him immediately so as to produce "a glow of delight among all the best supporters of the Administration." He even supplied the President with a copy of a letter from Chase, promising to accept the Chief Justiceship if it were offered.[9]

When Lincoln did not respond, both Sumner and Chase drew the desired inference from his silence, and both took vigorously to the stump to urge that the President be reelected. At towns in Massachusetts, at Hartford and New London, Connecticut, at Newark, New Jersey, and in New York City, before a gigantic rally at Cooper Union, Sumner spoke. He still found it easier to attack the Democrats than to praise the Republicans, and he spent much of his time ridiculing the pretensions of the South to be an aristocracy, when in fact the region had been originally settled by "convicts and wretches" and ever since had been "kept in barbarism by an oligarchy of man-stealers." Still, he did manage to say that the Republican presidential candidate had "never uttered a word of duplicity."[1] No doubt he hoped Lincoln would keep that record in mind and remember his promise when he named the next Chief Justice.

On election day Massachusetts went heavily for Lincoln, and Sumner promptly telegraphed the news to the White House.

[9] Sumner to Lincoln, Oct. 12 and 24, 1864, Lincoln MSS.; Sumner to Duchess of Argyll, Dec. 29, 1863, Argyll MSS.; Sumner to Lieber, Oct. 14, 1864, Sumner MSS.; Sumner to Chase, Oct. 14 [1864], Chase MSS., Lib. of Cong.

[1] Sumner: *Works*, IX, 110–11, 129.

Earlier in the day, however, he had analyzed for a friend the real meaning of the contest: "Mr. L's re-election is certain by an immense and unprecedented vote; but I know many who are anxious to have it, understood, that they vote *against* McClellan rather than *for* Lincoln." [2]

· 6 ·

During most of the 1864 campaign Sumner was in an ugly temper. He lashed out at anyone who dared to cross him. In September, accidentally encountering the Senator in the Boston Athenaeum, his old friend Palfrey cordially invited him to call upon his family. In a harsh, loud voice that could be heard all over the library, Sumner refused, asserting that he could not visit the Palfreys "consistently with self-respect" because Palfrey during the past two years had never come to his house in Hancock Street. Astounded, Palfrey, who had known Sumner since he was a Harvard student, had helped him form the Free Soil party in Massachusetts, and, more recently, had been made postmaster of Boston at Sumner's urging, replied that he had regularly called on the Senator every time he returned to Boston, and he even detailed the subjects he had discussed with him on those visits. Sumner denied any recollection of these calls, refused to listen further, and stamped off angrily. "It was the very madness of the moon," Palfrey concluded. "He has fine qualities, as well of character as of mind. But his irritability and arrogance have become extreme." [3]

Indeed, Sumner was, and remained, in a highly excitable state. Tired and unwell, he had been forced to accept a candidate he did not really want and to campaign for a party that he could only endorse as being better than the Democrats. Since the failure of his efforts in 1863 to take over direction of foreign and domestic policy, his political position had been steadily deteriorating, and the reelection of Lincoln weakened him still further. His most devoted political friends like Bird and Howe blamed

[2] Dennett (ed.): *Lincoln and the Civil War*, p. 234; Sumner to J. C. Welling, Nov. 8, 1864, copy, Dawes MSS.

[3] Palfrey to Dana, Sept. 12, 1864, Dana MSS.; Palfrey: Journal, Sept. 9, 1864, Palfrey MSS.

him for failing to stand on principle and openly fight against Lincoln's candidacy. When Robinson in the Springfield *Republican* began praising Henry Wilson and lamenting that Sumner was "growing more and more politic and less and less a statesman,"[4] there was evidence of dangerous disaffection among the antislavery men who had hitherto been the backbone of Sumner's political following. On the other hand, since his coolness toward Lincoln's candidacy was well known, his influence was also slipping in Washington. Furthermore, since the public issues now involved domestic, not foreign, policy, Sumner could no longer act the part of friend of the administration while attacking the Secretary of State. When the new session of Congress began in December 1864, Sumner, much against his wishes, was certain to be flushed out into open opposition to the President, a President enormously strengthened by successes of the Union armies and by his own triumphant reelection.

Adding to the discomfort of this position was Sumner's recognition that the war was nearly at an end. Like most Northerners he saw in Sherman's slash through Georgia, in Sheridan's victories in the Shenandoah, and in Grant's tenacious grip on Petersburg and Richmond sure signs that the "death-grapple" with the Confederacy was at hand, and it hardly seemed possible that the war could last longer than the summer of 1865. While welcoming peace, Sumner knew that only during war, with its mobilization of public sentiment and its concentration of power in national government, was there much chance of realizing major social reforms. "This is a moment for changes," he wrote Lieber. "Our whole system is like molten wax, ready to receive an impression."[5]

As Congress opened, therefore, Sumner had a desperate sense of urgency. Now was the time to sweep from the statute books all remaining references to slavery and all discriminations based upon race. He begged, he demanded, an immediate end to segregation on Washington streetcars. Now was the time to secure a Chief Justice who would not "require arguments of

[4] Springfield *Weekly Republican*, Jan. 14, 1865.

[5] Sumner to Duchess of Argyll, Oct. 4, 1864, Argyll MSS.; Sumner to Lieber [May] 15 [1864], Sumner MSS.

counsel in order to convert him to Liberty every where under the Constitution." Sumner continued to press Lincoln to name Chase, and at the swearing in of his friend as Chief Justice on December 13, Sumner occupied the most conspicuous position in the Supreme Court chamber, leaning against a marble column at the front of the room and looking, as a newspaperman thought, like "the guardian of the new life and honor of the Court."[6] Now was the time explicitly to overturn the infamous Dred Scott decision. No sooner had Chase taken his seat than Sumner petitioned to have one of his Negro constituents, John S. Rock, admitted to practice before the Court, which only eight years before had declared that Negroes were not citizens of the United States.[7] Now, too, was the time to make sure that Taney, author of the Dred Scott majority opinion, was not honored in the conventional way by having his bust placed in the Supreme Court room but to insist instead that the name of the late Chief Justice should be "hooted down the pages of history" for a decision "more thoroughly abominable than anything of the kind in the history of the courts."[8]

Behind Sumner's passionate urging of these symbolic actions was his unhappy awareness that he would have only a small share in the major decisions that must be made before the return of peace and inertia. He could do nothing to promote the constitutional amendment abolishing slavery. The Senate had

[6] Sumner to Chase, Nov. 20, 1864, Chase MSS., Hist. Soc. of Penn.; Boston *Commonwealth*, Dec. 24, 1864.

[7] Sumner to Chase, Dec. 21, 1864, Chase MSS., Hist. Soc. of Penn.; Rock to Sumner, Dec. 17 and 24, 1864, Sumner MSS.; Chase to Sumner, Dec. 21, 1864, and Jan. 6, 1865, ibid.; Nevins and Thomas (eds.): *Diary of George Templeton Strong*, III, 549.

[8] *Cong. Globe*, 38 Cong., 2 Sess., p. 1012; Sumner: *Works*, IX, 272. Walker Lewis, a recent biographer of Taney (*Without Fear or Favor* [Boston: Houghton Mifflin Company; 1965], pp. 477–92), attempts to prove that Sumner wrote an anonymous 1865 pamphlet attacking Taney: *The Unjust Judge—A Memorial of Roger Brooke Taney, late Chief Justice of the United States*. Mr. Lewis's charge is based, first, upon Sumner's bitter hostility toward Taney, which, however, was shared by virtually every Radical Republican. It rests, second, upon alleged stylistic resemblances between the pamphlet and Sumner's speech against honoring Taney. There are, indeed, a number of phrases which appear in both—as they had regularly appeared in abolitionist attacks upon Taney since 1857. Taken as a whole, the pamphlet appears definitely not to be in Sumner's quite distinctive style. There is no positive evidence to support Mr. Lewis's accusation. There are no letters between Sumner and the New York publishers of the pamphlet, Baker & Godwin. No letter by Sumner mentions the pamphlet, and none of his correspondents attributed it to him.

approved the measure during the previous session, and its fate now lay in the House.[9] Even if the Representatives endorsed it, Sumner feared it would never be ratified. It would be almost impossible to persuade three-fourths of all the states, including the eleven in the Confederacy, to accept the amendment; if only two border states rejected it, it would be blocked. Yet Sumner could rally little support for a plan to require ratification by three-fourths of only the loyal states. Doolittle, who was rapidly emerging as the Senate leader of Conservative Republicans, rasped that such a scheme would be rejected by "nine tenths, if not ninety nine out of every hundred, of the people of the United States," and even Lincoln thought that ratification under such a rule was "questionable, and sure to be persistently questioned."[1]

Nor could Sumner do much to forward the Freedmen's Bureau, desperately needed to supervise and protect the former slaves. Since the Senate in the previous session had voted to place this agency under the Treasury Department and the House had insisted that it belonged under the War Department, the bill went to a conference committee, on which Sumner was the principal Senate member. After long wrangling the conferees in February 1865 reported out a new version of the measure, authorizing an independent Department of Freedmen and Abandoned Lands, which, Sumner explained, would be "not unlike that of Agriculture" and "should not be subject either to the Treasury or the War [departments]." Anticipating some opposition from Democrats, Sumner was confident that most Republicans would accept the compromise and demanded immediate consideration of the bill. "I shall press it," he wrote General Butler, "and I think I have the votes."[2]

He was wrong. The Democrats did oppose, but so did many

[9] Sumner received sly hints that if he dropped his proposed bill to regulate the Camden & Amboy's "vampire monopoly" on railroad transportation between New York and Philadelphia the New Jersey Democrats in the lower House, who were in the pay of that railroad, might cast the deciding vote in favor of the amendment. Nicolay and Hay: *Lincoln*, X, 84–5. Cf. the erroneous account of this episode in Albert G. Riddle: *Recollections of War Times* (New York: G. P. Putnam's Sons; 1895), p. 325. For the story of Sumner's running battle with the Camden & Amboy see David F. Trask: "Charles Sumner and the New Jersey Railroad Monopoly during the Civil War," *N.J. Hist. Soc. Proceedings*, LXXV (1957), 259–75.

[1] *Cong. Globe*, 38 Cong., 2 Sess., p. 1010; Lincoln: *Works*, VIII, 404.

[2] Sumner: *Works*, VIII, 516; Sumner to Butler, Feb. 11, 1865, Butler MSS.

Republicans. The bill showed how sharply the majority party was divided over the issue of special protection for Negroes. It was not necessary to create "this vast machine" to supervise the freedmen and to subject them to the "system of fraud and swindling" that would surely result from it, urged Henderson of Missouri; "if you turn loose the negroes of the southern States and tell them to take care of themselves, they will do it." John P. Hale announced that he was against this coddling of black men at the expense of whites. He was as willing as Sumner himself to do anything needful to eradicate slavery, but "when he asks me to neglect my own kith and kin to legislate for the exclusive protection and benefit of colored men he goes a little further than I am willing to go." Henry S. Lane agreed: "I have an old-fashioned way of thinking which induces me to believe that a white man is as good as a negro if he behaves himself."

Vainly Sumner protested that Republican critics of the bill were echoing "a tone from the worst days of the olden time, when slavery filled this Chamber with its voice." Passionately he pleaded for justice for the blacks: "Whose sweat is it that has fertilized these lands? Whose rights lie at the very foundation of the war in which we are now engaged? Whose rights have for generations been assailed? It is fit that the freedmen should enjoy the first-fruits of returning justice, and they need them." [3] When the vote came, the Senate rejected the proposed independent Freedmen's Department. Joining the Democrats in defeating the bill were the men who were to become the major leaders of the Moderate Republicans during reconstruction: Doolittle, Grimes, and Trumbull.

Since it was clearly impossible for Sumner to sponsor a bill on this subject that the Senate could accept, Vice President Hamlin appointed a new conference committee, from which Sumner's name was dropped and Wilson's substituted. When the Freedmen's Bureau was established, it was not through Sumner's exertions.

Sumner also felt the reconstruction issue slipping out of his control. Strengthened by the election returns, Lincoln was pushing ahead with his reorganization of the Southern states. After

[3] *Cong. Globe,* 38 Cong., 2 Sess., pp. 962–3, 984–5, 989.

the establishment of a reconstructed government in Louisiana, General Banks came to Washington to lobby for its recognition, and at the President's request he remained in the capital all winter, using his prestige as a general and his influence as a former Speaker of the House of Representatives to urge the seating of the newly elected Louisiana Congressmen.

Though Sumner was positive that the Louisiana regime was not "strong enough in loyalty and freedom for an independent State," he was obliged to recognize the increasingly conservative temper of Republicans in Congress and the growing effectiveness of presidential pressure. During December 1864 he, along with other party leaders, had repeated talks with Lincoln and worked out a compromise that would preserve harmony between the President and the Congress. They agreed to readmit Louisiana under the regime Banks had helped create—"which ought not to be done," Sumner grumbled privately to Lieber—and at the same time to adopt for all the other Southern states a reconstruction act "giving the electoral franchise to 'all citizens,' without distinction of color." Sumner thought the plan a fair one: "Much as I am against the premature recognition of Louisiana, I will hold my peace, *if I can secure a rule for the other States*. . . ." In the long run he was confident that Louisiana could not stand out alone on the Negro suffrage issue, but "that the refluent waves from the other States would roll over her and she could be compelled into the same desired condition." [4]

During the Christmas recess the compromise so laboriously worked out during the previous weeks unraveled. As news of the plan leaked out, there were objections from all sides. Conservative Republicans thought that imposing Negro suffrage upon all the seceded states except Louisiana amounted to a capitulation to the Radicals; the compromise, gibed the New York *Herald*, was one in which "one side yields a little, and the other almost everything." Radical antislavery men found the plan equally objectionable. "If Congress allows the President to determine the conditions on which Louisiana shall return to the Union," asked the Boston *Commonwealth*, "what resistance can it make when

[4] Sumner to Lieber [Dec. 1864], Sumner MSS.; Sumner to Bright, Jan. 1, 1865, Bright MSS.; Boston *Advertiser*, Jan. 7, 1871.

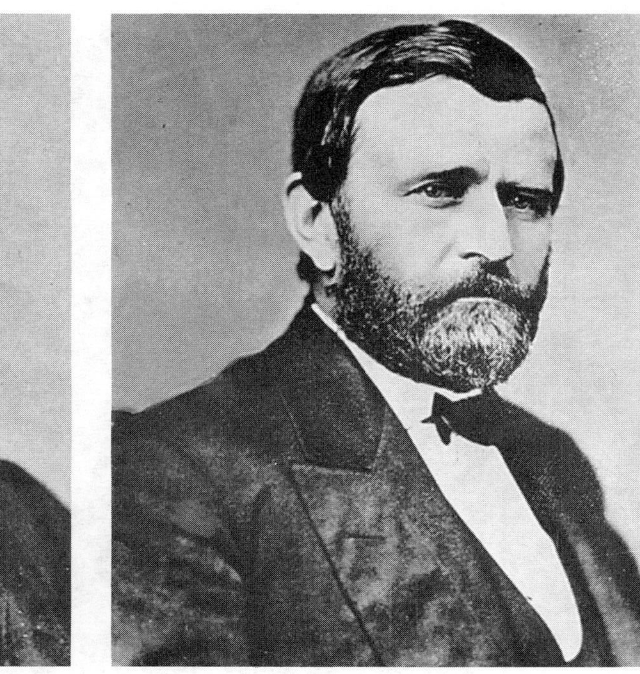

Andrew Johnson

Ulysses S. Grant

PRESIDENTIAL ENEMIES OF SUMNER

THE NATIONAL ARCHIVES

"I'm Not to Blame, for Being White, Sir!"
A Contemporary Caricature of Sumner's Concern for Blacks

THE LIBRARY OF CONGRESS

he brings Florida and Alabama along?" In January, when legislation to implement the compromise reached the House of Representatives, both Radicals and Conservatives sabotaged it, and by the middle of February it was clear that the plan was dead.[5]

If Sumner shed no tears for the compromise, neither had he reason to rejoice over its demise. Promptly the President's supporters moved to seat the two Senators from Louisiana. On the surface this proposal seemed an exact duplicate of the one rejected a year before, when the Senate declined to admit Fishback. In fact, however, the situations were quite different, because the Louisiana provisional government was clearly more viable than that of Arkansas had been, because the President was now politically powerful, and because, in a surprising shift, Trumbull, chairman of the Judiciary Committee, favored seating the Louisiana claimants. Declaring that the Louisiana provisional regime was "the legitimate government" of that state, Trumbull on February 18 moved that it was "entitled to the guarantees and all other rights of a State government under the Constitution of the United States" and urged that its Senators be given seats.

• 7 •

Trumbull's move to readmit Louisiana put Sumner in a dangerously embarrassing situation. If he agreed, he would help set a precedent for reorganizing all the Southern governments without Negro suffrage. If he opposed, he would have to come out in direct opposition to the President, at a time when his own political influence, even in Massachusetts, was at a low point. Characteristically he first tried to avoid the issue by begging Trumbull not to inaugurate the "dance of debate" upon so controversial a subject. Scornfully the Illinois Senator replied in his dry, schoolmasterish voice: "If a single negro is expelled from the cars in the District of Columbia, the voice of the Senator of Massachusetts is heard in this hall; he will repeal charters and take up the time of Congress about the rights of the negro, but when more than ten thousand voters, representing hundreds of thousands of loyal Union men, ask the protection of your laws and the rights

[5] Belz: *Reconstructing the Union,* pp. 257–8; McPherson: *The Struggle for Equality,* p. 308; Boston *Commonwealth,* Mar. 11, 1865.

guaranteed them by the Constitution, the Senator from Massachusetts says they shall not be heard. . . ." Doolittle harshly chimed in that nothing could be more practical than readmitting Louisiana, since its vote would be necessary to ratify the Thirteenth Amendment.[6]

Aware that an immediate vote would almost certainly seat the Louisiana claimants, Sumner and his fellow Radicals stalled for time. "Our constituents at home at this time," Howard noted, "are . . . very ignorant of the nature and qualities of this State government in Louisiana." Sumner hoped that delay would encourage "the discussion of the question and . . . appeal to the sober second thought of the people." [7] He began making dilatory motions. First he proposed a series of substitutes for Trumbull's proposal, all of which were intended to guarantee impartial suffrage in Louisiana. Finding that only seven or eight Senators were ready to back him, he tried to shift the debate to other issues, such as railroad regulation, which, in an unwonted mood of practicality, he called the only really urgent business before the Congress. Repeatedly defeated, he kept trying until several Senators shouted: "Give up." "Senators say, 'Give up,' " he responded. "That is not my habit." [8]

The debates over the readmission of Louisiana, which occupied most of the Senate's time from February 24 through February 27, exhibited Sumner in an angry and overbearing mood. The controversy made him desperately unhappy. First of all, in order to resist the recognition of the Louisiana regime, he and the seven or eight other Radicals who agreed with him were obliged to seek the cooperation of the Democrats, who were equally opposed to readmission, but for precisely opposite reasons. Sumner distrusted and disliked most Democratic Senators, especially those from the border states; they, in turn, regarded him as a personification of abolitionist ultraism. Hitherto his personal relations with them had not even been polite. Shortly before the Louisiana debates, for example, while he sat in the Senate anteroom with the visiting Frenchman, Auguste Laugel,

[6] *Cong. Globe*, 38 Cong., 2 Sess., pp. 1009–10.

[7] Ibid., p. 1128; Sumner to George Bancroft, Feb. 28, 1865, Bancroft MSS., Cornell Univ.

[8] Sumner: *Works*, IX, 312.

Lazarus Powell of Kentucky strode up to denounce him in an angry tirade. "You are a handful of fanatics engaged in destroying the country," Powell announced, just missing Sumner's shoe with the wad of tobacco he spat on the carpet. "It is very nice of you still to talk about the Constitution; why not frankly trample it under foot?" [9] Yet it was with this same Powell, and others like him, that Sumner and the Radicals must now work. When Powell denounced the Louisiana regime as "not a government formed by the people," Sumner followed by calling it only "a shadow"—only to have Garrett Davis, another extreme Democrat, embarrassingly echo: "but a shadow." Republicans taunted Sumner for collaborating with his own party's worst enemies, but doubtless he found more painful Powell's patronizing praise that the Senator from Massachusetts, so "seldom right on issues of this kind," was unexpectedly exhibiting "a lucid interval." [1]

A second reason for the ugly ill temper Sumner exhibited in the debates on Louisiana was the necessity of exposing, more fully than he was yet prepared to do in public, the details of his own reconstruction plans. Like every other Northern leader, he had long had difficulty in finding a constitutional basis for imposing conditions upon the Southern states when they sought readmission.[2] His "state suicide" resolutions of 1862 had been designed to show the existence of such authority in the federal government, but the phrase aroused so much antagonism that he dropped it. Then for a time, along with other Republicans, he spoke of the seceded states as having reverted to a territorial status, but when this theory also alarmed conservatives he was willing to renounce it since "strictly speaking, this rebel regime is not 'territory' of the U. States. It is only by analogy that we call it so." Increasingly, he, like most Radicals, came to depend upon the constitutional guarantee of a republican form of government as the basis for requiring drastic social changes in the South. But this position, too, offered problems: If Louisiana must free its

[9] Laugel: *United States During the Civil War*, p. 314.

[1] *Cong. Globe*, 38 Cong., 2 Sess., pp. 1061, 1064, 1106.

[2] Quotations in the following paragraphs are drawn from two letters in which Sumner most fully explained his constitutional theories about reconstruction: Sumner to Parke Godwin, Mar. 23 [1864], Bryant-Godwin MSS., and Sumner to "My dear Sir," Dec. 27, 1865, MS., New York Hist. Soc.

slaves in order to have a republican form of government, why should not Kentucky have to take the same step? If Negro suffrage was an essential to a republican form of government in South Carolina, was it not equally obligatory in Illinois, which disfranchised blacks?

Aware of these difficulties, Sumner for more than a year had been begging his friends not to be too precise in defining the constitutional status of the conquered South. Like Lincoln himself, he urged that it would not do to get "lost in a discussion, only worthy of schoolmen, on the metaphysical entity of a State." Instead, all should agree upon the "great unquestionable FACT" that the old governments in the South had ceased to exist with secession, that the rebel governments which replaced them could not be recognized, and that, therefore, new governments had to be set up in that section. The main point was *"to establish the jurisdiction of Congress over this region."* To secure this end, he wrote, "I accept any theory. . . . Call it 'territory'; say that we must exact security for the future; declare that we must require republican governments; in each of these cases the power of Congress cannot be easily disputed."

Now, however, the controversy over Louisiana put an end to this comfortable vagueness. Supporters of the provisional government tried to confront Sumner with a dilemma. In a heated exchange, Henderson maintained that drastic conditions could be imposed upon the Southern states only if they had been out of the Union—in other words, if their claimed right of secession was legitimate and if the Confederacy was a genuine independent nation at war with the United States. To this view Sumner vigorously objected: "No act of secession can take a State out of this Union." With Sumner thus committed, Henderson then announced that since everybody agreed that Louisiana was still part of the Union its government obviously had all the rights guaranteed to the states by the Constitution, including the right to regulate its own suffrage. Awkwardly Sumner, amid laughter from his colleagues, had to backtrack: "It is [in the Union] and it is not. The territory is in; but as yet there is no State government that is in." [3]

[3] *Cong. Globe,* 38 Cong., 2 Sess., p. 1103; Sumner: *Works,* IX, 314.

Beneath this constitutional issue was a more sensitive question, that of Negro suffrage. For at least a year Sumner had privately favored enfranchising the blacks. Of the abstract justice of allowing Negroes to vote he never had any doubts, and he was accustomed to seeing them at the polls in Massachusetts, where they were among his most devoted supporters. He had earnestly fought to enfranchise them in the District of Columbia and even in territories like Montana, where there were almost no black inhabitants. He had, however, hesitated before demanding that the huge numbers of politically inexperienced and mostly illiterate Negroes in the South be immediately given the vote. For a time he thought that impartial, rather than universal, suffrage might be desirable, a system that would forbid racial discrimination but would allow some educational or literacy test. But, he discovered, "there are very intelligent persons, especially among the freedmen, who cannot read and write." Even a minimal educational test would certainly exclude more blacks than whites; anyway, he recognized, "you *cannot get votes* of Congress to *disfranchise*" the illiterate Southern whites who already had the ballot. The result of "impartial" suffrage, then, would be to give political control of the South once more to those who had for the past four years been fighting against the Union. Since at least 1864, then, Sumner had been convinced that there would be "more harm in refusing than in the conceding the franchise" to the blacks, who, he observed, were about "as intelligent as the Irish just arrived." "Without their votes we cannot establish stable governments in the rebel states," he explained to Bright, who had reservations about enfranchising this large, unlettered electorate. "Their votes are as necessary as their musquets. . . . Without them, the old enemy will reappear and, under forms of law, take possession of the governments—choose magistrates and officers—and, in alliance with the Northern democracy, put us all in peril again, postpone the day of tranquility, and menace the national credit by assailing the national debt." "To my mind," he concluded, "the nation is now bound by self interest—aye, *self-defence*—to be thoroughly just." [4]

[4] Sumner to Lieber, Aug. 14, 1865, Sumner MSS.; Sumner to Bright, Mar. 13, 1865, Bright MSS.

The difficulty lay in discovering an acceptable constitutional rationalization for this policy. The only way Sumner could simultaneously insist that the Southern states were still in the Union and that the federal government could compel them to enfranchise Negroes was to argue that any state which excluded blacks from the polls lacked a government republican in form. But from this argument it followed that Kansas, Illinois, New York, and a dozen other Northern states which discriminated against Negro voting were as subject to reconstruction by the federal authority as were Louisiana and Virginia. Since racism ran deep in the North and except in New England there was an ugly hostility to Negro suffrage, this whole argument contained political dynamite for Radicals. Just to make Sumner's position entirely clear before the people, Henderson repeatedly pushed him to define his terms. When Sumner objected that the Louisiana regime did not have a truly republican form of government because it failed to ensure "complete freedom to every citizen, immunity from all oppression, and absolute equality before the law," the Missouri Senator pressed him to tell just how one would tell whether a government was truly republican. "If the loyal men, black and white, recognize it," Sumner explained, "then it will be republican in form." When cornered still further as to what such recognition meant, Sumner was obliged finally to avow his true view: The Louisiana government would be republican in form only after it adopted a guarantee that henceforth there should be "no denial of the electoral franchise or of any other rights, on account of color or race" and pledged that "all persons shall be equal before the law." [5]

Displeased at having to be so explicit on this dangerous issue, unhappy at having to cooperate with the hated Democrats, Sumner grew overbearing and intemperate as the Louisiana debates went on. Now that he was thoroughly angry, his opponents succeeded in goading him into a display of poor logic. Reverdy Johnson ridiculed the "fundamental condition" which Sumner wanted to impose upon Louisiana, pointing out that the state, once readmitted, could promptly repeal any such legislation, just as Ohio now could set aside the Northwest Ordinance prohibit-

[5] Sumner: *Works*, IX, 315, 317.

ing slavery. Sumner rose to the bait: "The Senator, then, thinks Ohio can enslave a fellow man?"

"Just as much as Massachusetts can," replied Johnson coolly.

"Massachusetts cannot," retorted Sumner.

"Why not?" Johnson queried.

"Massachusetts cannot do an act of injustice."

"Oh, indeed!" sneered Johnson, amid laughter. "I did not know that." [6]

Not since the debates over the Kansas-Nebraska act in 1854 had Sumner felt so desperate and so cornered. Indeed, as the debate progressed, he tended to equate the two struggles in his own mind. Both involved moral issues of enormous consequence. In 1865 as in 1854 it was a Senator from Illinois who was promoting an immoral measure. Like Stephen A. Douglas before him, Trumbull—after what Wade called "the most miraculous conversion that has taken place since St. Paul's time"—was now "proudly, confidently, almost menacingly" demanding the recognition of Louisiana, ready "to cram his resolution down the throats of the Senate." Equally culpable in Sumner's mind was Trumbull's co-adjutor, Doolittle, who was throwing "himself in the way of the march of human progress," exhibiting in his defense of the Louisiana government a "monomania which made him [thus] link himself with the slave power." [7]

Though a majority of Republican Senators were ready to readmit Louisiana, Sumner vowed to prevent a vote. The end of the session was near and the Senate still had to pass important laws needed to sustain the everyday operations of the government. Unless Trumbull agreed to drop the Louisiana question, Sumner threatened that no legislation would be adopted; he, along with a few other Radicals and their Democratic allies, would filibuster right up to March 4. "Does he hold in his hand the Senate of the United States," Trumbull stormed, "that, in his omnipotence, he is to say when votes shall be taken and public measures shall be passed? Has it come to this?" "What arrogance, what assumed superiority on the part of one man over

[6] Ibid., 316.
[7] *Cong. Globe*, 38 Cong., 2 Sess., pp. 1109–10.

his equals and peers. . . !" echoed Doolittle. Unabashed, Sumner replied: "I assure the Senator it is utterly impossible to take a vote." As Wade and Grimes moved in to assail the Louisiana bill, it became evident that Sumner was right. Trumbull surrendered when Sumner himself launched into another full-scale attack upon the "pretended State government in Louisiana." "To describe it," he announced, "I must use plain language. It is a mere seven-months' abortion, begotten by the bayonet in criminal conjunction with the spirit of caste, and born before its time, rickety, unformed, unfinished—whose continued existence will be a burden, a reproach, and a wrong." [8] At this point Sherman moved that the Senate turn to the appropriations bill, and for this session, at any rate, the admission of Louisiana was defeated.

Sumner's victory outraged conservative Republicans. "Whatever claims to the character of an honorable statesman Mr. Sumner may have heretofore held," the Springfield *Republican* announced, "he has forever destroyed them by this vulgar resort to the trickery of a pot-house politician." In private, Bowles, editor of that journal, fumed that Sumner's conduct was "perfectly unjustifiable . . . undignified, disgraceful." Dana felt that Sumner acted "like a madman . . . in the positions he took, the arguments he advanced, and the language he used to 20 out of 25 Republican Senators who differed from him." "If I could here [*sic*] that he was out of his head from opium or even N. E. rum . . . ," Dana added, "I should be relieved . . . his answers to questions were boyish or crazy. I don't know which." [9]

Among Radicals, on the other hand, the chorus of praise was equally ardent. "Thanks! thanks! thanks!" cheered Robinson, who was now firmly back in Sumner's camp. Sumner's success in keeping out "the *sham* State of Louisiana," exulted the abolitionist Elizur Wright, was "worth any three average military victories." "The friends of Freedom all over the country . . . ," wrote Frederick Douglass, "will look to you all the more, now that peace dawns, and the final settlement of our national trou-

[8] Ibid., pp. 1107, 1109, 1126, 1129.

[9] Springfield *Republican* quoted in Boston *Commonwealth*, Mar. 18, 1865; Merriam: *Life of Bowles*, I, 419; Dana to C. F. Adams, Mar. 3, 1865, Adams MSS.

bles is at hand." "We have watched your white plume with a fearful delight," wrote Wendell Phillips. "Could we only hope this defeat would be final, our joy would be unmixed." [1]

Aware that the victory was only a temporary success, Sumner was already preparing for the next struggle. "I think that during the summer and autumn, before the next Congress, the country can be rallied . . . ," he told Bird.[2]

• 8 •

Sumner was aware of Lincoln's displeasure with his course. Deeply committed to the regime Banks had set up in Louisiana, the President grew angry when Sumner blocked its recognition and growled to his private secretary that the Senator was attempting "to change this Government from its original form and make it a strong centralized power." He concluded that Sumner was obsessive on the question of Negro rights and told the cabinet: "Had the Louisianians inserted the negro in their Constitution, and had that instrument been in all other respects the same, Mr. Sumner would never have excepted to that Constitution." The extent of the President's dissatisfaction with the Senator became a matter of speculation in the newspapers, and the New York *Herald* announced that the intimate personal relations which had hitherto existed between the two men must now end since Sumner had "kicked the pet scheme of the President down the marble steps of the Senate Chamber." [3]

In fact, there was no break, and on March 5, only a few days after Sumner had talked the Louisiana bill to death, he received a note from Lincoln:

> I should be pleased for you to accompany us to-morrow evening at ten o'clock, on a visit of half an hour to the Inaugeral-ball. I inclose a ticket. Our carriage will call for you at half past nine.[4]

[1] Sumner: *Works*, IX, 324–8.

[2] Mar. 1, 1865, MS., Harvard Univ.

[3] Boston *Advertiser*, Jan. 7, 1871; Nicolay and Hay: *Lincoln*, X, 85; Pierce, IV, 219, note.

[4] Lincoln: *Works*, VIII, 334. The repetition of this invitation, dated the following day (ibid., VIII, 337), is puzzling, if it is indeed authentic.

Though Sumner had had no intention of attending the ball, he joined the presidential party at the appointed hour. Shortly after ten o'clock guards cleared a path through the crowds in the central hallway of the huge Patent Office building, and, as the band played "Hail to the Chief," President Lincoln, accompanied by Speaker Schuyler Colfax, entered. Holding Sumner's arm, Mrs. Lincoln, richly dressed in white moire ornamented with lace, immediately followed. As the spectators broke into applause, the party strolled down the long hall. When they returned to the central dais, Sumner tried to excuse himself, saying that people really wanted to see only the President, but Lincoln insisted that he remain seated. After an hour Sumner escorted Mary Lincoln to supper, and shortly after midnight the presidential party of four left.

Inevitably there was comment about the conspicuous attention the President paid Sumner. The Marquis de Chambrun, who attended the ball, saw the episode as a scene in a morality play: "Abolitionism victorious thus made its entry together with the great force which had annihilated the enemy." [5] The same New York *Herald* which only a few days earlier had predicted a break between Lincoln and Sumner now concluded that "the President had indorsed his Reconstruction theories."

The *Herald*'s second verdict was almost as erroneous as its first. What Sumner's presence at the inaugural ball did symbolize was a determination on the part both of the President and of the Senator to avoid a break in personal relations even though they differed over political issues. Neither man minimized the significance of those differences. Lincoln believed that the President, acting under the war powers, must take the initiative in reconstruction; Sumner, originally indifferent as to what agency of the federal government undertook the process, was now firmly committed to Congressional control over the reorganization of the South. Lincoln favored using the military to set up provisional regimes in the conquered South, but Sumner, reverting more and more to his original pacifism as the war neared an end, insisted that "a government founded on military power, or hav-

[5] Adolphe de Chambrun: *Impressions of Lincoln and the Civil War* (New York: Random House; 1952), pp. 33–4.

ing its origin in military orders, cannot be 'republican in form,' according to the requirement of the Constitution."[6] Aware of the weaknesses of the provisional regimes set up in the South, Lincoln felt that these embryos should be protected and encouraged on the grounds that ". . . we shall sooner have the fowl by hatching the egg than by smashing it." Sumner's reply was: "The eggs of crocodiles can produce only crocodiles; and it is not easy to see how eggs laid by military power can be hatched into an American State."[7]

Though these differences were real and at times sharp, both Senator and President were resolved that they should not be exaggerated. Sumner and Lincoln agreed upon many questions concerning reconstruction. Both insisted that there could be no peace without the death of slavery. Both recognized that conditions would have to be imposed upon the Southern states before they could be readmitted, and both now found authority for such conditions in the constitutional guarantee of a republican form of government in each state. Both wanted to avoid the "practically immaterial" or "metaphysical" question of whether the Southern states were really in or out of the Union.[8]

Lincoln and Sumner were also agreed upon the necessity of protecting Southern Unionists once the war ended. The President thought of Southern loyalists as being chiefly white, while Sumner believed the only trustworthy Unionists in the South were black; but both men saw that the problem was, as Lincoln remarked as early as November 1863, how "to keep the rebellious populations from overwhelming and outvoting the loyal minority" once peace was restored and federal troops were withdrawn.[9] Slowly both Senator and President came to conclude that the only realistic guarantee was to give the former slaves the ballot. After investigating the possibility of requiring impartial suffrage, Sumner now insisted upon immediate universal enfranchisement; Lincoln, moving more slowly, wanted to

[6] Sumner: *Works*, IX, 331.

[7] Lincoln: *Works*, VIII, 604; Sumner: *Works*, X, 44. Sumner probably derived this retort from a letter by several North Carolina freedmen urging: "Better 'smash the egg' than permit it to produce a viper." Ibid., IX, 363.

[8] Cf. Sumner to Parke Godwin, Mar. 23 [1864], Bryant-Godwin MSS., and Lincoln: *Works*, VIII, 403.

[9] Dennett (ed.): *Lincoln and the Civil War*, p. 113.

give the vote to "the very intelligent [Negroes], and especially those who have fought gallantly in our ranks," and in the last public speech he ever made announced his regret that the reconstructed government of Louisiana had failed to enfranchise any blacks.[1]

That President and Senator should agree upon so many basic issues was not surprising, for both men drew their political ideas from the same well. It was not until after Lincoln's death, when Sumner had to restudy his speeches and letters in order to prepare a eulogy, that the Senator came to understand how much both their political philosophies derived from the Declaration of Independence.[2] When Lincoln in his debates with Stephen A. Douglas said that he never had an idea, politically, which did not spring from the Declaration, he used words which Sumner could have echoed; when Lincoln in his 1860 Cooper Union address argued that the Union dated not from the Constitution but from 1776, he was voicing an idea basic to Sumner's antislavery philosophy. When Sumner in turn announced during the Louisiana debates: "We shall insist upon the Declaration of Independence as the foundation of the new state governments,"[3] he could hardly fail to hope that a President who believed with equal fervor in that Declaration would ultimately see the justice of his arguments.

Practical self-interest as well as philosophical agreement impelled the President and the Senator to continue working together despite differences. Aware that Sumner had few followers and fewer friends in the Senate, Lincoln knew that the Senator was the voice of a large, articulate element with great moral influence throughout the North; with Sumner at his side, the President could ignore the sniping from ultra-abolitionists. There was, then, perhaps an undertone of command in his

[1] Lincoln: *Works,* VII, 243; VIII, 403. An alleged letter from Lincoln urging universal suffrage (ibid., VIII, 101) is spurious.

[2] The most important and interesting part of the eulogy Sumner delivered on Lincoln in Boston on June 1, 1865, is that which traces the significance of the Declaration of Independence in the President's thought. Sumner: *Works,* IX, 380–93.

[3] Sumner to George Bancroft, Feb. 28, 1865, Bancroft MSS., Cornell Univ.

urgent invitation for Sumner to attend the inaugural ball as a member of the presidential party.[4]

For Sumner, too, there were practical advantages in staying on good terms with a President who had just been chosen to remain four more years in the White House. The feeling was widespread that, with the beginning of the new term or at least with the end of the fighting, Lincoln would reorganize his cabinet. Only a few of the original appointees remained. Both Chase and Blair had been dropped before the 1864 election; Attorney General Bates resigned shortly after it; and Fessenden left the Treasury Department in March 1865 to return to the Senate. Naturally Sumner watched all these changes with close attention in order to make sure that any new cabinet appointee, especially from New England, should be friendly and well disposed.

The strongest New England contender was a man, Sumner feared, who was neither. Having served four terms as governor of Massachusetts and having just been reelected to a fifth, John A. Andrew was ready to move onto the national stage, and he believed that, if named Attorney General, he could bring to the Lincoln administration that "coherence, method, purpose and consistency" which it had hitherto lacked.[5] The vigorous campaign to put Andrew into the cabinet had support from diverse elements—from the Bird Club, whose members remembered Andrew's stalwart antislavery record; from Boston businessmen, impressed by Andrew's zeal and efficiency; from nine of the Massachusetts congressional delegation; from Western Congressmen; from the powerful Blair family; and from Conservative Thurlow Weed.

When Andrew's backers came to Washington in February, they learned they could not count on Sumner's support. To Bird, Sumner hinted that he was not sure that Andrew was a loyal friend. To be sure, he admitted, the governor had finally helped in the 1862 campaign, but his efforts had been belated and mini-

[4] Margaret Leech: *Reveille in Washington, 1860–1865* (New York: Harper & Brothers Publishers; 1941), p. 372.

[5] Andrew to Thurlow Weed, Feb. 6, 1865, Weed MSS.

mal. Since that time Andrew had allowed his liaison man in Washington, A. G. Browne, Jr., to attack and abuse Sumner. Anyway, there were half a dozen strong Massachusetts candidates for a cabinet post, including General Butler, Representative Samuel Hooper, whom Lincoln himself had mentioned in connection with the Treasury Department, and Boutwell, with whom Sumner was "in habits of daily and most friendly intercourse." As senior Senator from Massachusetts it would be unbecoming for him to play favorites. Besides, he did not think Andrew ought to leave Massachusetts, where he was badly needed and where he had a kind of "contract with the people" because of his recent reelection. It was, Sumner told Andrew's friends, the Governor's "best interest . . . not to come" to Washington.[6]

Though furious, Andrew's supporters were unable to budge Sumner and they rightly suspected that he had another motive, which he let slip in remarking that if the Governor came to Washington he would be entering "a field here *belonging to others.*" Rumor had it that Seward would shortly resign, for he was supposed to have told Butler that "he had *accomplished his object as Secretary of State in keeping foreign powers out of our conflict—that a man should not repeat himself.*"[7] Sumner was most often mentioned as his likely successor, and he had the energetic backing of the Conservative Blair family, who were moved less by ideology than by personal hatred for Seward but who also had the cynical notion that if Lincoln gave offices to Radical Republicans they in turn would give the President a free hand in reconstruction.[8]

Unquestionably Sumner was receptive to the idea of becoming Secretary of State. With the end of the war he was certain that the United States would turn its attention to settling diffi-

[6] Bird to Sumner [Feb. 27, 1865], Sumner MSS.; W. L. Burt to Andrew, Feb. 1, 1865, Andrew MSS.; J. M. Forbes to Andrew, Feb. 12, 1865, ibid.; Sumner to E. P. Whipple, July 3, 1871, Whipple MSS.

[7] W. L. Burt to Andrew, Feb. 1, 1865, Andrew MSS.; F. P. Blair, Sr., to Lincoln, Feb. 22, 1865, Lincoln MSS.

[8] The Blairs were willing to support either Andrew or Sumner for the cabinet, though they tended to favor making Sumner Secretary of State and Andrew his successor in the Senate. J. M. Forbes to Andrew, Feb. 11 and 13, 1863, Andrew MSS. For the Blair strategy, see Montgomery Blair to Andrew, Feb. 18, 1867, ibid.

culties with Great Britain and France, and he believed that the ensuing negotiations were "destined to be of importance in the history of International Law." [9] Though his relations with Seward had mellowed, he still held the Secretary in contempt, since "he knew nothing of international law," [1] and he thought himself eminently qualified to conduct such delicate diplomacy. After all, he was the one American who had powerful contacts in the British government and who really knew how to get along with Englishmen. Insensitive to the feelings of others, Sumner did not realize how completely his 1863 speech on foreign relations had outraged the British, and he had no idea that the members of the British mission in Washington regarded him as a dangerous enemy. "If that man ever gets into power," the reticent Lord Lyons predicted, "he will, under some highly moral pretence, sacrifice the highest public interests to his personal position. Of all your public men, he is the one for whom I have brought away the least respect." [2] So long as there was a possibility that Sumner himself might become Secretary of State, he could not back Andrew or any other New Englander for the cabinet. Since Lincoln had not actually offered him the position and since Sumner could never permit himself to appear a seeker for office, he could not candidly explain his difficulty to Andrew's friends. He hinted that he had been "indirectly offered" the State Department through the Blairs—but promptly hedged by observing that he was not sure he wanted a cabinet post "*this year*, having some more speeches to make in [the] Senate." [3]

Blunt and outspoken, Andrew exploded when he learned of Sumner's cautious ambiguity. "If Massachusetts can be properly represented in the Cabinet she ought to be," he raged. "And it is extraordinary that Mr. Sumner should not see its importance. . . . But it is nothing to the purpose for Mr. Sumner to be talking about Mr. Hooper, with an *if*, and about Mr. Boutwell

[9] Sumner to Duchess of Argyll, Mar. 21, 1865, Argyll MSS.

[1] Sumner's words were thus reported by the Earl of Airlie, who visited him in Newport in August 1864. New York *Evening Post*, Jan. 27, 1865. Sumner was furious at this breach of confidence. J. V. L. Pruyn: Diary, Jan. 28, 1865, Pruyn MSS.

[2] Goldwin Smith to C. E. Norton, Dec. 29, 1864, Norton MSS.

[3] J. M. Forbes to Andrew, Feb. 12, 1865, and W. L. Burt to Andrew, Feb. 1, 1865, Andrew MSS.

with a *but,* and estimating my duties at home, with a parenthesis concerning himself, when the delegation can unite on neither of them, and when he will not agree to accept, should he be agreed upon." If Sumner could and would take the State Department, Andrew announced he would not be a candidate for any other cabinet post. The governor's friends thought this statement would force Sumner either to become an open applicant for a cabinet appointment or to throw all his support to Andrew.[4] Instead, to their fury, he joined with Wilson in procuring for the governor a relatively minor appointment to a federal district judgeship, which Andrew curtly rejected.

As one of Andrew's aides cynically noted, all these intricate negotiations served to bind Sumner to the President at a time when the policies of the two men on reconstruction seemed diametrically opposed. "I have really come to the conclusion," this friend wrote Andrew in early February after studying the Washington scene, "that the President is deliberately fooling and cheating him [Sumner] in this cabinet matter to get his aid on the admission of Louisiana—and he has been caught by these tricks." [5] Whether Lincoln followed such a calculated policy is dubious; if he did, it is certain that it failed to win Sumner's support for the readmission of Louisiana. But there is no doubt that the possibility of a cabinet appointment was one of the forces which kept Sumner from going into outright opposition.

During the winter of 1864–65 both the Lincolns continued to shower the lonely bachelor Senator with social courtesies.[6] The invitation to the inaugural ball was simply the most conspicuous of these occasions. Repeatedly they singled him out as their guest at the theater or the opera; sometimes he and a member of the diplomatic corps were the only other members of the presidential party, though, as the official responsible for Lincoln's

[4] Andrew to W. L. Burt, Feb. 6, 1865, copy, ibid.; J. M. Forbes to Andrew, Feb. 26, 1865, ibid.; Springfield *Weekly Republican,* Mar. 4, 1865. A copy of Andrew's statement, from the Boston *Evening Transcript,* Mar. 1, 1865, found its way into Lincoln's papers.

[5] W. L. Burt to Andrew, Feb. 1, 1865, ibid.

[6] The belated recollection of a White House guard that Lincoln gave orders "that Senator Sumner should not be admitted to the White House" is obviously erroneous. William H. Crook: *Through Five Administrations,* ed. Margarita S. Gerry (New York: Harper & Brothers Publishers; 1910), pp. 34–7.

safety warned the President, "neither . . . could defend themselves against an assault from any able-bodied woman in this city."[7] Just as the debates over Louisiana began, Sumner was invited to the White House for a state dinner.

Always closer to Mary Lincoln than to her puzzling husband, Sumner saw even more of the President's wife than usual while Congress was in session. She consulted with him upon several appointments, which were of course, none of her business, and warmly agreed with his suspicions of General Banks, whom both feared as a possible cabinet appointee. So similar were their views on reconstruction that Mrs. Lincoln wrote a friend: "Mr. Sumner says he wishes my husband was as ardent an abolitionist as I am." It was natural, then, that on April 3 when Mary Lincoln learned of the fall of Richmond she should dash off a note to Sumner: "This is almost too much happiness to be realized!" That evening Sumner and Baron Gerolt, the Prussian minister, came to the White House to celebrate the victory in the absence of the President, who was at City Point near Grant's army, and, buoyed by the excitement, the Senator had a gay time and laughed immoderately.[8]

The next day Sumner, along with Secretary of the Interior Harlan, Attorney General Speed, and others, set out with Mrs. Lincoln for City Point. Before they arrived, the President's wife received news that Seward had suffered a grave injury in a carriage accident and, alone in the early morning hours, she turned to Sumner for advice as to whether to proceed or to return to Washington. "The more I think of it, the more I feel that we must wait for the President," Sumner replied.[9] They went ahead to City Point, where they received the cheering news that Seward's injuries, though serious, were not fatal and the disturbing information that the President, almost without escort, had already been in captured Richmond. Mary Lincoln was angry that her husband had made his dramatic entrance into the Con-

[7] Ward H. Lamon to Lincoln, Dec. 10, 1864, copy, Lamon MSS.

[8] Mary Lincoln to Sumner [Nov. 1864], Nov. 24 [1864], Mar. 19, 1865, and April 3 [1865], Sumner MSS.; Ruth P. Randall: *Mary Lincoln*, p. 355; Mary Lincoln to Abram Wakeman, April 4 [1865], MS. in private hands.

[9] Mary Lincoln to Sumner [April 6, 1865], Sumner MSS.; Sumner [to Mary Lincoln, April 6, 1865], MS. owned by Mr. Victor Jacobs, of Dayton, Ohio.

federate capital without waiting for her, and Sumner, who feared an assassination attempt upon himself during this trip, was worried that the President had taken such an unnecessary risk. Both were relieved to learn that Richmond whites had either fled or had bolted themselves in their houses during Lincoln's visit and that the only people who showed themselves were Negroes.[1]

Encouraged by the President's boldness, Mrs. Lincoln's party pushed on to Richmond, with a cavalry escort, and they visited both the Confederate White House, where, as Mrs. Lincoln reported, " 'the banquet halls' of Jeff Davis looked sad and deserted" and the capitol, where Sumner made particular inquiry about the fate of the Southern archives. Jubilant and high-spirited, the whole party had a merry time, and, Mary Lincoln wrote, "even our stately, dignified Mr. Sumner acknowledged himself transformed, into a lad of sixteen." [2]

Sumner returned to Washington with President and Mrs. Lincoln aboard the *River Queen.* Once again Lincoln exhibited his skill in the delicate art of managing the Senator. He steered conversation away from controversial issues of reconstruction and did not discuss his decision to permit the reconvening of the Virginia Confederate legislature in order to take that state out of the war. Instead, he reminisced in a mellow, retrospective tone about the events of the past four years and once again neutralized Sumner's anticipated opposition by talk of cabinet appointments. Lincoln could not understand, he said, how people could think that Seward's had been the paramount influence in his administration. "I have counselled with you," he told Sumner, "twice as much as I ever did with him." The tone of the President's remark suggested to Sumner that he might soon "be called to decide the question, whether to quit the Senate." [3]

Sumner did not see Lincoln during the days following their

[1] Chambrun: *Impressions of Lincoln and the Civil War,* p. 108; Sumner to Chase [April 1865], MS., Henry E. Huntington Lib.

[2] Mary Lincoln to Abram Wakeman, April 13 [1865], MS. in private hands. During this visit Sumner picked up the gavel used by the speaker of the Confederate House of Representatives. Lincoln insisted that he give it to Speaker Colfax. A. Belin Sarmiento (ed.): *Obras de D. F. Sarmiento* (Santiago de Chile: Imprenta Gutenberg; 1887–1903), XXVII, 271.

[3] Sumner to Bird, April 16, 1871, Bird MSS.

return from City Point. Though Mrs. Lincoln invited him to the White House on April 11, when the President was expected to speak to serenaders celebrating Lee's surrender at Appomattox, Sumner did not go. Anticipating that Lincoln would make some new pronouncement upon the subject of reconstruction, he had no intention of again allowing his presence to be used, as it had been at the inaugural ball, to give symbolic approval. "I . . . was unwilling," he explained to Chase, "to put myself in the position of opposing him at his own balcony or assenting by silence." The President's remarks, strongly defending the reconstructed government of Louisiana, were precisely what he feared, and the speech, when linked with Lincoln's willingness to recognize the Confederate authorities in Virginia, seemed to augur ominous "confusion and uncertainty in the future—with hot controversy." "Alas! Alas!" he lamented, and could take comfort only from the fact that Lincoln's low-keyed, thoughtful address had "fallen very dead" and that the proposal to reconvene the Virginia legislature was likely to fail so completely that the President could still act "without any embarrassment in adopting a just and safe system" of reconstruction.[4]

On the evening of Friday, April 14, Sumner was still in this depressed mood when he stopped by the rooms of John Conness on Thirteenth Street to have a glass of wine with the California Senator and William M. Stewart, Senator from the newly admitted state of Nevada.[5] After the three had been talking for fifteen or twenty minutes, Conness's Negro servant burst in, shouting: "Mr. Lincoln is assassinated in the theatre. Mr. Seward is murdered in his bed. There's murder in the streets." The three Senators rushed to the White House, Stewart, the youngest, taking the lead, and Sumner, who was not in good physical trim, trail-

[4] Sumner to Chase, April 12, 1865, Chase MSS., Lib. of Cong.; Sumner to Chase, April 13, 1865, MS., Univ. of Chicago; Sumner to Chase [April 1865], MS., Henry E. Huntington Lib.; Sumner to Lieber, March [i.e., April] 13, 1865, Sumner MSS.

[5] The following account of Sumner's course during the night after Lincoln's assassination rests on Moorfield Storey: "Dickens, Stanton, Sumner, and Storey," *Atlantic Monthly*, CXLV (1930), 463–5; William M. Stewart: *Reminiscences*, ed. George R. Brown (New York: The Neale Publishing Company; 1908), pp. 191–2; Welles: *Diary*, II, 286–8; Sumner to Duchess of Argyll, April 24, 1865, Argyll MSS.

ing behind. They found that the White House sentinels had not yet heard the news.

Gathering up Robert Todd Lincoln, the President's oldest son, they jumped into a hack and drove rapidly to Ford's theater, where they learned that the injured President had already been moved to a house across the street. Meeting them at the door, the surgeon-general told them that the injuries were mortal, that too many people had already crowded into the room with the dying President, but that, since they were Senators, they could go in if they chose. Stewart and Conness retired, but Sumner exclaimed: "I will go in!" In the second room he found Lincoln lying diagonally across the bed, breathing heavily, with his eyes half open. Sumner took his hand and tried to speak to him, but one of the physicians said: "It's no use, Mr. Sumner—he can't hear you. He is dead." "No, he isn't dead," Sumner insisted. "Look at his face; he is breathing." But the doctors explained that there was no hope that he could regain consciousness.

Nevertheless Sumner remained at Lincoln's bedside from a quarter till eleven until after seven the next morning, holding the President's hand in his own and sobbing with his own head bowed until it almost touched the pillow. At about seven it was clear that death was near. Mary Lincoln paid her last visit, and Robert gave way to overpowering grief, crying aloud and resting his head on Sumner's tall shoulder for support.

After Lincoln breathed his last breath, Sumner left, saying: "Now for Mr. Seward." He had heard nothing of the condition of the Secretary of State, who, already injured in his carriage accident, had been the subject of an assassination attempt, or that of his son Frederick, the Assistant Secretary of State, who had also been attacked. At the Secretary's house he found Mrs. Seward, long his friend and his ally in his early struggles against slavery, seated, dazed, on the stairs leading to the third floor. "Charles Sumner," she said, seizing his hand, "they have murdered my husband, they have murdered my boy." After a few more words she suddenly rose, exclaimed: "I must fly," and disappeared. Sumner never saw her again, for, though both the Secretary of State and his son ultimately recovered from that night of horror, Frances Seward did not. She died within a few weeks.

It was still early in the morning when Sumner returned to his rooms on the corner of F and 13th Streets, to find that Secretary of War Stanton, fearing that he too might have been marked for assassination, had posted a guard outside. Before his untasted breakfast he sat haggard and stern as he contemplated "the rebellion defeated and degraded to assassination."[6] He had always said that Southern slavery led inevitably to barbarism.

[6] Pierce, IV, 238.

CHAPTER VI

Very Like Robespierre

SUMNER had no idea what to expect from the new President. Though he had served in the Senate with Andrew Johnson from 1857 to 1862, the two men were hardly acquainted. During the first two years of Johnson's term, Sumner was mostly absent, still recovering from the Brooks assault. Anyway, Johnson, a Democrat, a Southerner, and a slaveholder, was not a man whose friendship he would seek. On the positive side, Sumner knew of the Tennessean's courageous decision to stand by the Union, even when his own state seceded, and of his strenuous efforts as military governor to restore loyalty in Tennessee. On the other hand, he remembered all too painfully the disgraceful public exhibition Johnson had made of himself, just a few weeks earlier, when he took his oath as Vice President. Weakened after a bout of typhoid fever, Johnson drank some whiskey just prior to the ceremonies, and he made a rambling, egotistical speech, to which the President, the cabinet, and the Congress had to listen in shame. Outraged by the wretched affair, Sumner thought it "the most unfortunate thing that had ever occurred in our history." Since the House of Representatives was not in session, there could be no move to impeach the Vice President, but he assembled the Senate Republican caucus and demanded that Johnson be forced to resign from the office he had so dishonored. His colleagues, however, feeling that Johnson's behavior, though unfortunate, was excusable and complaining that nobody would have paid much attention to his intoxication "if Sumner hadn't been so exquisite about it," voted down his motion.[1]

It was to this same Andrew Johnson that Sumner paid his respects on the evening of April 15, 1865, on the pretext of needing to make arrangements for presenting the new British minister, Sir Frederick Bruce. Of course neither man referred to their past differences. Feeling overwhelmed by his new responsibilities, Johnson was nevertheless composed and resolute. A stocky, stalwart man, with swarthy complexion, jet-black hair, piercing dark eyes, and a firm mouth, the new President made an excellent impression. The message of courtesy and good will which he asked Sumner to convey to Bruce was all that could be asked. Then Sumner turned the conversation to the real object of his visit—Johnson's policy toward the defeated rebels. "I found him careful in what he said," he reported to Bright, "but very determined." [2]

In a second interview, on the following evening, Sumner came to have an even better opinion of the President. Before going to the White House he was disheartened by a meeting in the War Office with Secretary Stanton, Speaker Colfax, and several other Republicans to discuss proposed proclamations declaring the fighting at an end in Virginia and North Carolina. Sumner found that Stanton's draft made no provision for enfranchising the Negro, because, the Secretary said, Republicans differed so sharply on that question. Considering the Negro's right to vote "the essence, the great essential," Sumner announced that he, for one, would not proceed a step in the whole question of reconstruction "unless the black-man had his rights," but he was unable to persuade the others.[3] To his enormous relief, when he and Chief Justice Chase later called on the President, Johnson seemed better to understand "the rights and

[1] J. V. L. Pruyn: Diary, Mar. 4, 1865, Pruyn MSS.; Henry Wilson: *History of the Rise and Fall of the Slave Power in America* (Boston: Houghton, Mifflin and Company; 1877), III, 578; Springfield *Weekly Republican*, Mar. 18, 1865; A. G. Browne, Jr., to Andrew, Mar. 21, 1865, Andrew MSS.

[2] Sumner to Duchess of Argyll, April 24, 1865, Argyll MSS.; Sumner to Bright, April 18, 1865, Bright MSS.

[3] Gideon Welles, untitled MS., Brown Univ. Lib. Cf. Welles: *Diary*, II, 291.

necessities of the case." Since the President thought it would "disarm party at home" for the Negro suffrage movement to "appear to proceed from the [Southern] people," Chase undertook to tour the war-torn region in order to inform the whites that Johnson wanted to promote organization of state governments without distinction of color. Though Sumner himself did not think "the work could be effectively done without *Federal authority,*" he regarded "the *modus operandi* as an inferior question" so long as the result was to secure "*Equality before the law* . . . for all without distinction of color." All three men were beaming when Johnson ended the protracted interview by declaring: "There is no difference between us." [4]

Lighthearted, Sumner and Chase left the White House "charmed by his sympathy, which was entirely different from his predecessor's." For the first time since the Republicans came into power, Sumner's perennial difficulty of having to reconcile his own principles and the interests of his constituents with the political necessities of the national administration appeared to have been resolved; his ideas and Johnson's were the same. Though there is nothing to suggest that Sumner—unlike Wade and some of the vindictives—ever rejoiced in Lincoln's assassination, it is clear that these early interviews with Johnson reconciled him to the death of an old friend. Perhaps, as he came to think, the murder of Lincoln was "a judgment of the Lord," which was "needed to lift the country into a more perfect justice and to inspire a sublimer faith." "Family and friends may mourn," he wrote Bright in an elegaic mood; "but his death will do more for the cause than any human life, for it will fix the sentiments of the Country—perhaps of mankind. To my mind few have been happier." [5]

Each successive interview with Johnson confirmed Sumner's conviction that Providence had ordained the elevation of the new President. On all important issues the two men seemed to agree. Despite Johnson's early, injudicious remarks about punishing traitors, Sumner was cheered to find that the Presi-

[4] Sumner to Bird, April 25, 1865, Bird MSS.; Sumner to Lieber, May 2, 1865, Sumner MSS.

[5] Sumner: *Works*, IX, 407; Sumner to Bright, May 1, 1865, Bright MSS.

dent shared his view that Confederate leaders should be sent into exile rather than executed. Because "the men who have made so many tombs and vacant chairs must not be allowed to govern us again," Sumner favored driving perhaps five hundred prominent ex-Confederates out of the country, starting with former Senator R. M. T. Hunter of Virginia. "So long as these people remain at home, even though shut out from office, they will be so many centers of influence, through correspondence, conversation and the subtle freemasonry of kindred ideas," he explained to Lieber. "Let them all go with their lives, and learn abroad how to appreciate the crime they have committed." [6] Like Johnson, he felt that only Jefferson Davis should receive a harsher treatment. Sumner was sorry that Union troops took the Confederate President prisoner. "I never cease to regret that Jeff. Davis was not shot at the time of his capture," he told Chase. But since Davis was a prisoner and since, according to evidence Stanton was amassing, he appeared to have been responsible for the atrocities at Andersonville prison and personally implicated in the plot to assassinate Lincoln, he had to be punished. "He is an assassin," Sumner assured Bright. "A man who serves Slavery must be an assassin." [7]

Sumner was pleased that Johnson also agreed with him about the timing of reconstruction. The President told Wade that, unlike Lincoln, he opposed the readmission of Louisiana under its provisional government. To Sumner he made it clear that he deprecated haste, saying "that no state can be *precipitated* into the Union; that rebel States must go through a term of *probation*." [8] So encouraged was Sumner that he made no objection when the President on May 9 announced that the United States would recognize and assist the Unionist government of Francis H. Pierpont in Virginia, although in the previous session of Congress Sumner had contemptuously termed that regime "little more than the Common Council of Alexandria." Even

[6] Sumner to Bright, April 18, 1865, ibid.; Sumner to Lieber, Aug. 2, 1865, Sumner MSS.

[7] Sumner to Chase, June 25, 1865, Chase MSS., Lib. of Cong.; Sumner to Bright, June 5 and Aug. 8, 1865, Bright MSS. Cf. Sumner to W. Greene, July 7, 1865, MS., Hist. and Phil. Soc. of Ohio.

[8] Sumner to Lieber, May 2, 1865, Sumner MSS.

when Thaddeus Stevens protested that Johnson's action "so bedeviled matters as to render them incurable" and urged the summoning of a special session of Congress, Sumner remained blandly optimistic.

What Sumner found most encouraging of all was Johnson's attitude toward Negro suffrage. "Justice to the colored race" was Sumner's constant theme in the frequent conversations he held with the President in late April and early May, and he understood they both desired "the rebel states to be organized without any distinction of color." "On this question, Mr. Sumner," Johnson told him, "there is no difference between us; you and I are alike." Jubilant, Sumner replied that in that event there could be no division in the Union party, and Johnson promptly announced: "I mean to keep you all together." [9]

There remained, Sumner recognized, the need to determine what "process, modes and machinery" would best secure Negro suffrage, but he thought this was essentially a procedural question, which time in any case would decide. Realizing that Johnson hoped impartial suffrage would be "brought about by a spontaneous movement on the part of the Southern States," which he promised to encourage "by refusing any assistance or protection by the Federal authorities, until [this step] is taken," Sumner expected that the President would be disappointed. It was not reasonable, he thought, for Southern whites "to take the initiative in such, to them, revolutionary changes in the social conditions of the South." Then, perforce, Johnson would see the need for active federal intervention.[1]

Confidently Sumner wrote his friends: "*In the question of colored suffrage the President is with us.*" Forgetting that in the previous session of Congress he had insisted that reconstruction was a function of the legislative, not the executive, branch of government, he was glad that Congress was not in session, because during the recess Johnson could take dramatic, decided action to ensure equal rights. "And then what a regenerated

[9] Sumner to Bright, May 1, 1865, Bright MSS.; Sumner to Duchess of Argyll, May 1, 1865, Argyll MSS.; Sumner: *Works*, XI, 20.

[1] James F. Rhodes: *History of the United States from the Compromise of 1850* (New York: The Macmillan Company; 1920), VI, 8; Sir Frederick Bruce to Russell, May 6, 1865, Russell MSS.

land!" he exulted. "I had looked for a bitter contest on this question; but with the President on our side it will be carried by simple *avoirdupois*." [2]

In this euphoric state Sumner returned to Boston in the middle of May 1865, looking forward to a summer uninterrupted by politics or public affairs. He expected to spend long afternoons in quiet conversation with Longfellow and in idly dozing, with a white handkerchief covering his face, in the poet's great armchair in Craigie House. So certain was he that the issues of reconstruction were satisfactorily settled that he began thinking ahead to the next area of probable danger and controversy, foreign relations. In the fall, he told Longfellow, he might have to make another major speech dealing with American war claims against Great Britain.[3]

• 2 •

It would be nearly four years before Sumner would find the time to prepare his proposed speech on foreign relations, for within two weeks of his return to Massachusetts he learned that his hopes for speedy reconstruction upon the basis of Negro suffrage were hopelessly misplaced. On May 29 Johnson appointed William W. Holden provisional governor of North Carolina and called for the election of a constitutional convention, to be chosen by the loyal white voters. Sumner at first could not believe that the President had decided to exclude Negroes from the polls; to do so was "inconsistent with what he said to me, and to others." But, as proclamation followed proclamation, reorganizing one Southern state after another on the basis of white supremacy, he was obliged to accept as genuine Johnson's "change, which seemed like a somersault or an apostasy." Surely, he thought, the President was suffering from some "strange hallucination." [4]

[2] Stearns: *Life . . . of George Luther Stearns*, p. 344; Sumner to Lieber, May 2, 1865, Sumner MSS. On the inconsistency of Sumner's positions in 1864 and 1865 see George H. Mayer: *The Republican Party, 1854–1966* (2nd ed.; New York: Oxford University Press; 1967), pp. 127–8.

[3] Longfellow to G. W. Greene, June 11, 1865, Longfellow MSS.

[4] Sumner to Carl Schurz, June 19, 1865, copy, Sumner MSS.; Sumner: *Works*, XI, 22; Carl Schurz: *Speeches, Correspondence and Political Papers*, ed. Frederic Bancroft (New York: G. P. Putnam's Sons; 1913), I, 264.

It did not occur to Sumner that he had all along allowed his hopes to deceive him as to Johnson's policy. With so limited a previous acquaintance with the new President, he did not know that it was Johnson's habit to listen without replying to those who disagreed with him, and Sumner had too often taken silence for consent. Then, too, because of Sumner's sweeping unconcern for constitutional niceties, he had failed to see the significance of the differences which had emerged when he talked with Johnson about reconstruction; considering the discredited doctrine of states' rights, a hydra which must be beaten to death,[5] he could not conceive that Johnson quite literally believed in the constitutional guarantee of states' rights, including the right to regulate suffrage.

More perceptive observers had all along been aware that there were real differences in the reconstruction policies of the President and the Senator. Though a newcomer to Washington, British minister Bruce had alerted his government as early as May 5 to the probability of a quarrel between the two men. When Johnson recognized the Pierpont government in Virginia and failed to use his influence to secure impartial suffrage in Tennessee, a number of Radical Republicans began to feel that he had betrayed them, and it took both Sumner and Wade to convince a caucus held at the National Hotel on May 12 that "the President was in no danger . . . and that he was in favor of negro suffrage." Despite such assurances, the Springfield *Republican* announced, nine days before Johnson issued his North Carolina proclamation, that Sumner's theory of reconstruction was "not the theory of the administration." [6]

Even so, there was justice in Sumner's complaint that Johnson changed his course during the last weeks of May. While the President had probably never intended to force universal suffrage upon the South, the independent testimony of Sumner, Chase, Wade, and Representative Samuel Hooper proves that during the first weeks of his administration he looked upon Negro

[5] Sumner to Lieber, May 2, 1865, Sumner MSS.

[6] Bruce to Russell, May 5, 1865, Russell MSS.; George W. Julian: *Political Recollections, 1840 to 1872* (Chicago: Jansen, McClurg & Company; 1884), p. 263; Springfield *Weekly Republican*, May 20, 1865.

voting as a positive good.[7] Yet by August Johnson suggested to Southern leaders the possibility of enfranchising a limited number of educated Negroes only in order "to disarm the adversary," by which he meant "the radicals, who are wild upon negro franchise."

Feeling betrayed, Sumner attributed Johnson's about-face to political pressure, particularly from the Blairs, who had sheltered the Vice President when he was drunk after his inauguration, and from Seward, who had slowly recovered from his wounds and resumed his duties as Secretary of State. In fact, political considerations did determine the President's course, but they were both more complex and less personal than Sumner imagined.[8] Johnson was simultaneously being tugged in three different directions: by Sumner and his fellow Radicals in one way; by Seward, Raymond, and Weed, who looked toward creating a new Union party of moderates, in another; by the Blairs and their allies, who wanted the President to rejoin the Democrats, in yet another. Only so long as Johnson took no action could he live up to the pledge he had given Sumner: "I mean to keep you all together."

"And so we have before us another controversy," Sumner lamented, as he learned of Johnson's proclamation. The announcement of the President's reconstruction policy obliged Sumner to revert to a familiar political role. Once more, if he was going to stand by his own principles and to represent the constituents who supported him, he had to differ with the national head of his own political party. Yet, if possible, he wanted to avert an open break with Johnson, just as he had always done with Lincoln. "He is our President," he wrote Chase in June, "and we must keep him ours unless he makes it impossible to go with him." It was essential to delay the reconstruction processes begun by the President or at least to prevent the readmission of the Southern states when Congress reassembled in December.

[7] Hooper to N. P. Banks, Aug. 27, 1865, Banks MSS., Ill. State Hist. Lib.

[8] The best analysis of the political forces operating upon the President, especially from the Conservatives and the Democrats, is LaWanda and John H. Cox: *Politics, Principle, and Prejudice, 1865–1866* (Glencoe, Ill.: The Free Press; 1963), Chaps. 2–3. See also David Donald: *The Politics of Reconstruction, 1863–1867* (Baton Rouge, La.: Louisiana State University Press; 1965), Chap. 1.

Meanwhile, it was necessary to mobilize public opinion against Johnson's program, and Sumner appealed to his fellow Radicals for speeches and public letters opposing the President's course. "I wish you would make a speech soon or write a letter," he implored Wade. "When shall you speak?" he asked Carl Schurz. "We must all speak." [9]

Sumner lost no time in following his own injunction. When he learned of Johnson's proclamations he had virtually completed the eulogy on Abraham Lincoln he was scheduled to deliver in Boston on June 1, but he promptly set to work upon an addendum arguing that only through Negro suffrage could "the war waged by Abraham Lincoln be brought to an end, so as to assure peace, tranquility, and reconciliation." Cheerfully he admitted that he was getting right with Lincoln. The urgent need, he explained, compelled him to sacrifice the artistic unity of his oration in order to make it frankly "a political tract." [1]

To voice further opposition to Johnson's policy, Sumner welcomed an invitation to preside over the Massachusetts State Republican Convention held at Worcester on September 14. Barely avoiding an open attack upon the President, he challenged the presuppositions of Johnson's reconstruction program.[2] To the President's assertion that the states of the former Confederacy were now peaceful, he countered with extracts from his voluminous Southern correspondence to prove that "the rebel spirit still prevails." To Johnson's claim that reconstruction was a function of the executive branch of the government, he replied by recapitulating the arguments, so often used to combat Lincoln's program, proving that Congress had "plenary powers over the whole subject." The President's assertion that he had no power to impose Negro suffrage he dismissed; if Johnson could require the Southern states to ratify the Thirteenth Amendment and to repudiate the Confederate debt, he could also insist that they give blacks the vote. Anyway, there was ample power for

[9] Sumner to Duchess of Argyll, June 20, 1865, Argyll MSS.; Sumner to Chase, June 25, 1865, Chase MSS., Lib. of Cong.; Sumner to Wade, June 12, 1865, Wade MSS.; Sumner to Schurz, June 19, 1865, copy, Sumner MSS.

[1] Sumner: *Works*, IX, 424; Sumner to G. W. Greene, July 1, 1865, Greene MSS.

[2] Sumner: *Works*, IX, 441–77.

positive action to compel universal suffrage; resurrecting his old arguments about state suicide and the territorial status of the Confederate states, Sumner continued to give primary stress to the more widely acceptable view that Congress could require Negro suffrage as part of its duty to guarantee a republican form of government in the Southern states. That phrase in the Constitution, he was earnestly convinced, meant something more than just a guarantee against monarchy; indeed, it meant something "which was not fully revealed to [the Founding Fathers] themselves; but which we must now declare in the light of our institutions." [3]

Whatever Republicans at Worcester thought of Sumner's constitutional arguments—and perhaps it ought to be said simply that the whole problem of reconstruction was extra-constitutional and that every theory of reconstruction required the twisting of the words in the Constitution to purposes never envisaged by the framers of that venerable document—his listeners found his appeals strongly persuasive. To support Negro suffrage in the South he skillfully invoked state pride: "Massachusetts means always to keep on the right road, and by unerring instinct knows the way." By warning that the South was still "full of spirits who have sworn undying hatred, not only to the Union, but to reason itself," he roused New England hostility to the whites of the former Confederacy. He rallied businessmen and bondholders to his cause by warning that there was "not a single ex-Rebel who would vote to pay the interest on the national debt." Holding a United States Treasury note before the audience, he declared that it would have no value if Johnson's plan was followed.[4] Finally, he appealed to sympathy for his own past struggles for human freedom: "This is not the first time that I have battled with the barbarism of Slavery. I battle still, as the bloody mon-

[3] Sumner to Lieber, Oct. 12, 1865, Sumner MSS.

[4] Some historians have cited this portion of Sumner's speech to prove that the Radical interest in Negro suffrage was largely a front for their plans to promote Northeastern economic interests through payment of the debt in gold, contraction of the currency, protective tariffs, etc. For a similar contemporary view by the British minister at Washington, see Bruce to Russell, Sept. 18, 1865, Russell MSS. A closer reading of Sumner's speech, together with his correspondence, shows that, far from speaking for Massachusetts businessmen, he was virtually blackmailing them into supporting Negro suffrage as the best way of defending their economic self-interest.

ster retreats to its last citadel; and, God willing, I mean to hold on, if it takes what remains to me of life."

Not content with the fact that more than 20,000 copies of his Worcester address were circulated, Sumner throughout the summer and fall of 1865 seized every opportunity to publish criticisms of Johnson's policy. He put together a collection of his resolutions, articles, and Senate speeches on reconstruction and had them published as a thirty-two-page pamphlet called *Security and Reconciliation for the Future*. In public letters to Negro correspondents he urged: "Work on. Fight on. When Congress meets, we shall insist upon JUSTICE." To Theodore Tilton's pro-Radical weekly, *The Independent,* he contributed a letter again identifying equal rights in the South with Northern economic self-interest: ". . . I would say to the merchant, who wishes to open trade with this region,—to the capitalist, who would send his money there,—to the emigrant, who seeks to find a home there,—begin by assuring justice to all men." For the non-political *Atlantic Monthly* he prepared a long, learned article ostensibly discussing the provenience of two Latin phrases but actually arguing against premature clemency to "belligerent traitors." [5]

At the same time Sumner tried to rouse the veterans of the antislavery movement against Johnson's reconstruction program. He deeply deplored William Lloyd Garrison's decision in May to withdraw from the American Anti-Slavery Society, on the grounds that the organization had no purpose now that slavery was ended, and he urged Garrison to reenter the battle for the freedmen's rights by exposing "this miserable and cruel experiment of the President." [6] Initially Sumner hoped to receive strong support from *The Nation,* the new weekly periodical launched in July 1865 with funds provided largely by Boston and Philadelphia abolitionists, but when the editor, E. L. Godkin, failed to appreciate the enormity of Johnson's actions and the necessity of Negro suffrage, Sumner begged one of its principal financial backers: "Suspend the *Nation.* It does more hurt than good." [7] He was delighted, however, when the Boston *Advertiser*

[5] Sumner: *Works,* IX, 432, 501, 544.

[6] Sumner to Garrison, July 22, 1865, Garrison MSS.

[7] Stearns: *Life . . . of George Luther Stearns,* p. 337. On the founding of *The Nation,* see William M. Armstrong: *E. L. Godkin and American Foreign*

"Free Soil Her."
Mailed to Sumner anonymously, this 1864 cartoon is typical of the scurrilous anti-Negro literature with which he was constantly barraged.

COLLECTION OF MR. VAN DYK MACBRIDE

John A. Andrew

THE NATIONAL ARCHIVES

Lyman Trumbull

ILLINOIS STATE HISTORICAL LIBRARY

CONSERVATIVE REPUBLICAN CRITICS OF SUMNER

promised to publish the letters written by Carl Schurz during the inspection tour he made of the South, at the instigation of Secretary Stanton and with the reluctant consent of the President. So eager was Sumner to see this salutary influence exerted upon Massachusetts antislavery opinion that he arranged to have friends pay the special premiums on Schurz's life insurance policy, required because he was traveling in such a troubled region, and he also secured the services of an excellent stenographer, who accompanied the German-American general on his trip.[8]

Throughout the summer of 1865 Sumner also did what he could to rouse other Congressmen to the dangers of Johnson's course. He did not confine his correspondence to Wade, Stevens, Winter Davis, and the other leading Radicals but approached moderate or uncommitted Republicans and even gingerly asked the views of one Democratic Senator with whom he was on good terms.[9] Recognizing how closely the new Congress would be divided, he made a special trip in October to consult with Senator E. D. Morgan, in the hope of arousing that phlegmatic New Yorker's concern over "so many late Rebels coming into power." In conversation and in correspondence he everywhere bore the same message: Johnson had broken his promises; as a result, "the rebels are springing into their old life, and the copperheads also"; the President's policy was illegal, "flagrantly unconstitutional, because it sets up a discrimination of color," and "also against common sense, common humanity, and openly against Almighty God."[1]

• 3 •

Sumner found the response to his entreaties discouraging. Despite his warnings, many Republicans worked to bring their state

Policy (New York: Bookman Associates; 1957), pp. 17–21; and John G. Sproat: *"The Best Men"* (New York: Oxford University Press; 1968), pp. 18–20.

[8] For Sumner's connections with Schurz's Southern tour, see Schurz: *Writings*, I, 265–6, 275–7, and Sumner to Schurz, June 29 and Aug. 28, 1865, Schurz MSS.

[9] Sumner to Charles R. Buckalew, Aug. 28, 1865, Buckalew MSS.

[1] James A. Rawley: *Edwin D. Morgan, 1811–1885* (New York: Columbia University Press; 1955), p. 215; Sumner to Wade, Aug. 3, 1865, Wade MSS.; Sumner to E. D. Morgan, July 12, 1865, Morgan MSS.

parties behind the President's policy. In Wisconsin through what a correspondent told Sumner was "the pernicious influence of Senator Doolittle" and through appeals to "low, unmanly prejudice" against blacks, the Republican convention ringingly endorsed Johnson's actions in the South; and in the fall elections in that state voters defeated a plan to give Negroes the vote. Connecticut also defeated a Negro suffrage proposal in the fall. In Negrophobic Indiana the prestigious war governor, O. P. Morton, vigorously campaigned against Negro suffrage on the ground that it would "result in a war of races." Strongly influenced by Secretary Seward's support of the President and by Senator Morgan's determination to be firm but also calm and concilatory, New York Republicans commended the "eminently wise and just" course of the President.[2]

Even the handful of Radical Congressmen disturbed by Johnson's policy felt powerless to change it. Nearing the end of a brilliant, bitter career, Winter Davis wrote Sumner that there was no way Republicans could compel Johnson to alter his course, and that the only possible salvation was for Congress to rush through an act or an amendment prescribing universal suffrage before the Southern states were readmitted. "But is there *nerve* for the work?" he asked dejectedly. "The *last* Congress was not equal to it: is the present Congress?" Equally despairing was Thaddeus Stevens. "Is it possible to devise any plan to arrest the government in its ruinous course?" he asked Sumner. "Is there no way to arrest the insane course of the President . . . ?" Early in the summer he hoped that the Radicals could "collect bold men enough to lay the foundation of a party to take the hold of this government, and keep it off the rocks," but by October he found that he could not even rally his own Pennsylvania State Republican Convention behind a resolution favoring Negro suffrage. "I fear we are ruined . . . ," he grieved. Wade, too, gave up hope. Learning during a hasty visit to Washington that he could do nothing to influence the President, he gave way to bloody speculation: "The colored people of the south will be compelled to hew out their own way to liberty

[2] Byron Paine to Sumner, Oct. 7, 1865, Sumner MSS.; Springfield *Weekly Republican*, Oct. 14, 1865; Morgan to Sumner, July 21, 1865, Sumner MSS.

by the power of their own right arm . . . if by an insurrection they could contrive to slay one half of their oppressors, the other half would hold them in the highest respect and no doubt treat them with justice."[3]

No more effective were Sumner's attempts to enlist members of the cabinet against the President's policies. To be sure, the Attorney General agreed with Sumner's views on Negro suffrage, but James Speed had very little influence upon Johnson. Secretary of the Interior Harlan also regretted Johnson's actions but warned Sumner that too vigorous criticism would drive the President into the arms of the Copperhead Democrats.[4] Always sympathetic to Radical objectives, Stanton fell increasingly under Sumner's influence when he visited Boston in September 1865. When the Senator appealed in his Worcester address for the continued military occupation of the South "until it smiles with the charities of life," the Secretary responded that Sumner "asked him to do only what he wanted to do." Characteristically Sumner exaggerated the extent of Stanton's endorsement and subsequently asserted that the War Secretary "approved of every sentiment, every opinion and word" in his speech.[5] In fact, Stanton proved an unpredictable ally, for he was concerned less with the humanitarian and political objectives of the Radicals than with the need to protect the army, and especially those troops occupying the South.

Other members of the cabinet gave Sumner even less satisfaction. He knew that Seward was so hostile to Negro suffrage that he did not even approach him. When Sumner tried to convince Gideon Welles that Johnson was reenacting "the conduct of Mr. Buchanan and his Cabinet when the Rebellion began to show itself," the sharp-tongued Secretary of the Navy responded in interminable letters deploring "Denunciation and proscription" and arguing that the Southern white working peo-

[3] Davis to Sumner, June 20, 1865; Stevens to Sumner, June 2 and 14, Aug. 17 and Oct. 7, 1865; and Wade to Sumner, July 29 and Nov. 1, 1865—all in Sumner MSS.

[4] Speed to Sumner, June 17, 1865, ibid.; Harlan to Sumner, Nov. 11 [1865], MS., New-York Hist. Soc.; Harlan to Sumner, Aug. 21, 1865, Sumner MSS.

[5] Benjamin P. Thomas and Harold M. Hyman: *Stanton: The Life and Times of Lincoln's Secretary of War* (New York: Alfred A. Knopf; 1962), pp. 457–8; Sumner to Lieber, Sept. 18, 1865, Sumner MSS.; Welles: *Diary*, II, 394.

ple were "not only not irreclaimable but . . . patriotic." No more successful was Sumner's attempt, through a friend, to persuade the Secretary to resign because he was no longer a true representative of New England opinions.[6] Even more hostile was Hugh McCulloch, the Secretary of the Treasury, who dismissed Sumner's attempt to link the commercial prosperity of the North with Negro suffrage in the South as demagogy. He warned bluntly: "Nothing can be more damaging to our credit than the openly expressed opinion by leading men, that there may arise contingencies in which the national debt will be repudiated." Facing the practical problem of establishing a network of Treasury agents in the South, McCulloch felt that his hands were tied by the Congressional requirement, adopted at Sumner's insistence, that all federal employees must swear the iron-clad oath. Since there were not enough qualified Southerners who had never borne arms against the Union or in any other way assisted the Confederacy, McCulloch, after consulting with the President, decided that the law had not been intended to apply to the present circumstances and went ahead making provisional appointments throughout the South. Angrily Sumner objected to this "open disregard of an Act of Congress," but he got no satisfaction from the stiff-backed Secretary, who condescendingly replied that he was sure Sumner's hasty protest did "not mean to express a legal opinion."[7] Angrily, Sumner gave up on the cabinet. "They are all courtiers unhappily," he grieved, "as if they were the counsellors of a king."

Even more distressing was the falling off in support that Sumner sensed among the groups that had hitherto formed his most loyal following. In 1865 Northerners were tired—tired of the demands the war made upon their time and money, tired of the emotional hysteria, tired of the high-flown rhetoric—and wanted nothing more than to be left alone with the everyday business of making a living. The issues of the Reconstruction era

[6] *The Collector,* LVII (1944), 133; Welles to Sumner, July 13, 1865, Sumner MSS.; Welles: *Diary,* II, 330; Charles Eames to Sumner, Aug. 3, 1865, Sumner MSS.

[7] McCulloch to Sumner, Aug. 16 and Sept. 11, 1865, ibid.; Sumner to McCulloch, Sept. 7 and 16, 1865, McCulloch MSS. See the excellent treatment of this whole episode in Hyman: *Era of the Oath,* pp. 51–5.

did not command their interest or arouse their zeal as had those of the war years. It was one thing to fight a necessary war to preserve the Union and to eradicate slavery; it was another to inaugurate a new domestic strife in order to guarantee rights to the freedmen. Garrison accurately sensed the new mood when he declared that antislavery societies served no purpose now that slavery was abolished and closed down the *Liberator*. Though a majority of abolitionists followed Wendell Phillips and voted to continue the American Anti-Slavery Society in order to battle for the rights of freedmen, the controversy left some of Sumner's stanchest backers divided and confused.

Equally disturbing was the refusal of the younger generation of educated New Englanders to become deeply involved in the issues of reconstruction. Sumner tried hard to win the support of the intellectuals who reached maturity at about the time of the Civil War. In the Senate he constantly promoted their interests. Concerned to make the United States part of the world scientific community, he worked for the adoption of the metric system and year after year tried to reduce tariffs on books and scientific equipment. There should be no tax upon knowledge, he insisted, to the derision of Senators who could see no difference between duties on imported iron and imported illuminated manuscripts. Determined also to protect the rights of American authors, he tried in almost every session of Congress to have the United States accept the international copyright agreement. Though markedly conventional in his artistic taste, he did more than any other Senator to see that the best in American painting and sculpture adorned the national Capitol. In order to provide public recognition for American intellectuals, he attempted to persuade Congress to incorporate an Academy of Literature and an Academy of Social Science, comparable to the Academy of Science created during the war. Though Gurowski predicted that the academicians would consist of "a few rhetors, editors of newspapers, lecturers, compilers, literary barators, translators, etc.," and though, in truth, Sumner's lists of proposed members included mostly his New England friends and left out both Walt Whitman and Herman Melville, the intent was simply to see that in the postwar world American thinkers and writers received due recognition. "When our triumph is won and Slavery dead," he wrote a young sculptor in 1864, "what a field there will be in our country for art and for every thing good, great and glorious." [8]

Despite these exertions, few of the New England intellectuals admired or trusted Sumner, and even fewer were ready to join him in a fight against Johnson's reconstruction policies. In the whole Boston area, it was reported, only the gentle, non-political Longfellow really endorsed Sumner's views. Charles Eliot Norton and the other members of the Loyal Publication Society, which had circulated pro-Union propaganda during the war, were generally critical of his plans, while *The Nation,* the authentic voice of the new generation, was virtually always hostile.[9] This new breed of intellectuals thought of themselves as rigorously and scientifically trained in the empirical school, and they veered away from Sumner's grand generalizations about human nature and progress. Considering Great Britain the nearly perfect society, they wanted, as did British reformers, minimal government and a civil service chosen by merit—and therefore from the ranks of educated men like themselves; and they objected to Sumner's dropping of the civil service reform question after one trial, to his indifference to the tariff question, to his sweeping advocacy of increased national power, and to his frequent invocation of French and Roman law. But more than anything else the new generation distrusted Sumner's unabated zeal for good causes. Many of them had fought in the war and had been touched with fire; their emotions and their rhetoric had been singed. They were distrustful of the high-sounding phrase, suspicious of the glorious cause. In particular, they were growing disillusioned about the Negro. Without for a moment regretting the end of slavery or doubting the necessity of a war to end it, they did not romanticize the black man as God's image in

[8] Sumner to Lieber, Jan. 31 and Feb. 3, 1864, Sumner MSS.; Gurowski: *Diary: 1863–'64–'65,* p. 271; R. W. Emerson to G. W. Curtis, Dec. 15 [1865], Curtis MSS.; Sumner to Harriet Hosmer, Sept. 23, 1864, MS., Providence Public Lib.

[9] Norton to Godkin, Mar. 20, 1866, Godkin MSS.; Norton to Pierce, Mar. 24, 1866, Sumner MSS.; Pierce to Sumner, Mar. 27, 1866, ibid.; Boston *Commonwealth,* Mar. 31, 1866. For a typical Godkin reaction to Sumner's speeches, see *The Nation,* II (Feb. 8, 1866), 163.

ebony. Now a free man, he must make his own way. Why Sumner should insist upon special protection for the Negro was incomprehensible.

Not only reformers and intellectuals were unmoved by Sumner's concern for the freedmen; practical politicians in Massachusetts were exhibiting a similar disinterest. Even the Massachusetts State Republican Convention, after applauding Sumner's address, failed to condemn Johnson's policy but instead passed wordy resolves which, as Gideon Welles remarked, reminded "one of the old woman who wished to scream but dared not." That sensitive political barometer in western Massachusetts, Henry L. Dawes, showed such a disturbing tendency to equate the reconstruction policy of Johnson with that of the martyred Lincoln that Thaddeus Stevens thought he might need to "reconstruct" Dawes off all important committees in the new Congress dealing with the South.[1]

Most significant of all was a passage-at-arms between Sumner and Andrew in November, which indicated a deep rift in the Massachusetts Republican leadership.[2] With an introduction from Secretary Stanton, Lewis E. Parsons, whom Johnson had named provisional governor of Alabama, came to Boston in the hope of persuading New England capitalists to invest in his state and, more specifically, to buy Alabama state bonds. Predisposed to distrust all Johnson appointees, Sumner called upon Parsons because Stanton requested it, and, though the governor appeared "intelligent and amiable," he outraged the Senator by declaring "that rather than allow negroes to vote he would emigrate." Two days later when Parsons, flanked by Governor Andrew and Henry Ward Beecher, appealed to Boston's Union Club for the purchase of Alabama bonds, Sumner was forewarned. As the governor finished, he rose to alert prospective investors "that Alabama was a very bogus state, not more than half converted from disloyalty, and though perhaps not intending to take up

[1] Welles: *Diary,* II, 373; Sumner to Dawes, July 20, 1865, Dawes MSS.; Stevens to Sumner, Aug. 26, 1865, Sumner MSS.

[2] Sumner to Stanton, Nov. 5, 1865, Stanton MSS.; Springfield *Weekly Republican,* Nov. 18, 1865; Boston *Commonwealth,* Nov. 25, 1865; Mrs. Annie Fields: Diary, Nov. 8, 1865, Fields MSS.

arms again, yet fully intending to re[e]stablish institutions as nearly as possible on the old basis of injustice and slavery to the black race."

Angry at this treatment of a guest, Andrew exclaimed: "Until this moment, he had hoped Gov. Parsons would be treated by gentlemen as a gentleman." Remembering all too well how Sumner had blocked his appointment to the cabinet, he then proceeded "in a very personal and offensive strain to reply to Mr. Sumner, concluding with an appeal for cooperation with, rather than antagonism to, the South."

As always, Sumner took disagreement badly. When Andrew a few days later tried to explain his position more fully and more temperately in a long letter, the Senator stiffly replied in the third person:

> Mr. Sumner . . . ventures to suggest that first and foremost "among the arts and methods of peace" which the Governor now wishes to cultivate, is justice to the oppressed, and he entreats the Governor not to allow any negro-hater, with his sympathizers, to believe him, at this crisis, indifferent to the guarantees of Human Rights or disposed to postpone his efforts in their behalf.[3]

• 4 •

Though discouraged by his failure to arouse opposition to Johnson's policy, Sumner did not allow himself to grow disheartened. "Some of our friends are in great despair," he wrote Bright. "I am not. The good cause cannot be lost." For a time he believed that Johnson himself might see that he had erred and "give up all idea of reconstruction" on the ostensible ground that "a question of such trans[c]endent magnitude should be referred to Congress." When the President did not oblige, Sumner then thought that the fact his program was "failing wretchedly" in the South might cause him to reconsider. By September, however, even that faint hope disappeared. Only Congress, overruling the Presi-

[3] Sumner to Andrew [Nov. 22? 1865], Andrew MSS. Cf. Pearson: *Life of John A. Andrew*, II, 272–6.

dent, could now save the Republic, yet, barely a month before the December session he was obliged to admit: "It is doubtful how Congress will stand. Those who are associated with the President in his policy think it will unite with them. Others . . . feel sure that it will be firm the other way. . . . I know many who I am sure will not yield. I shall not. . . . If the President perseveres the Union party is broken up." [4]

On Saturday, December 2, 1865, two days before the opening of the Thirty-Ninth Congress, Sumner returned to Washington and went that evening to the White House. Ostensibly his purpose was to beg Johnson to change his course, but he was now convinced that the President was irreclaimable. Considering a rupture between Johnson and the Radicals inevitable, Sumner wanted to make sure, as he told Lieber, "that the President shall break with us and not we with him." [5] He received a chilly reception. Ignoring George Bancroft's hint that Sumner could be won around by flattery and some confidential talk about foreign policy,[6] Johnson also anticipated a clash with the Radicals, and he was determined to provoke Sumner into firing the first shot.

For two and one-half hours the men circled each other warily, looking for openings.[7] Both had to be on guard, for both were vulnerable. Having earlier rejoiced that Johnson was taking the whole reconstruction issue in hand and would settle it before Congress met, Sumner was in no position to complain that the President was usurping power or that he should have summoned Congress into special session. On the other hand, Johnson's position was equally difficult, for he had repeatedly declared that he favored Negro suffrage but then had permitted every Southern state to reorganize on the basis of white supremacy.

Since Johnson was host, he could afford to maintain a coolly defensive reticence until Sumner erupted into an angry accusation that the President "had thrown away the fruits of the

[4] Sumner to Bright, Aug. 8, Sept. 26, and Nov. 5, 1865, Bright MSS.; Sumner to Chase, June 25, 1865, Chase MSS., Lib. of Cong.

[5] Oct. 8, 1865, Sumner MSS.

[6] Bancroft to Johnson, Dec. 1, 1865, Johnson MSS.

[7] My account of this interview is based on the four following letters: Lewis D. Campbell to Johnson, Mar. 9, 1868, ibid.; Sumner to [P. W.] Chandler, Jan. 3, 1865, MS., Chicago Hist. Soc.; Sumner to Lieber [Dec. 3, 1865], Sumner MSS.; Sumner to George Bancroft [Dec. 3, 1865], Bancroft MSS., Cornell Univ.

victories of the Union army." When Johnson asked him to be specific, the Senator replied that "the poor *freedmen* in Georgia and Alabama were frequently insulted by rebels." Caustically Johnson inquired: "Mr. Sumner, do murders ever occur in Massachusetts?"

"Unhappily yes, Mr. President."

"Do people ever knock each other down in Boston."

"Unhappily yes, Mr. President, sometimes."

"Would you consent that Massachusetts should be excluded from the Union on this account."

"No, Mr. President, surely not."

By the end of the interview it was clear that the differences between the two men were irreconcilable. Finding Sumner's manner arrogant and dictatorial, Johnson understood him to intimate that the Radicals in Congress would open war upon the President's policies. Sumner, for his part, thought Johnson "ignorant, pig-headed and perverse" in pursuing a program sure to ruin the country. As the Senator rose to leave he picked up his silk top hat, which had rested on the floor beside his chair during the interview, and was disgusted to discover that the President, in his excitement, had used it for a spittoon.

"But thank God Congress will do its duty," Sumner exclaimed when reporting on his conversation with the President. To make sure that it did so, on the opening day of the session, even before the President's annual message could be received, Thaddeus Stevens in the House moved the creation of a joint committee to which all measures on reconstruction would be automatically referred. Simultaneously Sumner seized the Senate floor to introduce a barrage of resolutions, bills, and constitutional amendments outlining the program of reconstruction he considered preferable to the President's. The difference in the techniques employed by these principal Radical spokesmen suggested the dissimilar roles the two men would play in the ensuing battles over reconstruction. For all his personal eccentricities and his sharp tongue, Stevens was an organization man, who worked through committees and exerted influence through his control of the machinery of the House of Representatives; when he could not get a majority of his party to support his favored positions, he accepted whatever compromises were necessary. Sumner, on the other hand, was, despite his seniority, a political outsider; he disliked committees, except when he was chairman, was ineffectual in caucus, and proved inept at drafting legislation. He announced principles, as from on Mount Sinai, and deplored the compromises needed to transform ideals into legislative reality.

The program Sumner announced called for broad changes throughout the South. Because Congress had the constitutional duty to guarantee to each state a republican form of government, it should sweep away the regimes Johnson had set up and insist that throughout the former Confederacy there must be "no denial of rights, civil or political, on account of race or color," so that "all persons shall be equal before the law, whether in the court-room or at the ballot-box." To secure this goal, a provisional governor in each Southern state should register all male citizens and allow them an opportunity to swear an oath repudiating secession, upholding the national debt, and pledging always to "discountenance and resist any laws making any distinction of race or color." Whenever a majority adhered to this oath, the state should hold a constitutional convention, but no soldier or officer of the Confederacy could vote in the election or be chosen as a delegate. The convention must then frame a new state constitution that would disavow secession, prohibit slavery, permanently disqualify all high-ranking Confederates from holding office, and pledge that henceforth there would be "no distinction among inhabitants . . . founded on race, former condition, or color." Only when this document was approved by a majority of eligible voters—a term which under Sumner's plan would include Negroes but exclude most ex-Confederates—could a state be readmitted to representation in Congress.

It is not certain what Sumner thought his program, if adopted by Congress, would accomplish. The terms were so rigorous that it was virtually inevitable they would be rejected by the whites in every Southern state, especially since for the past six months President Johnson had led them to anticipate a far more generous peace. In anticipation of just such a response, Sumner's plan further provided that, until all his stipulations were accepted, the Southern states should remain under provisional governments directed to preserve the Negroes' rights. This perhaps is what Sumner expected and desired.[8] Under his plan civilian appointees would succeed military officers, whom he distrusted, as the governors of the South; all the principal Confederate leaders and, indeed, most Southern whites would be excluded from any share in political life, whether in the state or the nation; and, for perhaps a generation, the blacks would have an opportunity, under federal protection, to grow in independence, in knowledge, and in political wisdom.

If Sumner expected this result from his proposals, he was quickly disillusioned, for his program was not taken seriously. The titters in the Senate gallery as he introduced measure after measure were to be expected, as were Democratic denunciations of his bills as absurd, fanatical, and visionary. Perhaps he also anticipated the criticism of *The Nation* that his proposals were couched in language so loose and unlawyer-like as to be meaningless. But the total silence with which even his Republican colleagues greeted his resolutions and bills, especially when contrasted to the warm welcome given the next day to Johnson's message, suggested that his role in this session of Congress would again be an uncomfortably lonely one.

As the session got under way, it became increasingly clear that it was not Sumner but Johnson who dominated the scene. It was the President's messages, not the Senator's resolutions, that set the tone for subsequent debates, and few Senators were impressed when Sumner denounced Johnson's report of peaceful conditions in the South as a "whitewashing message," comparable to that of Franklin Pierce condoning proslavery outrages in Kansas during the 1850's. To be sure, Congress did set up a Joint Committee of Fifteen on Reconstruction, but this was hardly contrary to the President's wishes. More significant was the vote of the Senate Republican caucus, made over Sumner's heated protest,[9] against Stevens's plan giving this committee the

[8] Cf. William C. Bryant to Mrs. Waterston, Mar. 3, 1866, Bryant MSS., New-York Hist. Soc.: "Mr. Sumner's plan is to force a negro suffrage upon the whites of the South, and to keep the late insurgent states under the arbitrary rule of the federal government until they submit to this change."

[9] New York *Herald*, Dec. 12, 1865.

power to decide whether to seat Southern Congressmen; the Senate clung to its prerogative of judging the qualifications of its own members. Most revealing of all was the quiet decision of Senate Republicans to exclude Sumner from this powerful committee. They named as its chairman his bitterest enemy in the party, Fessenden, who wanted to cooperate with the President and was fearful lest the "yelping of the dogs" of radicalism might drive Johnson into the Democratic camp.[1]

There is no evidence that the Joint Committee ever considered any of Sumner's numerous reconstruction proposals. Just as Trumbull, another of Sumner's Republican foes, took complete charge of the Freedmen's Bureau Bill, broadening and continuing the work of the agency that Sumner had helped create, and also of the Civil Rights Bill, giving to freedmen the legal guarantees that Sumner so long had advocated, so Fessenden was in command of the constitutional amendment which would provide a long-range solution to the problems of reconstruction. Once more Sumner was shut out.

During the two months while the Joint Committee was deliberating Sumner grew more and more agitated. Everything appeared to be going wrong. The President proceeded with his reconstruction program; Southern state after Southern state reorganized its government and promptly passed a "Black Code" which did not secure even minimal civil rights to the freedmen; congressional committees failed to come up with any worthwhile proposals; and Congress endlessly debated without accomplishing anything. Adding to Sumner's anguish were the scores of letters he received every week from Southerners, warning: "In most places the freedmen are worse off than when slaves, being exposed to the brutality and vindictiveness of their old masters, without the old check of self-interest." Convinced that continuing the President's policy meant surrendering "our 'wards' white and black the true Unionists to a terrible fate," Sumner told Welles that, "while he could not denounce it as the greatest

[1] Jellison: *Fessenden of Maine*, p. 197. Fessenden wrote: "Mr. Sumner was very anxious for the place, but, standing as he does before the country, and committed to the most ultra views, even his friends declined to support him, and almost to a man fixed upon me." Fessenden: *Fessenden*, II, 20.

crime ever committed by a responsible ruler, he did proclaim . . . it the greatest mistake which history has ever recorded." [2]

Day after day in the Senate Sumner denounced Johnson in language so intemperate as to astonish even those who had known him for years. Welles could hardly credit the "impetuous violence" of his speeches, and Stanton, whom Sumner thought a wholehearted supporter, dismissed his views as "absurd and heretical." Senator Morgan thought he was acting "as if demented." Observing the hostility that Sumner and other Radicals exhibited toward Southern whites, former Attorney General Bates tried a bit of amateur psychoanalysis: "They feel that they deserve to be hated by the southern people for their cruel conspiracy to degrade and ruin the southern States, and, naturally enough, they conclude that their bad passions are imitated, and their malicious hatred reciprocated at the South." [3]

While no such complex explanation of Sumner's motives is justified, it is important to remember that he was during the winter of 1865–66 acting under severe political pressure. His break with the President encouraged all the conservative elements in Massachusetts and aroused the hopes of Republicans envious of Sumner's position. Increasingly John A. Andrew began to loom as a formidable rival. Just completing a fifth consecutive term as governor of Massachusetts, Andrew had little cause to think kindly of Sumner, who had blocked his chances of a cabinet appointment from Lincoln. Once an admirer of John Brown, Andrew had mellowed much during his years in office, and he now distrusted Sumner's doctrinaire rigidity on reconstruction. Friendly to Negro rights, he believed they could best be guaranteed by the responsible whites of the South. He was delighted by the support that former Confederates gave to the Johnson regimes, declaring: "A rebel vote is the best of all if it is only cast in the right way." Recognizing that Andrew was a popular political figure of unimpeachable antecedents and unquestioned ability, a Republican hostile to Radical reconstruction schemes, Johnson's friends began to woo the governor, and

[2] Sumner to Duchess of Argyll, Dec. 26, 1865, Argyll MSS.; Sumner to A. G. Coffin [1866], MS., Hist. Soc. of Penn.; Welles: *Diary*, II, 415.

[3] Ibid., pp. 400, 405; Bates: *Diary*, pp. 528–9.

the Blairs, in the name of the President, promised him in return for his support "the disposition of every office in Massachusetts or New England" as well as assistance in "organizing a new party or manipulating the old one in just such way as might seem fit." [4]

At any time during the past four years Sumner would have found it hard to fight off a bid by Andrew to take over leadership of the Massachusetts Republican party, but in the winter of 1865–66 his position was especially vulnerable. Absent from the state for long periods of time, he lacked the popularity of the war governor, whether among the local politicians, the returning veterans, or the Boston businessmen. In addition, Sumner's reconstruction plans opened him to serious challenge. Republicans in Massachusetts, proud that their state had the first public school system in America and distrustful of the Irish and other unlettered immigrants, found it hard to accept Sumner's view that all the former slaves of the South ought to be enfranchised, regardless of ability or even literacy.[5] Andrew spoke for a majority when, declaring himself a "radical believer in the *suffrage* for all men of competent capacity, irrespective of color or national origins," he deplored "the raising of the general question of the suffrage for colored men in the South, as yet." Certainly the Negroes must be guaranteed equal civil rights, Andrew argued, but the suffrage was a privilege, to be distributed "according to capacity and desert," and before receiving it the freedmen needed to demonstrate their ability to grow "in knowledge and in admitted capacity for exercising the political functions of citizenship."

On still another count Sumner's reconstruction program opened him to dangerous attack. After consulting Lieber, he introduced in February 1865 a constitutional amendment in-

[4] Pearson: *Andrew*, II, 264–5, 270, 280; W. L. Burt to Andrew, May 24, 1866, Andrew MSS.

[5] Sumner tried to straddle this issue. As late as August 14, 1866, he told the Duchess of Argyll that he favored *"impartial* suffrage. I have never said *universal* suffrage" (Argyll MSS.). Yet, he added, any educational requirement was "of doubtful value, especially where patriotic votes are needed to crush treason or counteract fraud." Therefore, he concluded with splendid obscurity: "What I ask especially is impartial suffrage, which is, of course embraced in universal suffrage. What is universal is necessarily impartial." Sumner: *Works*, X, 220.

tended to solve an urgent problem caused by the end of slavery. Before the war in determining the number of Representatives to which a state was entitled, only three-fifths of the slaves were counted. After emancipation, all blacks would be counted. Ironically, then, one result of the war would be to increase the representation of the Southern states in Congress. Designed to neutralize this increase, Sumner's amendment proposed to make representation proportional, not to total population, but to the number of voters. If adopted, either the amendment would force the South to enfranchise the Negroes, or it would reduce the number of Southern Congressmen. Though Sumner had never thought through the implications of his proposal, he reintroduced it among the bills and amendments that he presented on the opening day of Congress in December 1865. He was thus doubly committed to a proposal which tacitly recognized that states could disfranchise Negroes, if they were willing to pay the price in reduced numbers of Representatives. His amendment would also probably cut down the number of Representatives from New England, and especially from Massachusetts, which had a disproportionate number of women and of unnaturalized aliens, who would no longer be counted in the allocation of Congressmen.[6]

Massachusetts politicians were outraged that Sumner favored a plan reducing their influence and the number of their jobs. When the legislature heard the news, it rumbled in revolt. Shrewdly Andrew in his widely publicized valedictory address on January 5, 1866, capitalized upon this resentment against Sumner's plan, which he boldly labeled "a delusion and a snare." Cleverly the governor argued his case not on the selfish ground of the self-interest of New England politicians but on the altruistic basis of principle. "By diminishing the representative power of the Southern States, in favor of other States," he predicted, "you will not increase Southern love for the Union. Nor, while Connecticut and Wisconsin refuse the suffrage to men of color, will you be able to convince the South that your amendment was

[6] Roscoe Conkling introduced elaborate statistics designed to prove that this plan would not adversely affect New England (*Cong. Globe*, 39 Cong., 1 Sess., p. 357), but most New England politicians continued to believe it would cost their states several seats in the House.

dictated by political principles, and not by political cupidity."

Already embarrassed by his hastily considered proposal, Sumner found his position exceedingly dangerous when, less than two weeks after Andrew's blast, the Joint Committee on Reconstruction came up with a constitutional amendment which, to be sure, continued the apportionment of representation according to total population but declared that "whenever the elective franchise shall be denied or abridged in any State on account of race or color, all persons of such race or color shall be excluded from the basis of representation." This proposal, in other words, accomplished precisely what Sumner had intended —though with no cost to New England. But Andrew's valedictory warned that, if Sumner accepted it, he would be charged both with agreeing to disfranchise the freedmen and with accepting an unworkable compromise. Already newspapers were whispering that he had all along been "among the advocates of the constitutional amendments dodging the negro suffrage question" and that, unlike Andrew, he was trying to perform "a politician's trick to get rid of the question, [rather] than a statesmanlike or philanthropic settlement of a great principle." [7]

To keep from being outflanked by Andrew, Sumner had no choice but to oppose the amendment when it reached the Senate, and to oppose it in such vehement language that everybody would forget that he had previously sponsored an almost identical proposal. Opening the debate on the amendment, he informed Fessenden that he intended to "put his foot on it and crush it," [8] and he tried to do just that in an oration titled "The Equal Rights of All," with which he occupied the Senate for three hours on February 5 and for two more on the next day. By any standards it was a remarkable production. The larger part of the speech, occupying sixty-seven printed pages in Sumner's *Works*, traced the history of the phrase "republican form of government," which, under the Constitution, was to be guaranteed to each state. Convinced for several months that "the debate which approaches on the meaning of a 'republican government' will be the greatest in our history," Sumner had prepared very carefully,

[7] Springfield *Republican*, Jan. 29, 1866.
[8] Fessenden: *Fessenden*, II, 25.

reading, as he told Welles, "everything on the subject from Plato to the last French pamphlet." [9] All his research was crammed into his speech, even though, as he admitted, the definitions of "republic" by ancient philosophers, European writers, and lexicographers anterior to the Constitutional Convention of 1789 were "absolutely fallacious and inapplicable."

Equally remarkable was the fact that, though this was supposed to be a speech against the proposed Fourteenth Amendment, it contained almost no arguments against its specific provisions. Sumner could not so argue, since the amendment he had twice introduced contained similar objectionable clauses. Instead, the oration was a grand discourse on principles which, he sweepingly asserted, were "equally applicable . . . to all measures of Reconstruction." Only a few attentive observers, like Representative Dawes, noted that it was "a wonderful production, full of splendid platitudes, crammed with book learning, but utterly void of any practical adaptation to the present exigency." [1]

Sumner disguised the irrelevance of his argument by the vigor of his language. He concluded with a denunciation of the doctrine of white supremacy—"the Gospel according to Calhoun"—and with one of his finest perorations in behalf of human equality:

> Show me a creature, with lifted countenance looking to heaven, made in the image of God, and I show you a MAN, who, of whatever country or race, whether browned by equatorial sun or blanched by northern cold, is with you a child of the Heavenly Father, and equal with you in all the rights of Human Nature. You cannot deny these rights without impiety. . . . It is not enough that you have given Liberty. By the same title that we claim Liberty do we claim Equality also. . . . One is the complement of the other. . . . The Roman Cato, after declaring his belief in the immortality of the soul, added, that, if this were an error, it was an error he loved. And now, declaring my belief in Liberty and Equality as the God-given birthright of all men, let me say,

[9] Sumner to Lieber [Dec. 3, 1865], Sumner MSS.; Welles: *Diary*, II, 393.
[1] Henry L. Dawes to Electa Dawes, Feb. 11, 1866, Dawes MSS.

in the same spirit, if this be an error, it is an error I love,—if this be a fault, it is a fault I shall be slow to renounce,—if this be an illusion, it is an illusion which I pray may wrap the world in its angelic forms.[2]

After "The Equal Rights of All" speech there was little possibility that Andrew or anybody else could accuse Sumner of bartering away principle. Though Massachusetts conservatives remained critical, talk of any real defection from Sumner's old antislavery following died. To Andrew's chagrin, Massachusetts voters believed that he had been following Sumner's lead, and not vice versa. Sumner himself dropped a patronizing note to a friend, certain to show it to the former governor: "I am glad to know that Andrew agrees with me in opposing the Amendment." Pleased that the speech had done its intended work, Sumner felt it was "the best thing of my life." [3]

• 5 •

Congressional Republicans, who knew and cared little about Sumner's political problems in Massachusetts, regarded his opposition to the Fourteenth Amendment as inconsistent to the point of indecency. On the day after his speech Fessenden publicly rebuked his "very violent—I had almost said virulent—attack" upon the amendment, and in private the Maine Senator stormed that "Mr. Sumner, with his impracticable notions, his vanity, his hatred of the President . . . is doing infinite harm." [4] Worried that Republican Senators might join Sumner in opposing the amendment, Chief Justice Chase appealed to him that it "may not be defeated and especially that it may not be defeated by your vote." Thaddeus Stevens also begged that, if the amendment was "to be slain it will not be by our friends." But, impelled by exigencies his associates in Washington could not appreciate, Sumner persisted in opposition, and he carried with him seven other Radical Republicans—just enough, when combined with the Conservatives loyal to Johnson and the Democrats, to prevent the necessary two-thirds vote for the amendment. Enraged,

[2] Sumner: *Works*, X, 236–7.
[3] Sumner to Horatio Woodman, Mar. 18, 1866, Woodman MSS.
[4] *Cong. Globe*, 39 Cong., 1 Sess., p. 707; Jellison: *Fessenden*, p. 199.

Stevens fumed over Sumner's "puerile and pedantic criticism" of the amendment and grieved that it had been killed by "the united forces of self-righteous Republicans and unrighteous Copperheads."[5]

The bitterness of Stevens's tone suggested the deep estrangement that existed between Sumner and his colleagues during the winter of 1865–66. More and more Senators came to distrust, when they did not detest, him. Democrats, of course, despised him, even when they voted with him to kill moderate reconstruction proposals. Among the Moderate Republican leaders, Trumbull considered Sumner devious and unscrupulous; Grimes called him "a cold-blooded, selfish, dangerous man"; and Fessenden regarded him as a "malignant fool." Fellow Radicals, too, sharply disagreed with him. Even the genial Wilson was unwilling to follow him in opposing the Fourteenth Amendment. Wade, after listening to one of Sumner's hyper-classic speeches which, he said, only proved the obvious, remarked disparagingly: "It's all very well, Sumner, but it has no bones in it." The equally Radical Zachariah Chandler could not endure Sumner's lecturing and when he began piling precedent upon precedent, quotation upon quotation, would leave the Senate chamber, growling: "Sumner is one of them literary fellows."[6]

Aware of his unpopularity, Sumner attributed these differences to disagreement over basic principles; he had chosen the high road of morality while his colleagues had fallen into the slough of compromise with slavery. In actuality there was not a great deal of difference among Republicans over the basic issues of reconstruction. All agreed that slavery must be abolished, that the former Confederates must be kept from returning to power, and that the rights of the freedmen must be protected. Virtually all equated the welfare of the nation with the continuing supremacy of the Republican party. There were, of course, significant disagreements over means and over timing. Moderate Re-

[5] Chase to Sumner, Mar. 9, 1866, Sumner MSS.; Stevens's endorsement on Charles A. Wardwell to Stevens, Mar. 3, 1866, ibid.; Sumner: *Works*, X, 246.

[6] Welles: *Diary*, II, 447; C. E. Norton to E. L. Godkin, Mar. 11, 1866, Godkin MSS.; Allan Nevins: *Ordeal of the Union* (New York: Charles Scribner's Sons; 1947), I, 395; Hoar: *Autobiography*, II, 76–7; Marian Gouverneur: *As I Remember* (New York: D. Appleton and Company; 1911), p. 241.

publicans favored working with the President so long as that was possible; Radicals like Sumner insisted upon a sharp break. In return for early readmission, the more conservative members of the party hoped Southern whites would agree gradually to give the freedmen the vote; extremists wanted to compel instant enfranchisement of blacks. These were not, however, irreconcilable conflicts, and in neither house of Congress did Republicans yet vote along fixed factional lines. That, despite disagreements and some sharp words, William Pitt Fessenden and Thaddeus Stevens got along harmoniously as the two principal members of the Joint Committee on Reconstruction symbolized the basic unity of the party.

Required by the exigencies of Massachusetts politics to distinguish his position from that of his Republican colleagues, Sumner voiced his disagreements with characteristic abrasiveness. Now that the war was over, most Republican Congressmen wanted, after basking a little in the victory their party and their martyred President had won, to have a quick end to sectional hostilities and to get on with the business of government. Sumner, on the other hand, was constitutionally unable to enjoy success. Since his childhood, when he discovered that nothing he could do would ever satisfy his father or endear him to his mother, he had found that his triumphs turned into ashes, and he needed to move constantly onward, from one achievement to the next.

Necessarily his position was an isolated one, for there were few other Congressmen who could lead the strenuous life of incessant moral endeavor. In Sumner's earlier years he had needed the reassurance of having friends and colleagues laboring alongside him, but after the Brooks assault he grew increasingly self-directed. If other Senators did not now come up to his position, it was evidence of their limitations. Should Sumner's self-confidence ever waver, he had but to open his daily mail to find how right he was. During a two-week period in January 1866, for instance, he received the tribute of a Connecticut girl: "Your name is to me a synonym for all that is noble," and the praise of a Massachusetts lady: "I thank God that I live in an age in which He speaks through you. . . ." A Michigan correspondent echoed the religious note: "It seems to me that God has raised you up as a special agent in our national reformation," and a long-time Massachusetts abolitionist agreed: ". . . I am sure you have the approval of all loyal men and *angels,* while struggling against the devices of the archenemy of God and man." In more secular imagery, a Westborough, Massachusetts, constituent declared: "You and such as you are our Gibraltars." [7] It was little wonder that, after reading such letters at breakfast every morning, Sumner should seem to be to his fellow Radical, Representative George W. Julian, to be suffering from "'the big head,' . . . [which] threatens to become a very offensive disease with him." [8]

It was not Sumner's egotism alone which offended his colleagues, for, as Henry Adams remarked, nearly all Senators were self-centered and self-important; it was his insensitivity to the needs and wishes of others. When he told Julia Ward Howe that he was no longer interested in individuals, he was voicing if not the literal truth, his aspiration. He deliberately tried to insulate himself from situations where he might have to adapt his general principles to specific cases. He was bitterly resentful, for instance, when in May 1865 Baron Gerolt tricked him into coming to dinner with a former governor and Congressman from South Carolina, William Aiken, once an immensely wealthy planter now destitute and aged. Finding escape impossible without rudeness to his host, Sumner tried to make conversation by asking about mutual friends in South Carolina, only to receive from Aiken the invariable responses: "He is dead, he is in hiding, he has nothing left." Then the old man amusingly told his own story, treating it almost as a joke: Confederate soldiers had drunk his six thousand bottles of old Madeira, and Sherman's men had tossed into their bonfire his magnificent English silver service, which cost seven thousand pounds before the war. Almost as an afterthought Aiken added that as a result of his trials his wife had gone mad. Embarrassed "to find himself so trium-

[7] See the following letters in the Sumner MSS.: "S. J.," Jan. 24, 1866; T. Dana, Jan. 9 [1866]; J. A. Wellman, Jan. 13, 1866; R. L. Storrs, Jan. 22, 1866; George N. Richardson, Jan. 19, 1866.

[8] Julian to Laura B. Julian, Mar. 19, 1866, Julian MSS.

phant before this human ruin," Sumner fled Gerolt's house as soon as dinner was over. As though afraid to show pity, he kept saying: "But this man is a traitor, he was involved in the affairs of the blockade-runners, his case is terribly bad." [9] Thereafter he took greater care to avoid any such encounters; he preferred to deal with categories rather than with men.

At times it seemed that Sumner regarded himself less as a man than as an embodiment of principle. "It is not I who speak," he assured the Senate during one debate. "I am nothing. It is the cause, whose voice I am, that addresses you." As the personification of principle, he announced that he naturally saw above the negotiations and compromises involved in the normal legislative process. Cassandra-like, he warned the Senators advocating the Fourteenth Amendment that their halfway measure was "the least practical mode of settling questions involving moral principle." If they hoped their plan would bribe the Southern whites into giving blacks the vote, "success is more than doubtful, while the means employed are unworthy." The whole amendment was bound to miscarry, he predicted, because "a moral principle cannot be compromised." [1]

What made Sumner's claim of moral superiority so insufferable was his colleagues' knowledge that he was perfectly willing to compromise or equivocate when it suited him. He would hold up the business of the Senate for weeks to block the territorial organization of Montana or Colorado on the ground that Negroes were excluded from the polls. When told that there were almost no blacks in those territories, he replied flatly: "If there were but one, that would be enough to justify my opposition." Yet he also declared that there was no need for Congress to require Negro voting in the Northern states because there the disfranchisement of blacks was "on so small a scale that it is not perilous to the Republic." Admitting that women had as much right as Negroes to demand the ballot, the Senator who held that principles were non-negotiable announced that it was "not judi-

[9] Chambrun: *Impressions of Lincoln and the Civil War*, pp. 130–2; Annie Fields: Diary, Oct. 1868, Fields MSS.

[1] Sumner: *Works*, X, 219, 119, 121.

cious for them at this moment to bring forward their claims so as to compromise . . . the great question of equal rights for an enfranchised race."[2]

Since any politician's career is strewn with inconsistencies, Sumner's claim to be the voice of truth and justice would probably have aroused little hostility had it been made in the heat of debate. But his major speeches were carefully written out, and he read them, sometimes from his manuscript, sometimes from printer's proofs, in his deep voice to the Senate. When he labeled the Fourteenth Amendment "uncertain, loose, cracked, and rickety," an "abomination," "a new anathema marantha," "the very Koh-i-noor of blackness," and "the most utterly reprehensible" measure ever brought before Congress, he was not carried away by passion; he was reading deliberately chosen phrases. He ransacked Samuel Johnson's ponderous writings to come up with his characterization of the amendment as "no better than the 'muscipular abortion' sent into the world by the 'parturient mountain.'"[3] Even Sumner's admirers objected to this habit of "elaborating sentences before delivery" like a rhetorician, but he defended himself on the ground that his formal orations were not really directed at his immediate listeners. "There are speeches for the Senate, and speeches for the country," he explained, "different in character, and in preparation. If, in making a speech intended for the country, I give to it that study, without which such a speech must fail, I do not think that my whole senatorial life should be described as that of a 'rhetorician.'" With mounting irritation, then, his colleagues had to suspend all other Senate business while, day after day, they listened to him deliver "a long, labored, written, printed oration, prepared carefully in the study, elaborated, proof corrected, all the thunderbolts forged."[4]

Although many Senators were irritated by Sumner's conduct, it was Fessenden, perhaps the most influential Republican

[2] Ibid., 357, 135; *Cong. Globe*, 39 Cong., 1 Sess., p. 952.

[3] *Cong. Globe*, 39 Cong., 1 Sess., p. 1279. The Koh-i-noor was the famous diamond that became part of the British crown jewels after the annexation of Punjab in 1849. Many of these phrases, found in the manuscript of Sumner's second speech on the Fourteenth Amendment, now in the Chicago Historical Society, were deleted before he published it in his *Works*, X, 282–337.

[4] Sumner to Theodore Tilton, April 12, 1866, Tilton MSS.; *Cong. Globe*, 39 Cong., 1 Sess., p. 1278.

in the chamber, who undertook to put him in his place. Relations between the two men had long been bad, no doubt because each regarded himself as the leader of the New England delegation to Congress. Though already overworked as chairman of the Senate Committee on Finances, Fessenden had accepted membership on the Joint Committee on Reconstruction in order to keep Sumner off it. The additional labor strained his already feeble health, and, always short-tempered, he had less patience than ever with Sumner's long-winded oratory. When the Massachusetts Senator began to speak, Fessenden made it his practice to leave his seat noisily, go over to the Democratic side of the chamber, and make slurring comments in a not very subdued tone upon Sumner's remarks. Then, as Sumner finished, Fessenden would berate him for delaying practical legislation, joyfully point out the inconsistencies and irrelevancies in his argument, and dismiss his broad, abstract principles by snapping: "My constituents did not send me here to philosophize." [5]

To Fessenden's needling, Sumner was as sensitive as he was vulnerable. Though during his years in the Senate he had gained some fluency in debate, he still tacked and veered with all the speed and dignity of a Spanish galleon. As an astute newspaperman noted: "He moved as if in armour. . . ." [6] He was so devoid of humor that when the irrepressible Senator Nye twitted him for mistaking "twinges of dyspepsia for constitutional scruples," he replied in solemn puzzlement: "I never had the dyspepsia in my life." [7] Always unconscious of the force of his own language, he was genuinely surprised that Fessenden felt offended when he branded one of his bills a "paragon and masterpiece of ingratitude," "abortive for all good," "shocking to the moral sense," having a "loathsome stench" like "bad mutton" or "disgusting ordure." "Grant that I have been positive and peremptory in debate," Sumner conceded privately to Pierce, who wanted to reconcile the two Senators. "I have never left my seat ostenta-

[5] *Cong. Globe*, 39 Cong., 1 Sess., p. 705. See Conness's account of the Sumner-Fessenden relationship in Placerville Corner (Calif.) *Gold Hill News*, June 18, 1865.

[6] George W. Smalley: *Anglo-American Memories* (New York: G. P. Putnam's Sons; 1911), p. 123.

[7] Sumner: *Works*, X, 506.

tiously when Fessenden rose to speak;—I have never sought to disturb him in debate; I have never talked in abusive terms of him while he was on the floor; I have never made an allusion to him, unless in direct reply." It was, then, Fessenden who was the aggressor, for he had adopted a course "so vindictive, so disorderly, and utterly in defiance of all rules of the Senate or good breeding." [8] As was Sumner's custom when he was very angry, he decided to cut off all personal relations with the Maine Senator and declined either to recognize or to speak to him.

• 6 •

Andrew Johnson saved Sumner from political ostracism. Even before Congress met, the President had determined to rally behind his program all those political elements, North and South, opposed to extremism. He hoped to construct a coalition of Moderate Republicans, Northern Democrats who had supported the war, and white Southerners who accepted their defeat on the battlefield. Whether Johnson, like Seward and Weed, looked for a revival of the old Whig party or, like the Blairs, hoped for a conversion of the Democratic party is not clear. What is certain is that he was determined, as he told a group of Virginians, to exclude from his coalition of the center "extreme men South, . . . and extreme men North." He desired to drive into political exile those Southerners unalterably devoted to slavery and secession and also those Northerners who exhibited "the counterpart or the duplicate of the same spirit." [9]

The Southern phase of Johnson's program was quickly accomplished. Eager to reorganize loyal governments in the South and prompt to grant pardon to the repentant, the President set his face against the obdurate "traitors" who had led the Confederacy. Toward Jefferson Davis himself, imprisoned in Fortress Monroe, he was vindictive, and he sought to humiliate other Southern leaders by excluding from his general proclamation of

[8] Sumner to Pierce [1865 or 1866], Sumner MSS.
[9] *Cong. Globe*, 39 Cong., 1 Sess., Appendix, p. 111.

pardon all who had estates worth more than twenty thousand dollars. So successful was the President in splitting the moderate whites of the South from their former leaders that Robert Toombs, the Confederate general and Secretary of State, still in exile in Cuba, lamented: "I see nothing in the conduct of President Johnson to approve, not a single act. And looking at his policy as carefully and as coolly as I am able I see no difference between him and Sumner and Co. . . ."[1]

Simultaneously the President worked to read the Radical wing out of the Republican party. His final interview with Sumner in December 1865, staged in front of a friendly witness,[2] was carefully planned to produce a break, just as was his equally hostile confrontation with Thaddeus Stevens at about the same time. Eagerly welcoming Conservative Republicans like Cowan, Dixon, and Doolittle to the White House and listening attentively to uncommitted Congressmen like John Sherman and James A. Garfield, Johnson took a hard line toward the Radicals. Even casual visitors to the executive mansion "heard him declaim in private against the radicalism of Stevens and Sumner and express the opinion that the great heart of the country was with him."[3] Unquestionably the President noted with pleasure the repeated rebuffs other Republicans gave Sumner during the early months of the session, and he must have taken a sardonic satisfaction in observing that Sumner's opposition to the Fourteenth Amendment both outraged the majority of Republicans and helped kill a measure which the White House opposed.

Doubtless the hostile reception Senate Republicans gave Sumner's speech on "The Equal Rights of All" encouraged the President to pursue his plan for cutting the Radicals adrift. On February 19, 1866, he vetoed the act, supported by nearly all Republicans in the House and the Senate, to extend the life of the Freedmen's Bureau. As the veto message was read, Sumner recognized that Johnson was declaring war against him and the

[1] Ulrich B. Phillips (ed.): *The Correspondence of Robert Toombs, Alexander H. Stephens, and Howell Cobb* (Washington; 1913), pp. 673–4.

[2] Lewis D. Campbell, an Ohio politician friendly to Johnson.

[3] Mark A. DeWolfe Howe: *James Ford Rhodes: American Historian* (New York: D. Appleton and Company; 1929), p. 20.

whole Radical wing of the Republican party. In the Senate gallery at the time, Sir Frederick Bruce, the British minister, caught his reactions: "Sumner's face was a picture of venom and defeat. He is a dangerous man. His vanity is unbounded, he has no human sympathies, and is remorseless in carrying out his doctrines. I should judge him to be very like Robespierre."[4]

The President's action was daring, since he offended not merely the Radicals but Republicans like Trumbull and Fessenden, with whom he had been cooperating; but it was successful. On the day following his message a Senate attempt to override the veto failed by two votes. Deeply unhappy, Sumner could scarcely conceal his distress when he attended Seward's annual dinner for the Foreign Relations Committee that evening, and he confessed to a young visitor whom he escorted to the table: "Oh yes, for myself I try to keep as quiet as possible, but I cannot help feeling very anxious."[5]

The President, on the other hand, was jubilant, and on Washington's birthday, addressing a large crowd that assembled at the White House, he publicly revealed his plan to read the extreme elements out of American political life.[6] "I fought traitors and treason in the South; I opposed the Davises, the Toombs', the Slidell's . . . ," he told the cheering audience; "now when I turn around, and at the other end of the line find men—I care not by what name you call them—who will stand opposed to the restoration of the Union of these States, I am free to say to you that I am still in the field."

"Give us the names at the other end," called out a listener, when the applause thinned. "Name them! Who are they?" echoed other voices.

"You ask me who they are," replied the President, exhilarated by the cordial response. "I say Thaddeus Stevens of Penn-

[4] Bruce to Clarendon, Feb. 20, 1866, Clarendon MSS. "He is no friend of ours," Bruce added. Characteristically insensitive to the reactions of others, Sumner reported that he liked Bruce, whom he found "agreeable and social." Sumner to Duchess of Argyll, Dec. 26, 1865, Argyll MSS.

[5] Mary Frier to Fannie Frier [Feb. 20] 1866, MS., Goshen (N.Y.) Hist. Soc.

[6] My account of Johnson's speech follows "Perley's" despatch in the Boston *Journal*, Feb. 23, 1866, and the account in the *National Intelligencer*, as given in Edward McPherson (ed.): *The Political History of the United States . . . during . . . Reconstruction* (2nd ed.; Washington: Solomons & Chapman; 1875), pp. 58–63.

sylvania is one; I say Mr. Sumner of the Senate is another; and Wendell Phillips is another."

During the long-continued applause, another voice shouted: "Give it to Forney!" referring to the secretary of the Senate, whose Philadelphia *Press* and Washington *Chronicle* had become increasingly critical of the President.

"In reply to that," responded Johnson, "I will simply say that I do not waste my time upon dead ducks."

When the laughter and cheers died down, Johnson referred to Radical talk of impeaching him, related this to threats of assassination which he had received, and asked passionately: "Are those who want to destroy our institutions and change the character of the Government not satisfied with the blood that has been shed? Are they not satisfied with one martyr? Does not the blood of Lincoln appease the vengeance and wrath of the opponents of this Government? Is their thirst still unslaked? Do they want more blood?"

Rarely has a speech by a President had such far-reaching consequences. For Sumner himself Johnson's foolish and intemperate remarks amounted to a vindication; here, finally, was proof that the President was as heartless and as unwise as Sumner had for months been saying. Resentful of the President's attack upon their Senator, Massachusetts voters deluged Sumner with letters approving his course. The Boston Board of Aldermen promptly passed resolutions praising his "eminent loyalty, patriotism and statesmanship" and condemning as "utter falsehood . . . any accusation, no matter by whom made, which likens him . . . to the traitor chiefs of the rebellion." Sumner's friends had to do a little lobbying in the state legislature, where Andrew's influence was strong, but the General Court too resolved that the President's accusations against Sumner were "unbecoming the elevated station occupied by him, an unjust reflection upon Massachusetts, and without the shadow of justification or defence founded upon the private or public record of our eminent Senator." So clearly was public opinion in Sumner's favor that Andrew, who for months had been negotiating with Johnson's friends, gave up hope of challenging the Senator's leadership and announced his retirement from politics, declaring that henceforth he would not "act at all, in *political,* still less, in partizan ways." [7]

At the same time the President's speech ended his hope of driving the Radicals out of the Republican party. It became clear that Johnson, who understood white Southerners so well, had completely misjudged the nature of Northern politics and had underestimated the ties of principle, of interest, and of shared experience which bound Republicans, even when quarrelsome and discordant, together. Except for a handful who drifted into the Democratic party, Republicans promptly closed ranks and took steps to guarantee that on the next test of strength they could overrule a President who was trying to divide the party. To keep Johnson from playing one house of Congress against the other, the Senate now reconsidered the vote it had taken in December, much against Sumner's wishes, and agreed that no Congressman from a Southern state would be seated until both the House of Representatives and the Senate consented to readmission. At the same time immense pressure was applied to Republicans of wavering loyalty, like Morgan of New York, who had voted to sustain the President's veto of the Freedmen's Bureau bill, and Stewart of Nevada, who finally, as Sumner happily announced, became a "new convert to the necessity of colored suffrage." [8]

Republican Senators also began to look closely at the credentials of their Democratic colleagues. Nudged by New Jersey Republicans, Sumner discovered that there were technical irregularities in the election of Senator John P. Stockton of that state, and, in a move designed to give Republicans the requisite two-thirds to override Johnson's votes, the majority attempted to unseat him. When it became evident that a motion to confirm Stockton in his seat would carry by one vote, Sumner and Fessenden loudly whispered to Lot M. Morrill to break the pair which he had established with an absent Democratic Senator

[7] F. W. Lincoln, Jr., to Sumner, Mar. 2, 1866, Sumner MSS.; Washington *Morning Chronicle,* Feb. 27, 1866; George B. Loring to Sumner, Feb. 26, 1866, Sumner MSS.; Sumner: *Works,* X, 268; Andrew to F. P. Blair, Sr., Mar. 18, 1866, copy, Andrew MSS.

[8] *Cong. Globe,* 39 Cong., 1 Sess., p. 1438. Stewart coupled universal suffrage with universal amnesty, which Sumner could not accept.

and, to the jubilation of the Radicals, he did so. Infuriated, Stockton, who had hitherto abstained, demanded that his own name be called and voted for himself. Then Sumner, earnestly appealing to "those principles of justice which will be a benefit to our country for all time," called Stockton's injudicious act a further reason for expelling him,[9] and the Republican majority, in a move so obviously partisan that thoughtful men like Trumbull could not support it, voted to oust the New Jersey Senator.

To rebuke Andrew Johnson, Sumner was prepared to sacrifice fair play and parliamentary usage, but not the principle of Negro suffrage. To the fury of his Radical colleagues, he opposed a scheme to admit Colorado, which, it was clear, would send two more Republican Senators to Washington, on the grounds that its constitution limited suffrage to whites. When advocates of admission reminded him that there were only ninety blacks in the whole territory—fewer than there had been in Kansas, which he had voted to admit with white suffrage; fewer than in many Northern states, which still denied the Negro the ballot—he professed a grand disregard for consistency: "We are not called to sit in judgment on those constitutions; we have no power to revise them; we are not to vote upon them. . . ." The main point was to establish, as both a principle and a precedent: "*No more States with inequality of rights!*" "Tell me not that it is expedient to create two more votes in this Chamber," he scolded his colleagues. "Nothing can be expedient that is not right." Though both houses finally voted to admit Colorado, Sumner, along with Fessenden and Grimes, announced he would help sustain the President's veto, so as to establish authoritatively "that, from this time forward, no State shall be received into the Union with a constitution disavowing the first principle of the Declaration of Independence."[1]

Before the Colorado bill was disposed of, Johnson on March 27, 1866, presented a fresh challenge to the Republican majority in his veto of the Civil Rights bill. Though Sumner had had little part in either framing or advocating the measure, a product of

[9] Sumner: *Works*, X, 400.

[1] Ibid., 367, 370–1. Cf. Sumner to "My dear Lieutenant," May 4, 1866, Claflin MSS.

the Judiciary Committee, he recognized how urgently it was needed to protect the rights of the freedmen. It would be a terrible calamity if Congress sustained the President's veto, he wrote the Duchess of Argyll, because defeat of the Civil Rights bill would leave "the new crop of Black Laws in full force" and thus give "to the old masters a new letter or license to do anything with the freedman short of making him a chattel." Recognizing how difficult it would be to muster the necessary two-thirds vote against the President, Sumner seemed to a reporter "well nigh ubiquitous" in Washington during the week after the veto message; forgetting for a moment his stately dignity, he rushed from one hotel to another to canvass for votes and spent his best efforts in attempting to persuade Morgan.[2] His exertions were not in vain. On April 6, by exactly the necessary margin, the Senate overrode Johnson's veto. Had Sumner and his colleagues failed either to unseat Stockton or to convert Morgan, the President's policy would have been sustained.

For Sumner it was a victory of sorts. At the outset of the session he and the President had each vowed to read the other out of the Republican party, and it was the Senator who had succeeded. Sumner could take a grim satisfaction in reminding his colleagues that Johnson had only fulfilled his direst predictions. Gloatingly the Boston *Commonwealth* reviewed his course: "Even Mr. Sumner, had he added the inspiration of a prophet to that of a statesman, could not have anticipated, when he took his firm stand in the Senate, that victory would so soon perch upon his standard." [3]

• 7 •

Victory, however, had its price. The narrow margin by which the Senate overrode Johnson's veto of the Civil Rights bill warned Republicans that they must remain united. With the President revealed as so dangerous an enemy, they could no longer afford to snarl and snap at each other. Even Fessenden and Sumner agreed to a surface reconciliation. The agent in bringing the two

[2] Sumner to Duchess of Argyll, April 3, 1866, Argyll MSS.; New York *Herald*, Mar. 28, 1866.

[3] April 14, 1866.

men together was the wife of Representative Samuel Hooper, at whose luxurious Washington house both were frequent callers. She found her opportunity in the genuine grief produced by the death of Solomon Foot, the veteran Vermont Senator, which served to remind antislavery Congressmen how long they had all been working together in the common cause of freedom. After the funeral she told Fessenden that he and Sumner should end their controversy and stand side by side in the Senate, just as they had done as pallbearers at Foot's funeral. The Maine Senator agreed but declined to make the first move. Mrs. Hooper then turned to Sumner. "No matter how or by whom it came," she urged, "let the separation be ended by you." Shortly afterward Sumner went up to Fessenden as he was leaving the Senate chamber, extended his hand, and smiled: "I wished to shake hands with you."

"What about?" Fessenden replied, with Down Eastern terseness.

"You understand it," Sumner insisted. "I have wished to shake hands with you ever since our friend's funeral. Do you understand me?"

"Precisely," was the ungracious response, and the two men shook hands. Once more the two most powerful New England Republicans were on speaking terms, though they hardly formed the team which, Sumner dreamed, "might rule the Senate." [4]

It was less easy to quiet political than personal disagreements among Republicans. With the end of the session drawing close, Congressional leaders were uncomfortably aware how little they had accomplished: they had by the closest of votes secured minimal civil rights to the freedmen; they had failed to extend the life of the Freedmen's Bureau; and because of internal dissension they had killed the proposed constitutional amendment. Unless they promptly agreed upon some reconstruction policy, voters would go to the polls in the fall and choose between the President's plan and the Congress's lack of a plan. Yet within the party, differences appeared irreconcilable. Except from a handful of Radicals, Sumner could not secure

[4] Anna L. Hooper to Sumner, Easter Monday [1866], Sumner MSS.; Fessenden: *Fessenden*, II, 341.

approval for his proposal that Congress should pass "a bill for *political* rights as well as for *civil* rights, and on precisely the same argument—that it was needful in the enforcement of the prohibition of slavery." [5] At the same time the Radicals had enough votes to defeat a constitutional amendment, originated by Robert Dale Owen of Indiana and favored by the Joint Committee on Reconstruction, which offered immediate guarantees of Negroes' civil rights and outlawed racial discrimination in voting after 1876. Such a plan, Sumner objected, would amount to a tacit recognition "that the ex-slaveholders have a right to withhold suffrage from the freedmen for ten years longer," and he would be obliged to oppose it. "I must do my duty," he warned Owen, "without looking to the consequences." [6]

When the Joint Committee, dropping Owen's scheme, put forward a new plan of reconstruction in the form of the present Fourteenth Amendment to the Constitution, most observers expected that "Sumner and his few followers" would oppose it also.[7] The proposal of the Joint Committee, revealed in late April, was in many essentials closely similar to the plan Sumner had helped defeat in early March; both provided for a reduction in a state's representation in Congress if it disfranchised voters. At the outset of the debate it appeared that Sumner would live up to expectations, for he announced that the Joint Committee's plan was "grossly inadequate to the occasion," since it failed to state "those principles which are essential to the peace and stability of the Republic." Charging, with a good deal of justice, that the "excellent Committee has listened too much to voices from without, insisting that there must be a political issue presented to the country," he urged that consideration of the amendment be postponed as long as possible "in order that all just influences may come to Congress from the country, and that Congress itself may be inspired by the fullest and amplest con-

[5] Sumner to Moncure D. Conway, July 30, 1866, Conway MSS. Cf. Sumner: *Works*, X, 322.

[6] Joseph B. James: *The Framing of the Fourteenth Amendment* (Urbana, Ill.: The University of Illinois Press; 1956), pp. 101–2. Cf. Leopold: *Robert Dale Owen*, p. 369.

[7] Washington *Morning Chronicle*, May 1, 1866. A few days earlier it was reported that "Messrs. Stevens and Sumner are at loggerheads about a reconstruction policy." New York *Herald*, April 23, 1866.

sideration of the whole question." [8] When the Senate, in deference to his objection, did delay debate until the last week of May, he hoped to improve the time by arousing Northern opinion against the amendment. If practical politicians took a second look at the proposal, he was sure that they would find the plan for proportional reduction in a state's representation unworkable —as, indeed, it has proved to be; if earnest friends of the Negro studied the wording, they could not consent to the implicit acknowledgment that for the price of reduced representation in Congress states could disfranchise black citizens.

Yet when the amendment came up for debate again at the end of May, Sumner made only a token opposition to it. At first he did ask for a further delay, because it would be "the highest statesmanship" to collect more evidence about the possible effects of the amendment. Fessenden sharply responded: "If we adopted the advice of the Senator from Massachusetts to wait until we got every particle that by any possibility might throw light on the subject, we should wait until the next century, perhaps. . . ." Sumner then meekly yielded. "I hope I was not understood to make any formal opposition to proceeding with this measure," he apologized. "Most probably I am in error; but I have performed my duty, and in a humble way satisfy myself by making this declaration." [9] As debate on the amendment progressed, Sumner continued to keep his own record straight by proposing supplementary bills to impose Negro suffrage as a means of enforcing the Thirteenth Amendment and to require from every Southern state a guarantee "that all persons shall be equal before the law," but he made no effort either to promote his own measures or to block the amendment. On June 8, 1866, when the Senate adopted the Fourteenth Amendment, it received Sumner's vote, together with those of three other Radicals who had opposed the earlier proposal in March.

To many contemporaries the inconsistency in Sumner's course toward the two amendments was baffling, and he repeatedly found it necessary to explain his actions. Admitting that he

[8] Sumner to "My dear Lieutenant," May 4, 1866, Claflin MSS.; Sumner: *Works*, X, 429.

[9] *Cong. Globe*, 39 Cong., 1 Sess., pp. 2763–4.

was not entirely happy with either version, he claimed that the second was a material improvement. The earlier proposal of the Joint Committee had specified that representation should be reduced when a state disfranchised citizens on account of color or race. For Sumner, who had worked so hard to purge the statute books of discriminatory references to Negroes, such language was intolerable; it "actually grafted into the text of the Constitution inequality and caste on account of color, and tied the hands of Congress against any exercise of power to remove it." The second version of the amendment fortunately had "nothing in it positively offensive."[1] In addition, unlike its predecessor, it contained other provisions Sumner welcomed, such as a guarantee of civil rights and the repudiation of the Confederate debt.

Since, however, both versions of the amendment had such similar intent and would have had such identical effects, Democrats brushed aside Sumner's explanations and claimed that he had capitulated before party pressure. Senator Thomas Hendricks of Indiana observed that during the final week of May, when Sumner and some other Radicals began to voice objections to the amendment, a Republican Senate caucus was promptly convened. What went on, Hendricks could only speculate, for the Republicans, meeting behind closed doors and darkened windows, swore each other to such a stringent obligation of secrecy that "not even the sharp-eyed men of the press, have been able to learn one word that was spoken, or one vote given."[2] The inference, however, was that the Republican majority voted to gag Sumner and those inclined to support him.

Though Hendricks's story was a malicious exaggeration, it contained an element of truth. Certainly no Republican caucus could have silenced Sumner; had such a gag been possible, his colleagues would have resorted to it long before. But Sumner, like every other Republican leader, was aware of the need for party unity, especially since the President was starting a rival political organization by summoning a massive National Union

[1] Sumner to "My dear Lieutenant," May 4, 1866, Claflin MSS.

[2] *Cong. Globe*, 39 Cong., 1 Sess., p. 2939.

convention to meet at Philadelphia in August. He was also planning an extensive "Swing Around the Circle" through the Northern and Western states so as to present himself and his policies to the voters. In order to help the Republican party block Johnson, that "infinite calamity to the country," [3] Sumner was willing to accept a Fourteenth Amendment he did not fully approve.

At the same time Sumner was under political pressure from Massachusetts to support the amendment. William Claflin, who was both lieutenant-governor of the state and the Massachusetts member of the National Republican Executive Committee, warned him that "people desire to have some position on which they can stand in opposition to the copperhead policy" of the President and that the amendment recommended by the Joint Committee was welcomed in Boston "with considerable favor as the only measure we are likely to get passed this session." Sumner also realized that accepting the amendment would not expose him to political risk. Since the President's outburst on Washington's birthday, criticism of Sumner among Massachusetts Republicans had virtually ceased. Nobody now remembered Andrew's attack upon the earlier version of the amendment and, by implication, upon the proposal that Sumner had twice introduced. The former governor had withdrawn from politics and settled down to the lucrative practice of law. Even the Springfield *Republican*, usually critical of Sumner, praised the "noble manner" in which he agreed to accept the Fourteenth Amendment "for the sake of harmony and the country." [4]

It would be a mistake, however, to think of Sumner's decision as a purely political one. Had his health permitted, it is quite conceivable that he would have continued his opposition to the Fourteenth Amendment in spite of its consequences to his party, but ever since the beginning of the session he had been working under enormous physical and emotional strain. Tense and angry over Johnson's apostasy, over the conduct of Congressional colleagues, and over threatened political danger in Massa-

[3] Sumner to Duchess of Argyll, June 25, 1866, Argyll MSS.

[4] Claflin to Sumner, May 1, 1866, Sumner MSS.; W. P. Phillips to Sumner, April 2, 1866, ibid., Springfield *Republican*, June 1, 1866.

chusetts, he was for months able to get little sleep. Though no longer a young man, he pushed himself to the limits of his strength and insisted upon being in daily and continuous attendance at the Senate. After adjournment each day, he returned promptly to his rooms to continue his laborious reading and research for his speeches, which for this single session of Congress filled 556 pages of his published *Works*. Taking no exercise and pausing only for dinner, he worked, either alone or with his secretary, until after midnight.

Adding to these strains was Sumner's concern for his mother, his last surviving close relative.[5] Ailing for the past four years, the old lady was gradually growing feebler, and Sumner was torn between his desire to be at her bedside and his duty to remain in the Senate. There was, of course, nothing he could do to help her, for she had an excellent physician and a capable paid companion in attendance, but he knew she was lonely and longed for his return. The tie between Mrs. Sumner and her son was close, though both were such formal, reserved persons that they could not express their feelings easily in letters or even in words. Only by his presence could Sumner reassure her of his affection, yet his presence was urgently required in a Senate where every Republican vote was needed to block Andrew Johnson.

Overstrained and exhausted, Sumner became seriously ill about the middle of May, when he had an excruciating recurrence of angina pectoris, which had afflicted him in times of stress since 1858. Unable to sleep except through anodynes, he turned as always to Dr. Brown-Séquard for help and was fortunate enough to find that itinerant specialist in the United States. Prescribing sedation, the physician urged a vacation, but Sumner was unwilling to leave his post of duty. He compromised by agreeing to make no further extensive speeches in the Senate. Along with the medicine, Brown-Séquard gave Sumner psychic relief by declaring that his agonizing pain derived from his

[5] His only surviving sister, Julia Hastings, lived in San Francisco. She had been back East only once during the past ten years and rarely corresponded with either Sumner or her mother.

"original injuries 10 years ago" at the hands of Preston S. Brooks.[6]

Too ill to play more than a passive role as the Senate proceeded to adopt the Fourteenth Amendment, Sumner remained in Washington until he received word that his mother was rapidly sinking. He arrived in Boston four days before her death and was with her during her placid last hours. With restraint he wrote the Duchess of Argyll of his loss: "She was an excellent and remarkable person, whose death leaves me more than ever alone." [7] Returning from her funeral, to which only a few old friends had been invited, to the empty house on Hancock Street, he exclaimed: "I have now no home!" [8]

[6] Sumner to "My dear Sir," May 29, 1866, MS., Ill. State Hist. Soc.; Brown-Séquard to Sumner [May 1866], Sumner MSS.; Sumner to Mrs. John E. Lodge, June 4, 1866, Lodge MSS.; Sumner to Longfellow, June 6, 1866, Longfellow MSS.

[7] Sumner to Duchess of Argyll, June 25, 1866, Argyll MSS.

[8] Elias Nason: *The Life and Times of Charles Sumner* (Boston: B. B. Russell; 1874), pp. 311–12. On Mrs. Sumner's funeral, see Julia Ward Howe: Diary, June 17, 1866, Howe MSS.

CHAPTER VII

My Name Was Dishonored

DURING the summer and fall of 1866 Sumner's fortunes, both political and personal, altered dramatically and, as it seemed, for the better. Andrew Johnson's threat to the Republican party was scotched, both through his own blunders and through the folly of his supporters. As scheduled, the President made an extensive speaking tour of the North and West, but he allowed his audience to bait him into making intemperate charges similar to those in his Washington's birthday speech, which, his loyal supporter Doolittle grieved, had "lost to our cause" 200,000 votes. Even before Johnson left the capital, riots in Memphis and New Orleans, during which whites terrorized the blacks and assassinated their leaders, discredited his claim that the South was peaceful and ready to accept the outcome of the war. At the National Union convention in August the ubiquity of former Confederate leaders, together with the conspicuous presence of notorious Northern Copperheads, lent credit to the fear that the President was about to betray the Union into the hands of its enemies. Invoking the "spirits of the martyred dead," Republicans hostile to Johnson swept to victory in the fall congressional races, and it appeared that the new Congress would be overwhelmingly Radical.

If Sumner took little public notice of these encouraging events, it was because an even more decided change occurred in his personal life before the elections: he found a wife. After living fifty-five years as a bachelor, he began to realize, with his severe illness in the spring of 1866 and the death of his mother in June, how painfully alone he was in the world. Before returning to Washington from his mother's funeral, he took a long carriage drive with E. L. Pierce, the young lawyer from Milton who was becoming his most trusted political confidant, and unexpectedly turned the conversation to "the conditions which inclined people to marriage." He remarked "that for the first time in his life he had now the means to support a family, and if he should meet someone who inspired him, he felt at liberty to marry." Then, checking the discussion, he swore Pierce to secrecy. He had also hoped to talk with Longfellow about his solitary state but, finding no propitious occasion before he had to go back to the Senate, wrote: "When we meet again, I may have something to tell you; and certainly I shall have much on which to seek your communion. I have come to an epoch in life. My mother is dead. I have a moderate competency. What next?" [1]

In fact, Sumner already had a pretty good idea of what was next, for he had already met the "some one" so hypothetically mentioned in his talk with Pierce. For several years a regular visitor in the Washington home of his Massachusetts Representative Samuel Hooper, he had during the previous winter seen a good deal of his colleague's widowed daughter-in-law, Mrs. Alice Mason Hooper.[2] Four years before the war Alice had married William Sturgis Hooper, and while her husband was serving as a military aide to General Banks in Louisiana she had lived with her father, Jonathan Mason, on Beacon Hill. The death of her husband in September 1863 left her bereaved and depressed, and the Hoopers insisted that, in order to raise her spirits, she and her seven-year-old daughter, Isabella, must spend the 1865–66 social season in the capital.

Before Alice came to live with the Hoopers, Sumner was hardly acquainted with her, though what little he did know about her was to her credit. To be sure, she was the granddaughter of

[1] Pierce, IV, 302; Sumner to Longfellow, June 24, 1866, Longfellow MSS.

[2] Charles H. Pope and Thomas Hooper: *Hooper Genealogy* (Boston: Charles H. Pope; 1908), p. 169.

an arch-conservative Federalist Congressman and Senator, who had made his fortune developing the exclusive residential section of Beacon Hill; and her sister was married to Charles H. Appleton, son of the William Appleton who had tried to block Sumner's election to the Senate in 1851 and had attempted to ostracize him from Boston society. But her father was a stanch Unionist, who early declared that only emancipation, and not "half measures," could end the war, and Alice herself was an equally loyal supporter of Sumner's views. So strongly did she oppose concessions to the South that, shortly after the attack on Fort Sumter, when she encountered a Boston acquaintance who favored compromise, she spurned his extended hand, drew herself up proudly, and announced: "I don't know you, Sir." During the summer after her husband's death she insisted upon coming to Washington as a volunteer nurse and, even when not on regular duty, never let more than a day or two pass without visiting the wounded in the military hospitals around the capital. Grateful to Sumner for securing the appointment and promotion of her brother as an army officer, she treasured the public documents and occasional photographs that the Senator sent her.[3]

Slender and shapely, with perfectly regular if somewhat sharp features, Alice was one of the most strikingly beautiful women in Washington. She had both elegance and charm. Though women sometimes thought she was "artful," most men praised her "grace, ease, and beauty of deportment." As her period of mourning ended, she inevitably attracted more and more male callers to the Hooper residence. Even the irascible Fessenden frequently came by to play bezique with her until, observing that she "looked prettier than ever," the happily married Maine Senator concluded that it would not be discreet for him to see too much of a widow who was clearly becoming once more available. Another of Alice's most constant attendants was

[3] Jonathan Mason to Sumner, Mar. 21, 1862, Sumner MSS.; F. B. Sanborn: *Recollections of Seventy Years* (Boston: Richard G. Badger; 1909), II, 493; Herbert St. John Mildmay (ed.): *John Lothrop Motley and his Family* (London: John Lane; 1910), pp. 222–3. See Alice's letters to Sumner, dated April 9 [1863], Jan. 5 [1864], and Dec. 22 [1865], Sumner MSS., and that dated July 8, 1862, G. B. Pierce MSS.

that handsome bachelor, the eternally smiling Speaker of the House of Representatives, Schuyler Colfax.[4]

"I begin to think Mr. Sumner is looking in that direction," Fessenden reported to his family early in 1866. "He is always in attendance [upon her and her companion] at the Senate, finding seats, and on hand to wait on them out—a most unusual thing for him." How serious were Sumner's intentions he himself probably did not know. Against any thought of his marriage there were formidable objections. He was by choice and by temperament a bachelor. Though he had carried on mild flirtations in his youth, he had never, so far as can be determined, been in love with a woman. The story that in his early manhood he "had failed in a suit in which his whole heart was enlisted"[5] was probably myth, perhaps started by Sumner himself to explain his unwed state. As he grew older, as public business absorbed more and more of his time, and as the Brooks assault purged him of inner doubts and fears, he felt less need for the comfort, the reassurance, and the love which friends had supplied in his younger days and which a wife might have given him in his maturity.

There were excellent financial as well as psychological reasons why Sumner should not consider marriage. He had no regular income except his Senate salary. Since he had no law practice and since he adhered rigidly to his rule to accept no donations or expensive gifts while in public life, he had to live on the three thousand dollars, plus travel expenses, he received for his government service. On this sum he could, as a single man, live very comfortably, renting the best rooms available in Washington, purchasing his large wardrobe from the best English tailors, and buying occasional rare books and autographs, and he had even been able to save about five thousand dollars, which he

[4] H. L. Dawes to Anna Dawes, Dec. 8, 1866, Dawes MSS.; John Bigelow: Diary, Mar. 27, 1867, Bigelow MSS.; Fessenden: *Fessenden*, II, 341.

[5] Pierce, IV, 303. As a young man Sumner frequently spoke of his "love" for male friends like Longfellow and Howe. Perhaps it ought to be explained that the word in nineteenth-century usage did not imply an overt homosexual relationship, of which I have found not the slightest evidence in Sumner's entire career.

invested in government bonds.[6] But he felt that he could not afford to support a family—especially since, every six years, there was a possibility that he might lose his Senate seat.

Finally, operating against this particular marriage, was the factor of age. Sumner was nearly three decades older than Alice. To some observers the difference seemed even greater, for she looked "like a young lady of 16,"[7] while Sumner, because of ill-health, overwork, and overeating, had become slow-moving and portly, and his hair was now almost entirely gray.

Probably Sumner would never have done more than dream of matrimony had he not fallen ill in 1866. Since he did not think he should follow Dr. Brown-Séquard's advice and leave the capital, he tried to rest and recover in his rooms, on the corner of F and Thirteenth Streets, where it was natural that Alice, an experienced nurse, should visit and help take care of him. With the young woman acting in such a maternal role, the difference in their ages somehow seemed less.

The death of Mrs. Sumner removed another barrier, for that frugal lady had so carefully managed her husband's estate —to which had been added over the years legacies from her several sons—that she left to Sumner and his sole surviving sister Julia securities and cash worth more than $65,000, to be divided equally between them, and to Sumner alone the house at No. 20, Hancock Street, valued at $10,500. Combining his own savings with his share of the estate, Sumner found himself worth a little more than $40,000 in cash and securities and also the owner of a three-storey, thirteen-room house in Boston.[8] For the first time he could afford to talk not of that abstract emotion which he gravely labeled "the tender passion," but of love.

Why Alice looked with favor upon Sumner's suit must remain a subject for speculation. Though she was a widow, she

[6] See the carefully preserved financial records in the Sumner MSS. and, especially, James T. Furness to Sumner [c. Nov. 14, 1863], ibid.

[7] Richard Yates and Catharine Y. Pickering: *Richard Yates: Civil War Governor,* ed. John H. Krenkel (Danville, Ill.: The Interstate Printers & Publishers, Inc.; 1966), p. 251.

[8] Estate of Mrs. Charles P. Sumner, Docket 47,122, Probate Court Records, Suffolk County, Mass.; F. V. Balch to Sumner, Jan. 8, 1866 [i.e., 1867], Sumner MSS.; "Estimate of income of Hon. Charles Sumner, May 16, 1866 to Jan. 1867," ibid.

was certainly neither lonely nor necessitous. In both Boston and Washington bachelors thought her a prize catch, and Speaker Colfax appears to have been earnest in his attentions to her. It was widely known that she was as wealthy as she was beautiful. Since Congressman Hooper was one of the richest men in Boston, her husband had been able to leave her and "Bell," as they abbreviated her daughter's name, about $75,000—worth perhaps five times that amount in terms of present-day purchasing power. In addition, Alice's father was wealthy, and her first husband's maternal grandfather, William Sturgis, had settled a large amount of money upon her during her widowhood.[9]

Though there is no reason to believe, as later gossips charged, that Alice thought Sumner would make her First Lady of the land,[1] she did know that she was marrying the most conspicuous, and still the most handsome, member of the Senate. Doubtless she saw him as a strong figure, whom she could respect as well as love. At the same time she knew that in helping, protecting, and, when necessary, nursing him, she would be reenacting the role she had found so rewarding in the military hospitals during the war.

In all probability it was Alice who led Sumner to take the irrevocable step of proposing. Although he returned to the capital from Boston with amorous and honorable intentions, his plans were vague. Vacationing in the White Mountains in August, he gaily wrote former New York Senator Hamilton Fish, who had asked him to Fishkill: "It will take much to make me give up the visit which you kindly invite. Civil war, or marriage or some other extreme case might interfere." Only ten days later, however, he was writing his friends of his engagement, in terms both rhapsodic and bewildered. "Do not be too surprised," he cautioned one correspondent to whom he broke the news; "but you cannot be more so than I am." "If you knew how little of design or will there was in what has occurred," he told Bancroft, "you would see the Providence which has ruled." Sumner's more cynical friends suspected that it was not Providence but Alice who

[9] Estate of William Sturgis Hooper, Docket 44,900, Probate Court Records, Suffolk County, Mass.; Edmund Quincy to Anne Quincy, Oct. 26, 1866, Quincy MSS.; New York *Herald*, Dec. 29, 1889.

[1] Dawes: *Sumner*, p. 262.

had prevailed, and his more perceptive correspondents noted with amusement tinged with apprehension that he failed to mention the name of the lady to whom he was engaged.[2]

Sumner too was apprehensive. No sooner had he taken the irrevocable step than, like any other bachelor, he began to have doubts. "Now, Alice," he said more than once to his fiancée, "unless we are both satisfied that this union is to be a happy one, we had better separate now." She refused to share his anxieties and went ahead with plans for the wedding, even though her relatives took "no pains to conceal how distasteful the whole affair was to them." "Let me confess that I am not without solicitude," Sumner wrote Bancroft as the day approached. "I tremble sometimes at the responsibility I assume. I am to make another happy; for unless I do this there can be no happiness for me. . . ."[3]

On October 17, 1866, a gloriously beautiful day, full of sunshine which made the autumn leaves blaze like torches, Charles Sumner and Alice Hooper were married by the Episcopal bishop of Boston in the home of her brother-in-law, with only a handful of nearest relatives present. "Only think of Charles Sumner being married in William Appleton's former house!" gibed abolitionist Edmund Quincy. "It were almost enough to bring him back from the grave, if he had soul enough to be visible to the naked eye." "Today at 3 o'clock . . . and at the age of 55 [I] begin to live," Sumner wrote Whittier just before the ceremony. By 4:30 the newlyweds, accompanied by Bell and her dog Ty, were on their way to Newport for a three-week honeymoon.[4]

"There must be an end to all things—even to this enchantment," Sumner lamented as the time came for him to return to what he now called his "obscure home . . . in Hancock Street" in

[2] Sumner to Fish, Aug. 21, 1866, copy, Fish MSS.; Sumner to Sarah Cleveland, Aug. 31, 1866, Cleveland MSS.; Sumner to Bancroft, Sept. 19, 1866, Bancroft MSS., Cornell Univ.; Dennett (ed.): *Lincoln and the Civil War,* p. 249; Abigail B. Adams to Sumner, Sept. 19, 1866, Sumner MSS.

[3] Statement of F. W. Bird on Sumner's marriage, 1893, Bird MSS.; C. F. Adams, Jr., to Mrs. C. F. Adams, Oct. 20, 1865 [i.e., 1866], Adams MSS.; Sumner to Bancroft, Sept. 19, 1866, Bancroft MSS., Cornell Univ.

[4] Quincy to Anne Quincy, Oct. 26, 1866, Quincy MSS.; Sumner to Whittier, Oct. 17, 1866, Whittier MSS., Essex Institute.

order to pack for Washington. It was a matter of public interest, to be reported in the newspapers, when the Senator, accompanied for the first time by his family, set out for the capital. "Just think of it," exclaimed Whittier. "Instead of taking his carpet-bag and starting off for the Washington [railroad] cars, as aforetime, he went this winter, filling a coach with his family:—Mr. Sumner and Mrs. Sumner, and Mrs. Sumner's child, and Mrs. Sumner's child's nurse, and Mrs. Sumner's [child's] little dog!" The furnished house at 322 I Street formerly occupied by Senator and Mrs. Pomeroy was waiting for them. "I hope to be very happy," Sumner wrote Mrs. Lodge. "Tardily I begin." [5]

Inevitably Sumner's first weeks in Washington were occupied with what he called "the trials of a young house-keeper." The furniture had to be rearranged; everyday supplies like coal and soap had to be bought; crystal and china had to be ordered. He had to find a French tutor for Bell and to rent a pew in the Church of the Epiphany for the devoutly Episcopal Alice. In Washington, a city of transients, both household furnishings and servants were handed along from one owner to the next. Observers considered it ironical that Sumner, regarded as one of the most anti-British Senators in the capital, should thus inherit the coach and horses once belonging to Lord Lyons, and Sumner himself thought it amusing that his dining-room servant should have been for thirteen years Chief Justice Taney's favorite employee. After about a month, when the household began to settle down, Sumner spoke proudly of his "little kingdom," where he hoped his "subjects" would be "content and happy." [6]

Callers were struck by the ease with which Sumner adapted himself to his new domesticity. Three members of the Massachusetts delegation who visited the Sumners just after the opening of the Congressional session in December 1866 thought the Senator was a changed man. "It was so strange," Dawes reported to his daughter, "to find him instead of a recluse, as he has always been before, up to his chin in documents and dust . . .

[5] Sumner to Mrs. John E. Lodge, Nov. 1, 1866, Lodge MSS.; Boston *Commonwealth,* Nov. 24, 1866; Whittier to an unidentified correspondent, Dec. 30, 1866, copy, Whittier MSS., Harvard Lib.

[6] Sumner to Mrs. John E. Lodge, Jan. 2, 1867, Lodge MSS.; Alice M. Sumner to Longfellow, Dec. 9 [1866], Longfellow MSS.

now neatly attired and nicely seated in a very comfortable easy chair by the side of a sofa, on which was reclining his wife, happy as he himself, opening his vast mail for him, and enjoying with him its contents." Aware of his correspondent's interest in things feminine, the Representative went on to describe Alice's "straw colored dress of some material we men dont know the name of, not silk with large steel buttons in front, and high neck with plain, smooth white col[l]ar and cuffs, an elegant pin and diamond ring." The impression made by Mrs. Sumner, continued Dawes, "was that she was a lady of excellent sense, of varied attainments and pleasing manners. . . . You could not discover a hair out of place or a superfluous wrinkle in the dress. . . . I was charmed." [7]

Eager to pay back the social obligations Sumner had accumulated during his bachelor years, the newly married couple began almost at once to invite his old friends, like Longfellow and Lieber, to visit them. Nearly every evening they had guests for dinner, for they planned to make their dining room a salon, where "men of ideas and women of the highest culture, . . . all embued with great national sentiments," could meet. "Mrs. Sumner," reported the Boston *Transcript,* "is remarkable for her genius as leader of this kind of society, and Mr. Sumner is evidently anxious to bring remarkable political or otherwise conspicuous characters en rapport with the diplomats, so as to make foreign governments understand in whose hands the strength of the country lies." [8] To this end, the Sumners invited Thaddeus Stevens to dine with Baron Gerolt and Sir Frederick Bruce; they asked Secretary Stanton and Senator Morrill on another occasion to meet the new French minister, M. Jules Berthémy; and on yet another evening presented the Marquis de Chambrun, the new attaché at the French legation, to Dawes and Colfax. Soon it became general report that "Mrs. Charles Sumner leads the 'ton' in Washington." [9]

Though Sumner comfortably declared he was happier at home than anywhere else, the newly married couple naturally

[7] Dawes to Anna Dawes, Dec. 8, 1866, Dawes MSS.

[8] Quoted in *The Independent,* Jan. 17, 1867, p. 4.

[9] Dawes to Electa Dawes, Jan. 15, 1867, Dawes MSS.; H. A. Wise to Hamilton Fish, Jan. 29, 1867, Fish MSS.

received many invitations during their first months in the capital. One which they did not accept was to a dinner at the White House. Everywhere they went, they were the center of attention, Sumner robustly handsome and beamingly happy, Alice coolly beautiful and stunningly dressed, appearing to one admirer "as graceful as a lily of Egypt—and gentle, and genial, and good as she is graceful." "Sumner and his beautiful wife are themselves history and romance," gushed the wife of Representative Ashley; "they ought to be handsomely bound and opened a page at a time." [1]

• 2 •

Politically as well as socially Washington was a pleasanter place for Sumner in the winter of 1866–67 than it had been for years. No longer did he have to resolve the dilemma of reconciling the concern of his constituents for equal rights with the indifference of the national administration to those rights. Johnson had, in effect, joined the Democrats, and if the Republican leadership, which now fell to the Congressional caucuses, was by no means so radical as Sumner desired, it was certainly sympathetic to the freedmen. Moreover, Sumner knew that the next Congress, chosen in the recent fall elections but not seated until March 1867, would be more radical still. Contentedly he worked with his Senate colleagues to undo Johnson's reconstruction program and to curtail his powers for future harm.

Sumner had nothing to do with framing the Tenure of Office bill, which Senator George H. Williams of Iowa introduced on the first day of the session, but he enthusiastically supported this attempt to control Johnson by limiting his power to remove his subordinates. Indeed, he wanted the restrictions upon the President made much stronger. Senator Sherman, he thought, erred in consenting to exclude the cabinet from the protection of the law, since "the power of appointing and removing members of the Cabinet more properly belonged to the Senate as a permanent body than to the President," because "the Senate was less

[1] Mary C. Ames, in *The Independent,* April 4, 1867, p. 1; Ashley to Sumner, Jan. 13, 1867, Sumner MSS.

liable to become depraved and bad than the President." [2]

Sumner was even more concerned over the willingness of some Republicans to exempt minor civil servants from the protection of the Tenure of Office bill, since the President was now carrying out his campaign threat to kick Radical Republicans out of federal offices. He proposed therefore to amend the bill by requiring the President to secure the approval of the Senate before removing any government employee earning more than a thousand dollars a year. To angry protests that his amendment would "lumber up and incumber the business" of the Senate so that there would be no time for other, important legislation, Sumner responded: "I am willing to act on an inspector or a night watchman; and if I could, I would save him from Executive tyranny." To Fessenden's objection that his amendment was unprecedented, he replied: "I am not a Chinese, to be swathed by traditions." If Congress had never before acted to protect petty officeholders it was because "there was no such duty on our fathers," who never had the responsibility of curbing a "President of the United States who had become the enemy of his country." [3]

Fiercely McDougall interrupted with a question of privilege, charging that it was unparliamentary for a Senator to use such language toward a President. As other Senators became embroiled in the tangled procedural question, Sumner angrily demanded the floor, voicing "excited and angry appeals to the Chair and brother Senators as to whether he was rightfully interrupted." When he was able to resume his speech, he could make it not just a defense of petty officeholders but a vindication of the complete freedom of debate. "Exposure of the powerful, and protection of the weak" were "not only invaluable liberties, but commanding duties." For this reason he felt obliged to hold Andrew Johnson up to judgment, but in so doing he announced: "I do not dwell upon his open exposure of himself in a condition of intoxication, while taking the oath of office—nor do I dwell upon the maudlin speeches by which he has degraded the country as it was never degraded before—nor do I hearken to any

[2] Dennett (ed.): *Lincoln and the Civil War,* p. 267.
[3] Sumner: *Works,* XI, 66–7.

reports of pardons sold, or of personal corruption." Then, having carefully done precisely what he declared he was not doing, he attacked the President as "the successor of Jefferson Davis," "the minister of discord," "an enormous and malignant usurper, through whom the Republic is imperilled." [4]

Sumner felt a special responsibility to save from this peril the members of the United States foreign service, particularly those whom he himself had been instrumental in having appointed. He was distressed, but not surprised, to discover that Seward, now recovered from his wounds, was cooperating with the President in a political purge of American diplomats abroad. In December 1866 the Secretary of State precipitated the resignation of John Lothrop Motley, Sumner's special friend and protégé who was serving as American minister to Austria. An obscure American citizen traveling abroad named George McCrackin wrote to the President and to several Congressmen that Motley professed to despise American democracy, proclaimed "that an English gentleman is the model of human perfection," and asserted "that the President has deserted his pledges and principles in common with Mr. Seward, who . . . is hopelessly degraded." Sumner threw his letter from McCrackin in the fire, but Seward, probably at the President's urging, felt it necessary to look into the allegations and asked Motley for an explanation. Indignant that his superior could believe such aspersions on his character, Motley not merely denied them but resigned. As always, Sumner rushed to the defense of an old friend, without considering the possibility that there might be truth in the charges against the Anglophilic, indiscreet Motley or the likelihood that Seward's letter of inquiry was designed to forestall, rather than to cause, the removal of Motley. Angrily he demanded publication of the Motley-Seward correspondence, including the original McCrackin letter. "When a stab is given at an eminent citizen abroad," he told his colleagues, "we ought to know who has dealt the blow," and he added that Seward's letter to Motley did "great dishonor to our country." [5]

[4] Boston *Post*, Jan. 18, 1867; Sumner: *Works*, XI, 70–80.

[5] *Cong. Globe*, 39 Cong., 2 Sess., p. 904. See the fuller treatment of the Motley removal in Sister M. Claire Lynch: *The Diplomatic Mission of John Lothrop Motley to Austria, 1861–1867* (Washington: The Catholic University of

Privately Sumner believed that Seward's course had been not merely dishonorable but perverse. Seward seemed to have lost his principles, and he had "done nothing but blunder" since 1860. *"He never understood our war,"* Sumner concluded, "and he does not now understand how peace is to be secured." Nothing Seward could do served to bring him around. The Secretary's publicized visits to Capitol Hill, where he conspicuously sat next to Sumner in the Senate chamber and engaged him in apparently cordial conversation, did little to lessen the ill feeling. Nor were invitations for both the Sumners to attend Seward's intimate little dinners more successful. Seward's Sèvres china, Sumner decided, was better than his principles, and the two men were hopelessly alienated.[6]

As resignations began to occur in the foreign service and the President attempted to fill the vacancies with men of his own persuasion, the full force of Sumner's resistance to his "usurpation" began to be apparent. Repeatedly he and the Foreign Relations Committee voted to reject Johnson's nominees. "Congress," he told John Bigelow, "should require friends in foreign as well as in domestic places." The same loyalty was due to Congress as had formerly been due to the President, "when we had one." "The present incumbent," Sumner announced, "is a nullity and will be treated as such." [7]

Many months earlier Sumner had privately made up his mind that Johnson must be not merely treated as a nullity but removed. The President still had enough power to frustrate Republican attempts to reconstruct the South. He could veto bills, though there was a dependable Republican majority for overriding most of his objections; he could encourage the Northern Democrats and the former rebels in the South; and, worst of all, he had, as Chief Executive, the power to render Congressional acts nugatory through non-enforcement. "If we go forward and

---

America Press; 1944), Chap. 6, and Marjorie Frye Gutheim: "John Lothrop Motley" (unpublished Ph.D. dissertation, Department of History, Columbia University, 1955), Chap. 13.

[6] Sumner to W. W. Story, Dec. 16, 1866, MS., Henry E. Huntington Lib.; Sumner to Mrs. John E. Lodge, Dec. 16, 1866, Lodge MSS.; Dennett (ed.): *Lincoln and the Civil War*, p. 262.

[7] John Bigelow: Diary, Mar. 2, 1867, Bigelow MSS.

supersede the sham governments set up in the rebel states," Sumner saw, "we encounter the appointing power of the President, who would put in office men who sympathize with him. It is this consideration which makes ardent representatives say that he must be removed." [8]

Ardent himself, Sumner tried not to take a public stand on the impeachment of Johnson, since there was already a House committee investigating charges against the President and the Senate might have to try the case. Throughout the session he cautiously refrained from urging "the full remedy" for the difficulties between President and Congress, though he left few listeners in doubt that he desired the removal not just of the President but of the Secretary of the Treasury and of certain members of the Supreme Court. But he vigorously denied Democratic charges that he was prejudging the President's case. Officially, he insisted, he did not know what was going on in the other House. "What right have I to know that the President is to be impeached?" he exclaimed. "How can I know it?" [9] In fact, of course, he and every other Senator did know that impeachment proceedings were under way. Republican Senator Howe offered a better defense when he observed that if Sumner's utterances against Johnson rendered him ineligible as an impartial judge of the President so did the pro-Johnson statements of the Democratic Senators.

Until Republicans could decide whether to impeach the President and until they could agree upon a plan for reorganizing the South, Sumner thought he could best serve the cause, as he had so often done in the past, by blocking any inadvertent or ill-considered action on the part of Congress that might serve as an unfortunate precedent. He insisted, therefore, upon enfranchising the Negroes in the District of Columbia, not simply because it was an act of justice for the residents of Washington but because it was a symbolic move to inaugurate "a policy not only strictly for the District of Columbia, but in some sense for the country at large." Similarly he sought to force Nebraska to enfranchise blacks before it could be admitted to the Union.

[8] Sumner to W. W. Story, Dec. 16, 1866, MS., Henry E. Huntington Lib.

[9] Sumner: *Works*, XI, 74, 80; *Cong. Globe*, 39 Cong., 2 Sess., pp. 490, 1883.

Recognizing that there were only a handful of Negroes in the territory, he would not admit that his objection to the Nebraska constitution was what Wade called "a little miserable technicality." "Sir," he asked, "can a question of human rights be a technicality?" Republicans must unite under the banner: "No more States with the word 'white' in their constitutions."[1]

Despite occasional acerbity and overstatement in these debates during the early weeks of the session, Sumner was not bitterly estranged from his colleagues, as he so often had been during the previous winter, and he acted with considerable political finesse. In the discussion of suffrage in the District of Columbia, for instance, he took very little part, except to urge the Senate to a vote. Seemingly he recognized that sometimes he increased hostility to a measure by advocating it and that, where the majority was already on his side, silence was his best policy. Accordingly, he refused to allow himself to reply to Cowan's twitting remarks about his recent marriage, and he ignored Garrett Davis's query as to why a true Radical would not have "selected a sable daughter of Africa" for his wife.[2] Similarly, he refused to become involved in side issues, such as a Democratic proposal, designed to kill the District suffrage bill, to enfranchise women in Washington as well as Negroes. This, said Sumner, was "obviously the great question of the future," but, unlike a number of his fellow Radicals, he was unwilling to have the District voting bill "clogged, burdened, or embarrassed" by a woman suffrage amendment.[3]

On the Nebraska bill, finding himself unable to secure the total rejection of the proposed constitution, Sumner showed he knew the value of compromise, and he accepted Senator George Edmunds's proviso making universal suffrage an irrevocable condition for the admission of the state. Although many supporters of Edmunds's plan admitted that such a condition was of doubtful constitutionality, to Sumner it was acceptable because, he declared, "whatever may be its validity," it would "have at

[1] *Cong. Globe*, 39 Cong., 2 Sess., pp. 38, 124, 195, 197.

[2] Ibid., pp. 58, 80.

[3] Sumner: *Works*, XI, 49.

least this efficacy: it will keep the Congress of the United States on the record clear and above reproach."[4]

Impractical as Sumner's insistence upon abstract principles sometimes seemed, more and more Republicans came to share his hostility to any measure which even implicitly recognized the white race as superior to the black. Painfully they learned that astute lawyers on the Democratic side of the Senate would exploit every concession made to Northern racism and use it as a precedent for Southern actions. Johnson's supporters made much, for instance, of the fact that many Northern states continued to deny the vote to the Negro while their Congressmen tried to require enfranchisement of the blacks in the South; they exploited the awkward fact that the proposed Fourteenth Amendment seemed to give states the right to exclude citizens from the polls if they paid the price of reduced representation; and they found a precedent in the decision made in the final days of the previous session of Congress to readmit Tennessee without requiring Negro suffrage. Almost alone of his colleagues, Sumner could reply that he had voted against the admitting of Tennessee and that he had constantly declared the Fourteenth Amendment was not a finality but only the first step toward real reconstruction. Even the hostile Doolittle was obliged to admit that Sumner's position was always consistent.

By early 1867 it began to appear that Sumner's very inflexibility was beginning to pay off. As President Johnson continued intractable, as the Southern states one after another rejected the proposed Fourteenth Amendment, and as the Supreme Court's decision in the Milligan case threatened to strip army officers in the South of protection against the provisional governments, more and more Republicans came to see the need for drastic action, both against the President and against the unrestored South. Moderate Senators like Fessenden and Grimes clearly disliked Sumner's views and chafed at his intractability, yet, as Gideon Welles said, "at a deadlock, unable to go forward and not manly enough to retreat," they seemed to have "no alternative

[4] *Cong. Globe*, 39 Cong., 2 Sess., p. 357.

. . . but to follow Sumner."[5] Exultantly, and with no attempt to conceal his satisfaction, he watched his colleagues assume positions which he had long held. By mid-January 1867 he could boast that the Senate had adopted his views in extending suffrage to Negroes in the District of Columbia, in requiring universal suffrage as an irrevocable condition for the admission of both Nebraska and Colorado as states, and in declaring that in future elections in other territories there should "be no exclusion from the suffrage on account of color." "And thus ends a long contest," he reported to Bird, "where at first I was alone. . . ." Stewart, of Nevada, who sat in a nearby seat and glanced over Sumner's letter, added: "It cannot be said now, that the Republican party is not committed to Negro suffrage."[6]

Ahead lay the next task, that of overthrowing the "sham governments" the President had set up in the South, "so that we can begin again and build on the loyal element." There would be a fight ahead, Sumner was sure, but "Congress is doing pretty well. Every step is forward."[7] Eagerly he watched the growing success of his principles. He was now "very arrogant with success," John Hay found, yet there was "no selfish exaltation in it" but "rather the fierce joy of a prophet over the destruction of the enemies of the Lord." "He is splendid in his present temper," Hay recorded; "arrogant, insolent, implacable—thoroughly in earnest —honest as the day."[8]

• 3 •

Eagerly waiting for the Joint Committee on Reconstruction to mature a Republican plan for dealing with the South, Sumner during the early months of the session did all that he could to mobilize public and Congressional sentiment for a truly radical approach toward reconstruction. Repeatedly he presented memorials to the Senate from loyalists, black and white, in the South, who begged Congress to strike down the provisional gov-

[5] Welles: *Diary*, II, 635–6.

[6] Sumner to Bird, Jan. 10, 1867, Bird MSS.

[7] Sumner to Mrs. John E. Lodge, Dec. 16, 1866, Lodge MSS.; Sumner to W. W. Story, Dec. 16, 1866, MS., Henry E. Huntington Lib.

[8] Dennett (ed.): *Lincoln and the Civil War*, pp. 271, 276.

ernments President Johnson had set up and to start afresh with universal manhood suffrage. Every time he could obtain the floor, he read to his colleagues extracts from his large daily budget of mail from the South, where, as his correspondents informed him, Negroes were the constant victims of "terrorism and extortion" and where the spirit of rebellion was "*fiercer and more intolerant than it was at the middle of 1861.*" He tried to stimulate general discussion of reconstruction issues by introducing elaborate resolutions demanding the complete eradication of the Johnson regimes throughout the South. When parliamentary procedures kept him from making a frontal attack upon the President's program, he endeavored to provoke discussion of other aspects of the Southern question—for instance, by urging that all former rebels be excluded from the protection of a new bankruptcy bill and that all cases involving Negroes in the South be heard before federal courts.[9]

Far more than any speeches of Sumner's, the actions of Southern whites spurred on Congressional Republicans. By almost unanimous votes, legislature after legislature in the South rejected the Fourteenth Amendment. Sumner, who had not hitherto been an admirer of that proposal, was jubilant, because he felt that in defeating the amendment the rebels had unintentionally become "instruments of Providence for the establishment of human rights." Eagerly he welcomed to his house visitors from the South who assured him that Johnson's "experiment" in the South now was a complete failure and begged "that Congress should interfere by an enabling act authorizing the people black and white to vote for members of a Convention which might form a state Constitution of Republican Government." [1]

Eventually two bills designed to overthrow Johnson's work in the South received the approval of the House of Representatives: Thaddeus Stevens's measure to put the unreconstructed states under military rule and Thomas D. Eliot's proposal to replace the existing Louisiana government with a new regime that would enfranchise the Negroes and disfranchise most of the

[9] Samuel L. Gardner to Sumner, Selma, Ala., Nov. 19, 1866, Sumner MSS.; *Cong. Globe*, 39 Cong., 2 Sess., pp. 16, 1005, 1135; Sumner: *Works*, XI, 44–7.

[1] Pierce, IV, 321; Chase to "My darling Nettie," Dec. 12, 1866, Chase MSS., Lib. of Cong.

whites. When these bills reached the Senate on February 13 Sumner, as Senator Hendricks observed, seemed "scarcely able to command language in which he could with sufficient earnestness express his admiration of both."[2] Actually, along with Wade, Howard, and other Radicals, he strongly preferred Eliot's more drastic proposal. After Senate Moderates succeeded in shoving that bill aside, Sumner watched with satisfaction the attempts to amend the Stevens bill. Its failure to brand the Johnson regimes in the South as "sham governments" made him suspect that the Stevens plan was "thoroughly vicious in every line and in every word from the first to the last."[3] He accordingly "preferred delay, and, therefore, was content with anything that secured this, believing that Congress must ultimately come to the true ground" of reconstruction—presumably in the next session.[4]

Anxious to conceal factional differences from the public eye and eager to act quickly so as to avoid the anticipated presidential pocket veto at the end of the session, Republican leaders called a Senate caucus on February 17 and appointed a committee of seven, headed by John Sherman, to devise acceptable amendments to the House reconstruction bill. Sumner was one of the members. He succeeded in persuading the rest of the committee that the Johnson governments must be declared invalid, but he was unable to block the Moderate plan to readmit the Southern states after they ratified the Fourteenth Amendment. Only one other member of the committee supported his demand that these states must also adopt new constitutions allowing "no exclusion from suffrage on account of color."

That evening, when Sherman presented the committee's report to the Republican caucus, Sumner submitted a dissent, stating more fully his view that the Southern states must be required to let all qualified citizens vote. "It was in our power to decide this question," he urged, "and to supersede its discussion in the Southern states; . . . if we did not decide it, every State and village between here and the Rio Grande would be agitated

[2] *Cong. Globe,* 39 Cong., 2 Sess., p. 1385.
[3] Ibid., pp. 1392–3.
[4] Sumner to Bright, Washington, May 27, 1867, Bright MSS.

by it." Though it was near dinner time and his colleagues were impatient, they heard him out, and then, on two stand-up votes, the caucus by a majority of two endorsed his plan to require universal suffrage in the South.[5]

Sumner had scored, he believed, "a prodigious triumph" in thus securing "the direct requirement of universal suffrage, without distinction of race or color," a triumph the more valuable in his eyes because it was "done by Act of Congress, without Constitutional Amendment." With obvious pleasure he noted the remarkable shift that had occurred in Republican opinion during the past twelve months. He did not claim to be responsible for the change, for he recognized that Southern recalcitrance, Johnson's war upon Congress, and Republican victories in the 1866 elections had influenced more minds than did any number of speeches. Not even the action of the Senate Republican caucus was due solely to his persuasiveness, for his colleagues there realized that the House of Representatives was not likely to accept a bill requiring anything less than universal suffrage in the South. Still it was Sumner who forced the caucus to listen and to vote, and he was entitled to triumph in this "grand and beneficent exercise of existing powers, for a long time invoked, but now at last grasped." His amendment to Sherman's bill, he was sure, was a veritable Magna Charta. "Since Runnymede," he told his fellow Senators, "there has been nothing of greater value to Human Rights." [6]

Characteristically Sumner remained dissatisfied even in his hour of victory. Excellent as he thought his requirement of universal suffrage in the South, he found other sections of Sherman's reconstruction bill—as the amended version of the Stevens bill was now called—"horribly defective," because they made no provision for education in the South and set up no agency by which "the freedmen can be secured a freehold for themselves and their families." Moreover, since Sherman's measure failed to specify who was to call for new voter registration in the South and to order new elections, Sumner correctly pre-

[5] Ibid. In this letter Sumner gave the vote as 17–15. Elsewhere he remembered it as 15–13. *Cong. Globe*, 40 Cong., 2 Sess., p. 496.

[6] Sumner: *Works*, XI, 109.

dicted that this was "Reconstruction without machinery or motive power." Consequently he took little interest in the final Senate debates during the protracted evening session of February 17, and he went home at midnight, long before the Senate, at 6:22 the next morning, adopted the Sherman bill. Later Sumner's absence on this final vote was to become the basis for the preposterous charge that he was indifferent to enfranchising the freedmen, a charge that was to gain some credence because of the lack of candor in the public explanation of his course. He was, he claimed, tired and unwell and did not think it necessary to "remain till morning to swell the large and ascertained majority which [the bill] was destined to receive." [7] In fact, he angrily stalked out of the Senate so as positively to dissociate himself from a measure which he did not fully approve,[8] and he took pleasure in announcing, during the next session of Congress, when the defects of the legislation became apparent, that he shared no part of the blame: "I did not vote for the act as it passed the Senate." [9]

Unlike most other Republican Senators, Sumner was not dismayed but pleased when the House on February 19 refused to concur in the Senate plan of reconstruction and adhered to its own strictly military bill. He hoped the Senate would agree to a conference committee, where the House version was likely to prevail, but his colleagues refused. In order to get any reconstruction bill adopted, the House was obliged to swallow the Senate measure, adding only an amendment providing that prominent ex-Confederates should be disqualified from voting for or holding office in the new Southern constitutional conventions. Since Sumner wanted the former rebels kept from the polls, he was delighted with the House amendment, and he voted, along with all other Republican Senators and one Democrat, for the final passage of the bill. When President Johnson, as expected, vetoed it, Sumner also on March 2 voted for its readoption. Nevertheless he lamented that the "law was a very hasty and crude act of legislation," which came "short of what a

[7] Ibid., XI, 110; XIII, 303–7.
[8] Welles: *Diary*, III, 46–7; Boston *Post*, Feb. 18, 1867.
[9] *Cong. Globe*, 40 Cong., 1 Sess., p. 35.

patriotic Congress ought to supply for the safety of the Republic." [1]

· 4 ·

Unhappy at the direction affairs were beginning to take on Capitol Hill, Sumner found little solace at home. Once the novelty of marriage was over, he felt the strain that so drastic a change in habits put upon a fifty-five-year-old man hitherto accustomed to the independence of bachelorhood. Worry over money was the first evidence of stress. Used to renting furnished rooms in Washington, he was appalled by the cost of running a household, complete with coachman and nursemaid, and as early as December 1866 he lamented that his expenses were "now very different from what they were in other days."

"I can for the present pay my debts," Sumner wrote on the day before Christmas, but there seemed no end to the financial drain.[2] Dissatisfied with the furnished house they leased and thinking the rent at $575 a quarter exorbitant, he and Alice decided to buy a home of their own. Nothing would suit their sense of style and elegance but the house being built on the corner of H Street and Vermont Avenue, facing across Lafayette Square toward the White House. The estimated cost was $30,000—ten times Sumner's annual salary as Senator. Though Alice had an income from her first husband's estate, from which she drew more than $3,000 during the first months of the Congressional session,[3] the burden of buying and furnishing the new house fell on Sumner, and reluctantly, for the first time since he entered the Senate, he agreed to give an extensive lecture series during the coming summer months in order to raise money.

Marriage was also a tax on his time and energy. Used to appearing only infrequently in Washington society, he at first enjoyed going to dinners and dances with his handsome wife. After the Senate settled down to work in January, however, there were more and more evening sessions, and he tired of the con-

[1] Sumner: *Works*, XI, 115.

[2] Sumner to J. B. Smith, Dec. 24, 1866, MS., Henry E. Huntington Lib.

[3] Second Executor's Report, July 12, 1875, Estate of William Sturgis Hooper, Docket 44,900, Probate Court, Suffolk County, Mass.

stant social whirl. By the end of the month he sharply cut down on the number of evening parties he gave to members of the diplomatic corps. But Alice, with half her husband's years and twice his energy, insisted upon accepting the frequent invitations which they continued to receive. By mid-February Washington gossips were saying that "the madam" kept Sumner "a going at every party and refuses to go home when he wants to." "My dear," said Sumner to her at one dance that had already gone on until midnight, "is it not time to go home?" "You may go when you like," Alice replied. "I shall stay." Soon she began appearing at parties without her husband, but when questions were raised, she showed no sympathy for his limitations. "I am always left alone," she complained to the Marquis de Chambrun. "Mr. Sumner is always reading, writing and snoring." [4]

When bored, Alice proved high-strung and quick-tempered. Even when in good spirits she adopted toward her elderly husband a teasing tone which he, devoid of humor and accustomed to reverential respect, could neither understand nor reciprocate. In her bad moods, as even her friends admitted, her temper was torrential. Shortly after their wedding one who knew Alice well mused: "I should like to see Sumner the first time Alice says to him—'Go to hell; God damn you—it is none of your business.' " [5] Sumner had his first storm warning when, tense and overtired, she lashed out at him in the carriage as they left for their honeymoon, but he was such a romantic idealist, seeing marriage "through visions" and giving himself to it "with a complete surrender," that he was not alarmed.[6] Though their first few weeks in Washington were relatively happy the newlyweds soon had an angry scene over Sumner's habit of inviting Hooper, the father of Alice's first husband, to dinner every week. Wanting to see fresh faces at her table, she protested violently that she could not bear Hooper, that she "would not have him near her, that he

[4] Gustavus V. Fox to Virginia L. W. Fox, Feb. 19, 1867, Fox MSS.; interview of E. L. Pierce with Kate Chase Sprague, undated, G. B. Pierce MSS.; interview of E. L. Pierce with the Marquis de Chambrun, Dec. 19, 1886, ibid.

[5] Statement of F. W. Bird concerning Sumner's marriage, 1893, typed copy, Bird MSS.

[6] Statement of E. L. Pierce concerning Sumner's marriage, undated, G. B. Pierce MSS.; Sumner to Mrs. John E. Lodge, undated [c. Oct. 1868], Lodge MSS.

was stupid and a nuisance." [7] When Sumner tried to remonstrate with her, she only became more excited, and in some of her temper tantrums she swore at him. Even when they were in public she could not always keep her tongue under control.

By February Washington rumor had it that Mrs. Sumner had a weakness more serious than her high temper and quick tongue. While her husband was more and more absorbed in the work of the Senate, with the frequent grueling evening sessions toward the end of the session, Alice was seeing more and more of the young and handsome Baron Friedrich von Holstein. An attaché of the Prussian embassy in Washington, this German nobleman had come to America in 1865 to observe the workings of representative government, which he believed might ultimately triumph in his own country. When he reached Washington in December 1866 he naturally called upon Sumner as chairman of the Senate Foreign Relations Committee. Promptly invited to all the best parties and dances in Washington, Holstein preferred, as he wrote home in January 1867, informal visiting, and he boasted that there were several homes in the capital where he knew he was welcome day or night. One of these was the Sumners'.[8]

Report was later to have it that Holstein and Alice fell madly in love, but this is doubtful. Very possibly sexually impotent, Holstein certainly had no serious intentions. In all probability he thought he was engaging in a lighthearted flirtation with a beautiful young woman, a flirtation which, if a bit unconventional according to European standards, was no more so than many other aspects of social life in democratic America. Nor was she in love with the Prussian.[9] Bored and angry with her

[7] Sumner to Mrs. John E. Lodge, July 19 [1868], ibid.

[8] Using the printed sources, George W. F. Hallgarten, in "Fritz von Holsteins Geheimnis," *Historische Zeitschrift*, CLXXVII (Feb. 1954), 75–83, makes the most of Holstein's alleged infatuation for Mrs. Sumner. A more restrained interpretation, based upon the unpublished papers of both Holstein and Sumner, is Norman Rich, "Eine Bemerkung über Friedrich von Holsteins Aufenthalt in America," ibid., CLXXXVI (1958), 80–6.

[9] Sumner to Mrs. John E. Lodge, July 14, 1868, Lodge MSS. ". . . she used him as a catspaw to annoy her husband," was the opinion of the Marquis de Chambrun, adding that when he teased Mrs. Sumner about Holstein as a possible lover she had sniffed: "that fool." Interview of E. L. Pierce with Chambrun, Dec. 19, 1886, G. B. Pierce MSS.

ponderous, busy husband, she wanted companionship of her own age, and the baron was handsome, elegant, and rich—but neither aggressive nor intelligent enough to become a nuisance.

Soon the two were frequently seen together in public, and Holstein accompanied Alice to "*matinees* and *soirees,* and in other public places, and occasionally escorted her from the Senate, where both had been to hear the Senator speak." [1] Sure she had no guilt to hide, Alice made no secret of their meetings. Once in the late spring, Sumner, returning home unexpectedly, found her about to get into a carriage with Holstein and another young couple from the diplomatic set. "Where are you going, Alice?" he asked.

"I am going to enjoy myself," she replied defiantly.

"But where are you going?"

"That does not concern you," she snapped, and off they drove. Humiliated, Sumner thereafter pretended not to see the two when they appeared in public, conspicuously turning his back to avoid them.[2]

In private Sumner made stately attempts to rebuke his wife, but these only inflamed her temper. Never able to argue convincingly, he doubtless fell victim to the rhetorical exaggeration to which he was accustomed in public speaking. The more insistently he urged her to be discreet, the more savagely she lashed back. "I never entered the carriage with her to drive to dinner," Sumner later recalled, "that she did not treat me so that I was obliged to find relief in tears." When, to avoid such scenes, he remained at home, she ignored Sumner's admonitions and went to parties with Holstein, snarling at her husband: "God damn you, 'tis none of your business, I will go where I please, with whom I please." To demonstrate her independence, she did not confine her flirtation with the baron to public occasions. Once she went off alone with Holstein to visit a cemetery two miles outside of Washington, and they remained so long that the servants had to unlock the door when she came home after

[1] New York *Express*, quoted in New York *World*, Oct. 22, 1867.

[2] Gustavus V. Fox to Virginia L. W. Fox, May 27, 1867, Fox MSS.; interview of E. L. Pierce with Mr. and Mrs. S. C. Pomeroy, Dec. 18, 1886, G. B. Pierce MSS.

midnight. "All the time, day and late in the night," Sumner later complained, "she was off with her paramour!" [3]

There was gossip that the crisis in the Sumner marriage came when the Senator discovered his wife was wearing a new and extravagantly expensive amber necklace. Holstein, so the story goes, had learned that her own beads were artificial and, declaring that she deserved only the best, had ordered the necklace for her from Prussia. When Sumner learned the facts, he is supposed to have demanded the bill and to have insisted upon paying for the bauble himself.[4] Whether this story was true cannot be proved, but the fact that it was being whispered about is evidence enough that Washington was alive with reports of the Sumners' domestic difficulties.

Sumner decided he could no longer tolerate this public humiliation, and he told Alice that they could not "continue to live together without a change on her part." "Life is utter misery to me," he remembered his words a few months later. "One of us must leave this house. I have already written half of a letter to my constituents resigning my place and will go and bury myself in some obscure Swiss valley where [there] is peace at least. I am unfit for work."

"No!" exclaimed Alice, "if one is to go, *I* will go but *how* do you send me from you—a degraded wife?"

"No!" replied Sumner. "You shall bear my name and I will go with you on board the steamer, engage your rooms and you shall have my countenance until that hour." [5]

This uneasy truce between the Sumners lasted until Holstein received orders, issued in Berlin on April 16, 1867, to return to Prussia "as soon as circumstances permit." In all probability Holstein's recall was simply routine. There is no document preserved in the Prussian archives to suggest that Sumner

[3] Sumner to Mrs. John E. Lodge, July 14, 1868, Lodge MSS.; statement of F. W. Bird concerning Sumner's marriage, 1893, G. B. Pierce MSS.

[4] Bigelow: *Retrospections*, IV, 20.

[5] This is Sumner's version of the conversation as given to Mrs. John E. Lodge and reported by her much later, in a letter to Longfellow, July 16 [no year], Longfellow MSS. For less detailed but more contemporary reports see Sumner to Howe, Feb. 17, 1868, G. B. Pierce MSS., and Sumner to Mrs. Lodge, July 14, 1868, Lodge MSS.

had any part in it.[6] Sumner himself vowed: "I had nothing to do in any way directly or indirectly with the recall. . . . I never made any suggestion or gave any hint on the subject to a human being."[7] There is no reason to doubt his word, though the possibility nevertheless exists that Holstein was summoned home because of his indiscreet behavior with Mrs. Sumner. Baron Gerolt, the Prussian minister at Washington, who was one of the oldest and shrewdest diplomats in the capital, undoubtedly knew precisely what was going on, and he may well have dropped a hint to Bismarck, who certainly did not want to antagonize the powerful chairman of the Senate Foreign Relations Committee.

Mrs. Sumner was sure her husband had procured Holstein's recall. Fiercely she resented Sumner's assumed role in the affair as a slur on her virtue, and her anger smoldered throughout May, while public business held them in Washington. As soon as the Senate adjourned, they took the train for Boston, and Sumner handed her, for reading on the long trip, a French novel about an immoral woman who had betrayed her husband. Always made tense and irritable by travel, Alice fancied Sumner wanted her to identify herself with the heroine of the story—as, indeed, he probably did—and by the time they reached Boston her rage had become explosive. As Sumner unlocked the Hancock Street house, she spat a "God damn you" at him, swept ahead to their bedroom, and slammed the door in his face. From this time she insisted upon separate sleeping quarters.[8]

Though the Sumners managed to present a public facade of peace when they had dinner with the unobservant Longfellow on June 9, the breach was irreparable. After a few days she took Bell to Lenox, where for a time she kept up the fiction that Sumner would join her later. Sumner never spoke to his wife again. Alone in the empty house in Boston, which he had already sold in order to pay for the still unfinished mansion in Washing-

[6] Norman Rich: *Friedrich von Holstein: Politics and Diplomacy in the Era of Bismarck and Wilhelm II* (Cambridge: Cambridge University Press; 1965), II, 36–7.

[7] Sumner's statement, written on the back of a letter from Horatio Woodman [Dec. 1867], G. B. Pierce MSS.

[8] Interview of E. L. Pierce with John B. Alley, Oct. 24, 1885, ibid.

ton, he sat, as Longfellow wrote, "gloomily like Marius on the ruins of Carthage." [9]

• 5 •

Outside of Washington the public knew nothing of Sumner's domestic unhappiness. Though there was some gossip that Mrs. Sumner's interest in Holstein "crowded rather close upon the honeymoon," [1] no newspaper breathed a hint of scandal. Sumner confided his troubles not even to his closest friends. Apparently Alice was equally silent, for at the end of April her father cheerfully wrote Sumner: "I hear from all visitors at Washington that yours is the Happy family, and that you and Bell are confederates." [2] It did, however, become common knowledge that Sumner was looking tired and unwell, and somehow the report leaked out that he contemplated retiring at the end of his present Senate term. Alarmed that what had been intended as a rhetorical threat to influence Alice might serve to encourage potential rivals for the 1869 election, Sumner promptly called in Forney, and authorized him to report in his Philadelphia *Press* and Washington *Chronicle* that the resignation rumor had "no foundation in fact." [3]

If personal troubles did not bring about Sumner's retirement, they undoubtedly did make him a more difficult Senate colleague. In the Fortieth Congress, which assembled on March 4, 1867, he succeeded in making himself more unpopular than ever before. Adopting a patronizing tone to the new Senators and a didactic manner toward the old ones, he insisted upon reminding both how often in the past he had been proved right: right in predicting that slavery must be abolished before the war could be won; right in early suspecting Andrew Johnson of collaboration with the rebels; right in rejecting the Fourteenth Amendment as a satisfactory reconstruction program; right in predicting that the recently enacted reconstruction act would prove unworkable.

[9] Longfellow to Charles Longfellow, June 10, 1867, Longfellow MSS.; Longfellow to G. W. Greene, Sept. 22, 1867, ibid.

[1] Bigelow: *Retrospections*, IV, 116.

[2] Jonathan Mason to Sumner, April 23, 1867, Sumner MSS.

[3] Forney to Sumner, Mar. 25, 1867, ibid.; Washington *Morning Chronicle*, April 1, 1867.

Sumner's habit of setting himself up as a prophet was not a new one, but in the wreck of his marriage he seemed to take greater satisfaction than ever in contrasting the "slowness and timidity" of his colleagues with "his own progressiveness and foresight." [4]

Even on procedural points Sumner spoke with an Olympian air. Most Republicans wanted only a brief session of the new Congress, hoping to remedy the deficiencies in the reconstruction bill just passed by setting up the machinery for the registration of voters and for the holding of elections in the South. A few, determined to keep an eye on the President's execution of their reconstruction plan, were willing to brave the summer heats of Washington and hold additional short sessions from time to time during the summer. But Sumner, doubtless aware that adjournment would force some resolution of his marital problems, urged Congress to remain in constant session. Republicans who wanted to get away from Washington were derelict in their duty, he thundered; they were forgetting that the President was "a bad man, the author of incalculable woe to his country," neglectful of the needs of the loyalists in the South, "counted by millions." [5] Unmoved by Sumner's oratory, the Congressmen voted to adjourn on March 20 (a special session of the Senate to consider the Alaska purchase treaty followed immediately), and they reconvened only for three weeks in July, when they passed still another supplementary reconstruction act, and again for the last ten days of November. Still, they squirmed under the tongue-lashing Sumner gave them for putting personal comfort before public duty, and doubtless more than one Congressman agreed with Dawes, who, knowing nothing of Sumner's domestic infelicity, grumbled that he wished the Senator had "six wives at home, all needing his immediate presence there." [6]

To most Republicans in the Fortieth Congress Sumner's course seemed not merely exasperating but willful and irresponsible. During the March session while Sherman, Trumbull, and Fessenden led the Senate in framing a supplementary reconstruction bill, Sumner took virtually no part in the debates ex-

[4] Springfield *Republican*, Sept. 7, 1867.
[5] Sumner: *Works*, XI, 168–70.
[6] Dawes to Electa Dawes, July 8, 1867, Dawes MSS.

cept to point out that he had correctly predicted the deficiencies in the original act. But once the new measure was perfected, he stepped forth as Cassandra to declare his "conviction that we shall regret hereafter that we have not done more" and to lament that under this act new Southern governments would be "born of the bayonet." Stewart remarked that Sumner's tactics could make of any man a prophet. By voting for the bill, he could claim to be responsible if it was successful, but by simultaneously denouncing its provisions, he could go before the country, in case it proved a failure, and "get the credit . . . of having advocated some things higher and better than we are willing to adopt." [7]

If Senators thought Sumner's criticisms of their reconstruction legislation unfair and unreasonable, they were appalled by the elaborate bill which he introduced on March 6. Ignoring the act which Congress had passed only four days earlier, Sumner returned to the reconstruction plan which he had proposed in December 1865 but which he now made even more rigorous. After sweeping away the regimes Johnson had set up in the South, his proposal called for the appointment of new provisional governors in all the Southern states. Recognizing that the President could not be trusted to nominate Radicals to these posts, Sumner guaranteed that they would be surrounded by men of his own persuasion by requiring each provisional governor to select a legislative council consisting of "thirteen of the most fit and discreet persons of the state," all of whom must prove their past loyalty to the Union, must pledge to "resist all laws making any distinction of race or color," and must promise to support education "by public schools open to all." As in Sumner's earlier plan, these provisional governments should register all "male citizens, of whatever color, race, or former condition," but this time he excluded from both voting and holding office not just the generals and politicians of the Confederacy but "authors, publishers, editors, contributors, or . . . speakers or preachers, [who] encouraged the secession of any State, or the waging of war against the United States." Once again Sumner demanded a new constitution in each Southern state which would guarantee impartial suffrage and declare that "all persons

[7] Sumner: *Works,* XI, 146–7; *Cong. Globe,* 40 Cong., 1 Sess., p. 167.

shall be equal before the law." Only when a majority of the eligible voters ratified such a constitution would Congress, if it determined that "the people of the State are loyal and well disposed to the Union," agree to readmission.[8]

Even if Sumner's bill had not brushed aside all that had already been so painfully accomplished, Republicans would not have accepted it. Moderates strongly objected to his proposal to disfranchise an undetermined but very large number of white Southerners, since they hoped to draw some of these "natural leaders" of the section into the Republican party. Most Republican Congressmen now accepted the Negro's right to vote, but Sumner's key phrase, "all persons shall be equal before the law," seemed to augur demands for further rights for the freedmen. Senator Williams challenged Sumner to explain his plan for public education in the South, asking whether it meant "that each and every school shall be open to children of both races." As Sumner had vigorously opposed segregated schools since the Roberts case of 1849, his real intention was plain, but he replied somewhat equivocally: "If I should have my way, according to the true principle, it would be that the schools, precisely like the ballot-box or the rail cars, should be open to all. But the proposition is necessarily general in its character; it does not go into details. . . ."[9] Clearly he hoped to commit Congress to the broad policy of requiring public education in the South; then, as the states applied for readmission, he could try to go a step further and ban segregated schools.

Even more unsettling to many Republican Congressmen was Sumner's proposal, not incorporated in his bill but in the resolutions which accompanied it and in several supplementary motions, that homesteads "must be secured to the freedmen, so that at least every head of a family may have a piece of land." Regretting that at the end of the war "the great landed estates of the South [had not] been divided and subdivided among the loyal colored population," he urged as a condition for all subsequent pardons "that every landed proprietor who has been engaged in

[8] *Senate Bill No. 7*, 40 Cong., 1 Sess.; Sumner: *Works*, XI, 150–2.

[9] *Cong. Globe*, 40 Cong., 1 Sess., p. 169. For Sumner's role in the Roberts case, see Donald: *Sumner*, pp. 180–1.

the Rebellion . . . should convey to the freedmen, his former slaves, a certain portion of the land on which they have worked." Sumner put more stress upon education than economics, but like Thaddeus Stevens, who reversed the priorities, he was convinced that reconstruction "would be incomplete, unless in some way we secured to the freedmen a piece of land." [1]

Disturbed by the revolutionary changes Sumner hoped to bring about in the South, Republican Congressmen were horrified when they learned that he proposed to extend them to the North as well. On March 26 he introduced a bill "to enforce the several provisions of the Constitution abolishing slavery, declaring the immunities of citizens, and guarantying a republican form of government, by securing the elective franchise to colored citizens." Being interpreted, that meant that Congress should impose Negro suffrage upon the Northern and border states. There was no need, he argued, to wait for "the slow process of a constitutional amendment." If Congress could require Negro suffrage in the South, so could it insist upon it in the North. Reminding his fellow Republicans of the approaching fall elections, he stressed the political gains from adopting his bill: "Every Northern state will move into line with the colored vote to strengthen the Republican cause. Maryland and Delaware will be saved—to say nothing of Kentucky." "One vote in Congress and the work is done!" he urged. *"The right of suffrage once given can never be taken away.* It will be immortal." [2]

Though Senate Republicans tried to ignore Sumner's proposals, ordering his bills to be printed and consigned to quiet death in committee, Johnson's supporters gave much publicity to each new extreme position he assumed. Dixon announced, with all appearances of solemnity, that Sumner's claim to be a prophet was abundantly justified, for "what he has announced, what he has declared, what he has said must be law, has become law upon many subjects." Eagerly Buckalew agreed that the

[1] Sumner: *Works,* XI, 125, 368, 127.

[2] *Cong. Globe,* 40 Cong., 1 Sess., pp. 245, 280, 407; Sumner: *Works,* XI, 175. Shortly after adjournment Sumner elaborated his views in two letters to Theodore Tilton, the editor of the *Independent.* One, dated April 20, is published in his *Works,* XI, 356–60; the other, which is more revealing, dated April 18, is in the Tilton MSS.

country should give Sumner's proposals serious attention, since "the propositions which the Senator from Massachusetts makes one year and which are criticized by his colleagues as extreme, inappropriate, and untimely, are precisely the propositions which those colleagues support with greater zeal and vehemence, if possible, than he, the year following." [3]

Partly to keep Radicals like Sumner from giving such openings to the Democrats, Senate Republican leaders held a caucus on July 5, two days after Congress reconvened, and proposed in the remaining weeks of the session to limit legislative business "to removing the obstructions which have been or are likely to be placed in the way of the fair execution of the Acts of Reconstruction." Not aware of their plan until he entered the caucus, Sumner bitterly fought this limit on his freedom of action, and when the caucus adopted the gag rule, he rose to announce: "I will not be bound by any such proposition."

"Then you should not have voted on the subject," replied Fessenden, "if you did not mean to be bound by the decision of the majority."

"I am a Senator of the United States," retorted Sumner, meaning that he could not "without a dereliction of duty" acquiesce in a curb upon his constitutional duty to introduce and discuss whatever legislation he thought needed.

From the caucus Sumner tried to take his case to the Senate floor, where Fessenden again rebuked him, declaring that "gentlemen who find themselves in the minority should not bring their warfare into this Senate Chamber." "It is a little singular to me," Fessenden went on, "that gentlemen who went into that consultation, argued their views in full and voted, should now come in here and say they are not bound by anything that took place in consultation with their friends." Sumner, he added, was playing his customary game: "Heads I win; tails you lose." [4]

Passionately Sumner protested the gag, and Wade stepped down from his chair as presiding officer to support him, but most Senators, weary of the Washington heat and irked by Sumner's

[3] *Cong. Globe*, 40 Cong., 1 Sess., pp. 51, 170.

[4] Sumner: *Works*, XI, 373, 388; *Cong. Globe*, 40 Cong., 1 Sess., pp. 488, 498; Springfield *Republican*, July 9, 1867.

pontifical manner, rallied behind Fessenden. Gleefully they killed every substantive amendment Sumner offered to the second supplementary reconstruction act, which was finally passed over the President's veto on July 19. Some of his proposals, dealing with homesteads and education, they rejected as dealing with topics not permitted by the caucus ruling. Others were defeated because, as Roscoe Conkling, one of the new Republican Senators, remarked, they could "not have the slightest effect" but would be "a mere bull at the comet." Sumner's only considerable success was in securing the adoption of an amendment declaring that all the provisions of the reconstruction act "shall be construed liberally, to the end that all the intents thereof may be fully and perfectly carried out" [5]—a proviso that was legally meaningless.

By the end of July, when Congress disbanded, Sumner was conspicuously alone. His wife, with whom he had had no communication whatever for two months, was still in the Berkshires. His house on Hancock Street had already been sold, but, with his Washington mansion unfinished, he could not remove his belongings. In Massachusetts powerful voices began to argue that the state needed a new Senator. In Washington the party which Sumner had helped to found scornfully rejected his policies.

Sore and weary, Sumner poured out his discontent to James Redpath, a stenographic reporter who interviewed him in Boston about a month after Congress adjourned. Now it was not the "perverse, pig-headed and brutal" President but the Congressmen, especially "some of the new recruits," who were blocking a true reconstruction of the South. His Republican colleagues in the Senate had been most wrongheaded, for even those who gave "the impression of personal purity" were indifferent to the sufferings of Southern loyalists. Edmunds had proved to be "a prodigy of obstructiveness and technicality," and Conkling, though "a young man of admirable talents and with a great future, if he does not get ship-wrecked at the beginning," had abetted him. Worst of all was Fessenden, whom chronic dyspepsia had driven to actions "akin to insanity." Paying his worst respects, Sumner told the reporter that Fessenden was only a

[5] *Cong. Globe,* 40 Cong., 1 Sess., pp. 582–3.

lawyer "of the *nisi prius* order"; this "drag on reconstruction" resembled Andrew Johnson "in prejudice and in talent for combativeness." [6]

Published in virtually all the major newspapers, Sumner's interview with Redpath appeared at an embarrassing time for the Republican party. With fall elections approaching, Republicans were supposed to point with pride to their excellent reconstruction legislation and to unite in horror because President Johnson suspended Stanton from the war office on August 5. Sumner's bitter lamentations interrupted this harmonious chorus. Fessenden, who claimed that he found the whole interview "exquisitely funny," was in fact fiercely angry. Edmunds bore Sumner's slurs with equanimity, but Conkling, much annoyed, threateningly announced he planned to "have a friendly talk" with Sumner when Congress reconvened.[7] In the future Sumner was to pay for his bad temper as the "new recruits" excluded him from policymaking in his own party.

• 6 •

The difficulties between Sumner and his fellow Republicans reflected a clash not merely of personalities but of ideas. Doubtless many Senators shared his desire "always to be generous in interpretation of the Constitution," [8] but by the summer of 1867 it seemed that Sumner's generosity had become prodigality. "In his eagerness to reconstruct the Union in the interest of the Negro," the New York *Times* criticized, "he is prepared to disregard the Constitution, deprive the States of powers expressly vested in them, and remodel everything according to his philanthropic inclinations." [9] Forgotten were the prewar days when Sumner had defended the duty of the states to pass personal liberty laws in seeming defiance of the Constitution and had spoken of a state's right to nullify unjust acts of Congress. His nationalism, which had been gradually increasing since the outbreak of the war, now reached new heights. It was as if Sumner, averting his

[6] Supplement to Boston *Advertiser*, Sept. 4, 1867.
[7] Fessenden: *Fessenden*, II, 145–6.
[8] Sumner: *Works*, XI, 179–80.
[9] Quoted in Boston *Post*, Nov. 23, 1867.

gaze from the broken shards of his unhappy personal life, found consolation in contemplating the perfection of American nationality.

The history of the United States, he insisted, was the story of how the knot of national unity had grown tighter and tighter ever since the founding of the British colonies. The Declaration of Independence had proclaimed the nationhood of the United States. Though there had been, under the Articles of Confederation, a humiliating sacrifice of nationality to the pretensions of state rights, the Constitution had in its very opening words reaffirmed national unity and power. The Civil War had tested that unity, and from the conflict Sumner, like Edward Everett Hale, James Russell Lowell, and Francis Lieber, believed that the national spirit had emerged not merely unscathed but soaring. War had welded the United States into "one sovereignty, one citizenship, one people." The national motto, "*E pluribus unum,*" suggested the growing unity of the United States. The American flag, "to be cherished by all our hearts, to be upheld by all our hands," was the symbol of nationality, and to its colors Sumner gave, quite erroneously, an often quoted interpretation: "White is for purity; red, for valor; blue, for justice."

Now it seemed to Sumner fortunate that his country had never chosen a distinctive name, like "Vinland" or "Freeland," but had retained the general name "America," for it was bound to extend its institutions and its government over the entire North American continent. A disciple of John Quincy Adams, Sumner had long believed that in time the other North American countries would be gravitationally attracted to the United States, and now, with the new economic and military strength mobilized by the war, he was sure the time had come for his country to exercise "predominance, if not exclusive power," throughout the hemisphere.[1]

If Sumner's high nationalism served as a solace for his domestic woes, it also led him into some strange political company. On Friday evening, March 29, 1867, just the day before

[1] Sumner: *Works,* XII, 223, 227, 235, 232. For the post-Civil War tide of national feeling, see Hans Kohn: *American Nationalism* (New York: The Macmillan Company; 1957), pp. 124–8.

Congress was to adjourn, he received a cryptic note from Secretary of State Seward: "Can you come to my house this evening? I have a matter of public business in regard to which it is desirable that I should confer with you at once."[2] Hurrying over to Seward's house, Sumner found that the Secretary had already left for the State Department. His son, Frederick W. Seward, who served as Assistant Secretary of State, was, however, at home, and he and Edward de Stoeckl, who arrived about the same time as Sumner, explained the Secretary's hasty note.

The Russian minister was carrying the rough draft of a proposed treaty ceding all of Russian America to the United States for the price of $7,200,000. It was Sumner's first inkling that such a purchase was even being considered. Desirous of dramatically recouping his political fortunes and aware of the ill will many Senators bore him, Seward had forbidden Stoeckl to confide in any member of Congress during the preliminary negotiations. Now that the treaty was drafted, the Secretary was ready to tip his hand, and Stoeckl and Frederick Seward informed Sumner of its provisions and showed him a map of the land to be ceded. Without expressing any opinion of his own, Sumner listened until about midnight, when young Seward and the Russian minister left for the State Department, where the formal engrossing and signing of the treaty were to take place. He did not accompany them but returned to his own home. "You will not fail us," Stoeckl half begged, half predicted, as they parted.[3]

The acquisition of Russian America posed a real dilemma for Sumner. An expansionist, he was not "so cold or philosophical as to regard with insensibility a widening of the bounds of [his] country." In the past he had helped to block schemes to seize Mexico and Cuba because they would extend slavery, but for many years he had hoped for annexation to the north. Rus-

[2] Sumner MSS.

[3] Stoeckl to Gortchakov, No. 30, Washington, April 7/19, 1867, Papers from the Russian Foreign Office (photostat, Department of State Records, National Archives); Sumner: *Works*, XI, 183. The familiar painting by Emanuel Leutze (e.g., in Frederick W. Seward: *Seward at Washington* [New York: Derby and Miller; 1891], III, facing p. 349) which shows Sumner as present at the actual signing of the treaty is, therefore, incorrect.

sian America he had never seriously thought of, but at least since 1849 he had longed for that day when "natural law" would sweep Canada "into the wide orbit of her neighbor" and during the secession crisis he had briefly considered the annexation of Canada as a counterweight to the seceded slave states. Now Seward's treaty revived his hopes, for he promptly saw that the purchase of Russian America would put the United States "face to face to England alone" in North America and that then the United States could begin to "squeeze England out of the continent." [4]

On the other hand Sumner felt that there was something peculiar, possibly unsavory, about this Russo-American treaty sprung upon him so unexpectedly. As soon as he had the chance he tried to pry out of Stoeckl the reasons for the Russian cession and the steps which had led up to the surprising negotiations, but all he could get from the minister was the bland assurance that his government had merely responded to the repeated initiatives of the Americans. As chairman of the Senate Committee on Foreign Relations, Sumner felt that Seward should have notified him of these negotiations in advance, and he was unhappily aware that approval of the treaty would imply endorsement of Seward's foreign policy, and perhaps of Andrew Johnson's administration as a whole. Knowing Seward, moreover, he was justifiably worried lest success in this negotiation lead the headstrong Secretary to attempt further projects of "indiscriminate and costly annexation." [5]

Unable to resolve his doubts, Sumner played for time. Though Seward himself came down to the Capitol on the morning the treaty was signed and urged immediate approval, Sumner blocked him by asking that it be referred to his committee. Doubtless Sumner intended his move as a slap at Seward, but it probably saved the treaty, for, as Stoeckl himself noted, "if it had been immediately submitted to a vote, it would have been

[4] Sumner: *Works*, XI, 219, 223; C. C. Beaman's notes of discussions of the Senate Committee on Foreign Relations, April 1, 1867, Sumner MSS., Mass. Hist. Soc. For Sumner's early longing for Canada, see Albert K. Weinberg: *Manifest Destiny* (Baltimore: The Johns Hopkins Press; 1935), p. 230, and Donald: *Sumner*, p. 367.

[5] Stoeckl to Gortchakov, No. 10, Washington, April 7/19, 1867, Papers from the Russian Foreign Office; Sumner: *Works*, XI, 232.

rejected."[6] Because of the Senate's action, President Johnson was forced to summon a special session of the upper House on April 1.

Sumner called a meeting of the Foreign Relations Committee on the same day, and fortunately his secretary, impressed by the importance of the occasion, took notes of the discussions that followed.[7] Senator Morton of Indiana alone was absent from the first meeting. "What have we been buying?" asked Fessenden to open the subject, referring caustically to Russian America as "Seward's Farm." In reply Sumner gave no hint of his own opinion but sketched what he knew of the negotiations. No member of the committee showed much enthusiasm for the treaty. When Sumner tried to suggest that by purchasing the Russian territory the United States would be in a better position subsequently to oust Great Britain from the North American continent, Reverdy Johnson retorted: "No squeeze without a war." Quickly Sumner agreed that the "time when [the] U.S. control[s] the whole continent" would come "better without pressure than with pressure." "I would have kept [the negotiation with Russia] in hand," he ventured, "but delayed it." The committee agreed to defer action until public opinion could crystallize.

Still undecided as to his own course, Sumner reported the decidedly unfavorable reaction of his committee to Seward. At about the same time he told Stoeckl that there was no chance for the treaty to be approved and begged him to withdraw it. Stoeckl firmly refused, and Seward, alert to the danger, began a systematic campaign to win the Senators over. Night after night he invited the Senate luminaries, usually including Sumner, to dine at his "elegant establishment," where, according to the newspapers, over brandy and cigars he conducted a "diplomatic symposium."[8]

Seward's dinners could not persuade Sumner, but other

[6] *Senate Executive Jour.*, XV, 588–9; Stoeckl to Gortchakov, No. 30, Washington, April 7/19, 1867, Papers from the Russian Foreign Office.

[7] This memorandum, in the handwriting of Charles C. Beaman, is in the Sumner MSS., Mass. Hist. Soc. Unless otherwise identified, all quotations in the following paragraphs are drawn from this source.

[8] New York *Herald*, April 9, 1867.

influences were gradually softening his aversion to the treaty. Letters from his constituents, especially those from the representatives of New England commercial and mercantile interests, strongly supported annexation. Scientists connected with the Smithsonian Institution wrote him of the valuable minerals, furs, and other natural resources of the territory. Louis Agassiz allayed his scruples about annexing land without the prior consent of its people by assuring him "that there is, as yet, hardly any population" in the Russian possessions. At the same time Sumner began to realize the adverse consequences of opposing the treaty. Rejection would imperil the long-standing friendship between the United States and Russia, for Sumner realized that "A bargain once made must be kept." More immediately it would also endanger the Republican party in the West, where annexation was popular.[9]

When the committee met again on April 3 there was still no consensus for the treaty. Fessenden was ready to postpone annexation or to vote against the treaty; Cameron was willing to vote for it but preferred to wait until the December session of Congress; Reverdy Johnson was equivocally "not prepared to vote against it." Only one member, probably Morton from the expansionist Northwest, really supported immediate annexation, bluntly announcing: "I want to report it to the Senate and act on it."

Unpersuaded, Fessenden joked: "I'll go for it with an extra condition . . . put in that the Secretary of State be compelled to live there, and the Russian government be required to keep him there."

"That will be carried unanimously," Johnson chimed in; "I'll go for it and lead off on our [Democratic] side."

Not amused, Sumner recalled his colleagues to duty. Up to this point he had been largely silent, speaking only when committee members asked for background information. Now he had

[9] The Sumner MSS. contain letters opposing annexation from George S. Boutwell (April 7, 1867), Lemuel Shaw (April 2), and Moses Pierce (April 8), but letters from John M. Forbes (April 6), Charles Bryant (April 8), John Rogers (April 16), and others warmly favored the treaty. For the scientists' views, see the following letters, all in the Sumner MSS.: Louis Agassiz (April 6); Spencer W. Baird (Mar. 31); G. V. Fox (April 2); M. C. Meigs (April 2); and J. E. Hilgard (April 5).

to give his opinion, and it was clear that he lacked enthusiasm about the whole project. He confessed that he still knew next to nothing about the resources of Russian America. He blamed Seward for failing to consult the Senate earlier. He was worried about the cost and feared Congress would be choosing whether it was "better to spend money for the South to help them or for this." Yet he felt he could not oppose it. "I wish there were not so many New England men on the committee," he complained; "if we should go against it, it would be put down against New England and I don't want to deal her such a heavy blow." Despite his reservations, he announced that he had made up his mind: "I regret very much to go for this treaty. I've a heavy load to carry." ("Yes and it's harder when you don't want to carry it," the clerk of the committee impertinently interjected.) Still, he would support it, and the wavering members of the committee fell in behind him. In the final vote Fessenden and J. W. Patterson of New Hampshire continued, "as at present informed," to oppose annexation, but the other four members joined Sumner in reporting the treaty favorably and without amendments.

On April 8 Sumner presented this report to the Senate and defended the treaty in a speech that lasted two and three-quarter hours. Having had no time to write out his remarks, he spoke extemporaneously from a single sheet of notes and drew upon his disciplined memory for an array of facts and figures on the history and boundaries of Russian America, the advantages to be gained by annexation, and the natural resources of the region.[1] Since the Senate met in secret session, with no reporters present, his exact words cannot be recaptured, nor is it possible to follow the course of the debate that followed. Fessenden on April 9 moved to delay further consideration of the treaty, but his proposal was voted down (12–29). Immediately afterwards, in a show of unity designed principally to emphasize American good will toward Russia, the Senators adopted Sumner's motion to approve the treaty (37–2).

[1] The sheet of notes from which Sumner spoke, preserved by C. C. Beaman, his secretary, is in the Sumner MSS., Mass. Hist. Soc. The date assigned to his speech in Sumner's *Works* is April 9, but it was in fact delivered the previous day. Hunter Miller, "Russian Opinion on the Cession of Alaska," *Amer. Hist. Rev.*, XLVIII (1942–3), 522, note 5.

"My course had a decisive influence," Sumner reported to Longfellow,[2] and there is no reason to doubt the correctness of his judgment. On domestic matters his opinion was often dismissed as extreme, but over the years many Senators had come to trust his learning and judgment on foreign policy. Even Fessenden, who frequently was at odds with Sumner and was one of the two holdouts on this occasion, generally followed his lead in diplomatic matters with great confidence. Most Republicans agreed with H. B. Anthony in feeling that on issues of foreign policy the attitude of Sumner, who had thoroughly informed himself, "ought to control those of us who have not given very particular attention to it ourselves." [3]

Feeling responsible for a treaty which, if not so unpopular as legend sometimes has it, did not rouse any vast enthusiasm among the people, Sumner unsuccessfully tried to get the injunction of secrecy removed from the Senate proceedings, so that he could publish his speech, but when Fessenden blocked him, he decided to write out and expand his arguments for annexation anyway. He called upon Agassiz, J. E. Hilgard of the Coast Survey, and Spencer Baird of the Smithsonian to tell him more about the resources of the new territory, and he himself, along with his secretary, began ransacking the libraries in Washington for further information. "I am living with seals, and walruses, and black foxes and martins in Russian America," he reported to a friend.[4]

By the middle of May he had completed a monograph which followed the outline of his Senate speech; in his published *Works* it occupies 163 printed pages. It was, as the New York *Herald* sarcastically noted, "unquestionably the most encyclopedic of all the encyclopedic works ever elaborated by the learned Senator and his private secretaries." Even an advocate of the purchase like General Henry W. Halleck felt that Sumner had "completely exhausted the *subject*, as well as his *readers*." [5] Lacking as it was in literary grace, Sumner's "speech"—as he persisted in calling it

2 April 15, 1867, Longfellow MSS.

3 *Cong. Globe*, 40 Cong., 2 Sess., pp. 1725, 959.

4 Bigelow: *Retrospections*, IV, 77.

5 New York *Herald*, May 29, 1867; Halleck to Lieber, July 5, 1867, Lieber MSS.

—was a remarkably accurate and well-informed conspectus of the history and natural resources of the new territory, and it was influential both in shaping public opinion at large and in persuading members of the lower House to appropriate the purchase price specified in the treaty. Of more lasting influence was Sumner's concluding injunction that the newly acquired land must not bear "any name borrowed from classical antiquity or from individual invention"; instead its name must be "indigenous, aboriginal, one of the autochthons of the soil" [6]—namely, Alaska.

In his speech before the Senate, Sumner listed as one of the great advantages to be gained from annexing Alaska the likelihood that it was "another step to the occupation of N. America" by the United States, since it "diminishes from N. America one of the monarchical powers." As he did research for his monograph he was impressed by the frequency with which previous writers had shared this continental vision. After the Alaska essay was published, he continued to scour the libraries for quotations and soon he had a collection ranging from Sir Thomas Browne and Bishop Berkeley to George Canning and Richard Cobden. He published his anthology, which he called "Prophetic Voices Concerning America," in the September 1867 issue of the *Atlantic Monthly*, so as to remind readers how many other statesmen, both in this country and abroad, had foretold that time "when the whole continent, with all its various states, shall be a Plural Unit, with one Constitution, one Liberty, and one Destiny." To James T. Fields, the editor of the *Atlantic*, he confided that his essay, though very long, was most important, because "its bearing on Canada and especially on Mexico make it of present practical interest—especially as regards Mexico." [7]

Further to spread his doctrine of continentalism—and incidentally to help meet his crushing household expenses—Sumner took to the lecture circuit in October 1867. In response to many

[6] Sumner: *Works*, XI, 347.

[7] Sumner to Fields, July 3, 1867, MS., Henry E. Huntington Lib. Sumner continued to expand and revise his anthology, and at the time of his death was just completing copy for a new edition to herald the approaching centenary of the Declaration of Independence.

requests he crossed the Appalachians for the first time since 1855 and delivered his lecture titled "Are We a Nation?" no fewer than twenty-two times during the next six weeks. Though the trip was financially rewarding, it was not very satisfactory in other ways either to Sumner or to his audiences. Afflicted with a cold, which made his voice rough and hoarse, he delivered his lecture rather mechanically, with awkward, forced gestures. Many listeners detected an irritating tone of condescension in his voice, for he was too tired and too unwell to conceal his conviction that he was bringing light to the heathen. Shortly before he left Boston he announced to the diners at the Saturday Club—among them Ohioans William Dean Howells and T. B. Read, the Cincinnati poet—that "he never met a well-educated man from the west." This, Howells observed, "appeared very felicitous, and endeared him to both the western men present, who, however, had previously known themselves to be ignorant." [8]

Sumner's Western itinerary was a chronicle of disasters. At Milwaukee the audience also grew restive before the end of the two hour oration, and some walked out, with Sumner suspending his reading so as to follow with his eyes each retreating figure.[9] Sick and exhausted, he had to cancel all his Iowa engagements, except that at Dubuque, and rest up a few days at Chicago. Changing trains at Elkhart, on the way to his final Western engagement, he accidentally stepped from a moving train and had a bad fall. The hard top hat he was wearing saved him from serious injury, but it was pressed down over his face and disfigured his nose with bruises. Despite the accident he appeared on schedule before his Toledo audience, and, according to the Toledo *Commercial*, delivered his speech "with the masterly manner for which the distinguished speaker has gained a world wide reputation." [1]

Returning to Massachusetts on November 9, still bruised and ill, Sumner gave his lecture in Boston three days later,

[8] Howells to C. E. Norton, July 31, 1867, Norton MSS.

[9] Boston *Post*, Oct. 22, 1867.

[1] David Mead, *Yankee Eloquence in the Middle West* (East Lansing, Mich.: Michigan State College Press; 1951), p. 221.

shortly afterwards repeated it in Providence and Portland, and gave it its final reading at the Cooper Institute in New York on November 19.

Like most of Sumner's major addresses, "Are We a Nation?" persuaded those who were already true believers and failed to convince those who were not. The Democratic Boston *Post* pronounced his effort "unmistakably tedious and . . . decidedly soporific," and the New York *World* called it "prolix . . . puerile and ostentatious." On the other hand, the Radical *Independent* declared that Sumner's "high and holy passion for the American nation" gave to the lecture "the harmony of an ode, the unity and rhythm of a poem, whose soul is patriotism." In the privacy of her diary Julia Ward Howe judged that Sumner's oration was "on the whole . . . valuable and instructive," and Pierce, Sumner's closest political adviser, praised its "tone, thought, sweep, general principle and aspiration" but warned the Senator that "it perhaps declares a somewhat higher Caesarism than some minds would assent to." [2]

• 7 •

By the time Sumner returned from his Western lecture tour the news of his marital difficulties had begun to seep out. As early as June 13 Charles Francis Adams learned from Dr. Samuel K. Lothrop, the Boston minister who was visiting in London, that Sumner "had made a mistake in his marriage." Not surprised, Adams agreed: "An ambitious and imperious temper, with thirty years difference of age, augured little chance of happiness." [3] By September rumors began to fly as Alice, who had spent the summer in the Berkshires without hearing one word from her husband, decided to go to Paris with Bell, where they planned to live with her sister, Mrs. Appleton. Though her relatives bought the steamship tickets under another name, inevitably more and more people were in on the secret. Still, nobody had much information. Some said that Mrs. Sumner had gone off in a huff,

[2] Boston *Post*, Nov. 13, 1867; New York *World*, Nov. 20, 1867; *Independent*, Nov. 28, 1867; Julia Ward Howe: Diary, Nov. 12, 1867, Howe MSS.; Pierce to Sumner, Nov. 19, 1867, Sumner MSS.

[3] C. F. Adams: Diary, June 13, 1867, Adams MSS.

expecting her husband to follow her and effect a reconciliation; others believed that she really was needed in Paris to care for an invalid kinsman.

In mid-October, however, the Sumners' problems became a matter of general public knowledge. The New York *Express*, a scurrilous paper edited by Congressman James Brooks, published a lurid account of the "Senator Sumner, Baron Holstein Affair," and other Democratic papers gave it wide currency. Detailing the "acquaintanceship,—it cannot be properly called intimacy"—between Mrs. Sumner and the Prussian attaché, the *Express* painted Sumner as a jealous and ridiculous husband. The Senator, so it claimed, had written Holstein a letter insinuating "something not honorable to the wife." In reply Holstein had denied any impropriety but declared himself ready to give Sumner "any such satisfaction as a man of honor demanded." Thereupon, the *Express* charged, Sumner wrote to Bismarck, who recalled Holstein. When Mrs. Sumner learned of this correspondence, she became "indignant beyond all power of description," especially over "that part . . . which . . . touched her honor." She left her husband and was now on her way to Europe. Such was the report in Boston, according to the *Express;* "it may possibly be erroneous in some of the details but in substance, probably correct." There was, the paper added ominously, "some scandal afloat beyond all this, relating both to the Senator and the Lady." [4]

Sumner's political opponents were quick to capitalize upon these reports, which seemed to indicate that he had improperly used his official influence for personal objectives. "It is undoubtedly a very enormous thing," scolded the New York *World* on October 23, "for any benedict to be afflicted with a rival at once more susceptible to loveliness and impervious to fear—who won't be bullied and who will admire—but in the elimination of such an intractible [*sic*] the prestige of a great country should not be used."

For Sumner's numerous personal enemies, especially those belonging to the Conservative Somerset Club in Boston, the news of his domestic infelicity was a godsend. Everybody who knew

[4] New York *Express*, quoted in New York *World*, Oct. 22, 1867.

the couple had to admit that Alice was in part to blame because "her temper is sharp," but the ill-disposed argued that Sumner "might have exerted a controlling influence, or at least have secured her respect." Generally they agreed that Alice had grown "disgusted and estranged" when she discovered her husband's "selfishness and over-bearing disposition." Sumner's course toward her was "unmanly and brutal," a further demonstration that he was "completely free from natural feelings and sympathies." [5]

During the fall and winter other rumors began to circulate to the effect that, as the *Express* had hinted, there was a deeper reason for the separation than incompatibility of tempers. In mid-October Charles Francis Adams was told that Mrs. Sumner was planning to sue "for a divorce on the ground of impotence." Soon this gossip was repeated as an unquestioned fact. To the ribald it explained not merely Sumner's separation from his wife but his long delay in getting married, and, indeed, his self-centered political course or anything else they objected to about him. College classmates now recalled—what nobody had ever previously suggested—that Sumner had always been known to be impotent and that at Harvard they had nicknamed him "The Stag" because of his alleged deficiency. A young friend wrote Moorfield Storey, who was about to take up his duties as Sumner's secretary: "Please ask Charley confidentially if his wife left him because he could not *perform the functions of a husband* owing to continued secret———. This is what Madame Rumor says." [6] For years to come Sumner's enemies would jeer at him as "The Great Impotent."

It is as difficult to determine what truth underlay this rumor of Sumner's sexual impotence as it is to ascertain what, if any, part his wife played in spreading it. At no time did Alice leave any record of the breakup of the marriage; there is not even family hearsay among her granddaughters to suggest her version of events. Certain it is, however, that there was no talk about Sumner's alleged impotence during the couple's

[5] Chandler Robbins to R. C. Winthrop, Sept. 22, 1867, Winthrop MSS.; C. F. Adams, Jr., to C. F. Adams, Sept. 29, 1867, Adams MSS.

[6] C. F. Adams: Diary, Oct. 23, 1867, Adams MSS.; Bigelow: *Retrospections*, V, 143; "Jack" to Moorfield Storey, Nov. 29, 1867, Storey MSS.

1866–1867 winter season in Washington, though there was a little gossip about Alice's indiscreet behavior with Holstein. Nor when the Sumners separated in bitterness for the summer—and, as it turned out, forever—was there any hint that impotence was the cause. Not until Alice, after a summer of being ignored by Sumner, concluded that the breach was irreparable did the rumor begin. It did not become a matter of general report until winter, when she came back from Europe, partly because she had had a surprising and embarrassing encounter there with Holstein, who was in Paris, partly because her sister was returning to America. Looking worn and haggard but holding her head high, Alice tried to resume her usual place in Boston society, only to find that many even of her friends thought she had been imprudent and perverse. Then for the first time did "such awful insinuations . . . as would make your hair . . . curl" begin to circulate about Sumner's deficiencies. Much disturbed, Howe tried to learn the source of the stories, and in February 1868, A. A. Lawrence, a good friend of the Mason family, told him that Alice justified her course on two grounds: "that what every matured woman considers a just desire, was not fully granted; —and that, when by reasons of that denial she desired separate apartments, that too was denied." The two grounds, as Howe observed, were somewhat contradictory, but, what was more important, they were "cunning; and apparently incapable of being disproved." [7]

To this day the charge that Sumner was impotent remains just that. If there was impotence, it was not physiological, as in the case of John Randolph of Roanoke, whose doctrinaire rigidity was in some respects similar to Sumner's; after Sumner's death two physicians examined the body and pronounced his genitals perfectly normal.[8] Moreover, Sumner's vigorous masculine appearance, his manly stride, and his deep bass voice belied any suggestion of hormone deficiency. Psychic impotence, however, is much more difficult to establish or to refute. Of course, Sumner himself swore that the charge was "shamelessly un-

[7] Howe to Sumner, Feb. 14, 1868, G. B. Pierce MSS.

[8] The physicians were Charles Edward Brown-Séquard and Thomas Johnson. Memorandum by E. L. Pierce on Sumner's Marital Difficulties, G. B. Pierce MSS.

truthful," and he branded it "an afterthought and an invention" on the part of his wife; [9] but, as a principal, he can hardly be regarded as impartial. But if Lawrence correctly stated Mrs. Sumner's position, she complained not so much of Sumner's total impotence as of his inability "fully" to satisfy "what every matured woman considers a just desire." That Sumner was at least occasionally able to complete the sexual act is suggested by his otherwise inexplicable bet, shortly after his marriage, that he would become a father before his friend Henry S. Sanford did, and by his surprising announcement to James T. Fields, after his honeymoon, that Alice was expecting a baby.[1]

At the same time, there is every reason to believe that sexual incompatibility was at the base of the Sumners' difficulties. For a man in his mid-fifties, who had a long record of heart trouble and who was constantly preoccupied with his public duties, to have the sexual drive of a wife scarcely more than half his age would be unusual indeed. Incompatibility of temperament was added to that of age. When Alice, who had sought in Sumner a father figure to whom she could give total respect and obedience, found that instead her husband needed her compassion and assistance, her sharp sadistic streak appeared. The more her actions moved him to entreaties, the more she scorned him; she despised him for breaking into tears.

Sumner could not play the domineering husband. There had always been a passive, essentially feminine element in his composition; even in his courtship it was Alice who had been the pursuer and he the pursued. She had the experience of a former marriage; though he had read Michelet's *L'Amour* and knew all the literature about sex, he was probably a virgin. Doubtless he proved an awkward and often ineffectual lover.

But his masculine vanity would not let him admit his limita-

[9] Sumner to Howe, Feb. 17, 1868, ibid. According to Theophilus Parsons: ". . . Sumner did not satisfy Mrs S's carnal requirements. Whether she was peculiarly egigeante [*sic*] or he wholly impotent was the only question in doubt apparently." Bigelow: Diary, Nov. 27, 1867, Bigelow MSS.

[1] Sanford to Sumner, Nov. 27, 1867, Sumner MSS.; interview of E. L. Pierce with James T. Fields, undated, G. B. Pierce MSS. Fields was almost certainly incorrect in thinking this conversation with Sumner occurred in June 1867. See Pierce to Mrs. Fields, Dec. 30, 1886, MS., Henry E. Huntington Lib.

tions or ask his wife for instruction in the mysteries of marriage. It would have gone against the pattern of his whole life to concede that he could learn anything from a woman, one of those charming, decorative creatures whose proper role was to listen to him discourse on fine china and laces. Indeed, during the past decade, Sumner had become increasingly unwilling to believe that he could learn from anyone. During his sufferings after the Brooks assault he had come to rank himself among the holy company of the martyrs, and thereafter he craved admiration more than instruction or even solace. His mind, as Henry Adams commented in one of his most penetrating passages, "had reached the calm of water which receives and reflects images without absorbing them; it contains nothing but itself." In his own way he loved his beautiful wife, but he loved her as a projection of himself. It seems never to have occurred to him that she might have ideas—and desires, as well—of her own. Shrewdly William Cullen Bryant diagnosed the root of the difficulties between the Sumners when he remarked: "A woman is not content with a husband who is exclusively occupied with himself and his own greatness." [2]

Wholly unprepared to discover that the woman he had honored with his name was a self-willed, independent-minded—not to say, imperious—creature, Sumner tried to handle his marital problem in the way he always dealt with personal difficulties. First he avoided doing or saying anything, in the hope that the situation would right itself. In all his letters about the breakup of the marriage "forbearance" was his most frequently used word. When this passivity, instead of curbing Alice, roused her to new extravagances of behavior, Sumner then resorted to the silent treatment, to which he had subjected so many of the friends with whom he had quarreled in the past. He ignored her teasing; he turned his back when she appeared in public with Holstein; instead of discussing their problems, he gave her a French novel which presumably pointed up a lesson for her; he refused to write to her during the long summer while she stayed in Lenox—though he marked correspondence which mentioned

[2] *The Education of Henry Adams,* p. 252; Bigelow: *Retrospections,* IV, 134.

her and mailed it to her without any covering comment, just as he had once sent marked copies of newspapers and speeches to Francis Lieber when they were at odds.[3]

In domestic as in political warfare Sumner had no thought of compromise, and he was determined to regard the break with his wife as final and irreparable. In his eyes Alice had been wicked, and he adopted toward her the strategy he always used when dealing with evil: the moral blockade. Since neither silence nor forbearance could change her course, he would preserve his own purity by cutting her totally out of his life. The restraint and dignity which he preserved during the early, painful months of his domestic unhappiness he broke only when Congressman Hooper and other well-intentioned friends tried to bring about a reconciliation. The thought that he might again be linked to one whom he considered wicked drove Sumner almost to desperation. For a time he thought of giving up his house in Washington, now nearing completion, lest his wife decide to return; he talked of going into lodgings, where there could be no room for her. Only when Hooper reassured him that Alice would prefer "to brave anything rather than continue to live with you"[4] did he finally take up residence in his still unfurnished house, where he hoped to find more privacy than rented rooms would afford.

Characteristically Sumner brooded over the blow which he had been dealt, until by repetition, amplification, speculation, and exaggeration his version of Alice's behavior became distorted beyond recognition. Nothing could have been more discreet or gentlemanly than his reticence until October 1867. Even his closest friends, like Longfellow and Howe, did not know of his misfortune. Necessarily he discussed Alice's misconduct with Hooper, but he did not suggest that she was guilty of anything more than indiscretion and complained only that by being seen so frequently in public with Holstein she "gave opportunity for coarse comments among habitues of drinking and gambling places and other vulgar and malignant persons." But after the newspapers spread the story, with its implication that Sumner

[3] Cf. Donald: *Sumner*, pp. 242–3.

[4] Hooper to Sumner, Thanksgiving Day, 1867, G. B. Pierce MSS.

had misused his official position to procure Holstein's recall, he began to look upon his wife's actions in a more severe light and concluded that she had contracted "an open liaison," "an illicit intimacy which demoralized her nature." [5]

By December, when reports of his alleged impotence were widespread, Sumner had convinced himself that Alice was a monster of depravity. Now he hardly knew whether more strongly to censure her original misdeeds or her present "effort to throw the blame upon an innocent person"—namely, himself. "You can have only a small idea of her character," he assured Mrs. John E. Lodge. "She is a bad woman—at home in the house a devil self willed and infernal; in every respect forgetful of her marriage vows. . . . She reminds me sometimes of Lady Ellenborough, who ran away with Schwarzenberg, and is now the wife of an Arabian Sheick; but Lady Ellenborough was never violent or unamiable. For these features we must go to Lady Halten of an earlier day. She is a compound of these two bad women." After this excursion into the history of feminine flagitiousness, he concluded: "No picture can adequately show the completeness of her vileness." [6]

Brooding over his injuries, real and fancied, Sumner constantly repainted the picture of his wife in blacker colors. He believed a report that Alice had been unfaithful during her first marriage; he now credited the tale—which had no foundation whatever—that she conceived a child by Holstein and, after his recall, had an abortion.[7] Positive that her behavior had been infamous, he was furious when Howe assured him that Boston society generally was "settling down to the belief that you were, in the main, right." "I am unwilling to be thought only 'in the main right,'" Sumner raged. "I know that there cannot be 'two sides' to the question. Reviewing the whole case I find nothing but too great forbearance and tardiness on my part . . . Her whole nature was poisoned by her intimacy with a foreigner. My

[5] Sumner's words, quoted in Hooper to Sumner, Nov. 30, 1867, ibid.

[6] Sumner to Mrs. Lodge, July 14 and 19, 1868, Lodge MSS.

[7] Sumner to Horatio Woodman, Feb. 17, 1868, MS., Mass. Hist. Soc.; interviews of E. L. Pierce with Mr. and Mrs. S. C. Pomeroy (Dec. 18, 1886), and with Mrs. W. D. O'Connor (Dec. 17, 1886), G. B. Pierce MSS.; A. B. Johnson to Pierce, Aug. 4, 1877, ibid.

house soon became an *Inferno,* and my name was dishonored." [8]

Cutting Alice out of his life altogether, Sumner never saw or wrote to her again. After an unhappy stay in Boston, she took her daughter abroad, where she remained, except for brief trips back to America, until her death in 1913. Calling herself "Mrs. Mason," she became a friend of Henry James, who announced that he adored "her great beauty (which on horseback is enormous)" and her "great honesty, frankness and naturalness"—but added that she was "limited by a kind of characteristic American want of culture." Imperious and high-tempered to the end, she quarreled bitterly with John Singer Sargent, whose portrait of her, she protested with justice, "made her look like a murderess." Indeed, as she put on weight, she became more formidable than handsome. In 1873 by mutual agreement she allowed Sumner to divorce her on grounds of desertion, and she did not remarry.[9] Nor, of course, did Sumner, who never after their separation again uttered her name but referred to her only as "that woman."

[8] Howe to Sumner, Dec. 15 [1867], and Sumner to Howe, Dec. 18, 1867, ibid.

[9] Leon Edel: *Henry James: The Conquest of London* (Philadelphia: J. B. Lippincott; 1962), pp. 105, 114; *Vernon Lee's Letters* (privately printed, 1937), pp. 177, 222. For the divorce proceedings, see letters from F. V. Balch to Sumner, Nov. 22, 1872, and Feb. 14, Mar. 1, April 27, and May 14, 1873, Sumner MSS., and Docket No. 1076, April 1873 term, Supreme Judicial Court of Suffolk County, Boston.

CHAPTER VIII

Life Is a Burden

"You cannot enter into the depths of my sorrows," Sumner confided to his friend Pierce. The twelve months after the breakup of his marriage were the bitterest in his life. Everything went wrong at once. His wife left him, publicly, scandalously. He had sold the old family residence on Hancock Street and was obliged to move out. To Longfellow he said: "I have buried from this house my father, my mother, a brother and sister; and now I am leaving it, the deadest of them all." [1] His new, empty, expensive Washington mansion seemed but a mockery of his past hopes. Politically, too, his prospects were no more satisfactory. Andrew Johnson continued to occupy the White House, impeachment failed, the Republican party forgot its former leaders to nominate an available candidate in 1868, and Sumner himself faced a dangerous reelection to the Senate. To add to it all, his health was bad. Sadly he wrote Longfellow: "Life is a burden hard to bear in such a desolation as mine." [2]

When Congress reconvened in December 1867, Sumner showed signs of weakness and fatigue. During most of the session he was not very active, and when he did bestir himself it

[1] Sumner to Pierce, Aug. 8, 1868, Sumner MSS.; Charles Francis Adams: *Richard Henry Dana* (Boston: Houghton Mifflin and Company; 1890), II, 339. As Pierce (IV, 337) points out, Sumner had, in fact, buried not one but three sisters from the house.

[2] Mar. 26, 1868, Longfellow MSS.

was with an uncertainty he had never before exhibited. For almost the first time in his long senatorial career he was obliged to ask his colleagues to postpone debate on a subject in which he was interested, once because he carelessly had forgotten to bring the necessary papers, and again because he had not had sufficient time to complete his study of the question. In debate he forgot the date of the Northwest Ordinance. As chairman of the Foreign Relations Committee he moved the payment of certain claims but, when questioned, was unable to remember how much they totaled. Challenged on the residence requirement for voters in Massachusetts, he had to reply lamely: "I wish I were better informed. . . . Whether that is the requirement in Massachusetts I am not able to say." [3]

Such inconsequential slips emboldened Sumner's enemies to attack him, even on matters of foreign policy, where heretofore his opinions had rarely been challenged. In advocating routine appropriations for the State Department, Sumner came under fire from brash, arrogant Roscoe Conkling, who saw an opportunity simultaneously to undermine Seward, his principal foe among New York Republicans, and to chastise Sumner for his much publicized interview of the previous summer. Bluntly he told the Senator "to pay more attention to what other members of this body says [*sic*], and particularly the humbler members of the body." No longer, he warned, could Sumner push through these bills for the State Department by talking in general terms of needs and costs. This "fountain of light" must tell the Senate just how the State Department officials spent their money and earned their keep. Senators, he warned, were tired of swallowing "in the lump these stately phrases which the Senator employs with a view to convincing the Senate that he knows more about this matter than anybody else." Conkling, for one, would no longer accept illumination from "the great orb of the State Department who rises periodically in his effulgence and sends his rays down the steep places here to cast a good many dollars into the sea." [4]

Bewildered and hurt by such personalities, Sumner com-

[3] *Cong. Globe,* 40 Cong., 2 Sess., pp. 1121, 1628, 1834, 2667, 3316, 2419.
[4] Ibid., pp. 3391–4, 3249.

plained that Conkling seemed to have "a passion for misunderstanding" him and attributed his venomous style of debating to the fact that the New Yorker had only recently come to the Senate from the lower House, where such tactics were more frequently indulged in. But the ill will Conkling vented had a deeper origin. Indifferent alike to idealism and ideology, devoted only to power and the promotion of Roscoe Conkling, the New York Senator represented the "new recruits" of whom Sumner had spoken in his newspaper interview, the politicos who were about to take over the Republican party. Already the giants of the Civil War years were passing. Thaddeus Stevens was near death; Chase had been pushed upstairs to the Supreme Court; Wade was fighting a losing battle for reelection; Stanton had only two more years to live. Many thought Sumner, ill and shaken by domestic tragedy, would be the next to fall, and Conkling was ready to hasten the day. To such an implacable enemy Sumner did not know how to respond. "I am sorry," was all he could say after Conkling's attack. "I wish it were otherwise. . . . I am seeking nothing but the public interest."

• 2 •

From the frustrations of Congress Sumner took refuge in his new Washington house. He had moved into it only with great reluctance. He knew it would entail enormous expenses, for the house itself finally cost $28,060 and Hooper estimated that he would require between $7,000 and $8,000 a year to run it. Equally troubling was the public advertisement that moving into his house without his wife would give to his marital disaster. "I took this house for another," he told Longfellow. "I have no heart about it or anything else." [5] For a long time he hesitated, with good friends like Howe urging him to sell the house before occupying it and with other good friends like Hooper insisting that he move in. Finally Sumner came to see that whatever he did his enemies were going to exploit his marriage fiasco. If he attended the theater in New York, the papers reported that when one of the actors delivered his line: "Good heavens, madam, to

[5] Dec. 2, 1867, Longfellow MSS.

whom can a man trust his wife in the present state of society?" the audience, aware of Sumner's presence, "turned their faces from the stage to him and had a double enjoyment of the passage." Or if Sumner opposed adjourning Congress because he was suspicious of President Johnson, the newspapers gibed: "Sumner will trust nobody, even his own family." "It would be difficult to imagine cruelty or brutality beyond what I have encountered," he concluded and decided that, if his life was to be tortured by personal publicity, he might as well endure it in the privacy and comfort of his own home.[6]

Privacy he achieved at once, but comfort was to come later, for like any new housekeeper he had to face the tedious and expensive task of furnishing his home. The house, as Edmund Quincy reported, was not very large but well contrived. A compact brick building, it had an air of expensive elegance as it stood behind its green-painted iron fence and looked out over Lafayette Square. Aside from the kitchen and pantries in the basement and small bedrooms for the servants and for Sumner's secretary under the mansard roof, it consisted of six large rooms, three on each floor. Beyond the entranceway on the ground floor, where Sumner placed a bust of Minerva, there were the parlor, the dining room, and a library, which, however, did not have enough wall space for Sumner's books. Sumner's study, with three large windows, occupied most of the second floor, with his own bedroom and a guest room opening into it from opposite sides.

To furnish his new residence Sumner brought some belongings from the old house in Boston as well as his "household companions"—his books, bronzes, and engravings—but these were barely a beginning. At the outset he estimated that it would cost him at least five thousand dollars to furnish his two floors properly, and, like all such estimates, this one fell far short of the mark. He had expensive tastes, and, though he was constantly aware of the financial drain, he felt that he owed himself the right to be a little extravagant in equipping the only house

[6] Boston *Post,* Nov. 22 and 28, 1867; Sumner to Longfellow, Dec. 18, 1867, Longfellow MSS.

Mrs. Charles Sumner

HOUGHTON LIBRARY, HARVARD UNIVERSITY

Sumner's House in Washington
H Street and Vermont Avenue

THE LIBRARY OF CONGRESS

that he had ever bought. Irritably he noted that bills arrived more promptly than the specially designed furnishings he had ordered. More than a month after Sumner moved in, his new secretary, Moorfield Storey, reported that "the house is given over to the demon of chaos." By this time Sumner's bedroom and study were almost finished and the dining room was nearly ready, but there had been a mix-up on the delivery of carpets and everything else was also in confusion.[7]

Gradually order began to emerge. The center of the house was Sumner's upstairs study. At one end was his large desk, always stocked with five basic books—Harvey's edition of Shakespeare, Hazlitt's *Select British Poets* (both of which he had bought with college prize money), Roget's *Thesaurus*, Hickey's edition of the Constitution, and the *Rules and Usages of the Senate*. At the opposite end he placed a smaller desk for his secretary. A long, flat worktable occupied the center of the room. Desks, table, and even the chairs were usually loaded with books, documents, issues of the *Congressional Globe*, maps, correspondence, and other papers. In order to seat a visitor Sumner frequently had to dump the contents of one of the chairs on the floor. The whole room gave an impression of inextricable confusion, yet, as one of his secretaries remembered, Sumner "was systematic in his disorder, and could always find the paper or book he wanted, provided it had not been misplaced by another person. He even knew the stratum it occupied." [8]

The rest of the house was kept tidy, but as Sumner over the years indulged his fondness for collecting bronzes and china and paintings, it assumed an increasingly cluttered appearance. With no genuine artistic eye, Sumner was all too often the victim of unscrupulous dealers, to whom he paid high prices for paintings of dubious merit and authenticity. He was fondest of his supposed Tintoretto, "The Rendition of the Slave," because it had inspired his first great antislavery speech, and at his death he left it to his devoted Negro friend, the Boston caterer, J. B.

[7] Quincy to "Mollie," April 19, 1868, Quincy MSS.; Storey to his mother, Jan. 5, 1868, Storey MSS.

[8] Arnold Burges Johnson: "Charles Sumner," *Cosmopolitan*, III (1887), 411.

Smith. Most of the rest of his paintings went to the Boston Museum of Fine Arts, which found only a few worth preserving and auctioned off the rest, usually for less than fifty dollars a canvas.[9] Sumner's taste in engravings was better, for he had made a careful study of the art during his long illness after the Brooks assault, but he selected them more for historical and literary connotations than for aesthetic merit. Apologizing that his simple stairway leading from the entrance hall to his study was "only a sort of ladder after all," he lined it with engravings of beautiful stairways from all over the world. He covered virtually every inch of the walls of his study with prints, which he grouped around six pictures of celebrated peace conferences. Thus an engraving of the "Second Treaty of Westphalia" held the central position on one wall, with portraits of worthies of the time and a picture of the cathedral arranged around it. Over Sumner's desk hung Godefroy's engraving of "The Congress of Vienna," surrounded by portraits of the Bonapartes, Grotius, and the like. An engraving representing "Modesty" hung on the bathroom door.[1]

As the furniture began to arrive and the domestic servants began to learn their duties, Sumner came to take delight in his new home. "I confess the pleasure of space and cleanliness in a beautiful situation," he wrote Howe, "with the independence of a house that is my own." He took conspicuous pride in being, for the first time in his life, a householder. When Storey, just out of Harvard Law School, arrived to take up his duties as secretary, Sumner rather fussily showed him to his room and made a minute inspection to see that everything there was arranged for the young man's comfort. "As he did it," Storey recalled, "he told me that Chancellor Kent had rendered him the same service and had told him that Alexander Hamilton had done it for him, so I became a link in a curious chain." Proudly but insistently he invited his Massachusetts friends, from whom he in the past had

[9] *Catalogue of Paintings and Engravings from the Collection of the Hon. Charles Sumner* (Boston: W. F. Brown & Co.; 1874); Boston *Commonwealth*, Dec. 12, 1874.

[1] Dawes: *Sumner*, pp. 301–4; A. B. Johnson: "Charles Sumner," pp. 411–12; Mrs. A. H. Howard, in Philadelphia *Press*, Sept. 5, 1871.

accepted so much hospitality, to visit Washington and stay in his beautiful guest room overlooking the White House.[2]

So content did Sumner seem in his new surroundings that Edmund Quincy, who visited him on several occasions in 1868, concluded that he was not sorry to be rid of his wife "and restored to his bachelor estate," and Sumner himself bluntly told Howe: "Once relieved I shall not be easily tempted into any such cruel bonds." Though he still winced when newspapers gibed about his difficulties with Alice, he did not truly miss her. After about a year of separation he wrote to Mrs. Lodge, who commiserated with him on his domestic misfortune: "As for that bad woman, do not believe that I have any sorrow, except from the sense of my solitude and disappointment. It is an infinite solace that she is outside of my house never more to disturb me by her presence or to degrade the house." [3]

Slowly he began making a new social life for himself in Washington. Now he very rarely went out to parties, but, once he was sure of his cook, he gave small dinners of his own, usually without women present. His most frequent guest, almost unbelievably, was Caleb Cushing, that Massachusetts chameleon of politics who had once branded him a "one-idead abolitionist agitator" but who now, a widower, practiced law in Washington and headed a commission to revise the United States statutes. They had renewed friendship after Cushing in a legal case had gone out of his way to laud Sumner's "all comprehensive knowledge of public law." Members of the diplomatic corps frequently dined with him, and so many foreigners came to him bearing letters of introduction that Sumner used to say to Carl Schurz: "Come and dine with me to-day, and I will show you another Englishman." When Charles Dickens returned to Washington in

[2] Sumner to Howe, Jan. 2, 1867 [i.e., 1868], G. B. Pierce MSS.; Moorfield Storey: "Autobiography," Storey MSS. Palfrey, Pierce, Howe, G. W. Greene, and J. B. Smith were among those who accepted Sumner's invitation. Not all his guests were happy with their reception, and Palfrey complained of "Sumner's rudeness of treatment in his own house" (C. F. Adams: Diary, Mar. 10, 1869, Adams MSS.)—of which the Senator himself was entirely unaware.

[3] Quincy to Anne Quincy, May 13, 1868, Quincy MSS.; Sumner to Howe, Jan. 5, 1868, G. B. Pierce MSS.; Sumner to Mrs. John E. Lodge [October, 1868], Lodge MSS.

1868 to deliver readings from his novels, Sumner's was the only dinner invitation which he accepted, and he was fascinated to hear his host and Secretary Stanton reminisce of the frightful night when Lincoln was assassinated.[4]

Even on informal occasions, when Sumner invited friends to accept potluck with him, he set a good table, and guests were impressed by both the excellent cooking and the handsome table service, expressly made for him, with his initials on each plate and goblet. They found their host invariably agreeable. Careful to steer dinner conversation away from controversial subjects, Sumner welcomed political opponents as well as friends to his table. He was not an amusing conversationalist, but he was willing to smile tolerantly when others were witty. On the other hand, he would not permit vulgarity or profanity at his table. When one of his guests began a story: "I suppose I can tell this, there being no ladies present," Sumner impulsively interjected: "But there are gentlemen present." With every intention of being a good listener, Sumner invariably monopolized the conversation around the dinner table. He had been so many places; he knew so many men; he had so much to say. An innocent question about the vintage of his wine or the painter of one of his pictures or, especially, the provenience of a choice autograph in his collection would start him on a monologue, which, even an unfriendly witness was obliged to report, had "not much play of words and little lightness of touch" but was "in every other sense . . . brilliant."[5]

Sumner had always been a great talker, but now he talked with a kind of desperation so as to keep his guests on and on, to stave off the inevitable hour when he would be left alone in his great house with his thoughts. The men to whom he showed his household treasures were impressed by "the ever-present evidences of care and tidiness in his rooms," where everything was "neat, clean, and sweet," but a shrewder woman concluded: "It is

[4] Pierce, IV, 341; Sumner to Stanton, Sunday morning [Feb. 1868], Stanton MSS.; George Dolby: *Charles Dickens, As I Knew Him* (London: T. Fisher Unwin; 1887), pp. 244–5; Walter Dexter, ed., *The Letters of Charles Dickens* (Bloomsbury: The Nonesuch Press; 1938), III, 614–15.

[5] Carl Schurz: *Charles Sumner: An Essay*, ed. Arthur R. Hogue (Urbana, Ill.: The University of Illinois Press; 1951), pp. 81–2; Dawes: *Sumner*, p. 305.

full of books and pictures, and many rare old engravings, but it looks like the home of a lonely man." [6]

Partly as an anodyne against loneliness, partly as an unconscious recognition that since he would have no heir of his own blood he must leave behind children of his brain, Sumner about this time began preparing a new, comprehensive edition of his writings and speeches, the first since the collection he had published in 1856. Originally he hoped that James T. Fields would issue a five- or seven-volume edition of his works, but Fields was obliged to decline, since "in these degenerate days it takes 2500 to *pay*" and the prospect for such sales seemed dim.[7] Next Sumner turned to the Boston firm of Lee and Shepard, which specialized in selling books by subscription. His friends subscribed money enough to pay for the plates of the first two volumes, and the sales from these were supposed to finance publication of the rest.[8]

While completing publishing arrangements, Sumner set earnestly to work revising and editing his writings, and he secured the assistance of George Nichols, of Cambridge, a learned and meticulous proofreader, who agreed to verify all his dates and quotations. Day after day Sumner amended and pruned his speeches until he sometimes thought it would have been as easy to rewrite as to revise. At times, in discouragement, he thought of giving up the whole project: "If I could throw them into the fire, I would, and have an end of them. . . ." But this was a passing mood. "These speeches are my life," he wrote Howe in a more characteristic temper. "As a connected series, they will

[6] John W. Forney: *Anecdotes of Public Men* (New York: Harper & Brothers; 1881), II, 259; A. Augusta Dodge: *Gail Hamilton's Life in Letters* (Boston: Lee and Shepard; 1901), II, 747.

[7] Fields to Sumner, April 28, 1867, Sumner MSS. As early as 1865 Sumner had approached John Owen, with a view to securing his assistance in preparing a new edition of his speeches. Sumner to Owen, Aug. 6, 1865, MS. in private hands. The next year he brought the project to Fields's attention (July 7, 1866, MS., Henry E. Huntington Lib.) but was told that the time was not propitious.

[8] Raymond Lincoln Kilgour: *Lee and Shepard: Publishers for the People* (Hamden, Conn.: The Shoe String Press, Inc.; 1965), pp. 97 ff.; Lee and Shepard to Howe, Dec. 31, 1868, Charles A. Phelps to Sumner, Jan. 3, 1869, and Fields to Sumner, Jan. 14, 1869—all in Sumner MSS.; Sumner to Fields, Jan. 16 [1869], MS., Henry E. Huntington Lib. Dr. Charles A. Phelps planned to prepare a biography of Sumner to accompany the new edition of his works, but Sumner's closest friends strongly opposed the project.

illustrate the progress of the great battle with slavery, and what I have done in it. I hope it is not unpardonable in me to desire to see them together," he added with a touch of pathos, "especially as I have nothing else." [9] For the rest of Sumner's life his spare hours were occupied with this reliving of the past—with careful insertion of newspaper comments on his addresses, of extracts from his correspondence, and of footnotes to document quotations and with some slight deletion of literary or factual excrescences which he now found embarrassing—and the set ultimately was to grow to fifteen volumes. For all the labor, of which Sumner frequently complained, the task was an absorbingly important one, and he talked of his "book" incessantly. "I think he loves the author of it," Fields was moved to comment.[1]

• 3 •

It was well that Sumner could find pleasure in his new house, for these days there was little pleasure for him in Congress. The principal—one might almost say, the sole—business of the second session of the Fortieth Congress (1867–68) was the unmaking of one President and the making of his successor. The two processes were closely interrelated, and neither progressed as Sumner wished.

To be sure, he was heartily in favor of the impeachment of Andrew Johnson, which occupied so much of the time and attention of Congressmen throughout the session. He had wanted Johnson ousted at least since his speech on Washington's birthday in 1866, when, according to Sumner, Johnson's "foul-mouthed utterances which are a disgrace to human nature" offered ample grounds for removing him from office. As Sumner throughout 1866 and 1867 denounced the President as the defender of slavery, the arch enemy of his country, and the betrayer of liberty, he from time to time threatened that the remedy for this evil was "the removal of its author from the Executive chair," and once he even argued that the Senate would

[9] Sumner to Longfellow, July 8, 1869, Longfellow MSS.; Sumner to Howe, Dec. 7, 1868, Sumner MSS.

[1] Fields to Longfellow, Oct. 8, 1868, MS., Henry E. Huntington Lib.

be only acting "in strict harmony with its constitutional place in the Government" if it reprimanded the House of Representatives for failing to bring impeachment proceedings.[2]

Nevertheless, he maintained the fiction that he was not committed to removing the President. "It is hard to be reserved and patient in presence of such an offender," he explained to the Duchess of Argyll. "But I am one of his judges, and must cultivate a tranquil disposition." With legalistic precision he defined his stand in September 1867: "I have never doubted that the President would be impeached. I do not say what judgment I should pronounce as a Senator if he were before us. . . ."[3]

This nice distinction fooled nobody, but it kept Sumner from actively egging on the anti-Johnson proceedings in the House of Representatives. With mounting anger he heard the House committee report in early 1867 that the President had not yet committed the "high crimes and misdemeanors" required by the Constitution for his removal. In August he began to take hope again when Johnson suspended Secretary of War Stanton, who had so long served as a Radical keyhole into the cabinet. The President's move, which Sumner branded as "a national calamity" and "a horrible blow at reconstruction," surely ought to convince the House that it should long ago "have put him . . . in a straight-jacket."[4] To his chagrin he discovered that most Representatives were less disturbed by the removal of Stanton, which was performed precisely according to the Tenure of Office Act, than by Democratic resurgence in the fall elections. When Wisconsin Republican Matthew H. Carpenter argued that Republican defeats in Ohio and Pennsylvania proved that "the voice of the people is against impeachment," Sumner snapped back: "Those elections only show more imperatively the necessity for impeachment."[5] But few of his colleagues were convinced, and the House in December 1867 again defeated a resolution calling for Johnson's removal.

[2] *Cong. Globe*, 40 Cong., 2 Sess., p. 2897; Sumner: *Works*, XII, 349–50, 383; XI, 420.

[3] Sumner to Duchess of Argyll, Feb. 11, 1867, Argyll MSS.; Boston *Advertiser*, Supplement, Sept. 4, 1867.

[4] Boston *Advertiser*, Supplement, Sept. 4, 1867.

[5] Milton: *The Age of Hate*, p. 471.

Abruptly, on February 21, 1868, the whole complexion of affairs changed. Rebuffed when the Senate refused to approve his suspension of Stanton, the President decided to bypass the Tenure of Office Act, to stand on the rights he believed the Constitution granted him, and to order the firing of the Secretary. When his message announcing his action reached the Senate, there was a gasp of incredulity. At last Johnson had played into the Radicals' hands; he had committed what the Tenure of Office Act had expressly defined as a high crime. Sumner rushed up to the desk of the presiding officer to make sure of the good news, and soon Wade—who, in the absence of a Vice President, was next in line for the presidency should Johnson be ousted—was surrounded by exultant Radicals. The one danger to impeachment now was the possibility that Stanton might obey the President's order and resign, and to prevent such an unlikely happening the Senate rushed through a resolution denying Johnson's right to oust the War Secretary. At the same time many Senators dashed off letters begging Stanton to keep his place. Sumner's terse message read, in full: "Stick." [6]

Stick Stanton did, and swiftly the House of Representatives went into action. On February 24 it adopted a resolution impeaching the President; then—belatedly, one might think—it approved eleven articles laying forth Johnson's alleged crimes and misdemeanors in wearisome detail and appointed a committee of managers to present their case before the Senate, which would try the great offender.

To many Senators the trial of Andrew Johnson, which began on March 13 and continued with interruptions through May 16, with one final session ten days after that, posed puzzling problems of law, logic, or, at the least, consistency, but not to Sumner. Desperately he felt the necessity of removing the President. Every morning his mail from the South bore alarming tidings. From New Orleans one correspondent wrote: "The Original Rebs and *'old Respectable Citizens'* never can and never will be conciliated, they must and will Rule or be ruled. . . ." From North Carolina the story was that "the malignants of the South are more bitterly adverse to the Union today, than at any

[6] Stanton MSS.

time since the collapse" of the Confederacy and that farmers were driving the Negroes off the land "(and in some cases defrauding them) because they voted the republican ticket." A Virginia correspondent told how he had had his left eye gouged out and had been imprisoned for teaching Negroes in a Sunday school, and a laborer from the same state wrote: "we have a hard time of it heer the rebels have combine to gethere her you canot git a days work to do unles you have ben in the rebel army." A Mississippi writer reported that the Negroes were "*induring* what no other *class* of men on earth would indure—there *characters* are *traduced* they are *robed* of there *wages* and *killed* . . . yet with all this . . . they are peacalbe and *Law abiding*. . . ."[7]

Like his correspondents, Sumner knew the author of these evils. He could not forget that the career of Andrew Johnson was "compounded of falsehood and usurpation; how, beginning with promises to make treason odious, he soon installed it in authority; how, from declared sympathy with Unionists, white and black, he changed to be their persecutor; how in him are continued the worst elements of Slavery, an insensibility to right and a passion for power; . . . how he patronized massacre and bloodshed, and gave a license to the Ku-Klux-Klan; . . . how he so far triumphed in his wickedness that in nine States no Union man is safe and no murderer of a Union man can be punished. . . ." The need for Johnson's removal was so desperate that Sumner found his "path as clear as day. Never in history was there a great case more free from all just doubt."[8]

Eagerly he tried to push the trial to a prompt conclusion. Repeatedly he urged his colleagues to hold more frequent meetings and to sit for longer hours. Other public business ought to be suspended during the trial, for it was a gross impropriety for Congress to receive messages and nominations from a President whom they were trying to expel from office. As the trial proceeded, he sat much of the time next to old Thaddeus Stevens, at the impeachment managers' table, and he conferred frequently

[7] All these letters are in the Sumner MSS.; A. Jervis, Dec. 3, 1867; J. M. Robinson, Dec. 5, 1867; Thomas Chase, Dec. 9, 1867; George Hadden, Dec. 10, 1867; and T. W. Stringer, Dec. 28, 1867.

[8] Sumner: *Works*, XII, 383–4, 405.

with Wade in hopes of hurrying the Senate along to a verdict against the Great Usurper.[9]

Passionately Sumner denounced all efforts to conduct the impeachment proceedings like a regular trial before a court. It was an enormous mistake, he argued, "to confound this great constitutional trial with an ordinary case of *Nisi Prius*"; a true reading of the Constitution would show that impeachment was "a political proceeding before a political body with a political purpose."[1] There was, therefore, nothing at all wrong in allowing Wade to vote, although his vote might determine the outcome of the trial and in effect make him the next President. Nor did Sumner think there would be anything amiss about admitting two new Republican Senators from the reconstructed state of Arkansas after the trial was already under way and giving these fresh judges the right to vote on Johnson's fate.

Since the trial was in Sumner's view a political proceeding, he did not hesitate to urge that all evidence against the President be admitted. When, however, it came to allowing cabinet members to testify as to President Johnson's intent in removing Stanton, that was another matter. In view of Sumner's willingness to hear second-hand and tainted witnesses against Johnson, he had not the effrontery to vote against allowing Gideon Welles to testify, but he sat silent while his colleagues gagged the Secretary of the Navy. Derisively John B. Henderson, the Missouri Senator who opposed impeachment, sent him a note; "Stick, Sumner, Stick."[2] But consistency was no hobgoblin for Sumner now, intent as he was on ridding the country of Johnson. He failed even to wince when William M. Evarts, one of the President's attorneys, defended his client's right to interpret the Constitution for himself, just as Andrew Jackson had done in a previous day—and, Evarts was careful to mention, just as Sumner had done in 1852 when he defied court and Congress to call the fugitive slave laws unconstitutional.[3]

Impatiently Sumner brushed aside the technicalities and

[9] Springfield *Republican*, May 2, 1868; New York *Herald*, May 17, 1868.

[1] Sumner: *Works*, XII, 320–3.

[2] *The Trial of Andrew Johnson*, supplement to *Cong. Globe*, 40 Cong., 2 Sess., pp. 195, 224, 231, 232; Welles: *Diary*, III, 335. Henderson's note is in the Sumner MSS.

[3] *Trial of Andrew Johnson*, p. 355.

legal quibbles that made Republicans like Trumbull and Fessenden hesitate before condemning Johnson. Some Senators were troubled by the fact that Johnson had not actually removed Stanton, who still occupied the War Office; that during debate on the Tenure of Office bill John Sherman had expressly declared that it would be intolerable to keep a man in the cabinet against the wish of the President; and that, in any case, Stanton, who had been appointed by Lincoln and had never received a formal commission from Johnson, was not covered by the act. To all these points Sumner had answers, some based on plausible arguments, some deriving from strained law and warped precedent, but to him these issues seemed essentially irrelevant. By higgling over such fine points with "enormous scholiasm" Republicans were forgetting the true face and front of Andrew Johnson's offending. Bitterly Sumner regretted that impeachment had been brought "on such narrow ground" as in the House articles. He admitted that Johnson's alleged infraction of the Tenure of Office Act "without connection with transgressions of the past" would not have justified his removal. It was that past record, the fact that "There is nothing of usurpation he has not attempted," which was impeachable.[4]

Whatever could be said of Sumner's legal learning, there was an element of common sense in his view of impeachment. Too rigid an insistence upon the letter of the law meant, as Ben Butler, one of the House impeachment managers, stated, that it was possible to remove a President for robbing a chicken house (because this legally was a crime) but not for misgoverning the country. Why all Senators could not grasp this elementary point was beyond Sumner's comprehension. The blindness of men like Trumbull and Fessenden he could only attribute to the fact that they had practiced law too long. "Give me a lawyer to betray a great cause," Sumner exploded. "He can always find an excuse. Technicality and quibble cannot fail." [5]

Justifying his own course on general grounds of policy, Sumner was characteristically unwilling to allow other Senators to make the same defense for defeating impeachment. Desirous

[4] Sumner to Dana, July 1, 1868, Dana MSS.; Sumner: *Works*, XII, 348, 350.
[5] Sumner to Howe, May 21, 1868, G. B. Pierce MSS.

himself of deposing Johnson, whether or not he had committed a specific crime, so as to safeguard reconstruction in the South, Sumner felt it grossly unwarrantable for men like Fessenden to oppose impeachment not only because they thought Johnson innocent but because they shuddered at the prospect of having Ben Wade in the White House. Doubtless their attitude seemed the less defensible because they also feared that once Wade became President he would name Sumner Secretary of State or, at the very least, minister to Great Britain.[6] Sumner himself denied the persistent report about his anticipated appointment in a fashion to indicate that it had a basis of truth. "Wade assures me that he had not spoken with a human being about appointments . . . ," he told Lieber, adding, however: "He has spoken with me on some possibilities of the future, telling me that I was the only person he had spoken with on the matter." To the Duchess of Argyll in faraway Britain Sumner could afford to be more candid: "Mr. Wade would have relied upon me and wished me to leave the Senate." [7]

Aware that Fessenden, Trumbull, Grimes, Henderson, and other Republicans were defecting, Sumner still thought that impeachment would prevail. He could not believe that, when the test came, a good Republican would vote for acquittal. When Senator Edmund G. Ross, of Kansas, stopped briefly by his desk to discuss the trial, Sumner could not understand his misgivings. "It was a very clear case, especially for a Kansas man," he assured Ross; it was surely inconceivable "that a Kansas man could quibble against his country." [8] Sure of Johnson's conviction, Sumner apparently feared the impeached President might become a rallying point for Democrats in the coming election, and he introduced a resolution affirming the Senate's right, once Johnson was ousted, to impose "further judgment" upon him—presumably barring him from national office.[9]

[6] Fessenden: *Fessenden,* II, 183; New York *Herald,* Mar. 7 and 18, 1868; George Bemis to Sarah Bemis, Mar. 8, 1868, Bemis MSS.; Sidney Brooks to C. F. Adams, April 7, 1868, Adams MSS.

[7] Sumner to Lieber [May 1868], Sumner MSS.; Sumner to Duchess of Argyll, June 30, 1868, Argyll MSS.

[8] *House Report,* No. 75, 40 Cong., 2 Sess., p. 30.

[9] *Trial of Andrew Johnson,* p. 410; David M. Dewitt: *The Impeachment and Trial of Andrew Johnson* (New York: The Macmillan Company; 1903), p. 519.

It was, therefore, with incredulity mixed with exasperation that Sumner tallied the votes on May 16 when the Senators recorded their positions on the last—the broadest and presumably most palatable—of the impeachment articles. Seven Republicans joined the Democrats to acquit the President by a margin of one vote. Hastily the trial was adjourned, and during the next ten days, when the Republicans were holding their nominating convention at Chicago, every conceivable pressure was brought upon the defectors. But after the impeachment trial resumed on May 26, the lines still held, and on further tests the President still escaped removal by one vote.

Passionately involved himself, Sumner was certain the seven recusant Republicans acted from the meanest of motives. He believed that Ross had been bribed, and forgetting his pride in the Senate's cherished prerogative of immunity for its members, he welcomed Butler's unscrupulous investigation of alleged frauds during the impeachment proceedings and even testified before the House committee himself. Far worse in Sumner's eyes than a venal Senator was a traitorous one like Fessenden, whose vote against impeachment he could only explain by the Maine Senator's "vindictive hate of Wade." [1] As for himself, he only regretted that the rules of the Senate required him to vote on the articles of impeachment one by one, for he wanted to vote; "Guilty of all, and infinitely more." [2]

• 4 •

The recess in the impeachment trial was designed to allow Republican Congressmen and their retinue, filling seventeen railroad cars, to attend their national convention in Chicago, where they nominated Grant for President. As usual Sumner did not attend, and as usual he was not satisfied with his party's candidate. Henry Wilson, who sought the vice-presidential nomina-

[1] Sumner to Howe, May 21, 1868, G. B. Pierce MSS.

[2] Sumner: *Works,* XII, 401. John B. Henderson, one of the seven Republican recalcitrants, many years later wrote that Sumner repented his stand on impeachment and confessed: ". . . you were right and I was wrong." (Henderson: "Emancipation and Impeachment," *Century Mag.,* LXXV [1912], 209.) I know of no evidence to confirm this story. Henderson's account, prepared long after the event, is filled with errors both of fact and of judgment.

tion and was angry because his colleague failed to back him vigorously, thought that Sumner had "the Presidency on the brain." [3] In fact, Sumner never seriously thought of himself, at this or any other time, as presidential timber. His long record of radicalism disqualified him, and, even had he been otherwise available, the scandal of his marital troubles would certainly have killed his chances.

Like a number of other Radicals, Sumner had hoped the 1868 Republican nomination would go to a political veteran who had proved his devotion to principle. His initial choice was Chase, who was restive on the Supreme Court. In midsummer of 1867 he and the Chief Justice conferred on presidential prospects and agreed "that our candidate should be a thorough republican, to whom the unionists of the South, white and black, can look with trust and confidence." To Sumner that requirement seemed pretty well to rule out Grant and to point to Chase himself, but when the practical Stanton heard of their deliberations he exclaimed: "How verdant Sumner seems." [4] That Sumner was indeed green when it came to President-making became apparent when the Democrats won major victories in the 1867 fall elections. The Republican party could not afford to nominate Chase or any other of its stalwarts; its salvation was "staked upon General Grant's epaulettes." [5] As Chase's chances for the Republican nomination vanished, the Chief Justice drifted toward the Democrats, and with sad bewilderment Sumner watched his old friend prove during the impeachment trial that he was now lost to the Republican party.

The absence of an alternative did not make Grant's nomination the more palatable to Sumner. The two men had always maintained amicable, if rather distant, personal relations, but temperamentally and intellectually they had almost nothing in common. Sumner could not forget that Grant had been a Buchanan Democrat, although not a very active one, before the war.

[3] Mrs. Child quoted Wilson's 1868 remark in her letter to an unnamed correspondent, Dec. 18, 1872, Shaw Family Papers.

[4] Sumner to Richard Yates, Aug. 30, 1867, MS., Ill. State Hist. Lib.; Hooper to Sumner, Sept. 2, 1867, Sumner MSS.

[5] Charles H. Coleman: *The Election of 1868* (New York: Columbia University Press; 1933), p. 53.

Nor could he fail to remember that in 1865 Grant's report on the peaceful condition of the South had encouraged Andrew Johnson to pursue his reconstruction program. Even more disturbing was Grant's willingness to serve as Secretary of War ad interim in 1867 when Johnson suspended Stanton. Failing to understand that the general was trying to protect the interests of the army, and especially of those officers stationed in the South, Sumner thought that Grant's course left the country "in harrowing uncertainty with regard to his opinions." Reviewing Grant's behavior during the whole Reconstruction era, Sumner inquired: "Who can say that, as President, he would give to the freedmen . . . that kindly and sympathetic support which they need?" [6]

The unexpected show of Democratic strength in 1867 convinced most Republicans—but not Sumner—that Grant must be the candidate. At a secret conference of Republican leaders held in Washington just after the fall elections he earnestly begged his colleagues to "spare the Republican party from what he claimed [was] a want of faith in its own doctrines, as well as a confession of weakness." From Grant's nomination, he soberly predicted, would "date the gradual disintegration of the Republican party." To prefer an untried military leader to one of the experienced statesmen in the party would be almost a sacrilege, like "the casting aside of the Holy Bible by the Christian Church, in search of some new experiment." But not one other Republican at the meeting supported Sumner's stand.[7] Though all present took an oath of secrecy, in all probability Grant learned of Sumner's hostility through his close friends, John A. Rawlins and Orville E. Babcock, both of whom were present. If he did not, any doubts he might have had as to Sumner's attitude were resolved when the Senator in December told a newspaper reporter that Grant was "a good soldier, and nothing more," since there "was no record of his ever having expressed a political axiom or an idea which could afford the people an insight of his capacity for statesmanship." [8]

[6] Boston *Advertiser*, Supplement, Sept. 4, 1867.
[7] Cincinnati *Commercial*, July 19, 1891.
[8] New York *Herald*, Dec. 15, 1867.

Like Wade, Stevens, and many of the other conspicuous Radicals, Sumner only slowly became reconciled to the inevitable. Grant's acrimonious quarrel with Johnson when he resigned his temporary control of the War Office did something to ingratiate him with the extreme wing of the Republican party. Still, some of them demanded more explicit evidence of Grant's repentance before he was allowed to join the Radical church—or, as Ben: Perley Poore put it, they wanted him "to be bucked and gagged by 'the nigger.'"[9] Positive assurances they never received, but they took comfort from the fact that Grant's most dedicated supporters, like Conkling, worked indefatigably for Johnson's impeachment.

Warned by William Claflin: "It is vain to think of anyone else, here at present . . . ," Sumner began to see hitherto unsuspected virtues in Grant. Shortly before the Chicago convention, when the general invited him and Stanton to an informal dinner and a frank exchange of views, he almost came to think favorably of his candidacy. Ungraciously he announced to a correspondent that he was supporting Grant: "The Presidential chair has not always been filled by the most suitable men, but . . . we must take the best man we can get to represent our principles, and trust to the influence of time and education to cure the evils of the present."[1]

Only the Democratic nomination of Horatio Seymour made Grant's victory seem important to Sumner, for he believed that the success of "the rebel party, which is the true name for our present democracy," would be "terrible for the country—as bad as the worst defeat in battle."[2] He nevertheless could not muster real enthusiasm for his party's nominee, and no doubt he welcomed his physician's order to stay out of the presidential canvass lest he further strain his overtaxed vocal cords. Except for very brief remarks at a flag-raising ceremony at the Grant and Colfax Club in his own Boston ward, Sumner delivered but one speech during the campaign, a speech chiefly distinguished by

[9] Poore to W. W. Clapp, Jan. 31, 1868, Clapp MSS.

[1] Claflin to Sumner, Feb. 1, 1868, Sumner MSS.; Sumner to J. W. Phelps, April 18, 1868, MS., Hayes Memorial Lib.

[2] New York *Herald*, Aug. 24, 1868; Sumner to Duchess of Argyll, Nov. 1, 1868, Argyll MSS.

the fact that he made only three passing references to the Republican presidential nominee and spent most of his time defending his own record as Senator.

• 5 •

The election that worried Sumner during 1867–68 was not Grant's but his own. His third term in the Senate was about to expire, and the legislature chosen in the fall of 1868 would, when it assembled the following January, reelect Sumner or name his successor. For all his talk about retiring to some quiet Swiss village, Sumner at no time was willing to relinquish his office, and he fought vigorously and shrewdly for reelection.

Aside from the predictable but impotent Democratic opposition, Sumner faced rival Republican candidates on both the left and the right. N. P. Banks, that perennial aspirant to any political office, hoped the Massachusetts Irish voters would remember that he, as chairman of the House Committee on Foreign Affairs, persuaded the Representatives to vote unanimously for a relaxation of the neutrality statutes that would aid the Fenian raiders, while Sumner, as chairman of the Senate Committee on Foreign Relations, killed the proposal by preventing it from coming to the floor. Far more dangerous was the subterranean attempt of Benjamin F. Butler to oust Sumner. In early 1867 Bird warned: "Butler aims at your seat," [3] and he seemed a formidable rival. A miltary hero in the eyes of many Massachusetts voters, Butler had a strong following among the Irish, and his opposition to specie resumption allowed him to stand as the spokesman for the workingmen against the mercantile and banking interests.

Sumner saw that the most damaging attack Butler could make upon him would be the charge of "aristocracy"—i.e., that he gave too much support and patronage to his friends among the Cambridge and Boston intellectuals. To avoid this danger he disregarded the urging of his advisers and allowed Butler to block the nomination to the Boston customs house of General George Henry Gordon, who was considered a snob because he had attended West Point and Harvard Law School—and who,

[3] Mar. 8 [1867], Sumner MSS.

besides, had accused Butler of military incompetence. Similarly, though critics accused him of cowardice, Sumner uttered no word in support of his old friend, Richard Henry Dana, Jr., who staged a hopeless campaign to defeat Butler's reelection to Congress in 1868.[4] While avoiding all public conflict Sumner worked skillfully to weaken Butler's political organization. Cooperating with John B. Alley, Butler's predecessor from the Essex district, he managed to divert federal appointments, including even the postmastership of Salem itself, to his own supporters.[5] In the end Butler recognized that he was not yet strong enough to challenge the Senator, but Sumner knew he could expect from him only tepid support for reelection.

More dangerous still was the threat of a strong conservative candidate against Sumner. Boston memories are long, and it was still easy to revive tales of Sumner's feud with Winthrop and the respectable Whigs and to renew charges that he was first chosen to the Senate by an unholy and corrupt coalition. Sumner's marital difficulties stirred up ancient animosities once more, and the Senator's public and private actions had few defenders in the Union Club, that stronghold of Beacon Hill conservatism. Behind this persistent animosity lay a very general feeling that Sumner was still a man of "one idea," who subordinated the legitimate business interests of Massachusetts to the cause of the Negro.

During the spring and summer of 1867 it seemed probable that Massachusetts conservative Republicans would rally around Andrew as the candidate to beat Sumner in the following year's elections. Though the former governor had announced his withdrawal from public life and was busily engaged in practicing law, he kept up an active interest in politics and let it be known that his views differed significantly from Sumner's. He favored, he said, "a generous, manly effort to reestablish the Union," rather than the mean-spirited Radical program of disfranchising

[4] Dana to Sumner, Oct. 3, 1868, ibid.; Merriam: *Bowles*, II, 93; John L. King to Edward Atkinson, Oct. 26 [1868], Atkinson MSS. See Samuel Shapiro: *Richard Henry Dana, Jr.*, Chap. 12.

[5] N. J. Holden to Butler, April 12, 1867, with a draft of Butler's reply on its back, Butler MSS.; Alley to Sumner, April 12, 1867, Sumner MSS.; Willard B. Phillips to Sumner, April 24, 1867, ibid.

large numbers of Southern whites. Both President Johnson's followers and "Republican Radicals of certain schools" were playing politics with the grave issue of reconstruction. Andrew contrasted Henry Wilson's level-headed pragmatism on Negro rights with the doctrinaire stand of Sumner, who, the former governor declared, was "at present engaged in the . . . labor of digging his own political grave."[6] It was clear that Andrew would be happy to help Sumner dig.

Andrew's unannounced candidacy for the Senate, which was supported by Winthrop and by the younger members of the Adams family, worried Sumner and his friends. Even after the former governor weakened his position by opposing a prohibition law for Massachusetts—and thereby opened the way to charges that he himself was an alcoholic—he was a dangerous rival, and Sumner tried to maneuver him out of the race. In a letter to Bird, which was obviously intended to be shown to Andrew, he stressed his continuing "affection and respect" for Andrew and recalled that he had been "one of the earliest and most determined to press him for Governor." Denying reports that he had spoken slightingly of his rival, Sumner added: "I have often said that whenever Andrew desires my place I shall not be in his way." Promptly, however, he effectively negated that pledge by stressing his desire before he retired from public life to secure the revision of international maritime law and "the establishment of our government on the principles of the Declaration of Independence"—objectives which were certainly not attainable before the 1868 elections.[7] When Andrew failed to withdraw from a contest he had never openly entered, Sumner's one reliable newspaper supporter, the *Commonwealth,* began a quiet campaign to undermine the confidence of Massachusetts antislavery men in the former governor. Andrew did not now enjoy "the sympathy and communion with his old friends that he once had," the paper argued; he had exhibited a "want of ardor" on

[6] Andrew to J. M. Forbes, Aug. 16, 1867, author's draft, Andrew MSS.; C. H. Hill to James A. Garfield, Mar. 17, 1867, Garfield MSS. See the excellent analysis of Andrew's position in Eric L. McKitrick: *Andrew Johnson and Reconstruction* (Chicago: University of Chicago Press; 1960), pp. 215–38.

[7] Sumner to Bird, Aug. 17, 1866, Bird MSS.; also cited in Pearson: *Andrew,* II, 316.

reconstruction issues. Doubtless Andrew's principles were still true, the *Commonwealth* conceded somewhat patronizingly, but "he has given conservative people here hope." [8]

That hope was dashed when Andrew died on October 30, 1867, and Massachusetts Moderate Republicans were left without an obvious candidate to run against Sumner.[9] That their hostility was far from dead, however, was evidenced by the public dinner Boston conservatives proposed to give to Fessenden in midsummer 1868, after the Maine Senator had helped to defeat the impeachment of President Johnson. The name of every prominent Republican critic of Sumner in the Boston area appeared on the list of sponsors, which was studded with Cabots, Eliots, Ritchies, Lees, Parkmans, and other Brahmin dynasties. Both Fessenden and Sumner promptly recognized the political implications of the occasion, and Sumner instantly accepted the challenge: "If this is the beginning of an issue with me,—very well! I think the people of Massachusetts are not for A. J. or for any of the 'quibbles' by which he was saved." Promptly the *Commonwealth* began to expose the motives behind the invitation to Fessenden. Of the seventy-two signers, Pierce pointed out in a pungent editorial, at least fifty-seven were members of the Union Club of Boston, that headquarters of Republican conservatism on Park Street. Fessenden's sponsors were "the Republicans of State street, Court street, and Harvard College"—the very elements that had opposed Sumner in 1851, in 1857, and in 1863.[1]

Out of the plans for the Fessenden dinner came agreement on a new candidate to lead the anti-Sumner forces, Charles Francis Adams. Ever since Andrew's death, Henry Adams had

[8] Boston *Commonwealth*, June 8, 1867.

[9] In early 1868 it seemed that Governor Alexander H. Bullock might try to head an anti-Sumner coalition, and, as a trial balloon, he nominated Benjamin F. Thomas, a conservative Unionist who had succeeded Charles Francis Adams in Congress, to be Chief Justice of the Massachusetts supreme court. Alerted by the Bird Club, Sumner used his influence to defeat the nomination and to deflate Bullock's candidacy. See Sumner to William Claflin, Jan. 13, 1868, Claflin MSS., and the following letters to Sumner in the Sumner MSS.: Howe, Jan. 7, 1868; J. M. Forbes, Jan. 8, 1868; Pierce, Jan. 20 [1868]; and Edward W. Kinsley, Jan. 30, 1868.

[1] Sumner to Bird, June 13, 1868, Bird MSS.; Boston *Commonwealth*, July 4 and 11, 1868.

speculated that his father might take the field against Sumner, and the name of Charles Francis Adams, Jr., was conspicuous among the signers of the invitation to Fessenden. Adams appeared to have great strength as a candidate. The bearer of the most famous name in Massachusetts history, he was now coming home after his brilliant diplomatic career—which gave him the added advantage of having been aloof from local and domestic political issues for seven years. He was known to be moderate in his views on reconstruction and was respected as a practical, businesslike public servant. Since his youngest son, John Quincy Adams, Jr., had been the Democratic gubernatorial candidate in 1867, presumably he could expect to attract Democratic as well as Republican votes. Sumner's friends warned that the elements uniting behind Adams were "diverse and very bad" and predicted that he would give the Senator "a *stronger* opposition . . . than [in] any previous Senatorial canvass." [2]

To the danger of defeat Sumner, as always, professed indifference. "If the people of Mass turn from me," he told Longfellow, "I shall not complain. I have done my duty." In actuality, however, he was worried, and he listened attentively to the advice of his political friends. After the impeachment trial he had little more to say about President Johnson, reconstruction, or the freedman, but he began giving close attention to bills wanted by Massachusetts merchants and shippers, among whom, as Pierce warned, he was "not so very strong." For instance, he worked hard to reduce federal excise taxes on the rum Boston shippers exported to Africa, in an effort to preserve a pattern of trade dating back to the colonial era.[3]

While Sumner was trying to project a new image of himself, his Massachusetts associates worked to undermine Adams's candidacy. Radicals ostentatiously ignored a public reception given to Adams when he returned to Boston in midsummer 1868, and, to his disgruntlement, they took him at his word when he said he wanted to retire into complete political isolation

[2] Charles W. Slack to Sumner, July 15, 1868, Sumner MSS.

[3] Sumner to Longfellow, Aug. 4, 1868, Longfellow MSS.; Pierce to Sumner, July 24, 1868, Sumner MSS.; *Cong. Globe*, 40 Cong., 2 Sess., pp. 3277–8, 3539, 3681.

at Quincy.[4] The *Commonwealth* sniped that Adams's career in diplomacy—"which is about the same thing as slinking into secret places of assignation"—unfitted him for public office. After all, Robinson wrote in one of his columns: "The most that can be said in favor of the Seward-Adams diplomacy is that in spite of it we did not get into a war with England and France." Furthermore, Robinson argued, Adams was probably not really a Republican at heart, since his own son was a Democrat and pro-Johnson papers like the *National Intelligencer* and the New York *Times* endorsed him.[5]

A more serviceable weapon against Adams's candidacy was Massachusetts businessmen's fear of inflation and their desire for a resumption of specie payments. Much as they distrusted Sumner, they disliked Butler, with his advocacy of workingmen's rights and of greenbacks, even more. Men like Edward Atkinson, the textile manufacturer and economic theorist who was about to become editor of the Boston *Advertiser*, concluded that the alternative to Sumner was not Adams but probably Butler, who would "sacrifice the Republican party if he can and try to get into power on the ruins." [6] To demonstrate to such businessmen that, though radical on questions concerning the South and the Negro, he was economically orthodox, Sumner voted against a bill establishing an eight-hour day for laborers in government arsenals, shipyards, and the like.[7] More important, he yielded to the importunities of Atkinson and to the political advice of Pierce and on July 11, 1868, surprised his Senate colleagues by making a long address not on either reconstruction or foreign policy but on "Financial Reconstruction through Public Faith and Specie Payments," in which he tried to prove: "Every greenback is red with the blood of fellow-citizens." The vigor of Sum-

[4] Pierce to Sumner, July 24, 1868, Sumner MSS.; Springfield *Republican*, July 25, 1868; C. F. Adams to Henry Adams, Oct. 22, 1868, Adams MSS.

[5] Springfield *Republican*, July 25 and 27, Aug. 1, 4, and 8, 1868.

[6] Atkinson to Sumner, June 16, 1868, Sumner MSS. See the numerous letters between Sumner and Atkinson in the Sumner MSS. and the Atkinson MSS. and also Harold Francis Williamson: *Edward Atkinson* (Boston: Old Corner Book Store, Inc.; 1934), pp. 83–4.

[7] *Cong. Globe*, 40 Cong., 2 Sess., p. 3429. Ira Stewart, head of the eight-hour movement, declared that this vote proved workingmen could "hope for no sympathy from the class of which Mr. Sumner is a representative." Boston *Commonwealth*, Aug. 22, 1868. W. W. Broon, however, defended Sumner's right to vote as he saw best. Ibid., Aug. 8, Sept. 5, 1868.

ner's imagery was always in direct ratio to his ignorance of his subject matter, but the fact that he endorsed the hostility of that "ingenious merchant, Mr. Atkinson, of Boston," to paper money was sufficient proof of his economic conservatism.[8] After the speech his mail began to be filled with letters from conservative Bostonians, like that from William Amory, an old Whig who had always opposed his domestic policies: "The country is largely indebted to you for such outspoken truth, so forcibly, plainly, and irresistibly set forth, by one whose influence is so great, if not always exerted in the right direction." [9]

Even with such evidence of changing opinion, Sumner's backers were unwilling to leave anything to chance. Though the Senator himself would have preferred to spend the summer in his new house in Washington or to go to Europe, they insisted that he return to Massachusetts, where he could "show enthusiasm for Grant" by being " 'rough and ready' in the campaign." [1] Resisting invitations to travel and to lecture, Sumner therefore returned to do battle with "the enemy . . . lying in wait to strike me in Mass." Homeless now in Boston, he had to make do with rooms in the Coolidge House, looking out over a stable and a machine shop, where he heard "constantly the tread of horses and the hiss of steam." [2] Though his doctor allowed him to make only two public appearances during the campaign, he could confer with politicians and plan strategy. At his urgent request William Claflin, who was chairman of the Republican national committee and was closely identified with Grant's success, agreed to seek the Republican nomination for governor, so as to be sure that Butler's associate, Dr. George B. Loring, would be blocked.[3] To prevent any last-minute miscarriage of plans, Pierce resorted to the 1862 strategy and inserted in the resolutions presented to the Republican state convention on September 9 a tribute to Sumner's "eloquent, fearless and persistent devotion to the sacred cause of human rights" and his "diligence and success

[8] Sumner: *Works*, XII, 447, 471.

[9] Springfield *Republican*, July 18, 1868; Amory to Sumner, July 24, 1868, Sumner MSS.

[1] Pierce to Sumner, July 24, 1868, ibid.

[2] Sumner to Theodore Tilton, Aug. 7, 1868, MS., New York Public Lib.; Sumner to Longfellow, Sept. 17, 1868, Longfellow MSS.

[3] Sumner to Claflin, Aug. 9, 1868, Claflin MSS.

as chairman of the Senate committee on foreign affairs" and a demand for his reelection because of "his fidelity, experience and honorable identification with our national history." Since careful strategy had undercut all opposition, the convention approved the endorsement with three rousing cheers.[4]

"So at last I have conquered; after a life of struggle," Sumner exulted.[5] As expected, Republicans carried the November elections, choosing not merely Grant but a General Court pledged to Sumner's reelection. When the legislators assembled in January 1869 some Republicans may still have preferred another senatorial candidate, but, as the Springfield *Republican* remarked, "very few of them will care to say so, for no political sin in this state is remembered so long, or punished so severely, as a vote against Mr. Sumner." On January 19 the House of Representatives gave Sumner 216 votes, to 14 for the Democratic candidate, Josiah G. Abbott, and 1 for Banks; and the Senate stood 2 for Abbott to 37 for Sumner.[6] From all quarters congratulations poured in, but none were more enthusiastic than those from abolitionists who had fought at Sumner's side from the beginning of his public life in the antislavery cause. Most ardent of all was the letter from William Lloyd Garrison: "This is no human, but a divine triumph; this is not in the wisdom of man, but in the power of God."[7]

[4] Boston *Commonwealth,* Sept. 12, 1868.

[5] To Longfellow, Sept. 17, 1868, Longfellow MSS.

[6] Springfield *Republican,* Jan. 6 and 29, 1869. Sumner's vote against the eight-hour law cost him the one vote that went to Banks. Boston *Commonwealth,* Jan. 23, 1869.

[7] Jan. 20, 1869, Sumner MSS.

CHAPTER IX

To Fill a Patriot with Despair

SUMNER promptly discovered that victory in Massachusetts did not bring influence in Washington. To be sure, he was now dean of the Senate, for when Wilson presented the certificate of his fourth consecutive election, Sumner became the Senator with the longest record of continuous service,[1] but seniority did not mean leadership. Indeed, when the new session of Congress opened in December 1868, he felt more than ever isolated. The veterans of the antislavery conflict, Republicans with whom he had often quarreled but from whom he had always received a degree of respect, were rapidly disappearing from Washington. In August Thaddeus Stevens had died. Wade was now a lame-duck Senator, serving the final months of his term. Fessenden and Trumbull were estranged from the party they had helped found. Control of the Republican party in Congress was falling to a new breed of politicians, whom Sumner did not understand and for most of whom he had little liking. In the Senate the powerful men now were Conkling, who was publicly contemptuous of Sumner, Simon Cameron, as unprincipled and as corruptible as when he had been Secretary of War, and Morton, the efficient Indiana war governor who considered Sumner an im-

[1] Wade, who entered the Senate at the same time as Sumner, was to retire on March 4, 1869. Cameron and Hamlin had entered the Senate earlier than Sumner, but their service had been interrupted.

practical idealist.[2] In the House the new Speaker was James G. Blaine, a political technician committed to no ideology, and two of the principal Republican spokesmen were former generals John A. Logan, of Illinois, and Ben Butler, neither of whom hid their conviction that they were men of action while Sumner was a pompous windbag.

These New Radicals [3] differed from their predecessors less over policies than over priorities. Sumner and Wade were as outspoken in their desire to keep the Republican party in power as were Conkling and Butler, and all four men were advocates of Negro suffrage. But to Republican leaders of Sumner's generation the hegemony of their party was necessary to preserve the rights of the freedmen; to their successors, the protection of the Negroes was required in order to assure the success of the Republican party. There was also a significant difference in rhetoric. Republican veterans of the antislavery conflict freely invoked ideals of liberty, justice, and equality—sometimes to cloak selfish purposes; the New Radicals, considering themselves practical men, eschewed high-flown oratory and appealed to expediency—even to justify disinterested causes.

In this new atmosphere Sumner felt ill at ease. Because of his continuing throat ailment he made no major speeches during the session, though he insisted on maintaining his nearly perfect record of attendance in the Senate. In the day-by-day proceedings of the Senate he took little part except to present petitions like that of John Cram of Boston, who desired an extension of his patent "for an improvement in the towel stand and clotheshorse, such being an invention of much value and importance." [4]

Even in minor legislative matters, designed to benefit his state or his special political friends, he had very poor success. Congress defeated his attempt to lower duties on certain dyes

[2] In the Cincinnati *Commercial,* Mar. 1, 1869, Don Piatt contrasted the effectiveness of Sumner and Morton as Senate leaders.

[3] The phrase is that of Louis M. Hacker in *The Triumph of American Capitalism* (New York: Simon and Schuster; 1940), pp. 380, 383. Professor Hacker's distinction between "Old Radicals" (like Sumner) and "New Radicals" (like Conkling) I find useful, though I do not share his views on the economic policies of either group. There was, of course, a good deal of overlapping in leadership, with Zachariah Chandler, for instance, moving easily from the "Old" to the "New" category.

[4] *Cong. Globe,* 40 Cong., 3 Sess., p. 974.

used in Massachusetts textile manufacturing, and Sumner found himself in the peculiar position of supporting Andrew Johnson's veto of this protective measure.[5] He had no better luck in defending a federal subsidy to New England shipping. He fought a long, angry, and fruitless battle to secure payment of accumulated interest on debts, the principal of which was long settled, owed by the United States to Massachusetts for contributions made during the War of 1812. Though Sumner protested that his was not the voice of Massachusetts but of justice, his colleagues rightly believed the money would be used for a questionable railroad scheme, and they rejected the proposed appropriation. Angrily Sumner objected that he and his state were being discriminated against: "I have had too much occasion . . . to see in this Chamber that a claim presented from Massachusetts hardly receives the favor that a claim from another State might expect and actually receives. . . . Senators are disposed to attack Massachusetts, to vote against her claims." [6]

Whether Senators were hostile to Massachusetts may be doubted, but that they were suspicious of Sumner was abundantly evident. The new leaders of his party objected to the extreme positions which he took, the result of that illogical logic that carries a premise to its utmost conclusion. On the specie resumption issue, for example, though Butler and Wade were tainted with the greenback heresy and even cautious John Sherman appeared willing to make concessions to the inflationists, most Republican Congressmen agreed with Sumner in opposing inflation or partial repudiation. But in the protracted debate which occupied so much of their time with so little profit they could not accept him as spokesman for the sound-money position because he had taken the anti-inflationist lessons of Edward Atkinson and other conservative financiers too closely to heart. Convinced that inflation, like slavery, was wrong, he concluded that it should be abolished, and the sooner the better. On the

[5] Ibid., p. 1509. Failing to recognize the special New England interest Sumner was trying to protect, Henry Adams commended his disinterested support of Johnson's veto. George Hochfield (ed.): *The Great Secession Winter of 1860–61 and Other Essays by Henry Adams* (New York: Sagamore Press, Inc.; 1958), p. 71.

[6] *Cong. Globe*, 40 Cong., 3 Sess., p. 1854.

very first day of the session he introduced a bill "to provide for the resumption of specie payments on the 4th of July, 1869," and he began collecting facts and figures for a long speech he planned to make in defense of his proposal. He was genuinely puzzled when sound-money Senators did not rally to his support and baffled when even Atkinson warned that immediate resumption would disrupt business. "I cannot think you are right," he replied to an economist who protested against his scheme, "and though I have had long conversations with eminent financiers opposed to my plan, and have received letters from many more, I have not yet been convinced of my error. Indeed I am only the more certain I am right." In deference to expert opinion, however, he did postpone further work on his proposed speech.[7]

Sumner behaved in much the same fashion when Congress considered a constitutional amendment guaranteeing the Negro the right to vote. His supporters expected to find him in the forefront of this battle. One of the earliest advocates of Negro suffrage, he had correctly predicted that the Fourteenth Amendment would not secure that objective, had insisted that new Southern state constitutions provide for Negro voting, and had stressed the political importance of the still largely disfranchised black voters in Northern and border states. Previously Senators had not been willing to listen to his arguments, but Democratic gains in the 1867 state elections and in the 1868 presidential contest, when only Grant's personal popularity led his party to victory, made the Republicans more sympathetic to nationwide Negro enfranchisement as the only way to prevent a future Democratic triumph.

Yet Sumner played virtually no role in drafting or adopting the Fifteenth Amendment.[8] Believing, as he had for many months past, that Congress could enfranchise all Negroes merely by passing a law, he saw no need for another constitutional amendment, which would drop "all the poisoned ingredients of prejudice and hate" in the political cauldron during the

[7] Ibid., p. 5; New York *Herald,* Dec. 24, 1868; Atkinson to Sumner, Dec. 9, 1868, Sumner MSS.; Sumner to Henry C. Carey, Dec. 14 [1868], E. C. Gardiner Collection.

[8] See William Gillette: *The Right to Vote* (Baltimore: The Johns Hopkins Press; 1965).

debates on ratification in every state. Furthermore, to propose an amendment implied that under the Constitution as it now stood "a Caste and an Oligarchy of the Skin may be set up by a State without any check from Congress." To critics who argued that the Constitution gave the individual states the right to regulate elections, Sumner replied that the alleged power to regulate was nowhere to be found in that document, which simply declared that the states could set up "the Qualifications requisite for Electors" in federal elections. A qualification, he insisted, could not be an unchangeable condition but "something that can be acquired." Consequently, unlike "residence, property, education, or character, each of which is within the possible reach of well-directed effort," race or color could not be a qualification. "Are we not reminded that the leopard cannot change his spots, or the Ethiopian his skin?" No amendment, therefore, was needed. Congress had ample power to act, both under the original Constitution and under the recently adopted Thirteenth and Fourteenth Amendments. Senators should leave off footling debate and pass a sweeping act to outlaw caste discrimination in voting. They should remember that "beyond all question" the true rule of constitutional construction was "that *anything for Human Rights is constitutional.*" [9]

Nothing could shake Sumner from his position. He was deaf to arguments of expediency. Most Republicans agreed with *The Nation* in believing that "the leaving of human rights dependent on an act, when a constitutional amendment is possible," would be "in practice an abandonment of them." [1] But Sumner was unmoved because it was "plain as the sun" that "under the power of making regulations you cannot disfranchise a race, you cannot degrade the country, you cannot degrade the age." [2]

Agreeing that Sumner was "an impracticable egotist," Re-

[9] Sumner: *Works*, XIII, 50–1, 40, 37–8. To a limited degree Sumner's constitutional point was valid. Clearly a state may not set up "qualifications" which permanently disfranchise classes of its citizens. But not all qualifications for voting and office must necessarily be "within the possible reach of well-directed effort." For instance, convicted criminals may be deprived of their vote and no subsequent good behavior requires its restoration. Furthermore, no amount of effort, however directed, can make a person not born a citizen of the United States eligible to be President.

[1] *The Nation*, VIII (Feb. 11, 1869), 102.

[2] *Cong. Globe*, 40 Cong., 3 Sess., pp. 986–7.

publican advocates of Negro suffrage looked elsewhere for leadership.[3] Boutwell sponsored the proposed amendment in the House, and Stewart defended it in the Senate. Sumner participated in the debates infrequently, though he unsuccessfully tried to add provisions objectionable to its sponsors. Unwilling to see the need for an amendment but unwilling openly to oppose it, he was absent on all the crucial roll calls. The adoption of the amendment on February 26, 1869, made it more than ever clear that Sumner had no significant following in the Senate on domestic political issues.

• 2 •

Only on questions of foreign policy did Sumner continue to exercise leadership during the last years of the Johnson administration. Alienated from the President and distrustful of Seward, most Republicans were still willing to follow Sumner on diplomatic issues. He so dominated the powerful Committee on Foreign Relations that Senator John Conness, who frequently objected to the decisions Sumner reported as coming from that body, complained that the other members were mere cyphers and that "the honorable Senator was the committee." [4]

Through his committee Sumner played a decisive role in determining the fate of the numerous schemes of territorial expansion that Seward devised. Just as he was able to speed the ratification of the Alaska purchase treaty, so he succeeded in blocking plans to annex lands in the Caribbean. By silence and delay he killed the treaty for the acquisition of the Danish West Indies, which was submitted to the Senate in December 1867. The situation was embarrassing, for Denmark was a friendly power, General Waldemar R. Raasloff, the Danish minister who negotiated the treaty, was a favorite in Washington diplomatic circles, and there was a moral obligation to ratify a treaty made at the instigation of the American government. On the other hand, there was little public sentiment for the proposed pur-

[3] William D. Kelley to Howard M. Jenkins, Jan. 25, 1869, MS., Hist. Soc. of Penn.

[4] *Cong. Globe*, 40 Cong., 2 Sess., p. 1011.

chase. The strategic need for the islands was not obvious; the proposed price was high; Republicans were indisposed to adopt any treaty favored by President Johnson and his Secretary of State; and, when the discussion of the treaty was at a critical stage, a hurricane, an earthquake, and a tidal wave flattened St. Thomas. Feeling, with the majority of his associates, that the treaty should not be approved but that rejection would put the United States government in a bad light, Sumner held it inactive but "pending" before the Foreign Relations Committee, "thinking that it were better to have it fail through oblivion rather than by an adverse vote." [5]

Ordinarily that would have been the end of the treaty, but Seward, gambling ever more desperately, persuaded the Danish government repeatedly to extend the deadline for ratification, and with each extension the fate of the Danish ministry inevitably became more closely linked with the completion of the purchase. Raasloff himself, now a member of the Danish cabinet, returned to the United States in 1868 to throw his personal influence behind ratification of the treaty. Fond of the Danish diplomat and aware that he was in a tight place, Sumner assisted Raasloff so far as he could with propriety and without surrender of his own conviction that the treaty should be rejected. Repeatedly he received long letters from Raasloff urging ratification; he arranged for the general to have private interviews with other members of the committee, whom he hoped to influence; and, at Raasloff's request, he allowed him twice to appear in person before the full committee to plead his case. The Senators heard, but they were not convinced. Following Sumner's lead, they continued to hold the treaty before them without making a formal report and thus quietly killed the project.[6]

[5] Sumner to G. W. Curtis, May 30, 1868, Curtis MSS. See the elaborate treatment in Charles Callan Tansill: *The Purchase of the Danish West Indies* (Baltimore: The Johns Hopkins Press; 1932), Chaps. 1–2. The treaty was signed on October 24, 1867.

[6] See letters from Raasloff to Sumner, Jan. 11, 17, 18, 19, and Feb. 1 and 8, 1869, Sumner MSS. Olive Risley Seward: "A Diplomatic Episode," *Scribner's Magazine,* II (1887), 585–602, charged that Sumner was guilty of misleading Raasloff as to his own opinion of the treaty, of deliberately holding up Senate action on the treaty, and, thereby, of causing the United States government to break its faith with Denmark. These arguments were effectively answered at the time by Pierce (IV, 613–24), and Tansill's study (p. 140) agrees that "Miss

At the same time Sumner and his committee blocked Seward's proposed purchase of Samaná, in the Dominican Republic, as an American naval base.[7] Believing in the continental destiny of the United States, Sumner thought Seward's piecemeal annexation plans as unnecessary as they were expensive. "Do we really want a naval station in the West Indies?" he asked. "Sooner or later we shall have one, in the course of political events and without purchase." [8] In the case of Samaná Bay, Sumner was the more dubious because the Dominican government would use the money to prosecute its long-continued war against the neighboring Negro republic of Haiti, in which he, like his father before him, took special interest.[9] He looked with equal suspicion on both the rival factions in Santo Domingo. President José Maria Cabral, who was prepared to sell or lease large parts of his country, seemed as questionable a character as his deposed rival, Buenaventura Baez, who turned up in Washington in December 1866 and hour after hour begged, in his bad French, for Sumner's support.[1] When Baez ousted Cabral in March 1868 the change did little to make the prospects for lease or annexation more acceptable to Sumner, and Seward could do nothing to persuade him. Warned by the fate of his Danish negotiations, Seward did not push the Dominican scheme to the point of signing a treaty, which Sumner and his committee would certainly have rejected.

If Sumner frustrated Seward's policy in the West Indies, he strongly supported the Secretary's handling of the Mexican question. Throughout the war Sumner had felt that Union victory

---

Seward's article is obviously faulty in its interpretations." Finally, on March 22, 1870, the Committee on Foreign Relations made an adverse report on the treaty.

[7] For a detailed treatment see Charles Callan Tansill: *The United States and Santo Domingo, 1789–1873* (Baltimore: The Johns Hopkins Press; 1938), Chap. 7. Aware of probable opposition, President Johnson on February 10, 1868, took the somewhat unusual course of asking the Senate to approve in advance the plan to acquire Samaná Bay. Richard W. Leopold: *The Growth of American Foreign Policy* (New York: Alfred A. Knopf; 1962), p. 83.

[8] Sumner to G. W. Curtis, May 30, 1868, Curtis MSS.

[9] See the following letters in the Sumner MSS.: G. H. Hollister, June 29, 1868; L. A. de Pitti-Ferrardi, Feb. 24, 1868; Cooper Elwood, Mar. 7, 1867; and Dexter A. Hawkins, Feb. 25, 1869.

[1] Sumner to George Bemis, Dec. 24, 1866, Bemis MSS. For Sumner's later account of this interview, see Sumner: *Works*, XIV, 187–8.

Sumner at about the Time of His Marriage

THE NATIONAL ARCHIVES

Sumner in the Study of His House in Washington

FRANK LESLIE'S ILLUSTRATED WEEKLY MAGAZINE

would inevitably doom the French adventure, and after Appomattox he was more than ever convinced "that Maximilian's throne will fall without any thing from us." Willingly, therefore, he joined forces with Seward to check hotheads, both in the army, where there were generals ready to enlist in Benito Juarez's army, and in Congress, where there was a strong movement to censure French intervention and even to send in United States troops to overthrow Maximilian. Any foreign embroilment, Sumner recognized, might turn the Republican party "away from guarding the poor freedmen" and lead to the immediate readmission of the Southern states. All that the American government could do was to exert constant, quiet pressure upon Napoleon III to withdraw his support from Maximilian, but the French evacuation must seem to come at their own initiative so "that there should be nothing to leave behind any heart-burning in the French people." [2]

During the two years after the war, therefore, Sumner cultivated a carefully ambivalent attitude on the Mexican question. In Congress, and especially in his committee, he did his best to prevent "any declaration . . . on the Mexican and French questions." But to the French minister in Washington he conveyed his fear that, unless something was done, the House of Representatives could get out of control and demand forthwith the expulsion of Napoleon's troops from the hemisphere. By September 1866, this policy of using private pressure and avoiding public threats began to pay off, for the French minister assured Sumner that there would be "substantial withdrawal of the French troops from Mexico before next winter." Sumner utilized this information to the fullest advantage. "It was on this assurance given by me in my Committee that Congress was kept still," he wrote—only to add: "I have let M. Drouyn de l'Huys [the French Foreign Minister] know this." With Sumner quietly controlling Congress and Seward exerting unremitting diplomatic pressure, the French withdrew the last of the troops in February 1867, and Maximilian's shadow empire began to vanish. Then,

[2] Sumner to "My Dear Sir," May 3, 1865, MS. owned by Mr. Charles Segal; Sumner to Bright, Nov. 5, 1865, Bright MSS.; Bruce to Clarendon, May 15, 1866, Clarendon MSS.; Pierce, IV, 297.

and only then, did Sumner encourage American action by proposing that the United States mediate between the rival factions in Mexico "in order to avert a deplorable civil war." Before his resolution could be adopted, however, Maximilian's support disappeared, and the hapless Emperor was captured and executed.[3]

• 3 •

By 1868 Sumner found that even on foreign policy questions Republicans were beginning to chafe against his leadership. Some found it easy to translate their dislike of his domestic programs into distrust of his diplomatic policies. Others were irked by the restraint he had succeeded in imposing upon Congress since 1865 when foreign affairs were debated. But chiefly the restiveness appeared because Sumner was unable to unravel the tangled and angry snarl of Anglo-American relations after the Civil War.

Basically Sumner's policy toward Great Britain was identical to the one he advocated toward France: he hoped through quiet but frank and relentless diplomatic pressure to make the British recognize the damage their unneutral behavior had done to the Union cause during the Civil War; meanwhile he sought to hold in check the rabid Anglophobes in the Congress. But Queen Victoria's government was not Napoleon's. Shortly after Appomattox Earl Russell curtly rejected Adams's proposal for a general arbitration of all claims arising from Civil War damages and thereby blocked the possibility of realistic negotiations at the very time when, as Sumner later said, the Americans in their "oblivious good nature" at the end of the conflict would have accepted anything.[4] When, toward the end of 1865, Palmerston died and Russell himself became Prime Minister, the British stand grew more rigid. Great Britain, Russell declared, could not "submit to a foreign power the question of our own good faith in putting the [neutrality] law in force or the adequacy of the law," for that involved "a question of our own honor and sincerity," a

[3] Sumner to Duchess of Argyll, Aug. 14, 1866, Argyll MSS.; Sumner to Bright, Sept. 3, 1866, Bright MSS.; Sumner: *Works*, XI, 354.

[4] Sumner to George Bemis, May 25, 1869, Bemis MSS.

point on which no nation could compromise. The accession of a Tory government, headed by the Earl of Derby, in 1866 marked no substantial change in the British position. Clearly desiring a settlement, Lord Stanley, the Foreign Minister, proposed an unacceptable form of limited arbitration, from which the question of premature recognition of the Confederacy was excluded.[5]

Like Seward and Adams, Sumner during the three years after the Civil War tried repeatedly to warn the British of the dangers resulting from their inflexibility. The longer the difficulties between the two countries remained unresolved, the more they would fester. Russell's refusal to consider arbitrating Civil War claims, Sumner told the British minister in Washington, after sounding other members of the Committee on Foreign Relations, "rendered it impossible at present to do anything . . . by way of negotiation" with Great Britain, even on entirely routine matters. "The game that Lord Russell began will doubtless be followed on this side," he predicted. Urgently he wrote his friends abroad of the rising resentment, both in Congress and in the army, toward Britain. Influential Republicans like Chandler and Stanton talked freely about annexing Canada as compensation for damages done to the United States by British-built naval raiders during the war. Others, like Butler and Banks, hoped there would not be a prompt settlement, so that when Great Britain was next at war the United States could follow her precedent and construct warships for her enemies. In August 1865 Sumner passed along to the British government, through John Bright, Grant's ominous view of the diplomatic situation: "he cared little whether England paid 'our little bill,' or not;—upon the whole he would rather she should not as that would leave the precedent of her conduct in full force for us to follow, and . . . he thought that we should make more out of 'the precedent' than out of 'the bill.' . . ."[6]

Sumner himself shared the general indignation over British

[5] The best modern treatments are Martin B. Duberman: *Charles Francis Adams, 1807–1887* (Boston: Houghton Mifflin Company; 1961), and Adrian Cook: "The Way to Geneva: United States Policy and Attitudes towards Great Britain, 1865–1872" (unpublished D. Phil. dissertation in history, University of Cambridge, 1965).

[6] Bruce to Clarendon, Feb. 5, 1866, Clarendon MSS.; Sumner to Bright, Aug. 8, 1865, Bright MSS.

conduct during the Civil War. He never ceased to deplore "that fatal alliance with slavery, which opened English workshops to the Rebellion, under the Hallucination of neutrality." "As I think of England now I feel more than ever the utterly foolish and wicked character which her government has played toward us," he told Bright frankly. "Her diplomacy towards us has been without a precedent. I solemnly believe that history must turn from it with shame. From beginning to end it went on the idea—'You are down; now I can kick you.'" Aware that such bluntness pained his British friends, he nevertheless persisted, adding: "I am so much of an Englishman that I feel this as a personal dishonor. . . ."[7]

It is scarcely surprising that Sumner's correspondents in Great Britain were not able to distinguish between his own views and the warlike threats of other Americans which he passed along in his letters. Ever since his 1863 speech on foreign relations, they had thought him dangerous and basically hostile, and now he seemed to be the ringleader of American warmongers. With the British ministers in Washington he had always been so candid as to seem belligerent, and Sir Frederick Bruce, like Lord Lyons before him, reported to his government: "We have no more bitter enemy than Sumner. . . ." Concluding that the Senator's intellect had been deranged since the Brooks assault, Russell declined even to consider his appeal for a prompt settlement of the Alabama claims and agreed with Lyons "that if we were to yield on this point there would be no limit to the concessions demanded." Should Sumner ever become Secretary of State, both Russell and his Foreign Minister, Clarendon, believed that it would become impossible to maintain peace.[8]

Ironically enough, during these same three years after the war Congressional fire-eaters attacked Sumner for being pro-British. Failure to settle the Alabama Claims—as the whole group of Civil War claims came to be called—left the door open for

[7] Sumner to Duchess of Argyll, May 1, 1865, Argyll MSS.; Sumner to Bright, May 1 and Nov. 7, 1865, Bright MSS.

[8] Argyll to Gladstone, May 26 and June 8, 1865, Gladstone MSS.; Bruce to Russell, June 24, 1865, Russell MSS.; Russell to Bruce, May 27, July 8 and 15, 1865, copies, ibid.; A. G. Gardiner: *The Life of Sir William Harcourt* (London: Constable & Company Ltd.; 1923), I, 166.

renewed agitation about other longstanding American grievances against Great Britain. Americans who hoped for eventual expansion to the north looked upon the consolidation of British North American provinces into the Dominion of Canada in 1867 as a slap in the face. Westerners brought up again the unsettled problem of the disputed boundary at San Juan Island. Some Irish-Americans demonstrated their traditional hatred for England by supporting Fenian raids upon Canada, while a few more daring ones returned to Ireland itself to help subvert British rule. Captured and clapped in prison by the British government, which still considered them its citizens, however traitorous, these naturalized Americans loudly called for the United States government to protect them. Opposition to any new reciprocal tariff agreement with Canada was another manifestation of this general anti-British feeling, as were the renewed disputes over access to the North Atlantic fisheries.

Sumner's policy on all these matters was to prevent any Congressional action that might irreparably damage Anglo-American relations. In July 1866, when Banks, hoping to woo the Irish vote and possibly desiring to embarrass Sumner, secured unanimous House approval of new neutrality legislation that would allow the sale of American-built ships to either belligerent in a foreign war in which the United States was not involved, Sumner expected as usual to kill it in his Senate committee. Learning on the next to the last day before adjournment that some virulently anti-English Senators planned to call the proposed legislation directly to the floor, he appeared at his desk with an armful of books and announced that he was "good for 5 hours at least" if the neutrality bill came up—and those five hours would, of course, prevent the adoption of other, essential legislation. All night, for twelve uninterrupted hours, he kept in his seat, prepared to begin a filibuster if the Banks bill was brought up. The next morning, after repeated efforts, Chandler, who strongly favored the bill, got the floor at 11:00 o'clock and moved to consider the change in neutrality statutes, whereupon Sumner, reminding his listeners that the session would expire at 4:00 P.M., gave notice that he would speak all the remaining hours if necessary to defeat it. That blocked Chandler, and the "absurd bill" was allowed to sleep the sleep of death in Sumner's committee room.[9]

During the next session of Congress Sumner was again able to defeat measures which could only antagonize the British. In March 1867, when Chandler, who proudly announced that from youth he had been educated to hate Great Britain, proposed once more to change the neutrality laws so as to permit the sale of American warships to "friendly belligerents," Sumner, with the unanimous support of his committee, blocked debate on the measure and had it consigned to "the sleep that knows no waking." At the same time he buried in committee another resolution, for which Banks had secured unanimous House approval and for which Nye now sought Senate endorsement, that expressed American sympathy for the Fenian movement. Desiring to expose "the encouragers of this imposture," Sumner knew that if he spoke he would open a general debate on Anglo-American relations, and he concluded that, for the time at least, "silence is the true rule."[1]

But in view of the unyielding British attitude Sumner found it increasingly difficult to control his colleagues. As he wrote Bright in May 1867, the settlement of American Claims could not be postponed indefinitely, and he predicted: "The next Congress will debate it fully, unless meanwhile in some way it is settled."[2] Since no progress occurred before Congress reassembled in December, criticism of Sumner's silent inactivity mounted. Symptomatic of the rising sentiment against Britain was Chandler's resolution calling upon the President, in view of the state of hostilities then existing between Great Britain and Abyssinia, to issue a neutrality proclamation couched in precisely the same phrases as the Queen's 1861 recognition of Confederate belligerency.

Sumner was able to defeat this farcical proposition, but he could not suppress the growing Congressional sentiment for strong United States action to protect Fenian agitators impris-

[9] Sumner to Lieber, Dec. 29, 1866, Sumner MSS.; Sumner to Duchess of Argyll, Aug. 14, 1866, Argyll MSS.

[1] *Cong. Globe*, 40 Cong., 1 Sess., pp. 291–2, 328; Bigelow: *Retrospections*, IV, 76.

[2] May 27, 1867, Bright MSS.

oned by Britain. Even some members of his own committee ignored his warning that the Senate ought not to be rushed "by any temporary pressure into a premature discussion of an important question." Conness, the Irish-born Senator from California, sharply pointed to the inconsistency of Sumner's defense of human rights: "When a single negro, male or female, is deprived of the high privilege of entering a common mode of conveyance on the public highways in the Republic, my honorable friend [Sumner] stands forth here as the exponent and defender of equal rights before the law. . . . But when a foreign-born citizen, taking the responsibilities . . . and . . . the rights of American citizenship, . . . is found in a foreign dungeon, there is no resolution proposed by the honorable Senator; there is no action of the Government urged by the honorable Senator. . . ."[3]

So strong was the pressure that Sumner was unable to smother in his committee Banks's bill requiring the President, in the event a foreign power unjustly arrested an American citizen, "to suspend, in part or wholly, commercial relations with the said Government" or "to order the arrest . . . [of] any subject or citizen of such foreign Government who may be found within the jurisdiction of the United States" by way of retaliation. Horrified that this proposal might lead to the arbitrary arrest of distinguished British visitors such as Charles Dickens, Sumner stalled for time. Simultaneously he hurried along the treaty George Bancroft was negotiating with North Germany, which recognized the right of German-Americans to drop their original citizenship and guaranteed the protection of both naturalized and native-born United States citizens traveling in Germany. The completion of this agreement, Sumner recognized, would probably spur the British government to sign a similar protocol, and in his hope to forestall action on the Banks proposal he even went so far as to show the British minister in Washington a draft of the North German naturalization treaty before it was released to the other members of his own committee.[4] His strategy proved successful. When Conness and other Senators at last forced a debate upon the proposed retaliatory legislation in July

[3] *Cong. Globe*, 40 Cong., 2 Sess., pp. 270, 4208.
[4] Thornton to Stanley, July 4, 1868, F. O. 5, PRO.

1868, Sumner staged a stunning *coup de théâtre.* Rising to oppose the bill as "a proposal of unutterable barbarism, which, if adopted, would disgrace this country," he prefaced his remarks by reading a cable just received from London to the effect that Lord Stanley was now "ready to accept the American views of the question" of naturalization. Supporters of the Banks bill were demoralized, and, on the strength of his telegram, Sumner was able to secure its defeat.[5]

So strong was anti-British feeling, however, that the Senate felt obliged to enact some legislation to show its true sentiments. Finally, over Sumner's repeated objections, it passed a mild and meaningless resolution requiring the President, "whenever an American citizen was unjustly deprived of his liberty by a foreign government, to use such means, not amounting to acts of war, as he may think necessary and proper to obtain . . . a release." Disapproving of the resolution but unable to kill it, Sumner abstained from the final vote.

• 4 •

While these debates were proceeding, Charles Francis Adams resigned as American minister to Great Britain, and in June 1868 the President appointed Reverdy Johnson, the Maryland Senator who had for so many years served on the Senate Foreign Relations Committee, to succeed him. Sumner did not expect Reverdy Johnson's mission to produce much by way of results, both because he felt that any real settlement with Britain would have to wait until a new President was inaugurated and because he knew that Johnson was seventy-two years old and half-blind. He thought that the Marylander would probably "have little more than an official visit in England." Nevertheless, he felt it was a good time to take advantage of the slight softening in the British attitude that Stanley's correspondence suggested, and he felt that Johnson's high standing as a lawyer, his amiable disposition, and his detestation of "the idea of war or wrangle with England" could help soothe feelings. Consequently he moved Johnson's prompt and unanimous confirmation by the Senate

[5] Sumner: *Works,* XII, 482, 494.

and wrote letters recommending the new minister to his British friends.[6]

To everyone's astonishment Reverdy Johnson achieved a brilliant and speedy success in London. Alarmed by the rise of Bismarck's Prussia and its threat to the European balance of power, the British government was now eager to settle its difficulties with the United States. Stanley not merely agreed to a naturalization protocol, patterned after the American agreement with North Germany, and to a commission for settling the disputed San Juan boundary, but on November 10 he and Johnson signed a convention which provided for the settlement of all outstanding claims between the two nations. From the American standpoint the agreement was technically deficient in a number of ways, and by the time modifications had been made to suit Seward the Derby ministry fell. Lord Clarendon, the Foreign Minister in Gladstone's cabinet, continued Stanley's policy and signed the new version of the claims convention on January 14, 1869.

So long as possible Seward withheld from Sumner and other Senators all but the most general idea of the treaties Johnson was negotiating. When Edward Thornton, the rather nervous new British minister in Washington, asked whether the Senators should not be informed, Seward snorted contemptuously "that he knew their opinions and what they could sanction 'better than they did themselves.'" In explaining the blackout of information to Sumner, the Secretary tried to be more tactful, arguing "that it was perhaps fairer to him that he should not acquaint him with the details of the matter, so that when they should be presented to the Senate, he (Sumner) might give an entirely independent opinion." [7] In actuality, of course, Seward feared Sumner and his fellow Republicans would block any treaty that might redound to the credit of Andrew Johnson's

[6] Sumner to Duchess of Argyll, June 30 and July 28, 1868, Argyll MSS. After Sumner was instrumental in rejecting the Johnson-Clarendon Convention, some of his British friends, especially Bright, protested that he had misled them by writing warm letters introducing the new American minister. In fact, while Sumner spoke flatteringly of Johnson in his private letters abroad, he was careful not to write formal letters of introduction for him. The distinction was clear in his mind but not to recipients of his letters.

[7] Thornton to Clarendon, Jan. 12, 1869, Clarendon MSS.

administration, and he hoped that if he caught them unawares, as he had done with the Alaska treaty, he might be able to rush the agreements through the Senate.

With a powerful distrust of Seward and a conviction that the Senate committee should play an active role in shaping foreign policy, Sumner was predisposed to question the merits of Reverdy Johnson's treaties. His doubts turned into certainties after he learned that Johnson, in his zeal to restore Anglo-American amity, had shaken hands with Laird, the builder of Confederate cruisers, and had greeted as his friend John A. Roebuck, the chief parliamentary defender of the Confederacy. When Seward submitted the treaties to the Senate, Sumner found the naturalization and San Juan agreements acceptable enough, but the more important claims convention was clearly unsatisfactory. By providing that in cases where the claims commissioners were evenly divided they should choose an arbitrator by lot, the Johnson-Clarendon Convention seemed to make the settlement of weighty national grievances something like a game of chance. Most important of all, the convention contained not one word of British apology or regret.

Even so, as Sumner admitted, opposition to the Johnson-Clarendon Convention did not derive mainly from objections to its specific provisions. For nearly four years since the end of the war American hostility toward Britain had been gradually building up until now neither Sumner nor anyone else could quench the fire. In 1865 the terms Reverdy Johnson secured would have been enthusiastically accepted; even in 1868 they would, Sumner told Thornton, "have been approved almost without a dissentient vote." But Johnson's subservient behavior, coming after prolonged British haughtiness toward America, doomed the agreement. "Our minister has made it impossible to adopt anything he has done," Sumner bitterly wrote Bright, who was now a member of the British cabinet. The real fault lay not so much with Reverdy Johnson as with Seward, for Sumner was convinced that the minister "had acted *according to his Instructions* . . . and was not in fault." "The feeling towards Mr. Seward will not help the treaties," he warned Bright, and he himself was eager to take advantage of this final opportunity to get even with his old rival, with whom he had for nearly a decade been contesting over control of American foreign policy.[8]

If a desire to discredit the outgoing administration accounted in part for Sumner's hostility toward the Johnson-Clarendon Convention, uncertainty as to the policy of the incoming Grant regime was at least equally important in shaping his course. The election of a new President of his own party, who was surrounded by advisers generally hostile to Sumner and the other veteran antislavery stalwarts in the Republican party, threatened a significant diminution of Sumner's influence, which had already been rejected in domestic policymaking and was now confined almost entirely to the field of foreign affairs. When Lord Clarendon made a personal appeal for him to ignore "the unfortunate tho' well intentioned indiscretion of Mr. R. Johnson" and to join his lifelong British friends "in establishing a cordial entente between our respective countries," Sumner was obliged to admit that the fate of the treaty was not really in his hands.[9]

The enigmatic Grant was now in control of Republican policy, though he would not yet become President for another two months. On January 11, 1869, Sumner had to tell Thornton "that he was not acquainted with Grant's views on the subject" of the treaty, and he indiscreetly added "that he believed no one knew his views . . . ; indeed that Grant was not capable himself of forming an opinion upon such a subject." During the next two weeks, however, he had an opportunity to talk with the President Elect, who expressed no opinion on the treaty but asked whether "he did not think it better that it should wait until the new Government is installed." To Sumner, all too acutely aware that his personal influence in the Senate was limited, no further hint was necessary, and he repeated Grant's words to Thornton "two or three times, as if that were a sufficient cause for its rejection." [1] An aroused public opinion, a Senate hostile to Sumner's leadership even in foreign affairs, and an untried executive

[8] Thornton to Clarendon, Jan. 19, 1869, ibid.; Pierce, IV, 368; John V. S. L. Pruyn: Diary, Feb. 19, 1869, Pruyn MSS.

[9] Clarendon to Thornton, Dec. 26, 1868, copy, Clarendon MSS.

[1] Thornton to Clarendon, Jan. 12, 1868, Jan. 26, 1869, and Feb. 9, 1869, ibid.

all threatened danger in the months ahead. "I think," Sumner wrote Bright in January, "that never at any time have I felt so powerless over the question." [2]

• 5 •

Behind Sumner's feelings of impotence lay his uncertainty about where he stood with Grant. In retrospect it seems inevitable that the two giants of the Republican party should clash. Sumner was a man of books and words; Grant was a man of actions and silences. World-traveled and long experienced in public life, Sumner unconsciously condescended to Grant as a provincial novice in politics. Quite as naturally the hero of Appomattox scorned a man who knew more of Latin quotations than of bayonets and mortars. Sumner's self-esteem was so great that it provoked Grant to one of his rare attempts at humor; informed that the Senator had no faith in the Bible, the President replied: "Well, he didn't write it." [3] Lacking ready wit, Sumner could not retort in kind, but he might have illustrated Grant's swollen egotism by quoting from the untrained, inexperienced chief executive's inaugural address: "The responsibilities of the position I feel, but accept them without fear."

In the winter of 1868–69 it was not yet clear that the two most conspicuous figures in the Republican party were bound to battle. Keeping complete secrecy about appointments, Grant uttered only ambiguous truisms about the policies his administration would pursue. After his arrival in Washington he voiced few opinions of his own but listened in silence while Sumner discussed weighty questions of foreign policy. Years later, asked whether he had listened to Sumner converse, Grant replied: "No, but I have heard him lecture." [4] At the time, however, he disguised his boredom behind a cloud of cigar smoke and made an effort to be agreeable to a man whom he instinctively disliked. Afterwards he was to say: "Sumner is the only man I was ever

[2] Pierce, IV, 368.

[3] Sara Norton and M. A. DeWolfe Howe (eds.): *Letters of Charles Eliot Norton* (Boston: Houghton Mifflin Company; 1913), II, 43.

[4] Boutwell: *Reminiscences of Sixty Years,* II, 215.

anything but my real self to; the only man I ever tried to conciliate by artificial means." [5]

Sumner, too, tried to be conciliatory during these difficult weeks before Grant's inauguration. Though "Grawnt"—as he persisted in pronouncing the general's name [6]—had not been his own preference for the presidency, he recognized that the new administration would have exciting opportunities to settle major problems at home and abroad. Since Grant's political experience was so limited, some veteran Republican would have to exercise behind-the-scenes leadership during his administration, and Sumner thought he might be just the man. Throughout the campaign friends had written that it would become his duty, once Grant was elected, to join the cabinet and give a true Republican direction to his policies. Both Samuel Bowles of the Springfield *Republican* and John Russell Young of the New York *Tribune* powerfully urged Sumner's appointment to the State Department, and their campaign received unexpected backing from *The Nation,* which forgot its usual hostility to Sumner and argued that "there is nobody who united a greater number of qualifications for it than he." Even Seward was heard to say that Sumner, along with Charles Francis Adams and himself, was one of the three men in the country "fit to be Secretary of State." [7]

On the very day after Grant's election Sumner wrote cautiously to Lieber of the possibility that he might be called to give up his Senate seat and the chairmanship of his committee which made him "equal in position to anything in our government under the President." "Nobody has ever heard me say that I would accept a place out of the Senate, if it were offered to me," he added cagily. "I admit, however, that my country has a right to determine where I can work best." [8] As always Sumner carefully concealed, perhaps even from himself, his aspirations for higher office, but it is impossible to believe that both his col-

[5] Charles Eliot Norton (ed.): *Letters of James Russell Lowell* (New York: Harper & Brothers Publishers; 1894), II, 233.

[6] Undated interview with Sumner, J. W. Schuckers MSS.

[7] Bigelow: *Retrospections,* IV, 244, 271–2; John Russell Young to Sumner, Sept. 28, 1868, Sumner MSS.; *The Nation,* VII (Dec. 24, 1868), 518.

[8] Sumner to Lieber, Nov. 4, 1868, G. B. Pierce MSS.

league Henry Wilson and his hand-picked governor of Massachusetts, William Claflin, could have urged his name upon Grant without his prior if tacit consent. A month after the election Sumner was still expecting "the possible or probable offer to him by General Grant of the office of Secretary of State," and, according to the acquaintance who reported his conversation: "He would dislike to leave the Senate, and still I fancy he would like the Secretaryship." [9]

Between November and March, while Washington gossips quoted Sumner's chances for a cabinet appointment like prices on the stock exchange, the Senator himself remained in a state of uncertainty. When the President Elect visited Boston in December, he made a point of seeing Sumner, but he also talked with Charles Francis Adams, his chief rival. Grant told nobody his plans. Even Mrs. Grant was kept in the dark. She asked Sumner if he knew anything about the cabinet, saying that she was afraid again to question her husband because he had warned: "Jule, if you say anything more about it I'll get leave of absence, go off West, and not come back till the 4th of March." [1] During these unsettling months Sumner, as if to remind Grant that he was not a man safely to be ignored, proved in a series of petty skirmishes in the Senate, that he still had enough power to make a President's life uncomfortable. First he blocked the use of the Capitol for the gala inaugural ball that Grant's admirers had planned. Then, more significantly, he took the lead, both in the caucus and on the Senate floor, in defeating an attempt to repeal the Tenure of Office Act, which Grant correctly believed infringed the Chief Executive's power.[2]

On March 5, 1869, when Grant announced his cabinet, Sumner was not in it. Though it contained some men of ability, like E. Rockwood Hoar, the Attorney General, its members were mostly mediocrities, like John A. Rawlins, Grant's army crony who became Secretary of War, and A. A. Borie, the Secretary of the Navy, whose only apparent qualification was having contrib-

[9] Pruyn: Diary, Dec. 12, 1868, Pruyn MSS.; Wilson to Claflin, Mar. 1, 1869, Claflin MSS.

[1] George William Curtis (ed.): *The Correspondence of John Lothrop Motley* (New York: Harper & Brothers; 1889), II, 302.

[2] New York *Herald*, Feb. 23, 1869; Sumner: *Works*, XIV, 259–60.

uted largely to Grant's campaign funds. The most conspicuous of the nominees was the wealthy New York importer and merchant, A. T. Stewart, whom Grant named Secretary of the Treasury—only to discover that a 1789 law prohibited any person engaged in trade or commerce from holding that office. A hasty message from the White House urged that Stewart be exempted from this act; and John Sherman was about to move immediate Senate action when Sumner sonorously objected that "the bill ought to be most profoundly considered before it is acted upon" and demanded that it be referred to a committee. Facing certain defeat, Grant was forced to withdraw the nomination and to name Boutwell to the Treasury Department. With Sumner there was as yet no open break, yet as George W. Julian observed, the episode doubtless increased "the President's personal hostility to him, which so remarkably developed itself during the following years." [3]

That indifference, if not hostility, toward Sumner was already present, Grant's plans for the State Department gave abundant evidence. His first nominee was his Galena friend and protector, Congressman E. B. Washburne, whose qualifications were invisible and who, in fact, wished to be Secretary of State only for a short time so that he would be received with more distinction when he resigned to become American minister to France. To succeed Washburne, Grant wanted to name the equally unqualified Senator George H. Williams. When he declined, the President sought the services of the retired New York patrician, Hamilton Fish. Sumner, in short, was not even on Grant's list of possible candidates for the office.

Hardly able to "conceal his wrath and indignation at Grant's course," [4] Sumner tried to take comfort from the fact that Fish was an old friend, who had served with him in the Senate during the 1850's. At a time when antislavery men were unpopular in Washington, Sumner had always been assured of a hearty welcome at the Fishes' Washington residence, and he had often visited them at their Fishkill, New York, estate as well. Sumner took solace too from the fact that Fish accepted office not be-

[3] Julian: *Political Recollections*, pp. 326–7.

[4] Welles: *Diary*, III, 428.

cause he wished power but because he hoped to save Grant from the embarrassment of another refusal. If the President had slighted the most distinguished Republican in the Senate, there was every reason to believe that the new Secretary of State would recognize his importance and ability. Fish, moreover, had a realistic sense of his own limited acquaintance with foreign affairs, and in one of his first letters after agreeing to serve, he wrote to Sumner: "I hoped that I could rely upon your friendship and your experience and ability, for your support and aid to supply my manifold deficiencies." [5]

Nevertheless Sumner felt, as he so often had in the past, the annoyance of trying to exercise power through an intermediary, even one who was amiable and well disposed. Once again he had to plead for appointments to the foreign service rather than demand them as a matter of justice and right. Sadly he learned that neither Grant nor Fish was prepared to give to Massachusetts enough diplomatic posts to satisfy her hungry applicants, and he was obliged to tell old friends like George W. Greene, James Russell Lowell, and even Howe that he could not secure appointments for them. Only by persistent importunities did he persuade the President to nominate John Lothrop Motley to the Court of St. James,[6] but over this appointment he specially rejoiced since it was at once a deserved tribute to a distinguished man of letters, a vindication of Motley from the charges Seward had leveled against him in Vienna, and a permanent block against any possibility that the Adams family might hope for further ventures in Anglo-American diplomacy.[7]

[5] Mar. 13, 1869, Sumner MSS.

[6] Later Sumner stated that he "never in any way asked or urged the appointment" of Motley. He had, he declared, spoken to Grant but twice on the subject, once "casually on the stairs of the White House" and later as part of his general recommendation that only men of "experience and culture" be sent abroad. Sumner to Whitelaw Reid, Jan. 12, 1871, Reid MSS. At the time, however, he jubilantly told the Duchess of Argyll that Motley "had been originally nominated by the President on my recommendation, and, as the Secretary of State informs me 'as a compliment' to me." Sumner to Duchess of Argyll, May 18, 1869, Argyll MSS. Certainly Grant, Fish, and other members of the administration felt that Sumner was urging Motley's appointment with all his force. See Boutwell: *Reminiscences,* II, 214; Memorandum of Hamilton Fish, June 13, 1893, J. C. B. Davis MSS.; and G. F. Hoar to Pierce, July 24, 1893, Hoar MSS.

[7] Gutheim: "Motley," p. 287; C. F. Adams: Diary, Mar. 16, 1869, Adams MSS.

Such a rare success was poor compensation for the tedious work Sumner's Committee on Foreign Relations spent in screening Grant's diplomatic appointees. Most of the names the President submitted were those of Westerners, unknown to Sumner and to most other members of the committee. Typical was Grant's nomination of one J. Russell Jones as minister to Belgium, a position in which Sumner had hoped to protect the incumbent, his friend Henry S. Sanford. Reluctantly bringing Jones's name before his committee, Sumner asked whether any of his associates could give any information about him. Morton, with a sarcastic smile, replied: "Well, Mr. Jones is about the most elegant gentleman that ever presided over a livery stable." The other members of the committee were convulsed with laughter, but Sumner failed to see the humor in the situation.[8] "Anxious to purge this branch of the public service from inefficiency and incompetency," Sumner delayed action upon many of the nominees until more could be learned about them. Repeatedly he sought to have the most objectionable of Grant's nominees withdrawn, but he found the whole task "wearisome—very," for he was "tired of dancing attendance and arguing these questions." To Lieber he lamented, less than two months after Grant's inauguration: "Our foreign list is poor enough to fill the patriot with despair."[9]

[8] New York *Herald*, April 15, 1869; Carl Schurz: *The Reminiscences of Carl Schurz* (New York: Doubleday, Page & Company; 1908), III, 309. Jones was, in fact, a respectable appointee. A Galena merchant and railroad president, he had served as United States marshal for northern Illinois since 1861, and during the war Lincoln used him as a confidential agent to ascertain Grant's political aspirations.

[9] Sumner to H. B. Anthony, April 29, 1869, MS., Brown Univ.; Sumner to Lieber, April 22, 1869, Sumner MSS.

CHAPTER X

The Massive Grievance

ON April 13, 1869, Sumner made a desperate bid to recapture the power that had been slipping through his fingers. Before a secret executive session of the Senate he appeared, as chairman of the Committee on Foreign Relations, to present a unanimous report against ratification of the Johnson-Clarendon Convention and then, in an hour-long speech titled "Claims on England,—Individual and National," went on to urge the rejection of the treaty.[1] It was one of the most influential addresses Sumner ever made, for it had profound consequences both upon his own career and upon American foreign policy.

First Sumner explained the reasons behind his unusual report opposing the treaty. Based upon faulty precedents, containing dubious provisions, hastily drawn up "as if the honorable negotiators were engaged in huddling something out of sight," the Johnson-Clarendon Convention failed to remove "the massive grievance under which our country suffered for years." It was time, Sumner said, for an American to state, with proper precision, the true ground of complaint against Britain, which was simply that "when Civilization was fighting a last battle with Slavery, England gave her name, her influence, her material resources to the wicked cause, and flung a sword into the scale with Slavery."

[1] Sumner: *Works*, XIII, 53–93.

The original British offense, Sumner charged in words that echoed where they did not repeat his 1863 speech on "Our Foreign Relations," was committed on May 13, 1861, when the Queen issued her proclamation of neutrality recognizing the belligerent status of the Confederacy.[2] Again Sumner stressed his familiar distinction between land and ocean belligerency. If there were at this time only dubious grounds for recognizing the Confederates as belligerents on land, there was no justification whatever for conceding ocean belligerency to a rebel, slaveholding government which in early 1861 had not a single ship nor prize court. "Unfriendly in the precipitancy with which it was launched," the Queen's "fatal Proclamation" was even "more unfriendly in substance." Without it "no Rebel ship could have been built in England . . . nor could any munitions of war have been furnished" to the South; without it, as the British law lords had admitted, "any Englishman aiding [the Confederates] by fitting out a privateer against the Federal Government *would be guilty of piracy.*" The British government compounded this first error by permitting the *Alabama* and her consort "pirate" ships to be built and fitted out in British ports. These raiders which looted and burned American shipping were "not only British in origin, but British in equipment, British in armament, and British in crews." The welcome, hospitality, and supplies subsequently given to these Confederate cruisers in British ports added a third degree of British complicity.

For four years the British government had obdurately refused to redress these wrongs. During that time, Sumner felt, had there been manifested a generous spirit and a just recognition of the wrong done, Americans would have been appeased and this great question would have been settled. But now, even when the British had been brought to conclude an agreement, the Johnson-Clarendon Convention contained no acknowledgment of wrong or even of liability, not "one soothing word for a friendly power deeply aggrieved," but only an unsatisfactory

[2] The Queen's proclamation was, properly speaking, a proclamation of British neutrality in the American civil conflict. Since it recognized the existence of a state of war and thereby conceded to the Confederates the status of a belligerent, Americans frequently referred to it as a "proclamation of belligerency" or a "recognition of Confederate belligerency."

procedure for adjudicating claims of individual shipowners and other citizens who had been injured.

Of course such claims had to be settled, Sumner knew, but beyond them lay the more difficult, and as yet untouched, claims that should be called "*national* in contradistinction to *individual.*" These included such losses as "the rise of insurance on all American vessels; the fate of the carrying-trade, which was one of the great resources of our country; the diminution of our tonnage, with the corresponding increase of British tonnage; the falling off in our exports and imports." Such damages were difficult to estimate, but Sumner thought they might total $110,000,000.

This sum was, however, "only an item in our bill," for there was "that other damage, immense and infinite, caused by the prolongation of the war." It was safe to say that, "through British intervention, the war was doubled in duration." In effect, "the United States paid for a war waged by England upon the National Unity." Since the total cost of prosecuting the Civil War was four billion dollars, it was only fair to hold the British "justly responsible" for perhaps half this amount. Here then, fully revealed, were the true American claims against Great Britain, "mountain-high, with a base broad as the Nation, and a mass stupendous as the Rebellion itself."

Some Americans, Sumner warned, hoped that these claims would "rest without settlement, so as to furnish a precedent for retaliation in kind, should England find herself at war." For himself Sumner disavowed any such attitude. In the interests of world peace American claims ought to be liquidated and canceled promptly. There must be a new negotiation, followed by a new treaty. The first step toward a just settlement would be a generous expression of regret and apology by the British government. After that, individual claims had to be equitably appraised, and then, according to both common law and Roman law, a reckoning must be made for the national claims. "It is not I who say this," Sumner assured his fellow Senators; "it is the Law."

No speech Sumner had ever made met with such immediate, almost unanimous approval. Even as he finished speaking,

Senator H. B. Anthony of Rhode Island, who was in the chair, sent him a note: "That was a *great* speech." When he sat down, Republicans and Democrats, Conservatives and Radicals, gathered around his chair to congratulate him. Even Fessenden praised Sumner's "temperate and instructive views," and Democratic leader Thurman said "that his words honored the Senate as well as the statesman who uttered them." [3] Promptly the Senate, with only one dissenting vote, rejected the Johnson-Clarendon Convention, and Chandler, who often in the past had complained of Sumner's pro-English bias, moved to lift the injunction of secrecy so that his "Alabama Claims" speech could be published.

The public at large reacted as the Senators had done. For days Sumner's mail was crowded with letters praising his "recent grand speech," which exposed with "force, eloquence and truth" the "perfidy, offensive arrogance, and grasping selfishness" of the British. "No *abler speech* has ever been uttered in the United States Senate," declared one admirer, and another found "justice, wisdom, research, and eloquence" all combined in Sumner's argument. "God bless you!" exclaimed another correspondent. "The speech cannot fail to do great good." [4]

Newspapers were almost unanimously laudatory. The Chicago *Tribune* gloried in the "transcendent merits" of Sumner's speech. "Now for the first time," gloated Caleb Cushing in the Washington *Chronicle*, "Great Britain receives a distinct impression of the nature and consequences of her hostile intervention in the affairs of the United States." [5] Even the New York *Herald*, usually critical of Sumner, endorsed his "firm and masterly speech." In fact, argued the *Herald*, Sumner's views were so "manly, outspoken and dignified" that Grant ought at once to make him Secretary of State.[6]

Impressive as was such applause, it counted for less than the fact that many Northern conservatives, long suspicious of

[3] New York *Herald*, April 14, 1869; Springfield *Republican*, April 17, 1869.

[4] For these remarks, in the order quoted, see the letters from the following persons in the Sumner MSS.: George Plitt, April 14, 1869; E. P. Jacobson, April 15, 1869; M. Wakeman, April 14, 1869; J. G. Dudley, April 15, 1869; E. E. Williamson, April 15, 1869; and C. W. Denison, April 15, 1869.

[5] Quoted in Springfield *Republican*, April 17, 1869.

[6] New York *Herald*, April 15 and 16, 1869.

Sumner's radicalism, also endorsed his "Alabama Claims" speech. Grumpily *The Nation,* which disagreed with both Sumner's law and logic, had to admit that his address received "the approval of a great majority of the people of the Northern States, including many who have no sympathy with his favorite ideas." The usually critical Gideon Welles recorded in his diary that there was "more manly vigor and true statesmanship in this speech than in all Seward's diplomacy with England." "Sumner makes our case against John Pecksniff Bull even stronger than I thought it," wrote New York diarist George Templeton Strong; his speech was "the best thing he ever did—generally applauded, puts him in a new light." "There was never anything like it!" rejoiced E. M. Furness from Philadelphia. "Army and navy officers, *Quakers,* Democrats and radicals are united in grateful praise." [7]

Even in Boston, where shippers and importers had suffered heavily from Confederate raiders, Charles Francis Adams found Sumner had "certainly gained might . . . among those who hate him." Edward W. Kinsley, one of the Senator's lieutenants, reported that now "the whole business community are congratulating themselves upon the great speech." Reporting from the intellectuals, James Russell Lowell declared: "Your speech gives entire satisfaction. . . . I think you have struck exactly the true note—expressing the *national* feeling with [good] temper and dignity." As Governor Claflin summarized: "No speech of yours ever gave such universal and heartfelt satisfaction. . . ." [8]

• 2 •

Very different was the British reception of Sumner's "Alabama Claims" speech. The rejection of the Johnson-Clarendon Convention came as no surprise to informed Britons, who reacted moderately to the first brief cable announcement of the Senate's action. "We cannot afford a big quarrel with America," the Liver-

[7] J. C. Hurd, in *The Nation,* VIII (April 22, 1869), 308; Welles: *Diary,* III, 579; Strong: *Diary,* IV, 244–5; Furness to Sumner, April 17, 1869, Sumner MSS.

[8] Charles Francis Adams to Henry Adams, April 28, 1869, Adams MSS.; Kinsley to Sumner, April 14, 1869, Sumner MSS.; Lowell to Sumner, April 22, 1869, ibid.; Claflin to Sumner, April 17, 1869, ibid.

pool *Post* declared; "perhaps it would be wise to pay the money and have done with it. . . ." Finding the American behavior "almost contemptuous," the London *Daily News* warned against getting excited: "Our cousins may be assured that their rejection of the treaty will neither diminish our desire to act honorably by them nor our readiness to treat on the bases of concessions already made when they shall be in the mood to negotiate a final settlement." [9]

But toward the end of April 1869, when reports of Sumner's speech became available, Great Britain blazed with anger. Justin McCarthy, the Irish politician and writer who was visiting in New York, correctly predicted the response. When asked: "What will the English people think of this speech?" he unhesitatingly replied: "They will regard it as a declaration of war." [1] For once British newspaper opinion was united.[2] Charging that Sumner confounded "legal considerations of the first importance with totally distinct moral considerations in a manner almost childish," the *Spectator* asked: "Was anything so monstrous ever proposed on this earth before by any man taking the rank of a statesman?" The *Economist* agreed that it was "a womanish speech, mixing up matters of feeling with matters of law." The *Saturday Review* held that Sumner was "wholly actuated by a spirit of revenge" and announced: "If it were Mr. Sumner's object to precipitate a war, he could not be more bitter or more unjust."

The *Times* did not notice Sumner's speech until April 30, when it gave a full summary of his views, but in the following days it carried a series of bitter editorials against the Senator. "Mr. Sumner had the questionable honor of contributing more than any other man to the war which broke up the Union, and to the differences which keep the breach open," began the fourth of its thundering leaders. Just as in the years before the war it became evident "that nothing human nature was capable of would have satisfied Mr. Sumner, and that what he demanded of

[9] Both papers quoted in New York *Herald,* May 1, 1869.

[1] McCarthy to the editor of the New York *Tribune,* May 12, 1869, undated clipping, Sumner Scrapbooks.

[2] Unless otherwise identified, all quotations in the following paragraphs are taken from clippings in the Sumner Scrapbooks.

the South was, in fact, moral and political self-annihilation," so it was now clear that he was equally unreasonable in his expectations from Great Britain. His argument was "of that intuitive sort which has been common in all the tribunals of despotism"; he needed no proof but assumed British guilt. But, concluded *The Times* firmly, the question was one of law, "not one of feeling," and "it remains to be shown that the British Government can be held answerable for any infraction of law."

In cartoons the more popular papers carried the same message, caricaturing the United States now as "a villainous looking ruffian with belt stuck full of revolvers and knives, calculating how much he can make John Bull pay—now a pack of ugly curs smelling about a mighty bull-dog that they are afraid to attack and now a scrubby-looking eagle watching a chance to steal Canada from a magnificent lion." "Not a word has been said in our defense," reported the New York *Tribune*'s London correspondent as the storm of abuse broke. "If . . . Mr. Sumner's speech represents fairly the general opinion and feeling in America on the Alabama question, we have no longer an advocate among the English journals." [3]

The fact that it was Sumner who led in rejecting the Johnson-Clarendon Convention gave special virulence to British criticisms. To many in the British Isles Sumner in the past had seemed the nearest thing to an English statesman the United States could produce. Some still remembered him as a young visitor to Britain, eager, admiring, and flushed with social success; others had first met him when, as an invalid-martyr after the Brooks assault, he went abroad to recover his health. Sumner's often expressed love for Great Britain, his broad knowledge of English law and history, and his wide acquaintance among the British governing classes should have made him the American who best understood the British position on the Alabama Claims. Had his speech come from a Chandler or a Banks, it would hardly have been noticed, but it seemed an enormous perversity that it should have been pronounced by the one American politician who most loudly professed to be Britain's friend.

[3] George W. Smalley to James A. Garfield, May 22, 1869, Garfield MSS.; Smalley's London despatch, dated May 1, clipping in Sumner Scrapbooks.

"How *could* he make that speech!" exclaimed the Duchess of Argyll.[4]

To other Britons, more closely connected with the day-by-day operation of the government, Sumner's authorship of the "Alabama Claims" speech carried a very different significance. Since 1861 every British minister in Washington had developed a profound detestation for the Massachusetts Senator. Lyons regarded him as the most offensive American he had ever met; Bruce felt he was Britain's bitterest enemy;[5] and Thornton believed his animating motive was hatred to England. In part their hostility toward Sumner reflected a justifiable indignation over his repeated use of foreign policy issues as a weapon in American domestic political warfare. They were also, as good bureaucrats, troubled over the direct access Sumner had to members of the British cabinet, and, at least in Thornton's case, over his acceptance in rarefied social circles from which the British minister himself was excluded. More basic was their failure to recognize that Sumner was playing a dual role. Except for the politically necessary outbreak in his "Our Foreign Relations" speech in 1863, he had done all he could during the previous eight years to calm American resentment against Great Britain; at the same time he felt it his duty to convey that resentment both to the British ministers in Washington and to his correspondents in England. Since the ministers were not aware of the placatory part Sumner took in the secret sessions of the Senate devoted to foreign affairs, they could only view as hypocritical his repeated professions of affection for Great Britain, and over the years they persuaded their superiors in the Foreign Office that he bore a rankling hatred for all things English.[6] Even before Sumner made his speech, Clarendon was convinced that he "must be placed as our arch enemy."[7] When they read the "Alabama Claims" address, British officials were already prepared to believe that Sumner was basically hostile to their country and secretly wished to humiliate it.

[4] Motley to Sumner, June 7, 1869, Sumner MSS.

[5] Bruce to Russell, June 24, 1865, Russell MSS.

[6] Russell to Bruce, July 8, 1865, copy, ibid.

[7] Gardiner: *The Life of Sir William Harcourt,* I, 166; Clarendon to Thornton, April 3, 1869, copy, Clarendon MSS.

The anger with which Britons condemned Sumner's speech reflected no political partisanship. To be sure, high Tories, always suspicious of American democracy, seized upon the address as an illustration of the inevitable consequences of extending the suffrage, as British Liberals were advocating. Now that John Bright was in the cabinet, the London *Morning Post* warned that England like America was at the mercy of "blatant demagogues." Democracy run wild was bound to produce extreme speeches like Sumner's, and the Senator's contumelious utterances proved to the *Pall Mall Gazette,* organ of the most conservative British aristocracy, "the fruitlessness of further negotiations, and the necessity of being prepared for war."

But Liberals felt equally outraged. Earl Russell, now in retirement, thought the speech justified his previous opposition to making any concessions to the United States, for it proved that Americans were insatiable. Men like Bright and Argyll, who had spoken out for the Union at a time when the Confederacy was popular and who had defended the antislavery purposes of the Lincoln government before these had been articulated as Union goals, fiercely resented Sumner's unfairness in refusing to recognize the loyal and long-suffering support they had given to the United States, and they were angry at his failure to charge the government of Napoleon III with equal wrongdoing. The best Bright could say for his friend's speech was "that the embarrassment which its publication produced served England very properly"; privately he thought that Sumner's speech was "hostile and vindictive," "not only absurd but devilish." [8] Even the Duchess of Argyll disapproved and concluded that Sumner was "a Fanatic, and never did see more than one side, which was well enough when he had to fight the devilry of American Slavery." [9] W. E. Forster, one of the stanchest friends of the Union throughout the war, read Sumner's speech as a demand for "an abject apology" and told his constituents at Bradford: "They have not a monopoly of patriotism in America, and . . . there is a line beyond

[8] R. A. J. Walling (ed.): *The Diaries of John Bright* (New York: William Morrow & Company; 1931), p. 340; Reverdy Johnson to E. L. Godkin, Sept. 8, 1869, Godkin MSS.

[9] Duchess of Argyll to Gladstone, May 17, 1869, Gladstone MSS.

which concession would be a crime, because it would be a sacrifice of that position amongst civilized nations, which alone makes England able to do her duty."[1] From Cornell University, where he was teaching, Goldwin Smith charged that Sumner insisted "upon being judge in his own cause, on pronouncing us guilty on any grounds which his inflamed fancy can suggest, and fining and humiliating us at his discretion," and he warned British laborers against emigrating to the United States at a time when diplomatic relations were so tense.[2]

The business community, too, was angered by Sumner's address and feared it portended war. United States bonds dropped three or four percent when reports of the speech reached London, and the price of gold rose eight points. Visiting London in the middle of May, John Jay could speak still of the "panic created by Mr. Sumner's speech, which seems to be the principal topic of discussion with the press and in social circles."[3]

No less offended, the British government fortunately responded less violently. Though the Foreign Office had received advance warning that Sumner would speak against the Johnson-Clarendon Convention, it was not until April 29 that the text of Sumner's address, as printed in the New York newspapers, became available in London. There is no evidence that most members of the cabinet ever read the whole speech, but they all received a précis prepared by the Under Secretary for Foreign Affairs, C. S. A. Abbott (later Lord Tenterden), which quoted the more striking passages of the address and concluded that Sumner urged "his countrymen to demand from England the payment of £425,000,000 and an ample apology." Sumner's argument was so defective that it could be easily answered, Abbott concluded, but he thought it would be better to "drop our powder

[1] Sumner wrote Forster on June 8, 1869, challenging his arguments, but Forster declined to pursue the matter further. Reid: *Life of the Right Honourable William Edward Forster*, II, 15–19.

[2] Goldwin Smith: *The Relations Between America and England. A Reply to the Late Speech of Mr. Sumner* (London: John Camden Hotten; 1869).

[3] F. H. Morse to W. P. Fessenden, May 15, 1869, Fessenden MSS.; G. C. von Rosen to H. C. Carey, May 23, 1869, E. C. Gardiner Collection; Jay to Fish, May 11, 1869, Fish MSS.

and shot until we see what sort of target Motley will present." The cabinet, meeting on May 1, agreed to this view.[4]

Clarendon, who felt he had gone to the utmost limits in making last-minute concessions demanded by the Americans, felt outraged both by the rejection of the treaty and by Sumner's "atrocious speech." Transmitting Abbott's summary to the Queen, the Foreign Minister warned her that it "breathes the most extravagant hostility to England." Bluntly he told Benjamin Moran, the secretary of the American legation who was serving as chargé d'affaires, that Sumner's speech was insulting. As reports came in of the enthusiastic reception Sumner's speech was receiving in the United States, Clarendon began to anticipate the worst. "The news from America is very bad," he wrote on May 9, "and I believe that Grant and Sumner mean war; or rather that amount of insult and humiliation that must lead to it." Further concessions by Great Britain were impossible, he declared; "we should sink into utter contempt if we allowed ourselves to be humiliated which is clearly the object of Mr. M[otley] Sumner and Grant." [5] Yet failure to reach agreement meant paralyzing British policy on the Continent, where Bismarck's Germany was visibly threatening the balance of power. As Clarendon ruefully informed the Queen: "There is not the smallest doubt that if we were engaged in a continental quarrel we should immediately find ourselves at war with the U. States." [6]

Soon, however, he concluded that the importance of Sumner's speech had been overrated. Secretary of State Fish was behaving reasonably; some American newspapers were beginning to dissent from Sumner's views; and Clarendon's son, who

[4] Katherine A. Wells: "The Settlement of the Alabama Claims: A Study of British Policy and Opinion, 1865–1872" (unpublished doctoral dissertation, Clark University, 1936), p. 168.

[5] Clarendon to Queen Victoria, May 1 and 8, 1869, Royal Archives; Benjamin Moran: Diary, May 13, 1869, MS., Lib. of Cong.; Herbert Maxwell: *The Life and Letters of George William Frederick, Fourth Earl of Clarendon* (London: Edward Arnold; 1913), II, 358; Clarendon to Thornton, May 8, 1869, copy, Clarendon MSS.

[6] Clarendon to Queen Victoria, May 1, 1869, Royal Archives. Sumner was fully aware of this effect of his speech. "Since William (William and Mary) was buried," he wrote Lieber on May 21, 1869, "England has never before been so powerless on the Continent. For the first time she is 'counted out' in the European balance of power."

had just returned from a visit to the United States, assured him that there was no danger of war, since in America "nothing but money making is really cared about and every body knows that on the first announcement of a war with England gold would go up [to] 300—all insurance houses would break and there would be ruin thruout the States." Confident that Sumner was engaged in international blackmail, Clarendon assumed a calm but uncompromising attitude. "Mr. Sumner's speech and the general approval with which it has been received in the U. S. have awakened here the spirit with which such insolence should be received," he wrote Thornton; "and if Mr. Motley, instructed by Mr. Sumner thinks he can bully us or, as we are told he expects to do, set the working classes of England against the aristocratic advocates of the South in the recent civil war he will find himself miserably and deservedly mistaken. . . ." [7]

Other members of the government followed Clarendon's lead. Assured by Sir Henry Bulwer, whose long diplomatic career had included service at Washington, that the importance of Sumner's speech had been much exaggerated since he did not speak "as the organ of the Government or of the Senate," Prime Minister Gladstone urged members of his party to refrain from debating the American question in Parliament, lest they give undue attention to Sumner, "a man of huge and distempered vanity." Convinced that Sumner was "our arch-enemy," Gladstone nevertheless thought that, in a perverse way, the Senator had assisted the British, because the extravagance of his demands would ultimately bring the American people to their senses and also help "our cause before the great tribunal of the civilized world." [8]

• 3 •

Though most Americans were surprised by the violent British reaction to Sumner's "Alabama Claims" speech, there were some

[7] Clarendon to Gladstone, May 20, 1869, Gladstone MSS.; Clarendon to Thornton, May 15, 1869, copy, Clarendon MSS.

[8] Bulwer to Gladstone, May 19, 1869, Clarendon MSS.; Gladstone to Clarendon, June 3, 1869, ibid.; Clarendon to Gladstone, June 10 and July 5, 1869, Gladstone MSS.; Gladstone to Duchess of Argyll, May 18, 1869, ibid.

who from the outset dissented from the Senator's views and recognized that his address imperiled further peaceful negotiations with Britain. E. L. Godkin, who had developed a special detestation of Sumner, disliked everything about the speech from the day it was issued. It was a work "perfectly characteristic" of Sumner, he observed, adding: "He works his adjectives so hard that if they ever catch him alone, they will murder him." [9] At once he made the columns of *The Nation* available to those who disagreed with Sumner. On April 22, arguing that Sumner erred in calling the recognition of Confederate belligerency an unfriendly or unlawful act, the publicist John C. Hurd predicted that the speech could not be "a foundation for future negotiation." The next week a writer who signed himself "*Pax Nobiscum*," observed that "Sentimental wrongs between nations, as between individuals," could not be "measured in currency," as Sumner seemed to propose. As reports of the hostile British response trickled in, *The Nation's* attacks upon Sumner's "sentimental" argument grew stronger, and on May 13 Godkin declared that if Sumner truly believed he was promoting a peaceful settlement by his speech he was "the victim of a monstrous delusion."

In private a number of American public men shared Godkin's views. Lyman Trumbull told his friends that he disavowed Sumner's speech altogether, and he agreed with Gustav Koerner: "It was well enough to reject the treaty, but not for some of the reasons assigned by Sumner." When Charles Francis Adams, now in retirement in Massachusetts, read the speech he at once confided to his diary that its practical result would be "to raise the scale of our demands of reparation so very high that there is no chance of negotiation left unless the English have lost all their spirit and character." Improbably enough, Banks, who had made a career of baiting the British, came to very much the same conclusion. There was a possibility, he told his wife, that the speech might have an effect exactly the opposite of that intended by Sumner; "destitute of reason," the Senator had made such an exaggerated statement of American grievances that "the

[9] Rollo Ogden (ed.): *Life and Letters of Edwin Lawrence Godkin* (New York: The Macmillan Company; 1907), I, 304–5.

country will be obliged to do hereafter exactly what he says they will not do and chiefly because he says they will not do it." "I have no doubt," Banks explained, "that he did not comprehend the effect of the words he used himself." [1]

On the whole, however, the critics at first kept their views largely to themselves, and, except in *The Nation,* there was very little public dissent from his arguments until Americans learned that Englishmen seriously thought war was in the offing. "The Senate did approve Sumner," Henry Adams wrote Bright; "so did the press; so did the people, and it was not till England began to scold, that our people began to hesitate." [2] Then the newspapers changed their tune, and, while many continued to call the speech "a masterly production," they began finding faults in it, so that, as Thornton reported on May 11, "they have pretty well pulled it to pieces." Edmund Hammond, the permanent Under Secretary in the British Foreign Office, viewed this American response as entirely characteristic: "They are always ready to bluster and bully when they think they can do so with impunity, but are no less eager to draw in their horns when they find their anticipations not realized." [3]

Americans visiting in Great Britain were among the first to sense the force of the British reaction and to see the need for disavowing Sumner's positions. William Beach Lawrence, the authority on international law, let Londoners know his belief that Sumner's argument had shaky foundations, and Cyrus W. Field, the promoter of the Atlantic cable, directly informed Gladstone of his regret over Sumner's utterance. After long talks with Bright and other friends of the United States, Senator James W. Grimes, of Iowa, who was in London for his health, concluded: "Sumner has greatly injured our cause by presenting so many perfectly absurd arguments, and urging them with so much bitterness." On May 10 Grimes attempted to set the record straight in a careful letter to *The Times,* declaring that Sumner

[1] Koerner to Schurz, May 20, 1869, Schurz MSS.; Charles Francis Adams: Diary, April 15, 1869, Adams MSS.; Banks to his wife, May 7, June 1, and December 22, 1869, Banks MSS.

[2] Adams to Bright, May 30, 1869, Bright MSS.

[3] Thornton to Edmund Hammond, May 11, 1869, Hammond MSS.; Hammond to Thornton, May 22, 1869, copy, ibid.

spoke for himself alone and not for the United States government.[4]

While the vulgar New York *Herald* lauded Sumner as "a great American statesman, a man of culture, dignity and large experience," the thinking constituency for whom the Senator usually spoke increasingly began to question his law and his logic. Typical of the shift in opinion were the reactions of James Russell Lowell. Cordially endorsing the speech at first, Lowell came by April 24 to feel that "our soberest heads do not think that Sumner is right in his statement of the law." By May 2 he explained: "Sumner's speech expressed the *feeling* of the country very truly, but I fear it was not a wise speech."[5]

As informed public opinion turned against Sumner's address more and more people began to ask why he ever made it. Some of the speculations were improbable and absurd. Bitterly hostile to Sumner, Thornton wrote Clarendon that the Senator was trying "to make a play for the next Presidency," and Reverdy Johnson, infuriated by the rejection of his treaty, also assured the Foreign Minister that Sumner was *"going in* for the next Presidency on the *anti-English platform."*[6] But chronology, if nothing else, ruled out that explanation. With Grant in office only one month, it would have been foolishly premature for Sumner or anybody else with presidential aspirations to begin campaigning for 1872. In any case, Sumner was always aware that his outspoken radical record made him unavailable for the presidency. Some years later Lord Tenterden tried to connect Sumner's "Alabama Claims" speech with his marital difficulties, suggesting that Sumner was trying to make up "by vigour of tongue for his want of capacity in other organs."[7] But had Sumner's purpose been to assert his masculinity, he would hardly have waited so long before making an attack which he could have launched at any day during the past two years. In fact, living in his solipsistic world, he had now virtually erased

[4] Benjamin Moran: Diary, April 29, 1869, MS., Lib. of Cong.; Field to Gladstone, May 10, 1869, Gladstone MSS.; William Salter: *The Life of James W. Grimes* (New York: D. Appleton and Company; 1876), pp. 368–71.

[5] Norton (ed.): *Letters of James Russell Lowell*, II, 26–9.

[6] Thornton to Clarendon, Private No. 20, April 20, 1869, Clarendon MSS.; Clarendon to Queen Victoria, May 1, 1869, Royal Archives.

[7] Cook: "Road to Geneva," p. 275.

all memory of Alice's existence. No more probable was Henry Adams's theory that the Senator had been deranged since 1856 and that his "Alabama Claims" speech was simply the maddest of "all the crazy acts our friend Sumner ever did, and they are many." [8] If Sumner was mad, so was the Senate of the United States which approved publication of his speech and the great American public which applauded that speech.

Sumner's own version of his motives was scarcely more convincing. Forced by a rising tide of criticism to explain and defend himself, he could not successfully argue that he had had to make the speech in order to expose the inadequacies of the Johnson-Clarendon Convention. Those were so obvious as to need no oratorical unveiling. Moreover Sumner himself admitted that it was less the provisions of the treaty than its timing and the conduct of Reverdy Johnson which made it so unacceptable; six months earlier, he had declared, the United States would gladly have accepted these very terms.

No more persuasive was his claim that he had felt obliged to lead in defeating the Johnson-Clarendon Convention so as to prevent Butler and other Anglophobes from seizing control of the issue. "If we abandon it," he told Bemis, "be assured the politicians will take it up." Of course a farmer can forestall an arsonist by burning down his own barn. Aware of the strong resentment, both in the Congress and in the army, over Great Britain's conduct during the Civil War, Sumner did fear that unless a settlement was reached animosity between the two countries would grow. There is, however, little in Sumner's correspondence prior to the delivery of his speech to suggest apprehension lest Butler, Chandler, or anybody else take the claims question out of his hands. In fact, Butler, though always anti-English, did not issue his own salvo against Great Britain, urging a proclamation of non-intercourse, until May 24, after Sumner had demonstrated that it was politically safe to twist the lion's tail.[9]

More difficult to evaluate was Sumner's repeated protesta-

[8] Adams to Schurz, May 16, 1871, Schurz MSS.

[9] Sumner to Bemis, July 7, 1869, Bemis MSS.; Cook: "Road to Geneva," p. 255.

tion that he had made the "Alabama Claims" speech only with reluctance, feeling it his duty, since the treaty was being rejected, "to state the case against England and make her see the wrongs under which we have suffered." [1] With another man and in other circumstances this purpose would seem a monstrous presumption, for such explanations, if required, would normally be made by the President or the Secretary of State. But since Sumner was used to conducting a kind of independent foreign office on Capitol Hill, he may well have felt an obligation pressing upon him. Yet the fact that he objected less to the treaty than to Reverdy Johnson's behavior weakened the force of this argument. So too did the fact that when Sumner reported adversely upon the treaty during the final days of Andrew Johnson's administration, he saw no need to expose its failings and made no remarks upon it. Not until March 8, just after Grant was inaugurated and failed to put Sumner in his cabinet, did the Senator decide that when the treaty came before the new Congress "he would himself have to draw up a detailed statement, showing the objections entertained by the Committee." [2]

If the timing of Sumner's speech gives some clue to his motives, so too does a close examination of what he hoped to achieve by his denunciation of Great Britain. He did not intend to provoke a war. Had his talk of a massive grievance and of damages totaling two billions of dollars come from Chandler, the purpose might well have been to invite hostilities, and Butler wanted to perpetuate American ill will until Britain was involved in a European war, when the United States would "sweep her commerce from the ocean and substitute in its place our own." [3] But for Sumner, proud of his services to the cause of international peace, such a course was not conceivable. Even to the

[1] Sumner to Longfellow, May 25, 1869, Longfellow MSS. Cf. Sumner to Duchess of Argyll, May 18, 1869, Argyll MSS.; Sumner to Lieber, May 24, 1869, Sumner MSS.

[2] *Journal of the Executive Proceedings of the Senate*, XVI, 442–3, 475, 483; Thornton to Clarendon, Private and Confidential, Mar. 8, 1869, Clarendon MSS. As early as January, however, Sumner was borrowing works on international law by Halleck, Heffter, Phillimore, and others, from the Library of Congress. A. W. Spofford to Sumner, April, 10, 1869, Sumner MSS.

[3] New York *Herald*, April 26, 1869.

hostile Thornton, Sumner seemed sincere when he exclaimed: "Oh no! . . . don't talk of war; we must not have war." However others regarded his speech, Sumner himself insisted that it was "rather pacific in tone." Though he had stated the American wrongs "as plainly but as gently as possible," he had never "menaced, suggested or thought of war." In fact, his "Alabama Claims" speech was only "a mild abstract" of his 1863 oration on "Our Foreign Relations"—"defecated, if I may so say, of every thing to give offense, except so far as the statement of our wrongs might give offense." That Britons were so aroused by his speech in 1869 he could only attribute to the fact that English newspapers failed to print it in full, "as if they were afraid to let the people read it before the papers had a chance to prejudice public sentiment against it." Anyway, "there never has been a time since the Conquest when England liked to be told the truth, especially if she happened to be in the wrong." [4]

Nor was Sumner's purpose to extract huge monetary reparations from Great Britain. Indignantly he repudiated Forster's charge that he demanded from England "an abject apology—and some untold sum of money besides." "I never had the idea," Sumner assured Adam Badeau, Grant's aide who accompanied Motley to London. "My *speech makes no* DEMAND, *whether apology or money,* not a word of apology, not a cent of money. It shows that we have suffered incalculable damages. . . . But I ask nothing." [5]

Since Sumner's speech presented no demand that Britain pay her two billion dollar debt to the United States, some observers concluded that he had some other kind of reparation in mind. When a grocer presents his bill to the housewife, he usually expects payment, not the establishing of an accurate record of indebtedness. Many thought that Sumner, like Grant, looked to the annexation of Canada as a settlement for what the President persisted in calling "our little bill." So plausible was this speculation that when Bostonians heard of the speech they

[4] Thornton to Clarendon, Feb. 9, 1869, Clarendon MSS.; New York *Herald,* May 3, 1869; Sumner to T. O. Howe, June 3, 1869, Howe MSS.

[5] Sumner to Badeau, July 26, 1869, MS., New-York Hist. Soc.

promptly concluded "that the end of it all was to be the annexation of Canada by way of full indemnity," [6] and Senator Chandler complained with some petulance that Sumner had stolen his favorite project. Sumner was not, of course, averse to this solution of the difficulty; he had for years looked to the day when Canada would become part of the United States, and he had justified the purchase of Alaska as a step toward that end. Before he denounced the Johnson-Clarendon Convention, he had discussed possible settlement of the American claims with the French minister at Washington in terms which led Berthémy "to think that the British possessions on the continent of America might be accepted"—though Sumner then hedged by adding that this "would depend upon circumstances." [7] Two years later Sumner was to insist upon the withdrawal of the British flag from North America as an indispensable condition for settling the Alabama claims. But by 1871 circumstances had greatly changed, and Sumner's views had hardened. At the time he made the "Alabama Claims' speech he apparently had no definite territorial concessions in mind but instead recognized the impossibility of an outright cession of Canada. "Territory may be conveyed," he declared, "but not a people." No one who knew England could suppose she would agree to such a transfer; "he knows our country little, and little also of that great liberty which is ours, who supposes that we could receive such a transfer." [8]

In short, Sumner was decidedly vague as to what concrete results might be produced from his speech. "How the case shall be settled—whether by money, more or less—by territorial compensation—by apologies—or by an amendment of the Law of Nations," he assured Lieber in May, "is still an open question." [9]

Coming from almost any other figure in American public life, such fuzzy and ambiguous pronouncements would be immediately suspected of concealing other objectives, but in Sumner's

[6] Charles Francis Adams: Diary, April 15, 1869, Adams MSS. Cf. Henry Cabot Lodge: *Early Memories* (New York: Charles Scribner's Sons; 1913), pp. 287–8.

[7] Berthémy's comments reported in Lord Lyons to Clarendon, No. 277, Mar. 11, 1869, copy, Royal Archives.

[8] Sumner: *Works*, XIII, 127.

[9] May 30, 1869, Sumner MSS.

case they have to be viewed as part of his characteristic pattern of political behavior. Throughout his career he had made it his business to announce principles rather than to propose solutions. Just as in the struggle against slavery extension before the war, in the fight for emancipation, and in the battle for Negro rights during reconstruction, his proper duty in the Alabama claims controversy was to expose error in its hideous shape. Once the British studied his speech and realized that their offense against the United States had been as grievous as, say, that of the slavemaster against the slave, they would feel obliged to right the error by making new proposals. It was not for Sumner to determine in advance what those proposals ought to be. His was the role of the Sibyl of Cumae, who had offered her nine books to Tarquin the Proud; when Tarquin refused, she burned three and offered the remaining six at the same price; and when he declined once more, she burned three more and asked—and received—the original price for the remaining three. "If our demands are larger now than at our first call," he warned in his speech, "it is not the only time in history when such a rise had occurred. The story of the Sibyl is repeated, and England is the Roman king." When the Duchess of Argyll, outraged by his speech, tried to pin him down as to the price he expected England to pay, she got only the sibylline answer: ". . . the justice of our claims had always been the same." [1]

That it might take time for the proud British Tarquin to become humble did not at all distress Sumner. The Alabama Claims controversy would doubtless become "one of the greatest international litigations in history," and he foresaw with some pleasure "protracted correspondence and discussion." "I should not be at all surprised," he informed Thornton, "that the question should lie over, and that six years hence you and I will be negotiating the settlement of it." [2] He contemplated nothing so sinister as Butler's scheme; instead, he envisioned a memorable and protracted negotiation, comparable perhaps to that leading

[1] Sumner: *Works*, XIII, 92; Sumner to Duchess of Argyll, May 18, 1869, Argyll MSS.

[2] Sumner to R. H. Dana, Jr., Jan. 26, 1869, Dana MSS.; John V. S. L. Pruyn: Diary, Feb. 19, 1869, Pruyn MSS.; Thornton to Clarendon, Mar. 8, 1869, Clarendon MSS.

to the Treaty of Westphalia, in which he might play a shaping role in establishing new rules of international law. To commemorate such a historic peaceful settlement Sumner might just possibly have found room on his crowded study walls for another set of engravings, from which his own likeness would not have been absent.

The fact that in 1869 such a general settlement seemed far distant had, moreover, certain practical advantages for Sumner in dealing with a President who had conspicuously snubbed him and had ignored his wishes. The speech and the ensuing controversy, as Thornton tartly observed, served Sumner's purposes admirably, "for there is no doubt that previously he was losing his prestige both in the country and the Senate. Now he is reinstated in as high a position as he perhaps ever held in the opinions of his countrymen, who admire his speech, knowing nothing of its real merits and caring still less, provided it satisfies their feelings of dislike to England." Both Sumner's timing and his rhetoric in the "Alabama Claims" speech, then, suggest that it was, among other things, a bid for power. By so clearly and forcibly expressing "the sentiment of nine out of ten of our people," as Charles Francis Adams shrewdly perceived, Sumner had put himself in a position so as to be able "to control the Executive, not in this instance merely, where . . . General Grant entirely concurs with him, but in all other cases in the foreign Department where they may not agree." [3]

• 4 •

Only gradually did it become evident how completely Sumner intended to control American foreign policy. At the time he delivered his "Alabama Claims" address he seemed to be working in close cooperation with the President, who shared his resentment at the conduct of the British during the Civil War and sometimes thought a bit wistfully of how easy it would be to conquer Canada in a single campaign. "I conversed with the President before I spoke, and found his views to be in strict

[3] Thornton to Clarendon, May 18, 1869, ibid.; Charles Francis Adams to Henry Adams, April 21, 1869, Adams MSS.

conformity with mine," Sumner confided to Bemis on May 25. "Since the speech, he has thanked and congratulated me." [4]

The Senator also appeared to be voicing the views of the State Department, where his old friend Fish, inexperienced in foreign affairs and endlessly busy with removals and appointments in the foreign service, was thought to share his opinion of the misconduct of the British. In fact, the untried Secretary of State had yet had little time to consider any issue, but he did agree that the Johnson-Clarendon Convention was inadequate because it proposed to settle only private and individual claims. The United States, he wrote a few days after Sumner's speech, had unassailable national claims against Great Britain for the loss of her merchant marine and for the prolongation of the war by at least one year, which would "amount to not less than a thousand million of dollars." Like Sumner, the Secretary did not anticipate monetary reparation. Perhaps the British would agree to a modification "in the doctrine and practise of international law, as it relates to the rights and duties of both neutrals and belligerents"; perhaps they might withdraw from Canada, which would then fall to the United States. Whatever the solution, Fish, like Sumner, felt that the British must make an apology, or at least express regret for their misconduct.

The appearance Sumner gave of being the administration's spokesman on the claims question was, however, superficial. Though both Grant and Fish agreed with him on most basic issues, they had not asked him to represent their views, nor did they assent in full to his argument. The importance Sumner attached to British recognition of Confederate belligerence was the principal source of his differences with the administration. Pressed by Secretary of War John A. Rawlins and other close friends, Grant took a deep interest in the civil war then raging in Cuba and on several occasions was prepared to aid the rebels against Spanish rule by recognizing them as belligerents. The President, therefore, was wary of censuring Britain for doing just what he himself expected to do. Though opposed to recognizing the Cuban insurgents, Fish, too, questioned Sumner's stress on the Queen's neutrality proclamation. Doubtless the

[4] Bemis MSS.

British had acted hastily, but Fish remembered that in the past the United States had often sympathized with popular uprisings and had always insisted that it alone had the right to decide whether to recognize a state of belligerency. "There are therefore," Fish wrote a friend on April 22, "two strong sides to this point of the question." [5]

Not until more than a month after the "Alabama Claims" speech did Fish awake to the fact that Sumner differed with him not simply over abstract points of international law but over the direction of American foreign policy. Burdened with unaccustomed labor during the early weeks of the administration, Fish had no time to prepare the necessary instructions for Motley, who was going abroad as American minister to Great Britain. After dinner at Samuel Hooper's one evening in April, the Secretary lamented the delay, and Sumner, who was a fellow guest, promptly suggested: "Why not levy on Motley? Let him write a memoir, to be used in whole or part, or not at all, as you see fit." Understanding that Motley desired the assignment, Fish gladly assented.[6] On April 26 he received the results of Motley's researches in the State Department's archives, in the form of a long, lurid "Memoir" recounting the whole catalogue of American complaints against Great Britain. In words that might have been cribbed from Sumner's speech, Motley announced that "the premature, superfluous and ostentatious" recognition of Confederate belligerency was "the fountain and origin" of American grievances, since it was an attempt "to doom to death, so far as an English decree could doom it, the American Republic." Like Sumner he argued that granting of belligerent rights on the ocean to a Confederacy which had "no rebel navy, no rebel port, no rebel prize court . . . no rebel dock yards, no ships" had been a

[5] Allan Nevins: *Hamilton Fish: The Inner History of the Grant Administration* (New York: Dodd, Mead & Company; 1936), pp. 159–160; Cook: "The Road to Geneva," p. 306. Professor Nevins holds (p. 154) that Sumner's speech came as "a complete and unwelcome surprise" to Fish. Possibly so, but except for one letter expressing doubts about Sumner's argument on the belligerency question, Fish said and wrote nothing critical of Sumner until May 17. The most recent student of the question, Adrian Cook, concludes: "Fish did not differ too much from Sumner in his view of the question at this time."

[6] Washington correspondence, July 21, 1870, of Boston *Journal*, undated clipping in Sumner Scrapbooks. Later Sumner and Fish quarreled over the extent to which Motley had been a volunteer. Fish to Sumner, July 18, 1870, Sumner MSS.; Sumner to Fish, [July 19, 1870], Fish MSS.

clear violation of international law. Omniously Motley's "Memoir" concluded: "The prodigious accumulation of debt owing to the protraction of the conflict . . . , the hundreds of thousands of slaughtered men . . . , who might now be alive . . . , cannot be measured" in monetary terms, "but the memory of the wrong must grow ever deeper until there had been recognition and atonement." [7]

Since Motley's "Memoir," for all its thundering rhetoric, concluded lamely with a suggestion that Great Britain and the United States should "pause for a season" before resuming negotiations, it was really not a dangerous document which might provoke war. With minor verbal revisions Fish might have accepted it in full, labeling it, however, as Lincoln had once done one of Seward's threatening despatches to Charles Francis Adams: "This paper is for your own guidance only and not [to] be read or shown to any one." [8] But if Motley's "Memoir" did not endanger international peace it did threaten Fish's control over American foreign relations. Recognizing that Motley's manuscript was only an echo of Sumner's speech, Fish gave a single emphatic comment after he read it and put it away in a drawer.

Then, with the help of the Assistant Secretary of State, J. C. Bancroft Davis, he drafted his own set of instructions for Motley, which, by stressing the one major point on which Sumner and Grant differed, would remind the erring minister of his proper loyalties. Though Fish himself had originally been undecided on the belligerency question, he now unequivocally rejected Sumner's position. "The President wishes it understood," Motley's new instructions read firmly, "that he does not complain of the fact of the accordance by Great Britain . . . of belligerent rights to the insurgent population during the late rebellion. . . . He recognizes the right of Every Power, when a civil conflict has arisen within another State, and has attained a sufficient complexity, magnitude, and completeness to define its own relations . . . toward . . . the conflict. . . . He does not rest the claims of this nation against Gt Britain upon the time of issuing the

[7] Copy, Fish MSS.

[8] Randall: *Lincoln the President,* II, 35–6. For Sumner's relation to this despatch, see above, pp. 20–21.

proclamation of neutrality by the latter Govt." Fish went on to add that the time and the manner of the issuance of the British neutrality proclamation entered the American case "only as they foreshadow subsequent events." Both in official and private conversation Motley was directed to follow these instructions to the letter.[9]

Sumner became very agitated when he heard of the shelving of Motley's "Memoir." Though he considered Motley's paper "a model of composition, covering absolutely the ground of my speech, in gross and in detail,"[1] he did not in fact think it suitable to serve as instructions for the American minister.[2] But that it should be so unceremoniously rejected was a slap less at Motley than at himself. Surely his old friend Fish could not have committed such a blunder, and Sumner blamed Bancroft Davis, who was, after all, the son of the conservative Massachusetts Whig, John Davis, Sumner's one-time colleague in the Senate, and the nephew of the Democrat George Bancroft. Three times on May 13 Sumner unsuccessfully called at Davis's house to protest, and when, on his fourth visit, he found the Assistant Secretary at home, he launched into "an animated conversation, more like a speech," denouncing the proposed new instructions for Motley with a tremulous manner and in a loud voice. Angrily he demanded: "Is it the purpose of this Administration to sacrifice me,—me, a senator from Massachusetts?" Davis replied that he was only a subordinate and had not yet seen the instructions, and he urged Sumner to call on Fish.

That evening Sumner did visit the Secretary at his home, where he was cordially received, and the two men talked until about ten thirty. Leaving, Sumner paused on the doorstep to

[9] The Manuscript Division of the Library of Congress contains a set of photographic reproductions, probably preserved by J. C. B. Davis, of all the documents pertinent to the framing of Motley's instructions: Fish's original draft; Sumner's first proposed revision; Sumner's second proposed amendment; Fish's revised draft; and the final version worked out by Fish and Caleb Cushing. Unless otherwise identified, all quotations in the following pages are drawn from this source.

[1] Sumner to Lieber, May 30, 1869, Sumner MSS.

[2] Fish declared that Sumner "partially if not wholly concurred" in his opinion of the usefulness of the "Memoir." Fish to Sumner, July 19, 1870, copy, Fish MSS.

reargue his case. Fish replied, and Sumner answered in his loud, angry senatorial voice. Presently the Secretary felt obliged to stop him. "Sumner, you roar like the bull of Bashan," he said. "The police will be after us. I think we had better adjourn." [3]

The next day Sumner went to the State Department to renew his argument. When Fish showed him the proposed new instructions for Motley, he promptly pronounced them "fatal,—very." [4] In his fury he allowed himself, as Fish possibly anticipated, to be maneuvered toward a position that was ultimately to prove his undoing. Up to this time though Sumner had always stressed that British concession of belligerent status to the South had been "precipitate, unfriendly, and immoral," the "first stage" in later British depredations upon American commerce, he had never argued that the Queen's neutrality proclamation was the legal foundation for United States claims. In recent months, in fact, he had been specially cautious upon this very point, partly because he knew the precedents in international law were obscure, chiefly because he was aware Grant wanted to extend similar recognition to the Cuban insurgents. But now, choked with wrath over Fish's slap at Motley, he permitted the British concession of belligerency to become more and more central in his thinking. Except for the *Alabama* itself, he declaimed, the evidence that Great Britain had been negligent in enforcing her neutrality laws was not conclusive. The only way to secure compensation for damages wrought by other British-built raiders was to challenge the Queen's neutrality proclamation, which had "opened to the rebels the ship-yards and store-houses of England, lifting from the assistance they might supply the criminal character which it would have had otherwise, and placing [it] under the smaller penalties of violated neutrality." [5]

Fish's instructions to Motley would thus throw away the whole case, and, pacing up and down the Secretary's office, Sumner denounced this surrender of American principles. Finally, flying into a passion, he announced: "Motley shall resign."

[3] J. C. Bancroft Davis: *Mr. Fish and the Alabama Claims* (Boston: Houghton Mifflin and Company; 1893), pp. 31–2.

[4] Pierce, IV, 405.

[5] Sumner to B. F. Butler, June 3, 1869, Butler MSS.

"Very well," replied Fish. "Let him. We'll get a better man in an hour." [6]

The exchange brought both men to their senses, for neither was yet prepared for an open break. As tempers cooled, Fish asked Sumner to write out what he believed Motley's instructions ought to include. Hastily Sumner drafted a paragraph in pencil which insisted that the British proclamation of neutrality was "the beginning of the unjustifiable conduct of England and . . . a part of that prolonged system which resulted so disastrously to the U. States." Since such a statement would be inconsistent with the proposed recognition of Cuban insurgents, Fish knew Grant would stand behind him in rejecting it outright. "I am too much excited now," Sumner granted, sensing that he had gone too far; "allow me to send you another paper." [7]

Calling in Caleb Cushing for advice, Sumner made a second attempt to draft suitable instructions for Motley. His new version showed that he was not yet inflexible on the question of damages resulting from the Queen's proclamation but that, rather than lose all control over the claims question through an outright rupture with both Fish and Grant, he was prepared to make concessions. The Queen's proclamation, so his substitute paragraph now read, was certainly of questionable propriety, but it was "a part of the case only so far as it shows the beginning of that course of conduct, which resulted so disastrously to the U. States. It is less important in itself than from what followed. If there were other Powers that made this concession, it was in England that the concession was supplemented by acts causing direct damages to the U. States."

Pleased to have brought Sumner to heel, Fish was prepared to accept Sumner's suggestions "almost 'in totidem verbis.' " [8] The fact was that he, Sumner, and Grant at this point still did not greatly differ over the claims question: all three disliked the Johnson-Clarendon Convention, felt the need for a new treaty, wanted an expression of regret from Great Britain, hoped for a

[6] Précis of Thornton's despatches, written for Queen Victoria by General Charles Grey, June 16, 1869, Royal Archives. Cf. Fish's memorandum, dated June 13, 1893, J. C. B. Davis MSS.

[7] Davis: *Mr. Fish and the Alabama Claims,* p. 33.

[8] Fish to Sumner, May 17 [1869], Sumner MSS.

revision of international law, and anticipated the ultimate acquisition of Canada. The real difference as yet was over who was to direct foreign policy, and Fish thought this little encounter had proved it was to be the Secretary of State.

On Monday, May 17, 1869, he learned better. The evening before, Sumner had dinner with Caleb Cushing, renowned for his ability to say precisely what his listener wanted to hear. To the attentive Sumner, Cushing reiterated his enthusiasm for his "Alabama Claims" speech, which he found "in complete conformity with the law of nations," and expressed regret over the paragraph Sumner had just sent Fish, because it "toned down the true doctrine and inadequately stated our case." "I knew it was so," Sumner confessed, "but I did it in order to harmonize the ideas of the Administration with our case." The next morning, with Cushing at his side to remind him of his historic duty, he withdrew his compromise draft and stiffly wrote to Fish: "It will be for Congress to determine hereafter how much shall be claimed and on what grounds. . . . Under these circumstances I am more than ever satisfied, that, as Chairman of the Senate Committee, I ought not in any way to be a party to a statement which abandons or enfeebles any of the just grounds of my country, as already expounded by Seward Adams and myself." The best course would have been to allow Motley "to speak according to his own enlightened discretion." Failing that, Fish must be prepared to submit to the judgment of Congress on the claims question, and Sumner ominously predicted: "It will not take any steps backward." [9]

For once Fish's composure was shattered. Neither he nor Grant was prepared to have a public quarrel with Sumner, especially when few would be able to understand the technical quibbles at stake and when public opinion, so far as there could be one on this complex question, was certain to favor the Senator. Moreover, Fish was not even certain that he had Grant's backing, for there is nothing to indicate that he consulted the President during the little game of bluff he had been playing with Sumner. He had no alternative but surrender. "I think you are scarcely doing justice either to me or to the Administration," he replied

[9] Pierce, IV, 406; Sumner to Fish [May 17, 1869], Fish MSS.

plaintively to Sumner's letter withdrawing his memorandum. "We have but one object and differ only as to some incidents—they may be of more importance than I suppose, or of less than you think. But can hardly be of sufficient importance to break up an effort at negotiation, or to break down an Administration." He begged Sumner to reconsider "the intimations" of his letter.[1]

Content with this recognition of his power, Sumner sent Cushing to the State Department to work out a compromise, and after four hours of negotiation a new draft of Motley's instructions was prepared and submitted for Sumner's approval. Finding that "the clause abandoning our position on belligerency is given up" and that the rest of the paragraph was pretty much as he had written it, the Senator accepted the new version,[2] which went out to Motley under the incorrect date of May 15.

As to who had won the war, the two principals were later to disagree. Sumner argued that Motley's final instructions varied "in no essential particular" from his own draft, while Fish claimed to have made only "a *slight* alteration in the last two paragraphs" of the instructions. So far as the wording of the instructions was concerned, the contest was in fact a draw.[3] The ideas of both men—never truly far apart—were somewhat imperfectly cemented together in the instructions. Fish had his way in asserting: "The President recognizes the right of every Power, when a civil conflict has arisen within another state, and has attained a sufficient complexity, magnitude, and completeness, to define its own relations and those of its citizens and subjects toward the parties to the conflict"; but Sumner also scored by adding that the United States regarded the British neutrality proclamation as being of questionable necessity and propriety and that it therefore became "part of the case" insofar as "it shows the beginning and animus of that course of conduct which resulted so disastrously to the United States. It is impor-

[1] Fish to Sumner, May 17 [1869], Sumner MSS.

[2] Pierce, IV, 406.

[3] Sumner: *Works,* XIV, 272; Nevins: *Fish,* p. 167. J. C. B. Davis says the final instructions show "a complete abandonment of the position for which Mr. Sumner had contended in his speech" (*Mr. Fish and the Alabama Claims,* p. 36), and Professor Nevins writes: "On all essential points Fish stood his ground." E. L. Pierce, on the other hand, states that "Sumner was content with the result."

tant, in that it foreshadows subsequent events." As to which portion of the instructions would carry greater weight, that would of course depend upon who was interpreting them.

But the point of the struggle was not phraseology but power, and Sumner emerged clearly the victor. So long as he did not insist upon wording that would prevent Grant from recognizing Cuban belligerency, he could make Fish do his bidding. He had demonstrated that he exercised not merely the customary senatorial veto over the conduct of American foreign policy; he had named the American minister to Great Britain and had dictated his instructions. So thoroughly defeated was Fish that he did not even tempt Sumner's wrath again by telling Motley he disapproved of his intemperate "Memoir." Transmitting instructions to the minister, Fish evasively declared that he might have drawn upon Motley's paper but for the fact that it now seemed best to have "some intermission of discussion" as to the claims, so that excitement and irritation on both sides of the Atlantic could subside.[4]

• 5 •

Sumner had won, and he knew it. Fully to exploit his victory he needed the President's backing, and during May and June he was a frequent visitor at the White House. Dining with Grant on May 26, he expressed the hope that the President had not been disturbed by the storm of English protest over his speech. "Not in the least," replied Grant grimly; "let it go on." After all, the President added, Britain was an enemy, whose conduct during the Civil War "could not be overstated in its mischief." At about this time, too, Grant, though still declining to base the American case against Britain on the Queen's neutrality proclamation, told Sumner that he now "was entirely satisfied that England made the concession of belligerency 'to injure us.'" Seeing the President alone for an hour again on June 7, Sumner once more received his endorsement, together with the comment that Motley was clearly "the best man for England now." Triumphant, Sumner promptly called on Thornton to inform him that Grant

[4] Fish to Motley, May 17, 1869, copy, Fish MSS.

"had expressed his approval of all his arguments," and the British minister sourly concluded that the Senator was now "so carried away by his illusions and his vanity that any reasonable discussion is out of the question." "England must listen, and at last yield," Sumner predicted; the prolonged debate would finally end "(1) In the withdrawal of England from this hemisphere; (2) In remodelling maritime international law." "Such a consummation," he grandly concluded, "would place our republic at the head of the civilized world." [5]

But Fish, though defeated, had not been displaced from his office, and he had already quietly set to work with Dutch doggedness to recapture control over American foreign policy. On the very day that Sumner dictated the terms of Motley's instructions, the Secretary, for the first time since he assumed office, began to look for allies. Regarding Fessenden as the most reasonable man in the Senate and knowing well his long animosity against Sumner, Fish wrote him confidentially on May 17: "Do you approve the argument of Sumner's speech on the Claims treaty—or do you think it would be safe to rest our case upon the general ground set forth in that speech?" At the same time he told Francis Lieber, Samuel B. Ruggles, and other New York friends that Sumner's speech, while distinguished for its "eloquence, and the display of learning and of research," rested upon flimsy legal foundations, and he hinted: "It would be well if some well considered articles in this direction could appear in some of the leading papers." Fish also let Robert C. Winthrop, still the most influential of Sumner's conservative critics in Boston, know that he regarded "recent utterings" on the claims question "not wholly tenable as expositions of public laws or as logical deductions, either in argument, or of fact." Most important of all, he told the British minister that "Mr. Sumner could not be considered as the exponent of the opinions of the people in general or of his colleagues." [6] By midsummer the Secretary was gratified that Godkin in *The Nation,* Lieber in the *Evening Post,* and James C.

[5] Pierce, IV, 393, 409–10; Thornton to Clarendon, June 14, 1869, Clarendon MSS.

[6] Fish to Fessenden, May 17, 1869, copy, Fish MSS.; Fish to Ruggles, May 18, 1869, copy, ibid.; Fish to Winthrop, May 25, 1869, Winthrop MSS.; précis of Thornton to Clarendon, May 17, 1869, copy, Royal Archives.

Hamilton in the *Tribune* were all attacking Sumner's law and logic.

He was, however, still far from being strong enough to challenge Sumner directly. When the newspapers carried reports that Fish had won the battle over Motley's instructions and was now chuckling over his success in having "completely checkmated the Senator, President Grant sustaining the Secretary in oppositon to the views of the Massachusetts legislator," Sumner called him to heel. "There should be union at home," he informed him.[7] Obediently Fish dictated a special despatch which promptly appeared in the New York *Evening Post* on June 19, denying differences between the Senator and the Secretary and affirming: "In fact, at no time has Mr. Sumner been in closer accord or in more direct sympathy with the policy of President Grant than at present, and rumors of disagreement are entirely unfounded."

Flushed with victory, Sumner may well have thought the announcement was true. At any rate, he could afford to be a good winner. Though he carped a little over the wording of Fish's statement, he accepted it as the surrender it was, and he was now prepared to believe that the Secretary had been not merely defeated but converted. Doubtless Fish's errors had been due to his lack of knowledge about foreign affairs. "With more experience at Washington," Sumner assured Motley, "our front would have been more perfect." Whatever the problems of the past, there was now unity behind Sumner's position, and he exulted: "*The President, Secretary of State, Minister to London and Chairman of Senate Committee are all of one mind. . . .*"[8] Satisfied that he was in complete control, Sumner left Washington in the latter part of June, and his Massachusetts friends found him happier than he had been since the breakup of his marriage, full of self-importance and grandly loquacious. He monopolized the conversation at several sessions of the Saturday Club and, attending a musical festival in Boston, "talked all the

[7] New York *Herald,* June 17, 1869; Pierce: *Sumner,* IV, 407. Cushing again served as Sumner's intermediary with Fish. Julius Bing to Sumner, June 16, 1869, Sumner MSS.

[8] Pierce, IV, 410; Sumner to George Bemis, July 7, 1869, Bemis MSS.

time during *Ole Bull's solo.*"[9] In August, possibly with the purpose of keeping an eye on the Secretary of State, who had returned to his New York home at Glenclyffe, Sumner visited old friends at Albany and at Fishkill-on-Hudson, and then he spent a few days with Fish himself.

The Secretary of State, however, was fully aware that his newspaper statement was not true, but an exposure of his difference with Sumner would reveal Fish's weak role in drafting Motley's instructions and would endanger the success of his mission. Moreover, important political considerations required Fish to hold his tongue. Warned by the closeness of Grant's victory in 1868 that hostility to the South and friendship for the freedman would not forever provide a winning coalition, some Republican leaders were restlessly looking for a new issue, and a few at least believed they had found it in Sumner's "Alabama Claims" speech. It was not surprising that Zachariah Chandler, always an expansionist, endorsed Sumner's argument, wryly noting that it was no more than what he himself had advocated for years, or that Ben Butler tried to go Sumner one better in proposing immediate non-intercourse with Britain followed probably by war when England was preoccupied elsewhere. But when cautious Republican politicians like Andrew G. Curtin, former governor of Pennsylvania, began thinking they could restore their political fortunes by stressing the anti-English theme, there was a real possibility for a realignment of American politics that might leave Grant's administration without support. On the one side would be grouped the Union veterans, who were wholeheartedly anti-English, "the whole Irish array," disappointed office-seekers, "southern adventurers," and large numbers from the Democratic rank and file; opposed to them would be only "the respectable classes of the republicans," the present officeholders, and some conservative Democrats.[1] For such a political reshuffling—which in fact was curiously like that attempted by the Liberal Republicans in 1872—Sumner's assent was essential. As newspapers carried stories of the tumultuous acceptance of his

[9] N. P. Banks to his wife, June 20, 1869, Banks MSS.

[1] Charles Francis Adams to Henry Adams, June 16, 1869, Adams MSS.; New York *Herald,* June 11–12, 1869; Boston *Advertiser,* June 3, 1869; Springfield *Republican,* June 11–12, 1869.

views by assorted Irish-American conventions and reports that he might make a grand tour of the West to rally further support, Grant and Fish felt obliged to appease him.[2] If Sumner wished a denial of differences with the administration, Fish had to issue it.

So great was the political danger in midsummer that Fish could not permit even open insubordination on Motley's part to cause a quarrel with Sumner. Though appointed by the President, Motley was quite aware that he owed his post to Sumner. Indeed, he could hardly forget that fact, since Sumner himself never mentioned Motley "otherwise than as *his* agent" and since the British government received him as "the bearer of Mr. Sumner's demands." "As you . . . hold such a commanding position in the country," the minister wrote Sumner shortly after he arrived in London, "I shall always be grateful to you for constant communications." The letters Sumner wrote Motley have not been discovered, but it is safe to guess that he urged the minister to defend his "Alabama Claims" speech as the authorized statement of American grievances. His instructions were, however, hardly needed, for Motley had read Sumner's speech no fewer than six times before it was delivered, and he accepted its arguments absolutely.[3]

Vaguely Motley was aware that there might be a conflict between his loyalty to Sumner and his duty to the State Department, but with characteristic impatience he brushed aside the difficulty, confident that his brilliance, charm, and literary grace could overcome any problem. In the compromise phraseology of his instructions, over which Fish and Sumner had so violently quarreled, he thought he saw a way to serve both masters. Directed not "to enter upon a renewed discussion, either of the objections to the lately proposed [Johnson-Clarendon] convention, or of the basis of a renewed discussion,"[4] Motley was not

[2] Note that Sumner's interview with Grant on June 7, while such political speculation was at its height, was a trading session. Sumner approved Grant's order to Curtin not to make an anti-English speech but at once to take up his duties as minister to Russia, and in return Grant said "very kind things" about Motley. Pierce, IV, 409.

[3] Clarendon to Russell, Aug. 10, 1869, Russell MSS.; Clarendon to Gladstone, May 2, 1869, Gladstone MSS.; Motley to Sumner, June 16, 1869, Sumner MSS.; Sumner to Lieber, May 30, 1869, ibid.

[4] *Senate Exec. Doc.*, No. 10, 41 Cong., 3 Sess., p. 4.

forbidden to discuss Sumner's "Alabama Claims" speech, which he found to be generally misunderstood in England. Of course there was some difficulty in defending Sumner's position "without going into the whole matter from beginning to end—a thing wh[ich] I am expressly told not to do at present." However, he wrote Sumner, "I can steer my way easy eno—Defend the speech—expose the wilful misrepresentation of the press and the stupid misunderstanding of the general public and exactly conform to my instructions." [5]

How exactly Motley intended to conform was revealed on June 10, when he had his first significant conversation with Lord Clarendon, the British Foreign Minister. Taking his official instructions as a point of departure rather than as a limitation upon his own views, Motley transformed Fish's statement that the propriety of the British neutrality proclamation was "not admitted" into it was "not considered justifiable." Where Fish had spoken of the British concession of belligerency as showing animus toward the Union cause, Motley complained that it was "the fountain head of the disasters which had been caused to the American people, both individually and collectively." Worst of all, the minister vaguely threatened the British and warned of "the contingencies of war and peace" that depended upon the successful outcome of his mission. The next day when Benjamin Moran, the permanent secretary of the American legation, copied out Motley's long despatch reporting the interview, he correctly surmised that his superior had not expressed Fish's views and that his statement to Clarendon had "more of Mr. Sumner than the President in it." [6]

When the news of Motley's indiscretion reached Washington on June 23, Grant declared he must be dismissed at once, but Fish persuaded him to change his mind. The Secretary of State realized that the United States could not afford another diplomatic fiasco in dealing with Great Britain, and he had already learned that Clarendon was more bored than irritated by Motley's presentation. More important, he recognized that a quarrel

[5] June 7, 1869, Sumner MSS.

[6] *Senate Exec. Doc.*, No. 10, 41 Cong., 3 Sess., pp. 5–10; Nevins: *Fish*, p. 205.

with Sumner now would be politically disastrous. That the Senator would war with the administration if Motley was removed was painfully apparent; but in case anybody missed the obvious, Sumner demanded that the State Department break all protocol and send him a copy of Motley's despatch reporting his interview. Though horrified State Department underlings exclaimed that "such a thing has never been done before," Fish approved Sumner's request.[7] He also retained Motley as minister, even commending his "general presentation" of his subject to Clarendon and noting that "if there were expressions used stronger than were required by . . . instructions, the excess was in the right direction." [8] He did, however, try to curb the impetuous minister by announcing that all further discussion of the claims question would be conducted in Washington, not in London. This new directive was, as the veteran Moran noted, "a censure and a rebuke which few men would stand and not resign," but Fish made it tolerable to the sensitive Motley and to Sumner, to whom the minister regularly reported, by explaining that, "however discreet he might have been, and however scrupulously he might have followed his instructions," subsequent exploration of the issues with Britain would nevertheless have been removed to the United States "*because* we think that when renewed, it can be carried on *here* with a better prospect of settlement." [9] In negotiations held at Washington, of course, Sumner himself, rather than his chosen minister, could expect to play a leading role.

In case Fish was ever tempted to assert his independence, Sumner kept reminding the Secretary, in frequent letters throughout the summer months of 1869, where the real control over American foreign policy now lay. There must be firmness in presenting the American case against Great Britain, he warned, or Congress would insist upon debating the whole issue. "The more I reflect upon our Case and confer with our best people

[7] William Hunter to Sumner, July 8, 1869, Sumner MSS.; Fish to Sumner, July 10, 1869, copy, ibid.

[8] *Senate Exec. Doc.*, No. 10, 41 Cong., 3 Sess., pp. 10–11.

[9] Fish to Sumner, Oct. 9, 1869, Sumner MSS. Possibly Sumner and Motley acquiesced the more easily in Fish's decision because the Secretary warned that "under any other Government than this" the minister's violation of his instructions would have been "followed by the most severe censure and probably by an immediate recall."

here," he wrote Fish from Boston on July 10, "the more I am satisfied that I did not go too far in the statement of our grevance [*sic*]. When the debate comes I think you will find that graves and epitaphs will count." There must, he insisted the next day, be a complete "statement of our case, *so that England may see its extent.*" "When England sees the grievance, as we see it—when she learns that our generals from the President down all believe that the war, with its deaths and its expenditures, with present taxation [to pay for these], was prolonged through her conduct, and that this is the conviction,—let her grasp this idea, and she will be ready for the remedy." [1]

There was, moreover, pressure of time, for Sumner heard ancestral voices prophesying war. "We must keep the case in our hands," he alerted Fish on July 21; otherwise "politicians"—presumably men like Chandler and Butler and Curtin—would take over. The precise distinction between Sumner himself and a politician might well have eluded the unimaginative Secretary, but he could not fail to understand the self-fulfilling prediction of the Senator that without a prompt exposition of American injuries there would be "dissatisfaction" when Congress assembled. Weary, Fish once more recognized Sumner's power and told him to write out the statement of grievances himself. Cautiously Sumner refused. He had already made his speech, he told the Secretary; he was too busy.[2] What he wanted was to dictate the policies of the State Department without being responsible for them. Once again Fish turned to Cushing, who he knew would draft a statement of American claims acceptable to Sumner.

When Cushing's memorandum, in the form of new instructions to Motley, was finished in September, Fish had not the strength to oppose it. The death of Rawlins on September 6 removed the principal supporter of the Cuban rebels and left Grant more amenable to Sumner's arguments about the British neutrality proclamation. Fessenden, the one Senator who might have assisted the Secretary by serving as a counterweight to Sumner, died two days later. To keep up the pressure on the

[1] Fish MSS.
[2] Pierce, IV, 412–13.

State Department, Sumner agreed to serve as chairman of the Massachusetts State Republican Convention, which met at Worcester on September 22, 1869, and in a speech on "National Affairs at Home and Abroad" renewed his complaints about Britain's "great transgression" during the Civil War.

Two days later the cabinet approved the instructions Cushing had drafted for Motley, and the extent of Sumner's power was once more clear. "I think matters with England are going to your mind," Attorney General E. Rockwood Hoar assured the Senator, "and that your speech and our acts will not trouble each other." [3] Though the new statement of American claims did not challenge the legality of the British recognition of Confederate belligerency, it earnestly condemned its unreasonable precipitancy as the sign of a purpose of unfriendliness to the United States, and of friendliness to the insurgents. "We complain that the insurrection in the Southern States . . . obtained its enduring vitality by means of the resources it drew from Great Britain," the despatch continued, and it concluded with a Sumnerian thrust: "Great Britain alone . . . founded on that recognition a systematic maritime war against the United States; and this to effect the establishment of a Slave Government!" When Motley presented the long communication to Clarendon, the British Foreign Minister correctly concluded that it was nothing but "a réchauffé of Sumner's last speech," now "framed in a most malignant spirit." "Mr. Sumner must be well pleased," Clarendon concluded, "as he evidently directs the foreign policy of his Government. . . ." [4]

Months before the receipt of this latest piece of evidence the British had already decided that Sumner, not Fish, was dominant in Washington.[5] As early as June Thornton had tried a quiet exploration of the claims question with the Secretary of State and had succeeded in eliciting from him the opinion that Sumner's positions were "impracticable"; but when it came to

[3] Hoar to Sumner, Sept. 24, 1869, Sumner MSS.

[4] "Correspondence Respecting the 'Alabama' Claims: 1869–1870," *British Sessional Papers*, XLIX, 443–448; Clarendon to Russell, Oct. 16, 1869, Russell MSS.; Clarendon to Thornton, Oct. 23, 1869, copy, Clarendon MSS.

[5] For a full account of these 1869 attempts at negotiation, see Nevins: *Fish*, pp. 212–14, 219, 221–22, 228–30.

concrete proposals for settlement, Fish, lacking power, evasively raised the possibility of annexing Canada. The reason for the Secretary's vagueness was his uncertainty about Sumner's expectations; all he could extract from the sibyl of the Senate was the oracular opinion that it was too early to assess damages and that the United States "should make no 'claim' or 'demand' for the present." [6] Nor was John Rose, the Canadian Minister of Finance, who visited Washington in July on his way to London, more successful in securing from the Secretary of State any clarification of American terms. Unable to predict what Sumner and the Senate might do, Fish could only express his personal dissent from some of Sumner's arguments and hope that another treaty might contain an expression of regret by the British along with some "agreement as to the laws of neutrality for the future."

Nor did Thornton have more luck when he tried again in November to get Fish to intimate what terms the United States might accept. The Secretary replied that he could not act without consulting Sumner, "for . . . however impossible some of his arguments . . . might be, his influence in the Senate was too great to be overlooked, and it would be necessary to bring him round to something reasonable." But when Fish passed along the British query to the Senator, he received the invariable reply: "I do not think that at the moment any body here can *formularize* any proposal to England. Time must intervene, in order to ascertain what the people will require." "This," he added ominously, "will be seen in the probable debates of Congress." Fish had to report back to the British minister that the time was not yet ripe. "I daresay," wrote Clarendon when he heard the news, "that the President and Mr. Fish dislike Sumner but as it is clear that they are afraid of him and don't dare move without his sanction . . . I see nothing before us but a prolonged disagreement." [7]

Both the probable length of that disagreement and the degree of Sumner's influence were revealed in the "careful, explicit and firm statement" of American grievances against Great

[6] Pierce, IV, 409–10.

[7] Thornton to Clarendon, Private, Nov. 2, 1869, Clarendon MSS.; Sumner to Fish, Nov. 9, 1869, Fish MSS.; Clarendon to Thornton, Nov. 27, 1869, Clarendon MSS.

Britain which Fish, at Sumner's insistence, inserted in the President's message to Congress in December.[8] Commending the "wisely taken" action of the Senate in rejecting the Johnson-Clarendon Convention, Grant was made to review the "grave wrongs" resulting from the British course, as revealed "in the increased rates of insurance; in the diminution of exports and imports . . . ; in its effect upon the foreign commerce of the country; in the decrease and transfer to Great Britain of our commercial marine; in the prolongation of the war and the increased cost (both in treasure and in lives) of its suppression."[9] The voice was Grant's, the pen was Fish's, but the thought was Sumner's.

[8] Sumner to Fish, Nov. 9, 1869, Fish MSS.

[9] James D. Richardson (ed.): *A Compilation of the Messages and Papers of the Presidents* (Washington: Government Printing Office; 1898), VII, 32–5.

CHAPTER XI

The Greatest Champion of Liberty

WHEN Congress reconvened in December 1869, Sumner was in a buoyant mood. For once he was in a position to exercise power commensurate with his seniority. The death of Fessenden had removed his major rival from the Senate. His summer skirmishes with Fish had reduced the State Department to following his orders. Most of all, widespread praise for his "Alabama Claims" address gave him the right to speak for a broader following than ever before. His correspondents addressed him as "the father of the Senate, and . . . the ablest man in it." Even his colleagues recognized that he was "emphatically the leader of this Senate."[1] With self-satisfaction Sumner clipped for his scrapbook an editorial from the obscure *Weekly Publisher* predicting that this long "acknowledged champion of the equal rights of all men under the law" was now "about to rise into the position of acknowledged leader" of the Senate. It bore the gratifying title: "Sumner, the Leader."

Visitors to Washington found him more than ever the most conspicuous member of the Senate. Now he was showing some signs of age. His thick hair was iron-gray, and he wore it very long, allowing it to hang "low over the forehead, as if to conceal the vast intellect hidden there." For all his regular features, his

[1] J. Watson Webb to Sumner, Dec. 6, 1869, Sumner MSS.; *Cong. Globe*, 41 Cong., 2 Sess., p. 4196.

face now had a certain coarseness and heaviness, and he wore eyeglasses when he read. From the too devoted services of his excellent cook he had developed a middle-aged paunch; finding that his clothes were too tight, he stepped on the scales to discover with astonishment that his weight had jumped from 203 to 234½ pounds. But there was still vigor in his burly, erect figure and in his thunderous, if hoarse, voice. No visit to the Capitol was complete without hearing Sumner speak or at least gazing at him from the gallery as he sat with "his legs stuck out straight to full length before him, his hands on the arms of his chair, his lips protruding dubitably, his brow half furrowed between listening and thought." [2]

There was much listening to do in the second session of the Forty-First Congress, for its deliberations lasted until July 15, 1870, and filled 6,435 pages of fine print in the *Congressional Globe*. Always regular in his attendance, Sumner seemed omnipresent during this session; a list of his activities occupied more than three columns of the *Globe* index. He made a speech on every important measure that came before the Senate, usually a carefully prepared address which he read to his colleagues from printed slips or galley proofs. Active as always on measures involving reconstruction and foreign affairs, he also spoke forty-one times on funding the United States debt and thirty-six times on the post office appropriation bill. More than in any previous session he was willing to engage in close parliamentary infighting; his persistent, indeed almost pertinacious, battle to secure a pension for Mary Lincoln, in the face of powerful opposition from the pension committee,[3] was simply one of his many successes, both small and large, in a session which he dominated. So numerous were Sumner's labors that it was only half sarcastically that Timothy O. Howe called him the Hercules of the Senate.

Of course Sumner did not always get his own way, even during the early months of the session. When he ventured outside his usual areas of legislative interest to produce plans for

[2] Chicago *Republican*, Mar. 13, 1870; Sumner to Longfellow, May 18, 1870, Longfellow MSS.

[3] See Ruth P. Randall: *Mary Lincoln*, pp. 416–20.

funding the national debt, his colleagues, along with *The Nation*, tended to ask in exasperation: "Why cannot men who do not understand finance, and whose mental powers and training do not fit them to deal with its problems, leave the finances alone?" Sumner's slogan: *"Down with the taxes!"* gained some applause, and thinking men agreed with his argument that payment of the national debt should be shared by "succeeding generations, for whom, as well as for ourselves, it was incurred." But few took seriously his more technical proposals, such as that for resuming specie payments on January 1, 1871, by substituting additional bank notes for the greenbacks, and the Senate followed John Sherman's lead on financial legislation.[4]

But on matters closest to his own heart Sumner, to an extraordinary extent, led the Senate during the first four months of the session. Foreign relations he clearly controlled, and Secretary Fish seemed reconciled to following his lead. So far as the Alabama Claims were concerned, Sumner was content to rest the American case upon the strong despatch of September 25, 1869, which he had forced Fish to send, and early in the session he called his colleagues' attention to this statement of American grievances as "one of the ablest and most masterly State papers in our history."[5] The next move he was willing to leave to England.

On the question of Cuba, too, the Senator and the Secretary cooperated closely. Like Fish,[6] Sumner sympathized with the Cuban rebels but strongly opposed recognizing them as belligerents. Since they controlled no town of importance and no port, he thought it would "be quite absurd for us to grant them belligerent rights." First of all, such an action would gravely prejudice the claims the United States was making against Great Britain, partly on the ground of hasty recognition of Confederate belligerency in 1861. Second, it would discourage the liberals in Spain, who in 1868 had deposed the profligate and immoral

[4] *The Nation,* X (Mar. 24, 1870), 183–4; Sumner: *Works,* XIII, 234–98.

[5] *Cong. Globe,* 41 Cong., 2 Sess., p. 302.

[6] For an approving view of the Secretary of State's course toward Cuba, see Nevins: *Fish,* Chaps. 9 and 11. Philip S. Foner: *A History of Cuba and Its Relations with the United States: Volume II, 1845–1895* (New York: International Publishers; 1963), Chaps. 17 and 18, is sharply critical.

Queen Isabella II. If not provoked by American intervention, they would inevitably come to see that "the day of European colonies has passed—at least in this hemisphere" and would free Cuba and Puerto Rico. Then the two islands, along with the other Antilles, would naturally "gravitate into independent relations with the United States" and become American protectorates. But if the United States recognized the Cuban insurgents, Spain might well declare war, and during the ensuing conflict many Americans would demand the annexation of the island, to which Sumner was strongly opposed. "The Cubans don't speak our language," he explained. "The mass of them know very little about our customs or our institutions. They would not be an intelligent acquisition, and I cannot see that they would be valuable in any respect." In consequence, the true course of the United States toward the Cuban insurrection was "to avoid involving ourselves in any way." [7]

During the summer of 1869 he and Fish collaborated to keep the President on that course,[8] but by fall, pressure for American intervention began once more to build up. On December 6, the first day of the new session of Congress, Simon Cameron presented a petition, bearing thirty thousand signatures, for the recognition of Cuban belligerency. Forewarned by Fish, Sumner was ready and promptly moved its reference, without discussion, to the Foreign Relations Committee, where he knew he could kill it, just as he had quietly buried a similar House resolution the previous April. For weeks Sumner's mail was filled with denunciations, and newspapers blasted him as "that Old Man of the Sea, who has mercilessly endeavored to crush the Cuban patriots," but he imperturbably kept the Senate from debating the Cuban question.

Furious, the friends of the Cubans tried to circumvent the Foreign Relations Committee. On December 15 freshman Republican Senator Matthew Hale Carpenter of Wisconsin made a

[7] New York *Herald*, Dec. 28, 1869, and Mar. 7, 1870; Sumner: *Works*, XIII, 120.

[8] For Sumner's connection with a project for the Cubans to purchase their independence, see Springfield *Republican*, Dec. 22, 1869; Springfield *Weekly Republican*, Mar. 18, 1870; *Cong. Globe*, 40 Cong., 2 Sess., p. 1920; Sumner to Fish, July 21, 1869, Fish MSS.

passionate plea for immediate action to prevent the sailing of gunboats being built in American shipyards at the order of the Spanish government, obviously for use in Cuban waters. There was no time, argued Carpenter, to refer his proposal to Sumner's Foreign Relations Committee, where "that honorable and honored Senator" would surely cause further delay; it was, therefore, necessary to breach "the traditional courtesies of the Senate" so that the United States could maintain its tradition of aiding "the oppressed and down trodden of all lands." Eighteen of the gunboats were preparing to sail, Carpenter concluded urgently; the Senate must act or be prepared to stand before "the bar of impartial history" charged with failing to do its duty.

At this emotional point in the proceedings Sumner claimed the floor for another *coup de théâtre*, comparable to his torpedoing of the Fenian agitation in 1867. He read a telegram, just received, to the effect that the gunboats in New York had already been turned over to the Spanish authorities, had their officers and crew on board, and were flying the flag of Spain. Carpenter was too late. Improving upon the occasion, Sumner went on to inform the Wisconsin Senator that he failed to understand international law, insofar as it related to the duties of neutrals, for the Cuban insurgents, having "no provinces—no towns—no ports—no prize courts," had "not reached the condition of belligerents." "I have no disposition to go into this subject at length," Sumner declared, with an air of finality. His colleagues, well aware that he was in fact prepared to go into it at great length and that he remained able to strangle any recognition of the insurgents, for the time let the Cuban issue drop.[9]

Still the question would not die, and in February John Sherman moved to recognize the existence of a state of war between Spain and its Cuban colony; his motive, according to British minister Thornton, was less concern for the plight of the Cubans than "hatred towards Sumner and because he thought it would annoy him with reference to our [Alabama Claims] question." Whatever Sherman's intent, his resolution went automati-

[9] *Cong. Globe*, 41 Cong., 2 Sess., pp. 140–5. For a review of the debate hostile to Sumner, see E. Bruce Thompson: *Matthew Hale Carpenter: Webster of the West* (Madison, Wis.: The State Historical Society of Wisconsin; 1954), pp. 128–31.

cally to the Foreign Relations Committee, where Sumner assured him with all apparent seriousness it would be carefully considered. Then he gave the game away by adding: "It has been."[1] Sherman's proposal, as anticipated, died in committee.

Less easy to kill was a resolution calling for the President to issue a proclamation of neutrality in the Cuban conflict, which the House passed in June 1870 by an overwhelming majority. Sumner and his fellow committee members worked over the House proposal and on June 23 reported out as a substitute a thundering set of resolutions that condemned the "barbarous outrage" going on in Cuba, denounced the continued existence of slavery on that island, deplored "the extraordinary efforts of the Spanish Government by violence and blood, to maintain unnatural jurisdiction of Cuba, forbidden by the great law of progress," and assured both the Cuban rebels and the Spanish liberals of American sympathy in their fight for liberty—and concluded, lamely, with a call for the President to transmit these worthy sentiments to the Spanish government. "*Vox et praeterea nihil,*" snorted Senator Allen Thurman; the resolutions offered not "one single practical aid that can be conceived" for the Cuban insurrection.[2] In fact, Sumner's strategy was masterly, for, with Fish's constant aid, he had transformed dangerous action into resounding words, and the move to recognize the Cuban rebels was dead for the session. Shortly afterward the collapse of the insurrection removed the issue from American politics for the rest of the decade.

• 2 •

On reconstruction measures, too, Sumner led the Senate during the early months of the session. Until late in 1869 it had been possible for many Republicans to believe that Southern whites were basically law-abiding citizens who had been temporarily misled by their slaveholding leaders during the Civil War and to argue that if Congress clearly spelled out the terms for readmis-

[1] Thornton to Hammond, Feb. 22, 1870, Hammond MSS.; *Cong. Globe,* 41 Cong., 2 Sess., p. 1206.

[2] *Cong. Globe,* 41 Cong., 2 Sess., pp. 4752–3, 4806.

sion to the Union—whether they be the abolition of slavery, the enfranchisement of the freedmen, or the creation of a public school system in the South—they would be accepted in good faith. The speed with which each state of the former Confederacy,[3] acting under the basic Reconstruction Act of 1867 and its subsequent amendments, drafted a new constitution and created a new government seemed to prove this theory, and in 1868 representatives from all except Texas, Mississippi, and Virginia had been admitted to Congress. Shortly after inauguration, Grant, confident that Virginia too was "now ready to cooperate with the National Government" and "to give all its people those equal rights under the law which were asserted in the Declaration of Independence," urged Congress to provide for an election in that state, and the legislative branch complied.

By December 1869, however, it was abundantly evident that if the Southern whites were prepared formally to assent to the conditions imposed by Congress they were far from being ready to reorganize their society to comply with Northern wishes. Congress could require state constitutions that gave paper protection to Negro civil rights, but the Southern whites, once back in control, would in effect nullify these provisions. Congress could give the Negro the vote, but all over the South the Ku Klux Klan and other terrorist organizations systematically intimidated the freedmen, flogged or slaughtered their leaders, and drove whites who worked with them into exile. Congress could require federal troops to supervise the registration of voters, but Negroes were waylaid and butchered on the roads to the registration offices. Congress could suppress outright violence by military force, but it could do nothing to protect Negroes from landlords who told them bluntly: "if you vote with that yankee party you shall not live on our land." [4]

Faced with what was in effect a massive campaign of civil disobedience throughout the South, some Northern Republicans were by 1869 ready to give up the whole reconstruction effort and to make the best terms possible with the Southern whites.

[3] Except Tennessee, which had previously been readmitted.

[4] G. Henry Seldon, of Westmoreland County, Va., to Sumner, April 23, 1870, Sumner MSS. Almost daily Sumner received letters describing both open and covert intimidation of Negroes throughout the South.

They reverted to the original thinking of the Conservative faction of the party, arguing that with kindly, considerate treatment the Southerners would acquiesce in at least the minimal guarantees to the Negroes secured in the new constitutional amendments. Anyway, under the Constitution of the United States, Congress could do nothing more. "Let us have peace," Grant had urged in accepting the presidential nomination, and such Republicans welcomed his plea. "When is this question of reconstruction to end?" Lyman Trumbull asked plaintively. "Mr. President, this country is tired of this question." "Reconstruction has been under consideration for five years," echoed William Stewart, of Nevada: "the country wants it terminated if it can be done with safety. . . . We want an end of reconstruction." [5]

Most Republicans were not yet ready to accept this Conservative view, which was both discredited by the experience of the past four years and tainted by association with Andrew Johnson. They were convinced that the former Confederates were still foes of the Union. "You know well that a *converted* rebel is not within the scope of Divine Power to make," the New York lawyer, Edwards Pierrepont, wrote Sumner. "The rebels, and their sons and their daughters, their wives are our *enemies*—they yield to force, but the will is unconquered." [6] Somehow they must be subdued through a new and even more stringent program of reconstruction. Yet for this task Grant seemed hopeless; his ideas on reconstruction were impenetrable, even to his closest associates. The New Radicals, political technicians devoid of ideology, could not devise effective measures against a resistance that derived from deep-seated Southern racial prejudice and long-cherished theories of state rights. Most of the Old Radicals, the men who had for the past four years been devising Republican strategy, were now gone from the Washington scene.

Sumner was one of the few who remained, and during the winter of 1869–70 he emerged, for the first time in his senatorial career, as the leader of his party in domestic legislation. He alone of the Republicans appeared to have a plan for dealing

[5] Mark M. Krug: *Lyman Trumbull: Conservative Radical* (New York: A. S. Barnes and Company, Inc.; 1965), p. 281; *Cong. Globe*, 41 Cong., 2 Sess., p. 2822.

[6] Feb. 16, 1870, Sumner MSS.

with the South, and he could argue for his program with greater force because he had all along predicted that the reconstruction measures hitherto enacted were too lenient. In addition, he was able to justify his policy by broad philosophical and constitutional arguments, which even before the opening of the new session he had begun to disclose in the lecture on "The Question of Caste," delivered in a dozen Northeastern cities. It was not enough, he maintained, to abolish slavery or to give the Negroes the ballot; so long as segregation remained they would still be regarded as members of an inferior caste, like the untouchables of India. Invoking the new prestige of evolutionary science, he declared that ethnology and anthropology proved the *"overruling Unity"* among the races of man, "by which they are constituted one and the same cosmopolitan species, endowed with speech, reason, conscience, and the hope of immortality, knitting all together in a common Humanity." At the same time he drew upon the old Newtonian world view of universal order and regularity and upon the even older theological argument that "God rejoices in Unity" to bolster his attack upon all racial discrimination as "a perpetual discord, a prolonged jar,—contrary to the first principles of the Universe."

The end of segregation in the United States would promptly end the present woes of the South. What was better, it would produce a new kind of society. When the bars of caste were lifted, the Negroes would exhibit their basic racial traits of "simplicity, amenity, good-nature, generousity, fidelity," and these, when added to the "more precocious and harder" characteristics of white Americans, would result in a civilization where "men will not only know and do, but they will feel also." In that triumphant day of human brotherhood there would be "no height of culture or of virtue . . . which may not be reached . . . no excellence of government or society which may not be grasped. Where is the stopping place? Where the goal?" [7]

Doubtless few Congressmen, practical men whose flights of fancy soared close to the ground, were ready to accept in full Sumner's vision of the good society, but many were obliged to agree that so long as the caste lines in the South were un-

[7] Sumner: *Works*, XIII, 152–3, 161, 175–8.

breached the Negro could never become more than a second-class citizen, a peon and a pawn in the hands of his former master. There might be nominal and grudging Southern compliance with formal legal requirements imposed by Congress, but reconstruction would be a failure. The rebels would have lost the war only to win the peace.

When such worried colleagues asked under what constitutional authority they could take further action in the South, Sumner answered that they had virtually complete control over questions hitherto regulated solely by the individual states. Congress could act, first, under the provisions of the several reconstruction acts and the new constitutional amendments. Then, too, the Constitution gave ample authority by requiring Congress to guarantee to each state a republican form of government. But, most important of all, the Declaration of Independence gave almost unlimited power. "Full well . . . I know that in other days, when Slavery prevailed . . . there was a different rule of interpretation," Sumner admitted, but "our war . . . changed all that." Indeed, the greatest victory of the Civil War had not been at Appomattox nor in Sherman's triumphant march; it had instead been "the establishment of a new rule of interpretation by which the institutions of our country are dedicated forevermore to Human Rights, and the Declaration of Independence is made a living letter instead of a promise." "Clearly, unquestionably, beyond all doubt," he reassured his fellow Senators, the Declaration now should "stand side by side with the Constitution, and enjoy with it coëqual authority."

It followed that Congress could and must act to secure the rights of Negroes even in those Southern states that had been readmitted to the Union. No legal technicality or quibble could defend segregation, discrimination, or disfranchisement. "The Congress of the United States will have forevermore the power to protect reconstruction," he sweepingly announced. "No one of these States, by anything it may do hereafter, can escape that far-reaching power." When opponents twitted Sumner for his willingness to intervene in the affairs of Southern, but not Northern, states, he replied with rigorous logic that he now made no such distinction. If Massachusetts should ever be so unrepublican as to abolish her desegregated public school system, Sumner announced that he would readily see the national government intervene to restore it.[8]

That federal intervention was necessary in the Southern states became obvious on the first day of the session in December 1869. Congress had to decide whether to seat Senators and Representatives from Georgia. After that state had been readmitted in 1868, its legislature, under Democratic control, proceeded to purge all twenty-eight of its Negro members and then, as Northern Congressmen were informed, to institute a "reign of anarchy, of cruelty, and of tyranny." Republican Governor Rufus B. Bullock urged Congress to remand the state to military rule, since it had proved its unwillingness to maintain a republican form of government, and, with Sumner in the lead, the Senate by a strict party vote [9] refused to seat its representatives.

More divisive was the issue of readmitting Virginia, which had held the election authorized by Congress and, with no more than the usual amount of fraud, had chosen as governor the Conservative candidate, Gilbert C. Walker, pledged to rid the Old Dominion of the "horde of greedy cormorants and unprincipled carpet-baggers who came to sap her very vitals." On the advice of the defeated Radical candidate, Grant urged that the state be readmitted. So, too, did Lyman Trumbull and other members of the Senate Committee on the Judiciary, who argued that Virginia had complied with every condition laid down by Congress; they believed that, even if the outcome of the election was distasteful, the federal government had no power further to intervene in the affairs of the state. To Sumner, on the other hand, the admission of Virginia was a test of whether a state could obey the letter and violate the spirit of the whole reconstruction program.

Against Trumbull's insistence that there was "no public reason why this measure should be postponed for a single day," Sumner took the lead in delaying the readmission of Virginia. Informed by his correspondents that the new Virginia constitution had been drawn up by rebels and Copperheads and that,

[8] Ibid., 220–1, 208; *Cong. Globe*, 41 Cong., 2 Sess., p. 1256.

[9] Only Joseph S. Fowler, of Tennessee, elected as a "Union Republican," broke with the Republican majority.

through failure to require an iron-clad test oath for officeholders, it would kill "loyalty and human rights . . . for the present generation," [1] he called Governor Walker a traitor and announced that the Virginia legislature was "composed of recent Rebels still filled and seething with that old Rebel fire." [2] Ably backed by Wilson, Edmunds, and Charles D. Drake, of Missouri, Sumner insisted that Virginia before readmission must accept a series of fundamental and irrevocable conditions—not merely the requirement imposed upon other Southern states never to abridge the voting rights guaranteed under the United States Constitution and its amendments, but additional stipulations that the state must ratify the Fifteenth Amendment, that it must make members of both races equally eligible to hold office, and that it must maintain a uniform system of public schools.

These proposals, which went far beyond any previous reconstruction legislation both in what was demanded of the states and in what was promised by way of long-range Congressional surveillance, at once split the Republican Senators into factions [3] divided along lines different from both the Radical-Conservative dichotomy which had existed during Johnson's administration and the Old Radical-New Radical split which marked the later years of the Grant era. One wing of the party consisted of some fifteen Senators who shared an aversion to Sumner's sweepingly nationalistic interpretation of the Constitution and wanted an end to reconstruction. As chairman of the Judiciary Committee, Trumbull was often the spokesman of this group, though Carpenter, Williams, John Sherman, and Conkling were in many ways as influential. The opposing group consisted of about twenty-two Senators, including a majority of those from the recently readmitted Southern states. Edmunds, Justin S. Mor-

[1] See the letters in the Sumner MSS., for the following Virginians: Thomas M. Brown, of Portsmouth, Dec. 11, 1869; Samuel F. Maddox, of Chester, Dec. 12, 1869; Charles H. Porter, of Richmond, Dec. 27, 1869; and B. W. Hunter, of Richmond, Dec. 29, 1869.

[2] Sumner: *Works*, XIII, 207.

[3] The following analysis is based upon my tabulation of seventeen roll-call votes held in the Senate between December 9, 1869, and January 21, 1870, on questions relating to the readmission of Georgia and Virginia. It should be stressed that the blocs here outlined were of only brief duration. David Rothman: *Politics and Power: The United States Senate, 1869–1901* (Cambridge: Harvard University Press; 1966) correctly points to the absence of consistent Republican leadership in the Senate during the Grant era.

rill, and Howard were powerful in this bloc, though, as Carpenter noted, Sumner was "the biggest ox in the herd." [4] In between was a smaller group of moderate and undecided Republicans, for whose support both extremes played.

In the debates on Virginia Sumner, for the first time in his legislative career, persuaded a majority of his Republican colleagues, and a majority of the entire Senate as well, to support his views on reconstruction. By close votes, with the Democrats backing the Trumbull wing of the Republican party, the Senate imposed the new and stringent fundamental conditions upon Virginia. With Wilson's aid, Sumner succeeded in stipulating that "the New England system of common schools is a part of the republican form of government as understood by the framers of the Constitution"—an idea, as Henry Adams sourly remarked, "that would have seemed to the last generation as strange as though it had been announced that the electric telegraph was an essential article of faith in the early Christian Church." With Drake's assistance he succeeded in persuading the Senate to endorse his theory that "the powers originally reserved by the Constitution in the States are in the future to be held by them only on good behavior and at the sufferance of Congress." In short, remarked Adams direfully, "the first, decisive, irrevocable step toward substituting a new form of government in the place of that on which American liberties have heretofore rested has been taken, and by it the American people must stand." [5]

Sumner, of course, took no such mournful view, but he would have agreed that the Senate had taken a first step. In February 1870 he persuaded his colleagues to take another, when they rejected Trumbull's bill to readmit Mississippi without imposing fundamental conditions. Arguing "that the Equal Rights of All must be placed under the safeguard of one uniform law which shall be the same in all parts of the nation," [6] Sumner got the Senate to go along with the House in requiring Mississippi to assent to precisely the same terms as Virginia.

[4] Thompson: *Carpenter*, p. 128.
[5] Adams: *The Great Secession Winter*, p. 205.
[6] Sumner: *Works*, XIII, 332.

When Mississippi, accepting those terms, chose as one of her Senators a Negro, Sumner's sense of triumph was complete. But before Hiram R. Revels was sworn in as the successor of Jefferson Davis, he was obliged to endure racist attacks, both in and out of Congress. Cartoonists portrayed the light-skinned graduate of Knox College as a wild, coal-black Zulu. The New York *Herald* gibed at the "distinguished darkey" and carried a story that the new Senator from Mississippi had called Sumner "a good fellow . . . so good, indeed, that I'm sorry his skin is white, but I think we have this consolation at least:—if Sumner's skin is white his heart is as black as any of ours." [7] Senator George Vickers of Maryland objected to seating Revels because, according to Chief Justice Taney's ruling in the Dred Scott case, he was not a citizen of the United States. But Sumner crushed all opposition. "The time has passed for argument," he announced. The Dred Scott decision, "born a putrid corpse, . . . a stench in the nostrils and a scandal to the Court itself," ought "to be remembered only as a warning and a shame." Now the Declaration of Independence prevailed as the basic American law, and in admitting its first Negro member the Senate was once again affirming: "All men are created equal." By so acting it would influence other public groups. "Doors will open, exclusions will give way, intolerance will cease, and the great truth will be manifest in a thousand examples," he exulted. "Liberty and Equality are the two express promises of our fathers. Both are now assured." [8]

"That swearing in of Senator Revels," John Greenleaf Whittier wrote Sumner, "must have been a sight compensating for much of the labor, trial and obloquy which thee and other pioneers in the march of liberty have endured." Even more gratifying was the tribute from Sumner's Negro constituent, J. B. Smith: "the Great Battle is over—victory has been proclaimed. . . . See how the chains are broken—the Mantle of Honour must rest upon your Shoulders as the Greatest champion of Liberty." [9]

[7] Feb. 21, 1870.

[8] Sumner: *Works*, XIII, 336–8.

[9] The two letters, dated March 8 and 31, 1870, are in the Sumner MSS.

· 3 ·

Power did not bring Sumner popularity among his colleagues. Self-important Senators were unaccustomed to party discipline, and they especially resented Sumner's leadership because few of them really accepted his objectives. The faction which he led was destined to be short-lived, for it was not Sumner's vision of the great society but the recalcitrance of the Southern whites that made most Senators vote with his bloc. Morton spoke for many colleagues in confessing that he found both Trumbull's proposal to turn the Southern states back to the native whites and Sumner's policy to guarantee eternal federal supervision of Negro rights "about equally impracticable."[1] Yet on the key votes Morton apparently felt he could not give over the whole South to the Democrats, and twelve out of thirteen times he lined up behind Sumner.

Sumner did nothing to make his followers' path easier. His manner was as tactless and as overbearing as ever. Conscious of his own rare culture, unquestionable honesty, and sound morality, he created ripples of resentment every time he gained the Senate floor. When read, his speeches were hardly more egotistical than those of his colleagues, but they were delivered with an air of patronizing condescension. Sumner was ostentatious in small virtues, such as always being in his seat even during debates in which he took no special interest. He frequently addressed his fellow Senators as though they were backward schoolboys and he a very patient teacher. Discussing the laying of another ocean cable, he replied to a question from Conkling: "I can explain to the Senator so that I think he"—and too carefully he refrained from saying "even he"—"will not mistake it." Condescendingly he informed Thurman that, as a new member, he could not be expected to understand the usages of the Senate. Constantly he stood ready to remind the Senators of their duty —as though, remarked the irate Daniel S. Norton, of Minnesota, "his idea of the duty of a Senator should be the idea of every other Senator."[2]

[1] *Cong. Globe*, 41 Cong., 2 Sess., p. 567.
[2] Ibid., pp. 199, 200, 547.

Even when Sumner was not attempting to instruct his colleagues, he managed to irritate them. He kept announcing that he was devoted to principle and that he would never abandon a just position once he had taken it. Rushing forward to report that Nebraska had ratified the Fifteenth Amendment, he offended the Senators from that state, hitherto among his warmest supporters, because they had expected to break the news to the country. His fondness for introducing into debate British precedents, often of dubious applicability, exasperated the precise lawyer Edmunds, who usually voted with him. "I wish, Mr. President," the Vermont Senator chided, "if it is not asking too much, that my distinguished friend from Massachusetts would read the cases he presents for himself before he cites them for our instruction." To his colleagues Sumner's behavior seemed the more offensive because, with his devout following among the Northern antislavery forces and the Southern Negroes and his new disciples won by his "Alabama Claims" speech, he appeared always able to secure uncritical applause for any measure he advocated. "A portion of our party press," Carpenter complained indignantly, "is ready to indorse a speech made by him even before they have seen it, and pronounce any principle unsound which they are informed by telegraph he has condemned." [3]

Other Senators were enraged by Sumner's habit of identifying opposition to his opinions with the defense of slavery. There had been some justice in making such a connection in the years before the Civil War, when slaveholders in Congress opposed nearly everything he favored, but now it seemed a low form of name-calling. Accustomed to thinking of "plots" by "rebels," Sumner saw proslavery conspiracies everywhere. Not merely did the opponents of his views on reconstruction speak with "the voice of Slavery"; so too did those who objected to his banking and currency proposals and even to his bill to lower postage rates. "Everything that does not suit the Senator is in the interest of Slavery!" Trumbull angrily protested. Noting Sumner's almost obsessive belaboring of the slavery issue, Nye of Nevada remarked that he was "in the position that the clown in the circus took when he pounded the wood-chuck with a club till he was

[3] Ibid., pp. 2347, 1001.

told it was dead. Said he, 'I know it.' Then he was asked, 'Why do you want to pound things after they are dead?' 'Well,' said he, 'I want to convince this particular wood-chuck that there is punishment after death.' "[4]

Even more galling, because more dangerous politically, was Sumner's lofty insistence that those Senators who disagreed with his policies were deserting the Republican party and joining the Democrats. When Trumbull and Stewart, along with the handful of Democrats in the Senate, on January 11, 1870, urged the prompt readmission of Virginia, Sumner responded that it was only natural that these Republicans "acting in this new conjunction" should show themselves indifferent to human rights. "When one begins to act with such allies," he continued, "I can well imagine that he loses something of his original devotion to the great fundamental principles of our Government." Then, concentrating on Stewart, he concluded with a rousing pledge: "Let the Senator from Nevada desert; let him, joining the Democrats, take the other course; but I stand firm by the plighted faith of this great Republic."

Goaded by Sumner's "haughty, domineering tone, the same tone that demands all the amenities for himself and none for his fellow Senators," Stewart bluntly retorted: "I do not fear that I shall be read out of the Republican party by the Senator from Massachusetts." Where, he asked, had Sumner's fear of Democratic contamination been back in February 1869, "at the only session at which we should ever have an opportunity of ingrafting into the Constitution that grand principle of equal rights known as the fifteenth amendment?" Then the Senator from Massachusetts had not hesitated to filibuster, along with the Democrats, in his vain effort to kill the amendment.[5]

On January 13 Trumbull joined in the attack and challenged Sumner's right to speak for the Republican majority: "Who inaugurated him as the leader of the loyal people of this country? Upon what sort of food does he feed that he comes here and talks about the loyal people . . . ? Has he any higher claims to patriotism or to loyalty or to devotion to the country than

[4] Ibid., pp. 1364, 391.
[5] Ibid., pp. 393–4.

anybody else?" To Sumner's charge that his opponents had not been "true on these subjects of reconstruction," Trumbull retorted that he had taken an active part in shaping every reconstruction law, whereas Sumner had objected to them all and had advocated his own "impracticable, unreasonable, unconstitutional, and ineffectual measures." [6]

Itching to strip from Sumner "the infallibility and superiority which he assumed in this body," Trumbull returned to the attack on January 21 with a detailed review of Sumner's voting record.[7] Adopting a deliberately insulting tone and wearing his cold, sarcastic smile, the Illinois Senator announced his intention to "expose the presumption and assumption and effrontery that from day to day have been displayed in this Senate." As the galleries filled and visitors from the other House began to flock into the Senate chamber, Trumbull read from the *Congressional Globe* to show how Sumner had absented himself from the crucial vote which made Negro suffrage a requirement under the 1867 reconstruction act. Similarly Sumner had failed to vote for the Fifteenth Amendment. "The future historian," Trumbull concluded, "will search the records in vain for the vote of the Senator from Massachusetts in favor of any of the great measures which have secured suffrage to the colored man." [8]

Taken wholly by surprise, Sumner squirmed uncomfortably in his seat while Trumbull spoke, and when he gained the floor for reply he could hardly control his voice. Too aroused to be coherent, "he could not get his sentences in right shape—his well rounded periods were all out of tune." [9] Confronting Trumbull directly, he shouted that he had in fact initiated the Negro suffrage provision in the 1867 act, though he had been too tired and ill to remain in the Senate for the final vote.[1] He had left in

[6] Ibid., pp. 421–2.

[7] For excellent descriptions of the Sumner-Trumbull-Stewart encounters see New York *Tribune*, Feb. 15, 1870, and *Wyandotte Gazette*, Feb. 3, 1870.

[8] *Cong. Globe*, 41 Cong., 2 Sess., pp. 635–8.

[9] New York *Herald*, Jan. 22, 1870.

[1] For an account of Sumner's role in shaping this legislation, see pp. 285–8 above. Trumbull was, of course, correct in stating that Sumner had introduced none of the major reconstruction acts and that he had frequently abstained from voting when they were finally adopted. On the other hand, Sumner had incessantly agitated for Negro rights, both in and out of Congress, and he had sought to make the reconstruction laws as liberal and far-reaching as possible.

the knowledge that he had made the requirement of Negro suffrage "safe against the assaults of the Senator from Illinois," that same Senator who had since protected "the greatest enemy of reconstruction, the President of the United States," from impeachment and was now willing to turn over the states of the South to "the Ku Klux Klan, with its bloody orgies." [2]

Scenting that Trumbull had drawn blood, other Senators leaped to the attack, and for the next three weeks one tried to outdo another in the improbable effort to show that Sumner had been faithless to the Negro race. Stewart, still smarting under Sumner's charge that he had defected to the Democrats, was perhaps the most extreme. "I have never questioned that the Senator from Massachusetts has been for long years the strenuous advocate of the abstract principle of equal rights," he grudgingly conceded; "but I never knew him to be for it when there was any chance to make it a law. . . ." Not merely had Sumner failed to support the Fifteenth Amendment and the 1867 reconstruction act; he had earlier opposed the Fourteenth Amendment and even the 1866 civil rights act. "He is a theorist," Stewart scornfully concluded, "a grand, georgeous [*sic*], extensive theorist, but he is not a practical man, and my experience is that he has failed utterly to help us to get practical measures." [3]

Though Sumner felt it necessary to present a long exposition and defense of his course upon reconstruction legislation, these attacks strengthened, rather than weakened, his leadership. Had Trumbull and Stewart confined themselves to criticizing Sumner's arrogance and his assumption of omniscience, many Senators would have thought their criticisms just. But it required only a moment's reflection, and no searching through the *Congressional Globe*, to recall how insistently Sumner had always argued for Negro rights. Even to suggest the contrary was so preposterous as to throw doubt upon both the honesty and the intelligence of Sumner's assailants. Moreover, the vituperative language of Sumner's opponents turned opinion against them. After Stewart's philippic, Drake solemnly remarked: "There can hardly be a Senator upon the floor . . . to-day who

[2] *Cong. Globe*, 41 Cong., 2 Sess., p. 640.
[3] Ibid., p. 1183.

does not feel that this is one of the days of the Senate's degradation before the country." More significant politically was the judgment of John Sherman, who spoke for the middle-of-the-road Republicans not firmly affiliated with either Sumner's bloc or Trumbull's group: "In my judgment it would be just as well for George Washington to defend himself against the charge of disloyalty to the American colonies . . . as for the honorable Senator to defend his record on this question."[4]

• 4 •

Senators restive with Sumner's leadership looked in vain to the White House for assistance. Indeed, during the winter of 1869–70 it seemed that Sumner dominated the executive as well as the legislative branch of the government. In foreign policy the President appeared to follow the Senator's lead, and his Secretary of State was Sumner's mouthpiece. In domestic affairs Grant watched Sumner spurn his proposal for the speedy readmission of Virginia and uttered no word of objection. Two of Sumner's close political associates, Hoar and Boutwell, were members of the cabinet, and the President tried to elevate Hoar to the Supreme Court. On lower levels of the civil service, Sumner's every nomination was assured of Grant's personal attention. "They say Sumner is very powerful with the President . . . ," Banks reported hungrily.[5]

Grant's attempt to conciliate Sumner puzzled many observers, who were aware that the two men were temperamentally incompatible. Every Washington gossip knew that Sumner had been cool to Grant's nomination in 1868 and that the President had passed over the Senator in appointing a Secretary of State. But Grant, though still a political novice, was learning rapidly. He early discovered that running the executive branch of the federal government was not quite like commanding an army; he

[4] Ibid., pp. 1183, 1181. In February 1870 Sumner also got into an acrimonious quarrel with Conkling, over the best method for taking the census. Since no substantive political issue was at stake, Senators felt free to express their personal hostility toward Sumner; only nine stood by him. New York *Herald*, Feb. 10 and 13, 1870; *The Nation*, X (Feb. 24, 1870), 116.

[5] O. E. Babcock to Sumner, Mar. 11, 1870, letterbook copy, Grant MSS.; Banks to his wife, Jan. 8, 1870, Banks MSS.

might appoint men to his cabinet, as to his staff, simply because he liked them, but they brought him no political support. The President also found that his own enormous personal popularity could not be translated into dependable political strength. Anyway, during the summer of 1869 that popularity visibly diminished when the President publicly consorted with the swindlers, Jim Fisk and Jay Gould, and it declined even further when the attempt of these gamblers to corner the gold market with the apparent connivance of his administration resulted in the disastrous "Black Friday" of September 24 on the New York stock exchange. By December Grant came to recognize that he had no choice but to work with the Republicans who controlled the key committees in Congress. In particular he sought to win Sumner's aid through consideration and favors. As one Democratic Congressman cynically put it, the President hoped to put Massachusetts and her Senators "under bonds to keep the peace with the Republican party under almost any circumstances likely to arise under party emergencies." [6]

In early January [7] Grant demonstrated how far he was willing to go. On Sunday evening Sumner was having dinner at his home, overlooking Lafayette Square, with two of his newspaper friends, Ben: Perley Poore and John W. Forney. The three men were discussing what could be done to aid James M. Ashley, one of the original impeachers, who was being superseded as territorial governor of Montana, when the door bell rang. As the servant answered, Poore recognized the visitor's voice and said: "Mr. Senator, the President is at the front door." Courteously Sumner rose and welcomed his unexpected guest, who had unceremoniously strolled over from the White House for a chat. Seating Grant at the table, Sumner offered a glass of sherry,

[6] *Cong. Globe*, 41 Cong., 2 Sess., p. 1937.

[7] Years later, rereading an ambiguous entry in his diary, Hamilton Fish concluded that the interview took place on December 31, 1869 (Fish to Ben: Perley Poore, Nov. 21, 1877, letterbook copy, Fish MSS.), and both Allan Nevins (*Hamilton Fish*, p. 311) and J. C. Bancroft Davis (*Mr. Sumner, the Alabama Claims, and Their Settlement*, p. 13) have accepted this date. But Grant explicitly stated that he called on Sumner "during the first week of January" (Grant to Zachariah Chandler, June 8, 1870, letterbook copy, Grant MSS.), and Poore agreed that the visit occurred "on the first Sunday in January, 1870" (Boston *Journal*, Oct. 21, 1877). In all probability the date was Sunday, January 2.

which the President refused. Poore scented that something important was in the wind and offered to excuse himself, but Grant said: "Don't leave, I recognize you and Colonel Forney as friends." Before the President could say more, Forney began to talk about Ashley's case, and he asked Sumner to read aloud a letter just received from the deposed radical. Flushing with anger, Grant announced that Ashley was "a mischief-maker and a worthless fellow" and warmly expressed his hope that Sumner would not oppose confirmation of his successor when the Senate Judiciary Committee reported.[8]

Then, as the party adjourned to the library, the President explained the cause of his visit, the treaty [9] for the annexation of the Dominican Republic which he was about to submit to the Senate. Grant had not come to argue the merits of the treaty. He brought no scrap of paper with him and was prepared to describe the provisions of the document only in general terms. In calling at Sumner's home he was simply and straightforwardly appealing to the Senator's vanity; no doubt Grant was entirely aware, that, as the protocol-conscious Bancroft Davis exclaimed, he was doing "what probably no President ever did before under the same circumstances." [1]

While Grant was extolling the natural resources of Santo Domingo and explaining how the treaty had come to be negotiated, Boutwell called, and the President seemed to feel that he had stayed long enough. "I will send the papers over to you in the morning by Gen. Babcock," he told Sumner. Promising to study them, Sumner detained his guest by again bringing up the subject of Ashley's removal, but Grant, evidently annoyed, made no

[8] Poore, in Boston *Journal*, Oct. 21, 1877.

[9] Babcock actually negotiated two treaties, both of which were submitted to the Senate. The first, strongly favored by the Grant administration, provided for the annexation of the whole Dominican Republic. The second, drafted in case the Senate should prove obdurate, provided for a ninety-nine year lease by the United States government of Samaná Bay. For details on Babcock's operations, and a careful study of the whole annexation issue, see Tansill: *The United States and Santo Domingo*, Chaps. 9–10. Sumner Welles: *Naboth's Vineyard: The Dominican Republic, 1844–1924* (New York: Payson & Clarke Ltd.; 1928), Vol. I, Chaps. 4–5, remains an invaluable account of the internal problems of the island Republic.

[1] Interview with Grant, Jan. 17, 1878, unidentified clipping. Grant-Fish Scrapbook, Sumner MSS.; Davis to George Bancroft, July 11, 1870, Bancroft MSS., Mass. Hist. Soc.

reply. As the President was leaving, Forney spoke up: "Of course, Mr. Sumner, you will support this treaty." "Mr. President," Sumner recalled his reply, "I am an Adminstration man, and whatever you do will always find in me the most careful and candid consideration." [2]

Later every detail of this conversation, destined to be the turning point in Grant's administration and in Sumner's career as well, became the subject of controversy. Without any evidence whatever it was alleged that Grant had been drunk during the interview; he was not. The President called on Sumner, so it was claimed, to beg him to support the treaty, but in fact he expected no opposition and simply was trying not to offend the Senator by submitting a major treaty to the Senate without warning. According to Sumner's own later recollection, Grant repeatedly addressed him as chairman of the Judiciary Committee, but the President emphatically denied doing so.[3] Much argument rose also over the connection between Ashley's removal and Sumner's support for annexation, and Senator Howe concluded that Sumner hinted to the President that "his support of the treaty [was] conditioned upon Ashley's restoration." But Grant himself spurned the suggestion that Sumner had in effect put his vote up for sale. "Mr. Sumner could never have been bribed in but one way," he said. "That would be by flattery." [4]

Most controversial of all were the exact words Sumner used to express his attitude toward the Santo Domingo treaty. Sumner claimed to remember exactly what he had said, for his language was "precise, well-considered, and chosen in advance." Moreover, he declared, he repeated his words the very next day to Carl Schurz, who regarded them as merely a "polite expression of generally friendly feeling." But Forney understood Sumner to say that "he would cheerfully support the Treaty," and on the basis of this assurance wrote an editorial favoring annexation. Some years later, however, he claimed a fuller recollection of

[2] Sumner: *Works*, XIII, 126.

[3] Cf. ibid., p. 125, and Grant to Fish, Nov. 14, 1877, Fish MSS.

[4] Timothy O. Howe to Fish, Nov. 8, 1877, and Grant to Fish, Nov. 14, 1877, Fish MSS. It is extraordinary that historians have sometimes taken Howe's charge seriously; his evidence consisted solely of the facts that Sumner was angry over Ashley's removal and that he held his tongue on the Dominican treaty until he was required to speak.

Sumner's words: "Well, Mr. President, I am a Republican and an Administration man, and I will do all I can to make your Administration a success. I will give the subject my best thought, and will do all I can rightly and consistently to aid you." According to Poore, Sumner declared "that he was a Republican and a supporter of the Republican Administration, and that he should sustain the Administration in this case if he possibly could, after he had examined the papers." Boutwell retained a flat New England recollection of Sumner's words: "I expect Mr. President to support the measures of your administration." [5]

In all probability no one of these conflicting versions is precisely correct. Time blurred them all. Forney's first account was not written until June 1870; Sumner's version was not put to paper until December; Forney's second account, like the recollections of Poore and Boutwell, was dated 1877. Before any one of them was recorded, hostilities between Grant and Sumner had opened, and all the witnesses were partisans in the ensuing battle. It is suggestive that Forney's first statement, claiming that Sumner pledged to support the treaty, was written while the editor was still friendly to Grant and hopeful for favors from his administration; his second version came after he had broken with the Republican party and had gone into the Liberal Republican movement. Poore and Boutwell, on the other hand, remained stalwartly Republican.

What is certain is that Grant, like three other witnesses to the conversation, left Sumner's house that evening convinced that the Senator was committed to supporting the Santo Domingo treaty. No doubt the President as he strolled back across Lafayette Square chuckled quietly to himself at how little sugar it took to make the medicine go down. He had come to disarm Sumner's suspicions of a treaty that had been negotiated without his knowledge and to secure for it a prompt and fair hearing; he returned with a pledge of the Senate leader's support. On the

[5] For these several accounts, see Sumner: *Works*, XIII, 126; Forney to Orville E. Babcock, June 6, 1870, facsimile, Lib. of Cong.; Pierce, IV, 435, note; Boston *Journal*, Oct. 21, 1877; Boutwell: "Memorandum," Nov. 12, 1877, Fish MSS. For Schurz's view, see Bancroft (ed.): *Speeches, Correspondence and Political Papers of Carl Schurz*, VI, 281–2, and Schurz: *Charles Sumner*, pp. 118–19.

very next day he sent his aide, Orville E. Babcock, to Sumner with a draft of the treaty, and when the Senator, reserving any general comment on the document, contented himself with suggesting a few verbal changes, the President was confident there could be no difficulty. On January 10 he submitted the annexation treaty to the Senate in executive session, and it was promptly referred to the Committee on Foreign Relations.

Equally certain is it that Sumner did not think he had promised to support the treaty. It would take more than Grant's flattery to persuade him to approve, sight unseen, a measure of such importance. With his rigid view of public propriety and with his high esteem for the Senate and for his own committee, he was not likely to make any agreement that would lessen their powers or bypass their procedures. Furthermore, he already had some reason to be suspicious of the Dominican treaty; as early as December 24, 1869, his correspondent Peter F. Stout, of Philadelphia, had written him that dictator Baez was swindling the American negotiators.

Assuredly, Sumner—if he remembered his own words accurately—did tell Grant that, as an "Administration man," he would give the annexation treaty his "careful and candid consideration." From Roscoe Conkling or Simon Cameron those words would have been a pledge of support; from Sumner they meant that the annexation treaty would receive precisely the same consideration as any other measure proposed by Grant. During the previous nine months Sumner, all the while an administration man, had defeated Grant's effort to repeal the Tenure of Office Act, had blocked his naming of A. T. Stewart to the Treasury Department, had held up numerous nominations in his committee, had frustrated the President's plans to assist the Cubans, and had overridden his Secretary of State on the Alabama Claims question; currently he was running roughshod over Grant's reconstruction program for Virginia. The Santo Domingo treaty could expect the same careful and candid consideration. But in making his promise to Grant, Sumner had not been deliberately deceitful. He was in fact a Republican and an administration man, but he labored under the belief that the policies of the Republican administration were determined on his side of Lafayette Square, not on Grant's.

Doubting the wisdom of the treaty from the start, Sumner resorted to the tactics of silence and delay, which he had so often used in previous years to frustrate Seward's expansionist schemes. Not until eight days after the treaty was sent to his committee did he call a meeting to discuss it. Only on March 11 did the committee question Babcock, who had negotiated the treaty. Recognizing that his colleagues paid great respect to his opinion, Sumner submitted the treaty without any preliminary statement or recommendation of his own. Throughout the discussions he tried to preserve "an entirely neutral attitude, giving his own opinion only after every other member had had abundant time for consideration and opportunity for expressing himself." Not for weeks did the other members of the committee get "the least hint that Sumner would oppose it." [6]

The initial reaction of the Foreign Relations Committee to annexation was hostile. Regardless of the merits of the case, its members tended to be suspicious of Executive initiative. "The Senate," Fish shrewdly observed, "has been for two or three years accustomed to originate measures and to resist what the Executive originated. The habit of criticism, if not of opposition, became somewhat fixed, and on the accession of a friend to the Executive Chair, the habit could not entirely and at once subside —it is difficult to voluntarily relinquish power." At the first discussion of the treaty only Morton had anything to say in favor of annexation; the others were opposed. Recognizing that an immediate rejection would anger Grant, Sumner urged the committee to take no formal vote against the treaty; it would be better to smother than to stab Grant's favorite project.[7]

With delay Sumner and his fellow Senators gained a chance to learn more about the proposed Dominican treaty and the circumstances surrounding its negotiation, and the more they learned, the less they liked the whole scheme. Sumner was

[6] Schurz: *Writings*, VI, 282; T. O. Howe to Fish, Nov. 8, 1877, Fish MSS.

[7] Nevins: *Fish*, p. 313 (the order of the two sentences has been reversed); Sumner: *Works*, XIII, 126–7.

shocked to discover that the original outline, or *projet,* of the treaty had been drafted by General Babcock, who by law could not serve in a civilian diplomatic capacity without having resigned his army commission. To make matters worse, Babcock had signed the document as "aide-de-camp to his Excellency General Ulysses S. Grant" and had pledged that the President would "use all his influence . . . among members of Congress" to secure ratification. Sumner was no more favorably impressed by the fact that it was the President and "Great Citizen" of the Dominican Republic who had agreed to the cession; he remembered Baez from the days he had frustrated Seward's attempt to annex the island, and, had he forgotten, several oily letters he received from the dictator during 1869 would have reminded him of his mercenary character. Equally disturbing was the fact that Baez's principal aides in the annexation scheme were two unsavory American speculators, General Joseph W. Fabens and General William L. Cazneau, whose claim to own about one-tenth of all the land in Santo Domingo, plus assorted mining, banking, and shipping monopolies, would become exceedingly valuable if the United States ratified the treaty.

Probing further, Sumner discovered that Baez's regime was about to collapse. Chronically bankrupt, the Great Citizen was currently operating on funds supplied, at an exorbitant rate of interest, by the English firm of Hartmont and on money from the United States secret service funds. Meanwhile a powerful insurrection against his dictatorship had been started under Gregorio, Luperon and Cabral, and it was receiving assistance from the new President of Haiti, Nissage Saget. Since midsummer of 1869 the Baez regime had been propped up not merely by American money but United States naval power. The Secretary of the Navy had ordered the U.S.S. *Tuscarora* into Dominican waters at the time of Babcock's visit in order to "lend the moral support of its guns" to the annexation scheme, and Rear Admiral C. H. Poor informed the Haitian President that, so long as annexation was pending, any attack upon the Baez regime would be considered "an act of hostility to the Flag of the United States," which would "provoke hostility in return." [8]

[8] Welles: *Naboth's Vineyard,* I, 273, 284.

A four-hour interview with the ubiquitous Fabens, now lobbying in Washington for the treaty, gave Sumner further reasons to oppose the treaty. Keeping his own feelings under control, Sumner allowed Fabens to rattle along about Dominican affairs and prospects. At one point he interrupted to ask whether Fabens thought annexation would stop with the Dominican Republic. "Oh, no!" replied Fabens guilelessly, "you must have Hayti too."

"And is that all?" asked the Senator.

Reflecting a moment, Fabens judged that the acquisition of Puerto Rico, Jamaica, Cuba, the Windward Islands, and, indeed, all the rest of the West Indies, would shortly follow.[9] Garrulous and unperceptive, Fabens did not realize that he had triggered Sumner's fear for the black republic of Haiti and that his prediction ran counter to Sumner's hope for an American protectorate over independent Caribbean states. Instead, he wrote his partner Cazneau that the interview with Sumner gave him "good grounds for hoping he will come round"; to President Baez he unwittingly revealed the truth by reporting that he had explained to the Senator "the measure of annexation." [1]

Increasingly hostile to annexation, Sumner still intended to kill the treaty through the inaction of his committee, but Grant had other plans. Fearing that the treaty would expire on March 29 before there was even a committee report upon it, the President sent a special message to Congress on March 14, urging speedy action. Then for several days he went in person to the Capitol, where he occupied the President's room, customarily used only on the last day of the session for the purpose of signing bills, and called in some fourteen Senators in order to urge the advantages and necessities of annexation. The faith of the United States was pledged, the President argued; the people of the Dominican Republic had already expressed their desire in an overwhelming plebiscite (15,169–11) for annexation; the resources of the island were boundless; it offered a superb naval base; and since other countries, notably France, were also inter-

[9] Tansill: *United States and Santo Domingo*, pp. 393–4.

[1] Fabens to Cazneau, May 4, 1870, Fabens MSS.; Fabens to Baez, May 4, 1870, ibid.

ested in annexation, the United States was required to act under the Monroe Doctrine.

Such pressure made it impossible for Sumner to hold the treaty indefinitely in committee. On March 15, speaking for the five-man majority of the Foreign Relations Committee, he adversely reported the treaty to the Senate in secret session; the other two members of the committee, Morton and Harlan, favored annexation.[2] Nine days later he took the floor to explain and justify the hostile report. For four hours on the twenty-fourth and for an additional hour and one-half the next day he spoke, not using a manuscript but referring frequently to his notes and to books he had collected on his desk. Since the Senate was in closed session, his argument was not recorded, but it was conceded to be "a very able, exhaustive and scholarly effort," which even Stewart, an advocate of annexation, termed "magnificent." [3] Admitting "the beauties, advantages and resources of the island," Sumner believed that annexation would raise great financial, political, and moral questions. In the first place, the expense would be enormous. Without an impartial commission of investigation nobody could know the full extent of the Dominican debt; it was uncertain, for instance, whether the United States would have to repay the extortionate Hartmont loan. Besides, since a bloody insurrection against Baez was already raging, the United States would, in effect, be buying a civil war. Pointing to the cost of the United States Indian policy, and specifically to the expenses caused by the Seminole War (1835–43), Sumner predicted that it would be a "very expensive business to maintain peace in the island."

Turning to higher grounds, Sumner argued, just as Fabens had suggested, that annexation of the Dominican Republic would be only the first step toward swallowing up all the West Indies. Haiti, already at war with its neighbor, would surely be the first. The United States was "an Anglo-Saxon Republic, and would ever remain so by the preponderance of that race." The

[2] *Senate Exec. Journal*, XVII, 392; New York *Herald*, Mar. 16, 1870. Not until March 24 did Sumner's committee report adversely upon the treaty to lease Samaná Bay.

[3] New York *Times*, Mar. 25, 1870; J. W. Forney to Sumner [Mar. 25, 1870], Sumner MSS.

West Indies, on the other hand, were "colored communities," where the "black race was predominant." They had, therefore, "a distinct nationality, . . . which should be preserved in its integrity." These islands "should not be absorbed by the United States, but should remain as independent powers, and should try for themselves to make the experiment of self-government." The best course would be for the United States to assume a protectorate over the Dominicans, "giving them moral support and counsel, as well as aid them in establishing a firm and energetic republican government of their own." In this way the Antilles would emerge as "a free confederacy, in which the black race should predominate." "To the African belongs the equatorial belt," Sumner concluded, "and he should enjoy it undisturbed." [4]

After Sumner had finished, Morton made the best possible case for annexation by stressing the desire of the Dominicans to join the United States, the strategic value of naval bases, and the probable destiny of the United States as a Caribbean power. To demonstrate the vast natural resources of the island, Morton produced samples of Santo Domingo hemp, which Senators Stewart and Ramsay proceeded to test in an impromptu and high-spirited tug-of-war on the Senate floor, and a huge block of Dominican rock salt, which, to the amusement of other members, black Senator Revels and Negro-hating Senator Garrett Davis licked simultaneously.

The debate on annexation continued inconclusively for a week, with Sumner commanding the opponents of the treaty. At his suggestion the Senate ordered Secretary Fish to submit copies of the instructions under which the treaty was negotiated, requested Grant for copies of orders given to American naval vessels in Dominican waters, and entered a translation of the complex Hartmont loan agreement upon the record. No votes were taken, but it was obvious that the enemies of annexation by joining with the Democrats, pledged to oppose any measure advocated by Grant, could kill the treaty. Few Republicans, however, wanted to force a test vote that might split their party.

[4] This reconstruction of Sumner's speech is drawn from the reports in the Chicago *Republican*, Mar. 25, 1870; New York *Tribune*, Mar. 25, 1870; New York *Herald*, Mar. 25, 1870; Boston *Advertiser*, Mar. 26, 1870; and New York *Times*, Mar. 25, 1870.

For a time it seemed that John Sherman, ever the conciliator, had worked out a compromise, picking up Sumner's suggestion for an impartial commission to look into the Dominican debt and transforming it into a commission to investigate both the advantages and disadvantages of annexing the island. But Sumner, aroused and implacable, had no desire to let Grant save face, and for the time the idea of a commission had to be dropped. The best the friends of annexation, and of the administration, could salvage was an informal recess in the debate on Santo Domingo that lasted through April and May. Once again, it seemed that Sumner had demonstrated he was master of the Senate.

• 5 •

Grant was furious. Always an expansionist, he had hoped to make the annexation of the Dominican Republic the glorious achievement of his otherwise lackluster administration. Babcock, Fabens, and other trusted advisers had convinced him that Santo Domingo had boundless natural resources, sufficient to pay off the entire United States debt. Samaná Bay was one of the best harbors in the world, and a naval base there would guard the entrance to the proposed isthmian canal. The President was unable to see any legitimate objections to the treaty. He would make no modifications and no concessions.

Against Sumner the President was especially indignant. He had secured, as he thought, a pledge of support for the treaty, only to have it stalled in the Committee on Foreign Relations for ten weeks and then adversely reported. He now ordered his subordinates to give Sumner no information beyond what the law required and to discuss with him no possible alterations in the wording of the treaty. Guessing that Sumner had, "probably without knowing it," been unfair and inaccurate in presenting the treaty to his colleagues, Grant concluded that he had from the start really been an enemy of the treaty, and of the administration.[5] Reports of Sumner's speech in secret session further inflamed the President's rage. Though, in fact, Sumner alluded to Grant as little as possible and, according to Schurz, spoke

[5] Grant to Fish, Mar. 22, 1870, Fish MSS.; Fish: Diary, Mar. 30, 1870, ibid.

"very gently of the President," he necessarily challenged his statesmanship in advocating such a treaty and his wisdom in choosing the subordinates who negotiated it. Particularly infuriating was Sumner's patronizing concession that even in supporting so unfortunate and wicked a treaty the President was "entirely honest." [6]

It would, however, be easy to overestimate the influence of these personal grievances in causing the intra-party warfare that ensued between Grant and Sumner. Certainly the President was very angry with Sumner—but in the past he had been equally angry with Edwin M. Stanton and Benjamin F. Butler and had still found it possible to work with them politically. Certainly Sumner's personality was particularly irritating to a man like Grant—but the Senator was no more objectionable when blocking the Dominican treaty than he had been in holding up the prompt readmission of Virginia or in defeating the confirmation of A. T. Stewart. Grant's mental processes are obscure, for in politics as in war he moved silently toward his objectives, but it seems reasonable to conclude that he saw in Sumner's defection on the Santo Domingo issue not merely a breach of faith on the part of one Senator but the final proof that it was impossible to work with the arrogant and self-righteous Old Radical element of the Republican party. Repeatedly he had tried to conciliate these zealous partisans, and his reward was a total disregard of his wishes. Sumner's stand on the Dominican treaty seemed of a piece with the unfair assault Massachusetts Representative Henry L. Dawes was making against the Treasury Department.

If Grant's administration was to achieve any success, the President clearly had to devise a new political strategy, and he went about the task with the same secrecy and persistence that he had showed in his campaign against Vicksburg.[7] Indeed, Sumner's stand on Santo Domingo simply speeded Grant's change of base. In early February one of Sumner's political associates reported that presidential appointments in New Jer-

[6] Schurz: *Sumner*, p. 119; Washington *Chronicle*, Mar. 26, 1870; New York *Herald*, Mar. 28, 1870.

[7] Of Grant's biographers, only William B. Hesseltine (*Ulysses S. Grant: Politician* [New York: Frederick Ungar Publishing Co.; 1957], Chap. 12) seems to have discerned this basic shift in his political strategy.

sey were going to "men who have no faculty of mind and no impulse of their souls in sympathy with *Republicanism* as you and I understand it." On February 22, Forney wrote Sumner that, according to Philadelphia rumor, the President had determined to control the Republican party himself by striking down "the Republican statesmen" and that Sumner in particular, was marked out for sacrifice.[8] Instead of Republican veterans, whose committee assignments and seniority allowed them to deal on almost equal terms with the President, Grant began to favor the New Radicals, young, hungry, and ambitious. As his principal adviser on New England appointments, he called in Butler, who might be venal but who could be relied upon to stay bought. Similarly Grant turned his back on antislavery veterans in New York to make an informal alliance with Conkling, whose frequent verbal clashes with Sumner in the Senate doubtless endeared him to the President; the price of the bargain was the appointment of Conkling's choice, Thomas Murphy, as collector of the customs in New York. In the former Confederate states Grant recognized that extreme Radicals, both Negro and white, owed Republicans like Sumner such political and emotional debts that he could never depend upon their loyalty; consequently he continued the course he had already begun of fostering more moderate Republican leadership in the South.

Just as many during the Civil War thought of Grant's military strategy as sheer butchery, so many contemporaries—and subsequent historians as well—misjudged the skill with which the President fought his political war. For instance, he recognized that Hamilton Fish, unenthusiastic about the Santo Domingo scheme and unhappy about the adventurers surrounding the President, wanted to retire, but the Secretary of State was needed to give an air of dignity and sobriety to an otherwise undistinguished administration. To keep Fish in the cabinet, then, Grant on June 13 reluctantly sent to Congress, under his own signature, a message that the Secretary had prepared, denying, once and for all, that the Cuban rebels had any claim to be recognized by the United States. Then, realizing that this mes-

[8] James M. Scovel to Sumner, Feb. 7, 1870, and Forney to Sumner, Feb. 22 [1870], Sumner MSS.

sage would be difficult for his new ally Butler to swallow, Grant followed it up two days later by an abrupt request for Attorney General Hoar's resignation; there was nothing to be gained by continuing this friend of Sumner's in office, and his removal was a small price to pay for Butler's support. As Hoar's successor Grant sought a Southern Republican, for such a nomination would give the Senators from the reconstructed states an excuse to break with Sumner on the Santo Domingo treaty. Moreover, by nominating the moderate Amos T. Akerman, of Georgia, as Attorney General, the President could help undermine the Radicals in the South, who were loyal to the Sumner wing of the party. So quietly, so gradually, were these steps taken that few were aware of Grant's grand strategy. In July, after they were completed, former Senator Ira Harris, of New York, wrote Sumner in some bewilderment: "It seems to me that the present administration is drifting away from us as its predecessor did." [9]

During the spring of 1870, there appeared to be only aimless drift. Yet after Sumner's speech on Santo Domingo (March 24–25) one can sense under the flotsam of the turgid *Congressional Globe* a new current among Senate Republicans. Without any overt urging from the White House, without any public pronouncements of any sort, more and more Senators began quietly to dissociate themselves from Sumner's bloc.

The first open evidence of a change came when Congress once again had to deal with the vexed question of Georgia. Readmitted in 1868, then excluded again because Negroes were not allowed in the state legislature, that state had once more reorganized itself, and its Representatives and Senators were asking for admission. The unsavory governor, Rufus B. Bullock, opposed unconditional readmission; if new elections were held, as scheduled, in the fall of 1870 Democrats would certainly triumph, but if they could be postponed he still had a gambler's chance of building a viable Georgia Republican party through an alliance of Negroes and business-oriented planters. Bullock's pecuniary and political motives were, however, too blatantly apparent, and his lobbying in Washington was too heavy-handed, and

[9] July 6, 1870, ibid.

the House bill readmitting Georgia contained John A. Bingham's amendment requiring new elections in 1870.

In April when the bill came up for serious discussion in the Senate, Sumner expected to dominate the proceedings, just as he had done with the other reconstruction measures passed earlier in the session. Unhesitatingly he endorsed Bullock's scheme for perpetuating his faction in office. Bingham's amendment, Sumner announced, was "only an engine of Rebel power." Those who advocated it were using the slaveholders' argument for state rights; they were ignoring the fact that "a State is not a turtle which can shut itself within its shell, and enjoy its own separate animal existence; but it is a component part of this great Republic." There could be no question that Congress possessed the power to regulate affairs in Georgia, even to the extent of postponing elections. "As well question that the sun shines or the river flows." Congress could act under the provisions of the 1867 reconstruction act, or under the guaranty clause of the Constitution, or "from the necessity of the case." Aside from, and in addition to, these sources of power, Congress "is a Court of Equity, bound to supply deficiencies in the existing law, to enjoin against threatening wrong, and generally to see justice done in spite of technicalities." "You have the power," Sumner informed his colleagues. "Then you must exercise it." [1]

Carpenter, who had cherished a grudge against Sumner since their clash over Cuba early in the session, decided this was the time to challenge the Senate leader. Sneering that Sumner was a "valuting logician," he asked him "to descend from his tripod, to emerge from his oracular and profane mysteries," and explain precisely where in the Constitution Congress was authorized to regulate the election of state officials. Sumner's fuzzy thinking on constitutional subjects, he declared, revealed just "how high the tides of intellectual license can rise. . . . All the loose thought and wild talk inspired by a civil war, confined hitherto to newspaper editorials and inflammatory speeches on the stump, at length have found utterance in this high place; all this extravagance and absolute wildness are sanctioned, sancti-

[1] Sumner: *Works,* XIII, 356–66.

fied, and canonized, by the indorsement of the Senator from Massachusetts."[2]

Angered, Sumner, as Senator Howe reported, "prepared himself deliberately to *punish* Carpenter," and on April 18 he delivered a formal, written-out speech, before a packed Senate chamber, denouncing the Wisconsin Senator for "assuming the antiquated, well-worn, and now blood-bespattered garments of John C. Calhoun." In vain would Carpenter challenge the right of Congress to act under powers conferred by the Declaration of Independence, one of the "two great title deeds which our country holds." "The idea that he champions," Sumner concluded, to applause from the galleries, "was buried under the apple tree of Appomattox."

"Carpenter rather staggered under the blow," Howe reported, for Sumner "meant to hurt him and he did." Unable to answer Sumner's bloody-shirt appeal, he could only predict that the Senator from Massachusetts would "find it impossible long to deceive the American people" and to protest Sumner's "propensity . . . to reduce every discussion, no matter what may be its subject, to the general head of slavery." In this respect, he added, Sumner's actions called "to mind the practice of the quack who always threw his patients into convulsions, because that was a disease within his healing power."[3]

If these exchanges were only a little sharper than those which had occurred between Sumner and other Senators earlier in the session, the votes which followed were markedly different.[4] The number of Senators Sumner could consistently rally behind his position on the Georgia bill had increased to twenty-three, but nearly one half of his following consisted of Southern Republicans, men of little influence either in the Senate Chamber or in the party. An equal number of Republican Senators now belonged to the faction opposing Sumner, and the large increase since January included not merely the corrupt and patronage-hungry, like Pomeroy of Kansas, but such powerful

[2] *Cong. Globe,* 41 Cong., 2 Sess., pp. 2424–5.

[3] T. O. Howe to Grace Howe, April 24, 1870, copy, Howe MSS.; *Cong. Globe,* 41 Cong., 2 Sess., pp. 2748–50.

[4] The following analysis is based upon my tabulation of nine roll calls held in the Senate between April 6 and April 19 on the readmission of Georgia.

party spokesmen as Harlan, Edmunds, and Morrill. So closely were the factions now balanced that the Democrats, along with a handful of uncommitted Republicans, had the balance of power, and in a series of exceedingly close votes (24–25; 30–31; 29–30), undermined the Bullock regime by requiring Georgia to hold new elections in 1870.

It was not, as some historians have claimed, the first time since 1865 that the Congressional Radicals had been defeated,[5] since, in fact, the Radical wing of the Republican party had rarely exercised effective control and Sumner's own plans for restoration had nearly all gone unheeded. But it was Sumner's first significant defeat in his attempt to lead the Senate during Grant's administration. Just how significant it was was not evident until May, when the Senate debated what was to become known as the First Enforcement Act, designed to put down the Ku Klux Klan and other terroristic organizations in the South. Sumner had no share in drafting the bill, and he had hardly a dozen words to say while it was being discussed. His own program for solving racial problems in the South, an elaborate civil rights bill to prohibit discrimination against Negroes by common carriers, innkeepers, churches, and cemetery associations, and to outlaw school segregation,[6] was quietly ignored. Referred without discussion to Trumbull's Judiciary Committee, it lay buried there for two months, only to be reported out adversely at the end of the session.

Just what role Grant himself played in this extraordinary diminution of Sumner's influence is hard to determine. The general was not accustomed to announce his plans in advance or to boast of his accomplishments in retrospect. But the behavior of Benjamin F. Butler served as a pretty good index to the administration's strategy. Early in March when the House debated the scheme to perpetuate Bullock and the Georgia Republicans in power for another two years, Butler had been its principal advocate, but shortly after Sumner made his speech on Santo

[5] Ellis Paxson Oberholtzer: *A History of the United States Since the Civil War* (New York: The Macmillan Company; 1922), II, 266.

[6] For the complete text, see Frankfort (Ky.) *Weekly Yeoman*, July 1, 1870. For a fuller discussion of this important measure and its subsequent history, see below, pp. 531–9, 545–7.

Domingo he appears to have received a remarkable revelation and by June was ready to require new Georgia elections in 1870. Taunted because of this astonishing change of front, Butler replied candidly that he was indeed sacrificing his personal preferences, but he added: "I reflect I am a party man; I have the good of my party to my heart; I believe in the necessity of party action and of acting together for the common good." [7]

Convinced that he had broken Sumner's power, Grant insisted upon renewing the fight over Santo Domingo. On May 31 he again urged the Senate to approve his treaty, adding as a special reason for prompt action the alleged fact "that a European power stands ready now to offer two millions of dollars for the possession of Samaná Bay alone." [8]

But if Sumner could no longer direct domestic legislation, he still had the power to frustrate the President's wishes on foreign policy. He and his friends responded to the President's new message with motions designed to harry the Chief Executive; they required him to divulge the name of the mysterious foreign power interested in Santo Domingo, authorized another investigation of the circumstances under which the Dominican treaty had been negotiated, insisted upon a further appraisal of the public debt of the insolvent republic, and demanded copies of the instructions sent to naval officers operating near the island. In public session the opponents of annexation made much of the case of Davis Hatch, a Connecticut businessman with interests in Santo Domingo, who was arbitrarily arrested and brutally imprisoned by Baez, largely for opposing annexation. When Senator Ferry on June 8 revealed that Babcock had been on the island during Hatch's imprisonment and had actually connived in it, Sumner impulsively ejaculated: "He ought to be cashiered at once." [9]

This attack upon a trusted aide infuriated Grant. He thought it characteristic of Sumner to assail the reputation of a man who had no way of replying. "I can defend myself," Grant raged, "but he [Babcock] is merely a major of engineers with no

[7] *Cong. Globe*, 41 Cong., 2 Sess., Appendix, p. 578.
[8] *Senate Exec. Journal*, XVII, 460–2.
[9] *Cong. Globe*, 41 Cong., 2 Sess., p. 4194.

opportunity to meet a Senator." The President urged his Senate followers to expose Sumner as a "man of very little practical sense, puffed-up, and unsound." He and his friends began collecting statements about Sumner's supposed pledge to support the Dominican treaty.[1] At the same time a majority of Senate Republicans authorized an investigation of the Hatch case, not by Sumner's Committee on Foreign Relations but by a special committee headed by Nye, who had already announced his belief that Babcock was "as pure as the waters of the mountain from melted snow."

But not even presidential pressure could make two-thirds of the Senators support annexation. On June 30, when the final vote came, the Senate divided evenly (28–28), and the treaty failed.[2] For Grant the vote was a clear-cut defeat. For Sumner it was a final but ominous victory. In the test ballots leading up to the final vote, only eight other Republicans stood solidly behind him; a majority of both Northern Republicans and Southern Republicans went against him on most of these roll calls. On the final count, there were eighteen other Republicans who voted with him, but, outside of the New England delegation, nearly every major party leader supported the treaty: Zachariah Chandler, Roscoe Conkling, Jacob M. Howard, Oliver O. Morton, William M. Stewart, and the rest. Highly significant was the vote of Simon Cameron, who had joined with Sumner in opposing the treaty when it was before the Foreign Relations Committee but who now voted for annexation; Grant had just appointed his son-in-law minister to Turkey.[3] Sumner's principal Republican allies in defeating the treaty were men like Trumbull, whose loyalty to the party Sumner had often questioned, and the united support of the Senate Democrats was essential for the success of

[1] Charles Richard Williams (ed.): *Diary and Letters of Rutherford Birchard Hayes* (Columbus, Ohio: The Ohio State Archaeological and Historical Society; 1924), III, 111–12; Orville E. Babcock to J. W. Forney, June 6, 1870, copy, Zachariah Chandler MSS.; Grant to Chandler, June 8, 1870, ibid.

[2] The following analysis is based upon my tabulation of seven roll calls held in secret sessions of the Senate between March 24 and June 30 on the treaty to annex the Dominican Republic.

[3] Erwin Stanley Bradley: *Simon Cameron: Lincoln's Secretary of War* (Philadelphia: University of Pennsylvania Press; 1966), p. 320.

Hamilton Fish

THE LIBRARY OF CONGRESS

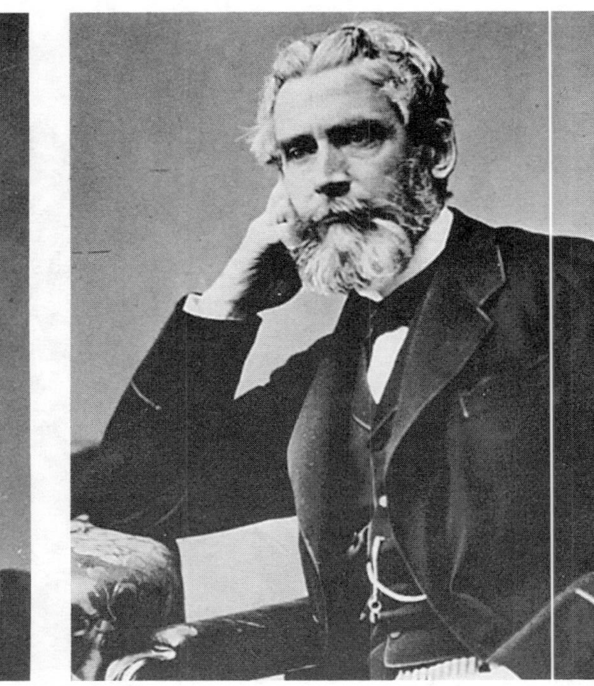

John Lothrop Motley

THE NATIONAL ARCHIVES

PRINCIPALS IN THE ALABAMA CLAIMS CONTROVERSY

"The Last Shot of the Honorable Senator from Massachusetts" Thomas Nast's View of Sumner's Speech on "Republicanism vs. Grantism"

HARPER'S WEEKLY, JUNE 22, 1872

"The Massive Grievance" A cartoonist uses a key phrase from the Alabama Claims speech to characterize Sumner himself.

VANITY FAIR, MAY 25, 1872

TWO HOSTILE VIEWS OF SUMNER IN 1872

his coalition against Grant.[4] Back in December 1869 Sumner had called Republicans who cooperated with Democrats traitors to their party; by June 1870 he was not merely voting with those same Republicans but was an ally of the Democrats himself.

[4] Because of this pattern of voting W. Stull Holt, in *Treaties Defeated by the Senate* (Baltimore: The Johns Hopkins Press; 1933), pp. 127–9, has suggested that Sumner's role in the defeat of the treaty has been exaggerated. The Democrats opposed it for party reasons and the Republicans who did so were independent-minded and progressive men who did not need Sumner's guidance. "Indeed," Professor Holt continues, "the negative votes were not due to Sumner's insistence, but the affirmative votes were due to Grant's." In view of the general unpopularity of the treaty, therefore, "the tie vote was a compliment to Grant's efforts and to the powers of the executive." Certainly this is a correct appraisal of Grant's influence. Professor Holt does less than justice, however, to Sumner's part in arousing public hostility to the annexation treaty; without his exertions it might have slipped through the Senate almost uncontested. He fails also to recognize that except for Sumner, four carpetbag Senators from the South would hardly have dared to vote against the treaty and that Sumner also brought along with him a number of Senators, like Thomas W. Tipton of Nebraska, who were strongly under his influence.

CHAPTER XII

An Act of Sheer Brutality

ON the day after the Senate rejected the Santo Domingo treaty, Grant ordered Motley recalled. If the move was sudden, it was also predictable. The President had never liked Motley, whom he had appointed at Sumner's insistence. The fact that the minister wore a monocle and parted his hair in the middle was simply outward evidence that he was unmanly and not wholly American. When Motley had disobeyed his instructions in his first interview with Clarendon on the Alabama claims, the President was ready to dismiss him, but it was imprudent then to break with Sumner. The Senator's opposition to the Santo Domingo treaty robbed Motley of that defense. As early as June 14, 1870, Grant informed the members of his cabinet that those Republicans who failed to support his policies were not "entitled to influence in obtaining positions," and he added pointedly that he would "not let those who oppose[d] him 'name Ministers to London,' etc., etc." [1]

If he could only find a first-rate replacement, Grant told Secretary Fish while the Santo Domingo treaty was still being considered, he would move. At once his advisers became involved in a series of comic-opera intrigues to name the ideal successor to Motley. Senators Chandler, Morton, and Carpenter, who had hitherto been fiercely critical of Fish, suddenly discov-

[1] **Fish: Diary, June 14, 1870, Fish MSS.**

ered that the Secretary of State was an admirable diplomat, just the man needed in London. If they removed him from the State Department, they knew they could soon persuade Grant to recognize the dying Cuban insurrection. Aware of this backstairs maneuver, Fish told the President that he could not accept the British mission and, once again, astutely offered to resign.

Hastily refusing to let his Secretary of State go, Grant then received an even more startling proposal—to replace Motley with Sumner himself. Fish seems to have originated this scheme some months earlier. The Dominican treaty severely tested his loyalties. He basically agreed with Sumner that it was not desirable to annex the Dominican Republic. Fish still retained much of his respect and affection for the Massachusetts Senator, regarding him as one of the elders of the Republican party, whose long services entitled him to indulge in excesses of egotism and of rhetoric. At the same time Fish was absolutely loyal to Grant. He could not oppose his chief on the Santo Domingo issue, and he even foresaw certain advantages from it, since the treaty diverted the President's attention from the more dangerous questions concerning Cuba and Great Britain. Always a compromiser, Fish had tried to avert a collision between Grant and Sumner. But the President bluntly rejected his proposed amendments that might make the Dominican treaty acceptable to its Senate critics, and Sumner proved equally unresponsive to the Secretary's earnest arguments for annexation.[2]

Calling at Sumner's house one evening in March, before the Dominican treaty had emerged from committee, Fish thought he discovered another solution. He found Sumner in "a morbid and disturbed condition of mind and temper," brooding over his loneliness, his physical exhaustion, and his lack of following in the Senate. He was, he told the Secretary, all alone in the world now, and in the dark hours of the night he often woke to realize his solitary, unhappy state. When Fish offered sympathy, Sumner rejected it: "You can't understand my situation. Your family relations are all pleasant. Why, many and many a night when I go to bed I almost wish that I may never awake." Genuinely touched, Fish advised him to go to Europe, where he would have

[2] Fish to Zachariah Chandler, June 8, 1870, copy, ibid.

the leisure for study and writing, but Sumner countered that he could not afford the additional expense; publishing his *Works* cost him $1,500 a year, and his house was an endless financial drain. At once Fish saw how to solve both Sumner's problems and his own. "There is the English mission," he urged. "Take it. It is yours."

Thoughtfully Sumner replied: "No, I would not like to interfere with Motley, who is my friend."

Forbearing to press the point, Fish left with the reassurance: "You are right; you should go without any official cares or duties." [3]

By June, when it was clear that Sumner's opposition would probably defeat the Santo Domingo treaty, this same solution to the difficulty occurred to other Republicans. Hearing of the impending removal of Motley, Butler warned Grant that Massachusetts Republicans would be badly upset, especially if as a result Sumner broke with the administration. Having no love for the "impractical and arrogant" Senator, Butler recognized that Sumner was "regarded by the Country as the Representative of the advanced sentiment of radical (Anti-Slavery) Republicanism" and that his defection could be politically dangerous. But if Sumner were to be offered the British mission and decline it, that would "deprive him of all appeal to sympathy on the score of persecution, or want of recognition." If he accepted and left the Senate, Santo Domingo might be annexed. Nor should the President be concerned about any damage Sumner might do in England; if any important negotiation should arise, Grant could always send a special envoy to Britain and thus Sumner would

[3] Fish's account of this conversation appeared in the Boston *Evening Transcript*, Oct. 31, 1877; Sumner's, in his *Works*, XIV, 260, and in his letter to Henry Wilson, June 2, 1871, Wilson MSS. It is not possible precisely to date the interview. Fish denied that he had "seriously tendered, or thought of tendering, to Mr. Sumner the British mission"; his offer was an offhand remark made to a friend in distress and he at once had realized how incautious he had been. Since there is no other instance in Fish's long public record of such effervescent friendship and since, only a short time later, he fully endorsed the plan of Butler and Cameron to send Sumner abroad, it is not possible to accept the Secretary's version; in fact, he was coolly calculating the best way to end the Santo Domingo impasse. It is equally impossible to accept Sumner's subsequent statement that he felt Fish was trying to bribe him; for months after this episode the two men worked amicably together and addressed each other in terms of great esteem and friendship.

"be effectually snubbed, and paid off for his arrogance and conceit exhibited . . . toward the President." Unmentioned was the possibility that Butler might secure the Senate seat Sumner would vacate. Simon Cameron, too, endorsed this plan; it would preserve a facade of party unity—and it would make Cameron, because of his seniority, Sumner's successor as chairman of the Senate Foreign Relations Committee.[4]

When Grant first heard this proposal, he grimly replied that he would nominate Sumner as minister to Great Britain only "on condition that he first resign his seat in the Senate, and with the understanding that he would remove him as soon as the nomination was confirmed." But when Fish recapitulated Butler's and Cameron's arguments, which so entirely coincided with his own, the President began to reconsider. "I don't like to do it," he grumbled, but he asked Secretary of the Treasury Boutwell how such a nomination would be received in Massachusetts. "The matter will be further considered," Fish with some satisfaction noted in his diary on June 28, "for it has at least acquired a lodgment as a question of expediency."

The defeat of the Dominican treaty, and more particularly Sumner's severe castigation of Babcock, put an end to this scheme, and Grant decided to replace Motley with Senator Frederick T. Frelinghuysen, of New Jersey. Still hoping to avoid an open break, Fish tried to dissuade the President, arguing that peremptory removal would have a bad effect upon the country, that it would be attributed to bad temper, and that, in any event, since Motley had done nothing in recent months to warrant recall, he ought to be allowed to remain in London until winter.

"That, I will not do," Grant firmly replied. "I will not allow Mr. Sumner to ride over me."

"But," said Fish, "it is not Mr. Sumner, but Mr. Motley, whom you are striking."

"It is the same thing," retorted Grant.

"The country will not so understand it," Fish objected.

"They will when the removal is made," snapped the President.

[4] **Fish: Diary, June 27, 1870, Fish MSS.**

The only concession the Secretary could secure was permission to write Motley that his resignation would be accepted.[5]

• 2 •

When Grant sent Frelinghuysen's nomination to the Senate on July 14, 1870, Sumner accepted it as a declaration of war. He was not surprised by the move, for the newspapers had been carrying rumors that Motley would be replaced; only the timing of the blow was unexpected. In the secret session of the Senate, where all appointments were considered, Sumner made it clear that he was not so much opposing Frelinghuysen, for whom he professed high regard, as defending Motley "as a generous American, an ultra-American, whose Americanism shone in all his writings and even in the selection of the subject of his history." To support his case, he read a letter which his colleague Wilson had written the President, in behalf of "the men of Massachusetts, who gave you more than 75,000 majority" in the 1868 election. Massachusetts Republicans remembered Motley's services to the Union cause abroad during the Civil War, his unjust treatment by Seward afterward, and his warm advocacy of Grant's candidacy in 1868, and they were "proud to number Mr. Motley among their most loved and honored sons." In Massachusetts, Wilson's letter concluded, the removal of Motley would certainly be interpreted as an attempt to punish Sumner for opposing the annexation of Santo Domingo.[6]

In reply Conkling spoke for the President. In order to minimize political repercussions, Grant had decided flatly to deny any connection between the removal of Motley and Sumner's fight against annexation. Instead, Conkling argued, Motley was asked to resign only because he had failed to present the administration's views on the Alabama Claims question to the British government. When appointed, he had volunteered to draft his own instructions, and the "one chief and pivotal point" of his elaborate paper had been that "the crime of England Consisted

[5] Ibid., July 1, 1870.

[6] Unless otherwise identified, quotations in the following paragraphs are drawn from the Boston *Advertiser*, July 18, 1870.

especially in her declaration of beligerancy [*sic*]." Since this was not the view of the administration, the State Department had given Motley quite a different set of instructions, but when the new minister arrived in Britain, he presented to Clarendon "his own position, and not that of his Government." From that moment his recall had been determined upon, though it had been "postponed out of Kindness and Consideration" until the present.[7]

Furious, Sumner tried to refute Conkling's charges. It was not true that Motley had volunteered to write his own instructions; Sumner, at the specific urging of the Secretary of State, had invited him to do so. In any case, Motley's views on the Alabama Claims question were precisely those of the State Department. His statement of the American position to Clarendon in May 1869 was "in entire harmony with the able and elaborate state paper of Secretary Fish of September 23 [1869]"—a paper which, Sumner neglected to add, had been written when he himself was all powerful in the State Department and had, therefore, vehemently restated his own views.[8] But even if Motley in an excess of patriotic zeal had exceeded his instructions back in May 1869, why was dismissal withheld until July of the following year? The only reason must be Sumner's opposition to the Santo Domingo treaty. To reinforce his point, Sumner had the clerk read from the official record the sequence of dates: June 30, the Senate's rejection of annexation; July 1, Grant's call for Motley's resignation.

Though only three Senators voted against confirming Frelinghuysen, with Sumner himself abstaining, Republicans were upset by the ousting of Motley. The minister himself had no political following, but party members who were not privy to the secret Senate debates were puzzled that the President had acted in a fashion that seemed both high-handed and devious. Throughout the summer there rose insistent demands that the administration "state formally and definitely and publicly the grounds of Mr. Motley's removal."[9] By fall the pressure was so

[7] Conkling's notes for his speech, attached to his letter to F. T. Frelinghuysen, July 15, 1870, Conkling MSS.

[8] See above, p. 411.

[9] Adam Badeau to J. C. B. Davis, Nov. 26, 1870, Davis MSS.

great that the quasi-official administration newspaper, the Washington *National Republican,* was finally obliged to announce: ". . . the removal of Mr. Motley had no connection whatsoever with Senator Sumner's course on the Santo Domingo question. . . . It was the continued disregard of instructions that finally brought things to that crisis. Mr. Motley, in his folly, neglected his duty. . . . His un-American conduct, his toadyism, his ridiculous apeing of the monarchical show and glitter . . . disgusted the President and Secretary Fish." [1]

Party stalwarts, like Senator Howe of Wisconsin, found it possible to swallow this explanation "that the removal of Mr. Motley was not an offense against Mr. Sumner," but the thinking element of the party remained unconvinced. Grant's action, George William Curtis felt certain, was "a blow at Sumner," and even Senators generally critical of Sumner, like Cornelius Cole of California, believed that it was "struck on account of Sumner's opposition to the Santo Domingo treaty." The President had taken "a very injudicious step," Cole concluded, lamenting: "Grant often forgets to act fairly. He is not always a wise politician." [2]

Sumner, least of all, could accept the pretexts given for replacing Motley. Even before he left Washington he was, according to Henry L. Dawes, passionate in his grief because "first, *his* friend and the elect of *the* pure that dwell in Athens is snubbed and *second* Sumner is himself in *dis*favor with royalty." [3] Upon his return to Massachusetts in late July, his anger boiled over. Surrounded by his political adulators in the Bird Club and by Motley's literary admirers in the Saturday Club, he grew increasingly indignant over the flimsy charges being brought against the historian. Point by point he labored to refute them. The accusation that Motley had volunteered to write his own instructions he branded as an outright lie, and he produced a statement from Representative Hooper to prove that Fish had asked the minister-designate to write out his views on the Alabama Claims question. Sumner also demolished the argument

[1] Oct. 25, 1870.

[2] T. O. Howe to Sumner, Aug. 23, 1870, Sumner MSS.; Curtis to C. E. Norton, July 24, 1870, Curtis MSS.; Cole to his wife, July 14, 1870, Cole MSS.

[3] Dawes to Electa Dawes, July 13, 1870, Dawes MSS.

that Motley was replaced because the death of Clarendon and the succession of Granville as British Foreign Minister made it desirable to begin negotiations afresh; he showed that the news of Clarendon's demise did not reach the United States until after Grant asked Motley to resign. The charge that the minister was un-American in behavior Sumner traced to the snubbing Motley had given hard-drinking, foul-mouthed Zachariah Chandler, who on his recent visit to England had wanted to be introduced into the highest British social circles.

Sumner was left, then, with his conviction that the sole reason for this "most atrocious crime . . . in diplomatic history" was the President's pique over rejection of the Santo Domingo treaty.[4] Going on a lecture tour in the fall, he had numerous opportunities to spread his version of the Motley affair in private talks with politicians in New England, New York, New Jersey, Pennsylvania, Michigan, and Illinois. Though James Redpath's highly organized, professional Lyceum Bureau made the venture a financial success, which netted Sumner seven thousand dollars he needed to maintain his expensive Washington household and to subsidize the publication of his *Works*, he found delivering thirty-eight lectures in as many days a heavy physical strain, doubtless increased by the unenthusiastic reception he received from some of his audiences. At Ann Arbor, for instance, the University of Michigan students gave such boisterous demonstrations of pleasure when, after two and one-half hours, Sumner reached his "In conclusion," that he declined his fee, and left the town sulking.[5]

The farther West Sumner traveled and the more fatigued he became, the more indiscreet did he grow. After his lecture in Chicago he visited former Congressman Isaac N. Arnold and, failing to notice that there was a newspaper reporter in the room, launched into a diatribe against the President. Accustomed to think of Grant as a kind of vacuum in the White House, Sumner could not believe that the President himself had instigated this "act of sheer brutality" toward Motley.[6] He was simply

[4] Sumner as quoted in J. C. B. Davis to Fish, Aug. 3, 1870, Fish MSS.
[5] Amelia Ormsby to Charles Croswell, Nov. 20, 1870, Croswell MSS.
[6] Sumner to T. O. Howe, Aug. 28, 1870, Howe MSS.

ignorant. Unlike Zachary Taylor, who also "was not a brilliant man or a statesman," Grant was unaware of his deficiencies and did not surround himself with capable advisers. In consequence, "those young military men whom the President had gathered around him or in his actual cabinet, by what warrant it was difficult to say," were exploiting the simple-minded chief executive. Seeing in the annexation of the Dominican Republic a good speculation, they had lured Grant, "honestly enough," into their scheme. Now, Sumner quoted an informant who had recently returned from Santo Domingo, "the whole coast of the Bay of Samaná is staked off into lots marked 'Cazneau,' and 'Babcock' and 'Baez,' " while "one or two particularly large ones are marked 'Grant.' " This last, Sumner conceded, was "most likely" done without the President's knowledge, for Grant was "no doubt . . . an honest man." [7]

Bad as was the President's course, malign as was the influence of Babcock and the other military aides surrounding Grant, even worse, in Sumner's opinion, was the behavior of responsible Republican leaders who had allowed themselves to become "compurgators" in the libelous assaults upon Motley. Though Senator Howe had to bear some of Sumner's wrath and Boutwell also felt his rebukes, Sumner came to be most fiercely angry with his old friend Hamilton Fish. Aware that the Secretary of State had not truly favored the Dominican treaty, knowing that he had signed the request for Motley's resignation with great reluctance, Sumner had expected from him neutrality, if not support, in his fight with the President. Instead, he came to feel, Fish was supplying arguments for Grant's apologists. The beginning of Sumner's disenchantment came shortly after the secret debate on Frelinghuysen's appointment, when he sought to correct the "absurd" accusation that Motley had volunteered to write his own instructions. Instead of agreeing with Sumner, the Secretary of State replied equivocally: "My recollection is not in precise accord

[7] Chicago *Republican*, quoted in Springfield *Weekly Republican*, Nov. 25, 1870. Later Sumner alleged that the newspaper report was "a stolen thing, with a mixture of truth, of falsehood, and of exaggeration, producing in the main the effect of falsehood" (*Cong. Globe*, 41 Cong., 3 Sess., p. 247), but there is abundant evidence from other sources to prove that it fairly accurately represented his views of Grant.

with yours. . . ." Sumner grew more suspicious when Conkling and Howe referred to Motley's "Memoir" as being in conflict with the views of the administration on the Alabama claims question; that document had been written for Fish's eyes alone, and presumably only he, Sumner, and the lesser officials at the State Department had access to it. When Sumner asked the Secretary point-blank whether others had made use of it, Fish replied uncandidly that "none outside the Cabinet" had known of its existence—though Fish's own diary proves that only two days earlier he had discussed the "Memoir" in detail with Senator Howe.[8]

Fish's position was, in fact, ambiguous and difficult. He knew, beyond doubt, that Grant had replaced Motley in order to punish Sumner. He also knew that the President for more than twelve months had had ample grounds for dismissing the minister. Only because of Fish's intervention had Motley been able to survive so long in London; when Grant's decision grew fixed, Fish had softened the order for recall by securing permission for Motley to resign, and he had accompanied his official request for that resignation with a personal note of warm sympathy. All these efforts both Sumner and Motley ignored. Flying into a rage when he received Fish's letter, the minister "swore at the President, damned his countrymen as vulgar and brutal, and wished the damned Government might be destroyed." He decided not to retire quietly but to force Grant to recall him. "I refused to resign," he explained to Sumner, "because it would be to confess that I had done something which would not bear examination—and I know I have been as faithful, loyal and diligent . . . as the President or Secretary of State. . . ." [9] Waiting for the official notice of his dismissal, which was issued on November 10, he began composing in his best polemical vein what he knew would be his last despatch.

Embarrassed by Motley's course, Fish was further exasperated by his inability to find a suitable successor. After confirma-

[8] Fish to Sumner, July 19, 1870, Fish MSS.; Fish: Diary, July 15 and 17, 1870, ibid.

[9] Benjamin Moran: Diary, July 15, 1870, MS., Lib. of Cong.; Motley to Sumner, Dec. 8, 1870, Sumner MSS. Cf. John Jay: "Motley's Appeal to History," *Internat. Rev.*, IV (1877), 838–54.

tion by the Senate, Frelinghuysen declined the appointment. Grant and Fish then began canvassing other possibilities and offered the mission successively to Senators Lyman Trumbull, Lot M. Morrill, George F. Edmunds, Oliver P. Morton, and Timothy O. Howe. When all of these refused, the President considered naming Senator George H. Williams, Representative James G. Blaine, President Andrew D. White of Cornell, and even Wendell Phillips. "It seems, the office is to go a begging, like the Spanish throne," Longfellow tartly observed, "and finally we shall have some Yahoo sent out to disgrace us." [1] Not until December 1870 was Motley's replacement found, in Robert C. Schenck, a competent but unimaginative former Congressman from Ohio.

During the summer of 1870 Fish must often have contemplated resigning as the simple way out of his difficulties, yet he held on. His loyalty to Grant and to the Republican party was so great that he would not consciously do anything to weaken it. Veteran party leaders, like Justin S. Morrill, begged him to remain in the cabinet, because only he could serve as the peacemaker between the President and the Chairman of the Committee on Foreign Relations; without Fish as intermediary, Sumner might defect and "if he should nurse his wrath undoubtedly he would draw off some of the most reliable members of the Republican party." Then, too, Fish knew that Grant was easily misled and that, with another man as Secretary of State, he might embark upon a Cuban adventure or exacerbate relations with England. This last consideration was especially weighty, for there was growing evidence that the British government genuinely desired a speedy settlement of its difficulties with the United States, an objective which Fish cherished as "the greatest glory and the greatest happiness of his life." [2]

There were also personal considerations, no doubt unconscious, which kept Fish in office. Slow to anger, he gradually came to feel that Sumner's touchiness and vanity were unbearable. After several months in office he grew restive under the Senator's constant lecturing, and he was wearied that Sumner

1 Longfellow to Sumner, July 18, 1870, Longfellow MSS.

2 Morrill to Fish, July 18 and Sept. 5, 1870, Fish MSS.; Charles Francis Adams: *Before and After the Treaty of Washington* (New York: n.p.; 1902), p. 93.

never ceased to fight battles even after they were already won. When Sumner demanded that Thomas H. Dudley be continued as American consul to Liverpool, where he had served since 1861, because removal would be considered a victory for the Confederates, the Secretary at last exploded: "How long is the rebellion to last? If death should overtake Dudley in the Consulate will it be a 'rebel triumph?'" Even worse was the constant, humiliating realization that Sumner, from his Foreign Relations Committee, was in effect conducting American foreign policy. Fish winced when Henry Adams, in a much quoted essay in the *North American Review,* described how Sumner virtually ignored the Secretary of State "and issued his orders with almost the authority of a Roman triumvir." Yet when British minister Thornton asked when the United States planned to ratify a treaty, Fish was obliged to make a humiliating admission of the Senator's power: "I don't know; I can't get Sumner to take up anything; there are a number of little things, but Sumner won't do anything." [3]

During the summer of 1870 Fish's relations with Sumner slowly deteriorated. So long as both men were in Washington they managed to remain on cordial terms, though sometimes in the course of friendly conversation Sumner would erupt with "outbursts of rhetorical denunciation" against not merely Grant but "every one connected with the Administration." [4] But by late July, when Sumner had returned to Massachusetts and Fish was taking a vacation in New York, the note of friendship began noticeably to quaver. Stung by attacks which appeared in the Boston papers, Fish charged Sumner with being their inspiration, if not their author. Sumner denied the accusation, and a long, acrimonious correspondence ensued.

Though the letters of both men were studded with references to their long friendship and with protestations that only "kindness" and "frankness and candor" compelled blunt statements of home truths, their tone became increasingly angry. The Secretary of State scored some debater's points in the epistolary

[3] Fish to Sumner, Feb. 28, 1870, Sumner MSS.; Henry Adams: *The Great Secession Winter,* p. 218; Thornton to Edmund Hammond, Feb. 15, 1870, Hammond MSS.

[4] Fish to T. O. Howe, Aug. 6, 1870, copy, Fish MSS.

exchange; he showed how Sumner had suppressed Fish's account of how Motley volunteered to write his instructions, and he proved that Sumner was, to say the least, disingenuous in denying that he provided the Boston papers ammunition with which to attack the administration. Yet on the whole Sumner clearly came off best. Recognizing that all the excuses offered for Motley's removal were transparently false, he challenged Fish: "Try to write a despatch, embodying the different reasons that have been assigned for M's disgrace—put them plainly as they should be put—and then read it over in a cool moment, and I am sure that [there] will not be a reason that you will not read with a smile of derision or with a blush of shame."

Gradually Sumner revealed what he thought Fish should have done in the circumstances. At first he tried to let the Secretary draw his own conclusions from the fact that "every one" of literary or academic prominence in New England was asking: "Why did not somebody resign rather than sanction an act of unjustifiable harshness by which the public service is such a loser?" Then he reported that when Boutwell had tried to defend Grant's action, his Boston dinner companions thought: "He should have resigned rather than see it go on." But when Fish did not take the hint, Sumner grew more explicit. Obviously the Secretary did not realize the "absolute eccentricity" of Grant's action against Motley. He must be afflicted with a kind of moral blindness which kept him from seeing that it was "unique—a paragon—a 'none-such.'" "Never before," Sumner insisted, "has the Department of State played the part of King Phyrrus's elephants and trampled down its own friends—trampled down an illustrious citizen abroad—also the senator and representatives of a Republican State, and still more the people of this faithful state and the sentiments of scholars and gentlemen throughout the country." Surely once Fish understood that this was the "most grievous *personal wrong* in the history of the Department of State," he would resign. He should have done so back in July, Sumner wrote bluntly. "Had you done this," he added, "there would have been no question as to your position—no question as to your sense of justice or friendship for Motley." [5]

[5] Sumner to Fish, Sept. 6, 14, and 29, 1870, ibid.

Angrily Fish denied Sumner's charges and rejected his suggested remedy, but he did so with an irritability of language and a moroseness of temper which suggested how unhappy he was at having to defend Grant's uncandid explanations for removing Motley. Instead of directing his hostility toward the President, however, he turned against Sumner and the other members of the Boston "Mutual Admiration Society." To a friend he remarked that the recent Vatican Council had erred in announcing the doctrine of papal infallibility. "If instead of the Pope," he jested, "they had proclaimed Boston literature, Boston Newspapers, etc., infallible, there would have been universal quiescence." By the time Congress assembled in December, Fish was hardly on speaking terms with Sumner, whom he now sneeringly called "the great Autocrat" of Massachusetts.[6]

• 3 •

Sumner was in no better favor with the Congressional leaders of his party. Grant's shrewd maneuvers during the previous session of Congress had eroded Sumner's following and by December 1870 the New Radicals were ready to take away his last remaining source of power, the chairmanship of the Foreign Relations Committee. Acting for the new Republican leadership, Zachariah Chandler, head of the Senate caucus committee responsible for making committee assignments, initially proposed to drop from the Foreign Relations Committee all three of the principal opponents of the Santo Domingo treaty, Sumner, James W. Patterson, and Carl Schurz, the scholarly German-American who had come to be Sumner's closest friend in the Senate and his most consistent supporter in the committee. Before moving he thought he had secured the backing of the President, for Babcock, Grant's aide, had deceitfully informed him that the "*old gentleman*" believed "that the Chairman of a Committee like that must be a friend to the Administration" and that, in consequence, "Mr. Sumner must leave the Committee."[7] In fact, neither Grant nor Fish favored Chandler's scheme,[8] for Fish had

[6] Fish to Carl Schurz, Sept. 5, 1870, Schurz MSS.
[7] Babcock to Chandler, Oct. 8, 1870, Chandler MSS.
[8] Memorandum of Hamilton Fish, June 13, 1893, Davis MSS.

a more devious strategy planned. Finding himself without administration support in the caucus, Chandler could not persuade his colleagues to overturn the seniority rules, and numerous Senators "denounced the hints thrown out that Mr. Sumner should be deposed from the chairmanship."

Foiled, Chandler then suggested dropping Schurz from the committee, on the ground that during the past summer he had helped to split the Republican party in Missouri and to elect an anti-administration Liberal, B. Gratz Brown, governor. He promptly learned that too many Senators had German constituents to risk ostracizing the principal German-American leader, and that plan had to be abandoned. Finally, Chandler tried to get his way by leaving both Sumner and Schurz on the committee and replacing Patterson with Conkling, a bitter foe of Sumner and a friend to annexation. Alerted to this maneuver, Sumner protested in caucus that such a change was "something extraordinary," and Patterson flatly declined to give up his post. After all Chandler's expedients were exhausted, Wilson on December 8 successfully moved that the committee be asked to bring in another slate of assignments, leaving the membership of the Foreign Relations Committee undisturbed.[9]

Taking the caucus decision as a vote of confidence, Sumner on the very next day renewed his attack upon the proposed annexation of Santo Domingo. Seizing upon a rhapsodic passage in the President's annual message which again urged annexation, argued that Santo Domingo was of vast strategic importance, and maintained that the island would one day become a huge consumer of United States farm and factory products, he demanded that Grant submit to the Senate all papers and correspondence regarding the treaty with the Dominican Republic.

Fully aware that the project of annexing Santo Domingo was dead beyond resuscitation, most Senators saw in Sumner's resolution only an outright affront to the President. In order to allow Grant to save face, most were willing to accept a motion that Morton immediately introduced, calling for the appointment of three commissioners to visit the island, investigate its

[9] Boston *Commonwealth,* Dec. 10, 1870; Washington correspondence, Dec. 8, 1870, in undated clipping from New York *Herald,* Sumner Scrapbooks.

resources and liabilities, and look into the terms and conditions by which annexation might be possible. Such a commission was, after all, rather like what Sumner himself had proposed at the very outset of the controversy over Santo Domingo. Everybody realized that adopting Morton's proposal would postpone further discussion of the touchy question for several months, until Grant's interests could be diverted elsewhere.

Sumner would not agree. He insisted that his own motion had priority over Morton's, which was not "simply a resolution in inquiry" but one which committed "the Congress of the United States to a certain extent to the policy of annexation." In pressing for his own motion Sumner, contrary to the opinion of his colleagues, was not merely insisting upon having his own way nor even attempting to celebrate his reinstatement in his chairmanship. Because of his position he had been privileged to read confidential despatches in the State Department, and he had also studied the secret instructions given by the Navy Department to vessels operating in Dominican waters, but he was not at liberty to make his findings public. If his proposal was adopted, he could bring forth these "vastly important" documents to demonstrate how unconstitutionally Baez was acting, how deviously Babcock had behaved, and how arrogantly United States naval officers had treated the government of Haiti. But since he could not produce much real evidence until after his motion to remove the bonds of secrecy was passed, most Republican Senators, who wanted nothing more than quietly to shelve the whole Dominican affair, were unconvinced, and they unceremoniously voted to give Morton's proposal first consideration.

Angry and frustrated, Sumner then tried to commit Morton's resolution to his own Foreign Relations Committee, where he could kill it. The game he was playing was a desperate one, he knew, especially for a chairman whose power had so recently been challenged, but he had now worked himself into a state of high excitement not equaled since the passionate antislavery debates of the 1850's. He believed that history was repeating itself. The proposal to annex the Dominican Republic was much like the Kansas-Nebraska bill and the Lecompton Constitution, "by which it was sought to subjugate a distant Territory to

Slavery." Sumner saw himself once more as the defender of freedom. Grant, on the other hand, was behaving like Pierce and Buchanan and was exhibiting "that same old heartlessness, and violence which prevailed against Kansas." [1] To make the parallels complete, Sumner expected that he would be the object of physical assault, as he had been in 1856. Babcock was reported to have threatened "that if he were not officially connected with the Executive he would subject Senator Sumner to personal violence," and Grant himself was supposed to have sworn that "if he were not President of the United States, he should hold Mr. Sumner personally responsible for his language, and demand satisfaction." [2]

Reliving in his mind the trauma of the Brooks assault, Sumner rose in the Senate on December 21 in the mood of a martyr prepared to make a final protestation of faith before burning at the stake. Speaking extemporaneously, with only a single sheet of notes and a pile of reference books before him, he may have let excitement carry him further than he had intended. Ignoring the fact that Morton's resolution only created a commission of inquiry, Sumner treated it as a scheme to commit the Congress "to a dance of blood" by tricking it into annexing the Dominican Republic.[3] Such a course was an outrage, he objected, first of all to the people of Santo Domingo, who were certainly not truly represented by that "political jockey" Baez, a man linked to those "other political jockeys, Cazneau and Fabens"; this unholy trinity had then "seduced into their firm" Grant's emissary, Babcock. Even at the time of the signing of the protocol Baez was not supported by his people; he was able to hold on to his office only because United States warships were in Dominican harbors. Thus he had been, and even now still was, "sustained in power by the Government of the United States that he may betray his country."

Annexation was equally an outrage to the Republic of Haiti. Not merely had United States naval guns menaced the Haitian

[1] Sumner: *Works,* XIV, 120; Sumner to W. L. Garrison, Dec. 29, 1870, Garrison MSS.

[2] *Cong. Globe,* 41 Cong., 3 Sess., pp. 217–18.

[3] Unless otherwise identified, quotations in this paragraph are drawn from Sumner: *Works,* XIV, 94–124.

government; by referring nine times in his December message to the acquisition not just of the Dominican Republic but of the island of Santo Domingo, Grant had unconsciously revealed his true purposes. As a Senator who had for years considered himself in a special sense the "representative of the African race," [4] Sumner could not endure this menace to the Negro republic. The United States should recognize that "the ordinance of Nature" had set aside the island of Santo Domingo as the possession of the colored people. "It is theirs by right of possession, by their sweat and blood mingling with the soil, by tropical position, by its burning sun, and by the unalterable laws of climate."

Enormously effective as oratory, Sumner's "Naboth's Vineyard" speech—as he titled the pamphlet version, after the Biblical story of the rich King Ahab who had coveted the vineyard of his humble neighbor—failed to convince his colleagues. After all, the Senate had already rejected the treaty to annex the Dominican Republic, and what it was considering was only Morton's mild resolution of inquiry. Few Senators were persuaded by Sumner's frequent references to his private sources of information about Santo Domingo; by his constant talk of confidential news from the South throughout the Reconstruction era he had overplayed that hand. Many members of the Senate were too young to remember vividly the antislavery battles of the 1850's, to which Sumner so often harked back, and they found it improbable to compare Grant with Pierce and Buchanan.

Indeed, the verbal excesses of Sumner's oration strengthened the Republican faction hostile to him, and, as the debate continued all night, both their power and their vindictiveness became evident. Ridiculing Sumner's "wild expressions upon this simple question of a reference to a committee," his enemies insisted that Morton's resolution was one "committing no man to anything." If the situation in Santo Domingo was as deplorable as Sumner had described, then surely there could be not the slightest danger from the proposed commission, for, as Morton reminded him, its duty was "simply to report the facts, and we are to pass upon them." [5]

[4] Sumner to Gerrit Smith, Dec. 29, 1870, Smith MSS.
[5] *Cong. Globe*, 41 Cong., 3 Sess., pp. 238, 240, 246.

Since Morton's proposed commission was innocuous, they alleged, Sumner must have had other motives which caused him to use this debate to launch an assault upon the President. Morton reminded the Senators that the Chief Executive whom Sumner had "treated with a bitterness of persecution and a torrent of calumny" was none other than Ulysses S. Grant. Sumner's reference to engaging in a "dance of blood" was indeed apposite, Nye added, for that was precisely what Grant had done during the war in order to save his country, with the result that before him "an admiring world bowed down almost in adoration." Since Sumner's charges were so unfounded, there must be behind his speech some "personal hostility, . . . some personal animosity, . . . some private grief." Chandler claimed that Sumner, like Seward and Chase before him, had been "bitten with the presidential mania," and he urged Sumner to take a lesson from "the lives and political death of those who from personal resentments or disappointments have left the Republican hosts to wallow with the Democrats."

Fiercely Sumner battled through the night hours, with little help save from the handful of Democrats. Once again he denied that he had ever promised Grant to support the annexation of Santo Domingo; once again he denied the authenticity of his newspaper interview attacking Grant; once again he denied that he had ever questioned the President's motives. Opponents brushed all his defenses away. "No sane man," charged Conkling, "no man of common sense, not maddened by passion or blinded by bigotry or hate" could have made such charges against the President. Nye chimed in that no man without a "heightened, quickened fancy" could have credited those rumors that Grant was going to beat up Sumner. By the morning hours the new Republican leaders had painted their verbal portrait of Sumner: he was not sane; he was not loyal; and he was not even a Republican.[6]

With votes as well as words the new leaders of the Senate rejected Sumner. First they defeated the proposal to refer Morton's resolution to the Foreign Relations Committee and then, strengthened by that victory, they pushed ahead to adopt Mor-

[6] Ibid., pp. 238, 240, 242, 246, 252.

ton's resolution itself by an overwhelming vote (32–9, with 30 absent or abstaining), just before the Senate adjourned at 6:37 A.M.

• 4 •

It was a defeat, but Sumner did not for some time realize its true dimensions. Indeed, he felt that he had more than held his own against Morton's "vaguely trifling" attack and against Conkling's "assault upon him and not upon his argument." Even Senator Howe, who had joined in assailing Sumner, conceded privately: "I have never known him to display more ability." [7] Most of Sumner's old friends from the antislavery crusade rallied promptly in support of the "sagacity, wisdom, and uncompromising loyalty to principle" shown in his speech. "Stand firm, the People are with you," was the theme of a hundred letters. Daily he received assurances from both New England and the West that "All intelligent republicans . . . who are opposed to official *jobbery* and *flunkeyism* endorse you on the San Domingo question." [8]

Though more critical, the newspapers, too, gave Sumner support. Many Republican journals naturally deplored the growing rift in the party, and several agreed with the Springfield *Republican* that both sides in the debate had used intemperate and injudicious language. But if Sumner was "imprudent, bitter, and unjust" in his remarks, the New York *Tribune* added, his opponents "behaved like Bowery boys at a Tammany primary." Sumner, most editors felt, had proved himself "impregnable in argument" on the Santo Domingo scheme. In the general praise for the Senator's course, there appeared a new note. Up to this time it had been generally assumed that major American figures were, however wrongheaded, men of integrity, but now there emerged an uneasy feeling that an upright politician was so

[7] New York *Sun*, Dec. 23, 1870; Howe to his wife, Dec. 27, 1870, copy, Howe MSS.

[8] These typical quotations are taken from letters in the Sumner MSS. from Edward Hopper, of Philadelphia, Dec. 28, 1870; George Glavis, of Terre Haute, Ind., Dec. 23, 1870; G. P. Griswold, of Traverse City, Mich., Dec. 31, 1870; Edward Kinsley, of Boston, Dec. 30, 1870; and W. D. Harriman, of Ann Arbor, Mich., Dec. 24, 1870.

exceptional as to call for admiration, whatever his policies. The Chicago *Tribune*'s editorial on Sumner expressed the public mood: "He may at times be unjust, or petulant, or dictatorial and domineering, or self-conscious, or one-sided, or mistaken, but he is always honest. Whatever he does, he believes in it, and sincerely believes that he is bound to believe in it as a man of honor and a man of sense." [9]

Even in the Senate it seemed that if Sumner had lost, his opponents had not won. When tempers cooled it became increasingly evident that the vote to send a commission to Santo Domingo reflected principally a desire "to give the President an opportunity to escape from the unpleasant position into which he has drawn himself." The slight support Republicans gave Sumner during the protracted debate did not prove they were ready to follow Chandler and Conkling; instead, it was a relatively harmless way of slapping down Sumner, so as to show "their personal dislike of the man and the insults they feel he has heaped upon them in the Senate chamber or in committee room." [1] Certainly the rebuff to Sumner was no indication of support for the annexation of the Dominican Republic. The true sentiment of the Senate on that point was revealed immediately after the Christmas holidays when, without even a roll-call vote, it adopted Sumner's resolution calling for all correspondence and papers in the executive branch of the government that related to Santo Domingo. On January 11, 1871, the Senate further showed its real feelings by approving, without a dissenting vote, an amendment to Morton's resolution explicitly announcing that the sending of United States commissioners to Santo Domingo should not be "held, understood, or construed as committing Congress to the policy of annexing the territory."

Annexation was now assuredly dead, and everybody knew it except Grant and Sumner. Implacably determined, the President proceeded to name the members of the United States commission in a fashion "to disarm Sumner and his immediate

[9] Springfield *Republican*, Dec. 23, 1870; New York *Tribune*, Dec. 23, 1870; Chicago *Tribune*, quoted in Boston *Commonwealth*, Jan. 21, 1871.

[1] New York *Sun*, Dec. 23, 1870.

advocates."[2] To interest the old abolitionists in the scheme, former Senator Benjamin F. Wade was made a member; President Andrew D. White, of Cornell, was added as a sop to the intellectuals; and Sumner's old friend, Samuel Gridley Howe, who most embarrassingly differed from the Senator upon this vexed question, was the third. To undercut Sumner's following among the Negroes, Grant named Frederick Douglass the secretary of the commission. But not even such clever politics could bring support for a plan that had been demonstrated to be a grand swindle. Long before the commissioners set sail, everybody knew that they would make a perfunctory investigation, that they would write a favorable report, and that Congress would fail to take any action upon it.[3] Santo Domingo would never become an American state.

But if annexation was dead, hostility toward Sumner was not. During the course of the fierce debate on Santo Domingo the new leaders of the Senate revealed their plans. Nye charged that Sumner intended "to hand this Administration over into the hands of the enemy." Chandler agreed and argued that Sumner had already defected to the Democrats. Then Conkling announced the remedy: "The time has come when the Republican majority here owes to itself to see that the Committee on Foreign Relations is reorganized and no longer led by a Senator who has launched against the Administration an assault more bitter than

[2] Fish: Diary, Jan. 13, 1871, Fish MSS. The reasons for Grant's insistence upon the annexation of Santo Domingo, aside from sheer obstinacy, are obscure. A general faith in the desirability of expansion, hope for an American naval base in the Caribbean, and loyalty to his subordinates who negotiated the treaties were all doubtless factors. In "Radical Republican Policy Toward the Negro During Reconstruction, 1862–1872" (unpublished Ph.D. dissertation, Yale University, 1963, Chap. 9), George Selden Henry, Jr., argues that Grant thought the island would be a refuge for many American freedmen, who were oppressed in the South and who were not wanted in the North. In his *Personal Memoirs,* written in the 1880's, Grant did state that he had expected American Negroes to emigrate to Santo Domingo "in great numbers, so as to have independent states governed by their own race," but, as Professor Henry notes (p. 300), in his several messages to Congress on this subject, the President "never referred publicly . . . to the possibility of American Negroes emigrating there." See also Jessie R. Grant's account of his father's motives (*In the Days of My Father, General Grant* [New York: Harper & Brothers Publishers; 1925], pp. 134–8).

[3] For a good account of the work of the commissioners, see Harold Schwartz: *Samuel Gridley Howe, Social Reformer, 1801–1876* (Cambridge: Harvard University Press; 1956), pp. 296–309.

has proceeded from any Democratic member of this body." [4]

It was the same plan Chandler had tried to follow in early December, but now the move to depose Sumner had a new and powerful supporter. The debates on Santo Domingo convinced Hamilton Fish that Sumner was "crazy—a monomaniac upon all matters relating to his own importance and his relations toward the President." For some time Fish had been edging toward this conclusion. Early in the summer he reported that Sumner was often carried away by his own rhetoric so that he was not fully "conscious of the extent and violence of his expressions, and . . . not wholly master of himself." After the increasingly acrimonious exchange of letters on Motley's removal, the Secretary of State confided to British minister Thornton that in his considered judgment "Mr. Sumner was going mad" and might very well commit suicide. When Sumner failed to justify Fish's prediction, which was also perhaps a hope, and went on to deliver his "Naboth's Vineyard" speech, the Secretary concluded that the Senator henceforth must be considered as "partially crazy": "upon a certain class of questions, and wherever his own importance, or influence are concerned, or anything relating to himself, or his views, past or present, or his ambition, he loses the power of logical reasoning and becomes contradictory, and violent, and unreasoning, and that is mental derangement." [5]

It hardly needs saying that Fish spoke not as a psychiatrist but as a harried Secretary of State, exasperated at the behavior of an old friend who had constantly bullied him and overshadowed him and who had too painfully pointed out to him the path of duty. Sumner was, most certainly, in a highly emotional state, to which resentment over his loss of power, anger over Motley's removal, and fear of another physical assault all contributed. Highly overwrought, he was in no mood to be fair to his opponents. Even friends who disagreed with him felt the "blind phrenzy" of his wrath, and some, like Samuel Gridley Howe, concluded that he was now "morally insane." [6] But Sumner in

[4] *Cong. Globe,* 41 Cong., 3 Sess., pp. 241–2, 246.

[5] Fish to T. O. Howe, Aug. 6, 1870, copy, Fish MSS.; Thornton to Granville, Sept. 27, 1870, copy, Thornton Letterbook; Fish: Diary, Dec. 23, 1870, and Jan. 8, 1871, Fish MSS.

[6] Schwartz: *Howe,* p. 311.

battle had always been passionate and violent. "It is my nature to stand by the down-trodden," he told Frederick Douglass; ". . . it was my duty to expose an act of wrong, one of the greatest in our annals, kindred to the outrage upon Kansas, and, if possible, of more historical importance." [7] Therefore he attacked the Santo Domingo project with the same fervor he had previously used to expose the opponents of prison reform, the advocates of the Kansas-Nebraska act, and the defenders of Andrew Johnson. Unless one is prepared to argue that Sumner throughout his public career was deranged, there is no justification for Fish's diagnosis of insanity. Very probably Sumner showed poor judgment in not recognizing that he had already defeated the annexation of Santo Domingo, but his obduracy upon this point was hardly more a sign of monomania than was Grant's continued advocacy of the discredited scheme.

Though untrue, Fish's insistence that Sumner was mentally incompetent provided him with an excuse for a course he had now decided to pursue. Sumner must be goaded into an action so unforgivable that he would be ousted from the chairmanship of his committee.[8] Fish's opportunity appeared the very day after Sumner delivered his "Naboth's Vineyard" speech, for on December 22 the State Department received Motley's long, final despatch from London, which he called "End of Mission." Outraged by his abrupt recall, Motley decided to have the last word, and after elaborately reviewing and refuting all the alleged grounds for his humiliation, he concluded that the true reason was "the opposition made by an eminent Senator who honors me with his friendship to the ratification of the San Domingo treaty." [9]

Now thoroughly embittered toward both Motley and Sumner, Fish determined upon a reply that would both squelch the minister and hoist the Senator from his chairmanship. In his

[7] Sumner to Douglass, Jan. 6, 1871, MS. owned by Dr. Joseph Douglass.

[8] Of course this explanation of Fish's course is speculative, but no other accords with the facts. Unless Fish's reply to Motley (see the following paragraph) was intended to provoke an open break with Sumner, it must be considered the result of a momentary outburst of frustration and ill-temper. But the fact that Fish read the despatch to Grant and to Colfax negates this explanation, which indeed would be out of keeping with everything else the cool and calculating Secretary of State did during his long tenure of office.

[9] *Senate Exec. Doc.*, No. 11, 41 Cong., 3 Sess., p. 25.

own hand he drafted a despatch to be sent to Benjamin Moran, the American chargé d'affaires in London, which flatly asserted that Motley was "utterly mistaken" in thinking that Sumner's stand on the annexation of the Dominican Republic had anything to do with his removal. "Mr. Motley must know," Fish wrote sharply, "or if he does not know it he stands alone in his ignorance of the fact that many Senators opposed the San Domingo treaty openly, generously and with as much efficiency as did the distinguished Senator to whom he refers and have continued to enjoy the undiminished confidence and the friendship of the President than whom no man living is more tolerant of honest and manly differences of opinions,—is more sincere or single in his desire for the public welfare,—is more disinterested or regardless of what concerns himself—is more frank and confiding in his own dealings—is more sensitive of betrayed confidence, or would look with more scorn and loathing upon one who uses the words and the assurance of friendship to cover a secret and determined purpose of hostility."[1] Just to make sure that his rebuttal was offensive enough, Fish read it to Grant and Vice President Colfax. The latter, always a compromiser, thought it might be too severe, but the President said firmly that he did "not wish a word changed in the whole paper."[2] The despatch was then sent, and, so that it would not lie buried in the embassy archives, on January 5, 1871, Morton, the administration stalwart, called for its publication.

Sumner did not at once read Fish's remarkable, untruthful, and indefensible attack, but the newspapers apprised him of its content. Since, as the Springfield *Republican* observed, the despatch read "more like the malignant effusions of Senator Conkling than the cautious statement of a diplomatist,"[3] he was at first baffled by it. Insensitive to the fact that he had trampled upon Fish's feelings beyond the point of endurance, Sumner could not believe that his old friend could treat him with such "ostenta-

[1] Fish's penciled draft of this despatch is in the Fish MSS. For the published version see *Senate Exec. Doc.*, No. 11, 41 Cong., 3 Sess., pp. 36–7.

[2] Fish: Diary, Jan. 2, 1871, Fish MSS.

[3] Springfield *Weekly Republican*, Jan. 13, 1871. Allan Nevins (*Fish*, pp. 455, 457) declares that the despatch was "uncandid" and that it should have been "more soberly phrased."

tious indignity," and for a time he thought that someone else in the State Department, perhaps that former Democrat J. C. B. Davis, must have written the offensive document.

On January 12 he was disabused of this idea when Fish sent Senator Patterson to inquire whether Sumner would be willing to receive the Secretary of State at his house to discuss official business. The circuitous approach convinced Sumner that Fish had a guilty conscience, but, in his slow-moving fashion, he could not immediately decide how to behave toward his friend of twenty years' standing who had now so unaccountably assailed him. Stiffly he told Patterson that he would welcome Fish kindly, though he could not conceal his feeling of pity that the Secretary had become the pawn of the Santo Domingo annexationists or his "deep sense of personal wrong received from him absolutely without reason or excuse." [4]

The interview passed off inconclusively enough, but Sumner continued to brood over Fish's gratuitous insult. By the end of another week he came to the conclusion that Fish deserved the silent treatment, with which Sumner in the past had tried to discipline so many of his friends—and even his wife—when they disagreed with him. Since he was "not the kind of man to maintain social relations with another after . . . a vile and gross personal indignity," he would impose a moral blockade against Fish and henceforth "decline, peremptorily decline, to hold any social intimacy with him whatsoever." In this case the procedure offered difficulties, Sumner recognized, because he was chairman of the Senate committee which necessarily did much business with the Secretary of State. The public interest must not suffer, but Sumner determined that he would draw a distinction between Hamilton Fish and the Secretary of State. The former he would cut off completely, but the latter he would meet "in a spirit of the greatest harmony and cordiality" on "all matters of official public duty, courtesy or intercourse." [5]

On January 20, at a dinner given by Robert C. Schenck,

[4] J. W. Patterson to Fish, Jan. 12, 1871, Fish MSS.; Sumner: *Works*, XIV, 265.

[5] Interview with Sumner, Mar. 14, 1871, quoted in clipping from unidentified Cincinnati newspaper, Longfellow MSS.; Sumner to Edward Eggleston, Mar. 17, 1871, clipping in Sumner MSS.

whose nomination as minister to Great Britain Grant was about to submit to the Senate, Sumner showed how he planned to behave. Since it was, by Sumner's definition, a social occasion, he exhibited marked coldness toward Fish, declining to speak or even to bow to him. Fish "at first endeavored not to notice the discourtesy; and addressed Sumner as if nothing had taken place, but this produced no change in his demeanour." Afterward, in case anyone had missed the demonstration, Sumner explained that he had deliberately cut Fish.[6]

Now Fish had grounds which any Republican could accept for removing Sumner from his committee chairmanship. To those who had been unwilling to oust Sumner because of his stand on the widely unpopular Santo Domingo question, there was now available a new and wholly acceptable rationalization. Obviously it was impossible to conduct the government if the members of the executive and legislative branches would not speak to each other. As Conkling summarized the situation: "Personal terms with the President, and with the Secretary of State, were quite broken off, and a pointed refusal to speak to the latter occurred, and was declared as intentional, to senators and other persons. Business, of course, ceased to be conducted, in the ordinary and suitable modes." [7]

• 5 •

In provoking Sumner to assume an untenable position, Fish ran a heavy risk. If his maneuver did not work and if Sumner retained his chairmanship, the Senator could dominate the negotiations with Great Britain, which were now at a critical point. For nearly twelve months after Sir John Rose's visit to Washington in July 1869 there had been little progress toward resolving Anglo-American difficulties, which seemed to grow greater with delay. Recurrent conflicts broke out between the United States and the recently created Dominion of Canada, which was taking

[6] Sir John Rose to Granville, Jan. 21 [1871], F. O. 5, PRO. Fish's own diary for January 20 simply records that Sumner at the party was "cold and distant evidently not wishing to converse with . . . me."

[7] Elizabeth Adams: "George William Curtis and His Friends," *More Books*, XIV, 357.

its privileges and duties very seriously. In a dispute over the rights of United States fishing vessels operating within what were claimed to be Canadian waters, the Dominion government seized ships without warning and sometimes sold them. Fierce animosity also existed in Canada over damages wrought by the Fenian raiders, who in the summer of 1870 again struck from bases in the United States. Canadians suspected that the United States had been behind the brief rebellion led by Louis Riel in the Red River settlement of Manitoba, while in faraway British Columbia settlers were angry over the still unsettled San Juan boundary dispute. Grant's annual message to Congress in December 1870 showed that the United States was equally irritated by the conduct of that "semi-independent but irresponsible" colonial authority known as the Dominion of Canada.[8]

The claims rising from the Civil War continued a festering issue. To remind the British that the United States still held the "firm and unalterable conviction" that Great Britain had been negligent in maintaining its neutrality, Grant's December message urged that the American government now pay these private claims so that, at a moment of final reckoning, it would have both "the ownership . . . as well as the responsible control of all the demands against Great Britain." The British government needed no such warning, for the outbreak of the Franco-Prussian War in July 1870 had caused the cabinet to recognize the dangerous precedent that had been set in allowing the *Alabama* to escape. As the Russians took advantage of the upset balance of power and tore up the treaty regulations which prohibited them from maintaining a fleet or constructing fortifications in the Black Sea, the British foresaw danger to the Ottoman Empire and, ultimately, to India.[9] In the event of a war with Russia they knew that the United States would be, at best, a dangerous neutral, from whose harbors would swarm raiders to sweep the

[8] On these Canadian-American problems, see W. L. Morton: *The Critical Years: The Union of British North America, 1857–1873* (Toronto: McClelland and Stewart Limited; 1964), Chaps. 12 and 13, and Lester B. Shippee: *Canadian-American Relations, 1849–1874* (New Haven, Conn.: Yale University Press; 1939), Chaps. 9–13.

[9] William L. Langer: *European Alliances and Alignments, 1871–1890* (2nd ed.; New York: Vintage Books; 1964), pp. 11–13; Goldwin Smith: *The Treaty of Washington, 1871* (Ithaca, N.Y.: Cornell University Press; 1941), pp. 24–5.

British merchant marine from the seas. For the British Foreign Office Lord Tenterden submitted to the cabinet a solemn memorandum urging the immediate settlement of all differences with the United States as "a matter of national exigency."

At the same time Fish was assuming a more conciliatory position. Gradually the Secretary of State came to feel that he had too closely followed Sumner's lead, that Sumner had been wrong not merely about Santo Domingo and Motley's removal but about the Alabama Claims as well. It was not entirely coincidental that just one day after Fish wrote his last long and angry letter to Sumner about the Motley affair on September 25, he inaugurated a new approach to the claims question. In a conversation with British minister Thornton he tacitly but quite clearly abandoned two positions which Americans had for more than a year insisted upon as essential: no longer would the United States object to arbitration of the Alabama Claims, and no longer would it insist upon Canadian independence.

When Thornton reported this about-face to his government, the British ministry at once decided to send Sir John Rose back to Washington as an unofficial emissary to explore the paths toward peaceful settlement. On January 9, 1871, Rose was in Washington, ostensibly to discuss a new United States bond issue to be floated by his banking firm. He spent less time with the Secretary of the Treasury than with the Secretary of State, and within three days he and Fish were close to agreement. Now Fish not merely abandoned all talk of Canadian independence but told Rose frankly that his government was "throwing over Mr. Sumner's extravagant ideas in reference to England's responsibility for the prolongation of the war by her premature recognition of belligerency." [1] Pleased, Rose conceded in return that the British were liable for the depredations of the *Alabama*, the only one of the Confederate raiders where British governmental negligence could be proved. Then, since the animosities stirred up by the rejection of the Johnson-Clarendon Convention kept either government from publicly initiating another round of

[1] Rose to Granville, Jan. 12, 1870 [i.e., 1871], printed copy for use of the Foreign Office, marked "Secret and Confidential," Royal Archives. For full discussions of the Fish-Rose negotiations, see Nevins: *Fish*, pp. 435–43, and Smith: *Treaty of Washington*, pp. 27–32.

negotiations, the negotiators agreed upon an elaborate formula: Great Britain would first propose the creation of a Joint Commission to settle all the problems connected with Canada—fisheries, San Juan boundary, and the like; the United States, in accepting, would suggest the inclusion of the Alabama Claims as well; and the British would then agree.

First securing the approval of the cabinet and of most Republican members of the Senate Foreign Relations Committee to these proposals, Fish had to decide how to handle Sumner. Grant said flatly that there was no need to consult the Senator at all, but Fish persuaded the President that it would be best at least to make the gesture of informing him, so as to indicate "the disposition of the Administration to respect the organized Committees of the Senate." [2] Since the Secretary of State had now no hopes of securing Sumner's cooperation, there were probably at least two other reasons behind his insistence that Sumner be approached.

First, as has already been indicated, he needed to goad Sumner into a public break with the administration in order to justify his removal from his committee chairmanship. Fish must have been puzzled and disappointed that Sumner at first made no response to the deliberate insult incorporated in the reply to Motley's "End of Mission" despatch. By insisting that the Senator be consulted and by sending Patterson to ascertain whether, "owing to some recent events," Sumner would speak to the Secretary of State, Fish forced him to react. Knowing the Senator so well, he must have anticipated that he would break off all social intercourse and thus give the necessary handle for removing him from his chairmanship.

But, as the letters of both Rose and Thornton show, Fish had a second purpose in consulting Sumner—that of strengthening his own hand in the Alabama Claims negotiations. Without asking, he knew what Sumner's response to a proposed treaty with Great Britain would be. The Senator would first play the sibyl, declining to name the price to be demanded of Britain. During his somewhat stiff interview with Fish on January 15 he acted out his frequently rehearsed role to perfection. Then Fish

[2] **Fish: Diary, Jan. 11, 1871, Fish MSS.**

remonstrated that he had come officially to him as Chairman of the Senate Committee on Foreign Relations to ask his opinion as to what reply should be given to Rose. Pinned down, Sumner replied that the subject required much reflection, and Fish rejoined that he must have Sumner's official reply within a day or two.[3]

Just two days later Fish received from Sumner a memorandum which must have contained precisely what the Secretary expected. Protesting that there must not be another failure in these negotiations, Sumner found the terms Fish and Rose had agreed upon unsatisfactory. Specific mention of the British government's responsibility for losses caused by the *Alabama,* he feared, would "dishonor the claims arising from the depredations of other ships, which the American Government cannot afford to do." But a real settlement with Great Britain must go beyond higgling over monetary damages. The greatest danger to Anglo-American peace was "from Fenianism which is excited by the proximity of the British flag in Canada." If, therefore, the British government sincerely wished to settle "all questions and sources of irritation between England and the United States . . . absolutely and forever," it must agree to "the withdrawal of the British flag . . . as a condition or preliminary." "To make the settlement complete," Sumner noted tidily, "the withdrawal should be from this hemisphere, including Provinces, and islands." Having stipulated the conditions, Sumner concluded: "No proposition for a joint Commission can be accepted unless the terms . . . are such as to leave no reasonable doubt of a favorable result. There must not be another failure." [4]

This remarkable memorandum, which is often cited as evidence of eccentricity or mental aberration on Sumner's part, was, in fact, little more than a restatement of views which he, along with many other Americans, had frequently expressed since at least 1863. In questioning the Fish-Rose agreement about Confederate cruisers, he was only repeating arguments

[3] Ibid., Jan. 15, 1871.

[4] Copy of Sumner's "Memorandum for Mr. Fish in reply to his inquiries," ibid., Jan. 17, 1871. Sumner's original manuscript is now missing, but there can be no doubt as to the authenticity of the copy Fish made. See J. C. B. Davis to William Dudley Foulke, Feb. 20, 1896, Foulke MSS.

Roscoe Conkling

William Lloyd Garrison

Oliver P. Morton

Frederick Douglass

FOUR REPUBLICANS WHO FOLLOWED GRANT INSTEAD OF SUMNER

THE NATIONAL ARCHIVES

Sumner in Old Age

THE LIBRARY OF CONGRESS

that both Seward and Adams had made and, indeed, that Hamilton Fish himself had held up to September 25, 1870; though the negligence of the British government could be demonstrated only in the case of the *Alabama,* most Americans felt that Great Britain was equally liable for the damages wrought by the other escaped cruisers.

In demanding the withdrawal of the British flag from North America Sumner was also simply reiterating, as he thought, a generally accepted American view, which now, with his customary illogical logic, he pushed to its extreme limits. Consistently Grant had favored the independence, if not the outright annexation, of Canada. Fish, too, had repeatedly pressed this point as an essential condition for a genuine settlement with Britain. His instructions to Motley on January 4, 1870, had directed the minister to press the issue of Canadian independence upon the British ministry. On March 22 the Secretary had told Thornton that by making the Canadian provinces independent Great Britain could remove the "cause of irritation and of possible complication" and assure a firm friendship between the two powers. Again in June he had informed the British minister: "I don't want your Canada, but I do want it to be independent." As late as September 18 he had complained to Thornton that the Canadians were stirring up trouble through mistreatment of United States fishing vessels in their offshore waters. "The best solution would be independence," he proposed. "Then the colonies would behave themselves and stop their annoyances." [5]

As Fish well knew, Sumner shared all these views. His letters from Canada convinced him that there was a genuine independence movement in the Dominion, and his correspondence with Englishmen persuaded him that the mother country would not be averse to parting with so troublesome a possession. At the time of his "Alabama Claims" speech he had thought that British withdrawal from Canada might be the easiest solution to Anglo-American difficulties, though he was prompt to disavow any intent to force a surrender or subsequently to compel annex-

[5] Nevins: *Fish,* pp. 397, 421, 423–4. For fuller documentation of United States interest in annexing Canada, see Doris W. Dashew: "The Story of an Illusion: The Plan to Trade the *Alabama* Claims for Canada," *Civil War Hist.,* XV (1969), 332–48.

ation. During the months since delivering that speech, he had gradually enlarged his views, partly under the influence of Caleb Cushing, partly under the inspiration of Elisha Mulford's expansionist book called *The Nation*. By late August 1870 he confessed to Senator Howe: "Our object—at least my object—*is the withdrawal of the British flag from this hemisphere*." [6]

If Fish easily anticipated the contents of Sumner's memorandum, he also understood that it was not necessarily intended to put an end to his promising negotiations with Rose. Blurred by anger, Sumner's thinking at this time was none too clear, but he appears to have anticipated two distinct stages in arriving at a settlement with Britain. First there would be an agreement to arbitrate the claims arising from the Civil War, and subsequently there would be a broader understanding, covering boundary disputes with Canada, fishing rights, tariff reciprocity, and all other points at issue. The claims question had precedence in his mind. Indicative of his priorities was a letter he sent to Fish just two days after his original memorandum; it made no reference to Canada or the British flag but reemphasized his "sense of the wrong done to good citizens" by giving any special preference to claims arising from the depredations of the *Alabama*.[7] Sumner seems always to have thought that his demand for British withdrawal from North America was one to be considered in subsequent, broader negotiations, and he branded as "pure invention" a newspaper story that he insisted upon territorial concessions as a precondition for settling the Civil War claims.[8] Carl Schurz, who saw the Senator almost daily and from whom Sumner had few secrets, believed that he never made the withdrawal of the British flag "a *conditio sine qua non*, while he did think of it as a desirable thing." To reinforce that opinion, Schurz stressed that at no time in the Senate debates upon the Treaty of Washington, which provided for the settlement of the Alabama Claims, did Sumner propose, or even mention, the annexation or independence of Canada.[9]

[6] Sumner to Cushing, Sept. 8, 1870, Cushing MSS.; Sumner to Howe, Aug. 28, 1870, Howe MSS.

[7] Sumner to Fish, Jan. 19, 1871, Fish MSS.

[8] Boston *Journal*, Jan. 14, 1878.

[9] Schurz: *Sumner*, pp. 122–3. ". . . Sumner repeatedly in his conversations with me spoke of the 'withdrawal of the British flag from the Western

But Fish by January 1871 was in no mood to explore the ambiguities of Sumner's position or to subject his proposals to semantic analysis. Now implacably hostile to his former friend and working eagerly to secure his removal from his committee chairmanship, he saw in his memorandum much practical utility. It was a powerful weapon to keep Grant in line. Though the President in the past had longed for Canada, the mere fact that Sumner insisted upon Canadian independence was enough to make him turn against his previous policy. Informed of Sumner's views, Grant instantly ordered Fish to push ahead promptly with the negotiations and he pledged that, in order to defeat Sumner, he would do "his utmost to carry through the Senate any settlement which it may be possible to make with England." [1]

Sumner's memorandum was equally useful to Fish in influencing the British. A week before Sumner wrote it, Assistant Secretary of State Davis was so certain of the Senator's views that he leaked news of this "absurd idea" of Canadian independence to Thornton, who promptly relayed it to Granville. Rose, too, was prepared for Sumner's extreme demands. In several long conversations with Rose before spelling out his conditions for Fish, Sumner had explained that, though utterly peaceful in intention, he was obliged to make aggressive noises against Britain so as to forestall the Anglophobes in Congress and keep *"the control of that question to himself in the future."* Convinced that the Senator was "almost a monomaniac on the Alabama Question," Rose was hardly surprised when Sumner jovially informed him that he had discovered an easy solution to all Anglo-American difficulties: "Haul down that flag and all will be right." [2] When, therefore, on January 24 Fish showed Rose Sumner's actual memorandum,[3] with its ultimatum of British with-

hemisphere' as the 'ideal' solution. . . . But I do not think he ever considered it a possible thing at the time, unless the negotiations then going on were so conducted as to make it *suggest itself* to the British statesmen. . . . I do not think he regarded it as a thing that could be *proposed*." Schurz to Moorfield Storey, April 7, 1900, Schurz MSS.

[1] Fish: Diary, Jan. 23, 1871, Fish MSS.; Thornton to Edmund Hammond, Jan. 24, 1871, Hammond MSS.

[2] Thornton to Granville, Jan. 10, 1871, copy, Thornton Letterbook; Rose to Granville, Secret and Confidential, Jan. 12, 16, and 19, 1871, F. O. 5, PRO.

[3] Fish had previously informed him of the substance of Sumner's demands.

drawal from the hemisphere as a precondition for settlement, the unofficial British envoy was prepared, as was Granville, to whom he promptly reported; and both were more than ever aware that, by way of contrast, the terms of settlement to which Fish was agreeing were exceedingly favorable. If the British government did not accept them, Sumner's more dangerous proposals would probably find a following in Congress.

Spurred by this knowledge, both Fish and Rose were eager to move quickly. After exhibiting Sumner's memorandum, Fish announced that his government was ready to proceed with the negotiations, and he pledged that if the British sent commissioners to Washington no effort would be "spared to secure a favorable result, even if it involved a conflict with the Chairman of the Committee on Foreign Relations." [4] Rose cabled this reassuring news to London, and at once the cumbersome diplomatic machinery got under way. By February 3 all the agreed-upon steps had been taken, and the way was open for the naming of a Joint High Commission to meet at Washington as soon as possible in order to settle all claims, British and American, arising out of the Civil War.

• 6 •

Throughout January 1871, with a growing sense of desperation, Sumner watched his enemies combine. Both the plan to remove him from his committee chairmanship and the proposal to conduct negotiations with Great Britain along lines very different from his own he traced back to a single origin: Santo Domingo. The hostility of his Senate colleagues he was used to, and he felt that he could overcome them if they were unaided. Fish he was prepared to write off as a political nullity, "a gentleman in aspect with the heart of a lackey." [5] But behind them all stood Grant, intent upon annexing the Dominican Republic whatever the cost.

Sumner had never understood the President, and even now

[4] John Bassett Moore: *History and Digest of the International Arbitrations to which the United States has been a Party* (Washington: Government Printing Office; 1898), I, 530.

[5] James Schouler: *History of the United States of America Under the Constitution* (New York: Dodd, Mead & Company; 1913), VII, 168.

he could not comprehend why Grant was so embittered toward him. Though he himself credited every rumor or even threat that was reported from the White House, he was astonished that the President could be influenced by the sharp attacks made upon his administration at Sumner's dinner table. Instead, Grant ought to know only the public record of the debates in Congress, during which, Sumner felt, he had always been entirely proper, even kindly, in his references to the Chief Executive. Indeed, it was ineffably absurd to think that his stand upon Santo Domingo was motivated by hostility toward the President. Unaware of the force of his own language, unable to understand that his condescending reference to Grant's honest ignorance was an insult, Sumner insisted that his speeches had contained "not one word of personality or personal imputation towards the President." [6]

Convinced that only Grant's monomania upon the subject of Santo Domingo could explain his unreasoning hostility, Sumner saw no alternative but to lash out again at that tawdry venture, and he began planning another oratorical denunciation of Grant's course. The speech, however, was not yet to be made. By the end of January Sumner was visibly affected by the prolonged mental excitement under which he had been operating, and his nervousness was intensified by fear of physical assault from Grant or one of his aides. He began to experience symptoms of the angina pectoris which had periodically affected him in the past. On the night of February 15 the pain in his chest and in his left arm was so great that he could not sleep, but, driven by a sense of duty, he insisted upon going to the Capitol the next day, where he remained for three hours. The following day he also attended the Senate session, but he was soon obliged to go home. That evening he suffered paroxysms in the chest and acute pain in his left extremities, and his physician could relieve him only by an injection of bromide.

Under doctor's orders, Sumner was obliged to remain at home and rest for the next two weeks. The malicious speculated

[6] Royal Cortissoz: *The Life of Whitelaw Reid* (New York: Charles Scribner's Sons; 1921), I, 191; Sumner to W. L. Garrison, Dec. 29, 1870, Garrison MSS.

that he was shamming in order to gain time to complete his new speech on Santo Domingo, but in fact he was seriously ill, unable to climb stairs or even to take the carriage rides which he so enjoyed. Significantly, Sumner himself in speaking of the attack ignored the several bouts of angina he had had in recent years and stressed that his suffering was a direct result of Preston S. Brooks's assault in 1856.[7]

But not even the Senator's suffering, nor his invocation of an ancient martyrdom, could deflect the punishment that was in store for him. The fact that the old Congress was expiring and that the new Forty-Second Congress was assembling immediately afterward on March 4, 1871, gave his opponents both their opportunity and their excuse to remove him from his chairmanship. At the beginning of every new session, committee assignments had to be made by the Democratic and Republican caucuses, each of which had a special committee for this purpose. The five-man Republican group consisted of two friends of Sumner's, Sherman and Morrill of Vermont, and of two enemies, Pool, of North Carolina, a scalawag who was under Grant's thumb, and Nye, of Nevada, for whose vulgarity and coarse anecdotes Sumner had showed marked distaste. Howe, of Wisconsin, once an admirer of Sumner but more recently an intimate of Fish, had the casting vote, and he was subject to intense pressure from all sides. Horace White of the Chicago *Tribune* and Representative W. B. Allison, of Iowa, tried to convince him that removal of Sumner would split the Republican party; Fish, assisted by Edmunds, insisted that the change was essential.[8] When the Republican caucus met on March 9, the committee, by a 3–2 vote, recommended that Sumner be dropped entirely from the Foreign Relations Committee and that, instead, he be named to chair a new Committee on Privileges and Elections.[9]

[7] Sumner to Longfellow, Feb. 22, 1871, Longfellow MSS.; Blanche Butler Ames (ed.): *Chronicles from the Nineteenth Century* (1957), I, 227.

[8] White to Sumner, April 12, 1872, Sumner MSS.; Fish: Diary, Mar. 8, 1871, Fish MSS. Howe originally favored neutralizing Sumner's influence by adding two more Republicans to the committee, but Fish dissuaded him. Ibid., Mar. 6, 1871.

[9] Newspaper accounts of the caucus differ slightly. I have followed chiefly an unidentified but detailed clipping in the G. F. Hoar MSS. (Vol. I, p. 42) and the summary in Pierce, IV, 470–1.

Present when the report was submitted, Sumner declared that he could not accept the new assignment, called upon his past associates in the Foreign Relations Committee to testify whether he had "ever failed in any duty of labor or patriotism," and withdrew from the caucus. In the ensuing discussion Sherman, assisted by Vice President Colfax, urged a compromise that would allow Sumner to remain chairman but would pack the committee with two additional Republican members, but the pressure from the State Department was inexorable. By a vote of 26 to 21 the caucus approved the committee recommendation. Sumner's backers were mostly those Northern Republicans who had stood with him in fighting the annexation of Santo Domingo; his enemies were the New Radicals who now surrounded Grant plus most of the Southern Republican Senators, who depended upon federal military assistance to maintain their places. So close was the vote and so numerous were the absentees that Sumner's friends moved to reconsider the decision when the caucus reassembled on March 10. This time they were defeated by a margin of only 2 votes, but the verdict was decisive.

From the caucus room the Republicans went directly to the Senate chamber, where Howe presented the slate of committee assignments. Sumner promptly asked to be excused from his new assignment. "I feel . . . ," he explained, "that after twenty years in this service I have a right to expect that my associates in this Chamber will not impose upon me a new class of duties when I expressly say that they are not welcome to me." [1]

Relieved as he requested, Sumner took almost no part in the subsequent debate, which centered about Schurz's demand: "What are the reasons for this change?" At first there was an evident unwillingness of the administration Senators to give any answer to the question, but finally Howe was obliged to make a defense. He could truthfully argue that the change had not been made at Grant's instigation, for the President shrewdly had taken no active role in the proceedings. Though many years later he was reported to have said that he would resign unless Sumner was ousted, at the time he maintained his magnificent taciturnity, which he had learned could be a political as well as a

[1] *Cong. Globe,* 42 Cong., 1 Sess., p. 34.

military asset. When a New Jersey Republican asked what his wishes on the subject were, Grant replied loftily: "I never asked to have any particular person put upon any one of the Senate standing Committees. All that I have asked is that the Chairman of the Committee on Foreign Relations might be some one with whom the Secretary of State and myself might confer and advise." [2]

Howe could not in honesty say that Fish was equally innocent, for the Secretary of State had conducted an active campaign for Sumner's removal. Weeks before the caucus met he had been explaining to Senators that he could not carry on diplomatic negotiations when his relations with Sumner were "such as to preclude . . . all social intercourse"; he neglected, of course, to add that this situation was the result of his own carefully planned insult to Sumner. When Senators pressed Howe for details, he adduced the snubbing Sumner had given Fish at Schenck's dinner, when "the Senator from Massachusetts . . . not only felt authorized to refuse to answer questions addressed to him by the Secretary of State, but . . . told of it after he left the presence of the Secretary." [3]

Many Senators were unconvinced. Promptly Sumner's defenders obliged Howe to admit that the snub to Fish had been on a social, not an official, occasion and that the Secretary had never "addressed a question to the Senator from Massachusetts upon official business which the Senator refused to answer." When the details became clearer, some of the shrewder Senators had a glimmering of the truth and inquired whether, in the future, a cabinet officer could not arrange the removal of a hostile committee chairman by outrageously insulting him. So weak was Howe's attack that Democratic Senator Bayard of Delaware proposed facetiously that henceforth the Committee on Foreign Relations bear the title "the Committee on Personal Relations." [4]

[2] Grant to A. G. Cattell, Mar. 21, 1871, copy, Grant MSS. For the rumor of Grant's threat to resign, see Horace White to E. L. Pierce, Oct. 14, 1888, Pierce MSS.

[3] *Cong. Globe*, 42 Cong., 1 Sess., pp. 35, 40. Howe gave a more elaborate version of this explanation in a letter to Theodore Tilton, published in *The Golden Age*, pamphlet copy in Howe MSS.

[4] *Cong. Globe*, 42 Cong., 1 Sess., pp. 40, 53.

Fish himself seems to have had an uneasy conscience over engineering Sumner's removal, and up until the year of his death in 1893 he kept going back over the whole episode, adducing new reasons why the Senator had to be ousted from his chairmanship. Confronted with the evidence that Sumner was at all times prepared to discuss public business with him, though not to renew a social acquaintance, Fish resorted to an outright lie. He charged that Sumner "systematically and (as I think) purposely" prevented Senate action upon eight treaties submitted during the 1870–71 session of Congress, as well as upon two others held over from the previous session. "This one fact of pocketing or locking up ten treaties," Fish claimed, "was of itself more than sufficient to justify his *removal* from the Chairmanship. . . ."[5] When the records of the secret sessions of the Senate were opened and it was demonstrated that in fact Sumner's committee had reported out all but one of the treaties Fish mentioned, usually within one month of receiving them, Fish changed his argument and claimed that Sumner had not been sufficiently diligent in urging ratification of the treaties once they were reported. Since the treaties in question dealt with extradition from Guatemala and Nicaragua, consular privileges in San Salvador, and commerce with Uruguay, Fish found it hard to justify his charge that the vital interests of the Republic were neglected by allowing these agreements to wait, as was customary at the end of a busy session, for approval from the new Congress.[6]

Aware that he was on shaky grounds, Fish and his defenders then proclaimed that the true ground for Sumner's removal

[5] Fish to Richard Smith, Mar. 23, 1871, copy, Fish MSS.

[6] Fish privately circulated these charges at the time Sumner was deposed, and he compiled a "List of Treaties unacted upon in the Senate of the U.S. in March 1871 when the change in the Chairmanship of the Com. on For. Relations was made" and entered it in his Diary (Vol. III, p. 419). After Sumner's death Grant, in an interview at Edinburgh, asserted that he "had hampered the business of the State Department by pigeonholing treaties for months" (Boston *Advertiser*, Sept. 26, 1877). When Wendell Phillips and others came to the defense of their dead friend, Fish supported Grant's accusation in a public letter (Boston *Evening Transcript*, Oct. 31, 1877). J. C. B. Davis repeated the charge in a letter to the New York *Herald* (Jan. 4, 1878), reprinted as *Mr. Sumner, the Alabama Claims, and Their Settlement* (New York: Douglas Taylor; 1878). E. L. Pierce decisively refuted Fish's allegations in "A Senator's Fidelity Vindicated," first published in the *North American Review* and reprinted as an appendix to his *Sumner* (IV, 625–38).

was his memorandum of January 17, 1871, demanding the withdrawal of the British flag from North America. According to J. C. B. Davis, proofs of whose book Fish read and revised, the Secretary had received that memorandum with astonishment; according to Charles Francis Adams, Jr., to whom the Fish family supplied elaborate documentation, he received it with dismay. In either case, Sumner's memorandum "would have shut the door to all settlement, had it been listened to." Then, for the first time, Fish is supposed to have decided that Sumner's deposition was necessary, and he privately showed Sumner's statement to Republican Senators Conkling and Edmunds and to Democratic Senators Thurman and Bayard, all of whom agreed that Sumner must be displaced so that differences with Britain could be settled.[7]

But in this plausible account, which was not made public until after Sumner's death, there were also errors. Fish's decision to force Sumner off the committee must have been made not when he received Sumner's memorandum of January 17 but after he read Sumner's "Naboth's Vineyard" speech on December 21; otherwise the insult he included in his rebuttal to Motley would have been pointless. Nor was Fish surprised by the terms Sumner proposed. As Adams admitted, Sumner had enunciated his views frequently since 1869 and was now simply insisting "upon adherence to a familiar policy long before formulated." That policy was, moreover, one in which up until September 1870 "the chairman of the Senate Committee on Foreign Relations, the President, the Secretary of State, and the members of the Cabinet generally had gone on in happy concurrence."[8] If Fish used Sumner's statement to influence any Senators, there is no contemporary evidence to prove it, and his detailed diary makes no reference to his alleged interviews with Conkling, Edmunds, Thurman, and Bayard.[9] Finally, it is not clear that

[7] Davis: *Mr. Fish and the Alabama Claims*, pp. 67, 137; Charles Francis Adams: *Lee at Appomattox and Other Papers* (2nd ed.; Boston: Houghton, Mifflin and Company; 1903), pp. 164, 235.

[8] Ibid., pp. 159, 163.

[9] Anti-British and expansionist sentiment was so strong in the United States (Shippee: *Canadian-American Relations*, pp. 322–3) that Fish well knew he could not rally a majority of Senate Republicans against Sumner because of his memorandum. It was doubtless for this reason that he did not—contrary to his

Sumner's memorandum, either in intent or in practice, would have impeded the negotiations with the British. Certainly the British negotiators, to whom—unlike the American Senators—Fish did show the document, did not think so. They believed that Fish had made a serious political blunder in forcing Sumner's deposition, one that was, furthermore, unnecessary since the Senator, "certainly now the vainest of Americans," could be easily won over by "judicious flattery." [1] Sumner's cordial endorsement of the Treaty of Washington supported their view, not that of Fish.[2]

Behind Fish's shifting explanations lay an unwillingness to admit the true reasons for his action. Though he unquestionably was worried about what Sumner as chairman of the Foreign Relations Committee might do to a treaty with Great Britain and though he undoubtedly found it difficult to do business with a man who snubbed him at social encounters, Fish in reality differed very little in principle or policy from Sumner. Their basic disagreement stemmed from the Secretary's understandable feeling that foreign policy should be conducted by the State Department rather than by the Senate, a feeling that became more acute as Fish, after an initial period of tutelage, grew restive under Sumner's didactic and overbearing treatment. Unconsciously there was truth in Fish's repeated assertion that the removal of Sumner had nothing to do with his stand on the

---

subsequent recollections—at this time disclose the document to any member of the Senate. He did show it to one Thomas C. Montgomery, of Rochester, New York (Montgomery to Fish, Feb. 14, 1878, Fish MSS.). More than a year later Roscoe Conkling referred to Sumner's "luminous communication" (Conkling to Fish, Aug. 7, 1872, ibid.), but there is nothing to indicate that he had seen it in 1871. Allan Nevins (*Fish*, p. 441) gives the impression that Fish showed Sumner's memorandum to Senators Morton, Harlan, Patterson, Cameron, Conkling, Chandler, and others, but the conferences to which he refers all occurred before Sumner wrote the document. This is not to argue that no one but Fish knew at least the general nature of Sumner's demands. The New York *Times* carried a fairly accurate summary of his memorandum (clipping in Gerrit Smith to Sumner, Feb. 20, 1871, Sumner MSS.), as did *The Nation* (Adams, p. 241). The Washington correspondent of the Boston *Advertiser* speculated (Mar. 13, 1871) that the displacement of Sumner had "some direct and notable connection with the negotiations . . . for the settlement of our controversy with England."

[1] De Grey to Gladstone, Mar. 21, 1871, Ripon MSS.; Thornton to Granville, Nov. 1, 1870, copy, Thornton Letterbook.

[2] For a review of the evidence, see D. H. Chamberlain: *Charles Sumner and the Treaty of Washington* (Boston: W. B. Clarke Company; [1901]).

Santo Domingo treaty; he was ousted because of the smoldering resentment of Hamilton Fish's outraged ego. Sumner could not, however, have been deposed without the backing of Grant, who learned from the Senator's opposition to the annexation of the Dominican Republic that he needed to reorganize the leadership of the Republican party just as he had once reconstituted the high command of the Army of the Potomac. And neither President nor Secretary of State could have been successful without the enmities and jealousies that had been building up for twenty years against Sumner in the Senate.

Naturally the debates could not explore these hidden, and sometimes unconscious motives, but they did bring close scrutiny of all the avowed reasons for the caucus decision. In defense of Sumner rallied not merely old friends like Wilson and Schurz, but former critics, like Lyman Trumbull. Admitting that in the past he and Sumner had differed frequently and unpleasantly, Trumbull protested against the thoughtless tyranny of the Republican majority: "I stood by him when he was stricken down in his seat by a hostile party, by the powers of slavery. I stand by him to-day when the blow comes from those who have been brought into power as much through the instrumentality of the Senator from Massachusetts as of any other individual in the country." [3]

But all argument was in vain. Defenders of the change argued somewhat contradictorily that the new committee assignments were a purely routine matter, hardly worth discussing, and that they were essential for the expeditious carrying on of the government. In any case the decision of the caucus was binding. As Cragin, of New Hampshire, who thought the change "impolitic and dangerous," lamely admitted: "I yield my judgment to the will of the majority of my political associates." Ignoring arguments that Sumner was the best qualified man for the chairmanship, ignoring appeals that Senators should stand up before executive pressure, ignoring warnings that the change was "the hardest blow ever struck at the present Administration or the Republican party of the country," [4] the majority moved

[3] *Cong. Globe*, 42 Cong., 1 Sess., p. 50.
[4] Ibid., p. 52.

inexorably to approve Sumner's removal. After four hours of argument, the Senate, with Sumner's friends abstaining and only nine Democrats voting in opposition, accepted the new list of committee assignments. For the first time in ten years Sumner had no control over American foreign policy.

CHAPTER XIII

He Stands on a Bridge

On the day the Republican caucus voted to oust Sumner from the Foreign Relations Committee, visitors at the White House found the President in a cheerful and, for so taciturn a man, almost garrulous mood. He told some Senators who called on him that it had been "necessary to make an example of Sumner in order to teach these men that they cannot assail an administration with impunity." After the momentary excitement died down, he predicted, the people would understand and sustain the action of the Republican caucus.[1]

True enough, expressions of support for the administration did begin to be heard. The ousting of Sumner delighted Massachusetts conservatives like former Governor John H. Clifford, who thought that he "ought under the circumstances to have declined to take the place [of chairman]—as he did not, it was eminently proper that the Senate should substitute a friend of the Administration in his stead." Outside the Bay State many Republicans professed indifference to the whole affair and called it "much ado about nothing." "I don't think the administration has suffered very much . . . ," a Connecticut correspondent wrote Cornelius Cole. Senator Howe advised his worried constit-

1 Stafford H. Northcote: *Diaries, 1869, 1870, 1871, 1875, 1882, of the First Earl of Iddesleigh* (1907), p. 189; Pittsburgh *Commercial*, Mar. 13, 1871.

uents that the commotion would soon be forgotten and reminded them: "I don't do very rash things." "Sumner's failure to be reappointed . . . has been seized upon to try and raise a little tempest," Secretary Fish reported coolly, "but I do not think that the Tea Pot is going to boil over in consequence—although Sumner does." [2]

Sumner had reason for so thinking, for his mail was filled with hundreds of letters praising his course and condemning those who had deposed him. "There is but one expression here and that is of deep indignation," Governor Claflin reported from Boston on March 13. "This attempted disgrace of you and the state . . . has served . . . to show you and the world, the unreserved confidence and esteem reposed in your statesmanship and spotless integrity." From all parts of the country Sumner's letters echoed the same refrain. His correspondents spoke of Grant's "prostitution of power," of the Senate's "spiteful and petty meanness," and of the "stupidity" of the Republican leadership. They voiced "indignation, nay fury" over Sumner's removal. "*Mad,* does not express the feeling of our people," wrote one Bostonian. "We feel personally outraged! *injured,* way down deep!" Eloquently Professor Moses Coit Tyler of the University of Michigan voiced the theme that ran through the letters: "Never before have so many millions of Americans been perfectly united in reverence, gratitude, and love, for you, as at this time." [3]

Newspaper opinion was more divided, but a majority of editors regretted the ousting of Sumner from his chairmanship. In varying tones of anger, Massachusetts Republican papers deplored the insult given to a distinguished native son, and Democratic journals gloated over the embarrassment the Senate's action caused the Grant administration. In New York City,

[2] Clifford to Fish, Mar. 13, 1871, Fish MSS.; Gaillard Hunt: *Israel, Elihu and Cadwallader Washburne* (New York: The Macmillan Company; 1925), pp. 126–7; John Johnston to Cole, Mar. 13, 1871, Cole MSS.; William H. Russell: "Timothy O. Howe, Stalwart Republican," *Wisconsin Mag. of Hist.,* XXV (1951), 96; Fish to E. B. Washburne, Mar. 21, 1871, copy, Fish MSS.

[3] See the letters from the following persons in the Sumner MSS.: Claflin, Mar. 13, 1871; Thomas L. Thornell, Mar. 10, 1871; J. B. Wilson, Mar. 11, 1871; W. I. Bowditch, Mar. 11, 1871; Adin Thayer, Mar. 10, 1870 [i.e., 1871]; Albert J. Wright, Mar. 11, 1871; and M. C. Tyler, Mar. 17, 1871.

though the *Times*, closely tied to Fish, remained silent and the *Herald* enjoyed both the deposition of Sumner and the resulting attacks upon his opponents, all the other papers condemned the course of the administration. "The Nation [is] Humiliated," announced the *Sun*, and the Democratic *World* lashed out at Grant as "stupid, vulgar, . . . incompetent, pig-headed." Elsewhere the press was neither so impassioned nor so unanimous. If the Cincinnati *Commercial* felt that the replacing of Sumner would make the Senate subservient to the President, the Cincinnati *Chronicle* felt that there was no such danger, since a man of Sumner's "vanity and ostentatiousness" would insist upon making himself heard anyway. A survey of small-town Michigan newspapers showed that fifteen deplored the Senate's action in varying terms of reprobation, six upheld the change, and three took a neutral stand.[4]

Even though some Republicans saw justification for ousting Sumner, most felt that the Grant administration had made a serious political blunder. Congressman James A. Garfield, thoroughly aware of Sumner's limitations, nevertheless concluded "that no act of either branch of Congress, since I have been a member, equals this in folly." Senator Cragin, who had voted for removing Sumner, believed that Grant's friends in Congress, "impracticable, headstrong, and destitute of good judgment," had insisted upon a step that would prove fatal to the party. The veteran Maine Republican, Neal Dow, protested not so much against the injustice as the impolicy of deposing Sumner at a time when "the utmost prudence, caution and wisdom are necessary . . . to carry the Republican Party successfully through the next Presidential campaign." A constituent asked Indiana Senator David D. Pratt to verify the rumors that "Sumners mind was affected—that he was threatened with softening of the brain and was doing all sorts of queer things"; otherwise, he said, there would be no way to defend the caucus action in the forthcoming elections. Charles Francis Adams, certainly no friend of Sum-

[4] See the summaries of press opinion in Boston *Advertiser*, Mar. 11, 1871, St. Louis *Democrat*, Mar. 13 and 14, 1871, and Detroit *Advertiser and Tribune*, Mar. 20, 1871; also a mass of clippings enclosed in S. E. DeWolfe to Fish, Mar. 17, 1871, Fish MSS.

ner's, took the action of the Senate to mean that "the doom of the republican party was sealed." [5]

During the excitement, Sumner, loquacious on all other topics, remained perfectly silent on his removal from the chairmanship. On this one subject he made no speeches in the Senate, wrote no public letters, and granted no newspaper interviews. Partly his reticence derived from his lifelong reluctance publicly to promote his own political advancement. Mostly, however, it reflected the fact that neither he nor his advisers knew what to say. Sumner was, in fact, in the most difficult position of his entire career. Up to this point he had managed, however precariously, to maintain a balance of political forces. In Lincoln's administration he had tried, with some success, to play off the President against the Secretary of State; in Johnson's, to counter the executive branch of the government with the legislative. Within the Senate he had received a hearing for his appeals in behalf of freedom and equality because of respect for his views on foreign policy. His influence in the national government had been enough to scotch discontent within the Massachusetts Republican party. The antislavery vanguard was less vehement in denouncing his occasional concessions to expediency because he so often exercised power for good in Washington, and even businessmen tended to condone his radicalism on Negro rights in view of his soundness on foreign policy.

Now all this was changed. The President and the Secretary of State stood as one man, and the Chief Executive and Republican Congressional leadership were also united. Ousted from the Foreign Relations Committee, Sumner lost control over American diplomacy as he had already lost influence over domestic legislation. Seeing the Senator powerless in Washington, disaffected elements in Massachusetts were readying to attack him, and one of his principal rivals, Butler, had the full backing of the national administration. To add to the difficulty, the Santo Domingo issue was not one that roused great enthusiasm among

[5] Garfield to Lieber, Mar. 11, 1871, copy, Garfield MSS.; Cragin to G. G. Fogg, Mar. 11, 1871, Fogg MSS.; Dow to Henry Wilson, Mar. 13, 1871, Norcross MSS.; James T. Bryer to Pratt, Mar. 14, 1871, Pratt MSS.; C. F. Adams: Diary, Mar. 28, 1871, Adams MSS.

Sumner's most loyal followers. Seeing that his position was so hazardous, his closest political advisers urged him to make no speeches and issue no statements.

His silence unnerved Grant's advisers. Edgily the cabinet received rumors on his state of mind as though they were bulletins on steps taken toward mobilization by some hostile foreign power. Sumner, they heard, was feeding newspaper reporters with facts and gossip against Grant and Fish; he was pleased with the generally hostile newspaper reaction toward his removal; he was collecting evidence to prove that Babcock really had threatened him; he was preparing henceforth to oppose any and all measures of the Republican party.

Behind this nervousness lay a well-grounded fear that Sumner might take the one possible step to recoup his political fortunes through assuming leadership of all the elements opposed to Grant's reelection in 1872. The first and essential step in this direction would be to torpedo the negotiations with Great Britain, which were then getting under way in Washington, and Fish desperately feared that Sumner might do just this. Another "Alabama Claims" speech would not only deprive the Grant administration of what it hoped would be its most solid accomplishment; it would rally the whole Democratic opposition behind Sumner and would perhaps also carry into his camp such Anglophobic Congressmen as Chandler and even Butler, both now leading Grant supporters. Anticipating that Sumner might make such a move, Fish during February 1871 sent out informal and unofficial warnings to American representatives abroad that a new crisis might be brewing. To Adam Badeau, Grant's former aide now serving as Secretary of Legation in London, he wrote: "Sumner's hostility to the President . . . has become so extreme and so morbid that he would ruin wherever he cannot rule. I have no doubt that he is insane. . . ." In a letter to Washburne, the American minister at Paris, Fish elaborated his charge: "Vanity, conceit, ambition have disturbed the equilibrium of his mind—he is irrational and illogical and raves and rants—no wild bull ever dashed more violently at a red rag than he goes at anything that he thinks the President is interested in." "His friends should subject him to treatment," Fish concluded, "that I think is the term they use in connection with the insane." [6]

Believing Sumner mad, Fish now tried to mollify the Senator. Since obviously Sumner himself could not be named as one of the American members of the Joint High Commission to settle the Alabama claims, his trusted friend, E. R. Hoar, became one of the United States delegation, and Fish saw to it that Sumner received from him frequent, but not very explicit, reports on the progress being made. On May 8, 1871, immediately after the commissioners signed the Treaty of Washington, intended to settle all outstanding claims between Great Britain and the United States, a copy was left at Sumner's door, inscribed: "The result of long and earnest labor is present and *dedicated,* with respect and confidence, by his friend, E. R. Hoar."

The British commissioners, who had come to Washington in February, also treated Sumner like a dangerous explosive. Despite the objections of the dyspeptic Thornton, who felt that no amount of conciliation could bring Sumner round, the Earl de Grey and Ripon, who headed the British delegation, Sir Stafford Northcote, who represented the British opposition party, and Mountague Bernard, the Chichele Professor of International Relations at Oxford, believed that deference and flattery would win him over. Realizing, as did John A. Macdonald, the Canadian member of the commission, that the fate of any treaty they drafted would "depend a good deal on Sumner's course," they paid him assiduous court, and on the very day they arrived in Washington, just after visiting Fish and minister-designate Schenck, they called on Sumner at his house. Fully briefed on the delicacy of the situation, they were prepared to cope with the awkward circumstance that the Senator and the Secretary of State were not on speaking terms. When Sumner, still looking unwell and showing "a touch of wildness in the eye which suggests the possibility he may go out of his mind," returned their call, Fish happened to be present. Without saying a word, the British commissioners in rushing forward to shake the Senator's hand formed a kind of human screen, behind which the Secretary of State contrived to slip out of the room without being

[6] Fish to Badeau, Feb. 24, 1871, McClellan Lincoln Collection; Fish to Washburne, Feb. 20, 1871, copy, Fish MSS.

either noticed or snubbed by Sumner.[7] So eager were the British commissioners to conciliate Sumner that they even forced themselves to read his celebrated "Alabama Claims" speech, which, two years after its delivery, they professed to find not so offensive after all. If the argument was "somewhat sharp," Northcote wrote Sumner, he would agree with its governing idea: "Great international differences are not to be disposed of by huddling them up and pretending not to look at them, nor to be treated as a man treats a bad shilling by trying to pass it among a handful of halfpence."[8]

Rather to their surprise, the British commissioners found Sumner himself charming. Expecting to deal with a crazy man, Northcote was delighted to discover that the Senator has "a negligent ease in his manner which is rather taking," and even that reserved Scot, Macdonald, reported that he had a good deal of pleasant talk with Sumner. In April, as negotiations were nearing an end, the British commissioners and their wives had dinner with the Senator and genuinely admired his china and crystal and enjoyed the special mandarin tea, which his friend Mrs. Lodge regularly supplied him. So successful was the evening that the commissioners returned for another dinner—this time without their wives—on the following evening.[9] When they left Washington, Sumner showered them with affectionate farewells, with advice to go West and see a prairie, and with *cartes de visite* bearing his latest photograph.

Though even the pessimistic Thornton believed all the attention had mollified Sumner, nobody could predict how he would react when the treaty came before the Senate in May. In fact, Sumner did not know his own mind. On May 6 he promised de Grey that he "would not attack any part of the Treaty without first giving him an opportunity of discussing it with him," but two days later he spoke of possible changes and warned that the Democrats "and some others" would probably oppose it. He

[7] Shippee: *Canadian-American Relations*, p. 374; abstract of De Grey's letter to Granville, Feb. 24, 1871, Royal Archives; Northcote: *Diaries*, p. 187. See also James P. Baxter, 3rd: "The British High Commissioners at Washington in 1871," *Mass. Hist. Soc. Proceedings*, LXV (1932–36), 350.

[8] April 27, 1871, Sumner MSS.

[9] Northcote: *Diaries*, p. 187; Springfield *Weekly Republican*, April 28, 1871; Dawes: *Sumner*, p. 306.

called upon Caleb Cushing and George Bemis for help in drafting amendments to the treaty, yet he assured the British commissioners that it would be ratified within a week after it was submitted. On a single day Thornton received reports from reliable sources that the flattery by the British High Commissioners had persuaded Sumner to support the treaty and that the Senator was going to cause trouble by adding "wicked" amendments to it.[1]

Sumner was facing one of the most difficult decisions of his life. As Northcote diagnosed his problem: "He is very anxious to stand well with England; but, on the other hand, he would dearly like to have a slap at Grant." Astutely Henry Adams judged that Sumner's dilemma was more complex: "If he resists the treaty and fails, he is done for. If he resists and succeeds, he will break himself down here, I think. If he accedes and votes for the treaty, Grant drags him in triumph at his chariot-wheels, as Sumner would say." [2]

Whatever the political dangers, Sumner could not oppose the Treaty of Washington without stultifying himself. Had he been Secretary of State, he could hardly have hoped for a more complete satisfaction of the demands made in his 1869 "Alabama Claims" speech.[3] Then he had insisted that any treaty must contain an acknowledgment of wrongdoing on the part of Great Britain; now the first article of the Treaty of Washington expressed "the regret felt by Her Majesty's Government for the escape . . . of the Alabama and other vessels from British ports, and for the depredations committed by those vessels." Sumner had condemned the "aleatory proceeding" provided in the Johnson-Clarendon Convention, which required that in case of deadlock an arbitrator should be chosen by lot; the Treaty of Washington agreed that all questions should be decided by a majority of the five-man tribunal of arbitrators. Sumner had wanted any settlement with Great Britain to advance international law; the

[1] Northcote: *Diaries*, pp. 224, 226–7; Thornton to Granville, May 23, 1871, copy, Thornton Letterbook; Thornton to de Grey, May 23, 1871, Ripon MSS.

[2] Andrew Lang: *Life, Letters, and Diaries of Sir Stafford Northcote* (Edinburgh: William Blackwood and Sons; 1890), II, 23; Worthington C. Ford (ed.): *Letters of Henry Adams (1858–1891)* (Boston: Houghton Mifflin Company; 1930), p. 208.

[3] Moore: *International Arbitrations*, I, 553.

treaty framed by the Joint High Commission included three rules binding neutral governments in the future to use due diligence to avoid the escape of other *Alabamas*.

The Treaty of Washington even included Sumner's specialty, the national claims of the United States government, in contradistinction to the claims of individual American citizens. To be sure, the British commissioners believed, as they jubilantly reported to London, that the Americans "had abandoned the claims of their country on account of the belligerent rights and all the constructive claims arising from the assistance rendered to the rebels," but the treaty they signed explicitly provided that all claims were to come before the arbitration tribunal. Going over the document line by line with Caleb Cushing, Sumner concluded that it fully covered all the claims for indirect and national damages mentioned in his speech. The Americans who negotiated the treaty agreed, and when Bancroft Davis drafted the *Case of the United States* to be presented to the arbitrators when they met at Geneva, it followed Sumner's argument almost completely, asking compensation for American expenditures in pursuit of the Confederate raiders, and for the damage done to the American merchant marine. It even concluded, in words Sumner himself might have written, with a claim against Britain for "the vast injury which these cruisers caused in prolonging the war," an injury which Davis suggested might include the costs of all military operations after the battle of Gettysburg.

The Treaty of Washington did not, of course, fulfill Sumner's long cherished dream that Canada would become part of the United States, yet its underlying assumptions and prompt effects served to eliminate Canada as an irritant in British-American relations. As a result of the treaty, the British military presence was removed from the St. Lawrence valley and from the middle of North America, and the withdrawal of troops implied a recognition of the military supremacy of the United States on the continent. The British flag was not hauled down, as Sumner had wished, but it was never again to wave so provocatively along the Canadian border as to incite further Fenian protests.[4]

[4] Morton: *The Critical Years*, p. 257.

In the circumstances, then, Sumner had no choice but to endorse the treaty. He grumbled that it might have done more to enlarge the concepts of international law, and he framed a series of amendments which would exempt "private property . . . from capture or seizure on the high seas, or elsewhere, by armed vessels or military forces." But, warned that any changes in the document might imperil the whole negotiation, he forebore pressing his amendments.[5] When the Senate considered the treaty on May 19 in closed session, he delivered a four-hour speech in its defense. His words were not recorded, and the only detailed account of his argument was that given in a newspaper report which Sumner branded a fabrication. It seems reasonable, however, to accept the journalist's summary that Sumner thought the treaty "was not such a document as he desired, yet he was not disappointed in it." [6] On the final vote he lined up with forty-nine other Republican Senators to consent to the treaty over the objection of the twelve Democrats.

If Sumner's conduct during the negotiation and ratification of the Treaty of Washington disproved Fish's report that he was insane, so his subsequent conduct belied the claim that he was really removed from his committee chairmanship because of his insatiable claims against Great Britain. In December 1871, when the Geneva tribunal received Davis's statement of the American case, the British were outraged to discover that it included claims for indirect and national damages. The British High Commissioners protested that Grant, Fish, and Davis were breaking their word; British newspapers raged against an arbitration which might impose upon their country a stiffer indemnity than Germany had exacted of France after the Franco-Prussian War; and members of the British cabinet called it "wholly incompatible with national honor to admit or to plead to [the American claims] before a Tribunal of Arbitration." Faced with the collapse of his work, Fish, who had hitherto endorsed every word of the case drawn up by his hand-picked associate, now declared

[5] Sumner enclosed copies of his proposed amendments in his letter to de Grey, May 23, 1871, Ripon MSS. Even the suspicious Thornton reported that he made no "factious opposition" to the treaty. Thornton to Granville, June 12, 1871, F. O. 5, PRO.

[6] New York *Herald*, May 20, 1871.

that reference to the indirect claims had only been included to prevent "an outcry from the people of the United States and from the majority of the Senators and Representatives." Subsequently he asserted that he had presented the claims for indirect damages out of political necessity "forced upon the Department by Mr. Sumner's speech, and the Hurrahs on one side, and the denunciation on the other side, which that speech excited." [7] When the British, feeling they had been tricked once, declined to accept Fish's word that the indirect claims were not intended to extort a monetary award and in May 1872 insisted upon adding an article to the treaty expressly excluding them, the President had reluctantly to go back to the Senate for approval of the change.

With the presidential election approaching, Sumner had a marvelous opportunity to rouse all the old anti-British hatred and to depict Grant as betraying his country's rights, but to Fish's astonishment he declined it. He did not vote for the new article outlawing indirect claims, for, as a newspaper reported, he "would do nothing further to cover the nakedness and protect the weakness of an administration that has shown its incompetence to be as gross as its malignity toward himself." Instead, he moved "that, without declaring any conclusion on the proposed withdrawal of certain claims, the Senate express the further opinion that the determination of this question belongs properly to the discretion of the President in the conduct of the case before the tribunal of arbitration." [8] But when his resolution was defeated and the amendment to the treaty was adopted, he made no further protest. Nor did he object when the British, finding the additional article inadequate, worked out with Charles Francis Adams, the principal American negotiator, an informal procedure for excluding indirect claims.

Even before the indirect claims were ruled out, Sumner had predicted to Thornton that the United States would receive "not

[7] Nevins: *Fish*, p. 520; Cook: "Road to Geneva," p. 555.

[8] Springfield *Republican*, May 22, 1872; *Senate Exec. Jour.*, XVIII, 262. Sumner labeled "absurd and ridiculous" a New York *Times* report that he said: "Great Britain should have been promptly notified, when she proposed to break up the tribunal, that the result would be war." *Cong. Globe*, 42 Cong., 2 Sess., p. 3864.

one cent" from them. Indeed, he insisted that he had never intended them to be "subjects of computation for pecuniary indemnification." He had, he declared, referred to the indirect damages in his 1869 "Alabama Claims" speech only in order "to show how much the U.S. had suffered from the conduct of England, so as to add force and weight to the Direct claims." Anyway, all claims were less important than the broad new guarantees of neutral rights under international law. "Such has been my interest always in this subject," he assured the British commissioners after their return to England, "that there has never been a time when I did not regard our claims as secondary, or at least as something to be pressed lightly, in comparison with an improvement by which civilization would gain." [9]

• 2 •

Estopped from attacking the Treaty of Washington, Sumner directed his mounting hostility against the Grant administration toward the President's continuing attempts to annex the Dominican Republic. Offended by the defeat of his annexation treaty, Grant was hurt even more by Sumner's imputation that "all concerned in negotiating it were . . . corrup[t] venal and guilty of a catalogue of crime." "Had the treaty been discussed fairly upon its merits and then rejected," the President explained, "as much as I might have differed with the Senate as to the wisdom of that action, it is not likely that the subject of Annexation would have come up again during this Administration." [1] Since his honor had been assailed and his motives impugned, he felt obliged to keep on advocating the project, and he denounced Sumner's opposition to it with uncharacteristic loquacity and vehemence. Sometimes the President was moved to sarcasm, as when he warned Chandler that there were men trying to disrupt the Republican party but declined to mention any names because, he declared: "I once said that I believed all men were

[9] Thornton to Granville, Mar. 12 and 26, 1872, copies, Thornton Letterbook; Fish to R. C. Schenck, Mar. 18, 1872, copy, Fish MSS.; Sumner to Northcote, July 18, 1871, Iddesleigh MSS.; Sumner to Ripon, July 18 [1871], Ripon MSS.

[1] Draft, in Grant's handwriting, of his message to Congress, April 5, 1871, Grant MSS. The passage was omitted from the final version, as sent to Congress.

wiser than any one man and immediately was accused of using personalities towards an old, distinguished and mild Senator who never said an unparliamentary thing in his life, nor used hard words about any one." More frequently he burst out in anger, and when he passed Sumner's house on his strolls around Lafayette Square he used to shake his clenched fist at it, exclaiming: "That man who lives up there has abused me in a way which I never suffered from any other man living." [2]

Incapable of sarcasm, Sumner reciprocated the wrath. Night after night he regaled his guests with tales of the swindles Grant's aides were perpetuating in Santo Domingo and, escorting his visitors to the door, he used to stand on the steps, looking out over Lafayette Square toward the White House, and denounce the President in ever louder tones until it seemed that "all Washington, including Mrs. Grant, must hear and the police would have to interfere." The more Sumner learned about the proposed annexation, the more convinced he grew that it was a wretched swindle. A former Foreign Minister of the Dominican Republic, Thomas Bobadilla Briones, who was in exile in Puerto Rico, wrote him that the true wish of the Dominican people was not for annexation but for assistance in settling their interminable civil wars. From the Haitian minister in Washington he heard how swaggering United States naval officers had threatened the independence of the black republic. Pouring over the State and Navy Department despatches concerning Santo Domingo, which the Senate at his insistence had ordered to be published, he grew ever more certain that ambitious military aides and corrupt speculators had gulled the incompetent President. Grant, Sumner told a New York *Herald* reporter, "doesn't know anything, sir. I do not accuse him of any knowledge whatever. He is not a man capable of understanding principles or of grasping anything in a comprehensive view." [3]

Desiring to undercut what everybody knew would be the

[2] Grant to Chandler, Aug. 4, 1871, Chandler MSS.; Hoar: *Autobiography,* I, 210–11.

[3] George H. Haynes: *Charles Sumner,* p. 359; *Boletin del Archivo general de la nacion* (Ciudad Trujillo), XIV (1951), 306–12; J. Duboile to Sumner, Mar. 10, 1871, Sumner MSS.; interview with Sumner in New York *Herald,* Mar. 14, 1871, clipping in Longfellow MSS.

favorable report of the United States commissioners, who were just returning from their perfunctory inspection of the Dominican Republic, Sumner went before the Senate on March 27 to present that principled, comprehensive view which the President had failed to give. His speech on "Violations of International Law, and Usurpations of War Powers" drew a large audience, for it had been widely publicized. Sumner himself had tried to secure a favorable reception for it by sending advance copies to the newspapers, and he gave a dinner party to selected Washington correspondents shortly before he spoke. When he made his appearance on the Senate floor, little suppressed currents of applause passed through the gallery, for he was clearly the hero of the hour. Arranging his desk systematically, with manuscript on the left and a pile of books on the right, checking to see that Schurz was sitting behind him, ready to forward more ammunition as needed, Sumner rose, tossed back his long mane of gray hair, which now almost reached his collar, checked that his pendant eyeglasses were properly in place over his massive chest, and sought recognition from the chair. Not for many years had he relied upon memory for his formal speeches, but this one had been so long in preparation and he was so familiar with all the details that during the three hours and fifteen minutes he held the floor he had rarely to refer to his manuscript as he "deliberately, forcibly, indeed, majestically," made his case. Scarcely moving from his place, he stood straight for the entire time, without leaning on a chair or desk. At climactic points in his address he lowered his left hand, in which he held his manuscript, and with his "long, stout, right hand and arm . . . made a gesture spontaneous and powerful, while his strong, full, yet husky voice had capacity, at earnest instances, to drop upon a word like a clap of thunder." A visiting Englishman remarked that more than ever before Sumner's head, face, and general bearing resembled those of Edmund Burke, and many in the audience seemed to feel that they were present at an occasion as momentous as the impeachment of Warren Hastings.[4]

At the outset Sumner announced that his purpose was not

[4] "Gath" [George Alfred Townsend], in an unidentified clipping, Mar. 27, 1871, Sumner Scrapbooks; London *Telegraph*, April 12, 1871.

to ask whether it was desirable to annex the Dominican Republic but "whether we are justified in the means employed to bring this acquisition." [5] He sought to prove, "first, that the usurper Baez was maintained in power by our Navy to enable him to carry out the sale of his country, and, secondly, that further to assure this sale the neighbor Republic of Hayti was violently menaced." These were, of course, precisely the same accusations he had previously made, in both open and secret sessions of the Senate, but now he could document his charges from the published documents of the State and Navy Departments. At elaborate length he quoted from them to show only too clearly that the United States had indeed supported a shaky dictatorship in the Dominican Republic while its agents bullied the government of Haiti.

Though much of the speech was technical, Sumner's audience followed him closely, and there were murmurs of approval when he scored hits on the Grant administration. So effective was he that the President's supporters in the Senate rustled papers, whispered noisily, and walked about rapidly to distract attention. After first making a pretense of writing letters, Conkling, sitting only three seats from where Sumner stood, began to talk with Howe and Hamlin, who occupied the intervening chairs, so loudly that Sumner was three times obliged to ask them to speak a little lower. Then Edmunds came up to Conkling and began a discussion which could be heard in the gallery. When Sumner requested that he lower his voice, the Vermont Senator snarled: "I'm not speaking at all." Invoking the rules, the Vice President required Sumner's hecklers to stop. Edmunds apologized curtly and then sat down and laughed, as if he had said something funny, and Conkling thereafter pretended to be wholly absorbed in scribbling letters.[6]

For most of his hearers, the high point of Sumner's speech was not so much his detailed account of the negotiations with the Dominican Republic as his allocation of responsibility for the whole fraudulent project. The initial blame, of course, fell upon Baez, that "adventurer, conspirator, and trickster, uncertain in

[5] Sumner: *Works*, XIV, 170–249.

[6] Brooklyn *Union*, Mar. 29, 1871; *Cong. Globe*, 42 Cong., 1 Sess., pp. 305–6.

opinions, without character, without patriotism, without truth." Equally culpable was the American negotiator Babcock, that "young officer, inexperienced in life, ignorant of the world, untaught in the Spanish language, unversed in International Law, . . . and unconscious of the Constitution of his country." But ultimately the guilt rested upon Grant, who had "seized the war powers carefully guarded by the Constitution, and without the authority of Congress . . . employed them to trample on the independence and equal rights of two nationals coequal with ours."

The impact of the President's illegal and immoral behavior, Sumner predicted, would be felt not merely abroad but at home, and, in a passage which he had not previously shown to his political advisers, he sought to equate the errors in Grant's foreign policy with his failure to guarantee civil liberty at home. "Pray, Sir," Sumner addressed the chair, "with what face can we insist upon obedience to Law and respect for the African race, while we are openly engaged in lawlessness on the coasts of San Domingo and outrage upon the African race represented by the Black Republic? . . . It is difficult to see how we can condemn, with proper, whole-hearted reprobation, our own domestic Ku-Klux, with its fearful outrages, while the President puts himself at the head of a powerful and costly proceeding operating abroad in defiance of International Law and the Constitution of the United States." Had the President tried "to bestow upon the protection of Southern Unionists, white and black, one half, nay, Sir, one quarter of the time, money, zeal, will, personal attention, personal effort, and personal intercession, which he has bestowed upon his attempt to obtain half an island in the Caribbean Sea," Sumner judged, "our Southern Ku-Klux would have existed in name only, while tranquillity reigned everywhere within our borders." As applause swept the gallery and the Vice President gaveled for silence, Sumner concluded with a fervent appeal not to dispossess "the African race . . . of its natural home in this hemisphere."

Sumner's accusations stung Grant's defenders into prompt counterattack. Half-paralyzed and confined to his chair but still fiercely combative, Morton charged that Sumner's purpose was less to kill an already rejected treaty than "to fix a crime upon the President of the United States." Professing pain at the sight of this "great man wrecked by his own misguided zeal or his misguided passions," Howe, too, claimed that Sumner's objective was to destroy the reputation of the President and protested that if he was determined thus to assail the Republican party he ought to "take off its colors, take his position in line with the common enemy, and strike like a man." [7]

As always after a major speech, Sumner found his mails full of laudatory letters, commending his "masterly words for the cause of Justice" and praising his oration as "not merely able—that is tame for it—but tremendous, and, in passages, sublime." William Lloyd Garrison, who was shortly to break with Sumner over Grant's policies, announced that the Senator had voiced "a judicial decision rather than a speech—dispassionate, grave, dignified, exhaustive, admitting of no appeal." [8]

Doubtless Sumner found such words of encouragement the more cheering because newspaper reaction to his speech was not, on the whole, favorable.[9] Of course, editors already hostile to Grant, like Samuel Bowles of the Springfield *Republican*, endorsed Sumner's "startling indictment of the executive," and the Democratic New York *World* thought the speech "convincing and unanswerable." But the New York *Times* reported that the speech was largely a rehash of "absurd" charges against the President; the New York *Commercial Advertiser* called it spiteful; and the Albany *Evening Journal* deplored Sumner's "acerbity of spirit and his exaggeration of utterance." "So much of the speech as is historical is harmless," the Baltimore *American* summed up the press response. "The other portions are childish."

The unfavorable reaction of the newspapers was less a

[7] *Cong. Globe*, 42 Cong., 1 Sess., pp. 306–7, 314–16, and Appendix, pp. 40–6. On March 29, 1871, the Senate, by a vote of 39 to 16, tabled Sumner's resolutions assailing Grant's naval cordon around the island as an illegal assumption of the legislature's power to make war. Though Sumner lost the vote, he won a victory, for soon afterward the American gunboats were withdrawn from Dominican waters. Leopold: *Growth of American Foreign Policy*, p. 102.

[8] See letters from the following in the Sumner MSS.: L. A. Tefft, Mar. 28, 1871; Edwin Morton, Mar. 27, 1871; and Garrison, Mar. 28, 1871.

[9] The Sumner Scrapbooks contain an an extensive sampling of newspaper editorials.

reflection of careful study given to Sumner's arguments than of a general boredom with the whole Santo Domingo question. Neither Sumner's denunciation of annexation nor the returning commissioner's report in favor of it stirred up much interest. Finally even Grant was persuaded that the project was dead. On April 5, submitting the final report of the commissioners to Congress, he announced an end to "all personal solicitude upon the subject" and gladly handed "over the whole matter to the judgment of the American people and of their representatives in Congress," at the same time advising that "no action be taken at the present session beyond the printing and general dissemination of the [commissioners'] report."

Sumner was more reluctant to give up the subject, on which, as Grant observed, he was "perfectly rabbid."[1] He thought the President's message "pretending to abandon the Santo Domingo folly" was filled with "most uncandid allegations and suggestions, [and] was not sincere." After all the United States government was still paying out money to support the Baez regime, and the flag of the United States was still flying over the harbor at Samaná Bay. "The Santo Domingo scheme is in full blast," he kept warning his correspondents. "The Santo Domingo ghost is still at work—saying 'Swear' like Hamlet's ghost."[2] But by midsummer of 1871 even Sumner recognized that the annexation project was dead beyond resuscitation and that there was nothing further to be gained by attacking it. "Here the tide is setting heavily against Mr. Sumner," Senator Howe wrote his wife from Washington. "The President's Message is received with acclaim. The temper of it is excellent and contrasts freely with the brutal temper exhibited in Sumner's speech." The effect of the message was "magical," reported another of Grant's friends; "it has completely taken the wind out of the sail of the Sumner-S[c]hurz party, and left them to drift ashore in a dead calm."[3]

[1] Grant to "Dear Jones," Feb. 8, 1871, MS., Chicago Hist. Soc.

[2] Sumner to Schurz, Aug. 1, 1871, Schurz MSS.; Sumner to G. W. Curtis, Aug. 3, 1871, Curtis MSS., Staten Island Inst. of Arts and Sciences; Sumner to Charles Nordhoff, Sunday [1871], MS., Yale Univ. Lib.

[3] T. O. Howe to Grace Howe, April 8, 1871, copy, Howe MSS.; Alexander G. Cattell to Fish, April 8, 1871, Fish MSS.

• 3 •

Sumner had no intention of lying becalmed, but it was not at all clear what political wind would again fill his sails. For a time he thought of arousing public sentiment against the Grant administration by reviving the controversy over his removal from the chairmanship of the Foreign Relations Committee. Convinced that the President was too stupid to have engineered such a stroke and that Secretary Fish was "the Mephistopheles who entrapped and led him stray," Sumner in March 1871 prepared a long review of his "Personal Relations with the President and Secretary of State." He had his proposed speech printed, and by mid-April newspapers carried stories that he held it in his desk, ready for delivery. Both Wilson and Butler, however, advised him not to reopen the old controversy, and the Marquis de Chambrun warned that Fish was prepared to answer any assault by publishing Sumner's own private letters, "which he should not like perhaps to read over again." [4] Even a more potent deterrent was Sumner's reluctant realization that nobody cared about the whole affair any more. With regret he pigeonholed his speech but sent out a few copies of the printed document to friends with the endorsement: "Unpublished—private and confidential—not to go out of Mr.———'s hands." [5]

A more effective way for Sumner to carry on his warfare against the Grant administration was to join with the reform elements in the Republican party which were gradually coalescing during 1871 into the Liberal Republican movement.[6] Sumner agreed with many of the principles of the reformers. Though he had not done much in recent years to oppose the spoils system, he could claim, with some justice, to be the father of civil service

[4] Fish: Diary, Mar. 19, April 21, 1871, Fish MSS.; New York *Tribune*, April 19, 1871; Wilson to Sumner, June 6, 1871, Sumner MSS.; Chambrun to Schurz, Sunday [1871], Schurz MSS.

[5] Both the Gerrit Smith MSS. and the Pierce MSS. contain copies so inscribed. After Sumner's death the document was published through the agency of Bird.

[6] On the social origins and political views of these reformers, see Sproat: *"The Best Men,"* Chap. 2; Eric F. Goldman: *Rendezvous with Destiny* (New York: Alfred A. Knopf; 1952), Chap. 2; and Matthew T. Downey: "The Rebirth of Reform: A Study of Liberal Reform Movements, 1865–1872" (unpublished Ph.D. dissertation, Princeton University, 1963), Chaps. 1–2.

reform in the United States because of the bill he introduced in 1864 for merit appointments.[7] He agreed with the Liberals in urging a return to specie payments; indeed, his hard-money proposals were so drastic as to make business-minded reformers like Edward Atkinson blanch. He was less interested in their appeal for a low tariff, for he had never formulated a consistent view on protection, but certainly his views were not in conflict with those of the Free Trade League, which in 1870 began a systematic attack upon Grant's policies.

On one basic issue, however, Sumner was wholly at odds with the reform elements in the Republican party. Saddened by the persecution which Southern Unionists, black and white, were suffering in the former Confederate states, he readily joined in April 1871 with the very Republicans who had ousted him from his committee chairmanship to support a new Enforcement Act, giving Grant powers to suppress the Ku Klux Klan and other terrorist organizations in the South. When Democratic Senator Thurman, eager to promote division among the Republicans, expressed surprise that Sumner could so easily forget how Grant had humiliated him and now vote for this measure giving the President "the power to make war upon the white people of America," Sumner reminded him that he had always insisted upon the full exercise of "national power, . . . coextensive with the National Unity and the Equal Rights of all." This "just centralism," this "generous imperialism," which acted "as the sunshine, with beneficent power, and, like the sunshine, for the equal good of all," he was prepared to defend against attacks from any party, "even if it falsely assume the name of Democrat." So ardent was Sumner's advocacy of the Enforcement Act that Howe, who during the debate on Santo Domingo had charged him with deserting the Republican party, now withdrew the accusation.[8]

But new enforcement legislation was the last thing the Liberal reformers wanted. They were tired of the perennial disturbances in the South; they were disillusioned over the progress of

[7] Ari Hoogenboom: *Outlawing the Spoils* (Urbana, Ill.: University of Illinois Press; 1961), pp. 9–11.

[8] *Cong. Globe*, 42 Cong., 1 Sess., pp. 651, 686; Sumner: *Works*, XIV, 282–3.

the freedmen; and they were shocked by the inefficiency and corruption of the carpetbag-Negro regimes. Increasingly they believed that control of the South should be returned to its "natural leaders" through removing all restrictions imposed upon the former Confederates. A broad program of amnesty would also have political advantages, especially in states where whites greatly outnumbered blacks; for the party or faction that succeeded in removing disabilities would certainly be rewarded by the votes of the ex-Confederates and their sympathizers. As early as 1869 Granville D. Hall, speaking for the "wisest and best Republicans" in West Virginia, had warned Sumner: "Our only hope of perpetuating Republican ascendancy in the State is by a magnanimous policy which shall bring a portion of the ex-rebels into co-operation with us when they become voters." Precisely the same political calculus operated in Missouri, where the reform Republicans, drawing upon former Confederate votes, elected B. Gratz Brown governor. In September 1871 Carl Schurz, representing the Missouri Liberal movement, made an important speech at Nashville, Tennessee, announcing that, though he had once been a Radical and an enemy of the Southern whites, he was now ready "to stretch out my hand to all men who, having stood against us during the civil war, are now ready to work for the 'restoration of universal peace, harmony, friendship and true brotherhood.' "[9]

Sumner was not convinced. Though he admired much of Schurz's argument, particularly his fierce denunciation of Grant, he could not agree that "Jeff. Davis and his compeers ought to have the license of officeholding again." After all, Southern Unionists were still under constant attack, and every day his mails were filled with pleas, especially from Southern Negroes, for protection and support. Even where the blacks could vote, they suffered from segregation and discrimination "in the courthouse,—in the public school,—in the public hotel,—and in the public conveyance, whether on land or water." To secure these rights was surely the first duty of Republicans. "I have always said that when the time had come, nobody should outdo me in

[9] Hall to Sumner, Sept. 14, 1869, copy, Hall MSS.; Schurz: *Speeches*, II, 257.

generosity to the South," he assured Schurz. "You insist that the time has come." Sumner could not believe it.[1]

Beside disagreement over reconstruction issues, a profound difference in personality or temperament divided Sumner from the leading Liberal Republicans. Though some of them were as old as he was, his long public service made him seem like a man of the previous generation, not merely an antique but a political primitive or grotesque. To most Liberals his concern for the rights of Negroes appeared archaic; his demand for broad national powers to protect individual rights ran counter to their belief in minimal government; his hostility toward England was incomprehensible to men who thought of the British government as the nearly perfect political order. Even in his prime Sumner had never had the full loyalty of "the best men"—as the postwar breed of reformer-politicians smugly thought of themselves—and now they tended to speak of him a bit patronizingly as a "poor fellow," for whose frailties and failings one might have compassion if only they were not so amusing. They forgot Sumner's achievements but remembered how at the Saturday Club he silenced casual conversation in order to tell about his own experiences, prefacing his remarks: "This is *history,* and you had better listen to it!" Like Henry James, who was not a politician but who shared most of the values of the New England reformers, they admitted feeling a sense of comfort that "while Sumner lived, . . . one uncorrupted soul at least was to be found in Washington." But, James promptly added, "when you came into personal contact with him, and felt yourself rapidly stifling under the weight of that insensate and implacable egotism, he almost made you suspect a public virtue which could be associated with what privately was so little admirable." [2]

If there were, then, reasons why Sumner and the Liberal reformers should not embrace, there were also powerful arguments against his further alienating himself from the main body of the Republican party. Not the least of these was sentimental, for Sumner had been one of the founders of that party and

1 Sumner to Schurz, Sept. 25, 1871, Schurz MSS.; Sumner: *Works,* XIV, 310.

2 Norton and Howe (eds.): *Letters of Charles Eliot Norton,* II, 39–40; Norton (ed.): *Letters of James Russell Lowell,* II, 181; James to G. W. Curtis, July 19, 1874, Curtis MSS., Staten Island Inst. of Arts and Sciences.

wanted to save, not scrap, it. Regarding the Democrats as proved traitors, he could not bring himself to take a step that would lead to their success in the next presidential campaign. "I am a member of the Republican party," he repeatedly protested in debate, "faithful to it always. . . ."[3] His most loyal personal and political friends shared that allegiance. Angered by the "astonishing meanness and folly" exhibited by Grant and his aides, Longfellow nevertheless urged Sumner to exercise great caution "lest we be thrown at the next election into the hands of the Democrats." Similarly Frederick Douglass, though often critical of Grant, protested that he would rather blow his brains out than lend himself "in any way to the destruction or defeat of the Republican party." "If you weaken the confidence of the country . . . in our President," asked one antislavery veteran just back from South Carolina, where the Ku Klux Klan was rampant, "will you not *palsy the arm* on which we depend to save life and liberty in the Southern States?"[4]

There were also practical political reasons why Sumner should not break with his party, even though it had treated him shabbily. With the President's support, Butler was becoming constantly more powerful in Massachusetts. Through him now were funneled most of the federal appointments in the state. In December 1870 Butler demonstrated his power by persuading the Massachusetts delegation to Congress to reject Sumner's choice for United States district attorney and substitute his own candidate. If Sumner's man were recommended, the delegation learned, "B.F.B. would transfer the contest and then the question would be between the nominee of a St. Domingo representative and that of an anti-St. Domingo senator, when B.F.B. would prevail." Stormily Sumner left the caucus, announcing: "I shall never go into another conference with the Massachusetts delegation."[5]

[3] *Cong. Globe*, 42 Cong., 1 Sess., p. 686.

[4] Longfellow to Sumner, Mar. 13, 1871, Longfellow MSS.; James M. McPherson: "Grant or Greeley: The Abolitionist Dilemma in the Election of 1872," *Amer. Hist. Rev.*, LXXI (1965), 49; H. C. Ingersoll to Sumner, Mar. 27, 1871, Sumner MSS.

[5] Sumner to Pierce, Dec. 15, 1870, ibid. Personal relations between Sumner and Butler had also deteriorated. In 1871 Sumner declared that he had not

By midsummer 1871 Butler was ready to seize the leadership of the Republican party in Massachusetts and announced that he was running for governor. Openly appealing for the labor vote and advocating both woman suffrage and prohibition, he actively went about the state corralling delegates in a style hitherto unknown in Massachusetts politics. Members of "the state house ring," as Butler scornfully labeled the party regulars who for years had followed the lead of Sumner and Wilson, appeared to be mesmerized while the general mobilized popular support for his candidacy. Butler, predicted Banks with some satisfaction, "will drive the governor out of his seat and then take Sumners place in the Senate. No one of the Radicals dare oppose him. I am glad he is the man—who[m] they have built up to destroy other men—who now beats their brains out. . . ." Sumner shared Banks's fears. "Why," he told a reporter, "this man has captured a [Congressional] district, is trying to capture the state, and if he succeeds will aim to capture the Presidency." [6]

Worried and confused, Sumner hardly knew during the summer of 1871 where to turn. Until August, long after the Senate had adjourned, he lingered in Washington, undecided in mind, unhappy in body, though apparently benefitting by the galvanic treatments his physician prescribed. "I am still here," he reported to Schurz. "Nobody is more surprised than myself. I am like that Genoese Doge taken to Versailles who when asked what he thought the most remarkable thing, said—'finding himself here.'" The cooler air of Massachusetts restored him somewhat, though he still looked feeble and unwell. When he tried hard, he could sometimes recapture his old form in conversation, "delighting every body by his varied knowledge" and holding forth as an expert "Lace Dealer—a Virtuoso on Old China—a dealer in Alderney stock—a Collector of Engravings—an Expert on Camel Hair Shawls." But now he tired easily, and his

met the general socially for three years. Sumner to Samuel Bowles, Mar. 3, 1871, Bowles MSS.

[6] Banks to his wife, May 10, 1871, Banks MSS.; Blanche Butler Ames (comp.): *Chronicles from the Nineteenth Century* (1957), I, 319. On the unorthodox aspects of Butler's race, see "Warrington" [W. S. Robinson]: "General Butler's Campaign in Massachusetts," *Atlantic Monthly*, XXVIII (1871), 742–50, and "The Butler Canvass," *North Amer. Rev.*, CXIV (1872), 147–70.

friends rightly concluded: "Something is weighing on his mind." [7]

That something was his still unresolved dilemma. If he remained within the Republican party, he would certainly be scorned and ignored by the Grant administration, but if he left it, he would give over control of Massachusetts to Butler. As the general's drive for the gubernatorial nomination gained ground, Sumner could no longer afford to hesitate, and in September he exerted all his strength to pull the Massachusetts Republicans back under control. After persuading Butler's numerous rivals to withdraw so that their votes could be concentrated upon William Washburn, Sumner induced Wilson, who also felt threatened, to join in a public statement, announcing that both the Massachusetts Senators "deeply regret and deplore the extraordinary canvass which Gen. Butler has precipitated upon the Commonwealth . . . and that in their opinion, his name as governor would be hostile to the best interests of the Commonwealth and the Republican party."

On the day after the statement was published, Butler stalked into Sumner's rooms at the Coolidge Hotel in Boston to ask whether it was authentic. Both Sumner and Wilson, who happened to be present, assured him that it was, and Sumner went on to add: "Had you allowed your name to go before the people as other candidates do, according to our usage, I should have quietly waited the action of the Convention. But you have come forward a self-seeker, attacking the Republican party and the existing State Government, making war on them for the purpose of elevating yourself."

Butler was all too aware that if he had behaved "according to our usage" he would have had no more chance at the Republican state convention than did Sumner's rivals in 1862 and 1868. Changing the subject, he took the offensive: "This all comes of your hostility to Grant; I am for him, and you are against him." He threatened to make public Sumner's opinion, repeatedly stated in private conversation, that Grant was "the lowest man

[7] Sumner to Schurz, Aug. 1, 1871, Schurz MSS.; Henry W. Sargent to J. O. Sargent, Nov. 15, 1871, Sargent MSS.; Longfellow: Journal, Aug. 31, 1871, Longfellow MSS.

who ever sat in the Presidential chair; lower intellectually than Andrew Johnson; lower morally than Franklin Pierce—lower socially, because Mr. Pierce was a gentleman."

"But, General," Sumner interjected, "to be frank do you think any better of General Grant than I do?" When Butler, who had consistently criticized Grant throughout the war, made no reply, Sumner pressed his advantage: "You are silent, General; you do not answer me. I ask you again, Do you think any better of Grant than I do? I know you do not. This I know." [8]

Unable to sway the Senators, Butler took his case to the Republican state convention at Worcester on September 26 and lost by a narrow margin. Though the relieved members of the Massachusetts business community, worried by Butler's inflationist and pro-labor policies, rallied in unprecedented endorsement of Sumner,[9] it was obvious that the cross-eyed general had developed immense political strength throughout the state. Angrily writing, "in memory of a former friendship," to rebuke Sumner for having lightly thrown away "the kindly feelings of twenty years," he was now an open enemy.[1] Should Sumner make any move to disrupt the national Republican party, he could expect an attack from Butler at home.

• 4 •

The only tolerable solution of Sumner's problem was to persuade the Republicans to nominate someone other than Grant in the next presidential election. During the summer of 1871 this did not seem an impossible endeavor. Though the worst scandals of the Grant years were yet to be exposed, the President's nepotism, his silent connivance with the unsavory Jim Fisk and Jay Gould, his advocacy of the corrupt Santo Domingo annexation scheme, and his support of the least reputable elements in the party alienated many thoughtful Republicans. At the same time the Grant administration did nothing to reform the currency, to

[8] Mrs. W. S. Robinson: *"Warrington" Pen-Portraits*, p. 133; *Atlantic Monthly*, XXVIII, 747–8; Boston *Evening Traveller*, Sept. 20, 1871.

[9] "I have not seen the Mercantile Community so stirred . . . for years." Alexander H. Rice to Sumner, Sept. 19, 1871, Sumner MSS.

[1] Butler to Sumner, Oct. 2, 1871, ibid.

lower the tariffs, to reduce governmental expenses, or to improve the civil service. Influential party spokesmen, like Horace White of the Chicago *Tribune,* concluded that if Grant was renominated hopes for a Republican victory in 1872 must be "well nigh abandoned." "His power is waning very rapidly," Garfield agreed, "and many of the best men . . . think his re-election is impossible." [2]

So strong seemed the current against Grant that there was much speculation about his possible replacement as the Republican candidate. Lyman Trumbull, Horace Greeley, Justice David Davis, and Gratz Brown were prominently mentioned. Sumner himself had some backing, partly from disgruntled Irish-Americans who liked his anti-British stand, but also partly from responsible Republicans like John Bigelow, who wrote to Whitelaw Reid, of the New York *Tribune:* "I marvel that his name has not been presented before. It is because, I suppose, he has more capacity for making friends for principle than for himself. . . . And yet of all our living statesmen I don't think of one whom Americans will be so proud of as of him when he has been buried as long as Jefferson." Though touched by such warmth, Sumner asked that his name not be mentioned in connection with the presidency: ". . . I beg you to believe that I do not consider myself a candidate for anything—unless it is the good will of good men." [3]

By fall, however, the administration had gained strength, and most observers concluded that the effort to defeat Grant's renomination was doomed. The President himself was superbly confident. "Everything seems to be working favorably for a loyal administration of the Government for four years after the 4th of March, 1873," he assured his friends. Party stalwarts like Forney and William E. Chandler, the New Hampshire boss, though still critical of the President, began to feel: "We must save the Republican Party and if Grant is the best man to do it, we must take him." "He has made a better President than . . . we . . . had any right to expect," Conkling argued. "With General Grant

[2] Downey: "Rebirth of Reform," p. 391.

[3] Bigelow's letter, dated Feb. 9, 1871, was quoted in Whitelaw Reid to Sumner, Feb. 22, 1871, Sumner MSS.; Royal Cortissoz: *The Life of Whitelaw Reid* (New York: Charles Scribner's Sons; 1921), I, 206.

as the candidate, our success is assured; with any other candidate, success is not certain; and hence the renomination and re-election of General Grant seem to me a foregone conclusion."[4]

Simultaneously Liberal Republicans came to the same verdict about Grant's renomination, though not about his reelection. Increasingly they began to see that their only hope of success lay in a third-party movement, a hope promoted by the growing tendency of Democrats, in both the North and the South, to accept, even though they did not approve, the constitutional amendments and the basic legislation of the reconstruction years. Still professing hope for reform within the Republican party, Schurz in September announced that the time had come "for a new organization to step forward—the truly National party of the future." "*You* ought to be the great leader of this movement . . . ," he urged Sumner. "It is the only manner in which the equal rights of all can be permanently secured in the South."[5]

Long after most reformers and regulars accepted Grant's renomination as inevitable, Sumner continued to believe that the Republicans would choose another candidate in 1872. Loyal to the party he had helped found, aware that by bolting it he would imperil his political position in Massachusetts, conscious that third-party movements in the United States are rarely successful, he clung desperately to his hope that he could persuade the Republicans to reject Grant. Confident that Grant "could not be nominated if it appears that he could not be re-elected," he wrote letters, day after day, exposing the limitations and failings of the administration. "'One term' is enough for any body," he urged his correspondents, "especially for one who, being tried, is found so incapable—so personal—so selfish—so vindictive—and so entirely pre-occupied by himself." Grant was "unhappily too great a soldier to appreciate harmony and good will among associates in the public service." He was the Great Quarreler in American history. He had "quarreled more than all other Presi-

[4] Earle D. Ross: *The Liberal Republican Movement* (New York: n.p.; 1919), p. 42; Leon B. Richardson: *William E. Chandler, Republican* (New York: Dodd, Mead & Company; 1940), p. 128; Alfred R. Conkling: *The Life and Letters of Roscoe Conkling* (New York: Charles L. Webster & Company; 1889), p. 336.

[5] Sept. 30, 1871, Sumner MSS.

dents," beginning controversies with "two members of the cabinet"—Hoar and Jacob D. Cox, both of whom resigned—"the chairman of a Senate Committee—distinguished senators—a minister to London," and others. Grant was "the lowest President, whether intellectually or morally, we have ever had." "Undoubtedly he is the richest since Washington," Sumner judged, adding by way of innuendo: "although he was very poor at the beginning of the War." Instead of enforcing the laws, this President spent his time "at entertainments, excursions [and] horse-races;" consequently, *"on him is that innocent blood"* shed by the Ku Klux Klan. "Such a man for President for a 2nd term," Sumner exploded; "God forbid." Republicans must see that Grant "is an incubus and mill-stone upon us" and they must tell him "plainly that he cannot expect a renomination." "I wish," he added, almost wistfully, "a President with a little common sense, common justice, and common liberality, who is not always brutal or vindictive." [6]

When Congress reassembled in December 1871, Sumner seized every occasion to expose Grant's failings. Working closely with Trumbull, Schurz, former Representative Julian, and other reformers, he devised a brilliant strategy of harassment. Day after day he introduced motions, neutral in tone and statesmanlike in purpose, in favor of purity in government, reduction of expenses, and the like, but in each case he prefaced his resolution with remarks suggesting that the whole Grant administration was guilty of fraud and corruption. Should Grant's supporters fail to reply, they seemingly acknowledged the correctness of Sumner's accusations; if they did respond, they apparently were opposing honesty and efficiency in the government. Sherman bitterly protested that Sumner's little prologues to his resolutions were indictments "by facts not yet proven, facts, that are to be submitted to examination, [of] high officers of this Government, and involving grave derelictions of public duty." Speaking for the Grant forces in the Senate, he complained: "We are treated like a bull in a Spanish bull-fight. These

[6] Sumner to Anna E. Dickinson, Mar. 25, 1871, Dickinson MSS.; Sumner to Gerrit Smith, Aug. 20 and 28, 1871, Smith MSS.; Sumner to E. D. Morgan [c. Nov. 28, 1871], Morgan MSS.; Sumner to Schurz, Sept. 25, 1871, Schurz MSS.

gentlemen enter with a red flag and wave it in our faces and demand, at their own time and in their own choice of their own methods, a political debate." [7]

One of Sumner's earliest and most successful efforts at Grant-baiting stemmed from the President's surprising announcement in his annual message that he wanted to reform the internal revenue service that had so proliferated during the war. Promptly Sumner responded by proposing to abolish all internal taxes and duties, except from the sale and use of stamps, and simultaneously to do away with "the offices of Commissioner, deputy commissioner, solicitor, collector and deputy collector, assessor and assistant assessor, supervisor, and detective, heads of division, and clerks, and employés under the Commissioner of Internal Revenue" by September 1872—i.e., just before the next presidential election. Should the President's friends in the Senate support this bill, they would, as the New York *World* observed, "destroy this powerful party engine, and cripple General Grant in the canvass of next year." If, as was more likely, they opposed the measure, they would reveal how hollow was Grant's protestation of interest in reform.[8]

In a further effort to embarrass Grant, Sumner proposed on December 21 a constitutional amendment to limit the President to one term in office. Embodying an idea that Sumner had cherished for many years, the resolution in its chaste wording seemed entirely non-political, for, if ratified, the amendment was not to take effect until after March 4, 1873. In actuality, however, the proposal was strictly a partisan maneuver, worked out by the Senator and George Wilkes, editor of the racy newspaper, *Spirit of the Times,* who was virulently hostile to Grant. The amendment was intended, as Wilkes said, to be "the first big gun to be sent booming over the surface of the land" to announce the drop-Grant movement within the Republican party. Immediately Grant's backers in the Senate saw that, though Sumner's proposal wore "a vail [*sic*] of preamble and a fig-leaf of benevolent postponement," it was really "a device, a make-weight, an expedient, to affect the reëlection of President Grant." If "the

[7] *Cong. Globe,* 42 Cong., 2 Sess., pp. 1009, 1011.
[8] Ibid., p. 45; New York *World,* Dec. 12, 1871.

American people . . . now pronounce for the one-term dogma," Conkling asked, "how can they stultify themselves, and straightway trample on the dogma by electing a President for a second term?" Sumner's amendment was, of course, killed, but not until the reformers got some political mileage from its preamble reminding the voters how Andrew Jackson, William Henry Harrison, Henry Clay, and Benjamin F. Wade had all favored a one-term presidency "for the plain reason that the peril from the Chief Magistrate, so long as he is exposed to temptation, surpasses that from any other quarter." [9]

Administration stalwarts felt more seriously threatened by Trumbull's proposal to establish a Joint Congressional Committee on Retrenchment, with power not merely to investigate recent reports of frauds in the New York customs house but to ferret out malfeasance in all branches of the public service. The dank odor of corruption was already beginning to seep out of the cellars of the Grant administration, and the President's lieutenants greatly feared that such a general investigation might uncover politically damaging scandals. At the same time they could not afford to oppose an investigation, lest they be accused of covering up fraud. After an unsuccessful effort in the open Senate to restrict the scope of Trumbull's proposed committee, they then agreed in caucus to appoint to it only Republicans averse to a far-reaching investigation and favorable to Grant's renomination. When Sumner bitterly protested that the caucus decision was "simply inexplicable on any ground of justice or parliamentary law," since it packed the committee with enemies of Trumbull's proposal and systematically excluded all its friends, Anthony, speaking for the administration forces, blandly assured him: "I do not know of a Senator in this body who is opposed to the most searching and thorough inquiry into any charges of corruption."

Angrily Sumner denounced the whole caucus system as "infinitely absurd and unconstitutional." As he had often done in the past, he insisted that a caucus was "simply a convenience" and that its rulings had no binding force. "A Senator has no right

[9] Wilkes to Sumner, Nov. 17 and Dec. 8, 1871, Sumner MSS.; *Cong. Globe*, 42 Cong., 2 Sess., pp. 354–5; Sumner: *Works*, XIV, 326.

. . . ," he protested, "to go into a secret chamber and there constrain himself in regard to the public business." In these secret conclaves, as he well knew, effective leadership was exercised by a handful of men, who really ran the Senate.[1] In former years when Sumner himself had been at times a member of that directory, he had objected to caucus rule; now, excluded from the seats of the powerful, he protested even more strongly against it. Speaking as "the oldest Senator in service here," as "one of the oldest members of the Republican party," as "one of its founders," he begged his colleagues to overthrow the oligarchy.[2] He knew that if it fell so would Grant's hopes for renomination.

· 5 ·

Delighted to help the reformers attack the Grant administration, Sumner could not support their plan to extend general amnesty to the former Confederates. The issue was at least as much symbolic as it was practical, for President Johnson had extended full pardon to the rebels on December 25, 1868, and, after the readmission of the Southern states, there were no federal statutes which kept ex-Confederates from voting. Under the Fourteenth Amendment, however, a few thousand prominent Southern whites, former high-ranking civil and military officers of the Confederacy, were forbidden to hold state or national office unless pardoned by a two-thirds vote of each house of Congress, and it was this disqualification which the Liberal Republicans now proposed to remove.[3] Many of them simply felt that the time had come to end reconstruction and to turn to pressing problems

[1] Cf. John A. Logan's observation: ". . . I think about five is the number in this Senate that does generally the business of the Senate, as far as arranging things is concerned—about five [laughter;] four or five; I may not be correct in the number, but not over five." *Cong. Globe,* 42 Cong., 2 Sess., p. 171.

[2] Ibid., pp. 160, 190. There is not room in these pages to discuss another attempt Sumner made to embarrass the Grant administration by charging that the War Department illegally sold surplus rifles and other equipment to the French government during the recent Franco-Prussian War. The political purpose of wooing the German-American voters away from Grant was obvious. See *Cong. Globe,* 42 Cong., 2 Sess., pp. 1008–11; Schurz: *Speeches,* V, 34; For Sumner's embarrassingly thin testimony before the investigating committee, see *Senate Report* No. 132, 42 Cong., 2 Sess., pp. 321–3, 335, 835–42.

[3] James A. Rawley: "The General Amnesty Act of 1872," *Miss. Valley Hist. Rev.,* XLVII (1960), 480–4.

elsewhere; others calculated that they would need the votes of the former Confederates and their sympathizers in order to defeat Grant in 1872.

Theoretically in favor of the broadest clemency, Sumner thought this concern for the rights of former rebels ill-timed. He was convinced that the reconstruction of the South had not gone far enough, for he regularly received reports from all parts of the former Confederacy detailing how the former slaveholders were gradually resuming power, driving out white Republicans, and reducing the blacks to second-class citizenship. As he had anticipated, not even the guarantee of universal suffrage protected the Southern Unionists. In every Southern state Negroes suffered from discrimination, whether in hotels or theaters, on streetcars or trains. Even in South Carolina, where a majority of the inhabitants were black, segregation of public facilities was common and, though there was a state civil rights act on the books, no one was ever convicted for violating it. Southern Negroes had to attend segregated, inferior schools, despite the express stipulation by Congress in 1870 that Virginia, Texas, and Mississippi would be readmitted only if they guaranteed that their schools would be open to all. Indeed, only a few months after Virginia's Congressmen took their seats, that state adopted a policy of mandatory school segregation.[4]

Drawing upon long political experience, Sumner also questioned the expediency of granting general amnesty at this time. If he advocated restoring the political rights of the former Confederate leaders, he was certain to alienate many blacks, his most consistent and enthusiastic supporters in the South. He doubted, moreover, that Southern white leaders, given again the chance to hold office, would flock to the Liberal Republican cause and help defeat Grant. He judged it more likely that they would lead their states back into the anti-Negro Democratic party.

[4] Alfred H. Kelly: "The Congressional Controversy over School Segregation, 1867–1875," *Amer. Hist. Rev.*, LXIV (1959), 540–2; James M. McPherson: "Abolitionists and the Civil Rights Act of 1875," *Jour. of Am. Hist.*, LII (1965), 496–9; Joel Williamson: *After Slavery: The Negro in South Carolina During Reconstruction* (Chapel Hill, N.C.: University of North Carolina Press; 1965), pp. 279–80.

When the House of Representatives passed the amnesty bill, he decided not to oppose it in the Senate but to add to it a sweeping guarantee of civil rights. He would thus link justice to generosity. His amendment provided that the federal government should guarantee to all citizens, without distinction of color, "equal and impartial enjoyment of any accommodation, advantage, facility, or privilege furnished by common carriers, whether on land or water; by inn-keepers; by licensed owners . . . of theatres or other places of public amusements; by trustees . . . , teachers, or other officers of common schools and other public institutions of learning . . . ; [and] by officers of church organizations, [and] cemetery associations." In addition, no person should be barred from jury service on account of race or color, and "every law, statute, ordinance, regulation, or custom, whether national or State, . . . making any discriminations against any person on account of color, by the use of the word 'white,'" should be repealed. All suits brought under this civil rights bill were to be heard in federal, not state, courts.[5]

Sumner designed his bill to be the "crowning work" of reconstruction. "Very few measures of equal importance have ever been presented," he was convinced. Once it was adopted, he announced: "I know nothing further to be done in the way of legislation for the security of equal rights in this Republic."[6] Reflecting his long advocacy of equal rights under the law, the bill brought together in a systematic fashion proposals which he had repeatedly advocated since the outbreak of the Civil War. He had first introduced the measure in May 1870 and had reintroduced it in January 1871 and again in March 1871. Carefully thought out and drafted with precision, it represented the fullest, and final, formulation of his equal-rights doctrine, and it was an accurate measure of both the strengths and the limitations of its author's mind.

The defects in Sumner's civil rights bill were obvious.

[5] *Cong. Globe*, 42 Cong., 2 Sess., p. 244.

[6] Sumner to Longfellow, Feb. 25, 1872, Longfellow MSS.; Bertram Wyatt-Brown: "The Civil Rights Act of 1875," *Western Political Quar.*, XVIII (1965), 764. For a recent review of Sumner's constitutional thinking on the civil rights question, see Ronald B. Jager: "Charles Sumner, the Constitution, and the Civil Rights Act of 1875," *New England Quarterly*, XVII (1969), 350–72.

Though he knew that his Senate colleagues liked to construe the Constitution literally, he did nothing to make his proposal more palatable to them. He might easily have eliminated, as Senator Carpenter privately urged him to do, the proposed regulation of churches, which appeared to be a clear violation of the First Amendment. He might, as the Supreme Court did subsequently, have cited the interstate commerce clause as giving the federal government authority to outlaw segregation on trains and in hotels, but he did not mention it. It is easier to understand why he placed little stress upon the Fourteenth Amendment's guarantee of equal protection of the laws; too many of his colleagues who had helped draft that ambiguous document would reply that they had never intended to outlaw segregation. Sumner's principal constitutional defense of his proposal was, peculiarly enough, the Thirteenth Amendment, which gave Congress power to enforce the abolition of slavery; though perfectly aware that most Senators did not agree with him in equating segregation and slavery, he declared grandly that clause was such a sweeping justification for his civil rights bill "as to make further discussion surplusage." When Senator Morrill insisted upon learning exactly where in the Constitution the federal government was given control over "matters of education, worship, amusement, recreation, entertainment, all of which enter so essentially into the private life of the people," Sumner replied that if Morrill were a Negro and had to suffer from injustice and discrimination he would readily enough "find power . . . in the Constitution to apply the remedy." For himself, Sumner discovered authorization in the Sermon on the Mount and in the Declaration of Independence, for which he again claimed a power higher than the Constitution, being "earlier in time, loftier, more majestic, more sublime in character and principle." [7]

Another weakness in the bill was Sumner's failure to provide effective machinery for enforcing it. He well knew that laws do not execute themselves. During the struggle to end segregation in the streetcars in the District of Columbia he had discov-

[7] *Cong. Globe,* 42 Cong., 2 Sess., Appendix, p. 4; Sumner: *Works,* XIV, 417–39; Pierce, IV, 501.

ered how little value there was in having a legal right for those too poor or powerless to assert it. The strategy by which the Southern states were effectively nullifying reconstruction legislation further proved that statutes alone were not enough to secure justice. Yet under Sumner's bill, the only way a Negro deprived of his civil rights could secure redress was by bringing suit in the federal courts—a process certainly too cumbersome and too expensive to afford general relief. It is not clear, however, that Sumner had any other option. In the 1870's the United States government had no means of compelling its citizens to obey the laws unless it was prepared to call out the army. There was no national police and only a rudimentary federal bureaucracy. In an age distrustful of all government and suspicious of all institutions, Congress would certainly never appropriate funds to support a permanent peacetime federal agency, with branches in every county of the South, to defend the rights of black men. It was no wonder, then, that Sumner—like most other Republican friends of the Negro—saw the only practical guarantee of civil rights in suits brought by individual citizens before the courts.

For all the lack of enforcement mechanism, Sumner's civil rights bill was a proposal of immense strength and of broad statesmanship. More than any of his political contemporaries, Sumner realized that the future of American democracy depended upon the ability of the white and black races to live together in peace and equity. Instead of huddling the sensitive question of race relations out of sight, he wanted it discussed fully and openly at a time when American institutions were still flexible enough to permit major social changes. He knew that it was possible to secure peace in his time by quietly abandoning the Negro and returning the South to the control of its "natural leaders" among the white race; but he was never deluded by the notion that, if generously treated, Southern whites would feel it was in their own best interest to see that Negroes were educated, well fed and housed, and secure. The subordination of the Negroes was less a matter of economics than of prejudice, deep-seated and ineradicable so long as black men legally were marked as belonging to an inferior caste. Only by securing equal rights to all citizens could the United States live up to its promise and become a land where even-handed justice ruled.

The civil rights bill also served to illustrate Sumner's style in politics, and it again showed that he was more astute politically than either his friends or his enemies were prepared to believe. This is not to argue that his motive in introducing the bill was political; his long advocacy of civil rights and his presentation of virtually this same bill on earlier occasions refute that notion. But by pressing the measure in the winter of 1871–72 he was able to serve his political purposes, and that fact may account for his greater concern for it than in previous sessions; in January 1871 he confessed that he had so entirely lost sight of his civil rights proposal that he was not even aware that the Judiciary Committee had adversely reported on it.[8] Now, however, by offering his civil rights measure as an amendment to the amnesty bill, he could test the sincerity of the Democrats in protesting that they were now willing to follow the "New Departure" and accept the changes wrought by the Civil War. Now, too, he could determine whether the Liberals were sincerely concerned for the rights of black men.

An even more important political consequence might be that of recalling the regular Republican party to its original principles. By so doing, he could strengthen his own position and weaken that of Grant, who had endorsed amnesty and was opposed to linking it with civil rights. Believing that the masses of black Republicans in the South were already distrustful of a President who lacked "genuine sympathy" for their cause,[9] Sumner intended, as Democratic Senator Joshua Hill of Georgia suspected, to present "himself more prominently, if possible, than he ever did before to the entire colored race of this nation as their foremost, if not their exclusive champion." "It is a vain thing for any gentleman in this body, or . . . in any section of the United States, to compete with the Senator from Massachusetts for honors with these people," Hill warned. "Sir, he will make and unmake men by the dozen who try to do this thing,"

[8] *Cong. Globe*, 41 Cong., 3 Sess., p. 616.
[9] Sumner to Duchess of Argyll, June 22, 1869, Argyll MSS.

because "as a political element . . . the colored people of America belong to-day to our Senator from Massachusetts." [1]

Grant's supporters were fully aware that Sumner's civil rights amendment to the amnesty bill posed a dangerous political dilemma. If they opposed his plan, they would alienate blacks, who in the deep South were the most numerous element in the Republican party, and would strengthen Sumner's charge that the President was indifferent to human rights. If they supported it, they would offend the Southern whites, from whom the party must secure support if it was to remain a viable political organization, especially in the upper South, and would also seem to recognize Sumner's leadership. After much consultation, Grant's friends in the Senate decided to support both amnesty and civil rights—in the expectation that both would fail. Their strategy was aided by the fact that, under the Fourteenth Amendment, the amnesty bill must receive a two-thirds vote in both houses, and they could count upon Sumner's civil rights amendment to make it so distasteful as to cause many Democrats to vote against the whole measure.

Aware of the danger, advocates of amnesty sought, when Sumner introduced his civil rights amendment in December 1871, to declare it out of order on the ground that it was not germane. Serving as President pro tempore of the Senate as it met in the committee of the whole, Anthony revealed the strategy of the Grant men by ruling in Sumner's favor. Upon appeal, every Democrat present and all the Republicans prominently identified with the reform cause except Sumner voted to overturn that ruling; Grant's supporters and the Southern Republicans voted successfully to uphold it. Immediately afterward, however, a slight shift of votes brought defeat to Sumner's proposal itself. "There will," he predicted, "be another vote on my amendment."

When the Senate went back into general session, he reintroduced his amendment, insisting that the amnesty plan had to have civil rights linked to it. "A measure that seeks to benefit only the former rebels and neglects the colored race does not deserve success," he argued; "it is an unworthy measure, it

[1] *Cong. Globe,* 42 Cong., 2 Sess., p. 880.

cannot be sustained by a righteous public sentiment." [2]

During the Christmas recess he set about creating that righteous sentiment. "Now is the time to assure this immense boon, which is the final fulfillment of the promise of the Declaration of Independence," he urged George William Curtis, whose influential *Harper's Weekly Magazine* he wanted to support the civil rights bill. "Will you not help my Bill for Equal Rights?" he begged Pierce, his loyal lieutenant in Massachusetts. ". . . it is the final measure for the safeguard of our colored fellow-citizens." "All possible help is needed to secure the passage of the Bill for Equal Rights," he implored George T. Downing, the wealthy Negro caterer, asking him to drum up support among other Northern blacks. "Besides petitions and letters there must be a strong Committee to visit every Republican Senator. Not a vote must be lost." To Southern Negroes planning to celebrate the anniversary of the final Emancipation Proclamation, he wrote: "You should pledge yourselves to insist upon Equal Rights and not to stop until they are secured." [3]

On January 15, 1872, Sumner made a formal speech in order to arouse further support for his civil rights proposal. The issue before Congress, he insisted, was none other than slavery, which was not dead but in its "barbarous tyranny stalks into this Chamber, denying to a whole race the Equal Rights promised by a just citizenship." Equality of rights, he asserted with doubtful accuracy, had been the objective of the North in the Civil War. "The victory of the war is vain without the grander victory through which the Republic is dedicated to the axiomatic, self-evident truth declared by our fathers [in the Declaration of Independence], and reasserted by Abraham Lincoln [in the Gettysburg Address]." To objections that his bill would compel the social mixing of the races, he replied: "This is no question of society, no question of social life, no question of social equality. . . ." To the argument that segregated but equal facilities could be supplied for Negroes, he responded, in words that anticipated

[2] Ibid., pp. 276, 278.

[3] Sumner to Curtis, Dec. 30, 1871, Curtis MSS., Harvard Univ.; Sumner to Pierce, Dec. 27, 1871, Sumner MSS.; Sumner to Downing, Dec. 28, 1871, MS. owned by Mr. H. DeGrasse Asbury of Hollis, N.Y.: Sumner to Charles N. Hunter, Dec. 29, 1871, Hunter MSS.

a Supreme Court ruling eighty-two years later: "The substitute is invariably an inferior article." Insisting that the Senate should first be just to its friends before it showed itself generous to its former foes, he demanded: "Let the record be made at last, which shall be the cap-stone of the reconstructed Republic." [4]

For the next three weeks virtually all other Senate business had to be suspended while the debate upon the civil rights amendment raged. Despite growing fatigue, Sumner was omnipresent and indefatigable. Over and over he made his points with such assiduity that "whenever he rose to urge his Civil Rights Bill, senators in their impatience would spring from their seats, wheel round and rush into the cloak-rooms, leaving him to make his speech almost alone to the President of the Senate." During the early stages of the discussion the galleries were thronged with both whites and blacks, but toward the end there were few in attendance but Negroes, who, according to the newspapers, "watched with breathless eagerness" a discussion "fraught with so much import to their welfare." To cheer Sumner on, Negro spectators one day presented him with a "colossal bouquet," which he placed conspicuously upon his desk as the debate proceeded.[5]

It was a complex controversy, in which Sumner was fighting on many fronts simultaneously. In the early stages of the discussion he had privately begged Northern Democratic Senators to support his amendment as proof of the sincerity of their "New Departure" program, but he was not surprised when they gave him no encouragement. Recognizing that he could not reach them with argument, he did not waste time in replying to Democratic charges that his measure was "palpably unconstitutional," a "plain usurpation of power that does not belong to Congress at all." With the Liberals, who were now steadily drifting away from the regular Republican organization, he also had few exchanges. These were now his closest friends in the Senate, with whom he had cooperated since the battle against annexing

[4] Sumner: *Works*, XIV, 369–414.

[5] *Dinner Commemorative of Charles Sumner and Complimentary to Edward L. Pierce, Boston, December* 29, 1894 (Cambridge: John Wilson and Son; 1895), pp. 56–7; Boston *Morning Journal*, Jan. 17, 1872; Boston *Commonwealth*, Feb. 17, 1872.

the Dominican Republic, and he would not give their enemies encouragement by attacking them. In mournful silence he listened as Schurz deplored the introduction of the civil rights issue and Trumbull charged that the real motive behind the advocates of Sumner's bill was to kill the amnesty plan.

Toward Southern Republicans who failed to support the civil rights amendment, he was severe. He took a fierce pleasure in attacking South Carolina Senator Frederick Sawyer, who had been born in Massachusetts. Elected largely by black votes, Sawyer was slowly drifting toward the white, more conservative wing of the South Carolina Republican party, and Sumner showed how hollow were his protestations of friendship for the Negro. When the carpetbag Senator replied in an equally abusive strain, Sumner reminded him where the loyalty of South Carolina black men lay: "Why seeks he now to liberate his soul against me? Is it to gratify the colored people of South Carolina? Does he think to win favor among them by striking at me while I am laboring to serve them?" [6]

The sharpest clashes during these prolonged debates were between Sumner and Republican Senators committed to Grant's renomination. Willing to vote for a civil rights amendment because it would probably defeat the amnesty bill, few of the New Radicals had any deep interest in the plight of the Negro. They regarded Sumner's proposal as "legislative buncombe," and after one of his exhortations ironically proposed that the Senate should sing the hymn "Old Hundred." Unwilling to give Sumner renewed importance in the public eye by appearing to follow his lead, they rigorously tested his constitutional theories and objected to his theory that the Declaration of Independence gave Congress any power to act. At the same time they tried to water down his proposal so that, if it should be passed, it would be less offensive to Southern whites and would cause less animosity among their own Negrophobic constituents. Carpenter, seeking revenge for an earlier encounter with Sumner, took the lead in trying to delete from the bill all reference to churches and the proposed regulation of juries, and he wanted to have suits heard before state, not federal, courts. Angrily Sumner fought back,

[6] *Cong. Globe*, 42 Cong., 2 Sess., p. 875.

denouncing Carpenter's "emasculated synonym of the original measure," launching into another tribute to the Declaration of Independence, whose "primal truths . . . are more commanding and more beaming now than when first uttered," and openly threatening: "I know that if I were a colored citizen . . . I would not forget those who, when my rights were in issue, neglect them. . . . I would bear them in mind, I would hold them to a strict responsibility." [7]

Sumner's oratory had less influence on the outcome of the civil rights controversy than did the exigencies of politics. Except perhaps for a few Southern Republican Senators, whom he persuaded or browbeat, few changed their opinions because of the debates. On February 9, 1872, Democrats and Liberals joined in voting against Sumner's amendment, but enough pro-Grant Republicans supported it to cause a tie. Then Vice President Colfax, aware that the Grant administration had to seem in favor of civil rights, gave his casting vote for Sumner's proposal. The now combined amnesty-civil rights bill was so objectionable to Democrats that, just as Grant's friends anticipated, enough Senators absented themselves from the final vote to prevent the measure from receiving the requisite two-thirds majority. The administration was now on record as supporting both amnesty and civil rights, and it could blame the Democrats and the Liberals for defeating these measures. Yet, since neither was passed, Grant did not have to receive the backlash of white resentment against Negro equality or of black hostility toward the rehabilitation of Confederate leaders. The main result of Sumner's efforts, then, was the strengthening of his chief enemy.

• 6 •

The debates over the civil rights bill made Sumner more than ever hesitant about joining the Liberal Republican movement, which was now acting like a third party and planned to hold a convention in Cincinnati on May 1. Though Trumbull, Schurz,

[7] Sumner: *Works*, XIV, 441, 451; *Cong. Globe*, 42 Cong., 2 Sess., p. 621. On the encounter between Sumner and Carpenter, see James A. Garfield: Diary, Feb. 5, 1872, Garfield MSS.; Boston *Advertiser*, Feb. 8, 1872.

Greeley, Gratz Brown, and other reformers thought they could absorb into their Liberal coalition all the political elements hostile to Grant, Sumner, with greater realism, recognized that the Democrats, with their numbers, their organization, and their experience, would become the senior partners in any such alliance. The unanimous vote of the Senate Democrats to kill the civil rights bill was a clear warning that their party was unregenerate.

Another reason for Sumner to exercise caution was the sharp division which the Liberal Republican movement created among his Massachusetts constituents. Bird led an influential segment of the Republican party in endorsing the Cincinnati convention, and Bowles, of the Springfield *Republican*, and Atkinson were also ardent Liberal partisans. On the other hand, both Hooper, Sumner's closest friend in the Massachusetts delegation, and Pierce, his most trusted political lieutenant in Massachusetts, announced they would support Grant if he was renominated. So too did Garrison, who spoke for most of the old abolitionists; admitting Grant's "paucity of . . . mind," his "coarse habits and utter lack of culture," the antislavery leader warned that any division among Republicans could "only inure to the advantage of the Democratic party . . . still so largely animated by its old negro-hating spirit." [8]

Adding to Sumner's uncertainty was his aversion for some of the politicians prominently mentioned as candidates on the Liberal Republican ticket. He could endorse Lyman Trumbull, despite their past bitter difference, but the austere Illinois Senator had little popular following and was not even master of his own state, where Justice David Davis, wholly unacceptable to Sumner, was also campaigning for convention delegates. For Horace Greeley, who was coming more and more to be spoken of as a presidential possibility, Sumner had little respect; for years there had been latent distrust between the two men, each of whom considered himself the principal spokesman of advanced Northern opinion, and Sumner knew well the personal and intellectual idiosyncracies of the New York *Tribune* editor.[9] Worst of

[8] Nov. 22, 1871, Sumner MSS.
[9] Bigelow: *Retrospections*, IV, 487–8.

all, in Sumner's eyes, was Charles Francis Adams, who in April began to be mentioned prominently as a likely Liberal candidate. Though the two former friends and bitter rivals were now on speaking terms, everybody recognized that the nomination of Adams would be "a personal trial and mortification" to Sumner as well as a "terrible blow" to his political power in Massachusetts.[1]

So obvious was Sumner's reluctance to accept any of the prominently mentioned Liberal candidates that his enemies began to think that he wanted to run for President himself. There had been scattered Sumner-for-President sentiment for several years, and in March 1871, just after he was removed from the Foreign Relations Committee, the influential New York *Sun* had argued that he would make an ideal candidate upon the Democratic ticket, who could carry all the New England states, all the South, and most of the rest of the country. In August Samuel J. Randall, one of the most powerful Pennsylvania Democrats in Congress, gave Sumner his endorsement. In December, Wilkes, the eccentric editor of *The Spirit of the Times*, began a more systematic campaign to have Sumner nominated by both the Democrats and the Liberal Republicans, arguing that he would be "a dignified and able officer in the Presidential chair; —a high-minded American, who would have exacted the whole of Canada from Great Britain in compensation for her Alabama wrongs; a statesman, whose honor is as spotless as a virgin's chastity." [2]

Believing that the presidency was not an office to be sought, Sumner did nothing to encourage this boomlet. He recognized that he was too old and ill for a strenuous campaign and that, after a generation of plain speaking on controversial issues, he had too many enemies. Doubtless he read without surprise former President Johnson's announcement: "The idea of the Democracy supporting Charles Sumner is too utterly preposterous to talk about. . . . Whenever you see the Democracy walking up to the support of Mr. Sumner and his principles, you will see

[1] Springfield *Republican*, May 14, 1872; Bird to Schurz, Aug. 7 [1872], Schurz MSS.

[2] New York *World*, Mar. 21, 1871; Thomas Fitzgerald to Sumner, Aug. 6, 1871, Sumner MSS.; *Spirit of the Times*, Jan. 20, 1872.

them going to their own funeral."[3] When, therefore, Bowles came to Washington in March 1872 to urge that the Liberals nominate Sumner and Trumbull, an unbeatable combination, he received no encouragement from the senior Senator from Massachusetts. With no regret Sumner told Wilkes unequivocally that he did not want his name presented to the Cincinnati convention, and he remained silent when Bird begged that he permit the Massachusetts delegation to vote for him.[4]

Refraining from any commitment to the Liberal Republican movement yet announcing that in no circumstances would he support the "venal, ambitious, vulgar, . . . obstinate and unmanly" Grant,[5] Sumner during the first six months of 1872 occupied an increasingly awkward political position. Supporters of the Cincinnati convention put great pressure upon him to declare himself. Bowles virtually demanded a public statement, as something due to those who had loyally supported Sumner in his attacks upon the Grant administration. Greeley, too, expressed his grave anxiety over "any prolonged delay in an authoritative expression from [Sumner] with reference to the combination against Grant" and added that if Sumner failed to support the Liberal Republicans, "it might then become necessary for The Tribune to take a different tack." Even August Belmont, the financier of the Democratic party, warned that only *"the most unequivocal attitude"* on Sumner's part could keep many Republicans from supporting Grant, and he scolded: "Sumner ought to have come out ere this and he certainly cannot afford to hold out any longer."[6]

By mid-April the pressure was so great that Sumner was on the verge of committing himself. David A. Wells, the tariff reformer, after consulting with friends in Boston and Washington, made a special trip to the capital in order to convince Sumner

[3] Chicago *Tribune*, Dec. 7, 1871.

[4] Boston *Morning Journal*, Jan. 22, 1872; Merriam: *Bowles*, II, 178; *Spirit of the Times*, May 11, 1872; Bird to Sumner, April 23 and 28, 1872, Sumner MSS.; Springfield *Republican*, May 2, 1872. For an elaboration of Bowles's position, see his letter to Sumner, May 21, 1872, MS. Yale Univ. Lib.

[5] Brooklyn *Union*, Feb. 23, 1872.

[6] Bowles to Sumner, Mar. 9, 1872, Sumner MSS.; Bowles to Sumner, March 30, 1872, MS., Yale Univ. Lib.; Whitelaw Reid to Sumner, Mar. 28, 1872, Sumner MSS.; Belmont to Schurz, April 1, 1872, Schurz MSS.

that his endorsement of Liberal Republicans was urgently needed. Finally capitulating, Sumner agreed as Wells left to draft a letter pledging that he himself would go to Cincinnati and support the movement. Just at this point, however, Professor John Mercer Langston, the distinguished Negro vice president of Howard University, called, and Sumner showed him the proposed letter. Fearing, as did Frederick Douglass, that any split in the Republican party would only ensure the triumph of the Democrats, Langston urged Sumner not to have anything to do with the Liberal movement and told Sumner he was imperiling the future of the blacks. That evening when Wells returned to pick up Sumner's promised letter, he discovered that the Senator had decided to maintain his silence.[7]

Angrily Massachusetts Liberal Republicans complained of Sumner's course. "Here in Massachusetts," as Bowles wrote Schurz in March, "we can make no demonstration until Sumner speaks his mind." "You have only to say the word," Bowles wrote the Senator himself, "and your friends will rally in great numbers at once." "Without your cordial cooperation and vigorous leadership," Bird agreed, "the movement will be a failure, here and elsewhere." "We fail . . . in Massachusetts without you," Bird again urged on April 28, warning: "You are shorn of power without us. I pray you, be prepared for that."[8]

When Sumner continued to be unresponsive, Bird went by Washington on his way to the Cincinnati convention. At first he could get little from Sumner except another statement of Grant's deficiencies, which the Senator promptly balanced by declaring that he could never do anything that would imperil Negro rights. Finally, however, he drafted for Bird a set of resolutions which he thought the Cincinnati convention ought to adopt, including a pledge to enfranchise "all citizens, so that there shall be no denial of rights on account of color or race, but all shall be equal before the law." Then, to Bird's fury, he declined to promise that he would support the Cincinnati nominees even if they ran on such a platform. Bird left with a hope that Sumner would send

[7] Wells to Schurz, Mar. 15 [1877], Schurz MSS. See also Wells to Sumner, April 14 [1872], Sumner MSS.

[8] Bowles to Schurz, Mar. 22, 1872, Schurz MSS.; Bowles to Sumner, April 14, 1872, Sumner MSS,; Bird to Sumner, April 15 and 28, ibid.

him a letter to be read to the convention, but all he received was silence. "I am pained that we get no word of encouragement from you," Bird complained on the opening day. "Urged by you to the perilous ridge, we are left to fight the battle alone." [9]

The decision of the Cincinnati convention to nominate Greeley and Gratz Brown did not force Sumner to declare himself. Though he doubtless preferred Greeley as nominee to Adams, whose candidacy Bird and other friends at Cincinnati helped defeat,[1] he could not help recognizing that the New York editor was not "our model" as a reformer; on the other hand, he was obviously "much better than Grant, who is without knowledge, justice, or decency." Sumner was pleased that the Liberal Republicans had adopted a platform calling for both equal rights and amnesty, for he hoped that the Democrats would accept both the Liberals' ticket and their principles. In that event, he predicted, the issue in the coming presidential contest "will be *personal* and not *political.* There will be no question between the Republican and Democratic parties, but between Greeley and Grant—between the two G's—the *GREAT* G and the little g." Surely most voters would choose the "kindly, true, and liberal" rather than the "personal and selfish" Grant. Yet, when asked how he himself was going to vote in the presidential contest, he promptly resumed his uncommitted stance and announced that he had "always been neutral." [2]

• 7 •

Behind Sumner's ambiguous response to the Liberal Republican nominations lay his continuing uncertainty whether the reformers, working in coalition with the Democrats, would live up to their promise to protect the rights of Negroes. Within a week of the Cincinnati convention he tested their platform pledge by

[9] Sumner's undated, three-point draft of a platform, ibid.; Bird to Sumner, April 29 and May 1, 1872, ibid.

[1] Bird to Sumner, May 7 [1872], ibid.; Bowles to Sumner, May 18, 1872, ibid.; Bird to Schurz, Aug. 7 [1872], Schurz MSS.; Charles Francis Adams: Diary, Mar. 12, 1874, Adams MSS.

[2] Sumner to Longfellow, May 16, 1872, Longfellow MSS.; Sumner to Pierce, May 12, 1872; Springfield *Republican,* May 18, 1872.

moving that the Senate substitute his civil rights bill for another amnesty proposal it was considering.

In the fierce three-day debate, which began on May 8, Sumner recapitulated all the arguments he had previously made for civil rights legislation. Again he insisted he was not opposed to amnesty for the ex-Confederates but that the removal of "the relics of generations of slavery" was more important than lifting "the disabilities of a few persons who drew their swords against their country." Pressing the need to integrate public schools, he called upon his fellow Senators "to decide whether you will give your sanction to a system of caste, which so long as it endures will render your school system a nursery of wrong and injustice." "How," he asked, "can you expect the colored child or the white child to grow up to those relations which they are to have together at the ballot-box if you begin by degrading the colored child at the school and by exalting the white child at the school?" To objections that the Constitution gave no power to Congress for such sweeping legislation, he replied: "I have . . . sworn to support the Constitution, and it binds me to vote for anything for human rights." [3]

Though Carpenter joined in criticizing Sumner's civil rights bill, the major opposition came from Liberal Republican Senators. Trumbull argued that there was no need for this legislation because under existing law the Negro had "the same right to travel, the same right to be entertained at a hotel, the same rights . . . exactly as a white person, and . . . the same remedies for their enforcement." The great difference, Orris S. Ferry of Connecticut added, was that a white man deprived of his rights would go into court while a Negro "rushes to a newspaper office and makes a statement of it for publication, and then sits down and writes a letter to the Senator from Massachusetts." The real trouble with Sumner's measure, Trumbull concluded, was that it was not really a civil rights but "a social equality bill." [4]

To Sumner both the debates and the frequent votes on his bill were ominous and revealing. For all the talk about a "New

[3] *Cong. Globe*, 42 Cong., 2 Sess., pp. 3264, 3259, 3263.
[4] Ibid., pp. 3264, 3257, 3254.

Departure," not one Senate Democrat supported the civil rights bill. On every significant roll call the prominent Liberal Republican Senators absented themselves or voted against the measure. As the New York *Times* remarked, the consistent opposition of Trumbull, Ferry, and Reuben Fenton, the New York Liberal Republican Senator, demonstrated that the "vote of the colored race is not desired or to be sought by the Greeley party." [5]

Though thirteen Senate Republicans, mostly from New England and the South, consistently supported the civil rights bill, Sumner learned that Grant's party was not a trustworthy friend of the Negro either. So long as there was a chance of driving a wedge between the Democrats, obdurately opposed to civil rights, and the Liberals, theoretically pledged to sustain them, or an opportunity to show up the contradiction between the Liberal Republicans' platform and their voting record on this issue, Grant's lieutenants let Sumner have his head. To Trumbull's fury, President pro tempore Anthony recognized Sumner's claim to the floor at every opportunity, and the President's friends talked encouragingly of reinstating Sumner in his old committee chairmanship. Once that game was played out, however, the New Radicals recognized that if no civil rights legislation was passed Sumner might use the issue to influence Negro voters, upon whom Grant's previous election had so largely depended. Determined to deprive Sumner of his position as the principal champion of the black man, Carpenter reintroduced his weakened version of the civil rights bill, which, among other things, failed to prevent racial discrimination in selecting juries, did not outlaw segregated schools, and left enforcement to the state courts. On May 21, when Sumner, still in poor health, left the Senate during a tedious all-night debate on the Ku Klux Klan, the Wisconsin Senator, in concert with other Grant supporters, pushed forward his toothless proposal and, despite some feeble protests that it was "unfair and unjust to take a vote upon this bill during the absence of the Senator from Massachusetts," pressed it to a successful vote.

Roused from his sleep at home, Sumner rushed to the Senate chamber but arrived just after Carpenter's bill passed.

[5] Selden Henry: "Radical Republican Policy toward the Negro," p. 337, note.

Bitterly he protested that "without any notice . . . from any quarter the Senate have adopted an emasculated civil rights bill," and he begged his colleagues to reconsider the vote. Eager to undercut Sumner's influence among black voters and impatient with this effort further to protract a sitting which had already extended for twenty-five hours, the Senators rejected Sumner's plea.[6]

"Sir, I sound the cry," Sumner warned as the long debate on civil rights closed. "The Rights of the colored race have been sacrificed in this Chamber where the Republican party has a large majority. . . . Let it go forth that the sacrifice has been perpetuated." Significantly he did not blame the Democrats or the Liberal Republicans for the death of his bill. It was the leadership of the Republican party which he found at fault. Though the time was short, since the Republican national convention was to meet in Philadelphia on June 5 and most of the delegates had long been selected, he planned one final attempt to persuade his party to reject that leadership.

On May 31, during a quiet discussion of the civil appropriation bill, which kept only a handful of Senators on the floor and bored the few sight-seers who yawned in the gallery, Sumner launched his thunderbolt. Introducing himself as "a member of the Republican Party, and one of the strictest of the sect," he began a four-hour oration, titled "Republicanism vs. Grantism," intended to read the President out of his party.[7] Grant, he charged, was guilty of nepotism. He was guilty of accepting presents while in the public service, to the extent that he was "now rich in houses, lands, and stock, above his salary, being probably the richest President since George Washington." He was guilty of an "ostentatious assumption of Infallibility," which caused him to ignore the advice of his party when selecting his cabinet, to surround himself with an illegal coterie of military aides in the White House, and to violate both international and constitu-

[6] *Cong. Globe*, 42 Cong., 2 Sess., pp. 3735–7, 3740–1. See also the account by John S. Mosby attached to a letter from Wade Hampton to Mosby, Dec. 11, 1876, John Warwick Daniels MSS. At the same time that the Senate passed the Carpenter version of the civil rights bill it adopted the General Amnesty Act of 1872, which had already been approved in the lower House. The civil rights bill failed to receive the approval of the House at this session.

[7] Sumner: *Works*, XV, 85–171.

tional law in trying to annex the Dominican Republic. He was "radically unfit for the Presidential office"; his whole presidency was "an enormous failure." The future historian would have to record that if Grant was first in war he was also "first in nepotism, first in gift-taking and repaying by official patronage, first in Presidential pretensions, and first in quarrel with his countrymen." He had completely fulfilled the prediction that Stanton confidentially made to Sumner in December 1869, shortly before his death: "I know General Grant better than any other person in the country can know him . . . now I tell you what I know: *he cannot govern this country.*"

When the news spread that Sumner was speaking, Senators quickly resumed their seats, the House of Representatives adjourned so that its members could listen, and the galleries were promptly filled. Aware that a number of delegates to the Philadelphia convention were among the auditors, administration Senators fidgeted and worried as Sumner spoke; as a newspaperman observed: "they pretended indifference, and took up newspapers and opened and answered letters; they sprung up suddenly and ran to conspire together." At one point their conversation at the rear of the chamber became so noisy that Sumner interrupted his oration to make the sarcastic request: "When that Conference Committee has ended, it will please make its report." Called to order, Conkling resumed his seat and spent the hours tearing the newspapers on his desk into bits; Carpenter sat stoically quiet, with an air of hopeless patience; Morton, crippled, listened in pale immobility; and only Chandler, who made frequent visits to his committee room for liquor, seemed cheerful. As soon as Sumner finished, Conkling and Morton rushed out to consult with Grant about the speech.[8]

Sumner had struck to kill, and after his speech he exultantly told Wilson that he had destroyed Grant's chance for reelection. "There will not be 3 states to vote for him," he predicted.[9] For a time it appeared that events might justify his hopes. He received hundreds of requests for copies of his speech,

[8] Washington correspondence of New York *Tribune,* June 6, 1872, in undated clipping, Sumner Scrapbooks; Chicago *Tribune,* June 1, 1872.

[9] Annie Fields: Diary, Thursday [June 1872], Fields MSS. Cf. *A Memorial of Charles Sumner* (Boston; 1872), pp. 241–2.

and his correspondents called it "the greatest oration . . . in our political history," "wonderfully able and statesmanlike," "so unambiguous, so cogent, so complete, . . . so true." Liberal Republican and Democratic newspaper editors, of course, joined in the chorus of praise. "Our greatest Senator," announced the ecstatic New York *Tribune,* had made "the greatest speech of his life."

Even before the plaudits died down, however, there were dissenting voices. As anticipated, the regular Republican papers denounced Sumner's speech. "The peerless one is peerless no more," jeered the Washington *Republican,* a Grant organ. "He crawls, bedaubed and bedraggled in the slime of our curbstone politics, retailing the curbstone slanders and scandals of the hour." More disturbing was the verdict of the New York *Evening Post,* which had favored the Cincinnati movement but could not endorse Greeley; its editors felt that Sumner had "consulted rather his resentments and prejudices than his judgment" in preparing the speech, that it did "not assail the administration in its most vulnerable places," and that it would in the long run "do the author . . . more harm than it will do the subject." Even the Liberal Springfield *Republican* feared that Sumner's portrait was "drawn in such colors that . . . the people will reject it as a truthful representation of General Grant's character," and concluded that Sumner's effort was "overdone, and hence a failure." [1]

Indeed, the speech was one of Sumner's poorest efforts, clearly reflecting the prolonged mental and emotional strain to which he had been subjected. Stylistically, it exaggerated all his characteristic faults. To condemn Grant's quarrelsomeness he adduced not one but two quotations from Shakespeare; to prove the President's arrogance, he recited two different translations of the same verses of Juvenal. He included a three-thousand-word digression on the origin and history of nepotism, especially among the Popes. His charges were sweeping, but his facts were thin. He confessed that he did not know how many relatives Grant had appointed to public office, and he made no effort to

[1] See summaries of press opinion in Providence *Patriot,* June 5, 1872, and Boston *Morning Journal,* June 3, 1872; also Springfield *Republican,* June 1–2, 1872.

prove that while in the White House he had accepted gifts. Finally, by insisting that Grant was the Great Quarreler in American history, Sumner roused some memories of his own far from pacific political life. "His career has been one long Philippic against everybody who did not agree with him, and he has cultivated invectives until he has become callous to the violence and offensiveness," observed his old enemy, Robert C. Winthrop. "He has a wonderful vein of vituperation, and really seems unconscious that he has described himself, when describing the Great Quarreler." [2]

Though Sumner's speech did nothing to influence the delegates to the Philadelphia convention, who had long ago been pledged to renominate Grant, it did have two practical effects. Hastily administration Senators abandoned their plan to adjourn the Senate and extended the session for another week so that they could reply to Sumner's charges. They claimed that Sumner made his oration because he was disappointed that he had not been named to Grant's cabinet and because he was disgruntled at having been removed from his committee chairmanship. He was, Cameron said, like an injured rattlesnake, which "in its frantic efforts to move out of the way bit itself and killed itself, destroyed . . . by its own poison." They challenged Sumner's account of Stanton's remarks, correctly noting that the former Secretary of War had enthusiastically campaigned for Grant's election in 1868.[3] But chiefly they waved the bloody shirt. Logan warned Sumner that he would "find an answer to that malignant speech of his in every crutch that helps and aids the wounded soldier to wend his way along in this land . . . in every wooden arm . . . in the bereaved heart of every widowed mother," since "the weeds of mourning . . . for the lost son and the lost brother will speak in . . . tones of thunder in defense of one of the most

[2] Winthrop to J. H. Clifford, June 7, 1872, Winthrop MSS. I have reversed the order of these two sentences.

[3] Providence *Patriot*, June 4, 1872. Sumner was in error in quoting Stanton as saying that during the 1868 campaign: ". . . I never introduced the name of General Grant. I spoke for the Republican party. . . ." Sumner: *Works*, XV, 100. There is, however, every reason to think that Stanton at the time of his interview with Sumner was disaffected toward Grant (Thomas and Hyman: *Stanton*, pp. 627–8, 634), and there is no question that he expressed a low opinion of the general's abilities. See Pierce, IV, 526, note.

gallant soldiers that ever led a gallant band for the preservation of a nation."[4]

The second result of Sumner's speech was the decision of the Republicans at Philadelphia, after renominating Grant by acclamation, to name the other Massachusetts Senator, Henry Wilson, as his running mate, in order "to *rebuke* Sumner for his speech against Grant" and to neutralize his influence in New England.[5]

• 8 •

At first incredulous that the Republican national convention, after his exposure of Grant's failures, should have renominated the general, Sumner was tempted to sit out the presidential contest in silence. Although he had made it publicly clear since March that he could not "on any account, support Gen. Grant for renomination or re-election,"[6] he still thought of himself as a Republican and of his party as the advocate of equal rights for the Negro. How wrong he was became apparent when on June 7, the day after Grant's renomination, he tried again to introduce his civil rights bill. Though unwell, he sat patiently through the all-night session, waiting for his chance, which did not come until 7:00 A.M., when he proposed his measure as an amendment to the pending appropriations bill. Abruptly Anthony—who earlier in the session had allowed Sumner to attach his rider to almost any bill—ruled the amendment out of order. Sadly taking up hat and cane, Sumner left the chamber and the Republican party.[7]

Even so, he hesitated to come out for Greeley. For a time he, along with Schurz and other Liberals, hoped that another candidate, more representative of reform ideas than the erratic New York editor, might be put in the field. After that scheme failed, Sumner still held off making any public announcement until after the Democrats, meeting at Baltimore on July 9, accepted

[4] *Cong. Globe*, 42 Cong., 2 Sess., pp. 4153, 4155, 4171, 4173.

[5] Ames (comp.): *Chronicles from the Nineteenth Century*, I, 361; N. P. Banks to his wife, June 7, 1872, Banks MSS.

[6] Boston *Morning Journal*, Mar. 19, 1872.

[7] *Cong. Globe*, 42 Cong., 2 Sess., p. 4393; Ames (comp.): *Chronicles from the Nineteenth Century*, I, 362.

Greeley as their candidate and also pledged to protect the equal rights of all citizens.

Not until July 29—at the last possible moment to influence the important elections in North Carolina [8]—did Sumner finally make his position public. In an open letter to Negro voters, he announced that it was his duty, and theirs, to support Greeley instead of Grant. "I have not taken this step without anxious reflection," he confided to Longfellow, "and I know the differences it will cause, but I cannot help it. I felt it my duty, which I could not avoid. . . ." With the eagerness of a new convert he argued that the 1872 election was going to be "the most remarkable in our political history," because "the Democrats have accepted a Republican Platform with a life-time Abolitionist as a candidate." Surely from this revolution would result "the final settlement of all the issues of the war." [9]

"You see that Sumner has spoken," Greeley wrote gleefully. " 'Was not that thunder?' I believe no utterance was ever more resonant and effective." [1] For Sumner the chief effect was to bring down upon him the anger of those with whom he had hitherto been associated in politics. During the months of his slow defection from the Republican party he had come increasingly in conflict with old political friends. He and Wilson were openly at odds, though both men tried to maintain their twenty-year friendship. With Boutwell he was able to maintain amicable relations only through a pact that neither would mention Grant's name. Most painful of all was the disagreement of former abolitionists, who had usually backed him in the past but who were convinced, as Wendell Phillips said, that Greeley was "wholly untrustworthy" and that he was "now surrounded by friends more objectionable than Grant's." Gerrit Smith published a broadside charging that Sumner's hostility toward Grant was that of a man "born in affluence and bred in elegance" to "a poor boy and a laboring man." Praising Grant's "patriotism, integrity, and general administration," Garrison sharply wrote that Sumner's "ill-judged, ill-timed, and . . . extravagant" attacks upon

[8] C. Delano to Zachariah Chandler, July 31, 1872, Chandler MSS.

[9] Sumner to Longfellow, July 13, 1872, Longfellow MSS.

[1] Greeley to M. H. Bovee, July 31, 1872, copy, Greeley MSS., Lib. of Cong.

the President made him the ally of those "who have heretofore been your deadliest enemies." [2]

In Boston every Republican newspaper was critical of Sumner's decision to endorse Greeley, including the long-faithful *Commonwealth,* whose editor grieved that Sumner, indulging in "his private and personal griefs," was joining in unholy union with the "vindictive, merciless, arrogant, rebellious" Democrats. In the South they were even "now violently opposing the constitutional amendments and civil and political rights of the blacks . . . carrying terror by night in reckless and secret bands." [3]

Elsewhere the Republican press embroidered the theme. With special vindictiveness Thomas Nast's caricatures in *Harper's Weekly* depicted Sumner as a modern Robinson Crusoe, about to desert his man Friday, the Negro people, as he went off to the Democratic rescue ship, or showed the Senator as an archer who, in trying to direct his arrow of hate and malice against Grant in the White House, stretched his bow until it broke. So scurrilous did Nast become that the editor, George William Curtis, who supported Grant himself and bitterly disagreed with Sumner over the election, insisted that he henceforth "not introduce Mr. Sumner in any way into any picture," since, with all his faults, the Senator was a "dear friend, a man whose services to the country and to civilization have been immense." [4]

Most painful of all to Sumner were the letters he received from blacks all over the country. "The alliance you have made, with the haters and persecutors of our race," wrote one New York Negro, "has struck the colored population of this city with astonishment. The democrats here hate us as bad as ever, and it is only through the Great Republican party that we are safe." [5]

[2] Phillips to Sumner, July 19, 1872, Sumner MSS.; *Speech of Gerrit Smith (To His Neighbors) in Peterboro, N.Y., June 22d, 1872,* broadside, Smith MSS.; Sumner to Smith, July 9, 1872, ibid.; Garrison to Sumner, June 1, 1872, Sumner MSS. Cf. John L. Thomas: *The Liberator: William Lloyd Garrison* (Boston: Little, Brown and Company; 1963), pp. 446–7.

[3] Aug. 3, 1872. Bird established in Boston a rival, pro-Greeley campaign sheet, *The Reformer,* which did not survive the election.

[4] Albert B. Paine: *Th. Nast: His Period and His Pictures* (New York: The Macmillan Company; 1904), pp. 236, 241; Curtis to Nast, Aug. 1, 1872, MS., New-York Hist. Soc. For Curtis's quarrel with Sumner, see Curtis to Charles E. Norton, June 30, 1872, Curtis MSS., Harvard Lib.

[5] J. G. Frisbie to Sumner, Aug. 3, 1872, Sumner MSS.

"The storm beats, but I could not have done otherwise," Sumner wrote Longfellow. "My present effort is the most important of my life. Besides bringing an original Abolitionist into the White House, I hope to obtain for the colored men then full recognition of their rights throughout the South." [6] During August he sought, simply by repetition, to convince himself of what was obviously untrue. Even the sympathetic E. R. Hoar judged him "manifestly insane" for believing Democratic promises to protect the Negro, and Longfellow lamented his alliance with "a Party that has always shown itself to be corrupt and dangerous." Astutely Lieber, who remained in the Grant camp, concluded that whoever won the election, Sumner would lose: The Republicans if successful would ostracize him, while the victorious Democrats would step on him like a beetle. "He stands on a bridge," Lieber wrote sadly, "and has set fire to both ends." [7]

Not until Sumner returned to Boston in late August did his friends become aware how desperate was his situation. They knew that he now had almost no following, except for the handful of politicians led by Bird, who seceded from the original Bird Club, and they knew that, just before his reappearance in Massachusetts, a Republican rally in Faneuil Hall had loudly hissed when his name was mentioned. But they were unprepared for the fact that Sumner was seriously ill. Still suffering from the effects of angina, debilitated by the long and strenuous Congressional session, he was so overwrought mentally and nervously that his physicians predicted that if he tried to campaign for Greeley he "might simply break down, bodily and mentally, and drag on years of maimed life."

Yielding to their persuasion, Sumner reluctantly gave up the idea of speaking out once more against Grant and agreed to go to Europe for his health. To avoid public notice, his friends booked his berth aboard the *Malta* in another name, and he did not come aboard at the Boston dock but was carried, with a small party of old friends, on a tug to join the steamer after it was at sea. Inevitably, however, the secret got out, and Grant soon

[6] Aug. 2, 1872, Longfellow MSS.

[7] Hoar to Garrison, Aug. 7, 1872, Garrison MSS.; Longfellow to William Greene, Aug. 1, 1872, copy, Longfellow MSS.; Lieber to Longfellow, Sept. 5, 1872, ibid.

heard the news. "Poor old Sumner is sick from neglect and the consciousness that he is not all of the republican party," the victor wrote. "I very much doubt whether he will ever get to Washington again. If he is not crazy his mind is at least so effected [*sic*] as to disqualify him for the proper discharge of his duties as Senator." [8]

[8] Grant to E. B. Washburne, Aug. 26, 1872, MS., Ill. State Hist. Lib.

CHAPTER XIV

So *White* a Soul

ON September 11, 1872, when Sumner arrived at Liverpool, he learned that during his voyage the Liberal Republicans and Democrats in Massachusetts had joined in nominating him for governor. The action was one which appalled most of his friends, for they saw that it would only result in his permanent estrangement from the Republican party and were painfully aware that the Senator's term had only two years to run. His enemies, on the other hand, were delighted. The nomination seemed to prove what they all along had been saying: that Sumner's attacks upon Grant were designed to promote his own political ambitions. At the same time, since Grant's reelection was now a certainty, they saw an opportunity to inflict upon Sumner a humiliating defeat. "For every other reason *than his own sake*," the abolitionist Samuel May wrote the embittered Garrison, "I wish he may accept it. It will teach him a lesson he sadly needs to learn—some self-distrust, and that the Massachusetts people are not *followers* . . . even of C. Sumner." [1]

The news of the nomination made Sumner indignant, almost frantic, and it cost him what progress he had made, despite seasickness, toward recovery while on shipboard. At once he cabled Bird, who had managed the nomination, that his name

[1] Pierce to Sumner, Sept. 13 [1872], Sumner MSS.; May to Garrison, Sept. 13, 1872, Garrison MSS.

must be withdrawn. "I could not and would not serve as Governor . . . ," he wrote. "Few things in my political life have troubled me more. Nothing has placed me in a position which . . . was so painful." When newspapers reported Sumner's declination with a hint that he might reconsider, he sent a second cablegram, peremptorily refusing to run. "I wish no letters on the subject," he told Bird. "It is too painful and disagreeable." When Bird, hoping that Sumner might have second thoughts, failed to act promptly, the Senator protested bitterly: "Why play with me—and do in my absence what would not be done if I were present. . . . Could I have anticipated any such thing I should have remained at home." [2] Only after Sumner's name was definitely dropped and that of Bird himself substituted as the Liberal Republican candidate did he begin to regain his health.

At the advice of his physicians, Sumner tried while abroad to remain wholly detached from the excitements of the presidential campaign, which had done so much to break down his health, but he was not altogether successful. Recognizing that Grant would be overwhelmingly reelected, he could not refrain from telling sharp stories about the President. Though he refused to read American newspapers, he could not erase the memories of the past few months, nor could he forget how many of his close associates had deserted him. Samuel Gridley Howe, the friend of his youth who had allowed himself to become Grant's ally in the Dominican annexation scheme, was a special object of his resentment. So was George William Curtis, who, despite the President's failure to support his work on the civil service commission, backed Grant's reelection. Angrily Sumner rejected Curtis's efforts in his influential *Harper's Weekly* to praise his character while differing from his political course. "I wish he would be silent about me, or stab me outright," he complained. "He kisses to betray. . . ." [3]

Saddened over "the heartlessness and falsehood of men," Sumner sought, with a sort of desperation, to busy himself while abroad. London he found as grand as ever, and he tried to visit

[2] Sumner to Bird, Sept. 15 and 18, and Oct. 4, 1872, Bird MSS.

[3] Sumner to Bird, Sept. 13, 1872, ibid.; Sumner to Pierce, Oct. 17, 1872, Sumner MSS.; Boston *Journal*, Mar. 11, 1876.

all the museums and palaces he had seen on his previous visits. He was, however, too feeble for such strenuous sight-seeing and soon contented himself with spending hours studying the paintings at the National Gallery.

This time Sumner encountered few of the notables whom he had met on his previous visits to Great Britain. Some of his former friends were embittered because of his "Alabama Claims" speech. Others, like John Bright and the Duke and Duchess of Argyll, were out of town for the season. Many more were no longer alive: the Duchess of Sutherland, Lord Brougham, Henry Hallam, George Grote, Lord Macaulay, Charles Dickens, Sydney Smith, William Makepeace Thackeray, and the rest. London was like a burial ground of his memories. "Constantly I think of the dead whom I have known and honored here," he wrote the Duchess of Argyll. Starved for recognition, he was extravagantly pleased when the landlord of the rooming house on Vigo Street where he had stayed in 1838 remembered him, and he derived great satisfaction from the fact that the attendants in the reading room of the British Museum recognized his name.[4]

He did see something of the Americans then in London, such as John Bigelow, former Secretary of the Treasury Hugh McCulloch, and Benjamin Moran, the veteran United States chargé d'affaires. All were struck by the fact that Sumner was a very sick man, with a thin, wrinkled face and watery eyes. Observing that he "spoke with a loudness of tone and vehemence of manner which [indicated] . . . that he had been drifting toward alienation of mind," Bigelow reported that he had "a certain difficulty in giving expression to his ideas, a want of fluency, in fact an absence of clear ideas which usually follow very great fatigue or an apoplectic attack." Acquaintances also commented upon his limited range of interests. Observing that Sumner in his conversation did not mention the name of a single commoner except that of Thomas Carlyle, Moran judged: "Lords

[4] Boston *Morning Journal*, Oct. 11, 1872; Bigelow: *Retrospections*, V, 81. The following year, declining to write letters of introduction for E. D. Morgan, who was going abroad, Sumner explained: ". . . in England I feel like one who has no longer available funds in [the] bank against which to draw . . . most with whom I was in intimate relations have passed away or are disabled by illness." Sumner to Morgan, May 5, 1873, Morgan MSS.

were uppermost in his mind." "He is more than ever the center of the system in which he lives," Bigelow concluded. "He did not ask a question that indicated the least interest in any mortal but himself." [5]

After a week in London, Sumner went with George W. Smalley, the foreign correspondent of the New York *Tribune,* for a brief vacation at Boulogne and then to Paris, where he settled for several weeks. Arriving unheralded, he received little attention at first in the French capital, but his vanity was somewhat assuaged by the fact that the French customs officials passed all his baggage without inspection because he was such a distinguished personage. As his health improved, he began ransacking the bookshops and art galleries of Paris with exhausting thoroughness. "I dare say," he remarked to Smalley, "you thought from my books at home that I cared nothing for books as books; or for bindings. But you will see." And he purchased set after set of books in fine bindings—which, as Smalley noted, "alas, were not so fine as they ought to have been." He spent too much money also on prints and bronzes of indifferent quality, for dealers in antiques found it easy to take him in. For all Sumner's genuine interest in art, William W. Story saw that he had "complete unsuccess" in appreciating it except on historical or literary grounds. "The world of art, as art, purely, was to him a locked world," Story wrote. "He longed to enter into it, and feel it as an artist does; but the keys were never given to him." [6]

Once Sumner's presence in Paris became known, he was deluged with invitations and attentions. De Corcelle, father-in-law of the Marquis de Chambrun, gave him a dinner, at which the French Minister of Foreign Affairs and the Minister of Finance were also guests, and Sumner's fluent command of the language made it possible freely to explore the problems facing the new republic. He met President Thiers at a reception and afterwards dined with him at the Champs d'Elysée palace. With Léon Gambetta he had a long discussion on the future of republi-

[5] Bigelow: *Retrospections,* V, 80–1; Moran: Diary, Sept. 21, 1872, MS., Lib. of Cong.

[6] Smalley: *Anglo-American Memories,* I, 112–13; C. H. Brainerd: "Reminiscences of Charles Sumner" [Dec. 1881], clipping in Pierce Scrapbooks; Pierce, IV, 541.

canism in France. "Ah, M. Sumner," exclaimed the Frenchman as he rose to leave, "il nous faut un Jefferson!"

"Trouvez un Washington, M. Gambetta," Sumner replied promptly, "et un Jefferson arrivera." [7]

To Sumner's surprise, the distances in Paris seemed greater than when he had raced about the city in his youth. "The garden of the Thuileries [*sic*] looked once very short compared with now," he reported in puzzlement to Longfellow. "But the garden has not changed." Sumner had. Though rest and the absence of public cares benefited his health, he continued to have fitful heart symptoms, and even short walks left him enfeebled.[8]

Still, he was able to visit Brussels, Antwerp, and The Hague, where he saw Motley, and by the end of October, when he returned to London, he seemed daily to grow in strength and vigor. The more completely he recovered, the more assiduously he set himself to buying books in leather bindings, autographs, bronzes, and wines to be shipped to his Washington cellar. He spent excessively, imprudently, almost desperately—as though he could not curb himself, as though he owed himself extravagant pampering, as though he had to create around him a world of belongings to comfort him in his loneliness. During his visit of a little more than two months abroad he expended more than six thousand dollars—a sum which he could ill afford at the best of times and which, he sadly learned just before leaving for home, he could spare even less just now, because the great Boston fire wiped out some of his capital.[9]

Unable to make the difficult trip to Inverary to visit the Argylls, Sumner did manage before leaving to see John Bright, his closest friend in Britain. Though the two men had recently differed over the Alabama Claims issue, they forgot all disagreements during Sumner's overnight stay at Rochdale and spent long hours comparing British and American society. Just as

[7] Boston *Morning Journal,* Oct. 22, 1872; Henry Cabot Lodge: *Early Memories* (New York: Charles Scribner's Sons; 1913), p. 281.

[8] Sumner to Longfellow, Sept. 27, 1872, Longfellow MSS.; Boston *Commonwealth,* Nov. 2, 1872.

[9] On these expenditures, see the detailed statement of Sumner's account submitted by Baring Brothers & Co., Nov. 19, 1873, and the numerous invoices and bills in the Sumner MSS. Sumner lost $3,500 through failure of the Fireman's Insurance Company. F. V. Balch to Sumner, Nov. 22, 1872, ibid.

Bright was warm in admiration of the United States, so Sumner was enthusiastic in praise of Great Britain. He could not help comparing the British government with his own and Prime Minister Gladstone with Grant, and he concluded: "a country was to be envied which could have in its highest positions men so eminent, of such great capacity, of such lofty purpose, and so conscientious." Overstimulated by the conversation, he had twinges of angina during the night, and he looked ill and depressed the next morning. Before he left, Bright's little dog tried to make friends with him, but Sumner did not know how to pet him for, he remarked, he "had never had time to play with dogs." [1]

The next day he was on the sea, bound for home. He knew that he would never again see England, and he felt that a longer stay might have produced a more thorough recovery. But to Story, who urged him to remain throughout the winter, he replied: "I must go. My duty requires it." [2]

• 2 •

Returning to New York on November 26, 1872, Sumner hurried to Washington, uncertain how he would fare in the session of Congress that was about to begin. There were some indications that partisan rancor against him had softened during his absence. Both the extent of Grant's victory in the election and Greeley's subsequent madness and death served to divert attention from Sumner's defection from the Republican party. With the exposure of the Credit Mobilier scandals—which were ultimately to implicate Vice President Colfax, Senator Patterson, and half a dozen Republican Congressmen, including Oakes Ames of Massachusetts, in frauds connected with the building of the Union Pacific Railroad—thinking members of the party recognized the need to bring back into its ranks men of unquestioned purity like Sumner. Wilson, now Vice President Elect, strongly urged reconciliation between Sumner and Grant, and

[1] Bright to Pierce, July 2, 1875, MS., Princeton Univ.; R. A. J. Walling (ed.): *The Diaries of John Bright* (New York: William Morrow & Company; 1931). p. 351.

[2] Pierce, IV, 542.

the stanchly Republican Boston *Journal* predicted that in the new session Sumner would prove himself "not only a Republican as ever, but one with the Republican party, in considerate and cordial support of the Republican Administration." When Sumner reached Washington, he reported as his initial impression that the "senators seem kindly." [3]

How mistaken he was quickly became apparent. The New Radicals had not forgotten that Sumner had deserted Grant and joined with the Democrats. Conkling, Morton, Carpenter, and Logan, the Grant spokesmen in the Senate, had no intention of accepting him back into the party. On the day after the session opened they made Sumner's position plain by sending him a printed announcement of the Republican senatorial caucus, to be attended only by those "who supported the platform and candidates agreed upon by the National Republican Convention held at Philadelphia."

With his own reelection coming up soon in an overwhelmingly Republican state, Sumner could not afford to be publicly read out of the party. Though he had always insisted that he was a genuine Republican—more so, indeed, than Grant's supporters—he ran a risk that the party caucus would humiliate him by denying him, as a renegade, any committee assignment, and he knew it would be political suicide to permit the Democrats to name him as one of their representatives on committees. Cleverly he escaped the trap by asking, before the Republican caucus reported, permission to follow the orders of his physician, who advised that he save his strength and serve on no committees.

Sumner's seeming withdrawal did not mean either that he intended to be a cipher in the Senate or that he was ready to accept the triumph of the Grant forces. Once again he was prepared to do everything he could to harass the administration. On the first day of the session he gave notice that he would again

[3] Boston *Morning Journal*, Nov. 28, 1872; Sumner to Cephas Brainerd, Dec. 2, 1872, Segal Coll. Some writers have alleged that Sumner by the time he returned from Europe had undergone a change of heart toward Grant and now longed for a reconciliation with the President. Dawes: *Sumner*, p. 316; Boutwell: *Reminiscences*, II, 217. Contemporary evidence does not sustain this view. Representative Henry L. Pierce, who saw much of Sumner during the winter of 1873–74, positively denied any change in Sumner's feelings toward Grant. H. L. Pierce to E. L. Pierce, Feb. 4, 1875, Pierce MSS.

bring up his civil rights bill, a measure which would not merely guarantee to the blacks desperately needed protection but would also prove to the Negroes how feeble was the President's interest in their welfare. Again he urged his bill for the speedy resumption of specie payments in order to end the present "derangement of trade, the lawlessness of speculation, the check to honest business, the high scale of prices, private losses, the bankruptcy of great houses, and general anxiety" over the monetary question. The bill would also, more than incidentally, drive a wedge between Grant, who advocated sound money, and Butler, who was an inflationist, and would show Massachusetts voters how conservative and businesslike Sumner's views were. He sought to embarrass the administration by protesting once more against the army of tax collectors who swarmed over the land and by complaining "that the taxes have been too numerous, too various in character, and assessed in different ways." [4]

For all these old and predictable maneuvers Grant's supporters in the Senate were prepared, but they were caught unawares by another proposal, relatively novel and seemingly innocuous, with which Sumner thought he might torpedo the administration. In order to promote "the national unity and good-will among fellow-citizens," he introduced on the opening day of the session a resolution ordering "that the names of battles with fellow-citizens shall not be continued in the Army Register, or placed on the regimental colors of the United States." At first sight nothing could seem more harmless. Back in 1862 Sumner had introduced an almost identical bill, which received the commendation of General Winfield Scott, and four years later he had, without incurring criticism, opposed commemorating Civil War battles in the paintings hung in the Capitol rotunda. He wanted his hearers to believe that his present resolution was nothing more than a continuation of his consistent efforts to bind up the nation's wounds.

Properly to be understood, however, Sumner's battle-flags resolution of December 1872 had to be interpreted in light of the farewell anti-Grant message he issued to his constituents before he sailed for Europe during the recent presidential canvass. "The

[4] *Cong. Globe*, 42 Cong., 3 Sess., pp. 142–3, 151.

time for the soldier has passed, especially when his renewed power would once more remind fellow-citizens of their defeat," he assured the Massachusetts voters. "Victory over fellow-citizens should be known only in the rights it assures; nor should it be flaunted in the face of the vanquished. It should not be inscribed on regimental colors, or portrayed in pictures at the National Capitol. But the present incumbent [i.e., Grant] is a regimental color with the forbidden inscription. . . . It is doubtful if such a presence can promote true reconciliation." [5] Incorporating precisely these partisan sentiments, Sumner's resolution was then, an anti-Grant bill, which during the months ahead he intended to use as an occasion for repeated denunciation of the Soldier-President.

Though clever, Sumner's tactic had a basic flaw. Having always had a low opinion of soldiers and feeling that the real victories of the recent war had been won in the Senate chamber, he failed to recognize the powerful bonds of loyalty which joined the hundreds of thousands of Union veterans in proud memory of their hard-fought battles. Thinking to attack the general, Sumner found he had engaged the whole army. Sensitive to the soldier vote now organized in the Grand Army of the Republic, Congressmen promptly damned Sumner's proposal, and the House whooped through a countermeasure forbidding the removal of the names of Civil War battles from the regimental colors on the ground that "the national unity cannot fail to be strengthened by the remembrance of the services of those who fought the battles of the Union in the late war of the rebellion."

In Massachusetts the reaction to Sumner's battle-flags resolution was equally prompt and more damaging. Mindful of Sumner's campaign manifesto which implied that Grant's name, like that of Civil War battles, ought to be expunged from the record,

[5] Sumner: *Works,* XV, 254. Of course Sumner never admitted a political purpose in introducing his battle-flags resolution. Indeed, once it became a matter of controversy, he let it out that its presentation to the Senate at this time was almost accidental. The newspaperman, Ben: Perley Poore, was looking through the pile of papers accumulated on his Senate desk. Coming upon the battle-flags resolution of 1862, he suggested that Sumner ought to reintroduce it then and there, and he did. Dawes: *Sumner,* p. 318; W. P. Phillips to Sumner, Dec. 27, 1872, Sumner MSS. Sumner would never have allowed a journalist to dictate his course on so important a matter, and his resolution was in fact part of his general campaign to harass the Grant administration.

administration partisans seized this opportunity to rebuke the Senator who had bolted. One of Butler's supporters, Hoyt, a member of the Massachusetts House of Representatives from Athol, introduced a motion strongly condemning Sumner's resolution, and, after an incredibly confused parliamentary tangle, the legislature voted that Sumner's proposal was "an insult to the loyal soldiery of the nation," that it met "the unqualified condemnation of the people of this Commonwealth," and that copies of this resolution of censure upon Sumner should be sent to the members of the Massachusetts delegation in Congress.[6]

Overreacting to a measure that passed the legislature at the dinner hour, when many members were absent and others were tired or unaware of what they were voting on, Sumner's friends leaped to the conclusion that Butler was behind the censure resolution. The most feared man in Massachusetts, the general seemed to respectable businessmen and lawyers a flaming radical, not, like Sumner, just on equal rights for Negroes in the faraway South but on the currency and the rights of labor, and he was thought to be so dangerous and so vindictive that even in private correspondence men tried not to use his name but referred instead to "the *able,* but corrupt and *audacious* General, whose *habits,* past, present and future, you so well know."[7] They assumed that Butler had a disciplined army of political supporters and were certain that he must have prompted Hoyt. In fact, the general's influence in the legislature at this time was by no means great, and one of his principal spokesmen, Dr. George B. Loring, was sure Hoyt's motion would backfire. "The ____ fools!" he exclaimed of those who rushed through the censure resolution; "if they don't look out, they will have Sumner re-elected when his term expires." Butler himself had no direct hand in the whole episode, though he was, of course, happy to make what political capital he could from it and issued a public statement: "I believe the exploits of our soldiers will tell in history whether Mr. Sumner's resolution to obliterate

[6] *House Report* No. 36, Massachusetts General Court, 1872, Extra Session. For a detailed history of the Hoyt resolution and how it was adopted, see three long articles by E. L. Pierce in the Boston *Commonwealth,* July 25, Aug. 1 and 8, 1874.

[7] John N. Barbour to Sumner, Dec. 20, 1872, Sumner MSS.

them from the army register is passed by the Senate of the United States or condemned by the Legislature of Massachusetts." [8]

If Butler's influence did not determine the action of the Massachusetts legislature, Republican resentment over Sumner's defection in the 1872 campaign did. During that canvass Massachusetts Republicans had been advised not to attack Sumner directly; he had too many friends, and an assault made during his illness might arouse widespread sympathy for him.[9] With Grant's reelection the gloves came off, and Republicans were ready to seize any pretext for an attack upon him. With memories of the war still fresh, many legislators were genuinely outraged over Sumner's battle-flags resolution, which demanded that the North "give up all of our glorious memories of battles fought for freedom." Others correctly connected Sumner's proposal with his hostility toward Grant. One legislator reminded his colleagues "that Mr. Sumner had previously announced . . . that no man who had become celebrated by faithful and successful service for the country in the army, during the war of the rebellion, should be nominated for any civil office because it would be flaunting a hostile regimental in the faces of fellow-citizens who were formerly rebels." [1] If Sumner could play politics with this issue, so could the legislature.

Understandable as was the action of the legislature, Sumner was deeply hurt, the more so because he was in feeble health. Though he had gained strength during his trip abroad, he still suffered from spasms of the bladder, probably caused by prostatitis, which obliged him to get out of bed twenty or thirty times each night to urinate, and he continued to have attacks of angina pectoris, which came upon him unexpectedly. Only a few days after the opening of Congress and the introduction of his

[8] Springfield *Republican*, Feb. 3 and Mar. 14, 1873; Boston *Commonwealth*, Dec. 28, 1872.

[9] Winthrop was amazed that Grant's backers handled Sumner with such care, making "special allowance for his 'honesty and integrity,' at a moment when he is maligning and misrepresenting all who differ from him." Winthrop to J. H. Clifford, Aug. 16, 1872, copy, Winthrop MSS.

[1] Boston *Commonwealth*, Dec. 28, 1872, and April 12, 1873; Vincent Y. Bowditch: *Life and Correspondence of Henry Ingersoll Bowditch* (Boston: Houghton, Mifflin and Company; 1902), II, 55.

battle-flags resolutions, he went out at night to hear a lecture by the British scientist, John Tyndall, and afterward, walking two blocks to catch the streetcar, had a violent seizure. Though looking quite feeble, he forced himself to go to the Senate the next day and continued to attend until December 19, when the attacks recurred so frequently and the pain became so great that he was obliged to absent himself for the remainder of the session.

His suffering was often intense. Usually an attack of angina was preceded by slight murmuring, or shooting pains, about the heart. Then came a paroxysm of pain, which, Sumner said, "seemed much like the sudden grasp of a cold hand, which gradually tightened, until it felt like a clasp of steel crushing his heart to atoms." [2] During the seizures the ulnar side of his left hand was almost paralyzed, and sometimes the numbness remained for hours afterwards. Almost as distressing as the pain was the uncertainty when the attacks would occur. Sometimes he could make a speech in the Senate, using his customary forcible gestures, with no ill effects, but at other times by suddenly turning in his chair, when he was quietly reading at night, he would bring on tearing agony. Since his bladder trouble prevented sleep, his suffering was all the more debilitating.

Dr. Brown-Séquard, who had presided over Sumner's recovery after the Brooks assault, was in general charge of his case and sent directives and prescriptions from New York, where he was now practicing, but for daily care Sumner relied upon a young Washington physician, Dr. Joseph Tabor Johnson. After auscultation, the two doctors made the erroneous diagnosis that Sumner's heart was perfectly sound. Autopsy was subsequently to prove that his left coronary artery, supplying blood to the muscles of the heart itself, was so badly ossified as to be reduced

[2] On Sumner's medical condition see Dr. Joseph T. Johnson: *Angina Pectoris, Illustrated by the Case of Charles Sumner* (Boston, 1874); Brown-Séquard in *Boston Medical and Surgical Journal,* May 21, 1874, pp. 510–12; report of autopsy upon Sumner, signed by J. B. S. Jackson and two other physicians and witnessed by six other physicians, including both Brown-Séquard and Johnson, dated Mar. 16, 1874, unidentified clipping, Pierce Scrapbooks; *Boston Medical and Surgical Journal,* Mar. 26, 1874, p. 318; A. B. Johnson to Pierce, Mar. 20, 1874, Pierce MSS.; and Brown-Séquard to Sumner, Dec. 2, 1872, (enclosing prescriptions), Sumner MSS. I am deeply indebted to Dr. E. Hunter Wilson, of Baltimore, for assistance in interpreting the medical evidence.

to only half its normal caliber and that his angina was, therefore, the result of a coronary insufficiency. But if medically unsound, the verdict of Drs. Brown-Séquard and Johnson was psychologically rewarding to Sumner, for they assured him that both his angina and his bladder trouble were consequences of the injuries Preston Brooks had inflicted upon him in 1856. So long as Sumner could believe that his suffering was part of his martyrdom for the cause of liberty, he could better endure the pain.

The treatment prescribed by Sumner's physicians was intelligent and in accord with the best practice of the day. Concentrating upon Sumner's bladder condition first, so that he could get some rest, Brown-Séquard first tried the bromides unsuccessfully and later prescribed atropine and then hyoscyamine. He predicted that through rest, relaxation, and returning general health Sumner would receive relief from the angina, but to alleviate the excruciating pain during the attacks he ordered hypodermic injections of morphine, to which a solution of salts of atropine and strychnine were added.

"I take medicines enough to cure a family," Sumner reported to Mrs. Lodge; "poison by phial, poison by pill, poison by powder and poison by injection." Confined to his house for several weeks after December 19, he was visited twice a day by Dr. Johnson, who at 10:30 P.M. each evening gave him an injection of morphine so that he could rest. "But this is not the sleep of which poets write," Sumner found sadly. "The next day I naturally suffer in strength." [3]

It was during this period of almost total prostration that Sumner learned the Massachusetts legislature had censured him. Though influential newspapers like the Boston *Advertiser* and the Springfield *Republican* promptly condemned Hoyt's resolution and lifelong associates like Wendell Phillips wrote to assure him that his "*real* old friends [never] waver a hair in their love and trust," Sumner felt rejected by his own state, and he was bitterly unhappy. "How a cultivated Heathen would differ from me I do not understand," he wrote angrily to James Freeman Clarke, the Boston Unitarian minister who denounced the legislature's action from his pulpit. "Where is Massachusetts

[3] Sumner to Mrs. John E. Lodge, Jan. 11, 1873, Lodge MSS.

civilization? Thus far our Commonwealth has led in the great battle for Liberty and Equality. By the blessing of God she shall lead again in smoothing the front of war." "Never did I deserve better of Massachusetts than now," he complained to another friend, "for never did I represent so completely that high civilization which is the pride of our beloved Commonwealth." [4]

Aware of the extent of Sumner's unhappiness, his supporters, organized by John Greenleaf Whittier,[5] began a campaign to have the resolutions rescinded. To the cause rallied with impressive solidarity all segments of the Massachusetts elite: businessmen like Amos A. Lawrence; educators like President Charles W. Eliot of Harvard College; authors like Longfellow and Oliver Wendell Holmes; lawyers like Sumner's former friend, long estranged by political differences, George S. Hillard. With Butler threatening in the wings, the Brahmins recognized Sumner, who had once been a social outcast, as one of their own. Expressing "a proud and grateful appreciation of the character and public services" of the Senator, the petitions called upon the new legislature, which assembled in January 1873, to repudiate the action of its predecessor. Governor William B. Washburn told the legislators that it had been dishonorable to condemn Sumner for standing by his principles and added pointedly: "No severer punishment could be offered to Mr. Sumner if his hands had been stained with the bribes that have been so freely offered in Washington, but which he has always spurned." Before the legislative committee James Freeman Clarke raised the same issue: "Shall Massachusetts, with members in Congress up to their ears in the Credit Mobilier, . . . select Charles Sumner, whom no one had ever dared to approach with a bribe, as the one on whom its censure should fall?"

Sumner's defenders overargued their case and made unnecessary enemies. Their praise of his services in the struggle against slavery aroused William Lloyd Garrison, who was sensi-

[4] Phillips to Sumner, Dec. 20, 1872, Sumner MSS.; Sumner to Clarke, Christmas Day [1872], Clarke MSS.; Elias Nason: *The Life and Times of Charles Sumner* (Boston: B. B. Russell; 1872), p. 328.

[5] On Whittier's role in organizing the campaign, see Whittier to William Claflin, Dec. 21, 1872, Claflin MSS., and Whittier to unidentified correspondent, Feb. 26, 1873, Whittier Collection, Haverhill Pub. Lib.

tive to any infringement upon his own claim to be the father of the abolitionist movement, and he insisted upon testifying before the legislative committee named to consider rescinding the resolutions of censure. Asking whether Sumner was really a reformer and whether during his whole public career he had ever exhibited any special courage, Garrison went on to inquire why if the Senator advocated unpopular notions he "should not be censured like the rest of us." To everyone's surprise, Julia Ward Howe, hurt by Sumner's failure to pay her attentions while she was in Washington, also testified against rescinding, not so much because she disagreed with his battle-flags resolution as because she deplored the "high handed and overbearing . . . man-worship" exhibited in the petitions defending his course.[6]

Inevitably the question got tangled in politics. After hearing all the influential and eloquent testimony in favor of expunging the censure, the legislative committee voted to take no action; the members explained privately that they were not so much condemning Sumner's battle-flags proposal as his anti-Grant speeches. On the floor of the legislature the committee's report became involved in the bitter contest to elect a Senator to succeed Wilson, who had become Vice President. Between the two almost evenly matched candidates, Representative Dawes from western Massachusetts, and Boutwell, who was still in Grant's cabinet, Butler's men in the legislature, though not numerous, held the balance, and they resolved to use their power so as to humiliate Sumner. When Dawes, despite warnings that his action would cost him badly needed votes, came out in favor of expunging the censure of Sumner, Butler made a tacit deal with Boutwell. The general's men in the legislature helped elect the Secretary of the Treasury to the Senate; promptly on March 19, 1873, Boutwell's supporters joined Butler's friends in defeating the bill to rescind the censure of Sumner.[7]

"No harm has come to our senior senator," the Springfield *Republican* whistled in the dark; "he is Charles Sumner to-day as he was yesterday, and as he will be to-morrow." Pierce and other

[6] Springfield *Republican*, Mar. 6–7, 1873; Julia Ward Howe: Diary, Mar. 5–6, 1873, Julia Ward Howe MSS. For Garrison's letter attempting to explain his position, see Boston *Morning Journal*, Mar. 8, 1873.

[7] Springfield *Republican*, Mar. 10 and 14, 1873.

advisers assured him that the vote of the legislature did not reflect the real sentiments of the people of Massachusetts and vowed to continue the fight. "We have met with a temporary defeat," J. B. Smith reported, but "our small army is in good spirits, and will carry it [the battle to rescind] into the field next Fall." [8]

• 3 •

Though greatly depressed when the legislature failed to retract its censure, Sumner, with rest and good medical care, began slowly to improve in health. By the end of February he was able to go for a carriage ride every day, and sometimes he took short walks in Lafayette Square. He made a point of being in his seat on March 4, when a special session of the Senate opened, and two weeks later, though he could not walk without heavily leaning upon his cane, he insisted upon presenting the credentials of his new colleague, Boutwell. As he rose to do so, Butler rather theatrically made his appearance on the Senate floor, as if to present a tableau of the past and the future of Massachusetts politics.[9]

Still very feeble, Sumner was further depressed during these months of his severe illness by having to think once more of his miserable marriage. He quietly began suit to divorce Alice on the grounds of desertion. The separation was something earnestly desired by both parties, and they were so eager to cooperate that their lawyers had to warn against the appearance of collusion. Finally, on May 10, after only a fifteen-minute hearing, the divorce was granted. "I rejoice that you are *free* at last," Pierce wrote him, and Sumner on the day he received the news reported "a certain sense of returning health." [1]

As he grew stronger, his friends rallied to keep him busy and entertained. Hooper, who lived next door, inquired daily

[8] Ibid., Mar. 20, 1873; Smith to Sumner, Mar. 20, 1873, Sumner MSS.

[9] New York *Times*, Mar. 18, 1873.

[1] Docket No. 1076, April 1873 Term, Supreme Judicial Court of Suffolk County, Boston; Sumner's "Memorandum of Law on Separation and Divorce," G. B. Pierce MSS.; F. V. Balch to Sumner, May 10, 1873, Sumner MSS.; Pierce to Sumner, May 10, 1873, ibid.; Sumner to Mrs. John E. Lodge, May 10, 1873, Lodge MSS.

about his health and made his horses and carriage available every afternoon. Representative Garfield, who shared Sumner's love for the classics, was equally attentive, and he listened patiently as the shattered Senator related the details of his travels in Europe. Lonely in his handsome house, Sumner begged friends to visit him, and, though he was sometimes obliged to receive them in his dressing gown, he felt buoyed by their affection. "Do not leave me yet," he would press his guests; "do stay a while longer, I want so much to speak with you!" [2]

Even when most seriously ill Sumner derived a grim satisfaction from watching the second Grant administration fulfill his prophecies. The Credit Mobilier affair was only the most notorious scandal that tarred the Republicans. There was corruption in the War Department, corruption in the Navy Department, corruption in the Indian Bureau. To all evidence of malfeasance Grant showed himself callously indifferent. "I have never known any person in public office whose sense of justice was so slight as Grant's . . . ," Sumner wrote Mrs. Child. "Such a President . . . is a trial to all who love their country and wish the establishment of Republican institutions." [3]

Only one of the scandals of the Grant era directly affected Sumner himself. The so-called "Salary Grab" Act, assiduously promoted by Butler, not merely increased the stipends of Congressmen and doubled the President's pay but gave each member of the expiring Forty-Second Congress a bonus of five thousand dollars. Sumner certainly could have used the money, which would almost have wiped out the debts incurred during his trip to Europe, but he quickly recognized that he must not accept it. At first he thought of donating the money to wounded soldiers, in a gesture that would counteract the ill will created among veterans by his battle-flags resolution, and then he thought of giving it to members of Negro regiments. At the advice of his friends in Massachusetts, however, he decided to return the money to the Treasury. His action, observed the Springfield *Republican*, "was no more than Massachusetts expected, and

[2] *Boston Memorial*, p. 160.

[3] Sumner's letter is quoted in Lydia M. Child to an unidentified correspondent, April 13, 1873, Shaw Family Papers.

had the right to expect, of her senior senator, whom she honors, to-day, in her heart of hearts more than ever before."[4]

That note of approbation suggested the reception Sumner was to receive when his health improved sufficiently for him to return to Massachusetts in August. He was greeted more warmly, and by a wider circle of admirers, than had welcomed him since the end of the Civil War. Sympathy for his protracted illness, disgust with the Grant administration, and, especially, fear of Butler's growing power buried old animosities and revived ancient friendships. As though to symbolize Sumner's return to the inner Brahmin circle, he was on September 10 elected to membership in the Massachusetts Historical Society, where his nomination had been repeatedly blackballed in years past, and on the same day Winthrop, the president of the Society, invited him to dinner, for the first time in nearly thirty years.[5]

At the same time Sumner renewed his ties with the aging Transcendentalists of Concord, as if to reaffirm the connection between their philosophical and his political idealism. There were curious parallels between his career and that of Ralph Waldo Emerson, for both had once been read out of Boston society as heretics and both were now, in their twilight years, recognized as New England's representative men. Sumner's friendship for Emerson was of long standing, and it was based upon mutual admiration and respect. Just as Sumner placed Emerson's name at the head of the list of charter members of his proposed American Academy of Arts and Sciences, so Emerson sponsored Sumner's election to the Saturday Club, the exclusive Boston group devoted to the discussion of ideas and letters. When Sumner returned to Massachusetts in the summers, he always tried to find time for a visit to Concord, and when Emerson came to Washington he was Sumner's guest. It was Sumner who had presented the sage of Concord to Abraham Lincoln in January 1862, and, exactly ten years later, Sumner took pleasure in entertaining Emerson in his own house on Lafayette Square,

[4] Springfield *Republican,* May 5, 1875. The amount Sumner received was $4,445.60. Receipt dated May 5, 1873, Sumner MSS.

[5] *Mass. Hist. Soc. Proceedings,* 1873–75, p. 104; Winthrop to Sumner, Sept. 10, 1873, Sumner MSS.

which the philosopher called "a library and a picture-gallery." Aware that Sumner was vain and sometimes pedantic, Emerson also recognized that he was a "clean, self-poised, great-hearted man, noble in person, incorruptible in life, the friend of the poor, the champion of the oppressed." "It characterizes a man for me that he hates Charles Sumner," he wrote; "for it shows that he cannot discriminate between a foible and a vice." [6]

Despite social attentions, Sumner during the summer of 1873 was more than ever preoccupied with his "book," as he insisted upon calling the volumes of his collected *Works*, which were slowly being published. Even when visiting Longfellow at the seashore, he would set up a table in a corner of a room and busy himself all day with preparing copy for the printer and reading proofs unless the poet was able to distract him with a short walk along the beach. During his illness the need for completing his task had come to have almost obsessive importance. "Life is very weary," he wrote to Mrs. Lodge at one low point. "But I do wish to finish that edition of my works. When that is done I shall ask to go beyond the reach of injustice and ingratitude."

The work, however, progressed at a turtle-like pace. Both John Owen, who helped Sumner make literary revisions and prepare annotations for his speeches, and George Nichols, that admirable but meticulous proofreader, took an exasperating amount of time for their labors. Sumner thought that Nichols, in particular, was doing unnecessary work in checking and rechecking his every word. "It was often," he complained to Longfellow, "as if a mason had taken up all the stones of your cellar, and, then finding them sound and verifying the quarries from which they came, replaced them." [7]

Editing and publishing the *Works* was also expensive, for Sumner had to pay Nichols alone $1,500 a year, and Owen also received a retainer. Already drained by heavy medical expenses,

[6] Ralph L. Rusk: *The Life of Ralph Waldo Emerson* (New York: Charles Scribner's Sons; 1949), pp. 414, 423, 450; Ralph L. Rusk (ed.): *The Letters of Ralph Waldo Emerson* (New York: Columbia University Press; 1939), VI, 197; Emerson: *Journals*, X, 291–5.

[7] Sumner to Mrs. John E. Lodge, Jan. 11, 1873, Lodge MSS.; Longfellow to G. W. Greene, Aug. 29, 1873, Longfellow MSS.; Sumner to Longfellow, Mar. 18, 1870, ibid.

Sumner could ill afford the costs, especially after depression struck the United States in late 1873, just when his note to cover the expenses of his European trip was about to fall due at the bank. Resolutely he decided to undertake another lecture tour in order to earn money. For many months he had been thinking of a speech defending his battle-flags resolution, and James Redpath, the best lecture agent in the country, promised that he would have crowded houses. "Only in the lecture field can I make anything," Sumner explained to his friends. "I know no senatorial way. This is my excuse." [8]

"What folly!" exclaimed Longfellow when he heard of Sumner's lecture tour. Though Dr. Brown-Séquard approved the plan, most of Sumner's closest friends saw that he was far too feeble for so strenuous an undertaking, and they begged him to reconsider. He was able to do so when Representative Henry L. Pierce, the brother of his trusted Massachusetts political lieutenant, E. L. Pierce, offered to meet his obligation to the bank, accepting a promissory note to be repaid whenever the Senator could afford to do so. Knowing that the lecture tour was beyond his strength, Sumner in one sense felt relief; but he was also sad, for he had to recognize that he was never again going to be fully restored in health. Picking up his pen to write a public letter explaining why he was canceling the tour, he sighed to the agent: "Mr. Redpath, this is the saddest act of my life." [9]

Both Sumner and his friends recognized that he must husband his small reserves of strength for the dangerous political contests that lay ahead. Butler was more of a menace than ever, for Grant was his ally, the Secretary of the Treasury, William A. Richardson, was his former aide, and the junior Senator from Massachusetts, Boutwell, owed his election to the general. Everybody considered Butler's candidacy for the governorship in 1873 as a steppingstone to Sumner's seat in the Senate. The general was now so powerful that Sumner did not dare come out in open opposition to him, as he and Wilson had done in 1871. Instead, while his aides worked assiduously, and successfully, to defeat

[8] Sumner to Howe, Sept. 18, 1873, Howe MSS.

[9] Nason: *Sumner*, p. 331; James Redpath to Elias Nason, April 10, 1874, MS. owned by Mr. Boyd C. Stutler.

Butler's nomination, he assumed an air of neutrality so convincing as to persuade even the general's daughter. When troubled Republicans asked the Senator's views on the several candidates for governor, he replied with comfortable vagueness: "I do not comprehend the political maze, and am happy to be out of it." [1]

In fact, of course, Sumner was never out of politics, but the race uppermost in his mind was not that for the governorship. It was imperative that he do nothing to offend the Republican members of the legislature, who would choose his successor in January 1875. At the same time it was urgently necessary for him to make frequent public appearances in order to give the lie to rumors that he was incapacitated or dying. During the fall of 1873, driving himself to the point of exhaustion, Sumner put on a magnificent demonstration of vitality. He seemed omnipresent as he turned up for the monthly dinners of the Saturday Club, attended the meetings of the Radical Club, where Boston intellectuals discussed such topics as the character of Portia in "Merchant of Venice," or introduced an abscure English writer, Edward Jenkins, to the Boston Lyceum.

He listened carefully to the advice of his political friends, who warned that Massachusetts voters were no longer concerned with reconstruction issues and cared nothing for his quarrels with Grant and Fish; they wanted their Senator to be concerned with everyday problems. Accordingly he spoke before a farmer's club, which met at former Governor Claflin's estate, and, though he had never owned more land than his city lot and could hardly distinguish between ox and horse, held forth for an hour on the glories of the agricultural life and the beauties of the various breeds of cattle. At the advice of former Representative Alexander H. Rice of Boston, he also made frequent demonstrations of his newly found solidarity with the business community. At the Commercial Club in Boston, for instance, his emphasis on the need for sound currency charmed bankers and merchants who had hitherto thought him exclusively concerned for the rights of the Negro.

Less overtly Sumner also cultivated other segments of the

[1] Ames (comp.): *Chronicles from the Nineteenth Century,* I, 529; Pierce, IV, 565.

populace that were beginning to exert political influence. Recognizing that he could not win the prohibitionist vote, which was loyal to Butler, he engaged in a cautious flirtation with Massachusetts labor, which had hitherto consistently supported the general. He had for some time corresponded with the most influential Massachusetts labor spokesman, Ira Steward, who persuaded him to end his opposition to the Eight-Hour Day movement and even to make a financial contribution to that cause. Sumner's supporters made sure that he also met some of the lesser labor leaders, so that they could gain from him "inspiration . . . as to the real motive [,] purpose and true philosophy of their social mission, and not be wholly absorbed by or confined to the organizations of . . . 'laboring men' as such, interesting as they are." Left unsaid was the assumption that he would gain from them something equally important if less inspiring—votes. At least in part the plan worked. When one group of labor spokesmen visited Sumner, their leader, Joseph Arch, began describing the evils from which the British workingmen suffered because of the crown and the hereditary nobility. When Arch paused for breath, one of his associates broke in: "Yes, Mr. Arch, we only elect *one Senator for life*," and the group broke into applause, which Sumner gracefully acknowledged.[2]

At the same time Sumner began to pay more attention to the advocates of woman suffrage. In an abstract way he had long believed that women ought to have the vote. When the major reconstruction legislation was under consideration, he later told Mrs. Elizabeth Cady Stanton, he had written "over nineteen pages of foolscap to get rid of the word 'male' and yet keep 'negro suffrage' as a party measure; but it could not be done." He had, therefore, for years deplored as "most inopportune" any agitation of this issue until Negro rights were secured. Now, however, that the Constitution guaranteed Negro suffrage he could afford to be more sympathetic to the women's rights movement, especially since both the independent Labor Reform party and a sizable

[2] John T. Sargent to Sumner, Nov. 4, 1873, Sumner MSS.; Lodge: *Early Memories*, pp. 284–5. According to Cesare Orsini, Sumner, along with Wendell Phillips and Horace Greeley, had joined the First International Workingmen's Association back in 1866. Minute Book of the First International Workingmen's Association, 1866–9, MS., Bishopsgate Institute, London.

minority in the Republican state convention favored giving women the vote. Urged by Susan B. Anthony to speak out "as grandly for *EQUAL RIGHTS TO ALL WOMEN* as to *all men,*" he permitted her to publish an account of an interview during which he expressed himself in favor of her cause. "Miss Anthony," he told her, handing her copies of his speeches on reconstruction, "put 'sex' where I have 'race' or 'color,' and you have the best and strongest arguments I can make for woman. There is not a doubt but women have the constitutional right to vote. . . . Sex cannot be a qualification [for suffrage] any more than size, race, color, or previous condition of servitude." [3]

But most of all, as the Senate election approached, Sumner tried to revive the loyalties of his long-term political allies. At the Banks Club—which included members from all parties and was appropriately named after Representative Banks, who had belonged to them all—he was non-controversial but made his point in reminiscing about the great statesmen Massachusetts had produced and about the loyalty she had always given them. Before the Massachusetts Club, composed of Republicans who had backed Grant's reelection, he was more overt, as he recalled his long services to the party and pointed toward the need for further civil rights legislation. "It may seem to you that I am speaking of things which I have often spoken of before," he conceded. "Perhaps, however, you have read of the bugle of Munchausen, in which the tunes were all frozen up, but when the warmth had thawed it the old tunes which once it had been accustomed to play rang out from it again. So, my friends, it is with me now. Warmed by your presence, the presence of my old friends and associates, the old bugle of my lifelong principles commences to play once more." [4]

[3] Elizabeth Cady Stanton, *et al.*: *History of Woman Suffrage* (Rochester, N.Y.: Charles Mann; 1887), II, 91, 96–7; Miss Anthony to Sumner, Dec. 9, 1872, and April 27, 1873, Sumner MSS.; Boston *Morning Journal,* April 9, 1873. See also Miss Anthony's endorsement, dated Feb. 15, 1903, on her pamphlet copy of Sumner's *Powers of Congress to Prohibit Inequality, Caste, and Oligarchy of the Skin . . . February* 5, 1869 (Washington: F. & J. Rives & Geo. A. Bailey; 1869), in the Library of Congress.

[4] Boston *Commonwealth,* Nov. 29, 1873; Boston *Morning Journal,* Nov. 3, 1873.

• 4 •

The tune Sumner wanted his bugle to play was taps for Ulysses S. Grant. His animosity toward the general in the White House was as fierce and unabating as ever. Though friends warned that further attacks upon the President might endanger his reelection to the Senate, he continued to look for opportunities to expose the weakness and the corruption of the administration. By the fall of 1873, after the onset of the depression and the revelation of the most notorious scandals, he believed the people were turning from Grant. "Is not the Administration very feeble?" he asked Schurz. "What can we do?" Unhesitatingly Schurz replied: "The hand of the Lord is upon the unrighteous. I think we shall be able to render the country some service this winter." [5]

The nature of that service became clear when Sumner on December 1, the opening day of the Congressional session, introduced, as he had so often done in previous years, a series of bills and resolutions designed to raise the major issues confronting the legislature, and to raise them in a manner calculated to embarrass the executive. Again he called for a single six-year term of office for the President, for the prompt resumption of specie payments, and for the end of segregation in District of Columbia schools. His major proposal, however, was once more his civil rights bill, which would erase the last legal distinctions between whites and blacks and would thus complete the work of reconstruction.

He was disappointed to discover that there was little support for his measure. Both the country and the Congress were tired of reconstruction issues and wanted an end of agitation. Grant's supporters in the Senate insisted that Sumner's bill go to the Judiciary Committee, where everybody knew it would be weakened if not destroyed. When Sumner protested, Edmunds sarcastically suggested that it was "just possible—I know it is a very remote possibility, but it is just possible—" that Sumner's civil rights measure was too strong for some Senators, including

[5] Sumner to Schurz, Nov. 6, 1873, copy, Schurz MSS.; Schurz to Sumner, Nov. 11, 1873, ibid.

those Liberal Republicans and Democrats with whom its author had so recently "clasped hands on a common political platform which would send this bill into the waste-basket in five months." Not even the Republican Congressmen from the South showed much interest in the bill. "I regret much to see how little pluck there is among colored representatives," Sumner complained to J. B. Smith. "They are considering how to surrender on the Civil Rights Bill, through fear of the President!" [6]

Sumner himself was without fear, but he was also without strength. On his way to Washington he had contracted a heavy cold, which he was unable to shake off, and his bladder trouble recurred. Feeble and unable to sleep at night, he reluctantly recognized after the first few days of the session that he could no longer play an active role in the day-by-day deliberations of the Senate. Frequently he was absent from his seat, and when he did appear it was usually to fire a few random shots at Grant's supporters. Several times he spoke against a proposal to change the centennial celebration of the signing of the Declaration of Independence into a world's fair at Philadelphia; when he had been chairman of the Senate Committee on Foreign Relations he had always urged American participation, even at great expense, in such international expositions, but now that Cameron, his successor as chairman, favored expanding the centennial observances, Sumner indignantly objected to inviting "the monarchies of the Old World to appear at our great banquet, and swell the pomp." [7]

Sumner's most embarrassing moment during the session came when the President in January 1874 nominated Caleb Cushing to succeed Chase as Chief Justice. Instinctively opposed to anything Grant favored and warned by antislavery veterans that Massachusetts still remembered Cushing as President Pierce's Attorney General and as Jefferson Davis's friend, Sumner had good reason to oppose the President's choice. On the other hand, in recent years Cushing had worked with Sumner in codifying the United States statutes, and he had been the Sena-

[6] *Cong. Globe,* 43 Cong., 1 Sess., pp. 947–8; Sumner to J. B. Smith, Jan. 1, 1874, Segal Coll.

[7] *Cong. Globe,* 43 Cong., 1 Sess., pp. 1830–3.

tor's close collaborator during the Alabama Claims controversy; he was also one of the Senator's favorite dinner companions. Believing that Cushing would announce constitutional "interpretations . . . large and strong—as my own—for Human Rights and sustained by learning and ability," Sumner decided to favor the nomination.[8]

When Grant was obliged to withdraw Cushing's name, after it became known that he had recommended a friend for a job in the Confederate government, Sumner was unquestionably relieved, because he was free to oppose the President's next choice, Morrison R. Waite, whom he regarded as a mediocre nominee. Too ill to lead a protracted fight against Waite, he made a long speech in the closed session of the Senate reviewing his recollections "of those who had occupied this exalted position, setting forth the qualifications necessary to make a good Chief Justice." By thus showing what Chief Justices had been in the past, he explained to Bowles, he wanted "to warn against an appointment of which the warmest praise was that he would be 'a respectable judge,' and whose opinions on vital questions were unknown." When the Senators, relieved to have Grant nominate a respectable candidate, voted to confirm Waite, Sumner pointedly abstained.[9]

He could do little else, for as the Washington correspondent of the Springfield *Republican* observed: "The senior senator from Massachusetts is counted a cipher by his associates. . . ." Just how slight his political weight was became apparent on February 16, 1874, when Grant named William A. Simmons, who had managed Butler's recent, unsuccessful gubernatorial campaign, as collector of customs at Boston.[1] To the Boston *Morning Journal* the appointment of Simmons was proof of "the progress of demagogical audacity here in Massachusetts"; to

[8] Sumner to Cushing [Jan. 9, 1874], Cushing MSS.; Sumner to Bird, Jan. 15, 1874, Bird MSS.; Sumner to P. W. Chandler, Jan. 15, 1874, Norcross MSS.

[9] Boston *Morning Journal*, Jan. 22, 1874; Sumner to Samuel Bolles [i.e., Bowles] [Jan. 1874], MS. in private hands.

[1] On Butler, Sumner, and the Simmons appointment see Springfield *Republican*, Feb. 28, Mar. 5 and 7, 1874; William D. Mallam: "Benjamin Franklin Butler, Machine Politician and Congressman" (unpublished Ph.D. dissertation, University of Minnesota, 1941), p. 438; Boston *Morning Journal*, Feb. 19–20, 1874; Boston *Commonwealth*, Mar. 7, 1874; Sumner to Samuel Bowles, Mar. 3, 1874, MS. in private hands.

Sumner, it was evidence that the Grant administration was about to take firm control over the Massachusetts Republican party, which was in a state of semi-revolt against the President, and to use its machinery to defeat his reelection to the Senate. Neither the protests of six Massachusetts Congressmen nor the petitions of influential Boston businessmen could shake the President's determination to take the most lucrative and powerful federal office in the state away from a friend of Sumner's and to give it to Butler's aide.

Desperately unhappy over the Simmons nomination, Sumner did not know how to defeat it. If he led in open opposition to the appointment he would only produce a public test of strength with Butler, which he would probably lose. If, on the other hand, he acquiesced in it and handed over to Butler control of the Republican party in Massachusetts, it was possible that the general, in return, might not try to block his reelection to the Senate. The Lawrence *American*, one of Butler's principal newspaper supporters, let it be known that, if Sumner was cooperative, he would "be his own successor to the Senate"—though, at the same time, it was also making similar tenders of support to other senatorial aspirants.

Only if Boutwell opposed the nomination could it be rejected without political danger to Sumner. As a member in good standing of the majority party, the junior Senator from Massachusetts could invoke senatorial prerogative; if he called any appointment in his state personally offensive, his colleagues would not override his wishes. Since Sumner was no longer considered a member of Grant's party, he, of course, was accorded no such veto. Appealing to Boutwell's self-interest in blocking Butler's imperial designs on Massachusetts politics, reminding him of the opposition of Boston businessmen to Simmons, and invoking the obligations of a friendship that dated from 1851, Sumner at first persuaded his colleague to oppose the nomination, and, on February 26, the Senate voted not to confirm Simmons. Since there was no quorum, however, the vote was not binding. Promptly the President's influence began to be felt, while Butler had fifty men at work for him, buttonholing Senators in the lobbies. Under such pressure Boutwell collapsed and announced that, while he personally was still opposed to Simmons's confirmation, he would waive his prerogative and not ask his colleagues to follow his example in voting. By a vote of 27 to 11 the Senate then confirmed Simmons's nomination. Jubilantly Butler announced that he was now the dominant force in Massachusetts politics and "that nobody will be re-elected who opposes him and Mr. Simmons."

• 5 •

Even before the nomination of Simmons, Sumner began to experience renewed attacks of angina, and during the excited controversy they became increasingly frequent, though less sharp and persistent than in earlier seizures. Only injections of morphine stopped the pain. The hypodermic needle "works upon me like magic," Sumner said. "It is like a commander-in-chief who cries 'halt.' "

Too ill to make more than an infrequent appearance in the Senate, he now had to admit that he was an invalid and spent nearly all his time quietly at home. When he was able, he continued to revise and annotate his *Works*, a task which now seemed more than ever "a load and mill-stone, under which time, income, strength, every thing seems to disappear." [2] Often he was desperately lonesome, and he besought friends to visit him. Former Governor Claflin and his wife stayed with Sumner when they came to Washington during the winter, as did Henry Adams and his clever young wife. Sumner most enjoyed visits from Wendell Phillips, who lectured in Washington in February and again in March, for the two veterans of the antislavery wars had endless topics for recollections. Well after midnight one evening when Phillips started to leave, Sumner insisted that he stay longer. When Phillips objected that it was late and that Sumner still had to have the hot footbath which the doctor ordered every evening before he went to bed, the Senator said, with almost childlike petulance: "Well, I will take it if you won't go." For another hour the two old friends talked of their early days in Boston while Sumner soaked his feet.[3]

[2] Sumner to Longfellow, Jan. 25 [1874], Longfellow MSS.
[3] Pierce, IV, 591.

Growing gradually feebler, Sumner now had only three interests: the completion of his *Works,* the passage of his civil rights act, and the rescinding of the Massachusetts legislature's censure of his battle-flags resolution. By the end of February 1874 his concern on the last count was nearly ended. His friends had organized a new campaign, and this time there was little resistance in the legislature. Even Butler professed neutrality, and legislators who talked of postponing the matter indefinitely were asked: "Do they really want to make it impossible for anybody to oppose Mr. Sumner's re-election, next year?" On February 11 the Massachusetts Senate voted overwhelmingly to repeal, and two days later the House did so as well. During the discussion one legislator voiced a concern that many of his colleagues had left unsaid: he urged "that the censure should be removed while Mr. Sumner was still with us." [4]

Sumner watched the course of the legislature with the intense, almost obsessive concern of the invalid. Privately some of his friends thought he "flattered himself by exaggerating the whole affair," and more than one correspondent reminded him that it was "quite immaterial whether the resolution be rescinded or not," since he could "afford to wait the vindication of time and the extinguishment of narrow prejudice and local partisanship." [5] But to Sumner the question was an important one, and he longed for public vindication of his course. It was with pain, therefore, that he learned that through inadvertence the legislature failed to order a report of its action be sent to every Massachusetts Congressman. In order to meet Sumner's wishes, the legislature passed the necessary supplementary resolution, and Governor Washburn named Sumner's Negro friend, J. B. Smith, to bring the official copies of the document to Washington. On March 7 Smith placed the resolution in Sumner's hands. "As he read them," Smith related, "he turned his head and wept as I never saw man weep before. He then said, 'I knew Massachusetts would do me justice.' " There remained only the public recording of his vindication, and Sumner insisted that

[4] Springfield *Republican,* Feb. 7 and 12, 1874.

[5] C. E. Norton to G. W. Curtis, Mar. 15, 1874, Norton MSS.; Chicago *Tribune,* quoted in Springfield *Republican,* Feb. 4, 1874.

Boutwell, who was also ailing, present the rescinding resolutions to the Senate on Tuesday, March 10.[6]

The excitement and anticipation were almost too much for Sumner, especially since the press carried, alongside the reports of the action of the legislature, the story that his divorced wife was considering remarriage. Late at night on March 8 he suffered an acute spasm of angina and was in excruciating pain for hours.[7] He continued to suffer the next day until a massive injection of morphine allowed him to sleep.

On Tuesday, however, he forced himself to go to the Senate in order to hear his colleague enter upon the Senate journal the resolutions of the Massachusetts legislature rescinding its earlier condemnation of him. Though outwardly calm, he was highly excited, and as he lingered in the Senate chamber he began to experience his familiar symptoms. "Ferry," he told the Connecticut Senator, who was also in bad health, "I have a toothache in my heart. I think I shall go home." [8]

By the time Hooper's horses and carriage were ready, however, Sumner had begun to feel better, and he invited Henry L. Pierce and Ben: Perley Poore to dine with him. When his guests arrived shortly before six, they found Sumner in his study, much exercised over a report that Samuel Gridley Howe was organizing a public dinner in Boston for Baez, the now deposed Dominican dictator. While the three men ate, they discussed public affairs, and Sumner seemed unable to get Baez off his mind, for he anticipated further efforts to annex Santo Domingo. Upon leaving the table, he dashed off an angry note urging Bird to cancel the proposed dinner. As for Baez, he wrote: "Something very different from a dinner should be his lot. There are many bad men in the world, but he is among the worst." [9]

Seeing that Sumner was out of sorts, Poore excused himself about nine o'clock, and Pierce soon left too. Sumner continued to

[6] *A Memorial of Charles Sumner,* p. 60; Boutwell: *Reminiscences,* II, 218.

[7] Except where otherwise noted, my account of Sumner's death is based upon Pierce, IV, 593–9; New York *Tribune,* Mar. 12, 1874; J. T. Johnson: *Angina Pectoris;* Samuel Ward to Longfellow, Mar. 11, 1874, Longfellow MSS.; and Boston *Morning Journal,* Mar. 12, 1874.

[8] G. F. Hoar to Pierce, April 18, 1896, Pierce MSS.

[9] Sumner to Bird, Mar. 11, 1874, Bird MSS. This was the last letter Sumner wrote.

work in his study until about eleven o'clock, when the servants heard him fall heavily to the floor. Summoning James Wormley from his hotel next door, they succeeded in lifting the Senator onto his bed and sent for the doctor. When Dr. Johnson arrived, he found Sumner in great pain, and his extremities were very cold. After giving an injection of morphine, he ordered the servants to bathe his feet in mustard water. When the pain persisted, he gave a second injection, and Sumner then dozed off for half an hour.

When he awoke, muttering the words "tired" and "weary," he was only half-conscious, and his pulse was so weak as to be almost imperceptible. Worried, Dr. Johnson called in another physician and also summoned Congressman Pierce. By one o'clock Sumner got some relief and slept quietly, but his skin was clammy, his breathing noisy, and his eyes glassy. The physicians aroused him every two hours during the remainder of the night in order to administer stimulants.

Through the morning Sumner lingered, in semi-conscious condition, while close friends like Pierce, Schurz, and Rockwood Hoar visited his bedroom and many others paid their respects in the study. In constant attendance at his bedside were his secretary and Wormley and Downing, representatives of the race he had tried to befriend. "I am so tired," Sumner would complain from time to time. "I can't last much longer." Though his mind wandered, he fixed on two subjects. "My book," he kept muttering, referring to his *Works*, "my book is not finished. . . ." Turning to his secretary, he said: "I should not regret this if my book were finished."

Even more insistent was the dying man's concern for his "bill." Thinking at first that Sumner was worried over some household debt, his secretary assured him it would be paid. "You do not understand me," Sumner mustered strength to explain; "I mean the Civil Rights Bill." When Hoar came to the bedside about ten o'clock in the morning, Sumner recognized him and managed to say: "You must take care of the civil-rights bill,—my bill, the civil-rights bill, don't let it fail." An hour later, when Frederick Douglass looked into the sickroom, Sumner returned to the subject once more, exclaiming with something of the old ring in his voice: "Don't let the bill fail."

At about 2:00 P.M. on March 11, in great pain, Sumner begged for another injection of morphine, but when the doctors convinced him that it might be harmful, he appeared to grow more quiet and comfortable. Some of his friends thought that the crisis was over and left the house. Half an hour later, however, he was seized by a violent spasm, followed by vomiting. Suddenly throwing himself back on the bed and gasping for air, he died.

Just before his death Sumner turned with complete lucidity to Hoar and said: "Judge, tell Emerson how much I love and revere him." Remembering Emerson's tribute to Sumner at the time of the Brooks assault, Hoar replied: "He said of you once, that he never knew so *white* a soul." [1]

[1] E. R. Hoar to Emerson, Mar. 11, 1874, Emerson MSS. For Emerson's exact words in 1856, see Donald: *Sumner*, p. 311.

PART I

List of Manuscript Collections and Scrapbooks Cited

THE PURPOSE of this list is to indicate the location of manuscript collections cited in the previous pages. It does not include numerous collections which I have searched but from which I have not quoted, nor does it enumerate detached or scattered manuscript items, the locations of which are given in the footnotes.

Adams Family MSS., Massachusetts Historical Society, Boston. Diaries and papers of John Quincy Adams and of Charles Francis Adams.

Aldrich, Charles, MSS., Iowa State Department of Archives and History, Iowa City.

Andrew, John Albion, MSS., Massachusetts Historical Society.

Appleton, Nathan, MSS., ibid.

Argyll MSS., Henry E. Huntington Library, San Marino, California. Papers of George Douglas Campbell, 8th Duke of Argyll, and of his wife, Elizabeth.

Armour, Alexander William, MSS., Library of Congress, Washington, D.C.

Bancroft, George, MSS., Massachusetts Historical Society.

Banks, Nathaniel P., MSS., Essex Institute, Salem, Massachusetts.

Bemis, George, MSS., Massachusetts Historical Society.

Bird, Francis W., MSS., Houghton Library, Harvard University, Cambridge, Massachusetts.

Brougham MSS., University College of London. Papers of Henry Peter Brougham, Baron Brougham and Vaux.

Butler, Benjamin F., MSS., Library of Congress.

Carlisle MSS., Castle Howard, Yorkshire. Papers of George William Frederick Howard, Lord Morpeth and later 7th Earl of Carlisle.

Chamberlain, Mellen, Jr., Diary, Boston Public Library.

Chase, Salmon P., MSS., Historical Society of Pennsylvania, Philadelphia.

Chase, Salmon P., MSS., Library of Congress.

Child, Lydia Maria, MSS., ibid.

Claflin, William, MSS., Rutherford B. Hayes Library, Fremont, Ohio.
Clarendon MSS., Bodleian Library, Oxford University. Papers of George Frederick Villiers, 4th Earl of Clarendon.
Clarke, James Freeman, MSS., Houghton Library.
Cleveland, Henry R., MSS., Berg Collection, New York Public Library.
Combe, George, MSS., National Library of Scotland, Edinburgh.
Crittenden, John Jordan, MSS., Library of Congress.
Curtis, Benjamin R., MSS., ibid.
Cushing, Caleb, MSS., ibid.
Dana, Richard Henry, Jr., MSS., Massachusetts Historical Society.
Daveis, Charles S., MSS., Columbia University, New York, N.Y.
Davis, John, MSS., American Antiquarian Society, Worcester, Mass.
Dawes, Henry L., MSS., Library of Congress.
Department of State, Appointment Papers, The National Archives, Washington, D.C.
Dix, Dorothea L., MSS., Houghton Library.
Dudley, Thomas H., MSS., Huntington Library.
Dunlap, Andrew, MSS., Essex Institute.
Ellis, G. E., MSS., Massachusetts Historical Society.
Everett, Edward, MSS., ibid.
Fields, James T., MSS., ibid.
Fillmore, Millard, MSS., Buffalo Historical Society, Buffalo, N.Y.
Fish, Hamilton, MSS., Library of Congress.
Folsom, Charles, MSS., Boston Public Library.
Fox, John, MSS., Duke University, Durham, N.C.
Fuller Family MSS., Houghton Library.
Papers of Margaret Fuller.
Garrison, William Lloyd, MSS., Boston Public Library.
Garrison, William Lloyd, MSS., Smith College, Northampton, Mass.
Giddings, Joshua R., MSS., Ohio Archaeological and Historical Society, Columbus, Ohio.
Giddings-Julian MSS., Library of Congress.
Greene, George W., MSS., Houghton Library.
Harvard College Faculty Records, Harvard University Archives, Cambridge, Mass.
Harvard College Library Charge Books, ibid.
Harvard College Papers, ibid.
Harvard College Records, ibid.
Hasty Pudding Club, Secretary's Records, ibid.
Hatherton MSS., Staffordshire County Record Office, Stafford. Papers of Edward John Littleton, First Baron Hatherton.
House of Baring MSS., Public Archives of Canada, Ottawa.
Howe Family MSS., Houghton Library.
Papers of Samuel Gridley Howe and Julia Ward Howe.

Kent, James, MSS., Library of Congress.
Lawrence, Amos A., MSS., Massachusetts Historical Society.
Library of Congress Records, Receipts for Books, Library of Congress.
Lieber, Francis, MSS., Huntington Library.
Lincoln, Robert Todd, MSS., Library of Congress.
Longfellow, Henry Wadsworth, MSS., Craigie House, Cambridge, Mass.
Loring, Charles G., MSS., Houghton Library.
Lowell, James Russell, MSS., ibid.
McLean, John, MSS., Library of Congress.
Mann, Horace, MSS., Massachusetts Historical Society.
Morton, Marcus, MSS., ibid.
Norton, Charles Eliot, MSS., Houghton Library.
Paine, Byron, MSS., Wisconsin State Historical Society, Madison.
Palfrey, John Gorham, MSS., Houghton Library.
Parker-Sumner Scrapbook, Boston Public Library.
Pierce, Edward L., MSS., Houghton Library.
Pierce Scrapbooks, ibid.
Prescott, William H., MSS., Massachusetts Historical Society.
Raymond, Henry J., MSS., New York Public Library.
Robie-Sewall MSS., Massachusetts Historical Society.
Robinson, William S., Scrapbooks, Boston Public Library.
Rockwell, A. F., MSS., Library of Congress.
Rockwell, Julius, MSS., New York Historical Society, New York, N.Y.
Sargent, Epes, MSS., Boston Public Library.
Sargent, John O., MSS., Massachusetts Historical Society.
Schouler, James, MSS., ibid.
Schouler, William, MSS., ibid.
Segal, Charles, Collection.
Over 100 letters from Sumner in the private possession of Mr. Charles M. Segal, Brooklyn. N.Y.
Seward, William H., MSS., University of Rochester, Rochester, N.Y.
Shattuck, George C., MSS., Massachusetts Historical Society.
Smith, Gerrit, MSS., University of Syracuse, Syracuse, N.Y.
Sparks, Jared, MSS., Houghton Library.
Stevenson, Andrew, MSS., Library of Congress.
Story, Joseph, MSS., ibid.
Stuart, George Hay, MSS., ibid.
Sumner Autograph Collection, Houghton Library.
Sumner, Charles, MSS., ibid.
Sumner, Charles Pinckney, MSS., Massachusetts Historical Society.
Sumner-Appleton MSS., Boston Public Library.
Thayer, William Sydney, MSS., Library of Congress.
Ticknor, George, MSS., Dartmouth College, Hanover, N.H.

Tilton, Theodore, MSS., Buffalo Public Library, Buffalo, N.Y.
Tower, Charlemagne, MSS., Columbia University.
Van Buren, Martin, MSS., Library of Congress.
Vaughan, Sir Charles, MSS., Codrington Library, All Souls College, Oxford.
Walker, Amasa, MSS., Massachusetts Historical Society.
Warden, David B., MSS., Maryland Historical Society, Baltimore.
Washburn Autograph Collection, Massachusetts Historical Society.
Waterston, Robert C., MSS., ibid.
Wayland, Francis, MSS., Brown University, Providence, R.I.
Webster, Daniel, MSS., Dartmouth College.
Webster, Daniel, MSS., Houghton Library.
Webster, Daniel, MSS., Library of Congress.
Weed, Thurlow, MSS., University of Rochester.
Weston, Maria (Chapman), MSS., Boston Public Library.
Whittier, John Greenleaf, MSS., Houghton Library.
Wilson, Henry, MSS., Library of Congress.
Winthrop, Robert C., MSS., Massachusetts Historical Society.
Woodman, Horatio, MSS., ibid.
Wright, Elizur, MSS., Library of Congress.

PART II

List of Manuscript Collections and Scrapbooks Cited

Adams Family MSS., Massachusetts Historical Society, Boston. Diaries and papers of Charles Francis Adams and his family.

Agassiz, Louis, MSS., Houghton Library, Harvard University, Cambridge, Massachusetts.

Andrew, John Albion, MSS., Massachusetts Historical Society.

Argyll MSS., Henry E. Huntington Library, San Marino, California. Papers of George Douglas Campbell, 8th Duke of Argyll, and of his wife, Elizabeth.

Atkinson, Edward, MSS., Massachusetts Historical Society.

Bancroft, George, MSS., Collection of Regional History and University Archives, Cornell University, Ithaca, New York.

Bancroft, George, MSS., Massachusetts Historical Society.

Banks, Nathaniel P., MSS., Library of Congress, Washington, D.C.

Bemis, George, MSS., Massachusetts Historical Society.

Bigelow, John, MSS., New York Public Library, New York, New York.

Bingham, Kinsley, MSS., Michigan Historical Collection, University of Michigan, Ann Arbor, Michigan.

Bird, Francis W., MSS., Houghton Library.

Bowles, Samuel MSS., in the possession of Mr. Richard Hooker, Springfield, Massachusetts.

Bright, John, MSS., British Museum, London.

Broadlands MSS. The papers of Lord Palmerston, owned by and cited through the kindness of Admiral of the Fleet the Earl Mountbatten of Burma.

Brougham MSS., University College of London. Papers of Henry Peter Brougham, Baron Brougham and Vaux.

Brownson, Orestes, MSS. University of Notre Dame, South Bend, Indiana.

Bryant, William Cullen, MSS., New-York Historical Society, New York.

Bryant-Godwin MSS., New York Public Library. Papers of William Cullen Bryant and Parke Godwin.

Buckalew, Charles R., MSS., in private hands.

Butler, Benjamin F., MSS., Library of Congress.

Chandler, Zachariah, MSS., ibid.

Chase, Salmon P., MSS., Historical Society of Pennsylvania, Philadelphia.

Chase, Salmon P., MSS., Library of Congress.

Child, Lydia M., MSS., ibid.

Claflin, William, MSS., Rutherford B. Hayes Library, Fremont, Ohio.

Clapp, William W., MSS., Library of Congress.

Clarendon MSS., Bodleian Library, University of Oxford, Oxon. Papers of George Frederick Villiers, 4th Earl of Clarendon.

Clarke, James Freeman, MSS., Houghton Library.

Cleveland, Henry R., MSS., Berg Collection, New York Public Library.

Cole, Cornelius, MSS., University of California at Los Angeles, California.

Conkling, Roscoe, MSS., Library of Congress.

Conway, Moncure D., MSS., Columbia University, New York, New York.

Crosswell, Charles, MSS., Burton Historical Collection, Detroit Public Library, Detroit, Michigan.

Curtis, George William, MSS., Houghton Library.

Curtis, George William, MSS., Staten Island Institute of Arts and Sciences, Staten Island, New York.

Cushing, Caleb, MSS., Library of Congress.

Dana, Richard Henry, Jr., MSS., Massachusetts Historical Society.

Daniels, John W., MSS., Duke University, Durham, North Carolina.

Davis, J. C. Bancroft, MSS., Library of Congress.

Dawes, Henry L., MSS., ibid.

Dayton, William L., MSS., New Jersey Historical Society, Newark, New Jersey.

Department of State Records, The National Archives, Washington, D.C.

Dickinson, Anna E., MSS., Library of Congress.

Emerson, Ralph Waldo, MSS., Houghton Library.

Everett, Edward, MSS., Massachusetts Historical Society.

Fabens, J. W., MSS., Essex Institute, Salem, Massachusetts.

Fessenden, William Pitt, MSS., Library of Congress.

Fields, James T., MSS., Massachusetts Historical Society.

Fish, Hamilton, MSS., Library of Congress.

Fogg, George G., MSS., New Hampshire Historical Society, Concord, New Hampshire.

Foreign Office Records, Public Records Office, London. The F. O. 5 file contains most papers relating to diplomatic relations with the United States.

Foulke, William D., MSS., Indiana State Library, Indianapolis, Indiana.

Granville MSS., Public Records Office. Papers of Granville George Levenson-Gower, 2nd Earl Granville.

Hammond, Edmund, MSS., British Museum.

Iddesleigh MSS., ibid. Papers of Stafford Northcote, 1st Earl of Iddesleigh.

Johnson, Andrew, MSS., Library of Congress.

Julian, George W., MSS., Indiana State Library.

Lamon, Ward Hill, MSS., Henry E. Huntington Library.

Layard, Austen Henry, MSS., British Museum.

Lewis, George Cornewall, MSS., National Library of Wales, Aberystwyth, Wales.

Library of Congress Records: Receipts for Books, Library of Congress.

Lieber, Francis, MSS., Henry E. Huntington Library.

Lincoln, Abraham, MSS., Library of Congress.

Lodge, Henry Cabot, MSS., Massachusetts Historical Society.

Longfellow, Henry Wadsworth, MSS., Craigie House, Cambridge, Massachusetts.

Loring, Charles G., MSS., Houghton Library.

Lowell, James Russell, MSS., ibid.

Lyons MSS., Arundel Castle, Sussex. Papers of Richard Bickerton Pemell Lyons, 2nd Baron and 1st Lord Lyons.

McClellan Lincoln Collection, Brown University, Providence, Rhode Island.

McCulloch, Hugh, MSS., Library of Congress.

Moran, Benjamin, Diary, MS., ibid.

Morgan, Edwin D., MSS., New York State Library, Albany, New York.
Norcross, Grenville H., MSS., Massachusetts Historical Society.
Norton, Charles Eliot, MSS., Houghton Library.
Palfrey, John Gorham, MSS., ibid.
Pierce, Edward L., MSS., ibid.
Pierce, George B., MSS., ibid.
Pierce Scrapbooks, ibid.
Pratt, David D., MSS., Indiana State Library.
Pruyn, J. V. S. L., MSS., New York State Library.
Quincy, Edmund, MSS., Massachusetts Historical Society.
Reid, Whitelaw, MSS., Library of Congress.
Ripon MSS., British Museum. Papers of George Frederick Robinson, 2nd Earl and 1st Marquis of Ripon.
Rockwell, Julius, MSS., New-York Historical Society.
Royal Archives, Windsor Castle, Windsor, Berks.
Russell MSS., Public Records Office, London. Papers of Lord John Russell, 1st Earl Russell.
Sargent, J. O., MSS., Massachusetts Historical Society.
Schuckers, J. W., MSS., ibid.
Schurz, Carl, MSS., Library of Congress.
Segal, Charles, Collection. Over 100 letters from Sumner in the collection of Mr. Charles Segal.
Seward, William H., MSS., University of Rochester, Rochester, New York.
Shaw Family Papers, New York Public Library.
Smith, Gerrit, MSS., University of Syracuse, Syracuse, New York.
Stanton, Edwin M., MSS., Library of Congress.
Storey, Moorfield, MSS., in the possession of Mr. Charles Storey of Brookline, Massachusetts.
Stuart, William, MSS., Public Records Office, London.
Sumner, Charles, MSS., Houghton Library.
Sumner, Charles, MSS., Library of Congress.
Sumner, Charles, MSS., Massachusetts Historical Society.
Sumner Scrapbooks, Houghton Library.
Tenterden MSS., Public Records Office, London. Papers of Charles Stuart Aubrey Abbott, 3rd Baron Tenterden.
Thornton, Edward, Letterbook, Bodleian Library, University of Oxford.
Tilton, Theodore, MSS., Buffalo Public Library, Buffalo, New York.
Tupper, Martin F., MSS., University of Illinois, Urbana, Illinois.
Wade, Benjamin F., MSS., Library of Congress.

Weed, Thurlow, MSS., University of Rochester.
Welles, Gideon, MSS., Henry E. Huntington Library.
Welles, Gideon, MSS., Library of Congress.
Whipple, E. P., MSS., Boston Public Library.
White Notes, University of Wyoming, Laramie, Wyoming. Notes and papers of Professor Laura White.
Whittier, John Greenleaf, MSS., Essex Institute.
Whittier, John Greenleaf, MSS., Houghton Library.
Wilson, Henry, MSS., Library of Congress.
Winthrop, Robert Charles, MSS., Massachusetts Historical Society.
Woodman, Horatio, MSS., ibid.

INDEX TO PART I

INDEX TO PART II

Other titles of interest

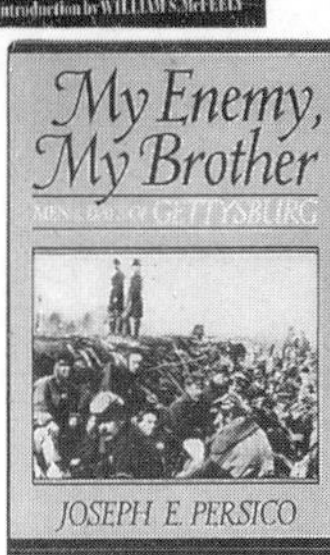

THE CIVIL WAR
In the Writings of
Col. G.F.R. Henderson
Edited by Jay Luvaas
336 pp.
9 maps and sketches,
1 illus.
80718-1 $14.95

THE CAMPAIGNS OF
GENERAL NATHAN BEDFORD
FORREST
and of Forrest's Cavalry
by General Thomas Jordan
and J.P. Pryor
New introduction by Albert Castel
736 pp., 14 illus.,
10 maps and sketches
80719-X $19.95

BLACK ABOLITIONISTS
Benjamin Quarles
310 pp.
80425-5 $13.95

THE BLACK PHALANX
African American Soldiers
in the War of Independence,
the War of 1812, and the
Civil War
Joseph T. Wilson
New introduction by
Dudley Taylor Cornish
534 pp., 64 illus.
80550-2 $16.95

THE BOOKS OF AMERICAN
NEGRO SPIRITUALS
Two volumes in one
J. W. and J. R. Johnson
384 pp.
80074-8 $14.95

A BRAVE BLACK REGIMENT
The History of the 54th
Massachusetts, 1863–1865
Captain Luis F. Emilio
New introduction by
Gregory J. W. Urwin
532 pp., 89 photos, 9 maps
80623-1 $15.95

ENCYCLOPEDIA OF
BLACK AMERICA
Edited by W. Augustus Low
and Virgil A. Clift
941 pp., 400 illus.
80221-X $35.00

FREDERICK DOUGLASS ON
WOMEN'S RIGHTS
Edited by Philip S. Foner
200 pp.
80489-1 $13.95

LINCOLN AND THE NEGRO
Benjamin Quarles
275 pp., 8 illus.
80447-6 $13.95

THE NEGRO IN THE
CIVIL WAR
Benjamin Quarles
New introduction by
William S. McFeely
402 pp., 4 illus.
80350-X $13.95

SLAVERY
A World History
Updated Edition
Milton Meltzer
584 pp., 251 illus. 3 maps
80536-7 $22.50

THOMAS MORRIS CHESTER, BLACK CIVIL WAR CORRESPONDENT: His Dispatches from the Virginia Front
Edited by R.J.M. Blackett
375 pp., 3 photos, 1 map
80453-0 $13.95

THE TROUBLE THEY SEEN
The Story of Reconstruction in the Words of African Americans
Edited by Dorothy Sterling
512 pp., 152 illus.
80548-0 $15.95

ABRAHAM LINCOLN
His Speeches and Writings
Edited by Roy P. Basler
Preface by Carl Sandburg
888 pp., 6 illus.
80404-2 $19.95

THE ABRAHAM LINCOLN ENCYCLOPEDIA
Mark E. Neely, Jr.
368 pp., more than 300 illus.
80209-0 $18.95

THE ANNALS OF THE CIVIL WAR
Written by Leading Participants North and South
New introd.by Gary W. Gallagher
808 pp., 56 illus.
80606-1 $19.95

THE ANTIETAM AND FREDERICKSBURG
General Francis W. Palfrey
New introd. by Stephen W. Sears
244 pp., 4 maps
80691-6 $13.95

BATTLE-PIECES AND ASPECTS OF THE WAR
Herman Melville
New introd. by Lee Rust Brown
282 pp.
80655-X $13.95

BY SEA AND BY RIVER
A Naval History of the Civil War
Bern Anderson
344 pp., 20 illus.
80367-4 $13.95

CAMPAIGNING WITH GRANT
General Horace Porter
New introduction by
William S. McFeely
632 pp., 32 illus.
80277-5 $12.95

CHANCELLORSVILLE AND GETTYSBURG
General Abner Doubleday
New introduction by
Gary W. Gallagher
269 pp., 13 maps
80549-5 $12.95

THE CIVIL WAR DAY BY DAY
An Almanac 1861-1865
E. B. Long with Barbara Long
1,135 pp., 8 pages of maps
80255-4 $19.95

THE CIVIL WAR PAPERS OF GEORGE B. McCLELLAN
Selected Correspondence 1860-1865
Edited by Stephen W. Sears
669 pp.
80471-9 $17.95

A CIVIL WAR TREASURY
Being a Miscellany of Arms and Artillery, Facts and Figures, Legends and Lore, Muses and Minstrels, Personalities and People
Albert A. Nofi
431 pp.
80622-3 $15.95

DESTRUCTION AND RECONSTRUCTION
Personal Experiences of the Civil War
General Richard Taylor
New introduction by
T. Michael Parrish
288 pp.
80624-X $14.95

GENERAL LEE
A Biography of Robert E. Lee
General Fitzhugh Lee
Introduction by
Gary W. Gallagher
478 pp., 2 illus., 3 maps
80589-8 $15.95

HERNDON'S LIFE OF LINCOLN
William Henry Herndon
and Jesse Weik
New introduction by
Henry Steele Commager
650 pp.
80195-7 $14.95

JEFFERSON DAVIS
Private Letters, 1823-1889
Selected and edited by
Hudson Strode
604 pp., 1 photo
80638-X $16.95

LINCOLN AND THE CIVIL WAR
In the Diaries and
Letters of John Hay
Selected by Tyler Dennett
362 pp.
80340-2 $13.95

THE LINCOLN READER
Edited by Paul M. Angle
608 pp., 40 photos
80398-4 $16.95

LINCOLN'S HERNDON
David Herbert Donald
442 pp., 11 photos
80353-4 $13.95

MEMOIRS OF GENERAL
WILLIAM T. SHERMAN
New introduction by
William S. McFeely
820 pp.
80213-9 $17.95

MY ENEMY, MY BROTHER
Men and Days of Gettysburg
Joseph E. Persico
288 pp., 8 illus., 1 map
80692-4 $13.95

MY STORY OF THE WAR
The Civil War Memoirs of the
Famous Nurse, Relief Organizer,
and Suffragette
Mary A. Livermore
New introd. by Nina Silber
710 pp., 20 illus.
80658-4 $19.95

THE OUTBREAK OF
REBELLION
John G. Nicolay
New introd. by Mark E. Neely, Jr.
246 pp., 8 maps
80657-6 $12.95

PERSONAL MEMOIRS OF
U.S. GRANT
New introd. by William S. McFeely
Critical Notes by E. B. Long
xxxi + 608 pp.
80172-8 $15.95

THE RISE OF U.S. GRANT
Colonel Arthur L. Conger
New introduction by
Brooks D. Simpson
432 pp., 12 photos and 14 maps
80693-2 $15.95

SINGING SOLDIERS
A History of the Civil War in Song
300 pp., 88 illus.
80021-7 $13.95

STONEWALL JACKSON,
ROBERT E. LEE, AND THE
ARMY OF NORTHERN
VIRGINIA, 1862
William Allan
New introd. by Robert K. Krick
755 pp., 16 maps, 1 photo
80656-8 $19.95

THE STORY OF THE
CONFEDERACY
Robert Selph Henry
Foreword by
Douglas Southall Freeman
526 pp.
80370-4 $14.95